TEXTBOOK ON
REVENUE LAW

For Ted and Alice

TEXTBOOK ON

REVENUE LAW

Adrian Shipwright
BCL, MA(Oxon), AIIT, FRSA, Barrister,
Visiting Professor, King's College, London

&

Elizabeth Keeling
LLB, LLM, Solicitor, Lecturer,
King's College, London

First published in Great Britain 1997 by Blackstone Press Limited,
9-15 Aldine Street, London W12 8AW. Telephone 0181-740 2277

© A. Shipwright, E. Keeling, 1997

ISBN: 1 85431 321 5

British Library Cataloguing in Publication Data
A CIP catalogue record for this book is available from the British Library

Typeset by Style Photosetting Ltd, Mayfield, East Sussex
Printed by Ashford Colour Press, Gosport, Hampshire

All rights reserved. No part of this book may be reproduced or transmitted in any form or by any means, electronic or mechanical, including photocopying, recording, or any information storage or retrieval system without prior permission from the publisher.

Contents

Preface xiii

Glossary xv

Abbreviations xxiii

Table of Cases xxv

Table of Statutes xliii

Part I GENERAL MATTERS   1

1 Introduction to Tax Law   1

1.1 Introductory matters   1.2 What is tax?   1.3 What are the aims of a tax system   1.4 What are the criteria for a 'good' tax system?   1.5 UK taxes   1.6 Territorial scope of UK taxation

2 Sources of Tax Law and Administration   23

2.1 Sources of tax law and administration   2.2 Cases and reports   2.3 Extra-Statutory Concessions, Statements of Practice etc.   2.4 Other   2.5 UK tax administration: structure and personnel   2.6 Self-assessment   2.7 Direct tax appeals   2.8 Appeal to Chancery Division   2.9 Law and fact   2.10 Further appeals   2.11 Other remedies   2.12 VAT and indirect tax appeals   2.13 Judicial review   2.14 Europe

3 The Interpretation of Taxing Statutes   50

3.1 Introduction   3.2 Method of legislation not conducive to clarity   3.3 Diversity of approaches   3.4 Impact of avoidance   3.5 Short or long legislation?   3.6 Legal theory   3.7 The approach(es) of the courts   3.8 'Rules' of interpretation   3.9 Ambiguity and obscurity   3.10 Parliamentary debates and *Pepper* v *Hart*   3.11 European influence   3.12 European principles and interpretation of UK domestic legislation   3.13 Summary   3.14 The European Court

4 Tax Avoidance   69

4.1 Introduction   4.2 What is tax avoidance?   4.3 How should tax avoidance be dealt with?   4.4 Anti-avoidance options and techniques   4.5 Shams   4.6 Avoidance, evasion and mitigation   4.7 Avoidance and case law   4.8 Subsequent cases   4.9 *Countess Fitzwilliam* v *IRC* [1993] STC 502   4.10 *Whittles* v *Uniholdings Ltd* [1996] STC 914   4.11 *IRC* v *McGuckian* [1994] STC 888   4.12 *Piggott* v *Staines Investment Co. Ltd* [1995] STC 114   4.13 What is the law?   4.14 Difficulties?   4.15 Official statements   4.16 Statutory anti-avoidance

PART II   INCOME TAX   135

5 Income Tax — General Principles   135

5.1 Income tax — introductory matters   5.2 History   5.3 The basic principles of UK income tax — source doctrine   5.4 Computation of the income tax charge   5.5 Charges on income   5.6 Reliefs   5.7 Rates of income tax   5.8 Assessment and collection

6 Schedule E — Income from Employment   153

6.1 Introduction   6.2 What is Schedule E concerned with?   6.3 Importance of history of Schedule E   6.4 The charge under Schedule E   6.5 What is an 'office'?   6.6 Offices as assets of a trade or profession   6.7 Summary: office   6.8 What is an 'employment'?   6.9 Statute and employment   6.10 Other cases   6.11 *Hall* v *Lorimer*   6.12 What are emoluments under the 'common law' of Schedule E?   6.13 Reality rules   6.14 Deduction from wages etc.   6.15 Trade-in value?   6.16 When is tax assessable? Deferral and waiver   6.17 Old rules   6.18 New rules   6.19 '. . . Perquisites and profits whatsoever', 'benefits in kind' and 'fringe benefits': General   6.20 Valuation of benefits in kind   6.21 Summary: benefits in kind and 'common law' of Schedule E   6.22 Contractual conditions   6.23 The rule in *Nicoll* v *Austin*   6.24 Payments compensating for lost or withdrawn fringe benefits   6.25 Extra-statutory concessions   6.26 Summary: emoluments   6.27 'Therefrom'   6.28 Some subsequent cases   6.29 Third party payments   6.30 Any relevant factors?   6.31 Inducements to take up an office or employment   6.32 'Golden handshakes'   6.33 Summary: Termination and the 'common law' of Schedule E   6.34 Statute   6.35 What Case?   6.36 Foreign emoluments   6.37 Place of performance of duties

7 Benefits in Kind — Statutory Modifications 211

7.1 Introduction   7.2 Statutory modifications applicable to all taxpayers   7.3 Vouchers   7.4 Living accommodation   7.5 Directors and employees earning more than £8,500 — benefits derived by company directors and others from their employment: Chapter II, Part V, TA

8 Schedule E — Expenses 240

8.1 Introduction   8.2 Section 198, TA relief for necessary expenses — general matters   8.3 Travelling expenses   8.4 Other expenses   8.5 Concessions etc.   8.6 Section 201, TA fees and subscriptions to professional bodies   8.7 Capital allowances   8.8 Interest on loan for plant   8.9 Business entertaining expenses   8.10 Miscellaneous

9 Schedule D Cases I and II — Profits from Trades, Professions and Vocations 254

9.1 General matters   9.2 Four major questions   9.3 Statute   9.4 'Badges of trade'   9.5 Asset stripping and dividend stripping — tax avoidance motive   9.6 Illegal trading   9.7 Mutual trading

10 Schedule D, Cases I and II — Computation 283

10.1 General   10.2 Cash and earnings basis   10.3 Trading receipts   10.4 The rule in *Sharkey* v *Wernher*   10.5 Deductions   10.6 Problem areas   10.7 The basis period rules   10.8 The new rules: FA 1994 as amended by FA 1995

11 Schedule D — Losses 337

11.1 Introduction   11.2 What is meant by a 'trading loss'?   11.3 Commencement losses — carry back of losses in the opening years: s. 381, TA   11.4 'Carry across' against other income: s. 380, TA   11.5 'Carry forward' against future profits of the same trade: s. 385, TA   11.6 'Carry back' against profits of the preceding three years (terminal loss relief): s. 388, TA   11.7 CGT

12 Capital Allowances 345

12.1 Introduction   12.2 Industrial buildings   12.3 Machinery and plant   12.4 Miscellaneous

13 Income Tax — Schedule D, Case III: 361
Interest, Annuities and Other Annual Payments

13.1 Introduction   13.2 Charges on income   13.3 The charge under Schedule D, Case III   13.4 Annuities, annual payments, interest and discounts   13.5 What is an 'annuity'?   13.6 What is an 'other annual payment'?   13.7 'Interest' and Schedule D, Case III   13.8 What are 'discounts'?   13.9 Basis of assessment for Schedule D, Case III   13.10 Deduction of income tax at source   13.11 Mortgage interest   13.12 Annuities and annual payments and deduction of tax at source   13.13 Section 348, TA   13.14 Section 349, TA   13.15 Donations to charity   13.16 Agreement not to deduct   13.17 Avoidance schemes   13.18 Who is chargeable under Schedule D, Case III?   13.19 Payment of tax   13.20 The international element   13.21 FA 1996 changes

14 Income Tax and Trusts 400

14.1 Introduction   14.2 The income tax liability of trustees   14.3 The income tax liability of beneficiaries   14.4 Non-resident trusts

15 Income Tax Anti-Avoidance Provisions on Settlements 413
— Part XV, TA

15.1 Introduction   15.2 Meaning of 'settlement'   15.3 Meaning of 'settlor'   15.4 The charging provisions

16 Income Tax and Death 423

16.1 Deceased's income   16.2 Income arising after death

17 Income Tax and UK Land 427

17.1 Introduction   17.2 Historical matters   17.3 General matters   17.4 The charge under the old Schedule A   17.5 Deductions and old Schedule A   17.6 Premiums and deemed premiums   17.7 Service charges   17.8 Capital allowances   17.9 Section 779, TA — sale and leaseback: limitation on tax reliefs   17.10 Section 780, TA — sale and leaseback: taxation of consideration received   17.11 Land as a trade   17.12 Non-residents and income from UK land and foreign land   17.13 The new Schedule A   17.14 Exemptions

18 Schedule D, Case VI 448

18.1 Introduction   18.2 The general charge   18.3 Specific charges   18.4 Basis of assessment   18.5 The international element

Contents

PART III CAPITAL GAINS TAX 453

19 Capital Gains Tax — General Principles 453

19.1 Introduction 19.2 Policy 19.3 History of capital gains taxation 19.4 Problems

20 Capital Gains Tax — The Charge 459

20.1 The charging section 20.2 Chargeable gains 20.3 Chargeable person 20.4 Assets 20.5 Disposal 20.6 Deemed disposals 20.7 Assets of negligible value 20.8 Hire purchase 20.9 Part disposal 20.10 Value shifting 20.11 Debts 20.12 Options 20.13 Time of disposal 20.14 Non-disposals 20.15 Rates of capital gains tax 20.16 Payment of tax

21 Computation of Gains and Losses 480

21.1 Introduction 21.2 Consideration 21.3 Allowable expenditure 21.4 Acquisition expenditure 21.5 Production expenditure 21.6 Enhancement expenditure 21.7 Title expenditure 21.8 Incidental costs of disposal 21.9 Modifications 21.10 Indexation allowance 21.11 Allowance for foreign tax

22 Capital Gains Tax — Losses, Exemptions and Reliefs 499

22.1 Losses 22.2 Exemptions 22.3 Reliefs

23 Capital Gains Tax on Death 527

23.1 Capital gains tax on death 23.2 Capital gains accruing during administration of the estate

24 Capital Gains Tax and Settlements 530

24.1 Introduction 24.2 Settled property 24.3 Transfer into a settlement 24.4 Settlor's liability to tax on the capital gains of the settlement 24.5 Disposals by trustees 24.6 Disposal of trust assets by the trustees 24.7 Absolute entitlement to settled property 24.8 Termination of a life interest in possession on death 24.9 Beneficiaries 24.10 Charitable trusts 24.11 Non-resident trusts

PART IV COMPANIES AND UK TAX 547

25 Companies and UK Tax — General Matters 547

25.1 Introductory matters 25.2 Outline of UK direct tax position 25.3 History 25.4 Problem areas 25.5 UK corporation tax — general matters   25.6 Some definitions   25.7 Rates of corporation tax   25.8 'Small companies' rate   25.9 Payment of corporation tax

26   The Charge to Corporation Tax   568

26.1 Introductory matters   26.2 What is chargeable to corporation tax?   26.3 Fiduciary receipts   26.4 Exclusion of income tax and capital gains tax   26.5 Liability of non-UK resident company to UK corporation tax   26.6 Basis of liability and computation   26.7 Deductions and charges on income   26.8 Charges on income etc. and corporation tax   26.9 Loan relationships

27   Advance Corporation Tax ('ACT') and Distributions   588

27.1 Purpose of chapter   27.2 Advance corporation tax ('ACT')   27.3 Distributions   27.4 Importance of company law   27.5 When is a distribution paid?   27.6 Important definitions   27.7 Matters which can be distributions   27.8 Qualifying distributions   27.9 'Non-distributions'   27.10 Stock dividends   27.11 Advance corporation tax   27.12 Reduction of corporation tax   27.13 Uses of surplus advance corporation tax   27.14 UK tax and recipients of distributions from UK companies   27.15 Resident corporate shareholders   27.16 Surplus franked investment income   27.17 Non-resident corporate shareholders receiving distributions from UK resident companies   27.18 Other resident shareholders   27.19 Other non-resident shareholders

28   Losses   605

28.1 Introduction   28.2 Commencement losses   28.3 Trading losses   28.4 Surplus capital allowances   28.5 Investment companies   28.6 Sections 242 and 243 and franked investment income   28.7 Case VI losses — section 396, TA   28.8 Other losses   28.9 Hivedowns etc.   28.10 Allowable losses   28.11 Group relief

29   Groups   615

29.1 Introductory matters   29.2 Outline of UK approach   29.3 Areas covered in this chapter   29.4 General matters   29.5 Group income   29.6 Deductible payments   29.7 Group relief   29.8 Surrender of advance corporation tax   29.9 Groups and chargeable gains   29.10 Anti-avoidance   29.11 Consortia

30   Reorganisations, Reconstructions and Repurchases   647

30.1 Introduction   30.2 CGT and reorganisation of share capital etc., ss. 126 and 127, TCGA   30.3 Paper for paper transactions — ss. 135 and 136, TCGA   30.4 Section 132, TCGA and section 473, TA: conversion of

Contents xi

securities 30.5 Demergers 30.6 Section 139, TCGA 30.7 Anti-avoidance 30.8 Consideration for the transfer 30.9 Relationship to other tax provisions 30.10 UK tax and redemption and purchase of own shares

PART V   INHERITANCE TAX   673

31   Inheritance Tax — General Principles   673

31.1 Introduction   31.2 History   31.3 Policy

32   Inheritance Tax — The Charge   678

32.1 The charge 32.2 Transfers of value 32.3 Transactions which are not transfers of value 32.4 Transfers of value on death 32.5 Gifts with reservation 32.6 Exempt transfers 32.7 All transfers 32.8 Lifetime transfers 32.9 Potentially exempt transfers 32.10 Conditionally exempt transfers

33   Inheritance tax — Computation   697

33.1 Introduction 33.2 Value transferred 33.3 The valuation of particular assets 33.4 Rates of tax 33.5 Quick succession relief 33.6 Aggregation 33.7 Payment of tax 33.8 Methods of payment 33.9 Variations and disclaimers

34   Inheritance Tax and Settlements   720

34.1 Settlement 34.2 Settlors 34.3 Trustees and beneficiaries 34.4 Interests in possession settlements 34.5 Settlements without interests in possession 34.6 Favoured settlements 34.7 Payment of tax

PART VI   FOREIGN ELEMENT   741

35   The Foreign Element   741

35.1 Introduction 35.2 UK residents with foreign income and gains 35.3 Schedule D, Cases IV and V 35.4 Income from overseas employments 35.5 Capital gains tax 35.6 Offshore trusts 35.7 Income tax and offshore trusts 35.8 Capital gains tax and offshore trusts 35.9 Inheritance tax and offshore trusts 35.10 Double tax relief 35.11 Miscellaneous

Index   761

Preface

The purpose of this book is to provide an outline of the parts of UK tax most commonly encountered in undergraduate and LLM courses on tax law. The task has become no easier since G.S.A. Wheatcroft described '. . . writing a . . . book on tax is like painting a picture of a sunset; as fast as a chapter is in draft the law has changed'. This is even more the case than in 1967 as some recent Finance Bills have needed to be published in two volumes.

This book is not intended to be an exhaustive treatise on UK tax law but is intended as a textbook to provide an introductory guide to the vast amount of material on UK tax and related matters. Although some may regard tax as a dry and difficult area it is one which raises some of the fundamental questions of law in a practical context. Given our backgrounds we hope we can bring some practical insights to the academic side of tax law. The contents of this book are based on materials available to us on 1 January 1997 with some later additions where this has been possible.

We are most grateful to many friends and colleagues for their help in the preparation of this book. The errors and omissions, however, remain our own unaided work. We owe our greatest debt of gratitude to our various pupils who have taught us more than they can ever realise. We are conscious that no work can ever be perfect and welcome constructive comment and suggestions for improvement in further editions.

Adrian Shipright
Elizabeth Keeling
King's College, London
May 1997

Glossary

This glossary is not meant to define the words and phrases set out below but is intended to give a general indication of the meaning of the word in question and the way it is used in this book. It is not, and is not intended to be, exhaustive and is subject to the 'context otherwise requiring' limitation.

Accruals 'Revenue and costs are accrued (that is recognised as they are earned or incurred, not as money is received or paid) matched with one another so far as their relationship can be established or justifiably assumed, and dealt with in the profit and loss account of the period to which they relate.' (See SSAP 20.)

ACT Advance Corporation Tax. A payment made earlier than the normal date for payment, i.e., in advance by a UK resident company making a qualifying distribution (qv). See s. 14, Income and Corporation Taxes Act 1988 ('TA').

Annuity 'An annuity means where an income is purchased with a sum of money and the capital has gone and ceased to exist, the principal having been converted into an annuity,' *per* Watson B in *Lady Foley* v *Fletcher* (1858) 3 H & N 769.

Assessment 'Assessment particularises the exact sum which a person liable [to tax] has to pay.' Lord Dunedin in *Whitney* v *IRC* (1925) 10 TC 88.

Avoidance	'The art of dodging tax without actually breaking the law'. Professor G.S.A. Wheatcroft (1955) 18 *MLR* 209.
Basic Rate	The basic rate of income tax under s. 1(2)(a), TA.
Board of Inland Revenue	Sometimes called The Board – the Commissioners of Inland Revenue who have the care of income tax etc. (See ss. 1 and 118, Taxes Management Act 1970 ('TMA') and ss. 1–3, Inland Revenue Regulation Act 1890).
Capital	The correlative of income.
Capital Allowance	By s. 832(1), TA any allowance under the Capital Allowances Acts (cf. s. 41(4), Taxation of Chargeable Gains Act 1992 ('TCGA'). Allowance for capital expenditure given in computing income in accordance with the Capital Allowances Act 1990.
Capital Allowances Acts	By ss. 832(1), TA the Capital Allowances Act 1990, including enactments which under the TA are so treated as contained in that Act.
Capital Gain	A chargeable gain, see ss. 1 and 15(2), TCGA.
Case Stated	(Stated Case in Scotland) means of appeal on a point of law whereby the tribunal states and signs a case for the opinion of the High Court; see s. 56, TMA.
Cash Equivalent	The amount on which benefits in kind are charged under the Code; see s. 156, TA.
Chargeable Gain	See Capital Gain above.
The Code	Sections 153 to 168G, TA.
Commissioners	The Special and General Commissioners who hear tax appeals and the Board of Inland Revenue above.
Company	Any body corporate or unincorporated association but does not include a partnership; see s. 832(1), TA and s. 288, TCGA.

Connected Person	See s. 839, TA, s. 286, TCGA and s. 270, IHTA.
Consultative or Consultation Document	Document published by the Revenue or Customs asking for views.
Contingent	Dependent on the happening of something.
Contingent Interest	Broadly an interest which will not come into existence unless and until some uncertain event occurs. A future right to future enjoyment which may arise if a condition precedent is fulfilled.
Contingent Liability	A liability which may arise if a condition precedent is fulfilled (cf. *Randall* v *Plumb* (1975) 50 TC 392 and s. 49, TCGA).
Control	See ss. 416(2) and 840, TA. Section 416 is applied for CGT by s. 288 TCGA.
Corporation Tax Acts	By s. 831(1)(a), TA the enactments relating to the taxation of the income and chargeable gains of companies and of company distributions (including provisions relating also to income tax).
Debenture	By s. 744, Companies Act 1985 ('CA') includes debenture stock, bonds and any other securities of a company, whether constituting a charge on the assets of the company or not. In *Levy* v *Abercorris Slate* (1887) 37 Ch D 260 Chitty J said '. . . a debenture means a document which either creates a debt or acknowledges it, and any document which fulfils either of these conditions is a "debenture" . . . [it is not] a term of art.'
Debt	As at a particular time a liability to pay a sum which is ascertained or capable of ascertainment (cf. Slade J in *Marren* v *Ingles* [1979] STC 637 at p. 639, quoted by Fox J in *Marson* v *Marriage* [1980] STC 177 at p. 188). A contingent unidentifiable sum, payable at an unascertained date, seemingly is not a debt (*Marren* v *Ingles* [1980] STC 500).
Debt on a security	'Defined' in s. 132, TCGA (see s. 251(1), TCGA) essentially something like loan stock. Category of debt on which a gain as well as a loss could be made. Description of class of debts chargeable to CGT.

Deduction	Sum deducted in computing profit or gain.
Deduction at source	Collection of tax by the payer so that the recipient receives a net sum, e.g., PAYE and certain interest payments. Also called withholding tax.
Defray	Provide money to pay (see *Concise Oxford Dictionary*).
Director	By s. 168(8), TA:

> (a) in relation to a company whose affairs are managed by a board of directors or similar body, a member of that board or similar body;
> (b) in relation to a company whose affairs are managed by a single director or similar person, that director or person; and
> (c) in relation to a company whose affairs are managed by the members themselves, a member of that company, and includes any person in accordance with whose directions or instructions ... the directors are accustomed to act ...

Distribution	A dividend and similar payments; see s. 209, TA et seq. (May also apply to distribution of an estate.)
Ejusdem generis	Rule of construction, literally 'of the same type'.
Emolument	By s. 131, TA '... the expression "emoluments" shall include all salaries, fees, wages, perquisites and profits whatsoever.'
Employment	... it seems to me that when the legislature took 'employments' out of Schedule D and put it into Schedule E alongside 'offices', the legislature had in mind employments which were something like offices, and I thought of the expression 'posts' as conveying the idea required. When a person occupies a post resting on a contract, and if, then, that is employment as opposed to a mere engagement in the course of carrying on a profession ... *Per* Rowlatt J in *Davies v Braithwaite* (1931) 18 TC 198.

Glossary

Evasion	Dodging tax illegally – usually a criminal offence.
Exemption	Something which takes a matter outside the charge to tax.
Expense	Expenditure which may be deductible in computing taxable profits or gains.
Gift with Reservation	GWR or GROB – gift with reservation of benefit on which IHT can be charged.
Gross up	The calculation used to work out the full or gross amount of a net sum. Thus if the amount is £60 net of 40% tax, the gross amount is: $£60 \times \frac{100}{(100-40)} = £100$
Hansard	The Official Report of the proceedings of the House of Commons.
Higher Paid Employee	Formerly the description of an employee earning a rate of £8,500 a year or more.
Higher Rate(s)	The higher rate(s) of income tax under s. 1(2)(b), TA.
Hivedowns	The transfer of business from one company to another company, usually within one group.
Income	Correlative of capital.
Income Tax Acts	By s. 831(1)(b), TA the enactments relating to income tax including any provisions of the Corporation Tax Acts which relate to income tax.
Interest	By s. 832(1), TA 'interest' means both 'annual and yearly interest and interest other than annual or yearly interest.' 'Interest means payment by time for the use of money,' *per* Rowlatt J in *Bennett* v *Ogston* (1930) 15 TC 374 at p. 379.
Judicial Review	Procedure for obtaining prerogative and private remedies against the administration; see RSC Ord 53 and Supreme Court Act 1981.
Lower Rate	The lower rate of income tax under s. 1(2)(aa), TA.

Mark to market	The mark to market basis involves valuing the debt at its fair value at the beginning and end of each accounting period. It is generally only used by banks and securities traders.
MCT	Mainstream Corporation Tax. The usage of the term MCT varies. Here it is used to mean the liability on the taxable profits rather than the difference between that and ACT, i.e., the extra amount to be paid.
Mitigation	Tax avoidance which is approved of.
Net	After deduction of tax.
Nothing	Something which has no tax effect, e.g., a payment which is not deductible.
OAP or Other Annual Payment	Matters which can fall within Schedule D, Case III as pure income profit, discussed in Chapter 13.
PAYE	Pay as you earn system of collecting income tax by deduction at source from employee's income; see s. 203, TA.
Pepper v *Hart*	House of Lords case setting out conditions when Hansard may be consulted.
Progressive	Tax system where the rate of tax increases with the amount of profits or gains etc.
Qualifying Distribution	A distribution (qv) which is made by a UK resident company and prima facie attracts a liability to ACT (qv).
Regressive	Tax system where the rate of tax decreases with the amount of profits or gains etc.
Relief	Something which postpones or reduces the charge to tax.
Remittance	Bringing profits or gains into the UK. Persons not domiciled in the UK are taxed on foreign source profits or gains etc. on a remittance basis, i.e., on what is received or treated as received in the UK. This can have an extended meaning; see ss. 65, 740(5), TA and s. 12, TCGA.

Roll-over	Reduction in acquisition cost of new asset – tax charge deferred.
Settlement	See s. 660G, TA inserted by sch. 17, FA 1995, Lord Wilberforce's speech in *Roome* v *Edwards* [1982] AC 279 discussed in Chapter 24 and s. 43(2), IHTA.
Shares	A share or proportion of the capital of a company, entitling the holder to a share in the profits of the company. Shares may be of different classes.
Tax Acts	By s. 831(2), TA, the TA and all the other provisions of the Income Tax Acts and the Corporation Tax Acts.
Withholding	Deduction at source (qv).

Abbreviations

AC	Appeal Cases
ACT	Advance Corporation Tax
All ER	All England Law Reports
BTC	British Tax Cases
BTR	British Tax Review
CA	Companies Act 1985
CAA	Capital Allowances Act 1990
CGT	Capital Gains Tax
Ch D	Chancery Division
CLJ	Cambridge Law Journal
ESC	Extra-statutory Concession
FA	Finance Act
FRED	Financial Reporting Exposure Draft
FRS	Financial Reporting Standard
HLR	Harvard Law Review
ICTA	Income and Corporation Taxes Act 1988 (also known as TA)
IHT	Inheritance Tax
IHTA	Inheritance Tax Act 1984
KCLJ	King's College Law Journal
LQR	Law Quarterly Review
LSG	Law Society's Gazette
MCT	Mainstream Corporation Tax
MLR	Modern Law Review
OTPR	Offshore Tax Planning Review
PCTA	Provisional Collection of Taxes Act 1968 (as amended)
PTPR	Personal Tax Planning Review
RSC	Rules of the Supreme Court
SJ	Solicitors Journal

SP	Statement of Practice
SSAP	Statement of Standard Accounting Practice
STC	Simon's Tax Cases
STI	Simon's Tax Intelligence
STP	Strategic Tax Planning
TA	Income and Corporation Taxes Act 1988 (also known as ICTA)
TC	Reports of Tax Cases
TCGA	Taxation of Chargeable Gains Act 1992
TMA	Taxes Management Act 1970
VAT	Value Added Tax
VATA	Value Added Tax Act 1994

Table of Cases

A-G's Reference (No. 1 of 1988) [1989] 2 All ER 1   133
A-G v Prince Ernest Augustus of Hanover [1957] AC 436   52
A-G v Wilts United Dairies Limited (1921) 37 TLR 884   2, 23, 50
Abbott v Philbin (1960) 39 TC 82   172, 175
Aberdeen Construction Group Ltd v IRC [1978] STC 127;
    [1978] 1 All ER 962   460, 464, 473, 480, 494, 533, 667
Adams v Lindsell (1818) 1 B & Ald 681   573
Administration des Douanes v Gondrand Frères [1981] ECR 1931   49
Agip (Africa) Ltd v Jackson [1990] Ch 265   279
Aikin v Macdonald's Trustees 3 TC 306   405, 406
Albeko Scuhmaschinen v Kamborian (1961) 111 LJ 619   573
Alexander v IRC [1991] STC 112   698
Alexander Ward and Co. Ltd v Samyang Navigation Co. Ltd [1975] 2 All ER 424   557
Allan v IRC [1994] STC 943   186
Allen v Farquharson (1932) 17 TC 59   322, 330
Alloway v Phillips [1980] 3 All ER 138   450, 452
American Leaf Blending Co. Sdn Bhd v Director General of Inland Revenue
    [1978] STC 561; [1978] 3 All ER 1185   517, 658
Amministrazione delle Finanze dello Stato v Simmenthal SA [1978] ECR 629   63
Amministrazione delle Finanze dello Stato v Srl Meridionale Industria Salumi
    [1980] ECR 1237   49
Anderton v Lamb [1981] STC 43   519
Anklagemyndigheden v Hansen & Sons I/S (case 326/88) [1990] ECR I-2911   65
Anson v Hill (1968) 47 ATC 143   39
Aplin v White [1973] 2 All ER 637   398
Argent v Minister of Social Security [1968] 1 WLR 1749   163
Asher v London Film Productions [1944] 1 All ER 77   257
Aspin v Estill [1987] BTC 553   48
Associated London Properties v Henriksen (1944) 26 TC 46   134
Associated Newspapers Ltd v Fleming [1973] AC 628   327
Attorney-General v Black (1871) LR 6 Ex 308   449

Attorney General v Eyre [1909] 1 KB 733	159
Attorney-General v Farrell [1931] 1 KB 81	722
Attorney-General v Lancashire and Yorkshire Railway Co. (1864) 159 ER 527	155
Automatic Self-Cleansing Filter Syndicate Co. v Cuninghame [1906] 2 Ch 34	556
Ayrshire Pullman Motor Services v IRC (1929) 14 TC 754	78
Aveling Barford [1989] BCLC 122	615
Aveling Barford v Perion [1989] BCLC 626	92, 615
Baden (No. 2), Re [1973] Ch 9	214
Baker v Archer Shee [1927] AC 844	402, 403, 742
Ball v Johnson (1971) 47 TC 155	196
Ball v National and Grindlays Bank Ltd [1973] Ch 127	580
Bamford v ATA Advertising (1972) 48 TC 359	330
Barclays Bank v Naylor (1960) 39 TC 256	182
Barker (Christopher) & Sons v IRC [1919] 2 KB 222	257
Barnes, Re [1939] 1 KB 316	699
Barron v Potter [1914] 1 Ch 895	557
Barry v Cordy (1946) 28 TC 250	260
Batey v Wakefield [1981] STC 521	506
Bayley v Rogers [1980] STC 544	462
Baylis v Gregory [1988] 3 All ER 495, HL	87, 88
Baytrust Holdings Ltd v IRC [1971] 3 All ER 76	660
Beak v Robson [1943] AC 352	205
Bean v Doncaster Amalgamated Collieries Ltd (1944) 27 TC 296	461
Becker, Re [1982] 1 CMLR 499	14
Beecham Group Ltd v Fair [1984] STC 15	161
Ben-Odeco Ltd v Powlson [1978] 2 All ER 1111	353
Bennett & others v IRC [1995] STC 54	692
Bennett v Ogston (1930) 15 TC 374	377, 379
Benson v Yard Arm Club Ltd [1979] 2 All ER 336	351
Bentley v Pike [1981] STC 360	482, 751
Bentleys, Stokes and Lowless v Beeson (1952) 33 TC 491	314, 326
Berry v Warnett [1982] STC 396	462, 471
Bhadra v Ellam [1988] STC 239	257
Bird v IRC [1985] STC 584	118, 123
Bird v Martland [1982] STC 603	183
Bispham v Eardiston Farming Co. (1919) Ltd (1962) 40 TC 322	260
Black Nominees v Nicol (1975) 50 TC 229; [1975] STC 372	80, 82, 167
Blackburn v Close Bros Ltd (1960) 39 TC 164	160
Blackpool Marton Rotary Club v Martin [1988] STC 823	555
Blackwell v Mills (1945) 26 TC 468	250
Bolton v International Drilling Co. Ltd [1983] STC 70	353
Bond v Pickford [1983] STC 517	540
Booth v Ellard [1980] STC 555	532, 534
Bourne v Norwich Crematorium Ltd [1967] 2 All ER 576	58, 346
Bowles v Bank of England [1913] 1 Ch 57	25, 32, 50
Brady v Hart [1985] STC 498	166
Bray v Best [1989] STC 159	137, 173
Bray v Best [1986] STC 96	184
Bridge House (Reigate Hill) Ltd v Hinder (1971) 47 TC 182	350
Bridges v Hewitt [1957] 2 All ER 281	195

Table of Cases

Brinkibon v Stahag Stahl [1982] 1 All ER 293	573
Bristow v William Dickinson & Co. Ltd (1946) 27 TC 157	328
Britannia Airways Ltd v Johnson [1994] STC 763	1
British Insulated and Helsby Cables Ltd v Atherton [1926] AC 205	315, 316
British Transport Commission v Gourley [1956] AC 185	465
Brockbank, Re [1948] Ch 206	531
Brocklesby v Merricks (1934) 18 TC 576	451
Brodie's Trustees v IRC (1933) 17 TC 432	407, 412
Brooklands Selangor Holdings Ltd. v IRC [1970] 2 All ER 76	659
Brown v Bullock (1961) 40 TC 1	249
Brown v Burnley Football and Athletic Co. Ltd [1980] 3 All ER 244	351
Brumby v Milner [1976] 3 All ER 636	185, 187
Brunnton v Commissioner for Stamp Duty (NSW) [1913] AC 747	59
BSC Footwear v Ridgway (1971) 47 TC 495	294
Buckingham v Securities Properties Ltd [1990] STC 166	346
Bull v Bull [1955] 1 QB 234	220
Bulmer v IRC [1967] Ch 145	415
Bunbury v Fuller (1853) 9 Exch 111	39
Burmah Steamship v IRC 16 TC 67	293
Burman v Hedges & Butler Ltd [1979] STC 136	626
Burston v IRC (1946) 28 TC 123	39
Butler v Wildin [1989] STC 22	417
Bye v Coren [1986] STC 393	488
C & E v P & O [1992] STC 809	46
C & E v Peachtree [1994] STC 747	41
Cairns v MacDiarmid [1983] STC 178	80, 378, 384
Calcutta Jute Mills v Nicholson (1876) 1 Ex D 428	557
Calvert v Wainwright (1947) 27 TC 475	191
Cameron v Prendergast (1940) 23 TC 122	199
Campbell v IRC (1968) 45 TC 247; [1970] AC 77	372, 374
Canada Safeway v IRC [1972] 1 All ER 666	651
Canadian Eagle Oil Co. Ltd v R [1946] AC 119	361
Capcount Trading v Evans [1993] STC 11	38, 482, 751
Cape Brandy Syndicate v IRC [1921] 1 KB 64	54
Cape Brandy Syndicate v IRC (1927) 12 TC 358	271
Capital and National Trust v Golder [1949] 2 All ER 956; (1949) 31 TC 265	577, 612
Carlisle and Silloth Golf Club v Smith (1913) 6 TC 48	281
Carmouche v Hearn 25 TC 425	195
Carr v IRC [1944] 2 All ER 163	255, 256, 257
Carr v Sayer [1992] STC 396	346
Carson v Cheyney's Executor (1958) 38 TC 240	302
Carter v Sharon [1936] 1 All ER 720	745
Carver v Duncan [1985] STC 356	406
Case of Ship Money (1637) 3 St. Tr. 825	23, 53
Case of Sutton's Hospital (1612) 10 Co Rep 1a	550
Cecil v IRC (1919) 36 TLR 164	257
Challenge Corporation [1986] STC 476	94
Chamberlain v IRC [1943] 2 All ER 200	415
Chaney v Watkis [1986] STC 89	492

Chapman, A.W. Ltd v Hennessey [1982] STC 214	633
Chick v Stamp Duty Commissioner [1958] AC 435	686
China Navigation Co v A-G [1932] 2 KB 197	2
Chinn v Collins [1981] 1 All ER 189	82, 416
Cie Continentale France v EC Council [1975] ECR 117	49
City Permanent Building Society v Miller [1952] Ch 840	438
Clark v IRC [1979] 1 All ER 385	128
Clarke v United Real (Moorgate) Ltd [1988] STC 273	437
Clayton v Gothorp (1971) 47 TC 168	196
Clayton v Lavender (1965) 42 TC 607	203
Cleary v IRC [1968] AC 766	125
Cleveley's Investment Trust Co. v IRC (1971) 47 TC 300	473
Cleveleys Investment Trust Co. v IRC (No. 2) 51 TC 26	490
Coates v Arndale Properties Ltd [1984] STC 637	87, 486, 639
Cochrane v IRC [1974] STC 335	529
Colquhoun v Brooks (1889) 2 TC 490, 14 App Cas 493; (1887) 19 QBD 490	14, 59, 255, 742
Commission v Greece (case 68/88) [1989] ECR 2965	65
Commissioner of Inland Revenue (New Zealand) v Challenge Corporation Ltd [1986] STC 548	76
Commissioners of Customs & Excise v APS Samex [1983] 1 All ER 1042	65
Commissioners of Customs & Excise v Top Ten [1969] 3 All ER 39	52, 60
Commissioners of Inland Revenue v Morris (1967) 44 TC 685	189
Committee of Directors of Polytechnics v C&E [1992] STC 873	255
Congreve v IRC [1948] 1 All ER 948	753
Conservative and Unionist Central Office v Burrell [1982] 2 All ER 1	554
Conservative Central Office v Burrell [1980] STC 400	689
Conservators of Epping Forest v IRC (1953) 34 TC 293	370
Cooke v Blacklaws [1985] STC 1	167
Cooksey and Bibbey v Rednall (1949) 30 TC 514	273
Cooper v Blakiston 5 TC 347	192
Cooper v Cadwalader (1904) 5 TC 101	17
Copeman v William Flood & Sons Ltd (1940) 24 TC 53	325
Corbett v IRC (1937) 21 TC 449; [1938] 1 KB 567	408, 424
Cordy v Gordon (1925) 9 TC 304	171
Coren v Keighley (1972) 48 TC 370	460
Cotman v Brougham [1918] AC 514	659
Council of Civil Service Unions v Minister of State for the Civil Service [1985] AC 374; [1984] 3 All ER 935	45, 190
Countess Fitzwilliam v IRC [1993] STC 502	94, 102
Cowan v Seymour 7 TC 372	195
Crane-Fruehauf Ltd v IRC [1975] 1 All ER 429	663
Craven v White [1987] 3 All ER 27; [1988] STC 476	56, 77, 87, 102
Croft v Sywell Aerodrome Ltd (1941) 24 TC 126	260
Crofters v Veitch [1942] AC 435	666
Crossland v Hawkins [1961] Ch 537	417
Crowe v Appleby [1975] STC 502	532, 533, 544
Cull v Cowcher (1934) 18 TC 449	137
Cunard's Trustees v IRC [1946] 1 All ER 159	407, 412
Currie v IRC (1944) 12 TC 245	255
Curtis v Oldfield (1925) 9 TC 319	322, 330

Table of Cases xxix

Customs and Excise Commissioners v Apple and Pear Development Council
  [1986] STC 193   65
Customs and Excise Commrs v Apple and Pear Development Council
  [1988] STC 221, ECJ   481
Customs and Excise v Thorn Electrical Industries Ltd [1975] STC 617   60

d'Abreu v IRC [1978] STC 538   415
Dale v IRC (1954) 34 TC 468   159, 161
Daphne v Shaw (1926) 11 TC 256   352
Davenport v Chilver [1983] STC 426   464
Davies v Braithwaite (1931) 18 TC 198; [1931] 2 KB 628   162, 256, 257
Davis v Powell [1977] 1 All ER 471   464
Daw v IRC (1928) 14 TC 58   425
Dawson v IRC [1988] STC 684; [1989] STC 473, HL   403, 405, 752
De Beers Consolidated Mines Ltd v Howe [1906] AC 455   550, 556
Dewar v IRC (1935) 19 TC 561   424
Dickinson v Abel [1969] 1 All ER 484; (1969) 45 TC 353   137, 148, 450
Dinshaw v Bombay Commissioner of Income Tax (1934) 13 ATC 284   329
Ditchfield v Sharp [1983] STC 590   380
Dixon v Fitch's Garage Ltd [1975] 3 All ER 455   351
Donald Fisher (Ealing) Ltd v Spencer [1989] STC 256   289
Dougal, Re [1981] STC 514   715
Doughty, Re [1947] Ch 263   592
Dracup v Radcliffe (1946) 27 TC 188   172
Drummond v Austin Brown [1984] STC 321   464, 465
Drummond v Collins [1915] AC 1011   370, 411
Duke v GEC Reliance Ltd [1988] 1 All ER 626   64
Dunmore v McGowan [1978] STC 217; [1978] 2 All ER 85, CA   381, 398, 743
Dunstan v Young, Austen and Young [1989] STC 69   648
Duple Motor Bodies v Ostime (1961) 39 TC 537   296
Durant v IRC (1921) 12 TC 245   257
Durrant v IRC (1995) Sp C 24   512

Earl Howe v IRC (1919) 7 TC 289; [1919] 2 KB 336   370, 371
Eastham v Leigh London and Provincial Properties Ltd [1971] Ch 871;
  [1971] 1 All ER   275, 476
Eckel v Board of Inland Revenue [1989] STC 305   275
Edwards v Bairstow [1956] AC 14; 36 TC 207   38, 46, 251, 259, 263, 342
Edwards v Clinch (1981) 56 TC 367   159
Egyptian Delta Land and Investment Co. Ltd v Todd [1929] AC 1   557
Ellis v BP Oil Northern Ireland Refinery Ltd [1985] STC 722   577
Ellis v Lucas (1966) 43 TC 276   159, 161
Elson v Price's Tailors (1962) 40 TC 671   298
Elwood v Utitz (1965) 42 TC 482   249, 252
Emery v IRC [1981] STC 150   122
Emmerson v Computer Time International Ltd [1977] 2 All ER 545   491, 494
English & Scottish Joint Co-operative Wholesale Society Ltd v
  Assam Agricultural Income Tax Commissioner [1948] 2 All ER 395   281
English Crown Spelter Co. Ltd v Baker (1908) 5 TC 327   322
English v Dedham Vale Properties Ltd [1978] 1 All ER 382   279
Ensign Tankers (Leasing) Ltd v Stokes [1992] STC 226   71, 91, 94, 277, 353

Eilbeck v Rawling [1981] 1 All ER 865	81
Entores Ltd v Miles Far East Corporation [1955] 2 QB 327	573
Erichsen v Last (1881) 8 QBD 414	259, 263
Erwin Behn v Hauptzollamt Itzehoe [1990] ECRI-2659.	64
Escritt & Barrell v IRC (1947) 26 ATC 33	257
Essex County Council v Ellam [1988] STC 370	372
Euro Hotel (Belgravia) Ltd, Re [1975] 3 All ER 1075	376, 377
EVC International NV v Steele [1996] STC 785	562
FA & AB Ltd v Lupton [1972] AC 634; (1971) 47 TC 580	276, 277
Fairman v Perpetual Investment Building Society [1923] AC 74	26
Fall v Hitchen [1973] 1 WLR 286	162
Farmer v Bankers Trust International Ltd [1990] STC 564	628
Faulconbridge v National Employers' Mutual General Insurance Association Ltd (1952) 33 TC 103	281
Ferguson v IRC [1970] AC 442	395
Fergusson v Noble (1919) 7 TC 176	177
Fiagel v Fox [1990] STC 583	192
Fielder v Vedlynn [1992] STC 553	481
Finsbury Securities Ltd v Bishop (1966) 43 TC 591	276
Firestone Tyre Co. Ltd v Llewellin (1958) 37 TC 111	572
Fitzleet Estates Ltd v Cherry [1977] 3 All ER 996	391, 580
Fitzpatrick v IRC [1994] 1 All ER 673	250
Fitzwilliam v IRC [1993] STC 502	680, 721
Fleming v Bank of New Zealand [1900] AC 577	481
Fletcher v CIR for Jamaica [1972] AC 414	280, 282
Floor v Davis [1979] 2 All ER 677; (1979) 52 TC 609; [1978] STC 436	82, 462, 472
Foster v Foster [1916] 1 Ch 532	557
Foster v New Trinidad Asphalt Co. [1901] 1 Ch 208	592
Frampton and Another (Trustees of Worthing RFC) v IRC [1987] STC 273	555
Francovich v Italian Republic C 6/90 and C 9/90 [1991] ECR I-5357	14, 61
Friederich Binder GmbH v Hauptzollamt Bard Reichenhall [1989] ECR 2415	64
Frost v Feltham [1981] STC 115	389
Fry & Shiels Trustees 6 TC 583	405
Fry v Salisbury House Estate (1930) 15 TC 266	139
Fuge v McClelland (1956) 36 TC 571	165
Furniss v Dawson [1984] STC 153	77, 85, 95, 102, 630, 650
Gallagher v Jones [1993] STC 537	1, 26, 30, 288
Gallic Leasing Ltd v Coburn [1992] 1 All ER 336	633
Garforth v Newsmith Stainless Ltd [1979] 2 All ER 73	172
Garland v Archer Shee [1931] AC 212	404
Gartside v IRC [1968] AC 553	543, 723
Gasque v IRC [1940] 2 KB 80	556
George Attenborough & Son v Solomon [1913] AC 76	425
Gillott and Watts v Kalhoun (1884) 2 TC 76	436, 440
Glantre Engineering v Goodhand [1983] STC 1	198
Glass v IRC [1915] SC 449	698
Glenboig Union Fireclay Co. Ltd, The v IRC (1921) 12 TC 427	290, 293
Gloucester Schomaster's Case, The (1410) YB Hil 11 Hen IV, 47, pl. 21	71

Table of Cases

Gold Coast Selection Trust Ltd v Humphrey [1948] AC 459	286
Golden Horse Shoe (New) Ltd v Thurgood 18 TC 280	297
Golding v Kaufman [1985] STC 152	475
Gordon & Blair Ltd v IRC (1962) 40 TC 358	342, 344, 609
Gordon v IRC [1991] STC 174	517
Graham v Arnott (1941) 24 TC 157	258
Graham v Green (1925) 9 TC 309	258
Grainger v Gough [1896] AC 325	571
Grant v United Kingdom Switchback Railways (1888) 40 Ch D 135	557
Gray v Seymours Garden Centre [1995] BTC 320	351
Great Western Railway v Bater (1922) 8 TC 231	155
Greenberg v IRC [1972] AC 109	115
Gregory v Hill (1912) 6 TC 39	370
Grey v Tiley (1932) 16 TC 414	451
Griffin v Craig-Harvey [1993] STC 54	508
Griffiths v Harrison [1963] AC 1	259, 276, 277
Griffiths v Jackson [1983] STC 184	261
Griffiths v Mockler (1953) 35 TC 135	252
Grosvenor Place Estates Ltd v Roberts [1961] Ch 148	394
Grove v YMCA (1903) 4 TC 613	264, 274
Hall v Lorimer [1993] STC 23; [1992] STC 599	162, 164, 168
Halliburton Services BV v Staatssecretaris van Financien [1994] STC 655	565
Hamblett v Godfrey [1987] 1 All ER 916; [1987] STC 60	184, 190
Hampton v Fortes Autogrill Ltd [1980] STC 80	351
Hanbury, Re (1939) 38 TC 588 CA	374
Harmel v Wright [1974] STC 88	744
Harrison, Re [1956] AC 14	342
Harrison v Nairn Williamson [1978] 1 All ER 608; [1978] STC 67	80, 480
Harry Ferguson Motors Ltd v IRC (1951) 33 TC 15	288
Hart v Briscoe [1978] 1 All ER 791	539
Harthan v Mason [1980] STC 94	545
Hartland v Diggines (1926) 10 TC 247	182
Hatch, Re [1919] 1 Ch 351	393
Hatton v IRC [1992] STC 140	722
Hawkins, Re [1972] 3 All ER 386	377
Hawks v McArthur [1951] 1 All ER 22	618
Heasman v Jordan [1954] Ch 744	172
Heather v P-E Consulting Group [1973] Ch 189; (1972) 48 TC 293	26, 30, 580
Heaton v Bell (1967) 46 TC 11	171, 178, 211
Hellenic & General Trust Limited, Re [1975] 3 All ER 382	651
Helvering v Gregory 69F (2d) 809 (2nd Cir. 1934), affd 293 US 465 (1935)	72, 79
Henley v Foster 16 TC 605	202
Henley v Murray (1950) 31 TC 351	202, 203
Herbert v McQuade 4 TC 489	192
Heydon's Case (1584) 3 Co Rep 7a	55
Higgs v Olivier [1952] Ch 311	289
Hinton v Maden and Ireland Ltd [1959] 3 All ER 356	350
HK, Re [1967] 2 QB 617	48
Hoare Trustees v Gardner [1978] 1 All ER 791	539

Hobbs v Hussey [1942] 1 KB 491   449
Hochstrasser v Mayes (1959) 38 TC 673; [1958] 1 All ER 369   185, 227
Hoechst Finance Ltd v Gumbrell [1983] STC 150, CA   577
Hofmann v Wadman (1946) 27 TC 192   202
Holland v Geoghegan (1972) 48 TC 482   184, 190
Holland v Hodgson (1872) LR 7 CP 328   354
Honour v Norris [1992] STC 304   507
Hood-Barrs v IRC [1946] 2 All ER 768   414, 415
Horne, Re [1905] 1 Ch 76   408
Housden v Marshall [1958] 3 All ER 639   450
Howells v IRC [1939] 2 KB 597   385
Hudson's Bay Company v Stevens (1909) 5 TC 424   271
Hudson v Kirkness (1955) 36 TC 28   60
Hughes v Viner [1985] STC 235   389
Humbles v Brooks (1962) 40 TC 500   250
Hunter v Dewhurst (1932) 16 TC 605   199
Hunter v Moss [1994] 1 WLR 452   536

ICI v Colmer [1996] STC 352   617
Ingle v Farrand [1927] AC 417   158
Ingram & another v IRC [1995] 4 All ER 334   686
Institute of Patent Agents v Lockwood [1899] AC 347   2
IRC (New Zealand) v Challenge Corporation [1986] STC 548   754
IRC v Aken [1988] STC 69, [1990] STC 497, CA   43, 279
IRC v Alexander von Glehn (1920) 12 TC 232   328
IRC v Anderstrom (1927) 13 TC 482   399
IRC v Barclay Curle and Co. Ltd [1969] 1 All ER 732   350
IRC v Berrill [1982] 1 All ER 867   406
IRC v Biggar [1982] STC 677   289
IRC v Blackwell [1921] 1 KB 389   408
IRC v Bowater Property Developments Ltd [1985] STC 783   87
IRC v Brackett [1986] STC 521   754
IRC v Brander and Cruickshank (1971) 46 TC 474   140, 159, 160
IRC v Brebner [1967] 2 AC 18   129
IRC v Buchanan [1958] Ch 289; [1957] 2 All ER 400   415, 680
IRC v Burmah Oil Co. Limited [1982] STC 30; [1981] STC 174   77, 83, 649
IRC v Chubb's Trustee (1971) 47 TC 353   491
IRC v Church Commissioners (1976) 50 TC 516; [1975] STC 546   368, 375
IRC v City of Glasgow Police Athletic Association [1953] 1 All ER 747;
   (1953) 34 TC 76   13, 59, 438
IRC v Clay [1914] 3 KB 466   698
IRC v Cleary (1967) 44 TC 399   114
IRC v Cock, Russell (1949) 29 TC 387   294, 295
IRC v Countess Longford, Pakenham and others (1928) 13 TC 573   405, 423
IRC v Crawley [1987] STC 147   381
IRC v Crossman [1937] AC 26   698
IRC v Europa Oil (NZ) Limited [1971] AC 760   83
IRC v Fraser (1942) 24 TC 498   267, 276
IRC v Frere [1965] AC 402   142, 364
IRC v Garvin [1981] STC 344; [1980] STC 295   117, 118, 121, 125, 488
IRC v Goodwin [1976] 1 All ER 481, HL   128

Table of Cases   xxxiii

IRC v Gordon [1952] 1 All ER 866	744
IRC v Hamilton (1931) 16 TC 213	382
IRC v Hamilton-Russell's Executors (1943) 25 TC 200	408, 409
IRC v Hawley (1927) 13 TC 327	424
IRC v Helical Bar [1972] AC 773	332
IRC v Henderson's Executors (1931) 16 TC 282	423
IRC v Hinchy [1960] AC 748; (1960) 38 TC 625	54, 58
IRC v Joiner [1975] 3 All ER 1050	26, 58, 115
IRC v Kleinwort Benson Ltd [1969] 2 Ch 221	120, 129
IRC v Land Securities Investment Trust Ltd (1969) 45 TC 495	375
IRC v Law (T W) Ltd (1950) 29 TC 467	714
IRC v Leiner (1964) 41 TC 589	415
IRC v Levy [1982] STC 442	416
IRC v Livingston (1926) 11 TC 538	270
IRC v Longmans Green & Co. Ltd (1932) 17 TC 272	59
IRC v Lord Rennell [1964] AC 173	693
IRC v Lysaght 13 [1928] TC 511	15
IRC v Mardon (1956) 36 TC 565	423, 424
IRC v Marine Steam Turbine (1920) 12 TC 171	517
IRC v Maxse (1919) 12 TC 41	255
IRC v McGuckian [1994] STC 888	76, 100
IRC v Miller [1987] STC 108	725
IRC v Mills [1974] STC 130	414, 417, 722
IRC v Montgomery [1975] 1 All ER 664; [1975] STC 182	463
IRC v Morris (1967) 44 TC 685	190
IRC v Morrison (1932) 17 TC 325	285
IRC v National Book League [1957] Ch 488	372
IRC v Nuttall [1990] STC 194	46
IRC v Parker [1966] AC 141; (1963) 43 TC 396	115, 116, 125
IRC v Pilkington (1941) 24 TC 160	425
IRC v Plummer [1979] 3 All ER 775	80, 391, 415
IRC v Priestley [1901] AC 208	59
IRC v Reid (1949) 30 TC 431	592
IRC v Reinhold (1953) 34 TC 389	263, 266, 273, 449, 454
IRC v Richard's Executors (1971) 46 TC 626	490
IRC v Rogers (1979) 1 TC 255	18
IRC v Saxone, Lilley and Skinner (Holdings) Ltd [1967] 1 All ER 756	346
IRC v Scottish & Newcastle Breweries Ltd [1982] 2 All ER 230	351
IRC v Slater (Helen) Charitable Trust Ltd [1981] STC 471, CA	501
IRC v Stannard [1984] STC 245	714
IRC v Stenhouse's Trustees [1992] STC 103	698
IRC v Turnbull (1943) 29 TC 133	165
IRC v Wachtel [1971] Ch 573	414
IRC v Whitworth Park Coal Co. Ltd (1957) 38 TC 531	369, 411
IRC v Wiggins [1979] 2 All ER 245	116
IRC v Willoughby [1995] STC 143	753, 754
IRC v Wilson's Executors (1934) 18 TC 465	433
Irving v Tesco Stores (Holdings) Ltd [1982] STC 881	632
Iswera v IRC [1965] 1 WLR 663	274, 454
J. P. Harrison (Watford) Ltd v Griffiths (1963) 40 TC 281	259, 279

Table of Cases

Jacgilden (Weston Hall) Ltd v Castle [1969] 3 All ER 1110	309
Jackson v Laskers Home Furnishers Ltd. (1956) 37 TC 69	490
Jackson's Trustees v IRC (1942) 25 TC 13	412
Jarrold v Boustead [1964] 3 All ER 76; (1964) 41 TC 701	198, 206, 467
Jarrold v John Good and Sons Ltd [1963] 1 All ER 141	350
Jay's The Jewellers Ltd v IRC (1947) 29 TC 274	299
Jeffs v Rington [1985] STC 809	320
Jenkins v Brown [1989] STC 577	532
Jenkins v Horn [1979] 2 All ER 1141	170
Johnson v Britannia Airways [1994] STC 763	26, 30, 284
Johnson v Jewitt (1961) 40 TC 231	75
Johnston v Heath [1970] 3 All ER 915; (1970) 46 TC 463	260, 263, 267, 276
Jones, Re [1933] Ch 842	396
Jones v Leeming [1930] AC 415	449
Keble v Hickeringill (1705) 11 East 574	71
Kelly v Rodgers 19 TC 692	403
Kelsall Parsons v IRC (1938) 21 TC 608	292, 293
Kenmir v Frizzell [1968] 1 WLR 329	518
Kidner, Re [1929] 2 Ch 121	684
Kidson v Macdonald [1974] Ch 339	534
Kildrummy (Jersey) Ltd v IRC [1990] STC 657	686
Kirby v Thorn EMI plc [1986] 1 WLR 851	467
Kirkham v Williams [1989] STC 333	272, 275
Kodak Limited v Clarke (1903) 4 TC 549	557
Kneen v Martin 19 TC 33	751
Lady Foley v Fletcher (1858) 3 H & N 769, 157 ER 678	368
Lagunas Nitrate Co. Ltd v Schroeder and Co. (1901) 85 LT 22	684
Laidler v Perry (1963) 42 TC 351	179, 187
Lake v Lake [1989] STC 865	718
Lang v Rice [1984] STC 172	463
Langley v Appleby [1976] 3 All ER 391	219
Law Shipping v IRC (1924) 12 TC 621	318, 323, 490
Lawson v Johnson Matthey [1992] STC 466	6, 320
LCC v Attorney General [1901] AC 26; (1901) 4 TC 265	138, 382, 454
Le Cras v Perpetual Trustee Co. [1967] 3 All ER 915	58
Leach v Pogson (1962) 40 TC 585	270, 273
Lee Ting Sang v Cheung Chi-Keung [1990] 2 AC 374	164
Leeming v Jones (1929) 15 TC 333	260
Leigh v IRC [1928] 1 KB 73	381, 382, 743
Levene v IRC [1928] 13 TC 486	16
Lewis v Lady Rook [1992] STC 171	507
Lim Foo Yong v Comptroller-General [1986] STC 251	5
Lindsay v IRC (1964) 41 TC 661	165, 277
Lindus and Hortin v IRC 17 TC 442	370, 407, 408, 411
Litster v Forth Dry Dock Company Ltd [1989] 1 All ER 1134	66
Liverpool and London and Globe Insurance Company v Bennett (1913) 6 TC 327	140
Lomax v Newton (1953) 34 TC 558	240, 251
Lomax v Peter Dixon [1943] KB 671	379

Table of Cases

London and Thames Haven Oil Wharves v Attwooll (1967) 43 TC 491   293
Londonderry's Settlement, Re [1965] Ch 918   531
Lord Inglewood v IRC [1983] STC 133, CA   738
Lord Tollemache v IRC 11 TC 277   408
Loss v IRC [1945] 2 All ER 683   257
Lowe v J.W. Ashmore (1970) 46 TC 597   430
Lowless v Beeson [1952] 2 All ER 82   326
Lucy and Sunderland v Hunt [1961] 3 All ER 1062; (1961) 40 TC 132   273, 275
Luke v IRC [1963] AC 557   56
Lupton v Potts (1969) 45 TC 643   250
Lurcott v Wakely & Wheeler [1911] 1 KB 905   325
Lynall v IRC [1972] AC 680; (1971) 47 TC 375   698
Lyon v Pettigrew [1985] STC 369   471, 476, 698
Lysaght v Edwards (1876) 2 ChD. 449   476

Macaura v Northern Insurance [1925] AC 619   547
Macfarlane v IRC 14 TC 532   410
Machon v McLoughlin (1926) 11 TC 83   171
Maclaine v Eccott (1926) 10 TC 481   572
Macpherson v IRC [1988] STC 362, HL   728
MacPherson v Bond [1985] STC 678   381, 743
Magnavox v Hall [1986] STC 561   87
Mairs v Haughey [1993] STC 569   184, 185
Makins v Elson [1977] STC 46   508
Mallalieu v Drummond [1983] STC 665   316, 322
Mangin v IRC [1971] AC 739   59
Mann v Nash [1932] 1 KB 752, 16 TC 523   278
Mannion v Johnston [1988] STC 758   511
Market Investigations Limited v Minister of Social Security [1969] 2 QB 173   163, 169
Markey v Sanders [1987] STC 256   506
Marleasing SA v La Comercial Internacional de Alimentación SA (case 106/89) [1990] ECR I–4135   64
Marshall v Kerr [1994] STC 638   527, 529
Marren v Ingles [1980] STC 500   461, 463, 473
Marsden v IRC (1965) 42 TC 326   248
Marsh v IRC (1943) 29 TC 120   165
Marson v Marriage [1980] STC 177   463, 473
Marson v Morton [1986] STC 463   260, 269
Martin v Lowry (1926) 11 TC 297   265
Mason v Innes (1967) 44 TC 326   310
McClelland v Commissioner of Taxation [1971] 1 All ER 969   275
McGowan v Brown and Cousins [1977] 3 All ER 844   293
McGregor v Adcock [1977] STC 206   511
McGregor v Randall [1984] STC 223   184
McMenamin v Diggles [1991] STC 419   159
McMillan v Guest (1942) 24 TC 190   158, 161
Melluish v BMI (No. 3) Ltd [1995] 3 All ER 453; [1995] STC 964   354, 355
Methuen-Campbell v Walters [1979] QB 525   507
Midland Bank Trust Co. Ltd v Green (No 2) [1981] 1 All ER 153   698
Miesegaes v IRC (1957) 37 TC 493   19

Mitchell and Edon v Ross (1961) 40 TC 11	140, 161, 165
Mitchell v Noble (1927) 11 TC 372	325
Moodie v IRC [1993] STC 188	373, 415
Moore & Osborne v IRC [1984] STC 236	724
Moore v Griffiths (1972) 48 TC 338	195
Moore v Thompson [1986] STC 170	508
Moorhouse v Dooland [1955] Ch 284	194
Morgan v Tate & Lyle (1954) 35 TC 367	7, 311, 314
Moriarty v Evans Medica (1957) 37 TC 540	301
Morley v Tattersall (1938) 22 TC 51	299
Morrice v Aylmer (1874) 10 Ch App 148	591
Moss Empires Ltd v IRC [1937] AC 785	371
Muir v Muir [1943] AC 468	540
Munby v Furlong [1977] 2 All ER 953	352
Municipal Mutual Insurance v Hills (1932) 16 TC 430	280
Munro & others v Commissioner of Stamp Duties [1934] AC 61	686
Murphy v Ingram [1973] STC 309	26
Murray v IRC 11 TC 133	411
Musgrave, Re [1916] 2 Ch 417	408
National Bank of Greece S.A. v Westminster Bank Executor and Trustee Co. (Channel Islands) Ltd [1971] AC 945	742
National Provident Institution v Brown (1921) 8 TC 57	137
National Smokeless Fuels Limited v IRC [1986] 3 CMLR 227; [1986] STC 300	61, 66, 67
Neild v IRC (1948) 26 ATC 33	257
Newhill Compulsory Purchase Order, 1937, Re [1938] 2 All ER 163	508
Nicoll v Austin (1935) 19 TC 53	182
Nobes and Co. Ltd v IRC [1966] 1 All ER 30	391
Nolder v Walters (1930) 15 TC 180	251
Norman v Golder (1944) 26 TC 293	255
North British Railway v Scott [1923] AC	182
Northern Ireland Commissioner of Valuation v Fermanagh Protestant Board of Education [1969] 3 All ER 352	219
Norton v Frecker (1737) Atk 524	699
Nuclear Electric v Bradley [1996] STC 405	607
O'Brien v Benson's Hosiery (Holdings) Ltd [1979] 3 All ER 652	461
O'Reilly v Mackman [1983] 2 AC 237	43
O'Rourke v Binks [1992] STC 703	57, 59
Oakes v Commissioner of Stamp Duties [1954] AC 57, PC	722
Odeon Associated Cinemas v Jones (1971) 48 TC 257	324, 490
Oram v Johnson [1980] 2 All ER 1	492
Ormond Investment Co. Ltd v Betts (1928) 13 TC 400	60
Overseas Containers (Finance) Ltd v Stoker [1987] STC 547	632
Owen v Burden (1971) 47 TC 476	250
Owen v Southern Railway of Peru (1954) 36 TC 602	288
Page v Lowther [1983] STC 799; (1983) 57 TC 199; [1983] STC 61	61, 131, 134
Paradise Motor Co. Ltd, Re [1968] 2 All ER 625	730
Park (deceased) (No. 2), Re [1972] Ch 385	693

Table of Cases   xxxvii

Parkside Leasing v Smith [1985] STC 63	381, 382, 743
Partington v A-G (1869) LR 4 HL 100	54, 78
Partridge v Mallandine (1886) 2 TC 179	257
Passant v Jackson [1986] STC 164	493
Pearson v IRC [1980] STC 318	40, 724, 725
Pennine Raceway Ltd v Kirklees Metropolitan Council [1989] STC 122	465, 467
Pepper v Daffurn [1993] STC 466	511
Pepper v Hart [1992] STC 898	30, 31
Peracha v Miley [1990] STC 512	743
Perry v Astor (1935) 19 TC 255	130
Peter's Exors v IRC 24 TC 45	370
Pettit, Re [1922] 2 Ch 765	395
Pexton v Bell [1976] STC 301	533, 544
Pickford v Quirke (1927) 13 TC 251	269, 454
Pickstone v Freemans plc [1988] 3 All ER 803	66
Pigott v Staines Investment Co. Ltd [1995] STC 114	102
Pilkington Brothers Ltd v IRC [1982] STC 103	630, 634
Pilkington v Randall (1966) 42 TC 662	274
Pitt v Castle Hill Ltd [1974] 3 All ER 146	318
Plummer v IRC [1979] STC 793	373
Police Authority for Huddersfield v Watson [1947] KB 842	203
Pook v Owen (1968) 45 TC 571	175, 244
Potel v IRC [1971] 2 All ER 504; (1970) 46 TC 658	590, 684
Poulson v Welbeck Securities Ltd [1986] STC 423, CA	475
Poynting v Faulkner 5 TC 145	192
Practice Note [1970] 1 WLR 1400	26
Practice Note [1995] 3 All ER 256	26
Precision Dippings Ltd v Precision Dippings Marketing Ltd [1986] Ch 447	590
Prenn v Simmonds [1971] 1 WLR 1381	83
Prest v Bettinson [1980] STC 607	529
Preston v IRC [1985] STC 282, HL	127
Pritchard v Arundale (1972) 47 TC 680	196
Procter & Gamble Ltd v Taylerson [1990] STC 624	599
Property Holding Co. Ltd v Clark [1948] 1 All ER 165	441
Pryce v Monmouthshire Canal & Rly Co (1879) 4 App Cas 197	55
Purchase v Stainer's Executors (1951) 32 TC 367	137
R v Commissioners for the Special Purposes of the Income Tax Acts ex parte Napier [1988] 3 All ER 166	47
R v Commissioners of Customs & Excise ex parte Tattersalls [1988] STC 630	44
R v Department of Social Security ex parte Overdrive Credit Card Ltd [1991] STC 129	45
R v Epping and Harlow General Commissioners ex parte Goldstraw [1983] 3 All ER 257	47
R v Home Secretary ex parte Ruddock [1987] 2 All ER 518	42
R v Hunt [1994] STC 819	11
R v IRC ex parte Commerzbank [1991] STC 271	43
R v IRC ex parte Fulford-Dobson [1987] STC 344	29
R v IRC ex parte ICI (1987) 60 TC 1	43
R v IRC ex parte ICI (1990) 60 TC 1	61

R v IRC ex parte MFK [1990] STC 873	27
R v IRC ex parte National Federation of Self-Employed and Small Businesses Ltd [1981] STC 260	42, 46
R v IRC ex parte National Federation of the Self-Employed [1981] STC 260	44
R v IRC ex parte Preston [1985] STC 282	29, 47
R v IRC ex parte T C Coombs [1991] STC 97	43
R v Ryan [1994] STC 446	11
R v Secretary of State for Home Affairs ex parte Ruddock [1987] 2 All ER 518	48
R v Secretary of State for Transport ex parte Factortame [1990] 2 AC 85	14, 61
R v University of Cambridge (1723) 1 Str 557	48
Rae v Lazard Investment (1963) 41 TC 1	5
Rainer Drexel (case 299/86) [1988] ECR 1213	65
Ramsay (WT) v IRC [1982] AC 300; [1981] 1 All ER 865; [1979] STC 582	54, 75, 77, 80, 90, 94, 100, 102, 473, 667, 680
Randall v Plumb [1975] STC 191	487
Rank Xerox Ltd v Lane [1979] 3 All ER 657	504
Rankine v IRC (1952) 32 TC 520	302
Ransom v Higgs [1974] 3 All ER 949; (1970) 50 TC 1	73, 131, 134, 263, 398
Ratti [1979] ECR 1629	64
Ready Mixed Concrete (South East) Ltd v Minister of Pensions and National Insurance [1968] 2 QB 497	163
Reed v Clark [1985] STC 323	17
Reed v Nova Securities Ltd [1985] STC 124	87, 273, 486, 641
Reed v Seymour 11 TC 625	193
Reed v Young [1986] STC 285	92, 94
Reference Re Saskatchewan Farm Security Act 1944, Section 6 [1947] 3 DLR 689	377
Reid's Brewery v Male (1891) 3 TC 279	322
Reid's Trustees v IRC 14 TC 512	402
Reynolds v Ashby [1904] AC 466	354
Richardson v Jenkins [1995] STC 95	338
Ricketts v Colquhoun [1926] AC 1; (1925) 10 TC 118	243, 750
Ridge Securities v IRC [1964] 1 All ER 275; (1964) 44 TC 373	370, 485
Riley v Coglan (1967) 44 TC 481	198, 206
Ripon (Highfield) Housing Order 1938, Applications of White and Collins, Re [1939] 3 All ER 548	39
River Wear Commissioners v Adamson (1877) 2 App Cas 743	56
RMC v Minister of Pensions [1968] 2 QB 497	168
Rolfe v Wimpey Waste Management Ltd [1989] STC 454	320
Rolls Royce v Bamford (1976) 51 TC 319	342
Rolls Royce v Jeffrey (1962) 40 TC 443	301
Roome v Edwards [1981] 1 All ER 736	539
Rose, Re [1952] Ch 499	477
Rose and Co. (Wallpapers and Paints) Ltd v Campbell [1968] 1 All ER 405	350
Russell v IRC [1988] STC 195	718
Rutledge v IRC (1929) 14 TC 490	265
Ryall v Hoare [1923] 2 KB 447	449
Rye and Eyre v IRC 29 TC 164	385

Table of Cases   xxxix

Sainsbury (J) Plc v O'Connor [1991] STC 318, CA   477, 618
Salomon v Salomon & Co Ltd [1897] AC 22   547, 549
Sandeman, Re [1937] 1 All ER 368   532
Sansom v Peay [1976] 3 All ER 353   505, 537, 543
Sargent v Barnes [1978] 2 All ER 737   320
Sargent v Eayrs [1973] STC 50   313, 315
Saunders v Vautier (1841) Cr & Ph 240   404, 409, 531, 692
Schmidt v Secretary of State for Home Affairs [1969] 1 All ER 904   48
Schnieder v Mills [1993] STC 430   718
Scoble v Secretary of State for India [1903] 1 KB 494   374
Scorer v Olin Energy Systems Ltd [1984] STC 141   608
Scott v Ricketts [1967] 2 All ER 1009   448
Secretan v Hart [1969] 3 All ER 1196   455
Severn and Wye and Severn Bridge Railway, Re [1896] Ch 559   684
Sharkey v Wernher (1955) 36 TC 275   15, 255, 304, 485, 492
Shaw v Tonkin [1988] STC 186   381
Shell-Berre, Re [1964] CMLR 462   68
Shepherd v IRC [1995] STC 240   117
Shepherd v Lyntress [1989] STC 617   91, 666
Shilton v Wilmshurst [1991] STC 88   206
Shott v McIlgorm [1945] 1 All ER 391   250
Sidey v Phillips [1987] STC 87   166
Simmons v IRC [1980] STC 350   264, 272
Simpson v Tate (1925) 9 TC 314   250
Sinclair v Lee [1993] STI 844   596
Skinner, Re [1942] 1 All ER 32   461
Smith v Abbott [1994] 1 All ER 673; [1991] STC 661   240, 250
Smith, F.L. & Co. v Greenwood (1922) 8 TC 193   571, 572
Smith v Smith [1923] P 191   370
Smith v Stretton (1904) 5 TC 36   172
Snook v London & West Riding Investments Limited [1967] 1 All ER 518   75
South African Supply and Cold Storage Co. Ltd, Re [1904] 2 Ch 268   659, 663
Southern-Smith v Clancy [1941] 1 KB 276   368
Southern v AB (1933) 18 TC 59   278
Southern v Aldwych Property Trust Ltd (1940) 23 TC 707   434
Spens v IRC (1970) 46 TC 276   424
Spiro v Glencrown Properties Ltd [1991] 1 All ER 600   477
St Aubyn v AG [1952] AC 15   686
Stamp Duties Commissioner of New South Wales v Perpetual
   Trustee Co. Ltd [1943] AC 425   686
Stanley v IRC [1944] KB 255; (1944) 26 TC 12   409, 424
Stanton v Drayton Commercial Investment Co. Ltd [1982] STC 585, CA   482
Stephenson v Barclays Bank Trust Co. Ltd [1975] STC 151   531, 534, 539
Stevens v Tirard [1939] 4 All ER 186   416
Stevenson Jordan & Harrison v MacDonald & Evans [1952] 1 TLR 101   163
Stevenson v Wishart [1987] STC 266, CA   407
Stokes v Bennett [1953] Ch 566   399
Stokes v Costain Property Investments Ltd [1984] STC 204   354
Strange v Openshaw [1983] STC 416   475, 485
Street v Mountford [1985] AC 809   430
Strong & Co. v Woodifield (1906) 5 TC 215   313, 314, 316

Strong, Re (1878) 1 TC 207	192
Stubart Investments Ltd v R [1984] CTC 294	73
Styles v Treasurer of Middle Temple (1895) 4 TC 123	53
Sugarwhite v Budd [1988] STC 533 (affirmed [1987] STC 491)	133, 134
Sun Life v Davidson (1958) 37 TC 330	612
Swedish Central Railways v Thompson [1925] AC 495	558
Swithland v IRC [1990] STC 448	659, 664
Taylor v Good [1974] STC 148	271, 273
Taylor v Provan [1974] 1 All ER 1201, 49 TC 579	246
Taylor v Taylor [1938] 1 KB 320	393
Temperley v Visibell Ltd [1974] STC 64	522
Tennant v Smith [1892] AC 150; (1892) 3 TC 158	54, 174
Thomas v Marshall [1953] AC 543	415
Thomas v Reynolds [1987] STC 135	351
Thompson v Magnesium Electron Ltd (1943) 26 TC 1	290
Thompson v Salah (1971) 47 TC 559	476
Thomson v Gurneville Securities [1972] AC 661; (1969) 47 TC 633	111, 276
Thomson v Moyse [1961] AC 967	745
Tilcon Ltd v Holland [1981] STC 365	617, 618
Ting Sang v Chung Chi-Keung [1990] 2 AC 374	169
Todd v Mudd [1987] STC 141	523
Tomadini [1979] ECR 1801	49
Tomlinson v Glyn's Settlement and Trustee Co. [1970] Ch 112	533, 539
Torbell Investments Ltd v Williams [1986] STC 397	341
Trustees of Earl Haig v IRC (1939) 22 TC 725	450
Tucker v Granada [1979] 2 All ER 801	318
Turner v Cuxson (1838) 27 TC 422	192
Turner v Follet [1973] STC 148	484
Turner v Last (1965) 42 TC 517	268
Tynewydd Labour WMC and Institute v Customs and Excise Commissioners [1979] STC 570	41
Tyrer v Smart [1979] 1 All ER 321; [1976] STC 521	175, 188
Union Corporation Ltd v IRC [1953] AC 482; [1952] 1 All ER 646	555, 557
Unit Construction Co. Ltd v Bullock [1960] AC 351	557, 558
Universities Superannuation Scheme Ltd v IRC [1995] STI 577	117
Ursula Becker [1982] ECR 53	64
Usher's Wiltshire Brewer Ltd v Bruce [1915] AC 433	311
Utica National City Bank v Gunn (1980) 118 N.E. 607	83
Vagliano v Bank of England [1891] AC 107	26
Van Arkadie v Sterling Coated Materials Ltd [1983] STC 95	353
Van Den Berghs Ltd v Clark (1935) 19 TC 390	154, 291, 293
Van Gend en Loos [1963] ECR 1	63
Vandervell v IRC [1967] 2 AC 91	70
Varty v Lynes [1976] 3 All ER 447	508
Vertigan v Brady [1988] STC 91	221
Vestey v IRC [1980] STC 10	29, 212, 228, 753
Vestey v IRC (No 2) [1978] STC 567	28
Vibroplant Ltd v Holland [1982] STC 164	345

Table of Cases

Vodaphone Cellular Ltd v Shaw [1995] STC 353 — 7
Von Colson and Kamann v Land Nordrhein-Westfaler (case 14/83) [1984] ECR 1891 — 64

Wahl v IRC (1933) 17 TC 744 — 425
Wales v Tilley 25 TC 136 — 201
Walker's Settlement, Re [1935] Ch 567 — 664
Walker v Carnaby [1970] 1 All ER 502; (1970) 46 TC 561; [1970] 1 WLR 276 — 159, 160, 161, 289
Walls v Sinnett [1987] STC 236 — 165
Walsh v Lonsdale (1882) 21 Ch D 9 — 430
Ward v Anglo-American Oil Co. Ltd (1934) 19 TC 94 — 384
Watkins v Ashford, Sparkes and Harward [1985] STC 451 — 315
Watton v Tippett [1996] STC 101 — 520
Webb v Conelee Properties Ltd [1982] STC 913 — 260, 261
Webster v IRC [1942] 2 All ER 517 — 257
Weight v Salmon (1935) 19 TC 174 — 177
Welbeck Securities v Poulson [1987] STC 468 — 462
Wells, Re [1940] Ch 411 — 395
West v Phillips (1958) 38 TC 203 — 271
Westminster Bank Exors & Trustee Co. (Channel Islands) Ltd v National Bank of Greece (1970) 46 TC 472 — 371, 377
Weston v Hearn and Carmouche v Hearn 25 TC 425 — 195
Whelan v Dover Harbour Board (1934) 18 TC 55 — 490
Whimster & Co. v IRC (1925) 12 TC 813 — 294
White v Carline (1995) Sp C 33 — 460
Whitney v IRC [1926] AC 37; (1925) 10 TC 88 — 33, 60
Whittles v Uniholdings Ltd [1996] STC 914 — 98
Whitworth Park Coal Co. Ltd v IRC [1961] AC 31 — 381, 451, 743
Wicks v Firth [1983] STC 25 — 238
Wilcock v Eves [1995] STC 18 — 191
Wilkins v Rogerson [1961] 1 Ch. 133; [1961] 1 All ER 358; (1960) 39 TC 44 — 177, 212, 223
William Esplen Son and Swainston Ltd v IRC [1919] 2 KB 731 — 574
Williams v Bullivant [1983] STC 107 — 470
Williams v Davis (1954) 26 TC 371 — 276
Williams v IRC [1980] 3 All ER 321; (1980) 54 TC 257 — 115, 125
Williams v Merrylees [1987] STC 445 — 506
Williams v Singer [1921] 1 AC 65 — 402, 742
Willingale v International Commercial Bank Ltd [1978] 1 All ER 754 — 286, 288
Willingale v Islington Green Investment Co. [1972] 3 All ER 849 — 578
Wimpey International Ltd v Warland [1989] STC 273 — 352
Wing v O'Connell [1927] IR 84 — 257
Wisdom v Chamberlain [1969] 1 All ER 332; (1969) 45 TC 92 — 263, 266, 274, 454
Wiseman v Borneman [1971] AC 297, HL — 127
Wood v Owen (1940) 23 TC 541 — 423
Wood Preservation v Prior [1969] 1 All ER 364 — 618
Woods v R. M. Mallen Engineering Ltd (1969) 45 TC 619 — 348
Woolwich v IRC [1992] STC 657 — 43
Wright v Boyce (1958) 38 TC 160 — 192

Yarmouth v France (1887) 19 QBD 647   349
Yates v Starkey [1951] Ch 465   416
Yoga Fruit Juices, Re [1969] CMLR 123   68
Young v Phillips [1984] STC 520   87
Yuill v Wilson [1980] STC 460   133

Zim Properties v Procter [1985] STC 90   461, 464, 466, 467, 468, 502

Table of Statutes

Administration of Justice
  (Miscellaneous Provisions) Act
  1938   44f
Agricultural Holdings Act   464, 466
Australian Acts Interpretation Act 1901
  55
  s.15AA   55

Bill of Rights 1689   24
  art.4   23, 50
Bills of Exchange Act 1882   213

Canadian Interpretation Act 1967–68
  s.11   55f
Capital Allowances Act 1990   345,
  348, 577
  Part I   141
  Part II   141, 350f, 354
  Part III   141
  Part IV-VI   141, 360
  Part VII   360
  s.3(1)   347
  s.3(3)   348
  s.4(1)   349
  s.4(3)-(4)   349
  s.4(10)   349
  s.9   347, 577, 578
  s.9(1)   347
  s.10(1)(b)   348
  s.10(3)(a)   348
  s.10(4)-(5)   348

Capital Allowances Act 1990 –
  continued
  s.11   348
  s.11(6)   348f
  s.15   343
  s.18   345
  s.18(3)-(4)   346
  s.18(7)   347
  s.20(1)   347
  s.20(2)   347f
  s.20(3)   348
  s.21(1)   347
  s.24   577
  s.24(1)   349
  s.24(1)(a)-(b)   353
  s.24(2)   356
  s.24(2)(a)(ii)   356
  s.24(2)(b)   357
  s.24(5)   357
  s.26   356
  s.26(2)-(3)   356
  s.27   349
  s.28   613
  s.31(2)(a)   359
  s.33A   359
  s.33B   359
  s.34   358
  s.36(1)   358
  s.36(2)   358f
  s.37(2)   358
  s.37(3)(a)   359

Capital Allowances Act 1990 – *continued*
  s.37(4)-(5)   359
  s.38   358
  s.39(6)-(8)   359f
  s.42   356f, 359f
  s.51(1)-(2)   354f
  s.51(3)   355
  s.52   345
  s.52(1)   354
  s.52(2)   355
  s.53   354
  s.57(2)-(4)   355
  s.57(6)   355
  s.59   356
  s.60(1)(a)-(b)   359
  s.61(1)(a)   360
  s.67A   353f
  s.79   357
  s.80   358
  s.140(2)   347, 355
  s.140(4)   355f
  s.141   141
  s.141(2)-(3)   355
  s.144   577
  s.145   577, 602
  s.145(3)   629
  s.145A   577
  s.159(1)(a)   345f
  s.159(3)-(6)   357
  s.161   577
  s.161(2)   347
  s.528(2)   141
  s.532   141
  Sch.17   577
  Sch.AA1   352
Capital Transfer Tax Act 1984   24f, 674
Chargeable Gains Tax Act 1979   459f
Companies Act   75, 159, 671
Companies Act 1948   159f
  s.2(4)   651
  s.110   159f
Companies Act 1981   669
Companies Act 1985   653
  Part XXIII   571
  s.2(5)   651
  s.23   625
  s.121-s.122   591f
  s.162-s.181   596
  s.263   589

Companies Act 1985 – *continued*
  s.263(1)   589, 593
  s.263(2)   593
  s.263(2)(d)   595
  s.263(3)   589, 592f
  s.265-s.267   589
  s.276   589f
  s.277   590
  s.311   182f
  s.652   595
Companies Acts   554
Contracts (Applicable Law) Act 1990   573f
Corporation Tax Acts   240f, 552, 568, 570, 576, 589, 590
Customs and Excise Management Act 1979   24
Customs and Inland Revenue Act 1874
  s.9   38
Customs and Inland Revenue Act 1876   174
  s.8   174

Employment Agencies Act 1973   166f
Employment Protection (Consolidation) Act 1978   166f
European Communities Act 1972   23f
  s.2   61
  s.2(1)   61
  s.2(2)   61-2

Family Law Reform Act 1969
  s.1   409f
Finance Act 1918   155f
Finance Act 1922
  s.18   155
Finance Act 1927
  s.55   659
Finance Act 1936
  s.18   130
Finance Act 1948
  Part IV   224
  s.31(1)   431
  s.38-s.46   224
Finance Act 1951
  s.32   74f
Finance Act 1956
  s.10   155
Finance Act 1960   131
  s.21-s.26   131
  s.28   111, 114

Table of Statutes

Finance Act 1960 – *continued*
  s.37-s.38 204
  Sch.4 204
Finance Act 1962 131
Finance Act 1963 428, 436
Finance Act 1965 459f
Finance Act 1966
  s.25 176
Finance Act 1971 137
  s.29-s.31 167
  s.32 137, 365
  s.33-s.39 137
  Sch.5 167
Finance Act 1972 549
Finance Act 1974 168
Finance Act 1976 224
  s.60-s.68 224
  s.69 224, 226
  s.70-s.72 224
  s.91 172f
  Sch.7 224
  Sch.8 224
Finance Act 1977 155, 665
  s.33 219
  s.35 226
  s.40 665
Finance Act 1978
  s.23 226
  s.29 167
Finance Act 1980 653
  s.79(1) 514
Finance Act 1981 468f
Finance Act 1982
  s.53 669
  s.53-s.56 669
  Sch.9 669
Finance Act 1983 239
  s.21 219
Finance Act 1984 386
  s.52(2) 599f
Finance Act 1985 633, 634
  s.39(2)(a) 634
  s.48 92f
  Sch.12 92f
Finance Act 1986
  s.100 24f
  s.100(1)(b) 674
  s.100(2) 674f
  s.102 686, 687, 719
  s.102(4) 694
  s.102(5) 688

Finance Act 1986 – *continued*
  s.103(1) 701
  s.103(5) 701
  Sch.20
    para.2 687
    para.2(4) 688
    para.2(6)-(7) 688
    para.6(1)(a)-(b) 687
    para.8 707, 709
Finance Act 1988 7, 150, 216, 218,
    363, 366, 481, 557
  s.36 366, 367, 383, 384
  s.37-s.39 366
  s.40 366, 367
  s.44 389
  s.66 556f, 557
  s.66(2) 557
  s.98 478
  Sch.7 556f
Finance Act 1989 155, 172, 173, 224,
    562, 624
  s.19 155
  s.53(2)(b) 224
  s.54-s.55 146
  s.56-s.57 146, 147
  s.59 373
  s.97 636
  s.102 637
  s.103 559
  s.106 561
  s.110 752
  s.151 405, 423
Finance Act 1990 387, 607
  s.25 394
  s.30 386
  s.77 167
  s.90(1) 143
  s.90(5) 143
  s.91 566
  s.97-s.100 566
  s.103 577
  Sch.5 386
  Sch.9
    para.10 585
  Sch.17 577
Finance Act 1991 611
  s.27-s28 388
  s.72 337, 344
  Sch.6 388
Finance Act 1992
  s.9 148

Finance Act 1993   102f, 233, 253,
    331, 585
  s.55   388
  s.60   461f, 482f, 503f
  s.67   395
  s.77   604f
  s.77(2)   746
  s.92-s.95   461f, 482f, 503f
  s.96   482f, 503f
  s.125-s.170   461f, 482f, 503f
  s.208   16
  Sch.15-Sch.18   461f, 482f
Finance Act 1994   102f, 333, 342,
    583, 588f
  Part IV   746
  s.7   41
  s.91   524
  s.93   498
  s.108(5)-(8)   206
  ss. 200 *et seq*   333
  Sch.11   524
  Sch.12   498
  Sch.19
    para.3   283
Finance Act 1995   333, 405f, 414,
    424, 427, 428, 436, 525
  s.35   148
  s.39(1)   445
  s.40(3)   443
  s.41   444
  s.43   233f
  s.46   524f
  s.70(2)-(3)   525
  s.74(2)   414
  s.75   424f
  s.86   387
  s.87   593
  s.126-s.127   443
  Sch.6   445-6
    para.5   445
    para.6-para.7   446
    paras.9-14   446
    para.17   446
    para.19   446
  Sch.17
    para.11   414
  Sch.18   424f
    para.2(1)   425
    para.3(1)-(2)   425
    para.4(1)   425f
    para.4(2)   426

Finance Act 1996   141, 147, 150,
    233f, 328, 361, 365, 366, 470,
    574, 578, 582, 583, 742f, 746
  Part IV   581
  s.73   399
  s.80   582, 649
  s.80(1)-(2)   582
  s.80(5)   582
  s.81   582, 649
  s.81(1)   582-3
  s.81(2)-(4)   583
  s.81(6)   583
  s.82   582, 584, 649
  s.82(1)-(3)   584
  s.83   582, 586, 602, 649
  s.83(2)   586
  s.83(2)(a)-(d)   587
  s.83(3)-(7)   587
  s.83(8)   586
  s.84   585, 649
  s.84(2)   584
  s.84(5)-(6)   585
  s.85-s.90   585, 649
  s.91-s.99   586, 649
  s.100-s.102   583, 649
  s.103-s.104   649
  s.105   399, 649
  s.184   708
  Sch.6   399
  Sch.8   586
    para.1-para.4   587
  Sch.9   585
    para.1-para.6   585
    para.11   585
    para.15   586
  Sch.10   586
  Sch.11   586
  Sch.12   583
  Sch.13   583
  Sch.14   399
Finance Act 1997   130, 241, 247, 248,
    352, 355, 359, 442, 503, 524, 577,
    635, 669, 753, 754
Finance Acts   25, 32f
Finance (No.2) Act 1987
  s.74   576
  s.82-s.90   566
Finance (No.2) Act 1992
  s.19   148
  s.35   651
  Sch.10   428

Housing Act 1936 39
　s.75 39
　Sch.2
　　para.2 39
Housing Act 1988
　s.136 440
　Sch.19 440
Housing Associations Act 1985 689

Income and Corporation Taxes Act
　1970
　s.258-s.264 92f
Income and Corporation Taxes Act
　1988 16, 24, 57, 120, 241, 284,
　　517, 589, 613, 684, 745
　Part II 431
　Part V 223
　Part VI 551, 588f
　Part X 113, 607
　Part XI 552
　Part XII 93, 552
　Part XIII 360
　Part XV 93, 113, 367f, 373f,
　　413–22, 414f, 421f, 483f, 535,
　　680f, 686f, 721
　Part XVI 424f, 424
　Part XVII 555
　s.1 32f, 135, 138, 144, 575
　s.1(1) 138
　s.1(2) 25, 559
　s.1(2)(a) 405
　s.1(2)(b) 399
　s.1(4) 148
　s.1A 148, 363, 391, 399, 405, 425,
　　746
　s.2 138, 575
　s.3 148, 390, 392, 575
　s.4 385, 387, 391, 392, 393, 575
　s.4(1A) 363
　s.5 575
　s.5(1) 149, 398
　s.5(2) 149, 331
　s.5(3)-(4) 149
　s.6 443, 548f, 552, 553, 568
　s.6(1) 118, 568
　s.6(2) 569, 573
　s.6(3) 570
　s.6(4) 118, 670
　s.6(4)(a) 559, 569
　s.7 552
　s.7(1) 574

Income and Corporation Taxes Act
　1988 – *continued*
　s.7(2) 574, 575
　s.8 443, 552, 568–9
　s.8(1) 552, 568
　s.8(2) 569
　s.8(3) 564
　s.8(8) 143
　s.9 552, 573–6, 606
　s.9(1) 573
　s.9(2) 573, 575
　s.9(3)-(4) 575
　s.9(6) 575
　s.10 552, 566
　s.10(1) 566
　s.10(3) 566
　s.11 552, 603
　s.11(1) 570
　s.11(2) 568, 569, 570
　s.11(3) 575
　s.12 552, 564f, 608
　s.12(1) 576
　s.12(2)-(3) 564
　s.12(3)(b)-(e) 564
　s.13 552, 559
　s.13(1) 565
　s.13(1)(a)-(b) 565f
　s.13(2)-(6) 565
　s.13A 112, 560, 562, 565f
　s.14 552f, 552
　s.14(2) 594
　s.14(3) 597
　s.15 150, 369, 429, 431
　　para.1 441, 442
　s.15(1) 445
　　para.1 445
　　para.1(c) 431
　　para.2-para.3 429, 445
　　para.4 429
　s.17 150
　s.18 150, 151, 254, 255, 288, 361,
　　366, 367
　s.18(1) 254, 366, 443, 444, 452
　　para.1(a)(i)-(ii) 452
　s.18(1)(b) 361f
　s.18(2) 254, 366
　s.18(3) 255, 361f, 366, 369, 399,
　　448, 741, 742
　s.18(3A) 366, 399, 582
　s.18(4) 366, 444, 448, 451

Income and Corporation Taxes Act
1988 – *continued*
  s.19 152, 153, 156, 184, 204f, 205, 206f, 208, 218, 228, 230
    para.1 153, 154, 208
    para.2–4 153
    para.4A 155
    para.4A(a) 198
  s.19(1) 154, 156, 169, 173, 741
  s.19(1)(4A)(a)-(b) 173
  s.20 363
  s.20(2) 363
  s.21(1) 401
  s.21(3)-(4) 446
  s.24 430, 438
  s.24(1) 437
  s.24(2) 438
  s.25 430, 431–3, 441
  s.25(1)-(2) 431
  s.25(3)-(6) 432
  s.25(6)(c) 432
  s.25(7)-(9) 432
  s.26 430, 431, 434, 445
  s.27 431, 434, 446
  s.28 431, 434–5, 442
  s.28(1) 435
  s.29 431, 435
  s.29(5) 435
  s.30 431, 435, 446
  s.31-s.32 431, 435
  s.33 341, 342, 435
  s.33A-s.33B 112, 431, 435
  s.34 112, 435, 436–9, 443, 613
  s.34(1)-(2) 438
  s.35-s.36 112, 435, 436, 439–40, 443, 613
  s.38 439
  s.38(1)(a)-(c) 439
  s.39 435, 436
  s.41 429
  s.42A 112, 443
  s.43 443
  s.53 112, 260
  s.53(1) 260, 443
  s.53(2) 260
  s.53(3) 260, 261, 443
  s.53(4) 260
  s.54 261
  s.55 112, 261, 443
  s.58 742
  s.59 398, 401

Income and Corporation Taxes Act
1988 – *continued*
  s.59(1) 398
  s.60 304, 331, 575
  s.60(1) 288, 333, 334
  s.60(2) 332, 333
  s.60(3) 333, 334
  s.60(3)(a) 335
  s.60(5) 333, 334, 335
  s.61 304, 331, 332, 333, 334, 335, 575
  s.61(1) 335
  s.61(3) 332
  s.62 304, 331, 332, 333, 334, 335, 575
  s.62A 335
  s.63 304, 331, 332, 333, 334, 336, 575
  s.63A 112
  s.64 380, 381f, 575
  s.65 575
  s.65(1) 743
  s.65(1)(a) 743
  s.65(4) 744
  s.65(5)(a)-(b) 744
  s.65(6)-(9) 745, 749
  s.65A 444
  s.66-s.68 575
  s.69 451, 575
  s.70 575
  s.71 381, 575
  s.72 332, 451, 575
  s.73 575, 578
  s.74 158, 240, 311, 312, 313, 326, 338, 442, 490f, 576
  s.74(a) 314
  s.74(b) 314, 316f
  s.74(c) 320, 323
  s.74(e) 321, 322, 330, 337f
  s.74(f)-(g) 320, 323
  s.74(j) 287, 302, 320, 322, 328, 329, 337f
  s.74(k) 337f
  s.75 433, 434, 576, 577, 602, 612
  s.75(1) 434, 612, 628
  s.75(3) 577, 612
  s.75(4) 578, 613
  s.76 577, 602, 612
  s.82 112
  s.86(1) 577
  s.87 440

Income and Corporation Taxes Act
    1988 – *continued*
s.94   302
s.96   303
s.96(1)-(3)   303
s.96(4)(a)-(b)   303
s.96(5)   304
s.96(7)   303
s.98   445
s.100   296, 491, 664
s.100(2)   295
s.101   296, 664
s.101(1)   664
s.102   296
s.103   302, 303
s.103(1)   303
s.103(3)-(5)   302
s.104   302, 303
s.104(1)   303
s.104(4)   287
s.105   302
s.105(4)   288
s.106   302, 303
s.107   302
s.108   288, 302
s.109   302
s.110   287, 302
s.110(2)   302
s.113   302
s.113(1)   303
s.117-s.118   92f, 112
s.118A   746
s.118E   746
s.118G(4)   746
s.120   313, 430
s.124   385
s.125   112, 373, 397, 415, 580
s.125(1)   367, 397
s.125(2)-(3)   397
s.130   563, 577
s.131   157, 169, 170, 171
s.131(1)   157, 240
s.131(2)   157, 209
s.132   210
s.132(1)-(3)   748
s.132(4)(a)-(b)   748f
s.132(5)   749
s.133   153
s.134   166, 167
s.135-s.136   176
s.140   176

Income and Corporation Taxes Act
    1988 – *continued*
s.141   112, 212, 213, 214, 216
s.141(1)   214, 216
s.141(2)(a)-(b)   215
s.141(3)   215, 216, 218
s.141(4)   215
s.141(6)   216
s.141(6A)-(6B)   216
s.141(7)   213, 217
s.142   112, 212, 216–17, 218
s.142(1)   217
s.142(2)   218
s.142(3A)-(3B)   218
s.142(4)-(5)   217
s.143   112, 212, 213, 218
s.143(3)   217
s.144   112, 217
s.144(4)(a)-(b)   214
s.144(5)   214, 216f, 217
s.144A   112
s.145   112, 219, 220, 221, 222, 224,
    229, 232, 238, 390
s.145(1)   220, 221
s.145(2)   220
s.145(3)-(4)   221
s.145(6)-(7)   220
s.145(7)(a)   220
s.145(8)(b)   220
s.146   112, 155f, 219, 221, 222–3,
    224, 229, 238
s.146(1)   222
s.146(3)-(4)   222
s.146(6)-(8)   222
s.146(11)   223
s.146A   112
s.148   51f, 51, 154, 158, 204f, 204,
    205, 206f, 206, 207f, 207
s.148(1)   204
s.148(2)   204, 205
s.148(3)   205
s.148(7)   205
s.149   229, 578
s.153   112, 224, 228, 246f
s.153(2)   228
s.154   224, 227, 228, 229, 231, 233,
    234, 235, 236, 239
s.154(1)   228
s.154(2)   229, 235
s.154(3)   230
s.155   224, 229, 230

Income and Corporation Taxes Act
  1988 – *continued*
  s.155(1)   229, 235
  s.155(1A)   216, 218, 229
  s.155(2)-(7)   229
  s.155A   229
  s.156   224, 230, 231, 232
  s.156(1)   229
  s.156(2)   230
  s.156(3)   231, 232
  s.156(4)   231
  s.156(5)   231, 232, 233
  s.156(5)(b)   232
  s.156(6)   231, 232
  s.156(8)   233
  s.157   224, 228, 229, 233, 234, 235
  s.157(1)   233f
  s.157A   171f, 233f
  s.158   224, 229, 235
  s.158(2)-(3)   235
  s.158(6)   235
  s.159   224, 234
  s.159(2)   233, 234
  s.159A   229, 235
  s.159AA   229, 235
  s.159AB-s.159AC   235
  s.160   223, 224, 229, 236, 238, 560
  s.160(1)-(2)   236
  s.160(6)   236
  s.161   224
  s.161(6)   237
  s.162   224, 229, 237
  s.162(2)(b)   238
  s.163   224, 228, 238
  s.164   224, 238
  s.165   224, 238–9
  s.165(3)   239
  s.165(6)(b)   225f
  s.166   224
  s.167   224, 226
  s.167(1)   224
  s.167(1)(a)-(b)   226
  s.167(2)   226
  s.167(3)   225, 227
  s.167(4)-(5)   225
  s.168   220, 224, 234
  s.168(2)   225f, 234
  s.168(3)   213, 227, 239
  s.168(4)   227
  s.168(5)   234
  s.168(7)   231, 232

Income and Corporation Taxes Act
  1988 – *continued*
  s.168(8)-(11)   225
  s.168A   112, 234
  s.168B-s.168E   112
  s.168F-s.168G   112, 234
  s.170(2)(a)   551
  s.188   51f, 154, 158, 159, 160, 204f, 205, 207
  s.188(1)(a)-(b)   205
  s.188(1)(d)-(f)   205
  s.188(4)   206, 207f
  s.189-s.190   206
  s.191A-s.191B   253
  s.192   156, 208, 209, 747, 748
  s.192(1)-(2)   209, 747
  s.193   209, 241, 253, 747, 748, 749
  s.193(1)   156, 208, 747f, 747
  s.193(2)-(6)   750
  s.194   749
  s.194(1)-(6)   750
  s.195   749
  s.195(2)-(3)   750
  s.195(5)-(7)   750
  s.198   32f, 52, 135, 158, 216, 221, 228, 233, 241–2, 243, 245, 246, 250, 252, 349f
  s.198(1)   241, 242, 243, 246, 749
  s.198(1)(a)   242, 248
  s.198(1)(b)   247, 248
  s.198(1A)   241, 248
  s.198(3)   241, 749
  s.198A   247
  s.198A(2)-(3)   248
  s.198A(4)   247
  s.201   216, 228, 233, 241, 253
  s.201A   167
  s.201AA   216, 228, 233
  s.202A   140f, 172, 173
  s.202B   173
  s.202B(8)-(11)   174
  s.203   156
  s.203A   155
  s.204   172f
  s.205   32
  s.208   104f, 548f, 552, 574, 600, 603
  s.209   113, 552f, 552, 589
  s.209(1)   589, 595
  s.209(1)(a)   311
  s.209(2)(b)   596, 669

Table of Statutes

Income and Corporation Taxes Act
1988 – *continued*
s.209(2)(c) 593, 594, 596
s.209(3) 596
s.209(4) 669
s.209(5) 593, 596
s.209(8) 593
s.210 113, 552, 596
s.210(1)(b) 596
s.211 113, 551, 552, 596
s.212 113, 552, 596
s.213 113, 552, 653
s.213(2) 653
s.213(3)(a) 654, 657
s.213(3)(b) 654
s.214 113, 552, 653, 657
s.215-s.218 113, 552, 653
s.219 113, 552, 596, 669, 670, 672
s.219(1) 670
s.219(1)(a) 670
s.219(1)(b) 672
s.219(2) 672
s.220 113, 552
s.220(1) 671
s.220(4)-(7) 671
s.221 113, 552, 671
s.221(3) 671
s.222 113, 552, 671
s.222(9) 671
s.223 113, 552, 671
s.224 113, 552, 672
s.225 113, 552, 669, 672
s.226-s.255 113, 552
s.227-s.228 671
s.229 669
s.229(1) 669, 670
s.229(2) 671
s.230 589, 596
s.231(1) 401, 600, 603, 604
s.231(2) 600
s.231(3) 604
s.231(3A)-(3B) 561, 563, 604
s.231(3C) 561, 604
s.231(3D) 561
s.231(4) 604
s.232(1)-(2) 604
s.232(3) 603
s.233(1) 604
s.238(1) 600
s.239 103
s.239(1) 597

Income and Corporation Taxes Act
1988 – *continued*
s.239(2) 598, 599
s.239(3)-(4) 599
s.240 589, 599, 617, 634, 635, 636
s.240(1) 634, 636
s.240(2)(a)-(b) 635
s.240(3) 635
s.240(4)-(7) 636
s.240(8) 637
s.240(9) 635
s.240(10) 634
s.240(11) 636
s.240(11)(a) 636
s.240(11)(b) 634
s.241 600
s.241(1) 600, 601
s.241(2) 601
s.241(3) 602
s.242 119, 602, 603, 606, 607, 613
s.242(5) 602
s.242(8) 602
s.243 119, 602, 603, 613
s.243(6) 603
s.244 613
s.244(2) 603
s.245 599
s.245(3A) 102f
s.245A 599, 635
s.245B 599, 635
s.246A-s.246Y 588f
s.247 104, 616, 617, 624, 626
s.247(1) 624
s.247(1)(b) 645
s.247(1A) 645
s.247(2) 104
s.247(3) 105, 626
s.247(4) 627
s.247(4)(a) 627, 645
s.247(5) 625, 627
s.247(8) 624, 627
s.247(8A) 624
s.247(9)(a) 645
s.247(9)(c) 645
s.247(10) 626, 627
s.248 617
s.249 596
s.251(2) 596
s.254(1) 591f, 591
s.254(2) 591
s.254(3) 589

Income and Corporation Taxes Act
1988 – *continued*
s.254(5)-(6)   591
s.254(7)-(8)   592
s.254(9)   591
s.254(12)   591
s.256   143, 405, 575
s.257-s.336   575
s.257(1)   144
s.257(5)   144
s.257A   144
s.257(A)(2)   144
s.257B   144
s.257E   144
s.259   145
s.259(1)(c)   145
s.259(2)-(3)   145
s.259(4A)   145
s.259(5)   145
s.260   145
s.260(1)   145
s.260(3)   145
s.261   145
s.262   146, 423
s.265(1)   146
s.276   143
s.278(1)   147
s.278(2)   604
s.313   205f, 205
s.314   167
s.323(3)   216, 228
s.329   378
s.331   238
s.332   241, 253
s.332(3)   221, 233
s.332(3)(b)   221f
s.333   504
s.334   17, 18
s.335   17, 19
s.335(1)-(2)   18
s.336   17
s.336(1)   18-19
s.336(2)-(3)   19
s.337   574
s.337-s.347   17, 552
s.337(2)(a)-(b)   574
s.337(3)   574
s.337A   574
s.338   578, 579, 602
s.338(1)   578, 581
s.338(2)   580

Income and Corporation Taxes Act
1988 – *continued*
s.338(2)(a)   580
s.338(3)   579
s.338(3)(a)   579, 580
s.338(5)(a)-(b)   580
s.338(6)   579
s.339   581
s.339(1)-(4)   581
s.339(6)   596
s.343   608, 613, 665
s.343(1)   665
s.347A   113, 362f, 363, 367, 384, 390, 398
s.347A(1)(a)   383
s.347A(1)(b)   384
s.347A(2)(a)   384
s.347A(7)   581
s.347B   417
s.348   17, 119, 143, 144, 148, 149, 151, 159, 313, 382, 384, 390, 391–3, 394, 395, 396, 397, 399, 404f, 404, 406, 575
s.348(2)(a)   390
s.349   17, 151, 313, 377, 382, 384, 393–4, 404f, 404, 575, 581
s.349(1)   119, 391, 393, 394, 395, 396, 399, 406, 575, 579
s.349(1)(b)   390
s.349(2)   363, 384, 385, 395, 396, 575, 579
s.349(2)(a)-(c)   384
s.349(3)   363
s.349(3)(a)-(b)   384
s.350   17, 151, 343, 382, 384, 404f, 404, 575
s.350(1)   385, 394
s.350(3)   385
s.350(4)   363, 385
s.351-s.368   17
s.352   363, 384
s.353   119, 343, 446
s.353(1)-(2)   237
s.354(1)   388
s.354(3)   388
s.355   389, 579
s.355(1A)   389
s.355(2A)   388
s.356   390
s.356A   388
s.356B-s.356D   389

Income and Corporation Taxes Act
1988 – *continued*
s.357   389
s.357(6)   389
s.359(4)   253
s.362   167f
s.367(1)   388
s.367(5)   388
s.368(3)-(4)   446
s.369   385, 388
s.369(1A)   388
s.370-s.379   388
s.373(5)   313
s.375(2)   313
s.375A(1)   446
s.379A   446
s.379A(2)-(3)   446
s.380   322, 337, 338, 339, 340, 341, 342, 343, 501
s.380(1)   340
s.380(2)   340, 341
s.381   337, 338, 339, 501, 607
s.381(1)-(2)   338
s.381(4)-(5)   338
s.384   341, 342
s.384(4)   341
s.384(9)   341
s.385   322, 337, 342, 343
s.385(4)   343
s.386   342
s.387   343
s.388   322, 337, 344
s.390   343
s.392   452
s.393   343, 608
s.393(1)   602, 603, 606, 607, 608
s.393(7)   606
s.393(8)   607, 608
s.393(9)   608
s.393A   606, 609, 612
s.393A(1)   602, 609, 610, 611, 628
s.393A(1)(a)   609, 610
s.393A(1)(b)   609, 610, 629
s.393A(2)   609, 611
s.393A(3)   609, 610, 611
s.393A(5)   612
s.393A(9)(a)   606
s.393A(10)   610, 611
s.394   552, 603, 607, 611, 612
s.395   552, 607
s.396   607, 613

Income and Corporation Taxes Act
1988 – *continued*
s.396(1)   613
s.396(2)   613
s.397   341, 342
s.401   446, 606, 607
s.401(1B)   446
s.402   92f, 552, 616, 617, 627
s.402(1)-(2)   627, 633
s.402(3)   616, 645
s.402(3)(a)-(c)   645
s.402(4)   616, 633
s.402(5)   633
s.402(6)   634
s.402(6)(b)   596
s.403   92f, 552, 617, 627, 628
s.403(1)-(8)   628
s.403(9)   645, 646
s.403(9)(a)   645, 646
s.403(10)   634
s.404   92f, 552, 558, 559, 617, 627, 632, 642
s.405-406   92f, 552, 617, 627, 634
s.407   92f, 552, 617, 627, 629
s.408   92f, 552, 617, 627, 646
s.408(1)-(2)   629
s.408(2)(a)-(b)   629
s.409   92f, 552, 617, 627, 629
s.409(5)-(8)   634
s.410   92f, 552, 617, 627, 629, 630, 632, 636, 646
s.410(1)   632
s.410(2)   646
s.411   92f, 552, 617, 627
s.411(1)-(2)   633
s.411(9)   633
s.412   92f, 552, 617, 627, 633
s.412(3)   634
s.413   92f, 552, 616, 617, 627
s.413(2)   627
s.413(3)(a)   627
s.413(5)   627, 628, 645
s.413(6)   645
s.413(7)   628, 645
s.413(8)-(9)   646
s.414(1)(c)   560
s.414(5)   559f, 560
s.414(6)   559f
s.415   560f
s.416   124, 126, 483f, 560, 565
s.416(2)   562

Income and Corporation Taxes Act
1988 – *continued*
s.417   560
s.417(1)   561
s.417(3)   561
s.417(7)   561
s.418-s.419   113, 560
s.420   560f
s.423-s.430   559
s.432   577
s.468   665
s.473   652
s.476   386
s.476(5)   386
s.476(5)(b)   386
s.476(6)   386
s.477A   387
s.477A(5)   381f
s.479(2)   386
s.480A   387
s.481   405f
s.481(1A)   387
s.481(2)   386, 387
s.481(3)   387
s.481(4)(d)   387
s.481(5)   386
s.481(5)(k)   387
s.481(5)(k)(iii)   405f
s.482(1)   381, 387
s.482(5)   405f
s.483   386
s.486(10)   575
s.490-s.491   575
s.497   598f
s.498   598f, 636
s.499   598f
s.503-s.504   428
s.505(1)(a)   447
s.505(1)(c)   387
s.505(1)(c)(ii)   581
s.505(1)(e)   581
s.506   225f
s.519(3)   555
s.519A   555
s.524   51
s.531   301
s.531(1)   301
s.531(3)   301
s.533   301
s.559   167
s.565   167f

Income and Corporation Taxes Act
1988 – *continued*
s.567   167f
s.573   614
s.574   500
s.574(3)(a)   500
s.574(3)(b)   501
s.576   501f
s.576(4)-(5)   501
s.577   251f, 313, 315, 320, 326
s.577(1)   253
s.577(1)(a)   577
s.577(5)   326
s.577(8)   253, 327
s.577(9)   327
s.577(10)   327
s.577A   279, 313, 328
s.580(3)   206
s.584   573, 743
s.585   553f, 746, 749
s.592(2)   447
s.596A(8)   206
s.617   153
s.656   368f, 368, 412f
s.656(3)-(6)   369
s.657(1)-(2)   369
s.657(2)(c)   412f
s.660   413f, 419
s.660A   397, 419, 420, 421, 422
s.660A(1)   404, 418–19
s.660A(2)   419
s.660A(6)   419
s.660A(8)   397
s.660A(9)(a)   397
s.660B   418, 420, 421, 422
s.660B(1)   420
s.660B(2)   404, 420
s.660B(3)   420
s.660B(5)   421
s.660B(6)(a)-(b)   421
s.660C(1)   422
s.660C(3)   422
s.660D(1)(a)-(b)   422
s.660E(2)-(5)   418
s.660G   401, 414, 417
s.660G(2)   417
s.671-s.674   419
s.674A   413f, 419
s.677   414, 421, 422
s.677(1)-(2)   421, 422
s.677(4)   422

Income and Corporation Taxes Act
1988 – *continued*
– *continued*
s.677(6)-(7)   422
s.677(9)(a)   422
s.677(9)(b)   421
s.677(10)   421
s.677   414f, 414, 421
s.678   414f, 414, 421, 422
s.678(1)   422
s.678(3)   422
s.679   414f, 414, 421
s.680-s.682   414f, 414, 421
s.682A   414f
s.683-s.684   419
s.686   406f, 406, 407f, 407, 536
s.686(1)   405
s.686(1A)   405, 536
s.686(2)   405, 406f
s.686(2)(b)   409
s.686(2)(d)   411
s.686(3A)-(3B)   425
s.686(4)   425
s.687   404f, 406f, 406, 407f, 407
s.687(2)(a)   406, 411
s.687(2)(b)   406
s.687(3)   407
s.687(3)(a)   406f
s.695(1)   425
s.695(2)   424
s.695(3)   425
s.695(4)(b)   742
s.695(5)   424f
s.696(3)   425
s.696(5)   425
s.696(6)   742
s.697(1)   425
s.697(1A)   425f
s.697(2)-(3)   426
s.700   426
s.701(2)   425
s.701(3)   424
s.701(3A)   425
s.703   73, 111, 112, 113, 114, 116, 117, 118, 124, 127, 129, 130, 672
s.703(1)   114
s.703(2)   115
s.703(3)   127, 128
s.703(4)-(6)   128
s.703(9)   127

Income and Corporation Taxes Act
1988 – *continued*
s.703(10)(a)-(b)   127
s.704   113, 118, 121, 130
s.704E(2)   126
s.705   113, 130
s.705(A)   128
s.705(1)-(3)   128
s.705(5)-(8)   128
s.706   113, 127, 130
s.707   27f, 113, 130
s.707(1)   130
s.707(1)(a)   130
s.707(2)-(3)   130
s.708   113, 127, 130
s.709   113, 117, 130
s.709(1)   116, 118
s.709(2)   115, 555
s.709(3)   125
s.709(4)   119
s.709(6)   119
s.710   113, 114f
s.711-s.737   113
s.738   113, 114f
s.739   20, 73, 101, 113, 114, 130–1, 752, 753, 754
s.739(1)   20
s.740   113, 753, 754
s.741   113, 754
s.742-s.746   113
s.743(1)   753
s.743(3)   20
s.744(1)   754
s.747-s.756   113
s.747(1)-(3)   760
s.757-s.764   113, 742f
s.765-s.767   113
s.767A   113
s.768   113, 608, 613
s.769   113
s.770   113, 301, 304, 760
s.770(1)   301
s.771-s.773   113
s.774   113, 555
s.774(4)(a)   555
s.775   113, 555
s.776   73, 113, 131–4, 275, 443, 444, 555
s.776(1)   131
s.776(2)   132, 133
s.776(2)(i)-(ii)   133

Income and Corporation Taxes Act
1988 – *continued*
s.776(3)   133
s.776(4)(a)   132
s.776(5)-(6)   133
s.776(8)   133
s.776(11)   27f
s.776(13)(a)   132
s.776(14)   134, 444
s.777   131, 555
s.777(2)-(3)   132
s.777(9)   134, 444
s.777(13)   133, 555
s.779   113, 442–3
s.780   113, 443
s.781-s.785   113
s.787   113
s.788   759
s.790   759
s.808A   113
s.811   758
s.812   603
s.813   603
s.813(2)   240f
s.814-s.816   603
s.817   240, 311
s.817(1)   451
s.817(1)(b)   390, 392
s.821   393
s.827   328
s.831(1)(a)   590f
s.832   2f, 57, 215f, 220, 259, 263, 379, 443, 553, 555, 617f, 650f
s.832(1)   260, 267, 376, 405, 554, 555, 569, 618
s.832(2)   555
s.832(3)   118, 671
s.833   5, 57
s.833(1)   5, 118
s.834   57, 564f
s.834(1)   571, 608
s.834(3)   590
s.835   140
s.835(1)   140
s.835(4)-(5)   149
s.835(6)   140–1
s.835(7)-(8)   141
s.837   232, 233
s.838   616, 617, 618
s.838(2)-(3)   618f
s.838(4)   618

Income and Corporation Taxes Act
1988 – *continued*
s.838(5)   619
s.838(6)   620
s.838(7)   620, 621
s.838(8)   620, 622
s.838(9)   621, 622
s.838(10)   621, 624
s.839   356f, 555
s.839(8)   555
s.840   630, 631, 632, 636
s.841   560
s.842   665
s.842A   555
Sch.1   435
Sch.3
  para.15   555
Sch.6   233f, 234
  para.1   234
  para.3   234
  para.5   234
  para.6-para.7   235
Sch.7   236
  para.1(1)   236
Sch.11A   253
Sch.12
  para.1A   747
  para.3(1)-(2)   747
  para.3(2A)   747f
  para.4   747
Sch.13   601
  para.1   601f
  para.4   601
Sch.16   363
  para.5   575
Sch.17A   633
  para.10(2)   633
Sch.18   625, 634, 645
Sch.29   166
Sch.A   138, 139f, 139, 141, 143, 150, 161, 254, 260, 261, 343, 347, 361f, 366, 369, 427, 428, 432, 433, 434, 436, 441, 442, 443, 444, 446, 447, 463f, 576, 578, 580, 612, 741
Sch.Aold   427, 428, 429, 441, 442, 445, 451
Sch.Anew   427, 429, 436, 443, 444–7, 451
Sch.B   150, 260, 366
Sch.C   141, 150, 366, 742f

Income and Corporation Taxes Act
1988 – *continued*
Sch.D 137, 138, 139f, 139, 140,
141, 150, 151, 155, 159, 161,
165, 166, 168, 337–44, 366,
383f, 430, 447, 517, 572, 575,
609, 741
case I 8, 139, 150, 154, 158, 161,
254–82, 283–336, 337, 339,
340, 343, 345, 374, 381f, 404,
405, 428, 431, 442, 443, 444,
446, 447, 449, 471, 486, 517,
553, 574, 576, 584, 608, 610,
742f, 744
case II 8, 137, 150, 154, 159,
160, 161, 162, 254–82,
283–336, 337, 340f, 343,
381f, 449
case III 137, 143, 151, 157, 159,
361–99, 402, 404, 405f, 411,
582, 584, 742, 746
r.1(a) 369
case III(b) 380
case IV 137, 151, 361f, 574, 579,
741, 742f, 742–6, 744f, 749,
752
case V 155, 255, 361f, 399, 402,
403, 428, 444, 548, 574, 579,
608, 609, 610, 611, 741, 742f,
742–6, 744f, 749, 752
case VI 127, 131, 133, 151, 287,
288, 303, 343, 369, 371, 422,
428, 429, 442, 443, 444, 445,
448–52, 605, 606, 608, 613,
634, 657, 741, 742f, 742, 753
case VII 455
case VIII 150, 428, 431
Part IV 563
Sch.E 32, 140, 141, 149, 152,
153–210, 155f, 212, 213, 216,
218, 223, 225f, 228, 235, 236,
240–53, 254, 257, 339, 340f,
349f, 356f, 366, 449, 573, 684,
741
case I 152, 156, 157, 169, 172,
173, 208, 209, 241, 746–8,
747f, 749, 750
case II 152, 156, 157, 169, 172,
173, 208, 209, 241, 748, 749,
750

Income and Corporation Taxes Act
1988 – *continued*
case III 152, 156, 157, 169, 172,
174, 208, 209, 241, 744f, 747,
748–9
Sch.F 140, 141, 147, 340, 399,
401, 404, 405f, 405, 548, 573,
588, 603, 604, 669, 361f.363
Income Tax Act 1803 135, 428
Sch.A 428, 431
Sch.B 428
Income Tax Act 1842 32, 382f
r.5-r.6 155f
r.10 155f
s.102-s.103 382f
Sch.D 382f
Sch.E
Sch.1
r.11 155f
r.12 155f
Income Tax Act 1853 382f
Income Tax Act 1888 382f
Income Tax Act 1918 266, 380
General Rules
r.12 307
Sch.B 306
Sch.D
Case I 306
Sch.E
r.9 243
Income Tax Act 1952
s.124(1) 315
s.152 315
s.179 431
Income Tax Acts 5, 51, 137, 138,
140, 141, 240f, 263, 279, 284,
402, 404, 460, 489, 604
Inheritance (Provision for Family and
Dependants) Act 1975 719, 730,
734
Inheritance Tax Act 1984 24f, 24,
674f, 674, 678, 682, 685, 697,
703, 721, 722, 723, 726, 727, 738
Part III 113
Part IV 113
s.1 678
s.2(1) 678
s.3(1) 679
s.3(2) 679, 723
s.3(3) 679
s.3A 113, 676

Inheritance Tax Act 1984 – *continued*
  s.3A(1)   693
  s.3A(1)(c)   721
  s.3A(2)   694, 721f, 727
  s.3A(4)   693, 710
  s.3A(5)   693
  s.4   685f, 738f
  s.4(1)   685, 701, 728
  s.5   701
  s.5(1)   681, 701
  s.5(3)   698
  s.5(4)   699
  s.5(5)   698
  s.6(1)   679, 757
  s.7(1)   709, 710
  s.7(2)   709
  s.7(4)   711f, 711
  s.7(5)   711f
  s.10   684, 728f
  s.10(1)   682, 683
  s.11   683f, 683, 684f, 730
  s.11(1)   683
  s.11(3)   683
  s.11(4)   683f
  s.11(6)   683f, 683
  s.12(1)-(2)   684
  s.13   685
  s.14-s.15   684
  s.16   685
  s.18(1)   688
  s.18(2)   689
  s.18(3)(a)-(b)   689
  s.19(1)-(2)   691
  s.19(3)   692
  s.19(3A)(a)-(b)   694
  s.20   692
  s.21(1)   692
  s.22(1)   693
  s.22(2)   693f
  s.23   689
  s.23(2)-(5)   691
  s.24   689
  s.24(3)-(4)   691
  s.24A   689
  s.24A(3)   691
  s.25   690
  s.25(2)   691
  s.26   690
  s.26(4)-(7)   691
  s.29(3)   692, 693
  s.29(5)   689f

Inheritance Tax Act 1984 – *continued*
  s.30(1)-(4)   694
  s.31(1)   694
  s.31(2)   695
  s.31(3)   695f
  s.31(4)-(4G)   695
  s.32(1)-(2)   695
  s.32(3)(a)-(b)   695
  s.32(4)-(5)   696
  s.33(1)(a)   696
  s.33(1)(b)   696f
  s.33(3)   696
  s.36-s.42   688
  s.43(2)-(3)   720
  s.44(1)   721
  s.44(2)   722
  s.47   723f
  s.48(1)   723
  s.48(3)   757
  s.49(1)   719, 726, 728
  s.50(1)-(4)   726
  s.50(5)-(6)   727
  s.51(2)   730
  s.52   729, 730, 731
  s.52(1)   727, 728, 729, 730
  s.52(2)-(3)   728
  s.52(4)   727f
  s.53(2)-(6)   729
  s.54A-s54B   730
  s.57   729, 736f
  s.58   731
  s.58(1)(a)   736
  s.58(1)(b)   737, 739
  s.58(1)(c)-(e)   739
  s.58(3)   739
  s.59   731
  s.59(2)   731f
  s.60   731
  s.61(1)   731
  s.62(1)   730
  s.63   732f, 734f
  s.64   731, 732
  s.65   734
  s.65(1)   732
  s.65(1)(a)-(b)   734
  s.65(2)   735
  s.65(4)-(6)   734
  s.65(7)   757
  s.66   732
  s.66(2)   732
  s.66(3)(a)-(b)   732

Table of Statutes

Inheritance Tax Act 1984 – *continued*
s.66(4)(a)-(c) 732
s.66(5) 732
s.66(6) 734
s.67(3) 733
s.68(1)-(2) 735
s.68(3)-(6) 736
s.69(1)-(2) 736
s.69(3) 736f
s.70(1) 737
s.70(2)(b) 737
s.70(3) 737f
s.70(5)-(6) 737
s.70(8) 737
s.70(9) 737f
s.71(1)-(2) 737
s.71(3)-(4) 738
s.71(5) 739
s.71(7)-(8) 738
s.76(1) 739
s.80 732
s.84 736f
s.86 739
s.86(1) 685
s.89 739
s.90 729
s.93 730
s.103(1) 736
s.104 707
s.104(1)(a) 707
s.104(1)(b) 708, 729
s.105 708
s.105(1)(a) 707
s.105(1)(cc) 708
s.105(1)(d) 708
s.105(1)(e) 729
s.105(1ZA) 708f
s.105(3)-(4) 707, 708
s.105(5) 708f
s.105(6) 708
s.105(7) 707
s.106-s.108 708
s.110 707f
s.112 708f
s.113(a) 709
s.113(b) 709f
s.113A 709
s.113B 709
s.114 113
s.114(1) 709
s.115(1) 736

Inheritance Tax Act 1984 – *continued*
s.115(2) 704
s.115(3) 705
s.115(4) 704f
s.115(5) 704
s.117(a)-(b) 705
s.118(1)-(2) 705
s.119(1) 705
s.120 705
s.122(1)-(2) 706
s.123(1) 706
s.124(1) 706
s.124A-s.124B 706
s.125(1)(a) 702f
s.126-s.130 702
s.131(1) 711
s.131(2)-(3) 712
s.132-s.134 712
s.137 712
s.139(1)-(3) 712
s.141 712, 731
s.142 730f
s.142(1) 718, 719f, 719
s.142(3) 719
s.142(5)-(6) 719
s.143 719
s.145 719
s.146 719
s.146(6) 730, 734
s.147 719
s.150 682
s.151 701, 739
s.152-s.153 701
s.154 685f
s.157 701
s.158(6) 759f
s.159 759f
s.160 697, 701
s.161 700
s.161(1)-(3) 700
s.162(1)-(2) 699
s.162(4) 699
s.162(5) 700
s.163 698
s.164 699
s.165(1) 676f
s.166 703
s.167(1) 703
s.168 704
s.170 727
s.171 703

Inheritance Tax Act 1984 – *continued*
 s.171(1)-(2)   702
 s.172-s.173   702
 s.176   702
 s.178-s.198   704
 s.186A-s.186B   704f
 s.191(1)-(2)   713
 s.199(2)   714
 s.200(1)   714
 s.200(1)(b)   740
 s.200(2)   715
 s.201(1)   740
 s.201(1)(d)   758
 s.201(3)   758f
 s.201(3A)   758f
 s.201(4)   758f
 s.201(5)   758
 s.201(c)   740
 s.203   713
 s.203(2)-(3)   713f
 s.204(2)   740
 s.204(3)   714, 740
 s.204(5)   740
 s.204(6)   714, 740, 758
 s.204(9)   714
 s.207(1)-(2)   716
 s.208   716
 s.211(1)-(2)   715
 s.216   715
 s.216(6)   715
 s.222   698
 s.226(1)   714, 715, 740f
 s.226(2)   715
 s.226(3)   714
 s.226(3A)   714
 s.226(3B)   740
 s.226(4)   716
 s.227   716
 s.227(1)   716
 s.227(3)-(4)   717
 s.230   717
 s.233   740
 s.234(1)-(4)   717
 s.236(1A)   740
 s.237(1)   718, 740
 s.237(2)-(3)   718f
 s.237(3A)   718
 s.237(6)   718
 s.238(1)   718
 s.265   713
 s.266(1)-(3)   713f

Inheritance Tax Act 1984 – *continued*
 s.267   679, 757
 s.268   113
 s.268(1)   680
 s.268(1)(a)   680
 s.268(2)   681f
 s.268(3)   681
 s.269   705
 s.270   682f, 683f
 s.272   57, 679, 681, 703f
 s.272(3)-(4)   703
 s.286   112
 s.286(1)(a)-(b)   681
 Sch.1   709
 Sch.2
   para.3   736
 Sch.3   690
 Sch.4   739
Inland Revenue Regulation Act 1890   24
 s.1(2)   32
 s.2   32
 s.13   32
 s.39   32f
Insolvency Act 1986   615f
 s.110   658, 667, 668
 s.110(2)   667
Interpretation Act 1978   14, 57
 s.5   57
 s.6   57
 Sch.1   13, 14, 57, 430
 Sch.2
   para.5   430
   Part I
     para.5   14

Landlord and Tenant Act 1954   462, 464, 465, 466
Law of Property Act 1925   57
 s.1(6)   533f
 s.53(1)(c)   680f
 s.61   57
 s.85(1)-(2)   477f
 s.149(6)   721f
Law of Property (Miscellaneous Provisions) Act 1989   438
 s.2   477f
Law Reform (Miscellaneous Provisions) Act 1934
 s.3   378

Laws in Wales Act 1535   14
  s.1   14
Local Government Act 1972
  Part 4   14
  s.1   14

Malaysian Income Tax Act 1967   658

National Insurance Act 1965
  s.1   163
New Zealand Acts Interpretation Act
    1924
  s.5(j)   55f

Parliament Act 1911   51
Partnership Act 1890
  s.1   554f
Provisional Collection of Taxes Act
    1968   24, 25, 32f, 135, 136, 568
  s.1   25
  s.1(1)   25, 568
  s.1(3)   25
  s.2   25
  s.5   25

Rentcharges Act 1977   430
  s.1   430
Road Traffic Act 1972
  s.190   234
Royal and Parliamentary Titles Act
    1927
  s.2(2)   13

Stamp Act 1891   24
Supreme Court Act 1981   44f
  s.31   44
  s.31(3)   44
  s.35A   378

Tax Acts   169, 171, 240, 452
Taxation of Chargeable Gains Act
    1992   24, 57, 436, 459f, 460,
    462, 471, 472, 475, 477, 480, 481,
    482, 493, 514, 517, 523, 529f,
    529, 533
  s.1   5
  s.1(1)   459
  s.2(1)   460, 741, 750
  s.2(2)(a)-(b)   499
  s.3(1)   502
  s.3(2)   537

Taxation of Chargeable Gains Act
    1992 – *continued*
  s.3(7)   529
  s.4(1)   529, 536
  s.5   536
  s.8   575, 576, 605f, 606, 614
  s.8(3)   606
  s.9(1)   460, 751
  s.9(3)   19, 751
  s.10   751
  s.10(1)   460f, 460
  s.10(5)   460f
  s.12   460
  s.12(1)   751
  s.13   113, 560
  s.15(2)   5, 459, 569
  s.16   605f
  s.16(1)-(2)   499
  s.17   80, 113, 483, 535
  s.17(1)   482, 525
  s.17(2)   468f, 483
  s.18   113
  s.18(1)   525
  s.18(2)   483, 525
  s.18(3)   484f, 500, 535, 542f
  s.18(4)   535f
  s.18(6)-(8)   483f
  s.21(1)   460
  s.21(1)(a)   463f, 472, 475
  s.21(1)(b)   482
  s.21(2)(a)   463, 471
  s.21(2)(b)   463, 469, 471
  s.22   437, 463, 464, 466
  s.22(1)   463f, 463, 464, 465, 467,
      475f, 477, 695f
  s.22(1)(a)   469, 477f
  s.22(1)(b)   469, 470, 477f
  s.22(1)(c)   448f, 467, 477f
  s.22(1)(d)   477f
  s.22(2)   477f, 477
  s.23(1)   468
  s.23(3)   468, 469
  s.23(4)-(5)   469
  s.23(6)   470
  s.24   469, 680f
  s.24(1)   470, 695f
  s.24(2)   470, 501
  s.24(2)(b)   470
  s.26(1)   477
  s.26(2)   478
  s.26(3)   487

Taxation of Chargeable Gains Act
1992 – *continued*
s.27   471
s.28   476f, 511f
s.28(1)   476, 492
s.28(2)   476f, 476, 477
s.29(2)   472, 484
s.30   113, 484
s.30(1)   472
s.30(1)(b)   472
s.30(3)-(4)   472
s.30(5)   484
s.31-s.34   113
s.35   481
s.35(3)   481
s.35(3)(a)-(c)   481
s.35(4)   481
s.35(5)   481, 497
s.35(6)   481
s.37   488
s.37(2)(a)   489
s.37(3)   489
s.38   494, 516, 575
s.38(1)   489f, 489, 495
s.38(1)(a)   490, 491, 496, 649
s.38(1)(b)   490, 492, 493, 496
s.38(1)(c)   496
s.38(2)   491, 545
s.38(3)   489f
s.38(4)   491
s.39(1)-(2)   489
s.40   489f, 575
s.41   642
s.42   471f, 498
s.42(2)   496
s.42(4)   496
s.43   494
s.44(1)   503
s.44(1)(c)   503
s.44(1)(d)   545f
s.45(1)-(3)   495, 503
s.45(4)   503
s.46(1)   495
s.48   487f
s.49   487
s.49(2)   468f, 487
s.51(1)   502
s.51(2)   378, 502
s.52(4)   490
s.53(1)   498, 499
s.54   497f

Taxation of Chargeable Gains Act
1992 – *continued*
s.55(1)   497
s.56(2)   525
s.58(1)   525
s.58(2)   525f
s.60   462, 530, 531, 533, 648
s.60(1)   530, 531, 533f, 533, 534, 538, 541, 544
s.60(2)   531, 534f, 538
s.62   676
s.62(1)(a)   527
s.62(1)(b)   478, 527
s.62(2)   499, 528
s.62(3)   527, 529
s.62(4)   528
s.62(4)(a)-(b)   528
s.62(5)   528
s.62(6)-(8)   529
s.62(10)   527f
s.64   545
s.64(2)-(3)   528
s.65(1)   529, 538
s.65(2)   529
s.68   530
s.69   671
s.69(1)   538, 541, 755
s.69(2)   755f
s.69(4)   542
s.70   535
s.71   539, 543, 545, 546, 756
s.71(1)   533f, 538, 539, 541
s.71(2)   542, 545
s.71(3)   538
s.72   542, 543, 544, 756
s.72(1)   543
s.72(1)(a)   543
s.72(2)   543
s.72(3)(a)   542
s.72(3)(b)   543f, 543
s.72(3)(c)   543
s.72(4)   543
s.72(5)   544
s.73-s.76   756
s.73(1)(a)   542f, 542
s.73(1)(b)   542
s.73(2)   542f
s.74   542f
s.76(1)-(2)   545
s.77(1)   535
s.77(2)   536

Table of Statutes

Taxation of Chargeable Gains Act
1992 – *continued*
s.77(8)   536
s.78   535f
s.79   536
s.80-s.98A   113
s.80(1)-(5)   756
s.85(2)-(3)   757
s.86   757
s.86(1)   756
s.87(1)-(2)   755
s.87(4)-(5)   755
s.87(7)   755
s.89(1)-(2)   756
s.91(1)-(2)   755
s.100   665
s.104   462, 498
s.105-s.114   498
s.115-s.117B   649
s.115(1)   503
s.117   503
s.122   589, 592, 657
s.126   647-9, 652, 657
s.126(1)(a)-(b)   647
s.126(2)   648
s.126(2)(a)   648
s.127   639, 647-9, 651, 652, 657
s.128   648, 649, 651, 652, 657
s.128(3)-(4)   649
s.129   649, 651, 652, 657
s.130   651, 652, 657
s.131   648, 651, 652
s.132   473, 474, 652
s.132(3)(a)   652
s.133-s.134   652
s.135   639, 649-52
s.135(1)(a)   651
s.136   649-52, 660, 662
s.137   73, 113, 652, 665, 667
s.138   27f, 652
s.139   552, 652, 657-65, 666, 667, 668
s.139(1)(c)   667
s.139(2)   664
s.139(5)   665, 666
s.139(9)   659
s.140A-140D   61f
s.144(1)   475
s.144(2)   485
s.144(3)-(4)   475
s.144(7)-(8)   475

Taxation of Chargeable Gains Act
1992 – *continued*
s.152(1)   523
s.152(3)-(4)   520
s.152(5)   523
s.152(7)-(8)   522
s.153   522
s.153(1)   522f
s.154   523
s.155   521
s.156   521f
s.157   523
s.158(1)   520
s.161   639, 640
s.161(2)   642
s.161(3)   485, 486
s.162   517, 518f
s.162(1)   517
s.162(2)   491
s.162(3)   518
s.163(1)   510
s.163(2)-(4)   511
s.163(5)   512
s.164   537
s.164(1)   513
s.164(7)   513
s.164A(8)-(9)   524
s.164B   538
s.164BA   524
s.164F   524
s.164G   524
s.164H   524f
s.164I   524
s.164L   113
s.164L(1)   524
s.165   515
s.165(1)   515
s.165(1)(b)   515f
s.165(2)   515
s.165(7)   516
s.166   516f
s.166(1)   515
s.167   516f
s.168   515
s.168(5)   516
s.168(7)   516
s.170   552, 617
s.170(3)(a)   637
s.170(3)(b)   638
s.170(6)   638
s.170(10)-(11)   638

Taxation of Chargeable Gains Act
 1992 – *continued*
 s.171   552, 616, 635, 638, 641, 668
 s.171(1)   638
 s.171(2)   639
 s.171(2)(a)   638
 s.171(2)(b)-(c)   639
 s.171(3)-(4)   639
 s.172-s.192   552
 s.173   639, 640, 641
 s.173(1)   639, 642
 s.173(2)   642
 s.174   642
 s.175   616, 642
 s.175(2)   642
 s.176-s.177   644
 s.177A   614, 644
 s.178   113, 668
 s.179   113, 616, 643, 644
 s.179(1)-(3)   643
 s.179(5)-(9)   644
 s.179(10)   643
 s.179(10)(c)   644
 s.179(11)   644
 s.179(13)   644
 s.180   113
 s.181   644
 s.185   559
 s.190   642
 s.190(1)   643
 s.190(3)   643
 s.192   653
 s.192(2)   657
 s.205   489f
 s.210(2)   504
 s.219-s.224   488f
 s.222(1)-(3)   505
 s.222(5)(a)   508
 s.222(5)(b)   509
 s.223(1)-(2)   509
 s.223(3)   510
 s.224(1)   510
 s.225   537
 s.226(a)   509
 s.227(a)   509
 s.237   504
 s.240   113
 s.242-s.243   497
 s.245-s.246   477
 s.251   503
 s.251(1)   473, 484

Taxation of Chargeable Gains Act
 1992 – *continued*
 s.251(3)   485
 s.252(2)   503f
 s.253(1)   500
 s.253(3)-(5)   500
 s.253(12)   500
 s.256(1)   501, 546
 s.256(2)   502
 s.257(2)   502
 s.257(3)   546
 s.260   515
 s.260(2)(a)   676
 s.260(7)   676
 s.262(1)-(2)   504
 s.262(3)   505
 s.262(4)-(5)   504f
 s.263   505
 s.268   505
 s.269   503
 s.274   527f
 s.275   752
 s.277   759f, 759
 s.277(1)   759f
 s.278   498, 758
 s.279   752
 s.280-s.281   478
 s.282   113
 s.286   484f, 682f
 s.286(2)   483, 525
 s.286(3)   483, 535
 s.286(4)-(5)   483
 s.286(6)-(7)   484
 s.286(8)   483
 s.288   57, 475
 Sch.1
   para.2(2)   502, 537
 Sch.5   757
 Sch.6
   para.1(2)   511, 512
   para.2   513
   para.3   510
   para.7-para.8   512
   para.13(1)   512
   para.15   512
 Sch.7
   para.2   537
   para.5   516
   para.7-para.8   516
 Sch.9   503

Taxes Acts 19, 183, 254, 255, 260, 396, 555
Taxes Management Act 1970 24, 566
  s.1 33
  s.1(2) 33, 37
  s.1(2A) 33
  s.2(3)-(5) 37
  s.4 37
  s.4(2) 37
  s.8(1) 35
  s.8(1A) 35
  s.8(1)(b) 35
  s.8(5) 35
  s.9(1)-(6) 35
  s.9A(1)-(2) 36
  s.11 566
  s.12B 283
  s.13 402f
  s.28C 35
  s.31 37
  s.31(5) 37
  s.35 172
  s.43 523
  s.44 37
  s.44(2) 38
  s.45-s.46 37
  s.46A 37
  s.56A 39
  s.59A 331, 336
  s.59A(1) 35
  s.59A(3)-(4) 35
  s.59B 336, 478
  s.59B(1) 35
  s.59C 35
  s.72 402f
  s.74 423, 529
  s.76 402f
  s.77 529
  s.78 402f
  s.86 35
  s.93 35
  s.94 566
  s.106 395, 396
  s.188(1) 32
  s.195-s.203 224f
  Sch.1
    Part III 33
  Sch.3 37
Tenures Abolition Act 1660 427f
Theft Act 1968 217

Town and Country Planning Act 1971 465
Tribunals and Inquiries Act 1992
  s.11 41
Trustee Act 1925
  s.31 406, 408, 409f, 409, 543, 738
  s.31(1)(ii) 409
  s.31(2) 409, 410
  s.32 538
  s.37 540

Unfair Contract Terms Act 1977
  s.11 42f
  Sch. 42f
Union with Scotland Act 1707 14
  art.1 14
  preamble 14

Value Added Tax Act 1983
  s.40 48
Value Added Tax Act 1994 24
  s.82-s.83 41
  s.84(2) 41
  s.85-s.86 41
  s.96 57
  Sch.11 283
    para.1 33
  Sch.12 41
Variation of Trusts Act 1958 718f

Wales and Berwick Act 1746 14
Welsh Language Act 1967 14
  s.4 14

European legislation
  Directive 77/338/EEC 24f, 46f
  EC Convention on Transfer Pricing 301
  EC Treaty *see* Treaty of Rome
  Single European Act 1986 61
  Treaty on European Union 23f
  Treaty of Rome 1957 62, 63, 65, 66
    art.5 62
    art.12 63
    art.100a 61, 552
    art.169 63
    art.170 63
    art.177 37, 68
    art.189 62
    art.190 67

French legislation
Code Civille
  art.1383 71f
Code Gènèrale des Impèts
  art.1653C 71f
  art.1729-3 71f

International legislation
UK/USA Double Tax Treaty 19, 593
  art.4 19
  art.11 604f

RULES

Companies (Tables A to G) Regulations 1985 (SI 1985/805)
Table A
  reg.70 556f

Deposit-Takers (Interest Payments) (Discretionary or Accumulation Trusts) Regulations 1995 (SI 1995/1370) 387

General Commissioners Regulations 1994 (SI 1994/1812)
  reg.20 38

Housing (Northern Ireland) Order 1981 Part VII 689

Income Tax (Building Societies) (Dividend and Interest) Regulations 1990 (SI 1990/2231) 387
  reg.3-reg.4 387
Income Tax (Sub-contractors in the Construction Industry) Regulations 1993 167f

Personal Equity Plan Regulations 1989
  reg.17(1) 504

Rules of the Supreme Court
  ord.53
    r.3 44f
    r.3(7) 44
  ord.55B
    r.71 39f

PART I
General matters

CHAPTER ONE
Introduction to tax law

1.1 INTRODUCTORY MATTERS[1]

This book is concerned with some of the more important aspects of UK taxation, but it is not intended to be, and could not be exhaustive. Tax is a statutory subject so it only makes sense when one talks about tax in relation to a particular legal system.[2] Accordingly, in the UK, tax is ultimately a matter of law rather than accountancy,[3] mathematics[4] etc. It is often to do with the rights of the state and the rights of the individual or subject[5] and the relationship between them.

1.2 WHAT IS TAX?

1.2.1 Long history

As good lawyers we should start by seeking to define and understand what it is that we are talking about. This prompts the question 'What is tax?' – an

---

[1.] See Kay and King, *The British Tax System*, 5th edn. 1990, OUP and James and Nobes, *The Economics of Taxation*, 1996/97 edn. for some of the economic background. The Inland Revenue and Customs and Excise produce a very useful series of booklets and pamphlets which have the great advantage of being free.
[2.] Cf. Dicey and Morris, *Conflict of Laws*, Rule 3: one state will not enforce the penal or revenue statutes of another.
[3.] Cf. *Britannia Airways Ltd* v *Johnson* [1994] STC 763 and *Gallagher* v *Jones* [1993] STC 537.
[4.] For example, 'The capital gains tax is a tax upon gains: it is not a tax upon arithmetical differences.' Lord Wilberforce in *Aberdeen Construction Group Ltd* v *IRC* [1978] STC 127 at 131.
[5.] See Adam Smith, *Wealth of Nations*, passim and H.H. Munroe, *Intolerable Inquisition? Reflections on the Law of Tax* (Hamlyn Lectures, 32nd series).

easy question to ask but a much harder question to answer. Certainly, tax is something which has been part of the human experience for a considerable time.[6] There is, for example, some evidence that tax was being levied amongst the Chaldeans.[7] It was certainly levied amongst the Egyptians.[8] Carol service readings also provide an example of tax being an all pervasive matter. It will be recalled that St Luke tells that 'it came to pass in those days that there went out a decree from Caesar Augustus that all the world should be taxed.'[9] Tax has been levied in the UK on a remarkable number of things. For example, servants,[10] windows,[11] plate[12] and dogs[13] have all, at some time, been taxed as have horses.[14] Those of a classical bent of mind may recall that Caligula taxed prostitutes even after they had married on 'as much as they received for one embrace each year.'[15]

1.2.2 Notoriously difficult to define

Despite its long history, tax is notoriously difficult to define. The relevant legislation contains no helpful definitions.[16] The case law (see, for example, *AG v Wilts United Dairies Ltd* (1921) 37 TLR 884, *Institute of Patent Agents v Lockwood* [1899] AC 347 and cf. *China Navigation Co v A-G* [1932] 2 KB 197) is not much more help. It does establish that since the Bill of Rights 'no money shall be levied to the use of the Crown except by grant of Parliament' (see Atkin LJ in *Wilts United Dairies* above). This has been tested in recovery and judicial review proceedings. In a pragmatic, English way, the question then is whether there was authority for what was done in the particular case, as tax and its imposition stem from statute.

If statute and case law do not help then the ordinary meaning of the word must be sought. The Shorter Oxford English Dictionary defines 'tax' as 'a legally levied contribution to state revenue.' However, this dictionary definition would include many things not usually considered to be taxation. For example, the purchase of a long-term government bond might fall within this definition. National Insurance contributions[17] certainly would be caught but perhaps they are properly to be regarded as taxation. National Insurance

---

[6.] See *Simon's Taxes* Vol A, Dowell, *A History of Taxation*, Sabine, *A Short History of Taxation*, Butterworth, 1980 and Parkinson, *The Law and the Profits*, Houghton Mifflin Co., 1960.
[7.] Ibid.
[8.] Ibid.
[9.] St Luke, Chapter 2, verse 1.
[10.] Introduced in 1777, see Sabine, *A Short History of Taxation*, p. 112 and in 1785 a tax on female servants, see ibid.
[11.] Introduced in 1696, see ibid.
[12.] Introduced in 1756, repealed 1777, see ibid.
[13.] Introduced in 1796, see ibid. The superior species of cats does not appear to have had such an indignity imposed on it.
[14.] See Sabine, op. cit.
[15.] See Suetonius, Book iv, Caligula, 40.
[16.] For example, s. 832, TA: 'Except so far as the context otherwise requires . . . "tax", where neither income tax nor corporation tax is specified means either of those taxes', is not very informative.
[17.] See D.W. Williams (1978) 41 MLR 404.

Introduction to tax law

contributions are levied as a percentage of income and for employees are collected by the same process and by the same people as income tax. National Insurance as far as employees are concerned is a very important matter.[18]

It thus seems almost impossible to produce a comprehensive definition of tax. Accordingly we should see if attempts to classify tax help to explain the concept.

1.2.3 Classification of taxes

There are many different ways in which taxes may be classified. Those that have been used are set out below. This approach allows us to follow Professor Hart's approach and seek elucidation of the word's meaning by its classification and description.

John Stuart Mill,[19] for example, in classifying taxes distinguished between direct and indirect taxes. A tax is said to be 'direct' when it is immediately taken from income or capital.[20] An example would be income tax. A tax is said to be 'indirect' when it is taken, for example, by making people pay for the liberty to use certain articles or to exercise certain privileges. An example of a modern indirect tax is value added tax.[21]

1.2.4 Tax bases

Other classifications of tax vary according to the base on which the tax is levied. By way of example, six possible bases will be considered. These are:

(a) income
(b) capital
(c) wealth
(d) expenditure
(e) transactions and documents
(f) inheritance

1.2.4.1 Income Income has been described as an obvious candidate for taxation. The payer has received the income out of which to pay the tax and 'income' is said to be fairly readily ascertainable, although those of you with accountancy knowledge may disagree since the precise meaning of income and its measurement are amongst the most difficult and controversial areas in accountancy.[22] Accountants at best only certify that the accounts give 'a true and fair view.'

---

[18] For reasons of space National Insurance is not considered further in this book.
[19] See J.S. Mill, *Principles of Political Economy*, Book V, Chapter 3.
[20] 'A direct tax is one which is demanded from the very persons, who it is intended or desired should pay it. Indirect taxes are those which are demanded from one person in the expectation and intention that he shall indemnify himself at the expense of the other: such as the excise or customs.' J.S. Mill, *Principles of Political Economy*, Book V, Chapter 3.
[21] Although it is probably wrong to describe it as a modern tax as it derives from the Spanish *al calaba* which led to the rebellion of the Netherlands in Charles V's time.
[22] See, e.g., *Cambridge Essays in Income Measurement*.

Equally those of you with a knowledge of economics may disagree with the statement that 'income' as opposed to, say, 'capital' is easy to compute. J.R. Hicks, the economist, defined a person's income as 'what he can consume during the week and still expect to be as well off at the end of the week as he was at the beginning.' This is not a very helpful definition for use as a tax base as it lacks certainty. The inspector and the taxpayer often have enough difficulty in agreeing what constitutes taxable income under the current law and it is difficult to imagine how the introduction of Hick's conception of 'income' would assist them.

Other economists' approaches have, however, been more helpful. R.M. Haig defined income as follows: 'Income is the money value of the net accretion to one's economic power between two points in time.' This was taken up by H.C. Simons and the Haig/Simons definition, which has been very influential, is as follows:

Professional income may be defined as the algebraic sum of:
(i) the market value of rights exercised in consumption; and
(ii) the change in value of the store of property rights between the beginning and the end of the period.

The Haig/Simons approach influenced the Canadian Royal Commission on taxation, the Carter Commission, in its report. The Commission considered that 'property gains', what we would call capital gains, should be taxed in the same way as other income receipts. The Haig/Simons approach also had considerable influence in the US and on the development of the comprehensive income tax base.[23] However, there are problems with the Carter Commission's approach in that it is not clear what types of monetary receipts are excluded. For example, would a receipt from great Aunt Agatha's estate on her death constitute 'income'? Would it be within the tax base?

The authors of an Institute for Fiscal Studies Report entitled, *The Structure and Reform of Direct Taxation* (chaired by Professor Meade and usually called the Meade Report) wrestled with this problem. It suggested two possible definitions of income. The first definition, definition A, is that 'The proper measure of a taxpayer's income in any one year is the value of what he could have consumed during the year without living on and so diminishing his capital wealth in the process.' Thus capital gains and windfall profits, for example from gambling, would be included. However, as is pointed out in the Meade Report, to accept this as the tax base would produce some very strange results. The Report gave the example of a millionaire who invested £1 million at 10% producing £100,000 per annum. If the national rate of interest rose to 11\frac{1}{9}% in one year, so that the capital value of his investment fell by £100,000 in the course of a year, his taxable income would be zero, thus wiping out his tax charge. Thus the effect of rises in interest rates in tax

---

[23.] See, e.g., Pechman 81 HLR 63; Andrews 87 HLR 1113 and 88 HLR 981 and *What Should be Taxed: Income or Expenditure?* ed. Pechman, Brooking Institution 1980.

Introduction to tax law 5

terms would be that the millionaire could become poverty stricken and claim supplementary benefit!

The second definition, definition B, is that 'A person's income is the amount which he could consume in any one year and yet be left with the resources and expectations at the end of that year which would enable him to maintain the same level of consumption indefinitely in the future.' However, this would also be impracticable as a tax base as it depends on future expectations.

The present UK income tax system conveniently avoids these difficulties by having no definition of 'income.' Instead it contains a list of sources giving rise to taxable profit or gains etc. As we shall see, this can be a great problem.

1.2.4.2 Capital

1.2.4.2.1 General Capital is the correlative of income but like income it suffers from a definitional problem. The most common analogy to distinguish between capital and income is that of tree and fruit for which Adam Smith is to blame. The tree is the capital which produces the fruit which is the income. In general terms this may be all very well, but what about the stalk? (see *Rae v Lazard Investment* (1963) 41 TC 1).

Statute does not give much guidance as to the meaning of income let alone capital. Section 833 TA 1988, for example, provides '(1) In the Income Tax Acts references to profits or gains shall not include references to chargeable gains . . .' A chargeable gain is a capital gain (see ss. 1 and 15(2), TCGA).

The following cases illustrate the difficulty of deciding what is income and what is capital.

The first case is *Lim Foo Yong v Comptroller-General* [1986] STC 251, a Privy Council case on appeal from Malaysia. In it a family company (whose objects included carrying on a hotel and restaurant business, purchasing property for investment and trafficking in property) built a hotel which it leased to a wholly owned subsidiary ('Sub 1'). The company then carried out a sale and leaseback of the hotel with a third party with a right of repurchase after ten years and transferred assets, including the right of repurchase, to a new company ('Sub 2') for an issue of shares as part of a reconstruction. The Revenue treated the value of the shares issued as a trading profit. The company argued it was capital. The Privy Council found that the transactions were entered into to raise finance for the company and retain the hotel as a profit earning asset. Therefore the transactions were on capital, not revenue, account. This may be illustrated as follows in figure 1.1.

Johnson Matthey PLC ('PLC') dealt in precious metals, particularly platinum. Its wholly owned subsidiary, Johnson Matthey Banking Limited ('JMB') carried on a banking business '. . . and thereby assisted the financing of . . . [PLC's] trade.' JMB experienced financial difficulties. It became clear over the course of one weekend that JMB could not pay its debts as they became due and so could not 'open for business' on the Monday. As a consequence PLC could not continue to trade. PLC could not afford to rescue JMB and the Bank of England ('Bank') was informed of the situation.

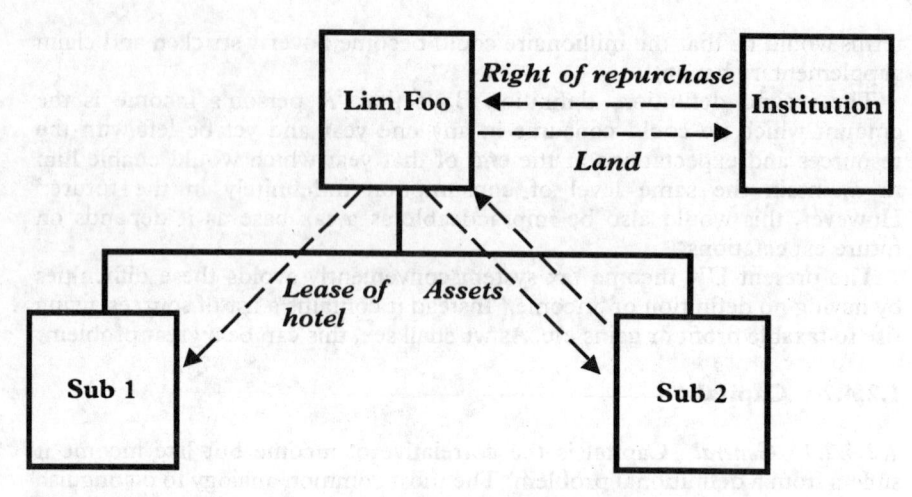

Figure 1.1

The second case is *Lawson* v *Johnson Matthey* [1992] STC 466 (and see Shipwright, Volume 4, 1993–94 KCLJ 118) the facts of which, according to Lord Templeman, were 'unprecedented'. This may be illustrated as follows in figure 1.2.

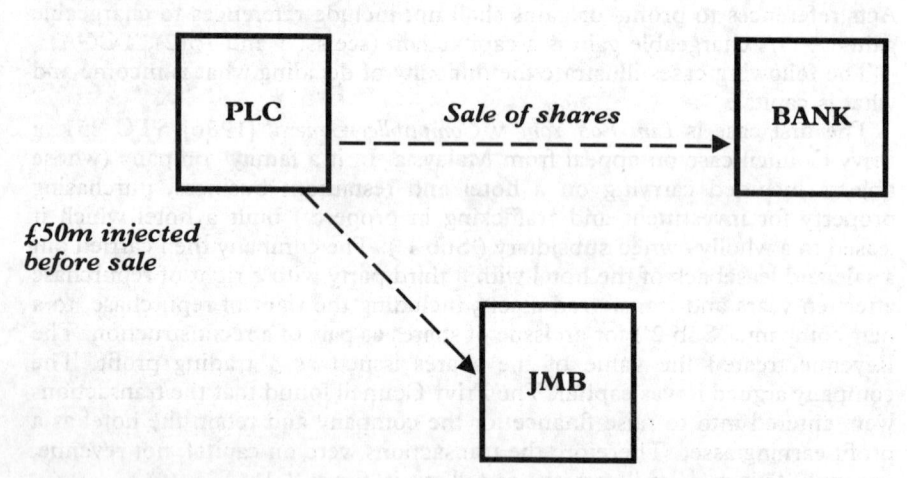

Figure 1.2

A non-negotiable offer was made by the Bank to buy JMB for £1 if £50 million were previously injected into JMB by PLC. A written agreement for the injection of £50 million was concluded. It did not mention any rescue of JMB by the Bank.

PLC claimed the £50 million as a trading expense arguing it was of a revenue nature. The inspector disallowed it as capital expenditure not laid out wholly and exclusively for the purposes of PLC's trade. PLC appealed. PLC was found by the General Commissioners to have made the payment of £50 million 'on the evidence . . . before [them] . . . to preserve the trade of [PLC] from collapse.' Apparently, '. . . even though the Bank did not (and no doubt could not) promise PLC that it would rescue JMB, nevertheless it was plainly planning to do so, . . . and it exacted the £50 million cash injection as PLC's contribution to that rescue. That explains why the sum was not payable to the Bank, but stipulated to be a cash injection into JMB before the shares were transferred . . . PLC knew that it could safely proceed . . . without any promise to rescue JMB, because matters had gone so far that the Bank was bound to mount that rescue as soon as JMB's doors were open . . . in these circumstances the payment cannot be described as money paid for the divestiture of the shares.'

Accordingly, the Commissioners found the payment *was* made for the purposes of PLC's trade. The case was appealed and ultimately reached the House of Lords. Duality, i.e., the payment was to preserve the capital asset (the JMB shares) for sale to crystallise a loss *and* preserve the trade, did not trouble the Lords although Lord Templeman concluded that the payment had been made solely to enable PLC to carry on its business. The nub of the case thus became the income/capital divide. If the payment were income it would be deductible as an income expense – if not, it would not be deductible (cf. *Vodaphone Cellular Ltd v Shaw* [1995] STC 353) for the purposes of corporation tax on income.

The parties accepted that the £50 million was a capital payment if it was made for the divestiture of a capital asset, i.e., the JMB shares. The essential question was, 'Was the payment to get rid of the JMB shares or in reality paid out to protect PLC's trade and so income?' Vinelott J and the Court of Appeal held it was paid to get rid of the shares and so was capital, as a first reading of the agreement suggests. However the House of Lords decided it was not paid for the transfer of the shares but as part of the wider purpose of saving PLC's business from collapse, although the House recognised the initial attraction of the alternative analysis. Lord Goff said that in those circumstances the payment could not be described as money paid for the divestiture of the shares. The reality was that it was a contribution to the rescue and a prerequisite to the share transfer.

However, the payment was not revenue simply because it was made to preserve the trade as the Commissioners had suggested. It also needed to be of an income nature. The characterisation did not depend upon PLC's motive but whether it was paid to dispose of a capital asset. Here it was not. It was paid, in effect, to enable PLC to continue earning profits and so was an expense of earning them (cf. *Morgan v Tate & Lyle* (1954) 35 TC 367).

As can be seen from these cases, the correct characterisation of a payment or receipt as income or capital can be difficult to determine. The precise facts are very important. The question whether the capital/income distinction matters is discussed below.

1.2.4.2.2 Does the capital/income distinction matter? In general UK tax rates for income and capital are the same. Since FA 1988 the highest marginal rate of UK tax is 40%. This is true of income tax, capital gains tax and inheritance tax. The rates of capital gains tax were increased from the former flat rate of 30%. CGT is now charged at rates determined by adding the chargeable gain to the taxpayer's taxable income. Accordingly, the maximum marginal rate of capital gains tax is 40% as for income tax. However, income tax and capital gains tax have not been amalgamated. The rates have been approximated or 'converged' but the tax base not been harmonised.

Thus, it is essential to determine which tax regime (i.e., income or capital gains taxation) applies since certain important differences remain, including the following:

(a) The bases of computation of liability differ (e.g., the Indexation Allowance is available for capital gains tax but not for income taxation).

(b) There is an annual exempt amount for CGT purposes of £6,500 (1997–98), whereas the personal allowance available as a deduction from total income is £4,045 for a single person (1997–98).

(c) Income losses may be used more extensively than capital losses.

(d) The dates for payment differ. Income tax under Schedule D, Cases I and II is due in January during the year of assessment and in July following the end of the year of assessment, in equal instalments, whereas CGT is due on 1 December following the end of the year of assessment.

(e) A non-resident who does not carry on a trade in the UK through a branch or agency is not within the charge to capital gains tax. However, a UK source may be sufficient for an income tax charge to arise.

(f) Different withholding tax requirements apply.

(g) Different reliefs apply for the purposes of the two tax regimes.

1.2.4.3 Wealth Some have argued that wealth, apart from providing a source of income which is compatible with a life of leisure, gives opportunity, security, social power, influence and independence. Equity, it is said, requires wealth to be included in the tax base.

The Labour government elected in 1974 announced its intention to introduce a wealth tax in the UK. A Green Paper was produced which was referred to a House of Commons Select Committee. However, the Committee was unable to agree and produced five minority reports (see J.F. Avery Jones and Erica Stary [1975] BTR 401 and A.R. Prest [1976] BTR 7).

The Green Paper put forward a tax capacity argument for a wealth base, i.e., wealth is a better indicator of taxable capacity than income. However, it is submitted that even this is not that clear. The owner of a stately home may have something that can be valued highly for wealth purposes but not much in the way of available resources because of the cost of keeping up the house and estate. The result was that capital transfer tax was introduced which became inheritance tax (IHT) (see Chapter 30 et seq).

1.2.4.4 Expenditure It has long been argued that it is wrong to tax 'income'; rather 'outgo' should be taxed. This was, for example, the argument of Thomas Hobbes in *Leviathan* (see in particular Part 2 of Chapter 30, 1651 edition) and his view was supported by John Stuart Mill.

Introduction to tax law

The Meade Report (see para. 1.2.4.1) suggested that such an 'out go' tax should be adopted. It was argued that such a tax would encourage saving by removing the discrimination of the 'double taxation' of savings, i.e., the taxation of income from savings made out of taxed income. However, there are certain practical difficulties in introducing such a tax base. For example, whose expenditure is to be relevant? Should it be the household? If so, only married families? What transitional provisions should be provided and on what basis?

1.2.4.5 Transactions and documents Particular transactions and documents can be used to trigger tax charges. Thus in the UK Stamp Duty is chargeable on documents and Stamp Duty Reserve Tax (SDRT) is chargeable on certain transactions.

1.2.4.6 Inheritance Inheritance can be a separate tax base or a particularised form of a capital or transactions base. In 1972 the then Conservative government issued a Green Paper (Cmnd 4930) considering an 'Inheritance Tax'. This was more of an acquisition tax (cf. the Irish Cumulative Accessions Tax) than a mutation tax (i.e., one charged according to the value of the property changing hands regardless of its destination) as estate duty was and as IHT may be considered. Again it was not a new idea. It had been considered in 1894 when estate duty was introduced and was the solution adopted by many continental systems.

1.3 WHAT ARE THE AIMS OF A TAX SYSTEM?

1.3.1 Expenditure

In earlier times, taxes were usually only levied occasionally to pay for some large expenditure such as a war.[24] For example, income tax was introduced by William Pitt in 1799 as a temporary measure to pay for the Napoleonic War (see Chapter 3). Taxation is still used as a means of raising money to meet government expenditure. Some people also think it has, or should have, other uses.

1.3.2 Nowadays?

Today governments claim to use taxation in some circumstances for purposes other than raising money to cover expenditure. For example, some governments claim that taxation should be used as an instrument for the redistribution of wealth. This was one of the stated objectives of capital transfer tax when first introduced.[25]

Tax is also thought by some to be available as a means of macroeconomic control. Whether this argument is accepted and, if it is accepted, whether it is desirable depends to a large extent on political belief.

[24.] See Dowell, *History of Taxation*, passim.
[25.] Denis Healey is alleged to have said that he wanted CTT to make the rich's pips squeak. Capital transfer tax has since mutated into inheritance tax which does not have redistributive aims, see Part V below.

1.3.3 Carter Commission (Canada)

The Canadian Carter Commission (see para. 1.2.4.1) said:

> Appraisal of the existing tax system and recommendations for its improvement must be predicated on a widely accepted set of goals or objectives that the nation is seeking, and on the knowledge of the potential role that a tax system can claim in the achievement of these goals.
> We believe that the four fundamental objectives on which the Canadian people agree are:
>
> (i) To maximise the current and future output and services desired by Canadians.
> (ii) To ensure that this flow of goods and services is distributed equitably among the individuals or groups.
> (iii) To protect the liberties and rights of individuals through the preservation of representative, responsible government and maintenance of the rule of law.
> (iv) To maintain and strengthen the Canadian Federation.
>
> Our task is nothing less than to try to design a tax system that will assist in the fullest possible achievement of all these goals simultaneously. This is indeed a difficult undertaking, but it is one that is inherent in our assignment.

The reader should consider whether these goals could be translated into a UK context. The authors would suggest that at present the UK tax system lacks any clear, coherent, underlying policies for taxation. To a large extent it is the result of history and the way in which our legislative process works or does not work.[26]

1.4 WHAT ARE THE CRITERIA FOR A 'GOOD' TAX SYSTEM?

1.4.1 Objectivity

If one is constructing or appraising a tax system the question arises, 'what makes for a "good"[27] tax system?'. To a large extent the answer to this question must be a subjective one as it is related closely to the individual's conception of what the aims of the state and the tax system should be.

[26.] For an illustration of the defects of the enactment of UK tax legislation, see the Armstrong Report, *Budgetary Reform in the UK* (1980) and the various reports of the Special Committee of Tax Law Consultative Bodies, most recently *Recommendations on the Development of Tax Legislation*, September 1993. For criticism of the UK legislative machinery in general, see *Making the Law*: the Report of the Hansard Society Commission on the Legislative Process 1992.

[27.] Good in the *1066 and All That* (Sellars and Yeatman) sense of being 'a good thing'.

Introduction to tax law

1.4.2 Adam Smith

Adam Smith set out four canons of taxation in his seminal work, *The Wealth of Nations*, which have been influential ever since. The first canon stated:

> The subjects of every state ought to contribute towards the support of the government, as nearly as possible, in proportion to their respective abilities; that is, in proportion to the revenue which they respectively enjoy under the protection of the state.

This is described in the modern tax literature as 'equity'. A good tax system on that basis must therefore be equitable. Adam Smith's view that only a proportional system (i.e., one with a fixed percentage for all) is equitable has, to a large extent, been rejected. However, it is interesting to note that it has recently resurfaced in New Zealand.

To be 'good' a tax system must be equitable in two senses:

(a) Horizontally equitable, which broadly means that like cases should be treated alike.[28] People in like circumstances with like taxable income should be taxed equally.

(b) Vertically equitable, which in simple terms means that those in unlike circumstances should be treated differently.[29]

The second canon is that:

> The tax which an individual is bound to pay ought to be certain and not arbitrary.

This makes for efficiency in the tax system in that it does not put arbitrary power in the hands of the tax gatherer. Further, it is likely to encourage what has been described as 'tax morality' as it makes tax evasion[30] more easily detectable.

The third canon is that:

> Every tax ought to be levied at the time, or in the manner in which it is most likely to be convenient for the contributor to pay it.

The modern jargon for this is that the tax should be neutral. By this it is meant that the system should be designed to minimise, as far as possible, the impact of the tax structure on the economic behaviour of agents in the economy and that it should avoid distortionary substitutional effects. This is not always the case in the UK where the tax system has been seen as a way

---

[28.] Cf. John Rawls, *Theory of Justice*, that one should only look to the welfare of the least advantaged. See discussion in Kay and King, *The British Tax System*, 5th edn, pp. 36–39.
[29.] Cf. H.L.A. Hart, *Minimum Content of Natural Justice*, OUP.
[30.] Evasion is a criminal offence; see *R v Hunt* [1994] STC 819 and *R v Ryan* [1994] STC 446. Avoidance or mitigation of tax is legal.

of providing incentives, for example, enterprise zones, or disincentives, for example, the luxury rate of VAT which was with us for a time. Neutrality demands that the tax system should distort the market as little as possible so as to enable profits etc. to be made in the best way commercially. The theory is that it is only when the income or gain has accrued that the recipient's thoughts should turn to taxation.

The fourth canon is that:

Tax should be so contrived as both to take out and to keep out of the pockets of the people as little as possible, over and above what it brings in to the public treasury of the state.

In other words, the tax must be administratively efficient.

1.4.3 Inefficiencies

Adam Smith lists four ways in which a tax system may be inefficient.

(a) A large number of officials may cost so much that they use up most of the tax-take in salaries and other incidental expenses.

(b) The officials may obstruct people from getting on with the business of making profits etc. 'which might give maintenance and employment to great multitudes.'

(c) Evasion may lead to ruin 'by the forfeitures and other penalties which those unfortunate individuals incur who attempt unsuccessfully to evade the tax, . . . and thereby put an end to the benefit which the community might have received from the employment of their capitals. An injudicious tax offers a great temptation to smuggling.'

(d) 'By subjecting people to the frequent visits, and the odious examination of the tax gatherers, it may expose them to much unnecessary trouble, vexation, and oppression; and though vexation is not, strictly speaking, expense, it is certainly equivalent to the expense at whichever man would be willing to redeem himself from it.'

1.4.4 Meade Report

The Meade Report (see para. 1.2.4.1) says that the following points are clear:

(a) A good tax system should be horizontally equitable, i.e., should treat like with like.

(b) A modern tax system must be so constructed as to be capable of use for vertical redistribution between rich and poor.

(c) There will almost inevitably be some clash between the criteria of economic efficiency (which requires low marginal tax rates) and of vertical redistribution (which requires high average rates of tax on the rich); but a good tax system is one which minimalises this clash and promotes a given redistribution with a minimum loss of efficiency.

Introduction to tax law 13

(d) The final choice of redistributional aims for a tax system involves a basic value adjustment about the nature of a good society, which are matters for political decision. However, a good structure is one which is sufficiently flexible to allow scope in a democratic society for different political choices, (for example, by variations in rates of tax).

You should consider whether you agree that this is so.

1.5 UK TAXES

1.5.1 The major UK taxes

The major UK taxes include:

(a) income tax
(b) capital gains tax
(c) corporation tax
(d) inheritance tax
(e) value added tax
(f) customs and excise duties.[31]

1.6 TERRITORIAL SCOPE OF UK TAXATION

1.6.1 Penal laws of another country?

Apart from rates (a local land based tax for businesses) and council tax (a local land based tax for individuals), UK tax is generally national in the sense of applying to the whole of the UK and being raised by national government. This can cause many difficulties as the English, Scottish and Northern Irish legal systems may have different underlying laws[32] while tax law has to be construed in the whole UK context. This is also true of other areas of the law, such as company law.

1.6.2 Meaning of 'United Kingdom'

As this book is concerned with UK tax, the question arises as to what is meant by the United Kingdom in this context. By s. 2(2), Royal and Parliamentary Titles Act 1927, United Kingdom means Great Britain and Northern Ireland unless the context otherwise requires. The Interpretation Act 1978 also states in sch. 1 that the United Kingdom means Great Britain and Northern Ireland in Acts passed on or after 12 April 1927. This includes most of the current provisions imposing tax in the UK.

[31.] These and stamp duty, petroleum revenue tax, air passenger duty and insurance duty are not considered in this book.
[32.] For example, as to charity and public trusts, see *IRC* v *City of Glasgow Police Athletic Association* [1953] 1 All ER 747.

Great Britain is not defined in the Interpretation Act. However, the preamble to the Union with Scotland Act 1707 and Art. 1 provide that the two kingdoms of England and Scotland shall be united into one kingdom by the nature of Great Britain. By virtue of the Wales and Berwick Act 1746 the reference in the 1707 Act to England includes a reference to Wales and accordingly 'Great Britain' means England, Wales and Scotland. The 1707 Act is not restrictive, its definition of Great Britain extends to Acts of Parliament.

By sch. 1 to the Interpretation Act, 'England' means, for the purposes of Acts passed on or after 1 April 1974 and subject to any alteration of boundaries under Part 4 of the Local Government Act 1972, the area consisting of the counties established by s. 1 of that Act, Greater London and the Isles of Scilly unless the contrary intention appears.

By para. 5 of Part 1 of sch. 2 to the Interpretation Act, in any Act passed before 1 April 1974 a reference to England also includes Berwick-upon-Tweed and Monmouthshire and, in the case of an Act passed before the Welsh Language Act 1967, 'England' also includes 'Wales'. Incorporation of Wales into the meaning of England also follows from the Laws in Wales Act 1535 in which s. 1 of the Act states that Wales is incorporated with England.

Section 4, Welsh Language Act 1967 provides that for those Acts passed on and after 27 July 1967 references to England in Acts of Parliament no longer include Wales, i.e., England and Wales must be used to impart this meaning of both countries.

The effect of this is that the United Kingdom means England, Wales, Scotland, Northern Ireland and the Isles of Scilly.

The Channel Islands do not form part of the United Kingdom. They are the residual vestiges of the Crown's claim to the Dukedom of Normandy. They thus have a different constitutional position from the constituents of the United Kingdom. The same is true of the Isle of Man where the Crown's claim derives from its right as the Lord of Man.

1.6.3 Income tax and territoriality

Tax is imposed by a legislature. How far does its jurisdiction run and what criteria should be the basis of that jurisdiction? Should an English court enforce a French tax liability? The answer is that, in general, the English courts will only enforce UK tax statutes. However, in some circumstances European Directives have direct effect.[33]

1.6.3.1 *Locus classicus* The most famous dictum on the territoriality of income tax is to be found in Lord Herschell's speech in *Colquhoun* v *Brooks* (1889) 2 TC 490 at p. 499. He said: 'The Income Tax Acts, however, themselves impose a territorial limit, either that from which the taxable income is derived must be situate in the UK or the person whose income is to be taxed must be resident there.' There are thus two alternative necessary conditions for the imposition of UK tax:

[33.] See *R* v *Secretary of State for Transport ex parte Factortame* [1990] 2 AC 85, *Francovich* v *Italian Republic* C 6/90 and C 9/90, *Becker* [1982] 1 CMLR 499.

Introduction to tax law 15

(a) The property must be located in the UK, for example, rent from land in the UK will be subject to UK tax no matter where the landlord is resident. Deduction at source is one way of avoiding the problem of collection in these cases.

(b) If a person is resident and/or ordinarily resident in the UK, he will generally be taxed on his worldwide income and capital gains. Generally, this will be on an arising basis, i.e., the tax liability arises as soon as the taxpayer is entitled to the income wherever it is, rather than on a remittance basis, i.e., the tax liability arises when the income is brought into the country. (However, as will be seen in para. 1.6.3.6 below, a person domiciled outside the UK can benefit from the remittance basis in respect of income and gains from a non-UK *situs* source – see further Chapter 35).

This may be stated formally as the proposition that there are two alternative necessary conditions for liability to UK tax to arise. These are that either:

(a) there must be a UK source, or
(b) there must be UK residence etc.

1.6.3.2 Connecting factors: 'residence', 'ordinary residence' and 'domicile' This leads us to the question what is meant by the words 'resident', 'ordinary resident' and 'domicile'. None of these terms is defined in the Taxes Act even though they are fundamental terms in UK taxation. Lord President Clyde has ventured the view that no exhaustive definition can be given.

Because of the lack of statutory help, we are therefore driven to look at the case law on the subject to try and extract some principles. However, residence and ordinary residence have been said to be a question of fact not law (see *IRC* v *Lysaght* 13 [1928] TC 511). This has led to the difficulty that in most of the cases which are generally treated as laying down principles, the judges have done no more than find that there was evidence before the Commissioners to justify the finding of the fact which therefore could not be interfered with. Many of the cases seem inconsistent and illogical but are explicable on this factual basis. So although we are told that there is no technical meaning to the words (see, for example, Lord Buckmaster in *Lysaght* v *IRC*), in extracting general principles an artificiality and technicality has arisen.

The decided cases do not cover the whole spectrum of the problem. The Revenue have therefore worked out their own administrative code based upon case law. This is set out in the Inland Revenue pamphlet IR 20 entitled *Residents' and Non-Residents' Liabilities to Tax in the UK* and was last revised in 1996. It has no statutory force but is applied in practice. It has been noted that the Revenue practice as set out in the code is: 'based on decisions in favour of the Revenue and consistently ignores those in favour of the taxpayer' (*Butterworths UK Tax Guide 1995–96*, para. 32:02).

The Revenue published a consultative document on 28 July 1988 which proposed changes to residence and the basis of taxation. However, Peter

Lilley subsequently announced that these proposals would not be proceeded with.

1.6.3.3 Residence The meaning of residence has developed with the case law. The concept of residence in the sense of the particular building in which an individual lives is not the one with which we are concerned. As Rowlatt J said in *Levene* v *IRC* [1928] 13 TC 486:

> The words 'resident' and 'residence' are in the first place quite clearly intended to describe . . . the attribute of the person. One must get out of one's mind altogether the use of the words resident and residence as applying to a building or anything of that kind.

The nearest thing to a definition of the word 'reside' comes from Viscount Cave LC in *Levene* v *IRC* where he says:

> . . . the word 'reside' is a familiar English word and is defined in the Oxford English Dictionary as meaning 'to dwell permanently or for a considerable time, to have one's settled or usual abode, to live in or at a particular place'.

No doubt this definition must for present purposes, subject to any modification which may result from the TA and Schedules, be accepted as an accurate indication of the meaning of the word reside. Two further points can be made:

(a) In strict theory, residence should be determined for a whole year. In practice the Revenue by concession split years of assessment for immigrants and emigrants who are resident during the course of the year (see para. 1.5 IR 20).

(b) It is possible to have dual residence (cf. domicile discussed below). A person may only have one domicile at a time.

Factors that have been treated as relevant to residence include the following:

(a) physical presence in the UK;
(b) nationality;
(c) past history as to residency;
(d) present habits and mode of life;
(e) frequency, regularity and duration of visits;
(f) purpose of visits and absences;
(g) family and business ties with the UK;
(h) whether or not a place of abode in the UK is maintained or is available for use.

The availability of accommodation is no longer as important as it used to be. Before the passing of s. 208, FA 1993 the availability of accommodation could, according to the Revenue, be determinative (based on a generous reading of *Cooper* v *Cadwalader* (1904) 5 TC 101). The present position is not that living accommodation is irrelevant, only that it is not to be taken into account for certain purposes. The ownership of a large house and estate in the UK may show a clear connection to the UK and so be relevant on that basis.

Sections 334–368, TA provide certain statutory modifications. Section 334 states:

> Every Commonwealth citizen or citizen of the Republic of Ireland:
> (a) shall, if his ordinary residence has been in the United Kingdom, be assessed and charged to Income Tax notwithstanding that at the time the assessment or charge is made he may have left the United Kingdom, if he has so left the United Kingdom for the purpose only of occasional residence abroad, and
> (b) shall be charged as the person actually residing in the United Kingdom on the whole amount of his profits or gains, whether they arise from property in the United Kingdom or elsewhere, or from any allowance, annuity and stipend, or from any trade, profession, employment or vocation in the United Kingdom or elsewhere.

This section is said to derive from s. 38 of the 1842 income tax legislation. Notwithstanding this, the first decision on the meaning of s. 334 is to be found in *Reed* v *Clark* [1985] STC 323. This concerned a Mr Dave Clark who was the 'leading light' in a five piece band which became known as the Dave Clark Five. As the Special Commissioners found:

> In the mid 1970s a new movement in popular music known as 'punk rock' (and later 'new wave') began in England; it had its origin in the more violent music of the 'Rock 'n' Roll' era of the early 1960s. Two of the original Dave Clark songs, 'Glad All Over' and 'Bits and Pieces' (which featured heavy stamping of feet to a loud musical accompaniment) became popular in clubs and dance halls.

Dave Clark and a company controlled by him owned the copyright in all the band's successful recordings. In late November 1977 agreements were entered into with a record company for a worldwide licence for two selected Dave Clark compilation albums. Dave Clark was a British subject domiciled in the UK. He was resident in the UK for all years except 1978–1979 during which time he went to the United States of America. He was advised that if he did not set foot in the United Kingdom during 1978–1989 and instead became resident (on UK tax rules) in the United States for that year he could receive the whole of the royalty payment free from UK and USA tax.

Dave Clark had for some time wished to go to the United States for a period as it fitted in well with his requirements and pattern of life. Thus he went to the USA and stayed there for 13 months. He was nevertheless assessed to income tax for the year 1978–1979 in respect of the payments. Two questions were at issue:

(a) Whether a person can be resident in the United Kingdom during the year of assessment in which he does not set foot in the United Kingdom.
(b) As to the effect of what is now s. 334, TA.

On the first issue, Nicholls J said that a taxpayer may 'reside' for tax purpose in the United Kingdom although physically absent from this country for a whole year. A master mariner in the East Indies maintaining a house on the Clyde, was an example of this (see *IRC v Rogers* (1979) 1 TC 255). His Lordship was attracted to the idea that residence normally required physical presence but there may be some exceptions to this for a wanderer such as a sea captain.

On s. 334, the learned judge concluded that it is a substantive charging provision. Where its conditions are satisfied, the person is to be charged as a person actually residing in the United Kingdom on the whole of his profits or gains. His Lordship considered that a person might be abroad for longer than a year for the purpose of 'occasional residence' and this would be a matter of fact and degree. However, he considered there had been a distinct break in Mr Clark's pattern of life and in the circumstances this was not occasional residence. The meaning of occasional residence was a question of law and was to be contrasted with ordinary residence.

Section 335, TA states:

(1) Where:
(a) a person works full-time in one or more of the following, that is to say, a trade, profession, vocation, office or employment; and
(b) no part of the trade, profession or vocation is carried on in the United Kingdom and all the duties of the office or employment are performed outside the United Kingdom;
the question whether he is resident in the United Kingdom shall be decided without regard to any place of abode maintained in the United Kingdom for his use.
(2) Where an office or employment is in substance one of which the duties fall in the year of assessment to be performed outside the United Kingdom there shall be treated for the purposes of this section as so performed any duties performed in the United Kingdom the performance of which is merely incidental to the performance of the other duties outside the United Kingdom.

Section 336, TA states:

(1) A person shall not be charged to income tax under Schedule D as a person residing in the United Kingdom, in respect of profits or gains received in respect of possessions or securities out of the United Kingdom, if—
(a) he is in the United Kingdom for some temporary purpose only and not with any view or intent of establishing his residence there, and
(b) he has not actually resided in the United Kingdom at one time or several times for a period equal in the whole to six months in any year of

Introduction to tax law

assessment, but if any such person resides in the United Kingdom for such a period he shall be so chargeable for that year.

Section 336(2) makes similar provisions for employees and with s. 335, the question is to be decided without regard to available accommodation (s. 336(3)).

Thus for certain purposes a person present in the UK for more than six months will be deemed resident in the UK (see also s. 9(3), TCGA 1992). The Revenue take the view that if a person is resident in the UK for six months or more in the year of assessment, he will always be regarded as resident for that year (see para. 8, IR 20). The Revenue approach is to regard six months as equivalent to 183 days whether or not there is a leap year. Under present practice days of arrival and days of departure are normally ignored.

1.6.3.4 Dual residence Although a person may only be domiciled in one country at any one time, it is possible to be resident for tax purposes in more than one country at any one time. This may cause problems in that it may lead to several tax liabilities in respect of the same income or gains. To avoid this, countries enter into agreements with other countries to allocate the rights to tax individuals, companies etc. between them. Most double tax treaties seek to allocate a person to one jurisdiction or another for tax purposes. For example, as far as individuals are concerned, the UK/US Double Tax Treaty provides a 'tie-breaker' for determining where an individual is resident in the case of possible dual residency (see e.g., Art. 4 of the UK/US Double Tax Treaty).

1.6.3.5 Ordinary residence There has been much judicial discussion of the difference between resident and ordinarily resident. Some judges suggest that they can see no real difference but from the context in which the two expressions are used in the Taxes Acts, it is clear that, at any rate, the draftsmen of the taxing statutes considered there was a distinction.

Again there is no statutory definition. However, it seems that ordinary residence denotes greater permanence than residence and is broadly equivalent to habitual residence (see old IR 20, para. 9 and cf. new para. 1.3). The most helpful judicial expression is that of Rand J in the Canadian case *Thomson* v *Minister of National Revenue* as applied by Wynn Parry J in *Miesegaes* v *IRC* (1957) 37 TC 493, that the expression 'ordinarily resident' carries a restricted signification, and although the first impression seems to be that of preponderance in time, the decisions on the UK Act reject that view. It is held to mean residence in the course of the customary mode of life of the person concerned, and this is contrasted with special or occasional or casual residence. The general mode of life is, therefore, relevant to a question of its application.

Paragraph 1.3 of IR 20 states:

You may be resident but not ordinarily resident in the UK for a tax year if, for example, you normally live outside the UK but are in this country for

183 days or more in the year. Or you may be ordinarily resident but not resident for a tax year if, for example, you usually live in the UK but have gone abroad for a long holiday and do not set foot in the UK during that year.

1.6.3.6 Domicile

1.6.3.6.1 Introduction Domicile may also affect an individual's liability to UK tax. This is partly for historical reasons and partly for the advantages that it gives the UK (e.g., foreign banks etc. basing themselves in the UK as their executives are willing to come to the UK). Someone who lives in the UK but is domiciled outside the UK has a special beneficial tax regime reflecting their foreign connections.

A person not domiciled in the UK is (inter alia):

(a) not liable to UK income tax on income from foreign securities (e.g., dividends from shares in General Motors) or from foreign possessions (e.g., rent on a flat in Gibraltar) unless the income is directly or indirectly received in the UK. This is known as the remittance basis for investment income;

(b) able to benefit from special rules excluding from UK income tax salary from an employment with a non-UK resident employer where all the duties of the job are carried on outside the UK unless that salary is received directly or indirectly in the UK. This is known as the foreign emoluments exemption. There are also special rules for foreign travel;

(c) only liable to UK capital gains tax on the capital gains accruing on the disposal of non-UK situate assets if the gain is directly or indirectly remitted to the UK;

(d) able to set up non-resident trusts without falling foul of the capital gains tax anti-avoidance legislation brought in in the 1980s and in 1991;

(e) entitled to the benefit of the 'excluded property' provisions in relation to UK inheritance tax. Broadly, excluded property is not taken into account when valuing the estate for IHT purposes. It consists (in general terms) of:

(i) property (other than an interest in a settlement etc.) situated outside the UK to which a person domiciled outside the UK is beneficially entitled; and

(ii) (in essence) property comprised in a settlement which is situate outside the UK and the settlement was made by a person domiciled outside the UK when the settlement was created. (There are special rules for determining the residence of settlements for IHT purposes.)

(f) outside the notorious anti-avoidance provisions (ss. 739, TA et seq) 'for the purpose of preventing the avoiding ... of liability to income tax by means of the transfer of assets by virtue ... of which ... income becomes payable to persons resident or domiciled outside the UK.' (Section 739(1) and s. 743(3), TA.) These are very widely drawn provisions which can provide a trap for the unwary.

Introduction to tax law

1.6.3.6.2 What is domicile? Domicile has been used for tax purposes as a matter of convenience. It is not a concept which has been specifically designed for tax purposes. The essential purpose of domicile is to connect an individual with the country in which he has his basis permanently or indefinitely, so that that country's law can be used in determining matters affecting that individual's personal status. This includes such matters as the essential validity of a marriage and matters concerning the individual's family, property, legitimacy, legitimation and adoption. Domicile is a technical legal construct used to link a person to a law system rather than 'a place of ordinary habitation; a house or home.'

1.6.3.6.3 The present rules – in outline Under the laws of the countries of the United Kingdom a person cannot be without a domicile and cannot be domiciled in two places at once. An individual acquires a domicile of origin at birth. For a legitimate child this will be that of the father at the time of birth. For an illegitimate child it will be that of the mother. This domicile or origin continues until the individual acquires a domicile of choice and revives if the domicile of choice is abandoned.

There are two necessary conditions for acquiring a domicile of choice. These are:

(a) residence (broadly physical presence) in that country; and
(b) having the intention to make his home in that country permanently or indefinitely. It seems that there must be a 'fixed and settled purpose' or *animus manendi* to abandon the country of his old domicile and to settle in the new country. However, more recently the rules seem to have been relaxed.

Long residence alone is not conclusive under the current rules. The age at which one can acquire a domicile of choice differs in different parts of the UK. Further the standard of proof in England to show that a domicile of origin has been replaced by a domicile of choice may be higher than the ordinary civil standard of the balance of probabilities. If a person abandons a domicile of choice without acquiring a new domicile of choice, then under English law his domicile of origin revives and applies unless and until he acquires a new domicile of choice.

Factors relevant to the retention of a foreign domicile include the following:

(a) Accommodation in the country of foreign domicile is a very helpful factor. It should be available for the individual to use, be furnished and be occupied by the individual at some time during each year.
(b) Passports, identity cards etc. for the foreign country should be retained and preferably no UK or other passport sought.
(c) Nationality of the foreign country should be retained and UK or other nationality should not be sought.
(d) A burial plot maintained in the foreign country should be continued.
(e) Membership of a club or clubs in the foreign country.

(f) Bank accounts should be maintained with banks in the foreign country and not in the UK.

(g) Credit cards should be issued from an institution in the foreign country with a foreign country address.

(h) Insurances should be through insurers in the foreign country.

(i) A pension should be maintained with an institution in the foreign country.

(j) A foreign country driving licence should be held (rather than a UK licence).

(k) Wills should be made under the law of, and in accordance with, the requirements of the foreign country.

(l) The non-UK domiciliary should register at the foreign country embassy.

(m) The non-UK domiciliary should join 'expat' clubs.

(n) Vacations should be taken in the foreign country.

(o) A diary should be kept of time spent in the foreign country.

(p) A declaration of the individual's foreign domicile should be made.

(q) A documented plan for return to the foreign country should exist.

CHAPTER TWO
Sources of tax law and administration

2.1 SOURCES OF TAX LAW AND ADMINISTRATION

This chapter is concerned with the sources of UK tax law and UK tax administration. Sources are dealt with first. There are a number of these.

2.1.1 Tax: a creature of statute

Tax in the UK is a creature of statute. Despite an outwardly feudal monarchy with extensive powers, the last time these were sought to be used to raise money without Parliamentary approval it led to the Civil War.[1] One consequence is that tax is thus usually imposed by an Act of Parliament in the UK.[2]

It seems now to be an accepted part of our constitution that the Crown may not tax the subject except by statutory authority. Article 4 of the Bill of Rights (1689) provides: 'That levying money for or to the use of the Crowne by pretence of prerogative without grant of Parlyament for longer time or in other manner than the same is or shall be granted is illegal.' Atkin LJ said in *A-G v Wilts United Dairies Limited* (1921) 37 TLR 884:

> No power to make a charge upon the subject for the use of the Crown should arise except by virtue of the prerogative or by statute, and the

---

[1.] See further, e.g., Clarendon's *History of the Great Rebellion* and *The Case of Ship Money* (1637) 3 St. Tr. 725.
[2.] Some of the Defence of the Realm legislation may have allowed exceptions to this. Membership of the EU and the consequent 'direct effect' etc. of some directives and articles of the EU Treaty has also impacted on the ability of the UK Parliament to create tax law, but even the applicability of EU law in the UK is theoretically based on a UK Act of Parliament, namely the European Communities Act 1972.

alleged right under the prerogative was finally disposed of by the Bill of Rights . . . though the attention of our ancestors was directed especially to abuses of the prerogative there can be no doubt that this statute declares the law that no money shall be levied for or to the use of the Crown except by grant of Parliament.

Although tax matters are often dealt with by non-lawyers, the courts remain the final determinants of what tax is due on the basis of legal interpretation of the statute applied to a correct legal analysis of the transactions. The interpretation of statutes is considered further in Chapter 3. The correct legal analysis of the transaction can often be the hardest part of the task.

2.1.2 Relevant statutes

The relevant statutes concerned with tax in the UK include:

(a) Income and Corporation Taxes Act 1988 ('TA'), the principal act, as its short title suggests, for income tax and corporation tax.[3]
(b) Taxation of Chargeable Gains Act 1992 ('TCGA'), the principal act, as its short title suggests, for chargeable or capital gains.
(c) Inheritance Act 1984[4] ('IHTA'), the principal act, as its short title suggests, for inheritance tax ('IHT').
(d) Value Added Tax 1994[5] ('VATA'), the principal act, as its short title suggests, for value added tax ('VAT').
(e) Stamp Act 1891, the principal act, as its short title suggests, for stamp duty.

There are also a number of statutes dealing with the administration of tax in the UK. These include:

(a) Taxes Management Act 1970
(b) Inland Revenue Regulation Act 1890
(c) Customs and Excise Management Act 1979
(d) Provisional Collection of Taxes Act 1968.

2.1.3 Need for annual Finance Act and provisional collection of taxes

A Finance Act is usually required each year to impose income tax and make other provisions and changes. This is discussed further in Part II. The government's proposals for each year are generally announced in the Budget. The Budget now takes place in November and covers both government

---

[3.] Corporation tax is charged on the profits of companies, i.e., income and chargeable or capital gains.
[4.] This was originally enacted as the Capital Transfer Act 1984. On citation etc. as the IHTA, see s. 100, FA 1986.
[5.] VAT is of European origin so reference must also be made to the European directives, especially the sixth directive, Dir 77/338 EC, 17 May 1977, OJ 1977 L 145/1.

expenditure and revenue. Previously the Budget had usually been in March and dealt only with the raising of revenue.

The Budget proposals have to be enacted into law. Until they are they would not normally have the force of law. Unusually, however, statutory force can be given to the Budget Resolutions of the House of Commons[6] allowing for the provisional collection of tax. The authority for this is the Provisional Collection of Taxes Act 1968. This derives from the 1913 Act enacted following *Bowles* v *Bank of England* [1913] 1 Ch. 57 a case arising out of the 1910–11 constitutional crisis which had delayed the passing of Finance Acts. A committee of the House of Commons passed a Ways and Means Resolution imposing income tax for 1912–13. Mr Bowles was the registered holder of £65,000 of Irish Land Stock. Before the Finance Act had been passed the Bank of England paid a dividend on the stock but deducted income tax from the payment. Mr Bowles sought a declaration that the Bank was not entitled to make the deduction and an order for the return of the money. Parker J granted the declaration and ordered the Bank of England to return the sums deducted.

The Provisional Collection of Taxes Act 1968 now governs such cases. Where a tax is renewed, or the House of Commons declares it expedient in the public interest, the resolution of the House of Commons can be given statutory effect (see s. 1, PCTA 1968). This is subject to a time restriction (see s. 1(3), PCTA). If the resolution is passed in November or December the resolution has effect until 5 May of the following year and in other cases four months. (For resolutions ceasing to have effect, see ss. 2 and 5, PCTA 1968.) The Provisional Collection of Taxes Act applies to income tax, corporation tax (including advance corporation tax), petroleum revenue tax, stamp duty reserve tax, value added tax, insurance premium tax, and duties of customs and excise (s. 1(1), PCTA).

2.1.4 Temporary tax

Income tax is still technically a temporary tax and has been since 1799. It therefore needs to be imposed each year in the annual Finance Act. This can be seen in s. 1(2), TA which provides for the rates of tax to apply ' where any Act enacts that income tax shall be charged for any year . . .' Not all UK taxes need to be imposed annually (see s. 1(1), PCTA above for those that do).

The annual Finance Acts usually introduce a broad range of changes in tax law, both as to substance and as to rates. The UK has not adopted the approach of some other countries which have one large 'parent' statute with 'spare' sections so that further provisions may be added as necessary (cf. USA and Australia).

It may well be necessary to look at more than one Act on any particular point in order to determine the applicable law. These problems arise from our system of legislation and the resultant speed and the means of drafting.[7]

[6.] See the annexes to each year's Red Book, i.e., the back-up document published with the Budget.

[7.] See, for example, the Armstrong Report, *Budgetary Reform in the UK* (1980).

2.1.5 Consolidating acts and case law

The principal UK taxing acts are consolidating not codifying statutes. Earlier case law therefore needs to be considered since it remains relevant even after re-enactment (see, e.g., *Vagliano* v *Bank of England* [1891] AC 107 and Chapter 3). This can cause problems in tracing provisions back but the published tables showing the derivation and destination of statutory provisions can help here.

A consolidation act is to be construed in the first place according to its actual language. If that is ambiguous the earlier legislation may be looked at and the presumption applied that a consolidation statute is not to make substantial changes to the law (see, e.g., *IRC* v *Joiner* [1975] 3 All ER 1050 at p. 1057).

Many of the basic 'principles' (e.g., the source doctrine, income, capital and residence) of UK taxation are found in case law and not in the taxing statutes themselves. This does not always make for clarity or ease of understanding (e.g., the distinction between capital and income, see para. 1.2.4.2). However, as was seen above, UK taxation remains fundamentally a creature of statute. Cases are merely interpretations of the legislation which is the source and origin of the tax. The interpretation of statutes generally is a question of law.[8]

2.2 CASES AND REPORTS

Tax statutes are subject to much interpretation in decided cases. Many of these are reported in the general series of law reports but they are also to be found (inter alia) in two special series of tax reports – the Official Reports of Tax Cases and Simon's Tax Cases. The Official Reports of Tax Cases are referred to by volume and the abbreviation 'TC'. Simon's Tax Cases are referred to by the year in square brackets and the abbreviation 'STC'.[9] The courts seem to prefer the citation of the Official Law Reports.[10] However, the Official Reports of Tax Cases have the advantage of having all the stages of a case reported in one place together with the case stated. Cases are sometimes reported in the STC or TC series which are not reported elsewhere.

2.3 EXTRA-STATUTORY CONCESSIONS, STATEMENTS OF PRACTICE ETC.

The Inland Revenue and Customs and Excise do much to let taxpayers know their views. They issue Extra-statutory Concessions and Press Releases and

---

[8] See Lord Denning MR in *Heather* v *P-E Consulting Group Ltd* (1972) 48 TC 293 at p. 322: 'The Courts have been assisted greatly by the evidence of accountants. Their practice should be given due weight; but the Courts have never regarded themselves as being bound by it. It would be wrong to do so. The question of what is capital and what is revenue is a question of law for the Courts.' Cf. *Gallagher* v *Jones* [1993] STC 537 and *Johnson* v *Britannia Airways Ltd* [1994] STC 763.

[9] Note square brackets are used in citing the STCs because the citation refers to the volume of the Reports not necessarily the year of decision of the case.

[10] See *Fairman* v *Perpetual Investment Building Society* [1923] AC 74, *Practice Note* [1970] 1 WLR 1400, *Murphy* v *Ingram* [1973] STC 309, *Practice Note* [1995] 3 All ER 256 and RSC Part 14 para. 4630, Citation of Authorities.

give 'rulings'[11] and 'clearances'[12] in some circumstances. Tax rulings and clearances are an important means of lubricating the tax system and easing its running given the imperfections of life and the imprecision of words. Taxpayers and tax officials need a practical way of resolving ambiguities and other difficulties with tax law and practice, which do not take up too much time or consume a disproportionate quantity of resources but which do provide practical certainty and finality. However, the basis and legality of rulings and clearances is not entirely clear.

As part of its statutory responsibility for the administration of the tax system there is a (*per* Judge J in *R* v *IRC ex parte MFK* [1990] STC 873 at p. 895):

> . . . long established practice by which the Revenue gives advice and guidance to taxpayers. This is sometimes done by public statements of the Revenue's approach to a particular fiscal problem. Sometimes advice is given in answer to a particular request from an individual taxpayer. The practice exists because the Revenue has concluded that it is of assistance to the administration of a complex system and ultimately to the benefit of the overall tax yield.

The Revenue is not generally obliged to give rulings '. . . it might stick to the letter of its statutory duty, declining to answer any question when not statutorily obliged to . . .' (Bingham LJ at p. 891).[13] But it is obliged by statute in some circumstances to give 'clearances' and so has to give an answer.

Tax rulings and clearances have assumed even greater importance as a means of facilitating the working of the tax system(s) with the changes being made and proposed to the UK tax system(s) taking the direct tax system more towards one of self-assessment which already operates for VAT. In a self-assessment system the taxpayer needs to be able to complete his or her tax return (or have it completed) and pay the tax easily. The tax officials need to be clear what the position is if the system is to function without the need to

---

[11]. 'Ruling' is used here to mean the provision of guidance by the Inland Revenue or Customs & Excise as to how it will treat certain matters for UK tax purposes. Generally, in the UK, these do not have a specific statutory basis. Rulings can range from what has been described as a private letter ruling given to an individual taxpayer to extra statutory concessions and statements of practice which are intended to be of more general effect. See now [1995] STI 886.

[12]. 'Clearance' is used here to mean a statutory based procedure for seeking confirmation that a particular provision will, or more usually in the context of an anti-avoidance provision, will not be applied if the transaction described by the applicant in the request for clearance is carried out and all material facts have been disclosed. If given, a clearance will be binding on the Revenue, for example, s. 138, TCGA and s. 707, TA.

[13]. It is sometimes obliged to answer, e.g., ss. 707 and 776(11), TA. The Revenue's attitude was set out in para. 6 of Mr Beighton's affidavit (p. 892). He said, '. . . the Board [of Inland Revenue] see it as a proper part of their function and contributing to the achievement of their primary role of assessing and collecting the proper amounts of tax and to detect and to deter evasion, that they should when possible advise the public of their rights as well as their duties, and generally encourage co-operation between the Inland Revenue and the public.' Bingham LJ did not think there was any reason to dissent from this judgment.

audit every case. Both taxpayer and official have an interest in doing this in the easiest way possible whilst maintaining the requisite degree of fairness to keep the system acceptable. A system of rulings allows the taxpayer to meet the obligations Parliament has imposed in a way acceptable to the Inland Revenue or Customs and Excise.

There have been a number of suggestions that the UK should introduce a formal, legally binding rulings system in the light of these proposed changes to the UK tax system: for example, The London Chamber of Commerce and Industry Taxation Committees: have published a persuasive document *Revenue Rulings: Proposals for the Introduction of a Formal Rulings Procedure in the UK*, December 1992.

The Inland Revenue announced a trial of a 'post-transaction rulings' scheme in 1994.[14] A Consultative Document on pre-transaction rulings was published on 9 November 1995 but is not now to be proceeded with.

2.3.1 Publication of Extra-statutory Concessions ('ESC')

ESC (as opposed to Statements of Practice see para. 2.3.2 below):

> . . . are departures from the strict letter of the law, but obviously always in favour of the taxpayer. Their purpose is to allow relief which is in the spirit of a particular piece of legislation but which, for some reason or other, is not actually given by it. There is a published list of these Extra-statutory Concessions which is brought up to date annually. They are reported to the Comptroller and Auditor General, and are subject to scrutiny by the Public Accounts Committee. They are therefore subject to Parliamentary examination and oversight. (1976 HC Vol 915 col 187, see also Press Release, 17 May 1985.)

ESC '. . . are few, tightly written and almost legislative in form'.[15] They have existed for many years. They were first reported to the Public Accounts Committee in 1897.[16] The first list was apparently published in 1944.[17] As the Radcliffe Commission ((1955) Cmd 9474) said: 'These concessions all look reasonable enough, and there is no attempt to make any secret about them; but if they are what they purport to be, extra statutory, it is a little disconcerting to find the statute being amended by this special and selective process' ((1954) Cmd 9474, para 240).

ESC are apparently reviewed twice yearly (Inland Revenue Press Release, 17 May 1985). They are intended to meet cases '. . . where a statutory remedy would be difficult to devise . . .'.

ESC are published in Inland Revenue Pamphlet IR [1]. They are subject to a general rubric that:

[14.] 12 May 1994 [1994] STI 611.
[15.] John Tiley, *Revenue Law*, 3rd edn., p. 170 para. 3.22. One could now quibble with the word 'few'; there are now over 200 published ESCs.
[16.] See The crown's case in *Vestey v IRC (No 2)* [1978] STC 567.
[17.] See D.W. Williams [1979] BTR 137 and Cmd 665.

The concessions described within are of general application, but it must be borne in mind that in a particular case there may be special circumstances which will require to be taken into account in considering the application of the concession. A concession will not be given in any case where an attempt is made to use it for tax avoidance.

Although the Revenue's 'primary duty is to collect, not to forgive, taxes' (*R v IRC ex parte Preston* [1985] STC 282, *per* Lord Templeman) concessions were treated as part of the concept of good management and administrative common sense in *R v IRC ex parte Fulford-Dobson* [1987] STC 344 relying on *Vestey* [1980] STC 10. It also held that the rubric did limit the application of the concessions. McNeill J considered that what was done in that case was done for the admitted purpose of tax avoidance which meant the concession did not apply, although he did not define what was meant by 'tax avoidance' in this context.

2.3.2 Statement of Practice ('SP')

A Statement of Practice is a description of the way the Revenue will in the general run of cases interpret and apply particular legal provisions. They are not legally binding. A Statement of Practice is a public statement of the Revenue's understanding of the law. It is open to any taxpayer who considers that its application to his own tax liability produces a result which cannot be upheld in law, to appeal against the assessment in the usual way. (See 1976 HC Vol 915 col 187.)

SPs are 'only slightly less formal' than ESCs.[18] The current series of SPs was introduced on 18 July 1978 by Press Release. Their introduction followed a review of the methods of publicising information on administrative practice with a view to making it available to the public in a uniformly accessible and more readily identifiable way.

2.3.3 Inland Revenue Interpretations

These are published in the Inland Revenue Tax Bulletin. The foreword says 'The content of Tax Bulletin offers some insight into the thinking of our technical specialists on particular issues. The Bulletin does not replace formal Statements of Practice.'

2.3.4 Inland Revenue Decisions

In the Tax Bulletin Issue 8, August 1993, the Inland Revenue said (on p. 77) that Revenue Decisions were effectively short case studies, intended to give some insight into the Revenue's approach in a particular case, but confined to the particular facts of that case. Unlike Interpretations, they are not intended to illustrate points of principle etc. of general application, as the 'health warning in each issue makes clear'.

[18.] John Tiley, *Revenue Law*. See note 15 above.

2.3.5 Press Releases

Like many other bodies, the Inland Revenue and Customs and Excise publish Press Releases. These often accompany new ESCs and SPs to introduce and explain them particularly to journalists. They can be an important source of information (for example, the Budget Press Releases).

2.3.6 Manuals etc.

The Revenue and Customs and Excise are in the process of publishing their internal manuals. These may be a useful source of information. They also publish Notes on Clauses to the Finance Bill and similar matters.

2.4 OTHER

2.4.1 Accounting practice

If income profits or capital gains are to be charged then the amount of the profit or gain chargeable needs to be ascertained. Initially this will be the province of accountants. However, accountancy has been described as more of a mystery than an art. It is certainly not an exact science.

The courts have increasingly come to accept accountancy practice in determining the amount of profit or gain which is to be subject to tax. In *Heather* v *P-E Consulting Group* [1973] Ch 189 evidence of accountancy practice was not considered to be conclusive but was thought to be persuasive. The more recent cases of *Gallagher* v *Jones* [1993] STC 537 and *Johnson* v *Britannia Airways* [1994] STC 763[19] have placed much greater emphasis on accountancy.

2.4.2 Hansard

When a court interprets a statute it is usually said to be seeking the intention of Parliament. However, until recently, there was 'a general rule that references to parliamentary material as an aid to statutory construction [was] not permissible' (Lord Browne-Wilkinson in *Pepper* v *Hart* [1992] STC 898 at p. 915). This was sometimes called the 'Exclusionary Rule'. It was a judge-made rule[20] and extended even to reports of Commissions etc.[21] The issue of the admissibility of Parliamentary material was central in the landmark case of *Pepper* v *Hart* [1992] STC 898. The case concerned the provision of education to the children of schoolmasters at Malvern College at

---

[19.] See Freedman, *Ordinary Principles of Commercial Accounting – Clear Guidance or Mystery Tour?* [1993] BTR 468 and *Defining Taxable Profit in a Changing Accounting Environment* [1995] BTR 434.

[20.] See in relation to tax statutes, Rawlinson, *Tax Legislation and the Hansard Rule* [1983] BTR 274.

[21.] But had been relaxed to permit reports of law commissioners and white papers to be looked at for the purpose of ascertaining the mischief the statute was intended to cure,

a reduced rate. This was a taxable benefit to the schoolmasters but the question arose whether the schoolmasters should be taxed on the 'average cost' (i.e., adding all the costs of the school together and dividing by the relevant number of pupils) or the 'marginal cost' (the extra cost, if any, of having the extra pupil in the school) which would be considerably lower than the average cost of providing the benefit? The Minister had in effect said in Standing Committee debates that the tax charge would continue to be on the marginal cost of the provision of the service ([1992] STC 898 at pp. 912–15). However, the assessment made by the Revenue was on an average cost base.

There were two hearings before the House of Lords. In the first, five Law Lords sat and in the second, seven Lords sat. The second was at their Lordships' invitation to consider whether there should be a departure from the previous authority that forbade reference to Hansard (see [1992] STC 898 at p. 901).

The majority[22] of the Lords held that one could look at Hansard in certain circumstances ([1992] STC 898 at p. 923). Broadly, these were where:

(a) the legislation is ambiguous or obscure or leads to an absurdity;

(b) the material relied on consists of statements by a Minister or other promoter of the bill together with such other Parliamentary material as is necessary to understand such statements and their effect;

(c) the statements relied on are clear. (No guidance is given as to the meaning of 'clear' in this context.)

This is an area which still seems to be developing. Its impact has not been confined to the tax field.[23]

2.5 UK TAX ADMINISTRATION: STRUCTURE AND PERSONNEL

2.5.1 Introduction

The mechanics and administration of most of the UK's direct tax system are somewhat old fashioned, dating mainly from the nineteenth century[24] and

---

[22] Lords Keith, Bridge, Griffiths, Ackner, Oliver and Browne-Wilkinson (who delivered the major speech with which the others agreed and/or concurred). Lord Mackay LC dissented on this point.

[23] For a discussion of the merits (or not) of *Pepper v Hart* see, inter alia, Baker (1993) 52 CLJ 353, Davenport (1993) 109 LQR 149, Oliver (1993) Public Law 5 and Styles (1994) 14 OJLS 151. In addition Bennion produced a supplement to the second edition of *Statutory Interpretation* in 1993.

[24] If not earlier. 'The administrative machinery was lifted directly from the land tax and so displayed that peculiarly English combination of central control and local executive power which still characterises it.' B.E.V. Sabine, *A Short History of Taxation*, Butterworths, 1980. Addington introduced the Schedular System and deduction at source which are still features of the modern UK tax system.

reflecting the needs and views of that time. 'The tax machinery of today is founded fundamentally on that provided in the Income Tax Act 1842.'[25] The 1842 Act[26] reintroduced income tax as a temporary measure[27] and was essentially a reprint of the 1806 Act.[28] The administrative machinery was virtually the same. It has formed the basis until the present day with some adjustment of the administrative machinery through various statutory consolidations and tinkerings. There are, however, special rules concerning assessments under Schedule E which deals with income from employment because of PAYE (s. 205, TA). There are also special rules for corporation tax and the introduction of 'self-assessment' (see para. 2.6) has been described as 'the most fundamental reform of the direct tax system since the introduction of PAYE' (*Self-Assessment: the legal framework*, Inland Revenue SAT2 (1995)).

2.5.2 'The Board' – care and management

By s. 188(1), Taxes Management Act 1970 ('TMA') 'The Board' means 'the Commissioners of Inland Revenue.' The administration and collection of income tax, capital gains tax, corporation tax and stamp duty are undertaken by the Commissioners of the Inland Revenue. Inheritance tax is also under the aegis of the Board via the Capital Taxes Office. The Board are '. . . to cause to be collected every part of the inland revenue[29] . . .' (s. 13, IRA). In the exercise of their duty they are subject '. . . to the authority, direction, and control of the Treasury . . .' (s. 1(2), IRA). The quorum for the Board is two (s. 2, IRA).

[25.] See *Simon's Taxes*, Revised Third Edition, Butterworths, Vol. A at A2.102. Much of this in turn was based on the 1806 Act's procedures. Some of it has changed with the introduction of pay and file for companies and self-assessment for individuals.

[26.] The legislation has since been consolidated (but not codified) and piecemeal changes have been made by annual Finance Acts. Some of the sections show their age, for example, the deduction for an employee for keeping a horse in s. 198, TA.

[27.] Technically it still is, see s. 1, TA, and the Provisional Collection of Taxes Act 1968 and *Bowles* v *Bank of England* [1913] 1 Ch 57 discussed at para. 2.1.3.

[28.] This was the Act that incorporated all the changes made by Addington and was reapplied until the tax was repealed in 1816 after the Napoleonic Wars, that caused its introduction, had ended. In the 1842 Budget speech, Peel introduced income tax so as to be able to reduce tariffs. He said: 'I propose that, for a time to be limited, the income of this Country should be called upon to contribute a certain sum . . . not exceeding 7d in the pound [2.917% approx] . . . for the same purpose of not only supplying the deficiency in the Revenue, but of enabling me with confidence and satisfaction to propose great commercial reforms, which will afford a hope of reviving commerce and such an improvement in the manufacturing interest as will react on every other interest in the country; and by diminishing the prices of articles of consumption and the cost of living will, in a pecuniary point of view compensate you for your present sacrifices . . .'. Queen Victoria expressed 'her determination that her own income should be subjected to a similar charge' to her subjects. Lord Melbourne advised her she was throwing away her money and her prerogative.' See Sabine op. cit. p. 122 and Tomkins and Shipwright, *Solicitors Journal*, 5 February 1993 at p.103. Gladstone proposed in 1853 that income tax should expire on 5 April 1860 but the needs of the Crimean War prevented this. The rate was reduced to 2d in the pound (about 0.8333%) in the 1870s but abolition seemed almost too much trouble.

[29.] The Inland Revenue Regulation Act ('IRA') 1890, s. 39, defines Inland Revenue as the revenue of taxes etc. placed under the Board's care and management.

Sources of tax law and administration

Value added tax is administered and collected by the Commissioners of Customs and Excise (para. 1, sch. 11, Value Added Tax Act (VATA) 1994). This is partly for historical reasons as its predecessor, purchase tax, was administered by Customs.

By s. 1, TMA income tax, corporation tax and capital gains tax are under 'the care and management' of the Board. The phrase 'care and management' is not entirely clear. It is considered in the context of judicial review below (para. 2.20).

The Board are to appoint inspectors and collectors 'who shall act under the direction of the Board' (s. 1(2), TMA).

Following the institution of the Citizens' Charter, the Revenue and Customs have issued taxpayers' charters and appointed adjudicators.

2.5.3 The inspector of taxes

Inspectors are appointed by the Board (s. 1(2), TMA) for general purposes or for such purposes as the Board think fit (s. 1(2), TMA). An inspector is required to make the declaration under Part III of sch. 1 to the TMA. Inspectors were originally called surveyors. The title was changed in 1922 supposedly because of their loyalty during the First World War.

2.5.4 The collector of taxes

Collectors are appointed by the Board (s. 1(2), TMA). They may be appointed for general purposes or for such purposes as the Board think fit (s. 1(2A), TMA). A collector is required to make the declaration under Part III of sch. 1 to the TMA.

2.5.5 Assessment

As Lord Dunedin has said (in *Whitney* v *IRC* (1925) 10 TC 88 at p. 110):

> ... there are three stages in the imposition of a tax: there is the declaration of liability, that is the part of the statute which determines what persons in respect of what property are liable. Next there is the assessment. Liability does not depend on assessment. That, *ex hypothesi*, has already been fixed. But assessment particularises the exact sum which a person liable has to pay. Lastly, come the methods of recovery, if the person taxed does not voluntarily pay.

It is against assessments that appeals are made. The way appeals are to be made is dealt with below after considering what is meant by, and involved in an 'assessment' and, more particularly, self-assessment.

2.6 SELF-ASSESSMENT

Income tax, capital gains tax and corporation tax have historically been assessed taxes[30] which depended on the Revenue having some information on which to base their assessment. Taxpayers were required to supply information to the Revenue so that the Revenue could issue an assessment which comprised the legal charge to tax and against which taxpayers had a right of appeal. However, in March 1993 the Chancellor of the Exchequer announced that the direct tax system would move to a system of 'self-assessment' with the aim of making the procedures for the assessment and collection of tax 'more straightforward, clearer and fairer for taxpayers and practitioners'.[31] The system applies from the 1996/97 tax year onwards. Under the self-assessment regime, taxpayers are obliged to provide all the information required to calculate their total taxable income (from all sources) and any chargeable gains. This information is supplied in a tax return. The taxpayer then has the option of choosing whether to calculate his or her own tax liability or whether to leave that calculation to the Inland Revenue. There are fixed dates for the filing of returns and the payment of tax and automatic penalties apply for failing to meet those deadlines.

Self-assessment is thus claimed to give taxpayers more control over their own tax affairs. Certainly it requires them to become more proactive. For the Revenue, their role will change from one in which large amounts of time and money were expended in issuing assessments (which could then be challenged by the taxpayer), to a role which accepts that the figures supplied by the taxpayer are *prima facie* accurate and collects tax on the basis of the information submitted. This will free up Revenue resources so that more time can be spent on ensuring that taxpayers are complying with their legal obligations. The direct tax system will thus become more like the VAT system in the way in which it is administered.

2.6.1 Personal returns

Under self-assessment a single return covers the taxpayer's income from all sources and capital gains for the tax year and takes account of any reliefs, allowances or repayments and any credit for tax deducted at source. In general, if the taxpayer has decided to calculate his or her tax liability, the return must be submitted by 31 January following the tax year to which the

---

[30.] An assessed tax is one where the government determines the amount of tax due on the basis of the information available to it. It can be contrasted with a self-assessment system under which the taxpayer makes the determination in the first instance. The UK is increasingly moving to a system of self-assessment – for example, VAT, pay and file for UK corporation tax and the introduction in 1997–8 of self-assessment for income tax, for a critique see A.J. Shipwright [1992] BTR 12.

[31.] Self-assessment: the legal framework, Inland Revenue SAT 2 (1995) para. 1.2; and see, *inter alia*, James [1994] BTR 204; Sandford and Wallschutzky [1994] BTR 213; and Sandford [1994] BTR 674.

Sources of tax law and administration

return relates (s. 8(1), (1A) and (5), TMA). For the 1996/97 year of assessment this will be 31 January 1998. If the taxpayer wishes the Revenue to calculate the tax due, the return must generally be submitted by 30 September following the tax year to which the return relates (s. 9(2)), i.e., 30 September 1997 for the 1996/97 tax year. If these time limits are not met fixed penalties automatically arise (s. 93) and the Revenue will estimate the tax due (s. 28C).

It may be necessary for the taxpayer to send in additional information with the tax return such as business accounts, although the forms have been designed so that, for many small businesses, account information can simply be transcribed onto the return and the accounts need not be sent to the Revenue. There is, however, a statutory requirement for taxpayers to keep records and the Revenue may ask to see these records at a later stage if they decide to open an enquiry into the accuracy of the taxpayer's tax return (see para. 2.6.3). Broadly, business records must be kept for five years from 31 January following the tax year to which they relate and records must be kept for one year in all other cases (s. 8(1)(b)).

If the taxpayer decides to assess his or her liability to tax, a figure must be included in the tax return and this will create the legal charge to tax (s. 9(1)). This figure will take into account any claims for tax reliefs, allowances etc. made in the return. Time is allowed for the correction (by either side) for any 'obvious' errors in the calculation such as arithmetic mistakes (s. 9(4), (5) and (6)). If the taxpayer does not wish to assess his or her own tax liability, no special procedure is necessary. The return must simply be filed by the earlier 30 September deadline without any calculations and the Revenue will do the calculations using the information in the return and notify this to the taxpayer (s. 9(3)).

2.6.2 Payment of tax

Under self-assessment, the taxpayer will be required to make two payments on account of income tax towards the tax due for the year and then a third balancing payment to meet any income tax still outstanding at the date when the tax return should be submitted (ss. 59A(1) and 59B(1), TMA). The balancing payment will also include any tax due in respect of capital gains realised by the taxpayer in the tax year in question. The first payment on account is due on 31 January of the relevant tax year and the second is due on 31 July following the tax year. Any balancing payment is due on 31 January of the year following the relevant tax year. The intention is that each payment on account should comprise approximately half the taxpayer's income tax liability for the year and a *de minimis* limit will apply so that no payments on account will be required if the taxpayer's liability is below a set threshold. Taxpayers will have the right to reduce or cancel payments on account if they have grounds for believing that this would lead to an overpayment of tax (s. 59A(3) and (4)). Interest and fixed penalties will, however, be charged on any due, but unpaid, tax (ss. 59C and 86).

2.6.3 Enquiries into returns

Under self-assessment, the Revenue will initially only check a taxpayer's tax return to the extent of correcting obvious mistakes such as arithmetic errors so that, in essence, the return is simply processed as it is submitted. However, the Revenue have the right at a later stage to check the accuracy of *any* tax return and need give no reasons for choosing to enquire into a particular taxpayer's return (s. 9A(1), TMA). This means that the Revenue can, if they wish, randomly select taxpayers' returns for inspection although it is likely that in many cases the Revenue will have some reasons for wishing to make further enquiries into a taxpayer's affairs. If a taxpayer's return is not selected for enquiry within the specified time limit, the return and the associated self-assessment are treated as 'final'. If the return is filed on or before 31 January following the tax year in question, this time limit expires on 30 January of the next year (s. 9A(2)).

2.7 DIRECT TAX APPEALS[32]

Appeal lies against a charge to tax to the General or Special Commissioners for the purposes of income tax. This is the first 'tax court'. Appeal by way of case stated from the General Commissioners and by way of originating motion from the Special Commissioners lies from the Commissioners on a

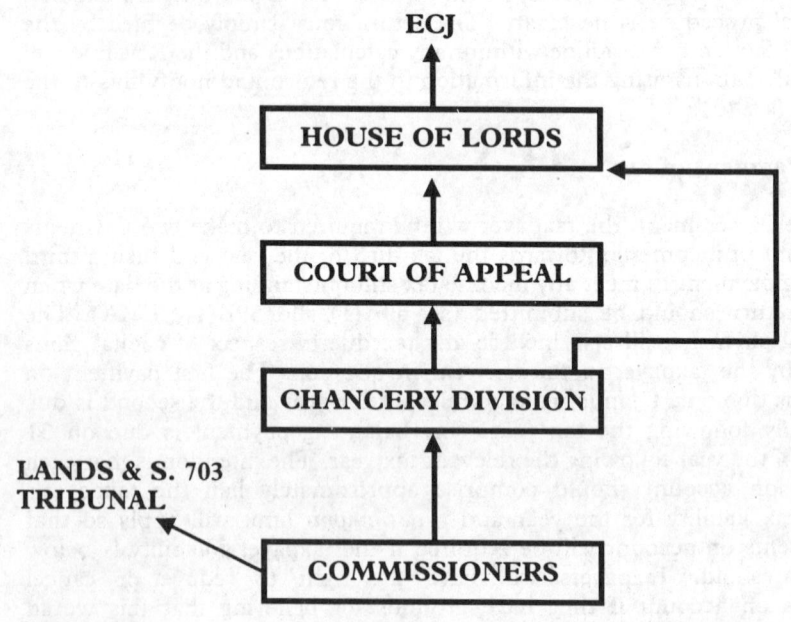

```
                    ECJ
                     ↑
            ┌──────────────────┐
            │  HOUSE OF LORDS  │◄─────┐
            └──────────────────┘      │
                     ↑                │
            ┌──────────────────┐      │
            │ COURT OF APPEAL  │      │
            └──────────────────┘      │
                     ↑                │
            ┌──────────────────┐      │
            │ CHANCERY DIVISION│──────┘
            └──────────────────┘
                     ↑
LANDS & S. 703
TRIBUNAL   ◄────┐
            ┌──────────────────┐
            │  COMMISSIONERS   │
            └──────────────────┘
```

Figure 2.1

[32.] See generally Potter and Prosser, *Tax Appeals*, 1991.

Sources of tax law and administration

point of law to the High Court and then above in the usual way. This may be illustrated as follows. It should be noted that a reference under Art. 177 of the EC Treaty may be made at any time but in cases of doubt the Lords regard themselves as bound to refer.

2.7.1 Commissioners – General and Special

There are two kinds of Commissioners:

2.7.1.1 General Commissioners – commissioners for the general purpose of the income tax General Commissioners are unpaid and part-time, although they may, with Treasury approval, be paid travel and subsistence allowances; see s. 2(5), TMA. They sit for local jurisdiction called a 'division'. The General Commissioners have a clerk who can give them legal advice. The clerk usually holds a legal qualification. General Commissioners are appointed in England and Wales and Northern Ireland by the Lord Chancellor and in Scotland by the Secretary of State (s. 2(2)–(4), TMA).

2.7.1.2 Special Commissioners Special Commissioners are remunerated and are generally full-time employees often with a highly specialist tax background. They are appointed by the Lord Chancellor after consultation with the Lord Advocate (s. 4, TMA). One is designated the Presiding Special Commissioner. Deputy Special Commissioners may be appointed (s. 4, TMA). This has allowed part-time Special Commissioners to be appointed and they are currently in the majority. No one may be appointed a Special or Deputy Special unless a barrister or solicitor of ten years standing (s. 4(2), TMA). They may sit singly (s. 45, TMA).

Generally appeals lie to the General Commissioner, subject to an election by the taxpayer to proceed before the Special Commissioners instead (ss. 46 and 46A, TMA).

For historical reasons Commissioners' hearings were secret. General Commissioners' hearings still are. However, under new regulations and rules the Special Commissioners sit in public and may publish selected decisions.

2.7.2 Appeals

Section 31, TMA (as amended) allows an appeal within 30 days of the date of a notice of assessment under the old system or an amendment to a taxpayer's self-assessment to tax or refusal of tax relief etc.

The notice of appeal must specify the grounds of the appeal but the Commissioners may allow the appellant to put forward any ground not specified in the notice if satisfied that the omission was not wilful or unreasonable (s. 31(5), TMA).

2.7.3 Jurisdiction

2.7.3.1 General Commissioners Section 44 and sch. 3 seek to deal with the question before which set of General Commissioners proceedings are to be brought. Broadly, appeals are to be to the Commissioners in whose division the business is carried on, or the employment is, unless there is an election for the place of residence. Where the value of land is in question, proceedings will be brought in the division in which the land is situate and otherwise to the Commissioners for the place of residence. It is, however, possible for the parties to agree that proceedings will be heard by a different set of General Commissioners notwithstanding these rules (s. 44(2), TMA).

2.7.3.2 Special Commissioners The Special Commissioners have a wide jurisdiction to hear tax appeals. There are restrictions on people seeking to abuse this.

2.7.3.3 Valuations etc. Certain matters do not go to the Commissioners on appeal but to other bodies. These bodies include the following:

(a) Lands Tribunal
(b) Board of Referees
(c) Section 703 Tribunal.

2.8 APPEAL TO CHANCERY DIVISION

Where a taxpayer or an inspector is dissatisfied with the General Commissioners' decision on a point of law the taxpayer may require the Commissioners to state a case for the High Court (or, exceptionally, the Court of Appeal; see, e.g., *Capcount Trading* v *Evans* [1993] STC 11). A case stated is a summary of the Commissioners' findings of fact and law and of their reasons for their decision. The party who loses before the Commissioners may appeal as of right to the High Court, i.e., no leave is required provided the appropriate procedure is complied with.

The case stated procedure was introduced by s. 9 of the Customs and Inland Revenue Act 1874. It used to apply also to appeals from the Special Commissioners. Appeal from them is now by originating motion.

The High Court may only reverse the Commissioners' decision in two sets of circumstances:

(a) where the Commissioners have made an *ex facie* error of law; or,
(b) where, in the words of Lord Radcliffe in *Edwards* v *Bairstow and Harrison* [1956] AC 14 at page 36 '. . . the facts found are such that no person acting judicially and properly instructed as to the relevant law could have come to the determination under appeal.'

In order to appeal to the High Court, the taxpayer or the inspector must request the General Commissioners to sign and state a case for the High Court. The taxpayer or inspector must be dissatisfied with the Commissioners' decision as being erroneous in point of law (reg. 20, General Commissioners Regulations 1994, SI 1994/1812).

A fee (currently £25) must be paid to the Clerk to the Commissioners before the party requesting the case 'is entitled to have the Case Stated'.[33] The importance of expressing 'dissatisfaction' and giving notice is shown by *Burston v IRC* (1946) 28 TC 123. Here a case was stated by Commissioners which was heard by Lawrence J. He allowed a new point of law to be taken on facts not stated in the case and the case was remitted to the Commissioners for further consideration. At the end of that hearing counsel for the taxpayer did not express dissatisfaction but, some ten months later, the taxpayer's agents requested that a stated case be prepared for appeal. At a further High Court hearing the Crown took preliminary objection to the fact that the taxpayer had not expressed dissatisfaction and had not given notice under the appeals procedures. Macnaghten J agreed with this and held he had no jurisdiction to hear the case in consequence. However this has recently changed.

2.9 LAW AND FACT

This area is a minefield. While the distinction between law and fact is relevant in many aspects of law, its importance in the tax field comes from the limitation on appeals from the Commissioners. Appeals from the Commissioners only lie by way of case stated to the High Court (or the Court of Appeal where s. 56A, TMA applies) on matters of law. In addition, for administrative law purposes, the fact/law distinction can be important in determining what type of remedial action, if any, may be available.

If a factual mistake is made this may also take a body of limited jurisdiction outside the scope of its jurisdiction. For example, in *Re Ripon (Highfield) Housing Order 1938, Applications of White and Collins* [1939] 3 All ER 548 the issue was whether the land over which the order had been made constituted part of a 'park'. If it was a park then the Council had no authority to make the order as s. 75 of the Housing Act 1936 provided (inter alia) that 'Nothing in this Act shall authorise the compulsory acquisition . . . of any land which . . . forms part of a park . . .'. There was no appeal procedure in the 1936 Act so the decision could only be challenged on ultra vires grounds. Paragraph 2 of sch. 2 to the Act allowed six weeks from publication of the order within which 'a person aggrieved' could 'question the validity thereof on the ground that it is not within the powers of this Act.[34] Luxmore LJ said (at p. 559), 'The first and most important matter to bear in mind is that jurisdiction to make the order is dependent on a finding of fact, for, unless the land can be held not to be part of a park . . . there is no jurisdiction to make . . . the order.' He also said that the exercise of the jurisdiction was open to review by the Court. His Lordship relied in part for this on *Bunbury v Fuller* (1853) 9 Exch 111 where Coleridge J delivering the judgment of the Court of Exchequer Chamber said:

[33.] On failure to pay promptly see *Anson v Hill* (1968) 47 ATC 143 where the fee was not paid for three years or so but the Crown took no objection.

[34.] This is what was done here under RSC Order 55B r. 71 and affidavit evidence led as the rules provided. See the report, p. 558 and report of Charles J's decision at [1939] 1 All ER 508.

... it is a general rule that no court of limited jurisdiction can give itself jurisdiction by a wrong decision on a point collateral to the merits of the case upon which the limit to its jurisdiction depends; and however its decision may be final on all particulars making up together that subject matter which, if true, is within its jurisdiction, and however necessary in many cases it may be for it to make a preliminary inquiry, whether some collateral matter be or be not within the limits, yet upon this preliminary question its decision must always be open to inquiry in the superior court. Then, to take the simplest case - suppose a judge with jurisdiction limited to a particular hundred, and a matter is brought before him as having arisen within it, but the party charged contends that it arose in another hundred, that is clearly a collateral matter independent of the merits. On being presented, the judge must not immediately forbear to proceed, but must inquire into that preliminary fact and for the time decide it, and either proceed or not with the principal subject-matter according as he finds on that point; but this decision must be open to question, and if he has improperly either forborne or proceeded on the main matter in consequence of an error on this, the Court of Queen's Bench will issue mandamus or prohibition to correct his mistake.

However, whether a matter is a question of fact or law is not always as simple as Coleridge J's example would suggest. In *Applications of White and Collins* above the matter could also be looked at as one of no evidence or as one of law on the basis that the meaning of the word 'park' as used in the statute was a question of law. It seems more sensible to regard the question whether or not a piece of land is 'part of a park' as a question of mixed fact and law, although the edges then become somewhat blurred. If a judge has jurisdiction to make a mistake of law, how is a question of mixed law and fact to be reviewed on circumstances similar to those in *White and Collins*?

2.10 FURTHER APPEALS

From the High Court an appeal may be made by the unsuccessful party to the Court of Appeal. Again no leave is required. Appeals from the Court of Appeal to the House of Lords will, however, require the leave of the Court of Appeal or of the House of Lords.

2.11 OTHER REMEDIES

It is open in some circumstances for the taxpayer to seek a declaration as to the parties' legal position. This is what was done in *Pearson v IRC* [1980] STC 318 the leading case on the meaning of interest in possession.[35] The Inland Revenue is also party to the Citizens' Charter and there is also an Inland Revenue Adjudicator who will review the way that the Revenue have handled a complaint or enquiry by a taxpayer.

---

[35] See Shipwright (1979) 123 *SJ* 87 and (1981) 125 *SJ* 535.

2.12 VAT AND INDIRECT TAX APPEALS

The structure for VAT appeals reflects its more recent introduction and the differences in its management and administration.

Section 82 of and sch. 12 to the VATA established the Appeals Tribunals. Section 7, FA 1994 renamed these as the VAT and Duties Tribunals. This was when the UK complied with its European obligations to provide for appeals in relation to Customs and Excise matters.

Section 83, VATA provides for appeals to lie to the tribunal. Appeal lies on the matters listed in s. 83, VATA. These include matters such as registration and the amount of VAT due. In order for an appeal to be entertained (s. 84(2), VATA):

(a) the appellant must have made all the returns required; and
(b) the amount shown in those returns must have been paid.

The tribunal does not have a general inquisitorial function in the way that the Commissioners seem to (see *Tynewydd Labour WMC and Institute* v *Customs and Excise Commissioners* [1979] STC 570). However the tribunal does have jurisdiction over costs and does seem to have a supervisory function as far as challenges to the exercise of the discretionary powers of Customs and Excise are concerned. The tribunal must consider the facts and matters which existed at the time the decision complained of was taken (see *C & E* v *Peachtree* [1994] STC 747). Section 85, VATA allows appeals to be settled by agreement.

An appeal lies from the tribunal to the Queen's Bench Division of the High Court (s. 11, Tribunals and Inquiries Act 1992). Section 86, VATA gives the Lord Chancellor power to prescribe that certain appeals may go straight to the Court of Appeal.

2.13 JUDICIAL REVIEW

English law has developed considerably in the recent past as far as control of the administrative decisions of public bodies is concerned. This reflects the increase in the role of the state during the twentieth century and the more recent response by the courts. A.J.P. Taylor's suggestion that 'until August 1914 a sensible law abiding Englishman could pass through life and hardly notice the existence of the state, beyond the post office and the policeman'[36] may be exaggerated but highlights the changes that have taken place.

The change in judicial attitudes to the control of administrative action has been considerable. Lord Woolf (speaking extrajudicially) has said: 'I find it difficult to believe that there has been any other period of our legal history where a sphere of law has developed in such a rapid and exciting manner as administrative law since I started practice.'[37]

---

[36] A.J.P. Taylor, *English History* (1914–1915), OUP, p. 25.
[37] 'Public Law - Private Law: Why the Divide?, [1986] PL 220. His Lordship was called to the Bar by Inner Temple in 1955.

This development has had an impact on the legal position of administrative law and enforceability of rulings and clearances. It is accepted by all concerned that the Inland Revenue and Customs and Excise should act fairly (see, e.g., *R v IRC ex parte National Federation of Self-Employed and Small Businesses Ltd* [1981] STC 260). The difficulty that arises from this is that it is not clear what 'fairly' means in this context (nor often in any other).[38] 'Fairly' is somewhat of a chameleon word.[39] Is it 'fair' that the Revenue should act otherwise than in accordance with what they said? Why is it 'unfair' if they are merely carrying out their statutory duty to collect tax although this is not in accord with what has been said before. This raises the question of, fair to whom? The case law is not clear on this. Is it to be 'micro justice' for the individual taxpayer or 'macro justice' for the body of taxpayers as a whole? Or are the Inland Revenue and Customs and Excise to act as a means of loss distribution?[40]

Accordingly, a number of questions arise as to the effect of a ruling, including the following:

(a) Is the ruling to be binding on the Inland Revenue and Customs and Excise?
(b) If so, in what circumstances and on what basis?
(c) Is the Inland Revenue or Customs and Excise obliged to give a ruling? Should they be?
(d) If enforceable, does the ruling create a right in the subject?
(e) Should the Inland Revenue and Customs and Excise be able to resile from rulings?
(f) If so, should they be liable for compensation and on what basis?

Depending on one's point of view the current arrangements either fail to provide consistent answers to these questions or are admirable for their flexibility and ability to do justice in the particular case. It is with some of these questions that this section is concerned.

2.13.1 Testing rulings etc. and remedies

When both taxpayer and tax official are happy with the approach taken in the ruling and/or clearance then, as between them, there is no practical problem.

---

[38] Cf. Craig, Legitimate Expectations: A Conceptual Analysis (1992) 108 LQR 79. Does it give rise to standing, a right to procedural fairness or something more, something in the nature of a substantive right of property?

[39] Cf. Unfair Contracts Terms Act 1977 especially s. 11 and the Schedule as amended. See also Taylor J in *R v Home Secretary ex parte Ruddock* [1987] 2 All ER 518 at 531 '. . . I conclude that the doctrine of legitimate expectation in essence imposes a duty to act fairly. Whilst most of the cases are concerned . . . with a right to be heard, I do not think the doctrine is so confined . . .' This suggests that fairness is to be determined within the context of the circumstances of the case. In other words it is all to depend on the circumstances.

[40] Cf. tort and insurance law, see Atiyah, *Accidents, Compensation and the Law*.

Sources of tax law and administration 43

The problems arise when there is a disagreement. The effect of rulings and clearances in a tax context can be tested before the English courts in a number of ways. These include:

(a) appeal against assessment, decision etc. to the Commissioners. Appeal beyond may be limited to matters of law by way of case stated to the High Court;
(b) disputing the debt when the Inland Revenue seek to enforce liability;[41] or
(c) judicial review.

The availability of different remedies having different requirements can cause difficulties for the taxpayer.[42] A distinction has also been drawn between public and private law rights[43] and when and how they can be enforced, which can add to the confusion. Overlaying this is the requirement of confidentiality as to a taxpayer's affairs and the fact that judicial review remedies are discretionary. They are not awarded as of right but are subject to judicial discretion which can sometimes include the relative behaviour of the parties.

Judicial review of administrative action is concerned with the 'legality' of, and authority for, a decision and the procedure by which the decision was made rather than the correctness or otherwise of the decision actually made on the merits. This makes each case even more dependent on its own facts than is generally the case and so impacts on the precedent value of a decision. A decision that an administrative act or omission was within the range of possible reasonable acts or omissions that the statute authorises confers a considerable degree of flexibility, but tends away from certainty in a system developed on a case by case basis. Judicial review is thus not an appeal on the merits allowing a new decision to be substituted by the court on its view of the merits. It is not for the court to make a decision, that Parliament has entrusted to another. Judicial review is a means of challenging the legality of administrative actions. The decision, act or omission is ineffective at law if the application is successful.

The remedy of judicial review is less than twenty years old (cf. *R v IRC ex parte ICI* (1987) 60 TC 1). It has only been on a statutory basis since 1981

[41.] Cf. *IRC v Aken* [1988] STC 69. Sometimes it may be appropriate to sue in debt to recover money, see *Woolwich v IRC* [1992] STC 657 and cf. *R v IRC ex parte Commerzbank* [1991] STC 271.
[42.] See, for example, Lord Mackay in *R v IRC ex parte T C Coombs* [1991] STC 97 at p. 99 expressing no view as to whether the applicant had the same task in challenging a matter by way of judicial review as opposed to raising a defence to penalty or enforcement proceedings and Lord Lowry at p. 111.
[43.] See *O'Reilly v Mackman* [1983] 2 AC 237. The Justice – All Souls Review 1988 have called for its reconsideration. See Wade, *Administrative Law* 7th edn ('Wade'), Chapter 18 for trenchant criticism.

(s. 31, Supreme Court Act 1981).[44] It is a two stage procedure requiring leave before an application is heard.[45]

The conventionally accepted rationale behind the supervisory function of judicial review is that the authority given by Parliament is not without limit and the interpretation of statutes is for the courts. If the authority conferred were limitless it would mean (according to an extreme view) that Parliament was no longer supreme or sovereign. It is thus for the courts to determine the bounds of the authority given by the statute when interpreting the statute. Something done outside the authority conferred by the statute is logically done outside that authority and so not supported by that authority. It is therefore, so the logic continues, ineffective at law, there being no legal authority or vires behind the act or omission.

2.13.2 Time limit

There is a time limit for challenging matters by judicial review which gives practical certainty and finality. Application generally has to be made within three months of the grounds arising although the court may extend the time if 'it considers there is good reason'. In practical terms, if not challenged, the act or omission is treated as effective.

2.13.3 Standing or sufficient interest

Further, to seek judicial review the applicant must have sufficient standing or *locus standi*. This requires a sufficient interest in the matter (see s. 31(3), Supreme Court Act 1981 and RSC Order 53, r. 3(7)). One taxpayer does not generally have sufficient interest in the tax affairs of another person other than in exceptional circumstances. So in *R v IRC ex parte National Federation of the Self-Employed* [1981] STC 260 the House of Lords held that the Federation did not have standing to challenge the immunity granted by the Revenue to the 'Fleet Street irregulars'. However, this general limitation that one taxpayer does not have sufficient interest in the affairs of another taxpayer has seemingly become less restricted in recent cases. For example, in *R v Commissioners of Customs & Excise ex parte Tattersalls* [1988] STC 630 bloodstock auctioneers based in Suffolk sought a declaration that Customs and Excise were wrong to grant temporary import exemption from VAT for racehorses acquired in Ireland. Their concern was that 'as a consequence of the interpretation, racehorse owners will tend to buy yearlings in Ireland, import them into the UK . . . and then re-export them within 24 months of import without becoming liable to pay Value Added Tax in the UK.'

[44.] See Gavin Dewry in Supperstone & Goudie (eds), *Judicial Review* ('Supperstone & Goudie') pp. 10 et seq.

[45.] See RSC Order 53, r. 3 and, e.g., Potter and Prosser, *Tax Appeals*, Chapter 16 and Vol. 1 1991/92 PTPR 3 et seq. Application for leave is made by notice in Form 86A supported by affidavit(s). This provides a 'control device' for the courts to filter cases. Before the enactment of the Supreme Court Act 1981 this process was thought to be required by the Administration of Justice (Miscellaneous Provisions) Act 1938.

Sources of tax law and administration 45

Tattersalls were not concerned with their own tax bill on importation but with the effect on their business. They were treated as having sufficient standing. In *R v Department of Social Security ex parte Overdrive Credit Card Ltd* [1991] STC 129, a case where the DSS tactics were said 'to resemble those of the Russian Army in 1812', the operators of arrangements for the use of fuel cards by employees of their corporate customers were able to seek judicial review of the issue of a DSS notice. The fuel cards were treated as free from Class 1 National Insurance contributions until the publication of an Aide Memoire in April 1990 described by the Court as a 'slovenly document'. There was no attempt by counsel for the DSS to defend it. The Aide Memoire purported to be retrospective to an earlier document which allegedly made it clear that National Insurance contributions would be charged. The Court said that it had not done any such thing. Lloyd LJ considered that Overdrive were clearly entitled to a declaration that the DSS should forthwith withdraw the Aide Memoire once it was accepted that it was erroneous. Overdrive was not the person paying the NICs but they were treated as having *locus standi* sufficient to strike down an erroneous general 'ruling' published by the DSS. There is no obvious reason why this decision should not equally apply to tax matters notwithstanding the *National Federation of the Self-Employed* case. It may be that where there is a competitive or economic interest in another taxpayer's affairs there is sufficient interest for judicial review.

2.13.4 When is judicial review available?

In broad simplistic terms, judicial review is a means by which a person having *locus standi* can require a public body given authority to do something by law to act reasonably and fairly in exercising their powers even if this is not expressly or explicitly stated in the legislation.[46] A doctrine of legitimate expectation has developed, discussed below, which can require a public body to stand by a legitimate expectation it has engendered that it will act in a particular way, for example by publishing a statement of practice.[47]

There are three broad categories in which judicial review may be available. Lord Diplock has said (in *Council of Civil Service Unions v Minister for the Civil Service* [1984] 3 All ER 935 at p. 950) that:

> Judicial review has I think developed to a stage today when . . . one can conveniently classify under three heads the grounds on which administrative action is subject to control by judicial review. The first ground I would

---

[46.] Unless there is other power to support it. However the decision is only struck down if it is challenged. An unchallenged administrative action is thus effective as it has not been upset. It is part of the consequence of the English system of litigation which determines matters between the parties to the action rather than in absolute terms. The maxim *Omnia rita praesumuntur esse acta*, i.e., all things necessary are presumed to have been done, would provide a cloak for this. There is a similar problem where a matter is challenged but the court declines in its discretion to grant a remedy.

[47.] See, for example, Craig (1992) 108 LQR 79.

call 'illegality,' the second 'irrationality' and the third 'procedural impropriety'. That is not to say that further development on a case by case basis may not in the course of time add further grounds. I have in mind particularly the possible adoption in the future of the principle of 'proportionality'[48] which is recognised in the administrative law of several of our fellow members of the European Economic Community . . .[49]

'Illegality' here is concerned with the 'vires' or authority for the action or omission and may subsume the other two heads. His Lordship said that:

> By 'legality' as a ground for judicial review I mean that the decision-maker must understand correctly the law that regulates his decision-making power and must give effect to it. Whether he has or not is par excellence a justiciable question . . .'[50]

'Irrationality' referred to the 'Wednesbury principle' is broadly the question whether the decision reached is within the range of reasonable decisions that could have been made. This is similar to the position on appeal on a matter of law by way of case stated where, in the words of Lord Radcliffe in Edwards v Bairstow and Harrison [1956] AC 14 at p. 35, the situation is that '. . . the facts found are such that no person acting judicially and properly instructed so as to the relevant law could have come to the determination under appeal'. The Court can also intervene on grounds of misconception of law.

'Procedural impropriety' includes a failure to observe the basic rules of natural justice (audi alteram partem, i.e., the right to a hearing, and nemo judex in causa sua, the rule against bias), a failure to act with procedural fairness towards the person who will be affected by the decision and a failure to observe the procedural rules laid down in the legislation (see [1984] 3 All ER 935 at p. 951). It is out of this that the doctrine of legitimate expectation (which is so important for tax rulings) developed. The extension is through

---

[48] The Committee of Ministers of the Council of Europe adopted the following principle in March 1980, Recommendation R(80)2: 'Proportionality. An appropriate balance must be maintained between the adverse effects which an administrative authority's decision may have on the rights, liberties, or interests of the person concerned and the purpose which the authority is seeking to pursue.' R.O. Plender QC has said: 'The principle of proportionality denotes that the means used to attain a given end should be no more than is appropriate and necessary for attaining that end.' Supperstone and Goudie (above, n. 52) at p. 294. VAT as a community derived tax based on the Sixth Directive 77/338 is particularly open to challenge on this basis. See, e.g., C & E v P & O [1992] STC 809 at 819 et seq. This decision was reversed on appeal: [1994] STC 259.
[49] It may be that it is inherent in the irrationality head. Proportionality along with equality (i.e., similar situations should not be treated differently unless differentiation is objectively justified), legal certainty (i.e., Community legislation must be unequivocal in its application and must be predictable for those who are subject to it), legitimate expectations (i.e., that assurances relied on in good faith should be honoured, which constitutes a superior rule of law for the protection of the individual and may entail liability) and solidarity (i.e., Community preference) are principles of Community law, see Supperstone and Goudie (above, n. 52) at pp. 294–95.
[50] Cf. the challenge in IRC v Nuttall [1990] STC 194 that there was no power in the Revenue to make such a contract. Although this was a case sounding in debt the Court relied on the judicial review case of R v IRC ex parte National Federation of Self-Employed [1981] STC 260.

Sources of tax law and administration

the idea of 'fairness'. Lord Scarman in *R v IRC ex parte National Federation of Self-Employed* was of the opinion that '. . . a legal duty of fairness is owed to the general body of taxpayers' (see [1981] STC 260 at p. 280). Lord Templeman (with whom the other Lords agreed) considered this correct and that 'the Commissioners must equally owe a duty of fairness to each individual taxpayer' in *R v IRC ex parte Preston* [1985] STC 282 at p. 292.

Not everything is subject to judicial review. Lord Diplock also said in the *Civil Service* case that:

> the subject matter of every judicial review is a decision made by some person (or body of persons) whom I will call the 'decision maker' or else a refusal by him to make a decision. To qualify as a subject for judicial review the decision must have consequences which affect some person (or body of persons) other than the decision-maker, although it may affect him too. It must affect such other person either (a) by altering rights or obligations of that person which are enforceable by or against him in private law or (b) by depriving him of some benefit or advantage which either (i) he has in the past been permitted by the decision-maker to enjoy and which he can legitimately expect to be permitted to continue to do so until there has been communicated to him some rational ground for withdrawing it on which he has been given an opportunity to comment or (ii) he has received assurance from the decision-maker that they will not be withdrawn without giving him first an opportunity of advancing reasons for contending that they should not be withdrawn.

This raises the question whether judicial review is concerned only with due process or goes further.

2.13.5 Alternative remedies

There is a further restriction on the availability of judicial review where there are alternative remedies. It is arguable that the courts are '. . . evolving a general principle that an individual should normally use alternative remedies where these are available rather than judicial review' ([1985] STC 282 at p. 292). Thus, for example, Donaldson MR said in *R v Epping and Harlow General Commissioners ex parte Goldstraw* [1983] 3 All ER 257 at p. 262, '. . . it is a cardinal principle that, save in the most exceptional circumstances, jurisdiction [i.e., the residual jurisdiction to grant leave for judicial review] will not be exercised where other remedies were available but have not been used.' This is usually justified on grounds of speed and certainty. The way in which this cardinal principle will affect the way a court will exercise its discretion to permit judicial review may depend on whether public law or private law rights are in issue. This is not always clear as, for example, breach of natural justice by the Commissioners seems to be a matter for appeal (see, e.g., *R v Commissioners for the Special Purposes of the Income Tax Acts ex parte Napier* [1988] 3 All ER 166), whereas vindication of public law rights involving legitimate expectation may be brought by way of application for judicial review. The distinction is not always clear cut. There is also likely to be a difference between the assessed taxes, where appeal only lies against an assessment, and certain specific matters such as VAT where appeal lies against a decision falling within s. 40, VATA 1983 which appears to be wider. Given the time limit for judicial review this can be problematic (cf. *Aspin* v *Estill* [1987] BTC 553).

2.13.6 Procedural fairness only?

The idea of 'fairness' in judicial control of administrative action can be traced back a long way. In one case it was noted, by Fortescue J, '. . . that even God himself did not pass sentence upon Adam, before he was called upon to make his defence' (*R* v *University of Cambridge* (1723) 1 Str 557 (*Dr Bentley's Case*)). This is the concept of procedural fairness or 'due process'. It was originally called 'natural justice' and consisted particularly of the rule against bias and the right to a fair hearing. 'Natural justice is merely a branch of the principle of *ultra vires*. Violation of natural justice is then to be classified as one of the varieties of wrong procedure, or abuse of power, which transgresses the implied conditions which Parliament is presumed to have intended.'[51]

The duty to act fairly has been said to be '. . . not rationally distinguishable from the rules of natural justice.' The duty to act fairly is said to have come to prominence in *Re HK* [1967] 2 QB 617 when Parker LCJ said (at p. 630): '. . . Good administration and an honest or *bona fide* decision must comprise not merely bringing one's mind to bear upon the problem but acting fairly.' This was still essentially concerned with procedural fairness into which the idea of legitimate expectation is tied. The early cases are concerned with the legitimate expectation of a hearing. Lord Denning MR seemed to have this in mind in *Schmidt* v *Secretary of State for Home Affairs* [1969] 1 All ER 904 at 907. Lord Diplock in the *Civil Service* case (see para. 2.20.4) talked of some matter being continued until grounds for withdrawing it had been notified and the applicant had been given an opportunity to argue against it. Lord Fraser (at pp. 943–44) put it more widely. He said:

> . . . even where a person claiming some benefit or privilege has no legal right to it, as a matter of private law, he may have a legitimate expectation of receiving the benefit or privilege, and, if so, the courts will protect his expectation by judicial review as a matter of public law . . . Legitimate, or reasonable, expectation may arise from an express promise given on behalf of a public authority or from the existence of a regular practice which the claimant can reasonably expect to continue. . . . Legitimate expectations such as are now under consideration will always relate to a benefit or privilege to which the claimant has no right in private law, and it may even be to one which conflicts with his private law rights . . .

That the duty to act fairly is no longer to be confined to procedural matters is confirmed by *R* v *Secretary of State for Home Affairs ex parte Ruddock* [1987]

---

[51] Wade (above, n. 51), p. 465.

Sources of tax law and administration 49

2 All ER 518. It is also important in that case that there was no actual reliance on the statements as the applicants did not know at the time that their phones were being tapped. Taylor J concluded (at p. 531) on the authorities that:

> ... the doctrine of legitimate expectation in essence imposes a duty to act fairly. While most of the cases are concerned, as Lord Roskill said, with a right to be heard, I do not think the doctrine is so confined. Indeed, in a case where *ex hypothesi* there is no right to be heard, it may be thought the more important to fair dealing that a promise or undertaking given by a Minister as to how he will proceed should be kept. Of course such promise or undertaking must not conflict with his duty ... I accept ... that ... [he] cannot fetter his discretion. By declaring a policy he does not preclude any possible need to change it. But then if the practice has been to publish the current policy, it would be incumbent on him in dealing fairly to publish the new policy, unless again that would conflict with his duties.

Ruddock is not a tax case but the analogy to Statements of Practice seems close.

2.14 EUROPE

There is a principle in Community law which requires that Community law 'must be unequivocal in its application and must be predictable for those who are subject to it.'[52] The authority usually cited for this is *Amministrazione delle Finanze dello Stato* v *Srl Meridionale Industria Salumi* [1980] ECR 1237. It has further been said that, 'In particular, rules imposing charges on taxpayers must be clear and precise so that he may know without ambiguity what are his rights and obligations and may take steps accordingly.'[53] There is also a principle of legitimate expectation in Community law by which assurances relied on in good faith should be honoured (see *Cie Continentale France* v *EC Council* [1975] ECR 117 at p. 140, and *Tomadini* [1979] ECR 1801 at pp. 1815–16).

[52.] See Supperstone and Goudie (above, n. 52) at p. 294
[53.] Supperstone and Goudie at p. 294 relying on *Administration des Douanes* v *Gondrand Frères* [1981] ECR 1931.

CHAPTER THREE
The interpretation of taxing statutes

3.1 INTRODUCTION

Tax is peculiarly the creature of statute. As has been seen in Chapter 2 and in *Bowles* v *Bank of England* [1913] 1 Ch 57 and *A-G* v *Wilts United Dairies Ltd* (1921) 37 TLR 884, statutory authorisation is needed in the UK in order to tax the subject. This requirement of statutory authority is to some extent protected by Art. 4 of the Bill of Rights which provides:

> That levying money for or to the use of the Crowne by pretence of prerogative without grant of Parlyament for longer time or in other manner than the same is or shall be granted is illegal.

As tax is imposed by statute the legislation needs to be interpreted[1] to see that tax is properly collected when it is due. Interpretation is the function of the courts and tribunals. A tax statute is generally to be interpreted in the same way as any other statute. This chapter is concerned with some of the difficulties of statutory interpretation in a fiscal context. It will be seen that the judges are not always consistent in their approach to statutory interpretation. It sometimes appears as if they are interpreting a statute in a way designed to achieve a particular result. This has been described as a 'creative' rather than a purely mechanical function. This approach causes difficulties of prediction and so potentially of certainty.

[1.] See Bennion, *Statutory Interpretation*, D.W. Williams (1978) 41 MLR 404, J Ward, 'A Comparative Study of the Interpretation of Tax Statutes in the UK and the Republic of Ireland' [1994] BTR 42 and 147 and Law Com 21 (1969).

The interpretation of taxing statutes 51

3.2 METHOD OF LEGISLATION NOT CONDUCIVE TO CLARITY

The method of creating tax legislation can produce difficulties[2] for those having to apply it. There are two aspects to this. First, the way in which the legislation is actually passed is far from ideal. Secondly, because much of the legislation is consolidation legislation, its language and approach are not always consistent. Tax legislation has been enacted at different times to deal with the problems of that period. It is subject to modification each year through the Finance Act.

The Finance Bill as a money bill is considered in detail only by the House of Commons (Parliament Act 1911).[3] Even this limited consideration of the Finance Bill is not as detailed as it could be. The committee stage deals with dozens of clauses, which can be long and complex, in twenty or so sittings. Because of the procedure of the House sittings often go on until the early hours of the morning. It is highly questionable whether consideration by non-experts[4] of a complex, detailed and probably lengthy clause at two or three o'clock in the morning is the most efficient way of legislating. Publication of draft clauses for advance consultation with the wider 'tax community' can help but is not always possible. The suggestion of a standing committee on taxation has much to commend it.

3.3 DIVERSITY OF APPROACHES

Another problem in interpreting taxing statutes is the diversity of approach apparent in the statutory language, particularly of the Income Tax Acts.[5] Some of the key concepts used in the legislation such as 'income', 'residence', 'trade', were left undefined in the original legislation, and have had to be interpreted by judges over the past almost 200 years. Statutory changes are often made to correct particular problems but frequently these are 'bolt on' provisions that presume an understanding of the previous law which continues subject to the new provisions (see, for example, ss. 148 and 524, TA). This can cause difficulties of construction especially where the previous law was unclear.[6]

---

[2] See H.H. Monroe, *Intolerable Inquisition* and the various reports of the Special Committee of Tax Law Consultative Bodies, including *Recommendations on the Development of Tax Legislation*, September 1993. More generally, see *Making the Law: The Report of the Hansard Society Commission on the Legislative Process*, 1992.

[3] If not passed without amendment by the Lords within one month, a money bill may be presented for Royal Assent.

[4] Most MPs are not tax specialists and rely on Treasury and other briefings as to the purpose or meaning of clauses without necessarily understanding them. This is only too evident from reading the 'debates'.

[5] Capital gains tax, inheritance tax and corporation tax, which have all been enacted since 1965, tend not to share this problem to such a degree.

[6] For example, payments for contingent rights and termination payments, see Chapter 6. Section 148, TA applies where the payment is not otherwise liable to tax so one needs to know when it would be taxable under the general rules. This can be important in practice as the relief in s. 188, TA depends on a charge under s. 148, TA.

3.4 IMPACT OF AVOIDANCE

As the perception of 'tax avoidance'[7] increased so Parliament responded with language and provisions of increasing complexity. This has changed the way in which more modern provisions are drafted. Thus, there are the older and very much more general provisions, the extent of which have to be determined and the modern, complex provisions, with complicated definitions in the same tax code. As much legislation is consolidation legislation, the old words are used in the consolidation legislation which are not always appropriate to modern conditions (e.g., the employee's horse in s. 198, TA, see Chapter 8 below and the change made by FA 1997).

3.5 SHORT OR LONG LEGISLATION?

Traditionally UK tax statutes are long and complex. For example, when first published, the 1994 Finance Bill was 414 A4 pages long, and had to be printed in two volumes. The length and prolixity comes from the intention to cover virtually all possibilities and potential situations. The draftsman seeks to cover not only the particular mischief but to stop 'abuse' of a relief by including 'anti-avoidance' provisions. This creates problems for courts in seeking to interpret the legislation. Should something not covered by the plain words but within the 'spirit of legislation' be charged? How does one discover the spirit or purpose of the legislation? Is there such a thing as the intention of Parliament? The courts have pointed out that if the drafting is too wide it may not be possible to give a sensible meaning to the words used.[8]

3.6 LEGAL THEORY?

There are also certain inherent difficulties with the interpretation of statutes. These concern matters which are not just the province of lawyers such as words and the concepts and meanings they seek to express. Ultimately the question is do statutory provisions lay down rules or principles?[9] Scholars of jurisprudence have written much on this. It is useful to recall H.L.A. Hart's approach in his inaugural lecture, *'Definition and Theory in Jurisprudence'* ((1954) LQR Vol. 70, p. 37) where he emphasised the importance of putting words in a context,[10] the problems of attempting to define a single word and the difficulty of defining rather than seeking to describe something. The

---

[7.] This is not easy to define, see Chapter 4. 'Tax avoidance' as a serious objective probably developed in the 1920s from the combination of heavy taxes and no foreign war to justify it.

[8.] See below and *Commissioners of Customs & Excise v Top Ten* [1969] 3 All ER 39 at p. 95: 'the courts may find themselves so totally unable to draw the line as to decide nothing more than that the subject has not clearly enough been taxed.'

[9.] Cf. Dworkin, *Hard Cases* and Popkin [1991] BTR 238 especially at p. 285.

[10.] Cf. *A-G v Prince Ernest Augustus of Hanover* [1957] AC 436 at 461, 'Words and particularly general words, cannot be read in isolation; their colour and content are derived from their context ... in its widest sense ... preamble, existing state of the law, statutes in pari materia and mischief which I can, by those and other legitimate means, discern that the statute was intended to remedy ...'

difficulties with words are that they are an imprecise tool and are used in different ways by different people. Words frequently have a core meaning that is clear and a surrounding penumbra or shadow where the meaning may vary with context or other matters.

In addition, there is a problem of devising 'rules' of statutory interpretation as such rules have to be formulated in terms of words and concepts that are often hard to give a meaning. There is also a difficult jurisprudential question as to whether the rules of statutory interpretation are rules of law. Since most of the canons of interpretation are found in decided cases, to that extent they are part of common law, though they are often obiter dicta and it is rare that a rule of construction will be the ratio decidendi of a case. However, there are often conflicting dicta.

3.7 THE APPROACH(ES) OF THE COURTS[11]

Tax statutes are Acts of Parliament and so have to be interpreted in the 'usual way' by the courts, although there is great difficulty in knowing what this is. There are no special rules of interpretation for tax statutes. As Wills J said in *Styles* v *Treasurer of Middle Temple* (1895) 4 TC 123:

> I am rather disposed to repudiate the notion of there being any artificial distinction between the rules to be applied to a taxing Act and the rules to be applied to any other Act. I do not think such artificial distinctions ever can help anybody arrive at the plain meaning of words.

Despite this the courts have long been a battleground in the area of taxation. It has been said that 'The judges, acting as Parliament's oracles, have a wide discretion in such areas of melancholy obscurity as taxing statutes.' The courts often talk about giving words their ordinary meaning.

Apart from the high drama of the seventeenth century with cases such as the *Case of Ship Money: R* v *Hampden* (1637) 3 St. Tr. 825, it seems the judges first dealt in detail with taxes and statute in the context of stamp duties. Stamp duties are broadly levies on instruments of certain kinds without which the documents cannot generally be used in court proceedings. These stamp duty cases often involved penalty provisions, so a strict approach tending against penalties was taken. This led to the somewhat restrictive approach, labelled the 'Literal Approach', which was to predominate in the Victorian period. This approach, broadly, meant that the subject was not to be taxed except by clear words and the words were to be given their plain and literal meaning without resort to the Mischief or Golden Rules of interpretation (described below). With the increase in the scope and complexity of taxation and the attempts to stop 'avoidance', the courts' approach changed and a less literal approach developed.[12] The UK's membership of the EU has also

---
[11.] See D.W. Williams (1978) 41 MLR 404.
[12.] For a comprehensive review of the House of Lords changing views towards tax law, see Robert Stevens, *Law and Politics: The House of Lords as a Judicial Body 1800–1976*, especially pp. 170–176, 204–208, 312, 392–396, 411–414 and 600–613.

introduced the UK to the more purposive or teleological approach of the civilian systems (see below).

3.8 'RULES' OF INTERPRETATION

3.8.1 General

Traditionally three 'rules' of interpretation have been used in the English courts.[13] These are the Literal, Mischief and Golden 'Rules.' These should be considered in the context of the various tax cases which the reader encounters to see which (if any) of these apply. One helpful approach to interpretation may be that of Lord Wilberforce in *W. T. Ramsay* v *IRC* [1982] AC 300, an avoidance case, who said (at p. 323):[14]

> A subject is only to be taxed on clear words, not on 'intendment' or the 'equity' of an Act. Any taxing Act of Parliament is to be construed in accordance with this principle. What are 'clear words' is to be ascertained on normal principles: these do not confine the Courts to literal interpretation. There may, indeed should, be considered, the context and scheme of the relevant Act as a whole, and its purpose may, indeed should, be regarded.

3.8.2 Literal rule

There are many dicta supporting the Literal Rule. Under the Literal Rule the words are to be given their plain and literal meaning.[15] Thus in *Partington* v *A-G* (1869) LR 4 HL 100 Lord Cairns LC said (at p. 122):

> If the person sought to be taxed comes within the letter of the law, he must be taxed, however great the hardship may appear to the judicial mind to be. On the other hand, if the Crown, seeking to recover the tax, cannot bring the subject within the letter of the law, the subject is free, however apparently within the spirit of the law the case might otherwise appear to be . . .

Lord Halsbury LC said something of similar effect in *Tennant* v *Smith* [1892] AC 150 at p. 154, 'Cases . . . under the Taxing Acts always resolve themselves into a question whether or not the words of the Act have reached the alleged subject of taxation' (see also Lord Reid in *IRC* v *Hinchy* [1960] AC 748 at p. 767). This gives some flexibility.

In discussing the Literal Approach H.H. Monroe (then the Presiding Special Commissioner) said in his Hamlyn lecture entitled *Intolerable Inquisition? Reflections on the Law of Tax*:

[13.] See J. Willis, 'Statutory Interpretation in a Nutshell' (1938) 16 *Can Bar Rev* 1.

[14.] This is partially based on Rowlatt J's dictum in *Cape Brandy Syndicate* v *IRC* [1921] 1 KB 64 that: 'In a taxing Act one has to look merely at what is clearly said. There is no room for any intendment. There is no equity about a tax.'

[15.] See Ogden and Richards, *The Meaning of Meaning*, 10th edn.

The interpretation of taxing statutes

This, then, appears to be the judge's dilemma. In looking for the meaning of a taxing statute he must reject as indications the intendment of the Act, the scheme of the Act, the purpose of the Act, the logic of the Act. His eyes must be fixed on the words, and the words alone, which he is called on to construe. If the words are clear, his task is over. He takes them, he applies them; down tumbles the sky, but the rules have been observed. If, however, the words are blurred, if they are not clear, then he may, nay he must, look at the context in which they are found and construe the Act as a whole.

The way at which the context may be looked at needs to be considered in relation to the other two 'rules.'

The use of a Literal Approach may be explained as Lord Cairns LC (the same Lord Chancellor as in *Partington* above) explained it in *Pryce* v *Monmouthshire Canal & Rly Co* (1879) 4 App Cas 197:

> ... The cases which have decided that taxing Acts are to be construed with strictness and that no payment is to be extracted from the subject which is not clearly and unequivocally required by Act of Parliament to be made, probably meant little more than this, that, in as much as there was not any *a priori* liability in a subject to pay any particular tax, nor any antecedent relationship between the taxpayer and the taxing authority, no reasoning founded upon any supposed relationship of the taxpayer and the taxing authority could be brought to bear on the construction of the Act and therefore the taxpayer has a right to stand upon a literal construction of the words used, whatever might be the consequence.[16]

3.8.3 Mischief rule

The mischief or purpose of the legislation may be important in its interpretation. *Heydon's Case* (1584) 3 Co Rep 7a is the classic authority for this. The '... mischief and defect for which the common law did not provide' is to be divined. This is to guide the interpretation of the statute. A provision inserted in 1980 into the Australian Acts Interpretation Act 1901, perhaps expresses this in more modern form. Section 15AA reads:

> In the interpretation of a provision of an Act, a construction that would promote the purpose or object underlying the Act (whether that purpose or object is expressly stated in the Act or not) shall be preferred to a construction that would not promote that purpose or object.[17]

---

[16] In an address given to the Statute Law Society's Corporation (reported [1982–83] *Statute Law Review* 78) Vinelott J said: 'Something of the same attitude is, I think, reflected in the initial reaction of the judiciary when first confronted with appeals from the Commissioners in the late nineteenth century. Taxing Acts were read as if they were written in a foreign tongue. The task of the judge was to retire to his room and to interpret the particular provision under consideration with no guide except a grammar book and a dictionary.'

[17] See also s. 11, Canadian Interpretation Act 1967–68 and s. 5(j), [New Zealand] Acts Interpretation Act 1924.

This is closely related to the Golden Rule discussed next.

3.8.4 Golden rule

The Golden Rule allows some note to be taken of absurd results that Parliament cannot have intended. Lord Blackburn said (at pp. 764–65) in *River Wear Commissioners* v *Adamson* (1877) 2 App Cas 743:

> I believe that it is not disputed that what Lord Wensleydale used to call the golden rule is right, viz. that we are to take the whole statute together, and construe it altogether, giving the words their ordinary signification, unless when so applied they produce an inconsistency, or an absurdity or inconvenience so great as to convince the court that the intention of Parliament could not have been to use them in their ordinary signification, and to justify the court in putting on them some other signification, which, though less proper is one which the court might think the words will bear.

The purposive approach is not always helpful. In *Craven* v *White* [1987] 3 All ER 27 Parker LJ said (at p. 61):

> ... the purpose does not appear to be of any assistance in the present appeal, for the detailed and elaborate provisions of the Act make it clear that the purpose was to tax some people and not others in respect of certain transactions and not others and one can only determine which people and which transactions by looking at the words of the section.

Luke v *IRC* [1963] AC 557 is probably the best illustration of the Golden Rule. Lord Reid said (at p. 579):

> In order to avoid imputing to Parliament an intention to produce an unreasonable result we are entitled and indeed bound to discard the ordinary meaning of any provision and adopt some other possible meaning which will avoid that result.

Professor Sir Rupert Cross described a unified approach to statutory interpretation which provides a useful summary of all of this. He said[18]

> 1. The judge must give effect to the ordinary or, where appropriate, the technical meaning of words in the general context of the statute; he must also determine the extent of general words with reference to that context.
> 2. If the judge considers that the application of the words in their ordinary sense would produce an absurd result which cannot reasonably be supposed to have been the intention of the legislature, he may apply them in any secondary meaning which they are capable of bearing.

---

[18]. R. Cross, *Statutory Interpretation*, Butterworths, 1st edn. The editors of the 2nd edition made some changes.

The interpretation of taxing statutes

3. The judge may read in words which he considers to be necessarily implied by words which are already in the statute and he has a limited power to add to, alter or ignore statutory words in order to prevent a provision from being unintelligible or absurd or totally unreasonable, unworkable, or totally irreconcilable with the rest of the statute.

4. In applying the above rules the judge may resort to . . . 'aids to construction and presumptions' . . .

3.8.5 Miscellaneous matters

3.8.5.1 Grammar and ordinary meaning The ordinary rules of grammar are to be applied in interpreting a statute. These are not a matter of law but more what might be described as a convention. Presumably judicial notice can be taken of the rules of grammar.

Words, in the first instance, are to be given their 'ordinary meaning'. Again this is not a matter of law. As Lord Reid said in *Brutus* v *Cozens* [1972] 2 All ER 1297 (at p. 1299):

> The meaning of an ordinary word of the English language is not a question of law. The proper construction of a statute is a question of law. If the context shows that a word is used in an unusual sense the court will determine in other words what the unusual sense is . . . It is for the tribunal which decides the case to consider, not as law but as fact, whether in the whole circumstances the words of the statute do or do not as a matter of ordinary usage of the English language cover or apply to the facts which have been proved. If it is alleged that the tribunal has reached a wrong decision then there can be a question of law but only of a limited character. The question would normally be whether their decision was unreasonable in the sense that no tribunal acquainted with the ordinary use of language could reasonably reach that decision.

(See also *O'Rourke* v *Binks* [1992] STC 703.)

3.8.5.2 Statutory matters Statutes sometimes give meanings to words for particular purposes. Thus the Interpretation Act 1978 provides definitions etc. to be applied to all statutes. The Law of Property Act 1925 also contains certain provisions applicable to deeds and other instruments. Thus a month means a calendar month (cf. s. 5 and sch. 1, Interpretation Act 1978), a person includes a corporation, the singular includes the plural and vice versa (cf. s. 6 Interpretation Act 1978) and the masculine embraces the feminine and vice versa (see s. 61, LPA 1925). Sections 832–834, TA provide definitions for the Income and Corporation Taxes Act. Section 288, TCGA is the interpretation section for that Act. The general interpretation provision for inheritance tax is in s. 272, Inheritance Tax Act 1984. Section 96, VATA is the definition section for VAT purposes.

3.8.5.3 Punctuation Punctuation is now found in statutes. It was not used in statutes before 1850. Lord Reid said in *IRC* v *Hinchy* (1960) 38 TC 625 (at p. 650):

> . . . before 1850 there was no punctuation in the manuscript copy of an Act which received the Royal Assent and it does not appear that the printers had any statutory authority to insert punctuation thereafter. So even if punctuation in more modern Acts can be looked at (which is very doubtful) I do not think that one can have any regard to punctuation in older Acts . . .

3.8.5.4 Consolidation A consolidation Act is to be construed in the first place according to its actual language. If that is ambiguous the earlier legislation may be looked at and the presumption applied that a consolidation statute is not to make substantial changes to the law (see e.g., *IRC* v *Joiner* [1975] 3 All ER 1050 at p. 1057 and Bramwell [1992] BTR 69). A statute may also be stated to be construed 'as one with'. This can reasonably be done in most cases but can cause difficulty.

3.8.5.5 Latin tags There are also certain Latin tags that can be applied by a court to the interpretation of statutory provisions. These include the following:

(a) *ejusdem generis*: Literally this means 'of the same type'. When there is a list of items of the same type followed by general words, the general words are to be limited to items of the same type as in the list (see, for example, *Le Cras* v *Perpetual Trustee Co.* [1967] 3 All ER 915 at p. 928).

(b) *noscitur a sociis*: Literally this means 'it is known by its friends'. This seems to mean that in interpreting a word the context may be taken into account. Stamp J said in *Bourne* v *Norwich Crematorium Ltd* [1967] 2 All ER 576 (at p. 578):

> English words derive colour from those which surround them. Sentences are not mere collections of words to be taken out of the sentence, defined separately by reference to the dictionary or decided cases, and then put back into the sentence with the meaning which you have assigned to them as separate words, so as to give the sentence or phrase a meaning which as a sentence or phrase it cannot bear without distortion of the English language. That one must construe a word or phrase in a section of an Act of Parliament with all the assistance one can from decided cases and, if one will, from the dictionary, is not in doubt; but having obtained all that assistance, one must not at the end of the day distort that which has to be construed and give it a meaning which in its context one does not think it can possibly bear.[19]

[19.] The question at issue was whether cremation of human remains was 'the subjection of goods or materials to any process for the purpose of claiming capital allowances.'

(c) *expressio unius est exclusio alterius*: Broadly, this means 'The inclusion of the one is the exclusion of the other'. If there is a list but no general words, the list is taken as exhaustive. Thus if one person or thing is mentioned but another person or thing is not, then that other is *prima facie* excluded (see *Colquhoun v Brooks* (1887) 19 QBD 490).

3.8.5.6 Scheme of the Act and *pari materia* Lord Halsbury said in *IRC v Priestley* [1901] AC 208 at p. 213, 'The scheme of the Act, of course, may be looked at where there are doubtful words.' This seems to tie in with the 'Golden Rule'.

3.8.5.7 Deeming provisions The drafting of tax statutes may deem certain things to be the case. For example, on a person becoming absolutely entitled against trustees, the trustees are deemed to dispose of the assets to which the beneficiary became absolutely entitled. These provisions are not always easy to apply.

3.8.5.8 Charging and machinery sections Tax will be imposed by one section and other sections may provide the machinery for the collection of the tax. This can alter the context in which the provision is to be applied as a charging section may require a different approach from a machinery provision. Finlay J recognised this in *IRC v Longmans Green & Co. Ltd* (1932) 17 TC 272. He said (at p. 282):

> It was pointed out . . . that you have got to get the charge imposed and you have got to get the necessary machinery for levying the tax. That is true, although, if you get the charge imposed, I see no reason why a specially rigorous construction should be imposed upon the machinery section. I should have thought if there was any intendment in the matter it would be rather the other way, but the truth of the matter is that I do not think these general rules with regard to construction help very much.[20]

3.8.5.9 Reading words in A court is usually unwilling to read words into a statute. Scott LJ (with whom Stuart-Smith LJ agreed) in *O'Rourke v Binks* [1992] STC 703 considered (at p. 709) that cases such as *Luke v IRC* (see para. 3.8.4) and *Mangin v IRC* [1971] AC 739 justify in some cases implying into a section a natural limitation as to its scope that would correspond with the obvious intention of the legislature. It can be difficult to persuade a court to do this though.

3.8.5.10 Applicable to all countries of the UK Generally, tax statutes apply to the whole of the UK. They should be interpreted in the light of this. Special provisions are often included to deal with differences in different parts of the UK, although this is not always the case (see, e.g., *IRC v City of Glasgow Police Athletic Association* [1953] 1 All ER 747).

---

[20] Cf. *Colquhoun v Brooks* (1889) 2 TC 490 at p. 507. See also *Brunnton v Commissioner for Stamp Duty (NSW)* [1913] AC 747 at p. 760 in particular.

3.8.5.11 Presumption against retrospection Viscount Simonds in *Hudson* v *Kirkness* (1955) 36 TC 28 (at p. 63) was of the view that:

> ... it is contrary to general principles of legislation in this country to alter the law retrospectively ... if Parliament alters the existing law retrospectively, it does so by an amendment which is an express enactment ... it will not do so by force merely of an assumption or an allusion in a later Act.

Rowlatt J described the argument to the contrary as 'a sinister and menacing proposition' (*Ormond Investment Co. Ltd* v *Betts* (1928) 13 TC 400 at p. 407).

3.9 AMBIGUITY AND OBSCURITY

It is sometimes said that if the legislation is ambiguous or obscure the court should favour the subject. This is often an aspect of the need for statutory authority for the imposition of tax; see Lord Simon in *Customs and Excise* v *Thorn Electrical Industries Ltd* [1975] STC 617 at p. 620. In *Commissioners of Customs & Excise* v *Top Ten* [1969] 3 All ER 39 at p. 93, Lord Donovan said:

> ... difficulty arises from the use of phrases of wide import such as 'benefiting from' and 'connected therewith' with no attempt to define these terms so as to avoid absurdities to which a literal interpretation inevitably leads. This is to shirk a responsibility which rests initially on the legal advisers of the commissioners, and persistence in this policy will one day lead to serious discomfiture for the department, when the obscurity of an enactment which it has sponsored, or the uncontrollable width of its language, compels a court to find that no reasonable construction is available and that the taxpayer is therefore not to be charged.

Lord Wilberforce said (at p. 95):

> ... the subsection uses words ... which are very general and capable of a very extensive meaning. And it is easy enough to give extreme instances which reduce their application to the absurd. In using them the legislator runs the risk that the courts may find themselves so totally unable to draw the line as to decide nothing more than that the subject has not clearly enough been taxed.

(Cf. Lord Reid in *IRC* v *Bates* (1966) 44 TC 225 at 263.)

Certainly, the court may favour an interpretation which makes the tax workable. In *Whitney* v *IRC* [1926] AC 37 Lord Dunedin (at p. 52) said:

> Once that it is fixed that there is liability, it is effective. A statute is designed to be workable, and the interpretation thereof by a court should be to secure that object, unless crucial omission or clear direction makes that end unattainable.

A court will also tend to favour an interpretation that does not breach international obligations. 'Where . . . the words of the statute are capable of more than one meaning, an English court must, in construing them, apply the presumption that Parliament does not intend to act in breach of the United Kingdom's international obligations', according to Warner J in *National Smokeless Fuels Ltd* v *IRC* [1986] STC 300. In the case of a European directive the UK's international obligations may require the court to give it direct effect. However, the Crown may not rely on direct effect to impose tax.

Side notes or headings in Acts are not usually to be used to resolve ambiguities (cf. *Page* v *Lowther* [1983] STC 61 especially at pp. 68–69).

3.10 PARLIAMENTARY DEBATES AND *PEPPER* v *HART*

The enormous impact of permitting the courts to refer to Hansard in construing legislation when certain conditions are met has already been discussed in Chapter 2.

3.11 EUROPEAN INFLUENCE

Since the UK joined what was then called the Common Market, Europe has had an increasingly greater influence over a number of matters in the UK. This includes tax, although on direct tax note Art. 100a of the Treaty of Rome, inserted by the Single European Act 1986; see, e.g., *R* v *Secretary of State for Transport ex parte Factortame* [1990] 2 AC 85 and *Francovich* v *Italian Republic* C 6/90 and C 9/90. European law can take precedence over domestic law. This European influence is particularly important as regards VAT.[21]

The supremacy of European law is incorporated into UK domestic law by s. 2 of the European Communities Act 1972. This provides:

> (1) All such rights, powers, liabilities, obligations and restrictions from time to time created or arising by or under the Treaties and all such remedies and procedures from time to time provided for by or under the Treaties, as in accordance with the Treaties are without further enactment to be given legal effect or used in the United Kingdom shall be recognised and available in law, and be enforced, allowed and followed accordingly; and the expression 'enforceable Community right' and similar expressions shall be read as referring to one which this sub-section applies.
> (2) Subject to Schedule 2 to this Act, at any time after its passing Her Majesty may by Order in Council and any designated Minister or department may by regulations, make provision:
>
> > (a) for the purpose of implementing any Community obligation of the United Kingdom or enabling any such obligation to be implemented, or of enabling any rights enjoyed or to be enjoyed by the United Kingdom under or by virtue of the Treaties to be exercised; or

---

[21.] It can be relevant for direct tax, e.g., cross-board and mergers, see s. 140A–140D, TCGA and cases such as *R* v *IRC ex parte ICI* (1990) 60 TC 1.

(b) for the purpose of dealing with matters arising out of or related to any such obligation or rights or the coming into force, or the operation from time to time, of subsection (1) above:
and in the exercise of any statutory power or duty, including any power to give directions or to legislate by means of orders, rules, regulations or other subordinate instrument, the person entrusted with the power or duty may have regard to the objects of the Communities and to any such obligations or rights as aforesaid.

The Treaty is to be treated as part of the domestic law of each member state. The European Court of Justice in *Costa* v *Enel* [1964] ECR 585 said:

By contrast with ordinary international Treaties, the EEC Treaty has created its own legal system which, on entry into force of the Treaty became an integral part of the legal system of the Member States and which their courts are bound to apply.

This follows in part from the application to domestic law of Art. 5 of the Treaty requiring member states to ensure the fulfilment of the obligations arising out of the Treaty. This has an effect on the way legislation arising out of EC obligations is to be interpreted.

Article 5 provides member states must take all appropriate measures, whether general or particular, to ensure fulfilment of the obligations arising out of the Treaty or resulting from actions taken by the institutions of the Community. They must facilitate the achievement of the Community's tasks and abstain from any measure which could jeopardise the attainment of the objectives of the Treaty.

Not all rules and regulations emanating from Brussels have the same force in domestic law. Some parts of European law have direct effect whilst others are directly effective. This is governed by Art. 189 of the Treaty. This authorises the making of regulations and the issue of directives. Article 189 provides:

In order to carry out their tasks and in accordance with the provisions of this Treaty, the European Parliament acting jointly with the Council, the Council and the Commission shall make regulations and issue directives, take decisions, make recommendations or deliver opinions.

A regulation shall have general application. It shall be binding in its entirety and directly applicable in all member-states.

A directive shall be binding, as to the result to be achieved, upon each member-state to which it is addressed, but shall leave to the national authorities the choice of form and methods.

Accordingly this Article authorises the making of regulations and the issue of directives. However it provides for a clear distinction between the two in that a regulation is to have general application and is binding in its entirety and is to have direct application in all member states, whereas a directive is binding as to the result to be achieved and is at most directly effective in whole or in part.

Direct application means that an EC regulation applies in each member state without the need for further implementation. Although it may be necessary for the member state to make further domestic or adjectival rules to ensure the enforceability of the regulations, regulations often make their own provisions as to the penalties for breach. Regulations not only confer rights on individuals but also impose obligations. Accordingly they can have 'horizontal effect' enabling one individual to sue another for failure to comply with the regulation. In *Van Gend en Loos* [1963] ECR 1 it was said:

> The fact that [Articles 169 and 170 of the Treaty] enable the Commission and the Member States to bring before the Court a State which has not fulfilled its obligations does not mean that individuals cannot plead those obligations, should the occasion arise, before a national court, any more than the fact that the Treaty places at the disposal of the Commission ways of ensuring that obligations imposed upon those subject to the Treaty are observed, precludes the possibility, in actions between individuals for a national court, of pleading infringements of those obligations . . . It follows from the foregoing obligations that, according to the spirit, the general scheme and the wording of the Treaty, Article 12 must be interpreted as producing direct effects and creating individual rights which national courts must protect . . . the objective of the EEC Treaty which is to establish a common market, the function of which is of direct concern to the parties in the Community, implies that the Treaty is more than an agreement which merely creates mutual obligations between the contracting States. This view is confirmed by the preamble to the Treaty which refers not only to governments but to people. It is also confirmed more specifically by the establishment of institutions endowed with sovereign rights, the exercise of which affects Member States and also their citizens . . . The conclusion to be drawn from this is that the Community constitutes a new legal order of international law for the benefit of which the States have limited their sovereign rights, albeit within limited fields, and the subjects of which comprise not only Member States but also their nationals. Independently of the legislation of Member States, Community law therefore not only imposes obligations on individuals but is also intended to confer rights upon them which become part of their legal heritage. These rights arise not only where they are expressly granted by the Treaty, but also by reason of obligations which the Treaty imposes in a clearly defined way upon individuals as well as upon the Member States and upon the institutions of the Community.

This decision gave rise to the concept of the Community legal order. It was said in the *Simmenthal* case (*Amministrazione delle Finanze dello Stato* v *Simmenthal SA* [1978] ECR 629):

> Furthermore, in accordance with the principle of the precedence of Community law, the relationship between provisions of the Treaty and

directly applicable measures of the institutions on the one hand and the national law of the Member States on the other hand is such that those provisions and measures not only by their entry into force render automatically inapplicable any conflicting provisions of current national law but – insofar as they are an integral part of, and take precedence in, the legal order applicable in the territory of each of the Member States – also preclude the valid adoption of new national legislative measures to the extent to which they would be incompatible with Community provisions.

Because regulations are directly applicable, errors by the member state in notifying its citizens of the effect of a regulation do not give rise to a defence in proceedings for the recovery of the right amounts of duty or tax. There is no defence of legitimate expectation engendered by the acts of the competent customs authority. The Commission jealously guards its right to its own resources; see *Friederich Binder GmbH* v *Hauptzollamt Bard Reichenhall* [1989] ECR 2415 and *Erwin Behn* v *Hauptzollamt Itzehoe* [1990] ECRI–2659.

A provision or article of a Directive which has direct effect must be implemented in domestic legislation by the member state. If the member state fails to implement the article or fails to implement it properly, the following consequences result.

A member state cannot rely on the directive to overcome its own failure when involved in proceedings against an individual (see *Ratti* [1979] ECR 1629). However the individual may rely on the article, rather than the ineffective legislation, if he or she so wishes in proceedings such as a VAT appeal against the member state. It was said in *Ratti*:

> it follows that a national court requested by a person who has complied with the provisions of a Directive not to apply a national provision incompatible with the Directive not incorporated into the internal order of a defaulting Member State must uphold that request if the obligation in question is unconditional and precise.

However, an individual cannot rely on the article as against another individual. In technical terms directly affected provisions have vertical but not horizontal effect. The case of *Ursula Becker* [1982] ECR 53 should be considered in this context.

A member state may be given a discretion as to the implementation of a provision of a directive. *Von Colson* ((case 14/83) [1984] ECR 1891, and *Marleasing* (case 106/89) [1990] ECR I–4135, established the principle that, in applying national law in an area where member states have an obligation to achieve the result envisaged by a directive the national court is required, so far as may be possible, to interpret the domestic legislation in the light of the wording and purpose of the directive, in order to achieve the results pursued by the directive. However, Lord Templeman said in *Duke* v *GEC Reliance Ltd* [1988] 1 All ER 626 that the *Von Colson* case '. . . is no authority for the proposition that a court of a Member State must distort the meaning of a domestic statute so as to conform with Community law which is not directly applicable.' Whether this would be the case as far as the European Court of Justice (ECJ) is concerned is a matter of conjecture.

The ECJ itself has a number of established principles which it applies. These include the principle of proportionality. This principle is that 'any Member State is only entitled to pass measures which are necessary to guarantee the application and effectiveness of Community law. Proportionality requires that where a Member State imposes penalties for infringement of Community law, those penalties must be effective, proportionate and dissuasive.' See *Commission* v *Greece* (case 68/88) [1989] ECR 2965, and *Anklagemyndigheden v Hansen & Sons I/S* (case 326/88) [1990] ECR I-2911.) Effective requires, amongst other things, that the member states endeavour to attain and implement the objectives of the relevant provisions of Community law. The phrase 'proportionate and dissuasive' means that the penalties must be sufficiently though not excessively strict, regard having being had to the objectives pursued (see the opinion of Advocate General van Gerven in *Hansen*).

In *Rainer Drexel* (case 299/86) [1988] ECR 1213, it was said:

> as the court has already held in another context concerning the free movement of persons, a system of penalties should not have the effect of jeopardising the freedoms provided for by the EEC Treaty. This would be the case if a penalty was disproportionate to the gravity of the offence so that it became an obstacle to the freedom guaranteed by Community law (see the judgment of 3rd July 1980 in *R* v *Pieck* [1980] ECR 2171, Case 157/79).

3.12 EUROPEAN PRINCIPLES AND INTERPRETATION OF UK DOMESTIC LEGISLATION

UK legislation which is derived from, or affected by, a Directive (such as VAT) cannot therefore be construed in a domestic vacuum. It is necessary to have regard to the purposes of the Directive and the result which the Directive is seeking to achieve in determining the meaning of the UK statutory provisions. This is the effect of *Von Colson* and *Marleasing*. Authority for this can be found in the decision of the House of Lords in *Customs and Excise Commissioners* v *Apple and Pear Development Council* [1986] STC 193. Here the word 'consideration' was used in both the UK statute imposing VAT and the Sixth Directive. The House of Lords did not assume that the word had its technical domestic meaning but referred the matter to the ECJ which found that it had a special European meaning.

It is not only necessary to refer to any relevant directives in construing the meaning of UK legislation, but in construing the directives and the UK legislation a purposive or teleological method of construction rather than the English literal method is to be applied. As Bingham J said in *Commissioners of Customs & Excise* v *APS Samex* [1983] 1 All ER 1042 at p. 1056:

The interpretation of Community instruments involves very often not the process familiar to common lawyers of laboriously extracting the meaning from words used, but the more creative process of supplying flesh to a spare and loosely constructed skeleton. The choice between alternative submissions may turn not on purely legal considerations but on a broader view of what the orderly development of the Community requires.

This can involve a court in adding words into a statute to ensure that the UK complies with its Treaty obligations. As was said by Lord Oliver in *Litster* v *Forth Dry Dock Company Ltd* [1989] 1 All ER 1134 at p. 1153:

> if this provision fell to be construed by reference to the ordinary rules and construction applicable to a purely domestic statute and without reference to Treaty obligations, it would, I think, be quite impermissible to regard it as having the same prohibitory effect as that attributed by the European Court to Article 4 of the Directive. But it is always to be borne in mind that the purpose of the Directive and of the regulations was and is to 'safeguard' the rights of employees on a transfer and that there is a mandatory obligation to provide remedies which are effective and not merely symbolic to which the regulations were intended to give effect. The remedies provided by the 1978 Act in the case of an insolvent transferor are largely illusory unless they can be exerted against the transferee as the Directive contemplates and I do not find it conceivable that, in so many regulations intended to give effect to the Directive, the Secretary of State could have envisaged that its purpose should be capable of being avoided by the transparent device to which resort was had in the instant case. *Pickstone* v *Freemans plc* [1988] 3 All ER 803 has established that the greater flexibility available to the Court in applying a purposive construction to the legislation designed to give effect to the United Kingdom's Treaty obligations to the Community enables the Court, where necessary, to supply by implication words appropriate to comply with those obligations.

Although the rule is that a taxing authority cannot rely on a directive where the UK has failed correctly to transfer the directive into UK domestic law, the European rules of interpretation can lead the court to give a generous interpretation to a statutory provision which, on UK principles, clearly fails to implement a directly effective article. Thus in *National Smokeless Fuels Ltd* v *IRC* [1986] STC 300 it was said:

> . . . if the words of a statute passed to fulfil an international obligation of the United Kingdom are so clear and unambiguous that they are capable of only one meaning, the terms of the international treaty or other instrument imposing that obligation cannot be invoked to modify that meaning. If, in such a case, the statute fails to fulfil the obligation, the remedy, subject to a well known exception, lies in a . . . forum other than Her Majesty's own courts. Where, on the other hand, the words of the

statute are reasonably capable of more than one meaning, an English court must in construing them, apply the presumption that Parliament does not intend to act in breach of the United Kingdom's international obligations. The well known exception . . . is, of course, that of a case . . . where the United Kingdom statute fails to fulfil an obligation contained in the provision of European Community law having direct effect in the Member States. That possibility does not arise for my consideration in the present case . . . Counsel for the Crown . . . does not [ask me to hold that the Directive has direct effect] because the principle on which an EC Directive may be held to have direct effect is such that it is not open to the Crown to rely on it.

Finally, in construing Community legislation the way in which the legislation is drafted is important. A Community instrument is to state the reasons which form its basis in fact and in law (see Art. 190 of the Treaty). The preamble will thus cite the powers and the factors giving rise to its propositions. This assists in the purposive construction of Community legislation. Warner J (formerly an Advocate General of the ECJ) said in *National Smokeless Fuels Limited* v *IRC* [1986] 3 CMLR 227 at p. 237 that the preamble of the directive must be taken into account when construing it. Reference may also be made to the text in different languages in interpreting a directive.

3.13 SUMMARY

In interpreting sections of a UK Act derived from a directive, such as the VATA, the procedure is as follows:

(a) Has the directive been clearly implemented? Even if it has been clearly implemented the court must still have regard to the European legislation in order to impose a construction on the UK legislation consistent with the purpose of the directive.

(b) If there is an ambiguity in the UK legislation the court is to have resort to the directive to resolve the ambiguity, whether the person seeking to rely on the provision is the taxpayer or the Revenue or Customs and Excise.

(c) If UK legislation fails to give full effect to Community law the court may still be willing to fill in the gaps whilst pretending to be 'interpreting' the statute. This may be done even if it favours the Revenue or Customs and Excise.

(d) Strictly it is not permissible for the court to impose a construction on domestic legislation which the legislation is incapable of bearing, merely because by doing so it will enable the UK to comply with its Treaty obligations. If there is a conflict between the legislation and the directive then Art. 189 must be considered. If the relevant European legislation is directly effective, the court must ignore the UK legislation if the proponent of the directive is the taxpayer. However the court must apply the UK legislation if the taxpayer so requests. If the article does not have direct effect then the court should properly apply the UK provision despite the breach of international comity.

3.14 THE EUROPEAN COURT

Many cases, particularly VAT cases, raise issues of construction of a directive particularly the Sixth Directive. If a decision on the construction of a directive is necessary to enable the court to give judgment, it may either try to resolve the issue itself or it may refer the issue to the European Court of Justice (ECJ). In practice a reference is not generally made unless one of the parties wishes such a reference. Provision for reference is made in Art. 177 of the Treaty. It provides:

> . . . the Court of Justice shall have jurisdiction to give preliminary rulings concerning:
>
> (a) the interpretation of this Treaty;
> (b) the validity and interpretation of acts of the institutions of the community . . .
> (c) the interpretation of the statutes of bodies established by an act of the Council where those statutes so provide.
>
> Where such a question is raised before any court or tribunal of a member state, that court or tribunal may, if it considers that a decision on the question is necessary to enable it to give judgment, request the Court of Justice to give a ruling thereon.
>
> Where any such question is raised in a case pending before a court or tribunal of a member-state against whose decisions there is no judicial remedy under national law, that court or tribunal must bring the matter before the Court of Justice.

Accordingly, courts below the House of Lords have a choice as to whether a reference is to be made. The House of Lords must make a reference where Art. 177 is relevant.

A domestic court of a member state is not obliged to make reference to the ECJ where the point of community law is free from doubt or uncertainty (see *Re Shell-Berre* [1964] CMLR 462 at 481 and *Re Yoga Fruit Juices* [1969] CMLR 123).

CHAPTER FOUR
Tax avoidance

4.1 INTRODUCTION

This chapter is concerned with what is often called tax avoidance.[1] As will be seen there is no clear consensus as to its meaning. The question of tax avoidance is closely related to the interpretation of the statute (discussed in Chapter 3), the problem for both being, what does the legislation actually cover and what should it cover? Should the statute be interpreted strictly so that what might otherwise not be within the spirit of the legislation is caught, or should it be interpreted according to its purpose, whatever that may be? This raises questions of constitutionality and fairness. On the one hand if the words used by the legislature do not cover the particular circumstances, why should the person be taxed if Parliament has not clearly imposed the tax? On the other hand it would be 'unfair' to other taxpayers if the person in question did not make their proper contribution and pay their 'fair' share towards the country's expenditure.

4.2 WHAT IS TAX AVOIDANCE?

One of the problems in any discussion of tax avoidance is what is meant by the phrase 'tax avoidance'. It seems implicit in the phrase that a comparison is to be made between what tax should have been paid and the tax consequences of what has actually been done. If it is to be of more than academic interest then what has been done must apparently result in a lower tax charge compared with something else. If so, is this necessarily something

---

[1]. See M.J. Gammie, *Strategic Tax Planning*, Vol. 2 (Ed, Shipwright), Part D Section 2, Millett J. (1982) 98 LQR 209, J. Tiley [1987] BTR 180 and 200 and [1988] BTR 63 and 108, also *Sham, Fraud and Mitigation* (ed. Shipwright) SPTL, 1997.

that should not be allowed to stand? Is it the consequence of what Parliament has enacted? Why is it objectionable? Many people think that it is objectionable but what is the rationale for this? What are the criteria for distinguishing between acceptable and unacceptable tax avoidance? Tax liability is *prima facie* a matter of law not of morality or of what ought to happen.

One person's tax avoidance may be another's evasion or another's sensible commercial arrangements. A gift of shares to a charity subject to an option to purchase them in favour of a trust of which the donor is the settlor can be perceived either as a means of avoiding income tax on dividends or as a means of maximising the gift to charity (cf. *Vandervell* v *IRC* [1967] 2 AC 91).

The English legal system, which has been very influential in shaping the UK tax system, has often taken the view that in so far as legislation or other law does not bite there is a residual liberty to do what one wishes. Certainly, the earlier approaches to tax avoidance reflect this. Nevertheless, if tax is the creature of statute and such statutes are the preserve of the Crown and Commons in Parliament assembled, what role do the judges have? Is it merely to apply the law in a strict way without 'any equity in a taxing statute' or is it to act as a guardian of 'fair contributions'? It is for consideration whether a return to strict literal interpretation could be a solution to the problem.

Further questions arise in this context. For example, should a taxpayer be entitled to set up a series of transactions intended to create, e.g., a deduction or loss which it is hoped can be used against other taxable profits or gains? What if the transactions are circular so that the money comes back to where it started from, the 'tax break' being the only advantage hoped for? This may be illustrated as follows.

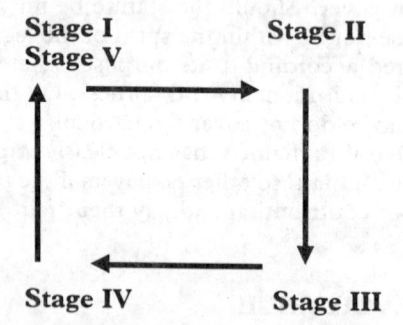

```
    Stage I          Stage II
    Stage V
       ↑ ──────────────→ │
       │                 │
       │                 ↓
       │ ←────────────── 
    Stage IV          Stage III
```

Figure 4.1

Many people might consider that a circular transaction such as this is objectionable. The problem is identifying why it is objectionable and deriving a principle from it. This is a matter which produces many views and much emotion. The question then arises whether transactions which are not circular, which might be described as 'linear', should be caught. This may be illustrated as follows.

Tax avoidance

Stage I → Stage II → Stage III → Stage IV

Figure 4.2

This appears to be a more acceptable series of transactions but the question again arises, why is it more acceptable? This is a very difficult question to answer objectively. Further, what is the distinction between linear and circular transactions? By introducing a company which the originator controlled, a circular transaction might apparently be opened up into a linear transaction. Should there be any distinction between the two? Should the taxpayer's motive be the determinative factor? If so how does one 'make a window into men's minds'? Should a *mens rea* be necessary for objectionable tax avoidance to be found?

Perhaps the important criterion to be found in this dictum of Lord Goff of Chieveley. He said:

> Unacceptable tax avoidance typically involves the creation of complex artificial structures by which, as though by the wave of a magic wand, the taxpayer conjures out of the air a loss, a gain or expenditure, or whatever it may be, which otherwise would have never existed. (*Ensign Tankers* v *Stokes* [1992] STC 226 at p. 244).

Ensign Tankers v *Stokes* is discussed in detail at para. 4.8 below.

4.3 HOW SHOULD TAX AVOIDANCE BE DEALT WITH?

Assuming one knows what tax avoidance is, the possible approaches to dealing with it are numerous. The civilian systems often have a general 'principle' in their law, sometimes called 'abuse of rights'[2] or '*fraus legis*' (e.g., in the Netherlands). It has been said that the abuse of rights doctrine 'is applied to cases in which one person has exercised a right with the intention or purpose of causing harm to another[3] . . . [and] thereafter found its way into many other fields of law . . .' including in some cases revenue law. English law not being a civilian system has no such general principle. It is interesting to consider whether EC law might develop such a doctrine which would then become part of the law applied in the UK.

[2.] See e.g., Art. 1383 of the French Code Civile and Arts. 1653C and 1729-3 of the Code Général des Impôts.
[3.] E.g., spite fences erected to interfere with another's enjoyment of light or land. See Ward *et al*, 'The Business Purpose Test and Abuse of Rights' [1985] BTR 68 at 70 citing André Tunc, 'The French Concept of Abus de Droit', The Cambridge Lectures 1981 at p. 151. It is interesting to compare some of the early English cases, e.g., *Keble* v *Hickeringill* (1705) 11 East 574n which has had much more influence in US tort law than in England and *The Gloucester Schomaster's Case* (1410) YB Hil 11 Hen IV, 47, pl. 21.

4.4 ANTI-AVOIDANCE OPTIONS AND TECHNIQUES

Brian Arnold and James Wilson have listed a number of anti-avoidance options or techniques by reference to common law approaches in an excellent article in three parts in the 1988 Canadian Tax Journal (CTJ). These can be summarised as follows.

4.4.1 Judicial anti-avoidance doctrines

A number of approaches can be taken by the courts including the following.

4.4.1.1 Sham and ineffective transactions The courts can strike down and/or 'recharacterise' transactions which pretend to be what they are not. We are not concerned with shams here as they are often related to fraudulent and deceitful transactions (see para. 4.5). This is likely to involve tax evasion and to be a criminal offence.

4.4.1.2 Substance over form It is sometimes said that tax consequences of a transaction should be determined by reference to the substance rather than its form. John Tiley has described this as 'insidiously attractive' ([1987] BTR at 226) but it is said 'to be little more than a convenient label that is used by judges to justify their conclusions' ([1988] CTJ 1137) without any specific criteria.

4.4.1.3 Step transaction doctrine A series of transactions may be entered into each of which is unobjectionable if looked at alone. However, if they are all put together they may be objectionable. This '. . . involves determining the tax consequences of a series of transactions either on the basis of its economic or commercial substance or on the basis that any steps that have no business purpose are disregarded notwithstanding that each step is legally valid'. This approach has been taken in the USA (see *Helvering* v *Gregory* 69F (2d) 809 (2nd Cir. 1934), affd 293 US 465 (1935) and the cases following it).

4.4.1.4 Business purpose test This allows a transaction to '. . . be disregarded for tax purposes if it lacks a business purpose, if the sole or dominant reason was the avoidance of tax.' This may form part of the process of statutory interpretation so the statute is to be interpreted as applying only to transactions that have some purpose other than the avoidance of tax. However, it suffers from the problem of what is meant by 'business purpose'. Many people in business would say saving tax *is* a business purpose. It has been said that such an approach '. . . all too often seems based on a "Freudian" view of extra-statutory morality' (Heward Stikeman QC, '*Furniss* v *Dawson*: The Canadian Approach' (1986) 7 *Fiscal Studies* 82 at p. 83).

4.4.1.5 Object and spirit The courts can seek to apply the 'object and spirit of the legislation'. The Canadian Supreme Court took this approach in

Tax avoidance

Stubart Investments Ltd v *R* [1984] CTC 294 (see Stikeman at para. 4.4.1.4). There are, however, problems in deciding what is the object and spirit of the legislation. It does not lead to certainty and it is not clear how it differs from a purposive construction. The Canadian courts have moved away somewhat from this approach in more recent times.

4.4.2 Legislative anti-avoidance techniques

A number of approaches can be taken by the legislature to 'tax avoidance' including the following.

4.4.2.1 Specific rules The legislature may use specific anti-avoidance rules to cut down particular forms of objectionable avoidance. UK legislation has many examples of these (see, e.g., ss. 703, 739 and 776, TA and s. 137, TCGA). The problems with specific rules are said to include the following matters:

(a) the drafting difficulty of foreseeing all the possibilities;
(b) the legislation may itself create new avoidance techniques;
(c) the rule is often 'overbroad' in seeking to catch similar matters and may affect legitimate activities;
(d) the legislation may provide a 'road map' for avoiders as it defines what is not caught as well as what is caught;
(e) much of the legislative complexity and prolixity comes from this type of legislation;
(f) early participants in a scheme benefit unless the legislation is retrospective, which is generally thought to be reprehensible;
(g) delay in implementation of specific rules may result in the loss of significant tax revenues.

Lord Simon of Glaisdale recognised some of this in *Ransom* v *Higgs* [1974] 3 All ER 949. He said:

In some fiscal systems there is a general provision that any transaction the paramount object of which is the avoidance of tax should be void for that purpose though valid for all other purposes. Our own fiscal system has no such provision, but rather attempts to deal with tax avoidance schemes specifically as they come to notice. The inevitable result of this and of other matters is a fiscal code of such complexity that many ordinary citizens, particularly those engaged in commerce and industry, seek the aid of experts in handling the tax affairs of themselves and the corporation for which they have responsibility; and, since the burden of taxation is heavy (in some circumstances punitive), and since there is generally some delay before tax avoidance schemes come to light (during which time a rich windfall may be garnered), there is a strong incentive for such experts to devote their talents to devising tax avoidance schemes for clients, actual or potential, and for such clients to adopt the schemes devised. . . . It may seem hard that a cunningly advised taxpayer should be able to avoid what appears to be his equitable share of the general fiscal burden and cast it on the shoulders of his fellow citizens. But for the courts to try to stretch the law to meet hard cases (whether the hardship appears to bear on the individual taxpayer or on the general body of taxpayers as represented by the Inland Revenue) is not merely to make bad law but to run the risk of subverting the rule of law itself. Disagreeable as it may seem that some taxpayers should escape what might appear to be their fair share of the general burden of national expenditure, it would be far more disagreeable to substitute the rule of caprice for that of law.

4.4.2.2 Ministerial discretion The Minister or the Revenue itself can be given power to decide whether or not there is 'avoidance' and what action to take against it. This is said by some to be contrary to the rule of law. Such discretion gives great power to the Revenue. It also offends Adam Smith's canon of certainty (see Chapter 1).

4.4.2.3 General rule A general anti-avoidance rule could be used.[4] This could be a statutory business purpose test or the like. It could be, for example, that no one must avoid the obligations the tax system seeks to impose, but this is somewhat question begging. Such a rule has not proved easy to apply and has tended to be very much restricted by the courts in the past although the Canadian and others' experience of relatively new rules of this nature may prove otherwise.

4.4.3 Statutory principles?

Arnold and Wilson (see para. 4.4) set out ten principles to be used in formulating a statutory approach (at pp. 1142 et seq).

1. A statutory general anti-avoidance rule should be broad enough to deal with all types of transactions that result in abusive tax avoidance.

2. A general anti-avoidance rule must distinguish between abusive tax avoidance transactions and legitimate tax avoidance transactions.

3. A general anti-avoidance rule should focus, if possible, on the results of a transaction rather than the taxpayer's purpose in carrying out the transaction. If, however, a purpose test is used, it should be an objective test.

4. A general anti-avoidance rule should be consistent with other anti-avoidance rules.

[4.] The UK has no such general rule at present. It has in the past for profits tax but it proved somewhat ineffective. See s. 32, FA 1951 which gave wide powers to the Revenue to recharacterise transactions.

5. A general anti-avoidance rule should prevail over other, specific statutory provisions in certain circumstances only.

6. A general anti-avoidance rule should minimise uncertainty for taxpayers.

7. A general anti-avoidance rule should apply as a provision of last resort.

8. Taxpayers must be entitled to appeal all aspects of the application of a general anti-avoidance rule.

9. The determination of the tax consequences of a transaction to which the general anti-avoidance rule is applied should be appropriate for the particular transaction.

10. A penalty should be imposed on taxpayers who engage in abusive tax avoidance transactions.

The basic problem still remains though of identifying abusive tax avoidance.

4.5 SHAMS

Shams are not really our concern in this chapter but it is convenient to deal with them here. 'Sham' is used in the sense of dissimulation and fraud. As Lord Wilberforce said 'to say that a document is a "sham" means that while professing to be one thing, it is in fact something different. To say that a document or transaction is genuine, means that, in law, it is what it professes to be, and it does not mean anything more than that' (in *W T Ramsay* v *IRC* [1981] STC 174 at p. 180). Shams are thus evasion not 'tax avoidance' or 'mitigation' (discussed at para. 4.6). The case of *Johnson* v *Jewitt* (1961) 40 TC 231 illustrates something short of this. It involved a partnership to promote companies. It was held not to be trading but 'a cheap exercise in fiscal conjuring and book keeping phantasy, involving a gross abuse of the Companies Act and having as its unworthy object the extraction from the Exchequer of an enormous sum which the Appellant has never paid in tax and to which he has no shadow of a right whatsoever' (Donovan LJ at p. 255).

The classic case on 'shams' is *Snook* v *London & West Riding Investments Limited* [1967] 1 All ER 518. This is not a tax case but is applicable in the tax context. In this case the plaintiff sought to raise £100 making use of his rights in respect of a car worth about £800, which he had acquired on hire purchase. About £160 of the instalments remained to be paid. There was a purported sale. The plaintiff claimed in conversion. He failed as he was estopped from denying title in the defendants (Lord Denning MR dissenting). Diplock LJ said (at p. 528):

As regards the contention of the plaintiff that the transactions between himself, [the HP company] and the defendants were a 'sham', it is, I think, necessary to consider what, if any, legal concept is involved in the case of this popular and pejorative word. I apprehend that if it has any meaning in law, it means acts done or documents executed by the parties to the 'sham' which are intended by them to give to third parties legal rights and obligations different from the actual legal rights and obligations (if any) which the parties intended to create. One thing, I think, however, is clear in legal principle, morality and the authorities (see *Yorkshire Railway Wagon Co v Maclure* (1882) 21 Ch. D. 309; *Stoneleigh Finance Limited v Phillips* [1965] 2 QB 537) that for acts or documents to be a 'sham', with whatever legal consequences follow from this, all the parties thereto must have a common intention that the acts or documents are not to create the legal rights and obligations which they give the appearance of creating. No unexpressed intentions of a 'shammer' affect the rights of the party whom he deceived.

(See also *IRC v McGuckian* [1994] STC 888 at pp. 930–31 discussed at para. 4.11.)

4.6 AVOIDANCE, EVASION AND MITIGATION

The terminology used in this context can be confusing. The expressions 'tax avoidance', 'evasion' and 'mitigation' have all been used in the case law. In simplistic terms the difference is that avoidance is legal and evasion is illegal often involving, for example, criminal offences such as fraud, forgery, theft, obtaining pecuniary advantage by deception and conspiracy to cheat.

Lord Templeman drew a distinction between tax avoidance and tax mitigation in the Privy Council case of *Commissioner of Inland Revenue (New Zealand) v Challenge Corporation Ltd* [1986] STC 548. He said (at p. 554):

Income tax is mitigated by a taxpayer who reduces his income or incurs expenditure in circumstances which reduce his assessable income or entitle him to reduction in his tax liability.

He gave a number of examples including a covenant to charity. He continued later:

Income tax is avoided and a tax advantage is derived from an arrangement when the taxpayer reduces his liability to tax without involving him in the loss or expenditure which entitles him to that reduction.

He also said (at p. 555):

In an arrangement of tax avoidance the financial position of the taxpayer is unaffected (save for the costs of devising and implementing the arrangement) and by the arrangement the taxpayer seeks to obtain a tax advantage without suffering that reduction in income, loss or expenditure which other taxpayers suffer and which Parliament intended to be suffered by any taxpayer qualifying for a reduction in his liability to tax.

This is somewhat question begging as it assumes one knows what Parliament's intention was.

Lord Templeman cited the *Westminster* case, *Black Nominees Ltd* v *Nicol*, *Chinn* v *Collins*, *Ramsay* v *IRC* and *IRC* v *Burmah Oil Co. Ltd* as examples of tax avoidance. These cases are discussed at paras 4.7.3 et seq.

Whilst the UK has a number of specific statutory anti-avoidance provisions, it has as yet no general statutory anti-avoidance provision (see para. 4.4.2.3). Further, until comparatively recently, taxation being purely the creature of statute, the general view was that a taxing statute should be strictly interpreted or construed. However, more recently the courts have been moving away from strict interpretation and the maxim that 'there is no equity in a taxing statute'. Instead, a purposive or teleological approach has to some extent been introduced into the interpretation of taxing statutes and their application to the 'factual matrix'. This approach is of uncertain ambit. Thus the present position with regard to the legitimacy of the avoidance of taxation is far from clear.

What was then called a 'new approach' to tax avoidance was gradually developed in the 1980s by the House of Lords by means, in particular, of four major cases. These were *Ramsay (WT) Ltd* v *IRC* [1981] STC 174, *IRC* v *Burmah Oil* [1982] STC 30, *Furniss* v *Dawson* [1984] STC 153 and *Craven* v *White* [1988] STC 476. Lord Templeman was particularly influential in this development.

In *Furniss* v *Dawson* it was said that a new approach to tax avoidance was emerging, the scope of which would have to be determined by subsequent cases. Despite the subsequent cases the principle remains of somewhat uncertain ambit and extent. The later cases shows the House of Lords at present following a restrictive approach to *Furniss* v *Dawson*. This may have something to do with changes in the personnel in the Lords as some of the current Law Lords were in the Court of Appeal and their judgments were reversed by previous Law Lords. It is also characteristic of the way case law develops in the common law (cf. *Donoghue* v *Stevenson* [1932] AC 562 and its subsequent development).

4.7 AVOIDANCE AND CASE LAW

4.7.1 Time and change

There are three periods that should be considered in this context. These are:

(a) the old approach and the *Duke of Westminster*;
(b) the position post-*Westminster* and pre-*Ramsay*;
(c) *Ramsay* and thereafter.

4.7.2 The old approach and the *Duke of Westminster*

The old approach to what is now called avoidance was that every man [sic] was entitled to arrange his affairs to minimise tax. Thus Lord Cairns LC said in *Partington* v *AG* (1869) LR 4 HL 100 (at p. 122):

> If the person sought to be taxed comes within the letter of the law, he must be taxed, however great the hardship may appear to the judicial mind to be. On the other hand, if the Crown, seeking to recover the tax, cannot bring the subject within the letter of the law, the subject is free, however apparently within the spirit of the law the case might otherwise appear to be. In other words, if there be admissible in any statute what is called an equitable construction, certainly such a construction is not admissible in a taxing statute, where you simply adhere to the words of the statute.

Lord President Clyde said in *Ayrshire Pullman Motor Services* v *IRC* (1929) 14 TC 754, '. . . No man in this country is under the smallest obligation, moral or other, so to arrange his legal relations to his business or to his property as to enable the Inland Revenue to put the largest possible shovel into his stores . . .'

These views may be reflective of the history of income tax. In the nineteenth century income tax was proportional (i.e., fixed rate) and at a relatively modest level affecting a relatively small percentage of the population (see Chapter 5). It was after the First World War that the UK first had high tax rates when there was no war. It was at this period that the issue of tax avoidance came to the fore with the higher rates in supertax and surtax. The increasing use of anti-avoidance provisions dates from this period to counter the government's loss of revenue. Also at this time a strict or literal approach was generally taken in the UK to the interpretation of tax statutes and to tax avoidance.

4.7.3 The *Duke of Westminster* case

IRC v *Duke of Westminster* [1936] AC 1 was probably the most important UK case before the 1980s on 'tax avoidance'. In this case the Duke of Westminster covenanted with various people who, for the most part, remained in his employ to pay them certain sums. The amounts paid under the covenants were in fact equal to the salary under their employment with the Duke of Westminster. A letter had been sent out to the employees explaining that whilst they still had the right to claim their salary it was hoped that they would make do with payment under the covenant. The reason for doing this was to reduce the Duke's surtax bill. The House of Lords held that the scheme was effective. The issue apparently turned on 'substance over form'.

The speeches in the House of Lords are not entirely clear. Lord Atkin said:

> . . . It was not, I think, denied at any rate it is incontrovertible that the deeds were brought into existence as a device by which the respondent might avoid some of the burden of surtax. I do not use the word device in

any sinister sense, for it has to be recognised that the subject, whether poor and humble or wealthy and noble, has the legal right so to dispose of his capital and income as to attract upon himself the least amount of tax. The only function of a Court of law is to determine the legal result of his dispositions so far as they affect tax . . .

Lord Tomlin said :

> . . . Apart, however, from the question of contract with which I have dealt, it is said that in revenue cases there is a doctrine that the Court may ignore the legal position, and regard what is called 'the substance of the matter', and that here the substance of the matter is that the annuitant was serving the Duke for something equal to his former salary or wages, and that therefore, while he is so serving, the annuity must be treated as salary or wages. This supposed doctrine (upon which the Commissioners apparently acted) seems to rest for its support upon a misunderstanding of language used in some earlier cases. The sooner this misunderstanding is dispelled, and the supposed doctrine given its quietus, the better it will be for all concerned, for the doctrine seems to involve substituting 'the incertain and crooked cord of discretion' for 'the golden and streight metwand of the law'. Every man is entitled if he can to order his affairs so as that the tax attaching under the appropriate Acts is less than it otherwise would be. If he succeeds in ordering them so as to secure this result, then, however unappreciative the Commissioners of Inland Revenue or his fellow taxpayers may be of his ingenuity, he cannot be compelled to pay an increased tax. This so called doctrine of 'the substance' seems to me to be nothing more than an attempt to make a man pay notwithstanding that he has so ordered his affairs that the amount of tax sought from him is not legally claimable. . . . There may, of course, be cases where documents are not *bona fide* nor intended to be acted upon, but are only used as a cloak to conceal a different transaction. No such case is made or even suggested here. The deeds of covenant are admittedly *bona fide* and have been given their proper legal operation. They cannot be ignored or treated as operating in some different way because as a result less duty is payable than would have been the case if some other arrangement (called for the purpose of the appellants' argument 'the substance') had been made . . .[5]

4.7.4 Post-*Westminster;* pre-*Ramsay*

The generally accepted view of the *Duke of Westminster's* case after the Lords decision was that each matter or step had to be considered in isolation and that other matters could not be considered. The assumed effect then of the *Duke of Westminster's* case was that the form took precedence over substance. It was assumed that the court could only look to individual steps and not the overall transaction. This is sometimes called a 'step by step' approach. On

---

[5.] Cf. *Helvering* v *Gregory* 69F (2d) 809 (2nd Cir. 1934), affd 293 US 465 (1935) decided at about the same time which introduced the step transaction doctrine into US tax law.

this basis very technical schemes were marketed in the 1970s. At that time the highest marginal rate on investment income was 98%. Further it was a period of high inflation and there was no indexation for capital gains tax purposes.

Companies such as Rossminster[6] acquired a degree of notoriety with the Revenue. The schemes they sold were technically correct in the main. However, they were very artificial and relied on a mechanical application of the rules.

The purpose of many of the avoidance schemes was to create an allowable 'loss' which could be set against a capital gain which had already accrued, rather than for any normal commercial purpose, assuming the avoidance of tax not to be a commercial purpose. These were often but not always circular schemes.

Schemes which were marketed were ones such as the following:

(a) Reverse annuities: An illustration of this kind of scheme is *IRC v Plummer* [1979] 3 All ER 775.

(b) Interest schemes: An illustration of this kind of scheme is *Cairns v MacDiarmid* [1983] STC 178.

(c) Offshore rollovers: *Furniss v Dawson* (see para. 4.7.7) is an illustration of this.

(d) Reverse *Nairn Williamson* schemes: The courts had decided a case (*Harrison v Nairn Williamson* [1978] STC 67) in favour of the Revenue holding that the base cost of a further subscription of shares was not what was paid for them but their value. In this case the market value was less than par and so the loss claim was restricted. However, the reverse was also true so that if shares were subscribed at par just before shares were sold at more than par the sale could appear to give rise to no capital gain as the base cost was increased by the market value of the new shares issued at par. Such an outcome was eventually reversed by statute (see what is now s. 17, TCGA).

(e) Complex corporate schemes: *Black Nominees v Nicol* [1975] STC 372 is an illustration of the kind of schemes which developed.

Templeman LJ (as he then was) described (in *Ramsay v IRC* [1979] STC 582 at p. 583 CA) the way in which some of these tax schemes had developed as being:

a circular game in which the taxpayer and four hired performers act out a play: nothing happens save that the Houdini taxpayer appears to escape from the manacles of tax. The game is recognisable by four rules. First, the play is devised and scripted prior to performing. Secondly, real money and real documents are circulated and exchanged. Thirdly, the money is returned by the end of the performance. Fourthly, the financial position of the actors is the same at the end as it was in the beginning save that the taxpayer in the course of the performance pays the hired actors for their success. The object of the performance is to create the illusion that something has happened, that Hamlet has been killed and Bottom did don

---

[6.] See Penrose, *The Tax Raiders*.

an ass's head so that tax advantages can be claimed as if something had happened. The audience are informed that the actors reserve the right to walk out in the middle of the performance but in fact they are creatures of the consultant who has sold and the taxpayer who bought the play; the actors are never in a position to show a profit and there is no chance they will ever go on strike. The critics are mistakenly informed that the play is based on a classic masterpiece called 'The Duke of Westminster' but in that piece the old retainer entered the theatre with his salary and left with a genuine entitlement to his salary and to an additional annuity.

4.7.5 Ramsay *et al*

It was against this background that the cases of *W T Ramsay Ltd* v *IRC* and *Eilbeck* v *Rawling* [1981] 1 All ER 865[7] came to be decided. In these cases two assets were to be created so that one asset's value could be decreased and the value of the other asset enhanced. The enhanced value asset would be sold and it was hoped to escape capital gains tax by falling within one of the exemptions. The diminished value asset would be disposed of and it was hoped to produce an allowable loss which could be set against a pre-existing gain. There was to be no change in overall value of the two assets in commercial terms. These were 'circular schemes' (see para. 4.2) and may be illustrated as follows.

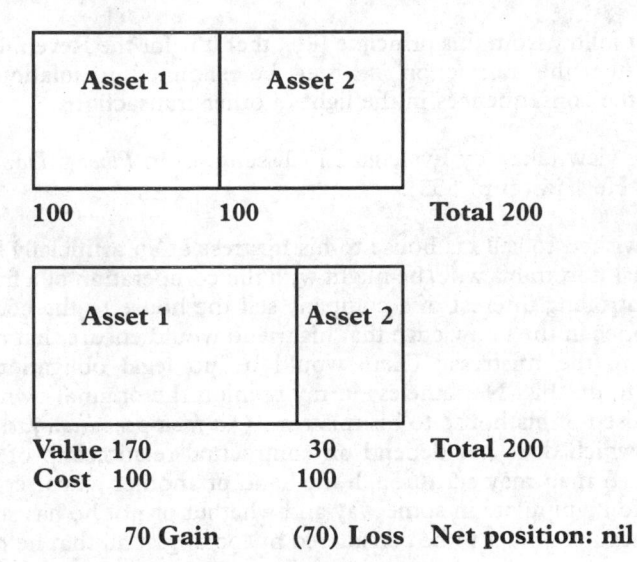

Asset 1	Asset 2	
100	100	Total 200

Asset 1	Asset 2	
Value 170	30	Total 200
Cost 100	100	
70 Gain	(70) Loss	Net position: nil

Change in overall value of assets: nil
Hoped for advantage (70) tax loss

Figure 4.3

[7.] Noted by Shipwright (1981) 125 SJ 227. The two appeals were heard together.

The taxpayer's scheme failed. Lord Wilberforce described the kind of thing that happened as follows:

> In each case two assets appear, like particles in a gas chamber with opposite charges, one of which is used to create the loss, the other of which gives rise to the equivalent gain which prevents the taxpayer from supporting any real loss . . . Like the particles, these assets have a very short life.

He added later that:

> capital gains tax was created to operate in the real world not that of make believe. Seemingly it was this judicial reality that the artificial schemes offended.

Lord Wilberforce's approach can be traced back to a number of earlier cases. For example in *Chinn* v *Collins* [1981] 1 All ER 189 the House of Lords took a fairly broad brush view and regarded the arrangement to buy back shares which had not been appropriated as being specifically enforceable in a jurisdiction where specific performance is not known.

Templeman J, as he then was, in *Black Nominees* v *Nichol* (1975) 50 TC 229 distinguished the *Westminster* case as not involving a 'disappearing trick' and said (at p. 281):

> It does not follow from this principle [i.e., that it is for the Revenue to show taxability] that the transaction . . . must be examined in isolation without regard to the consequences in the light of other transactions.

This was the view taken by Eveleigh LJ (dissenting) in *Floor* v *Davis* (1979) 52 TC 609. He said (at p. 633):

> If a man wished to sell his house to his mistress at an artificially low price and conceal it from his wife, he might with the co-operation of a friend who held a controlling interest of a company sell the house to the company at that low price in the knowledge that his friend would ensure that the house was sold to the mistress. There would be no legal obligation on the company to do this. Nonetheless in my opinion the original owner would have disposed of his house to his mistress. *Qui facit per alium facit per se* is a maxim which does not depend on contractual relationship of principal and agent. A man may act through the hand of another whose conduct he manages to manipulate in some way and whether or not he has so acted is often a question of fact to be considered by looking at all that he has done.

Ramsay, it is suggested, was not authority for the proposition that substance is to prevail over form. Lord Wilberforce had stated that the *Westminster* case was a cardinal principle. However, that does not require any steps in the scheme to be looked at individually. The wider approach allows the courts to determine the legal nature of the whole series of transactions.

Tax avoidance 83

This was the approach even in the *Duke of Westminster* case. Their lordships were not absolute in their opinion that each matter or step had to be considered in isolation and that other matters could not be considered. They did construe the contract. Lord Atkin's dissent was on the basis that there was a collateral contract.

Lord MacMillan said (at p. 526):

> Whereas previously Ullmann was entitled to 38 shillings per week as wages, he is now entitled to payment of this weekly sum whether he is employed by the respondent or not. That is the effect of the deed of covenant. The arrangement embodied in the two collateral documents does not alter that effect, whatever else it does . . . If the collateral documents had affected the absolute independent nature of the obligation under the deed of covenant different considerations might have arisen.

In other words one had to construe the documents to see what the real transaction was.

There is commercial law authority in *Prenn* v *Simmonds* [1971] 1 WLR 1381 that external evidence including previous documents is admissible to assert 'the genesis of the contract'.[8] This was also echoed by Lord Wilberforce in *IRC* v *Europa Oil (NZ) Limited* [1971] AC 760. He said (at p. 771):

> It is not legitimate . . . to disregard the separate corporate entities or the nature of the contracts made and to tax Europa on the substantial economic or business character of what was done.

Similarly in *Ransom* v *Higgs* (1979) 50 TC 1 it was said: 'It is legitimate to consider the scheme as a whole where there is evidence as there is here that each step is dependent on others being carried out.'

What was new in *Ramsay* was that by considering the whole of the arrangement an 'allowable loss' was created at no real cost (apart from the fees of the consultant) to set against an accrued and ascertained gain and the court was able to look at the whole series of transactions to disallow the claimed loss.

After *Ramsay* it was possible to argue that not all tax avoidance schemes are to be regarded as artificial and ineffective. However, their Lordships gave little guidance as to a test to discover what schemes were fiscally ineffective.

4.7.6 Burmah

IRC v *Burmah Oil Co. Ltd* [1981] STC 174 was the first opportunity for the House of Lords to consider *Ramsay* again. This was what was then known as a reverse *Nairn Williamson* scheme (see para. 4.7.4). It was a tailored or bespoke scheme to convert a loan into shares to obtain an allowable loss so as to maximise 'overspill relief' (which has since been repealed).

[8.] This is similar to Cardozo J in *Utica National City Bank* v *Gunn* (1980) 118 N.E. 607.

Lord Diplock in this case warned that:

It would be disingenuous to suggest, and dangerous on the part of those who advise on elaborate tax avoidance schemes to assume, that *Ramsay's* case did not mark a significant change in the approach adopted by this House in its judicial role to a preordained series of transactions (whether or not they include the achievement of a legitimate commercial end) into which there are inserted steps that have no commercial purpose apart from the avoidance of a liability to tax which in the absence of those particular steps would have been payable . . . The kinds of tax avoidance schemes that have occupied the attention of the courts in recent years, however, involve interconnected transactions between artificial persons, limited companies without minds of their own but directed by a single mastermind.

In the *Burmah Oil* case, Burmah Oil had, in 1969, sold some shares to a subsidiary for their then market value of £380 million, though the purchase price was left outstanding. In 1971, the subsidiary transferred these shares back to Burmah Oil for their then lower market value of £221 million. This left the subsidiary owing Burmah Oil some £159 million, which was an unallowable capital loss to Burmah Oil. Burmah Oil then entered into a series of transactions which were designed to convert this loss into an allowable loss. Burmah Oil lent £159 million to Manchester Oil Refinery Holdings Ltd (another of its subsidiaries). On the same day, Manchester Oil lent the same amount to the subsidiary, and the subsidiary used the loan to repay its debt to Burmah Oil. As a result, the subsidiary now owed £159 million to Manchester Oil, rather than to Burmah Oil. Six days later, the subsidiary made a rights issue, and Burmah Oil paid £159 million to the subsidiary to acquire shares under the issue. The subsidiary used the £159 million proceeds of the rights issue to repay Manchester Oil, and Manchester Oil then repaid the £159 million which it owed to Burmah Oil. The money had therefore gone round in a complete circle (actually, two complete circles), and ended up with Burmah Oil. However, the subsidiary no longer owed Burmah Oil. Instead, Burmah Oil had paid £159 million for shares in the subsidiary, and when the subsidiary went into liquidation shortly afterwards, the shares were worthless because it had no assets. Burmah Oil claimed that the £159 million loss on the shares was an allowable capital loss. There was no agreement that all the steps would be completed though of course the transactions all took place within the group. Real money was provided and passed between the parties.

The House of Lords accepted that if they were to adopt a step-by-step approach, the transaction would result in an allowable loss for Burmah Oil. However, as in *Ramsay*, they refused to do this. Burmah Oil had suffered no real loss so the question of it being allowable or not did not arise. That left Burmah Oil still holding an unallowable loss on the original share transactions. Lord Fraser, with whom Lords Scarman, Roskill and Brandon agreed, relied on what Eveleigh LJ had said in *Floor* v *Davis* (see para. 4.7.5) to reach this result. If the loan had originally been made by way of loan stock (a 'debt on a security' for capital gains tax purposes) then the House of Lords would

Tax avoidance

have accepted that there was a real loss. However, he did not consider that there was a 'real loss' here.

4.7.7 Furniss v Dawson

The House of Lords was able to consider the extent of the *Ramsay* doctrine further in *Furniss* v *Dawson* [1984] STC 153. The facts in this case were that the Dawson family owned shares in UK incorporated and resident companies (the 'Operating Companies'). Negotiations took place between the Dawsons and Wood Bastow Holdings Limited. It was agreed in principle that Wood Bastow would acquire the whole issued share capital of the Operating Companies. Negotiations were on the basis that there was to be no binding contract until solicitors had reviewed the matter and prepared all formal contracts. It was then decided to mitigate the impact of capital gains tax by deferring it using a technique well known at that time. This was to interpose a non-resident company over the operating company.

An Isle of Man company ('Green Jacket') was incorporated. Green Jacket issued shares to the Dawsons in return for their shares in the Operating Companies. The acquisition of the shares in the Operating Companies by Green Jacket was completed. Green Jacket then agreed to sell the shares in the Operating Companies to Wood Bastow. This was then completed. The transactions may be illustrated as follows.

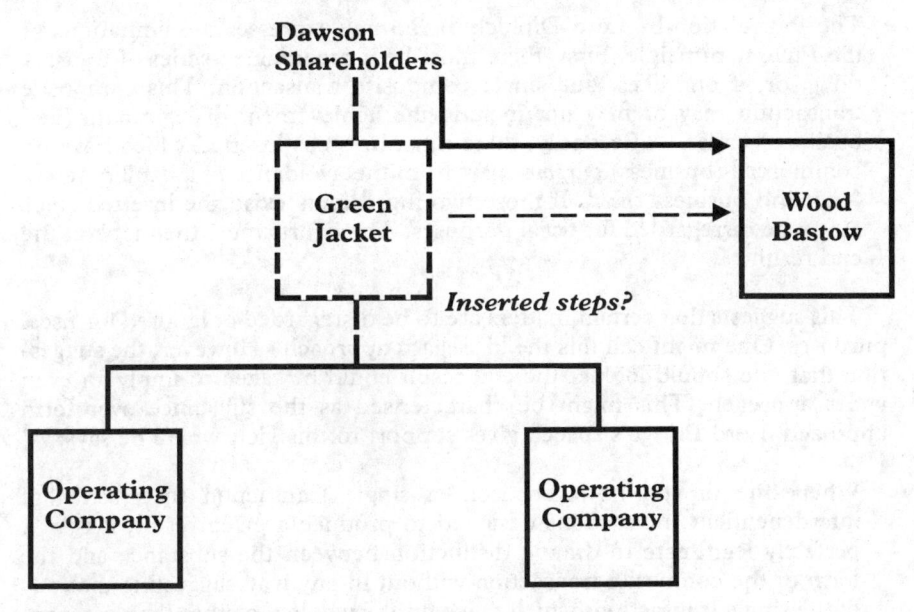

Figure 4.4

The Commissioners found the transactions were designed to achieve a particular fiscal result. They found nothing in the scheme or in the steps taken to implement it which could be designated a 'sham' in the sense that a transaction purporting to have a particular legal effect was in fact never intended to have that effect (see para. 4.5). They found that Green Jackets did acquire control of the Operating Companies and was not a mere nominee for the Dawsons.

The House of Lords decided that the scheme fell within the *Ramsay* approach and that the Dawsons had made the disposal and were therefore to be taxed.

Before their Lordships' speeches were delivered it had been hoped that the *Furniss* case would clarify *Burmah*. Unfortunately this did not happen. Lord Scarman did not seem to think that the Lords' function was even to attempt to do this. He said:

> Speeches in your Lordships' house and judgments in the appellate courts of the United Kingdom are concerned more to chart a way forward between principles accepted and not to be rejected than to attempt anything so ambitious as to determine finally the limit beyond which the safe channel of acceptable tax avoidance shelves into the dangerous shallows [of what he describes] as unacceptable tax evasion [sic].

The most important speech was given by Lord Brightman. The crux of his speech is to be found in the following passage:

> The formulation by Lord Diplock in *Burmah* expresses the limitations of the *Ramsay* principle. First, there must be a preordained series of transactions; or, if one likes, one single composite transaction. This composite transaction may or may not include the achievement of legitimate (i.e., business) ends ... Secondly, there must be steps inserted which have no commercial (business) *purpose* apart from the avoidance of a liability to tax – not 'no business *effect*'. If those two ingredients exist, the inserted steps are to be disregarded for fiscal purposes. The courts must then look at the end result.

This suggests that certain matters are to be disregarded or ignored for fiscal purposes. One might call this the 'disregard approach'. However, the suggestion that one should look at the end result could be taken to imply an even wider approach. This might be characterised as the substance over form approach. Lord Bridge's speech gives support to this view where he says:

> When one moves, however, from a single transaction to a series of interdependent transactions designed to produce a given result, it is ... perfectly legitimate to draw a distinction between the substance and the form of the composite transaction without in any way suggesting that any of the single transactions which make up the whole are other than genuine.

Whilst it may be possible to treat the end result approach of Lord Brightman as still falling within the disregard approach, the way in which Lord Brightman resolves the problems of the base cost of the Green Jacket's shares seems inconsistent with this and might suggest that he wishes to go more towards a remoulding or reanalysis or recharacterisation of the transactions. It would seem that he considers the transaction to have been a tripartite contract under which the consideration for the sale of the shares by A to B is paid to C. That consideration then in effect is used to pay up the shares in Green Jackets. If so this is more than a straight disregard.

The *Furniss* case raised a number of questions including the following:

(a) What is a composite transaction?
(b) When is it preordained?
(c) What is the end result and how is it to be determined?
(d) Who decides when the new approach applies?

The reader should consider to what extent the subsequent cases have clarified the answers to all or any of these questions.

4.8 SUBSEQUENT CASES

The case of *Furniss* v *Dawson* remained the leading authority in this area until the House of Lords decided the consolidated appeals of a group of three cases[9]. These were *Craven* v *White*, *IRC* v *Bowater Properties Developments Ltd* and *Baylis* v *Gregory* [1988] 3 All ER 495, HL. The speeches in these cases, whilst not unanimous, reviewed the previous cases in this area, and slightly redefined the principles to be applied.

In *Craven* v *White* itself, the facts were very similar to *Furniss* v *Dawson*, except that when the Isle of Man investment company was formed and acquired the shares from the vendors, the negotiations with the ultimate purchasers were not complete, and there was a possibility that the shares might be sold to a different purchaser (although in the event this did not happen). At first instance ([1985] 3 All ER 125), Peter Gibson J refused to apply the new approach because he could not find a preordained series of transactions, and his approach was supported by the Court of Appeal.

The approach taken in this case at first instance was followed by Warner J in *IRC* v *Bowater Property Developments Ltd* [1985] STC 783. Here the taxpayer company was negotiating to sell land, but before the intended sale the taxpayer actually sold the land to five associated companies with the object of taking advantage of the £50,000 exemption from development land tax which each would be able to claim. The intended purchaser withdrew from negotiations to purchase, but did later agree to buy the land on slightly different terms. The taxpayer was assessed to tax on the basis there was a single disposal. The appeal that there had been a disposal by the five

---

[9.] Earlier cases such as *Young* v *Phillips* [1984] STC 520 were decided on technical grounds but Nicholls J would have allowed the Crown's argument on *Ramsay* principles had it been necessary to do so. See also *Coates* v *Arndale Properties Ltd* [1984] STC 637 where the Lords found it unnecessary to consider the new approach as the scheme failed on technical grounds; *Reed* v *Nova Securities Ltd* [1985] STC 124 where the new approach was not applied to relief provided by Parliament; and *Magnavox* v *Hall* [1986] STC 561.

companies was allowed by the judge, and by the Court of Appeal ([1987] 3 All ER 27).

In *Baylis* v *Gregory*, the facts were again very similar to *Furniss* v *Dawson*, in that the shareholders of a family company were negotiating to sell it, and in anticipation arranged to exchange the shares in their company with shares in an Isle of Man company to defer capital gains tax. In fact, the original proposed purchaser withdrew from negotiations, but the shares were sold to another buyer some 18 months later. The shares were sold by the Isle of Man company, and the proceeds distributed as interest-free loans to the members of the family. Vinelott J held ([1986] 1 All ER 289) that the transactions were not linked so as to call for the application of the new approach, and this decision was upheld by the Court of Appeal ([1987] 3 All ER 27).

The judgments in all three cases were upheld by the House of Lords, who declined to apply the new approach in *Craven* v *White* by a majority of 3 to 2, and in the other cases unanimously. Their Lordships made it clear that the principle evolved in *Ramsay* v *IRC* and *Furniss* v *Dawson* is applicable where there is a preordained series of transactions entered into with no purpose other than to mitigate tax, but does not apply in cases where the whole scheme is not preordained.

The meaning of a 'preordained series of transactions' was discussed at some length in the speeches, but unsurprisingly without complete agreement, though there was a general consensus that the question was whether the transactions constituted a single and indivisible whole. The series would not be preordained if, at the time the first transaction was entered into, it was not clear that the whole series would be followed through. Therefore there was not a series of transactions in these cases (subject to some disagreement in the case of *Craven* v *White*) as in each of them, when the first step in the scheme was performed, it was not clear that the other steps would necessarily automatically follow. The decision in *Craven* v *White*, in that its effect was to uphold the strategic schemes devised by the taxpayers, has been generally seen as a slight watering down of the new approach.

While there was some suggestion that *Furniss* v *Dawson* was being limited to its own facts, it is clear that the judges did not intend the new approach to be undermined, but rather that they were seeking to clarify the principles in *Ramsay* v *IRC* and in *Furniss v Dawson*. As Lord Templeman said:

> Adapting the words of Lord Diplock in *Burmah*, it remains disingenuous to suggest, and dangerous on the part of those who advise taxpayers to assume, that *Ramsay* and *Dawson* did not mark a significant change in the approach adopted by this House in its judicial role to artificial tax avoidance schemes (whether or not they include the achievement of a legitimate commercial end) which include steps that have no commercial purpose apart from the avoidance of a liability to tax which in the absence of those particular steps would have been payable.

The question of when there is a preordained series of transactions greatly exercised the minds of their Lordships in *Craven* v *White*. They considered

Tax avoidance

many factors, such as the legal obligations, the time intervals involved, and any temporary interruptions.

Lord Keith considered that:

> In all these cases it is clear that the owner of the shares has so arranged matters that if and when a sale of the shares does take place it will not be a direct disposal of the shares by him, but a disposal by an intermediary company which he controls. But I do not think that the transaction embodied in the final disposal can be said to be preordained, a matter to be ascertained as at the time of the share exchange, when at that time it is wholly uncertain whether that disposal will take place, or a fortiori when neither the identity of the purchaser nor the price to be paid nor any of the other terms of the contract are known. In my opinion the transactions in the series can properly be regarded as preordained if, but only if, at the time when the first of them is entered into the taxpayer is in a position for all practical purposes to secure that the second also is entered into.

Lord Oliver expresses clearly the wider approach to what should be regarded as a preordained series of transactions. He said:

> The wider view interprets preordained simply as 'preconceived' or 'planned to take place in the future' so that all events which occur sequentially, which contain a tax-saving element and which result from the same initial conscious volition or contemplation on the part of the taxpayer form part of a scheme, are therefore preordained and accordingly fall to be construed as part of, and indivisible from, the ultimate disposition whether or not, at the time of the transaction in question, the ultimate disposition was certain, uncertain, anticipated or merely hoped for, provided that there was some particular disposition in view.

But he dismissed this wider view to suggest a broadly similar view to Lord Keith saying:

> In each case, one or more of the salient features in the *Dawson* transaction is missing. In particular the transactions which, in each appeal, the Revenue seeks now to reconstruct into a single direct disposal from the taxpayer to an ultimate purchaser were not contemporaneous. Nor were they preordained or composite in the sense that it could be predicated with any certainty at the date of the intermediate transfer what the ultimate destination of the property would be, what would be the terms of any ultimate transfer, or even whether an ultimate transfer would take place at all.

In laying down rules for what will be considered a series of transactions, Lord Templeman was even more specific (with a list effectively endorsed by Lord Oliver). He said:

In the case of a *Dawson* scheme where the tax-avoidance transaction precedes the taxable transaction four essential conditions must be satisfied. First, the taxpayer must decide to carry out, if he can, a scheme to avoid an assessment of tax on an intended taxable transaction by combining it with a prior tax-avoidance transaction. Second, the tax-avoidance transaction must have no business purpose apart from the avoidance of tax on the intended taxable transaction. Third, after the tax-avoidance transaction has taken place, the taxpayer must retain power to carry out his part of the intended taxable transaction. Fourth, the intended taxable transaction must in fact take place.

Lord Jauncey also provided a list of factors to take into account when deciding whether transations were preordained which is rather more general: These include (1) the extent to which at the time of the tax step negotiations or arrangements have proceeded towards the carrying through as a continuous process of the remaining transactions, (2) the nature of such negotiations or arrangements, (3) the likelihood, at the time of the tax step, of such remaining transactions being carried through, and (4) the extent to which, after the tax step, negotiations or arrangements have proceeded to completion without genuine interruptions.

While the indications given by all their Lordships are very helpful and will undoubtedly form the basis of argument in cases to come, there will still be some difficulties in deciding what is a preordained transaction on a particular set of facts, and one must have sympathy with the point raised by Lord Goff that there is some difficulty in distinguishing the case where A plans a scheme to sell to B and carries it through, and where A plans to sell to B but in fact sells to C using the same scheme. The position now seems to be that the first scheme would fail but the second would succeed. If one is to take into account the speed at which transactions have proceeded and the extent to which there have been interruptions, there is also the problem that one may not be able to know in advance whether a scheme will succeed, one can only decide when it is over. Putting too much stress on the importance of speed and the lack of interruptions also leaves open the possibility that a tax-avoidance scheme might succeed purely because it was held up by commercial difficulties, or simply because of the inefficiency of those involved.

Craven v *White* has been said to show a difference of judicial approach. However, this may not be as great as is sometimes thought. As M.J. Gammie has said the Inland Revenue's initial formulation of the *Ramsay* principle was:

> In applying a taxing statute to a transaction which is effected with the sole intention of avoiding tax on some other transaction then in their view the former is to be treated as having no independent fiscal effect but as a single indivisible transaction with the latter, if and when the latter takes place.

That formulation was unanimously rejected by the House of Lords. The Law Lords, however, divided into the majority who favoured a narrow approach to preordination and the minority who preferred a broader formulation. The difference between the two approaches is, however, not as great as might appear at first blush; even the minority were unable to accept the Inland Revenue's initial formulation and rejected the appeals. Both the majority and the minority were also agreed that the nature and extent of preordination in relation to any particular transactions are questions of fact for the Commissioners. On that basis, the difference between the broad and the narrow approach to preordination is to some extent a difference of view as to the weight that should be accorded to the evidence of what actually took place and, for example, of the time that elapses between the transactions. Both Lord Templeman ([1986] STC 476 at p. 490) in respect of the broad approach and Lord Oliver (at p. 507) in respect of the narrow approach identified four essential elements to their view of the new approach exemplified by *Dawson*.

These were (it seems) that:

(a) there must be a preordained series of transactions to avoid tax on an intended taxable transaction including an 'intermediate step';
(b) there must be no business purpose apart from tax avoidance for the intermediate step;
(c) there was no practical likelihood that the events would not take place;
(d) those events did in fact take place.

The disagreement seems to be on what was the preordained series of transactions.

From the later case of *Shepherd* v *Lyntress Ltd* [1989] STC 617 it appears that there is not a pre-ordained series of transactions where, when the first step in the scheme is performed, it is not clear that the other steps will necessarily automatically follow, for example because the purchaser is not identified. In *Shepherd* v *Lyntress* a large company held shares on which a substantial gain had accumulated. This company purchased Lyntress Ltd, which had £4,000,000 in tax losses, making it part of the purchaser's group. The shares with the accrued gains were then transferred to Lyntress Ltd, which sold them and set its losses against the gains. Vinelott J held that these steps did not amount to a single composite transaction. There was a sale on the market when the purchaser was not identifed.

The *Furniss* principle was also in issue in *Ensign Tankers* v *Stokes* [1992] STC 226. Ensign Tankers (Leasing) Limited ('Ensign'), a UK incorporated and resident company, was a member of the Thomas Tilling group of companies. It had been involved unsuccessfully in ship chartering and had then moved into leasing plant and machinery. The Inland Revenue published on 10 August 1979 SP9/79 in which the Revenue said 'capital allowance claims for film production will be accepted, provided the master print can properly be regarded as a capital asset in the business. In practice, a master print would be regarded as meeting this condition if it is retained by the production company and has an anticipated potential life of not less than two years.'

Ensign entered into 'equity deals' to finance the production and exploitation of two films[10] through the medium of a limited partnership with other companies. The partnership was called 'Victory Partnership'. A limited partnership was used so that, very broadly, limited partners such as Ensign would not be liable for any partnership debts over and above its capital contribution to the partnership. The Commissioners found that 'Ensign's motive for investing in those two films is to be found in its belief that by doing so it would obtain a fiscal advantage which would benefit the Tilling group as a whole.[11] This would be by obtaining capital allowances and surrendering any surplus capital allowances by way of group relief to other UK resident members of the Tilling group.[12] Put very simply, under the arrangements the limited partners contributed $3.25m of their own money towards the cost of the films. The remaining funds necessary to make the films (some $10.75m) were lent to Victory Partnership by Lorimar Productions Company ('LPI'), the film production company, and re-credited to LPI by Victory Partnership as payments made by Victory Partnership to LPI to finance the production of the films. Victory Partnership then claimed capital allowances on the basis that it had expended $14m on the making of the films.

The two films in question were 'Escape to Victory' and 'Outland'. Neither of these films was a financial success and both ran over budget. Neither film seems to have had an independent completion guarantor.[13]

Perhaps not surprisingly, the Revenue refused Victory Partnership's claim and succeeded before the Commissioners on the grounds that Victory Partnership was not carrying on a trade. On appeal, Millet J held that Victory Partnership had incurred capital expenditure of $14m and its activities did

---

[10] Under which the investors sought to claim first year capital allowances as owners of plant or machinery (i.e., the master print or negative) used in the trade in the same way that a widget manufacturer might claim a capital allowance in respect of the capital expenditure on a widget making machine. See, e.g., *Reed v Young* [1986] STC 285 which the Revenue lost in the House of Lords on the issue whether a limited partner could only claim losses up to the amount of his capital contribution to the limited partnership. This amount was generally small because of the capital duty that had (at that time) to be paid on such capital and to counteract the disincentive of effective subordination to other creditors. If the bulk of the capital went in by way of loan then that would rank with other creditors rather than behind them. The House of Lords decision that there was no such limitation on loss claims was reversed by s. 48 and Sch. 12, FA 1985, see now ss. 117 and 118, Income and Corporation Taxes Act 1988. This together with the loss of 100% first year allowances made the equity finance route unattractive.

[11] See [1989] STC 750. The effect of *Aveling Barford v Perion* [1989] BCLC 626 on this is an interesting question to contemplate in this context. Strictly Ensign invested in the partnership not the films.

[12] Group relief provisions at the time were to be found in ss. 258–64, Income and Corporation Taxes Act 1970 now ss. 402–413, TA. Group relief in effect allows losses to be consolidated for tax purposes rather than looking solely to the individual company thus supposedly providing a degree of neutrality between operating as a group or through divisions.

[13] In very broad terms a person who guarantees that there will be suffient funds to complete the film in the event of a budget overrun. According to the case stated there were at the time 'two well-known commercial firms specialising in the business of granting such completion guarantees' [1989] STC 739. Neither of these were involved. The partnership's position was secured through by the financial arrangements with the makers LPI and Ladd which in fact met the cost overruns. 'This was an important (and indeed essential) safeguard to Victory Partnership which effectively insulated it from the risk of budgetary overruns' [1989] STC at 759.

amount to the trade of making and exploiting films. The Court of Appeal reversed Millet J's decision. On appeal to the House of Lords, the Lords found, as regards part of the expenditure, that Victory Partnership was trading and entitled to allowances, but as regards the rest apparently it was not.

The leading speech was given by Lord Templeman (with whom the other Lords agreed). He considered, if the taxpayer's argument (that the taxpayer may enter into a transaction in any form he chooses and that the court is not entitled to contradict or ignore the form of that transaction and cannot have regard to the rights and obligations which flow from the transaction because the court cannot consider the substance of the transaction) were right, then 'although Victory Partnership incurred no expenditure in excess of $3.25m it achieved the apparently magic result of creating a further tax expenditure of $10.75m that was not a real expenditure.'

Lord Templeman's approach to the case is shown by his opening words '... this is a tax avoidance scheme ...'. This was admitted by the parties but it is respectfully submitted that it is irrelevant to the partnership's position and the purpose of its expenditure. Lord Templeman's view was based on his 'proper construction' of the transactions that the limited partners were not liable beyond their capital contributions. This is not necessarily correct, as the discussion of clause 10 in the lower tribunals shows. It seems at least arguable that the limited partners could be liable for up to $13 million. Nevertheless, Lord Templeman considered the legal effect of the documents was to create a trading transaction whereby Victory Partnership expended $3.25 million towards the production of a film in which Victory Partnership had a 25% interest. He does not mention what the nature of the other expenditure was nor by whom it was incurred. His Lordship also quoted from Millett J at first instance but seems to misunderstand Millett J's dictum. He agreed with Millett J as to the financial effect of the transaction but said that 'unfortunately, the judge continued' that 'in legal terms LPI, was not an equity participant, for it was making its contribution by way of loan'. He considered that such an 'analysis ignores the fact that by reason of the non-recourse provision of the loan agreement, the loan was not repayable by Victory Partnership or anyone else'. In the authors' view the fact that the legal position and the economic effect differ does not necessarily mean something underhand is going on. Indeed statute sometimes seeks to achieve this (e.g., Part XV, TA). It is submitted that if this issue was so important then an analysis of the loan agreement and clause 10b of the partnership agreement was required.

In addition, if Lord Templeman was correct in deciding that there was a joint venture with LPI and no element of loan, then is LPI entitled to losses in the UK through its permanent establishment which it could use to shelter UK profits? Or is there a collective investment scheme for FSA purposes which is an unapproved unit trust for UK tax purposes? His Lordship does not seem to have considered these issues (see Chapter III, Part XII, TA).

Returning to the principal point, Lord Templeman held that there was 'a tax avoidance scheme, a single composite transaction whereunder the tax advantage claimed by the taxpayer is inconsistent with the true effect in law of the transaction.' However, as $3.25 million had been contributed by the limited partners they were entitled to allowances in respect of that but not the 'avoidance money' as the arrangements were 'leveraged' (i.e., allowances of more than it contributed were sought by Ensign). It is this to which his Lordship seemed to have objected notwithstanding that the Lords had decided in *Reed* v *Young* [1986] STC 285 (since reversed by statute) that limited partners could have tax losses in excess of their capital contributions. If there were a single composite transaction would not this also have denied allowances on the $3.25 million as the lower tribunals found on the basis that there was no trade? On this point Lord Templeman said (at p. 241):

> Victory Partnership expended capital of $3.25m for the purpose of producing and exploiting a commercial film. The production and exploitation of a film is a trading activity. The expenditure of capital for the purpose of producing and exploiting a commercial film is a trading purpose. [Under the then Capital Allowances legislation] capital expenditure for a trading purpose generates a first year allowance. The [legislation] is not concerned with the purpose of the transaction but with the purpose of the expenditure. It is true that Victory Partnership only engaged in the film trade for the fiscal purpose of obtaining a first year allowance but that does not alter the purpose of the expenditure. The principles of *Ramsay* and subsequent authorities do not apply to the expenditure of $3.25m because that was real and not magical expenditure by Victory Partnership.

Lord Templeman considered the emerging *Ramsay* principle applied to the case, citing his speeches in a number of earlier cases, notwithstanding the Commissioners' findings and the decision of Millett J (who had been counsel for the Crown in *Furniss*) that the principle did not apply here. His Lordship raised again his distinction between 'tax avoidance' (a 'bad thing') and 'tax mitigation' (not always a 'bad thing') which he launched in *Challenge Corporation* [1986] STC 476. This has been criticised on the basis that it is effective planning if Lord Templeman says it is, but not, if he does not. That this is an easy principle to grasp can be illustrated by his Lordship's example of 'bed and breakfasting' which, as far as the taxpayer is concerned, is effective tax mitigation because the taxpayer has actually suffered that loss, notwithstanding that he owns effectively the same shares and has undertaken a composite transaction purely for a tax benefit. According to his Lordship this is not a 'magic loss' in contrast to the $10.75m expenditure in *Ensign*.

4.9   COUNTESS FITZWILLIAM v IRC [1993] STC 502

This case was unusual in that it involved a capital transfer tax ('CTT') 'deathbed' type of scheme and some vituperative remarks. The facts were complicated. Broadly, steps were devised to avoid tax at 75% on a residuary estate of about £11 million if the 81-year-old widow were to die. The approach was to take advantage of provisions which allowed consideration received for the termination of an interest under a settlement in some circumstances to be deducted from the amount liable to CTT.

The steps were as follows.

1. Part of the residuary estate was appointed under powers to do so under the will trusts to the widow, Lady Fitzwilliam.
2. A cheque for £2 million was given to her daughter, Lady Hastings, by the widow.
3. A further part of the residuary estate was appointed to the widow to pay the income to the widow to the earlier of her death or 15 February 1980 and part inter alia to Lady Hastings contingent on her being alive at the time of the widow's income interest ceasing.
4. The contingent interest was assigned to Lady Hastings by the widow for £2 million.
5. £1,000 was settled on trust to pay the income to the widow till the earlier of her death or 15 March 1980 and subject to this for Lady Hastings absolutely.
6. Lady Hastings assigned to her trustees her reversionary interest.

This may be illustrated as follows in figure 4.5.

The Revenue issued a determination that CTT should be paid as if there were a single composite transaction having the same effect as if there had been appointments to Lady Hastings and the widow respectively absolutely, notwithstanding the contingencies etc.

The Special Commissioners found that the steps satisfied the *Ramsay* principle. Vinelott J allowed the taxpayer's appeal which was upheld by the Court of Appeal. The Crown's appeal was dismissed by the Lords (Lord Templeman dissenting).

Lord Keith (with whom Lords Ackner and Mustill agreed) after quoting from Lord Brightman (at p. 166) in *Furniss* v *Dawson* [1984] STC 153 (see para. 4.7.7) said that it:

> demonstrates the intellectual basis on which the House was able to reach the conclusion that the fiscal consequences which would ordinarily have resulted . . . were not attracted. All the parties involved had informally agreed on what was to happen but were not formally bound to bring that about. The *Ramsay* principle made it possible to hold that the final result for fiscal purposes was the same as if the parties had been so formally bound.

He also considered that in *Craven* v *White* the House of Lords decisively rejected the argument for the Crown that any transaction entered into for the purpose of avoiding tax on some later transaction was on that ground alone to be disregarded for fiscal purposes. He said (at p. 513):

Figure 4.5

Trust — Power of appointment for 23 months

Lady Fitzwilliam 81 affected by death of H and sister

1 → £4m appointed on trust as to capital and income for Lady F absolutely

3 → £3.8 of residue on trust to pay income to Lady F till earlier of 15.2.1980 or death subject thereto one moiety for Lady H absolutely and the other moiety contingent on her being alive at the end of Lady F's income interest and subject thereto on trust for the son absolutely

2 Lady H daughter ← Lady F
post dated cheque for £2m

latter outright gift intended to be net of CTT

4 31.1.1980 Lady F assigned interest in contingent moiety to Lady H for £2m then paid

Lady H assigned her interest in the vested moiety

5 5.2.1980 £1,000 settled on trust to pay the income to Lady H till earlier of 15.3.1980 or death subject thereto to Lady H absolutely

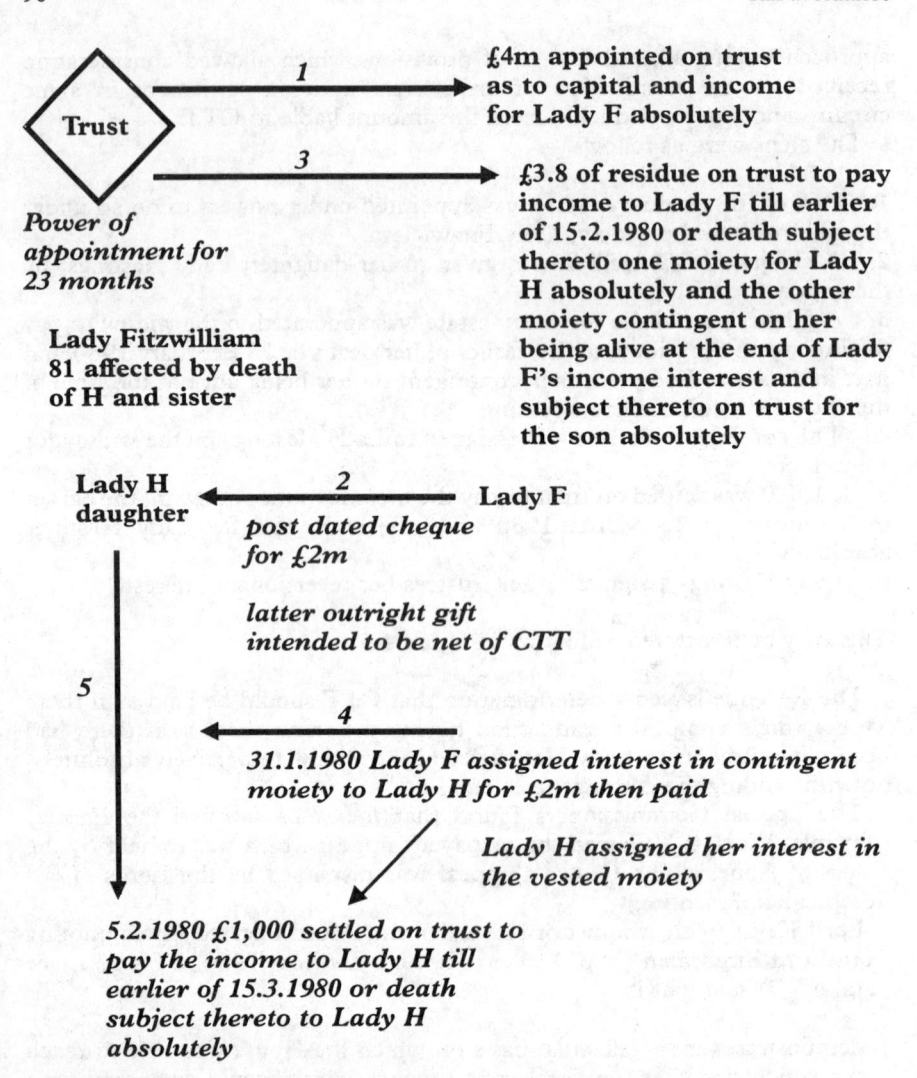

Figure 4.5

... the correct approach to a consideration of the ... steps ... which the Crown says were ineffective ... is to ask whether realistically they constituted a single and indivisible whole in which one or more of them was simply an element without independent effect and whether it is intellectually possible so to treat them.

He considered (at p. 514) that the Crown's postulation of a single composite transaction

Tax avoidance

... cannot be regarded as a realistic or intellectually possible view of the matter. It does not depend on disregarding for fiscal purposes any one or more of the transactions involved in steps 2–5 as having been introduced for fiscal purposes only and as having no independent effect for those purposes, nor on treating the whole series of steps as having no such effect. Each of the steps 2, 3, 4 and 5 had the fiscal effect of giving rise to a charge to income tax on Lady Hastings or on Lady Fitzwilliam for a period of time, and there was a potential charge to capital transfer tax if either had died while in enjoyment of the income.

He considered (at p. 515) that:

No case applying the *Ramsay* principle has yet held it legitimate to alter the character of a particular transaction in a series or to pick bits out of it and reject other bits. In *Furniss* v *Dawson* the transfer to the intermediary company Greenjacket was disregarded for fiscal purposes because of the pre-existing informal agreement and of the manner in which the two transactions were carried out, which made it intellectually possible to hold that Greenjacket never had control of the operating companies within the meaning of the statute. No comparable exercise is possible here.

Lord Keith also considered the meaning of 'preordained'. He considered the concept started off in self-cancelling transactions but was picked up by Lord Brightman in *Furniss* and applied to non-self-cancelling transactions.

... By treating 'preordained' as equivalent to 'precontracted' he was able to reach the conclusion that the true effect of the two transactions was that of a single tripartite contract, so that the intermediate company never obtained control of the family companies within the meaning of the relevant legislation. In the present case I would accept that steps 2, 3, 4 and 5 were preordained in the sense that they all formed part of a preplanned tax avoidance scheme, and that there was no reasonable possibility that they would not all be carried out, notwithstanding the pause while Lady Hastings as an individual took independent legal advice. But the fact of preordainment in this sense is not sufficient in itself, in my opinion, to negative the application of an exemption from liability to tax which the series is intended to create, unless the series is capable of being construed in a manner inconsistent with the application of the exemption. The series in *Furniss* v *Dawson* was capable of being so construed, for the reasons explained by Lord Brightman [i.e., that their true effect was that of a tripartite contract]. In my opinion the series in the present case cannot be... There is no question of running any two or more transactions together, as in *Furniss* v *Dawson*, or of disregarding any one or more of them. I am unable to perceive any rational basis on which steps 2, 3 and 4 can be treated as effective for the purpose of creating a charge to tax under paragraph 4(2) of Schedule 5 to the 1975 Act but ineffective for the purpose of attracting the exemption in paragraph 4(4) and that in paragraph 4(5).

Lord Templeman dissented vigorously. He considered that use was made of
'. . . two separate devices. The first consists of self-cancelling payments
[*Ramsay*] . . . The second device consists of carrying out one transaction by
means of two transactions . . .'

He said of the majority view '... I have read a draft of the speech of . . . Lord
Keith. I am unable to follow his reasoning or to agree with his conclusions.'
'The material points on which I differ from Lord Keith are six in number.'
He then set them out at p. 532. No attempt is made here to summarise these
material points for fear of misrepresenting them. However, Lord Templeman
comes close to saying there was a sham despite the findings of fact to the
contrary.

His Lordship considered (at p. 534) that:

> All decisions of this House are founded on justice, principle and precedent.
> If an individual taxpayer employs a device to avoid tax the result is unjust
> because the Revenue are deprived of money intended by Parliament to be
> available for the common good.

It is suggested that this is the crux of Lord Templeman's approach.

Lord Browne-Wilkinson, whilst agreeing with Lord Keith that the appeal
should be dismissed, considered that one had to identify the real transaction.
He continued (at p. 535):

> The provision of the taxing statute is to be construed as applying to the actual
> transaction the parties were effecting in the real world, not to artificial forms
> in which the parties chose to clothe it in the surrealist world of tax advisers.

In his view:

> . . . the whole scheme was not preordained until after step 1 was taken.
> Therefore one of the essential *Ramsay* requirements was not satisfied. The
> Crown did not appeal that decision. Instead the Crown have sought to
> extract tax on the basis of a 'mini-*Ramsay*'.

The case shows how reasonable people can come to different conclusions
in this area. It is suggested though that *Countess Fitzwilliam* v *IRC* is not much
more than an application of *Craven* v *White*.

4.10 *WHITTLES* v *UNIHOLDINGS LTD* [1996] STC 914

This is a complicated case involving swaps. Essentially the taxpayer was
trying to argue that the taxpayer could apply *Ramsay* as well as the Revenue.
The Court of Appeal held that although the principle was capable of being
invoked by the taxpayer, it did not apply in the particular case as the two
transactions were not sufficiently linked. The transactions may be represented
as follows in figures 4.6 and 4.7.

Tax avoidance

```
      ┌────────┐
      │  Bank  │
      │        │
      └────────┘
         │  ╲
         │    ╲  Loan
         │      ╲ US$ 25.6m
         │        ╲ accepted
         │          ╲ 4.5.1982
         │            ╲
         │             ↘
         │          ┌──────────┐
         │          │   Uni-   │
         └──────────│ holdings │
                    │   Ltd    │
                    └──────────┘
   Forward Purchase
   of US$25.6m at           Investment
   £13.9m instructed        £14m in TIH
   14.5.1982
```

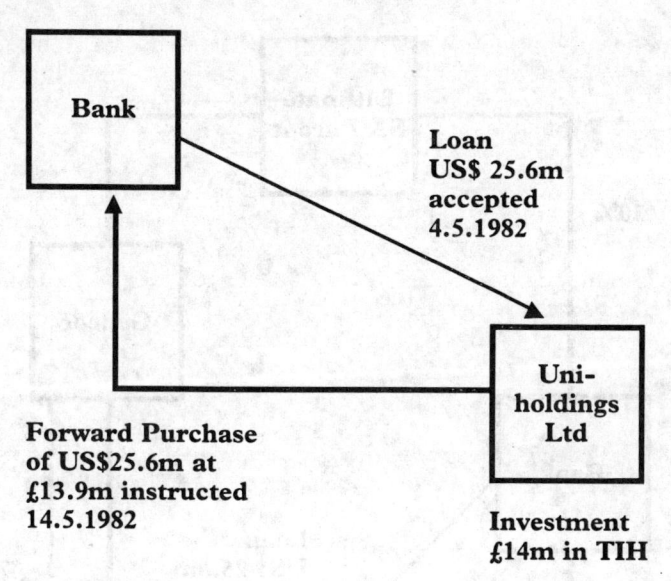

Figure 4.6

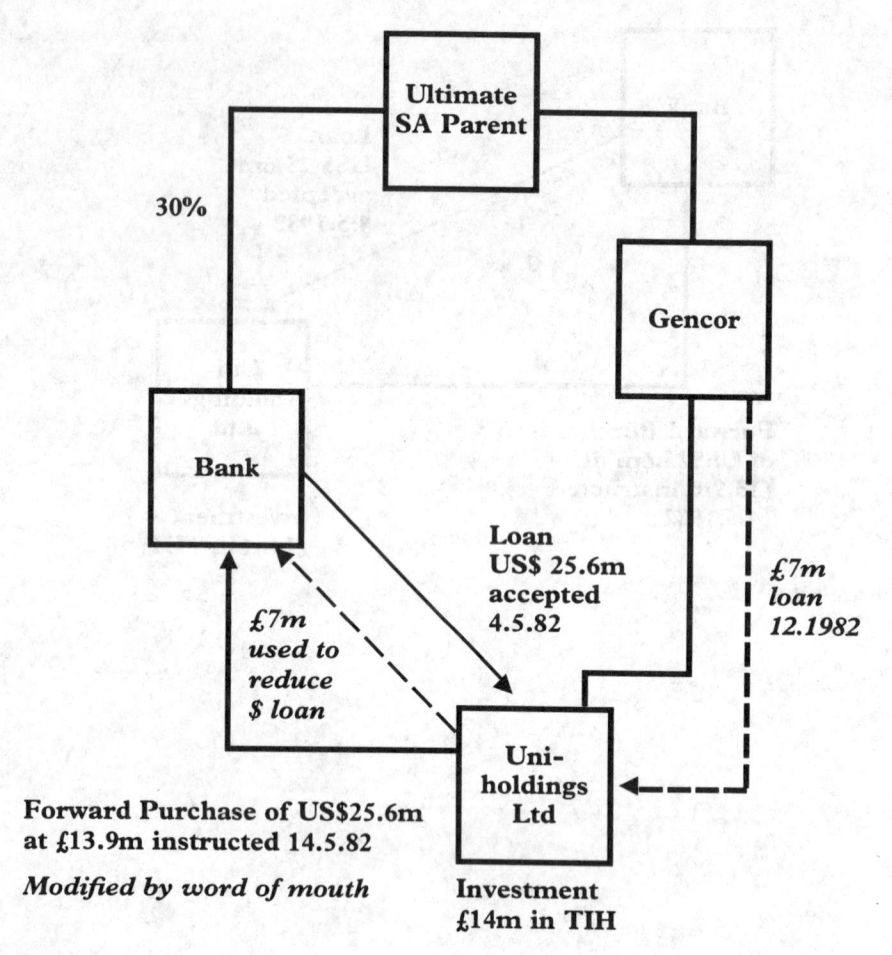

[Figure 4.7: Diagram showing Ultimate SA Parent with 30% link to Bank, and link to Gencor. Gencor gives £7m loan 12.1982 to Uni-holdings Ltd. Bank makes Loan US$ 25.6m accepted 4.5.82 to Uni-holdings Ltd. £7m used to reduce $ loan from Uni-holdings Ltd to Bank. Forward Purchase of US$25.6m at £13.9m instructed 14.5.82. Modified by word of mouth. Uni-holdings Ltd: Investment £14m in TIH.]

Figure 4.7

The following dictum of Nourse LJ (at p. 924) is probably the most important matter to come out of this case:

> Decisions subsequent to *Ramsay* itself, especially *Craven v White* have shown that the principle is still in the process of development. Differences of opinion amongst their Lordships in *IRC v Fitzwilliam* have shown that it is still uncertain where it has got to and to where it might go next.

4.11 IRC v McGUCKIAN [1994] STC 888

This is an important case from Northern Ireland which considers the relationship between *Ramsay* and specific legislative anti-avoidance provisions (a point left open in *Fitzwilliam* by Lord Browne-Wilkinson). The Court of

Tax avoidance 101

Appeal considered it inappropriate to invoke *Ramsay* to disregard a valid assignment and reconstitute a capital payment into an income payment so as to apply s. 739, TA. The facts may be represented diagrammatically as follows.

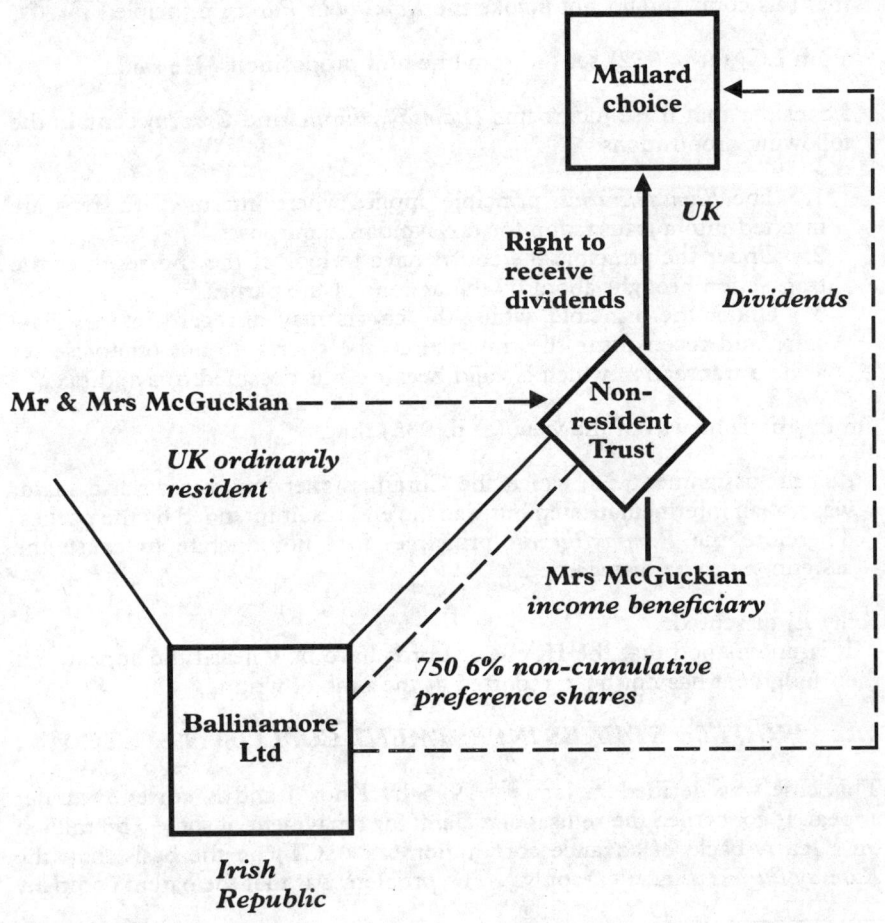

Figure 4.8

Carswell LJ said (at p. 917) that the Crown relied strongly on the argument:

> that the transaction should be reconstructed for fiscal purposes in such a way that the assignment of the right to receive the dividends is disregarded and the trustees are treated as if they themselves received the dividends . . .

He considered this inappropriate as (at p. 922):

the substance of the transaction was ... what it purported to be, the sale of trustees' rights to dividends for a capital sum. It was not in my opinion a case where that was wrapped up in some other transaction or where there was any pretence. Nor do I find it easy to regard that sale as an inserted step, like that in *Furniss*. I accordingly conclude, not entirely without hesitation, that this court should not invoke the *Ramsay* or *Furniss* principle ...

Hutton LCJ (at p. 932) set out some helpful propositions. He said:

> I consider that these judgments [*Ramsay, Furniss* and *Craven*] contain the following propositions:
>
> 1. The *Ramsay/Furniss* principle applies where intermediate steps are inserted into a transaction for tax avoidance purposes.[14]
> 2. Under the principle the courts have to look at the end result of the transaction brought about by the actions of the parties.[15]
> 3. Under the principle, whilst the courts may disregard intermediate steps and reconstitute the transaction, the courts do not otherwise set aside a transaction which is valid because it is designed to avoid tax.[16]

On this basis he was of the view (at p. 935) that:

> ... the assignment ... which the Commissioner found was not a sham, was not an intermediate step but was the end result intended by the parties. Therefore the *Ramsay/Furniss* principle does not operate to cause the assignment to be disregarded.

Kelly LJ dissented.

It is understood that the House of Lords have now heard the appeal, but their judgment has not been reported at the time of writing.

4.12 *PIGOTT* v *STAINES INVESTMENT CO. LTD* [1995] STC 114

This case was decided in January 1995 by Knox J and is currently under appeal. It concerned the refusal of a claim for repayment of some £58 million on a 'carry-back' of advance corporation tax (ACT) on the basis that 'the *Ramsay/Furniss* principles' apply.[17] The problem was that the parent company

---

[14.] Relying for this on *Furniss* v *Dawson* [1984] STC 153 (Lord Brightman at p. 166), *Craven* v *White* [1988] STC 476 (Lord Oliver at p. 503, Lord Goff at p. 512), *Countess Fitzwilliam* v *IRC* [1993] STC 502 (Lord Browne-Wilkinson at p. 535).
[15.] Relying on the passages cited for the first proposition and *Craven* v *White* [1988] STC 476 (Lord Oliver at p. 503) '*Ramsay* as developed in *Dawson*, merely established that the fiscal consequences of a preordained series of transactions carried to their preordained conclusion are generally to be determined by looking at the preordained result of the series.'
[16.] Relying for this on *Ramsay* v *IRC* [1981] STC 174 (Lord Wilberforce at p. 179) and *Craven* v *White* [1988] STC 476 (Lord Keith at p. 480, Lord Oliver at p. 498).
[17.] The law has changed since then. No repayment claim would now be possible because of s. 245(3A), TA inserted by FA 1993 and the introduction of the foreign income dividends (FIDS) by FA 1994.

Tax avoidance 103

of the BAT group, BAT Industries plc, effectively had too much overseas income with tax credits for it to be able to use all its ACT on its qualifying dividends against mainstream corporation tax ('MCT') (see Chapter 27).

The steps taken were as follows.

Step 1 On 14 February 1991 BAT purchased the whole issued capital of a company called Staines from Tesco. There was deferred consideration dependent essentially on the amount of corporation tax recovered. Staines was a company which had paid corporation tax in the past which would, under the then law, be available for a repayment claim under s. 239, TA.

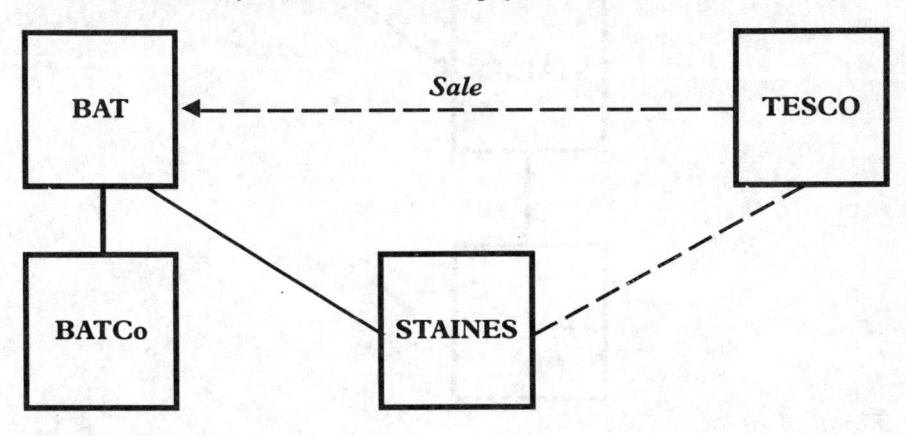

Figure 4.9

Step 2 On 15 February 1991 BAT transferred all the shares in BATCo (a member of its group) to Staines for an issue of shares in Staines. There was no dispute that the insertion of this layer was to pave the way for a future repayment claim from carried back surplus ACT (see [1995] STC 114 at p. 132). Staines was then in a position to receive a dividend from BATCo.

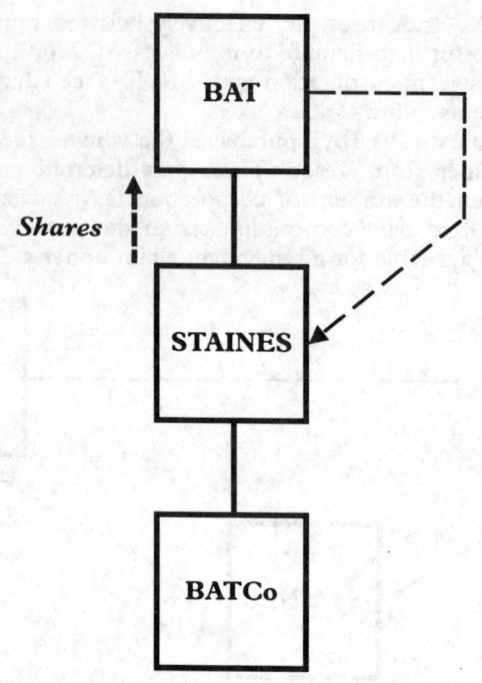

Figure 4.10

Step 3 On 18 December 1991 BATCo paid a dividend of some £176 million to Staines out of pre-acquisition profits and nearly all was paid under a group income election. Staines therefore received income that was not liable to corporation tax[18] and carried no tax credit (see s. 247, TA especially subsection(2)).

[18.] Section 208, TA corporation tax is generally not chargeable on dividends from a UK company received from another UK company. See Chapter 27 generally.

Tax avoidance

```
      ┌─────────┐
      │   BAT   │
      └────┬────┘
           │
      ┌────┴────┐
      │ STAINES │
      └────┬────┘
    ▲      │
Dividend   │
    ┊      │
      ┌────┴────┐
      │  BATCo  │
      └─────────┘
```

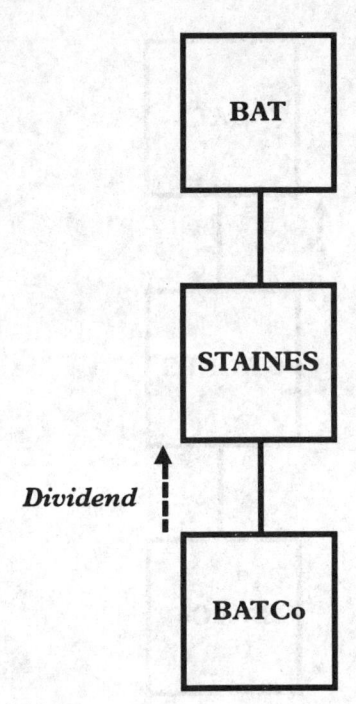

Figure 4.11

Step 4 On 19 December 1991 Staines paid a dividend to BAT outside the group income election. The ACT on this dividend was the subject of the dispute. On paying the dividend Staines became liable to account for ACT as it was paid outside the group income election (see s. 247(3), TA). Staines then claimed to carry back this ACT against its MCT in earlier years with a consequent repayment of tax.

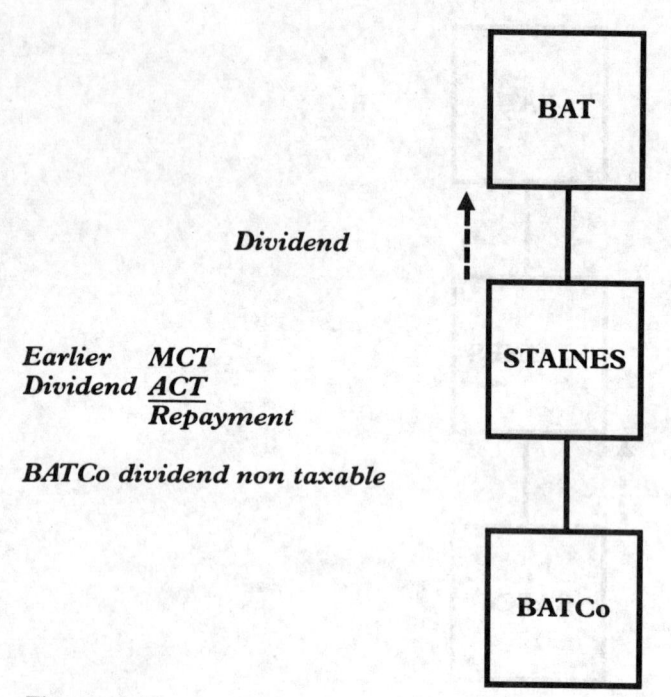

```
Earlier    MCT
Dividend   ACT
           Repayment

BATCo dividend non taxable
```

Figure 4.12

The Revenue refused the repayment claim on the basis that the *Ramsay/Furniss* principles applied. They argued that the four steps were a series of preordained steps effected solely for tax mitigation [sic] purposes which constituted a composite transaction, the end result of which was a payment to BAT of the £176 million or so which on its proper interpretation was not a dividend payment by Staines. This may be illustrated as follows.

Tax avoidance

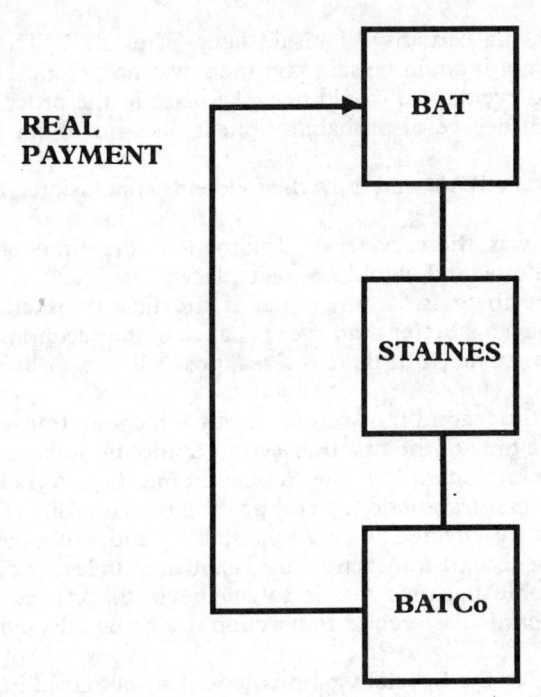

```
                    ┌──────────┐
         ┌─────────▶│   BAT    │
REAL     │          └────┬─────┘
PAYMENT  │               │
         │          ┌────┴─────┐
         │          │  STAINES │
         │          └────┬─────┘
         │               │
         │          ┌────┴─────┐
         └──────────┤  BATCo   │
                    └──────────┘
```

Figure 4.13

The Special Commissioner who heard the case found that:

(a) the four steps were a series of preordained steps effected solely for tax mitigation purposes; but

(b) there was no rational basis by which those four steps could be recharacterised in a way which excluded Staines' repayment claim.

The taxpayer argued that it was wrong to find a composite transaction, taking essentially two points:

(a) that the wrong test as to the degree of certainty had been applied; and

(b) that the time interval prevented there being a composite transaction.

Knox J rejected the taxpayer's argument that the wrong test had been applied in concluding that there was a single series of preordained transactions. It was agreed that the test was that there is a preordained series of transactions if 'it can be said that there is no practical likelihood that the transaction which actually takes place will not take place' ([1995] STC 114 at p. 134, quoting Lord Oliver in *Craven v White*). This was called the double negative test in the case and differed from the positive test put forward by the taxpayer, i.e., is it likely that the later step will take place? Knox J described the difference between these as 'roughly equivalent to the difference between

a favourite and a racing certainty.' He said later (at p. 137) 'The question
... was whether or not it could be said that there was no practical likelihood
that the pre-planned events . . . would not take place in the order ordained.
That requires a high degree of probability but it does not require absolute
certainty.'

He analysed *Craven v White* and drew the following conclusions (at p. 138).

(1) The test is, was there no real likelihood at the time of the first
transaction that the second would not take place?
(2) The fact that there is, at the time of the first transaction, active
contemplation or even a better than evens chance of the second transaction
taking place, is not sufficient if there is a real possibility of a different event
taking place.
(3) The fact that the second transaction exactly matches a transaction that
was planned at the time of the first transaction cannot be sufficient to bring
the totality of transactions within the *Ramsay/Furniss* principles if there is,
at the time of the first transaction, a real possibility that a different second
transaction might be effected. Contemplation of, and probability of the
occurrence of, the second transaction are insufficient unless it can also be
said that the double negative test is satisfied, viz that there is no real
possibility of the particular second transaction not being effected.

Knox J considered that the Special Commissioner had not erred in law here.

The submisson that a time interval (in the instant case, ten months)
necessarily prevented the events at either end of the period being treated as
a single composite transaction was rejected (see p. 139). Knox J accepted that
the 'existence of an extended interval is relevant to the factual question, was
there is a preordained series of transactions' and agreed that 'Lord Oliver did
not intend in *Craven v White* to state as a universal principle that a long
interval inevitably prevents a series of steps from being a preordained series'
(at p. 139). He continued, 'The passage of time is in my view only conclusive
if it has the effect of preventing the transactions before and after the interval
from forming a single continuous process . . . [see *Craven v White* [1988]
STC 476 at pp. 520–2, *per* Lord Jauncey]. Whether this is so must be a
matter of degree' (at p. 139). He did not consider that the break prevented
a series of transactions here.

The Crown argued that the Commissioner was wrong to find that although
the four steps were a series of preordained steps effected solely for tax
mitigation purposes, there was no possibility of a realistic and intellectually
defensible way of treating the series of transactions as a composite whole in
a way which excluded Staines' repayment claim.

The Crown, however, accepted that 'enduring steps taken in the preordained series of transactions had to be taken account of and not disregarded'.
Knox J considered that '. . . it is clear from the decisions in both *Furniss v
Dawson* and *Craven v White* that the court in recharacterising steps only taken
for a fiscal advantage has to look at and take account of the end result of the
composite transaction.' The Crown agreed that in this case the end result

included the existence of Staines as the subsidiary of BAT and holding company of BATCo. Accordingly Knox J considered that excluded any recharacterisation which altogether ignored Staines and treated the overall transaction as a payment of dividend by BATCo to BAT.

The Crown argued before Knox J for a recharacterisation, postulating a quadripartite contract between BAT, BATCo, Staines and Tesco under which Staines accepted a contractual obligation to hand over to BAT the dividend which BATCo was to declare and pay to Staines. Knox J did not consider this to be 'a logically defensible transaction'. To do otherwise would be 'not so much to recharacterise as to denature a perfectly ordinary transaction'. He also considered that the contract postulated would not turn the dividend into anything other than a dividend.

Overall Knox J considered that:

> the application of the *Ramsay/Furniss* principles to the normal operation of the three-tier structure of BATCo, Staines and BAT, which the Crown accepts as one of the enduring consequences forming part of the end result of the scheme, seems to me to go further than has been done in any other decided case, in that it involves a recharacterisation of a perfectly normal and straightforward commercial transaction into a thoroughly abnormal and unusual transaction whose only merit (if that is the right word) is that it attracts a tax disadvantage. That seems to me to be going far beyond disregarding steps only taken for a tax advantage and not for any commercial purpose.

Accordingly he dismissed the appeal.

4.13 WHAT IS THE LAW?

It is suggested that the following may represent the present position in UK tax law.

(a) The charge to tax is to be by reference to the legal nature of the real transaction rather than its economic effect, i.e., the real legal transaction is to be charged. This does not seem to require recharacterisation but analysis to find what the real deal was rather than recharacterising it as something different from what the parties intended.

(b) The tax law is to be applied by reference to the end result where there is a preordained series of transactions (in the sense of there being no real likelihood of all the transactions in the series not being carried through).

(c) The new approach is concerned with the fiscal effects of real transactions, not with shams.

(d) There is no general anti-avoidance test which automatically brings the emerging principle into play but an avoidance motive may be relevant in putting a transaction(s) in its context in determining the real deal. Generally, the intention of a taxpayer to avoid tax is not relevant to the decision of a tax case. The court is concerned with what the taxpayer has done and whether what he has done has attracted tax. Such an intention may be a relevant factor though in ascertaining what was done especially if the existence of a composite transaction is to be regarded as a question of fact.

(e) If the tax advantage arises as part of the real deal it may be allowed to stand, but if the tax advantage does not arise as part of the real deal then it will not be allowed to stand.[19]

4.14 DIFFICULTIES?

A number of difficulties following the cases still arise, namely:

(a) uncertainty which includes:

 (i) What is a composite transaction?
 (ii) When is it preordained?
 (iii) What is the end result and how is it to be determined?
 (iv) Who decides when the new approach applies?

(b) the effect when the new approach applies (for example, when does the transaction(s) under consideration take place?);
(c) *mens rea*;
(d) retrospection;
(e) relationship to legislation:

 (i) with its own anti-avoidance provisions;
 (ii) legislation which gives tax incentives.

The reader should consider which cases can be considered as giving what answers to which of these questions.

4.15 OFFICIAL STATEMENTS

The Inland Revenue have been particularly reticent about the way in which they view the new approach, though inspectors will use discretion in applying it to particular facts (see [1982] STI 556). In the House of Commons, the Chief Secretary to the Treasury has said that the new approach does not in any way:

> call in question the tax treatment of covenants, leasing transactions and other straightforward commercial transactions. Nor is there any question of the Inland Revenue challenging, for example, the tax treatment of straightforward transfers of assets between members of the same group of companies. I also assure the House that, in accordance with normal practice, the Inland Revenue will not seek to reopen cases when assessments were properly settled in accordance with prevailing practice and became final before that decision [i.e., *Furniss* v *Dawson*].

---
[19]. Cf. M.J. Gammie, *Strategic Tax Planning* (ed. Shipwright), Vol. 2, Part D.

The operative word in this statement is obviously 'straightforward'. The exclusion of covenants from the new approach is justified on the basis that a covenant will normally be a single-step transaction into which nothing has been, or can be, inserted. This is also sometimes used to justify the continued validity of the decision in the *Westminster* case. However, in *Furniss* v *Dawson* Lord Roskill declined to express any view as to whether, were the *Westminster* case to arise for decision again, the Duke or the Revenue would emerge as the ultimate victor. Given that the Duke's transaction was not as 'straightforward' as the normal deed of covenant (because the gardener also 'understood' that he would not claim his wages), this doubt is understandable.

In 1985, the Inland Revenue met representatives of the Law Society and the Institute of Chartered Accountants, and as a result of that meeting correspondence took place between the Inland Revenue and those bodies. The correspondence is reproduced in [1985] STI 568, and sets out the Revenue's views on certain transactions.

4.16 STATUTORY ANTI-AVOIDANCE

4.16.1 Introduction

4.16.1.1 General Statutory anti-avoidance provisions have been with us for centuries.[20] For example, the Statute of Uses in the sixteenth century was an anti-avoidance deeming provision for tax purposes. The reason that the 'use' was executed was so that the heir took the land as heir and had to account for any of the feudal servitudes for which he was liable. There have been large numbers of deeming provisions ever since and there are many anti-avoidance provisions in current UK tax legislation (see the Table in para. 4.16.1.4).

Probably the widest anti-avoidance section is to be found in what is now s. 703, TA discussed in para. 4.16.2. This section was introduced to counteract dividend stripping and was originally s. 28, FA 1960. Dividend stripping had many variants but one way was to buy an asset-rich or cash-rich company, liquidate it, extracting the assets as cash, hopefully in a tax free way, and then claim that, as a trader, you had made a loss on the shares because on liquidation the shares were destroyed and had a nil value. This loss could then be set against other income.

Dividend stripping was counteracted by the courts, particularly the House of Lords, in a line of cases starting with *Thompson* v *Gurneville* (1969) 47 TC 633 which held that such transactions were not part of the trade and so did not give rise to a trading loss. However, anti-avoidance legislation had already been introduced.

This is a common theme throughout the anti-avoidance provisions. Often tax avoidance schemes have been struck down by the courts, particularly the superior courts, after the Revenue have introduced legislation that is designed

---

[20] Deeming provisions can be found in the legislation of Henry VII: see Simpson, *An Introduction to the History of Land Law*, OUP, p. 173.

to counteract the scheme which is being attacked. This was the case in *Furniss v Dawson* [1984] STC 153 where the anti-avoidance legislation had been introduced in 1977.

4.16.1.2 Statutory rules of general application and UK tax As already noted, there is no anti-avoidance statutory rule of general application for UK tax purposes nor any general statutory rule allowing for recharacterisation. The nearest to this in UK legislation is to be seen in s. 703, TA discussed in para. 4.16.2. The UK does have, for certain taxes and certain purposes, statutory provisions allowing various transactions or operations to be linked together or associated. Thus s. 286, IHTA allows certain matters to be associated for inheritance tax purposes. However, the charge remains the same, it is merely whether the facts are to be considered together or separately that these provisions affect. They are there to deal with indirect methods of achieving something that would otherwise be taxable and which, because of the UK's lack of purposive construction, until recently might not have been held to be within the strict wording of the legislation.

4.16.1.3 Anti-avoidance rules related to specific fields There is much of this in UK tax. Long, detailed tax legislation with wide anti-avoidance provisions is a characteristic of UK tax legislation. The UK does not have a tradition of a Code as in civil law systems but of statute interpreted in minute detail in various cases. The courts do not generally see themselves as laying down grand principles but doing what is necessary to answer the particular question before the court. The response of the legislature has been to introduce long, detailed legislation in an attempt to cover every possibility (particularly where a tax incentive has been introduced) so it is not 'abused'.

The UK legislation of this kind ranges from an extended meaning of 'dividend', to market value substitution for capital gains tax purposes, to transfer pricing and group provisions. Paragraph 4.16.1.4 below sets out some of the provisions.

4.16.1.4 Illustrative table of some UK specific anti-avoidance provisions (This table is not exhaustive and is for illustrative purposes only.)

TA

13A	Close investment holding companies
33A & B	Connected persons and rent
34–38	Premiums, leases etc.
42A	Payment of rent to non-residents
53 & 55	Some land receipts treated as trade
63A	Overlap profits
82	Interest paid to non-residents
117–118	Limited partnership restrictions
125	Annual payments for non-taxable consideration
141–144A	Vouchers
145–146	Living accommodation
153–168G	Employee benefits

Tax avoidance

209–255	Distributions
347A	Annual payments
Part X	Loss reliefs and group relief
418–419	Extension of distributions
Part XV	Settlements
703–709	Transactions in securities; cancellation of tax advantages
710–738	Accrued income etc.
739–746	Transfer of assets abroad
747–756	Controlled foreign companies
757–764	Offshore funds
765–767	Migration of companies
767A–769	Effect of change in ownership of company
770–774	Transfer pricing
775	Sale by individual of income derived from his personal activities
776	Transactions in land: taxation of capital gains
779–785	Leasing etc.
787	Restriction of relief for payment of interest
808A	Interest: special relationship
TCGA	
13	Attribution of gains to members of non-resident companies
17	Market value substitution
18	Transactions between connected persons
29–34	Value shifting
80–98A	Non-resident settlements
137	Restriction of ss. 135 and 136 relief
164L	Re-investment relief; anti-avoidance
178–180	Companies leaving groups
240	Leases
282	Recovery of tax from donee
IHTA	
3A	PETS
Part III Chapter II	Discretionary trusts
Part IV	Close companies
114	Avoidance of double relief
Chapter IV	Transfers within seven years before death
268	Associated operations

(VAT and other indirect taxes are not considered further here because they tend to be of European origin.)

4.16.1.5 Do the rules affect what is taxable or do they affect the assessment powers of the tax authorities? The UK statutory and case law rules do not generally rely on an economic analysis of a contract etc. (cf. the civil law approach). Instead they try in general to discover what the real transaction is and tax it.

Some of the anti-avoidance provisions give the Revenue power to counteract a tax advantage (e.g., s. 703, TA which gives extended powers of assessment etc. to the Revenue). In the UK the burden of proof is on the taxpayer to show that the taxpayer is not liable to the tax levied etc. This is extended further in some provisions such as s. 739, TA (discussed in para. 4.16.3). The escape clause for the application of some of the provisions requires the Revenue to be satisfied that the transaction or transactions were carried out for *bona fide* commercial reasons and that none of them has as their main object, or one of their main objects, to obtain a tax advantage.

4.16.2 Section 703

4.16.2.1 Introduction As noted above, these provisions started life as s. 28, FA 1960 and were enacted to stop a number of avoidance schemes, in particular 'dividend stripping'.[21] However, they are not limited to this. Viscount Dilhorne said of these provisions ((1966) 43 TC at p. 431):

> I do not agree that the general mischief which s. 28 [now s. 703] was designed to hit was dividend stripping. It was, to my mind, designed to hit other forms of tax avoidance as well. I do not think one should restrict the general and unambiguous words . . . by reference to the mischief which it is thought the section is aimed at. Nor do I think it is right to seek to interpret the general words in the light of the particular instances given in the section. It is a familiar choice of a draftsman to state expressly that certain matters are to be treated as coming within a definition to avoid an argument whether they did or not.

IRC v *Cleary* (1967) 44 TC 399, for example (see para. 4.16.2.5.5), illustrates the width of these provisions which were held to apply by the House of Lords on a sale of shares in a company with accumulated profits.

4.16.2.2 Conditions for application of s. 703 For s. 703, TA to apply three conditions must be satisfied:

(a) there must be a transaction in securities;
(b) as a result a person must obtain or be in a position to obtain a tax advantage;
(c) one of the prescribed circumstances must be present.

Once these three conditions are satisfied, the provisions of s. 703 apply unless the person concerned can show that the transaction was carried out either for *bona fide* commercial reasons or in the ordinary course of making or managing investments and that the tax advantage was not his main objective (s. 703(1)). If the provisions of s. 703 are applied, the tax advantage can be cancelled (see para. 4.16.2.6).

[21.] The practices known as 'bond washing' and 'coupon stripping' are not considered in this book, but are subject to their own anti-avoidance rules in ss. 710 to 738, TA 1988.

4.16.2.3 'Transaction in securities' 'Transaction in securities' is very widely defined for these purposes. Securities includes stock and shares and any interest of a member in a company. Transactions in securities include transactions of whatever description relating to securities and in particular:

(a) the purchase, sale or exchange of securities;
(b) the issue or securing the issue of, or applying or subscribing for new securities;
(c) the alteration or securing the alteration of the rights attached to securities (s. 709(2)).

The necessary causal connection between a transaction in securities and a tax advantage is far from clear. In most of the cases though the tax advantages come to the taxpayer through a transaction in securities itself.

In *Williams* v *IRC* (1980) 54 TC 257 Viscount Dillon said at p. 309:

> It is not, I think, necessary to list the many transactions coming within the definition which were entered into from the inception of the scheme. They were all necessary ingredients, those gains do not cease to be in consequence of those transactions if one or more links in the chain of operations does not come within the definition.

The tendency in the cases is to give the expression 'transaction in securities' the widest meaning. Thus, in *IRC* v *Parker* [1966] AC 141, Lord Guest said:

> It was said that the particularisation which followed the wide inclusion of transactions of whatever description relating to securities in some way qualified the general words and that as the issue of securities was mentioned and nothing was said of the redemption of securities it must be presumed to have been excluded. There is, in my view, no substance in this argument. The words 'of whatever description relating to securities' are extremely wide and are apt to cover the redemption of a debenture.

In addition to redemptions, the House of Lords have held that loans come within the definition of transactions in securities (*Williams* v *IRC*) and, where the purchase price for the sale of shares is paid by instalments, each instalment is a transaction relating to securities (*Greenberg* v *IRC* [1972] AC 109). However, the House has held that the liquidation of a company cannot, by itself, be a transaction in securities (*IRC* v *Joiner* [1975] 3 All ER 1050).

It is worth recalling in this respect that the tax advantage must be obtained or obtainable in consequence of a transaction in securities (or of the combined effect of two or more such transactions). However, a tax advantage is deemed to be obtained or obtainable in consequence of a transaction in securities (or of the combined effect of two or more such transactions) if it is obtained in consequence of the combined effect of the transaction or transactions and of the liquidation of the company (s. 703(2)). It was on the basis of this provision that the House of Lords in *IRC* v *Joiner* held that a liquidation on its own was not sufficient to amount to a transaction in securities.

As far as the meaning of the word 'security' is concerned, in *IRC* v *Parker* (1963) 43 TC 396 at p. 408, Ungoed-Thomas J at first instance reviewed the authorities and concluded:

> These cases indicate, to my mind, (1) that prima facie security is limited to security for the payment of a debt as contrasted with shares in the capital of the company; (2) that the context may extend its meaning to include shares; (3) that security by a document establishing personal liability and without charge on property is recognised as a form of security; (4) that it is questionable whether security in that sense would be within its prima facie meaning; but (5) even if is not within the prima facie meaning of security, yet such security is a less extended meaning of that word than are shares.

4.16.2.4 Tax advantage For s. 703 to apply, a person must obtain a 'tax advantage' as a result of a transaction in securities. By s. 709(1) 'tax advantage' means:

(a) relief or increased relief from tax; or
(b) repayment or increased repayment of tax; or
(c) the avoidance or reduction of a charge to tax or an assessment to tax; or
(d) the avoidance of a possible assessment to tax.

In the case of an advantage within (c) or (d) above, the avoidance or reduction may be effected either by accruing receipts in such a way that the recipient does not pay or bear tax on them, or by a deduction in computing profits or gains.

Lord Guest said in *IRC* v *Parker* that '"receipt" is in my view a deliberately wide term and "accruing" does not necessarily import payment'.

Lord Wilberforce in the same case said (at p. 441) that the definition of tax advantage:

> ... presupposes a situation in which an assessment to tax, or increased tax, either is made or may possibly be made, that the taxpayer is in a position to resist the assessment by saying that the way in which he received what it is sought to tax prevents him from being taxed on it and that the Crown is in a position to reply that if he had received what it is sought to tax in another way he would have had to bear tax. In other words, there must be a contrast as regards the 'receipts' between the actual case where these accrue in a non-taxable way with a possible accrual in a taxable way, and unless this contrast exists, the existence of the advantage is not established.

This may be illustrated by the decision in *IRC* v *Wiggins* [1979] 2 All ER 245, where the taxpayers were shareholders in a company engaged in restoring and selling picture frames.

The facts of this case were that in 1955, the company, in the ordinary course of its trade, acquired for £50 a frame with a picture in it. Ten years later, the picture was identified as *The Holy Family* by Poussin and was then valued at £130,000. The company wished to sell the picture to Knoedler Ltd, and rather than selling the picture directly, entered into a scheme. The company sold its stock (with the exception of the picture and a few other items) and transferred its staff to another company owned by the taxpayers. Knoedler Ltd then purchased the entire share capital of the company, thus providing the taxpayers with a capital receipt representing consideration for the shares. Walton J held that since the picture could have been sold direct to Knoedler Ltd and the company's resulting profit distributed by way of dividend to the taxpayers, there was another possible way in which the profits accruing to the company from the sale of the picture might have reached the taxpayers (although as a distribution the dividend would have been treated as income and, as such, subject to tax at a then higher rate than a capital profit). The sale of the company's shares to Knoedler Ltd was accordingly a transaction in securities resulting in a tax advantage to the taxpayers.

The flavour of the meaning of 'tax advantage' in this context can be gleaned from the judgment of Buckley LJ in *IRC v Garvin* [1980] STC 295. His Lordship, having looked at earlier case law, said:

> The common features of all these cases are (a) that a taxpayer owning shares in a company replete with profits so arranged his affairs, either on his own or in cooperation with others, that he received something in such a way that the receipt did not attract income tax; (b) that the value of what he received was at least in part attributable to the accumulated profits of the company; (c) that he could have so arranged matters that he received the same subject-matter from the company by means of a distribution in cash or in kind of its accumulated profits which would have attracted income tax; and (d) that consequently the way in which he arranged his affairs was advantageous to him as regards income tax. These four features are, in my judgment, together sufficient to satisfy the definition of 'tax advantage' contained in section [709].

There is apparently a distinction between a 'relief' and an 'exemption' for these purposes (see *Shepherd v IRC* [1995] STC 240 and *Universities Superannuation Scheme Ltd v IRC* [1995] STI 577). Aldous J said in *Shepherd v IRC* (at p. 254):

> The word 'relief' would normally indicate the alleviation of an obligation, whereas 'exemption' would denote removal of the obligation altogether ... A person who relieves himself from tax obtains a tax advantage but a person who has no obligation to pay tax does not obtain a tax advantage by taking steps which result in him paying no tax.

Accordingly s. 703 did not apply.

A further problem relating to the definition of tax advantage is, which taxes are caught? By s. 832(3), TA, 'tax' means income tax and corporation tax. Capital gains tax is therefore not expressly included, and although s. 709(1) refers to 'profits or gains', this cannot include a reference to chargeable gains for capital gains tax purposes (833(1), TA). However corporation tax applies to both profits of a revenue nature and to chargeable gains (ss. 6(1) and (4), TA) and and for this purpose corporation tax on chargeable gains and capital gains tax are to be treated as one tax. It would therefore seem that s. 703 is to be limited to income tax and to corporation tax on income. This conclusion is supported by the quotation of Buckley LJ in *IRC* v *Garvin* above, which refers only to income tax.

It is possible that a liability to capital gains tax will have arisen in respect of the transaction in securities which is subsequently subject to the application of s. 703. Where this is the case, it is understood that the Inland Revenue, as a matter of concession, credit the capital gains tax paid against any income tax charge under s. 703. In *IRC* v *Garvin* [1981] STC 344, the House of Lords expressed concern that the elimination of this possibility of double taxation should rest only on concession, and suggested that the law should be reviewed so that the element of double taxation could be excluded as a matter of law.

In carrying out the transactions which fall foul of s. 703, the taxpayer might incur some tax liabilities in order to create the tax advantage which is subsequently cancelled. Thus, in *Bird* v *IRC* [1985] STC 584, Vinelott J said:

> It is now well settled that in order to ascertain whether a taxpayer has obtained a tax advantage by means of a transaction in securities and the amount of any advantage so obtained the proper course is to contrast the receipt which in fact accrued in a non-taxable way with a similar receipt which might have accrued in some other taxable way. The question that arises in this case is whether in making the contrast account must be taken of other liabilities to tax that may have fallen directly or indirectly on the taxpayer in consequence of the transactions which he in fact carried out.

Vinelott J held that the other liabilities to tax must be taken into account. Thus, when the taxpayers in that case were assessed under s. 703, the Inland Revenue had to give credit for a due proportion of the tax paid by a company of which the taxpayers were shareholders as a result of a transaction affected by the operation of s. 703. This decision has now been supported by the House of Lords ([1988] 2 All ER 670).

4.16.2.5 The prescribed circumstances

4.16.2.5.1 Introduction The 'prescribed circumstances' are set out in s. 704, TA. They are broadly as follows:

(a) distribution of profits or sale or purchase of securities followed by purchase or sale as a result of which a person receives an abnormal amount by way of dividend;

(b) a fall in the value of securities resulting from a payment of the dividend or from any other dealing with company assets as a result of which the taxpayer becomes entitled to a deduction;

(c) payment of an abnormal amount by way of dividend leading to receipt of a consideration on which no tax is paid;

(d) the person in question receives a consideration representing the value of the assets available for distribution or future profits of a closely held company;

(e) transactions between two (d) companies.

4.16.2.5.2 Circumstance A The first prescribed circumstance relates to straightforward dividend stripping (see para. 4.16.1.1 above). In normal circumstances, the receipt of a dividend will represent investment income, possibly taxable at the higher rates of income tax. However, if the recipient were exempt from tax, the gross amount could be received with no adverse tax consequences; similarly, if the recipient were a share dealer, the dividend income (which would represent trading income) could be used to absorb other trading losses. Taking this a stage further, if a share dealer buys a company's shares, and then strips out the company's distributable profits by declaring higher than normal dividends in his own favour, subsequently selling the shares at a lower amount (because the company now has no or significantly reduced distributable profits), the loss on the subsequent share sale could be used to absorb the dividend income, thus allowing a claim to be made for the repayment of the tax notionally deducted from the dividend. This, and other forms of dividend stripping, would now be caught by circumstance A, which applies where in, connection with either a distribution of profits or a sale or purchase of securities, the person concerned receives an abnormal amount by way of dividend which is then taken into account for any of the following purposes:

(a) any exemption from tax;
(b) the setting-off of losses against profits or income;
(c) the giving of group relief;
(d) the application of franked investment income in calculating a company's liability to pay advance corporation tax;
(e) the application of a surplus of franked investment income under ss. 242 and 243, TA;
(f) the computation of profits or gains out of which payments are made falling within s. 348 or s. 349(1); or
(g) the deduction from or set-off against income of interest under s. 353.

Broadly, a dividend is abnormal if it 'substantially exceeds' the dividend which would normally be expected in respect of the securities concerned, having regard to the market value of the securities, and the length of time for which the securities have been held (s. 709(4) and (6)).

4.16.2.5.3 Circumstance B This second circumstance also applies to dividend stripping, but does not require the payment of an abnormal dividend.

However, it is effectively restricted to share dealers. Thus it applies where, in connection either with the distribution of profits or with the sale or purchase of securities which is followed by the purchase or sale of the same or other securities, the person concerned becomes entitled (in respect of securities either held or sold by him, or formerly held by him whether sold by him or not) to a deduction in computing profits or gains by reason of a fall in the value of the securities resulting from the payment of a dividend or from any other dealing with any assets of the company.

The Inland Revenue attempted to apply circumstance B in *IRC v Kleinwort Benson Ltd* [1969] 2 Ch 221. The taxpayer company was a share-dealing merchant bank which acquired certain debenture stock for some £300,000 (the price being based on the principal amount and premium due together with interest arrears). The debtor company subsequently paid off the debenture stock in full, as a result of which the taxpayer company received principal and a premium of nearly £150,000 plus interest. However, being a share dealer, the taxpayer company did not enter the interest in its profit and loss account, with the result that it showed a loss on the transaction which it set against its taxable profits. In holding that circumstance B did not apply, Cross J said:

> The question may be stated thus: did the taxpayer company in connection with the payment off of the stock and arrears of interest become entitled as a holder of the stock to a deduction in computing its profits and gains by reason of a fall in value of the stock resulting from the payment of the interest? If words are to be given their ordinary meaning the answer must be 'no'. There was never any fall in the value of the stock by reason of the payment of interest. Principal, premium, and arrears of interest were paid off on the same day. All rights of the stock holders were extinguished and the stock ceased to exist.

4.16.2.5.4 Circumstance C Circumstance C applies if:

(a) the person concerned so receives a consideration that he does not pay or bear tax on it as income, and that consideration either:

(i) is, or represents the value of, assets which are (or apart from anything done by the company would have been) available for distribution by way of dividend, or

(ii) is received in respect of future receipts of the company, or

(iii) is, or represents the value of, the company's trading stock; and

(b) the consideration is received in consequence of a transaction whereby another person:

(i) subsequently receives, or has received, an abnormal amount by way of dividend, or

(ii) subsequently becomes entitled, or has become entitled, to a deduction in computing profits or gains by reason of a fall in the value of the securities resulting from the payment of a dividend or from any other dealings with the company's assets.

The purpose of circumstance C was explained in *IRC* v *Garvin* [1981] STC 344 by Lord Bridge of Harwich. He said:

> I do not think it is very difficult to visualise the kind of tax avoidance scheme at which the language of paragraph C . . . is directed. A and B ('the persons in question'), individual income tax and surtax payers, between them hold all the shares in company X, which has large undistributed profits available for distribution by way of dividend. If X pays a large dividend to A and B, they will incur heavy liabilities to income tax and surtax. If they can find a buyer, company Y ('any other person'), which will be in a position, for one reason or another, having acquired company X, to extract the profits in the form of an abnormal dividend without incurring any tax liability, they may be able to sell their shares for a price which substantially represents the value of the undistributed profits. This will be a capital receipt which, apart from paragraph C of section [704] and assuming that no other paragraph of the section applies, will attract no liability to income tax or surtax in the hands of A and B. If the . . . provisions of paragraph C can never apply to counteract the tax advantage which A and B obtain in such circumstances as I have indicated, I find it difficult to see how they serve any useful purpose at all in the scheme of the Act. If I have correctly identified the statutory target, how can the statutory language be construed to give it the intended effect? The difficulty arises from the use of the words 'transaction' and 'whereby'. In my example, if 'transaction' is given its ordinary meaning, the sale by A and B of their shares in company X to company Y is one transaction, the declaration and payment of an abnormal dividend by company X to company Y is quite another. In the context in which it is used in paragraph C, I do not think it is possible to construe the word 'transaction' as equivalent to 'series of transactions', or to stretch its meaning to embrace both the sale of shares and the subsequent payment of a dividend in a single transaction. This would introduce more problems than it would solve. If the reasoning is sound so far, it must follow that 'whereby' cannot be used in its narrowest sense, since, on that reading, the only transaction whereby Y receives the abnormal dividend, would be the declaration and payment of the dividend itself. Accordingly, 'whereby' must at least be wide enough to denote some kind of causal connection between the transaction of sale and purchase of shares in X, in consequence of which A and B receive a tax-free consideration of the kind to which paragraph C applies, and the subsequent receipt of an abnormal dividend by Y. The kernel of the problem is to determine what kind of causal connection is contemplated. It cannot, in my opinion, be required that one should find that the receipt of the abnormal dividend is a necessary consequence of the share transaction, for this requirement could seldom, if ever, be satisfied. I was at one time much attracted to the view that there was a sufficient causal

connection if the purchase of the shares by Y enabled Y to procure the subsequent payment of an abnormal dividend by X. But on further reflection I appreciate that this would make the liability of A and B potentially dependent on an event which was outside their knowledge or control. This can hardly have been intended. Counsel for the taxpayer submitted that the taxpayer could not be liable under paragraph C unless he was a 'party' to payment of the abnormal dividend. I do not accept this formula, but I accept, at least in part, what I take to be the idea underlying the submission. To revert to the characterisation used in my example, to establish that the sale of shares by A and B to Y was a transaction 'whereby' Y subsequently received an abnormal dividend, it would be necessary, in my opinion, to show that Y's purpose or one of Y's purposes, in purchasing the shares was to produce in due course the payment of an abnormal dividend by X to Y, and that A and B were, at the time of the sale, aware of this purpose. These are, of course, matters which will seldom be susceptible of direct proof but will often be plain by inference from circumstances.

The Inland Revenue successfully applied circumstance C in *Emery* v *IRC* [1981] STC 150. The taxpayer here was the owner of all the share capital in Mersey Industrial Estates Ltd. Mersey carried on business as a property dealer and developer and by selling some land, realised a profit of £261,500 which the taxpayer wanted to extract from the company. Extracting the profit by way of dividend would have resulted in a significant income tax charge. The taxpayer therefore tried to use a different method to extract the profit. He sold his shares in Mersey to Tishmear Investment Co. Ltd (a company controlled by the taxpayer's advisers) for £233,409 payable in instalments over 101 years. A second company owned by his advisers, Kopley Investment Co. Ltd, borrowed £233,409 from Mersey to allow it to buy from the taxpayer for the same amount the right to receive the future instalments: as a result, therefore, the taxpayer now had £233,409 capital in his hands. Mersey then declared a dividend of £260,500 to Tishmear, £233,409 of which Tishmear lent to Kopley and which Kopley used to repay its loan to Mersey: the amount of the loan had thus gone round in a circle. At the end of these transactions, therefore, the taxpayer was left holding cash of £233,409, Mersey had been stripped of the profit, and Tishmear and Kopley were left with, respectively, an obligation to pay and the right to receive, £233,409 payable in instalments over 101 years.

For circumstance C to be satisfied, the Inland Revenue (in the words of Nourse J) would have to show:

That the person in question (Mr Emery) received, in consquence of a transaction whereby some other person (Tishmear) subsequently received an abnormal amount by way of dividend (£260,500), a consideration (£233,409) which represented the value of assets which, apart from anything done by the company in question (Mersey), would have been available for distribution by way of dividend; and that the said person (Mr

Emery) so received the consideration that he did not pay or bear tax on it as income.

The issue in the case turned on whether there had been a 'transaction whereby' Tishmear had received an abnormal dividend. In supporting the Inland Revenue, Nourse J said that the transaction in question was the whole series of operations down to and including the payment of the abnormal dividend by Mersey and the simultaneous loan by Tishmear to Kopley and repayment of the loan made by Mersey to Kopley. Once this transaction was identified, Norse J was satisfied that there was a sufficient causal link between that transaction and the subsequent receipt by Tishmear of the abnormal amount by way of dividend.

The question of a causal link fell to be considered again by Vinelott J in *Bird* v *IRC* [1985] STC 584 (a complicated case). Part of the scheme in this case involved the sale of shares in Croydon Centre Development Ltd (CCD) to Tishmear Investment Co. Ltd. Vinelott J referred to counsel for the taxpayers' submission that the fact that neither the taxpayers nor their advisers were aware that following the sale of their shares to Tishmear substantially the whole of the distributable reserves of the relevant company would be distributed by way of dividend, was fatal to the claim that the relevant transaction (the sale of the shares of CCD) was one whereby the dividend was declared. He said (at pp. 634–5):

> I think there is considerable force in the submission of counsel for the taxpayers that it is implicit in the analysis of paragraph C in . . . *Garvin* that the transaction relied on as one in consequence of which a consideration of the kind mentioned is received by the taxpayer and as one whereby an abnormal amount by way of dividend is received by another person must be a transaction to which the taxpayer was a party and also something other than (though not necessarily antecedent to) the payment of the dividend and the receipt of the consideration . . . It is clear that the word 'cause' is used in the speeches in the House of Lords and in the judgments in the Court of Appeal in a teleological and not a purely mechanistic sense [that is, the word was given the meaning which the courts thought most served its purpose or design]. In that sense of the word 'cause' the necessary causal link between the transaction and the receipt of an abnormal amount of dividend is to be found in a design or structure of which the transaction and the receipt of the dividend are functioning parts.

The question is: were the transaction (the sale of the shares of CCD) and the payment of the dividend conceived as part of a single design to a pre-arranged end?

Vinelott J thought that they were, and continued:

> If that is right then the only question is whether the Crown must also show that the taxpayers knew that it was part of the overall scheme . . . that the available assets would be extracted from CCD by way of dividend . . . I

think there is support in the speech of Lord Wilberforce [in *IRC* v *Garvin*] for the proposition that the Crown does not need to show in a case of this kind knowledge on the part of the taxpayer at the time he sells his shares that the purpose of the purchaser is to declare a dividend of an abnormal amount. Even if I am wrong in finding implied support for this proposition in the speech of Lord Wilberforce, there is nothing in his speech which shows positively that he shared Lord Bridge's opinion that such knowledge is necessary. In these circumstances, although I must of course give the greatest weight to the opinion expressed by Lord Bridge, I am not bound to follow it. I have come to the conclusion after careful consideration that I ought not to do so. In the instant appeals (as in *Emery*) the taxpayers bought a scheme consisting of a number of related and . . . closely interlocking steps. Indeed, they paid £300,000 for it. The scheme was designed and sold to them as one which would avoid all taxation on the commercial profit to be made from the sale of the Croydon property, including corporation tax on the profit realised by CCD. I cannot see that the taxpayers' liability to a counteracting assessment under section [703] can depend on whether they troubled to investigate every part of the scheme to see how that end would be achieved. The causal link between the sale of the shares and the declaration of the dividend is to be found in the purpose and design of those who throughout controlled the operation of the scheme, calling on the taxpayers only to play such part as it was necessary for them to play.

4.16.2.5.5 Circumstance D This circumstance is designed to apply to the distribution by a company of its assets otherwise than as a dividend taxable as income. The conditions are that:

(a) in connection with the distribution of profits of a company:

(i) which is under the control (as defined in s. 416, TA) of not more than five persons; or
(ii) whose shares or stocks are not authorised to be dealt in on a stock exchange in the United Kingdom; and

(b) the person concerned so receives a consideration that he does not pay or bear tax on it as income, and that consideration:

(i) is, or represents the value of, assets which are (or apart from anything done by the company would have been) available for distribution by way of dividend, or
(ii) is received in respect of future receipts of the company, or
(iii) is, or represents the value of, the company's trading stock.

Circumstance D does not, however, apply to a company which is controlled by one or more companies which do not fall within paragraph (a)(i) or (ii) above. References to 'distribution of profits' include references to the transfer or realisation (including an application in discharge of liabilities) of income, reserves or other assets (s. 709(3)). The House of Lords held in *IRC* v *Garvin* [1981] STC 344 that the control required by circumstance D must be shown to exist at the date when either there is a distribution of profits or a realisation of assets.

Circumstance D has also been considered by the House of Lords on three other occasions.

In *IRC* v *Parker* [1966] AC 141, the company capitalised £35,002 from its profit and loss account and issued debentures of that amount (which were not charged on any of the company's assets, and did not carry interest) to shareholders in proportion to their holdings of paid-up shares. Some eight years later, the debentures were redeemed, and the taxpayer received £18,002 in respect of his debentures. The House of Lords held that circumstance D applied for the reasons given by Viscount Dilhorne:

> the only object of capitalising the £35,002 and of the issue of debentures was to secure at some date the distribution of £35,002 to the members of the company without liability to surtax. The issue of the debentures was a necessary stage in the achievement of this object. It was not achieved until the debentures were redeemed, and in my opinion the respondent then received a consideration which was the value of the assets of the company which apart from anything done by the company would have been available for distribution by way of dividend, and received it in such a way that he did not pay tax upon it.... Was the £18,002 received by him in connection with the distribution of the profits of the company? It is provided ... that references to distribution include applications in discharge of liabilities. In my opinion, the sum received by the respondent was received in connection with the distribution of profits of the company. It was received by him as a result of two transactions by the company, first, the capitalisation of the £35,002 of the profits of the company and the issue of debentures for that sum and, secondly, by the redemption of those debentures.

In *Cleary* v *IRC* [1968] AC 766, the taxpayer and her sister each owned half of the shares in two companies, one of which held accumulated profits of £180,000 of which £130,000 was represented by cash at the bank. The sisters sold to this company for full value a number of their shares in the other company, thereby extracting £60,500 in cash each. The sisters argued that, because there had been no diminution in the amount available for distribution (since full value had been given for the shares), there could not have been a distribution of profits. The House of Lords rejected this argument, and held that circumstance D applied.

In the third case, *Williams* v *IRC* [1980] 3 All ER 321, a company owned by the taxpayers (Kithurst Park Estates Ltd) had profits of £422,255 when it stopped trading. In order to extract this profit with a minimal liability to income tax, the taxpayers acquired the shares of Gristrim Investment Co. Ltd (specially incorporated for the purpose). Kithurst subsequently paid a dividend of £422,000 to Gristrim. A third company, Dolerin Investment Co. Ltd (initially independent of the taxpayers), then agreed to lend £84,216 to each of the taxpayers. Using its dividend income, Gristrim acquired the share capital of Dolerin for £421,250, and the taxpayers then became directors of Dolerin. The taxpayers thus received £84,216 each by way of a loan from a company of which they became shareholders and directors. The House of Lords held that, in connection with the distribution of Kithurst's profits, the taxpayers received a consideration which represented the value of assets which would have been available for distribution to them by way of dividend but for the steps taken by Kithurst.

4.16.2.5.6 Circumstance E Circumstance E applies to the receipt of non-taxable consideration in the form of shares or securities representing distributable assets. More particularly, the requirements of circumstance E are as follows:

(a) there are at least two companies, each of which satisfy one of two conditions:

(i) the company is under the control (as defined in s. 416, TA) of not more than five persons; or
(ii) the company's shares or stocks are not authorised to be dealt in on a stock exchange in the United Kingdom;

this requirement is not satisfied if one of the companies is under the control of one or more other companies which do not satisfy these requirements;
(b) the person concerned receives a non-taxable consideration which is or represents the value of assets available for distribution by one of those companies and which consists of any share capital or security (including a security which does not create or evidence a charge over property) issued by one of them;
(c) that consideration is received in connection with either:

(i) the direct or indirect transfer of assets of one of those companies to another such company, or
(ii) any transaction in securities in which two or more of those companies are concerned.

For this purpose, consideration is non-taxable if the recipient does not pay or bear tax on it as income (a liability to capital gains tax would therefore be ignored); and assets are available for distribution if they are, or apart from anything done by the company in question, would have been (i) available for distribution by way of dividend, or (ii) the company's trading stock. Where the consideration represents share capital other than redeemable share capital, circumstance E applies only to the extent that the share capital is repaid, whether in a winding-up or otherwise (s. 704E(2)).

4.16.2.6 Cancellation of a tax advantage The Revenue are given wide powers to counteract a tax advantage.

Section 703 only applies if the Board of the Inland Revenue first notify the person concerned that they have reason to believe that the section may apply to him in respect of a transaction or transactions specified in the notice (s. 703(9)). The Board's decision may be subject to judicial review (*Preston* v *IRC* [1985] STC 282, HL). If the recipient of a notice believes that the section does not apply to him, he has 30 days from the issue of the Board's notice to make a statutory declaration to the effect that s. 703 does not apply to him, stating the facts and circumstances upon which his opinion is based (s. 703(9)). If the Board agree with the opinion expressed in the statutory declaration, or see no reason to take the matter further, s. 703 does not then apply to the declarant (s. 703(9)). If, however, the Board do see reason to take further action, they must refer the matter to a tribunal (s. 703(10)(a)), consisting of a chairman and two or more persons appointed by the Lord Chancellor as having special knowledge of, and experience in, financial or commercial matters (s. 706). The Board must send to the tribunal a certificate to the effect that they see reason to take further action, together with the statutory declaration and (if they wish) a counter-statement by them (s. 703(10)(a)). The function of the tribunal is to consider the declaration and certificate (and any counter-statement) and to determine whether or not there is a prima facie case for proceeding further (s. 703(10)(b)). Since the tribunal need only decide whether there is a prima facie case, it is not acting unfairly or contrary to the rules of natural justice if it refuses to allow the taxpayer to see the Board's counter-statement (*Wiseman* v *Borneman* [1971] AC 297, HL). If the tribunal decide that there is no prima facie case, then s. 703 cannot apply to the declarant (s. 703(10)(b)). If the tribunal determine that there is a prima facie case for proceeding further, or if the recipient of a notice under s. 703(9) does not make a statutory declaration, the Board must next specify by written notice the requisite steps for counteracting the tax advantage which the taxpayer has obtained or may obtain (s. 703(3)). It should be noted in this connection that the Board have the power to require any person to whom they think that s. 703 might apply to provide information in his possession which relates to the transaction or any of the transactions which may be subject to s. 703. The request to provide information must be made in writing and must give the person concerned at least 28 days in which to respond (s. 708).

The Board must specify in any notice given under s. 703(3) which of the following bases of adjustment they propose to counteract the tax advantage (s. 703(3)):

(a) an assessment;
(b) nullifying a right to repayment of tax;
(c) requiring the return of a repayment already made (by way of a charge under Case VI of Schedule D);
(d) the computation or recomputation of profits or gains;
(e) the computation or recomputation of liability to tax.

The recipient of a notice under s. 703(3) may appeal to the Special Commissioners within 30 days if he believes that s. 703 does not apply to him or that the adjustments chosen by the Board are inappropriate (s. 705(1)). If an appeal is made, and the taxpayer or the Board are dissatisfied with the determination of the Special Commissioners, either party may within 30 days require the appeal to be reheard by the tribunal which, like the Special Commissioners, may cancel or vary the s. 703(3) notice or vary or quash any assessment (s. 705(2), (3) and (5)). An appeal against the decision of the tribunal then lies to the High Court and beyond in the usual manner (s. 705(A)).

Where a tax advantage obtained in circumstance D or circumstance E is cancelled by an assessment to income tax, provisions exist, if the Board are of the opinion that it is just and reasonable in the circumstances to do so, to treat the tax paid as having been paid by way of advance corporation tax (cf. ss. 703(4), (5), and (6), and 705(6) to (8)).

4.16.2.7 Exemptions

4.16.2.7.1 Introduction The tax advantage obtained cannot be counteracted if the taxpayer can show:

(a) that the transaction or transactions in securities were carried out either:

(i) for *bona fide* commercial reasons; or
(ii) in the ordinary course of making or managing investments; and

(b) that none of them has as their main object, or one of their main objects, to enable a tax advantage to be obtained.

There is a clearance procedure (see para. 4.16.2.8 below).

4.16.2.7.2 Commercial reasons The reasons for carrying out a transaction or transactions are a question of subjective intention to be proved by the taxpayer and determined as a matter of fact by the Special Commissioners. A higher court will only interfere with such a finding of fact if the only reasonable conclusion is inconsistent with their determination (*IRC* v *Goodwin* [1976] 1 All ER 481, HL).

In *Clark* v *IRC* [1979] 1 All ER 385, the taxpayer and his brother each owned half of the shares in an investment company, Highland Finance Ltd, whose principal investment was in a quoted company (Caledonian Associated Cinemas Ltd) of which the taxpayer's father was chairman and managing director. The taxpayer was a farmer, and he decided to buy a farm which adjoined his own. To finance the purchase, he decided to sell his shares in Highland. The taxpayer's brother also decided to sell his shares in that company, and in order to comply with their father's wish that control of Caledonian should remain with the family, the brothers sold all their shares in Highland to another investment company controlled by the company.

Fox J held that the taxpayer had carried out the sale for the *bona fide* commercial reason of acquiring the adjoining farm, and, since the reason need not be intrinsic to the transaction, he was entitled to the benefit of the escape clause.

4.16.2.7.3 Ordinary course of investing The second limb of the escape clause, which is an alternative to the first (described in para. 4.16.2.7.2 above), is designed to except from the operation of s. 703 share dealers and the like who engage in transactions in securities in the ordinary course of their business operations. Provided a tax advantage was not the main object or one of the main objects of these transactions, those transactions will escape the effect of s. 703. In *IRC* v *Kleinwort Benson Ltd* [1969] 2 Ch 221, Cross J held that, had circumstance B applied, he would have applied the escape clause:

> As the purchaser was a dealer he was entitled to keep the interest element out of his tax return and so was able to pay a higher price than an ordinary taxpayer would have been able to pay. Similarly, a charity, because it would have been able to reclaim the tax would have been able to pay an equally large price and still make a profit. . . . I do not think that one can fairly say that the object of a charity or a dealer in shares who buys a security with arrears of interest accruing on it is to obtain a tax advantage, simply because the charity or the dealer in calculating the price which they are prepared to pay proceed on the footing that they will have the right which the law gives them either to recover tax or to exclude the interest as the case may be.

4.16.2.7.4 Obtaining a tax advantage To benefit from the escape clause, the taxpayer also has to establish that he, she or it did not have as their main object the obtaining of a tax advantage to the satisfaction of the Special Commissioners. By way of example, in *IRC* v *Brebner* [1967] 2 AC 18, the taxpayer and others were shareholders in two companies, one of which supplied coal on favourable terms for consumption by the other's coal-burning ships. Faced with a take-over bid for the coal-supplying company, the taxpayer and others made a counter-offer at a price based on the need to defeat the original bid. The cash for the counter-offer, which proved successful, was raised by way of a bank loan. In order to repay the loan, the taxpayer and others arranged for the company, first, to capitalise distributable reserves, and secondly, to reduce the company's capital to its original level by repaying the surplus to shareholders. The House of Lords refused to interfere with the Special Commissioners' finding that this transaction in securities had been entered into for *bona fide* commercial reasons and the ensuing tax advantage was not the main object of the transaction.

It is interesting to note that Lord Upjohn said:

> My Lords, I would conclude my judgment by saying only that when the question of carrying out a genuine commercial transaction, as this was, is considered, the fact that there are two ways of carrying it out, one by paying the maximum amount of tax, the other by paying no, or not much, tax it would be quite wrong as a necessary consequence to draw the inference that in adopting the latter course one of the main objects is for the purposes

of the section avoidance of tax. No commercial man in his senses is going to carry out commercial transactions except on the footing of paying the smallest amount of tax involved. The question whether in fact one of the main objects is to avoid tax is one for the Special Commissioners to decide upon the consideration of all the relevant evidence before them and the proper inferences to be drawn from that evidence.

4.16.2.8 Clearance procedure There are many commercial instances where taxpayers enter into transactions which might later be challenged as transactions in securities to which s. 703 applies. It will now be appreciated that the provisions of ss. 703 to 709 are very widely drawn and that any transaction involving securities may be fraught with danger. However, a clearance procedure does exist whereby the Board can be required to state in advance that they are satisfied that s. 703 will not apply (and see Statement of Practice SP 3/80, 26 March 1980 and Press Release, 9 August 1989). The procedure requires the taxpayer to make full and accurate disclosure to the Board of all material facts and considerations relating to any transaction or transactions in respect of which the taxpayer requires clearance (s. 707(1) and (2)). If the Board believe that the particulars supplied are not sufficient for them to satisfy themselves that s. 703 does not apply, they may require the taxpayer to furnish further information (s. 707(1)(a)). Any notification given by the Board that s. 703 does not apply to the taxpayer will be void if the particulars (and any further information supplied by the taxpayer) do not make full and accurate disclosure of all material facts and considerations (s. 707(2)).

Finally, s. 703 can still apply to a transaction or transactions which have been cleared pursuant to s. 707 if they also include another transaction or other transactions not so cleared (s. 707(3)).

4.16.3 Section 739, TA

This provision dates from between the two World Wars. Income tax rates just after the First World War were, comparatively, very high. Consequently, the practice of transferring funds to a trust or company outside the UK which could invest in securities outside the UK tax net began to become popular with wealthy individuals with large incomes and a consequent high income tax liability. Such an individual could, for example, set up a foreign trust to take advantage of the remittance basis then in force or could sell capital assets (there being no CGT at that time) in return for a consideration which could be linked to the purchasing company's or trust's income in such a way as to be capital in the recipient's hands and so on general principles outside the income tax charge (cf. *Perry* v *Astor* (1935) 19 TC 255).

Legislation to counter both the income and capital schemes was introduced by s. 18, FA 1936 and was strengthened in 1938. These provisions (as amended) are now to be found in s. 739, TA. This section is very widely drafted (and has been extended in the Finance Act 1997) and its precise ambit is somewhat unclear.

Section 739, TA is discussed further in Chapter 35.

4.16.4 Section 776, TA

4.16.4.1 Introduction This section is an anti-avoidance section designed to prevent taxpayers turning quasi-trading profits into capital profits. It has far less relevance today with similar tax rates applying whether income or capital gains are realised. Nevertheless differences between the different tax charges remain so that the question of whether the section applies will continue to have relevance in certain circumstances.

Section 776, TA was aimed at transactions such as *Ransom* v *Higgs* (1970) 50 TC 1 (see particularly Lord Wilberforce's speech). It was originally introduced to deal with loopholes in the 1960 and 1962 Finance Acts concerned with stock stripping. In this connection it should be noted that there was no general capital gains tax till 1965. Roy Jenkins's Budget speech introducing the provisions was not particularly illuminating. He said:

> the Finance Bill has retained provisions to counter tax avoidance in three fields. The first relates to the profits arising from land, where the provisions of Sections 21–26 of the FA 1960 have been found to be inadequate to deal with some of the devious schemes for avoiding a charge on dealing although it is abundantly clear that dealing has in fact taken place.

An elephant gun approach was taken in the drafting of what is now s. 776, TA. The section is very widely drafted and expanded still further by s. 777, TA. It must have some limits but these are not obvious. The Revenue have tended in the past, it seems, to use this section where they consider something abusive to have been going on.

Section 776, TA was formerly headed 'artificial transactions in land'. However, it applies to more than this. Its new heading in the TA, 'transactions in land: taxation of capital gains' reflects this. Although subsection (1) provides that s. 776 is enacted to prevent avoidance of tax by persons connected with a development of land, it seems that no intention to avoid tax is necessary for the section's application (see *Page* v *Lowther* [1983] STC 799). Thus a claim that the transaction was a *bona fide* commercial transaction is not of itself a defence but may be relevant to the Revenue's attitude.

Where the section applies the gain is treated as Schedule D, Case VI income for the chargeable period in which the gain is realised and as the income of the person who realised the gain. However the section is wider than this as the provision of an opportunity to someone else to make a gain can also be taxed.

The section seems most likely to apply in circumstances where there is:

(a) an indirect realisation of the land (e.g., a sale of shares in a land-owning company);
(b) a 'slice of the action' is retained;
(c) a passing on of profit to someone else, especially where they are non-UK resident.

These are considered at para. 4.16.4.4. 'Land' includes buildings for these purposes (s. 776(13)(a), TA), as well as any estate or interest in land, so equitable interests are included.

4.16.4.2 When does s. 776 apply?

4.16.4.2.1 General In broad terms there needs to be a gain of a capital nature obtained from the disposal of land or property deriving value from land (e.g., shares in a property company) for the section to apply. 'Disposal' is widely defined for these purposes. By s. 776(4)(a), TA:

> . . . land is disposed of if, by any one or more transactions or by any arrangement or scheme, whether concerning the land or property deriving its value from the land, the property in the land, or control over the land, is effectually disposed of . . .

Thus property in, or control of, the land is caught.

In case this meaning is not wide enough for these purposes it is extended by:

(a) s. 777(2), TA so that any indirect transmission or transfer or alteration in the value of the property may be an occasion of charge; and

(b) s. 777(3) which gives particular examples of what may fall within s. 777(2) such as transactions of option, consent or embargo.

4.16.4.2.2 Conditions for application of s. 776, TA For s. 776, TA to apply there are two sets of conditions in s. 776(2), TA that need to be satisfied. Both conditions need to be satisfied if the section is to apply.

Condition I
Where:

(a) land or property deriving its value from land is acquired with the sole or main object of realising a gain from disposing of the land etc.; or

(b) land is held as trading stock; or

(c) land is developed with the sole or main objects of realising a gain from disposing of the land when developed;

Condition II
Then if a gain of a capital nature is obtained from the disposal of the land:

(i) by the person who acquired, held or developed the land or any connected persons; or

(ii) a scheme or arrangement has been effected allowing a gain to be realised by an indirect method by any person who is a party to or concerned in the arrangements of the scheme;

section 776, TA can apply.

By s. 777(13), TA 'capital amount' means:

> any amount in money or money's worth which . . . does not fall to be included in any computation of income for the purposes of the Tax Acts and other expressions including the word capital shall be construed accordingly.

Consequently, an income profit of a UK trader in land is outside the charge. Vinelott J in *Sugarwhite* v *Budd* ([1987] STC 491 at 501 affirmed [1988] STC 533) said, 'In the absence of evidence to the contrary from the taxpayer these gains must be assumed . . . to be of a capital nature.' 'Obtained' is seemingly a word of wide meaning (see *A-G's Reference (No. 1 of 1988)* [1989] 2 All ER 1).

It should be noted that it does not matter whether a person obtains the gain for himself or for another, the charge can still arise (see s. 776(2) and (8), TA).

4.16.4.2.3 *What is chargeable?* Section 776, TA charges the 'gain of a capital nature' under Schedule D, Case VI (see s. 776(3), TA). Where the section applies the charge arises under Schedule D, Case VI and '. . . such method of computing a gain shall be adopted as is just and reasonable in the circumstances . . .' (s. 776(6), TA). The liability arises when the gain is 'realised' (see s. 777(13), TA and *Yuill* v *Wilson* [1980] STC 460), i.e., when it is effectively enjoyed or the land is disposed of.

4.16.4.3 Who is liable under s. 776? The persons liable under s. 776, TA include:

(a) a person acquiring, holding or developing the land or any person connected with him (s. 776(2)(i), TA);

(b) if there is a scheme or arrangement, any person involved in it (s. 776(2)(ii), TA);

(c) persons transmitting the opportunity of making a gain.

The transmission of the opportunity to make a gain still requires a disposal to trigger the charge.

The concluding words of s. 776(2), TA show that it is immaterial whether the gain is acquired for the person in question or another. Section 776(5) and (8), TA extend this although it seems the better view is that a person who is a bare trustee from the start is to be ignored for these purposes as he has not transmitted the opportunity to make the gain which was always the beneficiary's.

Non-residents can also be caught, see para. 4.16.4.5.

4.16.4.4 Three areas where s. 776 is particularly applicable

4.16.4.4.1 Indirect realisation of land Two cases decided before the section was introduced illustrate what is involved here. In *Ransom v Higgs* (1979) 50 TC 1 there was a complicated 'partnership' scheme for 'stock stripping'. Mr. Higgs procured others to enter into the scheme but was not himself trading. Lord Wilberforce said such an indirect realisation would fall within what is now s. 776, TA.

Associated London Properties v Henriksen (1944) 26 TC 46 involved the indirect realisation of the development value of land by the sale of shares in a property dealing company. The sale was held to be a trading transaction. If it were not trading, s. 776, TA could apply.

4.16.4.4.2 'Slice of the action' *Page v Lowther* (1983) 57 TC 199 is the classic case here. For good commercial and trust reasons, trustees leased land in Kensington to a development company for a premium on the grant of the lease, plus a proportion of the price at which underleases of the properties to be built on the land were granted. This was held to be caught by s. 776.

4.16.4.4.3 Passing profit on Sugarwhite v Budd [1988] STC 533 (affirmed [1987] STC 491) is an example of the kind of transaction caught here. In this case a solicitor arranged transactions via Bahamian companies. The taxpayer was found to be an active party to the arrangements under which he had diverted a capital sum to a Bahamian company to which s. 776 applied.

4.16.4.5 Non-UK residents
Section 776 is not limited to UK residents. Section 776(14), TA provides: 'This section shall apply to all persons, whether resident in the UK or not . . .'

Withholding at basic rate (23%) from the consideration can be directed by the Board if it appears to the Board that the recipient is not resident in the UK (see s. 777(9), TA). This is harder to apply in England than in Scotland as entries in the proprietor section of the land register are made in England only after the transaction is completed.

4.16.4.6 Exceptions
There are three specific exceptions from s. 776. These are:

(a) trading profits;
(b) transactions involving an individual's principal private residence; and
(c) shares in a company disposing of land in the normal course of its business.

PART II
Income tax

CHAPTER FIVE
Income tax – general principles

5.1 INCOME TAX – INTRODUCTORY MATTERS[1]

Income tax is an annual tax, which has to be imposed each year by Parliament (see s. 1, TA and Chapter 2 above on PCTA). The income tax legislation has been consolidated a number of times but still bears the marks of its ancient origins, e.g., the deduction for an employee's horse in s. 198, TA. Accordingly it is necessary to understand some of its history to appreciate its modern form.

5.2 HISTORY[2]

Income tax was introduced from 1 January 1799 by William Pitt the Younger to pay for the Napoleonic Wars, despite his earlier opposition to the idea of an income tax. However Pitt's Triple Assessment of 1798 proved unpopular even though no tax was payable on incomes below £60. It was said to be 'remarkable how large a number of persons declared their income as just under £60.' The tax produced half its expected yield.

Income tax was considered to be a serious infringement of privacy. One of the reasons for this was that a general return of income had to be made under 19 'cases'. The tax was also easily evaded.

Addington succeeded Pitt in 1801. He introduced the Income Tax Act of 1803 which contained two important changes to the structure of the tax. These are still with us today:

---

[1] See Whiteman, *Income Tax*; *Simon's Taxes*, Volume A, passim.
[2] See generally H.H. Monroe, '*Intolerable Inquisition? Reflections on the Law of Tax.*' (Hamlyn Lectures, 32nd series).

(a) Deduction of tax at source by a disinterested third party.[3]

(b) The Schedular system. Instead of a general return, separate returns for different sources of income were to be made to different officials. This 'sweetened the bitter pill of disclosure'.

The different sources were enumerated in Schedules (and the Schedular system is still the basis of our income tax notwithstanding that the main reason for its introduction has gone).

Income tax was abolished as from 6 April 1816. When it was reintroduced in 1842 by Peel it was intended as a temporary tax. Gladstone later intended to end it but the Crimean War made this inexpedient. So, despite its contemplated abolition in the 1870s, income tax remains with us. However, even to this day, it is a temporary tax imposed only a year at a time. Potential difficulties in respect of the collection of tax are overcome by the Provisional Collection of Taxes Act 1968 (see Chapter 2 above).

The major twentieth century changes to income tax have concerned the rate structure and the proportion of the population covered by the tax. The tax has been transformed from:

> a primitive tax imposed at low rates on the few citizens who had relatively high incomes, to a modern sophisticated tax which is imposed at rather higher rates on the many citizens, including those who have relatively low incomes.[4]

Until 1911 income tax was a proportional tax, i.e., everyone paid tax at a fixed rate subject to exemption below a certain limit and an abatement for income above it. A distinction was introduced in 1907 between 'earned' and 'unearned' income. Earned income relief reduced the amount of the income brought into charge, although tax remained proportional on that income. 'Differentiation', i.e., treating income from investments and employment differently, was recommended by a Select Committee chaired by Sir Charles Dilke.[5] 'Graduation', i.e., taxing larger incomes at a higher rate, was one of the reforms proposed in Lloyd George's Budget of 1909 although Gladstone in earlier times had rejected it as 'tending towards communism'. Graduation took the form of an additional tax called 'supertax' and was introduced by Lloyd George as part of his 1909 War Budget against poverty.

Winston Churchill (Chancellor of the Exchequer from 1922–1928) turned supertax into surtax in 1927. Surtax was to be part of income tax but payable a year later. However, the tax base of surtax differed from that of income tax so that income could be subjected to both income tax and surtax. The two

---

[3.] This seems to owe much to the Land Tax under which deduction and retaining of tax from rental payments had been permitted since the fourteenth century according to Sabine, *A Short History of Taxation*, Butterworths (1980).

[4.] James and Nobes, *The Economics of Taxation*, 1996/97 edn, p. 150.

[5.] A colourful character who resigned after a scandal (see the biography by David Nicholas, *The Lost Prime Minister*, Hambledon Press). He was involved in an infamous divorce case as the man who was in bed with two women, one of whom was shocked by his knowledge of 'French practices'.

taxes were finally amalgamated by Anthony Barber by the Finance Act 1971 as from 6 April 1973 in the 'Unified System' (see ss. 32–39, FA 1971).

5.3 THE BASIC PRINCIPLES OF UK INCOME TAX – SOURCE DOCTRINE

5.3.1 Income

One consequence of the Schedular system is that there is no definition of 'income' as such in the UK tax legislation. To be liable to income tax, 'income' must fall within a taxable source listed in the statute. If it is not within one of the sources made taxable by the legislation no income tax is due in respect of that income.[6]

This effect may be illustrated by a number of cases. In *Dickinson v Abel* (1969) 45 TC 353 payment to a person, who made an introduction, by way of a gift was held not taxable by Pennycuick J. Viscount Haldane said in *National Provident Institution v Brown* (1921) 8 TC 57:

> ... My lords, in *London County Council v The Attorney General* [1901] AC 26 it was decided by this House that the Income Tax Acts ... do no more than impose a single tax on profits and gains brought into charge by the Income Tax Acts. There is no special or peculiar tax under each Case of Schedule D and the other Schedules or their branches, whatever be the idiosyncrasies of the methods prescribed for collection. The expression Income Tax, as used by the legislature, was a generic description of the tax which was levied under all the Schedules alike and it was not meant to be anything but a tax on income. There was imposed under the Schedules no collection of taxes distinct from each other, but simply one tax with standards for assessment which varied according to the sources from which the taxable income was derived ...

In *Cull v Cowcher* (1934) 18 TC 449 Cull was held to have been properly assessed as the source, money on deposit, had not ceased. The case of *Purchase v Stainer's Executors* (1951) 32 TC 367 (see also *Bray v Best* [1989] STC 159) concerned earnings of Leslie Howard (Stainer), 'the well known film actor'. He made several films, including 'The 49th Parallel', on the basis that he would be paid a percentage of the gross receipts. The sums due to him could not be ascertained for some considerable time; in some circumstances they could not be determined till after he was dead. His executors were assessed on payments they received after his death notwithstanding that no assessments could have been raised under Schedule D, Case II. The Special Commissioners' decision to discharge the assessment as the sums did not fall within Schedule D, Cases II, III or IV was upheld.

[6.] See, for example, *NPI v Brown* (1921) 8 TC 57 (see para. 5.3.1) and *Bray v Best* [1989] STC 159 (now reversed by legislation). Trustees made an allocation to an employee on the winding up of a trust. The taxpayer was assessed on the basis of emoluments from his employment for the last year or over the period employed, although he was not an employee of the relevant company at the time of allocation.

5.3.2 *Situs*

It was seen in Chapter 1 that UK tax may be imposed on the income of non-UK residents if their income is generated from a UK source.[7] The determination of the situs of a source of income is generally made in accordance with the normal rules of private international law, although in some circumstances the statute may make special provision.

5.3.3 Capital and income

Clearly, *income tax* can only be imposed on *income*. Thus, the distinction between capital and income is one of the essential distinctions in tax law. It determines which tax regime applies to the profit or gain in question. Some of the difficulties of distinguishing between income and capital have been considered in Chapter 1.

Lord Macnaghten said in *LCC* v *A-G* (1900) 4 TC 265 (at p. 293, which has been quoted ever since):

'Income Tax, if I may be pardoned for saying so, is a tax on income. It is not meant to be a tax on anything else. It is one tax not a collection of taxes essentially distinct. There is no difference in kind between the duties of income tax assessed under Schedule D and those assessed under Schedule A or any of the other Schedules of charge. One man has fixed property, another lives by his wits, each contributes to the tax if his income is above the prescribed limit. The standard of assessment varies according to the nature of the source from which taxable income is derived. In every case the tax is a tax on income, whatever may be the standard by which the income is measured.

5.3.4 The charge to income tax

Section 1 of the Income and Corporation Taxes Act 1988 ('TA') provides (inter alia):

The charge to income tax
(1) Income tax shall be charged in accordance with the provisions of the Income Tax Acts in respect of all property, profits or gains respectively described or comprised in the Schedules A, D, E and F, set out in sections 15 to 20 or which in accordance with the Income Tax Acts are to be brought into charge to tax under any of those Schedules or otherwise.

The various Schedules are summarised in the chart at the end of this chapter.

Proportions of a pound are charged (s. 2, TA) but no tax can be charged on amounts of less than one penny. In practice, liability is rounded down to the nearest pound after calculation to the nearest pound.

[7.] See also Stephen Edge, Taxation – By Source or Residence? in *Recent Tax Problems* (ed. Dyson) 1985.

Income tax – general principles

5.3.5 Year of assessment

Income tax (and capital gains tax) are assessed in respect of each 'year of assessment'. The year of assessment runs from 6 April one year to 5 April the following year. The reason for this is historical and it would cost over £1 billion to change according to the Treasury Select Committee. Originally the tax year started on Lady Day, 25 March.[8] When the calendar was changed the government did not wish to lose any tax so the start of the tax year was changed.

5.3.6 'Annual profits or gains'

The Schedules are mainly concerned with 'profits' or 'gains'. These words have been taken to mean profits or gains of an annual nature (see, e.g., Lord Macnaghten in *LCC v A-G* at para. 5.3.3).

5.3.7 The mutual exclusivity of the Schedules

The Schedules are mutually exclusive and although the Revenue may not, generally, elect to assess a taxpayer under one Schedule rather than another in order, for example, to raise more revenue, it may be able to elect between cases within the same Schedule. This may be illustrated by the following three cases.

The first case is *Fry v Salisbury House Estate* (1930) 15 TC 266. This concerned a company which owned a property of about 800 rooms in central London let as offices. In addition to rent, the company also received moneys from the ancillary services it provided such as porters and cleaners. The company agreed that its profits from the ancillary services fell within Schedule D, Case I, but challenged the Revenue's assertion that the rental income was also subject to tax as the profits of a trade under Schedule D, Case I as opposed to Schedule A. The company won. Viscount Dunedin said (at p. 308):

> ... it being imperative to deal with rents under Schedule A there is no possibility of subsequently dealing with them under Schedule D ... when income is dealt with in the property Schedule the same income cannot be dealt with again under another Schedule ... once assigned to its appropriate Schedule, the same income cannot be attributed to another Schedule.[9]

[8.] The Feast of the Annunciation of the Blessed Virgin Mary. This had been inherited from the Land Tax, much of the administration of which was derived from the Church.

[9.] See also Lord Atkin (at p. 319): 'The scheme of the Income Tax Acts is and has always been to provide for the taxation of specific properties under Schedules appropriated to them and under a general Schedule D to provide for the taxation of income not specifically [covered] ... nothing could be clearer to indicate that the Schedules are mutually exclusive; that the specific income must be assessed under the specific Schedule.' Lord Tomlin said (at p. 325): '... as between Schedule A and other Schedules the Revenue authority has no option to select the Schedule to be applied ...'

The second case is *Mitchell and Edon* v *Ross* (1961) 40 TC 11. The issue here was the deductibility of expenses of doctors who held part time NHS appointments (taxable under Schedule E) and carried on private practice (taxable under Schedule D). In Viscount Simond's view the single question was whether expenses incurred in earning Schedule E profits were deductible for Schedule D purposes. He considered they were not, regarding it as settled law that the Schedules are mutually exclusive and each Schedule affords a complete code for its relative class of income.

However, the Revenue may elect between two or more cases in a Schedule if income could fit into either of them. So in *Liverpool and London and Globe Insurance Company* v *Bennett* (1913) 6 TC 327, Lord Shaw of Dunfermline said (at p. 376): '. . . it is well settled that if a sufficient warrant be found in the Statute for taxation under alternative heads the alternative lies with the taxing authority . . .' (See also *Fry* v *Salisbury House* above.)

5.3.8 Summary

(a) The Schedules are mutually exclusive.[10]

(b) If income is not within any Schedule it escapes income tax altogether.[11]

(c) Income is classified and taxed according to its source. If income has no source in a particular year it is not liable to income tax in absence of special provisions.[12]

(d) Different bases of computation apply under each Schedule.

5.4 COMPUTATION OF THE INCOME TAX CHARGE

Income tax is not a collection of different taxes but one tax charged on different sources of income (see Lord Macnaghten in *LCC* v *A-G* (para. 5.3.3). The 'total income' of the taxpayer from all sources has to be calculated.

Section 835, TA defines 'total income' for the purposes of the Income Tax Acts. It provides:

> (1) In the Income Tax Acts 'total income', in relation to any person, means the total income of that person from all sources estimated in accordance with the provisions of the Income Tax Acts . . .
>
> (6) In estimating the total income of any person:
>
> (a) any income which is chargeable with income tax by way of deduction at the basic rate or lower rate in force for any year or which for the purposes of Schedule F comprises an amount . . . equal to a tax credit calculated by reference to the rate of advance corporation tax in force for any year shall be deemed to be income of that year, and

---

[10] *Mitchell and Edon* v *Ross* (1961) 40 TC 11 applied in *IRC* v *Brander & Cruickshank* (1971) 46 TC 574.

[11] For example, *Dickinson* v *Abel*.

[12] For example, on post cessation receipts, s. 202A, TA.

Income tax – general principles

(b) any deductions which are allowable on account of sums payable under deduction of income tax at the basic rate in force for any year out of the property or profits of that person shall be allowed as deductions in respect of that year;

notwithstanding that the income or sums, as the case may be, accrued or will accrue in whole or in part before or after that year.

(7) Where an assessment has become final and conclusive for the purposes of income tax for any year of assessment:

(a) that assessment shall also be final and conclusive in estimating total income; and

(b) no allowance or adjustment of liability, on the ground of diminution of income or loss, shall be taken into account in estimating total income unless that allowance or adjustment has previously been made on an application under the special provisions of the Income Tax Acts relating thereto.

(8) The provisions of subsection (7) shall apply in relation to:

(a) any relief under section 353 [interest set off against income subject to income tax];

(b) any relief by reason of the operation of an election for the herd basis under Schedule 5; and

(c) any allowance under Parts I to VI of the Capital Allowances Act 1990 to be given by way of discharge or repayment of tax and to be available or available primarily against a specified class of income (that is to say any capital allowance to which section 141 of the Capital Allowances Act 1990 applies, or, as provided by section 532 of this Act, any capital allowance to which section 528(2) of this Act applies);

as it applies in relation to allowances or adjustments on the ground of diminution of income or loss.

So income computed in accordance with the rules in Schedules A, C (now repealed by FA 1996), D, E and F is added together to form the taxpayer's total income. Certain expenses may be allowed in computing the income of each Schedule. Since some income is subject to deduction of tax at source, that income must be 'grossed up' to take account of the tax paid. The taxpayer is then given a credit for the tax paid.

Example

If A, a basic rate taxpayer receives £77,000 of income because £23,000 of tax has been withheld from the gross amount of £100,000 the position is as follows:

	£,000
Receipt	77
Tax credit	23
Gross amount to be included in taxpayer's total income	100
A is then given credit for the tax paid so:	
Total income	100
Tax @ 23%	23
Tax credit	23
Tax payable	NIL

Once the taxpayer's total income has been computed, it is subject to a number of adjustments to take account of any deductions from total income ('charges on income') and any personal reliefs etc. to which the taxpayer is entitled. The resulting figure will be the taxpayer's 'taxable income'.

5.5 CHARGES ON INCOME

In some circumstances a taxpayer can 'alienate' income so that it will not be regarded as his for income tax purposes even though it is initially received by the taxpayer. A lawyer would normally regard as income that which 'came in' and would not be concerned with what was done with the income, i.e., how it was appropriated. However, in some circumstances it may be right to regard the receipt as belonging to someone else, for example, in the case of an annuity charged by legal right upon property.

The classic statement on charges on income is the speech of Viscount Radcliffe in *IRC v Frere* [1965] AC 402. He said:

> This recognition of a division of ownership between two or more persons entitled to rights in a single 'fund' of income was not, however, confined to such cases as those where there was trust income or an annuity charge. There was also the case of 'annual' or 'yearly' interest – I do not distinguish between the two adjectives – payable under a mortgage, the characteristic feature of which seems to have been that in setting up the mortgage situation, the borrower had in effect divided the gross income of his estate between himself and the mortgagee. Up to this point it could fairly be said that the division corresponded with and followed the lines of enforceable legal rights in an identifiable fund of property, the accruing income. But the tax system can be seen to go further than this, for it applied the same idea of division of proprietary right to situations in which legal distinctions draw no dividing line. Thus an annual payment secured by personal covenant only, involving no charge on any actual security, whether income or capital, was treated in the same way for tax purposes. It had to be 'annual' and it had also to be payable 'out of the profits or gains brought into charge' in order to rank as income for payee not of payer, because it was the division of taxable income with which the code was dealing; and it may well be asked what at this stage is the significance of the words 'out of' as applied to a payment, the obligation for which was merely the personal one to find the money required out of whatever resources the payer might mobilise for the purpose. The answer was provided by the application of what is in truth an accountant's, not a lawyer's conception, for it was accepted that, so far as the payer was found to have in the relevant year a taxable income larger than the gross amount required to make the payment, to that extent he was entitled to claim that he had made the payment 'out of profits or gains brought into charge' and to deduct and retain for his own account tax at what in due course (after 1927) became the 'standard rate'.

Charges on income may be illustrated as follows. In 1980 John covenanted to pay £100 p.a. for seven years to Jane. John's income is £1,100 paid as rent by Lee. The diagram represents this.

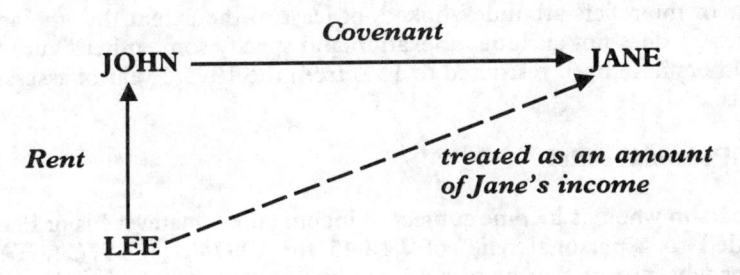

Figure 5.1

John has a liability to income tax under Schedule A on £1,100. Jane has a liability on £100 received from John under Schedule D, Case III. John should be entitled to a reduction in his total income of £100 as he has passed the income directly on to Jane. The deduction is called a charge on income. The rules as to covenants have changed since 1980 for individuals but remain for charities.

Thus certain receipts are regarded for tax purposes as not being income of the recipient but as income of someone else, i.e., the income has been alienated to the other. However, in some cases the recipient may have to act as unpaid tax collector (see para. 5.7.3). The old s. 8(8), TA (since substituted by FA 1990, s. 90(1), (5)) defines 'charges on income' as 'amounts which fall to be deducted in computing total income' for return purposes.

5.6 RELIEFS

5.6.1 General

A certain part of every taxpayer's total income is exempt from income tax because of the existence of certain income tax reliefs. These days the reliefs are given because of his personal situation not because of the type of income involved, as sometimes in the past. The effect is to reduce the taxpayer's average rate of tax.

The reliefs must be claimed (s. 256, TA). These details will be included in the forms for self-assessment. Reliefs can only be claimed up to the amount of the taxpayer's total income. They cannot be used to create losses. Unused reliefs cannot be carried forward or back to other years.

Reliefs cannot be set against charges on income. Payments made under deduction of income tax under s. 348, TA are included in total income for the purposes of charging basic rate income tax only (s. 276, TA). This is because the income is not treated as belonging to the taxpayer. The taxpayer is simply acting as tax collector for the Inland Revenue and if, in the case of a s. 348 payment, the income on which the Inland Revenue are allowed to collect basic rate tax were to be absorbed by reliefs, the Inland Revenue would not be able collect the tax due to them.

Some of the reliefs are index-linked, at least to the extent that the annual Finance Act does not exclude indexation and specify some other figure (s. 1, TA). Others have been restricted to 15% from the 1995/6 year of assessment onwards.

5.6.2 Personal relief

Every person who has income subject to income tax (whatever his or her age) is entitled to a personal relief of £4,045 for 1997/8, (s. 257(1), TA). A taxpayer who proves that he was 65 or older at any time during the year of assessment is entitled to a higher personal allowance of £5,220 for 1997/8. If he can prove that he or his wife was 65 or older at any time during the year of assessment, he is entitled to the higher married allowance of £3,185 for 1997/8 restricted to 15%, provided that his wife is living with him or is wholly maintained voluntarily by him (s. 257(A)(2), TA). However, if the taxpayer's total income exceeds £15,600 for 1997/8, these higher figures are reduced by one-half of the excess of total income over that figure, but in any event, the reduction will not deprive the taxpayer of the general personal allowance (s. 257(5), TA).

An increased personal relief is available for those aged 75 and over. The relief is £5,400 for a single person over that age, and a married couple's allowance of £3,225 (restricted to 15%) is available where either spouse in a married couple is over that age. This is instead of the higher relief for those aged 65 or over, but the limits for a high total income are similar.

From 1990–91, age allowances are available depending on the age of either spouse, the married woman being entitled to an age allowance in her own right (s. 257A, TA). There are also transitional provisions to protect couples where the age allowance is currently available on the basis of the husband's age rather than the wife's (s. 257E, TA).

The independent taxation of spouses from 1990–91 involved changes in the personal reliefs available to married people. Both spouses now have their own single person's allowance. In addition, a married man is entitled to an extra allowance (currently £1,830) (but restricted to 15% from the 1995/6 year of assessment onwards) (s. 257A, TA 1988). To the extent that the husband's income is too low to make use of this extra allowance, the spouses can elect that it be set against the wife's income, though the husband's basic personal allowance will not be transferable (s. 257B, TA). The fact that the extra allowance goes primarily to the husband does of course mean that married couples will not become entirely equal and separate in tax terms. However from 1993–94 it is possible for the couple together or for the wife alone, to elect that half of the extra allowance should go to the wife (s. 257B TA). Also from 1993–94, any part of the extra allowance which is not used because it exceeds the husband's income can be claimed by the wife (s. 257B, TA).

5.6.3 Additional personal relief

The plight of 'one-parent' families has attracted attention in recent years, and s. 259, TA represents an attempt to alleviate the problem. The 'parent' who is alone is entitled to the single person's allowance of £4,045 plus an additional relief of £1,830 (restricted to 15%) for 1997/8. The relief is not confined to 'parents' in the natural sense, but applies to any man or woman who is not married and living with her or his spouse. Thus the claimant need not be living alone; it is sufficient that the person living with him or her is not a spouse.

The relief is given to a claimant who has a 'qualifying child' resident with him for the whole or part of the year of assessment (s. 259(2), TA) though the amount of the relief is the same no matter how many qualifying children there are (s. 259(3), TA). A qualifying child is a child who:

(a) is

    (i) born in the year of assessment, or
    (ii) under the age of 16 at the beginning of the year, or
    (iii) 16 or over at the beginning of the year and is receiving full-time instruction at any university, college, school or other educational establishment or is undergoing training by an employer for any trade, profession or vocation in such circumstances that the child is required to devote the whole of his time to the training for a period of not less than two years; and

(b) is

    (i) a child of the claimant: this includes a stepchild, an adopted child under the age of 18 at the time of adoption, and an illegitimate child if the claimant has married the other parent after the child's birth; or
    (ii) born in, or under 18 at the beginning of the year and maintained at the claimant's expense for the whole or part of the year (s. 259(5), TA).

The relief is also available to a married man who is entitled to the married man's allowance but whose wife was totally incapacitated by physical or mental infirmity throughout the year of assessment (s. 259(1)(c), TA).

It will be appreciated that because a qualifying child need only reside with the claimant for part of the year, there may be two or more claims in respect of the same child. In these circumstances, s. 260 apportions the relief between the claimants either in the proportion agreed by the claimants themselves or in proportion to the length of the periods for which the child is resident with them during the year of assessment (s. 260(1) and (3)). From 1993–94 it is possible to claim relief in the year in which a couple separate (s. 261, TA). In the past, it was possible when an unmarried couple lived together and had more than one child, for each to claim the additional personal relief. From 1989–90, this is no longer possible as in such a case they will only be able to claim relief in respect of the youngest relevant child (s. 259(4A), TA).

5.6.4 Widow's bereavement allowance

Where a married man dies and he was or would have been entitled to the married couple's relief for the year of assessment in which he dies, his widow may claim a relief of £1,830 for 1997/8 (restricted to 15%) for the year of assessment in which he dies and (unless she remarries in the year of assessment in which he dies) for the following year of assessment (s. 262, TA).

5.6.5 Blind persons' relief

If the taxpayer is a registered blind person for the whole or part of the year of assessment, he is entitled to a relief of £1,280 for 1997/8 (s. 265(1), TA). If the taxpayer is married and his or her spouse lives with him or her but the taxpayer has insufficient income to absorb the relief, the relief may be deducted from the spouse's income.

5.6.6 Medical insurance

Tax relief for premiums paid for medical insurance was introduced from 6 April 1990 by ss. 54–57, FA 1989. For the relief to be available:

(a) the premium must be paid by an individual under a contract for private medical insurance which is eligible for relief;
(b) the payment must not be made out of resources provided by another person for that purpose; and
(c) the payment must not otherwise attract tax relief.

The relief is only available if the contract insures an individual who at the time the payment is made is aged 60 or over and is resident in the United Kingdom, or more than one person, each of whom satisfies this condition. If the policy insures a married couple, at least one of whom is aged 60 or over, and both are resident in the United Kingdom, relief will be available.

The relief is given by allowing the premium to be deducted from the payer's income in the year in which the payment is made, so long as a claim is made to that effect. Since the person making the payments does not have to be the insured person, the government hope to encourage people to take advantage of the tax relief to make provision for their older relatives. Regulations provide that payments attracting tax relief may be paid net of basic rate tax, the recipient insurer being able to reclaim the amount deducted from the Inland Revenue. Tax relief can be withdrawn if necessary.[13] If relief is due at the higher rate, it will be dealt with by the individual's tax office.

The requirements for eligible contracts are set out in s. 55, FA 1989. The scheme must be run by an approved insurer, and can only offer approved

---

[13.] SI 1989/2387 and SI 1989/2388.

Income tax – general principles

benefits. The period of insurance must not exceed one year from the date the policy is entered into, and the contract must not be connected with any other contract. The contract must be in a standard form and must be certified under s. 56, FA 1989, for which it must only provide indemnity in respect of all or part of the costs of treatments, medical services, cash benefits, and other matters specified in regulations made by the Treasury, and the premium must be reasonable. There are provisions for certification to be revoked. Further regulations about the availability of tax relief on medical insurance policies may be made under s. 57, FA 1989, including what variations from the standard form of medical insurance contracts may be allowed.

5.6.7 Non-residents

An individual not resident in the UK is not entitled to reliefs (s. 278(1), TA) unless he or she:

(a) is a Commonwealth citizen or an EEA (European Economic Area) national; or
(b) is resident in the Isle of Man or the Channel Islands; or
(c) has previously been resident in the United Kingdom but is now resident abroad for the sake of his or her health or the health of a member of the family resident with him or her; or
(d) is or has been in the service of the Crown, or is the widow of such a person (s. 278(1), TA).

The foreign income of a wife who is not chargeable to tax in the United Kingdom does not form part of the husband's income.

5.7 RATES OF INCOME TAX

5.7.1 General

Since the introduction of the 'Unified System' (see para. 5.2) income tax has been charged at different rates namely 'Lower Rate', 'Basic Rate' and, above a certain level, 'Higher Rate'. Previously income above a certain level was liable to an investment income surcharge which could be justified on the grounds that, unlike earned income, unearned income did not involve the 'pain' of earning it. This has now been abolished. The position now is the opposite in that, generally 'savings' or investment income is charged at a lower rate than earned income.

The economic theory on tax and savings is complex and diffuse. Some argue that on the basis that savings equal investment, in retrospect investment should be taxed at lesser or nil rate. Others argue that the source of the income is irrelevant as it is the possibility of expenditure that gives power.

There are special rules for dividends (now extended to other investment income by FA 1996). These are taxable under Schedule F but carry an additional 20% tax credit to reflect the tax paid by the company on the payment of the dividend (see Chapter 27). An individual recipient of a dividend is subject to tax on the dividend plus the tax credit, however, any income which is not chargeable at the higher rate of tax is chargeable at the lower rate of tax, i.e., at 20% (s. 1A, TA). The tax credit thus satisfies the full liability of basic rate taxpayers, although higher rate taxpayers will have additional tax to pay.

The thresholds and bands of higher rate tax are indexed by reference to the Retail Price Index unless Parliament decides otherwise (s. 1(4), TA).

5.7.2 Lower rate

From 1992–93 a new lower rate of tax was introduced (s. 9, FA 1992 and s. 19 F(No.2)A 1992). This rate applies to the first £4,100 of taxable income and the rate is set at 20% (s. 35, FA 1995). The government has announced a desire to move to a 20% basic rate of tax when circumstances allow and this is intended to be a first step, giving most benefits to low earners.[14]

5.7.3 Basic rate

The basic rate of income tax for 1997–8 is 23%. This rate is applied to the second (up to £26,100) band of taxable income. However, if the taxpayer makes any payment subject to deduction of income tax under s. 348, TA 1988 which is required to be included in his total income for the purposes of basic rate tax only, the amount of the payment will effectively increase the figure of £26,100. This is because the amount of the payment will be deductible as a charge on income when computing higher rate tax liability, and will not therefore be taken into account when computing whether total income exceeds £26,100 and yet s. 3, TA 1988 only allows the Inland Revenue to collect basic rate income tax on the payment. This somewhat tortuous process reflects the legal position: the taxpayer is not legally entitled to the income and therefore ought not to be taxed as though the income were his; he acts only as a tax collector on behalf of the recipient of the payment. In other words, he is paying the recipient's income tax, not his own, and in effect the deduction as a charge on income for higher rate tax purposes and s. 3 achieve the separate taxation of the payment at basic rate.

5.7.4 Higher rate

Formerly, once the taxpayer had income in excess of the basic rate band, he was taxed progressively in five higher rate 'bands' rising to a top rate of 60%. From 1988–89, these bands were replaced by a single higher rate of 40% on all income in excess of the basic rate limit, currently £26,100. This substantial change caused some controversy, and has altered many considerations in tax planning. Tax avoidance is less important with a top rate of 40%, and with

---

[14] The downside of this commitment to a general 20% rate is that the government have restricted many reliefs to 15% from 1995/6, see para. 5.6).

Income tax – general principles

capital gains being charged to tax at an individual's marginal rate of income tax; planning based on distinctions between income and capital gains has lost much of its point.

As noted above, for the purposes of higher rate tax, taxable income does not include s. 348, TA payments, which are charges on income for this purpose and liable only to basic rate income tax.

The existence of a progressive rate of income tax makes it inevitable that taxpayers will want to set their reliefs against that class of income which is subject to the highest rates of tax. Generally the taxpayer is entitled to make the deduction that will result in the greatest reduction of his liability (s. 835(4), TA) though deductions for personal reliefs are to be made last (s. 835(5), TA). However, government policy in the last two years has been to restrict certain reliefs, initially to 20% and, in 1995/6, to 15%. This has been discussed at para. 5.6.

5.7.5 Rate applicable to trusts

A special rate of tax is applicable to certain income of discretionary trusts. This is 34%. The income tax treatment of discretionary trusts is discussed in Chapter 14 below.

5.8 ASSESSMENT AND COLLECTION

Having applied income tax at the lower, basic and higher rates, as appropriate to the taxpayer's taxable income, the inspector of taxes will send the taxpayer an assessment detailing the amount of tax due. Before he does this, however, the Inspector will deduct from the tax due any income tax which has been collected at source on the taxpayer's behalf (see above). The amount of income tax due may also be reduced by 'top-slicing' relief, where available and by double taxation relief. This will change with the move to self-assessment.

Income tax is payable on or before 1 January in the year of assessment for which it is due or, if it is later, at the expiration of 30 days from the date of the issue of the assessment (s. 5(1), TA) although income from any trade, profession or vocation is due in two equal instalments, the first on or before 1 January and the second on or before the following 1 July or, if in either case it would be later, at the expiration of 30 days from the date of the issue of the assessment (s. 5(2) and (3), TA). Any higher rate tax due in respect of a payment from which basic rate income tax was deducted at source is due on or before 1 December in the year of assessment after that for which the tax is due (s. 5(4), TA). Payments under the Pay As You Earn scheme are made at the time a payment of income is made to the taxpayer. This scheme takes into account all the factors discussed in this chapter through the coding mechanism, and if the taxpayer is assessed only under Schedule E no further assessment or payment of tax will be due.

The Main Charging Provisions for Income Tax – Charged by Assessment

Schedule	Nature of Income Chargeable	Person Chargeable	Basis of Charge
SCH A s. 15	Income from property in land (after 1969–70) previously charged under Case VIII of Sch. D.	Recipient	On profits arising in the relevant tax year.
SCH B	Commercial woodlands (when occupier has not elected for Sch. D). **REPEALED FA 1988**	Occupier	On one-third of annual value.
SCH C s. 17	Dividends and interest on government securities, with certain exceptions (see charge by deduction below). **REPEALED FA 1996**	Paying bank or agent	On dividends of current year.
SCH D s. 18			
Case I	Profits of trade, including 'concerns' transferred to Sch D, farming and woodlands (if elected for Sch. D).	Trader	On profits of current account year.
Case II	Profits of a profession or vocation.	Professional person	On profits of current account year.

The Main Charging Provisions for Income Tax – Charged by Assessment

Schedule	Nature of Income Chargeable	Person Chargeable	Basis of Charge
SCH D s. 18			
Case III	Interest, annual payments etc.	Recipient (Case III) or payer (ss. 348, 349, 350)	On profits arising in the current year (or profits received in the current year if the remittance basis applies).
Case IV & V	Foreign income.	Recipient	On profits arising in the current year (or profits received in the current year if the remittance basis applies).
Case VI	Miscellaneous special types of income.	Recipient	On profits arising in the current year (or profits received in the current year if the remittance basis applies).

The Main Charging Provisions for Income Tax – Charged by Assessment

Schedule	Nature of Income Chargeable	Person Chargeable	Basis of Charge
SCH E (Cases I–III) s. 19	Emoluments from offices and employments (see charge by deduction below).	Recipient	On receipts attributable to current year.
SCH E (gen charge)	Pensions (see charge by deduction below).	Recipient	On receipts attributable to current year.
	Income arising to trustees of discretionary trusts applicable to trusts.	Trustees	On income received in current year.

CHAPTER SIX
Schedule E – income from employment

6.1 INTRODUCTION

This chapter is concerned with the taxation of income from offices and employments[1] – income tax under Schedule E. Schedule E is generally the most important of the Schedules under which income tax is charged. Its importance is in both in terms of the number of people it affects and the amount of revenue raised under it.

6.2 WHAT IS SCHEDULE E CONCERNED WITH?

Schedule E is concerned with income from offices and employment. In general terms there are three matters which are charged under Schedule E. These are:

(a) wages, salaries, directors fees etc. from offices or employment (para. 1, s. 19, TA);

(b) most annuities, pensions and stipends derived from employment (paras 2–4, s. 19, TA);

(c) a miscellaneous collection of benefits which are directed to be charged under Schedule E. This specifically includes such matters as pensions (para. 3, s. 19, e.g., a voluntary pension under s. 133, TA and strictly termination payments), some social security payments (s. 617, TA) and similar matters.

The charge under Schedule E will be considered later in greater detail. However, before that it is necessary to look briefly at the history of Schedule

---

[1.] See Whiteman, *Income Tax* and *Simon's Direct Taxes*.

E as it explains the present structure of Schedule E and its relationship to other Schedules.[2]

Four general points about Schedule E should first be noted. These are as follows.

(a) Schedule E is on a current year basis, in other words, it is charged on the emoluments for the year (see para. 1, s. 19(1), TA).

(b) Most tax under Schedule E, as anyone who has been employed will be only too painfully aware, is collected by deduction of tax at source by the employer under the pay as you earn or PAYE system. The employers by acting as unpaid tax gatherers save much government time and money.[3]

(c) Schedule E has limited expense rules (compared with, e.g., Schedule D, Case I see Chapter 10).

(d) Schedule E has special provisions dealing with termination payments (see s. 148 and s. 188, TA). This can have the effect of charging what might otherwise be thought of as capital payments to income tax.[4]

6.3 IMPORTANCE OF HISTORY OF SCHEDULE E

As will be recalled, income tax was introduced as a temporary measure in January 1799 by Pitt the Younger to pay for the Napoleonic war. The schedular system was introduced by Addington to remedy some of the defects of the original system. Originally tax under Schedule E was charged on the income of all *public* offices or employments of profit within the UK. These included offices of either House of Parliament,[5] of any court of justice in the UK, offices or employments of profit under any company or society whether corporate or not and most helpfully of all, 'all other public offices or employments which are of a public nature'. These, generally, were occupations where the annual profits of the office or employment could be readily ascertained and where the employer or paymaster was a trustworthy disinterested party on whom the obligation to deduct tax at source could be placed with confidence. By 1918 payments by railway companies and to public officials were subject, in practice, to deduction of income tax at source. Income tax was also charged under Schedule E in respect of annuities, pensions or stipends payable by the Crown or out of public revenue.

Income tax in respect of employments other than public employments was then chargeable under Schedule D, Case II.[6] The word 'public' and the need for some element of 'publicity' in Schedule E caused some difficulty but few

---

[2.] Neither of these would be the way one chose to set up a system from scratch. They have emerged over the years.

[3.] See, for example, the various Institute of Fiscal Studies pamphlets by Profesor Cedric Sandford. The PAYE system is not discussed in this book for reasons of space.

[4.] Termination of one's only full time employment might be thought of as equivalent to the cancellation of one's entire profit making apparatus cf. *Van den Berghs Ltd* v *Clark* (1935) 19 TC 390.

[5.] MPs were not paid at the time and were not concerned with matters now discussed in Lord Nolan's report.

[6.] See Shipwright, *Trade, Profession, Employment or Vocation?* 123 *SJ* 679.

Schedule E – income from employment

cases came before the courts on this point in the 19th century.[7] Those that did gave little guidance. Thus the Court of Exchequer in *Attorney-General* v *Lancashire and Yorkshire Railway Co.* (1864) 159 ER 527 said that the Schedule did not extend to railway workmen and artisans but gave no guidance as to where to draw the line between Schedule D and Schedule E. However, in 1922 a case came before the courts which gave a greater guidance and upset a Revenue practice which had continued for about 60 years. This was the case of *Great Western Railway* v *Bater* (1922) 8 TC 231. The question at issue here was whether GWR were required to deduct income tax from the salary of one W. H. Hall, a clerk in their employ. It was held that Mr Hall did not hold a public office, or office of a public nature or exercise a public employment of profit or an employment of profit of a public nature within Schedule E. The Revenue had been taxing persons such as Mr Hall under Schedule E rather than under Schedule D for 60 years or more.

As is often the case in Revenue matters the upset for the Crown was short-lived as, by s. 18, FA 1922, all employments were brought within Schedule E from the year of assessment 1922–3. There were then two types of employment within Schedule E, namely:

(a) those that had always been there, i.e., those of a public nature; and
(b) employments formerly within Schedule D, Case II.

Income from employments which constituted foreign possessions remained chargeable at that time under Schedule D, Case V on a remittance basis (see *Davies* v *Braithwaite* at para. 6.8). Following the recommendations of the final report of the Royal Commission on the taxation of profits and income in 1955 s. 10, FA 1956 brought all offices and employments within Schedule E as a single category but divided into three cases according to the residence status of the employee and the place of performance of the duties of the office or employment. However, the retention of the remittance basis in cases with a foreign element (i.e., only charging income when it was remitted to the UK) gave considerable scope for tax avoidance. As a result of certain aspects of 'the Lonrho affair' in the early 1970s – 'the unacceptable face of capitalism' according to Sir Edward Heath in a speech in 1973 – the taxation of income from foreign offices and employments was put on to an arising basis instead with certain fixed rate deductions. This scheme which was introduced in 1974 was, despite opposition from the Revenue, to some extent relaxed by the 1977 Finance Act. However, the Revenue got their revenge in the 1980s when this relaxation was removed and with the change in the basis of taxation introduced by the Finance Act 1989 (see s. 203A and para. 4A, s. 19, FA 1989). This will be dealt with later on.

One feature, which has been mentioned before, that is now well established in the collection of income tax under Schedule E – the PAYE system, Pay As You Earn. Schedule E has long been associated with deduction at source,[8] the

---

[7.] The case stated procedure for appeals was only introduced in 1874; see Chapter 2.
[8.] See, e.g., Rules 11 and 12. Schedule 1 Schedule E, FA 1918 derived from s. 146 and rules 5, 6 and 10, Income Tax Act 1842.

method of collection beloved of governments because of the cheapness and efficiency for the benefit. Despite Lord Buckmaster's view in *GWR* v *Bater* dissenting (at p. 244) that 'tax at the source of weekly wages was impracticable', such a system was introduced from the year of assessment 1940–41 for the deduction of tax from current pay in respect of past periods. This had certain practical difficulties and unfortunate effects where incomes fluctuated. From 1944–45 PAYE applied on the basis that tax on current income is deducted from current pay (see s. 203, TA, the regulations made thereunder and the helpful Revenue pamphlets).

Special statutory provisions have gradually expanded the scope of Schedule E. The most important of these was the code introduced in 1948 to tax under Schedule E the cost to the employer of the fringe benefits, expenses allowances etc. for directors and higher paid employees. This was considerably strengthened in 1976. It will be dealt with in detail later in Chapter 7.

6.4 THE CHARGE UNDER SCHEDULE E

The specific charging provisions for Schedule E need to be considered in detail next. The charge under Schedule E is set out in s. 19, TA. It reads (in so far as relevant) as follows:

(1) The Schedule referred to as Schedule E is as follows:

SCHEDULE E

1. Tax under this Schedule shall be charged in respect of any office or employment on emoluments therefrom which fall under one, or more than one, of the following Cases —

Case I: any emoluments for any year of assessment in which the person holding the office or employment is resident and ordinarily resident in the United Kingdom, subject however to section 192 if the emoluments are foreign emoluments (within the meaning of that section) and to section 193(1) if in the year of assessment concerned he performs the duties of the office or employment wholly or partly outside the United Kingdom

Case II: any emoluments, in respect of duties performed in the United Kingdom for any year of assessment in which the person holding the office or employment is not resident (or, if resident, not ordinarily resident) in the United Kingdom, subject however to section 192 if the emoluments are foreign emoluments (within the meaning of that section);

Case III: any emoluments for any year of assessment in which the person holding the emoluments is resident in the United Kingdom (whether or not ordinarily resident there) so far as the emoluments are received in the United Kingdom;

and tax shall not be chargeable in respect of emoluments of an office or employment under any other paragraph of this Schedule.

The emoluments referred to in Cases I and II as foreign emoluments are emoluments of a person not domiciled in the United Kingdom from an office or employment under or with any person, body of persons or partnership resident outside and not resident in, the United Kingdom.

2. Tax under this Schedule shall be charged in respect of every annuity, pension or stipend payable by the Crown or out of the public revenue of the United Kingdom or of Northern Ireland, other than annuities charged under paragraph (c) of Case III of Schedule D. . . .

4A. Where (apart from this paragraph) emoluments from an office or employment would be for a year of assessment in which a person does not hold the office or employment, the following rules shall apply for the purposes of the Cases set out in paragraph 1 above —

(a) if in the year concerned the office or employment has never been held, the emoluments shall be treated as emoluments for the first year of assessment in which the office or employment is held;

(b) if in the year concerned the office or employment is no longer held, the emoluments shall be treated as emoluments for the last year of assessment in which the office or employment was held.

5. The preceding provisions of this Schedule are without prejudice to any other provision of the Tax Acts directing tax to be charged under this Schedule, and tax so directed to be charged shall be charged accordingly . . .

Section 131, TA helps with the meaning of chargeable emoluments for this purpose and the relationship between the cases. It provides:

Chargeable emoluments

(1) Tax under Case I, II or III of Schedule E shall, except as provided to the contrary by any provision of the Tax Acts, be chargeable on the full amount of the emoluments falling under that Case, subject to such deductions only as may be authorised by the Tax Acts, and the expression 'emoluments' shall include all salaries, fees, wages, perquisites and profits whatsoever.

(2) Tax under Case III of Schedule E shall be chargeable whether or not tax is chargeable in respect of the same office or employment under Case I or II of that Schedule, but shall not be chargeable on any emoluments falling under the said Case I or II.

In general terms, as noted above, there are thus three matters which are charged under Schedule E namely:

(a) wages, salaries, directors' fees etc. from offices or employment;
(b) most annuities, pensions and stipends derived from employment;
(c) a miscellaneous collection of benefits which are directed to be charged under Schedule E.

There are four questions in particular which arise from s. 19, TA, the main charging section for Schedule E. These are:

(1) What is the meaning of:
  (i) office; and
  (ii) employment?
(2) What is the meaning of emoluments and how are they to be calculated?
(3) What is the meaning of the word 'therefrom' in this context?
(4) What is the appropriate Case?

Each of these questions will be considered below. As ever there is a lack of statutory definitions applicable here. Accordingly, one is often driven to the case law which is not always as clear as one would wish.

There have been many cases concerning the Schedule E and Schedule D, Case I borderline because Schedule D, Case I is often more favourable to the taxpayer (see *Fall* v *Hitchin* and *Hall* v *Lorimer* discussed at para. 6.11) This is (inter alia) for the following reasons.

(a) Most tax on emoluments from an office or employment is collected on a current year basis which applies for Schedule E whereas collection by reference to last year's tax and adjustment applies for Schedule D, Case I.

(b) PAYE applies for Schedule E payments whereas direct assessment or self-assessment applies for Schedule D, Case I.

(c) There are different expense rules for Schedule E and Schedule D, Case I. The deduction rules in s. 198, TA have been described as 'niggardly' because of the 'necessary in the performance of duties' requirement (see Chapter 8). The requirements of s. 74, TA are seemingly less restrictive.

(d) Termination payments under Schedule E can attract favourable treatment (see ss. 148 and 188, TA). There is no equivalent for Schedule D, Case I purposes. However, as this can be regarded as an example of capital being taxed as income this may be unnecessary.

(e) The rules concerning the foreign element are different.

6.5 WHAT IS AN 'OFFICE'?

The emoluments from (inter alia) an office are taxable under Schedule E. It is therefore necessary to know what an office is for these purposes. Mr Justice Rowlatt gave some guidance on the meaning of 'office' in *GWR* v *Bater* (the railway clerk case) which gave rise to the 1922 changes. He said (at p. 235) that:

'. . . an office [is] a subsisting, permanent, substantive position which had an existence independent of the person who filled it, and which went on and was filled in succession by successive holders.'

Lord Atkinson concurred in this view (see p. 246). This was assumed to be the correct approach in *Ingle* v *Farrand* [1927] AC 417 where a London County Council clerk was considered not to hold public office. Lord Atkinson in *McMillan* v *Guest* (1942) 24 TC 190 at p. 201 (where a UK resident director held an office) treated Mr Justice Rowlatt's statement in *GWR* v *Bater* as 'a generally sufficient statement of the meaning of the word [office]'. Statutory authority seems to be unnecessary to create an office. In *IRC* v *Brander and Cruickshank* (1971) 46 TC 474 the House of Lords held that Scottish advocates who acted as secretaries and registrars of various companies were office holders in respect of their registrarships notwithstanding there was no requirement under the Companies Act for a company to appoint a registrar[9] They were thus entitled to the relief in what is now s. 188, TA in respect of payment on termination of their appointment.

Trustees and executors can also be said to be office holders. Their position has been considered in cases concerning succession and estate duty and the 'special contribution'. Channell J in *Attorney General* v *Eyre* [1909] 1 KB 733 (an estate duty case) said that:

> a trusteeship is often spoken of as an office . . . in my opinion that is the correct expression. The question is what does office mean in that section. I cannot help thinking that the legislature had in their minds the case of an office in which there was an immediate successor . . .

This was applied in *Dale* v *IRC* (1954) 34 TC 468 where the real question was whether or not income paid to a trustee of the Wellcome Foundation under a will was earned income, that is income arising in respect of remuneration from an office of profit (there was then a different rate for such income). Lord Normand said that 'office is an apt word to describe a trustee's position or any position in which services are due by the holder and in which the holder has no employer'. The House of Lords held that the trustee's remuneration in the circumstances of the case was earned income. However, it seems that the current practice of the Revenue as regards trustees and executors is not to tax them under Schedule E but to tax ordinary trustees and executors under Schedule D, Case III and professional trustees under Schedule D, Case II. A barrister's clerk was held not to hold an office in the particular circumstances of *McMenamin* v *Diggles* [1991] STC 419. It may be that this case turned on its special facts.

The question has arisen more recently whether Rowlatt J's dictum quoted above is still good law. This was at issue in *Edwards* v *Clinch* (1981) 56 TC 367. This case arose because of a change in practice by the Revenue in the way local planning inquiry inspectors were taxed. Previously they had been charged under Schedule D. It was now sought to charge Mr Clinch and others under Schedule E rather than Schedule D. PAYE would then be applicable.

[9.] Lord Morris: 'A duty is imposed upon a company to keep a register of members: Companies Act 1948, s. 110. Even though the Companies Act does not require that there should be an appointment as registrar, a company must arrange that some person or persons should on its behalf perform the statutory duties of maintaining its register. In doing so, it may establish a position which successively will be held by different persons. If it does so the company may have treated what could rationally for income tax purposes be called an office.' See also *Ellis* v *Lucas* (1966) 43 TC 276 and *Walker* v *Carnaby* [1970] 1 WLR 276.

Mr Clinch was one of a panel of about 60 people from amongst whom the Minister invited inspectors at a daily fee. The invitation was for a specific enquiry. It was found that the enquiry was held independently without direction or guidance from the Ministry.[10] A National Insurance card was stamped as self-employed. The General Commissioners were of the opinion that the inspector did not hold an office. Walton J reversed this, holding that Mr Clinch did hold an office. He based himself upon the *Oxford English Dictionary* definition of the word office. He said that it was after all:

> an ordinary English word usable in many different ways, – one can take the following definitions: 'a position or place to which certain duties attach, specially one of a more or less public character; a position of trust, authority, or service under constituted authority; a place in the administration of government for direction of a corporation, company, society etc'.

Walton J was reversed by the Court of Appeal. The House of Lords split three to two on the matter. The majority held that the appointment of the taxpayer to be the inspector for a public local enquiry was a temporary, ad hoc appointment personal to the taxpayer and had no quality of permanency about it. Consequently, the taxpayer was not liable under Schedule E in respect of his fees for conducting the public local enquiries. An interesting question is whether this judgment would cover private arbitrators.

6.6 OFFICES AS ASSETS OF A TRADE OR PROFESSION

An office may be held by someone who is also a trader or a professional. It is sometimes argued that an office is an asset of the trade or profession. This may be so as to get the benefit of wider expense rules and/or different taxation of termination receipts. There have been a number of cases on this matter including the following.

In *Blackburn* v *Close Bros Ltd* (1960) 39 TC 164 a sum was paid on termination of a contract for provision of managerial and secretarial services for a fee. Pennycuick V-C held that this was a revenue payment assessable under Schedule D, Case II and not a capital payment even though sums paid under the contract qualified as emoluments.[11] In *Walker* v *Carnaby* (1970) 46 TC 561 Ungoed Thomas J took a similar approach but reached a different conclusion on the facts. The position was further considered by the Lords in *IRC* v *Brander & Cruickshank* (see para. 6.5) who treated termination payments for registrars as taxable under Schedule E and so entitled to termination relief under the predecessor of s. 188, TA.

6.7 SUMMARY: OFFICE

In summary it seems that the following can be said of 'office' in the present context.

---

[10] Cf. Farmer, *Tribunals and Government*, Law in Context Series.
[11] NB Lord Morris doubted this was correct in *IRC* v *Brander & Cruickshank* (see para. 6.5).

Schedule E – income from employment

(a) The starting point is still Rowlatt J's dictum in *GWR* v *Bater* about a subsisting, permanent, substantive position independent of the holder for the time being which is filled by successive holders.

(b) This dictum may give an example of the core meaning of the word in the current context but it is not exhaustive.

(c) Office has been held to include (inter alia):

  (i) a director of a UK resident company in *McMillan* v *Guest* (1942) 24 TC 190;
  (ii) trustees and executors in *Dale* v *IRC* (1954) 34 TC 468;
  (iii) NHS consultants in *Mitchell and Edon* v *Ross* (1961) 40 TC 11;
  (iv) auditorships in *Ellis* v *Lucas* (1966) 43 TC 276 and *Walker* v *Carnaby* [1970] 1 All ER 502.

(d) An inspector at a public inquiry is not an officeholder; see *Edwards* v *Clinch* (in para. 6.5).

6.8 WHAT IS AN 'EMPLOYMENT'?

The emoluments from (inter alia) an employment are taxable under Schedule E. It is therefore necessary to know what an employment is for these purposes. As with the word office there is no statutory definition of the word 'employment' for these purposes. Until 1922 (see para. 6.3) the majority of employments fell within Schedule D, Case II with professions and vocations. There was thus no distinction in their tax treatment between an employed assistant solicitor and the senior partner of a firm of solicitors which employed him. As will be seen much difficulty has arisen as to where to draw the line between an engagement in the course of a Schedule D profession and an employment the emoluments of which are taxable under Schedule E with the consequent differences in the applicable rules. In the authors' view it would be better if there were a uniform system. Functions carried out by a doctor do not differ so drastically, or should not, when the doctor is employed to operate on a national health patient or operates in his or her private capacity on a private patient.

Although cases on the distinction from other Schedules usually concern Schedule D, Case I, sometimes other charges are involved as in *Beecham Group Ltd* v *Fair* [1984] STC 15 which concerned the distinction between Schedule E and Schedule A.

Two approaches have been taken in the past to the construction of 'employment':

  (a) the analogy to a post; and
  (b) the approach in the National Insurance and tort cases on contract of service rather than contract for services.

The distinction between a contract of service and a contract for services is familiar in other parts of the law as, for example, in social security and tort.

The most important approach now though is that in *Hall* v *Lorimer* (discussed at para. 6.11 after some of the earlier case law and statutes have been dealt with to set *Hall* v *Lorimer* in context).

The meaning of the word 'employment' was considered by Rowlatt J in *Davies* v *Braithwaite* (1931) 18 TC 198. This case concerned Miss Lilian Braithwaite, a well known actress and film star of the 1920s. Miss Braithwaite was a UK resident during the years of assessment in question. She acted in the USA. Employment income was then charged on a remittance basis (i.e., on what was brought into the UK. If it was not brought into the UK there was no charge to UK income tax). It was argued, inter alia, by Miss Braithwaite that so far as her overseas performances were concerned she appeared under a contract which established the relationship of master and servant and so was taxable under Schedule E (and at that time chargeable on a remittance basis) and, as there had been no remittances of income to the UK, she was not liable to UK income tax in respect of the income from the overseas activities. The court held that Miss Braithwaite exercised one profession including the overseas performances all the annual profits of which were assessable under Schedule D, Case II.

Mr Justice Rowlatt said that the criterion was not skill nor was it duration. He continued:

> where one finds a method of earning a livelihood which does not consist in the obtaining of a post and staying in it but consists of a series of engagements and moving from one to another . . . then each of those engagements cannot be considered an employment but is a mere engagement in the exercise of the profession.

It follows from this and other of his remarks that the word 'employment' means something akin to a 'post'. Lord Denning's favourite reference work, the *Shorter Oxford English Dictionary* defines 'post' inter alia as 'an office or situation to which anyone is appointed; position; place; employment'. It seems that it is the meaning of post when used in a sentence such as 'he was appointed to a teaching post at the school' that one is concerned with . This is not the most modern usage (see Nolan LJ in *Hall* v *Lorimer* [1993] STC 23 at p. 31).

The taxpayer tried to argue that he was outside Schedule E in the later case of *Fall* v *Hitchen* [1973] 1 WLR 286. Here the taxpayer wanted to fall within Schedule D with the less restrictive expense rules and (at that time) the preceding year basis of assessment. This case concerned a ballet dancer at Sadler's Wells as it then was. He was engaged under the Esher standard form of contract for ballet. The contract provided that it was for a period of rehearsals and thereafter for a period of 22 weeks' work determinable by either side on two weeks' notice. Remuneration was to be in accordance with the schedule which also contained a restrictive covenant that he should not appear elsewhere without permission during the contract term, and provision as to sickness etc. In accordance with the usual theatrical practice the dancer paid social security contributions etc. as an employed rather than a self-

Schedule E – income from employment

employed person. This was to allow him to claim unemployment benefit whilst 'resting'. Pennycuick V-C took the view that there was an employment for the purposes of Schedule E where there was a contract of service. He considered the expressions 'contract of service' and 'employment' to be coterminous. He also thought that this was consistent with *Davies v Braithwaite*. He considered that the question as to whether there is a contract of service is for all practical purposes one of law. He then considered the various cases on this and concluded that there was a contract of service and so an employment within Schedule E. These cases on 'contract of service' need to be considered first and *Fall v Hitchen* will then be discussed further.

What test is to be applied to determine when there is a contract of service? As noted above, the concept is familiar in at least two other areas of law, namely tort and social security law. The usual distinction is between a contract of service and a contract for services. The old test in tort for vicarious liability purposes is control but in *Stevenson Jordan & Harrison v MacDonald & Evans* [1952] 1 TLR 101 Denning LJ (as he then was) introduced the 'integration' test. It may be accurate to say that today's test is not so much submission to orders but whether the person in question is part and parcel of the organisation.

Social security law has also been important in this context. Section 1 of the National Insurance Act 1965 was concerned with persons gainfully employed under a contract of service. There are a number of important cases on this matter. In *Argent v Minister of Social Security* [1968] 1 WLR 1749 an actor who was also a part time teacher of music and drama was held not to be an employed person. It was said that no single factor was decisive but all the circumstances had to be examined and in the particular circumstances he was not employed. A similar approach was taken in *Ready Mixed Concrete (South East) Ltd v Minister of Pensions and National Insurance* [1968] 2 QB 497 which concerned 'owner-drivers' of ready mixed concrete lorries. The owner-driver scheme replaced employees driving such lorries. Mackenna J considered that the terms of the contract were all important (at p. 516). He considered that in the particular circumstances there was a contract of carriage rather than employment because of the freedom the owner-driver has as to the running of the business, the obligation to provide a substitute in case of illness or holiday and the element of risk on the owner-driver.

It is interesting to contrast another social security case which has been very influential. *Market Investigations Limited v Minister of Social Security* [1969] 2 QB 173 concerned a Mrs Irving who was a part time interviewer for a market research company. Cooke J considered that she was gainfully employed. After reviewing the relevant case law Cooke J said that:

> the fundamental test to be applied [in distinguishing between a contract of service and a contract for services] is: 'is the person who has engaged himself to perform these services performing them as a person in business on his own account?' If the answer to that question is yes (i.e., he is performing on his own account) then the contract is a contract for services. If the answer is no then the contract is a contract of service. No exhaustive

list has been compiled and perhaps no exhaustive list can be compiled of considerations which are relevant in determining that question, nor can strict rules be laid down as to the relative weight which the various considerations should carry in particular cases. The most that can be said is that control will no doubt always have to be considered, although it can no longer be considered as the sole determining factor; the factors that may be of importance are such matters as the man performing the services provides his own equipment etc.[12]

It was said in *Lee Ting Sang* v *Cheung Chi-Keung* [1990] 2 AC 374 that 'the matter had never been better put than by Cooke J'. This case involved an employee's compensation claim from Hong Kong. The Privy Council considered that in the particular circumstances there was a contract of service.[13] The test was whether the person who is performing the services was a person in business on his own account as in *Market Investigations*.

The remarks of Cooke J in *Market Investigations* set out above were cited and applied by Pennycuick V-C in *Fall* v *Hitchen* (the ballet case). He considered that virtually all the factors in the case pointed to a contract of service rather than a contract for services and in particular:

(a) the minimum period of 22 weeks;
(b) the provision for notice;
(c) the specified hours of work for a specified regular salary set out in the schedule to the agreement; and
(d) the fact that it was full time work.

These were all factors pointing to a contract of service rather than a contract for services. The judge considered that once it had been established that the emoluments arose from a contract of service it followed that they arose from an employment within Schedule E under which Schedule they were properly assessable.

There are seemingly three things that could be concluded from *Davies v Braithwaite* and *Fall* v *Hitchen*. These are:

(a) that an employment is something in the nature of a post;
(b) the expressions 'contract of service' and 'employment' are coterminous; and the fundamental test is whether the person performing these activities is performing them on their own account;
(c) in considering the questions and the existence of an employment all the circumstances must be considered.

It is for consideration whether this represents the law.

Whilst these statements may seem reasonably clear in the abstract their application in practice to a given set of facts can sometimes be a little difficult.

[12.] But even this is not determinative, see, e.g., *Hall* v *Lorimer* where Mr Lorimer did not provide the studio equipment.
[13.] This may have been to ensure that there was compensation. The scheme only applied to employees.

Schedule E – income from employment

It is instructive to contrast two excess profit tax cases. An employee was not assessable to excess profit tax but a self-employed person was liable. In both these cases the taxpayer appealed against an assessment to excess profits tax contending inter alia that the taxpayer was the employee.

In *IRC* v *Turnbull* (1943) 29 TC 133 Mr Turnbull was a member of the Institute of Marine Engineers who acted as the London representative of the Dartmouth Ship Building Company and of a Manchester engineering firm. He received salary and commission. He had his own office in London and a secretary whose salary he paid himself. The General Commissioners' conclusion that he was not assessable to excess profits tax was upheld by Macnaghten J who said that the taking of the second representativeship was insufficient to change his position to that of a person carrying on a business on his own account.

The opposite conclusion was reached in *Marsh* v *IRC* (1943) 29 TC 120. The facts here were that Mr Marsh was a commercial traveller for a firm of flour merchants. With their permission he also acted as a traveller for four other firms who sold products associated with the bakery trade. He received salary and commission from three of the firms and commission only from the other two firms. Mr Marsh arranged his own journeys but frequently received instructions to call on a particular customer. He used a room in his house as an office and had the services of an employee of the flour firm as an assistant. On these facts it was held that the taxpayer carried on a business within the charge to excess profits tax and thus was not an employee. It is interesting to consider what would be the position of a commercial traveller with a similar factual background but only three representativeships? Would he be an employee or a person engaged to perform activities who is performing them on his own account?

Upjohn J (as he then was) indicated the test in *Mitchell and Edon* v *Ross* (1962) 40 TC 11 (the NHS consultant's case) where he asked (at p. 35) does the taxpayer in respect of the particular activity in question '(a) occupy an office; or (b) undertake an employment; or (c) does he merely render services in the course of the exercise or practice of a profession?' This sounds a relatively easy distinction but difficulties arise where a person carries on a profession or has an employment and also engages in activities of a similar nature, e.g., the part time NHS consultant in *Mitchell and Edon* v *Ross*. He was held to be employed and carrying on a profession. It is a question of fact and degree whether a person is exercising two employments or vocations or the activity of one employment or vocation. In *Fuge* v *McClelland* (1956) 36 TC 571 a daytime teacher giving evening classes under a separate agreement with the same employer was held assessable under Schedule E. Similarly in *Lindsay* v *IRC* (1964) 41 TC 661 a full time radiologist at a teaching hospital was paid separate fees by the hospital board, his employers, for lectures at the hospital to students. He was held assessable on these under Schedule E. *Walls* v *Sinnett* [1987] STC 236 concerned a professional singer who lived in Sussex, who was a part time lecturer at a technical college and who had previously been assessed under Schedule D but was changed to Schedule E. Vinelott J said that:

what is striking about this case is that the engagement, to use a neutral word, is full time . . . [Mr Walls] says that, although full time, he was able to carry on a great deal of other work, but that does not assist him in the context of this case; the engagement, as I have described it, or employment was as a very senior teacher or lecturer, and such teachers frequently have relatively light teaching load and are encouraged to engage in other activities which can add to their experience and which may be of benefit to the college.[14]

In general terms then it seems that we can say that if a person resident in the UK holds a subsisting permanent substantive position (with an independent existence filled by successive holders) or has been appointed to a post or is employed under a contract of service then the emoluments therefrom will be taxable under Schedule E.

6.9 STATUTE AND EMPLOYMENT

Statute has also provided that in certain circumstances the earnings of some types of workers should be taxable under Schedule E rather than under Schedule D as they might claim. In effect statute deems them to be employees for income tax purposes so that deduction at source applies.

6.9.1 Section 134 and Schedule 29, TA – workers supplied by agencies

Some people who 'temped' or acted in a freelance capacity obtained their work through agencies but claimed to be carrying on a trade, profession or vocation. Section 134 now provides that in certain circumstances the services which the worker (i.e. the taxpayer) renders or is under an obligation to render to the client (i.e. the person to whom the services are supplied) and the agency are to be treated as if they were duties of an office or employment held by the worker, and remuneration receivable under or in consequence of the contract is to be treated as emoluments of that office or employment and assessable under Schedule E.[15] PAYE is thus applicable. Where the worker is under no obligation to the agency to render the services, the section is inapplicable.

6.9.2 The construction industry[16]

There is a separate and special scheme for the construction industry. There had been concern about the 'Lump' system or as it is more delicately called

---

[14.] Cf. *Sidey* v *Phillips* [1987] STC 87 which concerned part time lecturing at a polytechnic by a non-practising barrister. His engagements were found to be employments in the Schedule E sense upheld by Knox J.
[15.] See *Brady* v *Hart* [1985] STC 498 for an example of s. 134 in operation and see also the Employment Agencies Act 1973 and the Employment Protection (Consolidation) Act 1978.
[16.] See Inland Revenue Pamphlet IR 14/15, Construction Industry Tax Deduction Scheme.

in the legislation, 'sub-contractors in the construction industry'. Sections 559 et seq, TA deal with the scheme. The scheme was introduced for 1972–73 by ss. 29–31 and sch. 5, Finance Act 1971 which required deduction of basic rate tax by contractors from payments to workers in the construction industry, other than from payments representing the direct cost of material, but it proved inadequate. For example, in early 1976[17] a company was fined £675,000 plus costs of £52,000 and its directors and officers suffered heavy prison sentences and/or fines on being found guilty of conspiracy to cheat and defraud the Inland Revenue by forging, uttering and falsifying documents. Those convicted had failed to deduct tax from payments to men on 'the Lump' as they were required to under the special scheme. A new scheme became effective in 1977 and is tighter and more toughly drawn. This is sometimes known as the 714 certificate scheme.

6.9.3 North Sea divers

Many North Sea divers and supervisors were caught by the provisions outlined in s. 134, TA (para. 6.9.1). A vigorous campaign was mounted which resulted in s. 29, FA 1978 (now s. 314, TA) being enacted. This treats the employment and the performance of the duties of an employment such as a diver as the carrying on of a trade and excludes the emoluments therefrom from the charge under Schedule E.[18]

6.9.4 Actors

The Revenue in the recent past have tried to rely on *Fall v Hitchen* (see para. 6.8) to say that all actors should be taxed under Schedule E and so more importantly fall within PAYE. Special deduction rules were introduced (see s. 201A, TA introduced by s. 77, FA 1990). Nevertheless, the Revenue have lost the argument before the Special Commisisoners on this. The law has not been changed to say that actors and actresses are employees and *Davies v Braithwaite* (see para. 6.8) remains good law. The position will thus depend on individual circumstances.

6.10 OTHER CASES

Tax avoidance does not deprive the receipts from a contract of employment of their taxability under Schedule E. In *Black Nominees v Nicol* (1975) 50 TC 229 (a case featuring Julie Christie) liability under a contract of employment was not displaced by a tax avoidance motive. Thus a charge under Schedule E can arise on payment from a 'Lend-a-star' company (i.e., on employment of a star which is a loan out by a company).

Similarly illegality does not necessarily prevent a Schedule E charge. *Cooke v Blacklaws* [1985] STC 1 shows that even if the contract of employment is

---

[17.] See Press Release 25 March 1976. See also ss. 362, 565 and 567, TA and the Income Tax (Sub-contractors in the Construction Industry) Regulations 1993.
[18.] See HL Written Answers, 3 February 1978, Vol 943 Col 59.

illegal the emoluments from the office or employment are still taxable under Schedule E. The taxpayer was a New Zealand domiciliary working as a dentist in England. As a self-employed practitioner he paid tax on all his income in the usual way. Following advice he entered into a contract of employment with DAI, a company incorporated in Panama, which made its services available to his practice. DAI then paid the taxpayer a salary. Since DAI was non-resident and the taxpayer was domiciled in New Zealand, he claimed foreign emoluments relief under the Finance Act 1974. The contract was in breach of the legislation applying to dentists. His appeal was successful before the Special Commissioners. Peter Gibson J declined to overturn their decision on appeal.

6.11 HALL v LORIMER

Hall v Lorimer [1992] STC 599 is the most important recent case on the meaning of employment. It concerned a taxpayer who had been employed as a vision mixer who went freelance and claimed to be taxed as a self-employed person. The courts held him self-employed. A vision mixer would work in a gallery control room with a vision mixing panel which was owned or procured by the studio company. The equipment was very expensive and was not provided by the taxpayer (see pp. 602–603, 610 and cf. *Market Investigations v Minister of Social Security* at para. 6.8).

The taxpayer had an office at home. His wife helped him with his paperwork till they were divorced. He solicited business. He built a client list of 22 in the first 14 months (see p. 603). He was registered for VAT. On a small number of occasions he provided a substitute. The engagements were usually of one or two days – the longest was ten days. His charges were higher than union rates. He did not share in the profit or losses of the production but was listed in 'the credits'. However, he could lose money if a client became insolvent. 'The taxpayer kept busy in what is a volatile industry'.

The Special Commissioner held that Mr Lorimer was not an employee and discharged the assessments. The Crown appealed.

Mummery J held that he could not interfere as there was no misdirection of law (see p. 610). It was common ground before him that whether or not there was an employment for Schedule E purposes depended on whether or not there was a contract of service (and it was also accepted that they were all either Schedule D receipts or Schedule E receipts). This was to be determined under the general law.

Mummery J considered *Davies v Braithwaite*, *Fall v Hitchen* and other of the tax cases discussed above and said:

> There is . . . a broad measure of agreement on the relevant law to be applied in distinguishing between a contract of service and a contract for services. The leading cases are *RMC v Minister of Pensions*,[19] *Market*

[19.] *RMC v Minister of Pensions* [1968] 2 QB 497 especially at pp. 515–525.

Investigations v *Minister of Social Security*,[20] and *Lee Ting Sang* v *Chung Chi-Keung*.[21]

He thought no checklist could be used to make the decision: one had to look at the overall effect and circumstances (see p. 612). One had to consider whether the taxpayer performed services as a person in business on his own account. Here the correct question to ask was, 'Why is the taxpayer not in business on his own account as a vision mixer?' (see p. 613).

The Crown's appeal to the Court of Appeal was dismissed with costs ([1993] STC 23). Nolan LJ accepted that the 'question whether the individual is in business on his own account' was often helpful but (at p. 30):

> may be of little assistance in the case of one carrying on a profession or vocation. A self-employed author working from home or an actor or a singer may earn his living without any of the normal trappings of a business. For my part I would suggest there is much to be said in these cases for bearing in mind the traditional contrast between a servant and an independent contractor. The extent to which the individual is dependent or independent of a particular paymaster for the financial exploitation of his talents may well be significant.

The effect of *Hall* v *Lorimer* seems to be that it all depends on the circumstances of the particular case. There is seemingly no one test. The *Market Investigations* approach may often be helpful as is the servant/ independent contractor approach. (The authors favour the *Market Investigations* approach as covering most of the other approaches and as the approach of the leading cases.)

6.12 WHAT ARE EMOLUMENTS UNDER THE 'COMMON LAW' OF SCHEDULE E?

This section of this chapter is concerned only with the general meaning of 'emoluments' in Schedule E and not with the statutory modifications (see chapter 7) that have extended it. Section 19(1), TA provides that 'tax under this Schedule should be charged in respect of any office or employment on emoluments therefrom . . .'. Section 131, TA tells us that 'tax under Case I, II, or III of Schedule E shall, except as provided to the contrary by any provision of the Tax Acts, be chargeable on the full amount of the emoluments falling under that case, subject to such deductions only as may be authorised by the Tax Acts, and the expression 'emoluments' shall include all salaries, fees, wages, perquisites and profits whatsoever.'

The phrase 'all salaries, fees, wages, perquisites and profits whatsoever' is probably not an exhaustive definition though it is difficult to think of matters which are not covered and it should be noted that the word 'includes' in a

---

[20.] *Market Investigations* v *Minister of Social Security* [1969] 2 QB 173 especially at pp. 184–185 considered at para. 6.8 above.
[21.] *Ting Sang* v *Chung Chi-Keung* [1990] 2 AC 374 at p. 382.

statute may be construed as giving an exhaustive definition. Apart from s. 131, TA and certain special statutory rules with particular purposes there is no further help in the statute as to the meaning of the word 'emoluments'.

The Shorter Oxford English Dictionary defines 'emolument' as 'profits or gain from station, office or employment; dues; remuneration; salary.' Thus the university lecturer's salary or a car worker's wages at a factory are within the definition of emoluments as are the director's fees of a director of ICI.

In *Pook* v *Owen* discussed at para. 6.19 Lord Guest said a 'perquisite' is merely a casual emolument additional to regular salary or wages. Lord Pearce said:

> The normal meaning of the word [perquisite] denotes something that benefits a man by going 'into his own pocket'. It would be a wholly misleading description of an office to say that it had very large perquisites merely because the holder had to disburse very large sums of money out of his own pocket, and is later wholly or partly reimbursed by the employer, nobody would describe him (or her) as enjoying a perquisite. In my view, perquisite has a known normal meaning, namely, a personal advantage, which would not apply to a mere reimbursement of necessary disbursements.

In broad terms therefore 'emoluments' include not only money but also any advantage, such as a fringe benefit, which is capable of being turned into money.

6.13 REALITY RULES

In deciding what is an emolument and its value, a realistic approach is to be taken. In *Jenkins* v *Horn* [1979] 2 All ER 1141 the taxpayer had been employed by a company for three or four years at a minimum weekly wage of £60. An arrangement for paying wages in sovereigns was entered into. The company purchased the required number of sovereigns each period. Cost was used in the company's accounts in accounting for the sovereigns. It was common ground between the parties that gold coins were legal tender at the relevant time. The argument that the employee was only taxable on the nominal value of the coins was rejected.

Browne-Wilkinson J said:

> The question which arises is whether . . . liability to tax is to be assessed on the sovereigns' . . . nominal value only, that is to say, £1 for each sovereign, or whether he is to be taxed on the basis that each sovereign is to be treated as having its actual open market value . . . In my judgment, looked at in any realistic sense at all, the perquisites and profits which the taxpayer received in any week when he received one or two sovereigns were not fully represented by the nominal value of each sovereign as being £1 sterling. The full amount of his emoluments was the amount for which he was able to realise, and indeed did realise, on the sovereigns that he

received. Therefore, on the simple wording of the . . . Act the full value of the gold sovereigns is the proper amount which is taxable in his hands.

6.14 DEDUCTION FROM WAGES ETC.

If money is deducted from wages this does not of itself reduce what is taxable. The problem of a deduction of a sum of money in respect of board, lodging, washing and uniform from the salaries of asylum attendants was considered in two cases by Rowlatt J.

In the first case, *Cordy* v *Gordon* (1925) 9 TC 304 the judge said that:

> . . In many cases it must be a mere question of words. £150 plus board and lodging or £200 less a deduction of £50 in respect of board and lodging, would be stating the same thing in different words. But in this case I think there is this distinction that he is expressed to be paid a gross salary and is to pay back out of that in respect of board and lodging which he is bound to take from his employers not a fixed sum but a sum varying with the cost of living so that the cost of living is his risk.

In the other asylum case *Machon* v *McLoughlin* (1926) 11 TC 83 which was on basically similar facts, Rowlatt J made the following comment. 'When you have a person paid a wage with the necessity – the contractual necessity if you like – to expend that wage in a particular way then he must pay tax upon the gross wage and no question of alienability arises.' It follows that income tax under Schedule E is charged on the gross emoluments and that, in the words of s. 131, they are subject only to the deductions authorised in the Taxes Acts.

6.15 TRADE-IN VALUE?

It may not always be easy to tell whether there is a deduction from the gross wage or an amendment of the wage for example by waiver. If wages are adjusted because of, for example, a fringe benefit which can be traded-in, what is taxable? This was the first question considered in *Heaton* v *Bell* (1967) 46 TC 11 a case to which we shall return.[22] This case concerned the craftsman car loan scheme introduced by John Waddington Limited, the manufacturers of *Monopoly* and playing cards. Under the scheme the taxpayer was provided with a new car for his use. He could use the car for pleasure purposes provided that, except in emergencies, he drove the car himself. On entry into the scheme the so-called conditions of the scheme provided that 'an amended wage basis will apply'. The effect of this was the taxpayer received about £2·50 per week less in cash than if he were not in the scheme. By a majority of four to one (Lord Reid dissenting) the House of Lords concluded that the sums payable by the taxpayer under the scheme were an agreed deduction from his gross wages. It is clear from this case that one has

---

[22.] See s. 157A, TA inserted to prevent exploitation of this Case to reduce employers' National Insurance contributions.

to look at the whole set of circumstances in deciding whether in these circumstances there is an agreed deduction from the gross wage, or an agreed reduction in the gross wage. It is also clear that an employee or office holder is liable to tax under Schedule E in respect of the gross wages or salary or fees which he receives from his office or employment.

6.16 WHEN IS TAX ASSESSABLE? DEFERRAL AND WAIVER

The basis of assessment under Schedule E was changed from 6 April 1989 by FA 1989. Under the old rules assessment under Schedule E was broadly on an 'earnings basis' (i.e., what was earned for the tax year was charged in that year). Emoluments for a period which were received in a later period were treated as income of the earlier period (see, e.g., *Heasman* v *Jordan* [1954] Ch 744). The Finance Act 1989 changed the basis of assessment under Schedule E to a 'receipts basis'. Receipt has a special meaning here as the following illustrates. From 1989–90 income tax is charged under Schedule E:

(a) under Cases I and II on the emoluments received in the tax year;.

(b) under Case III income tax is charged on emoluments received in the UK in the year of assessment (s. 202A, TA).

This will be considered further after the old rules have been outlined.

6.17 OLD RULES[23]

Broadly under the old rules an employee was taxed on emoluments when he became entitled to receive them (cf. Lord Denning dissenting in *Abbott* v *Philbin* (1960) 39 TC 82 at p. 128 set out at para. 6.19). *Edwards* v *Roberts* 19 TC 618 illlustrates this. The case concerned a 'deferred remuneration scheme' under which an amount was invested in shares to which the taxpayer was entitled after five years. He was held correctly assessed in the year of receipt rather than over the five year period (see also s. 35, TMA 1970).

In *Dracup* v *Radcliffe* (1946) 27 TC 188 the taxpayer was appointed a director of a company on 18 May 1942. The company's year end was 30 June. She was assessed on the remuneration voted to her at the company's AGM for the year ended 30 June 1942 and on a proportion of the remuneration voted to her at the next AGM for the company's year ended 30 June 1943 on a time basis. This remuneration was voted to the directors on 27 July 1943 and apportioned amongst them on 28 July 1943. She argued that at the termination of the year of assessment 1942–43, i.e., midnight on 5 April 1943, she was not entitled to any remuneration at all in respect of her services during the previous nine months and was therefore not taxable in respect of the year 1942–43. This was rejected and she was held properly

---

[23.] See inter alia *Smith* v *Stretton* (1904) 5 TC 36. Dulwich schoolmaster's provident retirement fund. Inland Revenue Press Release, 11 November 1975 (now s. 91, FA 1976). *Garforth* v *Newsmith Stainless Ltd* [1979] 2 All ER 73. Crediting of director's bonus 'payment' for s. 204, TA.

Schedule E – income from employment

assessed in respect of the remuneration which could be related back to the year for which it was paid.

The changes in FA 1989 followed the decision in *Bray* v *Best* [1989] STC 159, decided under the old rules. Here sums paid to a former employee on the winding-up of an employee trust fund after a takeover and liquidation of the company to which it related, were held not to be taxable under Schedule E. The payments were made after employment with the company taken over had ceased. The Special Commissioners held that although the sums were emoluments from the taxpayer's employment, they were not attributable to any particular year of assessment during which he was employed, i.e., when the source existed. The House of Lords held that the period to which any given payment was to be attributed was a question of fact and that the Commissioners' finding could not be interfered with.

This is an example of the application of the source doctrine. The decision in *Bray* v *Best* was reversed by FA 1989.

6.18 NEW RULES

The FA 1989 substituted a new paragraph into s. 19(1), TA. This provides:

(4A) Where (apart from this paragraph) emoluments from an office or employment would be for a year of assessment in which a person does not hold the office or employment, the following rules shall apply for the purposes of the Cases set out in paragraph 1 above—
    (a) if in the year concerned the office or employment has never been held, the emoluments shall be treated as emoluments for the first year of assessment in which the office or employment is held;
    (b) if in the year concerned the office or employment is no longer held, the emoluments shall be treated as emoluments for the last year of assessment in which the office or employment was held.

This reversed *Bray* v *Best*. Under paragraph 4A(b) the payments out of the trust would be related to the last year of the employment. Paragraph 4A(a) prevents the argument succeeding that there could be no charge on payments before the office or employment in effect has commenced as such payments are related to the first year of employment.

Thus pre-employment payments are now treated as emoluments of the first year of employment and post-employment payments are treated as emoluments of the last year of employment (s. 19(1)(4A), TA).

Section 202A puts Schedule E assessment on a receipts basis. Emoluments are treated as received (s. 202B, TA) for Cases I and II on the earliest of:

    (a) payment of the emoluments; or
    (b) payment of the emoluments to an account;
    (c) when a person becomes *entitled* to payment, or payment on account;
    (d) in the case of a director, when sums on account of the emoluments are credited in the company accounts or the end of the emolument period.

There are special provisions. Section 202B(8)–(11), TA determine when benefits in kind are treated as received. The remittances rule for Case III is unchanged.[24]

6.19 '... PERQUISITES AND PROFITS WHATSOEVER', 'BENEFITS IN KIND' AND 'FRINGE BENEFITS': GENERAL

It is clear that an employee or office holder's liability to tax under Schedule E is by reference to the gross wages or salary or fees which the taxpayer receives from his office or employment. It is now necessary to consider what else falls within the definition of emoluments and in particular within the words 'perquisites whatsoever'. This will bring us into contact with what is sometimes called benefits in kind and/or fringe benefits. Fringe benefits can be an emotive subject.[25]

The leading case on the subject of 'fringe benefits' dates from 1892. This is the case of *Tennant v Smith* 3 TC 158. The matters to which this case related in the particular have now been changed but the speeches in the House of Lords have long been treated as of importance. The question of immediate concern to the taxpayer was whether he was entitled or not to an abatement of £120 on incomes under £400 provided for in s. 8, Customs and Inland Revenue Act 1876. The taxpayer was the agent for the Bank of Scotland at Montrose. As the headnote says, he was bound to occupy a house as custodier of 'the whole premises as part of his duty'. The point at issue between the taxpayer and the surveyor of taxes was whether or not the value of occupation of the house estimated at £50 should be added to his salary of £374 in ascertaining whether or not his income exceeded £400 for the purposes of the abatement under the 1876 Act.

The House of Lords allowed the taxpayer's appeal, holding that the value of the residence was not an emolument of the office in respect of which the taxpayer was chargeable with income tax and was not to be included in the total amount of income for the purposes of a claim to abatement. The taxpayer was thus entitled to abatement under the 1876 Act.

Lord Halsbury, the Lord Chancellor, considered that the occupation of the house was not income. He said that:

> I come to the conclusion that the Act refers to many payments made to the person who received them, though, of course, I do not deny that if substantial things of money value were capable of being turned into money they might for that purpose represent money's worth and be therefore taxable.

He said later 'I am of the opinion . . . that the thing thought to be taxed is not income unless it can be turned into money'. Lord Watson made similar remarks to those of Lord Halsbury. He said:

[24.] Technical Release, Institute of Chartered Accountants in England and Wales, TAX11/93.
[25.] For an illustration see the extract from Hansard for 18 December 1975 set out in para. 7.5.1.

is the residence a perquisite or profit of his office? I do not think that it comes within the category of profits, because that word in its ordinary acceptation appears to me to denote something acquired of which the acquirer becomes possessed of, and can dispose of to his advantage, in other words money, that which can be turned to pecuniary account.

He did not think there was a perquisite here. Lord MacNaghten said that:

on examining Schedule E it became obvious that it extends only to money payments or payments convertible into money. A person is chargeable not on what he saves from his pocket but on what goes into his pockets.

In *Pook* v *Owen* (1968) 45 TC 571 Lord Pearce made similar comments. He said that 'the normal meaning of the word [perquisite] denotes something that benefits a man by going into his pocket . . . "perquisite" has a normal meaning, namely, a personal advantage.' In the same case Lord Guest said that 'perquisite' is merely a casual monument additional to regular salary or wages. Lord Salmon in *Tyrer* v *Smart* [1979] 1 All ER 321 at p. 326 said 'a perquisite is any advantage which has any value and which he receives from the employment.'

This approach was recognised and affirmed in the speeches of the House of Lords in *Abbott* v *Philbin* (1960) 39 TC 82. The test, said Lord Simonds, was whether it was by its nature capable of being turned into money.

Abbott v *Philbin* concerned an option granted to the secretary of a public company under which he could purchase 2,000 ordinary shares at the market price at the date of the grant of the option, namely 68 shillings and 6 pence per share being the middle market price on the Bristol Stock Exchange on the day of grant. The taxpayer paid £20 for this option which was expressed to be non-transferable and was to expire after ten years or upon the earlier death or retirement of the taxpayer. The taxpayer exercised the option over 250 shares when the middle market price was 82 shillings. The taxpayer was assessed for the year of assessment in which he exercised the option for 250 shares on £166, being the difference between 250 shares at the prevailing middle market price at the date of acquisition and of 250 shares at the option price plus a proportionate part of the cost of the option.

The Crown argued that the option was not a perquisite or emolument which was convertible into money but that the shares acquired on the exercise of the option were money's worth and therefore taxable. The Special Commissioners felt themselves bound by a Scottish case (*Forbes Executors*) to find in favour of the Crown. Roxburgh J considered that he could distinguish the Scottish case and found in favour of the taxpayer. The Court of Appeal felt unable to distinguish the Scottish case and followed it, reversing Roxburgh J's judgment.

The House of Lords by a majority of three to two overruled the Scottish case and held that the assessment was bad. The option itself was taxable as when granted it could, notwithstanding its expressed non-transferability, be converted into money or money's worth by arrangement with a third party that after the exercise of the option the shares would be transferred to the third party (see in particular Lord Reid's speech). One learned commentator said that 'a much more convincing analysis is to be found in the consenting judgment of Lord Denning, based on the wholly plausible assertion that a bird in the hand is taxable, but a bird in the bush is not.' The same commentator considers that the option was of indeterminable value when granted but this seems to ignore Lord Simonds's statement that 'if it had no ascertainable value, then it was a perquisite of no value – a conclusion difficult to reach since £20 was paid for it'. Lord Simonds goes on to compare the option to a provisional letter of allotment which the Revenue are certainly capable of valuing and which can be converted into cash in the way suggested by their Lordships that the option could be.

A different approach could be taken to the option but as noted above did not find favour with the majority. Lord Denning said in the course of his dissent:

> My Lords, I ask myself, what is the difference, for tax purposes, between the case I have just put, where nothing is paid for the option, and the case we have before us, where a nominal sum is paid? The difference is that in the one case he has only an expectation of profit: whereas in the other he has a right to make profits in the future, if the opportunity arises. But in either case, until the option is exercised, he has not the profits themselves. And as I read the Act, it is not the expectation to salary, not the right to salary, which is taxable, but only the salary itself. A bird in the bush is not taxable, even if you have the right to get it in the future, if it is still there. You must have it in hand before you can be taxed on it. And when you come to consider what 'profits' the servant receives from his employment by virtue of the option, surely it makes no difference whether he pays a nominal sum or not. In either case the employer grants him the option as a reward or return for his services, and the profits he makes out of it are the same save for this: if he paid nothing, it is all profit; if he paid a peppercorn, it is all profit less the value of a pepper berry; if he paid 1s., less 1s.; if he paid £20, less £20.

Following this decision share options schemes became very popular but were limited by s. 25, FA 1966 (now ss. 135, 136, 140, TA) which gave partial effect to Lord Denning's approach.

It follows from the case law that if some non-convertible amenity or benefit is made available to an employee, then that amenity or benefit is not as a matter of general law taxable as an emolument under Schedule E. If, for example, Ms Rita Chevrolet's employer, under a contract between Lord Gnome and a beauty salon, were to pay for her beauty treatment to ensure her continued delectable appearance which costs, say, £3,200 a year, then since (it is assumed) Ms Rita Chevrolet could not convert her beauty treatment into cash this benefit will not be liable to tax under general Schedule E principles. This is so even if there was a cost to Lord Gnome who would presumably be able to claim a deduction for the costs as a trading expense! If an increased salary had been paid to Ms Chevrolet to spend on beauty treatments the salary, including the increased salary, would be liable to tax (see *Fergusson v Noble* (1919) 7 TC 176). It is not enough that the benefit has a monetary value which can be assigned to it if it is not convertible into money. It is therefore necessary to determine whether a fringe benefit is convertible into money, and if so what its value is, to determine its taxability.

Weight v Salmon (1935) 19 TC 174 supports the view that one must look to what is received and what it can be converted into for the purposes of the general part of Schedule E (statutory modifications may change this, see Chapter 7). Mr Salmon was a managing director of J. Lyons & Co. Ltd. He was given the opportunity by resolution of the board of directors to subscribe for shares in the company at par when the value of the shares on the open market was in excess of this. The granting of such an opportunity was repeated over a number of years. The resolution originally expressed the opportunity to be given because of his 'eminent and special services' as managing director. He was assessed on the difference between the market value and the par value of the shares.

Lord Atkin said:

I think it is really impossible to appreciate the argument which suggests that that was not an immediate profit in the nature of money's worth received by the Director as remuneration for his services. It appears to me to correspond very closely in substance to a case where a company might have sold 1,000 tons of its product, if the company were a colliery company, to a director who was in the coal trade, at a price which was one-third of the market price of the day. There no question could arise that the person was receiving profit in the nature of money's worth to the extent of the difference between the price he could get for it and the price he had actually paid.[26]

6.20 VALUATION OF BENEFITS IN KIND

Even if something can be turned to pecuniary account so as to amount to an emolument, one still needs to know how much to bring into charge to income tax. The question thus arises, 'how is the value of benefits in kind to be ascertained?' The question of the amount to be included in the Schedule E assessment of a benefit in kind was considered in *Wilkins v Rogerson* (1960) 39 TC 44. It was decided there that the basic principle was that where an employee receives a benefit in kind, the taxpayer is chargeable on the amount which could be obtained by the disposal of the benefit – the cost to the employer is in these circumstances irrelevant. It is the resale value to the employee that matters.

Wilkins v Rogerson concerned a suit which was given to the taxpayer by his employers, Anglo-Oriental and General Investment Trust Limited. In 1955

[26.] His Lordship advised that the appeal be dismissed. Lords Tomlin, Russell, MacMillan and Wright agreed.

the directors decided to give all the company's male staff (other than executives) a Christmas present of clothes up to the value of £15 for wear at the office, drawn from a choice of a suit, overcoat or raincoat. According to the case stated 'the clothes were to be purchased by the employer from Montague Burton Limited. Thus the employees were to choose the article they wanted and Burtons would bill Anglo-Oriental. The taxpayer chose a suit marked £14.15s.' The Special Commissioners found that the suit formed part of the emoluments of the taxpayer but that the assessment which included the cost of the suit was bad. He should have been assessed not on the cost of the suit to the company but on the price he would get for it if he sold it, which the parties agreed to be £5.00. This decision was upheld by Danckwerts J and in the Court of Appeal.

Harman LJ said:

> ... this perquisite is a taxable subject matter because it is money's worth. It is money's worth because it can be turned into money and, when turned into money, the taxable subject matter is the value received. I cannot, myself, see how it is connected with the cost to the employer ... Income Tax is a tax levied on income. The taxpayer has to pay on what he gets. Here he got a suit. He can realise it only for £5. The detriment to his employer has been considerably more, but that seems to me to be irrelevant, and I do not see that it makes any difference that no property in the suit would ever pass to the employer.

After citing *Tennant* v *Smith* Harman LJ continued, 'this can be realised in cash, and it is that realisable quality which is the measure of the taxpayer's liability'.[27]

The valuation of a benefit is a most important matter in two respects. First in determining whether the benefit is taxable since, if the benefit is not convertible into money because it has no resale value, it is not taxable as it is not an emolument. For example, a service provided to an employee, such as free conveyancing to the solicitor's secretary, has no residual value and thus is not taxable on general Schedule E principles. It is money saved, not money going into the pocket. The contention that tax is chargeable on money saved was rejected in *Tennant* v *Smith* and subsequent cases. Secondly, the valuation of a benefit in kind determines the extent of the liability in respect of it on general Schedule E principles.

Both these questions were discussed in the House of Lords in *Heaton v Bell* 46 TC 211, (a case already met in connection with gross salary subject to a deduction or a reduced salary). Their Lordships considered a second question which arose, namely if there was a reduction in the salary whether the benefit of the use of the car was taxable as an emolument. Except in the case of Lord Reid this discussion was obiter but it is certainly of persuasive authority. It should be remembered that the employee alone was allowed to drive the car under the scheme except in cases of emergency. It was not a

---

[27] The Code could change the measure of liability, see Chapter 7.

benefit which could be assigned within the so-called conditions of the scheme. Lord Reid's view was that one must ask what money would have come in and gone into the taxpayer's pocket if he had surrendered his right to use the car. He considered that the taxpayer was liable to tax on the basis of the increase of wages to which he would have been entitled on surrendering his right to the car. He said that by surrendering the right he had disposed of it to his advantage, he had turned it to pecuniary account and as a result of this surrender money came in and went into his pocket. Lord Morris of Borth-y-Gest, when considering what he called the alternative construction of the agreement, considered that the assessment made would still have been correct on the basis that the use of the car would have been a perquisite to be included in the full amount of the emoluments chargeable to tax. He considered that the taxpayer could at any time convert his right to use the car into money, by saying to his employers that he relinquished in their favour his right to the use of the car and in exchange could require that an ascertained sum of money should be paid to him. He was in a position to choose to have an ascertained sum of money and no car or not to have that particular ascertained sum of money but to have a car. This perquisite represented money's worth.

Lord Diplock accepted the contention of the Crown that the free use of the car for the taxpayer's own purposes under the company's loan scheme was a perquisite from his employment in respect of which Mr Bell was chargeable to income tax under Schedule E because, if he had chosen to forgo it, he could have received a higher money wage instead.

Lord Hodson and Lord Upjohn dissented on this point. Lord Hodson found himself unable to escape from the conclusion that the use of the motor car was not convertible into money for it could not be converted in the ordinary sense of the word by sale or assignment to another. Lord Upjohn considered that the taxpayer could not turn the perquisite, which was no more than the personal use of the car, into money or anything which could be equated with money; all he could do would be to give up his perquisite and obtain higher wages. These views seemed to find some support from the speeches in *Tennant* v *Smith* but when one considers that convertibility had already been extended in meaning in *Abbott* v *Philbin* it does not seem to be too extreme a decision. The decision in *Wilkins* v *Rogerson* was that one should tax the value of the benefit to the taxpayer when, as here, the benefit had a cash-in value which the employee could have enforced. On that basis this case accords with the line of authority stretching from *Tennant* v *Smith*. *Wilkins* v *Rogerson* was cited with approval by Lords Reid, Morris and Hodson in *Heaton* v *Bell* (see also *Laidler* v *Perry* (1963) 42 TC 351).

6.21 SUMMARY: BENEFITS IN KIND AND 'COMMON LAW' OF SCHEDULE E

In summary it seems possible to make four points in regard to benefits in kind and the general part of Schedule E:

(a) In order to be taxable the benefit must be capable of being turned to pecuniary account, that is it must be money's worth with the quality of convertibility into money. It seems that it is not necessary that what is received should itself be convertible into money by assignment or the benefit received itself. If the non-assignable option can be turned into shares which can be sold that may be sufficient.

(b) If the benefit has no residual value, for example, the provision of a service and is not convertible into money then it is not a taxable emolument.

(c) If the benefit has a 'cash-in' value then it is convertible into money.

(d) The amount on which tax is chargeable in respect of the benefit in kind is its value to the recipient which will often be its second-hand value though where the benefit is not assignable or saleable but is capable of being cashed in, then the cash-in value will be the amount included in the assessment.

6.22 CONTRACTUAL CONDITIONS

A further problem was raised in *Heaton* v *Bell* which had been raised earlier in *Abbott* v *Philbin* ((1960) 39 TC at p. 125) by Lord Radcliffe where he said that:

> ... it has generally been assumed that this decision [i.e., *Tennant* v *Smith*] does impose a limitation upon the taxability of benefits in kind which are of a personal nature, it is not enough to say that they have a value which can be assigned some monetary equivalent. If by their nature they are incapable of being turned into money by the recipient they are not taxable, even though they are of value to him. It is obvious that this conception raises many attendant uncertainties which are not, so far as I know, cleared up except where some particular class of benefit has offended the eye of the legislature and has been dealt with by special legislation. Must the inconvertibility arise from the nature of the thing itself or can it be imposed by mere contractual stipulation? Does it matter that the conversion into money is a practical though not a theoretical impossibility; on the other hand, that conversion, though forbidden is the most probable assumption?

He left these matters open.

The question being raised seems to be capable of being rephrased as whether the benefit has to be completely non-assignable in its nature or whether it is sufficient to escape liability that the terms of use of the benefit, for example a season-ticket on British Rail, provided that the benefit is non-assignable. Suppose in breach of the conditions of use the employee was able to sell the ticket to someone else, would that make it convertible? Further, can an employer reduce the value of the benefit to his employee by imposing contractual conditions? For example, what is the effect of the employer imposing a condition that only the employee should drive the car? Lord Reid in *Heaton* v *Bell* suggests that contractual conditions if they are genuine are sufficient. He says in his judgment:

the recipient of a benefit other than a sum of money can be assessed and can only be assessed on the amount of money which he could have got by some lawful means by the use or in place of the perquisite. I say by lawful means for I see no ground for the Revenue being entitled to disregard a genuine condition restricting the recipient's right to use or dispose of the perquisite. But of course if any restrictive condition is a sham or is inserted simply to defeat the claims of the Revenue it can be disregarded.

This seems to require us to look at the realities of the situation. Lord Diplock left unanswered the question whether the inconvertibility must arise from the nature of the thing itself. He considered it unnecessary to answer that question for the purposes of the appeal before him. But he continued:

it must not be supposed that I assent to the proposition that the benefit in kind can escape all charges to tax as a perquisite by limitations upon the employee's right to deal with it imposed by a contract collateral to the contract of employment which he enters into of his own volition.

It is submitted that Lord Reid's approach should be regarded as the correct view of the matter and that one should look to the realities of the situation and disregard sham conditions. But this still does not solve the problem if, for example, someone pays to use a season ticket in breach of the conditions?

6.23 THE RULE IN *NICOLL* v *AUSTIN*

One form of 'perk' from an employment, known as a benefit in kind, has been considered above but a benefit to an employee or officeholder can take other forms such as the discharge of an employee's liability to a third party by the employer.

The discharge of an employee's debt to a third party by the employer is clearly of benefit to the employee but is it merely a saving to the employee's pocket and so not an emolument? Should this be taxable under Schedule E? The answer to this is, 'yes' as it is a benefit to the employee and it is this that Schedule E seeks to tax under its 'common law' principles. The next question is, what should the measure of taxable emolument be? Should it be the cost to the employer or the benefit to the employee? It cannot be the resale value as there is no possibility of resale. The general part of Schedule E looks to the benefit to the employee as the measure, rather than the cost to the employer which is the general measure in the Code (see Chapter 7). UK tax law treats the measure of the benefit as being the amount of the loan discharged. This is sometimes called the rule in *Nicoll* v *Austin*.

This rule is to the effect that an employee will be charged to tax where the employer meets an obligation incurred by the employee, for such payments are regarded as money's worth to the employee. However, the value to the employee is regarded as the sum paid by the employer to discharge the obligation. The measure of the taxable emolument is effectively in most cases the cost to the employer of discharging the obligation.[28] This contrasts with the benefits in kind rules where under the general law the measure of the taxable emolument is usually the second-hand value of the benefit. If the employer in *Wilkins* v *Rogerson* (see para. 6.20) had discharged an obligation incurred by the employee to Burtons, the employee would have been taxable on the amount paid by the employer, probably £14.15s, rather than on £5 as the second-hand value of the suit. It is thus the benefit to the employee that matters. As always in tax matters it is vital to get the analysis of the underlying transaction sorted out before trying to apply the tax law to the transactions in question.

In *Nicoll* v *Austin* (1935) 19 TC 53 the life governing director and principal shareholder of a company found that he was unable to continue to pay for the upkeep of his house, Debden Hall at Loughton in Essex, and that he would have to vacate it. The company entered into an agreement with him under which the company agreed that if a director continued to reside in the house it would pay the cost of upkeep of the house. The company paid the rates and discharged the cost of heating, lighting, telephone and the upkeep of the garden. Finlay J held that this was an emolument from the director's office or employment as it constituted money's worth and that the director was correctly assessed on the value of the benefit which is what the company had paid to discharge the obligation. Thus if a lecturer incurs a substantial bill at the local gastronomic restaurant entertaining undergraduates but the college pays the bill then the lecturer would be taxable on an amount equal to the obligation of his that the college discharged. If on the other hand the college had provided the meal, statutory provisions apart, the lecturer would be taxable on the second-hand value of those meals which in the case of many colleges might well be nil.

This principle extends to the payment by the employer of an employee's tax. The employee is regarded as having received gross emoluments equivalent to the amount he actually received plus the tax on that sum. The grossing up only takes place once.[29]

The rule in *Nicoll* v *Austin* does not always apply where an employer apparently discharges an obligation. Thus in *Barclays Bank* v *Naylor* (1960) 39 TC 256 the trustees of the ICI scheme to assist in the education of the children of overseas employees of ICI paid sums under deduction of tax into the name of such a child. On a claim to repayment of the tax deducted, the question arose as to whose income it was. The father's liability in respect of the school fees was settled by the trustees of the fund by transfer to the school of income from the fund which was payable to the employee's child.

Cross J held that the payment did not constitute income of the employee. 'The way in which the employer contributed to the education expenses was not by paying school bills but by providing the child with an income out of

---

[28.] What if the employer discharges a larger sum at a smaller cost by providing, for example, 'a hawk or a robe' to discharge a £1,000 debt of the employee? It seems the better view would be that £1,000 is taxable on the employee as this is the benefit to the employee.

[29.] See *North British Railway* v *Scott* [1923] AC and *Hartland* v *Diggines* (1926) 10 TC 247 and note the position at company law on directors and tax free payments: see in particular s. 311, CA.

which the bills could be met.' This again illustrates the importance of analysing the underlying transactions carefully to ascertain their precise legal effect before seeking to apply the provisions of the Taxes Acts to them.

The discharge of a debt to a third party is similar to the forgiving of a debt to the employer. Such forgiveness was held taxable on the value of a debt forgiven in *Clayton v Gothorp* (1971) 47 TC 168.

6.24 PAYMENTS COMPENSATING FOR LOST OR WITHDRAWN FRINGE BENEFITS

The broad principle is that where a benefit in kind or a right to commission is withdrawn from an employee and the employer pays a compensatory sum to the employee in lieu of the lost benefit, that payment is an emolument taxable under Schedule E (but cf. *Mairs v Haughey* below). The argument that such sums are capital, and thus not liable to income tax, does not seem to have held much sway with the courts.

In *Bird v Martland* [1982] STC 603 the taxpayers, Martland and Allen, had been provided with a company car in an unusual way by their employer contributing £350 a year towards the cost of hire. The expenses of running the car were met by the employee as was the remainder of the hire charge. The scheme was withdrawn after a takeover of the employer. The taxpayers were awarded a compensatory payment approximately equal to the second-hand value of the cars hired. They were assessed on this as an emolument. The General Commissioners upheld the taxpayers' appeal. The Crown's appeal to Walton J was, however, successful.

Walton J said:

> So we come back (as I think in all these cases we always come back in the end) to the formulation by counsel in the case of *Brumby (Inspector of Taxes) v Milner* ([1975] STC 215 at 231): does the employee receive the sum in question 'because he is an employee without any other qualification than that he was an employee at a particular date'? The formulation here is not quite the same, but it is very parallel indeed: that the employees received the money because they were employees having perquisites which were going to be taken away from them for the future. Once one is driven to that as the true analysis of what took place, on the facts as found by the General Commissioners is there anything that can be put in the scales against it? Really, the only matter that can possibly be put in the scales against it is that there was no obligation put on the employees concerned to remain in the company's employ after receipt of the payment, and that is of such slight weight that it cannot possibly, in my judgment, justify a contrary conclusion to that which I think any sensible person, uninstructed, would reach: that this sum of £2,110 paid to each of these taxpayers was paid to them as a perquisite of their employment in substitution for (or, to use the words that the General Commissioners themselves used, 'as recompense for') the deprivation of the perquisite which they had hitherto enjoyed.

There have been many other cases on such compensatory payments including the following.

McGregor v *Randall* [1984] STC 223 (compensation for loss of commission);
Hamblett v *Godfrey* [1987] STC 60 (compensation for loss of rights to belong to a trade union) discussed at para. 6.28;
Bray v *Best* [1986] STC 96 (lump sum paid upon the termination of an employee trust);
Holland v *Geoghegan* (1972) 48 TC 482 (compensation paid to refuse collector for loss of salvage rights).

In the relatively recent case of *Mairs* v *Haughey* [1993] STC 569 the taxpayer agreed to forgo a contingent right to be paid a non-statutory enhanced redundancy payment on the privatisation of Harland & Wolff for a payment of £4,506. The courts held him wrongly assessed. The Special Commissioner did not regard the payment as an inducement for a new employment nor did the House of Lords and dismissed the Crown's appeal. They considered that the emoluments to be taxable must come from the employment not just from the employer.

6.25 EXTRA-STATUTORY CONCESSIONS

There are certain Extra-statutory Concessions which are relevant in this context. They are not the law but they do represent the Revenue's practice. Examples are:

A2 meal vouchers
A6 miners' coal
A57 suggestions schemes
A58 travel etc. when public transport disrupted.[30]

6.26 SUMMARY: EMOLUMENTS

In summary it can said that an employee will in general be taxable:

(a) on the second-hand or cash-in value of the benefits in kind;
(b) on the cash-in value of payments in lieu of such payments; and
(c) on the cost to the employer of discharging an obligation of the employee to a third party.

6.27 'THEREFROM'

Section 19, Taxes Act taxes the emoluments 'therefrom'. It is thus a necessary condition of charge that the emoluments be 'therefrom'. It is not entirely clear what this means or what test is to be applied to determine whether a payment is 'therefrom'.

[30.] See further Inland Revenue Pamphlet IR 1; written answer 23 May 1979, Hansard Vol 967 Col 147, [1979] STI 220 and *Simon's Taxes* Vol G.

Schedule E – income from employment

The first matter to consider is 'from what?'. Broadly, payment must be derived from the office or employment, i.e., there must be a causal link between the emolument and the office or employment. The problem is, what is the necessary link? How is it to be tested? The reader should consider when reading what follows whether the question to start with is, 'is the payment for acting as or being an employee?' Is it to be extended to becoming an employee? (cf. Lord Templeman in *Mairs* v *Haughey* [1993] STC 569).

It should be remembered that this section is concerned only with the 'common law' of Schedule E and not the special statutory provisions considered in Chapter 7. These have their own causal test which may be different!

The leading case on the meaning of 'therefrom' is still *Hochstrasser* v *Mayes* (1959) 38 TC 673. This case concerned a payment under an ICI scheme guaranteeing employees against loss on the sale of a house on a transfer required by ICI. The taxpayer, Mayes, was employed by ICI, a large company with plants situated in several parts of the country. In addition to his contract of employment, the taxpayer had entered into a 'housing agreement' with the company. The agreement, which was optional, provided inter alia that when an employee moved house at the company's request and sustained a loss on the sale of his previous home the company would indemnify the employee in respect of the loss. The Revenue argued that £350 paid by ICI to Mayes pursuant to the housing agreement was a taxable emolument. The taxpayer appealed successfully.

Upjohn J (at p. 685) said in the High Court on the question of the necessary link:

> In my judgment, the authorities show this, that it is a question to be answered in the light of the particular facts whether or not a particular payment is or is not a profit arising from the employment. . . . not every payment made to an employee is necessarily made to him as a profit arising from his employment. Indeed in my judgment the authorities show that to be a profit arising from the employment the payment must be made by reference to the services and it must be something in the nature of a reward for services past, present or future.

The learned judge found in favour of the taxpayer on the grounds that the payment was not part of the employee's remuneration or contract of service and was not an inducement to enter into the employment. The House of Lords reached the same conclusion. Viscount Radcliffe neatly summed up the position by saying an emolument received by an employee 'is assessable if it has been paid to him in return for acting as or being an employee' (p. 707). The House of Lords unanimously gave judgment against the Crown upholding the decisions of the court below.[31]

The first judgment in the House of Lords was delivered by Viscount Simonds. He cited the above passage from Upjohn J's speech with approval saying that:

[31.] The phrases '*causa causans*' and '*causa sine qua non*' were used in the Court of Appeal and House of Lords but have been criticised; see e.g. Lord Simon of Glaisdale in *Brumby* v *Milner* [1976] 3 All ER 636 at p. 639 set out in para. 6.28 below

Mr Justice Upjohn before whom the case first came, after a review of the relevant case law, expressed himself thus in a passage which appears to sum up the law in a manner that cannot be improved upon. 'In my judgment,' he said, 'the authorities show this, that it is a question to be answered in the light of the particular facts of every case whether or not a particular payment is or is not a profit arising from an employment. Disregarding contracts for full consideration in money or money's worth and personal presents, in my judgment not every payment made to an employee is necessarily made to him as a profit arising from his employment. Indeed in my judgment the authorities show that to be a profit arising from employment the payment must be made in reference to the services the employee renders by virtue of his office, and it must be something in the nature of a reward for services past, present or future.' In this passage the single word 'past' may be open to question, but apart from that it appears to be entirely accurate.

Viscount Simonds went on:

> if in such cases as these the issue turns as I think it does upon whether the fact of employment is the *causa causans* or only the *causa sine qua non* of the benefit which perhaps is only to give the natural meaning to the word therefrom in the statute it must often be difficult to draw the line and say on which side of the line a particular case falls.

His lordship pointed out that the salary of the employees compared favourably with salaries elsewhere.

Lord Radcliffe agreed with Viscount Simonds's conclusion and his reasons for advancing that conclusion. He considered the test to be applied as contained in the statutory requirement, i.e., the payment if it is to be the subject of assessment must arise from the office or employment. He continued that:

> in the past several explanations have been offered by judges of eminence as to the significance of the word 'from' in this context. It has been said that the payment must have been made to the employee as such. It has been said that it must have been made to him in his capacity of employee. It has been said that it is assessable if paid by way of remuneration for his services, and said further that this is what is meant by payment to him 'as such'. These are all glosses and they are of value as illustrating the idea which is expressed by the statute. . . . But it is perhaps worth observing that they do not displace the words. Their meaning is adequately conveyed by saying that whilst it is not sufficient to render a payment assessable that an employee would not have received it unless he had been an employee, it is assessable if it has been paid to him in return for acting as or being an employee.[32]

[32.] This was approved and applied in *Allan* v *IRC* [1994] STC 943.

Schedule E – income from employment

This seems to be the *causa causans* test expressed in English rather than Latin. Lord Radcliffe considered that the £350 here was not paid for being or acting as an employee.

Lord Cowen considered that the court must be satisfied that the service agreement was the *causa causans* and not merely the *causa sine qua non* of the receipt of the profits. He accepted Jenkins LJ's proposition that the employment here was only the *sine qua non* and not the *causa causans*. Lord Keith of Avonhome merely agreed.

Lord Denning took a characteristically bold approach and tried to decide the case by the touch stone of common sense which even he admitted was perhaps rather a rash test to take in a Revenue matter. He said that in the last resort one must come back to the test of the statutory words. He considered that the £350 received by Mr Mayes was not a profit from his employment for the simple reason that it was not a reward or remuneration or return for his services in any sense of the word.

It is thus clear from their Lordships' speeches that there must be a causal connection between the payment and the employment if it is to be assessable to tax under Schedule E.

On the case law at that time it seemed that a payment made to an employee or office holder would be 'derived from' the office or employment if:

(a) the payment is being made to him for acting as or being an employee rather than merely that the opportunity to receive the payment arose because the recipient was an employee. The employment or office must be the *causa causans* not merely the *causa sine qua non*; and (which probably amounts to the same thing);

(b) the payment must be made in reference to the services which the employee renders by virtue of his office and be in the nature of a reward for his present or future services. If made for past services the position is not entirely clear.

In considering the following cases the reader should consider whether or not the above represents the current law.

6.28   SOME SUBSEQUENT CASES

The House of Lords applied the *Hochstrasser* test in *Laidler* v *Perry* (1965) 42 TC 351. This was a case which concerned vouchers given by a company to its employees at Christmas. The position would now be covered by statute.

However, the causation test had one critic in the House of Lords, Lord Simon of Glaisdale who did not think that the issue could be determined by 'outmoded and ambiguous concepts of causation couched in Latin'.[33] He subsequently said in *Brumby* v *Milner* [1976] 3 All ER 636 at p. 639 that:

> the distinction between a *causa causans* and a *causa sine qua non* was formerly much used in other branches of the law; this was found to confuse

---

[33] Cf. Hart and Honore, *Causation in the Law*.

rather than illuminate and it has been generally abandoned. Causation has been debated by metaphoricians and magicians throughout the recorded history of philosophy; the debate continues, with more sophisticated tools of analysis than the term *causa causans* and *causa sine qua non*. These would rarely if ever assist the law where they have frequently been used without definition or analysis.

He cited Lord Radcliffe in *Hochstrasser* and Lord Reid in *Laidler* as laying down, in his words, a far less question begging test and asked, was it paid to him as an employee? However, he seems to ignore Lord Reid's discussion of the *Hochstrasser* case and in *Laidler* v *Perry* his example of a gift to an employee where he says the employment was not the *causa causans*, and Lord Radcliffe's whole approach in the *Hochstrasser* case and his agreement with Viscount Simonds's conclusions and the reasons advanced for that conclusion.

Brumby v *Milner* above concerned the taxability under Schedule E of distributions of the surplus on the winding-up of a profit sharing scheme which had been set up for the benefit of employees. The distributions were interim distributions to the employees and pensioners entitled under the trust deed. Disagreement arose between the Revenue and the company and led to a test case being taken to the House of Lords. It was contended on behalf of the recipients that the payment's effective cause was not the employment but the decision to terminate the scheme and the payment was not from the office or employment. It was held that the scheme was fundamentally one based on reward for services by the employee and accordingly the payments thereunder were rewards to the employees for their services and so taxable as emoluments of their employment. Lord Simon's criticism did not seem to shake the authority of *Hochstrasser* and the *causa causans* type of approach.

Lord Simon's criticism did not have much sway in the subsequent case of *Tyrer* v *Smart*. Mr Justice Brightman talked in terms of *causa causans* and *causa sine qua non*. The Court of Appeal either approved or used similar language in upholding his judgment on appeal. Lord Edmund Davies approved Brightman J's summary in the Lords though the case was decided in the Lords on the issue as to whether the court could interfere with the Commissioners' findings. Following *Edwards* v *Bairstow* they could not. This is not the most helpful way of proceeding for those concerned to establish the meaning of 'emoluments therefrom'. *Tyrer* v *Smart* [1976] STC 521 concerned an employee who availed himself of an opportunity to acquire 5,000 shares at a price of £1 per share under a special scheme giving preference to employees on a sale by tender of a number of the shares in the parent company by his employer. A certain proportion of the shares were reserved for the employees at a fixed price of £1 per share. The market price on the day of allotment of the shares was between 23 shillings and 24 shillings per share. The taxpayer was assessed to income tax under Schedule E on the difference between the market price and his acquisition price for the 5,000 shares that he acquired on the basis that the preferential right to apply for the shares was an emolument of his employment.

There was a specific finding by the Commissioners that the company's purpose in making shares available for employees was to encourage employees to identify with the company and to induce loyalty towards the company. It is also worth noting that one of the directors' memorandums sent to employees stated, inter alia, 'by this means all members of the staff will have the opportunity of purchasing readily marketable shares through The Stock Exchange and for that matter will be able to sell them quickly at the market rate if they so wished' (see pp. 522–9 (case stated)).

Brightman J held that the employment although the *causa sine qua non* of the benefit was not the *causa causans*. The *causa causans* was a combination of several facts including the view the taxpayer took of the market, his willingness to risk his own money in a venture that was speculative in the sense that its outcome was uncertain and his completion of the application form.

The House of Lords restored the Commissioners' decision that there was an emolument from the employment, essentially on the ground that the decision was reasonable so they could not interfere with it (relying on *Edwards v Bairstow*).

Lord Diplock (with whom Lord Russell of Killowen agreed) said that the test for taxability was well established. It was whether the benefit represents a reward or return for the employee's services, whether past, present or future, and whether it was bestowed on him for some other reason. The border line he considered might be a very fine one. He also thought that where the employer creates the benefit, as opposed to a third party, the employer's motive is an important factor. Lord Edmund Davies took a similar view.

An interesting case on this particular matter of causation and Schedule E, which at first sight seems strange in result, is the case of *Commissioners of Inland Revenue v Morris* (1967) 44 TC 685. This case concerned a chief engineer of the UK Atomic Energy Authority who was seconded to the South of Scotland Electricity Board. After the work for which he was seconded was completed he left the Authority and joined the Board. The following Christmas the Board paid him £1,000 stating that it was to mark their appreciation of his work during his period of secondment. The taxpayer had not expected such a payment. At the same time the Board gave amounts ranging from £150 to £750 to 15 of the 33 other employees of the Authority seconded to the Board. The Commissioners' decision that the payment was not an emolument from the taxpayer's employment was upheld by the First Division of the Court of Session. The Lord President said that:

> the circumstances in which the question has arisen in the decided cases are infinitely various, and no single criterion can be extracted from the decision conclusively to determine on which side of the line the payment falls . . . no two cases are precisely alike but it is possible to find factors pointing in favour of or against liability.

He then set out the factors which he considered supported the Commissioners' decision.

(a) It is usually easier to infer that a payment is assessable to tax if the recipient's office or employment has not yet terminated when the payment is made. Here this factor points to an expression of gratitude and not to remuneration for services.

(b) The payment was not made by the employers at the time the work was performed. This makes it harder to infer a reward for services.

(c) Here there was a once and for all payment, not recurring periodical payments which are more likely to be derived from the employment.

(d) The accompanying letter in this case also pointed in this direction.

Although many Schedule E cases have concerned actresses, actors, dancers and sportsmen the most important recent case on this is *Hamblett* v *Godfrey* [1987] 1 All ER 916. This had an interesting political background as it concerned the payments to staff at GCHQ in Cheltenham when trade union recognition was withdrawn (see *Council of Civil Service Unions* v *Minister of State for the Civil Service* [1985] AC 374). To the annoyance of the recipients the Inland Revenue decided to tax the payments. The decision that the receipt was liable to income tax was thought by many to extend Schedule E by taxing such compensation. However, it is suggested that the case was merely an application of the *Hochstrasser* principle to the particular facts. It was a payment made to those who stayed on and so was essentially a reward for being an employee or continuing so to be. The payment was for the loss of rights that were not personal rights but were directly connected with the employment.[34] The source of the payment was an employment.

In *Hamblett* the payment was made by the employer. In *Shilton* v *Wilmhurst* (see para. 6.34.2) it was made by the 'former' employer. However, merely because a payment is made by someone other than an employer, it does not mean it is not from the employment and so not taxable under Schedule E. The fact that a payment is made by an employer makes it more likely that a payment is taxable as it is more likely to be made for acting as or being an employee and so derived from the employment (see, e.g, *IRC* v *Morris* (1967) 44 TC 685). However, a voluntary payment from a third party may, depending on the circumstances, amount to an emolument derived from the employment. In contrast a payment made because of the personal qualities or circumstances of the recipient is unlikely to be derived from the employment.

In *Mairs* v *Haughey* (the Harland & Wolff restructuring payment case, see para. 6.24) the House of Lords relied on Viscount Radcliffe's speech in *Hochstrasser* where he considered the test was whether the payment had been made for acting as or being an employee. This was not the case when the payments were properly analysed here. Lord Woolf said (at p. 580) 'The distinction between the deferred payment of wages or salary and a redundancy payment may be narrow but is none the less real. In the case of a deferred payment once the employment comes to an end the right to payment will inevitably accrue. In the case of a redundancy payment, the sum is only

---

[34] Cf. *Holland* v *Geoghegan* (1972) 48 TC 482.

Schedule E – income from employment

payable in limited circumstances and there will be no entitlement if for example the employee leaves the employment of his own accord.

Finally, *Wilcock* v *Eves* [1995] STC 18 may have extended the meaning of 'therefrom'. Carnwath J said (at p. 25) that, 'One thing that is clear from the recent authorities is that the concept of an emolument from employment is not confined to something in the nature of a reward for continuing employment'. He considered 'on the facts of this case' there was no distinction between the common law test and the test under the Code of 'by reason of employment'. It has yet to be established whether this case has extended the test beyond those laid down in the earlier cases of higher courts.

6.29 THIRD PARTY PAYMENTS

6.29.1 General

Two general points need to be made first. These are as follows.

(a) That to be referable to services the payment does not have to be made by the employer. A voluntary payment from a third payment may, depending on the circumstances, amount to an emolument derived from the office or employment. However it is, in practice, easier to show that a payment from a third party is not 'from' the employment than is the case with a payment from the employer.

(b) A payment made because of personal qualities or circumstances of the recipient is unlikely to be an emolument from his office or employment.

This distinction can be very difficult to apply in practice.

6.29.2 Areas to consider

There are many cases on this subject. However, there are four areas, in particular, in which third party payments have been considered. These are in connection with:

(a) tips;
(b) the clergy;
(c) bonuses; and
(d) inducement payments.

6.29.3 Tips

Are tips paid to an employee by a third party taxable under Schedule E? *Calvert* v *Wainwright* (1947) 27 TC 475 concerned tips paid to an employed taxi driver. Atkinson J held that the normal tips paid to such a cabbie were taxable. He said (at p. 478):

> Some people take the same taxi every morning to take them to their work ... It comes in the morning as a matter of course and then takes him home

at night. The ordinary tip given in those circumstances would be something that was assessable, but supposing at Christmas, or when the man is going for a holiday, the hirer says: 'You have been very attentive to me, here is a £10 note', he would be making a present, and I should say it would not be assessable because it has been given to the man because of his qualities, his faithfulness, and the way he has stuck to the passenger, and has always been available in that sort of way. In those circumstances . . . it would be a payment of an extraordinary kind and so not taxable. The payment was for personal qualities and not a payment to the driver qua taxi driver.

(See also *Wright* v *Boyce* (1958) 38 TC 160 (huntsman's tips), and *Fiagel* v *Fox* [1990] STC 583 (tronc arrangements).)

6.29.4 The clergy cases

The clergy cases concern collections made for clergymen particularly at Easter and payments from clergy sustentation funds. The cases turn on the distinction between payments made to an officeholder qua officeholder and payments made to the clergyman which was personal to the recipient. (See, e.g., *Herbert* v *McQuade* (1902) 4 TC 489 and *Turner* v *Cuxson* (1838) 27 TC 422.) The fact that the qualities had been displayed while in Holy Orders did not make the payment a reward for services.

In *Re Strong* (1878) 1 TC 207 the Christmas gift of money raised by subscription and made annually to the clergyman responsible for a parish in Scotland was held assessable under Schedule E. The payment might be voluntary but was one made to the clergyman as their clergyman and received by him in respect of the discharge of his duties. A similar decision was reached in *Cooper* v *Blakiston* 5 TC 347. This concerned the Reverend Blakiston who was the vicar of St Swithin's, East Grinstead. He received the collections taken in church at Easter together with certain voluntary payments as a freewill offering to his own use. This followed an appeal by the Bishop recommending such offerings supported by the churchwardens. The House of Lords held these receipts were assessable.

In *Herbert* v *McQuade* 4 TC 489 a grant from the Queen Victoria Clergy Sustentation Fund which related to the office was held taxable. Stirling LJ said that a profit accrues by reason of an office when it comes to the holder of an office as such – in that capacity – and without the fulfilment of any further condition on his part. He considered that there was a capacity case here.

Turner v *Cuxson* should be contrasted with this. Here a payment from the Curates Augmentation Fund was held not assessable as, to qualify, the curate had to be a deserving curate of 15 years' standing and was paid because of the individual's personal qualities and circumstances. It was given '*donatio honoris causa* because for 15 years he has worked hard and borne a good character and borne a high character in his sacred profession'. The payment was made because he was a 'good chap' rather than because of his office according to their Lordships. (See also *Poynting* v *Faulkner* 5 TC 145.)

6.29.5 The bonus cases

The bonus cases cover a wide area and in this context the cricket and football cases are of particular interest.

6.29.5.1 The cricket cases

Reed v *Seymour* 11 TC 625 was the first of the benefit cases. James Seymour was a noted Kent cricketer. As he neared the end of his career in 1920 he was granted a benefit match by Kent. The player had no right to a benefit match and the benefit was granted by the club and the exercise of their absolute discretion. The benefit was granted only on condition that the proceeds were invested in the name of the club's trustees and used for approved purposes. The net gate money received at the match amounted to some £939. This was invested in securities together with money raised by certain public subscriptions, the income from which was paid to the player annually under deduction of tax. In 1923 the securities were realised and the proceeds handed over to the player with a view to their being applied to the purchase of a farm. The player was assessed on the gate money from the match but not on the public subscription. Rowlatt J considered that there was no distinction between the gate money and public subscriptions and that the public subscriptions had been excluded from assessment by the inspector to blunt the edge of any criticisms. Rowlatt J upheld the General Commissioners' decision to discharge the assessment. He considered the question was whether the receipt was in the nature of a remuneration or a personal gift. The learned judge, echoing the words of Lord Lorburn in *Cooper* v *Blakiston*, said that in the circumstances the payment was a testimonial of which it must properly be said that it was a mere present. He considered that the size of the sum and the once only nature of the payment were important factors. This was a very large and exceptional sum given on quite an exceptional occasion to a professional of a well known club, a hero in a great many people's eyes, a valiant cricketer! His decision was reversed by the Court of Appeal (Sargant LJ dissenting) but was restored on appeal to the House of Lords (Lord Atkinson dissenting).

Viscount Cave, the Lord Chancellor, said that it must now be taken as settled, that all payments made to the holder of an office or employment as such, that is to say by way of remuneration for services, even though such payments might be voluntary, were chargeable to tax. They did not include a mere gift or present (such as a testimonial) which was made to him on personal grounds and not by way of payment for his services. The question to be answered, as Rowlatt J put it, 'is it in the end a personal gift or is it remuneration?' If the latter, it is subject to tax; the former is not. The benefit's purpose was not to encourage the cricketer to further exertions but to express the gratitude of his employers and the cricket loving public for what he had already done and their appreciation of his personal qualities.

Lord Phillimore distinguished what he called the 'religious cases' on the basis that although the offering might be voluntary it was not spontaneous. His lordship, who was well versed in ecclesiastical law, then discussed the common law as to Easter dues. Having considered these cases and certain other authorities, he said that he did not feel compelled by any of the authorities to hold that an employer could not make a solitary gift to his employee without rendering the gift liable to taxation under Schedule E. Nor did he think that it mattered that the payment was made during the period of service and not after its termination or that it was made in respect of good and faithful service. This was a plain gift. It was not taxable in his view under Schedule E.

Moorhouse v *Dooland* [1955] Ch 284 concerned Bruce Dooland, an Australian cricketer who was employed under a contract of service made between him and effectively the East Lancashire Cricket Club, one of the member clubs of the Lancashire Cricket League. The contract provided that the player should be paid a salary, receive talent money and expenses and that a collection should be made for any (meritorious) performance with the bat or the ball in specified matches in accordance with the rules of the Lancashire League for the time being. Bruce Dooland appeared in 25 matches in 1951 and received collections totalling £48.15s made on 11 occasions. He was assessed under Schedule E on this amount. The Court of Appeal held that the proceeds of these collections were taxable under Schedule E.

Lord Evershed MR pointed out three things:

(a) the performances in respect of which the collections were made were in the course of playing as the club's professional;

(b) the performances were in Rowlatt J's words in *Reed* v *Seymour* exceptional in the sense of being outstanding but they were not exceptions in the sense of being very rare and unlikely to be repeated. The recurrence was an important fact;

(c) it was a term of his contract enforceable at law that the collection should be taken if certain conditions were fulfilled. They were not spontaneous collections for a batting or bowling feat. A Christmas box might be taxable if the fact of the payment was essentially attributable to the circumstances that the payee was an employee.

He continued that in his view a gift or present made upon some special occasion such as a wedding, a century at cricket, a birthday or a season of the year when it is customary to make presents, does not necessarily cease to be non-taxable merely because the ties that link the recipient to the giver are, or substantially are, those of service and not those of blood or friendship; and this may be so although the present is, for example, given whenever another century is made or according to the custom, e.g., at Christmas (i.e., repeated). He distinguished *Seymour* v *Reed* principally on the grounds of contractual entitlement in this case.

Birkett LJ reached a similar conclusion. Jenkins LJ made a most important speech in this case which should be read in full. He said that it was long settled that payments made voluntarily by a third party to the holder of an office or employment may, in some circumstances, be taxable as profits arising to such holder therefrom, although the immediate source from which they proceeded consisted in the generosity of persons on whom he had no legal claim. Each case has to be judged on its facts.

6.29.5.2 Footballers Footballers have mainly been assessable because they received payments for accrued benefits on transfer. A payment to a footballer was held not taxable in *Moore* v *Griffiths* (1972) 48 TC 338 where a payment of £1,000 by the Football Association and £750 from Radox to Robert Frederick Moore, the captain of the 1966 World Cup winning side, were held not taxable. It was a payment to him in his personal capacity on an exceptional event and not 'in return for acting as or being an employee' (at p. 349).

6.30 ANY RELEVANT FACTORS?

There seem to be four factors which come out of the cases, which we have looked at so far, as being relevant in deciding whether a payment is taxable or not under Schedule E. These factors are as follows:

(a) The degree of anticipation of the payment. The unsuccessful taxpayer in *Moorhouse* v *Dooland* had a contractual right to the benefit. The successful Kent cricketer in *Seymour* v *Reed* had no legal right to a benefit match. It was given to him as a matter of the exercise of the club's discretion. The only provisions in his contract of service related to what was to be done to the proceeds of a benefit match if one were granted. The difficult question now is the effect of *Hamblett* v *Godfrey*, on this. If the test has been expanded, does this expanded test catch such payments? Should it?

(b) The second factor is the exceptional nature of the event or payment. Thus a payment made as a publicity stunt by Radox to the winning England World Cup side in 1966 along with the FA testimonials were held non-taxable in *Moore* v *Griffiths* above. However, a payment on an exceptional event may not always be unanticipated. Long service awards of cash and savings certificates were held assessable as gratuities or bonuses for the services given in *Weston* v *Hearn* and *Carmouche* v *Hearn* 25 TC 425. The position is now covered by published concession A22.

(c) The third consideration is whether or not the payment has a voluntary character. This seems to have been important in *Seymour* v *Reed* though Lord Phillimore did point out that the mere fact payment is voluntary does not automatically free the payment from income tax under Schedule E. Thus a tip to an employed London taxi driver would be taxable.

(d) The character of the payer and the relationship of the recipient to the payer can be an important factor. In *IRC* v *Morris* it appears to have played a part. Lord Migdale said the fact that the board was not the employer at the relevant time was an important though not conclusive factor. It was also a relevant factor in *Cowan* v *Seymour* 7 TC 372 where the shareholders of a company voted the liquidation surplus to the liquidator of the company who had also acted as its unpaid secretary. Lord Sterndale MR considered it significant that the payment was not made by the employer, the company, but the shareholders individually. It was also relevant in *Bridges* v *Hewitt* [1957] 2 All ER 281. Here the children of the founder of Meccano Limited fulfilled the expectations of those who helped their father by transferring shares to them under a strangely drawn deed. Morris LJ said (at p. 299):

The circumstance that a large payment is to be made by someone other than an employer may be a considerable indication, though by no means a conclusive one, that the payment is not by way of remuneration . . . Where some payment, and particularly some non-recurring payment, is received from someone other than an employer, it will probably only have the attributes of remuneration in those classes of cases where it is reasonable to expect that remuneration would come from some other source than from the pocket of an employer.

There are two other miscellaneous cases which should also be mentioned. The first is *Clayton* v *Gothorp* (1971) 47 TC 168. This case concerned a loan made by a local authority to a woman to enable her to take a course leading to the certificate of health visitors in the UK. It was provided that the loan was to become recoverable if she did not serve the council for 18 months after the course. She completed the necessary period of service and her husband was assessed to tax on the amount of the loan forgone as an emolument of his wife's employment. Plowman J held that he was properly assessed. What turned the loan into an absolute payment was the 18 months' service. It was a reward for past services and as such an emolument arising from Mrs Gothorp's employment. There is difficulty with the case, however, in that it seems to ignore the words of Lord Simonds when approving Upjohn J's statement of the principle to be applied in *Hochstrasser* v *Mayes* that the word 'past' may be open to question. Plowman J had cited this earlier in his judgment. The fact that Mrs Gothorp was fully remunerated during that period does not seem to have carried any weight, though it was apparently a relevant factor in *Hochstrasser* v *Mayes*. The past services problem has not been considered in the later cases, for example, *Tyrer* v *Smart*.

The other case is *Ball* v *Johnson* (1971) 47 TC 155. This case concerned the taxability of discretionary payments made to an employee who passed the Institute of Bankers' exams and received a payment from the Midland Bank. Plowman J reviewed the authorities extensively especially *Hochstrasser*, *Laidler* and *Morris*. He considered the employment was the *sine qua non* of the payment, it was not the *causa causans* of the payment which was accordingly not taxable.

6.31 INDUCEMENTS TO TAKE UP AN OFFICE OR EMPLOYMENT

6.31.1 General

A payment may be made to induce a person to take up an office or employment, sometimes called a 'golden hello'. Is this taxable? For there to be a charge there needs to be a causal connection between the payment and the job.

The most helpful case here is *Pritchard* v *Arundale* (1972) 47 TC 680 but this case turned on its peculiar facts, namely that the taxpayer could have kept the shares whether he joined the company or not and that he was moving

Schedule E – income from employment

from self-employed to employed. Arundale was a partner in a firm of accountants and was an adviser and friend of his client, Mr Lowe. Lowe invited Arundale to come and run his group of compaies. An agreement dated 19 June 1962 was entered into between Arundale and Lowe.

Clause 2 of the agreement provided:

> In consideration of Mr Arundale undertaking to serve the company as aforesaid Mr Lowe shall forthwith after the execution of this agreement transfer to Mr Arundale 4,000 of Mr Lowe's shares in the company.

The appointment as managing director was to begin not later than 1 January 1963.

The Commissioners who heard the case, relying on Upjohn J's dictum in *Hochstrasser* v *Mayes*, found that the transfer of the 4,000 shares, although connected with Mr Arundale's proposed employment, was not something in the nature of a reward for his future services with the company and discharged the assessment.

Megarry J considered that it was the word 'therefrom' which provided the central core of the case. He reviewed the relevant case law extensively. He also referred to Upjohn J's dictum in *Hochstrasser* v *Mayes* that:

> ... it is the question to be answered in the light of the particular facts of every case whether or not a particular payment is or is not a profit arising from the employment ... to be a profit arising from the employment payment must be made in reference to the services the employee renders by virtue of his office and thus must be something in the nature of a reward for services ...

Megarry J pointed out that there were two elements in Upjohn J's words:

(a) The payment has to be in reference to the employee's services; and
(b) The payment must be a reward for services.

In both cases the payment must be in reference to services and the connection had to be, not merely with the office, but with the services. Whether or not this was so was primarily a question of fact. Megarry J accepted that for the payments to be taxable they had to have a cause or connection with the office or employment, though he preferred an Anglicised formulation to one in Latin. He pointed out that consideration and causation are by no means identical. The contractual expression and consideration is not conclusively determinable as causation. He pointed out that clause 2 of the Agreement referred not to the rendering of services to the company but to the undertaking to serve the company. These pointed not to continuous rendering of services but to the initial entering into of the obligation to serve.

Mr Arundale had given up a secure livelihood in order to serve the company full time. To that extent the concept of compensation for loss made Mr Arundale's case akin to *Hochstrasser* v *Mayes*.

Further, the shares had been transferred to him on an out-and-out basis and were to be transferred on execution of the Agreement under which the employment did not start immediately (see now s. 19, TA, para. 4A(a)). There was no provision on death for the return of the shares or if Mr Arundale did not take up the appointment. In addition the transfer was made by his potential employer – that would have been impossible in the UK but by a third party.

His Lordship did not consider the word 'from' meant 'for'. In other words the payment must be made in reference to the services rendered under the employment as a reward for them, and so in that sense flow from the employment; this is not the same as a payment made 'for' undertaking the employment. He said that if Schedule E is to apply, what the payment must relate to and reward is not the mere existence of a contract of services nor merely entering into such a contract for the services rendered or to be rendered under the contract.

On the facts before him Megarry J said that the Crown had failed to establish that the transfer fell within the words imposing the charge to tax. There was no emolument from any office or employment nor was the transfer in the nature of a reward for services or made in reference to services. In reaching this conclusion the judge briefly considered two other inducement cases sometimes known as the Rugby League cases (see para. 6.31.12).

The more recent case of *Glantre Engineering* v *Goodhand* [1983] STC 1 concerned the position of a payment where a person moved from one employment to another. Warner J held the payment taxable there. His Lordship thought the question was essentially one of fact. There was no delay in taking up the position. The payment was not from a third party. Accordingly, it was not on all fours with *Pritchard* which was distinguished.

6.31.2 The Rugby League cases

These are the cases of *Jarrold* v *Boustead* (1964) 41 TC 701 and *Riley* v *Coglan* (1967) 44 TC 481. These illustrate the point that a payment not connected with or referable to services or a reward for services is not taxable but a payment for services and a reward for them is taxable.

At the time, Rugby Union was apparently an exclusively amateur game. Rugby League was played by amateurs and professionals. If one turned professional one could not take part in Rugby Union or amateur athletics and, further, on becoming a professional some degree of social discrimination was experienced. One was not allowed to visit Rugby Union clubs and if one was discovered on a Rugby Union ground one might be asked to leave.

The Court of Appeal in *Jarrold* v *Boustead* held that the signing on fee paid to the player was paid as a consideration for relinquishing his amateur status which he relinquished for life. Lord Denning then said:

> the player gave up all the advantages of being an amateur for the rest of his life and in return he got the payment at the beginning. He considered that the commissioners were quite entitled to find that it was a capital sum in

Schedule E – income from employment

compensation for what was a permanent asset in his hands. The remuneration for services (of so much a match) was an entirely different thing. It was remuneration for services whereas the signing on fee was for giving up a permanent advantage.

He considered that the position was the same as in the example of £500 paid to a golfing organist on his taking up of the position as Church organist if he gave up golf on Sundays for the rest of his life.

In *Riley* v *Coglan* the payment was held to be an emolument because it was specifically related to the playing period during which he was to serve the club. The payment covered the whole period of the contract, irrespective of when it was received and was in consideration of the taxpayer's services and was therefore taxable remuneration.

So an inducement is subject to the same tax as any other emolument and if there is a causal connection it is paid as remuneration for services and so it is taxable. If it is not so paid it is not taxable under Schedule E.

6.32 'GOLDEN HANDSHAKES'

Termination payments or golden handshakes can be taxable on general principles but there are also special statutory provisions (see para. 6.34).

The 'common law' cases can be broadly grouped for the purposes of exposition under three non-exclusive headings. These are:

(a) variation payments etc.
(b) termination payments made in accordance with a prior agreement;
(c) payments before all obligations to serve have ceased.

Each of these will be considered in turn.

6.32.1 Variation payments etc.

In *Cameron* v *Prendergast* (1940) 23 TC 122 the taxpayer was paid £24,000 in consideration of his not serving a notice of resignation as a director of the company, Higgs & Hill Limited, and continuing to serve the company though for less time and at a reduced salary. He was assessed under Schedule E on £24,000.

Viscount Caldecote LC could see no difference between a promise not to resign and a promise to continue to serve. Continuance in office of the taxpayer was the essence of the bargain. The payment was thus a reward for his services and was taxable therefore as a profit from his office under Schedule E.

In reaching their decision in *Prendergast* all the members of the House of Lords distinguished the earlier case of *Hunter* v *Dewhurst* (1932) 16 TC 605. This was one of a number of appeals and concerned the directors of a company, George & R Dewhurst Limited, who were cotton brokers. The taxpayer had been a promoter of the company. The articles of association of the company in question provided (inter alia) that in the event of any director who had held office for not less than five years, dying, resigning or ceasing to hold office for any reason other than misconduct, bankruptcy, lunacy or incompetence, the company should pay to him or his representatives, by way of compensation for loss of office, a sum equal to the total remuneration received by him in the last five years.

Commander Dewhurst wished to retire from the active management of the company of which he was chairman and a director. His circumstances fell within the provisions of the retirement article so that, had he retired, he would have been entitled to a payment under the terms of that article. His co-directors did not wish him to resign and if he did resign they wished to be able to consult him. It was agreed that Commander Dewhurst should resign from his office as chairman but remain on the board as a director at a reduced remuneration. It was also agreed that he should receive a lump sum as 'compensation' in lieu of the amount which he would have received under the articles had he resigned as director and that he should waive any future claim under the relevant article.

Commander Dewhurst was assessed for tax under Schedule E on the lump sum he received. His appeal eventually reached the House of Lords. Their Lordships (Viscount Dunedin and Lord McMillan dissenting) held that the sum paid to Commander Dewhurst was not assessable to income tax.

Lord Atkin said that Commander Dewhurst entered into:

. . . no bargain to serve the company for any particular time . . . the £10,000 was not paid for past remuneration for the condition of its becoming payable, for instance, loss of office was never performed. He was not paid for future remuneration that was expressed to be £250 per annum which was to be the sole remuneration.

His Lordship went on:

. . . it seems to me that the sum of money paid to obtain a release for contingent liability under a contract cannot be said to be received under the contract of employment, it is not remuneration for services rendered or to be rendered on the contract of employment and is not received on the contract of employment.

Lord Warrington said that the case might be decided against the Crown on the very special circumstances under which the payments were made. In his view no part of the sum paid represented remuneration either past or future. He decided under the special circumstances that the sums in question were purely capital. Lord Thankerton considered the payments were not in the nature of income at all and were isolated payments once and for all.

The distinction that is drawn between *Cameron* v *Prendergast* and *Hunter* v *Dewhurst* was that in *Prendergast* the payment was a reward for services whereas the payment in *Hunter* was not a reward for services but a payment to release a contingent liability. This is not always a very clear distinction and

Schedule E – income from employment

can be a very difficult one to apply in practice. Imagine trying to advise clients on the precise boundaries of contingent and other liabilities in this context.

Both *Prendergast* v *Cameron* and *Hunter* v *Dewhurst* were followed in *Wales* v *Tilley* 25 TC 136. The facts of this case were that the taxpayer was employed by a company as its managing director under a contract of service which provided inter alia that he should be paid an annual salary and after his ceasing to be a managing director he should be paid an annual pension for ten years. Subsequently a new agreement was entered into under which the taxpayer agreed to release the company from the obligation to pay the pension and to continue to serve the company as managing director at a reduced salary. In consideration the company agreed to pay him £40,000.

The Revenue assessed the taxpayer on the £40,000 under Schedule E. The General Commissioners discharged the assessment. The Crown's appeal was upheld by Lawrence J. His judgment was upheld by the Court of Appeal. The taxpayer's appeal to the House of Lords was unanimously allowed in part.

Their Lordships held that so much of the consideration as represented consideration for the reduction in salary was taxable, following *Cameron* v *Prendergast*. The amount of the consideration relating to the release of the pension was held not to be taxable, following *Hunter* v *Dewhurst*, the sum for the release of an obligation to pay the pension was said to be a contingent obligation.

The precise legal effect of an agreement to pay someone money in return for an apparent variation of the contract of service thus has to be considered very carefully before applying the general income tax law. If the payment is for the discharge of a contingent liability, and not as a reward for services, it is not taxable under the general income tax law applicable to the general charge under Schedule E. The construction of the documentation in question may, however, be far from easy. It is worth noting that certain special provisions apply in respect of share offers.

It should also be noted here that wages in lieu of notice will not usually be taxable under Schedule E principles, since they are paid to discharge a contingent liability. However, they will probably be caught by the statutory provisions but unless they exceed £30,000 they will be taken out of the charge to tax under the special exemptions of the statutory rules (see para. 6.34).

6.32.2 Termination payment in accordance with prior agreement

The second class to consider is payments made on the termination of an office of employment in accordance with a prior agreement. The general rule is that payment made pursuant to a term of the service agreement, or under the articles of association of the company to an office holder or an employee on termination, will be taxable under Schedule E income tax principles.

Dale v *De Soissons* (1950) 32 TC 118 is an example of a payment made pursuant to a provision in the service contract. Colonel De Soissons was employed as an assistant to the managing director of Gallagher Limited. The company had power under the service agreement to terminate the employment on giving three months' notice at specified dates and paying a specified sum. The company exercised this option and paid Colonel De Soissons £10,000 'by way of compensation for loss of office' pursuant to the service agreement. Colonel De Soissons was assessed on the £10,000 under Schedule E. He was held properly assessed.

Evershed MR said that 'cases of this character were never easy and . . . the line between those in which the taxpayer had succeeded and those in which he had failed may be described as "a little wobbly".' The argument that the sum was paid in consideration of a cancellation of rights which Colonel De Soissons would otherwise have had was rejected. The basis of the Court of Appeal's decision that the sums were taxable under Section E was that '. . . the Colonel surrendered no rights. He got exactly what he was entitled to get under his contract of employment.' Accordingly the payment was taxable.

The case of *Henley* v *Murray* (1950) 31 TC 351 was said to be in a different class because the payment there was for the total abrogation of Mr Henley's contract of employment. *Henley* v *Foster* 16 TC 605 is an example of a payment made pursuant to a company's articles of association. This involved the same company and the same article as *Hunter* v *Dewhurst*. The appeals were joined. However, the facts here were different. Mr Foster resigned and received the payment he was entitled to under the relevant article. He was assessed on this sum. The Court of Appeal held that he was correctly assessed. Lawrence LJ said:

> . . . the determining factor in the present case is that the payment to the Respondent whatever the parties may have chosen to call it was a payment which the company had contracted to make to him as part of his remuneration for his services as a director . . . a sum agreed to be paid in consideration of the Respondent accepting and serving in the office of director, and consequently is a sum paid by way of remuneration for his services as director.

Lawrence LJ is in effect saying that it was deferred remuneration.

The payment in both cases was part of the reward for being an employee and was so taxable on normal, general Schedule E principles.

6.32.3 Payment before all obligations to render services have ceased

The third type of case to consider is the type where payments are made before all obligations to render services have ceased. This is a rather odd course, but *Hofmann* v *Wadman* (1946) 27 TC 192 illustrates it. The facts of *Hofmann* v *Wadman* were that a director's contract of employment was cancelled forthwith and the company were to be able to call upon the employee's services for a further period. The taxpayer's remuneration was continued after determination! Norton J held that stipulations to the rendering of the services during the transition period were immaterial and that even if he was in fact under no obligation to render services he would have been assessable under Schedule E in respect of the payment.

Evershed MR has described the bargain here that:

the employers should remain liable under the contract for the remuneration they had contracted to pay although they gave up their right to call on Mr Hofmann, their works manager, to perform the duties under the contract which he was bound to perform.

Stamp J (as he then was) declined to follow *Hofmann* in the later case of *Clayton* v *Lavender* (1965) 42 TC 607. Here the employee was bound for five years and thereafter subject to six months' notice. The employee did not wish to serve beyond five years and his employers offered to terminate his employment as soon as he intimated this on the terms that he would be paid £4,000 for one year forward and £2,000 for the year after that.

Stamp J held that since there was no requirement in the contract under which the payments were made requiring performance of the duties of an office or employment, it was not a contract of employment and the payments were not remuneration but were payments made in consideration of the surrender of rights. The judge went on to say that the case was indistinguishable from *Hofmann* v *Wadman* which he refused to follow.[35] Stamp J said that the correct approach was that set out in *Henley* v *Murray* (1950) 31 TC 351 by Jenkins LJ where he says (at p. 367):

> as the many cases on this topic show it is often very difficult to determine the character of a payment made to the holder of an office when his tenure of office is determined or the terms on which he holds it are altered. The question in each case is whether on the facts of the case the lump sum paid is in the nature of remuneration or profits in respect of the office or is in the nature of a sum paid in consideration for surrender by the recipient of his rights in respect of the office.

This may be a good summary of the position but does not reconcile the two cases of *Hofmann* v *Wadman* and *Clayton* v *Lavender*.

It is submitted that *Clayton* v *Lavender* is to be preferred since, as Stamp J says, payment is agreed to be made to an employee in consideration of his agreeing that he will not in future perform any obligations for his employer and the employer will not be entitled to require his services. The contract of employment does seem to be at an end.

6.33 SUMMARY: TERMINATION AND THE 'COMMON LAW' OF SCHEDULE E

The position as to the general income tax law regarding termination or variation payments can, it seems, be summarised broadly in the following three propositions.

[35.] As a matter of precedent one High Court judge is not bound to follow the decision of another. '... a judge of first instance, unless he is convinced that the judgment is wrong, would follow it as a matter of judicial comity. He certainly is not bound to follow a decision of a judge of equal jurisdiction' (*Per* Lord Goddard in *Police Authority for Huddersfield* v *Watson* [1947] KB 842 at p. 848.)

(a) Where there is a pre-arranged agreement either in the contract of service or in the company's articles that the payment will be regarded as a form of deferred remuneration then it is fully taxable under general Schedule E principles;

(b) A payment made in respect of future services, e.g., as in *Cameron v Prendergast* the payment for not serving the resignation notice and continuing to serve at a reduced salary, is regarded as an advance remuneration for services under the office and is thus fully taxable under Schedule E as an emolument from the office of employment. The necessary connection between the payment and the office of employment is regarded as established.

(c) A payment made not under a service agreement etc. but as a consideration for the release from or the surrender of the employee's rights under a service contract is not a taxable emolument under general income tax law and, apart from statutory provisions, is free from income tax.

6.34 STATUTE

6.34.1 General

As can be imagined, with such a framework of rules it was possible, by structuring the matter in the right way, to get a payment on the termination of an office or employment to the former holder free from income tax. For example, voluntary ex gratia payments made to a former employee on the termination of, or the variation of the function of the office or employment, could normally be structured in such a way as to avoid liability to income tax. If, for example, six months after his resignation and not pursuant to any prior agreement, an ex gratia payment were made by a company to the former managing director of the company, the payment would not have been taxable.

Such widespread opportunities to avoid liability to tax were bound to attract the Revenue's and the government's attention sooner or later. Provisions were enacted in 1960 to withdraw these payments from immunity in ss. 37 and 38 and sch. 4, Finance Act 1960 (now s. 148, TA).[36] This was not a root and branch reform of the whole area but a tacking on of a charging provision to the existing law. Consequently, both the previous law and the statute need to be known.

Section 148, TA applies to payments within the section 'not otherwise chargeable to tax' (s. 148(2)). Accordingly, if the payment is within the general Schedule E charge it is not within s. 148.[37] This preserves the old law and tacks on a charge to payments not taxable under the pre-existing law. It can also be important for relief purposes.

Section 148, TA applies to 'any payment to which this section applies' made to the holder or past holder of an office or employment whether made by the employer or any other person (s. 148(1), TA). It does not matter

---

[36]. See Shipwright, 123 *SJ* 191, 208, 227.
[37]. This may matter for relief purposes. Section 188, TA only applies to payments falling within s. 148, TA not those caught by s. 19, TA. The £30,000 relief under s. 188, TA would thus not be available if there were a s. 19, TA charge.

Schedule E – income from employment

whether the payment is made in pursuance of any legal obligation or not. A gratuitous payment can thus be caught. It does not matter whether the payment is made directly or indirectly. However, for s. 148 to apply it must be made 'in consideration or in consequence of, or otherwise in connection with, the termination of the holding of the office or employment' (s. 148(2)). The section also applies to any change in the functions or emoluments of the employment, including any payment in commutation of annual or periodical payments (whether chargeable to tax or not) which would otherwise have been made (s. 148 (2)).

For these purposes any payments made to the spouse or any relative or dependant of a person who holds or has held an office or employment, or made on behalf of, or to the order of, that person, are treated as made to the present or past officeholder or employee (s. 148(3)).

Any valuable consideration other than money (which is already caught) is to be treated as a payment of money equal to the value of that consideration at the date when it is given (s. 148(3). For example, the transfer of a company car; see ICAEW Technical Release TR 851, 6 November 1991).

The person making the payment must notify the inspector in writing within 30 days of the end of the tax year (s. 148(7)).

6.34.2 Relief and exemptions from s. 148, TA

Section 188, TA sets out a number of exemptions from s. 148, TA. The exemptions only apply to a charge which would otherwise have arisen under s. 148, TA. Accordingly, they do not apply to a charge under s. 19, TA.

By s. 188(1)(a) payments made on the death of the holder of an office or employment, or on account of his injury or disability, are not charged to tax under s. 148 (see further SP 10/81). Thus if Hilary falls off a ladder at work and is unable to work again a payment on account of the disability would not be charged under s. 148. The Revenue apparently accept that 'disability' covers not only a condition resulting from a sudden affliction but also continuing incapacity to perform the duties of an office or employment arising out of the culmination of a process of deterioration of physical or mental health caused by chronic illness' (para. 3, SP 10/81). Payments not falling within this may be treated as relevant benefits under a retirement benefits scheme.

By s. 188(1)(b) sums chargeable under Schedule E by virtue of s. 313, TA[38] in respect of a restrictive covenant are also not charged under s. 148.

By s. 188(1)(d) certain lump sums paid under retirement benefit schemes are not taxed under s. 148.

By s. 188(1)(e) terminal grants, gratuities or other lump sums paid to members of the armed forces are not taxed under s. 148.

By s. 188(1)(f) a benefit provided under a superannuation scheme established by a foreign Commonwealth government for the benefit of its employees is not taxed under s. 148.

[38.] What is now s. 313, TA was introduced to reverse *Beak* v *Robson* [1943] AC 352 and originally only charged at the higher rate. Basic rate is now also charged as it was used as a planning device on termination. Section 313, TA is quite wide in its scope.

The first £30,000, reduced by any statutory redundancy money paid, is exempt from charge under s. 148. (ss. 188(4), 580(3)). Thus if A is paid £50,000 on the termination of his employment then if s. 148 would otherwise apply A would be charged on £20,000 (i.e., £50,000–30,000).

By s. 189, TA a lump sum paid under an approved retirement benefit scheme and certain statutory and foreign schemes is not taxed under s. 148 and neither is a payment under a personal pension arrangement.

Statutory redundancy pay is also outside s. 148 TA, (s. 596A(8), TA, s. 108(5)–(8), FA 1994).

It is to be noted that certain grants and payments made to a person ceasing to be an MP or MEP are exempt from income tax without limit (s. 190, TA).

The case of *Shilton* v *Wilmshurst* [1991] STC 88 draws much of this together. The Shilton in this case is the famous footballer, former England goalkeeper, Peter Shilton. The case (case stated reported at [1988] STC 868) concerned the taxability of a payment by one club to a footballer for him to join another club in addition to the signing on fee paid by the new club.[39]

The General Commissioners found him taxable on the payment and considered (inter alia) the following facts proved. Peter Shilton had been employed by Nottingham Forest during the period from September 1977 to August 1982. In July 1982 Forest were approached about a transfer of their goalkeeper by Southampton Football Club. Terms were agreed between Forest and Southampton for Peter Shilton to be transferred from Forest to Southampton subject to terms being agreed between Shilton and Southampton. Brian Clough, the then Forest manager, indicated that should Peter Shilton agree terms with Southampton, Forest might be willing to make him a payment for agreeing to the transfer. The Forest board resolved to pay Shilton £75,000, which was paid subject to deduction of PAYE, after he had entered into his new contract with Southampton including a signing-on fee of £80,000 payable over four years which it was accepted was taxable. It was found that at the time 'the deal was negotiated . . . there was some pressure on Nottingham Forest to raise money by the sale of players and to reduce their wage bill . . .'. The General Commissioners considered that 'The payment by Nottingham Forest to the taxpayer was an inducement to him to play football for Southampton and as such was an emolument flowing from that service which he was to render to Southampton'. This put the Inland Revenue in a strong position.

The issue in the case was whether the payment to Peter Shilton by Forest for agreeing to the transfer was an 'emolument' from Peter Shilton's employment and so liable to income tax on general principles[40] or whether it was chargeable under what is now s. 148, TA[41] when certain exemptions could

---

[39]. Signing on fees linked to a period of service (as this was here) are usually taxable; see e.g. *Riley* v *Coglan* (1967) 44 TC 481 and *Jarrold* v *Boustead* (1964) 41 TC 701. It may be different if something personal such as amateur status is given up.
[40]. I.e., ignoring any statutory modification and looking only to s. 19, TA 1988.
[41]. Section 148 applies to 'any payment (not otherwise chargeable to tax) which is made . . . in connection with, the termination of the holding of an . . . employment or any change in its functions . . .'

apply.[42] Lord Templeman said: 'I sympathise with the conclusion which absolves the taxpayer from part of the tax claimed by the Revenue but if that conclusion is to be upheld it must be consistent with the logical construction and application of the taxing statute.' Since the payment was from a third party (Forest) in respect of an employment with another (Southampton Football Club), the case was of vital importance as far as tips, bonuses, awards and the like paid by third parties to people such as sportsmen and entertainers were concerned. It differs from the usual 'golden hello' cases in that the payment is by the former employer and is more akin to a 'golden goodbye'.

The decisions at first instance and in the Court of Appeal are a tribute to the powers of advocacy of Andrew Thornhill QC, counsel for Peter Shilton. At first instance Morritt J said (at p. 878):

'... Forest were only concerned that the taxpayer should enter into a contract of employment with Southampton in order that Nottingham Forest should obtain the agreed transfer fee from Southampton. Thereafter Nottingham Forest had no concern or interest direct or indirect in the performance of that contract.' He concluded that consequently it was not an emolument '*from*' the employment with Southampton. If this were right it is hard to see how an inducement payment (a payment to enter into a contract of employment) could ever be taxable. It is hard to see how such a conclusion fits in with the findings of fact. The analysis in the Court of Appeal ([1979] STC 55) also leaves something to be desired. The discussion of *Pritchard* v *Arundale* (see para. 6.31.1) fails to recognise the special facts and seems to concentrate on performance of service. The House of Lords in *Hochstrasser* (see para. 6.27) referred to 'a payment for acting or being an employee' as being assessable under Schedule E. Peter Shilton, even on the judge's and the Court of Appeal's analysis, was being paid for being an employee.

The House of Lords, it is submitted, merely applied the *Hochstrasser* principle as enunciated in *Hamblett* v *Godfrey* (see para. 6.28) and applied the normal principles to the facts as found by the Commissioners.

On the facts as found by the Commissioners, the answer to the question, 'was this payment from his employment with Southampton' it is hard to see how it could be said it was not, as it was 'an inducement to him to play football with Southampton'. It was the Southampton employment that had to be looked to as the source and not that with Forest. It was a payment for acting as, or agreeing to act as an employee of Southampton. The unusual feature was that the payment had come from the previous employer. If the payment had come from a rich Southampton supporter it would still have been taxable. The fact that Forest paid for Shilton to go to play for Southampton does not seem sufficient distinction. The interesting question is whether the payment could have been structured differently and so attracted the exemption (now of the first £30,000) for a termination payment not otherwise taxable, by virtue of ss. 148 and 188, TA 1988. However, this was not how it was done, so the taxpayer was liable.

[42.] By s. 188(4), TA, where s. 148, applies the first £30,000 is exempt. For s. 148 to apply the payment must not otherwise be chargeable to income tax, e.g., under general Schedule E principles.

6.35 WHAT CASE?

6.35.1 General

By s. 19, TA Schedule E paragraph 1 income tax is charged under three cases. Which case applies depends on the residence (see Chapter 1), status of the taxpayer and the place of performance of the duties. It provides (in so far as is relevant for these purposes):

> Case I: any emoluments for any year of assessment in which the person holding the office or employment is resident and ordinarily resident in the United Kingdom, subject however to section 192 if the emoluments are foreign emoluments (within the meaning of that section) and to section 193(1) if in the year of assessment concerned he performs the duties of the office or employment wholly or partly outside the United Kingdom.
> Case II: any emoluments, in respect of duties performed in the United Kingdom for any year of assessment in which the person holding the office or employment is not resident (or, if resident, not ordinarily resident) in the United Kingdom, subject however to section 192 if the emoluments are foreign emoluments (within the meaning of that section).
> Case III: any emoluments for any year of assessment in which the person holding the office or employment is resident in the United Kingdom (whether or not ordinarily resident there) so far as the emoluments are received in the United Kingdom;

and tax shall not be chargeable in respect of emoluments of an office or employment under any other paragraph of this Schedule.

The emoluments referred to in Cases I and II as foreign emoluments are emoluments of a person not domiciled in the United Kingdom from an office or employment under or with any person, body of persons or partnership resident outside and not resident in, the United Kingdom.

This may be summarised as follows

Case	Persons covered?	What charged?
I	UK resident and ordinarily resident	Any emoluments for any year of assessment wherever earned
II	Either not UK resident or, if resident, not ordinarily resident	Emoluments for any year of assessment in respect of duties performed in the UK
III	UK resident (whether ordinarily resident or not)	Any emoluments received in the UK for any year of assessment or any earlier such year when the person was a UK resident

6.35.2 Case I

Where the employee or office holder is resident *and* ordinarily resident in the UK then the employee or office holder is liable to UK income tax on any emoluments under Case I. It does not matter where the duties are performed as the tax is charged on a worldwide arising basis. Residence and ordinary residence are the connecting factors. This is subject to a foreign emoluments deduction under s. 192, TA. Section 193, TA allows a deduction for certain travel expenses.

6.35.3 Case II

This case applies in two circumstances to emoluments in respect of duties performed in the United Kingdom. The place of performance is thus important here. The circumstances are that for the year of assessment the employee or office holder is:

(a) resident but not ordinarily resident in the United Kingdom; or
(b) is not resident in the UK.

subject, however, to s. 192 if the emoluments are foreign emoluments (within the meaning of that section). This contrasts with Case I which requires the employee or officeholder to be resident *and* ordinarily resident in the UK.

If a person comes to the UK for a short period and works as an employee, then Case II would be applicable if Case I were not. If the duties had been outside the UK then Case II would be inapplicable.

Case II is subject to a foreign emoluments deduction under s. 192, TA.

6.35.4 Case III

If the employee or office holder is resident in the United Kingdom (whether or not ordinarily resident in the UK) so far as the emoluments are received in the United Kingdom they are liable to UK income tax under Case III. This can apply where a person is both resident and ordinarily resident in the UK so that prima facie Case I would apply if the emoluments are foreign emoluments. They are then excepted from Case I by s. 192(2), TA.

The effect of s. 131(2), TA is that Cases I and II take precedence over Case III (hence the need for s. 192(2)).

6.36 FOREIGN EMOLUMENTS

These are defined in s. 192(1), TA. Where an employee or office holder is not domiciled in the UK and is employed by or holds office with a person, body of persons or partnership resident outside and not resident in the UK, then the emoluments from it are 'foreign emoluments'. This does not include an employment or office with a person, body of persons or partnership resident in the Republic of Ireland. It seems arguable at least that this is in breach of EU law.

In the past there were greater deductions for foreign emoluments but in the main these were abolished from 1989–90.

6.37 PLACE OF PERFORMANCE OF DUTIES

This is dealt with by s. 132, TA. The effect is that 'merely incidental duties' may be treated as performed outside the UK in some cases. This is discussed in Chapter 35.

CHAPTER SEVEN
Benefits in kind – statutory modifications

7.1 INTRODUCTION[1]

This chapter is concerned with the provision of benefits (generally otherwise than in cash) to an employee (including an office holder) and the statutory modifications to the general charge designed to bring the cost of the benefit into charge. These rewards are often referred to as 'benefits in kind'. Taxing benefits in kind on their second-hand value (as discussed in Chapter 6) made them very attractive as a way of maximising benefit to the employee at as low a tax cost to the employee as possible and low cost to the employer.[2]

Benefits in kind became a growth sector in the UK during times of high tax rates (until 1979 the highest marginal rate of income tax on earned income was 83%). The 'grabbag' or 'cafeteria' approach to executive pay became common. The executive could take his remuneration how he wished up to a certain cost to the employer. The 'common law' rules which required convertibility and charged the second-hand value were useful to maximise the value of benefits taken by the employee. Successive governments have considered this unsatisfactory from a policy perspective. Accordingly various modifications have been made to the 'common law' rules (especially in the light of free petrol schemes and similar planning). The broad thrust of these

---

[1.] See, generally, *Whiteman on Income Tax* and *Simon's Direct Taxes*.
[2.] Having the use of a £10,000 car for a year might have a cost and resale value of £1,000. At current rates this would give rise to a charge on a higher rate employee of £400. If it cost the employer £1,000 gross to provide the benefit then it would cost £667 net of 33% corporation tax for a corporate employer. In contrast, to provide the employee with £1,000 net in cash would require a gross payment of £1,667, a net cost to a corporate employer of £1,167. If there were no possibility of allowing use by another and no cash value there would be no charge on the employee; cf. *Heaton* v *Bell* (1967) 46 TC 211 (see Chapter 6).

rules is to tax the cost to the employer rather than the value of the receipt by the employee or office holder.[3]

Some of the statutory modifications apply to all taxpayers whatever their level of earnings. Others are more limited and apply to those holding certain positions or earning £8,500 a year or more (formerly called higher paid employment). The rules applicable to all employees and office holders will be considered first and other provisions afterwards.

7.2 STATUTORY MODIFICATIONS APPLICABLE TO ALL TAXPAYERS

This section is concerned with those modifications that apply to all employees and office holders whatever their level of income. As noted above, the 'common law' rules for Schedule E gave rise to difficult distinctions and anomalies. In particular, the use of company vouchers and credit cards for petrol and other goods and services; the provision of accommodation and the payment of insurance premiums became targets for legislation.

7.3 VOUCHERS

7.3.1 General

Providing an employee with a voucher exchangeable only for goods or services (but not for cash and having no trade-in or assignment value) could be a tax efficient way of paying an employee and still allowing a fair degree of flexibility as to the benefit the employee obtained. Under the 'common law' rules the benefit was only taxable on the second-hand value of the goods or services (see, e.g., *Wilkins* v *Rogerson* [1961] 1 All ER 358). Provisions were therefore introduced in the mid 1970s to deal with the provision of vouchers to employees. These sections are as follows:

(a) non-cash vouchers   s. 141, TA
(b) credit tokens   s. 142, TA
(c) PAYE and cash vouchers s. 143, TA.

The relationship between these sections is not always as clear as one might wish. The precise wording of the actual sections needs to be carefully considered in applying them to any particular case.

The *Concise Oxford Dictionary* defines a 'voucher' inter alia as a 'document which can be exchanged for goods or services as token payments made or promised by a holder or another'. It is broadly this kind of matter with which these provisions are concerned.

[3.] The statute often does not expressly exclude a double charge on the second-hand value of the benefit as well as the cost to the employer. However, it is considered that the principle in *Vestey* [1980] STC 10 that the same income should not be taxed more than once would probably cover this.

7.3.2 Non cash vouchers

7.3.2.1 Section 141, TA Section 141 applies where certain conditions are met. These are:

(a) a non cash voucher;
(b) provided for an employee;
(c) by reason of his employment; and
(d) is received by the employee.

Each of these conditions will now be considered in turn.

7.3.2.2 Non cash vouchers By s. 141(7) a non cash voucher does not include a cash voucher (as defined in s. 143 (see para. 7.3.4). This is not the most logical of drafting. However, subject to the exclusion of cash vouchers, a non cash voucher '. . . means any voucher, stamp or similar document or token capable of being exchanged . . . for money, goods or services (or any combination of two or more of those things) and includes a transport voucher and a cheque voucher . . .' (s. 141(7)). Examples might be book tokens, store vouchers, vouchers for health clubs, hotels, holidays etc.

The dictionary definition of a voucher has been considered above. 'Stamp' seems to be used to mean something like a trading stamp or holiday stamp. The *Concise Oxford Dictionary* defines a 'token' inter alia as 'a piece of metal like and used instead of a coin but worth much less than nominal value and issued by tradesmen, banks etc. without sanction of government; device like coin bought for use with machines etc. or for other payment where money is not to be handled.' It is presumably in this broad sense that token is used here.

'Transport voucher' is defined in s. 141(7) as '. . . any ticket, pass or other document or token intended to enable a person to obtain passenger transport services . . .' Thus a travel warrant provided to an employee would be a transport voucher as would a season ticket or pass on the railways or buses.

'Cheque voucher' is defined in s. 141(7) as '. . . a cheque [as to the meaning of which, see the Bills of Exchange Act 1882] provided for an employee and intended for use by him wholly or mainly for payment for particular goods or services . . .'

7.3.2.3 Provided for an employee For a charge to arise the provision of the non cash voucher must be 'for an employee'. This implies that the provision needs to be made to a person in his capacity as an employee. This raises the question whether the section could catch the provision of a book token by a mother to her son if she employs her son in her business? Is the provision then for the employee or the son? The legislation is not entirely clear but it seems the better view is that it would be caught (cf. para. 7.3.2.4). There is no specific exemption for family provision as there is in the Code (see s. 168(3), TA discussed at para. 7.5).

'Employee' here means 'the holder of any office or employment the emoluments in respect of which fall to be assessed under Schedule E . . .'

(s. 144(5)). If the charge only applied to the provision *to* an employee it would be easy to avoid the charge by, for example, providing the benefit to the employee's spouse or child. This obvious avoidance device is covered by s. 144(4)(b). Under this subsection reference to the provision of a voucher for an employee includes '. . . it being provided for or received by a relation of his . . .'. 'Relation' here means the spouse, parent or child, such a child's spouse, or dependant (cf. *Re Baden (No. 2)* [1973] Ch 9) of the employee.

7.3.2.4 By reason of his employment

By s. 144(4)(a) 'a non cash voucher . . . provided for an employee by his employer shall be deemed to be provided for him by reason of his employment.' Read pedantically it could be argued that the voucher needs to be provided 'for an employee' rather than to a person who is an employee. In other words the provision has to be made to the taxpayer in his or her capacity as an employee. The hairsplitting could affect the book token example in para. 7.3.2.3. If capacity is relevant then, if the provision is to the son and were a birthday present rather than 'for an employee', s. 144(4)(a) might not apply and so the benefit might not be taxable under s. 141.

Third party provision also seems to be caught by the section. However, there is no clear authority as to what the test should be. It seems 'by reason of employment' is a wide test. This is also a problem with the Code (see para. 7.5).

7.3.2.5 Received by the employee

As noted at para. 7.3.2.4 by s. 144(4)(a) if a voucher is '. . . provided for an employee by his employer it shall be deemed to be provided for him by reason of his employment.' But the employee must also receive it. The time of receipt is the time of charge for most non cash vouchers. This is discussed at para. 7.3.2.6.

Where a non cash voucher is appropriated to an employee by attaching it to a card for the taxpayer or in some other way, the employee is treated as receiving the voucher at the time it was appropriated.

7.3.2.6 What is charged?

What is charged under s. 141 is 'the chargeable expense'. By s. 141(1) 'the chargeable expense' is treated as emoluments of the employee for 'the relevant year of assessment'.

The 'chargeable expense' is an amount equal to the expense incurred by the person at whose cost the voucher and the money, goods or services for which it is capable of being exchanged are provided, in or in connection with that provision. This is not always the easiest of drafting to apply.[4] The reference to goods etc. seems to be a reference to the cost to the employer of acquiring the goods etc. exchanged for vouchers if the employer does acquire them. If a third party is used, the third party fees are included as all or part of the chargeable expense. However, in practice, management time in devising and running the scheme is not generally caught. Retail vouchers

---

[4.] See, for example, the practice statement which the Revenue have had to issue in connection with incentive awards, SP 6/85.

bought from a shop etc. will usually give rise to a charge on the cost of purchase of the vouchers.

By ESC A 2 luncheon vouchers are exempt from tax, up to 15p a day (the cost of a ham sandwich when luncheon vouchers were introduced!). ESC A 70 provides that small gifts (less than £100 including VAT) from a person other than the employer (or connected person) consisting of a voucher only capable of being used to obtain goods are exempt from tax.

The actual goods, services or money obtained in exchange for the voucher are disregarded for income tax purposes. This stops there being a double charge on the cost of providing the voucher and on the second-hand value of the goods obtained on exchange of the voucher.

The charge is for 'the relevant year of assessment'. This (except for a cheque voucher) is the later of the year of assessment[5] in which the expense is incurred or, if later, the year of assessment in which the employee receives the voucher (s. 141(2)(b)). For a cheque voucher the relevant year of assessment is the year of assessment in which the voucher is handed over for money, goods or services (s. 141(2)(a)). If it is posted the time of posting is taken.

7.3.2.7 Reductions in amount chargeable It would be unfair to tax an employee on the cost of the vouchers if he made good the whole cost of them. Equally, if the employee had paid a quarter of the cost it would be unfair if the full cost of the vouchers were taxed. Similarly if the vouchers were used to pay for something that would otherwise be a deductible expense (see Chapter 8) it would be unfair not to allow a deduction. Subsections (3) and (4) of s. 141, TA deal with this.

By s. 141(4) the amount taxable, 'the chargeable expense', is 'treated as reduced by any part of [the chargeable] expense made good to the person incurring [the expense] by the employee. To whom does the payment have to be made to reduce the charge? The answer is, to the person incurring it. This is not always the employer.

Example
A Co provides B with a voucher exchangeable for goods at a number of shops including A Co. B pays £10 for these vouchers with an exchange value of £110. B spends £60 of vouchers at A Co's shop and £50 elsewhere. A Co has to pay the other shops £50 for the goods supplied but the goods A Co itself supplied only cost £40. B's tax position in respect of this will be:

A Co vouchers cost	£40
Other vouchers cost	£50
Total	£90
Less amount made good	£10
Taxable	£80

[5.] See s. 832, TA: 6 April one year to 5 April following. This seems applicable even if the employer is a company.

Section 141(3) deals with deductible expenses. This provides for a deduction from 'the chargeable expense' (the amount treated as emoluments under s. 141(1)) for necessary expenses under Schedule E (s. 198), for fees and subscriptions to professional bodies etc. (s. 201); for certain liabilities and indemnity insurance (s. 201AA); and for expenses of ministers of religion (s. 323(3)), as if the cost of the goods or services in question had been incurred by the employee out of his emoluments. Fulfilment of the other conditions for deduction is still necessary for an allowable deduction (see Chapter 8). The effect is, broadly, that if the employee uses a voucher to obtain goods or services the cost of which, if purchased directly, would have been a deductible expense it is allowed as a deductible expense. Thus if a firm of solicitors provides an assistant solicitor with a travel warrant to travel from the office to court in the performance of the assistant's duties then, provided the expense of travelling was necessarily incurred in the performance of those duties, there would be a deduction from the voucher charge. Thus if the voucher cost £50 and the allowable fare was £50 there would be no tax charge[6] on the assistant.

7.3.2.8 Exceptions Section 141 itself provides certain exceptions from the charge. These include the following.

(a) Certain transport vouchers are taken out of charge if they are provided to an employee of a passenger transport undertaking under arrangements in operation on 25 March 1982. The arrangements must be intended to enable the employee or a relation[7] to obtain passenger transport services from the employer, a subsidiary or parent company of the employer or another passenger transport undertaking (s. 141(6)). Thus if X works on the buses and his daughter Y receives a free travel pass for the cross channel ferry as a result, no charge would arise if the arrangements were in operation on 25 March 1982.

(b) A non cash voucher, if it is used to obtain the use of a car parking space at or near the employee's place of work is taken outside the charge (s. 141(6A)). This reflects the exemptions in s. 155(1A) introduced by FA 1988.

(c) Certain entertainment and hospitality obtained through the use of a non cash voucher by the employee or a relation of the employee is taken out of charge (s. 141(6B), TA).

7.3.3 Credit tokens

7.3.3.1 Section 142 These provisions date from 1981. They were introduced as part of the tussle over the taxation of certain benefits particularly for the provision of petrol. Section 142 applies on each occasion where:

[6.] The chargeable expense of £50 would be reduced by an allowable expense of £50. Accordingly there would be nothing to tax (£50 − £50 = nil). A problem would arise where the expense and the fare did not match.

[7.] By s. 144(5) 'relation' with respect to an employee means the employee's spouse, parent or child, the spouse of his child and any dependant of that employee.

Benefits in kind – statutory modifications

(a) a credit token;
(b) provided for an employee;
(c) by reason of his employment;
(d) is used by the employee to obtain money, goods or services.

These conditions are considered in turn.

7.3.3.2 Credit token By s. 142(4), TA a credit token does not include a non cash voucher (see s. 141(7) and s. 144(5)) or a cash voucher (see s. 143(3) and s. 144(5)). However, it does include:

> ... a card, token, document or other thing given to a person who undertakes:
> (a) that on the production of it (whether or not some other action is also required) he will supply money, goods or services (or any of them) on credit; or
> (b) that where, on the production of it to a third party (whether or not some other action is also required) the third party supplies money, goods or services (or any of them), he will pay the third party for them (whether or not taking any discount or commission).

The meaning of non cash voucher has been considered at para. 7.3.2.

A credit token is 'a card, token, document or other thing given to a person ...' The difference between what is involved here and a voucher is not crystal clear. It seems to go to function in that in exchange for a non cash voucher, the taxpayer obtains the goods etc. themselves, whereas the exchange of a credit token procures the supply of goods on credit or provides that the issuer will pay the third party supplier. The distinction is not always obvious in practical situations.

By s. 142(5) the use of an object to operate a machine provided by the person giving the object, or by a third party, is treated as the production of the object to the person in question. This is to prevent the argument that the supply was by the machine rather than the operator of the machine (see Theft Act 1968 and amendments).

7.3.3.3 Provided for an employee Section 144, TA also applies here. This has the same meaning as for the non cash voucher provisions discussed at para. 7.3.2.

7.3.3.4 By reason of his employment Section 144 also applies here. This has the same meaning as for the non cash voucher provisions discussed at para. 7.3.2.

7.3.3.5 What is charged? On each occasion the credit token is used, the employee is treated as receiving an emolument from his employment of an amount equal to the expense incurred by the person at whose cost the money, goods or services are provided in, or in connection with, that provision (s. 142(1)).

7.3.3.6 Reductions As with non cash vouchers, it would be unfair to tax an employee on the cost of the credit token if he made good the whole or part of the cost of provision. Equally if the credit token were used to pay for something that would otherwise be a deductible expense, it would be unfair not to allow a deduction. Accordingly s. 142(2) also allows a reduction in the tax charge in such circumstances.

7.3.3.7 Exceptions Section 142 provides certain exceptions from the charge. These include the following:

(a) A credit token used to obtain the use of a car parking space at or near the employee's place of work is taken outside the charge in s. 142(3A). This reflects the exemptions in s. 155(1A), TA introduced by FA 1988.

(b) Certain entertainment and hospitality obtained by a credit token by the employee or a relation of the employee is also taken out of charge under s. 142(3B), TA.

7.3.4 Cash vouchers taxable under PAYE

Almost by definition a 'cash voucher' is easily convertible into cash and so chargeable on general principles. Section 143, TA does not therefore introduce a new charge but ensures collection of tax through PAYE. It ensures, broadly, that tax is charged on the face value of the cash voucher.

Section 141(3) defines a cash voucher as:

> ... any voucher, stamp or similar document capable of being exchanged (whether singly or together with such other vouchers, stamps or similar documents, and whether immediately or only after a time) for a sum of money greater than, equal to or not substantially less than the expense incurred by the person at whose cost the voucher is provided (whether or not it is also capable of being exchanged for goods or services), except that it does not include:
>
> (a) any document intended to enable a person to obtain payment of the sum mentioned in the document, being a sum which if paid to him directly would not have been chargeable to income tax under Schedule E; or
>
> (b) a savings certificate the accumulated interest payable in respect of which is exempt from tax (or would be so exempt if certain conditions were satisfied).

7.4 LIVING ACCOMMODATION

7.4.1 Introduction

A general Schedule E charge is difficult to apply if the property is not actually transferred to the taxpayer. In these circumstances, if the accommodation cannot be turned to account (i.e., is not convertible into money) there is nothing on which a s. 19 charge can bite. This has been seen in *Tennant* v

Benefits in kind – statutory modifications 219

Smith (see Chapter 6), the bank house case, and is also illustrated by *Langley v Appleby* [1976] 3 All ER 391. In that case, 12 appeals by Essex police officers against assessments on the provision of police houses by the police authority were heard by Fox J. The appeals were allowed because the officers were representative occupiers obliged to live there under the terms of their employment. Fox J approved Lord Upjohn's test of representative occupation in *Northern Ireland Commissioner of Valuation* v *Fermanagh Protestant Board of Education* [1969] 3 All ER 352 at p. 359. To establish representative occupation it must be established:

> either (a) that it is essential to the performance of the duties of the servant that he should occupy the particular house or (b) that it is an express term of the employment that the servant shall occupy the premises and that by doing so he can better perform his duties as a servant to a material degree.[8]

Following this case specific provisions were introduced to charge living accommodation. Two charges may apply. These are:

(a) the general charge introduced by s. 33, FA 1977 and now contained in s. 145, TA; and
(b) the charge in s. 146, TA for expensive houses derived from s. 21, FA 1983.

The second charge depends on the first charge. If s. 145, TA does not apply (otherwise than by reason of a sum made good by the employee) s. 146, TA does not apply. Thus if no s. 145 charge arises because one of the exceptions discussed below applies, s. 146 does not apply.

7.4.2 Section 145, TA

Section 145 applies where:

(a) living accommodation;
(b) is provided for a person in any period;
(c) by reason of his employment; and
(d) is not otherwise made the subject of any charge to him by way of income tax.

If the house had been transferred outright to the employee then a charge could arise under other provisions. Condition (d) thus prevents a double charge.

7.4.2.1 Living accommodation
The charge only applies to the provision of living accommodation. There seems to be no statutory definition of living accommodation for these purposes although some accommodation is not

---
[8.] See *Langley* v *Appleby* [1976] 3 All ER 391 at pp. 409–410. However, the payment of a housing allowance to the officers was taxable.

relevant for these purposes (see exclusions in para. 7.4.2.6). The *Concise Oxford Dictionary* defines 'accommodation' (inter alia) as 'lodgings, living premises'. It is this that is of concern here.

7.4.2.2 Provided in any period For a charge to arise the accommodation must be 'provided' for the employee. What does this mean? What if the employee has an existing right to be on the property as a joint owner? A joint owner has a right to be on the property having an undivided right in the property.[9]

Section 832, TA defines chargeable period as an accounting period of a company or a year of assessment. Here it is usually thought to mean a year of assessment.

7.4.2.3 By reason of employment If the accommodation is provided by the employer for the employee, it is deemed to be provided by reason of the employee's employment (s. 145(7), TA). Provision for a member of the taxpayer's family or household is included by s. 145(6). If this were not so there would be an obvious avoidance device. 'Family' and 'household' bear the same meaning as for the Code (see para. 7.5, definitions in s. 168 applied by s. 145(8)(b)). This is subject to two 'social exceptions'.

The first exception is where the employer is an individual and it can be shown that the provision is made in the normal course of the individual's domestic, family or personal relationships (s. 145(7)(a)). Thus a son employed in the family unincorporated firm living at home would not normally be subject to tax on his living accommodation nor would a secretary who moved in with the individual worked for. If the business is incorporated the exception does not apply but the provision then might not be by the employer.

The second exception is for accommodation provided for employees of a local authority where it can be shown that the terms are no more favourable than for persons not so employed. This was introduced so that the provision of council houses, particularly to teachers who moved from cheaper areas of housing to more expensive areas when recruited and who were housed in council accommodation, would not be caught.

7.4.2.4 Amount charged Section 145(1), TA states that the amount subject to tax is 'the value to [the taxpayer] of the accommodation for the period, less so much as is made good . . .' to the provider. Broadly, 'the value to [the taxpayer] of the accommodation for the period' is an amount equal to the rateable value of the property and this is charged as additional emoluments of the taxpayer where s. 145 applies. This is the effect of s. 145(2) although it is not entirely clear from its drafting.

If the provider of the accommodation rents the property and pays a rent higher than the annual value of the property, then this rent is substituted for the rateable value of the property in determining the taxpayer's liability.

[9.] Four unities for joint tenants of possession, interest, term and time and see, e.g., *Bull* v *Bull* [1955] 1 QB 234.

7.4.2.5 Reductions

Section 145(1), TA provides that there is to be deducted from the annual value '. . . so much as is made good . . .' to the provider. Thus if the employee pays some rent for the property this is deductible provided it is paid to the right person, i.e., the provider of the accommodation.

Section 145(3) provides for the deduction of such amounts under ss. 198 or 332(3)[10] as would have been so deductible if the accommodation had been paid for by the employee out of his or her emoluments.

7.4.2.6 Exceptions

By s. 145(4), TA three situations are taken out of the s. 145 charge (and so the s. 146 charge). These are as follows:

(a) Where it is necessary for the proper performance of the employee's duties that the employee should reside in the accommodation. The lighthousekeeper (in the days of manned lighthouses) or school caretaker are the usual examples given of this.

(b) Where accommodation is:

(i) provided for better performance of the employee's duties of employment; and
(ii) it is customary for it to be so provided.

This exception was introduced following the decision in *Langley* v *Appleby*, the police officer case and considered in *Vertigan* v *Brady* (1988).

(c) Where there is a special threat to an employee's security and special security arrangements are in force which involves the employee residing in the accommodation provided by the employer as part of those arrangements.[11]

The exceptions from charge in (a) and (b) above were considered in *Vertigan* v *Brady* [1988] STC 91. In this case Brian Herbert Alfred Vertigan was a very experienced nurseryman who was found to be a 'key worker'. His employer purchased him a bungalow in which Mr Vertigan lived rent free as he could not afford to buy one himself. He was assessed under what is now s. 145, TA. He appealed against this on the basis that the provision was either:

(a) necessary for proper performance of his duties to reside there; or
(b) for better performance of the duties of his employment and was the kind of employment in which it was customary to make such provision.

Knox J rejected both these arguments. He said (at p. 99) as regards the 'necessary proper performance' exception that it:

. . . is directed by a necessity based on the relationship between the proper performance and the dwelling house, and not to a necessity based on the

---

[10.] Expenditure of ministers of religion. Section 332(3)(b) allows certain rent as a deduction.
[11.] This was introduced to exclude Ministers and other government employees from charge but was widened during the Bill's passage as No. 11 Downing Street was being refurbished.

personal exigencies of the taxpayer in the shape of his inability to finance the acquisition of suitable accommodation . . .

As regards the second exception it was accepted that the provision was for the better performance of the duties but although the practice of providing accommodation might have been prevalent if it had not become customary. Knox J considered (at p. 101) that the approach in construing (b) was 'to seek to identify what is involved in the conception of a practice being customary for employers to follow.' There seem to be three constituent factors. First, there is the statistical evidence. How common is the practice statistically? Secondly, there is the question of how long the practice has gone on. A custom can hardly come into existence overnight. Thirdly, there is the question, has it achieved acceptance generally by the relevant employers? The Commissioners' findings did not meet these tests even though there was evidence that two out of three key workers were provided with accommodation. The question whether or not the provision had become customary was a matter of fact for the tribunal.

7.4.3 Section 146 – additional accommodation charge

7.4.3.1 General The charge under s. 145, TA could be on a comparatively very low amount since the charge is by reference effectively to rateable value which can be comparatively very low even if the house were very expensive. For example if the rateable value of a property in Eaton Square which cost £2 million was only £2,000 it might not be thought an adequate amount to charge only the rateable value.

Section 146 applies where:

(a) s. 145 applies or would but for the sum made good by the employee (s. 146(1)); and
(b) the cost of providing the accommodation exceeds £75,000.

The effect of s. 146 applying is that extra emoluments are deemed to the employee calculated on a deemed loan and interest basis. The drafting of these provisions is not lucid.

7.4.3.2 Cost of provision The definitions here are somewhat confusing. By s. 146(4) the cost of providing any living accommodation is the aggregate of (a) the expenditure incurred in acquiring the estate or interest in the property and (b) the expenditure on certain improvements. Section 146(6) – (8) expands on this. If this cost of provision exceeds £75,000 then s. 146 can apply.

7.4.3.3 Charge The charge on the employee is the additional value of the accommodation to the employee occupying the accommodation. By s. 146(3) this 'value' is an annual 'rent' calculated in a special way. This is somewhat confusing as essentially it is a notional interest charge on a notional loan of the excess of the cost of provision over £75,000 rather than a true rent. In effect the 'rent' = (cost less £75,000) × the appropriate percentage. The appropriate percentage is the same as for s. 160 for employee loans (see s. 146(11) and para. 7.5.20).

Example
(10% is assumed to be the appropriate percentage for this example).
Megacoy PLC provides its chief executive officer, Evelyn, with a house which costs £475,000.

Section 145 charge is, say,	£1,000
Section 146 charge is: (£475,000 − £75,000) × 10/100 =	£40,000
Total charge	£41,000

7.5 DIRECTORS AND EMPLOYEES EARNING MORE THAN £8,500 – BENEFITS DERIVED BY COMPANY DIRECTORS AND OTHERS FROM THEIR EMPLOYMENT: CHAPTER II, PART V, TA

(NB: references in para. 7.5, unless the context otherwise requires, are to Chapter II, Part V, TA (the 'Code') as amended.)

7.5.1 Introduction

The charge on general Schedule E principles does not tax all that might be regarded as remuneration of an employee or office holder or necessarily charge tax on the 'right' amount. Generally only benefits (other than cash and discharge of debts) convertible into money and then the resale value rather than the costs of provision (see *Wilkins* v *Rogerson* [1961] 1 Ch. 133) are taxable under general Schedule E principles. This leads to the possibility of much 'tax mitigation' by using benefits in kind. This became somewhat political as can be seen from these extracts from Hansard for 18 December 1975.

> *Mr Ashley*: Is my hon. friend aware that we receive many loud complaints from wealthy Conservatives shouting through the windows of their Rolls-Royces about abuses of the tax system by people on unemployment pay and social security benefits? But is he aware of the abuses of the tax system by a large number of upper management who receive 'perks' worth millions of pounds, including interest-free loans, housing, entertainment and a variety of other things? Does he realise that while the Chancellor does nothing the broadest backs get the biggest gift packages? Will he now stop acting as Santa Claus to these people and don the robe of Robin Hood?

Mr Davis: As my hon. friend says, there are abuses throughout the tax system and people at the higher levels have a better opportunity to reduce their tax burden than people at the lower levels. As I said, my right honourable friend [the Chancellor of the Exchequer] is looking at this matter urgently but I could not anticipate his Budget Statement.

As it turned out, new provisions were introduced by ss. 60–72 and schs 7 and 8, FA 1976. However, the 1976 changes were not the first attempt to deal with the problem. Taxation by reference to the cost to the employee was introduced for 'higher paid employees' (£2,000 was the limit then) by ss. 38–46, (Part IV) FA 1948[12] (the 'Old Code'). However, the Old Code did not cover all matters and still provided much scope for 'mitigation' which led to dissatisfaction and the 1976 changes referred to above.

If there was no cost to the employer in providing the benefit then the Old Code did not apply. Only actual costs gave rise to a charge. An interest free loan out of the employer's own resources (for example, without getting a bank loan to do so) was thus not caught. Similarly, the 'opportunity cost' of providing the benefit was not taxed:

(a) the Old Code applied only to benefits to employees from their employers and not benefits from third parties;[13]

(b) the Old Code applied only to employers who were trading or investment concerns. Thus, for example, central and local government employees were not caught;

(c) the Old Code did not have specific provisions dealing with cars. The treatment of company cars by individual inspectors varied across the country. In general company cars received very lenient treatment. People became quite agitated about this.

The New Code introduced by FA 1976, was consolidated in the 1988 Taxes Act as ss. 153–168 (inclusive). This New Code makes a significant inroad into the *Tennant* v *Smith* principle. However it does not apply to all employees, unlike ss. 145 and 146 TA, as the New Code is limited to directors and what used to be called higher paid employees. The FA 1989 changed the nomenclature from 'higher paid employees' to employees earning more than £8,500 (see s. 53(2)(b), FA 1989).

7.5.2 To whom does the Code apply?

The formal answer to the question 'To whom does the New Code apply?' is that the Code applies to 'directors or employees with emoluments at the rate of £8,500 a year or more'. By s. 167(1), TA this is now described in the title to the section as 'Employment to which this Chapter applies'.

The section provides that the Code applies:

[12.] These became ss. 195–203, TA 1970.
[13.] Although special provision was made for groups of companies; see s. 41, FA 1948.

(a) to employment as a director of a company (subject to subsection (5) below); and

(b) to employment with emoluments at a rate of £8,500 a year or more.

The rate of pay is calculated on a special basis. This is discussed at 7.5.4 and 7.5.5 below.

Subsection (5) of s. 167, TA allows escape from (a) if the taxpayer does not own more than 5% of the ordinary share capital of the company (see s. 168(11), TA) and is director of a non-profit making or charitable organisation or a full-time working director. However, such a director can still fall within the Code via (b) if the director is paid at a rate of £8,500 a year or more.

An office holder is included within the Code. This is because 'employment' for these purposes includes an office and an employment the emoluments of which fall to be assessed under Schedule E.[14]

One cannot avoid the Code by having various separate employments with the same employer. Section 167(3), provides that if the emoluments of one of the employments is at a rate of £8,500 a year or more, or the total emoluments of all the employments is at a rate of £8,500 a year or more, the Code applies to all the employments with that employer.

By s. 167(4) all employees of a partnership or body over which an individual or another partnership or body has control are treated as employments with the individual, partnership or body having control. Thus if E works for the X Partnership controlled by Y Co Ltd which is 100% owned by Z and also is employed by Z directly, then in determining E's earnings level E will be treated as being employed for both jobs by Z.

7.5.3 What is a director?

The expression 'company director' covers a multitude of sins. Somewhat more precision is needed for these purposes. By s. 168(8) 'director' includes members of a board of directors and a single director and '. . . any person in accordance with whose directions or instructions . . . the directors are accustomed to act . . .' By s. 168(9) there is an exclusion for certain professional advisers.

It has already been noted that if the director does not own more than 5% of the ordinary share capital of the company and is a director of a non-profit making or charitable organisation or a full-time working director the director provisions do not apply.

By s. 168(10) 'full-time working director' means a director who is required '. . . to devote substantially the whole of his time to the service of the company in a managerial or technical capacity.'

By s. 167(5) a 'non-profit making company' is one that does not carry on a trade nor do its functions consist mainly in holding investments or other property. 'Charitable purposes only' bears its usual meaning.[15]

[14.] Section 168(2), TA. Cf. the scholarship provisions in s. 165(6)(b) where an emolument also includes emoluments which would be assessable under Schedule E if the taxpayer was UK resident etc.

[15.] Cf. s. 506, TA and cases on it; see, e.g., A.J. Shipwright, *UK Tax and Trusts*, Key Haven, Chapter 9.

7.5.4 Employees earning more than £8,500

A lower earnings limit of £8,500 must be met or exceeded for the Code to apply to employees. This limit only applies to employees. There is no lower earnings limit for the directors' limb in s. 167(1)(a).

The limit for the Code has been changed from time to time. The position is as follows:

Pre 1977–78	£5,000	s. 69, FA 1976
1977–78	£7,500	s. 35, FA 1977
1979–80 onwards	£8,500	s. 23, FA 1978

The effect of inflation on the limit has been considerable.[16]

It should be noted that s. 167(1)(b), TA applies to employments with emoluments 'at the rate of £8,500 a year or more'. The Code therefore cannot be avoided by a series of short employments at less than the overall limit in the amount paid but in excess of it on an annualised basis.

Example
If X is employed by Y Ltd for six months at £750 a month plus certain benefits, in order to work out if X is caught by the Code it is necessary to work out X's annual rate of pay.

6 months' employment at £750 per month:
Earnings: £750 × 6 = £4,500
Annual rate   £750 × 12 = £9,000
X would thus be within the Code.[17]

7.5.5 Calculation of s. 167, TA limit

It is a necessary condition of the Code applying that emoluments are at a rate of £8,500 a year or more. To ascertain whether the Code applies it is necessary to work out the employee's total emoluments, not just the employee's cash receipts. In doing this the taxpayer is to be treated as if the Code applied with no deduction for expenses necessary or otherwise (s. 167(2)). This is quite Draconian but is aimed at an obvious avoidance device. If one had a salary of say £8,000 a year in cash and benefits costing £100,000 then without this provision the Code would not apply. The disallowance of expenses, however, can operate in a harsh manner as the following example illustrates.

[16.] The Old Code's £2,000 limit would in 1992 on *true* basis of average earnings need to be £73,000. The £8,500 limit would then have been £27,000 on that basis. H.L. Written Answer, 10 November 1992, Vol. 540, Cols 9–10 [1992] STI 975.
[17.] If the annual rate of pay were below the limit it would be necessary to work out the emoluments on the basis that the Code applied; see paras. 7.5.5 below.

Example
Harry is employed by Tourist Enterprises Limited (figures for illustrative purposes only).

Salary:	£6,000
Car	£2,140
Loan interest	£260
Allowable expenses reimbursement	£1,000
Total	£9,400
Less expenses	£1,000
Taxable income (without Code)	£8,400

The Code is thus applicable as the total receipts of £9,400 exceed £8,500 whereas only £8,400 would be taxable on general principles.

By s. 167(3) two or more employments with the same employer are aggregated.

7.5.6 Summary

In summary it can be said that the Code applies to:

(a) directors and certain other persons in controlling positions whatever their emoluments, although certain full-time working directors are excluded; and

(b) employees (including full-time working directors excluded under (a) above and other office holders) remunerated at the rate of £8,500 a year or more including all expense payments and benefits before the deduction of any allowable expenses.

7.5.7 To what benefits does the Code apply?

The following general comments can be made about the benefits to which the Code applies. By s. 154 the Code applies (subject to exceptions) to all 'benefits or facilities' provided by reason of employment to an employee or a member of the taxpayer's family or household. Section 168(4) provides that 'references to members of a person's family or household are to his spouse, his sons and daughters and their spouses, his parents and his servants, dependants and guests'. The inclusion of dependants and guests renders the charging provision one of wide scope. These matters are considered in greater detail below.

By s. 168(3) a benefit is deemed to be made 'by reason of employment' if it is made by the employer (cf. *Hochstrasser* v *Mayes* [1958] 1 All ER 369). A proviso to s. 168(3) makes an exception for provision by an individual employer in the normal course of domestic, family or personal relationships. This covers such matters as birthday presents, pocket money, housekeeping etc.

7.5.8 Expense payments

Section 153 makes special provision for payments in respect of expenses where the Code applies. Sums put at the employee's disposal and paid by the employee for such expenditure are to be treated as emoluments taxable under Schedule E. This is without prejudice to a deduction under ss. 198, 201, 201AA or 323(3) (s. 153(2)).

7.5.9 What amount is chargeable in respect of benefits or facilities provided?

The 'cash equivalent' is generally what is chargeable in respect of benefits or facilities provided which fall within the Code. Much of the Code is concerned with establishing what the cash equivalent is. The structure of the legislation goes from the general to the specific. The Code imposes a general charge in s. 154 and certain specific charges, for example, on cars (see s. 157).

7.5.10 General charge

The general charge is to be found in s. 154(1). It provides:

> Subject to section 163, where in any year a person is employed in employment to which this Chapter applies and —
> (a) by reason of his employment there is provided for him, or for others being members of his family or household, any benefit to which this section applies; and
> (b) the cost of providing the benefit is not (apart from this section) chargeable to tax as his income,
> there is to be treated as emoluments of the employment, and accordingly chargeable to income tax under Schedule E, an amount equal to whatever is the cash equivalent of the benefit.

This provision raises a number of questions including the following:

(a) To what employments does the Chapter apply? (See paras 7.5.2–7.5.6.)
(b) When is provision by reason of employment?
(c) What is a person's family or household? (See para. 7.5.7.)
(d) To what benefits does s. 154 apply? (See para. 7.5.11.)
(e) What is the cost of provision?
(f) What is the cash equivalent of a benefit?

To the extent that these questions have not been answered in the preceding paragraphs, they are considered below.

There is no specific exclusion for the charge on the second-hand value under s. 19, TA. Presumably *Vestey* [1980] STC 10 would stop the double jeopardy of charge under both sections.

7.5.11 What benefits are caught by the Code?

Section 154(2) deals with the benefits caught by the Code. It provides:

> The benefits to which this section applies are accommodation (other than living accommodation), entertainment, domestic or other services, and other benefits and facilities of whatsoever nature (whether or not similar to any of those mentioned above in this subsection), excluding however —
> (a) any benefit consisting of the right to receive, or the prospect of receiving, any sums which would be chargeable to tax under section 149 [sick pay]; and
> (b) any benefit chargeable under ss. 157, 158, 159A, 159AA, 160 or 162; and subject to the exceptions provided for by ss. 155 and 155A.

Further exceptions are set out in s. 155.

In summary the exceptions from s. 154 include the following:

(a) living accommodation (ss. 145 and 146 already impose a charge);
(b) sick pay (s. 149 already imposes a charge);
(c) cars and vans (ss. 157 and 159AA already impose a charge);
(d) car fuel (s. 158 already imposes a charge);
(e) mobile telephones (s. 159AA already imposes a charge);
(f) beneficial loan arrangements (s. 160 already imposes a charge);
(g) employee shareholdings (s. 162 already imposes a charge);
(h) benefits in connection with car or van (which are taxed under ss. 157 and 159AA) other than the provision of a driver for the car or van (s. 155(1));
(i) car parking space at or near work (s. 155(1A));
(j) accommodation, supplies or services used by the employee solely for the performance of duties of employment (s. 155(2));
(k) repairs and alterations etc. to living accommodation (s. 155(3));
(l) pensions and death benefits etc. (s. 155(4));
(m) canteen meals for staff generally (s. 155(5));
(n) medical treatment outside the UK etc. (s. 155(6)) but otherwise taxable;
(o) certain limited forms of entertainment (s. 155(7));
(p) child care provided by employer etc. on non-domestic premises (s. 155A).

Items (a) to (g) are otherwise taxable under specific provisions and so are there to prevent double taxation.

7.5.12 Cash equivalent

The charge under the Code is on the 'cash equivalent'. This raises the question what is meant by the cash equivalent. By s. 156(1):

> The cash equivalent of any benefit chargeable to tax under s. 154 is an amount equal to the cost of the benefit, less so much (if any) of it as is made good by the employee to those providing the benefit.

By s. 154(3), 'For the purposes of this section and sections 155 and 156, the persons providing a benefit are those at whose cost the provision is made.'

7.5.13 Cost of a benefit

The rules for determining the cost of providing a benefit depend on the transaction and asset concerned. Relevant factors include:

(a) whether or not title to the asset has passed to the employee;
(b) whether or not the asset is new or used;
(c) whether or not its use has already been taxed.

These will be considered in turn below.

The general rule is that the cost of provision and any associated administrative cost are to be taxed. By s. 156(2):

Subject to the following subsections, the cost of a benefit is the amount of any expense incurred in or in connection with its provision, and (here and in those subsections) includes a proper proportion of any expense relating partly to the benefit and partly to other matters.

(See *Pepper* v *Hart* [1992] STC 898 discussed at para. 2.4.2.)

7.5.14 Transfer of asset

7.5.14.1 General The transfer of title of an asset to an employee would give rise to a charge on the second-hand value of the asset under s. 19. Section 156 reflects this rule but makes special provision to charge the cost of providing the benefit in certain cases. It deals with three situations. These are the transfer of:

(a) a new asset;
(b) a used asset;
(c) an asset after taxable use.

7.5.14.2 New asset When a new asset is transferred s. 156(2) applies, i.e., the cash equivalent of the benefit less so much (if any) as is made good to the provider of the benefit by the employee.

Example
Megacoy buys Evelyn a stereo and gives it new to Evelyn. Evelyn will be charged on the cost to the employer, Megacoy, of providing the stereo rather than on the second-hand value.

7.5.14.3 Used asset If an asset has been used by others before transfer to the employee, and so is not now new, its value is likely to have gone down. If the stereo in the example in para. 7.5.14.2 had been used for six months before being given to Evelyn then its value would be lower. The question then arises as to what amount should be taxed.

Section 156(3) deals with this. It provides:

Where the benefit consists in the transfer of an asset by any person, and since that person acquired or produced the asset it has been used or depreciated, the cost of the benefit is deemed to be the market value at the time of transfer.

In other words the 'market value' is to be taxed. What is meant by 'market value'? Section 168(7) provides: 'For the purposes of s. 156, the market value of an asset at any time is the price which it might reasonably have been expected to fetch on a sale in the open market at that time'. This rule could be a licence to taxpayers to ensure that assets are used by employees before transfer so as to reduce the employee's tax charge. However, s. 156(3) is subject to s. 156(4) discussed below which imposes a charge in some cases by reference to the cost when the asset was first applied to taxable use.

Example
An employer buys a TV set for £150. It is used for a year by Jo who is not an employee. Then the employer gives the set to his higher paid employee, Hilary at a time when its market value is £15. The cash equivalent will be £15 (leaving s. 156(4) out of account).

7.5.14.4 Transfer after taxable use The general rule is that if a used asset is transferred its market value at the time of transfer is taxed. However, if there has been a taxable use before transfer, s. 156(4) applies to tax the benefit by reference to the cost or provision when the asset was first used. Section 156(4) provides that where a charge has been made in respect of an asset put at an employee's disposal (within s. 156(5)) and property in the asset is then transferred to an employee, the cost of the benefit is deemed to be the market value of the asset at the time it was first applied as a benefit under s. 154 (i.e., the original cost of the asset and not its second-hand value), less the aggregate of s. 156(5) charges levied in respect of it to date. (The calculation of s. 156(5) charges is discussed in para. 7.5.15 below.) It should be noted that s. 156(4) only applies if the cost of the benefit apart from the section would be less than the figure produced by that section's application.

Example
An employer provides a suit of clothes to his employee without transferring property in it. The purchase price of the suit is £500. The cash equivalent charged to tax under s. 156(5) and (6) (see para. 7.5.15) will be 20% of £500 = £100. If in year two the employer decides to transfer ownership of the suit to the employee then s. 156(4) ensures that the cash equivalent is:

Original cost (£500) less aggregate of 2 years' s. 156(5) charges (£200) = £300.

Without this provision the only charge which would arise on the transfer of title to the suit from employer to employee would be the s. 156(3) charge on the second-hand value of the suit. Further if such sum (invariably small in the case of all but the most exceptional clothes) were reimbursed by the employee to the employer as the purchase price of the (second-hand) suit, no charge would arise.

7.5.15 Asset placed at disposal without transfer of title

If there is no transfer of title to the asset to an employee but only permission to use it then the special provisions apply. To charge an employee who only has the use of an asset on the full cost of the asset would be inequitable. A different measure of charge is needed.

This is to be found in s. 156(5) which provides for the measure in these circumstances to be 'annual value' plus expenses in connection with providing the asset (s. 156(5)(b)). The question then arises as to what is meant by 'annual value'? The answer to this is to be found in s. 156(6). The effect of this is that cash equivalent is:

(a) in the case of land, the annual value determined under s. 837 TA (cf. s. 145 discussed at para. 7.4.2) which broadly equates to the rateable value of the land in question;

(b) in other cases 20% of the market value of the asset (10% in the case of assets first so applied before 6 April 1980) at the time it is first applied in the provision of a benefit by reason of employment. Section 168(7) states: 'For the purposes of s. 156, the market value of an asset at any time is the price which it might reasonably be expected to fetch on a sale in the open market at that time.'

Example
Megacoy PLC places at Evelyn's disposal (without transfer of title):

(a) land for Evelyn's daughter's pony at an annual value of £300; and
(b) a suit which originally cost £500.

The effect of this would be that Evelyn would be taxable on:

(a) £300 as the annual value of the land within s. 837; and
(b) £100 (20% of £500) in respect of the suit.

The rules where an asset is first put at the disposal of an employee and later transferred have been discussed above. However, another example might be instructive.

Example
Megacoy had a suit costing £500 which it made available to Evelyn for four years. Megacoy then transferred the suit to Evelyn on the fourth anniversary of its provision to Evelyn. Evelyn would be taxed on:

The cost of benefit = market value   £500
              Less (£500 × 20%) × 4   £400   Four years' cost
                                               ----   of benefit
                                               £100

The cost of the benefit would thus be £100 so that Evelyn would be taxed on £100 in respect of this.

Where rent or hire is payable by the provider of land then, under s. 156(5) the rent or hire is to be substituted for the annual value under s. 837 as provided by s. 156(5) if it is higher than the annual value under the earlier subsection (s. 159(2)).

Section 156(8) allows as expenses deductible under ss. 198, 201, 201AA or 332(3) such amounts (if any) as would have been deductible if the cost of the benefit had been incurred by the employee out of his emoluments.

7.5.16 Cars

The arguably unsatisfactory taxation of cars provided by an employer to his or her employees was one of the reasons for the introduction of the 1976 changes. These introduced a fixed scale charge based on the age and cylinder capacity of the car which was relatively generous. The rules were changed by the FA 1993 to one more closely related to the market value of the benefit so that employees are now taxed on 35% of the 'price of a car as regards a year'. This is a higher charge than it used to be but is not necessarily the same as the tax charge on the amount that would be necessary to put the taxpayer in a position to provide the car for the year out of the taxpayer's own resources.

An employer can provide a car to an employee either by outright transfer or by making it available to the employee. If an employer gives a car to an employee outright (i.e., there is a transfer of title) then s. 154 (discussed at para. 7.5.10) will apply to the provision of that benefit. Indeed were the car to be so unusual or rare that its second-hand value would be equal to, or greater than, its purchase price, then the rule in *Tennant* v *Smith* could apply so that, in practice, s. 154 would be inapplicable. Section 157 would also be inapplicable.

In contrast, where:

(a) by reason of his employment;
(b) a car is made available to an employee;
(c) without transfer to him of property in it; and
(d) the benefit[18] is not otherwise chargeable to tax,

s. 157 applies so that the cash equivalent of the car (i.e., 35% of its price, see below) is to be treated as emoluments of the employee's employment.[19]

---

[18] Section 157(1), TA refers to benefit rather than cost because the cash equivalent is dealt with in Sch. 6. See also FA 1996.

[19] An avoidance device of providing a trade-in value for the benefit to avoid the Code charge has been stopped by s. 43, FA 1995 which inserts a new s. 157A, TA.

There is an exemption from charge in s. 159 for what are called 'pool cars'. Where the car provided for the employee is a 'pool car' no charge, under either s. 154 or s. 157, will arise in respect of it. A pool car is, broadly, a car which is available for use by more than one employee, which is not normally garaged overnight at an employee's home and which is used predominately for business purposes (s. 159(2)).

A car for these purposes is 'any mechanically propelled road vehicle' (s. 168(5)). This is subject to a number of exceptions. These include:

(a) a vehicle primarily for the conveyance of goods or burden;
(b) a vehicle of a type not commonly used as a private vehicle and unsuitable to be so used (e.g., a fire engine but what about a hearse? There are also sections dealing with vans, see below);
(c) a motor cycle as defined in the Road Traffic Act 1972 (s. 190, RTA, now repealed: 'a mechanically propelled vehicle having fewer than four wheels and weighing less than eight hundredweight');
(d) an invalid carriage.

The charge to tax under s. 157 is on the cash equivalent of the car. The cash equivalent of any particular car is to be ascertained in accordance with the tables in sch. 6. Paragraph 1 of sch. 6 provides that 'the cash equivalent of the benefit is 35% of the price of the car as regards the year'. There is a cap on the price of a car as regards a year currently of £80,000 (see s. 168G, TA. The Treasury is given power to increase this cap.).

The price of the car as regards the year is defined in s. 168A, TA. This is the car's price if there is one or its notional price if there is no list price. There is a list if a price was published by the car's manufacturer, importer or distributor as the inclusive price for a car of that kind if sold in the UK singly in a retail sale on the relevant day (s. 168(2)). There are complicated rules dealing with accessories.

Since a classic car would have, in historic terms, a very low list price, s. 168F makes special provision in respect of such cars. Section 168 applies to a car which is more than 15 years old and the market value of the car is £15,000 or more. Broadly, in such circumstances the market value of the car is the used rather than the list price.

The cash equivalent is reduced by one-third where the car is four years old or older (para. 5, sch. 6, TA). If the employee is required by the nature of his employment (e.g., a travelling salesman) to use, and did so use, the car for at least 18,000 miles of business travel in the year in question then the cash equivalent is reduced by two-thirds. If the business mileage in those circumstances is between 2,500 and 18,000 the cash equivalent is to be reduced by one-third. The figures are reduced proportionately if the car is not available to the employee for part of the year (see para. 3, sch. 6). If the employee has more than one car taxable under s. 157 concurrently available for his or her use, then the cash equivalent for the car used to the greatest extent is to be reduced by one-third instead of two-thirds if it is used for more than 18,000 business miles and not at all below that mileage.

Where an employee is required, as a condition for the car's being made available for his or her use, to pay a sum to the employer for the use of the car, it is provided that the cash equivalent is to be reduced by the sums so paid (para. 7, sch. 6). Further, the cash equivalent is to be reduced proportionately where the car is unavailable for use by the taxpayer at any time during the year of assessment (see para. 6, sch. 6 on the meaning of 'unavailable').

7.5.17 Car fuel

Where fuel is provided in respect of a car which is subject to a s. 157 charge, the employee in question is to be treated as having received extra emoluments to the value of the cash equivalent of the fuel so provided. It is further provided in s. 158(3) that fuel is deemed to have been provided where the employer pays any bill in connection with the provision of fuel, provides a non cash voucher or a credit card to purchase fuel or reimburses the employee for any expenses incurred in the provision of fuel for the car. This extension of the ordinary meaning of the provision of fuel means that, usually, whatever mechanism is adopted to ensure that the employer pays for the fuel for the car, s. 158 will operate to impose one of its standard charges in connection therewith. Further, s. 158 ensures that the provision of fuel for a s. 157 car will not give rise to any charge under any other Schedule E charging provision, so the possibility of a double tax charge in respect of the provision of fuel is avoided. A charge in respect of fuel under s. 154 is excluded by s. 154(2) and s. 155(1).

The cash equivalent under s. 158 is to be found by reference to tables provided in s. 158(2).

Where an employee reimburses his employer a sum in respect of a car, that sum is taken to reduce the cash equivalent attributable to the car (para. 7, sch. 6). This rule does not apply to partial reimbursement of fuel costs. Where, however, an employee makes good the whole of the expenses of fuel provided for his private use, the cash equivalent of fuel provided is reduced to nil (see s. 158(6)).

7.5.18 Vans

There are similar rules to those for company cars for 'company vans' available for private use in ss. 159AA–159AC. If the van is available for private use by an employee then a standard charge is applied of £500 for a van less than four years old and £350 for an older van.

7.5.19 Mobile telephones

Norman Lamont, when Chancellor of the Exchequer, introduced a charge on mobile telephones, now contained in s. 159A. Where it applies, s. 159A deems emoluments chargeable under Schedule E of £200 to the taxpayer.

Section 159A applies where:

(a) a person is in employment to which the Code applies;
(b) has a mobile phone made available (without transfer of title) to him or her or a member of his or her family or household;
(c) which is available for private use; and
(d) is not otherwise liable to tax.

7.5.20 Beneficial loan arrangements

7.5.20.1 Introduction Section 160 deals with beneficial loan arrangements for taxpayers within the Code. Section 160 imposes two charges. These are:

(a) a charge by reference to the annual interest saving to the employee or office holder; (s. 160(1)); and
(b) a charge on the writing off or release of the whole or part of a loan (s. 160(2)).

Section 160 has its own causation test. Paragraph 1(1) of sch. 7 states that 'the benefit of a loan is provided by reason of a person's employment if it was made by his employer.' This is narrower than the causation test applicable to s. 154 benefits.

7.5.20.2 The interest charge By s. 160(1) an amount, the cash equivalent, is to be treated as emoluments of an employment taxable under Schedule E where:

(a) a loan to the employee or a relative of the employee;
(b) is obtained by reason of employment;
(c) is outstanding for the whole or part of a year when the employment is within the Code; and
(d) no interest or interest at less than an officially prescribed rate is paid.

There are certain exceptions.
'Relative' is defined in s. 160(6) for these purposes. It means a person's spouse, parents, grandparents and other ancestors and that person's children, grandchildren and remoter issue of the taxpayer's spouse. Brothers and sisters of the person in question and that person's spouse are included as are the brothers' and sisters' spouses. The cash equivalent of benefits falling within s. 160 is to be found by reference to the provisions of sch. 7. The cash equivalent is the amount of interest which would have been payable in respect of the loan, had interest been payable at the official rate, less interest actually paid, if any. Detailed provision is made in sch. 7 for the calculation of interest at the official rate. Where the loan itself is £5,000 or less, no charge is to be made under s. 160, replacing the previous *de minimis* exception calculated on the basis of the interest which would have been payable. This ensures that interest free loans made by employers for the purchase of season tickets will not, generally, be caught. Thus if X Co Ltd lent its chief executive £100,000

Benefits in kind – statutory modifications

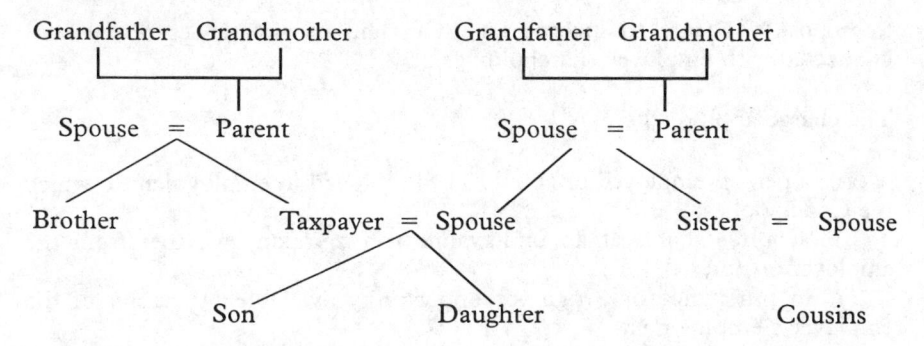

```
Grandfather  Grandmother          Grandfather  Grandmother
      └──────┬──────┘                    └──────┬──────┘
             │                                  │
      Spouse = Parent                    Spouse = Parent
            ╱ ╲                                ╱ ╲
  Brother   Taxpayer = Spouse          Sister = Spouse
              ╱ ╲
           Son    Daughter                      Cousins
```

All but cousins caught.

at 5% p.a. when the official rate was 10%, X's tax position would be as follows:

Interest at official rate	£100,000 × 10%	£10,000
Amount paid	£100,000 × 5%	£5,000
Amount Taxable		£5,000

There is no charge where the interest on the loan would be eligible for relief under s. 353(2) (or would be so eligible apart from s. 353(1)).

7.5.20.3 The writing off charge Where a loan to a person in employment to which the Code applies (or a relative), obtained by reason of the employee's employment, is written off or released in whole or in part, the amount written off or released is brought into charge as emoluments of the employment. The employee is treated as being in receipt for Schedule E purposes of extra emoluments to the value of the amount released or written off.

A loan continues to be one to which the Code applies even if the employment has terminated or ceased to be an employment to which the Code applies for the purposes of this charge. This section applies to impose a charge even where the write off or release of the loan occurs upon the termination of the employee's employment. The only exception to this rule is a write off or release which takes effect on death (s. 161(6)).

7.5.21 Employee shareholdings – s. 162

This section deals with employee shareholdings. A common feature in the past of share schemes for employees was the use of:

(a) partly paid shares or shares acquired at less than market value; and
(b) 'stop loss' arrangements, i.e., arrangements to protect against a fall in the value of the shares after the employee acquired them, for example, by giving the employee an option to require the company to buy the shares back at his acquisition cost. Section 162 was introduced to tax these benefits and

to impose a charge to income tax in certain circumstances on benefits connected with employee shareholdings.

The charge applies where:

(a) a person employed or about to be employed in employment to which the Code applies;
(b) acquires shares at an undervalue in a company whether from the employer or not;
(c) in pursuance of a right or opportunity available by reason of the employee's employment.

The charge applies by deeming there to be a loan called in the section 'the notional loan' to which s. 160 (beneficial loan arrangements) applies. The amount of the notional loan is the amount of the undervalue. By s. 162(2)(b) the amount of the undervalue is the market value of those shares on acquisition if fully paid up, less any payment then made for the shares. Thus if X acquired 100 shares at £1 each when they had a market value of £11 each the undervalue would be:

Market value	100 × £11	£1,100
Amount paid	100 × £1	100
Initial amount of notional loan		£1,000

7.5.22 Other matters

7.5.22.1 Section 163 – expenses connected with living accommodation Directors and employees earning in excess of £8,500 a year are within ss. 145 and 146 but also incur an extra charge under s. 163 on heating, cleaning, repairs to their living accommodation etc. provided by their employer.

7.5.22.2 Section 164 – directors' tax paid by employer Section 164 provides that where a director receives his income gross in circumstances where income tax should have been deducted under the PAYE system and someone other than the recipient pays the tax, the sum received by the director is to be treated as a sum net of tax, so that it will need to be grossed up to the rate or rates applicable to find the tax due. This section does not, it seems, apply to employees earning in excess of £8,500 per annum. Nor does it apply where the director has no material interest in the company and either the director is full-time or the company is a charitable or non-profit making organisation.

7.5.22.3 Section 165 – scholarships Scholarship income is exempted from income tax by s. 331. In *Wicks* v *Firth* [1983] STC 25 the Revenue put to the House of Lords the proposition that the exemption was limited to the holder of the scholarship. Therefore, the argument ran, where an employer awards an employee's child a scholarship, s. 154, because it applies to benefits provided to members of an employee's family or household as well as to the employee, operates to charge the employee in respect of the cash equivalent of the scholarship. Since the s. 154 charge was on the employee and not the scholarship holder, the exemption was of no avail to the taxpayer. The House of Lords rejected this argument, holding that the exemption's wording was wide enough to protect both the scholarship holder and the employee from a charge to tax in respect of the scholarship.

In the FA 1983 provisions were introduced to reverse in part the effect of *Wicks* v *Firth*. Section 165 now provides that any scholarship provided for a member of a person's family shall be taken to be provided by reason of a person's employment if it is provided under arrangements entered into by that person's employer or any person connected with his employer. Thus s. 154 applies to such benefits. Excepted from s. 165 are 'excluded scholarships' within s. 165(3).

Scholarships are excluded if:

(a) they are provided from a trust fund or scheme;
(b) they are held by persons undergoing full time instruction at an educational establishment;
(c) they would not be regarded as being provided by reason of a person's employment leaving s. 168(3) out of account; and
(d) not more than 25% of the total amount of the payments made out of the fund in question in respect of educational scholarships is attributable to scholarships awarded by reason of a person's employment.

CHAPTER EIGHT
Schedule E – expenses

8.1 INTRODUCTION

This chapter is concerned with some aspects of deductible expenses for Schedule E purposes.[1] Schedule E allows for some, albeit restricted, deductions from 'emoluments' in calculating the amount taxable under Schedule E. What constitutes emoluments from an office or employment under the general rules of Schedule E has been considered in the preceding chapters. The expenses rules for Schedule E are not generous. As Vaisey J said of the rules in *Lomax* v *Newton* (1953) 34 TC 558, they 'are notoriously rigid, narrow and restricted in their operation [and] . . . when examined they are found to come to nearly nothing at all'. Warner J described them as '. . . to some extent unfair . . .' in the recent case of *Smith* v *Abbott* [1991] STC 661 at p. 664.[2]

Section 131(1), TA provides that:

> tax under . . . Schedule E shall, except as provided to the contrary by any provision of the Tax Acts, be chargeable on the full amount of emoluments falling under that Case, subject to such deductions only as may be authorised by the Tax Acts . . .

Accordingly, all the emoluments are taxable unless statute authorises a deduction (cf. ss. 817 and 74, TA discussed in Chapter 10). It is therefore necessary to consider what deductions are authorised by the Tax Acts.[3]

[1.] See Whiteman, *Income Tax*, 3rd edn, Sweet & Maxwell, and see *Simon's Taxes*, Butterworths.
[2.] And see E. Keeling, KCLJ (1994) Vol. 5, p. 179.
[3.] The expression Tax Acts is defined in s. 831(2) as, so far as the context otherwise requires, this Act and all other provisions of the Income Tax Acts and the Corporation Tax Acts.

Schedule E – expenses

There are five groups of deductions for Schedule E provided by the Taxes Act which need to be mentioned in particular here. These are:

(a) s. 198, TA relief for necessary expenses;
(b) s. 201, TA deduction for fees and subscription to professional bodies etc;
(c) capital allowances;
(d) interest on loans for plant and machinery;
(e) business entertaining expenses.

There are also some special rules for matters such as foreign travel for employments performed outside the UK during the year in s. 193, TA and for the accommodation and related expenses of ministers of religion in s. 332, TA.

8.2 SECTION 198, TA RELIEF FOR NECESSARY EXPENSES – GENERAL MATTERS

The Finance Act 1997 has made a number of changes to s. 198, TA with regard to travelling expenses. The changes are intended to make the rules 'simpler and fairer' (Budget Press Release, 26 November 1996). Whether they will in fact do so remains to be seen. The amendments also finally remove the extremely outdated reference to the expenses incurred in keeping and maintaining a horse which has appeared in the TA for many years.

The 'new' s. 198(1) takes effect as from 6 April 1998 and reads as follows:

if the holder of an office or employment is obliged to incur and defray out of the emoluments of that office or employment—
(a) any amount necessarily expended on travelling in the performance of the duties of the office or employment,
(b) any other expenses of travelling which are not expenses of ordinary commuting but are attributable to the attendance of the holder of the office or employment at any place on an occasion when his attendance at that place is in the performance of the duties of the office or employment, or
(c) any amount not comprised in expenses falling within paragraph (a) or (b) above but expended wholly, exclusively and necessarily in the performance of the duties of the office or employment,
then (subject to subsection (1A) below) there may be deducted from the emoluments to be assessed the amount which is so incurred and defrayed.

Section 198(1A) is discussed in para. 8.3.4 below.

The 'old' s. 198(1) will therefore continue to apply for the 1997/98 year of assessment.

Before looking at s. 198 in detail, it should be noted that s. 198, TA only applies for Cases I and II of Schedule E. Section 198(3), TA makes provision for the deduction of expenses from emoluments taxable under Case III of Schedule E. However, this is by reference to s. 198(1), TA.

Section 198(1), TA thus breaks down into two parts, namely:

(a) travelling expenses;
(b) other expenses.

Both of these will be considered in turn.

8.3 TRAVELLING EXPENSES

8.3.1 Introduction

This section is concerned with the deductibility of travelling expenses for Schedule E purposes. It is worthwhile repeating the new statutory wording (so far as relevant):

> if the holder of an office or employment is obliged to incur and defray out of the emoluments of that office or employment—
> (a) any amount necessarily expended on travelling in the performance of the duties of the office or employment,
> (b) any other expenses of travelling which are not expenses of ordinary commuting but are attributable to the attendance of the holder of the office or employment at any place on an occasion when his attendance at that place is in the performance of the duties of the office or employment, . . .

Under the 'old' s. 198(1), travelling expenses are deductible:

> if the holder of an office or employment is necessarily obliged to incur and defray out of the emoluments of that office or employment the expenses of travelling in the performance of the duties of the office or employment, or of keeping and maintaining a horse to enable him to perform those duties, . . . there may be deducted from the emoluments to be assessed the expenses so incurred and defrayed.

Travelling expenses thus need only to be incurred 'necessarily' or (from 1998/99 onwards) be expenses which are not expenses of 'ordinary commuting' but which are 'attributable' to the attendance at a place of work rather than 'wholly, exclusively and necessarily' incurred as is the case for the deductibility of other expenses discussed in para. 8.4.

In order to obtain a deduction for travelling expenses under the existing law and the new s. 198(1)(a) there must be:

(a) a necessary obligation to incur the expenses;
(b) the expense must have been incurred in performance of the duties of the office.

A trilogy of House of Lords' cases used to dominate this area of the law.[4] They illustrated both requirements and are considered below chronologically.

[4.] For a review of all three cases see P.F. Smith [1977] BTR at p. 290 and the reply from Graham McDonald [1978] BTR 79.

8.3.2 Trilogy of cases

8.3.2.1 *Ricketts* v *Colquhoun*

The first of these cases is that of *Ricketts* v *Colquhoun* (1925) 10 TC 118. Mr Ricketts was a well-known barrister at the time practising in the Temple. He held the part-time office of the Recorder of Portsmouth. He claimed, inter alia, a deduction under Rule 9 of Schedule E of the Income Tax Act 1918 (now s. 198(1), TA) a sum in respect of his travel from London to Portsmouth for the start of quarter sessions and from Portsmouth to London at the end of quarter sessions. The Commissioners disallowed his claim to deduct travelling expenses. Rowlatt J held that upon the authorities he had to find for the Crown and deny the deduction. He said (at p. 121) 'the place where the taxpayer practises is really, in point of law, as much as the place where he resides, at his own discretion to select'. The barrister could have resided in Portsmouth. The travel was not in the performance of the duties.

The Court of Appeal affirmed Rowlatt J's decision (Warrington LJ dissenting). Pollock MR said he attached importance to the words 'necessarily obliged'. He thought (at p. 124) they were:

> ... to be read as meaning this, that where an obligation is imposed upon a holder of an office or employment which *ex necessitate* of the office compels him to make outlays, it is in those cases, and after you have fulfilled that condition that you first begin to consider what is the possible expenditure that may be deducted.

Warrington LJ in his dissenting judgment considered the travelling expenses and the cost of living in Portsmouth were incurred in the performance of the Recorder's duties. He considered that the word 'necessarily' did not have to be considered in the abstract. It meant necessary or necessarily in regard to the circumstances of the individual concerned.

Warrington LJ's view was rejected in the House of Lords which upheld the view of the majority in the Court of Appeal. Lord Cave, the Lord Chancellor,[5] considered that the expenses were not necessarily incurred, in the sense of 'obliged' by the fact that Mr Ricketts held the office, nor were they incurred in the performance of the duties of the office. The expenses were incurred not in the course of performing the duties but partly before Mr Ricketts started to perform them and partly after he had fulfilled them. In other words they were expenses of travelling to and from work and so not in the performance of the duties of the office or employment.

Lord Blanesburgh delivered the only other reasoned speech. He thought that the language of the section was generally a restricted language, some of it repeated apparently to heighten its effect.

He went on to say (at p. 135) in a most important passage:

> ... the language of the rule points to the expenses with which it is concerned as being confined to those with which each and every occupant of a particular office is necessarily obliged to incur in the performance of

---

[5.] Lords Atkinson, Buckmaster and Carson concurred or agreed.

its duties, to expenses imposed upon the holder *ex necessitate* of his office and to such expenses only. It says if the holder of an office – the words be it observed are not 'any holder of an office' is obliged to incur expenses in the performance of the duties of an office – the duties again are not the duties of his office; in other words the terms employed as strictly, and, I cannot doubt, purposely, not personal but objective. The deductible expenses do not extend to those which the holder has to incur mainly and it may be only because the circumstances in relation to his office which are personal to himself were as the result of his own volition.

Thus his Lordship considered that one could not interpret the rule as Warrington LJ had done as having a personal element. Lord Blanesburgh also considered that the expenses were not incurred in the performance of the duties.

8.3.2.2 *Pook v Owen* Travelling expenses were again considered by the House of Lords in *Pook v Owen* (1968) 45 TC 571. The taxpayer was a GP in Fishguard and also held part-time appointments as an obstetrician and anaesthetist at a hospital in Haverfordwest 15 miles away. He was reimbursed part of his expenses for travelling to and from the hospital. There was a special finding by the General Commissioners that his responsibility for a patient began as soon as he received a telephone call and on occasions he had to be on stand-by call. On receipt of a call he gave instructions to the hospital staff and usually set out immediately by car for the hospital. However, he sometimes 'applied treatment by telephone' and awaited a further report.

Two questions were argued before the House of Lords. These were:

(a) whether the money he received in reimbursement of the travelling expenses constituted 'emoluments' of his employment; and
(b) whether the excess of the travelling expenses incurred over the amount of reimbursement was deductible.

It was held (Lord Pearson dissenting) that the reimbursements, being reimbursements of actual expenses, were not part of the emoluments of his employment.

By a majority of three to two (Lords Donovan and Pearson dissenting) the House of Lords held the excess travelling expenses incurred over reimbursements were deductible.

Lord Guest said that the basis of the Crown's arguments was *Ricketts* v *Colquhoun* and in particular Lord Blanesburgh's speech. This was considered in para. 8.3.2.1. Lord Guest considered that *Ricketts* v *Colquhoun* could be distinguished because in that case there was only one place of employment, Portsmouth. In *Pook* v *Owen* Lord Guest considered that it was shown that there were two places where Dr Owen's duties were performed, the hospital and his home by telephone. His Lordship continued 'if he was performing his duties in both places then it is difficult to see why on the journey between the two places he was not equally performing his duties'. The travelling expenses were in his opinion therefore incurred 'in the performance of the duties of his office'.

Schedule E – expenses

Lord Pearce wished their Lordships to reconsider *Ricketts v Colquhoun*. He considered it very unsatisfactory both in result and reasoning. However, he agreed that *Pook v Owen* could be distinguished from *Ricketts v Colquhoun* on the basis that there were two places of employment so the Commissioners' decision allowing a deduction was correct.

Lord Wilberforce also considered that *Ricketts v Colquhoun* could be distinguished on the facts. In *Pook v Owen* there were two places of employment. He said that what is required is proof to the satisfaction of the fact finding Commissioners that the taxpayer in the real sense had two places of work, and that the expenses were incurred in travelling from one place to another. He compared Dr Owen with the well-known Australian flying doctor! In discussing *Ricketts v Colquhoun* Lord Wilberforce agreed that the rule was drafted in an objective form so as to distinguish between those expenses which arose from the nature of the office and those which arose from the personal choice of the taxpayer. He continued: 'that this does not mean that no expenses can ever be deductible unless precisely those expenses must be incurred by each and every holder of the office'. The objective character of the deductions relates to their nature and not to their amount. He said further:

> ... in this case the hospital management committee required the services of doctors on a part time basis for emergencies and had found that there was a difficulty in obtaining suitable men. Unless a suitable retired doctor could be appointed (and that case might be different) the committee would have to appoint a doctor with a practice of his own who might live within 15 miles, 1 mile or a hundred yards of the hospital; the choice in the matter, if any exists, lies not with the doctor who was there in his practice but with the committee, which decides however near or far he works, to appoint and to require him to discharge a part of his duties at his practice premises . . .

Lord Wilberforce considered irrelevant the undemonstrated possibility that a nearer practitioner might have been selected. Lord Wilberforce's approach thus seems less restrictive than that of Lord Blanesburgh.

The dissenting Lords Donovan and Pearson in contrast considered the case fell within *Ricketts v Colquhoun* which they thought was indistinguishable. In the light of the majority view in *Pook v Owen* and the decision in the next case to be considered, *Taylor v Provan*, it appears that the courts may be taking a slightly less restrictive approach to the construction of s. 198, TA.

An interesting question in *Pook v Owen* is why the expenses of Dr Owen's return journey from the hospital were deductible. If Dr Owen had done what was necessary, why was he not just going home from work?[6]

[6.] Presumably the answer in favour of deduction is that 'home' was also a place of work and he could be required to take responsibility for another patient by a telephone call as he walked through the door. The argument against is that he travelled to the hospital at a time when he was responsible for a patient. He travelled home at a time when he was not. What if he stopped off on the way or went somewhere else before going home? Would a mobile phone make all his travel deductible?

8.3.2.3 Taylor v Provan   *Taylor* v *Provan* [1974] 1 All ER 1201, 49 TC 579 concerned a Canadian who undertook brewery amalgamation as a kind of business recreation. He became involved as an unpaid consultant in a series of amalgamations which led to the formation of Bass Charrington. For prestige reasons he was appointed a director of the company but took no part in the usual functions of a director. Because of the taxpayer's other business commitments it was arranged that he would do as much of his work as possible in Canada. When it was necessary for him to visit the UK the company reimbursed his air fare. He received no remuneration for his services. The taxpayer was assessed to UK income tax under Schedule E on the reimbursements under the special provisions regarding directors' expenses in the Code.[7] It was held by the House of Lords that the reimbursements were emoluments of the taxpayer's office but by a majority of three to two (Lords Wilberforce and Simon of Glaisdale dissenting) that the air fares were deductible expenses under what is now s. 198(1), TA. The air fares were travelling expenses necessarily incurred in the performance of the duties of the taxpayer's office since in the circumstances of the case the taxpayer was regarded as having two places of employment.

Lord Reid referred to the fact that s. 198, TA authorises the keeping and maintaining of a horse to enable the taxpayer to perform the duties of the office or employment:

> The holder of the office would keep his horse at his home, so he would use it to get from his home to the various places where his duties had to be performed. So this part of the rule must mean to enable the holder of the office to get from his home to the place where his duties are to be performed as well as to enable him to get from one place to another in the course of performing his duties. There is no suggestion of a distinction between travelling from his home to the place of work and travelling between places of work. He can deduct the whole cost of keeping his horse – not merely part of it.

This part of Lord Reid's speech might be taken as casting doubt on Lord Cave's approach in *Ricketts* v *Colquhoun*. Lord Reid also considered that the basis of his own decision was that there had to be a part-time appointment and it was therefore necessary that whoever was appointed should incur travelling expenses. One should look at the realities of the situation. Lord Reid therefore thought that *Taylor* v *Provan* was covered by *Pook* v *Owen*. The essential feature was that it was impossible for the company to get the work contracted to be done by the taxpayer done by anyone else. This has been described by one learned commentator as a novel proposition which it is submitted will be adjudged in time as a herring of the brightest scarlet.

Lord Morris also considered that *Ricketts* v *Colquhoun* was distinguishable on the facts. In *Taylor* v *Provan* the office here could probably have been filled by no one else. Further the feature of there being in a real sense a dual location of the duties he considered more pronounced than in *Pook* v *Owen*.

[7.] See now s. 153, TA and Chapter 7 above.

Lord Salmon preferred practical reality to theoretical possibility and thought that one should not rigidly apply Lord Blanesburgh's *dictum* in *Ricketts v Colquhoun* which at any rate he considered afforded little guidance as to how *Taylor v Provan* should be decided.

Lord Wilberforce dissented saying that travelling expenses can only be deducted if the job itself required the taxpayer to travel so that the travelling is *on* the taxpayer's work as distinct from travelling *to* his work. That a taxpayer has two places of work is a variant of this accepted travelling on his job. But for this to apply the travel must be required by the nature of the job which requires the work to be done in two places. He said that his words in *Pook v Owen* showed that the matter must be viewed objectively and were intended to provide a test whether the office or employment was such as to require its duties to be performed in two places. He considered that in *Taylor v Provan* the element of necessity in the objective sense did not exist. However, in the authors' view, if the taxpayer's job is specially created for him as the only person who can do it it is hard to see the distinction from *Pook v Owen*. It is interesting to compare Lord Wilberforce's speech in *Pook v Owen*, with his later speech in *Taylor v Provan*.

Lord Simon of Glaisdale (the other dissenting Lord) considered that the two places of work distinguished *Pook v Owen* from *Taylor v Provan*.

8.3.3 Site based employees and 'triangular travel'

Section 198(1)(b) has been inserted by the Finance Act 1997 and will take effect from 6 April 1998 onwards. It covers travelling expenditure which does not comprise 'ordinary commuting' but which is attributable to attendance by the employee at 'any place' where his or her attendance at that place is in performance of the duties of the office or employment. Section 198(1)(b) will thus enable those employees who do not have a normal place of work but who perform their duties at a number of different sites to get relief for their travelling expenses. It will also determine the availability of relief where, instead of travelling from the normal workplace to a temporary workplace, an employee travels directly from home to that temporary workplace (so called 'triangular travel').

'Ordinary commuting' is defined in new s. 198A. Broadly it comprises travel between a 'permanent workplace' and any of the following places provided they do not constitute places where the employee is performing the duties of his or her office or employment:

(a) the employee's home or place of permanent or temporary residence;
(b) any place that the employee is visiting for social or personal reasons;
(c) any place which the employee attends for the purposes of a trade, profession or vocation he or she carries on;
(d) any place attended in performance of another office or employment (s. 198A(4)).

A 'permanent workplace' is the place where the employee regularly attends to perform his or her duties and which is not his or her home or other place of permanent or temporary residence (s. 198A(2)). Where necessary, a permanent workplace can include a geographical area if the employee does not work at a single defined place (s. 198A(3)).

8.3.4 Quantum

Even if the taxpayer can satisfy the tests discussed in paras 8.3.2 and 8.3.3, there may still be a question as to the quantum of expenditure allowed, i.e., could the taxpayer have travelled more cheaply?

A case on this which has been described as a case of the 'biter bit' is *Marsden* v *IRC* (1965) 42 TC 326. This case concerned an Inland Revenue investigator who was required to visit a number of towns in Lancashire. He travelled by car and claimed an allowance for the excess cost over his reimbursement at the official rate. It was not a condition of his employment that he should travel in his own car and there was no evidence that he could not have travelled by public transport. It was held that the excess was not an expense which the taxpayer was necessarily obliged to incur and therefore it could not be deducted. Pennycuick J said:

> . . . There appears to be no reported case in which the Court has had to consider the scale of travelling expenses; that is to say, how far travelling expenses wholly and exclusively incurred [sic] in the performance of the taxpayer's duties were necessary, having regard to the availability of cheaper transport. The question must be one of everyday occurrence, for example, as between car and train, self-drive car or chauffeur-driven car, aeroplane or ship, first or second class, and the like. [Counsel for the Crown] submits that this must be a question of fact and degree depending on all the circumstances of any particular case, including not only the price of the transport but such considerations as speed, convenience, the purpose of the journey, the status of the officer, and so forth. I agree with that contention.

As there was no evidence that Mr Marsden could not have travelled on his work by public transport there was no reason for interfering with the Commissioners' decision denying the deduction.

The Finance Act 1997 amendments to the deductibility of travelling expenses also contain some additional rules which go to quantum. Under a new s. 198(1A) which will take effect from 6 April 1998 if the employee incurs deductible travelling expenditure under 'new' s. 198(1)(a) or (b) and, in consequence of doing so, does not incur the expenses of ordinary commuting that he would otherwise have done, the deductible amount is reduced by the amount of ordinary commuting expenditure that the employee has saved.

8.3.5 Summary: travelling expenses

In summary, for a travelling expense to be deductible from emoluments it must be incurred:

Schedule E – expenses

(a) necessarily in the sense of being:

(i) a necessary expense; and
(ii) a necessary amount; and

(b) incurred in the performance of the duties.

This will generally exclude the cost of travel to work as such expenses will not be in the course of the performance of the duties of the office or employment. The money will be spent to put one in position to carry out the work. The situation may be different if there are two places of work. Travelling between two places of work is likely to be in the performance of the duties (see *Pook* v *Owen* at para. 8.3.2.2).

8.4 OTHER EXPENSES

8.4.1 General

Other expenses (i.e., expenses other than travelling expenses) must meet three conditions to be deductible for Schedule E purposes. These are as follows:

(a) the taxpayer must be necessarily obliged to incur the expenditure;
(b) the expenditure must have been incurred in the performance of the duties of the office or employment; and
(c) the expenditure must have been wholly, exclusively and necessarily incurred in the performance of the duties.

8.4.2 'Necessarily obliged'

The first condition for deduction is that the expenditure must have been 'necessarily obliged' to be incurred by the taxpayer. This is apparently to be determined on an objective test.

In *Brown* v *Bullock* (1961) 40 TC 1 Donovan LJ said that the test was not whether the employer imposes the expense but whether the duties do in the sense that, irrespective of what the employer may prescribe, the duties cannot be performed without incurring that particular outlay. In *Brown* v *Bullock* it was virtually a condition of the bank manager's appointment that he should join a Pall Mall club but the cost of joining and subscribing to the club was disallowed under Donovan LJ's test as not being an expense imposed by the duties of the employment but by the employer. However, *Brown* v *Bullock* was distinguished in *Elwood* v *Utitz* (1965) 42 TC 482 which also concerned a club subscription. McDermott LJ said in the Northern Ireland Court of Appeal that the decision in *Brown* v *Bullock* was simply that the duties of the bank manager did not necessitate the outlay on the subscription because he did not need to be a club member in order to discharge his duties. That, he thought, was an altogether different case from the instant one in which the subscriptions were paid, not to gain membership as an end in itself, but to obtain accommodation which an appellant had to get if he was to perform the duties of his office. Thus the necessity, although objective, seems to be judged in the particular context of the taxpayer's employment.

8.4.3 'In the performance of the duties'

The second condition for deductibility under s. 198, TA is that the expenses must be incurred 'in the performance of the duties' of the office or employment. An expenditure merely to put one into a position to perform one's duties is not incurred in the performance of one's duties. Thus a commission paid to an employment agency to obtain a job is not deductible expenditure (see *Shott* v *McIlgorm* [1945] 1 All ER 391). Similarly the cost of the headmaster's attendance at a history course to prepare for lectures at his school was not deductible (see *Humbles* v *Brooks* (1962) 40 TC 500; *Blackwell* v *Mills* (1945) 26 TC 468; and *Owen* v *Burden* (1971) 47 TC 476) nor were an articled clerk's exam fees paid to the Law Society (see *Lupton* v *Potts* (1969) 45 TC 643). For the same reason subscriptions to learned societies and professional bodies were not deductible. This has been partially reversed by statute (see para. 8.6).

This problem can be put in a different way, namely that any expense which is incurred prior to or after performing the duties of the office or employment is not deductible. In *Simpson* v *Tate* (1925) 9 TC 314 a county medical officer failed in his claim to deduct the cost of subscriptions to the Royal Society of Medicine and other learned societies which he had joined to keep himself abreast of the latest developments in medicine. Rowlatt J held that the expense was not incurred in the performance of his duties and was therefore not deductible.

The recent consolidated appeals of *Fitzpatrick* v *IRC* and *Smith* v *Abbott* [1994] 1 All ER 673 considered when expenditure was incurred in the course of the office or employment. These were conflicting English and Scots decisions at the lower level. The taxpayers in both cases were journalists. Each received reimbursement of the cost of newspapers and periodicals read to gain current information and to provide ideas as to issues and presentation. There was some evidence that journalists were expected to read widely and that the quality of their work could suffer if they did not read widely. The findings of fact in the two cases differed. In the English case, *Smith* v *Abbott*, the General Commissioners found as a fact that:

(a) the reading of newspapers and periodicals was *necessary* because each taxpayer had to be equipped with ideas for editorial meetings and the like; and

(b) the employers and employees regarded such reading as an essential part of their duties.

There were no such findings of fact in the Scots case of *Fitzpatrick* v *IRC*. The Court of Session had rejected the journalist's claim for a deduction whereas the English Court of Appeal had allowed it.

The House of Lords (Lord Browne-Wilkinson dissenting) held that no deduction was possible in either case. Lord Templeman delivered the leading speech. He considered that both decisions could not be right. The question in each case was whether the reading was carried out in the performance of the duties. Lord Templeman considered that the journalists' duty was the production of their employer's newspaper. Reading other newspapers was not producing their newspaper and so was not in the performance of their duties. Lord Templeman thought that if the deductions were allowed 'there would be no end to it' (at p. 608). As the newspapers were read at home and on the train the expenditure on the newspapers contained elements of personal choice and benefit. It was as if they had wined and dined to keep themselves up to date.[8] There are a number of problems with this approach. How can it be reconciled with the Commissioners being the final arbiters of fact as the House of Lords held in *Edwards* v *Bairstow* [1956] AC 14? His Lordship's mixed fact and law approach is far from convincing. As one commentator has said, 'It was not legitimate for the House to disregard the findings of fact made by the Commissioners or to seek to characterise as a question of law what in reality was a question of fact.'[9] The different findings of fact distinguished the cases. The result is highly unsatisfactory as it tends away from certainty and the established jurisdictions of the court and tribunal. Nevertheless, the restrictive approach to 'in the performance of the duties' remains.

8.4.4 'Wholly, exclusively and necessarily'

The third condition is that the expenditure must be 'wholly, exclusively and necessarily' incurred. These are most restrictive words. Vaisey J said in *Lomax* v *Newton* (1953) 34 TC 558 that 'an expenditure may be necessary for the holder of an office without being necessary to him in the performance of the duties of that office; it may be necessary in the performance of those duties without being exclusively referable to those duties; it may perhaps be both necessarily and exclusively but still not wholly so referable. The words are indeed stringent and exacting; compliance with each and every one of them is obligatory if the benefit of them is to be claimed successfully.'

He continued, in a well-known passage, that 'they are, to my mind, deceptive words in the sense that when examined they come to nearly nothing at all'. The *Lomax* case concerned certain mess expenses of an army officer. If he had refused to meet them he would have been asked to resign his commission. Nonetheless the expenses were held not deductible as they were not incurred wholly, exclusively and necessarily in the performance of his duties.

Nolder v *Walters* (1930) 15 TC 180 is an interesting case. Rowlatt J refused to allow deductions to a pilot for the expense of installing a telephone, keeping a motor car, and buying special flying clothes, books etc. However,

---

[8.] This is counterfactual and is at any rate dealt with by a specific provision in s. 577, TA discussed at para. 8.9 below.
[9.] E. Keeling (1994) 5 KCLJ 181.

the pilot was held to be entitled to claim the extra cost of staying away from home. This seems to be the position for others who incur expenses as a result of being away on business such as long distance drivers and commercial travellers.

Where the taxpayer derives some element of personal benefit from the expenditure in issue, the sum spent will not be allowable as a deduction since it would not be true to say of such a sum that it was spent 'wholly and exclusively' in the performance of the duties of the office or employment. In *Griffiths* v *Mockler* (1953) 35 TC 135 the taxpayer was a Major in the Royal Army Pay Corps. He claimed to deduct the amount of his annual mess subscriptions from his emoluments. He was obliged to make the subscription under the King's Regulations then in force. Vaisey J rejected the taxpayer's claim: the payment 'provided an element of private benefit to the Respondent' (at p. 137). Equally, since the bank manager in *Brown* v *Bullock* (at para. 8.4.2) derived some personal benefit from his membership of London clubs, the cost of membership did not satisfy the exclusivity requirement.

Where the personal benefit is incidental, however, the exclusivity requirement may be held to have been met so that the expense will be deductible. In *Elwood* v *Utitz* (1965) 42 TC 482 the taxpayer claimed to be able to deduct the cost of subscriptions to London clubs. He was managing director of a Northern Ireland company and his post caused him to visit London frequently. By using the accommodation facilities of London clubs his company was saved substantial sums compared with the cost of hotel accommodation. The Northern Ireland Court of Appeal held that the cost of subscriptions was a deductible expense for Schedule E's purposes. Lord MacDermott CJ distinguished *Brown* v *Bullock* saying (at p. 498):

> In that case the subscriptions were paid in order that the taxpayer should become a club member and so make social contacts and keep in touch with other members who were customers of the bank. There was nothing incidental about these benefits, and the question of 'wholly' or 'exclusively' did not arise for consideration . . . that, to my mind, is an altogether different case from the present one in which the subscriptions were paid not to gain membership as an end in itself but to obtain accommodation and facilities which the Appellant had to get if he was to perform the duties of his office.

8.5 CONCESSIONS ETC.

The rigours of s. 198, TA are mitigated by several Extra-statutory Concessions. They include the following:

ESC A1:
This makes substantial provision for flat rate allowances in connection with expenditure on the cost or upkeep of tools or special clothing in connection with particular employments;

Schedule E – expenses

ESC A4:
This deals with the travelling expenses of directors and employees earning £8,500 or more a year;

SP 16/80:
This statement of practice makes special provision for the deduction of expenses by lorry drivers in connection with meals purchased away from home.

8.6 SECTION 201, TA FEES AND SUBSCRIPTIONS TO PROFESSIONAL BODIES ETC.

Subscriptions to such bodies would normally not be incurred in the course of the performance of the duties of the office or employment since it would be classified as expenditure to put a person into a position to carry out the duties of the office or employment and so not allowable.

Section 201, TA allows certain subscriptions and other payments by solicitors, architects, opticians, patent agents and members of bodies approved by the Inland Revenue for the purpose, to be deducted for Schedule E purposes.

8.7 CAPITAL ALLOWANCES

An employee may be entitled to capital allowances. The availability of capital allowances is discussed in Chapter 12.

8.8 INTEREST ON LOAN FOR PLANT

Section 359(4), TA allows interest on a loan used for the purchase of plant which qualifies for capital allowance treatment to be claimed as a deduction.

8.9 BUSINESS ENTERTAINING EXPENSES

By s. 577(1), TA no deduction is permitted for Schedule E purposes for any expense incurred in providing 'business entertainment'. 'Business entertainment' means entertainment, including hospitality of any kind, provided by an employee in connection with his employer's trade. Thus if an employee takes a customer to lunch the cost of the lunch is not deductible from the employee's emoluments under Schedule E. This section also applies to the provision of gifts to customers (s. 577(8), TA).

8.10 MISCELLANEOUS

There are special rules for certain foreign travel (s. 193, TA), for removal expenses (ss. 191A and 191B and sch. 11A inserted by FA 1993) and ministers of religion (s. 332, TA).

CHAPTER NINE
Schedule D, Cases I and II – profits from trades, professions and vocations

9.1 GENERAL MATTERS

This chapter is concerned with the general aspects of income tax and profits from trades, professions and vocations.[1] The profits and gains of trades, professions and vocations are charged under Schedule D, Cases I and II. The charging provision is set out in s. 18, TA. It provides (so far as relevant) as follows:

(1) Tax under this Schedule shall be charged in respect of —
 (a) the annual profits or gains arising or accruing —
  (i) to any person residing in the United Kingdom from any kind of property whatever, whether situated in the United Kingdom or elsewhere, and
  (ii) to any person residing in the United Kingdom from any trade, profession or vocation, whether carried on in the United Kingdom or elsewhere, and
  (iii) to any person, whether a Commonwealth citizen or not, although not resident in the United Kingdom, from any property whatever in the United Kingdom, or from any trade, profession or vocation exercised within the United Kingdom, and
 (b) all interest of money, annuities and other annual profits or gains not charged under Schedule A or E, and not specially exempted from tax.
(2) Tax under Schedule D shall be charged under the Cases set out in subsection (3) below, and subject to and in accordance with the provisions of the Tax Acts applicable to those Cases respectively.

[1.] See generally Whiteman *Income Tax*, 3rd edn, Sweet & Maxwell and *Simon's Taxes*.

(3) The Cases are —
Case I :
   tax in respect of any trade carried on in the UK or elsewhere . . .;
Case II :
   tax in respect of any profession or vocation not contained in any other Schedule . . .

The effect of this is that Case I deals with the profits of a trade and Case II deals with the profits of any profession or vocation. This used to matter more as there were differences in the charge between the Cases. Broadly, the Cases are now taxed on the same basis.[2] The main distinction now is not between Schedule D, Case I and Schedule D, Case II but between a capital gain and a trading etc. profit (see Chapters 19 et seq on capital gains tax).

Notwithstanding the wording of Case I ('tax in respect of any trade carried on in the UK or elsewhere') it does not apply to trades controlled and carried on wholly abroad (see, for example, *Colquhoun* v *Brooks* (1889) 2 TC 490, 14 App Cas 493). Profits from such a trade are normally taxed under Schedule D, Case V (see Chapter 35).

9.2 FOUR MAJOR QUESTIONS

Section 18, TA gives rise to four major questions in relation to Schedule D, Cases I and II. These are:

(a) What is a 'profession'?
(b) What is a 'vocation'?
(c) What is a 'trade'?
(d) How is the profit for the year to be calculated? (see Chapter 10).

(a) to (c) will be considered in turn.

9.2.1 What is a 'profession'?

There is no definition of a 'profession' in the Taxes Acts.[3] Accordingly the case law needs to be considered. This can be problematic as it has been said that it is a question of fact whether or not a profession exists.[4]

The starting point in considering the meaning of profession is usually *IRC* v *Maxse* (1919) 12 TC 41. The question at issue here was whether the editor

---

[2.] Differences still include that an isolated transaction may be an adventure in the nature of a trade. There is no equivalent of an adventure in the nature of a profession. The rule in *Sharkey* v *Wernher* (1955) 36 TC 275 (discussed at para. 10.4) may not apply to professions. There can seemingly be differences as to expenses, see *Norman* v *Golder* (1944) 26 TC 293 at p. 297 that it is '. . . not untrue to say the incidence of the Income Tax Acts on professional men in respect of expenses is not always, perhaps, quite as fair as one would wish it to be, as compared with the incidence on persons carrying on trades or businesses; but unfortunately we all have to live under it'.
[3.] See also in the VAT context, *Committee of Directors of Polytechnics* v *C&E* [1992] STC 873.
[4.] See *Carr* v *IRC* [1944] 2 All ER 163. Sterndale MR said in *Currie* v *IRC* (1944) 12 TC 245, 'there is a very large tract of country in which the matter becomes a question of degree'.

and publisher of the *National Review* was carrying on a profession – if he were he would not be liable to Excess Profits Duty. Scrutton LJ said at p. 61:

> The next question is, what is a 'profession'? I am very reluctant finally to propound a comprehensive definition. . . . But it seems to me, as at present advised, that a 'profession' in the present use of language involves the idea of an occupation requiring either purely intellectual skill, or if any manual skill, as in painting and sculpture or surgery, skill controlled by the intellectual skill of the operator, as distinguished from an occupation which is substantially the production, or sale, or arrangements for the production or sale of commodities. The line of demarcation may vary from time to time. The word 'profession' used to be confined to the three learned professions – the Church, Medicine and Law. It has now, I think, a wider meaning. It appears to me clear that a journalist whose contributions have any literary form, as distinguished from a reporter, exercises a 'profession', and that the editor of a periodical comes in the same category. It seems to me equally clear that the proprietor of a newspaper or periodical, controlling the printing, publishing and advertising, but not responsible for the selection of the literary or artistic contents does not exercise a profession, but a trade or business other than a profession.

The decision in *IRC* v *Maxse* should be compared with *Davies* v *Braithwaite* [1931] 2 KB 628, the film star case, considered in Chapter 6 in connection with Schedule E. It will be recalled that Lillian Braithwaite was treated as carrying on a profession.

Du Parcq LJ set out the approach to take as to the existence of a profession in *Carr* v *IRC* [1944] 2 All ER 163. He said (at p. 166):

> Ultimately one has to answer this question: Would the ordinary man, the ordinary reasonable man – the man, if you like to refer to an old friend, on the Clapham omnibus – say now, in the time in which we live, of any particular occupation, that it is properly described as a profession? I do not believe one can escape from that very practical way of putting the question; in other words, I think it would be in a proper case a question for a jury . . . Times have changed. There are professions today which nobody would have considered to be professions in times past. Our forefathers restricted the professions to a very small number, the work of the surgeon used to be carried on by the barber, whom nobody would have considered to be a professional man. The profession of the chartered accountant has grown up in comparatively recent times, and other trades, or vocations, I care not what word you use in relation to them, may in future years acquire the status of professions. It must be the intention of the legislature, when it refers to a profession, to indicate what the ordinary intelligent subject, taking down the volume of the statutes and reading the section, will think that 'profession' means. I do not think that the lawyer as such can help him very much.

However, this 'Clapham omnibus' approach can sometimes be misleading. For example, a solicitor *prima facie* is a professional assessable under Schedule D, Case II but may be employed, in which case the income would be assessable under Schedule E (see Chapter 6). A taxpayer who carries on a profession (such as a doctor) may also have some income from employment (for example, from part-time employment in hospital, *Bhadra* v *Ellam* [1988] STC 239). It is thought that the commercial background of the occupation is much more important than Scrutton LJ's words in *IRC* v *Maxse* would suggest. Du Parcq LJ's comments in *Carr* v *IRC* would seem to support this.

The following have been accepted as professionals by the courts:

(a) actor (*Davies* v *Braithwaite* [1931] 2 KB 628);
(b) optician (*Carr* v *IRC* [1944] 2 All ER 163; see also *Neild* v *IRC* (1948) 26 ATC 33 and compare *Webster* v *IRC* [1942] 2 All ER 517, a case concerning an ophthalmic optician);
(c) Journalist (*IRC* v *Maxse* above).

The following have not been considered professionals in the cases:

(a) photographer (*Cecil* v *IRC* (1919) 36 TLR 164);
(b) stockbroker (*Christopher Barker & Sons* v *IRC* [1919] 2 KB 222);
(c) insurance broker (*Durant* v *IRC* (1921) 12 TC 245);
(d) dance band leader (*Loss* v *IRC* [1945] 2 All ER 683);
(e) film producer (*Asher* v *London Film Productions* [1944] 1 All ER 77).

A difficult question to consider these days is whether a management consultant or an estate agent (cf. *Escritt & Barrell* v *IRC* (1947) 26 ATC 33) is a professional for these purposes (the authors have experience of them being accepted as such by the Revenue).

9.2.2 What is a 'vocation'?

As ever there is no definition of a 'vocation' in the TA. The *Shorter Oxford Dictionary* defines 'vocation' inter alia as 'one's ordinary occupation, business or profession'. In normal usage it often has a religious or idealistic quality to it. This is not so in tax law where the leading cases concern bookmaking.

The case of *Partridge* v *Mallandine* (1886) 2 TC 179 concerned Partridge and Hancox who attended race courses as bookmakers or betters on races (on jockeys, see the Irish case of *Wing* v *O'Connell* [1927] IR 84). They had no other profession or employment. They were assessed on their profits. The Commissioners upheld the assessments as did the High Court and so they were treated as having a vocation. Denman J said in this case:

> ... A man may employ himself in order to earn money in such a way as to come within that definition, but I think the word 'vocation' is a still stronger word. It is admitted to be analogous to the word 'calling', which is a very large word; it means the way in which a person passes his life, and

it is a very large word indeed. These persons go to races and they systematically bet, and for this reason, it must be assumed, make profits. Does it lie in their mouths to say that they are not to be assessed to income tax because they cannot bring an action in respect of the bets which they make? Every year they have so many of their bets paid as puts, say, £1,000 a year in their pockets; and to say that because they cannot bring an action to recover the bets they make, betting being made illegal by Act of Parliament, therefore they do not carry on a vocation, it seems to me is putting a construction upon the Act which would be giving a very undue favour to persons with whom the Legislature is by no means supposed to deal with favour, inasmuch as the thing they do is a thing which is hampered by the Legislature because it is supposed to be mischievous, . . . But I go the whole length of saying that, in my opinion, if a man were to make a systematic business of receiving stolen goods, and to do nothing else, and he thereby systematically carried on a business and made a profit of £2,000 a year, the Income Tax Commissioners would be quite right in assessing him if it were in fact his vocation. There is no limit as to its being a lawful vocation, nor do I think that the fact that it is unlawful can be set up in favour of these persons as against the rights of the Revenue to have payment in respect of the profits that are made. I think this does come within the definition of the word 'vocation' according to common sense and according to the ordinary use of language, and therefore I think the Income Tax Commissioners were right.

The *Partridge* case should be contrasted with *Graham v Green* (1925) 9 TC 309 (distinguished in *Graham v Arnott* (1941) 24 TC 157) where the contributor of a betting system to a newspaper was held properly assessed. This concerned 'Punters'. Graham bet on horses from home. He was successful at it and made a profit. For many years it was his sole means of livelihood apart from some bank interest. He was assessed on the profit. The General Commissioners upheld the assessment but were reversed on appeal. Rowlatt J said:

'. . . It has been settled that a bookmaker carries on a taxable vocation. . . . Now we come to the other side, the man who bets with the bookmaker, and that is this case. These are mere bets. Each time he puts on his money, at whatever may be the starting price. I do not think he could be said to organise his effort in the same way as a bookmaker organises his. . . . I think all you can say of that man, in the fair use of the English language, is that he is addicted to betting. It is extremely difficult to express, but it seems to me that people would say he is addicted to betting, and could not say that his vocation is betting. The subject is involved in great difficulty of language, which I think represents great difficulty of thought. There is no tax on a habit . . .

The real explanation of these cases may be that since the bookie sets the odds and usually wins and the punter usually loses, tax is maximised by taxing the bookie and not allowing a deduction for betting losses.

9.2.3 What is a 'trade'?

As has been seen in para. 9.1, Schedule D, Case I, charges the profits or gains from a trade. Accordingly, one needs to know what a 'trade' is for these purposes. As ever there is no general helpful definition of trade for these purposes (notwithstanding s. 832, TA considered below). Like a monkey or an elephant, one is supposed to recognise a trade when one sees it (cf. Lord Denning in *J. P. Harrison (Watford) Ltd* v *Griffiths* (1963) TC 281 at p. 299). However, certain specific matters are dealt with by the statute. These are considered at para. 9.3 below. The most important is the extension to an 'adventure in the nature of trade'.

Whether a trade exists is usually said to be a question of fact (*Edwards* v *Bairstow* [1956] AC 14; 36 TC 207). However, the meaning of the word 'trade' in the statute is a matter of law. There is an added difficulty in that in most of the cases the question is not whether the Commissioners were wrong but whether their decision was unreasonable (cf. Lord Reid in *Griffiths* v *Harrison* [1963] AC 1 at p. 6). The primary facts are for Commissioners alone to decide. However, there is an open texture to what constitutes primary facts. Matters can, if the court so wishes, be characterised as law and so appealable. All of this can make it difficult to decide the precise authority of a decision.

Lord Denning has said (in *J. P. Harrison (Watford) Ltd* v *Griffiths* (1963) TC 281 at p. 299):

> Try as you will, the word 'trade' is one of those common English words which do not lend themselves readily to a definition but which all of us think we understand well enough. We can recognise a trade when we see it, and also an 'adventure in the nature of trade'. But we are hard pressed to define it . . . Short of a definition, the only thing to do is to look at the usual characteristics of a 'trade' and see how this transaction measures up to them.

It is hard to disagree with this. In reality the position is that trade is not susceptible of one definition to cover all circumstances. There is no single definition or rule as to trade. Trade is a complex phenomenon with no single characteristic which is essential for its existence. As Jessel MR said in *Erichsen* v *Last* (1881) 8 QBD 414 at p. 416, 'There are a multitude of things which together make up the carrying on of a trade . . . it is a compound fact made up of a variety of incidents'. In other words all the circumstances need to be considered.

A particular problem can arise with 'one-off transactions'. Should, for example, the profit from the sale of one item for several million pounds be taxable as a trading transaction? Most people would be likely to say that it all depended on the circumstances. The Act takes this approach in s. 832, TA.

Section 832 provides that 'trade' includes every trade, manufacture, adventure or concern in the nature of a trade (see para. 9.3 below and note 'in the nature of a trade' governs both a concern and adventure; see Goff J in *Johnston v Heath* [1970] 3 All ER 915 at p. 922). An adventure in the nature of a trade can thus amount to a trading transaction for these purposes. So an isolated, one-off transaction can be a trading transaction. In *Leeming v Jones* (1929) 15 TC 333 Lawrence J said (at p. 354) '. . . it seems to me that in the case of an isolated transaction of purchase and resale of property there is really no middle course open. It is either an adventure in the nature of a trade, or else it is simply a case of sale and resale of property.' (cf. *Marson v Morton* [1986] STC 463). It seems that 'adventure' in this context does not necessarily connote that there must be risk (*Johnston v Heath* [1970] 3 All ER 915 at p. 922). But it also includes 'a pecuniary risk', a venture, a speculation, a commercial adventure (see Scott LJ in *Barry v Cordy* (1946) 28 TC 250 at p. 258 relying on the *Oxford Dictionary*).

9.3 STATUTE

Some guidance as to the meaning of 'trade' is given in the Taxes Act. It has already been seen that s. 832(1) provides that 'trade' includes every trade, manufacture, adventure or concern in the nature of a trade. However, this is not particularly helpful. Certain specific matters are dealt with by ss. 53–55.

Section 53(1) provides (inter alia) that all farming and market gardening is to be treated as trading and taxed accordingly. This is to prevent an argument that farming profits are only taxable under Schedule A (before 1963 this was an occupational charge). 'Farm land' is defined in s. 832(1) to mean 'land in the United Kingdom wholly or mainly occupied for the purposes of husbandry, but excluding any dwelling or domestic offices, and excluding market garden land, and "farming" shall be construed accordingly.'

Husbandry is defined in some dictionaries inter alia as farming! All farming carried on by any particular person or body of persons is to be treated as one trade (s. 53(2)). This can be important, for example, for loss relief (see *Bispham v Eardiston Farming Co.* (1919) Ltd (1962) 40 TC 322).

'Market garden land' is defined in s. 832(1) to mean 'land in the United Kingdom occupied as a nursery or garden for the sale of the produce (other than land used for the growing of hops) and "market gardening" shall be construed accordingly.'

By s. 53(3) the occupation of land (other than farm land and woodlands – see s. 53(3) and (4)) managed on a commercial basis and with a view to the realisation of profits is to be treated as trading and taxed accordingly. The scope of the type of situation this section is concerned with was considered in *Croft v Sywell Aerodrome Ltd* (1941) 24 TC 126. This case concerned a company which owned an aerodrome which it let to an aviation company. The owning company was assessed under Schedule D, Case I. It appealed successfully against the assessment. Its liability to tax was exhausted in the circumstances by Schedule A (and Schedule B as then in force).

Lord Greene MR (at p. 139 quoted with approval by Warner J in *Webb v Conelee Properties Ltd* [1982] STC 913) said:

When the owner of land grants a licence to another to come upon his land he is exercising his rights of property just as much as when he is granting a lease. It is by virtue of his proprietary rights that he has power to grant the licence and this is equally true of the freeholder or leaseholder. The fact that a licensee carries on a trade on the strength of his licence has nothing in the world to do with the owner who grants the licence. It does not convert him for tax purposes into a person carrying on a trade any more than in the case where a lessee carries on a trade. . . . If the grant of one licence is merely an exercise of such rights I cannot see that the grant of half-a-dozen licences bears a different character.

Thus some exploitation other than leasing the land is needed for s. 53(3) to apply. Using land for a car park might be sufficient though. Some help on the distinction can be gained from Warner J in *Webb* v *Conelee Properties Ltd* [1982] STC 913. He said (at p. 910):

It was I think common ground between counsel that [the] authorities establish that the owner of land may carry on activities on the land that go beyond the mere exploitation of his proprietary rights in the land and which constitute a trade. Where it is shown that there have been such activities, it is a matter of fact and degree whether they are sufficient to amount to the carrying on of a trade.

The letting or subletting of property, whether furnished or not, is not therefore a trade even if certain ancillary services are provided (though the profits of those ancillary services might be separately charged under Case I). Vinelott J in *Griffiths* v *Jackson* [1983] STC 184 (at p. 191) considered that the *Sywell Aerodrome* case graphically illustrated the distinction between 'income derived from the exploitation of the owner's rights of property and his rights of occupation on the one hand, and income derived from carrying on a trade . . .' He also considered it '. . . a cardinal principle of United Kingdom tax law that "income derived from the exercise of property rights properly so called" by the owner of land (freehold or leasehold) is not income derived from the carrying on of a trade . . .'

By s. 55 the profits arising out of land in the case of mines, quarries etc. are to be taxed under Schedule D, Case I. Again this is to stop a claim that tax should only arise under Schedule A. (Section 54 dealing with woodlands managed on a commercial basis has been repealed.)

Statute gives no further real help in identifying the meaning of trade. Accordingly one is driven back to the case law. There is an enormous amount of this. Some of it will be considered below.

9.4 'BADGES OF TRADE'

There have been many cases on whether a trade was carried on or not. Before the introduction of capital gains tax, if a profit was not taxable as a trading profit it was often not taxable at all. Whether or not there should be a fixed rule or a number of criteria varying in importance with the context has been considered as a matter of policy and the latter has been favoured. The Royal Commission in considering this set out in its Final Report (Cmd 9479 para. 116) six 'badges of trade' which have often been referred to in deciding whether or not there is a trade.

The Report reads as follows.

116. We concluded that, it was better that there should be no single fixed rule. This means that each case must be decided according to its own circumstances. The general line of enquiry that has been favoured by appeal Commissioners and encouraged by the Courts is to see whether a transaction that is said to have given rise to a taxable profit bears any of the 'badges of trade'. This seems to us the right line, and it has the advantage that it bases itself on objective tests of what is a trading adventure instead of concerning itself directly with the unravelling of motive. At the same time we have noticed that there has been some lack of uniformity in the treatment of different cases according to the tribunals before which they have been brought. This seems to us unfortunate and, for the sake of clarity, we have drawn up and set out below a summary of what we regard as the major relevant considerations that bear upon the identification of these 'badges of trade'.

(1) The subject matter of the realisation. While almost any form of property can be acquired to be dealt in, those forms of property, such as commodities or manufactured articles, which are normally the subject of trading are only very exceptionally the subject of investment. Again property which does not yield to its owner an income or personal enjoyment merely by virtue of its ownership is more likely to have been acquired with the object of a deal than property that does.

(2) The length of the period of ownership. Generally speaking, property meant to be dealt in is realised within a short time after acquisition. But there are many exceptions from this as a universal rule.

(3) The frequency or number of similar transactions by the same person. If realisations of the same sort of property occur in succession over a period of years or there are several such realisations at about the same date a presumption arises that there has been dealing in respect of each.

(4) Supplementary work on or in connection with the property realised. If the property is worked up in any way during the ownership so as to bring it into a more marketable condition; or if any special exertions are made to find or attract purchasers, such as the opening of an office or large-scale advertising, there is some evidence of dealing. For when there is an organised effort to obtain profit there is a source of taxable income. But if nothing at all is done, the suggestion tends the other way.

(5) The circumstances that were responsible for the realisation. There may be some explanation, such as a sudden emergency or opportunity calling for ready money, that negatives the idea that any plan of dealing prompted the original purchase.

(6) Motive. There are cases in which the purpose of the transaction of purchase and sale is clearly discernible. Motive is never irrelevant in any of these cases. What is desirable is that it should be realised clearly that it can be inferred from surrounding circumstances in the absence of direct evidence of the seller's intentions and even, if necessary, in the face of his own evidence.

9.4.1 General comments

The problem of the fact/law distinction (see Chapter 1) must be borne in mind in considering the case law more than ever in the context of trading. The cases often seem conflicting and confusing. However, it should be remembered that strictly the ratio decidendi is often that there was evidence on which a reasonable body of Commissioners could have reached the conclusion they did. This makes it hard to construct rules or principles determinative of the result.[5] This is further compounded, since as was seen in para. 9.2.3, whether a trade exists is usually said to be a question of fact (cf. *Edwards* v *Bairstow* [1956] AC 14, 36 TC 207 and para. 9.2.3). However, the meaning of the word 'trade' in the statute is a matter of law although no conclusive definition can be given. As Jessel MR said in *Erichsen* v *Last* (1881) 8 QBD 414 'trade is a compound fact made up of a variety of incidents', so each case depends on its peculiar facts. This can allow cases such as *IRC* v *Reinhold* and *Wisdom* v *Chamberlain* (see para. 9.4.2) to be reconciled.

It is also important to remember the extension of the meaning of trade to include 'adventure in the nature of trade' here (s. 832, TA). 'In the nature of trade' governs both a concern and an adventure (see Goff J in *Johnston* v *Heath* [1970] 3 All ER 915 at p. 922 (para. 9.2.3)). Thus an isolated, one-off transaction can be a trading transaction.

It is important to identify *who* is the trader in the circumstances. Each person involved in the transaction is to be considered separately. This is true even in the case of a partnership in deciding who is a member of the partnership. This was crucial in *Ransom* v *Higgs* [1974] 3 All ER 949 where a complicated scheme organised by Higgs was intended to shelter development profit. Higgs was not an actor in relation to the scheme but procured others to do things. He was assessed on the basis that he was a trader. The House of Lords upheld his appeal. Lord Reid said (at pp. 954–957) that the Crown argued:

> that in procuring the steps taken by the companies and individuals, Mr Higgs was carrying on a trade within the meaning of the Income Tax Acts

---

[5.] Cf. Dworkin, 'Is law a system of rules?' in *Essays in Legal Philosophy* (ed. Summers), Blackwell. 1968, p. 25 and Dworkin, *Taking Rights Seriously*, Duckworth, 1977.

... As an ordinary word in the English language 'trade' has or has had a variety of meanings or shades of meaning. Leaving aside obsolete or rare usage it is sometimes used to denote any mercantile operation but it is commonly used to denote operations of a commercial character by which the trader provides to customers for reward some kind of goods or services.

The contexts in which the word 'trade' has been used in the Income Tax Acts appear to me to indicate that operations of that kind are what the legislature had primarily in mind.

... I have come to the conclusion that it would be unreasonable to hold that Mr Higgs was trading. Mr Higgs did not deal with any person. He did not buy or sell anything. He did not provide anyone with goods or services for reward. He had no profits or gains. Under this scheme he never could have had any, and it was I think for that reason that it was admitted in this House that he could not be assessed personally. I can find no characteristic of trading in anything which Mr Higgs did ... No doubt Mr Higgs engaged in an adventure but for the reasons which I have given I cannot agree that it was an adventure in the nature of trade. I am therefore of opinion that the appeal ... must be allowed.

Since trade is infinitely varied its categories are not closed. Case law gives some help as to the elements that may be involved in a trade. In *Ransom* v *Higgs* Lord Wilberforce said (at p. 357):

Trade involves, normally, the exchange of goods, or services, for reward, [although] not all services, since some qualify as a profession, or employment, or vocation, but there must be something which the trade offers to provide by way of business. Trade, moreover, presupposes a customer (to this too there may be exceptions, but such is the norm), or, as it may be expressed, trade must be bilateral – you must trade with someone.

In *Simmons* v *IRC* [1980] STC 350 Lord Wilberforce emphasised the need for an intention to trade. He said (at p. 352):

Trading requires an intention to trade: normally the question to be asked is whether this intention existed at the time of the acquisition of the asset. Was [the asset] acquired with the intention of disposing of it at a profit, or was it acquired as a permanent investment? Often it is necessary to ask further questions ...

This raises the question whether there are circumstances when a profit is made but there is no intention to trade and no investment? Lord Wilberforce seemed to think not (see para. 9.4.7 below). It is hard to conceive of many examples. Perhaps *Grove* v *YMCA* (1903) 4 TC 613 would be one where a profit was made by accident.

9.4.2 Subject matter dealt in

(1) The subject matter of the realisation. While almost any form of property can be acquired to be dealt in, those forms of property, such as commodities or manufactured articles, which are normally the subject of trading are only very exceptionally the subject of investment. Again property which does not yield to its owner an income or personal enjoyment merely by virtue of its ownership is more likely to have been acquired with the object of a deal than property that does.

This badge, when found, can often be conclusive of the question whether a trade is being carried on. If the taxpayer buys certain property which is obviously intended neither for personal enjoyment nor as a long term investment, then the taxpayer stands an extremely high chance of being found to be trading.

In *Martin* v *Lowry* (1926) 11 TC 297 the taxpayer was an agricultural machinery merchant. He bought almost 45 million yards of parachute linen from the government as surplus. Before this he had no connection with the linen trade. He tried to sell it to manufacturers and failed. Accordingly he set up an organisation so he could sell it to the public. The disposal took place by a number of sales over several months to the public of an item which was a *one-off* purchase. He made a profit of almost £2 million and was assessed under Schedule D, Case I. The House of Lords held he was trading even though the taxpayer had indulged in one 'single gigantic speculation'.

In *Martin* v *Lowry* there had been work on the single purchase. However, even if the single purchase is followed by a single sale, there still can be trading. Timing may be important here. The best known example is *Rutledge* v *IRC* (1929) 14 TC 490. Rutledge was a moneylender and company director who, whilst on business in Berlin in 1920, bought one million toilet rolls for £1,000. He was offered threepence a roll delivered at London Dock by 'an East-End Jew' [sic at p. 491] which he accepted. Rutledge made a profit of approximately £10,895. The Commissioners found the profits liable to income tax as profits of a concern in the nature of a trade. The Court of Session unanimously found in favour of the Crown, holding that a trade was carried on here on the facts. This was a speculation, an adventure in the nature of a trade. The toilet rolls were bought with a view to resale at a profit. Lord Sands considered that (at p. 497):

> The nature and quantity of the subject matter dealt with exclude the suggestion that it could have been disposed of otherwise than as a trade transaction. Neither the purchaser nor any purchaser from him was likely to require such a quantity for his private use.[6]

Although there might not have been a trade *simpliciter* the question was whether there was an adventure in the nature of trade. Lord President Clyde said (at pp. 496 and 497):

[6.] There is an apocryphal story that the subject matter was condoms rather than toilet paper. This may have influenced his Lordship's comments.

An adventure it certainly was; for the Appellant made himself liable for the purchase of this vast quantity of toilet paper obviously for no other conceivable purpose than that of re-selling it at a profit and that is just what he did. . . . it seems to me to be quite plain:

(1) that the Appellant, in buying the large stock of toilet paper entered upon a commercial adventure or speculation;

(2) that this adventure or speculation was carried through in exactly the same way as any regular trader or dealer would carry through any of the adventures or speculations in which it is his regular business to engage; and therefore

(3) that the purchase and re-sale of the toilet paper was an 'adventure . . . in the nature of trade' within the meaning of the Income Tax Act, 1918. If that is right the appeal cannot succeed.

The transactions in *Martin* v *Lowry* and in *Rutledge* v *IRC* were found to be trading transactions because the trader was buying large quantities of a tradeable commodity with a view to a commercial success in the way of profit.

The profit making objective was in issue in *Wisdom* v *Chamberlain* (1969) 45 TC 92. Here Norman Wisdom, the comedian, bought £200,000 of silver as a hedge against inflation and the loss of value in the currency which resulted from it. Later in the same year Wisdom sold the silver at a profit. He was assessed on this as the profits of a trade. He was held correctly assessed on the basis that this was 'an adventure in the nature of trade'. The purchase was not for his personal use but as a hedge against inflation and was not an income-producing, long-term investment. As Harman LJ said:

The whole object of the transaction was to make a profit. It was expected that there would be devaluation, and the reason for wanting to make a profit was that there would be a loss on devaluation; but that does not make any difference, it seems to me, to the fact that the motive and object of the whole transaction was to buy on a short-term basis a commodity with a view to its resale at a profit. That, as it seems to me, is an adventure in the nature of trade . . .

This should be contrasted with *IRC* v *Reinhold* (1953) 34 TC 389. Reinhold bought four houses near Watford in January 1945 and sold them at a profit in December 1949. It was admitted they were bought to make a profit. He had bought and sold a hotel some ten years earlier at a profit. The General Commissioners were equally divided and so discharged the assessment. The Court of Session held that the profits were not assessable.

Lord Carmont said (at p. 392):

The Lord Advocate accepted that all was well with an investment which the purchaser bought in the hope and expectation of a rise that would subsequently justify the sale: that would leave the profit as an accretion of capital. He argued, however, that if at the time of purchase the purchaser had resolved to sell on the happening of certain conditions, and *multo magis* if he at the time of purchase instructed his agent to sell on the happening of that selected event, the transaction could never be treated as an investment; it must be viewed as an adventure in the nature of trade and the profit or accretion treated as income. I cannot accept this argument as valid. . . . we find that the Respondent is a warehouse company director and not a property agent or speculator, and that the only purchases of property of which we are made aware are two separated by ten years, and that the first heritage was acquired without intention to sell, which only arose fortuitously. I would therefore say that the Commissioners of Inland Revenue have failed to prove – and the onus is on them – the case they sought to make out.

His Lordship distinguished *Fraser* (see below) and *Rutledge* and continued:

. . . although in certain cases it is important to know whether a venture is isolated or not, that information is really superfluous in many cases where the commodity itself stamps the transaction as a trading venture, and the profits and gains are plainly income liable to tax.

Here it was not.

There can, however, be an isolated transaction involving land which is a trading transaction particularly if entered into in the line of the taxpayer's own trade. *Johnston v Heath* [1970] 3 All ER 915 concerned a taxpayer who was employed by a building company. Informally he agreed to buy some land from the company for £15,000. He contacted three possible purchasers and sold to one of them at £25,000. He was held to be trading (reversing the General Commissioners) as, on a true construction of what is now s. 832(1) TA, the isolated purchase and single transaction constituted an adventure in the nature of trade because:

(a) 'in nature of trade' governs not only a 'concern' but an 'adventure' as well (at p. 922);

(b) land is no different from any other commodity *per se*, rather one should have regard to the nature and quantity of land and surrounding circumstances – in other words the subject matter, placing reliance on *Rutledge* (at p. 920), and

(c) it was easier to conclude that the taxpayer was 'trading' here because:
   (i) the taxpayer contracted to sell before buying;
   (ii) the transaction bore a clear relation to the taxpayer's usual line of business (at p. 921);
   (iii) the taxpayer offered land to several prospective buyers (see p. 921).

Goff J in *Johnston v Heath* also relied on *IRC v Fraser* (1942) 24 TC 498. Here a woodcutter with no special knowledge of the whisky trade bought a large quantity of whisky. It was too large a quantity for him alone to drink. He did not take personal delivery of the whisky but acted through an agent. The whisky was resold at a profit. The question at issue was, was this an adventure in the nature of a trade, as the reason for buying the whisky was *speculation* about profit? The Court of Session held that it was an adventure in the nature of trade.

Lord President Normand said (at p. 502):

> It is in general more easy to hold that a single 'transaction' entered into by an individual in the line of his own trade (although not part and parcel of his ordinary business) is an adventure in the nature of trade, than to hold that a transaction entered into by an individual outside the line of his own trade or occupation is an adventure in the nature of trade. But what is a good deal more important is the nature of the transaction with reference to the commodity dealt in. . . . the purchaser of a large quantity of a commodity like whisky, greatly in excess of what could be used by himself, his family and friends, a commodity which yields no pride of possession, which cannot be turned to account except by a process of realisation, I can scarcely consider to be other than an adventure in the nature of a trade . . .

The Lord President considered that *Rutledge* was the closest case and treated it as an authority binding on him.

As a result of these cases it seems possible to say that the subject matter is relevant particularly where taxpayers speculate or buy large quantities of goods of a commercial nature with an eye on the profit or resale. These are caught as a trade because it includes 'every . . . adventure in the nature of trade'. This is to be contrasted with the owner of an ordinary investment who merely chooses to realise it. The increase in the value of the investment (if say the taxpayer buys at £1,000 and sells at £1,500) will be a capital gain and not income of a trade. It seems it is the aim to resell at a profit which is the crux of this badge. The type and quantity of the subject matter can indicate this.

9.4.3 Length of the period of ownership

> *(2) The length of the period of ownership. Generally speaking, property meant to be dealt in is realised within a short time after acquisition. But there are many exceptions from this as a universal rule.*

Length of ownership *per se* as a matter of theory is really neither here nor there in the characterisation of a transaction. However, if the taxpayer is keeping property for a short period of time so that he has a rapid turn over, it might lead to the conclusion that there is a trade. A trader will often want to buy cheaply and sell quickly at a high price so as to maximise the profit although this will not always be the case.

In *Turner* v *Last* (1965) 42 TC 517 the appellant was a farmer who had been assessed to tax in respect of the profit on the sale of some fields. He bought a total of 13 or so acres in one transaction but sold them off (with planning permission) at a considerable profit in two transactions, soon after purchase. The taxpayer said that he never intended to sell the fields, that he did not purchase them with a view to resale but with a view to farming and that therefore he was *not* a property trader. It was held by Cross J that the taxpayer *was* trading. He commented (at p. 523):

> Of course, the mere fact that when you buy property, as well as intending to use and enjoy it, you have also in your mind the possibility that it will appreciate in value, and that a time may come when you will want to sell it and make a profit on it, does not of itself make you a trader; but if the position is that you intend to sell it as soon as you can to recover the cost of the purchase, the position is obviously very different . . .

In *Marson* v *Morton* [1986] STC 463 the piece of land was only owned by the potential taxpayers for about three months, but it was held they were not trading largely because the land was bought as a long term investment by people who did not regularly invest, and was sold as a whole. The fact of rapid resale was not conclusive of the trading question. But, it was said that where someone does resell rapidly after purchase it 'leads one to scrutinise the evidence very carefully'.

It should be noted that in *Rutledge* v *IRC* and *Johnston* v *Heath*, the subject-matter acquired was disposed of within a short time of acquisition.

9.4.4 Frequency or number of transactions

(3) The frequency or number of similar transactions by the same person. If realisations of the same sort of property occur in succession over a period of years or there are several such realisations at about the same date a presumption arises that there has been dealing in respect of each.

Once a taxpayer has been involved in a number of similar or identical transactions the fact that he repeatedly engages in such transactions may bring him within Schedule D and prevent him claiming that he is merely making a capital gain. A number of cases illustrate this.

In *Pickford* v *Quirke* (1927) 13 TC 251 a director formed a company for buying up the shares in a mill. He duly bought the shares and sold the mill's assets to another company at a profit. This is known as asset stripping. He did this four times in all. The question at issue was, was he trading? At first instance and in the Court of Appeal the taxpayer was held to be trading. Rowlatt J said (at p. 263):

> . . . one transaction of buying and selling does not usually make a man a trader, but if it is repeated and becomes systematic, then he becomes a trader and the profit of the transactions, not taxable so long as they remain isolated, become taxable as items in a trade as a whole.

This view was endorsed by the Court of Appeal. This should not be taken to mean, however, that an isolated transaction cannot be a trading transaction within Schedule D, Case I. Again, both *Rutledge* v *IRC* and *Johnston* v *Heath* were cases of isolated transactions held to be adventures in the nature of trade.

A similar question was at issue in *Leach* v *Pogson* (1962) 40 TC 585. Here the taxpayer formed driving schools. They were successful. He sold each one to newly formed companies in return for shares and money. There were some 30 transactions in all. By 1959 he had received £65,000. Were these capital gains or trading receipts? The taxpayer argued that the sales were on capital account and that he was not in the business of selling goodwill. The Special Commissioners did not accept this and upheld the assessment. They were upheld by Ungoed-Thomas J who considered that the frequency of the transactions and the repetition of the transactions led to the conclusion that there was a trade and the receipts were trading receipts. The Commissioners were entitled to take subsequent events into account in determining the nature of the original transaction.

In *Martin* v *Lowry* (discussed in para. 9.4.2) it will be recalled that the taxpayer could not sell the entire stock in one transaction, so he set up a selling organisation to dispose of it. It then took him about a year to sell off the linen, and he made a profit of almost £2 million. The House of Lords held that he was trading.

It should be remembered that the subject matter dealt in may offset the conclusion which one would normally draw from frequently repeated transactions. Thus where an investor owns investments he may well frequently change those investments. The fact that he buys and sells a lot of (say) shares during the year will not necessarily make him a trader in respect of his investments. A different conclusion may well follow if what is dealt in is silver or antiques however (see subject matter dealt in para. 9.4.2 above).

9.4.5 Work done on subject matter dealt in

(4) Supplementary work on or in connection with the property realised. If the property is worked up in any way during the ownership so as to bring it into a more marketable condition; or if any special exertions are made to find or attract purchasers, such as the opening of an office or large-scale advertising, there is some evidence of dealing. For when there is an organised effort to obtain profit there is a source of taxable income. But if nothing at all is done, the suggestion tends the other way.

The court will more readily infer that the taxpayer was trading where work is done by the taxpayer or at the taxpayer's request to make the property concerned more readily marketable. Equally, where the taxpayer takes steps to find purchasers, that will help the court to draw the inference of 'trade' (see, e.g., *Martin* v *Lowry* in para. 9.4.2).

In *IRC* v *Livingston* (1926) 11 TC 538 three taxpayers bought a cargo ship. They converted it into a steam drifter and sold it. This was held to be a trade and seems to be archetypally 'an adventure in the nature of trade'.

This badge, it seems, is not of itself determinative. It is often true of anyone selling property of his own that he will put it into better condition: it does not *automatically* follow from that that he is engaged in a trade.

The test is more useful if the work done on the property changes its character. For example, if pig iron is turned into steel it is more likely that its sale will be a trading transaction. Thus in *Cape Brandy Syndicate v IRC* (1927) 12 TC 358 three taxpayers joined together to buy a large quantity of brandy. This was shipped to the UK and duly blended with other brandy bottled and sold over an 18-month period. It was held that this constituted 'trading'. Rowlatt J said that the taxpayers did far more than buy the brandy cheaply and resell it dearly:

> They bought it with a view to transport it, with a view to modify its character by skilful manipulation, by blending, with a view to alter not only the amounts by which it could be sold . . . but by altering the character . . . so that it could be sold in smaller quantities. They employed experts – to dispose of it over a long time . . . They bought it to turn over at once obviously and to turn over advantageously . . . In other words, look to what they did to the goods and ask yourself – is that the sort of thing traders do?

The test according to Lord Clyde in *Livingston* is 'whether the operations involved in it are of the same kind, and carried on in the same way, as those which are characteristic of ordinary trading in the line of business in which the venture was made' (11 TC at p. 542 and see also *Taylor v Good* [1974] STC 148).

9.4.6 Circumstances surrounding realisation

> *(5) The circumstances that were responsible for the realisation. There may be some explanation, such as a sudden emergency or opportunity calling for ready money, that negatives the idea that any plan of dealing prompted the original purchase.*

This is linked to the question of motive. It requires one to ask, why did the vendor sell? If it was to pay off an overdraft or to buy something else then it is likely that it is not without more (such as acquisition as trading stock) in the course of a trade.

In *Hudson's Bay Company v Stevens* (1909) 5 TC 424 a company acquired large amounts of land in exchange for surrendering their Charter. They sold off property from time to time *as offers were made*. It was held, by the Court of Appeal, that this was not assessable to income tax because the company was only acting like a normal landowner in selling at a judicious time. They did not buy and sell land, they merely sold the land they had every now and again as fast as they could get rid of it. They were merely realising a capital asset. It seems that the fact that the land had not been acquired with a view to resale was an important factor here.

Another example of the sort of case where this badge can be of some relevance is *West v Phillips* (1958) 38 TC 203. The taxpayer was a builder. He built some houses for investment and others for sale at a profit. Later on he decided to sell the houses he had built for investment purposes as well.

The reason he sold these was that rent control made the properties a less sound investment, his taxes were getting to be too much for him and the increases in the cost of repairs were making renting out his investment houses less profitable than he had hoped.

The Court of Appeal reversed the Commissioners and held that, because the builder had decided to sell the houses for reasons unconnected with his trade, the sale did not give rise to a trading profit.

9.4.7 Motive and intention

(6) Motive. There are cases in which the purpose of the transaction of purchase and sale is clearly discernible. Motive is never irrelevant in any of these cases. What is desirable is that it should be realised clearly that it can be inferred from surrounding circumstances in the absence of direct evidence of the seller's intentions and even, if necessary, in the face of his own evidence.

This should be contrasted with what was said earlier in the Royal Commisson's Report:

The [badges of trade approach] seems to us the right line, and it has the advantage that it bases itself on objective tests of what is a trading adventure instead of concerning itself directly with the unravelling of motive.

The Commission was concerned that all the circumstances should be taken into account not just some guess made as to motive.

Nevertheless motive is bound to be an important factor in determining what is going on. Thus in *Kirkham* v *Williams* [1989] STC 333 Vinelott J relied on Lord Wilberforce in *Simmons* v *IRC* [1980] STC 350 who as quoted in para. 9.4.1 said:

Trading requires an intention to trade: normally the question to be asked is whether this intention existed at the time of acquisition of the asset. Was it acquired with the intention of disposing of it at a profit, or was it acquired as a permanent investment? Often it is necessary to ask further questions: a permanent asset may be sold in order to acquire another investment thought to be more satisfactory; that does not involve an operation of trade, whether the first investment is sold at a profit or loss. Intentions may be changed. What was first an investment may be put into trading stock, and, I suppose vice versa. If findings of this kind are to be made precision is required since to shift an asset from one category to another will involve changes in the company's accounts, and, possibly a charge to tax [cf. *Sharkey* v *Wernher* para. 10.4 below]. What I think is not possible is for an asset to be both trading stock and permanent investment at the same time, nor to possess an indeterminate status, neither trading stock nor permanent investment. It must be one or the other, even though, and this seems to me legitimate and intelligible, the company in whatever character it acquires the asset, may reserve an intention to change its character.

The taxpayer's intention at the time of purchase was also important in *Taylor* v *Good* [1974] STC 148 (and cf. *Cooksey and Bibbey* v *Rednall* (1949) 30 TC 514 and Lord Templeman in *Reed* v *Nova* [1985] STC 124 at p. 130). Difficult questions arise as to whether this is the same as motive. In *Taylor* v *Good* Mr Taylor bought Marle Hill Court at a public auction. His parents had worked there in service. The Commissioners found that he had not decided what to do with the property if he bought it, but he had in mind going to live in it with his wife. His wife and daughter vetoed the idea of living there and he abandoned it. He applied and eventually obtained planning permission to demolish Marle Hill Court and to erect 90 houses on about nine acres. He then sold the property with the benefit of planning permission. His intention was thus unclear at the time of purchase. The Court of Appeal held that Mr. Taylor was not trading in these circumstances, reversing the decision of the Commissioners. The Crown conceded in the High Court and above that there was no evidence of adventure in the nature of a trade. Megarry J considered that there was a supervening intention to trade and so a Schedule D, Case I liability. Rusell LJ (with whom Stamp and Orr LJJ agreed) said (at p. 297):

if of course you find a trade in the purchase and sale of land, it may not be difficult to find that properties originally owned (for example) by inheritance, or bought for investment only, have been bought into the stock in trade of that trade. To such circumstances I would relate the dicta relied upon in the other three cases referred to by Megarry J.[7] But where, as here, there is no question at all of absorption into a trade of dealing in land or lands previously acquired with no thought of dealing, in my judgment there is no ground at all for holding that activities such as those in the present case designed only to enhance the value of the land in the market, are to be taken as pointing to, still less as establishing, an adventure in the nature of a trade. Were the Commissioners, on a remission to them, to decide otherwise, it seems to me they would be wrong in law.

Motive as a badge is not of itself decisive. The courts seek to test objectively whether there is in fact trading. Suppose, for example, that the taxpayer does *not* intend to make a profit, but that in fact the transactions are more successful than the taxpayer may think they would be and he does in fact make a gain. The fact that he did not intend a profit will not necessarily prevent the court finding that there was 'trading'.

It will be recalled that in *IRC* v *Reinhold* (1953) 34 TC 389 (see para. 9.4.2), the taxpayer had bought four houses and then sold them at a profit three years later. He admitted that he had bought the property with a view

---

[7.] These were *Cooksey & Bibby* v *Rednall* (1949) 30 TC 514 at p. 519, *Lucy & Sunderland Ltd* v *Hunt* (1961) 40 TC 132 at p. 138 and *Leach* v *Pogson* (1962) 40 TC 585 at pp. 593–4 (see [1973] 1 WLR 1257).

to resale, and he had instructed his agents to sell whenever a suitable opportunity arose. The Commissioners were equally divided and therefore allowed the taxpayer's appeal against a Case I assessment. In the Court of Session, which held that the Commissioners' decision was justifiable, Lord Keith said:

> It is not enough for the Revenue to show that the subjects were purchased with the intention of realising them some day at a profit. This is the expectation of most, if not all, people who make investments. . . . The intention to resell some day at a profit is not *per se* sufficient . . . to attract tax.

IRC v *Reinhold* may be contrasted with *Pilkington* v *Randall* (1966) 42 TC 662. The taxpayer and his sister were entitled between them to their father's residuary estate of several acres of land in respect of which outline planning permission for development had been given. The taxpayer purchased his sister's interest, developed the property and sold it at a profit. The Commissioners held that the profit was a trading profit, and the Court of Appeal reluctantly affirmed their decision. Lord Denning MR said:

> The Commissioners heard Mr. Pilkington's evidence. They said they were in no doubt that the reason he had bought his sister's share was to make a profit by reselling it off. They held that he had embarked on a trade. The decision of the commissioners is not such an unreasonable conclusion that this court should interfere with it.

In *Wisdom* v *Chamberlain* [1969] 1 All ER 332, discussed in para. 9.4.2, the taxpayer's motive in selling the silver bullion was important. However, it must not be thought that a profit motive is essential to a finding of trade. In *Grove* v *YMCA* (1903) 4 TC 613 Ridley J found that the Association ran a restaurant according to the 'usual commercial principles', but 'would indeed carry it on even without a profit'. Yet, his Lordship could not 'escape from the conclusion that the object is to carry that restaurant on as a trade'.

Difficulties of categorisation related (inter alia) to motive can also arise where a larger piece of land is acquired but a smaller plot is what the purchaser wishes to retain and the surplus is sold on. Is this to be treated for tax purposes as a trading transaction? If so, is this to be a trading transaction as far as all the land is concerned or just to the part sold on? (Cf. *Pilkington* above). Such transactions were held to be trading in *Iswera* v *IRC* [1965] 1 WLR 663. The taxpayer, in this case, bought a 2·5 acre site close to her daughters' school. It was a larger area than she wanted but the vendor would sell only the whole and not just the part the taxpayer wanted. The taxpayer divided the land into twelve plots. She sold off nine and reconveyed one to the vendor. The surplus land was sold off to finance the purchase of the larger area. She was assessed on the basis that this was an adventure in the nature of trade. Lord Reid described this as a borderline case but the assessment was upheld by the Privy Council. It was treated as a trading transaction notwith-

Schedule D, Cases I and II – profits from trades, professions and vocations 275

standing that the land retained was not bought for trading purposes. It has been said that the fact finding tribunal found that:

> The dominant motive was to divide the land and to sell the lots so as to make a profit, and obtain a lot for herself at below market value . . . and Mrs Iswera intended from the first to divide up and sell off the greater part of the land (see *Eastham* v *Leigh London and Provincial Properties Ltd* [1971] 1 All ER at p. 976).

Accordingly she was held to be trading and on an appeal on a point of law this could not be upset.

What though of the position of a person who wanted to keep the land but on whom circumstances force a sale? Are they to be regarded as trading? *McClelland* v *Commissioner of Taxation* [1971] 1 All ER 969 was such a case. The taxpayer and her brother became jointly entitled under their uncle's will to land in Western Australia with development potential. She wished to retain the land but her brother did not. He granted her an option over his interest. She did not have the money to exercise the option. Accordingly, she decided to sell part of the land in order to raise the money. A potential purchaser was found for the part she wished to sell and the option over her brother's land was exercised. The sale and the option transaction were completed. The sale raised more than three times the amount she needed to exercise the option. She was assessed to income tax on the profit she made on the sale of the part under Australian legislation which is similar to, though not the same as, the UK statute. Windeyer J discharged the assessment as she had 'not acquired property for the purpose of profit making by sale'. She acquired an undivided half-share through the bounty of the testator. She acquired the other half by purchase from her brother but her dominant purpose in doing this was to ensure that as far as she could do so the land would not be sold until some time in the future. The appellant – so far as she had been obliged to sell – had done no more than realise a capital asset. The full court allowed the Commissioner's appeal and held her taxable. The Privy Council (by majority) allowed her appeal. As Lord Donovan said, 'judicial decisions, whether in the Commonwealth, or in the United Kingdom, yield no touchstone by which all cases may be easily resolved.' (See also *Eckel* v *Board of Inland Revenue* [1989] STC 305 and *Kirkham* v *Williams* [1989] STC 333.)

If there is not a trade or an adventure in the nature of trade then the possible impact of s. 776, TA must be considered. This is discussed below. A tax avoidance motive may stop there being a trade; see *Ensign* v *Stokes* para. 9.5 below (see also *Marson* v *Morton* in para. 9.4.3 and *Lucy and Sunderland* v *Hunt* [1961] 3 All ER 1062).

9.4.8 Business knowledge

The fact that the taxpayer has 'business knowledge', in other words the taxpayer has inside knowledge or previous experience of a particular trade, is evidence that he is 'trading' for Schedule D purposes when he does something about which he has specialised knowledge. In *IRC* v *Fraser* (1942) 24 TC 498 Lord Normand put this clearly. He said 'It is . . . more easy to hold that a single "transaction" entered into by an individual in the line of his own trade (although not part and parcel of his ordinary business) is an adventure in the nature of trade' than to hold that a transaction entered into by an individual outside the line of his own trade or occupation is an adventure in the nature of trade (see also *IRC* v *Reinhold* and *Johnston* v *Heath* (1970) 46 TC 463). This is an additional badge of trade not identified by the Radcliffe Commission.

9.4.9 Summary

All the circumstances are relevant in determining whether or not there is a trade. Relevant factors include the following:

(a) was profit the sole object? (*Leeming* v *Jones*);
(b) were the transactions in the course of trade or outside? (*Marson* v *Morton*, *Williams* v *Davis* (1954) 26 TC 371);
(c) what was the intention at the time of acquisition? (*Taylor* v *Good* and *Reed* v *Nova*);
(d) was it a forced sale? (*Hudson Bay* and *West* v *Phillips*);
(e) was it an isolated transaction or not? (*Leeming* v *Jones*);
(f) was a special method adopted for sale? (*Martin* v *Lowry*);
(g) has the taxpayer carried out similar transactions before? (*Pickford* v *Quirke*);
(h) was it a 'deal' or realisation of investments? (*Marson* v *Morton*);
(i) was it within a corporate taxpayer's company objects?
(j) what was the comparison of rental and investment and resale? Was there an income? (not essential for capital; see *Marson* v *Morton*);
(k) what was the motive? (*Taylor* v *Good*).

9.5 ASSET STRIPPING AND DIVIDEND STRIPPING – TAX AVOIDANCE MOTIVE

A tax avoidance motive can also affect the question of whether or not a trade is carried on. Motive was seemingly the distinction between genuine share transactions (e.g., *Griffiths* v *Harrison* [1963] AC 1) and artificial devices intended to obtain a tax advantage such as asset and dividend stripping (see *FA & AB Ltd* v *Lupton* [1972] AC 634 and *Thomson* v *Gurneville Securities* [1972] AC 661). In *Finsbury Securities Ltd* v *Bishop* (1966) 43 TC 591, a dividend stripping case it was said (by Lord Morris at p. 627, Lords Reid, Pearce, Upjohn and Pearson concurring):

> The various shares which were acquired ought not to be regarded as having become part of the stock in trade of the company. They were not acquired for the purpose of dealing with them. In no ordinary sense were they current assets. For the purpose of carrying out the scheme which was devised the shares were to be and had to be retained.

Schedule D, Cases I and II – profits from trades, professions and vocations 277

Accordingly there was no adventure in the nature of trade as the necessary motive was missing. (Note that *Griffiths v Harrison* [1963] AC 1 was distinguished.)

Lord Morris in *FA & AB Ltd v Lupton* (1971) 47 TC 580 said that some transactions can be so affected by fiscal considerations that the shape and character of the transaction is no longer a trading transaction. Fiscal considerations naturally affect the taxpayer's evaluation of a transaction. Capital allowances and the like are financial inducements to engage in commercial activities which would be financially unattractive or unacceptably speculative without them. An overriding fiscal motive does not stop something being a trading transaction, its commerciality must also be affected so that it is no longer a commercial transaction. This is a question often of fact and degree depending on the precise circumstances.

The position has been considered more recently in *Ensign Tankers (Leasing) Ltd v Stokes (Inspector of Taxes)* [1992] STC 226 (for the background and facts of the case see (1991–2) 2 KCLJ 95). The House of Lords considered that the Victory Partnership was trading and entitled to allowances as regards part of the expenditure, but as regards the rest apparently it was not trading. This was because of the tax avoidance motive and the way the transactions were funded. *Ensign Tankers v Stokes* is discussed in more detail at para. 4.8 above.

9.6 ILLEGAL TRADING

Certain activities which can result in profit are illegal. A regular course of burglary might be profitable but would be criminal, as would buying and selling goods known to be stolen or living off immoral earnings. The question arises whether profits of illegal activities should be liable to tax. If the state levies tax on the profits of illegal transactions is it not condoning or participating in the illegality? Or should the participant be denied the further advantage of escaping tax altogether on his or her illegal profits?

The courts have usually distinguished between the profits themselves and the way the profits were made for tax purposes if they are merely illegal. The position may be different if they are the profits of a crime[8] which may not be regarded as a trade.

It does not usually matter that the profits of a trade are illegally obtained (for example by fixing slot machines to cheat customers). The Revenue can

---

[8.] See *Lindsay v IRC* (1932) 18 TC 43 which concerned selling whisky to the US during prohibition and committing a fraud on Customs (*quaere* whether this type of smuggling is really a crime?) Lord Sands said at p. 56: 'The third question is whether the profits of the adventure are exempt from Income Tax because their acquisition was tainted with an offence against the criminal law. The tax is imposed upon profits of trade. Crime, such as housebreaking, is not trade, and therefore the proceeds are not caught by the tax. It does not follow, however, that there cannot be a business answering to the description of trade, albeit it is tainted with illegality. Trafficking in drugs, for example, is of the nature of trade, albeit such trafficking may in the circumstances be illegal. I respectfully adopt the dictum of Lord Haldane, in delivering the judgment of the Privy Council in the case of *Smith*, that once the character of a business has been ascertained as being of the nature of trade, the person who carries it on cannot found upon elements of illegality to avoid the tax'.

still tax them if the trade itself in these cases is legal. But what if the trade itself is illegal? There is nothing in the definition of trade which suggests that trades must be legal. However, the better view appears to be that systematic crime is in fact not a trade as it is only systematic crime. This has the undesirable policy effect that the more serious the crime the less likely a tax charge. A second problem arises in connection with the deductibility of illegal payments (for example payments made out of a slush fund) or of fines (see Chapter 10).

In *Mann* v *Nash* [1932] 1 KB 752, 16 TC 523 the taxpayer was an amusement caterer (providing amusement machines for public use). He provided machines to people who would use them for unlawful gaming. The question at issue was, did this element of illegality prevent his profits being assessable? It was held by Rowlatt J that it did not. The profits were merely tainted with illegality and that did not stop the taxpayer from being a 'trader'.

Rowlatt J said:

... I myself cannot see why this letting out of the machines in a commercial way, with a view to the reception of profits in a commercial way, is not trade, adventure, manufacture or concern in the nature of trade. On the words, it clearly is. The question really is whether as a matter of construction those words are to be cut down by an overriding consideration that the trade is tainted with illegality. The great mainstay of Mr Field's argument, quite rightly from his point of view, was the case of *Hayes v Duggan* [1929] IR 406 decided in the Irish Free State, and that decision of the Supreme Court seems to have gone upon this principle, that no construction could be admitted which recognised that the State should come forward and seem to take a profit from what the State prohibited ... But, in truth, it seems to me that all that consideration is misconceived. The Revenue representing the State is merely looking at an accomplished fact. It is not condoning it; it has not taken part in it; it merely finds profits made from what appears to be a trade, and the Revenue laws happen to say that the profits made from trades have to be taxed, and they say: 'Give us the tax.' It is not to the purpose in my judgment to say: 'But the same State that you represent has said they are unlawful'; that is immaterial altogether and I do not see that there is any conflict between the two propositions.

Finlay J followed this decision in *Southern* v *AB* (1933) 18 TC 59 a case involving a betting business which was wholly illegal. Finlay J reversed the Special Commissioners' decision and held that the business constituted a trade the profits of which had been properly assessed. Finlay J said:

The illustration of the burglar – which is an extreme illustration, but extreme illustrations are sometimes useful – was taken. I express no opinion upon a case which is quite unlike the case which is before me, but I desire to point out exactly why, assuming as I am quite willing to assume, the burglar does not come within the purview of the Income Tax Acts: if he does not come within the purview of the Income Tax Acts, it is because what he does is not the carrying on of a trade within Case I, and it is not because, carrying on a trade within Case I, he is taken out by some considerations of morals or anything of that sort. The question always is, I think, a short question of construction: is there a trade – I use 'trade' compendiously; trade, or the other words referred to – carried on within the meaning of Case I? Lord Sands refers to a dictum of Lord Haldane, which I do not go back to because I have said I would not deal with the authorities prior to Mr Justice Rowlatt's judgment, but the observations made by Lord Haldane in delivering the opinion of the Privy Council in *Smith's* case seem to be in accord with the view I am taking.

In *Mann* v *Nash* the illegality was incidental. Where the illegality is inherent in the activity alleged to be a trade, however, the courts may take a different view. In *J. P. Harrison* v *Griffith* (1969) 40 TC 281 Lord Denning said obiter:

> Take a gang of burglars. Are they engaged in a trade or an adventure in the nature of trade? They have an organisation. They spend money on equipment. They acquire goods by effort. They make a profit. What detail is lacking in their adventure? You may say it lacks legality, but legality is not an essential characteristic of a trade. You cannot point to any detail that it lacks. But still it is not a trade, nor an adventure in the nature of trade . . . it is burglary and that is all there is to say about it.

The issue of illegality was raised in *IRC* v *Aken* [1988] STC 69, [1990] STC 497, CA, where, following a television appearance by a prostitute known as 'Lindi St Clair', the Inland Revenue made enquiries into her income resulting in assessments for a six year period amounting to a total of £58,751 in tax. The taxpayer argued that her activities as a prostitute involved illegality so she should not be taxed. This argument was not accepted and the assessments were upheld by the High Court and by the Court of Appeal.

The practical difficulties of ascertaining the income of a taxpayer where there is an element of illegality of course remain, let alone the possibilities of what might be claimed or allowed as deductions (NB s. 577A, TA discussed in Chapter 8). It should be remembered, that, if the activity is illegal albeit incidental to a legal trade, a constructive trust (see, for example, *Agip (Africa) Ltd* v *Jackson* [1990] Ch 265) may be imposed on any profit received, so that there is no profit to which the taxpayer is entitled in respect of which he could be assessed. It is not clear how sympathetic the court would be to the argument that there should be no tax because of the lack of entitlement caused by the constructive trust. It may be that the consequences imposed by a constructive trust in these circumstances would not include liability to tax of the constructive trustee (cf. *English* v *Dedham Vale Properties Ltd* [1978] 1 All ER 382). The income is not beneficially that of the constructive trustee who is in the position of a bare trustee.

9.7 MUTUAL TRADING

Mutual trading describes the phenomenon which occurs when a group of people contribute to a fund for a purpose common to them all, for example, a mutual assurance society. Where such a society enjoys an excess of income over expenditure (contributions received exceed benefits paid) it could be said to have made a trading profit. However, the members of the society are really only trading with themselves and a person cannot logically trade with himself/herself. Therefore such profits escape tax under Schedule D, Case I. As Lord Wilberforce has said, 'trade must be bilateral, you must trade with someone' (*Ransom* v *Higgs*, see para. 9.4.1).

If people combine together to achieve a common purpose for example in a club, (i) they may not be trading if there is any surplus of subscriptions over expenditure; or (ii) the contributions may not be a profit since they may still belong to the members. There may then be mutual trading. As Lord Wilberforce said in *Fletcher* v *CIR for Jamaica* [1972] AC 414:

> Cases in which groups of persons making contributions towards a common purpose have been held not liable for tax on any surplus over expenditure fall under a number of heads. The expression 'the mutuality principle' has been devised to express the basis for exemption of these groups from taxation. It is a convenient expression, but the situations it covers are not in all respects alike. In some cases the essence of the matter is that the group of persons in question is not in any sense trading, so the starting point for an assessment for income tax in respect of trading profits does not exist. In other cases, there may be in some sense a trading activity, but the objective, or the outcome, is not profits, it is merely to cover expenditure and to return any surplus, directly or indirectly, sooner or later, to the members of the group. These two criteria often, perhaps generally, overlap; since one of the criteria of a trade is the intention to make profits, and a surplus comes to be called a profit if it derives from a trade. So the issue is better framed as one question, rather than two: is the activity, on the other hand, a trade, or an adventure in the nature of trade, producing a profit, or is it, on the other, a mutual arrangement which, at most, gives rise to a surplus? The three main fields in which the mutuality principle has been applied are insurance, rating and clubs.

Before the taxpayer may claim the benefits of this doctrine of mutual trading all contributors must be entitled to share in the surplus of the club's funds and the only people who are entitled to share in that surplus must be contributors: 'all and only the contributors'. As Lord MacMillan said in *Municipal Mutual Insurance* v *Hills* (1932) 16 TC 430:

> The cardinal requirement is that all the contributors to the common fund must be entitled to participate in the surplus and that all the participators in the surplus must be contributors to the common funds in other words there must be complete identity between contributors and participators.

The complete identity required is not, however, identity of individuals but of class of persons: *Faulconbridge v National Employers' Mutual General Insurance Association Ltd* (1952) 33 TC 103. This requirement will be satisfied in the case of mutual insurance societies, as in *Faulconbridge* itself, where every policyholder was a member of the association, and the association's only income came from premiums on policies paid by members. If any person ceased to be insured by the association, his membership was terminated. Upjohn J affirmed the decision of the Commissioners that despite a varying membership the association was a mutual concern not assessable to tax on its surpluses.

The requirement of identity will likewise be satisfied in the case of a members' club. Thus in *Carlisle and Silloth Golf Club v Smith* (1913) 6 TC 48 and 198 the subscriptions of members of a golf club were not assessable because of the mutuality principle although green fees paid by visitors were liable to income tax. Hamilton J said:

> I think, therefore, that at the outset the club has, for considerations sufficient in its own view, annexed to its ordinary enterprise of a golf club the rendering of services systematically to strangers for the purpose of obtaining, among other advantages to itself, the revenue that those strangers provide. It is not a case where, thanks to the relations of membership or family bonds, people club together and reduce the common expenditure on some common object by contributions which they fix roughly with some reference to the cost. It seems to me that it is not a case in which the members as an aggregate (for they are not incorporated) dispose of their surplus because they have no necessity to consume it; it is a case it seems to me at the outset in which this aggregate of gentlemen, who may for practical purposes be treated as one person, annexed to their club for the purposes of recreation an enterprise which is separate from it and which results in pecuniary receipts to themselves.

Not all common ventures meet the requirements of mutual trading. In giving the advice of the Privy Council in *English & Scottish Joint Co-operative Wholesale Society Ltd v Assam Agricultural Income Tax Commissioner* [1948] 2 All ER 395, Lord Normand said:

> What kinds of business other than mutual insurance may claim exemption from liability to income tax under the principle of [mutual trading] need not be here considered, but their Lordships are of opinion that the principle cannot apply to an association, society or company which grows produce on its own land or manufactures goods in its own factories, using either its own capital or capital borrowed whether from its members or from others, and sells its produce or goods to its members exclusively. In the present case the appellant society is not bound by its rules to sell its tea only to its members, but it could make no difference if it were. No matter who the purchasers may be, if the society sells the tea grown and manufactured by it at a price which exceeds the cost of producing it and rendering it fit for

sale, it has earned profits which are, subject to the provisions of the taxing act, taxable profits . . . for there is no common fund to which the members of the appellant society contribute and in which they participate.

It should be noted that there must be a 'reasonable relationship' between what each member puts into the club and what each member gets out of it. For example, in *Fletcher* v *CIR for Jamaica* [1972] AC 414, a bathing club claimed exemption from tax in respect of sums paid to the club by its 'hotel members' on the grounds that this was a case of 'mutual trading'. The club owned a beach. It had 900 members who paid the club a subscription and thereafter bathed free. Non-members used the beach for three shillings per day. These non-members were guests at nearby hotels. Later a new scheme was devised. The *hotels* would join the club for £1.10.0 each and two shillings for each guest. The guests would then bathe free.

The Privy Council decided that the club was trading with the hotels and that 'mutual trading' did not apply. When the figures were looked at, the hotel members paid six times as much as all the 900 individual members put together. However, supposing there were 20 hotels, each hotel would receive only $1/920$ of any surplus profit. It was held that this relationship stretched the doctrine of mutual trading too far. In reality there was no mutuality.

It should be noted that if an association which is otherwise a mutual concern has dealings with outsiders any profit from those dealings will be assessable under Case I in the usual way (see *Carlisle and Silloth Golf Club* v *Smith* discussed above).

CHAPTER TEN
Schedule D, Cases I and II – computation

10.1 GENERAL

The purpose of this chapter is to consider some of the general matters involved in computing the profits and gains liable to income tax under Schedule D, Cases I and II. (The computation of profits under Case I and Case II is essentially the same, so that the two may be considered together.) In many countries this is done on the basis of the business's accounts. For historical reasons this is not the case in the UK.[1] There are special rules for the computation of the profits and gains liable to income tax under Schedule D, Cases I and II which differ from the way in which accounts are generally drawn up in accordance with normal accountancy principles (e.g., depreciation and capital allowances – see Chapter 12). Surprisingly, until recently there was no general requirement for a trader to keep accounts for income tax purposes (cf. VAT; see sch. 11, VATA, especially para. 6) though the trader usually will so as to see how the business is doing and how it should be managed. A new s. 12B, Taxes Management Act 1970 (TMA) was inserted by para. 3, sch. 19, FA 1994, which requires a person who may be required to make a return etc. to keep all '... such records as may be requisite for the purposes of enabling him to make and deliver a correct and complete return for the year or period ...' and preserve them until 'the relevant day' (which may be for up to six years from the end of the period).

It is easy to state that the general rule is that what is taxed is receipts less allowable expenses. The problems with this are in knowing which receipts are taxable and which expenses are allowable and for what period and how to

---

[1.] It seems that there were only nine accountants practising in London in 1803 (cf. Kelly's Directories for the period). The Institute of Chartered Accountants in England and Wales only received its Charter in 1880. The Scottish Institute predated it.

work out the difference. This is not as simple as it sounds. There are no clear hard and fast rules as to how the excess (if any) of receipts over expenditure is to be calculated.

Whiteman and Wheatcroft said of 'profits and gains' in their first edition[2] that:

> both bear the same meaning, that is the net profits of the trade or profession computed for the relevant period on normal commercial principles in accordance with established legal concepts, and subject to any specific qualifications imposed by the Income and Corporation Taxes Act.

This still seems to be a good general summary of the position but accountancy principles have of late, seemingly, become of much greater importance (see, e.g., *Johnson v Britannia Airways Ltd* [1994] STC 763). Knox J said at p. 782 that:

> The court is slow to accept that accounts prepared in accordance with accepted principles of commercial accountancy are not adequate for tax purposes as a true statement of the taxpayer's profits for the relevant period. In particular, it is slow to find that there is a judge-made rule of law which prevents accounts prepared in accordance with the ordinary principles of commercial accountancy from complying with the requirements of the tax legislation . . . As long ago as 1957 Lord Radcliffe in *Southern Railway of Peru Ltd* v *Owen* said that he would view with dismay the assertion of legal theories as to the ascertainment of true annual profits which were in conflict with current accountancy practice and were not required by some special statutory provision of the Income Tax Acts[3] . . . Equally, the reluctance of appellate tribunals to interfere with factual determinations by tribunals to whom issues of fact are entrusted by relevant legislation was reasserted by the Privy Council in the context of accountancy matters in *Southern Pacific Insurance* v *IRC* [1986] STC 178.

These statements illustrate the tension between the legal and accounting approach. It should be noted that few judges have any accountancy experience.

It should also be remembered that we are here only concerned with income or revenue receipts and expenditure. Accordingly, capital receipts and expenditure are generally excluded from 'profits and gains' for these purposes (an exception might be capital allowances discussed in Chapter 12).

10.2 CASH AND EARNINGS BASIS

10.2.1 General

There are many bases upon which accounts may be drawn up to give a true and fair view of the position. Three bases in particular are in common use. These are:

[2.] Para. 6–26, *Whiteman and Wheatcroft on Income Tax and Surtax*, 1971, Sweet & Maxwell.
[3.] See (1954) 36 TC 602 at p. 645.

Schedule D, Cases I and II – computation

(a) the earnings basis;
(b) the cash basis;
(c) the bills delivered basis.

These are broadly concerned with when receipts and expenditure should be brought into account so as to reflect them properly in determining the profits attributable to a particular period. This is not as easy as it sounds. Should one look at what is left in the money box at the end of the period (a simplified cash basis)? Alternatively, should one look at what work has been completed in the period so that nothing more has to be done to earn the profit notwithstanding that payment has not yet been received? How should one deal with say a quarterly electricty bill when part of the accounting period is within the relevant accounting period and part outside?

Lord President Clyde said in *IRC v Morrison* (1932) 17 TC 325 at p. 330:

In assessing the profits of such a professional business as this, one or other of two modes of computation are in use, which have, no doubt, been found alternatively convenient and appropriate according to particular circumstances. It is obvious that the usual mode which applies to the assessment of the profits of a trading business which buys and sells, or to a manufacturing business which buys raw material and makes it up and sells the finished product, would not be practically capable of application to an ordinary professional business in which the professional man markets nothing but his own services and ingathers nothing but his professional fees. The two alternative modes of computation are known as the 'cash' basis mode and the 'earnings' basis mode. According to the first, the profits of the business are estimated according to the excess of the actual cash receipts during the year over the cash outlays and expenses actually disbursed or paid during the year. This mode takes no account of what are called 'outstandings', that is, fees earned but not yet ingathered, either at the beginning or at the end of the year. According to the 'earnings' basis mode the actual cash receipts during the year and the actual cash outlays during the year are treated in the same way as before; but, to the favourable balance thus brought out, there is added the amount of the fees earned but not yet collected at the end of the year, and then there is deducted the amount of the fees earned but not yet collected at the beginning of the year. Both modes appear to be somewhat rough and ready; but I suppose that – one year with another – they are found to work out with sufficient accuracy. The first has the merit of avoiding all the trouble which the second imposes on the taxpayer in calculating the 'outstandings' on current jobs.

10.2.2 Earnings basis

The most common basis of calculation uses what is called 'the earnings basis'. This is the basis which virtually always applies to traders. The only Schedule D, Case I and Case II individual taxpayers who escape this basis *altogether* are barristers[4] and authors.[5] Others (such as solicitors) will be on the earnings basis for years 1–3 inclusive, and thereafter may be permitted to change to, for example, a bills delivered basis (see para. 10.2.4).

Under the earnings basis it is irrelevant whether a sum has actually been received or not. The principles underlying this basis of accounting are those of liability and entitlement. The accounts are drawn up to reflect those sums which become due to the taxpayer in the course of the accounting period and those which become due from the taxpayer in respect of the accounting period. Such a basis is appropriate to most traders who carry stock and who operate on a system of credit. In many cases, of course, sums become due and are paid instantly so that a taxpayer's receipts will reflect his earnings either completely or almost completely. Sometimes his earnings are then referred to as 'receipts'. However, that should not be permitted to confuse one into thinking that a basis other than the earnings basis applies. It is merely true that in such cases the best guide to the taxpayer's earnings are his receipts.

The earnings basis may broadly be described as:

	sums owed to the trader of a revenue nature
less	sums owed by him of a revenue nature
equals	**Profit or gains** (i.e., *equals* entitlements *less* liabilities)

If the taxpayer is assessed on the earnings basis, and he receives moneys worth instead of cash, the market value of the asset received is entered in the accounts (see *Gold Coast Selection Trust Ltd* v *Humphrey* [1948] AC 459). In this case, the taxpayers sold a mining concession in return for a holding of shares having a par value equal to the value of the concession. The House of Lords held that the shares must be valued at market and not par value, but that the market value could be reduced to take account of the fact that the sale of such a large shareholding would depress the value.

Sums are only earned when all the conditions attached to payment are fulfilled, so that if there are any contingencies to be satisfied, the payment is earned at the time of the satisfaction of the contingency. For example, if goods are sold in one accounting period on the condition that payment is to be due on delivery, and delivery takes place in the next accounting period, the price of the goods is earned at the time of delivery and will be entered into the later accounts.

In *Willingale* v *International Commercial Bank Ltd* [1978] 1 All ER 754, the Inland Revenue sought to include a fractional part of the profit to be earned by the taxpayers on the maturity of certain bills of exchange held by them, on the basis that the value of the bills increased as the maturity date approached. The House of Lords held (by a 3 to 2 majority) that the

---

[4.] Seemingly on the theory that in the past barristers could not sue for their fees.

[5.] Seemingly because they cannot know in advance how much royalties they will earn. It would be churlish to note that higher judges are almost always barristers many of whom may have been authors.

taxpayers did not realise any profit on the bills until they were sold or they matured, and that accordingly no part of the anticipated profit on sale or maturity could be included in the accounts. The profit was not therefore earned until the bills were sold or paid off on maturity and could not be assessed until that time.

In relation to a sale on credit, the purchase price is earned in the year of sale, and ought therefore to appear in the accounts at that time. However, in practice, the taxpayer is allowed to discount the original price when accounting for his earnings, though if he subsequently receives more than the discounted value his accounts for the year of receipt will be reopened and the excess will be added in and taxed accordingly. Relief is available for bad or doubtful debts proved to be such (s. 74(j), TA see para. 10.6.11).

10.2.3 The cash basis

Broadly, this is the money box approach. What is actually received and what is paid is what matters in computing the profits or gains. In other words it is cash in *minus* cash out that is relevant. Liabilities, debts and credits are all irrelevant. The cash basis thus only takes account of cash actually received and actually spent. This basis is applied automatically to barristers and to authors. The cash basis can be applied to others if they can satisfy the Inland Revenue that there is some reason why the basis should be applied. However, they must wait until they have been carrying on business for at least three years before they will be allowed to change to this basis.

10.2.4 Bills delivered basis

The bills delivered basis requires items to appear in the accounts at the time an invoice, bill or fee note is sent out or received. This may be later or earlier than a sum is earned or becomes due and later or earlier than the receipt of payment. This basis is appropriate for professional men such as solicitors and architects. It resembles the earnings basis but no account is taken of work-in-progress.

10.2.5 Change of basis

The taxpayer is entitled to change the basis on which he prepares his accounts from earnings to bills delivered or to cash, or to cash from bills delivered, or vice versa. For this purpose, s. 110, TA distinguishes between the earnings basis and the 'conventional' basis (meaning profits 'computed otherwise than by reference to earnings', and therefore the cash or bills delivered basis). If there is a change from the conventional basis to the earnings basis, or a change of conventional basis which results in receipts dropping out of computation, a charge under Case VI of Schedule D is applied to sums received after the change of basis which were not included in any accounts before the change (s. 104(4), TA). This charge would therefore apply to a change from either bills delivered or cash to earnings in respect of payment for goods supplied or work performed before the change for which no bill had been delivered or no payment received before the change. It would also apply to a change from cash to bills delivered if payment was received after the change in respect of goods supplied or work done before it. As an alternative, the taxpayer may elect to have sums received within six years of the change treated as though they had been received on the day before the change, and he would then be charged by reference to his tax position at the time of the change rather than the time of actual receipt (s. 108, TA). It is provided by s. 105(4) that expenses for which no allowance was made in accounts prepared before the change (because, for example, no bill had been received or no payment actually made) may be allowed against sums chargeable under Schedule D, Case VI (s. 105(4)).

10.2.6 Anticipation of profit, losses and expenses

This problem will not arise when a cash basis is adopted. However, it will arise where the profits of a trade are computed on an earnings basis so that receipts are to be brought in when they are earned and expenses are brought in when they are incurred notwithstanding when they are actually paid. This is relatively easy in the case of a merchanting activity but much more difficult in a service or financial context.[6] Where a fungible is bought and sold in a short time (as in most merchanting actvities) the position is relatively simple but if one is concerned with a 15 year loan then the position may be more complex as questions such as spreading over the 15-year period arise. Issues relating to the anticipation of a profit (or losses) are discussed further at paras 10.3.5 and 10.4.

10.3 TRADING RECEIPTS

10.3.1 Introduction

The next question to be addressed is, what incomings are taxable? Section 18, TA imposes the charge to income tax on the '. . . annual profits or gains . . . from any trade, profession or vocation . . .' Section 60(1), TA provides that the 'full amount of the profits or gains' for the period are to be taxed. These provisions require the receipts to be of an income nature.

MacDermott LCJ said in *Harry Ferguson Motors Ltd* v *IRC* (1951) 33 TC 15 at p. 42:

> It should be remembered that income tax is a tax on income. Accordingly only receipts of an income nature are taxable. There is no single infallible test for settling the vexed question whether a receipt is of an income or capital nature.

The price received for the sale of goods during the course of a trade is clearly to be included. The difficulties arise in connection with what else should be

---

[6.] See *Willingale* v *ICB* (para. 10.2.2) and *Owen* v *Southern Railway of Peru* (1954) 36 TC 602 on future deductions and *Gallagher* v *Jones* [1993] STC 537.

included. However, it is clear that the receipt must arise in or accrue from the trade, profession or vocation.

There are thus two necessary characteristics for a trading receipt:

(a) it must be derived from the trade; and
(b) it must be an income receipt not a capital one.

10.3.2 'Derived from the trade'

If the payment is made to the taxpayer for goods or services supplied in the course of the taxpayer's trade it is a trading receipt. If it is made for some other reason, it is not (e.g., a payment made for personal motives only). In *Higgs* v *Olivier* [1952] Ch 311 Sir Laurence Olivier entered into an agreement with Two City Films Ltd in connection with the making of 'Henry V'. A deed of covenant was later entered into whereby in consideration of £15,000 Sir Laurence agreed not to appear in or produce any film for 18 months (other than for Two City Films Ltd). He was assessed under Schedule D, Case II on the £15,000. The Special Commissioners considered that the sum came from refraining from carrying on his vocation and in their opinion was a capital receipt. Both Harman J and the Court of Appeal dismissed the Crown's appeal. It may be that this was a case that turned on its particular facts. This was certainly the view of the Scottish court in *IRC* v *Biggar* [1982] STC 677 when it reviewed *Higgs* v *Olivier* (see also *Walker* v *Carnaby* [1970] 1 All ER 502).

10.3.3 Capital/income distinction

This can be a very difficult matter. Suppose X teaches people to drive and owns his own driving school. He is paid £10 per hour by customers. Those sums are trading receipts. Suppose he also has a shop selling motoring accessories. Receipts from sales of motoring accessories are also trading receipts. If, however, X sells the school and the shop, these are not trading receipts, they are purely capital receipts from the sale of capital assets.

It should be noted that to confuse this area further there is difficult terminology. One often refers to the stock in the shop as *circulating* capital and to the shop itself as *fixed* capital. The distinction is thus often expressed as one between profits from sales of circulating capital and profits from sale of fixed capital. Only the *former* (circulating capital profits) are trading receipts (see further para. 10.3.6).

10.3.4 Compensation payments

10.3.4.1 General Problems have arisen as to how to treat compensation payments (see also *Donald Fisher (Ealing) Ltd* v *Spencer* [1989] STC 256). It is important to analyse properly what the payment is made for. The cases can be divided into three broad categories.

(a) sterilisation of assets;
(b) cancellation of contracts;
(c) filling a hole in the taxpayer's profits.

The difficulty is often working out in the particular circumstances what the payment is really for. This difficulty is compounded because, for example, a payment for the cancellation of a contract may also be an aspect of filling a hole in profits.

10.3.4.2 Sterilisation of assets In *The Glenboig Union Fireclay Co. Ltd* v *IRC* (1921) 12 TC 427 the company was inter alia the lessee of a fireclay field. The railway company lessor required the company to desist from working close to their railway line. The lessee received compensation from the railway company for not working these beds. This was held to be a capital rather than an income receipt. Lord Buckmaster said:

> In truth the sum of money is the sum paid to prevent the Fireclay Company obtaining the full benefit of the capital value of that part of the mines which they are prevented from working by the Railway Company. It appears to me to make no difference whether it be regarded as a sale of the asset out and out, or whether it be treated merely as a means of preventing the acquisition of profit that would otherwise be gained. In either case the capital asset of the Company to that extent has been sterilised and destroyed, and it is in respect of that action that the sum of £15,316 was paid. It is unsound to consider the fact that the measure, adopted for the purpose of seeing what the total amount should be, was based on considering what are the profits that would have been earned. That, no doubt, is a perfectly exact and accurate way of determining the compensation, for it is now well settled that the compensation payable in such circumstances is the full value of the minerals that are to be left unworked, less the cost of working, and that is, of course, the profit that would be obtained were they in fact worked. But there is no relation between the measure that is used for the purpose of calculating a particular result and the quality of the figure that is arrived at by means of the application of that test. I am unable to regard this sum of money as anything but capital money, and I think therefore it was erroneously entered in the balance sheet ending 31st August, 1913, as a profit on the part of the Fireclay Company.

The decision in *Glenboig* should be compared with the case of *Thompson* v *Magnesium Electron Ltd* (1943) 26 TC 1. Here a company was formed to carry on the manufacture of magnesium by electrical means. Chlorine was necessary for this process. Negotiations took place and a settlement was reached under which the company agreed to abandon its intention of manufacturing chlorine and buy the gas from ICI at a basic price of £10 per ton delivered. ICI also agreed to indemnify the company against certain expenses incurred in its preparations for the manufacture of chlorine. ICI further agreed to pay the company £6.15s. in respect of each ton of caustic soda they would have produced if the company had manufactured its own chlorine so long as the company observed a restrictive covenant not to manufacture chlorine or caustic soda. This worked out at £7.10s. per ton of chlorine delivered. The sums received were held to be correctly assessed under Schedule D, Case 1 as trading receipts.

10.3.4.3 Cancellation of contracts There have been a number of cases concerned with payments connected with the cancellation of contracts.

In *Van Den Berghs Ltd* v *Clark* (1935) 19 TC 390 a payment relating to the cancellation of a contract was held to be capital as it related to the structure of the business. Here, the company carried on business as a margarine manufacturer. It had long been in competition with a Dutch producer. An agreement was entered into by the two of them in 1908 for profit sharing and pooling in a 'friendly alliance'. Payments were made under the agreement until 1913 and were treated as trading receipts. During the First World War these profits could not be calculated. A dispute arose between the parties as to the amounts due under the agreement. In 1927 a settlement was reached whereby the agreement was cancelled and all claims withdrawn in consideration of the payment of £450,000 as 'damages'. This sum was assessed under Schedule D, Case I. The General Commissioners found that the damages were to be brought in in computing the balance of profits and gains of the appellant for the period in question.

Finlay J allowed the company's appeal thus treating the payment as a capital but this was reversed by the Court of Appeal. The House of Lords allowed the company's appeal thus treating the payment as a capital receipt. Lord Macmillan (with whom Lords Atkin, Tomlin, Wright and Russell agreed) said:

> The reported cases fall into two categories, those in which the subject is found claiming that an item or receipt ought not to be included in computing his profits and those in which the subject is found claiming that an item of disbursement ought to be included among the admissible deductions in computing his profits. In the former case the Crown is found maintaining that the item is an item of income; in the latter, that it is a capital item. Consequently the argumentative position alternates according as to whether it is an item of receipt or an item of disbursement that is in question, and the taxpayer and the Crown are found alternately arguing for the restriction or the expansion of the conception of income. [His Lordship then referred to Viscount Cave's dictum in *British Insulated and Helsby Cable Ltd* v *Atherton* [1926] AC 205.] My Lords, if the numerous decisions are examined and classified, they will be found to exhibit a satisfactory measure of consistency with Lord Cave's principle of discrimination. With the guidance thus afforded I now address myself to the question whether £450,000 received by the Appellants in the circumstances already narrated can properly be described as an item of profit arising or accruing to them from the carrying on of their trade, which ought to be credited as an income receipt. It is important to bear in mind at the outset that the trade

of the Appellants is to manufacture and deal in margarine, for the nature of a receipt may vary according to the nature of the trade in connection with which it arises. The price of the sale of a factory is ordinarily a capital receipt, but it may be an income receipt in the case of a person whose business it is to buy and sell factories. My Lords, the learned Attorney-General stated that he was content to take the agreements of 1927 as meaning what they say. The sum of £450,000 is accordingly to be taken as having been paid by the Dutch Company to the Appellants in consideration of the Appellants consenting to the agreements of 1908, 1912 and 1920 being terminated as at 31st December, 1927, instead of running their course to 31st December, 1940. If the payment had been in respect of a balance of profits due to the Appellants by the Dutch Company for the years 1914 to 1927, different considerations might have applied, but it is agreed that it is not to be so regarded. Now what were the Appellants giving up? They gave up their whole rights under the agreements for thirteen years ahead . . . The three agreements which the Appellants consented to cancel were not ordinary commercial contracts made in the course of carrying on their trade; they were not contracts for the disposal of their products or for the engagement of agents or other employees necessary for the conduct of their business; nor were they merely agreements as to how their trading profits when earned should be distributed as between the contracting parties. On the contrary, the cancelled agreements related to the whole structure of the Appellants' profit-making apparatus. They regulated the Appellants' activities, defined what they might and what they might not do, and affected the whole conduct of their business. I have difficulty in seeing how money laid out to secure, or money received for the cancellation of, so fundamental an organisation of a trade's activities can be regarded as an income disbursement or an income receipt . . . In my opinion that asset, the congeries of rights which the Appellants enjoyed under the agreements and which for a price they surrendered, was a capital asset.

An example of a case where the payment was not for termination of part of the structure of the business but an incident in the trade and so treated as income is *Kelsall Parsons* v *IRC* (1938) 21 TC 608. In that case the taxpayers carried on business as agents for sale of various manufacturers' products in Scotland. One of their agency agreements which only had a year to run was terminated at the manufacturer's request in consideration of £1,500. The taxpayers treated the sum as a capital receipt. The General Commissioners considered that the sum should be included in the calculation of the taxpayers' profits. This was upheld by the Court of Session. Lord President Normand said:

Each case depends upon its own facts, and in this case the facts, which seem to me not to be closely analogous to the facts in any of the cases cited to us, lead me to the conclusion that the determination of the Commissioners should stand. The sum which the Appellants received was, as the Commissioners have found, paid as compensation for the cancellation of the agency contract. That was a contract incidental to the normal course of the Appellants' business. Their business, indeed, was to obtain as many contracts of this kind as they could, and their profits were gained by rendering services in fulfilment of such contracts. The Appellants' business is entirely different from the business carried on by someone who, under contract, acts exclusively as agent for a single principal . . . In my opinion the agency agreements entered into by the Appellants, so far from being a fixed framework, are rather to be regarded as temporary and variable elements of the Appellants' profit-making enterprise.

10.3.4.4 Filling a hole in profits The case of *London and Thames Haven Oil Wharves* v *Attwooll* (1967) 43 TC 491 is the case of a payment made to make good a hole in the taxpayer's profits. This was held to be an income receipt. The company owned and operated one of the largest oil storage installations in Europe. One of their jetties was damaged when a supertanker was docking. The company recovered £77,875 from the owners of the ship, and received £26,738 from their insurers, making a total of £104,613 (plus interest). The company was assessed on £21,404 being the amount by which the sum recovered exceeded the physical damage. The Special Commissioners considered that the £21,404 'was paid to the company to fill the hole created in the company's profits and is a trading receipt'. Buckley J allowed the taxpayer's appeal on the ground that the sum received was in respect of the sterilisation of a capital asset. This was reversed by the Court of Appeal.

10.3.4.5 Summary

(a) if a taxpayer agrees to restrict his, her or its trading activities for a payment, the payment will be a trading receipt but this is a question of construction (*Higgs* v *Olivier*). The greater the restriction on a taxpayer's activities the more likely the receipt is to be held to be capital not income;

(b) sums paid for 'sterilisation of an asset' of the trader are capital even if calculated by reference to profits (see *Glenboig* v *IRC* (1921) 12 TC 427 and *Burmah Steamship* v *IRC* 16 TC 67. For a more recent example see *McGowan* v *Brown and Cousins* [1977] 3 All ER 844) unless the sterilisation of the asset is temporary);

(c) compensatory sums paid for cancellation or non-performance of business deals are likely to be dealt with as follows:

(i) if the contract relates to the business structure the compensation is likely to be capital (see *Van den Berghs Ltd* v *Clark* (1935) 19 TC 390),

(ii) if the contract is not structural the compensation is likely to be income (*Kelsall Parsons* v *IRC* (1938) 21 TC 608).

The major problem is knowing when the contract is structural. There is no clear guidance in either the legislation or case law on this.

10.3.5 Trading stock, work in progress

10.3.5.1 General In order to ascertain the profits of a period (otherwise than on a cash basis) stock must be included if the figure computed is to approach the true profit or gain of the period. The cost of goods sold (including those in possession at the beginning of the period) must be included in the computation and the cost of goods unsold must be written out of the accounts so that the costs are allocated to the appropriate period. It is important that the receipts and expenses be allocated to the appropriate period of account as income tax is an annual tax and is charged on the full profits of the year in question. Hence the many cases after the First World War about the allocation of stock for Excess Profits Duty since the year of allocation could drastically affect the tax bill.

Generally accountants as a matter of prudence do not allow profits to be anticipated but do allow provision to be made for known or expected future losses (see, e.g., Lawson, *Accountancy for Solicitors*, Butterworths, p. 34). A fall in the realisable value of stock would be such a loss. This is normally taken into account by valuing the stock at the lower of cost or market value (see Lord President Clyde's 'two commonplaces' in *Whimster & Co.* v *IRC* (1925) 12 TC 813 at p. 823 and *IRC* v *Cock, Russell* (1949) 29 TC 387).

Lord Reid considered the use of lower of cost or market value was an exception to the 'cardinal principle' that profit should not be taxed until realised. 'It is no doubt good conservative accountancy but is quite illogical'.

Russell LJ (as he then was) explained his understanding of the practice of including stock in the profit and loss account in *BSC Footwear* v *Ridgway* (1971) 47 TC 495. He said (at p. 513):

> In my view the accepted practice of entering stock in hand at cost at the terminal date of the first period and the opening date of the second period arises from the fact that the expenditure has not contributed anything directly to the figures of gross profit in the first period. It is unused expenditure, to be carried forward into the second period, in which it is estimated that it will contribute on sale to the gross profit of that period. But if it is estimated that on sale it will not contribute to the gross profit of the second period – that is, if it is estimated that it will sell below cost – the shortfall is to be regarded in the course of stock valuation as irrecoverable and may properly be treated as a loss incurred in the first period. This I believe to be the basis of the principle that for tax purposes market value if below cost may be taken as the value of stock in hand. The principle relates to loss of all gross profit and more, and not to diminution.
>
> The Crown's figures of valuation are based upon the taxpayers' estimate of retail selling prices in due course: but they allow a deduction for salesman's commission. This, it is suggested by the taxpayers, reveals a fallacy in the Crown's approach, for, they say, all kinds of overheads will be involved in producing these sales, overheads that will be absorbed in the mark-up involved in the taxpayers' method of valuation. I do not myself think that this shows a fallacy. Granted that market value means that which

the stock is expected to produce at retail sale, it seems to me logical and reasonable to look for the money expected to reach the till as a result of sales: in effect, the salesman's commission does not reach the till, though in practice he does not abstract it from money handed over the counter and pocket it before paying the balance into the till.[7]

In arriving at a figure for closing stock value does the trader use cost to him or market value? In *IRC v Cock, Russell* (1949) 29 TC 387 the courts sanctioned the rule that the taxpayer may use the lower of cost or market value. The trader may thus, in drawing up his 1996 accounts, choose either cost price for closing stock or market value whichever is lower. He may make this choice item by item (he may 'pick and choose'). This permits him in effect to lower his profits. The figure entered into account for a particular item of trading stock at closing becomes next year's opening stock figure. Since trading stock is added in as a trading receipt it operates to alter profits (i.e., the lower the trading stock figure, the lower the profits).

Examples
G sells tapes.
Year 1   he buys 10,000 @ £1
          he sells 5,000 @ £2

Accounts
Sales 5,000 @ £2   10,000
and value closing stock (5,000 @ £1)   5,000
                                                           15,000
less expenditure 10,000 @ £1   10,000
                                                           £5,000

What if market value of tapes is 50p each at the end of the accounting period?

Substitute market value for cost
Sales 5,000 @ £2   10,000
and value closing stock (5,000 @ 50p)   2,500
                                                           12,500
less expenditure   10,000
                                                           £2,500

What if the trader is an artisan engaged in work on, say, a hand crafted table at the end of the accounting year? Is that by analogy with the trading stock rules, to be brought into account? The answer to this is 'yes' as it is clearly caught by the definition of 'trading stock' in s. 100(2), TA.

10.3.5.2 How is the 'market value' to be determined? This is clearly awkward and practice varies from trade to trade. Broadly speaking the market

---
[7.] Note the relevance of trading stock in valuing accounts on earnings basis.

value of the work in progress at the end of the year is found by adding up the direct costs (i.e., materials and labour) and adding a suitable proportion of overheads (e.g., electricity). This method is referred to as the 'on cost' method of valuing work in progress. The taxpayer may, however, merely use the 'direct costs' method leaving overheads out of account in an appropriate case (see *Duple Motor Bodies* v *Ostime* (1961) 39 TC 537).

It should be noted that:

(a) the higher the figure for work in progress, the higher the taxpayer's profits for the year since it is entered into earnings basis accounts as a trading receipt just like trading stock at closing;

(b) on a discontinuance of the trade, profession or vocation the valuation of work in progress is subject to special rules contained in ss. 100–102, TA.

Further example – inclusion of stock in trader's accounts
(Current prices are assumed in this example.)

A is a trader who makes up his accounts on an earnings basis. In the year in question he had stock at the beginning of the year left over from the previous year of £10,000 ('Opening Stock'). He bought £12,000 of stock during the year. He had £2,000 of stock left at the end of the year ('Closing Stock'). His receipts from sales were £40,000, his wage costs etc. were £10,000 and his other overheads and expenses etc. were £8,000.

His trading and profit and loss account on a simplified basis for the period would look as follows.

	£		£
Opening Stock	10,000	Sales	40,000
Purchases	12,000		
	22,000		
Less Closing Stock	2,000		
Cost of Sales in the year			20,000
Gross Profit			20,000
Gross Profit c/d			20,000
Wages	10,000		
Other overheads	8,000		
			18,000
Net Profit for year			2,000

In this computation the cost of purchasing stock in earlier years is taken into account in the year of sale as opening stock. The cost of purchases is also included. However, the costs of goods unsold at the end of the year are taken out of the computation for this year since these are costs which are properly referable to future sales. This is done by deducting closing stock so as to arrive at the cost of sales during the year. If this were not done there would be no profit in the year in question (since net profit and closing stock are equal) because costs had been attributed to the wrong period. The following year's accounts would also be distorted. The closing stock figure of one year becomes the opening stock figure of the following year. This system works well enough during times of constant prices but can cause great difficulties and inequities in times of fluctuating prices.

10.3.6 Excursus – what is stock?

Stock is often equated with circulating capital (cf. Adam Smith). The following extract from Romer LJ's judgment in *Golden Horse Shoe (New) Ltd v Thurgood* 18 TC 280 at p. 300 may help to explain this.

> The reason for this distinction being drawn between fixed and floating or circulating capital is not far to seek. In assessing a trader to Income Tax under Schedule D, Case I, the Revenue authorities are only concerned with his annual gains and profits; that is, gains and profits in the year of assessment, or whatever may be the other material interval of time. They are not in the least concerned with his financial position at the end of that time, as compared with his financial position at the beginning. Changes in the value of his fixed capital are therefore disregarded except where it is otherwise expressly provided in the Act. On the other hand, changes in his floating or circulating capital must be taken into consideration in ascertaining his annual gains and profits. For the profits or losses in a year of trading cannot be ascertained unless a comparison be made of the circulating capital as it existed at the beginning of the year with the circulating capital as it exists at the end of the year. It is, indeed, by causing the floating capital to change in value that a loss or profit is made.
>
> Unfortunately, however, it is not always easy to determine whether a particular asset belongs to the one category or the other. It depends in no way upon what may be the nature of the asset in fact or in law. Land may in certain circumstances be circulating capital. A chattel or a chose in action may be fixed capital. The determining factor must be the nature of the trade in which the asset is employed. The land upon which a manufacturer carries on his business is part of his fixed capital. The land with which a dealer in real estate carries on his business is part of his circulating capital. The machinery with which a manufacturer makes the articles that he sells is part of his fixed capital. The machinery that a dealer in machinery buys and sells is part of his circulating capital, as is the coal that a coal merchant buys and sells in the course of his trade. So, too, is the coal that a manufacturer of gas buys and from which he extracts his gas. For the purpose of ascertaining his profit in a year, it is clear that he must debit his profit and loss account with the purchase price of the coal that he treats in the course of that year, and that, too, whether he buys it

in that year or buys it in advance. It is part of the cost of producing the gas that he sells. Such cases as these cause no difficulty. But now suppose that the gas manufacturer, instead of buying his coal from outside sources, purchases a coal mine and produces the coal that he requires by mining. The cost of extracting from the mine the coal treated will, of course, be a permissible deduction in ascertaining the profits of his business in the year. But he may not debit his profit and loss account with the sum by which the value of his mine has depreciated in consequence of the extraction of that coal, for the mine is regarded as being fixed capital – see *Coltness Iron Company* v *Black* 1 TC 287, and *Alianza Company* v *Bell* [1904] 2 KB 666; [1905] 1 KB 184. If, on the other hand, instead of buying the mine, the gas manufacturer had bought a quantity of coal already extracted from the mine and stacked on the surface, the price of the coal would have been regarded as part of the circulating capital. The reason for this distinction is not, at first sight, very easy to discover. It must, as it seems to me, be found in this: that, in the former case, the purchase of the mine is not a purchase of coal but a purchase of land with the right of extracting coal from it. The land is regarded merely as one of the means provided by the manufacturer for causing coal to be brought to his gasworks, and, therefore, as much part of his fixed capital as would be any railway trucks or lorries provided by him for the same purpose. The land is regarded as a capital of the same nature as the coal contracts that were held to be fixed capital in *Smith* v *Moore* [1921] 2 AC 13. In that case, Lord Sumner said: 'The business carried on was not that of buying and selling contracts, but of buying and selling coals, and the contracts, which enabled the seller of the coals to acquire the coals were no more the subject of his trading as a stock in trade, for sale than a lease of a brickfield would be the subject of a sale of bricks.

10.3.7 Unclaimed deposits and released debts

An unclaimed deposit can be a sum of money which a purchaser of goods has placed with the trader which is forfeited because the purchaser never completes the purchase. The legal analysis of the payment is important in determining the amount and timing of the trader's tax liability. When does the taxpayer become entitled to what?

Elson v *Price's Tailors* (1962) 40 TC 671 concerned a payment as an 'earnest of performance'. This was held to be a trading receipt in the year of payment. The company carried on business as tailors. Customers paid 'deposits' when ordering garments. In some cases the garments were not collected. The question at issue was whether the unclaimed deposits were taxable as trade receipts. The Special Commissioners' decision was that the unclaimed deposits were not taxable but this was reversed on appeal. Ungoed Thomas J considered that the 'deposit' was a true deposit in the sense of a security for the completion of the purchase and so taxable as a trading receipt.

However, if the deposit has a different function so that it does not belong to the trader when it is received, e.g., deposits taken by auctioneers (which are their clients' income), then if it is forfeited because it is unclaimed it does not thereby become a trading receipt: *Morley* v *Tattersall* (1938) 22 TC 51 (thus it escapes tax). In that case, Messrs Tattersall were a firm of auctioneers dealing mainly with racehorses. No money was, under the conditions of sale, to be paid or remittance sent by post without a written order. Some vendors neglected to send such an order and the money remained in Tattersall's hands to the credit of the vendors as 'unclaimed balances', which the firm regarded itself as liable to pay when claimed. Balances not claimed within six years were credited to the partners. The Crown sought to assess these unclaimed balances as trading receipts. The Special Commissioners discharged the assessments. Lawrence J found in favour of the Crown but was reversed by the Court of Appeal.

Greene MR (with whom Scott and Clausen LJJ agreed) said:

What was distributed to the partners was not an asset item, but a liability item. As I have pointed out, this liability was cut down by a certain sum. That sum was then used to feed the partners' account, but it was a liability, not an asset; it is on the left-hand side of the balance sheet, not on the right, and there was no dealing with any balance in the sense of an asset at all. It seems to me quite impossible, with the greatest deference to the learned Judge's view, to treat that accountancy transaction *inter socios*, by which they effected the re-arrangement of the liabilities side of their balance sheet, as a distribution of trading profits. It was not.

Now the learned Judge further treated the liability as a merely contingent liability which could be disregarded. I have difficulty in accepting that view, at any rate in the sense in which the learned Judge appears to have used it. This money, of course – using a colloquial and business expression rather than a legal expression – was never Messrs Tattersall's money; it was the customer's money; it remains the customer's money; the customer can call for it at any moment, and the fact that a demand in writing has to be made before a liability to pay accrues, so as to make the Statute of Limitations run, does not make the liability a mere contingent liability in the sense in which the learned Judge appears to regard it. It is an existing liability which can only be enforced when the creditor has made a demand. But treating it as a contingent liability, he says: here is a receipt – receipt, be it observed, at the date of the alteration in the accounts, not at the date when the money was originally received, but a receipt at that date – with (tied to it, so to speak) a mere contingent liability which may never become effective, and, for Income Tax purposes that contingent liability can be disregarded.

Another case, *Jay's The Jewellers Ltd* v *IRC* (1947) 29 TC 274 concerned pawnbrokers. If the pledgee did not demand the excess, the question was whether the pawnbroker was taxable on it. If a pledge was sold the surplus over the amount due to the pawnbroker could be demanded by the pledgee within three years. The Special Commissioners found that the pawnbroker obtained an absolute right in the property on the failure of the pledgee to make a demand in time which became a taxable receipt at the time.

On appeal, Atkinson J said:

Now I cannot see any principle on which the Crown can claim that surpluses are trade receipts in the year in which they come into existence. The position can be tested thus . . . you must look each sum as it comes in. Supposing there was only one sale, which produced a surplus of £x, can the Crown say: 'You must treat that as your own money, as a trade receipt augmenting your taxable profit'? Surely the pawnbroker could say: 'But it is not mine. I owe that money to my client. He may come to me for it at any date'. I think the answer to the Crown's appeal is that these surpluses are not trading receipts in the year in which they are received. I think that the case is completely governed on this point by *Tattersalls'* case . . . As a matter of law, these monies when received were not their monies at all; they belonged to their clients, and if a client came in the next day and demanded his money they would have to pay it away.

I think the Commissioners were right in holding that these sums could not be deemed to be trade receipts of the year in which they were received. Therefore the Crown's appeal fails. Then comes the more difficult question: Can a surplus be treated as a trade receipt of the year in which, it not having been claimed by the pledger, the pawnbroker becomes entitled to retain it as his own? . . . What the partners did in this case, as I have said, was to decide among themselves that what they had previously regarded as a liability of the firm they would not, for practical reasons, regard as a liability: but that does not mean that at that moment they received something, nor does it mean that at that moment they imprinted upon some existing asset a quality different from what it had possessed before. I have already indeed held that these sums cannot be regarded as trade receipts, and if that be right, if follows that it is unsound to regard all that follows as merely the elimination from the liabilities side of the balance sheet of a liability to clients. The true accountancy view would, I think, demand that these sums should be treated as paid into a suspense account, and should so appear in the balance sheet. The surpluses should not be brought into the annual trading account as a receipt at the time they are received. Only time will show what their ultimate fate and character will be. After three years that fate is such, as to one class of surplus, that in so far as the suspense account has not been reduced by payments to clients, that part of it which is remaining becomes by operation of law a receipt of the Company, and ought to be transferred from the suspense account and appear in the profit and loss account for that year as a receipt and profit. That is what it in fact is. In that year Jays become the richer by the amount which automatically becomes theirs, and that asset arises out of an ordinary trade transaction. It seems to me to be the commonsense way of dealing with these matters, and it is the way in which the Special Commissioners have dealt with them. But it is argued that I cannot give effect to that view because of *Tattersalls'* case. . . . But here the position is quite different. Here, at the end of three years, the money in question, the three-years-old surplus, did attain a totally different quality; a different quality was imprinted on surpluses three years old. I think there was then a definite trade receipt. At the end of the three years a new asset came into existence, an asset which had arisen out of a trade transaction, and it seems to me that what the Master of the Rolls was dealing with in that case was a situation quite different from that which exists here.

10.3.8 Know-how payments

Know-how is a peculiar item.[8] It covers matters such as methods of manufacturing particular goods. Sections 531 and 533, TA provide two rules for its tax treatment upon a sale.

(a) where know-how is sold alone, s. 531(1) treats the receipt as a trading receipt;
(b) where know-how is sold together with a business, s. 531(3) treats the receipt as a capital receipt.

This 'clarifies' the decisions in *Moriarty* v *Evans Medica* (1957) 37 TC 540 and *Rolls Royce* v *Jeffrey* (1962) 40 TC 443.

10.3.9 Transfer pricing – s. 770

These provisions apply particularly to trading companies. It is possible to manufacture a trading loss by selling stock in trade to, say, a connected company which, when it sells the stock, will make a non-taxable profit (because, for example, it is non-resident). This dodge is struck at by s. 770 which provides that market value is to be substituted for actual sale price in certain circumstances.

Example
Company A sells stock in trade to company B.
Company A is UK resident.
Company B is not and is not within the charge to UK tax (and therefore it is not taxed under Schedule D).
If the stock cost £250,000 and is sold to Company B for £100,000 at a time when market value is £500,000 then (in the absence of s. 770, TA) Company A can claim a loss of purchase price *less* sale price i.e., £250,000 – £100,000 = £150,000. And Company B can sell for £500,000 and make a £400,000 profit tax free.

Section 770, TA requires that the sale by A to B be treated as at market value, i.e., producing a profit of £250,000. A will be taxed on that profit. Section 770 applies to all sales between associated bodies of persons (see s. 770(1)). If the 'bodies' are unconnected the section will not apply. Section 770 can operate harshly. Therefore a recent EC convention on transfer pricing was agreed to mitigate the consequences in certain circumstances.

[8.] See Shipwright and Price, *Intellectual Property and UK Tax*, 2nd edn, Sweet & Maxwell, 1996.

10.3.10 Post cessation receipts – ss. 103–110

On general principles, the permanent discontinuance of a business ends the 'source' from which taxable receipts arise, so that any sums received after the cessation of business are tax-free: see *Carson* v *Cheyney's Executor* (1958) 38 TC 240. In *Rankine* v *IRC* (1952) 32 TC 520, the taxpayers were civil engineers who were assessed on a cash basis. Their business was discontinued. They subsequently received money earned before the discontinuance, and the Inland Revenue raised a further assessment to income tax on the earnings basis. The Court of Session held that these post-cessation receipts could not be assessed since the profits of the taxpayers before discontinuance had already been assessed and the assessment could not be disturbed by altering the basis of assessment from cash to earnings. Perhaps not surprisingly, this general rule has been subject to statutory modification by ss. 103 and 104, TA. These provisions apply where a trade, profession or vocation is permanently discontinued, but this can include, by virtue of s. 110(2), any event treated as a discontinuance under s. 113.

Where accounts have been drawn up on an earnings basis (see para. 10.2.2), any sums received after the discontinuance which were not included in the accounts before the discontinuance are chargeable under s. 103, and such sums are deemed to include the release or payment of bad or doubtful debts after the discontinuance for which relief under s. 74(j) had been given before it (see para. 10.6.11 and cf. s. 94 and s. 103(4) and (5)).

Where accounts have been drawn up on a conventional (meaning bills delivered or cash) basis (see paras 10.2.3 and 10.2.4), any sums received after the discontinuance which were not included in the accounts before it, and which would not have been included even if the accounts were drawn up on an earnings basis because they were not due or ascertained before then, are also chargeable under s. 103. Three types of sums are excluded from s. 103 by subsection (3):

(a) sums received by a person not resident in the United Kingdom in respect of income arising abroad;

(b) lump sums paid to an author's personal representatives for the assignment in whole or in part by them of the copyright in a literary, dramatic, musical or artistic work;

(c) sums realised by the transfer of trading stock or work-in-progress at the time of discontinuance.

Further, if accounts are prepared on a conventional basis and s. 103 does not apply or would have applied but for exceptions (a) and (b) above, then s. 104 applies a charge to sums received after the discontinuance in respect of which no entry appeared in the accounts before the discontinuance, and sums received for work-in-progress are included. Thus the taxpayers in *Rankine* v *IRC* would now be liable under s. 104. Any expenses, losses or capital allowances for which relief has not been given which would have been deductible had the business not ceased, are deductible from chargeable post-cessation receipts (s. 105).

Since a charge under ss. 103 and 104 depends upon receipt of a chargeable sum, tax could be avoided by selling the right to receive sums after discontinuance to a third party. However, such transactions are frustrated by s. 106 which treats the consideration for the transfer (or the market value of the right in the case of a transfer not at arm's length) as a post-cessation receipt to which ss. 103 and 104 apply.

The charge on post-cessation receipts is made under Case VI of Schedule D (ss. 103(1) and 104(1)), and they are treated as received at the time of actual receipt. However, if a sum is received in a year of assessment beginning within six years of the discontinuance, the taxpayer may elect within two years of the end of the year of assessment in which the sum is received to have the sum treated as though it had been received on the day of discontinuance (s. 108); he will then be taxed by reference to his tax position at the time of discontinuance rather than the time of actual receipt.

10.3.11 Fluctuating profits

Taxpayers who carry on the trades of farming or market gardening are subject to the vagaries of the weather and other seasonal factors, and so their profits may fluctuate markedly from year to year. To help them over this problem, s. 96 allows the profits for two consecutive years of assessment to be averaged out (s. 96(1)). Profits for this purpose means profits before loss relief or stock relief (s. 96(7)).

There are three major restrictions on the availability of this relief:

(a) The profits for one year must not exceed 70% of the profits for the other (s. 96(2)); thus, to take an extreme example, if the profits for one year are £200 and for the next year £17,000, the profits for each year will be averaged to give £8,600; if the profits for one year are more than 70% but less than 75% of the profits for the other year, the averaging process does not take place: instead one finds the difference between three times the excess of higher profits over lower profits and 75% of the higher profits, and deducts this amount from the higher profits and adds it to the lower (s. 96(3)). For example, if the profits of one year are £7,200 and of the next year are £10,000 (so that the total is the same as before), the excess of profits is £2,800 which, multiplied by three (£8,400) less 75% of £10,000 (£7,500), gives a figure of £900; the profits for each year are then adjusted by adding £900 to the first year's profits (£8,100) and deducting £900 from the second year's profits (£9,100).

(b) Once a claim has been made for a year of assessment, no claim may then be made in respect of an earlier year of assessment (s. 96(4)(a)).

(c) No claim may be made in respect of a year of assessment in which the trade is set up and commenced or permanently discontinued or is treated as such by s. 113(1): s. 96(4)(b). It is submitted that a claim for the second year of assessment (or penultimate year) is not precluded by this provision even though it will involve averaging the profits of that year with those of the year of commencement (or discontinuance). The claim for relief under the section is made in respect of the second (or penultimate) year and not in respect of the opening (or closing) year. If a claim is made for three successive years, the profits of the second year for the purposes of averaging them with those of the third year are the profits as reduced or increased by averaging with the first year (s. 96(5)).

It should be mentioned here that if a taxpayer sustains a loss in an accounting period, the assessment on him for the year of assessment for which those accounts form the basis period in accordance with ss. 60 to 63 will be nil. If he is entitled to claim loss relief (see Chapter 11) in respect of other accounting periods the assessment will be reduced by the loss relief.

10.4 THE RULE IN *SHARKEY* v *WERNHER*

10.4.1 General

The theory of the 'Just Price' went out of fashion in mediaeval times. Thus traders are not usually obliged to sell at the best or most profitable price. Nothing even obliges them normally to break even. There are exceptions to this rule (one of which is s. 770 (see para. 10.3.9). The rule in *Sharkey* v *Wernher* (1955) 36 TC 275 may apply to reverse, for tax purposes, the presumption that a trader need not sell for a particular, or the best price, as when the rule applies its effect is to substitute market value.

In *Sharkey v Wernher* (1955) 36 TC 275 Lady Zia Wernher owned a stud farm which constituted a statutory trade of farming assessable under Schedule D, Case I. She also trained and raced horses as a purely recreational activity which was admitted not to be taxable. Lady Zia sometimes transferred horses (five in all) from her stud farm to her stables. The cost of breeding these horses had been debited in the stud farm accounts and it was common ground that some sum should be brought into the stud farm accounts in consequence of the transfer. The Special Commissioners decided that to bring into account the horses at market value would be to include a profit which had not been realised. They concluded the proper course was to bring into credit the relative figures of 'cost' so as to eliminate the costs of the horses charged therein – in effect a sort of 'contra' entry.

Vaisey J allowed the Crown's appeal. This was reversed by the Court of Appeal. The House of Lords (Lord Oaksey dissenting) allowed the Crown's appeal. Viscount Simonds said:

> . . . since it is the Respondent's case that Lady Zia did not dispose of the transferred horses in the way of trade, I do not understand why it is admitted that she should be credited as a receipt with the cost of production. In fact as a trader she received no more the cost of production than the market value: I do not understand, therefore, why the argument did not proceed that, as she received nothing, her trading account should be credited with nothing; that she suffered, so far as her trade was concerned, a dead loss in respect of these animals, and that the accounts

of the stud farm should be made up so as to show this like any other dead loss. I do not understand how the adjustment could take the form of the fictitious entry of a receipt which had not been received.

My Lords, I am more puzzled by the basis on which this case has proceeded because learned Counsel for the Respondent has throughout insisted on what is an elementary principle of Income Tax law that a man cannot be taxed on profits that he might have, but had not made: see, for example *Dublin Corporation* v *M'Adam* 2 TC 387; *Gresham Life Assurance Society* v *Styles* 3 TC 185. But this is only saying in another way that a trader is not to be charged with the receipt of sums that he might have, but has not, received, and this is equally true whether the sum with which it is sought to charge him is market value or production cost, whether it will result in notional profit or a notional balancing of receipts with expenditure and whether the reason for his not in fact receiving such a sum is that the goods which are his stock-in-trade have perished in the course of nature or that he has chosen to use them for his own pleasure or otherwise dispose of them. The true proposition is not that a man cannot make a profit of himself but that he cannot trade with himself. The question is whether and how far this general proposition must be qualified for the purposes of Income Tax law.

An attempt has been made to justify the notional receipt of a sum equal to the cost of production by treating such a receipt as the equivalent of an expenditure which in the event proved not to have been for the purpose of trade, since the article was not disposed of in the way of trade. But this is pure fiction. Up to the very moment of disposition, in this case the transfer of a horse from stud farm to racing stable, the article was part of the trader's stock-in-trade and the cost of its production was properly treated as part of his expenditure for Income Tax purposes. I see no justification for an ex post facto adjustment of account which in effect adds to a fictional receipt a false attribution of expenditure.

This is, however, the position with which we are faced. Your Lordships may not think it necessary to express any opinion on the question whether, if the Crown is not right in requiring market value to be brought into account in the present case, it is nevertheless entitled to require the cost of production to be brought in. This is said to be of no importance in this case, though it might well be of great importance in other cases. Yet I cannot refrain from calling attention to what must be fundamental to the solution of the question. For I cannot escape from the obvious fact that it must be determined whether and why a trader, who elects to throw his stock-in-trade into the sea or dispose of it in any other way than by way of sale in the course of trade, is chargeable with any notional receipt in respect of it, before it is asked with how much he should be charged.

It is, as I have said, a surprising thing that this question should remain in doubt. For unless, indeed, farming is a trade which in this respect differs from other trades, the same problem arises whether the owner of a stud farm diverts the produce of his farm to his own enjoyment or a diamond merchant, neglecting profitable sales, uses his choicest jewels for the adornment of his wife, or a caterer provides lavish entertainment for a daughter's wedding breakfast. Are the horses, the jewels, the cakes and ale to be treated for the purpose of Income Tax as disposed of for nothing or for their market value or for the cost of their production?

It is convenient at this stage to refer to *Watson Bros v Hornby* 24 TC 506 which I have already mentioned. In that case the taxpayers, who were the appellants in the appeal, carried on a business of poultry dealers and breeders of poultry at a hatchery belonging to them which was conceded to be an enterprise chargeable as a trade under Case I of Schedule D of the Income Tax Act, 1918. The business of the hatchery was to produce and sell day old chicks. They also carried on farming activities which were conceded to be for Income Tax purposes a separate enterprise from the hatchery business and, as the law then stood, were an Income Tax source chargeable under Schedule B of the Income Tax Act, 1918. Most of the produce of the hatchery was sold, but a substantial number of day-old chicks were from time to time transferred to the farm and became part of the stock of poultry of the farm. The question in the appeal was whether, in computing the profits of the hatchery business, the day-old chicks transferred to the farm should be brought in at cost or market value. The market value was at the material times much below cost, namely, 4d, as against 7d per chick. It was contended for the taxpayers that market price and for the Crown that cost of production should be adopted as the appropriate figure in the accounts. It was decided by Macnaghten J, that the taxpayers' contention was right, and they were accordingly chargeable upon the footing that as traders in respect of their hatchery business they received 4d only per chick. This decision, which your Lordships were told has ever since been adopted as the basis of assessment by the Revenue in similar cases, involves two things, first, that the taxpayer may in certain cases be subject to a sort of dichotomy for Income Tax purposes and be regarded as selling to himself in one capacity what he has produced in another, and, secondly, that he is regarded as selling what he sells at market price. It is a decision upon which the Appellant relies in the present case, and which, as I have said, Vaisey J regarded as an authority binding him . . .

My Lords, how far is this principle, which is implicit in the judgments that I have cited and in the admission upon which this case has proceeded, supportable in law? That it conflicts with the proposition, taken in its broadest sense, that a man cannot trade with himself is, I think, obvious. Yet it seems to me that it is a necessary qualification of the broad proposition. For if there are commodities which are the subject of a man's trade but may also be the subject of his use and enjoyment, I do not know how his account as a trader can properly be made up so as to ascertain his annual profits and gains unless his trading account is credited with a receipt in respect of those goods which he has diverted to his own use and enjoyment. I think, therefore, that the admission was rightly made that some sum must be brought into the stud farm account as a receipt though nothing was received and so far at least the taxpayer must be regarded as having traded with himself. But still the question remains, what is that sum to be. I suppose that in the generality of cases in which the question arises in a farming or any other business, for example, where the farmer supplies his own house with milk, or a market gardener with vegetables, an arbitrary or conventional sum is agreed. The House was not given any information as to the prevailing practice . . . I see no reason for ascribing to it any other sum than that which he would normally have received for it in the due course of trade, that is to say, the market value. As I have already indicated, there seems to me to be no justification for the only alternative that has been suggested, namely, the cost of production. The unreality of this alternative would be plain to the taxpayer, if, as well might happen, a very large service fee had been paid so that the cost of production was high and the market value did not equal it.

Lord Radcliffe said:

. . . To begin with, I am not prepared to forget that the code already achieves this fictitious separation in various ways. The owner-occupier of business premises charges against his trade receipts the annual value of those premises for the purposes of his Case I, Schedule D assessment (Income Tax Act, 1918, Rules applicable to Cases I and II of Schedule D, Rule 5). No money passes, but he is treated as his own lessor. The non-resident producer or manufacturer, who is liable to tax because he markets in the United Kingdom is entitled to have his assessment based on merchanting profit only (Income Tax Act, 1918, General Rules, Rule 12). For the purposes of assessment he is treated as if he, as producer or manufacturer, had sold to himself as merchant or retailer, and had made the sale on trade terms. The provisions which are contained in treaties for relief against double taxation habitually set up a system under which the profits made by the producer or manufacturer of the one country but sold through a 'permanent establishment' of his in another are divided between the two taxing jurisdictions on the basis of a similar fictitious division of the taxpayer's personality and a similar fictitious trading with himself. My Lords, it may be objected that these situations are all provided for and regulated by statutory enactment, that these indeed are planned departures from what would otherwise be the general rule, and that it is just because there is no provision which deals with the present type of case that our decision should be for the Respondent. I do not see great force in this. The statutory enactments have, of course, settled the matter wherever they operate by providing definite rules for their particular occasions: but what we are looking for is some principle to determine the Respondent's assessability to taxation, and I think it is a wrong sort of approach to look for principles in judicial decisions only and to treat the whole Income Tax code as if it made law but could not itself contain principle. But, apart from that, it seems to me that we are dealing with a problem that must have arisen in hundreds of thousands of cases under various forms, and I think that there are traces that the Courts have not found this general proposition that a man cannot trade with himself or make profit out of himself a satisfactory guide for all purposes.

To begin with, there is *Watson Bros v Hornby* 24 TC 506, which explicitly decided that it may be necessary, for a proper assessment of trade profits under Case I of Schedule D, to treat a man who supplies himself in his trade as trading with himself on ordinary commercial terms. The decision was given in 1942: it laid down a principle that must continually affect a great many taxpayers: and only now is it said that the case was wrongly decided.

My Lords, with these considerations in mind, I must now say what I believe to be the right way to deal with the present case. When a horse is transferred from the stud farm to the owner's personal account, there is a disposition of trading stock. I do not say that the disposition is made by way of trade, for that is a play on words which may beg the question. At least three methods have been suggested for recording the result in the stud farm's trading accounts. There might be others. Your Lordships must choose between them.

First, there might be no entry of a receipt at all. This method had behind it the logic that nothing in fact is received in consideration of the transfer, and there is no general principle of taxation that assessed a person on the basis of business profits that he might have made but has not chosen to make. Theoretically, a trader can destroy or let waste or give away his stock. I do not notice that he does so in practice, except in special situations that we need not consider. On the other hand, it was not argued before us by the Respondent that this method would be the right one to apply: and a tax system which allows business losses to be set off against taxable income from other sources is in my opinion bound to reject such a method because of the absurd anomalies that it would produce as between one taxpayer and another. It would give the self-supplier a quite unfair tax advantage.

Secondly, the figure brought in as a receipt might be cost. That is what the Respondent contends for. It is not altogether clear what is to be the basis of such an entry. No sale in a legal sense has taken place nor has there been any actual receipt: the cost basis, therefore, treats the matter as though there had been some sort of deal between the taxpayer and himself but maintains that in principle he can only break even on such a deal. I do not understand why, if he can be supposed to deal at all, he must necessarily deal on such self-denying terms. But then the Respondent argues that the cost figure entered as receipt is to be understood as a mere cancellation of the cost incurred to date. The item of stock transferred to the owner's private account is shown by that very event to have been 'withdrawn' from the trade and the only practical course is to write out of the trader's accounts the whole of the cost *bona fide*, but mistakenly, entered in respect of it. I think this a very attractive argument, but its weakness is that it does not explain why such cancellation should take place. This is not put to us as a case in which, there being no market, cost is the best available estimate of value. The fact that an item of stock is disposed of not by way of sale does not mean that it was any the less part of the trading stock at the moment of disposal. On the contrary, it was part of the stock of the venture at every moment up till then and whatever was spent upon it was rightly entered as a part of the costs and expenses of the trade. Its disposal does not alter that situation. The trade of which the receipts and expenses are in question is the whole activity of farming and the disposal of the produce is only one, though a very important incident of that activity. I think it a fallacy, therefore, to suppose that the method of disposal can give any warrant for treating costs hitherto properly charged to the trade as if, ex post facto, they never ought to have been charged at all. Yet, if a cancelling entry is not to be made there must either be a figure entered as a receipt which, admittedly, does not represent any actual legal transaction or the costs incurred up to the date of disposal must remain on the books to create or contribute to a 'loss' of income which common sense suggests to be a fiction.

In a situation where everything is to some extent fictitious, I think that we should prefer the third alternative of entering as a receipt a figure equivalent to the current realisable value of the stock item transferred. In other words, I think that *Watson Bros* v *Hornby* was rightly decided and that its principle is applicable to all those cases in which the Income Tax system requires that part of a taxpayer's activities should be isolated and treated as a self-contained trade. The realisable value figure is neither more nor less 'real' than the cost figure, and in my opinion it is to be preferred for two reasons. First, it gives a fairer measure of assessable trading profit as between one taxpayer and another, for it eliminates variations which are due to no other cause than any one taxpayer's decision as to what proportion of his total product he will supply to himself. A formula which achieves this makes for a more equitable distribution of the burden of tax, and is to be preferred on that account. Secondly, it seems to me better economics to credit the trading owner with the current realisable value of any stock which he has chosen to dispose of without commercial disposal than to credit him with an amount equivalent to the accumulated expenses in respect of that stock. In that sense, the trader's choice is itself the receipt in that he appropriates value to himself or his donee direct, instead of adopting the alternative method of a commercial sale and subsequent appropriation of the proceeds.

Lord Porter agreed with the opinions of both Viscount Simonds and Lord Radcliffe. Lord Tucker agreed with the reasoning of Lord Radcliffe. Lord Oaksey dissented.

10.4.2 Exceptions

There are two particular exceptions to the rule in *Sharkey* v *Wernher*. These are:

(a) if a disposal at an undervalue can be justified commercially (so that the transaction *is* a genuine commercial one) then *Sharkey* v *Wernher* does not apply (see *Jacgilden (Weston Hall) Ltd* v *Castle* [1969] 3 All ER 1110);

(b) the rule has no application to professions, see *Mason* v *Innes* (1967) 44 TC 326 below;

It should be noted that:

(a) *Sharkey* v *Wernher* is an exception to the rule that what is taxed is what is received or earned, not what might have been received or earned;
(b) the cash basis is however not conclusive of the non-applicability of the *Sharkey* v *Wernher* principle. (The reader should compare the reasoning in *Mason* v *Innes* below.)

In *Mason* v *Innes* Ralph Hammond Innes the author gave the rights in a book of his subsequently to be published and called *The Doomed Oasis* to his father. The market value of the rights at the time of disposal was £15,425. His accounts were prepared on a cash basis. The Special Commissioners discharged the assessment levied on the basis of *Sharkey* v *Wernher*. Goff J found against the Crown as did the Court of Appeal. Lord Denning MR said:

> I start with the elementary principle of income tax law that a man cannot be taxed on profits that he might have, but has not, made: *Sharkey* v *Wernher* [1956] AC 58. At first sight that elementary principle seems to cover this case. Mr Hammond Innes did not receive anything from 'The Doomed Oasis'. But in the case of a trader there is an exception to that principle. I take for simplicity the trade of a grocer. He makes out his accounts on an 'earnings basis'. He brings in the value of his stock-in-trade at the beginning and end of the year: he brings in his purchases and sales; the debts owed by him and to him; and so arrives at his profit or loss. If such a trader appropriates to himself part of his stock-in-trade, such as tins of beans, and uses them for his own purposes, he must bring them into his accounts at their market value. That is established by *Sharkey* v *Wernher* itself. Now, suppose that such a trader does not supply himself with tins of beans, but gives them away to a friend or relative. Again he has to bring them in at their market value. That was established by *Petrotim Securities Ltd* v *Ayres* [(1963)] 41 TC 389 . . . the Crown contends that that exception is not confined to traders.
>
> I cannot accept [the] proposition. Suppose an artist paints a picture of his mother and gives it to her. He does not receive a penny for it. Is he liable to pay tax on the value of it? It is unthinkable. Suppose he paints a picture which he does not like when he has finished it and destroys it. Is he liable to pay tax on the value of it? Clearly not. These instances – and they could be extended endlessly – show that the proposition in *Sharkey* v *Wernher* does not apply to professional men. It is confined to the case of traders who keep stock-in-trade and whose accounts are, or should be, kept on an earnings basis whereas a professional man comes within the general principle that when something is received there is nothing to be brought into account.

Davies and Russell LJJ delivered judgments in favour of dismissing the appeal.

10.5 DEDUCTIONS

10.5.1 Introduction

In order to arrive at the annual profits or gains, the cost of earning the sales etc. has to be taken into account by deducting them from sales etc. Broadly to be deductible the item:

(a) must be of an income nature; and
(b) must not be disallowed by statute.

The authority for deduction of expenditure is not entirely clear. Section 817, TA provides inter alia that 'In arriving at the amounts of profits or gains for tax purposes . . . no other deductions shall be made than such as are expressly enumerated in the Tax Acts . . .'

Lord Sumner said in *Usher's Wiltshire Brewer Ltd* v *Bruce* [1915] AC 433 at p. 436, 'The paradox of it is that there are no allowable deductions expressly enumerated at all, and there is in words no deduction at all unless indirectly.'

Some allowable deductions have been introduced since he spoke and the Tax Acts do contain certain prohibitions on certain deductions. The courts have decided that by necessary implication the 'disallowance section' (s. 74, TA, and see para. 10.5.2) allows items not within this disallowance to be allowed if they are of a revenue nature and in general terms of a type allowed in ordinary commercial accounting.

Jenkins LJ in *Morgan* v *Tate & Lyle* (1954) 35 TC 367 at pp. 393-4 said:

The curiously negative structure of these provisions, or their predecessors, has been the subject of much comment. Section 209 (1)(a) [now s. 817] enjoins that in arriving at the amounts of profits or gains for the purpose of Income Tax no other deductions shall be made than such as are expressly enumerated in the Act. But turning to the Rules applicable to Cases I and II of Schedule D one finds in Rule 3, instead of an enumeration of permitted deductions, an enumeration of items the deduction of which is prohibited with certain exceptions from or qualifications of those prohibitions. Thus Rule 3(a) does not provide that money wholly and exclusively laid out or expended for the purposes of the trade may be deducted, but that no sum shall be deducted in respect of any disbursements or expenses not being money wholly and exclusively laid out or expended for the purposes of the trade. It is, however, obvious that if no deduction at all of expenses from gross receipts was allowed, it would be impossible to arrive at the balance of the profits and gains of a trade upon which tax under Case I of Schedule D is to be assessed. Accordingly, it has long been well settled that the effect of these provisions as to deductions is that the balance of the profits and gains of a trade must be ascertained in accordance with the ordinary principles of commercial trading, by deducting from the gross receipts all expenditure properly deductible from them on those principles, save in so far as any amount so deducted falls within any of the statutory prohibitions contained in the relevant Rules, in which case it must be added back for the purpose of arriving at the balance of profits and gains assessable to tax. (See *Usher's Wiltshire Brewer Ltd v Bruce* (1915) 6 TC 399, *per* Lord Loreburn at p. 419, Lord Parker of Waddington at p. 429, Lord Sumner at pp. 435–6, and Lord Parmoor at p. 440.)

10.5.2 Section 74

Section 74 provides as follows:

General rules as to deductions not allowable
Subject to the provisions of the Tax Acts, in computing the amount of the profits or gains to be charged under Case I or Case II of Schedule D, no sum shall be deducted in respect of

(a) any disbursements or expenses, not being money wholly and exclusively laid out or expended for the purposes of the trade, profession or vocation,

(b) any disbursement or expenses of maintenance of the parties, their families or establishments, or any sums expended for any other domestic or private purposes distinct from the purposes of the trade, profession or vocation,

(c) the rent of any dwelling-house or domestic offices or any part thereof, except such part thereof as is used for the purposes of the trade, profession or vocation, and where any such part is so used, the sum so deducted shall not, unless in any particular case it appears that having regard to all the circumstances some greater sum ought to be deducted, exceed two-thirds of the rent *bona fide* paid for the said dwelling-house or offices,

(d) any sum expended for repairs of premises occupied, or for the supply, repairs or alterations for any implements, utensils or articles employed, for the purposes of the trade, profession or vocation, beyond the sum actually expended for those purposes,

(e) any loss not connected with or arising out of the trade, profession or vocation,

(f) any capital withdrawn from, or any sum employed or intended to be employed as capital in, the trade, profession or vocation, but so that this paragraph shall not be treated as disallowing the deduction of any interest,

(g) any capital employed in improvements or premises occupied for the purposes of the trade, profession or vocation,

(h) any interest which might have been made if any such sums as aforesaid had been laid out at interest,

(j) any debts except

(i) a bad debt;
(ii) a debt or part of a debt released by the creditor wholly and exclusively for the purposes of his trade, profession or vocation as part of a relevant arrangement or compromise; and
(iii) a doubtful debt to the extent estimated to be bad, meaning, in the case of the bankruptcy or insolvency of the debtor, the debt except to the extent that any amount may reasonably be expected to be received on the debt;

(k) any average loss beyond the actual amount of loss after adjustment,
(l) any sum recoverable under an insurance or contract of indemnity,
(m) any annuity or other annual payment (other than interest) payable out of the profits or gains,
(n) any interest paid to a person not resident in the United Kingdom if and so far as it is interest at more than a reasonable commercial rate,
(o) any interest in so far as the payment of interest is or would be, otherwise than by virtue of section 375(2), either

(i) a payment of interest to which section 369 applies, or
(ii) a payment of interest to which that section would apply but for section 373(5);

(p) any royalty or other sum paid in respect of the user of a patent, or
(q) any rent, royalty or other payment which is, by section 120, declared to be subject to deduction of tax under section 348 or 349 as if it were a royalty or other sum paid in respect of the user of a patent.

10.5.3 General or specific?

In dealing with specific items of expenditure s. 74 lists some items, other items may be deductible because incurred wholly and exclusively 'for the purposes of trade'.

10.5.4 General conditions and s. 74

The relevant conditions of deductibility are:

(a) the expense must be incurred for business purposes, i.e., it must not be 'too remote';
(b) the expense must be incurred only for business purposes. This is sometimes called the duality or exclusivity rule (see *Sargent v Eayrs* [1973] STC 50 and para. 10.5.6);
(c) the expense must be incurred to earn a profit or facilitate earning of profits (*Strong v Woodifield* (1906) 5 TC 215);
(d) the expense must be of an income nature not capital (see *Law Shipping v IRC* in para. 10.5.8.2);
(e) the expense must not be disallowed by ss. 74, 577 or 577A.

10.5.5 The remoteness test

This test was thoroughly explored in *Morgan* v *Tate and Lyle* (1954) 35 TC 367. Tate and Lyle spent considerable sums on propaganda against what was believed to be the imminent nationalisation of the sugar industry. The question in the case was, was the expenditure deductible? It was held, by the Court of Appeal (Jenkins and Hodson LJJ, Singleton LJ dissenting) that they were deductible. Jenkins LJ said that the crucial question was whether the funds were wholly and exclusively laid out for the purpose of the company's trade.

The Court derived the following principles from the earlier case law:

(a) in order to be deductible a disbursement must be wholly and exclusively laid out for the purpose of enabling the trader to carry on and earn the profits of the trade (*per* Lord Davey in *Strong & Co.* v *Woodifield* (1906) 5 TC 215);

(b) disbursements need not, however, be immediately productive of profit to be allowable expenses;

(c) payments made for the purpose of preserving the business or protecting the trader from being deprived of the means of carrying on the trade may be deductible;

(d) payments made with a view to preventing the transfer from one person to another of the right to receive profits when earned are not deductible.

In *Morgan* v *Tate and Lyle*, the primary aim of the propaganda was to prevent the company losing its assets and business and facilitating the continued earning of profits. It was irrelevant that by so doing the expenditure protected the capital assets of shareholders.

10.5.6 The rule against duality of purpose

This is sometimes called the 'exclusivity test'. Section 74(a) and (b) is especially relevant here. It provides as follows.

> Subject to the provisions of the Tax Acts, in computing the amount of the profits or gains to be charged under Case I or Case II of Schedule D, no sum shall be deducted in respect of
>
> (a) any disbursements or expenses, not being money wholly and exclusively laid out or expended for the purposes of the trade, profession or vocation,
>
> (b) any disbursement or expenses of maintenance of the parties, their families or establishments, or any sums expended for any other domestic or private purposes distinct from the purposes of the trade, profession or vocation . . .

There is a famous dictum on the nature of the exclusivity test in *Bentleys, Stokes and Lowless* v *Beeson* (1952) 33 TC 491. The taxpayers who were solicitors had incurred expenses in entertaining their clients. The question was, were such expenses wholly and exclusively incurred for professional purposes? (Nowadays the position would be covered by s. 577). The Revenue contended that the 'wholly and exclusively' test was not satisfied.

The Revenue argued that one could not say that the sole purpose of the entertainment was business purposes. Part of the purpose was the ordinary 'I want to entertain a guest purpose'. However, the Court of Appeal considered otherwise. Romer LJ's judgment is particularly useful:

If the activity be undertaken with the *object* both of promoting business and also with some other *purpose*, for example, with the object of entertaining a friend or stranger or of supporting a charitable or benevolent subject, then the paragraph is *not* satisfied although in the mind of the actor the business motive may *predominate*. For the statute so prescribes *per contra*, if in truth the *sole object* is business promotion, the expenditure is not disqualified because the nature of the activity *necessarily involves some other result*, or the attainment or furtherance of some other objective, since the latter result or objective is necessarily inherent in the Act.

In *Sargent v Eayrs* [1973] STC 50 the taxpayer was a UK farmer. He claimed deduction in 1969/1970 of £1,093 expenses incurred in visiting Australia to investigate farming conditions there. The taxpayer was considering the possibility of emigrating. The taxpayer argued that the expenses were deductible within s. 124(1), ITA 1952 since it had been incurred for the extension of farming activity and under s. 152 ITA 1952, all farming was to be treated as *one* trade.

It was held that the taxpayer was not entitled to deduct the expenses because:

(a) the provision deeming all farming to be a single trade was to be treated as referring to UK farming only. Thus the expenditure was not deductible because it was not incurred wholly and exclusively by reference to UK farming;

(b) alternatively, the expenditure was not deductible because it was not of a revenue character, but of a capital character being for the purpose of initiating or extending a business: *British Insulated* v *Atherton* [1926] AC 205.

In *Watkins* v *Ashford, Sparkes and Harward* [1985] STC 451 a solicitors' firm in Devon had offices in four towns. Certain meetings were held at which meals were provided. They were as follows:

(a) local office meetings – weekly or fortnightly at lunch time;
(b) plenary meetings – occasional, evening dinner being provided;
(c) annual firm's weekend conferences which involved a one night stay at a hotel with families (the firm's conference), (no claim was made in respect of the families' costs);
(d) some partners also attended a conference of West Country solicitors' firms (the solicitors' conference). The firm contributed to the cost of the conference.

The question at issue was, were these expenses deductible? It was held by Nourse J:

(i) (a) and (b) were meals provided at a time when taxpayers would have eaten anyway and therefore were not exclusively for a business purpose. Thus such expenses were not deductible.

(ii) (c) and (d), the cost of partners' accommodation at the firm's annual conference and the firm's contribution to the solicitors' conference were wholly and exclusively for business purposes. No distinction should be made between accommodation and food/drink for these purposes. Thus such expenses were deductible.[9]

(See also *Mallalieu* v *Drummond* discussed at para. 10.6.5.)

10.5.7 The expenditure must be incurred to earn or facilitate the earning of profits

This is sometimes called the rule in *Strong* v *Woodifield* 5 TC 215. In that case an injured customer successfully sued Strong & Co. who owned an inn, in tort when a chimney fell on him. The question at issue was whether the damages (some £1,490) recovered by the customer were deductible in computing Strong & Co.'s profits. It was held by the House of Lords they were not. The loss did not arise out of the trade. The money was not wholly and exclusively laid out or expended for the purpose of the trade of being an innkeeper.

Lord Loreburn LC said 'The Act allows deductions for losses arising wholly and exclusively for the purposes of the trade. Here the taxpayers incurred the loss as householders not as innkeepers. Thus the loss is not really incidental to their trade of innkeeping and therefore not deducible.'

10.5.8 The revenue/capital test

10.5.8.1 General For an expense to be deductible it must be of an income or revenue nature. Capital expenditure may not generally, under s. 74, be set against income profits in the computation of income tax liability. This is a question of law, ultimately to be decided by the court. The basic proposition is that expenditure made once and for all is *capital* whilst recurrent expenditure is *revenue*.

A dictum of Viscount Cave LC in *British Insulated and Helsby Cables Ltd* v *Atherton* [1926] AC 205 is the most quoted matter in this connection (see para. 10.5.8.2 below). He said:

> When an expenditure is made, not only once and for all, but with a view to bringing into existence an asset or an advantage for the enduring benefit

---

[9.] It seems *per curiam* from this case, that maintenance in s. 74(b) is not restricted to domestic expenditure but could apply to a taxpayer when away from home.

of a trade, I find that there is a very good reason . . . for treating such an expenditure as properly attributable not to revenue but to capital.

The problem here is essentially the one we have already dealt with in relation to trading receipts.

10.5.8.2 Miscellaneous cases In *British Insulated and Helsby Cables Ltd* v *Atherton* the company established a pension fund for its employees. It agreed to pay £31,784 to form the nucleus of the fund. The question was whether this was an allowable deduction. The Special Commissioners determined that it was an allowable deduction. Rowlatt J upheld this decision but was reversed by the Court of Appeal. The Court of Appeal's decision was confirmed by the Lords.

Viscount Cave LC said:

But there remains the question, which I found more difficult, whether apart from the express prohibitions, the sum in question is (in the words used by Lord Sumner in *Usher's* case), a proper debit item to be charged against incomings of the trade when computing the profits of it; or, in other words, whether it is in substance a revenue or a capital expenditure. This appears to me to be a question of fact which is properly to be decided by the Commissioners upon the evidence brought before them in each case; but where, as in the present case, there is no express finding by the Commissioners upon the point, it must be determined by the Courts upon the materials which are available and with due regard to the principles which have been laid down in the authorities. Now, in *Vallambrosa Rubber Company* v *Farmer*, 1910 SC 519, 5 TC 529, Lord Dunedin, as Lord President of the Court of Session, expressed the opinion that 'in a rough way' it was 'not a bad criterion of what is capital expenditure as against what is income expenditure to say that capital expenditure is a thing that is going to be spent once and for all and income expenditure is a thing which is going to recur every year': and no doubt this is often a material consideration. But the criterion suggested is not, and was obviously not intended by Lord Dunedin to be, a decisive one in every case; for it is easy to imagine many cases in which a payment, though made 'once and for all', would be properly chargeable against the receipts for the year. Instances of such payments may be found in the gratuity of £1,500 paid to a reporter on his retirement which was the subject of the decision in *Smith* v *Incorporated Council of Law Reporting*, [1914] 3 KB 674, and in the expenditure of £4,994 in the purchase of an annuity for the benefit of an actuary who had retired which, in *Hancock* v *General Reversionary and Investment Company*, [1919] 1 KB 25, was allowed, and I think rightly allowed, to be deducted from profits. But when an expenditure is made, not only once and for all, but with a view to bringing into existence an asset or an advantage for the enduring benefit of a trade, I think that there is very good reason (in the absence of special circumstances leading to an opposite conclusion) for treating such an expenditure as properly attributable not to revenue but to capital. For this view there is already considerable authority.

In *Law Shipping* v *IRC* (1924) 12 TC 621 (Court of Session) Law Shipping had bought a second-hand ship in a state of disrepair. One long voyage was undertaken at the end of which the company was obliged to spend a large sum in repairs. Was the whole cost of repairs deductible in computing the profits of a trade for income tax (and therefore for Excess Profits Duty)? It was held that it was not. The expenditure was of a capital rather an income nature.

Lord President Clyde said (at p. 625):

It is clear that had the taxpayer's predecessors in title not sold the ship the cost of repairs (£51,558) would have been deductible in computing *their* profits. Is the sum deductible in computing the taxpayer's profits though? No: the expenditure was capital (not revenue) expenditure because the total cost of purchasing the ship was: purchase price plus cost of repairs.

In *Pitt* v *Castle Hill Ltd* [1974] 3 All ER 146 the taxpayer owned some warehouses. The warehouses needed a new access by road because the old access caused disturbance to neighbours. The company surrendered some of its land to the local authority who in turn permitted the company to build a new access road on local authority land. The local authority then granted the taxpayer an easement over the land. The road cost £5,227. The question at issue was, was this deductible? Megarry VC held it was not. In determining whether the expenditure was revenue or capital it was necessary to consider:

(a) was it a single lump sum or were there recurrent payments (e.g., commensurate with time periods)?
(b) was an enduring asset obtained for the payment or was an intangible or ephemeral asset obtained (or was an asset obtained at all)?
(c) what was the manner of use of the new asset – would it be static or possess the quality of recurrence?

In *Tucker* v *Granada* [1979] 2 All ER 801 Granada operated a motorway service area. The rent was £15,000 a year plus a percentage of annual gross takings (including tobacco sales) ('AGT'). As tobacco duty increased, the AGTs increased, but Granada's profits diminished. The effect of increasing AGTs was to increase the rent payable. The company therefore agreed with the Ministry of Transport (the landlord) that tobacco duty would henceforth be excluded from AGT for the purpose of rent calculation if the company paid the Ministry of Transport £122,220. The question that arose for determination by the courts was whether the £122,220 was deductible.

The Special Commissioners upheld the taxpayer's claim. Templeman J, the Court of Appeal and the House of Lords reversed it.

It was held by the House of Lords that the payment to the Ministry of Transport was a once and for all expenditure on a capital asset (the lease) to make it more advantageous. The fact that the purpose of the expenditure was to improve profitability was irrelevant. Lord Wilberforce (with whom Lords Edmund-Davies and Keith agreed) said:

Schedule D, Cases I and II – computation   319

So how is the £122,220 to be regarded? On the one hand the payment was designed to enable the appellants to earn more profits: from this point of view it might be thought that the payment should have a revenue character. On the other hand, the payment produced a modification in the lease, which could be regarded as an identifiable asset, making the lease less disadvantageous: from this point of view it might be thought that the payment should be regarded as a capital payment. It is common in cases which raise the question whether a payment is to be treated as a revenue or as a capital payment for indicia to point different ways. In the end the courts can do little better than form an opinion which way the balance lies. . . .

I think that the key to the present case is to be found in those cases which have sought to identify an asset. In them it seems reasonably logical to start with the assumption that money spent on the acquisition of the asset should be regarded as capital expenditure. Extensions from this are, first, to regard money spent on getting rid of a disadvantageous asset as capital expenditure and, secondly, to regard money spent on improving the asset, or making it more advantageous, as capital expenditure. In the latter type of case it will have to be considered whether the expenditure has the result stated or whether it should be regarded as expenditure on maintenance or upkeep, and some cases may pose difficult problems.

It is in this connection that so many discussions start from the well-known phrase of Viscount Cave LC in *British Insulated and Helsby Cables Ltd v Atherton*: '. . . when an expenditure is made, not only once and for all, but with a view to bringing into existence an asset or an advantage for the enduring benefit of a trade.' . . . Nearest to this line is the case in this House of *Inland Revenue Comrs v Carron Co* 45 TC 18. There the expenditure was incurred in order to procure a modification of the company's charter in such a way as to enable it to trade more properly and to facilitate day-to-day operations. This House held that the payment had a revenue character. Unless indeed it could be said that the charter was a capital asset, it is difficult to see what other decision could have been given. In the course of my opinion I used these words:

'. . . the disposition of a source of liability may be equivalent to the acquisition of a source of profit – an extension perhaps of, but not an exception to, the principle that in some sense or other, an asset of a capital nature, tangible or intangible, positive or negative, must be shown to be acquired. If this is correct – and until a case arises which constitutes a true exception, I shall continue to think that it is – the present expenditure cannot be brought with the capital class.'

With due caution against using these words as if they were statutory, I adhere to them. They were, of course, directed to excluding cases where no capital asset could be seen or identified, which was so in that case; I had not intended to narrow the conception of capital payment to the case of the acquisition of an asset . . . So it remains to decide the present case. For myself I cannot doubt where it lies: it is a case of once and for all expenditure on a capital asset designed to make it more advantageous. It is true that the lease was non-assignable, so it had no balance sheet value before or after the modification. But it was nonetheless an asset and a valuable one for the appellants' trade, and, if an asset, was a capital asset. It appears to me to be impossible to divorce the payment from the lease and to regard it as simply a payment intended to increase the appellants' share of the profits. That it may have done, but the parties chose to do it through the medium of a lease, just as in the petrol filling stations cases, the object of increasing gallonage sales was effected through a lease. Nor in my opinion can the payment be regarded as payment of rent: that would be to confuse the measure, or basis of calculation, of the payment with its nature. I agree therefore with both courts below in regarding the payment as of a capital nature.[10]

The case of *Lawson* v *Johnson Matthey* [1992] STC 466 illustrates again the narrow capital and income divide and the importance of findings of fact for UK tax. In that case the House of Lords decided that payments to allow a company to continue to trade by removing the danger of a subsidiary's insolvency could be treated as a trading expense notwithstanding it was a one-off. The case is discussed in detail in Chapter 1.

10.6 PROBLEM AREAS

10.6.1 Introduction

There are a number of problem areas concerning deductible expenditure. These include the following.

(a) travelling expenses;
(b) tort damages;
(c) legal and accountancy costs;
(d) clothes;
(e) rent: see s.74(c);
(f) repairs and improvements: see s.74(f), s.74(g);
(g) salaries etc.;
(h) entertainment expenses: see s.577;
(i) fines and illegal payments;
(j) bad debts: see s.74(j);
(k) employee theft.

Each of these will be considered below.

10.6.2 Travelling expenses

In *Sargent* v *Barnes* [1978] 2 All ER 737 Mr Barnes was a dentist. He lived near Cheltenham, had a dental laboratory in Cheltenham and his surgery in

---

[10.] See also *Jeffs* v *Rington* [1985] STC 809, *Rolfe* v *Wimpey Waste Management Ltd* [1989] STC 454, *Lawson* v *Johnson Matthey* [1992] STC 466 (HL) discussed at para. 1.2.4.2.1.

Winchcombe. Each day he travelled by car from his home to his laboratory (about 1 mile) and thence to his surgery (about 11 miles). He collected completed work from the laboratory and discussed matters with the technician. He delivered articles to the laboratory on the return journey. The question at issue was whether the expenses of travelling between the laboratory and the surgery were deductible expenses. The General Commissioners found that it was absolutely necessary for the taxpayer to travel back and forth from his laboratory in order to carry out his profession as a dentist. However, the Crown's appeal was allowed by Oliver J who said:

> In asking themselves, therefore, whether it was necessary for the taxpayer to travel back and forth, the commissioners were, quite simply, asking themselves the wrong question, because the fact that expenditure is necessary is no guide to whether it is exclusively incurred for the purposes of a trade . . . The question in this case arises in relation to journeys from and to a point intermediate between the principal place of work and the taxpayer's home, because, although, no doubt, visits to the laboratory involve some relatively insignificant deviation from the direct route between home and surgery, effectively I have to deal with a straight line from residence via laboratory to surgery, and vice versa.
>
> Counsel for the taxpayer submits that the true analysis is that, on the commissioners' findings, the taxpayer had two places at which he carried on his professional practice, the laboratory and the surgery.
>
> In the instant case, on the facts found it would in my judgment be a travesty to say that the taxpayer was in any relevant sense carrying on his practice as a dentist at The Reddings [the laboratory]. He had established a facility at The Reddings, and he was merely utilising his journey between his residence and the base of operations where the practice was carried on to avail himself of this facility; that is to say, to visit this intermediate point, where he had arranged for an independent contractor to carry out an activity, no doubt a necessary activity, referable to the practice. But the journey did not thus assume a different purpose once the intermediate point was passed, or cease to be a journey for the purpose of getting to or from the place where the taxpayer chose to live. I do not therefore think that, however necessary to the practice the activity pursued at The Reddings may have been, the commissioners could properly have arrived at the conclusion that the expenses claimed were incurred wholly or exclusively for the purposes of the practice; and the appeal therefore succeeds.

It is an interesting question whether apportionment of the expenses should have been allowed.

10.6.3 Tort damages and losses generally

Section 74(e), TA provides that: '. . . any loss not connected with or arising out of the trade, profession or vocation' is not deductible. (See *Strong* v

Woodifield (para. 10.5.7) and see also *Curtis* v *Oldfield* (1925) 9 TC 319 (director's 'borrowings' outside the trade and so not deductible) and *Mitchell* v *Noble* (para. 10.6.8).)

Here the word loss has a meaning akin to or similar to 'expense': a sum disbursed or lost in the course of trading. Section 74(e) and (j) are concerned with losses arising out of *particular* transactions and are not concerned with the overall post-deductions question of whether or not the trader has made an operating profit on his Schedule D, Case I income. Contrast this with s. 380, TA which permits a loss in the sense of overall trading loss to be set against income derived from other sources and to be carried over where necessary; see also ss. 385 and 388.

Since a loss which is not connected with, or arising out of the trade is not deductible this excludes:

(a) non-business, i.e., personal losses; and
(b) losses incurred ancillary to the trade pursued but not actually incurred in the course of the trade of the taxpayer.

Thus losses which are insufficiently closely or intimately connected with the trade or for the purpose of earning profits are excluded.

In *English Crown Spelter Co. Ltd* v *Baker* (1908) 5 TC 327 the taxpayer's company spent money acquiring a new company to work zinc mines in Wales so as to supply the taxpayer with zinc. The new company failed. Was this a s.74(e) loss? The court held it was not. The money was capital employed in a separate concern.

In *Reid's Brewery* v *Male* (1891) 3 TC 279 the taxpayer company were brewers. They sustained losses on loans to third parties made in connection with the third parties' purchases of pubs. The loans were not repaid. Were such losses deductible? It was held that the losses were deductible because they were incurred as part of the taxpayer company's trade.

10.6.4 Legal and accountancy costs

As a matter of strict law these are not normally deductible but may be in practice (see, e.g., *Allen* v *Farquharson* (1932) 17 TC 59).

10.6.5 Clothes

The leading case on this matter is *Mallalieu* v *Drummond* [1983] STC 665. This concerned the deductibility for a 'lady barrister' of a 'wardrobe of clothes . . . suitable to be worn under her gown during her court appearances . . .' Were these 'exclusively' for the purposes of her profession? It was accepted that a private advantage did '. . . not necessarily preclude the exclusivity of the business purpose'. However, the Commisioners found there was a dual purpose, namely:

(a) a business purpose; and

(b) to enable her to be properly clothed for 'warmth and decency'.

The House of Lords considered that this was the only possible conclusion. However, their Lordships' discussion of a nurse's uniform and a self-employed waiter's 'tails', which seemingly would be allowable, may give pause for thought as were not the barrister's court clothes a sort of uniform? However, their Lordships considered that there should not be a problem with 'uniforms' as 'it is a matter of degree'. This still leaves open the question as to what precisely the rule is.

10.6.6 Rent

Section 74(c), TA provides that:

> the rent of the whole or any part of any dwelling-house or domestic offices, except any such as is used for the purposes of the trade or profession, and where any such part is so used, the sum so deducted shall not, unless in any particular case it appears that having regard to all the circumstances some greater sum ought to be deducted, exceed two-thirds of the rent *bona fide* paid for the said dwelling-house or those offices.

This allows rent of the flat above a shop to be deductible in some cases.

10.6.7 Repairs and improvements

Section 74(f) and (g) provide that the following expenses are not deductible:

> (f) any capital withdrawn from, or any sum employed or intended to be employed as capital in, the trade, profession or vocation, but so that this paragraph shall not be treated as disallowing the deduction of any interest,
> (g) any capital employed in improvements of premises occupied for the purposes of the trade, profession or vocation . . .

Two cases illustrate the effect of these subsections. These are *Law Shipping v IRC* and *Odeon Associated Theatres v Jones*.

In *Law Shipping v IRC* (1923) 12 TC 621 the company purchased the SS *Duns Law* for £97,000. It was then put through a Lloyd's survey which resulted in expenditure of £51,558 on repairs. When the ship was purchased the survey was overdue but exemption from it was obtained in respect of a voyage then in contemplation. It was agreed that if the former owner had incurred the expenditure on repairs he would have been entitled to deduct the cost of the repairs.

The Special Commissioners allowed only the proportion of the cost attributable to the company's period of ownership as a deduction. The balance was to be treated as capital expenditure in respect of which 'wear and tear will be admissible at the usual rate'. The Court of Session rejected the taxpayer's appeal.

Lord President Clyde said:

The expense laid out in keeping a ship, which is employed in trade, in proper repair is certainly an expense necessary for the purposes of the trade. It is made for the purpose of earning the profits of the trade. Repairs may be executed as the occasion for them occurs; or, if they are such as brook delay, they may be postponed to a convenient season: but, in either case, they truly constitute a constantly recurring incident of that continuous employment of the ship which makes them necessary. They are therefore an admissible deduction in computing profits, and, as is admitted in the case, if the ship had not been sold, the purchasers' predecessors would have been entitled to deduct the whole of the £51,558 in returning their profits for Income Tax. Accumulated arrears for repairs are, in short, none the less repairs necessary to earn profits, although they have been allowed to accumulate.

In the present case, however, the accumulation of repairs represented by the expenditure of £51,558 required to overtake them, was an accumulation which extended partly over a period during which the ship was employed, not in the purchasers' trade, but in that of the purchasers' predecessors. And the question relates to the computation of the purchasers' profit only.

The purchasers started their trade with a ship already in need of extensive repairs. The need was not so clamant as to make it impossible to employ her (as she stood at the time of the purchase) in the voyage she was then about to commence. So much is clear from the fact that she was allowed exemption from survey for the purposes of that voyage. But, while some portion of the repairs executed after her return was no doubt attributable to her employment in the purchasers' trade between the date of their purchase and the return of the ship – and while such portion was therefore necessary to the earning of profits by them in that and subsequent voyages – it seems plain that a large portion of them was attributable solely to her employment by the purchasers' predecessors, in whose profits the purchasers had no interest whatever. The admissibility of deduction of the latter portion thus appears to be negatived by the terms of Rule 3 of Cases I and II . . .

Again, when the purchasers started trade with the ship, the capital they required was not limited to the price paid to acquire her, but included the cost of the arrears of repairs which their predecessors had allowed to accumulate; because, while their own trading with her would – in ordinary course – provide a revenue out of which the repairs incidental to such trading would be met it would be unreasonable and abnormal – in any commercial sense – to saddle such trading with the burden of arrears of repairs, incidental to the trading of their predecessors from which the purchasers derived no benefit.

Lords Skerrington, Cullen and Sands delivered speeches to similar effect.

In *Odeon Associated Cinemas* v *Jones* (1971) 48 TC 257 Odeon Associated Cinemas Ltd were film exhibitors. In the immediate post-war years they bought many cinemas and cinema owning companies. On 8 January 1945 Odeon bought the Regal Cinema at Marble Arch for £240,000. Because of restrictions only small sums could be spent on repairs during the war. Consequently the cinema was somewhat run down but was still a full, effective, profit-earning asset. Between 1945 and 1954 substantial sums were spent on repairs and renewals. There was accountancy evidence that it was within the established principles of commercial accountancy to charge this expenditure to revenue.

Salmon LJ said:

The evidence of a number of exceptionally distinguished accountants, accepted by the Special Commissioners, was that in accordance with the established principles of sound commercial accounting the disputed items of expenditure were a charge to revenue. The learned Vice-Chancellor held that in law these items were properly chargeable to revenue and that the profits for the years in question should be assessed for tax on that basis. . . . In my judgment the true proposition of law is well established, namely that, in determining what is capital expenditure and what is revenue expenditure in order to arrive at the profit for tax purposes in any particular year, the Courts will follow the established principles of sound commercial accounting unless they conflict with the law as laid down in any statute.

(See also *Lurcott* v *Wakely & Wheeler* [1911] 1 KB 905.)

10.6.8 Salaries etc.

In general the costs of paying staff etc to run the business are deductible provided the expenditure is wholly and exclusively for the purposes of the trade. This is illustrated by *Copeman* v *William Flood & Sons Ltd* (1940) 24 TC 53. Miss Mary Flood was appointed a director of the company when she was 17. G.A.M. Flood, her brother, was also a director. Each was credited with £2,600 by way of remuneration as directors. Miss Flood's duties consisted of dealing with telephone calls made to her father's private residence. G.A.M. Flood's duties consisted mainly in calling on farmers to purchase pigs from them. The Revenue contended that the whole of the payments made to the Flood children could not be regarded as disbursements or expenses wholly and exclusively laid out or expended for the purposes of the company's trade. The General Commissioners decided that they could not interfere with the prerogative of the company in paying such sums as remuneration to directors as the company thought fit.

Lawrence J allowed the Crown's appeal and remitted the case to the Commissioners to find as a fact whether the sums in question were laid out wholly for the purpose of the company's trade. He said: 'It does not follow that because the sums of money were paid to the directors as remuneration that they were necessarily wholly and exclusively laid out for the purposes of the trade.'

Mitchell v *Noble* (1927) 11 TC 372 concerned a company of insurance brokers. Directors were appointed for life but could be dismissed for misconduct. Considerable personal friction arose between one director and the rest of the board. The company might have been justified in exercising its power of dismissal. Anxious that the matter should not become public and to avoid a scandal affecting the reputation of the company, negotiations were entered into for the director's retirement. He agreed to go if the company paid him £19,200 payable in five annual instalments.

The question at issue was whether such sums were allowable deductions. The Special Commissioners decided that they were. Rowlatt J thought that a payment to get rid of a servant in the interests of the trade was a proper deduction and upheld the decision of the Special Commissioners. The Court of Appeal affirmed Rowlatt J's decision.

Sargant LJ said:

> Now, first, as to the question whether this was a disbursement wholly and exclusively laid out or expended for the purposes of the trade, it seems to me that there is nothing at all to show that it was not so exclusively laid out. The object, as disclosed by paragraph 9 of the Case, was that of preserving the status and reputation of the Company, which the directors felt would be imperilled either by the other director remaining in the business or by a dismissal of him against his will, involving proceedings by way of action in which the good name of the Company might suffer. To avoid that and to preserve the status and dividend earning power of the Company seems to me a purpose which is well within the ordinary purposes of the trade, profession or vocation of the Company. . . . Then comes the next point: whether this very large payment was a payment which was so exceptional in its nature that it must be considered as a capital payment and not a payment by way of deduction from annual outgoings. With regard to that, I entirely agree with the view of the learned Judge, that the dismissal of a servant, or compensation paid to ensure the dismissal of a servant (which, of course, this director was – a servant of the Company) is a payment which would in the ordinary course be attributed to the year in which the payment was made, and I see no reason for thinking in this case that it was of the nature of a capital expenditure.

10.6.9 Entertainment expenses

The cost of business entertainment was held deductible under s. 74, TA in *Bentleys, Stokes and Lowless v Beeson* [1952] 2 All ER 82. This was seen as an abuse and restrictions were introduced. Accordingly, s. 577, TA disallows business entertainment expenses incurred by a person carrying on a trade, profession or vocation or by members of his staff.

'Business entertainment' is defined by s. 577(5), TA as:

> entertainment (including hospitality of any kind) provided by a person or a member of his staff in connection with a trade, profession or vocation, but does not include anything provided for *bona fide* members of staff [such as office parties] unless its provision for them is incidental to its provision for others.

This is extended by s. 577(8), TA to include gifts, though gifts other than food, drink, tobacco or a voucher exchangeable for goods, which incorporate a conspicuous advertisement for the donor, and which do not cost (together with other gifts) more than £10 for each donee in each year of assessment are excluded. Thus cheap calendars or pens which advertise the trader's business can be given away and still be deductible.

Section 577(9), TA excepts from s. 577(8) (i.e., allows) the deduction of expenditure incurred in making gifts to charitable bodies. Extra-statutory Concession B7 extends this still further. It provides:

Section 577(8), TA provides that in general the cost of gifts is not an admissible deduction in computing profits chargeable under Schedule D or in management expenses claims. Section 577(9), TA removes this restriction for Schedule D in the case of business donations to registered charities (provided the deduction would otherwise be allowable) and a similar approach is taken to management expenses claims. Other expenditure on gifts is not regarded as within section 577 provided that:

(a) it is allowable under section 74(a) or section 75(1), TA;

(b) the gift is made for the benefit of a body or association of persons established for educational, cultural, religious, recreational or benevolent purposes, and the body or association is (i) local in relation to the donor's business activities; and (ii) not restricted to persons connected with the donor;

(c) the expenditure is reasonably small in relation to the scale of the donor's business.

The payment of an ordinary annual subscription to a local trade association by a non-member is similarly not regarded as a gift provided condition (a) is met.

Section 577(10) excludes from the operation of the section 'the provision by any person of anything which it is his trade to provide, and which is provided by him in the ordinary course of that trade for payment or, with the object of advertising to the public generally, gratuitously.' This subsection was considered by the House of Lords in *Associated Newspapers Ltd* v *Fleming* [1973] AC 628. The taxpayers' journalists were reimbursed by the company for money spent on drinks and meals for informants. The taxpayers claimed that s. 577(10) applied to the payment. The House of Lords held that it did not. The expenses had been incurred on the provision of entertainment, and it was the taxpayers' business to provide newspapers, not entertainment (!). Lord Reid's first impression in *Associated Newspapers Ltd* v *Fleming* was that s. 577(10) was 'obscure to the point of unintelligibility'.

10.6.10 Fines etc.

A trader may incur a fine in the course of carrying out the trade. For example, a parking fine may be incurred in delivering goods to a customer. The question then arises whether a deduction should be allowed for the payment of the fine. As a matter of policy, should the fine be effectively reduced by the taxpayer's marginal rate? This was considered in *IRC* v *Alexander von Glehn* (1920) 12 TC 232. Here Customs sought penalties for breach of wartime legislation. A settlement was reached on a payment by the company. The Court of Appeal held the payments were not deductible. The rationale seems to be that the fines were not incurred in the course of earning profits (cf. Scrutton LJ at p. 244 and Warrington LJ at p. 241). By s. 827, TA VAT penalties etc. are not allowed as deductions.

Section 577A, TA disallows certain illegal payments as deductions.

10.6.11 Bad debts

Section 74(j), TA provides that any debts except:

(i)   a bad debt;
(ii) a debt or part of a debt released by the creditor wholly and exclusively for the purposes of his trade, profession or vocation as part of a relevant arrangement or compromise; and
(iii) a doubtful debt to the extent estimated to be bad, meaning, in the case of the bankruptcy or insolvency of the debtor, the debt except to the extent that any amount may reasonably be expected to be received on the debt.

If a trader has included a sum to which the trader is entitled (e.g., in respect of goods supplied) in the profit computation for the period in which the sum falls due but is not paid the sum, then the UK tax system allows a deduction for debts proved bad.[11] The wording of s. 74(j) was amended by the FA 1996. However, it is submitted that the following remains good law.

This was considered in *Bristow* v *William Dickinson & Co. Ltd* (1946) 27 TC 157. Here the company inter alia exported coal and coke to Spain. As a result of the Spanish Civil War the company regarded its debts of about £10,000 owed by Spanish customers as bad debts. It debited £4,000 in the company's profit and loss account as 'Provision for Bad and Doubtful Debts'. The following year the provision was increased to £6,710. These provisions were allowed as deductions for income tax purposes for the years in question. In 1940 the British government advanced £2 million for the payment of such debts and a clearing house was set up. The company recovered £5,115.9s.6d and £333.3s.11d through this scheme. These sums were credited in the profit and loss account as 'Transferred from Reserve for Bad and Doubtful Debts as no longer required'.

Lord Greene MR (with whom Somervell and Cohen LJJ agreed) said:

The only statutory provision which bears on this question to which I need refer is [s. 74(j)]. The first question which falls to be decided, in examining

---

[11.] This would not apply in cases where the cash basis is used as the amount would not have been brought into account in the first place.

this matter, is one on the true construction of that Sub-rule. In the case of *The Gleaner Co Ltd* v *Assessment Committee* [1922] 2 AC 169, a case in the Privy Council on appeal from Jamaica arising out of the Jamaica Income Tax law, it is said that a provision similar in terms to this one did not justify the giving of an allowance in respect of a doubtful or bad debt save on the occasion when the debt was first brought into the account . . . But in the recent case of *Absalom* v *Talbot*, in the House of Lords, [1944] AC 204 (26 TC 166), the effect of the Sub-rule was considered in that connection . . . Viscount Simon LC, Lord Atkin and Lord Porter, emphatically and clearly dissented from the view which had been expressed by the Privy Council in the *Gleaner* case, and held – I repeat by way of dictum only – that it was legitimate for the Revenue to make allowance in a subsequent year in respect of a debt which, in the earlier year, had been treated as a perfectly good debt . . . in my opinion, the views expressed by those three members of the House in *Absalom* v *Talbot* are correct. When one looks at the language, it starts, first of all, by prohibiting a deduction in respect of a debt. That would appear to mean, as I have said, that a taxpayer cannot come and say: 'Exclude this debt from the computation because it has not yet been paid.' But in this case, in the years 2 and 3 the Company was in effect saying to the Revenue: 'We claim a deduction in those two years in respect of this debt, the reason being that in those years 2 and 3 something has happened to it which has had the result, first, of reducing it in value and subsequently, destroying the value altogether on the ground that it was bad.' The Company, claiming to make that deduction in respect of the debt in the years 2 and 3, is entitled to the relief which the Sub-rule allows, namely, that, if it is a bad or doubtful debt proved to be such to the satisfaction of the Commissioners, a deduction may be made.

That is exactly what happened.

The Court of Appeal considered that there was no reason for saying that, as between the taxpayer and the Revenue, the receipt must be attributed to the year 1.

The following points can be made about bad and doubtful debts.

(a) Bad and doubtful debts are deductible because the sums owed to the taxpayer will generally already have been treated as taxable income in the taxpayer's accounts because of the earnings basis method of drawing up accounts.

(b) A bad debt is one which is not repaid on time. When is a debt bad? Section 74(j) says that in the case of bankruptcy or insolvency of that debtor, a doubtful debt is estimated to be bad to the extent that any amount may reasonably be expected to be received on the debt.

The clearest way to prove a debt bad is to take action on the debtor and fail to recover despite judgment. But this is not essential. Whether a debt is bad is a question of fact. A debt may be bad even though the debtor is still trading as a going concern (see *Dinshaw* v *Bombay Commissioner of Income Tax* (1934) 13 ATC 284).

(c) A bad debt is taken into account in the year in which it becomes bad.

(d) A bad debt subsequently recovered is a trading receipt in the year in which it is repaid. Previous assessments in which the debt appeared as a s. 74(e) deduction are not reopened; see *Bristow* v *William Dickinson & Co. Ltd.*

10.6.12 Employee theft

A problem arises as to how to treat sums stolen by an employee.[12] If an employee takes money out of the till or otherwise obtains what is really the business's money for himself, should that amount be allowed as a deduction? This was considered in *Bamford* v *ATA Advertising* (1972) 48 TC 359. Here credit arrangements that had been entered into with Forward Trust allowed a director to obtain company money for himself. The director went bankrupt and the £15,000 he had obtained for himself was written off by the business as a bad debt. This was disallowed as a deduction by the Revenue. This disallowance was upheld on appeal as a controller of the business got the money.

Brightman J said:

... there is a distinction [between petty theft by a subordinate employee and massive defalcation by a director]. I can quite see that the Commissioners might find as a fact that a £5 note taken from a till by a shop assistant is a loss to the trader which is connected with and arises out of the trade ... That ... is quite a different case from a director with authority to sign cheques who helps himself to £15,000 which is then lost to the company. I find it difficult to see how such a loss could be regarded as 'connected with and arising out of the trade.' In the defaulting director type of case there seems to me to be no relevant nexus between the loss of the money and the conduct of the company's trade. The loss is not as in the case of the dishonest shop assistant an incident of the company's trading activities. It arises altogether outside such activities. That I think is the true distinction.

It is a question to consider as to how obvious this distinction is and whether it should exist as a policy matter.

10.7 THE BASIS PERIOD RULES

10.7.1 Introduction

Historically the basis of assessment for Schedule D, Case I and Case II was the preceding year basis (or an average of the preceding year's profits). This meant that income tax was charged on the profits of the preceding tax year. Under new rules this has recently been changed to what is called in the

---

[12.] *Allen* v *Farquharson* (1932) 17 TC 59, and *Curtis* v *Oldfield* (1924) 9 TC 319.

Schedule D, Cases I and II – computation 331

legislation a current year basis so that income tax is theoretically charged on the profits of the tax year itself. As will be seen later tax on a 'current year' basis is a misdescription.

Schedule D, Cases I and II tax is a direct matter, and unlike Schedule E is not by deduction at source through PAYE.

The new current year basis applies:

(a) from the 1994/95 year of assessment onwards to all businesses which were (or are treated for tax purposes as) set up and commenced after 6 April 1994;
(b) from 1997/98 onwards for all other businesses. For these businesses special transitional rules apply for the 1996/97 year of assessment but these transitional rules are not included in this book for reasons of space.

The dates for payment of Schedule D, Cases I and II tax under the preceding year basis were as set out in s. 5(2), TA, namely:

(a) half on or before 1 January in the year of assessment;
(b) half on or before the subsequent 1 July.

The introduction of self-assessment has meant a change in these dates from the 1st to the 31st of the month in question (see s. 59A, TMA as inserted by FA 1993 and see para. 2.6).

The payment dates are the cause of much of the difficulty in this area. There is a problem of knowing what the profit for a period is before it has ended. The preceding year basis allowed a figure for the payment of tax to be found but resulted in the need for special rules for the early years of a trade (the commencement or opening provisions) and special rules for the end of a trade (the closing or discontinuance provisions). The current year basis does not solve this problem so that effectively tax is paid by reference to last year's figures subject to adjustment.

10.7.2 The old system

10.7.2.1 Introduction
The rules governing this were found in the following provisions:

(a) general rule: s. 60, TA;
(b) opening years: s. 60–62, TA;
(c) closing years: s. 63, TA.

10.7.2.2 General rule – old system
The general rule was that income tax under Schedule D, Cases I and II was to be charged on the full amount of the profits or gains of the year preceding the year of assessment – s. 60, TA. Thus if a trader drew up his accounts from 6 April one year to 5 April the year after then these profits would have provided the figure of profits to be assessed for the following year of assessment.

Example
Assessment for 1993–94, i.e., 6 April 1993 to 5 April 1994
Preceding year 1992–93, i.e., 6 April 1992 to 5 April 1993

	1993–94
1992–93	AMJJASONDJFMA
AMJJASONDJFMA	

Thus in this example, the trader would pay tax in 1993/94 on what he had earned in 1992/93.

Example
However, if the accounts were made up to a date ending in the preceding year the profits for the accounting period ending in the preceding year were taken as the taxable profits in the year of assessment. Thus if accounts were made up for the calendar year ending on 31 December 1992 they would form the measure of profits for year of assessment 1993–94. This may be illustrated as follows.

	1993–94
1992–93	AMJJASONDJFMA
AMJJASONDJFMA	
JFMAMJJASOND	
(Accounting period 1992)	

If the trader did not make up accounts, or made them up for a period of less or more than 12 months, the Inland Revenue was given a discretion by s. 60(2) as to what period of 12 months to take (see *IRC v Helical Bar* [1972] AC 773).

Special provision had to be made for the opening and closing years. This was done in ss. 61–63, TA. The opening year rules are briefly discussed in para. 10.7.2.3 below.

10.7.2.3 Opening years – old system Obviously, when the trade is first started there is no preceding year to use. If special provision were not made there could be no tax charge as there would be no preceding year on which to determine taxable profits. Section 61, TA set out the rules which were to be applied in this context.

If the trader did not make up accounts as at 5 April (and he was not required to) the profits of the first 12 months would be apportioned on a time basis using months; see s. 72, TA. For the second year the basis period was the period of 12 months from the commencement of the business (s. 61(3), TA). For the third year the normal preceding year basis could apply. Section 62, TA gave an election to the taxpayer to prevent injustice as a result of using the opening period profit as a basis of assessment for several years although if, as is generally the case, the profits of the first year's trading were low or nil, these rules were advantageous to the taxpayer.

10.8 THE NEW RULES: FA 1994 AS AMENDED BY FA 1995

10.8.1 Charge on current year basis

Sections 200 et seq, FA 1994 substituted new sections into TA. The most important of these is a new s. 60, TA headed 'Assessment on current year basis'. It provides:

> (1) Subject to subsection (2) below and section 63A, income tax shall be charged under Cases I and II of Schedule D on the full amount of the profits or gains of the year of assessment.

The reader should consider in reading the following paragraphs whether the new system has in fact achieved a current year basis when (inter alia) tax is paid by reference to the previous year and opening and closing rules are included.

10.8.2 Profits or gains of the year of assessment

It is thus intended that, in any tax year, income tax will be charged on the profits arising in that tax year. However, this will only work if the taxpayer draws up his accounts so that his accounting period ends at the end of the tax year, i.e., 5 April. Many businesses will not do this. It is therefore necessary for the legislation to specify specific basis periods, the profits of which are treated as if they were profits of the tax year in which the basis period ends. Accordingly, s. 60(2) provides:

> Where, in the case of a trade, profession or vocation, a basis period is given by subsection (3) or sections 61 to 63, profits or gains of that period shall be taken to be profits or gains of the year.

10.8.3 Basis period

By s. 60(3):

> Subject to sections 61 to 63, the basis period for a year of assessment is as follows—
> (a) if the year is the first year of assessment in which there is an accounting date which falls not less than 12 months after the commencement date, the period of 12 months ending with that accounting date; and
> (b) if there is a basis period for the immediately preceding year and that basis period is not given by s. 61, the period of 12 months beginning immediately after the end of that basis period.

This raises some questions of interpretation.

10.8.3.1 'Commencement date'
By s. 60(5) this is the date on which the trade, profession or vocation is set up and commenced.

10.8.3.2 Section 61 etc. Section 61 is headed 'Basis of assessment at commencement' (see para. 10.8.5 below). Sections 62 and 63 deal with a change of basis period and discontinuance.

10.8.3.3 'Accounting date' By s. 60(5) in relation to a year of assessment this means a date in the year to which the accounts are made up or, where there are two or more such dates, the latest of those dates.

10.8.4 General rule

If the accounting date is 5 April the basis period will be actual 12 months' profit. This may be illustrated as follows.

$$\text{6 April} \underline{\quad \textit{Tax Year} \quad} \text{5 April}$$

$$\text{6 April} \underline{\quad \textit{Accounting Period} \quad} \text{5 April}$$

Thus the basis period and the tax year are the same and a true current year basis has been achieved.

If a date other than 5 April is used then the 12 months' profit for the accounting period ending in the tax year is taken as the basis period for the year of assessment. Thus, one has to look to the taxpayer's accounting period. This may be illustrated as follows.

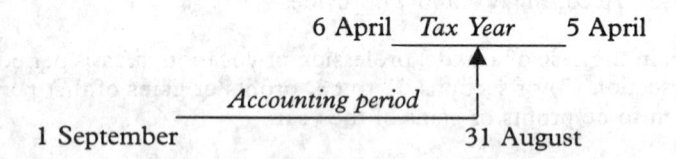

$$\text{6 April} \underline{\quad \textit{Tax Year} \quad} \text{5 April}$$
$$\underline{\quad \textit{Accounting period} \quad}$$
$$\text{1 September} \qquad\qquad \text{31 August}$$

Thus the profits of the accounting period ending on 31 August will be taken to be the profits subject to tax in the tax year in question.

Thus in summary income tax will be charged on:

(a) the full amount of the profits of the tax year where accounts are made up to 5 April (s. 60(1)); and
(b) on the profits of the twelve month period ending in the year of assessment where accounts are made up to a date other than 5 April (s. 60(3)).

10.8.5 Commencement provisions

Because the system of payment is not on a true current year basis it has to have commencement provisions for essentially the same reasons as the 'old' preceding year basis. If taxpayers were really taxed on current year profits then by definition commencement provisions would be unnecessary.

Schedule D, Cases I and II – computation

By s. 61 if the year of assessment is the 'commencement year' (defined in s. 60(5)) then the actual profits from the start of the business to the following 5 April are to be taken. This may be illustrated as follows.

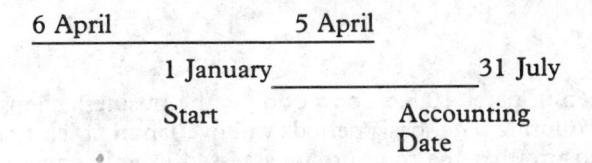

```
6 April              5 April
         1 January_____31 July
         Start            Accounting
                          Date
```

Tax will therefore be charged on the profits arising from 1 January to 5 April. The basis period for the second year will depend on the accounting date adopted by the business. If the accounts are drawn up to an accounting date which falls 12 months or more after the date of commencement, the basis period will be the 12 months to the accounting date (s. 60(3)(a)). However if, as in the above example, the accounts are made up to a date in the second year which is less than 12 months later, then tax is based on the actual profits for the 12 months from commencement. The consequence in this case is that two years' actual profits are used as the basis of assessment, something criticised in the old system in the Revenue's consultative document which preceded the introduction of these changes, although this is subject to 'overlap relief' discussed in para. 10.8.8 below.

Thus in summary tax will be charged here:

(a) on the profits from the start of the business to 5 April following (s. 61(1));
(b) by reference to the first 12 months' trading;
 (i) 12 months from the commencement if the commencement to the accounting date is less than 12 months;
 (ii) the same if there is a change of accounting date in the second year so that from the commencement to the new date is less than 12 months;
 (iii) otherwise 12 months to the accounting date ending in year 2 (which will generally be the first 12 months' profits in any event).

10.8.6 Change of accounting date

Sections 62 and 62A apply special rules so that a change in a business's accounting date will only result in a change in the basis period if certain conditions are met. The rules are apparently necessary to prevent double taxation etc.

10.8.7 Discontinuance

When a business ends its final accounting period will usually be less than 12 months. There will usually be a normal 12 month accounting period followed by a shorter accounting period up to the date on which the business ceases.

The broad effect of s. 63 is to tax the profits from the end of the preceding (12 month) basis period to the date of cessation. (There is an exception if the cessation is in only the second year of the business when the profits from 6 April to date of cessation are taken.)

10.8.8 Overlap relief

Finally, as has been seen in para. 10.8.5 above, unless the business chooses to use 5 April as its accounting date, basis periods will overlap in at least one tax year. In order to ensure that the total profits assessed exactly equal the total profits made 'overlap relief' will be given in a subsequent tax year. In essence, the amount of profits which have been included in the computations for two successive years of assessment will be identified and relief will be given.

10.8.9 Payment of tax

Following the introduction of self-assessment the dates for payment of income tax have been changed to 31 January and 31 July (see para. 10.7.1). Interim payments are to be made in two instalments on account for that year (s. 59A, TMA). Each instalment is intended to cover half the taxpayer's income tax liability for the year. Where necessary an adjustment by reference to the actual profits of the period in question will be made on 31 January following the relevant tax year (s. 59B).

10.8.10 Conclusion

The main reason given for introducing the change to a current year basis of assessment was that it would be clearer and simpler than the old preceding year basis. The reader may wonder whether such a result has been achieved.

CHAPTER ELEVEN
Schedule D – losses

11.1 INTRODUCTION[1]

In the nature of things some businesses make losses, not profits.[2] The treatment of such losses from a trade, profession or vocation for income tax purposes must now be considered. It is the use of losses from a trade, profession or vocation (called trading losses in this chapter) with which this chapter is concerned. If the rules of a particular Schedule or Case result in a person having allowable expenses in excess of his chargeable receipts, he will have suffered a loss. A loss will result in a nil liability (as there are no profits to charge) under Schedule D, Case I or II for the relevant year of assessment. There may, however, be special provisions which allow a loss to be set against any profit chargeable to tax in a previous or succeeding year of assessment. A trading loss can also be used in various other ways which must now be considered.

The ways in which such losses can be used include the following:[3]

(a) carry back of losses in the opening years: s. 381, TA;
(b) carry across against other income: s. 380, TA;
(c) carry forward against future profits of the same trade: s. 385, TA;
(d) carry back against preceding three years' profits (terminal loss relief): s. 388, TA;
(e) trading losses used against capital gains: s. 72, FA 1991.

[1.] See *Whiteman on Income Tax* and *Simon's Direct Taxes*.
[2.] See s. 74(e), TA: deductible losses connected with or arising out of the trade (Chapter 10) and cf. also 'bad debts', s. 74(j) and 'average losses', s. 74(k).
[3.] These are set chronologically by reference to the stages of the business which is not the way it is set out in the legislation.

Claims for relief are generally necessary for the use of such losses (see *Richardson v Jenkins* [1995] STC 95).

11.2 WHAT IS MEANT BY A 'TRADING LOSS'?

A loss for these purposes is the net deficit which results from a calculation of income under the Schedular rules where deductions exceed receipts. 'Loss' in this context does not refer to expenses in the course of earning profits in the s. 74, TA sense but a deficit at the end of the calculation. It refers to the overall situation where a trader ends up with negative taxable income from the trade. Where the taxpayer shows such a negative figure there will be a nil tax liability (see s. 380, TA).

Example
T, a trader, draws up accounts on a calendar year basis (i.e., 1 January to 31 December).
Suppose his accounts are as follows:

1 January 1990 – 31 December 1990 £10,000 profit
1 January 1991 – 31 December 1991 (£10,000) (loss)

The 1990 figure will form the basis of assessment in 1991–92 (the old preceding year basis of assessment then being applicable, and the 1991 figure in 1992–93 etc.). Thus in 1991–92 T pays tax on £10,000 but in 1992–93 there will be a nil assessment and T will have £10,000 of trading losses which he can use in one of the ways set out in this chapter.

The loss must arise in the course of a trade. A tax avoidance scheme may prevent there being a trading loss on the basis that there is no trade (see *Ensign* discussed at para. 4.8 above).

11.3 COMMENCEMENT LOSSES – CARRY BACK OF LOSSES IN THE OPENING YEARS: S. 381, TA

By s. 381, TA losses sustained in the first four years after the commencement of a trade can be carried back three years from the year of loss and set against the taxpayer's income of that period. For this relief to be available the trade must be carried on on a commercial basis and with a reasonable expectation of profit (s. 381(4)). The relief is given by setting any loss incurred in a trade, profession, or vocation against the taxpayer's income from any other source arising in the three years of assessment before that in which the loss was sustained, taking the earlier of those years before the later ones (s. 381(2)).

A claim for relief under s. 381 must be made on or before the first anniversary of 31 January next following the year of assessment in which the loss is sustained for the 1996–97 years of assessment onwards (s. 381(1)). The period of the relief under s. 381 cannot be extended from the first four years of assessment to the first eight years by transferring the trade to a spouse after four years (s. 381(5)).

Schedule D – losses

Example
T started trading on 6 April 1991. His trading results have been:

Year ending 5 April 1992: £ 8,420 profit
Year ending 5 April 1993: (£32,960) (loss)

Before starting his own business, T was employed at a salary of £14,500. In addition, he received gross investment income of £1,740 a year. The trading loss of £32,960 sustained in 1992–93 will be relieved under s. 381 as follows:

1989–90
Schedule E income	£14,500
Investment income	£ 1,740
	£16,240
Less s. 381 relief	£16,240
Taxable income	Nil

Loss of £16,660 left (£32,900 – £16,240)

1990–91
Schedule E income	£14,500
Investment income	£ 1,740
	£16,240
Less s. 381 relief	£16,240
Taxable income	Nil

Loss left £420 (£16,660 – £ 16,240)

1991–92
Schedule D, Case I income	£ 8,420
Less s. 381 relief	(£420)
	£ 8,000
Investment income	£ 1,740
Taxable income	£ 6,260

This can be a useful way of financing the commencement of a trade.

11.4 'CARRY ACROSS' AGAINST OTHER INCOME: S. 380, TA

11.4.1 Introductory matters

The rules here differ according to when the business was commenced. However, the broad effect remains the same and allows trading losses to be set against other income of the taxpayer for that period and one other. The changes are because of the move to a supposed current year basis discussed in Chapter 10. 'Carry across' relief allows a loss to be used earlier than if it were carried forward against future profits of the trade. If the trader has taxable income from other sources (for example, rents or dividends), the trader can obtain immediate relief for a trading loss by setting it against his other, general, income. Section 380(1), TA applies if a person sustains a loss in any trade, profession, *employment*[4] or vocation. The claim for the relief must be made (for 1996–97 onwards) within 12 months from 31 January next following the end of the year of assessment in which the loss is sustained. The relief will reduce income of a corresponding class first, i.e., earned income before investment income if an 'earned' loss. A loss is deemed to occur in the year of assessment in which the accounting period ends.

In addition to a claim under s. 380 to set the loss against his *general* income for that year a trader may also claim, where the loss is sufficient, to carry the loss:

(a) under the old rules forward and set it against his *general* income for the succeeding year (s. 380(2)); and

(b) under the new rules back one year and set it against the general income of the preceding year.

Thus, for example, under the old rules if T makes up his accounts as shown below and he has in addition £2,000 of income derived from a source other than his trade (say, investment income) then his tax position would be this:

Accounting Period	Year of Assessment	DI income	F income	Total Taxable
1989	1990–91	10,000	2,000	12,000
1990	1991–92	(10,000)	2,000	Nil
1991	1992–93	10,000	2,000	4,000

In 1991/92 T used £2,000 of his Schedule D, Case I loss to offset his taxable Schedule F income and in 1992/93 he used the remaining £8,000 of his trading loss to reduce his total taxable income from £12,000 to £4,000. Strictly, relief under the old form of s. 380, TA is to be given by reference to the year of assessment. By ESC A 87, however, the Revenue will allow an accounts basis.

11.4.2 New s. 380

The new s. 380(1), TA reads as follows:

Where in any year of assessment any person sustains a loss in any trade, profession, vocation or employment carried on by him either solely or in

---

[4.] Sic. This appears to be a result of consolidation and the move of employment from Schedule D, Case II to Schedule E. It is understood that the Revenue do not accept that a loss can ever arise even where expenses exceed emoluments, see *Butterworths UK Tax Guide 1995–96*, para. 5.17.

Schedule D – losses

partnership, he may, by notice given within twelve months from 31 January next following that year, make a claim for relief from income tax on –

(a) so much of his income for that year as is equal to the amount of the loss or, where it is less than that amount, the whole of that income; or

(b) so much of his income for the last preceding year as is equal to that amount or, where it is less than that amount, the whole of that income but relief shall not be given for the loss or the same part of the loss both under paragraph (a) and under paragraph (b) above.

This allows the taxpayer on making a claim to claim relief for so much of the income of that year as the trading loss covers. Income of the year puts this on an 'accounts' basis with provision to prevent double use of losses. The Revenue view is that partial claims will not be allowed. In other words the claim has to be in respect of the whole loss or, if the loss exceeds the income, the whole income.

The subsection also allows the taxpayer to make a claim to set the relief off against the income of the 'last preceding year'. As seen in para. 11.4.1 this is a change from the previous position which effectively allowed the loss to be carried against income of the next following year provided the same business was being carried on. It seems one does not have to claim the loss for the current year first. If no claim is made for the current year then one can claim wholly in respect of the preceding year.

Subsection 380(2) deals with priority where claims are made for different years in respect of the same loss or two claims are made in respect of the same loss.

11.4.3 Restrictions on s. 380

Sections 384 and 397 restrict the relief available under s. 380. Section 384 provides that losses shall not be available for carry across unless it is shown that the trade was carried on on a commercial basis and with a view to the realisation of profits in the year in question. However, s. 384(9) provides that the fact that a trade was at any time carried on with a reasonable expectation of profit is conclusive proof that it was conducted with such a view.

Section 384, like the corresponding restriction on a claim in respect of commencement losses (see para. 11.3), prevents a taxpayer from engaging in a hobby trade for the purpose of setting his trading losses against his regular taxable income. It would seem that the Inland Revenue cannot rely on hindsight (normally the fact that losses are made) in determining whether or not the taxpayer was trading with a view to realising a profit (cf. *Torbell Investments Ltd* v *Williams* [1986] STC 397).

Where during a year of assessment a business is in fact or, by reason of a change of partners, is treated as being, set up or discontinued, it will be treated as having been carried on in the way in which it was carried on at the end of the year of assessment or at the time of deemed discontinuance in respect of which the loss was sustained (s. 384(4)).

Section 397 imposes further restrictions on claims by farmers and market gardeners. Loss relief under s. 380 will be lost if the farmer or market gardener has incurred a loss in each of the preceding five years, unless he can show that his activities are of such a nature and are carried on in such a way as to justify a reasonable expectation of profit if they had been undertaken 'by a competent farmer or market gardener'. Query if competence lies in making a profit every fifth year!

Where the owner-occupier of a farm in the United Kingdom makes a loss but, under s. 384 or s. 397, cannot claim loss relief because he does not carry on farming on a commercial basis with a view to realising profits, or because he has sustained a loss in each of the last five years, he will be allowed, by concession, to claim the same relief for the cost of maintenance, repairs and insurance of his agricultural land as may be claimed by a landlord of agricultural land under s. 33, TA.[5]

11.5 'CARRY FORWARD' AGAINST FUTURE PROFITS OF THE SAME TRADE: S. 385, TA

By s. 385 the loss can be carried forward and set against future profits of the same trade, profession or vocation. It should be noted that s. 385 relief is restricted to profits arising from the same trade. Whether or not the same trade is involved is primarily a question of fact (see, e.g., *Gordon & Blair Ltd v IRC* (1962) 40 TC 358). The loss may be carried forward indefinitely until it is all used up.

Section 385, TA loss treatment applies to sole traders and partnerships. It can be used instead of carry across relief under s. 380. If s. 380 relief is claimed but the profits prove insufficient to use it all up then s. 385 may apply to the excess. But the same loss cannot be used under *each* provision.

If a trade changes s. 385 relief is lost (see *Gordon & Blair* v *IRC* discussed below). Whether there is a material change is a question of fact: *Rolls Royce* v *Bamford* (1976) 51 TC 319. In other words it is a question for the Commissioners and the 'rule' in *Edwards* v *Bairstow* and *Harrison* [1956] AC 14 that the courts may only reverse a decision of the Commissioners if 'the facts found are such that no person acting judicially and properly instructed as to the relevant law could have come to the determination under appeal' (*per* Lord Radcliffe at p. 36) applies to it.

The FA 1994 made no changes of real substance to this relief but altered the claims procedure.

Section 386 preserves s. 385 relief where a trade is incorporated, for example where a trade is transferred to a company in return for shares therein.

Example

T creates T Ltd and acquires shares and transfers business to T Ltd. Section 386 applies, even if the taxpayer's interest in the newly incorporated business is not controlling. The effect of s. 386 is that any trading losses can be set against income of the taxpayer (T) which is derived from the company (e.g., dividends or other distributions).

[5.] See Extra-statutory Concession B5.

Payments under s. 350 (i.e., certain charges on income of a business nature) may create losses for s. 385 purposes (see s. 387).

Under s. 353 certain interest payments are deductible for income tax purposes. If a taxpayer's income is insufficient in any one year to meet all the deductible interest then the interest so paid may be treated as a trading loss and carried forward under s. 385 (s. 390).

Finally, if the taxpayer cannot fully relieve a trading loss under s. 381 or s. 380, s. 385 will allow him to carry the loss forward to future years of assessment in which he is carrying on the same trade, profession, or vocation to be set against the earliest profits in those years.

Example
T makes up his accounts to 31 December each year. His recent accounts have shown the following profits and losses:
Year ending 31 December 1990 (£4,000) (loss)
Year ending 31 December 1991 £3,000 profit
Year ending 31 December 1992 £5,000 profit
The income tax assessments for the relevant years of assessment would be:
1991–92 Schedule D, Case I (£4,000) loss therefore taxable income nil
1992–93 Schedule D, Case I £3,000 profit
Less relief under s. 385 (£3,000) so taxable income nil
1993–94 Schedule D, Case I £5,000 profit
Less unrelieved loss relief under s. 385 (£1,000) so taxable on only £4,000

As noted above, a loss carried forward under s. 385 can only be set against future profits assessed under Case I or II of Schedule D, and not against any other income. In computing those profits, it is customary to exclude income taxed at source; however, for the purposes of a claim under this section, there may be included in the profits against which the loss may be set any interest or dividends on investments held for the purposes of the trade (that is, investments of a share dealer), if the profits would otherwise be insufficient to relieve the loss (s. 385(4)).

By Extra-statutory Concession B19:

Where a trader sells an industrial building after the cessation of the trade in which it has been used, any balancing charge is assessable under Schedule A or Case VI of Schedule D (s. 15, Capital Allowances Act 1990), and, in consequence, unused trading losses cannot in strictness be carried forward under section 385 or section 393 TA to set off against it. In practice such losses may be set off against a balancing charge arising in these circumstances. This treatment also applies where the balancing charge arises in respect of an event other than a sale. . . In the case of individual traders, unused capital allowances as well as trade losses may be set against such balancing charges since for income tax, but not corporation tax, purposes capital allowances are carried forward separately from losses.

Capital allowances are discussed in Chapter 12.

The question of whether or not the same trade was being carried on following a change of business was considered in *Gordon & Blair Ltd* v *IRC* (1962) 40 TC 358. The taxpayers were brewers making losses. They decided to stop brewing, and to buy beer from another brewer which they could bottle and sell as their own. This was more successful and profits were made. The court held that the brewing formerly carried on by the taxpayers and the bottling and selling which they were subsequently engaged in were not the same trade. The taxpayers accordingly could not carry forward their brewing losses and set them against their bottling profits.

11.6 'CARRY BACK' AGAINST PROFITS OF THE PRECEDING THREE YEARS (TERMINAL LOSS RELIEF: S. 388, TA)

A taxpayer who makes a loss in the last year of trading etc. may claim to have the loss set against the profits charged to Schedule D of that trade of the last three years of assessment using the profits of later years first. The trade, profession or vocation must have been 'permanently discontinued'. If a partner in a partnership retires, there will be a discontinuance in relation to that partner only if the remaining partners elect to continue the business.

11.7 CGT

An alternative to a deduction of a trading loss for income tax purposes was introduced from 1991–92 by s. 72, FA 1991, by which trading losses can be set against capital gains (a form of relief already effectively available for companies). Relief is available under this section to the extent that an income trading loss cannot be set against income for a particular year, and is not being used for income tax relief for any other year. The amount of the trading loss must be finally determined for relief against capital gains tax to be given, and the trade must not have ceased.

CHAPTER TWELVE
Capital allowances

12.1 INTRODUCTION

It was seen in Chapter 10, that only revenue expenses may be deducted in computing the profits of a trade for the purposes of Schedule D, Case I and therefore any allowances a business makes in its accounts for the depreciation in the value of a capital asset over time will not be deductible. This approach has been relaxed over the years and special provision has been made to permit depreciation of capital assets to be written off against income tax. The relevant legislation is now contained in the Capital Allowances Act 1990 (the 'CAA') and its operation is discussed in this chapter.[1]

12.2 INDUSTRIAL BUILDINGS

Capital allowances may be claimed in respect of the capital expenditure incurred on the construction of an 'industrial building or structure'. A building will be an industrial building or structure if the following activities are carried on there (s. 18, CAA):

(a) A trade carried on in a mill, factory or other similar premises. A manufacturing or processing process must be going on, so in *Vibroplant Ltd*

---

[1] Prior to the introduction of capital allowances, the Inland Revenue allowed businesses to deduct as ordinary trading expenses the cost of replacing assets which have a short working life. The practice, which persists to the present day, is known as the 'renewals basis'. Some businesses may still prefer a full deduction against trading receipts under the renewals basis, rather than capital allowances against trading profits. Where the renewals basis has been claimed for expenditure, strictly, capital allowances are not available, s. 159(1)(a), CAA. However, if a taxpayer changes from the renewals basis to capital allowances, he will be allowed to claim capital allowances as if his expenditure qualified (ESC B1).

v *Holland* [1982] STC 164, depots used by a plant hire contractor to clean, service and repair plant after it had been returned from hiring did not qualify as industrial buildings.

(b) A transport, dock, inland navigation, water, sewerage, electricity or hydraulic power undertaking.

(c) A tunnel, bridge or highway undertaking.

(d) A trade which consists of the manufacture of goods or materials or the subjection of any goods to any process. The Court of Appeal held in *Vibroplant Ltd v Holland* that the cleaning etc. of plant was not the subjection of goods to a 'process' since the word implied a substantial measure of uniformity of treatment which was not satisfied by the individual attention given to each item of plant. Section 18(3) now provides that the subjection of goods or materials to any process may include maintaining or repairing those goods or materials, although it cannot include the maintenance or repair of any goods or materials employed by the taxpayer in his trade unless that trade falls within headings (a) to (h). Since the trade of plant hire does not fall within those headings, the taxpayer in *Vibroplant Ltd v Holland* would not have been helped by this provision.[2]

(e) A trade which consists in the storage of any goods or materials:

(i) which are to be used in the manufacture of any other goods or materials;

(ii) which are to be subjected in the course of a trade to any process;

(iii) which have been manufactured, produced or subjected to any process and are awaiting delivery to any purchaser;

(iv) on their arrival in the UK by sea or air. Premises will only fall within category (iv) if they are at, or near, a seaport or airport (*Copol Clothing Ltd v Hindmarch* [1984] STC 33).[3]

(f) A trade which consists of the working of any mine, oil well or other source of mineral deposits or of a foreign plantation.

(g) A trade which consists of the ploughing or cultivating of land or threshing crops.

(h) A trade which consists of the catching of fish or shell fish.

It is specifically provided that dwelling houses, retail shops, showrooms and offices are not industrial buildings or structures (s. 18(4)). However, if a building is being used for more than one purpose, and one of the purposes falls within (a) to (h) above, the whole building qualifies as an industrial building or structure. So in *IRC v Saxone, Lilley and Skinner (Holdings) Ltd*

[2.] It was held in *Buckingham v Securities Properties Ltd* [1990] STC 166 that notes and coins handled by a security firm were not 'goods' for these purposes. The term has also been held to exclude the bodies of dead human beings, *Bourne v Norwich Crematorium Ltd* [1967] 2 All ER 576.

[3.] The facilities must be required in the ordinary process of transporting goods, so quarantine kennels will not qualify as industrial buildings or structures for these purposes, *Carr v Sayer* [1992] STC 396.

[1967] 1 All ER 756 a central warehouse used to store shoes qualified as an industrial building, despite the fact that the taxpayer company only manufactured some of the shoes, the remainder being purchased from other manufacturers. However, a distinction must be drawn with the case where a qualifying purpose is carried out in a defined part of the premises. In such a case, the capital expenditure is apportioned and capital allowances can only be claimed in respect of the expenditure relating to the part of the building used for the qualifying purpose. Nevertheless the whole of the building will qualify for capital allowances if the capital expenditure on the non-industrial part does not exceed 25% of the whole (s. 18(7)).

12.2.1 Allowances

Capital allowances (known as 'writing down' allowances)[4] are available where any person is, at the end of a 'chargeable period', entitled to a 'relevant interest' in an industrial building or structure in relation to capital expenditure incurred on the construction of all or part of that building or structure (s.3(1), CAA).[5] A chargeable period is an accounting period of a company or a period of account (s. 161(2)). This takes account of the move to the supposed current year basis of income tax. The allowance is 4% of the cost of the building or structure on a straight-line basis (which means that the allowance is spread over the period in equal instalments). Thus if a taxpayer spent £100,000 on constructing an industrial building or structure, he would be entitled to a £4,000 writing down allowance each year so that the cost of the building would be fully written off after 25 years. However, it should be noted that only the expenditure on the building or structure qualifies; the cost of buying the land on which the building or structure stands is specifically excluded (s.21(1)). Allowances are generally given to the taxpayer in taxing his trade, i.e., they are treated as a trading expense (ss. 9(1) and 140(2)).[6] If the taxpayer's interest in a building is subject to a lease, the allowances are given by discharge or repayment of tax primarily against Schedule A income (s. 9 and see para. 12.2.2).

The 'relevant interest' means the interest to which the person who incurred the expenditure on the construction of the building or structure was entitled when he incurred it (s. 20(1)).[7] Thus if a freehold owner of land constructs a building and then leases that building, the tenant cannot claim capital

---

[4] Historically, first year allowances permitting a large write off in the first year have been granted but these were abolished in 1986 save for certain exceptions such as expenditure on industrial buildings within Enterprise Zones. First year allowances were temporarily revived between 31 October 1992 and 1 November 1993 but have now lapsed again.

[5] The reader should consider whether capital expenditure incurred on extending a building or work done to strengthen an existing building qualifies for capital allowances.

[6] These rules apply to businesses established after 6 April 1994 and for existing businesses for the year 1997/98 and thereafter. Existing businesses currently use a basis period which takes account of the preceding year basis of assessment and allowances are given against the profits of that basis period.

[7] If a person has more than one interest in a building, for example, as freeholder and sub-lessee, the superior interest (in this illustration the freeholder) is taken to be the relevant interest, s. 20 (2), CAA.

allowances for the costs he incurs in (say) extending the building because the landlord has retained the relevant interest throughout (*Woods* v *R. M. Mallen Engineering Ltd* (1969) 45 TC 619). However, a taxpayer will not cease to hold a relevant interest if it is surrendered or merged, for example, if the relevant interest was a leasehold interest and the tenant subsequently acquires the freehold (s. 20(3)).

Where the person who incurred capital expenditure on the construction of the building sells his relevant interest in it, the purchaser can claim writing down allowances in respect of it. The computation of the allowances will vary according to whether or not the building is used before the relevant interest is sold. If the building has not been used, writing down allowances are given to the purchaser on the expenditure actually incurred on the construction or the purchase price if less (s. 10(1)(b)). Special provision is made for the sale of a relevant interest in an industrial building or structure by a property developer. This provision is needed since the developer's costs of construction will, strictly, be revenue and not capital expenditure as required. The CAA grants writing down allowances to the purchaser of the relevant interest on the price paid by him for the relevant interest (s. 10(3)(a)).

If, in contrast, the building or structure has been used before the relevant interest is sold, the purchaser can claim writing down allowances on the unrelieved cost of construction after taking into account any balancing allowances or charges (see para. 12.2.2) spread evenly over the remaining 25 year period (s. 3(3)). If the vendor is a property developer, writing down allowances will be available to the purchaser as if he had purchased the building from an owner who has incurred capital expenditure on its construction and to whom all appropriate writing down allowances and balancing allowances or charges have been made (ss. 10(4) and (5)).

Special provisions are also made when a landlord who has incurred capital expenditure on the construction of an industrial building or structure, grants a lease of more than 50 years in respect of that building. If the landlord and the tenant jointly elect within two years of the date the lease takes effect, the tenant will be able to claim capital allowances (s.11). The mechanism by which this is done is that the grant of the lease is treated as a sale of the relevant interest and any capital sum paid by the tenant is treated as the purchase price on sale. The tenant can thus claim capital allowances in respect of that capital sum (s. 11).[8] One effect of this provision is to assist those who finance the construction of industrial buildings but have no capacity to absorb the available capital allowances because of, say, trading losses or exemption from tax, for example, a pension fund.

12.2.2 Balancing allowances and charges

If before the end of the writing down period, i.e., within 25 years, the relevant interest is sold, or the building is demolished or destroyed or ceases to be

---

[8] The rule does not apply if the landlord and the tenant are connected or it appears that the sole or main benefit which might be expected to accrue is the obtaining of a balancing allowance, s. 11(6), CAA.

used altogether, the amount of any unrelieved expenditure is allowed as a balancing allowance (s. 4(1), CAA). Where sale, salvage, compensation or insurance moneys are received, only the excess of the unrelieved expenditure over these moneys is allowed as a balancing allowance (s. 4(3)). If the sale, insurance etc. moneys exceed the previously unrelieved capital expenditure a balancing charge is made on the excess (s. 4(4)). However, the balancing charge cannot exceed the capital allowances given to the taxpayer in respect of the building or structure (s. 4(10)). The rationale for these provisions is to ensure that the capital allowances given correspond to the actual depreciation suffered by the taxpayer.

Example
Harold built a factory at a cost of £100,000. The factory was demolished in 1995 when it was declared unsafe following a fire. At the time of demolition, Harold had claimed capital allowances of £40,000. Harold received £150,000 compensation from his insurance company in respect of the loss of the building.

	£
Cost of building	100,000
Capital allowances	(40,000)
Unrelieved expenditure	(60,000)
Insurance moneys	150,000
Potential balancing charge of:	90,000
But as this exceeds the capital allowances given to Harold, the balancing charge is limited to:	40,000

12.3 MACHINERY AND PLANT

Section 24(1), CAA also grants capital allowances where:

(a) a person carrying on a trade has incurred capital expenditure on the provision of machinery or plant wholly and exclusively for the purposes of the trade, and

(b) in consequence of his incurring that expenditure, the machinery or plant belongs or has belonged to him.

The allowances are extended to employments, professions, vocations and offices, but in the case of employments and offices allowances can only be claimed in respect of machinery or plant which is necessarily provided for use in the performance of the employment or office (s. 27).[9]

There is no statutory definition of the phrase 'machinery or plant'. In *Yarmouth v France* (1887) 19 QBD 647, (a workman's compensation case) Lindley LJ said:

---
[9] This wording corresponds with that used for the deduction of Schedule E expenses in s. 198, TA.

There is no definition of plant in the Act but in its ordinary sense, it includes whatever apparatus is used by a businessman for carrying on his business – not his stock-in-trade, which he buys or makes for sale; but all his goods and chattels, fixed or moveable, live or dead, which he keeps for permanent employment in his business.

Thus 'machinery or plant' means the apparatus used by a person for carrying on his or her trade. Lindley LJ's use of the word 'permanent' has since been explained as connoting long-term employment in the trade or durability (*Rose and Co. (Wallpapers and Paints) Ltd* v *Campbell* [1968] 1 All ER 405).[10]

The cases on the meaning of 'machinery or plant' distinguish between items used for the purposes of a business which are 'plant' and items which are merely the setting in which the business is carried on, which are not.[11] This is because the concept of 'plant' has overtones of movability even if, in the particular case, the plant may have become fixed to the building in which it is situated. For example, in *Jarrold* v *John Good and Sons Ltd* [1963] 1 All ER 141, moveable partitions were used for dividing up the space in an office building so that accommodation within the building could be varied from time to time. Pennycuick J thought that moveable partitions merited the title of apparatus used for carrying on business and accordingly the partitions qualified as plant. This decision was upheld by the Court of Appeal. Ormerod LJ said:

> I would agree, however, that there may be cases . . . where an asset or some article can be excluded from the definition because it is more a part of the setting than part of the apparatus for carrying on the trade. In the present case, however, the contrary is found. These partitions are required by the nature of the taxpayer's trade.

The distinction between the setting *in* which an activity is carried on and the apparatus *with* which the activity is carried on can also be seen in *IRC* v *Barclay Curle and Co. Ltd* [1969] 1 All ER 732. In that case, the taxpayer company built a dry dock at its shipyard for the purpose of enabling it to repair ships. Lord Reid said:

> It seems to me that every part of this dry dock plays an essential part in getting large vessels into a position where work on the outside of the hull can begin, and that it is wrong to regard either the concrete or any other part of the dock as a mere setting or part of the premises in which this operation takes place. The whole dock is, I think, the means by which, or plant with which, the operation is performed.

The courts have considered that an item cannot be plant where it is not, strictly, 'involved' in carrying on the taxpayer's business. So in *Bridge House*

---

[10]. In *Hinton* v *Maden and Ireland Ltd* [1959] 3 All ER 356 lasts and knives used by a shoe manufacturer which had a useful life of about three years qualified as plant.

[11]. Hence the need for specific provisions granting capital allowances in respect of expenditure on matters such as fire safety and thermal insulation, Chapter VII, Part II, CAA.

(Reigate Hill) Ltd v *Hinder* (1971) 47 TC 182 the taxpayers, who were restaurateurs, contributed to the cost of connecting drains to the public sewer, and claimed capital allowances in respect of their contribution. The Court of Appeal held that this was not expenditure on the provision of plant or machinery for the taxpayers' trade. Lord Denning MR said:

> It is very much a matter of impression. Are sewerage and drainage pipes part of the apparatus for carrying on the business? I think not. They are an essential ancillary to the house itself, just as much as the chimney stack. Every house, large or small, has to have a chimney stack to carry away smoke, and it has to have pipes to carry away the effluent. None such is 'plant'. They are part of the setting in which the business is carried on.

For the same reason, allowances have been refused in respect of an illuminated canopy covering the service area of a petrol filling station (*Dixon* v *Fitch's Garage Ltd* [1975] 3 All ER 455), a false ceiling in a restaurant (*Hampton* v *Fortes Autogrill Ltd* [1980] STC 80), a spectators' stand at a football ground (*Brown* v *Burnley Football and Athletic Co. Ltd* [1980] 3 All ER 244), an inflatable air dome to protect a tennis court used by a tennis coach (*Thomas* v *Reynolds* [1987] STC 135) and a 'planteria' used to display plants to customers of a garden centre (*Gray* v *Seymours Garden Centre* [1995] BTC 320).[12]

Difficulties have arisen when the expenditure incurred is partly functional and partly used to create a particular atmosphere in a building. In *Benson* v *Yard Arm Club Ltd* [1979] 2 All ER 336 the taxpayers claimed capital allowances for the purchase and conversion of a ship into a floating restaurant moored in the Thames. The Court of Appeal dismissed the claim. Templeman LJ (as he then was) said:

> The authorities disclose a distinction between premises in which a business is carried on and the plant with which the business is carried on. There are borderline cases in which a structure forming part of the business has been held to be plant because it does not merely consist of premises providing accommodation for the business but it also performs a function in the carrying on of the business. Premises or structures forming part of premises, which have characteristics and perform functions of plant, merit the claim for capital allowances. In my judgment, it follows that if a chattel, such as a ship or a hulk, only provides accommodation for a business and has the characteristics and only performs the function of premises, that chattel does not qualify as plant for the purposes of capital allowances ... For the present purposes I can see no distinction between a restaurant in the Thames and a fish and chip shop in Bethnal Green.

Nevertheless in *IRC* v *Scottish & Newcastle Breweries Ltd* [1982] 2 All ER 230 the taxpayers successfully claimed capital allowances in respect of electric

---

[12] The fact that the planteria also preserved the plants in a saleable condition while they were on display could not turn it into something other than the premises in which the taxpayer's business was carried on.

light fittings and various decorative items in their hotels. The House of Lords held that these items constituted plant and thus qualified for allowances because it was part of a hotelier's function to create an attractive atmosphere. Lord Lowry explained the decision in *Benson v Yard Arm Club Ltd* as follows:

> The Crown relied on the case because of the fact that the ship was used to create a 'shipboard feeling' in other words, a certain kind of atmosphere, among the patrons. But the distinction is that the ship, although a chattel, was the place in which the trade was carried on and was therefore the equivalent of the various premises in which the present taxpayer company carried on their trade and not of the apparatus used as an adjunct of the trade carried on in those premises.

It is, however, clear that the cases in which capital allowances may be claimed for atmospheric lighting and the like will be rare. A claim by the Wimpey chain of fast-food restaurants for its expenditure on, *inter alia*, floor and wall tiles, fire doors and suspended ceilings in its restaurants was rejected (*Wimpey International Ltd v Warland* [1989] STC 273). Fox LJ stated that floor tiles chosen to appeal to prospective customers were still part of the floor of the premises and were therefore not plant for the purposes of capital allowances. The expenditure on floor tiles simply made the floor more attractive in the same way as the choice of a beautiful building for a hotel would make the hotel more attractive to potential guests.

Expenditure incurred after 30 November 1993 on plant and settings is additionally subject to the rather odd provisions in Schedule AA1 to the CAA. This provides that expenditure on the provision of machinery or plant does not include expenditure on the provision of 'buildings' or 'structures'. Buildings and structures are defined to include items specified in an associated table which contains two columns of items. Items which fall into the first column do not qualify as machinery or plant. They include floors, walls, waste disposal systems and fire safety systems. Items in the second column may, however, qualify as plant if they would do so under the existing case law. The aim of these provisions was to make it clear that land, buildings and structures could not qualify as plant but ensure that expenditure on buildings and structures which previously qualified for relief would continue to do so (Budget Press Release IR 30, 30 November 1993). The reader is left to consider for him or herself whether these provisions actually meet this objective. The Finance Act 1997 introduced some changes in the legislation concerning fixtures to deal with some anomalies the Revenue considered were being exploited.

12.3.1 Books

In *Munby v Furlong* [1977] 2 All ER 953 the Court of Appeal held that a barrister could claim capital allowances in respect of law textbooks and reports for use in his practice.[13]

[13.] Thus overruling *Daphne v Shaw* (1926) 11 TC 256.

12.3.2 'Expenditure on the provision of . . .'

The capital expenditure must be incurred on the provision of machinery or plant (s. 24(1)(a), CAA). This will not, however, include finance costs such as interest and commitment fees on loans raised to finance the purchase of machinery or plant (*Ben-Odeco Ltd v Powlson* [1978] 2 All ER 1111),[14] but will include the loan itself. Some doubts as to whether expenditure financed by so called 'non-recourse' loans could qualify as capital expenditure were raised by the House of Lords decision in *Ensign Tankers (Leasing) Ltd v Stokes* [1992] STC 226). In that case the taxpayer unsuccessfully claimed capital allowances in respect of a loan made to a partnership in which the taxpayer was a limited partner. The loan was made by the company producing the film and was expressed to be repaid out of the profits of the film; the loan was non-recourse because the lender could not look to the taxpayer for payment. However, the 'loan' was immediately passed back to the production company under the guise of payments made to finance the production of the film. Lord Templeman concluded that capital allowances could not be claimed for this 'magical' expenditure by the taxpayer, i.e., expenditure which it was never intended that the taxpayer should repay. Nevertheless it is submitted that *Ensign Tankers* does not lay down a general proposition that non-recourse borrowing does not involve the incurring of expenditure. In the authors' view, it does not matter where or on what terms the money is borrowed so long as it is really spent.[15] In *Ensign Tankers* there was never really a loan at all. All the 'loans' to the taxpayer were made on the same day, and went through the same bank account, so that the bank account was never in credit or debit at the end of the banking day.

12.3.3 'Belonging'

In addition to showing that he has incurred expenditure on the provision of plant and machinery, the taxpayer must also show that 'in consequence of his incurring the expenditure, the machinery or plant belongs or has belonged to him' (s. 24(1)(b), CAA).[16]

The words 'in consequence of' were considered in *Bolton v International Drilling Co. Ltd* [1983] STC 70. The taxpayer company supplied an oil rig to Amoco under a contract which gave Amoco an option to purchase the rig before the expiration of the contract. Towards the end of the contract period, it became apparent that the option price was significantly less than the market

---

[14.] Cf. *Van Arkadie v Sterling Coated Materials Ltd* [1983] STC 95 where the extra sterling cost of a foreign currency purchase price was allowed.
[15.] This conclusion is bolstered by the speech of Lord Goff who said 'the mere fact that such a loan is a non recourse loan in the sense that the taxpayer is not personally liable for its repayment, the loan being repayable out of property or proceeds in the hands of the taxpayer, will not of itself prevent the transaction from constituting what is in truth a loan, or the expenditure so financed qualifying for capital allowances.'
[16.] Special rules deem computer software to be machinery or plant and treat computer software acquired under a licence as belonging to the taxpayer as long as he is entitled to the software under that licence, s. 67A, CAA.

value of the rig and the taxpayer company agreed to pay Amoco £530,000 for the cancellation of the option. Vinelott J held that the payment of this sum represented capital expenditure and that 'in consequence of' the payment the company had acquired ownership of the rig. The taxpayer company thus qualified for capital allowances.

The requirement that the plant or machinery must belong to the taxpayer can create difficulties where taxpayers carry on businesses in premises that are leased to them and who expend money on machinery or plant that becomes fixed to the premises. It was held in *Stokes v Costain Property Investments Ltd* [1984] STC 204 that if machinery or plant becomes the property of the landlord under English land law, it does not 'belong' to the tenant for the purposes of the capital allowances legislation. A similar problem can occur in reverse. In *Melluish v BMI (No. 3) Ltd* [1995] 3 All ER 453, HL it was held that (prior to the introduction of the statutory provisions discussed below) the taxpayer company could not claim capital allowances in respect of central heating and other equipment which it had leased to a number of local authorities. The equipment was leased on terms that it would become fixed to the local authorities' properties (subject to repossession by the taxpayer in the event of non-payment of rent). The House of Lords held that once the equipment became a fixture it was owned by the owner of the land and therefore belonged to the owner of the land (the local authorities) not the taxpayer for the purposes of the capital allowances legislation.

This difficulty has been partially overcome by Chapter VI of Part II of the CAA which permits capital allowances to be claimed in respect of fixed machinery or plant. The taxpayer must have incurred expenditure on machinery or plant:

(a) either for the purposes of a trade carried on by him or for leasing otherwise than in the course of a trade; and

(b) that machinery or plant has become a fixture;[17] and

(c) the taxpayer has an interest in the relevant land at the time the machinery or plant becomes a fixture (s. 52(1)).

Thus an equipment lessor (such as the taxpayer company in *Melluish v BMI (No. 3) Ltd*) can claim capital allowances in respect of the leased equipment if capital allowances would have been available to the lessee under s. 52 had the lessee incurred the expenditure (s. 53).

A taxpayer will have an interest in land if he has a freehold or leasehold estate (or an agreement to acquire the freehold or leasehold), an easement (or

---

[17.] A 'fixture' is defined as machinery or plant 'which is so installed or otherwise fixed in or to a building or any other description of land as to become, in law, part of that building or other land', ss. 51(1) and (2), CAA. However, the meaning of fixture for the purposes of English land law is not entirely clear. 'The question whether a chattel has been so affixed to the land so as to become part of it is sometimes exceedingly difficult to answer. It is a question of law for the judge, *Reynolds v Ashby* [1904] AC 466, but the decision in one case is no sure guide in another for everything turns upon the circumstances and mainly, though not decisively upon two particular circumstances, namely the degree of annexation and the object of annexation, *per* Blackburn J, *Holland v Hodgson* (1872) LR 7 CP 328 at p. 334,' Cheshire and Burn, *Modern Law of Real Property*, Butterworths, 15th edn, at p. 143.

Capital allowances

agreement to acquire an easement) or a licence to occupy the land (s.51(3)). In Scotland there will be an interest in land if the taxpayer has the estate or interest of the proprietor of the *dominium utile* (or in the case of property other than the feudal property, the owner) or any agreement to acquire such an estate or interest. Where the machinery or plant could be treated as belonging to more than one person, there are rules which treat it as belonging to the person with the most subordinate interest (s. 52(2)).

A fixture will be treated as ceasing to belong to the taxpayer when his interest in land comes to an end by transfer, surrender, expiry or otherwise (s. 57(2)). Where a lease or licence comes to an end, the fixture is then treated as belonging to the landlord or licensor (s.57(6)). However, a fixture is not treated as ceasing to belong to the taxpayer when his interest comes to an end by acquisition of the relevant freehold, leasehold or easement (s. 57(3)); nor when a lease or licence comes to an end and is replaced by a new lease or licence to the taxpayer or the taxpayer remains in occupation (s. 57(4)).

The Finance Act 1997 has introduced changes to deal with some anomalies in the legislation which the Revenue considered were being exploited. Broadly, the effect is:

(a) to limit allowances to the original cost of the fixtures;

(b) to allow for an election to be made by the vendor and purchaser as to the amount of consideration to be attributed to fixtures;

(c) to restrict allowances as plant leased to non-taxpayers reversing *Melluish* v *BMI (No. 3)* [1995] STC 964;

(d) to restrict the acceleration of allowances.

12.3.4 Allowances

Where all the necessary conditions are satisfied, the taxpayer will be entitled to capital allowances in respect of his qualifying capital expenditure in that chargeable period. As with allowances for industrial buildings or structures, a chargeable period is an accounting period of a company or a period of account. The allowances are given in taxing the trade, that is they are treated as a trading expense of the trade in that period (s. 140(2), CAA).[18] If there are no business profits to absorb capital allowances or the profits are not sufficient to absorb all the allowances due, the unrelieved allowances can be carried forward to the next chargeable period and relieved against profits of that period (s. 141(2)). There is no limit on the time for which unrelieved losses can be carried forward. As an alternative, any surplus of allowances over balancing charges can be set off against the taxpayer's income from other sources for that year of assessment (s. 141(3)).

Qualifying expenditure on machinery or plant is placed in a common 'pool' and a writing down allowance of 25% is allowed on the outstanding balance

---

[18] For professions, vocations, employments and offices see s. 140(4), CAA. These rules apply after 6 April 1994 and for existing businesses for 1997/98. For the position with regard to existing businesses see n. 6.

of the pool year by year (s. 24(2)).[19] This method of giving allowances is often referred to as the 'reducing balance basis' and its effect is to grant larger allowances in the early years.[20] For example, if a taxpayer spent £1,000 on machinery and plant, capital allowances would be available as follows:

Year 1	£1,000 @ 25%	= £250
Year 2	£750 @ 25%	= £187.50
Year 3	£562.50 @ 25%	= £140.62

And so on.

If a business has only been carried on for part of a chargeable period, the 25% allowance is proportionately reduced (s. 24(2)(a)(ii)). Each year the value of the pool will be increased by any new qualifying capital expenditure incurred.

The value of the pool will be reduced by the 'disposal value' of any machinery or plant in a chargeable period. The disposal value is:

(a) the net proceeds of sale of any machinery or plant, together with any insurance money and capital compensation received by the taxpayer. If, however, the sale is at a price lower than the market value of the machinery or plant, the disposal value is the market value;[21] or

(b) if the machinery or plant is destroyed or demolished, the disposal value is the net amount received by the taxpayer for the scrap, together with any insurance money or other capital compensation; or

(c) if the taxpayer permanently loses possession of the machinery or plant (other than on destruction or demolition) the disposal value is any insurance money or other capital compensation received by the taxpayer; or

(d) if the taxpayer starts using machinery or plant for non-business purposes or gives it away, he is treated as though he had disposed of it for its market value (s. 26).

The disposal value of machinery or plant cannot exceed the capital expenditure incurred by the taxpayer on it (s. 26(2)), although if the taxpayer acquired it from a connected person,[22] the capital expenditure is deemed to be the highest amount of expenditure incurred by any of the connected persons involved in the transaction (s. 26(3)). Where fixed machinery or plant is a fixture and the taxpayer's interest in the land comes to an end, special rules determine the disposal value of the fixture (s. 59).

If in any chargeable period, the taxpayer's qualifying expenditure is less than the disposal value he has to bring into the pool, the excess is charged as

---

[19] First year allowances were revived on a temporary basis at the rate of 40% between 1 November 1992 and 31 October 1993 but these have now lapsed. Capital allowances are restricted to 10% if the asset, i.e., the machinery or plant, is leased abroad, s. 42, CAA.
[20] Although, of course, if further qualifying capital expenditure is incurred the value of the pool as a whole will go up.
[21] Unless the disposal at undervalue results in a benefit in kind assessable under Schedule E.
[22] As defined in s. 839, TA 1988.

Capital allowances

a 'balancing charge' (s. 24(5)). Thus, to the extent that the taxpayer has been granted capital allowances for the depreciation of machinery and plant which has not actually occurred, the excess is treated as additional profit assessable to income tax.

Where a business is permanently discontinued, or deemed to be permanently discontinued, the balance of any unrelieved capital expenditure in the pool (i.e., expenditure remaining after the appropriate disposal value has been brought into account) is allowed as a 'balancing allowance' (s. 24(2)(b)). If the disposal value exceeds the value of the pool a balancing charge will arise instead.

Capital expenditure on machinery or plant is added to the pool in the chargeable period in which it is incurred. Generally, capital expenditure is taken to be incurred on the date when the obligation to pay for the machinery or plant becomes unconditional even if part of the amount due will actually be paid later because (say) it is payable in instalments (s. 159(3)). This rule was introduced to bring the capital allowance rules more into line with accountancy practice. However, if the taxpayer acquires title before the obligation to pay becomes unconditional, and the obligation to pay becomes unconditional within a month of the end of the chargeable period, the expenditure is treated as incurred at the end of that period (s. 159(4)). The effect of this provision is to accelerate the claim for capital allowances which might result in capital allowances being claimed before the asset is used in the business. To prevent exploitation, the rule is modified in certain situations. First, if the capital expenditure or any part of it need not be paid until more than four months after the obligation to pay has become unconditional, the expenditure is treated as incurred at the time when it is 'required' to be paid (s. 159(5)). Secondly, if the obligation to pay becomes unconditional earlier than would be expected according to normal commercial usage, and the sole or main purpose of this is to accelerate the claim to capital allowances to an earlier chargeable period than would otherwise be possible, the expenditure is treated as incurred at the time it is required to be paid, rather than at the time when the obligation to pay became unconditional (s. 159(6)).

12.3.5 Separate pools

In some circumstances, qualifying capital expenditure does not form part of the normal pool and is dealt with separately.

12.3.5.1 Use of machinery or plant for non-business purposes Where the taxpayer incurs capital expenditure on machinery or plant which is used partly for business and partly for non-business purposes, that expenditure is assumed to have been wholly and exclusively incurred for the purpose of a separate, notional trade carried on by him and so not part of the normal pool (s. 79, CAA). The writing down allowances that would otherwise be due on the whole of the capital expenditure are reduced to 'such extent as may be just and reasonable' having regard to the business and non-business use.

12.3.5.2 Subsidies for wear and tear
Where a taxpayer receives a subsidy or other payment which partially takes account of wear and tear to any machinery or plant, the capital expenditure on that machinery or plant is treated as having been incurred for purposes of a separate, notional trade carried on by the taxpayer, and so is not part of the normal pool (s. 80, CAA).[23] The writing down allowances that would otherwise be due on the whole capital expenditure are reduced 'to such extent as may be just and reasonable having regard to all the relevant circumstances of the case'.

12.3.5.3 Motor cars costing more than £12,000
Capital allowances can be claimed in respect of 'motor cars', defined as any mechanically propelled road vehicles, unless of a construction primarily suited for conveying goods, or of a type not commonly used as a private vehicles and unsuitable to be used as such, or provided wholly or mainly for hire to, or the carriage of, the public in the ordinary course of a trade (s. 36(1)).[24] Thus the provisions apply principally to private cars and will not include vans, taxis or hire cars.

When the capital expenditure incurred on the provision of a motor car exceeds £12,000, the taxpayer is treated as though that expenditure was incurred for the purposes of a separate trade carried on by him (s. 34). The writing down allowance for such a car is restricted to £3,000 a year (proportionately reduced if the allowance is claimed for a period of less than a year).

12.3.5.4 Short life assets and long life assets
The 25% writing down allowance allows the bulk of the cost of machinery or plant to be written off for tax purposes over eight years. This rate of depreciation is appropriate for many assets but the useful working life of others can be much shorter. If these 'short life' assets remained in the normal pool, their actual depreciation would be much faster than their tax depreciation, and the taxpayer would still be claiming capital allowances on them long after they had been replaced. To alleviate this problem the taxpayer can now elect to pool short life assets separately. The advantage of so doing is that balancing allowances may be claimed at an earlier date if the disposal value of the asset is less than the unrelieved capital expenditure. In the case of income tax, the election, which is irrevocable, must be made before 31 January next following the year of asssessment in which the chargeable period in which the expenditure was incurred ends (s. 37(2), CAA). The election is not available for certain types of assets, such as private motor vehicles and machinery or plant used for non-business purposes or for which subsidies for wear and tear have been received (s. 38). Technically the election should identify each short life asset separately. However, where this is impossible or inappropriate (because, for example, there are too many short life assets) the election may be made for a batch of acquisitions, and the costs of those assets can be aggregated and

---

[23] If the subsidy takes into account the whole of the wear and tear, no capital allowances are available.

[24] The period of hire to any one person, or anyone connected with him, must normally be less than 30 consecutive days or 90 days a year, s. 36(2), CAA.

shown in the election in one sum (Inland Revenue Statement of Practice SP 1/86).

Where the election is made, the expenditure on the short life asset is treated as incurred for the purposes of a separate, notional trade carried on by the taxpayer. However, any capital allowances due in respect of that asset are given against the profits of the actual business (ss. 37(3)(a) and (4)). The asset is kept in the separate pool for five years. If it still belongs to the taxpayer at the end of that period it is transferred to the general pool (s. 37(5)).

The Finance Act 1997 has introduced a new Chapter IVA dealing with long life assets. This replaces the 25% writing down allowance with a 6% allowance for assets (subject to certain exceptions such as ships) which have an economically useful life of 25 years or more for expenditure of more than £100,000 incurred after 26 November 1996.

12.3.5.5 Ships If a taxpayer acquires a ship for the purposes of his, her or its trade, the expenditure is deemed to have been wholly and exclusively incurred for the purposes of a 'single ship trade' (s. 31(2)(a), CAA). When the ship is disposed of special provisions allow any balancing charges to be deferred (ss. 33A and 33B, CAA).

12.3.5.6 Hire purchase Where a taxpayer incurs capital expenditure on the provision of machinery or plant for his business under a hire purchase contract, that machinery or plant is treated as belonging to him and not to any other person for as long as the contract subsists (s. 60(1)(a), CAA). All the capital expenditure incurred by the taxpayer after the machinery or plant is brought into his business is treated as though it is incurred at the time the asset is bought into business use (s. 60(1)(b)). This means that writing down allowances are based on the full cash price paid for the asset irrespective of the dates on which instalments are paid. Capital allowances are not therefore affected by buying machinery or plant on hire purchase terms rather than outright.[25]

12.3.5.7 Leasing Where a trade consists of the leasing of machinery or plant, capital expenditure on the provision of machinery or plant will generally qualify for 25% writing down allowances as part of the lessor's normal pool of capital expenditure.[26] However, where the lessor does not lease the machinery or plant as part of a leasing business, the capital expenditure incurred by the lessor in providing equipment is treated as

---

[25.] The interest element of any payments is, of course, excluded from a claim for capital allowances but should be deductible in computing profits of the business as an ordinary trading expense in the period in which it is payable.

[26.] Capital allowances are restricted to 10% if the machinery or plant is leased abroad, s. 42, CAA. However, this restriction will not apply to UK traders who are in the business of chartering ships or aircraft abroad who can claim the full 25% writing down allowance unless the main purpose of the transaction is to obtain 25% allowances, i.e., the trader has a tax avoidance motive, ss. 39(6), (7) and (8), CAA.

though it was incurred for a separate leasing trade (s. 61(1)(a), CAA). The capital expenditure is therefore placed in a separate pool for the purposes of calculating the writing down allowances and balancing allowances or charges.

12.4 MISCELLANEOUS

In addition to the allowances for industrial buildings and machinery and plant considered above, capital allowances are also available in respect of mines, oil wells and other sources of mineral deposits (Part IV, CAA), dredging (Part VI, CAA), agricultural land and buildings (Part V, CAA), scientific research (Part VII, CAA) and patents and know-how (Chapter 1, Part XIII, TA).

CHAPTER THIRTEEN
Income tax – Schedule D, Case III: interest, annuities and other annual payments

13.1 INTRODUCTION

13.1.1 General

This chapter is concerned with Schedule D, Case III.[1] Schedule D, Case III deals broadly with income[2] received without the 'real expense' of earning that income in the usual sense of earning it.[3] The charge is found in s. 18, TA set out (so far as is considered relevant) below. However, essentially it covers interest, annuities and other annual payments. Such receipts will usually be investment (or savings) income.[4] FA 1996 has made some significant changes to tax rates etc. in this context which are considered in para. 13.21.

---

[1] See Whiteman, *Income Tax*, 3rd Edn, Sweet & Maxwell, *Simon's Direct Taxes*, Pamphlets IR 11 & 30, E.C.D. Norfolk, *Taxation Treatment of Interest*, 2nd edn, Butterworths.
[2] Other than from UK land dealt with under Schedule A (see s. 18(3) Case III (a)), dividends etc. from UK resident companies dealt with under Schedule F for individuals (they have in the past fallen within D III, see, e.g. *Canadian Eagle Oil Co. Ltd v R* [1946] AC 119), foreign possessions and securities dealt with under Schedule D Cases IV and V. Public revenue previously dividends dealt with under Schedule C (repealed by FA 1996, see s. 18(3) Case III (c)) are now included. See also s. 18(1)(b), TA. The proper approach though is to look at what the charge actually covers rather than what it excludes, see source doctrine para. 5.3.
[3] E.g. buying in stock to sell. What is involved here is at most an opportunity cost. It is sometimes called 'pure income', see footnote 5.
[4] This used to be more important as there was an investment income surcharge. It is still relevant for matters such as relevant earnings for pensions etc. However, for basic rate taxpayers, the distinction with earned income has again become important as such income is now taxed at the lower (20%) rate, see para. 13.21.

13.1.2 Matters within Schedule D, Case III

The charge under Schedule D, Case III includes, inter alia, the following heads of income:[5]

(a) interest
(b) annuities
(c) 'other annual payments'
(d) discounts.

13.1.3 Alienation of income

In the past payments falling within Schedule D, Case III in the recipients' hands were often treated as reducing the payer's taxable income as a deduction from it called a 'charge on income'. In other words such payments were regarded as giving rise to an alienation of income from the payer to the recipient and the recipient's tax was collected by deduction at source (discussed in para. 13.10). This is still the case for payments such as covenanted donations to charity but has changed for many other payments. The change confuses some of the underlying logic to Schedule D, Case III and makes it a collection of somewhat disparate rules. It is these disparate rules that this chapter seeks to outline.

13.1.4 Original questions

Schedule D, Case III was originally concerned with two closely linked questions. These were:

(a) when is income taxable on a recipient as being 'any interest of money, whether yearly or otherwise, or any annuity or other annual payment'? and
(b) when may a person making such a payment deduct the payment in computing his total income for income tax purposes? Deductibility is now restricted as is explained below.

Tied into this was the question of whether the payer had to withhold income tax from the payment. As noted above, these rules have now been modified. Nevertheless, deduction at source continues to be an important feature of Schedule D, Case III.

[5.] These heads of charge are sometimes described as having the nature of 'pure income' or 'pure profit income'. This is to do with the lack of actual cost in earning the income rather than a pure theory of taxation or of law such as Kelsen's (Kelsen, Hans, *Pure Theory of Law* (1967), University of California: Berkeley). They have in common the fact that they do not have revenue expenses of earning them, for example lending money may have an opportunity cost but not a real cost. Thus if a fixed percentage of tax is deducted at source the right amount of tax will generally be collected for the Revenue in a proportionate system, i.e., where there is only one rate of tax as there was in the UK until 1911 (see Chapter 5). Much Schedule D Case III income was subject to the deduction of basic rate tax at source, i.e., income is paid 'net' of basic rate income tax and the tax collected by the payer. This is now less the case than it was; see s. 347A discussed at para. 13.3.2.

13.1.5 Example of deduction at source

In seeking to understand the workings of Schedule D, Case III and some of the cases on it, it is necessary to have some awareness of the mechanics of deduction of tax at source. The present example is intended to give an overview. Deduction at source is discussed in more detail at para. 13.10.

A company,[6] A Ltd, agrees to pay 10% interest a year on a loan of £10,000 (i.e., interest of £1,000 a year) to an individual, B,[7] the lender. B has no revenue cost of earning the interest. When A Ltd makes the payment it is required to deduct 'a sum representing the amount of income tax thereon' from the payment (s. 349(2), TA). As A Ltd is not a bank, s. 349(3) is inapplicable). For 1997/98 this will be the lower (20%) rate (see ss. 4(1A) and 1A, TA).

A Ltd will pay £800 to B and £200 to the Inland Revenue (in accordance with sch. 16, TA; see s. 350(4)). B will be entitled to a tax credit for the amount deducted. A Ltd will usually give B a certificate of tax deducted (s. 352 – strictly B needs to ask for it).

B's tax position will be as follows:

Actual Receipt	£ 800
Tax credit	£ 200
Taxable	£1,000

(The recipient is entitled to the full £1,000 and is taxable on that amount. The £200 is effectively treated as merely an application of part of the £1,000 on behalf of the recipient.)

If B is liable to income tax at 40% B would be liable to pay £400 of income tax on the receipt of £1,000. B is treated as having already paid £200 because of the deduction at source and is given credit for this against the £400 liability. Accordingly an extra £200 will be due from B so that B's tax bill of £400 is paid as to £200 of tax by deduction at source and as to £200 by B. If B is only a basic rate or lower rate taxpayer the right amount will have been deducted. If B has a nil rate, B may be able to reclaim the amount deducted.

It can be a complex matter to determine whether the deduction of tax at source rules apply or not, especially in the light of changes in FA 1988 (see now s. 347A, TA). This is considered at para. 13.10 below. Broadly, it depends on the date the obligation was entered into and characterisation of the payment and the recipient.

Dividends and other qualifying distributions made by UK resident companies are outside Schedule D, Case III, falling instead within Schedule F (see s. 20, TA especially subsection (2)). In the past such payments fell within the collection mechanism of Schedule D, Case III. Schedule D, Case III has considerable relevance to income paid by trustees to beneficiaries. (For a discussion of the income tax rules applicable to trusts, see Chapter 14.)

[6.] Not carrying on a banking business when special rules may apply.
[7.] Who is not a financial trader etc., when different rules may apply.

13.2 CHARGES ON INCOME

As noted above, in the past certain payments falling within Schedule D, Case III for the recipient could be deducted from total income and so reduce the tax liability of the payer. These were called 'charges on income'. The best description of charges on income is that of Lord Radcliffe in *IRC v Frere* [1965] AC 402. He said:

> ... in principle it is irrelevant to the determination of a person's taxable income that some part of it has been expended by him on what would normally be regarded as his own income account, in paying rent, wages, mortgage interest, rates, insurance, for example, or that the payments that he makes for such purposes will themselves constitute or contribute to assessable income in the recipient's hands. Under our system payments may run to and fro many times in the course of a single tax year, creating new taxable income at each separate point of receipt. The idea of double taxation does not even arise in these multiple assessments. The mere fact, then, that part of a taxpayer's income has been used to pay interest on a loan during the year, even assuming that you visualise 'income' as a separate spending fund, would not in itself set up a reason for reducing the assessment of his taxable income. The payment of the interest, whether long or short, would be no more, for this purpose, than an 'application' of his income. On the other hand, it is notorious that, quite apart from fixed reliefs for such kinds of expenditure as support of dependants or life assurance premiums [since abolished], the code does make provision for certain 'charges' on income being treated for tax purposes as if the income of the payer was, to the extent of the charge, not his income but the income of the recipient. To take the crudest case, that of the income received by a trustee for his beneficiary, probably the holder of a life interest under a settlement. If you wanted to calculate the 'total income' of those two persons for the purpose of working out their rights to tax relief, as individuals, you would not, nor does the tax code, stop at the bare fact that the income payments received by the trustee were actually charged to tax in his hands either by direct assessment or by the machinery of deduction. You would say that, when it came to arriving at a 'total income' under the tax scheme, such payments must not be attributed to the trustee, through whose hands they passed, but must on the contrary be attributed to the beneficiary, whose hands they were from the beginning destined to reach. That is straightforward. But now take the next most straightforward case, that of the annuity which is by legal right charged upon property, income primarily, capital by way of resort. A man comes in to the right to that income subject to the charge of the annuity. Under the tax system, as in ordinary thinking, his own income is reduced by the amount of the charge. The gross income accruing to him is divided in ownership rights, a part equal to the annuity figure belonging to the annuitant, the balance to him. The reality of this situation was recognised and allowed for by the tax system, because, while the payer of the annuity was assessed and charged on the gross income, he was from the earliest days allowed to deduct from his

Income tax – Schedule D, Case III: interest, annuities etc. 365

payments a proportionate part of the tax which he had borne or was to bear on the total. By this means his true taxable income was treated as being the residue left after the charge of the annuity, the burden of the tax being shifted from payer to recipient by the former's statutory right to recoup himself out of the payment due to the latter. This recognition of a division of ownership between two or more persons entitled to rights in a single 'fund' of income was not, however, confined to such cases as those where there was trust income or an annuity charge. There was also the case of 'annual' or 'yearly' interest – I do not distinguish between the two adjectives – payable under a mortgage, the characteristic feature of which seems to have been that in setting up the mortgage situation, the borrower had in effect divided the gross income of his estate between himself and the mortgagee. Up to this point it could fairly be said that the division corresponded with and followed the lines of enforceable legal rights in an identifiable fund of property, the accruing income. But the tax system can be seen to go further than this, for it applied the same idea of division of proprietary right to situations in which legal distinctions draw no dividing line. Thus an annual payment secured by personal covenant only, involving no charge on any actual security, whether income or capital, was treated in the same way for tax purposes. It had to be 'annual', and it had also to be payable 'out of the profits or gains brought into charge' in order to rank as income of payee not of payer, because it was the division of taxable income with which the code was dealing; and it may well be asked what at this stage is the significance of the words 'out of' as applied to a payment, the obligation for which was merely the personal one to find the money required out of whatever resources the payer might mobilise for the purpose. The answer was provided by the application of what is in truth an accountant's, not a lawyer's, conception, for it was accepted that, so far as the payer was found to have in the relevant year a taxable income larger than the gross amount required to make the payment, to that extent he was entitled to claim that he had made the payment 'out of profits or gains brought into charge' and to deduct and retain for his own account tax at what in due course (after 1927) became the 'standard rate'.

(For 1973–74 and subsequent years the basic rate (see s. 32, FA 1971) and, since the FA 1996, either the lower or the basic rate depending on the nature of the payment.)

This may be represented as follows:

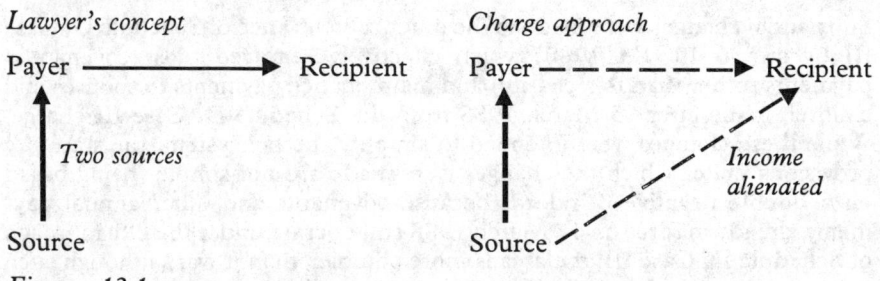

Lawyer's concept
Payer ⟶ Recipient
↑
Two sources
Source

Charge approach
Payer – – – – ⟶ Recipient
↑ ↗
Income alienated
Source

Figure 13.1

13.3 THE CHARGE UNDER SCHEDULE D, CASE III

13.3.1 General

Section 18, TA imposes the charge under Schedule D, Case III. It provides (inter alia)

(1) Tax under this Schedule shall be charged in respect of – . . . (b) all interest of money, annuities and other annual profits or gains not charged under Schedule A, [B, C now repealed] or E, and not specially exempted from tax.
(2) Tax under Schedule D shall be charged under the Cases set out in subsection (3) below, and subject to and in accordance with the provisions of the Tax Acts applicable to those Cases respectively.
(3) The Cases are – . . .
Case III
tax in respect of –
   (a) any interest of money, whether yearly or otherwise, or any annuity or other annual payment, whether such payment is payable within or out of the United Kingdom, either as a charge on any property of the person paying the same by virtue of any deed or will or otherwise, or as a reservation out of it, or as a personal debt or obligation by virtue of any contract, or whether the same is received and payable half-yearly or at any shorter or more distant periods, but not including any payment chargeable under Schedule A, and
   (b) all discounts, and
   (c) income from securities which is payable out of the public revenue of the United Kingdom or Northern Ireland.

Certain other income is also directed to be charged under Schedule D, Case III (s. 18(4), for example certain patent receipts).

FA 1996 has substituted a new Schedule D, Case III by reference to 'loan relationships' for corporation tax purposes (see s. 18(3A), TA as substituted).

13.3.2 1988 changes

Substantial changes were made to the practical relevance of Schedule D, Case III by ss. 36–40, FA 1988, which effectively removed most covenanted payments (other than to a charity) and maintenance payments to spouses and children made after 15 March 1988 from the Schedule D, Case III charge. While these changes were intended to simplify the tax system, the statutory provisions under which the changes were made are not simple (being based on a double negative!). Indeed, because covenants and other annual payments already in force on 15 March 1988 still operate under the old approach of Schedule D, Case III, the area is more complex than it was, although such payments are now dying out. The changes in the Finance Act 1988 mean that formerly popular covenants in favour of students[8] and of grandchildren[9] are no longer tax effective if entered into after 15 March 1988. The removal of maintenance payments made after that date from Schedule D, Case III gives rise to some real drawbacks for those paying and those receiving maintenance following a separation or divorce.

From 15 March 1988, only limited categories of annual payments effectively remain within the charge under Schedule D, Case III (see below). This is the effect of s. 347A, TA inserted by s. 36, FA 1988. As a result of s. 347A, TA no annual payment is deductible from the income of the payer or taxable in the hands of the recipient if it is not in the following categories. These are:

(a) payments of interest;
(b) covenanted payments to charity (subject to certain conditions);
(c) payments made for *bona fide* commercial reasons in connection with an individual's trade, profession or vocation;
(d) payments under s. 125(1), TA (that is, payments within Schedule D, Case III, other than interest, which are made under a liability incurred for money or money's worth all or any of which is not required to be brought into account in computing income tax or corporation tax liability for the person making the payment).

However, annual payments made under existing obligations entered into before 15 March 1988 will continue to be taxed under the Schedule D, Case III system while they remain enforceable so long as the Inland Revenue was notified of the obligation before 30 June 1988 (s. 40, FA 1988).

13.4 ANNUITIES, ANNUAL PAYMENTS, INTEREST AND DISCOUNTS

Since the 1988 changes operate by effectively excluding from Schedule D, Case III certain payments that would otherwise be within it, the starting point is always to determine whether or not a payment is within Schedule D, Case III. The charging section, s. 18, TA (set out in para. 13.3.1) covers annuities, annual payments, interest and discounts and so raises four questions in particular to consider, namely:

(a) What is an annuity?
(b) What is an annual payment?
(c) What is interest?
(d) What is a discount?

---

[8]. In the days of grants if the parental contribution were covenanted to an adult student then, if drafted in the right way, the student could claim basic rate income tax back so maximising the position. The Inland Revenue even issued their own pack to do this.
[9]. These covenants could be outside Part XV, TA for basic rate purposes and the grandchild could use the personal allowance to recover tax deducted.

13.5 WHAT IS AN 'ANNUITY'?

There is, as usual, no general statutory definition of an 'annuity' in the UK tax legislation. The classic definition of 'annuity' is that of Watson B in *Lady Foley* v *Fletcher* (1858) 3 H & N 769, 157 ER 678. He said: 'An annuity means where an income is purchased with a sum of money and the capital has gone and ceased to exist, the principal having been converted into an annuity.'

Some further guidance may be found in Stamp LJ's speech in *IRC* v *Church Commissioners* [1975] STC 546, CA (for House of Lords see [1976] STC 339). He said (at p. 551):

> ... if a principal sum be paid as the price of the purchase of a terminable annuity, the whole of each payment is to be regarded as income and liable to income tax. As Greene MR pointed out in *Southern-Smith* v *Clancy* [1941] 1 KB 276, in such a case the legal nature of such a contract is beyond question. The property in the principal sum passes absolutely to the recipient of that sum. No relationship of debtor and creditor with regard to that sum is ever constituted. The sum as a sum ceases to exist once it is paid. Its place is taken by the promise to pay the annuity and the annuitant's only right is to demand payment of the annuity as it accrues due. The financial results of the transaction will, however, be that the recipient of the annual payments will receive by the end of the period of years a sum equal to the amount which he paid together with a sum in respect of interest, and if each annual payment is struck with tax he will in one sense be paying tax on capital. 'Nevertheless' remarked Greene MR 'it has throughout been assumed by the courts that such payments are liable to tax: *Coltness Iron Co* v *Black*, *Jones* v *IRC* and *Perrin* v *Dickson*. The reasoning in *Scoble's* case [[1903] 1 KB 494] seems to be based upon the same view.[10]

This would cover the house equity income schemes to be seen advertised in the Sunday newspapers aimed particularly at those without a mortgage or negative equity. Although the calculation of the annuity may be based on the return of the capital sum with interest, no account is taken of this on general principles. In *Southern-Smith* v *Clancy* [1941] 1 KB 276 Sir Wilfrid Greene MR said:

> If the law were that, in the ordinary case of an annuity for a term of years, the nature of the financial calculation involved stamped part of the payment as a capital payment, leaving only the interest element to be taxed, on the ground that an annuity is taxable only in so far as it is a profit, the position would be simple and perhaps not unjust ... However, I do not feel myself at liberty in this court to adopt any such principle.

A measure of simplicity and justice has now been achieved in relation to 'purchased life annuities' by s. 656, TA, which allows such an annuity to be

---

[10.] Section 656, TA lays down a special scheme for purchased life annuities.

dissected into a capital and income element with only the latter subject to income tax. A 'purchased life annuity' is a life annuity granted for money or money's worth in the ordinary course of an annuity business, and a 'life annuity' is an annuity payable for a term ending with (or at a time ascertainable only by reference to) the end of a human life which need not necessarily be the annuitant's life (s. 657(1)). The section does not apply to an annuity which would otherwise be treated as capital, or which was purchased in pursuance of a will or settlement, or which was bought by payments made by the annuitant which qualified for retirement annuity relief (s. 657(2)). The capital element of the annuity, which will be constant for all payments of it, is calculated by taking the lump sum paid by the annuitant and dividing it by his life expectancy at the time the annuity is first paid (s. 656(3) to (6)).

Example
A pays £18,000 in return for an annuity of £1,900. At the time the first annuity payment becomes due, A's life expectancy is 12 years. The capital element of each annuity payment is therefore one twelfth of £18,000, which is £1,500. The income element of each annuity payment is therefore £1,900 minus £1,500, i.e., £400.

13.6 WHAT IS AN 'OTHER ANNUAL PAYMENT'?

13.6.1 General

Again, there is no general statutory definition of 'other annual payment' (see Lord Radcliffe in *IRC* v *Whitworth Park Coal Co. Ltd* (1957) 38 TC 531 at p. 575). The statute does provide that annual payments 'reserved in respect of, or charged on or issuing out of land' are chargeable under Schedule A (see s. 15, TA) and so are not assessable under Case III (see s. 18(3)). However, there is no further guidance. Accordingly, it is necessary to turn to the case law. The usual starting point in any discussion of 'other annual payment' is Jenkins LJ's propositions in *IRC* v *Whitworth Park Coal Co*. This was a case about tax on interim compensation for the loss of income paid under the relevant legislation on nationalisation. The actual question at issue has now become obsolete – it concerned close company apportionment. In essence the question was '... whether these receipts are chargeable to Income Tax under Case III or Case VI of Schedule D ...' (see Harman J at 38 TC 531 at p. 537).

13.6.2 Jenkins LJ's propositions

Jenkins LJ said: *'There have been many judicial pronouncements as to the scope of Rule 1 (a) of Case III and the following propositions can be regarded as established.'* Each of these propositions will now be considered in turn.
 (The propositions are set out in italics.)

(i) To come within the Rule as an 'other annual payment' the payment in question must be ejusdem generis with the specific instances given in the shape of interest of money and annuities . . .'

The effect of the *ejusdem generis* approach is that to be an annual payment the payment must be of an income rather than a capital nature. Even if it is of an income nature the payment must still be similar to interest and annuities. Accordingly payments of life assurance premiums were not 'other annual payment' in *Earl Howe* v *IRC* (1919) 7 TC 289 nor was rent in *Gregory* v *Hill* (1912) 6 TC 39.

(ii) The payment in question must fall to be made under some binding legal obligation as distinct from being a mere voluntary payment: see Smith v Smith [1923] P 191, per Lord Sterndale, MR, at p. 19, and Warrington, LJ, at p. 202.

This seems to be consonant with the words 'personal debt or obligation' in Schedule D, Case III itself as drafted. Thus a series of voluntary payments such as a £5 gift every Christmas from an aged aunt would not be an annual payment for income tax purposes. Such gifts are not liable to income tax if there is no binding legal obligation as there is no source for the income (*Smith* v *Smith* [1923] P 191 at p. 197; *Peter's Exors* v *IRC* 24 TC 45). However, this is not the case for payment under a discretionary trust. Once the income has been appointed to the beneficiary there is a legal obligation which it is said is sufficient for these purposes (see *Lindus and Hortin* v *IRC* 17 TC 442 and see the speech of Lord Wrenbury in *Drummond* v *Collins* [1915] AC 1011).

If the agreement is defective in any way then the question arises whether payments under it can be an 'other annual payment'. An ultra vires payment by a company seemingly was not in *Ridge Securities* v *IRC* (1964) 44 TC 373 (see pp. 395–96).

(iii) The fact that the obligation to pay is imposed by an Order of the Court and does not arise by virtue of a contract does not exclude the payment from . . . Case III. 'The words in Case III, 1 (a) "whether such payment" and so forth do not in my opinion limit the annual payments to those there mentioned but merely provide that they at all events shall be included', per Warrington, LJ, in Smith v Smith, at p. 201, and Lord Sterndale, MR, to the same effect, at p. 197.

Payments made pursuant to a trust, under a court order (cf. *Smith* v *Smith* [1923] P 191) or pursuant to statute (e.g., *Conservators of Epping Forest* v *IRC* (1953) 34 TC 293) can thus be caught.

(iv) The payment in question must possess the essential quality of recurrence implied by the description 'annual'. But that description has been given a broad interpretation in the authorities . . .

Income tax – Schedule D, Case III: interest, annuities etc. 371

This does not require that the payments recur in fact. What is needed is a capacity to recur. However, this is not a sufficient condition on its own (see *Moss Empires Ltd* v *IRC* [1937] AC 785). Lord Radcliffe in *Whitworth Park Co.* v *IRC* (see para. 13.6.1) said:

> The word 'annual' has not been found to admit of any significant interpretation. To the Courts it means no more than 'recurrent' . . . – or even 'capable of recurrence'. That may be so, but I think that it would be both bad logic and bad law to deduce that merely because a payment is in fact recurrent or capable of recurrence it is therefore to be treated as an annual payment.

It seems though that payments may meet this requirement in some cases where the payment is contingent and variable in amount (*Whitworth Park Co.* v *IRC*).

Because, in particular, of the deduction at source requirements, casual payments are more likely to be held by the courts to fall within Schedule D, Case VI rather than Case III. (On the location of the source, cf. *Westminster Bank Exors & Trustee Co. (Channel Islands) Ltd* v *National Bank of Greece* (1970) 46 TC 472.) Lord Radcliffe in the *Whitworth Park Co.* case said:

> Such temporary and casual incomes appear to me to fit less naturally into Case III, with interest of money, annuities and other annual payments, than into Case VI, which has always been regarded as the Case that covers what I may call the oddities of Schedule D.

> (v) *The payment in question must be in the nature of a 'pure income' profit in the hands of the recipient.* By way of authority for this proposition we need only refer to *Earl Howe* v *Commissioners of Inland Revenue*, 7 TC 289, at p. 303, where Scrutton, LJ, said: 'It is not all payments made every year from which Income Tax can be deducted. For instance, if a man agrees to pay a motor garage £500 a year for five years for the hire and upkeep of a car, no one suggests the person paying can deduct Income Tax from each yearly payment. So, if he contracted with a butcher for an annual sum to supply all his meat for a year, the annual instalment would not be subject to tax as a whole in the hands of the payee, but only that part of it which was profits . . .'

That the payment be 'pure income' is a requirement of an 'other annual payment' is beyond argument. The question is, what does it mean? Jenkins LJ refers to *Earl Howe* v *IRC* [1919] 2 KB 336 as authority for his fifth proposition requiring 'pure income profit' and Scrutton LJ's examples in the *Earl Howe* case.[11] In those examples[12] the annual instalment would not be subject to tax as a whole in the hands of the payee, but only that part of it which was profits. The point here is that income from trading or professional

---
[11] Earl Howe was attempting to deduct insurance premiums for surtax purposes.
[12] An agreement to pay a motor garage £500 a year for five years for the hire and upkeep of a car, and a contract with a butcher for an annual sum to supply all his meat for a year.

activities does not represent 'pure income' profit as there is a cost of earning it, and so is not within Schedule D, Case III. The profit in such cases can only be ascertained by taking expenses from the receipts, not simply by taking the receipts themselves. In *Campbell* v *IRC* [1970] AC 77 Lord Donovan said that Scrutton LJ's approach was the correct one, and explained that:

> One must determine, in the light of all the relevant facts, whether the payment is a taxable receipt in the hands of the recipient without any deduction for expenses or the like – whether it is, in other words 'pure income' or 'pure profit income' in his hands, as those expressions have been used in the decided cases. If so, it will be an annual payment under Case III. If, on the other hand, it is simply gross revenue in the recipient's hands, out of which a taxable income will emerge only after his outgoings have been deducted, then the payment is not such an annual payment.

A useful illustration is *IRC* v *National Book League* [1957] Ch 488, where the National Book League received subscriptions from members under deeds of covenant, to whom the League's facilities were then made available. It was held that these subscriptions did not fall within Case III, since they were made in return for the provision by the League of goods and services. Here the 'pure income profit' requirement became confused with a requirement that there should be no condition or counterstipulation for making the payment. The misunderstanding was set straight by the House of Lords in the *Campbell* case. Only if the condition or counterstipulation amounts to a quid pro quo given by the payee to the payer, the cost of which to the payee is deductible from the amount of the payment in computing the payee's income for tax purposes, will the payment cease to qualify as an annual payment within Schedule D, Case III.

Essex County Council v *Ellam* [1988] STC 370 affirmed [1989] STC 317 shows the current approach. Here the local authority arranged for the payer's child to attend a special school. The payer covenanted to pay the net amount of the school fees to the authority, who then sought to reclaim tax under the covenant, arguing it was separate from the school fees. This argument was rejected by Hoffmann J who held that the payments were not pure profit and therefore not annual payments. Hoffman J considered that the payments would not have been taxable gross if the Council had been liable to tax (see [1988] STC 370 at p. 385). The payments were made in return for the Council having arranged for the child to go to the special school and continuing to pay his fees while he was there (at p. 385). There was thus a cost to the Council. The Court of Appeal agreed.

The decision in *Campbell* v *IRC* set the seal on a very simple and effective method of turning taxable income into non-taxable capital. A taxpayer would sell an annuity to a charity for a lump sum. The capital sum would not be liable to either income tax or capital gains tax in the taxpayer's hands. The annual payments he made to the charity in respect of the annuity would cost him only a fraction of their gross amount as he would be saved income tax thereon. Provided the payments were applicable and applied to charitable purposes only, the charity would be exempt from tax on the amount of payments. That such 'reverse annuity schemes' were not affected by the then anti-avoidance legislation was confirmed by the House of Lords in *Plummer* v *IRC* [1979] STC 793 (but now see *Moodie* v *IRC* [1993] STC 188 which held that the decision in *Plummer* was out of step with the later *Ramsay* line of cases discussed in Chapter 4). Anticipating the adverse decision, the Revenue secured the enactment of s. 125, TA which prevents the payer of any annual payment obtaining any tax relief in respect of the making of it. The section applies where the payment is made under a liability incurred for consideration in money or money's worth all or any of which is not required to be brought into account in computing, for the purposes of income tax, the income of the payer. The section contains certain limited exceptions.[13]

As was seen above it used to be thought that to constitute pure income profit, annual payments must not have been made with conditions or counterstipulations attached. It must nearly always follow that, if the condition or counterstipulation is enforceable (for example, by contract), the income is not 'pure profit' income. However, as Lord Donovan pointed out in *Campbell* v *IRC*:

> The truth is, in my opinion, that one cannot resolve the problem whether a payment is an annual payment within Case III simply by asking the questions 'Must the payee give or do something in return?' or 'Did the payer make some counterstipulation or receive some counter-benefit?' or 'Was it pure bounty on his part?' . . . The test must be applicable to all annual payments; and the problem must continue to be resolved, in my opinion, on the lines laid down by Scrutton LJ in the *Earl Howe* case. The crux of the matter, therefore, is not whether there is a condition or counterstipulation, but whether the taxpayer can claim any sum as an expense of earning the income.

13.6.3 Charities and counterstipulations

For some years, the general view that there must be no enforceable counterstipulation proved a problem for some charitable bodies wishing to provide limited special benefits for those who signed covenants in their favour. The position has been clarified for certain payments due after 14 March 1989 by s. 59, FA 1989. This section provides that if a body is a charity and has as its sole or main purpose the preservation of property for the public benefit or the conservation of wildlife for the public benefit, certain types of consideration provided to those who sign covenants will be ignored. The considerations that will be ignored are, a right of admission to view property the preservation of which is the sole or main purpose of the charity, or to observe wildlife the conservation of which is the sole or main purpose of the charity, such a right being either free or at a reduced charge for the covenantee or for a member of his family. This would apply, e.g., to covenanted payments for family membership of the National Trust.

[13.] The settlement provisions in Part XV must also be considered in this context; see Chapter 15.

13.6.4 Income or capital?

The requirement is that the payment be pure *income* to amount to an 'other annual payment'. A payment of capital would not be 'pure income' on general principles. However, the fact that a lump sum is paid does not necessarily make it capital any more than payment by instalments makes it income. It may be a mixture of income and capital (cf. an annuity and see *Scoble* v *Secretary of State for India* [1903] 1 KB 494).

In *Re Hanbury* (1939) 38 TC 588 CA the question at issue was whether a lump sum payment of some £22,700 as compensation for the use of certain chattels constituted income taxable under Schedule D, Case III and so subject to deduction of tax at source. Here it was held that the sum was income but it was not 'pure'. Sir Wilfred Greene MR said:

> . . . From the point of view of the recipient, his position may be summarised. Being the owner of chattels the use and enjoyment of which has been had by the Respondents against payment, is he bound to submit to having the sum he so receives treated as pure income profit in relation to which as between himself and the Revenue he would be entitled to no item of deduction at all on the other side of his profits account, or is it a sum in respect of which he is liable to direct assessment and upon such assessment would be entitled to put forward such claim, if any, as he may have on the other side of the account? It seems to me that the nature of the payment brings it within the second class quite clearly. The matter, I think, can be tested in this way. If the Appellant had been carrying on a business of letting out plant for reward, the receipt which he obtains under the present circumstances would have been an item to be taken into account in ascertaining the profits of that business for the purpose of assessment under Case I of Schedule D. Nobody could suggest in such a case, it seems to me, that this payment would be a thing which must be segregated from the receipts of his business and subjected to some special treatment. If that be right – and I have no doubt that it is right – it appears to me to show the quality of this payment to be such that by its nature it is merely an element in the ascertainment of profits and is not a pure profit to be taken by itself.

In *Campbell* v *IRC* (1968) 45 TC 247 the House of Lords held that the sums were capital receipts in the trustees' hands. As a result, the trustees were unable to reclaim income tax deducted from the payments. Here Davies (Tutors) Ltd ('Tutors') entered into a deed of covenant to pay annually to Davies Educational Trust (a registered charity) 80% of its net profits. A few days later Davies' Educational Developments Ltd ('Developments') was incorporated as a company wholly owned by the Trust. Tutors and Developments entered into a partnership for carrying on a tutorial business hitherto owned by Tutors. Developments was to purchase from Tutors one-fifth of the goodwill in the business for £10,000 and to have the option of purchasing further one-fifths at the same unit price. Money paid under the covenant was

Income tax – Schedule D, Case III: interest, annuities etc.   375

given by the Trust to Developments who used it to buy a further share in the goodwill. The Trust claimed repayment of the tax notionally deducted by Tutors on the grounds that they constituted Schedule D, Case III income in the Trust's hands. This failed as the payments were not income and so could not be pure income.

In *IRC v Church Commissioners* (1976) 50 TC 516 the Church Commissioners owned land leased to the Land Securities group, a property investment concern. The Church Commissioners agreed to sell the property subject to the leases to Land Securities in consideration of rentcharges, i.e., periodic payments charged on the land. It was common ground that there had never been any legally enforceable agreement between the parties to sell for a lump sum. The question at issue was whether tax had been properly deducted in paying the rentcharges and therefore whether Church Commissioners could reclaim the tax deducted. (The agreement had already been the subject of litigation. In *IRC v Land Securities Investment Trust Ltd.* (1969) 45 TC 495 it had been held that the rentcharges were not deductible in computing Land Securities profits for tax purposes.)

The Crown contended:

Where a capital asset is transferred, or a capital obligation discharged, or a capital payment is made, in consideration of a series of cash receipts of fixed amounts over a fixed period so that the total debt may be immediately calculated, then those cash receipts are in the hands of the recipient partly income and partly capital, whether the parties call the series of cash receipts 'rent' or 'annuity' or 'annual sums' or 'rentcharges' or 'instalments' and whether the payments are secured or unsecured.

Nonetheless the Special Commissioners decided in favour of the Church Commissioners. Megarry J upheld this decision as did the Court of Appeal. The House of Lords unanimously gave judgment against the Crown.

Lord Wilberforce (with whom Lord Salmon agreed) said (50 TC 516 at pp. 565–6):

English [sic] tax law has consistently taxed, as revenue, periodical payments of the kinds enumerated in [the section], in spite of the fact that they may be payments for wasting assets – i.e., assets the capital value of which is to disappear after time, and without any distinction (such as the Crown seeks to draw here) between perpetual payments or payments for an indeterminate period . . .

His Lordship continued (at p. 568):

. . . except in particular cases where a different rule is stated, all payments which fall within the charging words are *prima facie* taxable as income notwithstanding that, as a matter of accountancy or prudence or trust administration, some part ought to be treated as capital. I have said '*prima facie*' because there are . . . cases in which the courts have held that although the payment appears to fall within this description income tax is not chargeable on the payment or not wholly chargeable. The first is where there is a sale for a consideration represented by a principal amount which is payable by instalments. The distinction between such a case and that where the sale is for an annuity or a rentcharge has been recognised by many authorities . . . I do not think that the Crown can succeed on the general argument without destroying this dichotomy, but in my opinion they attempt the impossible. On general, logical grounds, and perhaps on considerations of an economic character, there may be much to be said for a rule which recognises the existence of an interest element in all deferred capital payments – I think that Cross J was attracted by this kind of argument in *Vestey* v *Commissioners of Inland Revenue* [1962] Ch. 861. But illogical or not (and the consequences of rejecting the dichotomy might introduce other illogicalities) it is too clearly and firmly rooted in the income tax law to be displaced except, in selected cases, by legislation. And it has been, if not without difficulty, at least with fair consistency, applied by the courts. Whether there are other possible cases of dissection, ie, apart from the case where a lump purchase price has been agreed upon, may be a debatable area. There is no doubt, in my opinion, that the plain case is recognised by authority – *Scoble* v *Secretary of State for India* [1903] AC 299.

He said later (at p. 569):

The essential feature of the negotiations and of the bargain, as shown by the documents, was that Land Securities did not wish, on any account, to pay a lump sum for the properties. . . . The bargain was always thought of in income terms, and was concluded on income terms, and there is nothing in the documents which gives to the transaction, or to any element in it, a capital character. The resemblance to the facts of *Vestey* (itself a borderline case), though at first sight striking, is, in the end, more superficial than real, and the essential 'true' character found to exist in *Vestey* is missing here. *A fortiori*, the present case differs from the clear factual situation in *Scoble's* case. In the end, the decision in the present case rests upon a narrow point but I find that it does not come within a dissection principle.

13.7 'INTEREST' AND SCHEDULE D, CASE III

13.7.1 General

By s. 832(1), TA 'interest' means both 'annual and yearly interest and interest other than annual or yearly interest'. This led Megarry J (as he then was) to quip 'interest in short means interest' (*Re Euro Hotel (Belgravia) Ltd* [1975] 3 All ER 1075 at p. 1081).

This raises three questions in particular. These are:

(a) what is interest?

(b) what is annual or yearly interest?
(c) what is short interest?

13.7.2 What is interest?

The most quoted description of interest is that of Rowlatt J in *Bennett v Ogston* (1930) 15 TC 374 at p. 379. He said 'interest means payment by time for the use of money'. It has been considered in many other cases. A few of these cases are considered below.[14]

In *Re Euro Hotel (Belgravia) Ltd* [1975] 3 All ER 1075 the question arose whether certain payments which fell to be made under a building agreement were 'interest of money' within s. 349, TA. The payments were made by way of compensation for delay in completion, were described as interest in the agreement and were to be calculated on a daily basis by reference to an annual percentage rate on a stated sum of money. Megarry J decided the payments were not interest. He referred to the Canadian case of *Reference Re Saskatchewan Farm Security Act 1944, Section 6* [1947] 3 DLR 689 on a subject far removed from the present, but of value for some words that Rand and Kellock LJJ uttered in the Supreme Court of Canada. Rand J said:

> Interest is, in general terms, the return or consideration or compensation for the use or retention by one person of a sum of money; belonging to, in a colloquial sense, or owed to, another.

Rand J added:

> ... the definition, as well as the obligation, assumes that interest is referable to a principal in money or an obligation to pay money. Without that relational structure in fact and whatever the basis of calculating or determining the amount, no obligation to pay money or property can be deemed an obligation to pay interest.

Kellock J said: 'There can be no such thing as interest on principal which is non-existent.'

Megarry J in *Re Euro Hotel (Belgravia) Ltd* said:

> To these authorities, which were duly put before me, I would add a passage from the speech of Lord Wright in *Riches v Westminster Bank Ltd* [1947] 1 All ER 469 at 472, a case concerned with 'interest of money' in the Taxing Acts. He said '... the essence of interest is that it is a payment which becomes due because the creditor has not had his money at the due date. It may be regarded either as representing the profit he might have made if he had had the use of the money, or, conversely the loss he suffered because he had not that use. The general idea is that he is entitled to

---

[14.] On whether payments of 'interest' by a guarantor are themselves interest, see *Westminster Bank v National Bank of Greece* (1970) 46 TC 472 where the point is left open and on payments under an indemnity which were held to be interest, see *Re Hawkins* [1972] 3 All ER 386.

compensation for the deprivation. It seems to me that running through the cases there is the concept that as a general rule two requirements must be satisfied for a payment to amount to interest, and *a fortiori* to amount to 'interest of money'. First, there must be a sum of money by reference to which the payment which is said to be interest is to be ascertained. A payment cannot be 'interest of money' unless there is the requisite 'money' for the payment to be said to be 'interest of'. Plainly, there are sums of 'money' in the present case. Second, those sums of money must be sums that are due to the person entitled to the alleged interest; and it is this latter requirement that is mainly in issue before me. I do not, of course, say that in every case these two requirements are exhaustive, or that they are inescapable. Thus I do not see why payments should not be 'interest of money' if A lends money to B and stipulates that the interest should be paid not to him but to X: yet for the ordinary case I think that they suffice.

13.7.3 What is yearly interest?

Lord Denning MR answered this question in *Corinthian Securities Ltd* v *Cato* (1969) 46 TC 93 saying (at p. 96):

Interest is 'yearly interest of money' whenever it is paid on a loan which is in the nature of an investment, no matter whether it is repayable on demand or not. An ordinary loan on mortgage is usually in point of law repayable at six months. But it is still 'yearly interest of money'. On the other hand, when a banker lends money for a short fixed period, such as three months, and it is not intended to be continued, such a loan is not in the nature of an investment. It is not 'yearly interest of money', but a short loan. That is shown by *Goslings and Sharpe* v *Blake* (1889) 23 QBD 324, where Lindley LJ said (at p. 330), referring to the ordinary mortgage: 'In point of business, therefore, a mortgage is not a short loan; but a banker's loan at three months is a totally different thing.'

Lord Denning's use of the word 'investment' has not met with universal approval. In *Cairns* v *MacDiarmid* [1983] STC 178 Sir John Donaldson MR said, after citing *Corinthian Securities* that he 'would personally wish to avoid the use of the term "investment" as providing any sort of test in the context of . . . annual interest . . .' He considered it well settled that the difference between what is annual interest and what is short interest depends on the intention of the parties (see [1983] STC 178 at p. 181). Did they intend the loan to be for a year or more?

Interest on damages for personal injuries or death awarded under inter alia s. 3. Law Reform (Miscellaneous Provisions) Act 1934, or s. 35A, Supreme Court Act 1981 is not taxable as income (s. 329, TA, cf. s. 51(2), TCGA).

13.7.4 Summary – yearly or short interest

In summary it seems that the following can be said:

(a) Interest is yearly when paid or payable on loans which are expressed or intended by the parties to last 12 months or longer.

(b) If interest is expressed and intended to last less than 12 months it is short interest. (Hence the useful definition in s. 832, TA).

(c) It is important to note:

(i) the impact of the intention of the parties;
(ii) the irrelevance of whether interest is expressed to be paid monthly, quarterly, half yearly, annually or at other times;
(iii) that it is irrelevant that capital is *repayable* before one year is up or on demand.

13.7.5 Interest or premium?

The courts distinguish 'premiums' from 'interest' (see *Lomax* v *Peter Dixon* [1943] KB 671). An example may help to illustrate this. Three situations should be considered.

(a) L lends B £1,000 which B is to repay over two years at a charge of 10% per annum. The charges paid by B are normally classified as interest because interest is 'payment by time for the use of money' (cf. Rowlatt J in *Bennett* v *Ogston* (1930) 15 TC 374 (para. 13.7.2)).

(b) L lends money to B on the same terms as to interest etc. but insists that B pays an extra £100 at the end of the loan to compensate L for the risk of lending the money to B. That £100 is a 'premium'.

(c) L may simply not charge interest at all but require the payment of a lump sum, say £700, when B returns the £1,000 at the end of two years. That lump sum is also a premium.

The difference is between:

interest: which is broadly payment by time for the use of money; and
a premium: which is broadly an insurance payment against the risk of loss of capital.

The important point is that premiums are not within the definition of 'interest' for general income tax purposes.

It is suggested that the following points may be derived from (inter alia) *Lomax* v *Peter Dixon*:

(a) whether the payment is 'interest' or 'premium' is a matter of law;
(b) if interest is charged at a rate which is 'reasonably commercial' on a reasonably sound security then any additional sum is probably a premium and not disguised interest;
(c) relevant factors in determining whether a payment is 'interest' or a 'premium' include:

(i) the terms of the contract;
(ii) the term (i.e., length) of the loan;

(iii) the rate of interest charged if any;
(iv) the nature of the risk taken (the riskier the venture the more likely any 'premium' is to be a 'premium' and not interest).

In broad terms the consequences of the difference are as follows:

(a) if there is a premium it is a capital sum and no income tax will be payable on it (capital gains tax may be payable), whereas if the sum is 'interest' income tax is payable;
(b) interest is deductible for the payer as a business expense whereas premiums, on general principles, are not.

13.8 WHAT ARE 'DISCOUNTS'?

Tax under Schedule D, Case III, is also charged on 'all discounts' (Schedule D, Case III para. (b)). This charge was considered in *Ditchfield* v *Sharp* [1983] STC 590. Bergers, the paint company, had issued a promissory note promising to pay a Dutch company £2,399,000 free of interest as part consideration for the sale of the entire share capital in the British Paints group of companies. The taxpayers subsequently bought the promissory note from merchant bankers. The promissory note was paid in full by Bergers on the due date, and the taxpayers realised a profit of some £460,000 which the Revenue sought to assess under Case III as a discount. Walton J at first instance made the following preliminary observation ([1982] STC 124 at p. 131):

> The bald phrase 'all discounts' is an extremely curious one. Down to the Income Tax Act 1918, the phrase used was 'profit on a discount' ... With this form of words it was easier than it is at present to translate them into 'profits arising from discounts received on discounting transactions', but it has not been suggested to me that the alteration in language involved any alteration of substance, so the question is for present purposes: was the excess a profit arising from a discount received on a discounting transaction?

The answer to this question was in the affirmative. The Court of Appeal held that the purchase of the promissory note from the merchant bankers before it matured for a price which was less than the full face value of the note was a discounting transaction and that the realised profit was a profit arising from a discount.

13.9 BASIS OF ASSESSMENT FOR SCHEDULE D, CASE III

The preceding year basis applied to Schedule D, Case III income other than for new sources arising on or after 6 April 1994 (see the 'old' s. 64, TA). A current year basis applies for new sources. The current year basis will apply to all sources from 1996–1997.

Where payments are assessed on a preceding year basis then, for example, the charge is made for 1993–94 on the payments arising in 1992–93.[15] Under the current year basis, income tax is charged on the full amount of the income arising within the year of assessment. Thus payments arising in 1996–97 will be charged to income tax in 1996–97.

Income 'arises' for these purposes when it is received by the taxpayer (*Whitworth Park Coal Co. Ltd* v *IRC* [1961] AC 31) for as Rowlatt J said in *Leigh* v *IRC* [1928] 1 KB 73, 'receivability without receipt is nothing'. It would seem, however, that on general principles[16] bank (and presumably building society) interest is received at the time it is credited to the taxpayer's account (cf. *Dunmore* v *McGowan* [1978] 2 All ER 85, CA, and see s. 482(1), TA for 'a relevant deposit' where any amount credited as interest in respect of a relevant deposit is to be treated as a payment of interest). However, where a bank deposit is charged in favour of the bank to secure another's indebtedness, and the bank can transfer money from the deposit to satisfy the indebtedness, interest on the deposit is never received by the depositor (*MacPherson* v *Bond* [1985] STC 678). Similarly, interest paid to the taxpayer by cheque is not received by him until the cheque is cleared and credited to his account (*Parkside Leasing Ltd* v *Smith* [1985] STC 63). Nevertheless, by virtue of s. 71, TA, a charge can be made on the preceding year basis even though no income arose from the source in the year of assessment in which the charge is made (as long as the source still exists).

Tax is payable on the full amount of income assessable under Schedule D, Case III without deduction – any expense might well prevent the payment being pure profit in any event. In *Shaw* v *Tonkin* [1988] STC 186, the taxpayer formed an association for teachers' widows, putting funds raised for it into a savings account. She sought to deduct from the income received from the account her expenses in running the association, but it was held that this was not possible.

A payment will be liable to be assessed when it is due (even if taxed on a preceding year basis)[17] whether or not it is actually paid then. This gave rise to a difficulty in *IRC* v *Crawley* [1987] STC 147, where a deed made in 1971 provided for payments of £5,000 a year to be made to a charity. The payments fell into arrears, and the sums due for 1974–76 were paid several years late, although the payer did then deduct tax at basic rate for the years when the payments should have been made. In 1984 the charity sought repayment of the basic rate tax from the Inland Revenue, but it was held this was not possible as the payments were assessable when they were due, and as more than six years had passed since then no repayment could be made. This is a clear warning to recipients of Schedule D, Case III payments to ensure that they do get the payment and make any claim for tax repayment within six years of the due date.

---

[15] Cf. the preceding year basis for Cases I and II, which is different, being based on an accounting period ending in the preceding year of assessment.

[16] See also s. 477A(5), TA, that tax is to be computed on the 'full amount of the income arising in the year of assessment'.

[17] This is the effect of the arising basis and 'old' s. 64, TA.

13.9.1 Summary

The general rule for all Schedule D, Case III income is that income is only taxed if it is received. Thus income due in year one is not taxed in year one unless received then.

There are three exceptions to this rule to note in particular:

(a) If interest is received in year two which was due in year one, it is taxed in year two as year two's income (*Leigh* v *IRC* [1928] 1 KB 73 (para. 13.9) and see also *Parkside Leasing* v *Smith* [1985] STC 63: If A sends B a cheque for interest, is that sum received when the cheque is received or when it is honoured? Held, when it is honoured).

(b) A current year basis of assessment applies to income falling within ss. 348–350, TA.

(c) A current year basis applies to bank deposit account interest and building society interest.

13.10 DEDUCTION OF INCOME TAX AT SOURCE

13.10.1 Introduction

The collection of tax by deduction at source[18] has long been popular with governments wherever it can be imposed. Historically, a cardinal feature of the taxation of income falling within Schedule D, Case III was deduction of tax at source. Lord Hanworth MR said in *IRC* v *Hamilton* (1931) 16 TC 213 (at p. 228) '. . . the root principle, or one of the root principles of the collection of Income Tax is deduction at source . . .' The history of the matter is well set out by Lord Macnaghten in *LCC* v *Attorney General* (1901) 4 TC 265.[19] When a payer paid a sum to the payee, the payer collected income tax

---

[18] See Revenue pamphlet on interest and E.C.D. Norfolk, *Taxation Treatment of Interest*, 2nd edn, (1992).

[19] He said (at pp. 295–7) 'In the Act of 1842 the charge upon annuities, yearly interest of money, and other annual payments, is not expressly included in Schedule D, where it was afterwards placed by the Act of 1853. It forms the subject of a distinct section. The charging section is section 102. It extends to all annual payments. The charge is to be according to, and under and subject to, the provisions by which the duty in the third case of Schedule D may be charged. There is a provision that "in every case where the same shall be payable out of profits or gains brought into charge by virtue of this Act," (your Lordships will note those words, they extend to income chargeable under each of the five schedules) no assessment is to be made upon the person entitled to the annual payment. The whole of the profits and gains are to be charged, and the person charged in respect thereof is entitled to deduct a proportional part of the duty when he comes to make the annual payment to which he is liable. In every other case the annual payment is charged with duty in the hands of the recipient. Then section 103 imposes penalties on persons refusing to allow the deductions authorised by the Act. It is only material as showing that these provisions with regard to annual payments extend to annual payments out of profits or gains chargeable under all the different schedules. Now, what has the Act of 1888 really done? It is no longer optional for a person who has to make an annual payment to deduct Income Tax. He is bound to make the deduction, and bound to pay over to the Crown the amount deducted unless the payment comes out of income which has already paid the duty. That is a substantial improvement, and a reasonable security for payment of duty in many cases where formerly it was

from the sum and paid the payee the net sum. In effect, because of charges on income an annual payment was regarded as income of the recipient, i.e., the income was regarded as being assigned or alienated to the recipient and was regarded as a charge against or deduction from the payer's income reducing the amount of the payer's taxable income.

The advantage, for the Revenue, of a system of deduction at source is that it is easy to require the person making the payment to deduct income tax from the payment and for the Inland Revenue to collect the tax deducted from the payer. The payer has no interest in not accounting for the money by deducting it and it avoids the possibility of the money being spent before the tax can be paid. It can also improve the Revenue's cashflow.

However, the system of charges on income was open to abuse. It was also very inefficient and expensive where the payee was not liable to income tax, since the payee would be forced to make a repayment claim or suffer tax to which the payee was not liable.

Therefore s. 36, FA 1988 took a wide range of payments out of Schedule D, Case III altogether, thereby taking the payments out of the deduction of tax at source rules. However, it did not effect a root and branch change and the two systems coexist for different purposes and payments. For example, the old system remains for payments to charities but not to individuals (where payments are made in respect of an obligation entered into after 15 March 1988).

The difference can be seen in the treatment of a covenant by A to pay £100 a year for seven years to his adult niece B.

Under the old system the position would be as follows.

A pays B   £ 77
A pays Revenue £ 23   A gives B certificate of deduction

Total   £100

A would have a charge on income of £100.
B would be taxable on £100 with a tax credit of £23 (using current rates).

Under the new system, i.e., if the covenant was entered into after 14 March 1988 (or a payment falling due on or after 15 March 1988 unless an 'existing obligation' as defined in s. 36, FA 1988), then the position would be as follows.

A would be taxable on the £100 with no charge on income. This is the effect of s. 347A(1)(a), TA which provides that A's 'income shall be computed without any deduction being made on account of the payment'.

---

liable to be evaded. But to read the enactment as imposing a double duty would be contrary to the whole scope of Income Tax legislation and whimsical in the highest degree, when you consider that the double burden would necessarily fall upon the fundholder, in whose case the collection of duty is certain, while a person chargeable under Schedule D would be expressly exempted from double duty.'

The £100 would not form part of B's income. This is the effect of s. 347A(1)(b) which provides that 'the payment shall not form part of the income of the person to whom it is made or of any other person'. Accordingly B would not pay tax on the £100 but A would be taxable in respect of it.

The £100 would be paid gross as it is not 'charged with tax under Case III of Schedule D' and so not within ss. 348 and 349.

For the exceptions from s. 347A, TA see para. 13.3.2 (for maintenance payments, see Shipwright, *Strategic Tax Planning*, Division B).

The general procedure for the deduction and collection of tax at source in respect of Schedule D, Case III income is contained in ss. 348, 349 and 350 (see below). There are a number of exceptions. The effect of s. 36, FA 1988 must be borne in mind (see above). A payer who is subject to these sections is under a duty (enforceable by legal action) to supply the taxpayer at his request with a written statement showing the gross amount of the payment, the amount of income tax deducted, and the actual amount paid to the payee (s. 352, TA). The payee can use this statement to prove to the inspector of taxes the payment and amount of income tax and receive credit for the tax deducted. This is because although the tax is collected by the payer, it is paid on the payee's behalf (ss. 348, 349 and 350 specifically so provide).

The rules applicable vary with the type of payment in question. These rules will be considered in the following paragraphs.

13.10.2 Interest and deduction of tax at source

Section 349(2), TA applies to 'any yearly interest of money' chargeable under Case III. The meaning of 'interest of money' was considered in para 13.7.2. To constitute 'yearly' interest, it seems that the obligation under which the liability to pay interest arises must continue for a year or more (see paras 13.7.3 and 13.7.4 and cf. *Ward* v *Anglo-American Oil Co. Ltd* (1934) 19 TC 94 and *Cairns* v *MacDiarmid* [1983] STC 178). The changes made by s. 36, FA 1988 do not apply to interest; see s. 347A(2)(a), TA.

Section 349(2) applies to the following matters:

(a) interest paid by a company or local authority (s. 349(2)(a));

(b) interest paid by or on behalf of a partnership of which a company is a member (s. 349(2)(b));

(c) interest paid by any person including an individual to a person whose usual place of abode is abroad (s. 349(2)(c)).

It does not apply to:

(a) non-yearly (or short) interest (s. 349(2));

(b) interest paid by a company or local authority in a fiduciary or representative capacity (s. 349(2)(a));

(c) interest paid by, or to, a bank carrying on a *bona fide* banking business in the United Kingdom (s. 349(3)(a) and (b) but the rules as to relevant deposits may apply, see para. 13.10.3.2);

(d) interest on advances made by deposit takers or mortgage interest paid under the MIRAS scheme (s. 369);

(e) interest paid on certain quoted Eurobonds (s. 124). In practice this can be a relatively cheap way of avoiding withholding of interest on a large loan because of the way the stock exchanges of some EU member states operate;

(f) interest paid by an individual other than to a person whose usual place of abode is outside the UK.

Where s. 349(2) applies, the 'person by or through whom' payment is made is required to deduct a sum representing the amount of income tax thereon for the year in which the payment is made. For 1997–98 this will be the lower (20%) rate (ss. 4 and 349(2)). A person who is acting in two capacities can make a payment 'through' himself. Thus, in *Howells* v *IRC* [1939] 2 KB 597 (and see also *Rye and Eyre* v *IRC* 29 TC 164), a solicitor, who had lent money to one of his clients, deducted interest due on the loan before paying the balance of certain money to the client. Although the solicitor had not retained income tax on the interest payable to himself, the court held that he was a person through whom the payment of interest to himself had been made, and he was accordingly liable to pay the tax to the Inland Revenue which *prima facie* the client was liable to pay on the solicitor's behalf. Such a result seems odd when it is remembered that the solicitor was the taxpayer who would ultimately be liable to be assessed on the interest under Case III. He was merely fulfilling his client's obligations to deduct and pay tax which would be treated as tax paid by the solicitor anyway.

Apart from the unusual facts in this case, it does illustrate that agents such as solicitors who make payments on their clients' behalf may be assessable under s. 349(2). If s. 349(2) applies, the person by or through whom payment is made must deliver an account of the payment to the inspector of taxes, and he is then liable to be assessed and charged to income tax on that payment (s. 350(1),(3) and (4)). In this way, the payer has paid the full amount of the interest (though some of it has gone directly to the Inland Revenue to satisfy the payee's liability to income tax under Case III on the interest), the payee has received the full amount of the interest (though some of it is already held by the Inland Revenue to satisfy his liability to income tax on the interest) and the Inland Revenue are assured of at least lower rate income tax on the interest.

Example

B borrows a sum of money from L who lives in Ruritania (with whom the UK has no double tax treaty). In 1997–98, B is liable to pay interest of £500 to L. Because s. 349(2) applies, B must deduct tax from the £500 before making any payment. Tax at the basic rate of 20% on £500 is £100; B will therefore pay only £400 to L. B must then account to the Inland Revenue for the tax deducted, which the Inland Revenue will hold on account of L's liability to income tax on all income chargeable to tax in the United Kingdom in 1997–98. Thus, B has parted with £500 by sending £400 to L and £100 to the Inland Revenue; L has received £500, though £100 of it is being held to his credit by the Inland Revenue to satisfy his income tax liability on the interest due to him.

13.10.3 Building society and bank interest

13.10.3.1 General Arrangements existed for many years under which building societies accounted to the Inland Revenue for tax at a special reduced rate ('the composite rate') on most interest which they paid or credited to investors (see s. 476, TA, now repealed). Depositors who received interest from building societies were then treated as though they had received interest net of basic rate income tax (s. 476(5)).

Taxpayers who were liable only to tax at the basic rate on their building society interest thus had no further liability to income tax. However, depositors who were not liable to pay income tax on their interest (typically widows, orphaned children and pensioners) could not reclaim the income tax paid on their behalf, and taxpayers who were liable to pay higher rates of income tax on their deposit interest were still liable to pay their excess liability (s. 476(5)(b) and (6)).

Similar provisions were introduced by the Finance Act 1984 in relation to interest paid by banks after 5 April 1985. Again, interest paid by banks was treated as a payment net of basic rate income tax, so that basic rate taxpayers had no further liability whilst higher rate taxpayers had to make good the excess liability and no repayment was made to those not liable to pay income tax on the deposit interest (s. 479(2), also now repealed). These provisions applied to interest paid or credited to the depositor's account by the Bank of England, any recognised bank, the Post Office through the National Girobank, any trustee savings bank, or a Scottish savings bank (s. 481(2)). However, deposits held at overseas branches of UK banks or at non-UK branches of foreign banks were excluded, as were the deposits of investors who are not ordinarily resident in the United Kingdom who made a declaration in the prescribed form to that effect to the bank (s. 481(5)). The composite rate was the same for building societies and banks and was fixed every year by statutory instrument (s. 483). Although composite rate was lower than basic rate, the drawback of the system was that an individual who was not liable to pay basic rate tax could not reclaim the tax withheld from interest payments.

This approach attracted some criticism, and from 1991–92 the scheme under which building societies and banks paid a composite rate of tax was stopped. From 6 April 1991 building societies and banks instead paid basic rate tax on interest payments (s. 30 and sch. 5, FA 1990). Any taxpayer who was not liable to pay all or part of that basic rate tax was able to reclaim it, and any individual who was not liable to pay tax at all could complete a form to this effect, and as a result could receive their interest gross. The system remains in force today, but such interest is now taxed at the lower rate of 20% (rather than the basic rate). The deduction of lower rate tax will be deemed to satisfy a basic rate taxpayer's liability, but a higher rate taxpayer will have

Income tax – Schedule D, Case III: interest, annuities etc. 387

to account to the Revenue for an additional 20% (being the difference between the higher rate of 40% and the 20% already deducted).

13.10.3.2 Banks etc. and relevant deposits – s. 480A, TA The FA 1990 introduced a new scheme for banks and similar bodies, called in the legislation 'deposit takers' (defined in s. 481(2) as applied by s 481(1A)). A deposit taker is to deduct income tax (lower rate income tax; see s. 4) on paying interest on a 'relevant deposit'. A deposit is defined in s. 481(3) (applied to s. 480A by virtue of s. 481(1A)) as 'a sum of money paid on terms under which it will be repaid with or without interest and either on demand or at a time or in circumstances agreed by or on behalf of the person making the payment and the person to whom it is made.' This is a very wide definition and would catch a bank deposit account. A deposit is a 'relevant deposit' if 'but only if' the person entitled to any interest in respect of the deposit is an individual or personal representatives. A deposit is not a relevant deposit if the individual is ordinarily resident outside the UK and has made the appropriate declaration (s. 481(5)(k)). By s. 482(1) any amount which is credited as interest in respect of a relevant deposit is treated as a payment of interest. Section 86, FA 1995 extended the tax deduction at source scheme for bank interest to cover deposits belonging to discretionary and accumulation trusts with effect from 6 April 1996. Regulations setting out the arrangements were laid before Parliament on 24 May 1995 ([1995] STI 887 and see Deposit-Takers (Interest Payments) (Discretionary or Accumulation Trusts) Regulations 1995 SI 1995/1370 [1995] STI 1018). (See s. 481(4)(d), TA.)

13.10.3.3 Building societies and deduction of tax at source The position as far as building societies and deduction at source is concerned is now governed by s. 477A, TA inserted by FA 1990 and the regulations made under it. The main regulations are the Income Tax (Building Societies) (Dividend and Interest) Regulations 1990 (SI 1990/2231, amended inter alia by SI 1992/11 and SI 1992/2915). The broad effect of regs. 3 and 4 is that (subject to exceptions) a building society is to deduct lower rate tax on paying a dividend or interest unless it falls into certain specified classes. These include (inter alia) payments to:

(a) individuals not ordinarily resident in the UK, including joint entitlement if only individuals are involved;
(b) trustees of a trust under which no person has an interest other than an individual who is not ordinarily resident in the UK and certain offshore discretionary and accumulation trusts where no person has an interest other than an individual who is not ordinarily resident in the UK;
(c) personal representatives if the investment formed part of the deceased's estate, if the deceased was not ordinarily resident in the UK;
(d) a charity entitled to exemption under s. 505(1)(c), TA;
(e) an exempt approved retirement benefits scheme;
(f) a company;

(g) a payment of interest on a bank loan;
(h) a payment in respect of certificates of deposit etc.;
(i) a payment in respect of an investment held at a branch of the building society outside the UK (for example the Channel Islands or the Isle of Man).

13.11 MORTGAGE INTEREST

Mortgage interest payable after 31 March 1983, provided the conditions set out below are satisfied, is subject to the procedure allowing mortgage interest relief at source (MIRAS). In outline, the scheme provides for the deduction of income tax from any payment of mortgage interest although relief is restricted to 15%. In this way, a taxpayer is given some relief against tax for the amount of any mortgage interest paid by him. This is the only way in which a taxpayer can claim mortgage interest relief since his total income is now subject to income tax without any reduction for the interest paid. Tax relief is available on a mortgage up to a maximum of £30,000 (s. 367(5), TA and s. 55, FA 1993). The details of the MIRAS scheme can be found in ss. 369 to 379, TA. A higher rate taxpayer has never been able to receive any relief against higher rate tax under MIRAS, such relief in the past being given by deduction of interest paid from income subject to the higher rate. However, from 1991–92 higher rate relief has been abolished, and only 15% relief as already outlined is available (s. 27 and sch. 6, FA 1991). In 1994–95 the relief was 20% (a reduction from basic rate relief which was previously available) and mortgage interest relief was restricted to 15% for 1995–96 and subsequent years (see s. 369(1A), TA).

In order for any interest to qualify for relief under MIRAS, it must satisfy certain conditions. Interest is eligible for relief if it is paid by the owner of an estate or interest in land in the United Kingdom or the Republic of Ireland on a loan to defray money applied in purchasing the estate or interest or in developing the land or any buildings on the land (s. 354(1), TA). Formerly relief was also available for loans for the improvement of land, but this is now only available for loans made before 6 April 1988 (a written offer made before that date confirmed in writing is sufficient); (s. 355(2A)). The relief is extended to include a caravan, and by s. 367(1) to include a houseboat designed or adapted for use as a place of permanent habitation. Certain qualifications that had to be satisfied in the case of a caravan under s. 354(3) have been removed from 1991–92 (s. 28, FA 1991). Interest relief was initially available to the individual taxpayer, so it was possible for more than one individual to join together in the purchase of a property and claim relief for a loan up to £30,000 each, but from 1 August 1988 the limit of £30,000 relates to the property, so that an overall limit of £30,000 applies even if there is more than one purchaser (s. 356A, TA). A loan will only be accepted as being made before 1 August 1988 if there is written evidence that the loan was offered before that date and a binding contract to buy the relevant property was entered into before that date. Loans made to joint borrowers before 1 August 1988 will continue to attract full relief for each borrower, but only for so long as the same loan continues. There are quite complicated provisions setting out how relief will be apportioned where there is more than one purchaser after 1 August 1988; *prima facie* the relief will be divided between them equally even if they are not buying in equal shares, but any relief that one purchaser does not actually use may be transferred to another up to the limit of £30,000 for each property (so long as that other is actually paying a larger proportion of the mortgage) (ss. 356B, 356C and 356D).

From 1990–91, it is possible for a husband and wife who are not separated to elect that qualifying interest paid by one may be treated as paid by the other (s. 356B). The land, caravan or houseboat must be used as the only or main residence (cf. *Frost* v *Feltham* [1981] STC 115) of the taxpayer (s. 355, TA) and interest relief is allowed only on a loan or loans must up to £30,000 (s. 357). For the purpose of calculating this limit, no account is taken of unpaid interest (up to £1,000) which has been added to the outstanding capital (s. 357(6)). Formerly relief was also available where the loan was in respect of a main residence for a dependent relative or a former or separated spouse of the taxpayer, but this is now only available for loans made before 6 April 1988 (s. 44, FA 1988).

The terms of the 'only or main residence' test are stringent. However, some relaxation is offered by Extra-statutory Concession A27 (as revised May 1995). Temporary absences of up to a year are in practice ignored in determining whether a property is used as an only or main residence. In addition, where a person is required by reason of his employment to move from his home to another place, either in the United Kingdom or abroad for a period not expected to exceed four years, any property being purchased with the aid of a mortgage which was being used as his only or main residence before he went away, will still be treated as his only or main residence, provided it can reasonably be expected to be so used again on his return. Where a person has acquired an estate or interest in a property, for example, by exchange of contracts, but is prevented by his move from occupying it as his home, he will nevertheless be regarded as having used the property as his home for the purposes of the concession. Relief will not be given beyond a period of four years but if there is a further temporary absence after the property has been re-occupied for a minimum period of three months, the four-year test will apply to the new absence without regard to the previous absence. If an individual already on an overseas tour of duty purchases a property in the United Kingdom in the course of a leave period and uses that property as an only or main residence for a period of not less than three months before his return to the place of his overseas employment, he will be regarded as satisfying the condition that the property was being used as his only or main residence before he went away. If an individual lets his property whilst he is away, at a commercial rent, the benefit of the concession may also be claimed, where appropriate, if this is more favourable than a claim for relief against letting income.

Where a taxpayer takes out a second or bridging loan to acquire a new home before he has disposed of his old one, interest paid on the loan for the old home continues to be eligible for relief for one year from the taking out of the second loan (s. 355(1A), TA), provided that the taxpayer does in fact occupy the new home (*Hughes* v *Viner* [1985] STC 235). The relief is also available to a person in 'job-related' living accommodation (which is defined either as accommodation within the three categories in s. 145 set out in para 7.4.2.6, or as premises or other land provided by a person (whether under a tenancy or otherwise), under a contract entered into at arm's length requiring the taxpayer or his spouse to carry on a particular trade, profession or vocation, and to live either on those premises or on other premises provided by the other person, provided that that other person is not a company in which the taxpayer or his spouse has a material interest or a business partner of the taxpayer or his spouse) (s. 356).

13.12 ANNUITIES AND ANNUAL PAYMENTS AND DEDUCTION OF TAX AT SOURCE

A taxpayer is entitled (unless some other rule applies) to be taxed in accordance with the legal form of his arrangements. If this is so, then the legal effect of an annuity or an 'other annual payment' (which must be made under a binding legal obligation and which from 15 March 1988 must not be caught by s. 347A, TA – see para. 13.10.1) is to create in someone else the legal entitlement to that income, and it would necessarily follow from this that the payer should not be assessed on the annuity or annual payment but that the recipient should. In theory, this is what happens, but the theory is distorted somewhat in practice by the system of collection of tax at source.

This system operates by treating the tax deducted by the payer as tax paid by the recipient (and therefore reflects the true legal position, since the recipient is entitled to receive the amount of the annuity or annual payment but is liable to pay tax on it, and the payer is liable to pay the full amount of the annuity or annual payment and it can hardly matter to him whether he pays the full amount to the recipient or part of it to the recipient and part to the Inland Revenue to discharge all or part of the recipient's liability to income tax). The distortion arises because of the way in which the Inland Revenue collect the tax deducted by the payer. In theory, the payer should not be assessed at all on the income because it belongs not to him but to the recipient, and therefore he ought to be able to deduct the full amount of the payment in computing his own liability to income tax. In practice, this is not so, for the Inland Revenue need some method of collecting from him the basic rate tax which he deducts. First, therefore, the taxpayer is prevented from deducting annuities and annual payments in computing his taxable income by s. 817(1)(b). Secondly come the methods of collection. If the taxpayer makes the payment of the annuity or annual payment out of income which the Inland Revenue would normally assess to tax, then they may as well continue to do so, and collect tax from him in this way (s. 348). It must be remembered, however, that the object of the system is to collect only basic rate income tax from the payer to be treated as tax paid by the recipient: in order to ensure that the Inland Revenue do not collect too much tax from the payer, s. 3 provides that where the payer has paid an annuity or annual payment (or patent royalty – see ss. 348(2)(a) and s. 349(1)(b)) from which he has deducted income tax, he is only to be charged to basic rate income tax on his own income from which the payment is made. If, on the other

Income tax – Schedule D, Case III: interest, annuities etc.

hand, the payer makes the annuity or annual payment out of money not normally assessable to income tax, the Inland Revenue will need to assess him directly and separately on the amount of the payment, but again only at basic rate (s. 349(1)). A distinction is accordingly drawn between payments of annuities, and annual payments or patent royalties 'payable wholly out of profits or gains brought into charge to income tax' (s. 348) and payments not so payable (s. 349(1)). It is therefore important to know when payments are or are not made out of chargeable income. This is also important to determine the rate at which deduction is to be made (see ss. 4 and 1A, TA).

According to Lord Wilberforce in *IRC v Plummer* [1979] 3 All ER 775, the general rule is that what is significant, when one is considering the application of the statutory rule, is not the actual source out of which the money is paid, nor even the way in which the taxpayer for his own purposes keeps his accounts, if indeed he keeps any, but the status of a notional account between himself and the Revenue. He is entitled, in respect of any tax year, to set down on one side his taxed income and on the other the amount of the annual payments he had made and if the latter is equal to or less than the former, to claim that the payments were made out of profits or gains brought into charge to income tax.

This general rule may, however, be disregarded where the taxpayer has treated the payment in his accounts in such a way as to produce practical results or consequences inconsistent with the payment being treated as made out of chargeable income. For example, in *Fitzleet Estates Ltd v Cherry* [1977] 3 All ER 996, the taxpayers borrowed money and charged the interest to their profit and loss account. The taxpayers subsequently decided, with the approval of the auditors, to capitalise the interest by transferring amounts equal to the interest paid to the capital cost of the property acquired as shown in the balance sheet. The effect of this capitalisation was to allow a greater dividend to be declared in the future. The House of Lords held that the capitalisation had practical consequences, and accordingly the taxpayers could not now claim that payments charged to capital could be treated as having been paid out of chargeable income.

In *Nobes and Co. Ltd v IRC* [1966] 1 All ER 30, the taxpayers were similarly precluded by their own actions from contending that payments had been made out of taxed profits. Lord Morris of Borth-y-Gest said that the mere form of the taxpayer's accounts would not be decisive, but the accounts were evidence of a decision upon which an action was taken which had positive results and which affected the rights of others. Resolutions as to the payment of dividends were passed and were acted upon in reference to the accounts which had as their basis that the annual payments were made out of capital and accordingly would not diminish the funds available for distribution. Accordingly, the annual payments had to be paid out of chargeable income.

13.13 SECTION 348, TA

Section 348, TA applies to the payment of an annuity, an effective annual payment, or patent royalty, but not interest, payable wholly out of profits or gains brought into charge to income tax.

There are three consequences of the application of s. 348:

(a) The taxpayer is assessed and charged to income tax on his taxable income 'without distinguishing' the payment. This confirms s. 817(1)(b). The words 'without distinguishing' are, however, misleading. If the payment were not distinguished, the payer would be assessed to income tax at basic and higher rates on income which, as stated above, is not legally his.

The object of s. 348 is to collect from the payer basic rate tax on behalf of the recipient. The payment is therefore distinguished to the extent that s. 3 only empowers the Inland Revenue to assess the payer to income tax at basic rate tax on that part of his income which represents the annuity, annual payment, or patent royalty. It must follow from this that the payer is not to be assessed to higher rate tax on that part of his income. The payer deducts basic rate income tax at the rate in force for the year of assessment in which the payment is due and not when it is paid (s. 4).

(b) If the payer, having paid basic rate income tax to the Inland Revenue, in accordance with (a) above, were to remain under his contractual liability to pay the full amount of the annuity, annual payment, or patent royalty to the recipient, he would ultimately be paying more than he agreed to. Therefore s. 348 allows the payer to deduct from the payment due to the recipient the amount of basic rate income tax which he will become liable to pay in respect of that payment, and the recipient is bound to allow such deduction. Suppose, therefore, that the payer covenants to pay to the recipient £100 a year for ten years. Every year, the payer will pay to the recipient £77 (assuming solely for purposes of illustration basic rate income tax to be 23%). The Inland Revenue will assess him to basic rate tax on £100, and he will be liable to pay £23 to the Revenue in tax. The payer finds this amount from the £23 that he has deducted and retained when making the payment. He is therefore paying the same total amount that he would by making the covenanted payment in full, and is paying no more income tax than if the covenanted payment were ignored altogether, because he has retained the amount of the extra tax as against the recipient.

(c) The basic rate income tax collected from the payer is treated as tax paid by the recipient, so that if the recipient is liable to pay more income tax on the payment than has been paid on his behalf (because he is liable to higher rate tax), the Inland Revenue will collect the difference from him. If the recipient is liable to pay less than the basic rate of income tax (because he is exempt from income tax on that income or his income is such that he is not within the full charge to tax), then the Inland Revenue will make a repayment to him of the tax overpaid.

Example

C has taxable income of £15,000, out of which he makes an annual payment to D (a registered charity) of £3,000. When making the payment to D, C deducts and retains basic rate tax at 23% (£690), and pays the balance (£2,310). The Inland Revenue assess C to income tax on £15,000 (cf. para. 13.12). His income tax liability is therefore 23% of £15,000, which is £3,450 (of which £690 is paid on behalf of D). Since C retained £690 when making the payment to D, he has only £2,760 to find to satisfy his tax liability. This is the sum which would be due in income tax if the annual payment were treated as though it did not belong to C (23% of £12,000 is £2,760). D is treated as receiving the annual payment of £3,000, although it is treated as if it had already paid income tax of £690.

Section 348 does not impose any obligation on the payer to deduct income tax when making the payment. It merely allows him to do so if he wishes, although of course, he will be paying more than he bargained for if he chooses not to make the deduction. If the payer fails to make the deduction in one year, he may not make the deduction for the earlier payment in later years (*Re Hatch* [1919] 1 Ch 351), although he may claim previously undeducted tax from payments due later in the same year of assessment, and in any event is not prevented by the failure to deduct in an earlier year from deducting tax for later years in those later years (*Taylor* v *Taylor* [1938] 1 KB 320). If, however, payment is made in arrears, the payer may deduct income tax at the rate in force when the payments were due (s. 4 and *Taylor* v *Taylor*). If the payer makes a payment from which he deducts income tax, and because of the subsequent passing of a Finance Act did not deduct enough, s. 821 allows him to deduct the deficiency from the next payment or, if there are no future payments, to recover it as a debt. Failure to deduct income tax does not affect the Inland Revenue, since they will collect the tax from the payer by assessing his taxable income.

13.14 SECTION 349, TA

Where any annuity, an effective annual payment, or patent royalty is paid out of profits or gains not brought into charge, s. 349(1) requires the person by or through whom (cf. *Howells* v *IRC* in para. 13.10.2) the payment is made to deduct income tax (s. 4). This will be 23%. Such a person must deliver an account of the payment to the inspector of taxes, who will then assess and charge him to income tax at the basic rate on the amount of the payment, or the amount which is not brought into charge to income tax. Where an annuity, etc., if paid in the due year, could have been paid wholly or partly out of taxed income (so that s. 348 would have applied) but is paid in a later year out of income which is not brought into charge, the Inland Revenue make an allowance when fixing the amount due to them under s. 349(1) for the tax which the payer would have been entitled under s. 348 to deduct and retain had the payment been made on time (Extra-statutory Concession A16).

Payments out of profits and gains not brought into charge will include payments made out of capital (unless they are special types of receipt taxable as income, such as receipts in respect of some intellectual property), payments made by companies (which are liable to corporation tax, not income tax), payments made by persons who are exempt from income tax, and payments out of profits against which a loss has been set.

Example

C is liable to make an effective annual payment to D of £3,000. He makes this payment out of his capital. Before making the payment to D, C must deduct tax at 23% (£690) and pay only the balance to D (£2,310). Unlike the s. 348 procedure, C cannot keep the £690 which he deducts, but must deliver an account of the payment to the Inland Revenue so that they can assess him directly on £3,000 and require the payment of the £690 as basic rate income tax on the annual payment. D is assessed on his taxable income from all sources, including the annual payment, but is treated as though he had already paid income tax of £690.

If C had paid D £1,000 out of taxable income, and £2,000 out of capital, s. 348 would apply to the payment out of income and s. 349(1) to the payment out of capital. Thus, C would deduct and retain £230 out of the £1,000 of income, and the Inland Revenue would assess his income in the normal way (but making sure that the £1,000 representing the annual payment was only charged at basic rate). He would also deduct £460 from the capital sum, but would be assessed directly under s. 349(1) for the payment of that amount. D would be deemed to have paid £690 in income tax (£230 + £460).

The obligation on the payer under s. 349(1) to deduct tax when making the payment to the recipient is mandatory, unlike s. 348. If he fails to make the deduction, he may recover the income tax from the recipient in the same way as under s. 348. The Inland Revenue are also interested in the failure to deduct, because they are relying on the payer to discharge the recipient's liability to basic rate income tax. If the payer fails to deduct tax the Revenue have a choice as to what to assess. They may assess the payer since an assessment on the payer under s. 349(1) does not depend on his having deducted income tax (see s. 350(1)). Alternatively, they may assess the recipient as the recipient remains liable on the full amount of the payment under Case III (*Grosvenor Place Estates Ltd* v *Roberts* [1961] Ch 148). The income is, after all, legally that of the recipient, and if the payer has failed to make the deduction, the recipient is the person who has the income from which the tax should have been deducted.

13.15 DONATIONS TO CHARITY

It has for many years been possible to make covenanted donations to charity and receive favourable tax treatment under the rules already outlined. However, the need to sign a covenant form and to make a commitment for at least three years are inevitably a disincentive. Therefore as from 1 October 1990 the rules for donations to charity made by individuals were widened so that a single donation might attract tax relief similar to that available for covenanted payments (s. 25, FA 1990). To qualify under this section, there must be a gift to a charity which involves the payment of a sum of money that is not subject to any condition for repayment, and which is not associated with the acquisition by the charity of property from the donor or someone associated with the donor otherwise than by gift. The donor must be resident in the United Kingdom, the sum paid must be not less than £250 (or £400 prior to 16 March 1993, s. 67, FA 1993) and prior to 19 March 1991 the maximum payable was £5,000,000, although from that date this upper limit has ceased to have effect. If the donor or any person connected with him derives any benefit from the gift, the value of that benefit must not exceed 2·5% of the value of the gift, and must not exceed £250 in value. The gift will not get favourable tax treatment under this section if it already does so because it is a covenanted payment, or because it falls within the payroll deduction scheme. The donor must provide the charity with an appropriate certificate stating that the gift satisfies these conditions, and that the donor has paid or will pay either directly or by deduction from profits or gains brought into charge to tax a sum equal to basic rate tax on the grossed up value of the payment. Basic rate for the year in which the payment falls to be made should be used for this purpose. The single gift will then be treated like a covenanted payment in that the donor will have to pay basic rate tax on the gift, but will be able to deduct the gross value of the gift for higher rate tax purposes. It will also be possible for the charity to reclaim the basic rate tax paid.

13.16 AGREEMENT NOT TO DEDUCT

The recipient may be unhappy at having tax deducted from the payments and may therefore wish to enter into an agreement with the payer to prevent the deduction being made. However, by s. 106, Taxes Management Act 1970, a person who refuses to allow a deduction of income tax authorised by ss. 348, 349(1) or 349(2), TA will incur a penalty of £50, and any agreement for payment in full without allowing an authorised deduction is void. It is important to realise that only 'agreements' are subject to s. 106 of the 1970 Act, and statutes, court orders and wills do not fall within that category.

It was held by the House of Lords in *Ferguson* v *IRC* [1970] AC 442 that a 'free of tax' clause in an agreement does not contravene s. 106. Such a clause imposes a liability on the payer to pay any tax that the recipient would be liable to bear on the gross amount of the payment which is expressed to be free of tax. Any similar phrase will achieve the same result provided that as a matter of construction, it is clear that the agreement refers to the deduction of United Kingdom tax. The phrase 'free of all deductions' does not meet this requirement (*Re Wells* [1940] Ch 411).

If a 'free of tax' clause is valid, the recipient is entitled to receive only the stated sum which is free of tax, and the payer is liable to pay that sum and the income tax which the recipient is liable to bear on the gross amount. This means that if the payer accounts for (say) basic rate tax and the recipient's position is such that he is not liable to pay as much income tax as the payer has paid on his behalf, the recipient is under a duty to reclaim the overpaid tax and (because he is only entitled to the stated amount) pay it to the payer as in *Re Pettit* [1922] 2 Ch 765.

The drawback with a 'free of tax' clause is that the payer's liability under the agreement providing for the payment will vary each year as the recipient's liability to income tax changes. Section 106, TMA refers to deductions authorised by the Taxes Acts, and ss. 348, 349(1) and 349(2), TA refer only to deduction at the basic or lower rate. The payer could therefore agree with the recipient to pay a stated sum 'less income tax at the basic or lower rate for the time being in force' and this would not contravene s. 106. The payer's liability would then be fixed and he would pay the same amount every year. The recipient suffers by receiving a net amount which varies as the basic rate of income tax changes. If this is not acceptable, a more sophisticated type of formula is one which provides for the payment of 'such a sum as after the deduction of income tax at the basic rate for the time being in force shall leave the sum of . . .'

Such a formula has the advantage that the recipient knows each year that the net amount of the payment is constant, and the payer's liability varies only with the basic rate of income tax and not with the recipient's liability to income tax as a whole. The effect of both types of clauses is to give the recipient the entitlement to the gross amount of the payment, so that the rule in Re Pettit does not apply to them (Re Jones [1933] Ch 842) and the recipient may claim any repaid tax for himself. Conversely, the payer agrees only to discharge the basic rate liability, and the recipient must accordingly pay any extra tax that is due in respect of the payment.

Example
(i) C agreed to pay D a tax-effective annual payment of '£1,000 a year less tax at the basic rate'. In 1987–88, basic rate tax was 27%; in 1993–94 it is 25%. In 1987–88, therefore, C deducted £270 tax and paid D £730; in 1993–94, C deducts £250 tax and pays D £750. In both years the cost to C is £1,000; but in 1993–94 D is better off because the tax rate is lower.
(ii) C agrees to pay D a tax-effective annual payment of 'such a sum as after the deduction of income tax at the basic rate for the time being in force shall leave the sum of £700'. The net sum payable therefore remains constant at £700, but C's gross liability varies with the basic rate. To find the gross sum C must pay, we must gross up the net figure of £700. With a basic rate of 27%, C was liable to pay a total of £958.90 (£700 × $^{100}/_{73}$) in 1987–88. In 1993–94, with basic rate at 25%, C is liable to pay a total of £933.33 (£700 × $^{100}/_{75}$). In both years, D receives £700, but in 1993–94 C is better off because the tax rate is lower.

13.17 AVOIDANCE SCHEMES

It has been seen that the legal alienation of income from one person to another is reflected (in a roundabout way) in the tax system, since the payer is assessed to income tax which he is entitled to retain from the recipient's payment and is therefore effectively not taxed on the amount of the payment, and the recipient receives a net amount in respect of which he is treated as though basic rate tax has been paid. Such an arrangement would be beneficial if a higher rate taxpayer could thus alienate his income to a person who paid no or much less tax. Provisions have existed for some time to prevent this sort of tax benefit being (in the eyes of the Inland Revenue) abused, and these provisions are considered in the context of the income tax treatment of settlements (see Chapter 15). But even these provisions could be avoided by entering into a transaction which had no element of bounty, in other words, where consideration was given for the payments.

For example, in *IRC* v *Plummer* [1979] 3 All ER 775, the taxpayer entered into an agreement with a charity whereby in return for a capital payment of £2,480, the taxpayer agreed to pay the charity an annuity of such a sum as would after the deduction of basic rate tax leave £500, the payments to continue for five years. The taxpayer therefore received a sum which was substantially returned to the charity over five years (although in legal terms it disappeared). In effect, the taxpayer was entitled to deduct the gross amount of the annuity when computing his liability to tax at higher rates and the basic rate tax which he paid under s. 348, TA on the charity's behalf could be reclaimed by the charity because it was exempt from tax on that income. The House of Lords held that the true form of the transaction was for the payment of income in return for capital, and not simply the return of capital, and allowed the deduction of the annuity from the taxpayer's taxable income and the claim for repayment by the charity. For a more recent case on similar facts, see *Moodie* v *IRC* [1993] 2 All ER 49.

Long before the Inland Revenue lost this case before the House of Lords, Parliament had stepped in and frustrated such schemes by enacting s. 125. The section applies to any annuity or annual payment chargeable under Case III which is made under a liability incurred for consideration in money or money's worth which is not taxable as income (s. 125(2)). The effect of the section is to prevent the deduction of income tax at source, so that the recipient is assessed and charged on the full amount of the payment and, tax not having been paid by the payer, no credit is given and therefore no repayment can be made for basic rate tax (s. 125(1)). Further, the payer is not entitled to deduct the payment in computing his taxable income, so he too will be liable to pay income tax on the full amount of his income (s. 125(1)). By s. 125(3), the section does not apply to an annuity granted in the ordinary course of a business of granting annuities, a payment made to an individual for the surrender, assignment or release of an interest in settled property to or in favour of a person having a subsequent interest (for example, a future life tenant or the remainderman), or to a payment excepted from s. 660A by s. 660A(8) and (9)(a). (For a discussion of s. 660A see Chapter 15.)

These provisions, however, still left open a variety of ways in which annual payments could be used to provide some tax advantage for the payer and/or the recipient. Particularly common was the use of a covenant where the payer would be making the payments from taxed income but the recipient had little or no income and thus had some unused personal allowance, for example a parent providing for a student at university, or a grandparent making payments to a grandchild. Such covenants were regarded as acceptable for many years but, in a climate of simplifying the tax system from 15 March 1988, such covenants are no longer effective since such annual payments may no longer be deducted from the income of the payer, or be subject to tax in the hands of the recipient (although covenants under existing obligations before that date will continue to be tax-effective while they are legally effective). The statutory limit on the types of annual payment that will be effective has not been uniformly welcomed. While grandparents may find other tax-effective ways of providing for their grandchildren, it may well be true to say that without covenanted payments some parents may find it more difficult to provide the required parental contribution for their child's grant for further education (although the amount of student grants has been increased to a small extent to take this into account). What is more serious is that s. 347A also takes maintenance payments outside the annual payments system, and it has been quite widely argued that this may result in less money being available for maintenance with limited tax relief being available to the payer.

13.18 WHO IS CHARGEABLE UNDER SCHEDULE D, CASE III?

By s. 59(1), TA, income tax assessed under Case III is to be charged on and paid by 'the persons receiving or entitled to the income' in respect of which the charge is made. It was held by the Court of Appeal in *Ransom* v *Higgs* [1973] 2 All ER 657, that 'entitled' meant legally (or, presumably, equitably) entitled. From 15 March 1988, only annual payments not excluded by s. 347A are taxable in the hands of the recipient. All other annual payments are free of basic rate tax in the hands of the recipient (but fully taxable to basic rate tax in the hands of the payer).

In *Aplin* v *White* [1973] 2 All ER 637, the taxpayer was an estate agent who collected rents on behalf of clients. These rents were then placed on deposit account and earned interest. The taxpayer found the apportionment of this interest amongst the clients too complicated and therefore retained it. He was assessed under Case III in respect of the interest. Megarry J held that although the taxpayer was not beneficially entitled to the interest, he had nevertheless received it and so had been correctly assessed under s. 59.

Similarly, in *Dunmore* v *McGowan* [1978] 2 All ER 85, the Court of Appeal held that the taxpayer was 'entitled' to the interest paid on sums in a deposit account in a bank's name, the principal of which guaranteed the indebtedness to the bank of a company in which the taxpayer was interested. The taxpayer failed in his argument that he should not be assessed under s. 59 until he received the balance in the account when the company's indebtedness was discharged, the bank in the meantime holding the money as trustee for him. There was on the evidence no express trust, and the court saw no reason to imply one. The taxpayer could have withdrawn the interest at any time.

13.19 PAYMENT OF TAX

Payment in respect of tax due under Case III is due on or before 1 January in the year of assessment to which the tax relates (s. 5(1), TA). However, in no event is payment to be due before the expiration of 30 days from the issue of the notice of assessment (s. 5(1)).

Income tax – Schedule D, Case III: interest, annuities etc.

13.20 THE INTERNATIONAL ELEMENT

If annual payments are made under an obligation governed by United Kingdom law, they are assessable under Case III, whether the recipient is resident in the United Kingdom or not, and notwithstanding that the payments may be made abroad (s. 18(3), TA). The payer will be subject to the s. 348 or s. 349(1) procedure in this situation whether he makes the payments out of income arising in the United Kingdom or elsewhere, although if he is not resident in the United Kingdom and he makes the payments out of income arising abroad, s. 349(1) may still apply to him, but it is a question of fact whether he has deducted tax at source. If he has, then the Inland Revenue may only assess him under s. 349(1); if he has not, the recipient will be assessed on the gross amount under Case III (cf. *Stokes* v *Bennett* [1953] Ch 566). If, on the other hand, annual payments are made under an obligation governed by foreign law, the recipient will be liable to income tax under Case V of Schedule D if resident in the United Kingdom (*IRC* v *Anderstrom* (1927) 13 TC 482).

13.21 FA 1996 CHANGES

A new Schedule D, Case III is introduced for corporation tax purposes (see s. 18(3A), TA substituted by s. 105 and sch. 14, FA 1996).

Section 73, FA 1996 inserts a new s. 1A into the Taxes Act. This provides for certain Schedule D, Case III income as well as Schedule F income to be charged at the lower rate rather than basic rate in accordance with the provision of the section and sch. 6, FA 1996. Higher rate above the limit can still apply (see s. 1(2)(b), TA).

CHAPTER FOURTEEN
Income tax and trusts

14.1 INTRODUCTION

For ease of exposition, the income tax provisions applicable to trusts will be discussed in this and the following chapter and those applicable to capital gains tax will be discussed in Chapter 24. However, in most cases, it will be necessary to consider both sets of provisions simultaneously since the trustees will be managing both income and capital investments. In addition, the application of inheritance tax should not be overlooked and the relevant inheritance tax provisions are discussed in Chapter 34.

The income tax rules applicable to trusts have been described as some of 'the most complicated and difficult areas of the tax system'.[1] There are a number of reasons for this. First, when a trust has been created, there are three types of persons who may be potential taxpayers in relation to the trust – the settlors, the trustees and the beneficiaries. Secondly, there may be a variety of different entitlements to property under the trust. This is because one function of a trust is to separate the management of trust property from its enjoyment; the trustees will be entitled to the income of the trust fund at common law and the beneficiaries will be entitled in equity. The situation is complicated if the beneficiaries have, as yet, no entitlement to the income of the fund because their entitlement is dependent on the exercise of a discretion in their favour by the trustees. Thirdly, a trust may be used to change the

---

[1.] This comment, which also applies to the capital gains tax rules, was made in an Inland Revenue Consultative Document, *The Income and Capital Gains Tax Treatment of UK Resident Trusts*, 1991. The proposals made in this document in relation to capital gains tax have now been withdrawn, but other proposals concerning the definition of a trust for income and capital gains tax purposes and the tax residence of trusts are still under consideration; see Inland Revenue Press Release dated 18 March 1993.

character of a payment from capital to income or vice versa. Trustees may make a deliberate decision to accumulate income with the result that it will become 'capitalised' and can be paid out of the trust fund as capital and not as income. Alternatively the trust capital can be charged with the payment of an annuity and this annuity may constitute income in the beneficiary's hands. Fourthly, trusts may be used as a method of passing income from a higher rate taxpayer to a lower rate or non taxpayer, for example, from parent to child. This obvious tax planning opportunity is restricted by a number of anti-avoidance provisions which are discussed in Chapter 15.

Before commencing the discussion of the substantive income tax provisions applicable to trusts, a few general comments can be made. The UK has not adopted a single coherent code for the income taxation of trusts. The legislative provisions that do exist do not conclusively determine whether trust income belongs to the trustees or beneficiaries for tax purposes and do not lay down the circumstances in which the trustees may be required to pay income tax on the beneficiary's behalf. It has been left to the courts to discover or invent principles of trust taxation and the reader must judge for himself or herself how well the judiciary has managed this task. Further, where legislative provisions do exist, they are phrased in terms of 'settlements' rather than 'trusts'. A settlement is not necessarily the same as a trust. For the purposes of the anti-avoidance rules discussed in Chapter 15, a 'settlement' includes any disposition, trust, covenant, agreement, arrangement or transfer of assets (s. 660G, TA). This is an extraordinarily wide 'definition'.

14.2 THE INCOME TAX LIABILITY OF TRUSTEES

14.2.1 General

As already noted, the various Schedules and Cases of the income tax code do not generally distinguish between legal and beneficial ownership. Thus Schedule A income tax is charged on the person 'receiving or entitled to' the profits so charged (s. 21(1), TA), Schedule D income tax is charged on the person 'receiving or entitled to' the income (s. 59) and under Schedule F the tax credit is available to the person 'receiving' the distribution (s. 231(1)). Although the failure to distinguish legal and beneficial ownership is somewhat surprising, the explanation can be found by an examination of the history of income tax.[2] Put simply, when income tax was first introduced it was a proportional, flat rate tax and it made little difference whether the income was taxed as income of the trustee (as legal owner) or of the beneficiary (as beneficial owner). The move towards a progressive income tax system with far higher rates of tax in the twentieth century changed this picture completely and the courts were accordingly called upon to resolve disputes as to the person who could correctly be subjected to tax.

It is sometimes said that trustees are taxable in respect of income of which they are in 'actual receipt or control'. The authority usually given for this

---

[2.] For a fuller discussion; see part II of Kerridge (1994), 110 *LQR*, pp. 85 to 91.

proposition is Viscount Cave's speech in *Williams* v *Singer* [1921] 1 AC 65. Although a Schedule D, Case V decision, the case is always cited as authority for both UK and non-UK source income although this is not self-evident from their Lordships' speeches. In *Williams* v *Singer* income from foreign investments was, at the direction of the UK resident trustees, paid directly to the beneficiary who was domiciled and resident abroad. The Revenue failed in their attempt to charge the trustees who had not themselves received any income.[3] Viscount Cave said:

> The fact is that, if the Income Tax Acts are examined, it will be found that the person charged with the tax is neither the trustee nor the beneficiary as such, but the person in actual receipt and control of the income which it is sought to reach.

This proposition was doubted in a later Scottish case, *Reid's Trustees* v *IRC* 14 TC 512. Trustees of the testator's will were assessed to tax on interest received under Schedule D, Case III. Under the will, two-thirds of the interest was to be accumulated and the remaining one-third to be paid to the testator's adult son. The trustees claimed that in the absence of an express provision in the Income Tax Acts imposing liability on them *qua* trustees, they escaped liability to tax.[4] This argument was quickly dismissed by the Court of Session which held that the trustees were 'entitled' for income tax purposes to the whole of the interest. Lord Morrison considered any other approach to be based on a misconception of the will. Lord President Clyde said that in his view the proper persons to be assessed were the trustees. There was nothing inconsistent with the Income Tax Acts in recognising and respecting the distinction between property owned by a person as trustee and property owned by him in his own right. He thought the ratio of *Williams* v *Singer* came to no more than that, in a great many cases, the trustees were the right persons to assess.

This decision has led many commentators[5] to explain *Williams* v *Singer* on the basis that the trustees are taxable in respect of trust income except where the income of the trust is paid directly to the beneficiary without passing through the hands of the trustees. However, dicta in another case, *Baker* v *Archer Shee* [1927] AC 844, suggest that a trustee may not be assessable in respect of the income of a trust if the beneficiary is *absolutely entitled* to the income even though the income is not paid directly to the beneficiary. These dicta were disregarded in *Reid's Trustees* v *IRC*, Lord Clyde (at p. 525) preferring an alternative explanation of *Williams* v *Singer*, namely that although the trustees would generally be liable:

[3.] The beneficiary was only taxable on income remitted to the UK, and as no income had been remitted, no tax was due from her. See Chapter 34 for a discussion of the remittance basis.

[4.] The only express provision is in respect of trustees for non-resident (s. 78, TMA) or incapacitated persons (s. 72, TMA). What are now ss. 76 and 13, TMA were relied on in *Williams* v *Singer* as preventing liability on the trustees. This is hard to reconcile with the wording of these sections which seem to be about the trustees' obligations to make returns and supply information about the *beneficiary's* (not the trustees') liability.

[5.] See, inter alia, *Whiteman on Income Tax*, 3rd. edition, Sweet & Maxwell, para. 20–02 and *Butterworths UK Tax Guide 1995–96*, para. 11:03.

Income tax and trusts   403

they may have a good answer to a particular assessment, as regards some share or part of the income assessed, on the ground that such share or part arises or accrues *beneficially* to a *cestui que trust* in whose hands it is not liable to income tax, e.g., a foreigner under Case V.

There are thus three possible bases on which trustees may be assessed to income tax:

(a) trustees are liable in respect of trust income except where income is paid directly to the beneficiary without passing through the hands of the trustees;
(b) trustees are liable in respect of trust income except where the beneficiary entitled to that income is not a UK taxpayer; or
(c) trustees are liable in respect of trust income except where the beneficiary is absolutely entitled to that income – entitlement to be determined by applying trust law principles.

It is submitted that option (c), an extension of the 'actual receipt and control' test, is to be preferred.[6] Option (b) suffers from the fact that the tax liability of a trustee is determined by reference to the tax (as opposed to the trust law) position of the beneficiary.[7] In addition, option (b), and to a lesser extent option (a), raise difficult questions as to the source of any subsequent payment to an absolutely entitled beneficiary. Is an absolutely entitled life tenant entitled to the same income as accrues to the trustees or does the life tenant's right derive from the settlement and so from a separate source? If the latter approach is right there are two sources of income each of which is assessable to income tax.[8] In practice, the Revenue do not take the point, regarding the life tenant as entitled to the income and so liable to tax but with a 'credit' for any tax paid by the trustees (see para. 14.3.2). But this practice is only really explicable on the basis that the beneficiary was entitled all along to the income and the tax paid by the trustees is, in fact, a pre-payment of the beneficiary's tax liability.

The facts in *Baker* v *Archer Shee* may help to explain the points that have just been made. Lady Archer Shee was a UK resident who had a life interest in a settlement consisting of foreign investments. She was assessed in respect of gross income received by the trustees in New York. She argued that she was assessable only in respect of the net payments made to her by trustees. On the assumption that the law of New York which governed the trust was

---

[6.] In addition to *Baker* v *Archer Shee*, support for this proposition can be gained from the judgment of Dillon LJ in *Dawson* v *IRC* [1988] STC 684, CA where assessment on the UK resident trustee (the two other trustees being non-residents) failed because the Revenue could not show that the UK resident trustee was in receipt or control of the trust income. The decision on the assessment of trustees has since been reversed by legislation (see para. 14.2.2).
[7.] *Butterworths UK Tax Guide 1995–96*, para. 11:04 goes so far as to argue that option (b) is not 'firmly grounded'. However, Lord Clyde's judgment on the point was approved by Lord Hamworth MR and the Court of Appeal in *Kelly* v *Rodgers* 19 TC 692 at p. 710.
[8.] As is the case with a company and its shareholders under a classical system.

the same as English law,[9] it was held that Lady Archer Shee was the 'sole beneficial owner of the interest and dividends of all securities, stocks and shares forming part of the trust fund' and was assessable in respect thereof (*per* Lord Carson at p. 870).[10] The decision was subsequently explained by Lord Tomlin in *Garland* v *Archer Shee* [1931] AC 212 at p. 222 on the basis that the House of Lords had:

> Founded themselves upon the view that according to English law . . . [the beneficiary] had a property interest in the income arising from the assets constituting the American trust.

Thus where the beneficiary is absolutely entitled to the income:

(a) the beneficiary will have to pay income tax at his or her marginal rate of tax with a 'credit' for any tax already paid by the trustees (see para. 14.3.2);

(b) the income in the beneficiary's hands is treated as deriving from the underlying source so if the trust receives Schedule D, Case I and Schedule F income, the beneficiary will be treated as receiving Schedule D, Case I and Schedule F income; and

(c) the trustees have no authority or obligation to apply ss. 348 to 350, TA to the income payments because the income will not constitute Schedule D, Case III income in the beneficiary's hands. The trustees will only be able to apply s. 348 if the income is already s. 348 income when they receive it, i.e., it is an annuity or other annual payment.[11]

Trustees will not be assessed in respect of any income which is deemed to be the settlor's under the anti-avoidance rules discussed in Chapter 15. The income is deemed to be the income of the settlor for all purposes of the Income Tax Acts and not of any other person (ss. 660A(1) and 660B(2), TA). Accordingly, the trustees do not have taxable income in respect of the trust.

14.2.2 Assessment on trustees

Where an assessment is properly made on the *trustees*, they are assessed on that income according to the source from which the income arises. So if the

---

[9.] This was assumed for lack of expert evidence. Foreign law is regarded as a matter of fact which must be proved – see generally Fentiman (1992), 108 *LQR*, 142. In the later case of *Garland* v *Archer Shee* [1931] AC 212, expert evidence of New York law established that Lady Archer Shee had only limited rights in the fund and not to the individual dividends. Rowlatt J said 'according to American law her right goes no further back than to ask the trustees to do something . . . she is entitled to the balance sum, and not entitled to the dividends as they arise.' Consequently, later assessments on Lady Archer Shee's husband failed.

[10.] The decision has been criticised as not being consistent with the traditional view that a beneficiary's interest under a trust is a right *in personam* not one *in rem*. However, that 'traditional' view has itself been criticised, see inter alia Hart (1899), 15 *LQR* 294 and Hanbury (1929), 45 *LQR* 196 and certainly a *sui juris* beneficiary may demand transfer of the legal title from the trustee and so obtain the trust property for himself under the principle in *Saunders* v *Vautier* (1841) Cr & Ph 240.

[11.] See paras. 13.13 and 13.4 for a discussion of ss. 348–350, TA. When trustees make a payment out of a discretionary settlement to a beneficiary s. 687, TA applies, see para. 14.2.3.

Income tax and trusts 405

income arises from carrying on a trade, the trustees will be assessed under Schedule D, Case I. If the income takes the form of dividends paid in respect of shares the trustees will be assessed under Schedule F and so on. The trustees may set against such income the expenses appropriate to the type of income in respect of which they are assessed. So, for example, trading expenses may be set against income chargeable under Schedule D, Case I. However, the trustees may not generally offset any of the expenses of managing the trust (*Aikin* v *Macdonald's Trustees* 3 TC 306). Nor are they entitled to use their own personal reliefs to reduce income assessable on them as trustees, since such allowances are only available to individuals (s. 256, TA) and trustees are 'persons' (see Viscount Sumner in *Baker* v *Archer Shee* (para. 14.2.1) and Lord Skerrington in *Fry & Shiels Trustees* 6 TC 583 at p. 586). Because they are 'persons' for income tax purposes, trustees pay tax at the basic rate of income tax (s. 1(2)(a), TA and see *IRC* v *Countess Longford, Pakenham and others* (1928) 13 TC 573) or, in the case of dividend and other savings income, at the lower rate (s. 1A, TA). Different rules apply to the trustees of discretionary or accumulation trusts (see para. 14.2.3).

The trustees are jointly, not jointly and severally, entitled to the assets. It was said in *Dawson* v *IRC* [1988] STC 684, HL that one consequence of this was that each joint tenant held nothing by himself yet held the whole property with his fellow trustees.[12] That rendered the Revenue's previous practice of making assessments on a single trustee incorrect. However, the law was changed by s. 151, Finance Act 1989 which provides that income arising to the trustees of a settlement may be assessed and charged on any one or more of the 'relevant' trustees. The 'relevant' trustees are trustees to whom the income arises and any subsequent trustees of the settlement. The provision is deemed always to have had effect.

14.2.3 Accumulation or discretionary trusts

As noted above, because trustees are persons not individuals, they are only liable to income tax at the basic or lower rate unless that tax has been deducted at source,[13] when that liability will already have been satisfied. This explains why trusts are such an attraction to higher rate taxpayers. To counter this a special rate known as the 'rate applicable to trusts', currently 34% (ss. 686(1), 686(1A) and 832(1), TA), is applied to trustees in respect of income which:

(a) is to be accumulated or payable at the discretion of the trustees (s. 686(2)), that is, generally, income accumulated under a general power to

---

[12] Romer J's dicta in *IRC* v *T W Law Ltd* (1950) 29 TC 467 at p. 471) support this.
[13] For instance, income arising under Schedule D Case III or Schedule F. As from 6 April 1995, bank interest on deposits belonging to discretionary and accumulation trusts is paid under deduction of tax, s. 481 TA as amended by FA 1995. Trusts with no connection with the UK can receive gross interest if the trustees make the appropriate declaration. The Revenue take the view that 'beneficiaries' in s. 482(5), TA only applies to identifiable beneficiaries, so trusts with non-UK resident beneficiaries but with power to add to the class of beneficiaries are not automatically excluded from making a declaration to receive gross interest under s. 481(5)(k)(iii), TA; see, *Law Society's Gazette*, 26 April 1995.

accumulate as well as income accumulated under a positive duty (*IRC v Berrill* [1982] 1 All ER 867) such as that imposed by s. 31, Trustee Act 1925 during the beneficiary's minority; and

(b) is not the income of any person other than the trustee and is not treated as the settlor's income for any purpose; and

(c) does not arise under a trust established for only charitable purposes or from investments, deposits or other property held for the purposes of a retirement benefits or personal pension scheme; and

(d) exceeds the income applied in defraying the expenses of the trustees which are properly chargeable to income (or would be but for a provision in the settlement directing them to be charged to capital).[14]

Where the trustees make any payment out of a discretionary settlement to a beneficiary, s. 687, TA applies instead of ss. 348 or 349(1). The payment is treated as a net amount which has had tax at the rate applicable to trusts deducted. The tax liability is assessable on the trustees (s. 687(2)(b)) but if the rate applicable to trusts has remained the same since the receipt of the income taxable under s. 686, the trustees will not be liable to any further tax.[15] If, however, the rate has increased, the trustees will be liable to pay the amount of the increase although apparently no rebate will be available if the tax rate has decreased.[16] The income tax paid by the trustees is treated as income tax paid by the beneficiary (s. 687(2)(a)). So if the beneficiary is a higher rate taxpayer, he will be liable to pay the extra tax due (currently 6% – the difference between the higher rate of 40% and the rate applicable to trusts of 34%). A beneficiary who has no tax liability in respect of the income will able to reclaim the tax deducted by the trustees from the Inland Revenue.

Example

Thomas and Terry are trustees of a discretionary trust. In 1997/98 the trust has £100 of income. Thomas and Terry decide to pay the whole of the net income of that year to Bernard, a higher rate taxpayer. The income tax position is as follows:

	£
Gross income received by trustees	100
Less: tax under s. 686	34
Net payment to Bernard	66

The payment to Bernard of £66 is treated as a gross amount from which tax at the rate applicable to trusts has already been deducted, i.e., £100 on which

---

[14] This reverses the decision in *Aikin v Macdonald's Trustees* in respect of such discretionary trusts. In *Carver v Duncan* [1985] STC 356 the House of Lords held that s. 686(2) only allows the deduction of income applied in defraying income as opposed to capital expenses, and will not allow the deduction of expenses which are only chargeable to income because of an express provision in the settlement.
[15] Since the tax paid under s. 686 can be set off against the liability under s. 687 (s. 687(3)(a)).
[16] As happened in the November 1995 Budget when the Chancellor of the Exchequer reduced the rate applicable to trusts from 35% to 34%.

£34 tax has been paid. As a higher rate taxpayer, Bernard would be subject to tax at 40% so he must pay an additional £6 of tax, leaving him with a net receipt of £60.

If the trustees make a payment to a discretionary beneficiary out of capital but which is income in the beneficiary's hands,[17] the payment must be grossed up for the purposes of s. 687 and the trustees are liable to pay tax at the rate applicable to trusts on it. If the payment was made out of accumulated income, that is out of 'capitalised income', it will have been subject to tax under s. 686 when received and the amount of tax paid by trustees under s. 686 can be set against the s. 687 charge on the payment to the beneficiary with the result that the trustees will only be liable for further tax if tax rates have increased. If, however, the payment is made out of 'pure' capital, s. 686 will not have been applied and so the trustees will be liable to the whole amount of the rate applicable to trusts at the time of the payment to the beneficiary (s. 687(3)).[18]

Care must be taken in applying this section since not all payments out of capital intended for use by the beneficiary for an income purpose will constitute income of the beneficiary. For instance, in *Stevenson v Wishart* [1987] STC 266, CA, trustees held property on trust, and had absolute discretion as to how that property and the income from it should be appointed amongst the beneficiaries. One of the beneficiaries was Mrs Henwood. For the last three years of Mrs Henwood's life, the trustees appointed trust capital to meet the cost of her medical expenses and the fees of a private nursing home. The Inland Revenue appealed against the Special Commissioners' refusal to uphold an assessment on the trustees under s. 687 on the amount of the appointed trust capital in each of the relevant years of assessment. Knox J rejected their appeal. Although Mrs Henwood was an object of a discretionary trust, the payments were being made under a power to appoint capital. This decision was supported by the Court of Appeal. While Fox LJ (at p. 272) accepted that the payments from capital could be income in the hands of a beneficiary, he was in no doubt that on the facts of the case the payments were capital:

> If, in exercise of a power over capital, [the trustees] choose to make at their discretion regular payments of capital to deal with the special problems of Mrs Henwood's last years rather than release a single sum to her of a large amount, that does not seem to me to create an income interest. Their power was to appoint capital. What they appointed remained capital.

14.2.4 Mistakes

It seems clear that a trustee who fails to deduct income tax from payments to beneficiaries through a mistake of law can deduct that tax from any future

---

[17.] Such as an annuity or where capital may be used to supplement the income of the life tenant for life; see *Brodie's Trustees* v *IRC* (1933) 17 TC 432, *Lindus and Hortin* v *IRC* 17 TC 442 and *Cunard's Trustees* v *IRC* 27 TC 122.

[18.] The trustees are allowed, however, to set against such tax, any tax paid by them under s. 686 on other income and in respect of which no deduction has been made for other payments out of the trust subject to s. 687.

payments he is liable to make to those same beneficiaries.[19] It has also been argued that the law of restitution is now sufficiently developed to allow a trustee to recover any payments to an overpaid beneficiary under a mistake of law, subject only to any defences to restitution (such as a change of position) that the beneficiary may have.[20]

14.3 THE INCOME TAX LIABILITY OF BENEFICIARIES

14.3.1 Absolute entitlement

The general rule is that income arising under a settlement to which the beneficiary is absolutely entitled is taxable in the beneficiary's hands (*Baker v Archer Shee* (para. 14.2.1). The rationale for taxing an absolutely entitled beneficiary was summed up by Sir Wilfred Greene MR in *Corbett v IRC* [1938] 1 KB 567:

> Where trustees are in receipt of income which it is their duty to pass over to the beneficiaries, either with or without deduction of something for the trustees' expenses on the way, that income is at its very inception the beneficiary's income.[21]

The criterion for taxation is simply entitlement so in *IRC v Hamilton-Russell's Executors* 25 TC 200, an absolutely entitled beneficiary was taxable even though he had not actually received any income. In contrast, if the beneficiary is not entitled to the income then the income will not form part of the beneficiary's income for income tax purposes.[22]

Sums applied for the benefit of a beneficiary or in accordance with his directions will form part of the beneficiary's taxable income. So if the beneficiary is entitled to live in a house, the expenses of which are met by the trust, he is taxable on all such outgoings (*IRC v Lady Miller* 15 TC 25 and *Lord Tollemache v IRC* 11 TC 277). Benefits in kind are also taxable, irrespective of whether they can be converted into money (*Lindus and Hortin v IRC* 17 TC 442). Where the trust is silent as to the distribution of trust income, s. 31 of the Trustee Act 1925 is critical. Sums actually paid for the maintenance, education or benefit of an infant beneficiary will form part of the total income of that infant (*IRC v Blackwell* [1921] 1 KB 389) but the position is more complicated when income is accumulated. As was seen in

---

[19.] *Re Musgrave* [1916] 2 Ch 417 but cf. *Re Horne* [1905] 1 Ch 76 if the trustee is also the beneficiary.
[20.] Goff and Jones, *The Law of Restitution*, 4th edn., Sweet & Maxwell, pp. 154–155.
[21.] It should be noted that the *Corbett* case concerned executors and the position of executors was held to be different from trustees. Sir Wilfred said that it was 'not true to say . . . that the income when received by executors pending the conclusion of the administration' was income of the beneficiaries. Thus at common law the income of an estate remains the executors' income until the administration is complete although this rule has now been overridden by statute; see Chapter 16.
[22.] The beneficiary will not be absolutely entitled to the income if he or she is only contingently entitled or is a discretionary beneficiary.

para. 14.2.3 above, trust income which is accumulated is generally subject to tax at the rate applicable to trusts (currently 34%) but this provision will not apply if the income is already the income of any person other than the trustee or the settlor (s. 686(2)(b), TA). Thus the income tax treatment of accumulated income turns on whether the beneficiary has a vested or a contingent interest in that income. If the beneficiary has a vested interest, the trust income forms part of his total income taxed at his marginal rates. If the interest is contingent, or the beneficiary's interest is liable to be divested, the income will be taxable in the hands of the trustees at the rate applicable to trusts.

In a case where s. 31, Trustee Act 1925 applies the following propositions can be made:

(a) If the beneficiary is over 18 and absolutely and beneficially entitled to the income then, even if there is a direction to accumulate income, the trust income belongs to the beneficiary. The beneficiary can call for the trust income to be paid to him so putting an end to the accumulation (*Saunders* v *Vautier* (1841) Cr & Ph 240). The trust income belongs to the beneficiary and forms part of his total income whether he receives it or not (*IRC* v *Hamilton-Russell's Executors* 25 TC 200). The beneficiary will also be taxable on the trust income on reaching 18 (even if his interest in the capital of the fund is still contingent) because of the effect of s. 31(1)(ii), Trustee Act 1925.[23]

(b) If the beneficiary is an infant and has a vested interest in both the income and the capital of the fund, the income will form part of the infant beneficiary's total income. This is because the income (and the capital) belongs to the beneficiary all along even though during his infancy he cannot give good receipt for the money. As Lord Greene MR put it in *Stanley* v *IRC* [1944] KB 255 at p. 259):

> It is [the beneficiary's] income even though he cannot give good receipt for it. On his death under 21 [now 18][24] income which has accumulated during his minority goes to his legal personal representatives. In such a case there can be no doubt the income accruing during minority is the income of the infant.

(c) If the infant beneficiary has no, or a contingent, interest in the capital but is a life tenant, then s. 31(2), Trustee Act 1925 provides that if the beneficiary attains the age of 18 or marries under that age, and his interest in the trust income during his infancy is a vested interest or he then becomes absolutely entitled to the trust capital, the trustees are to hold the accumulations in trust for that beneficiary absolutely. In any other case, the trustees hold the accumulations as an accretion to the capital of the trust fund. It was

---

[23] Section 31 can, of course, be excluded by necessary implication.
[24] Section 1, Family Law Reform Act 1969.

held by the Court of Appeal in *Stanley* v *IRC* that the effect of s. 31(2) was that an infant beneficiary with a vested life interest was 'for all practical purposes in precisely the same position as if his interest were contingent'. Lord Greene MR said (at p. 261):

> The infant does not during infancy enjoy the surplus income. The title to it is held in suspense to await the event, and if he dies under [18] his interest in it (whether or not it can be truly described as a vested interest) is destroyed.

The court concluded that to treat the rights of the infant as other than contingent in such circumstances would mean that the infant would be assessable to income tax in respect of income which might never become his. Thus, in such a case, the surplus income is taxed at the rate applicable to trusts during the accumulation period. When the accumulated income is paid out to the beneficiary on reaching majority, that payment cannot be taxed as income of the year of receipt because it is then a capital receipt of the beneficiary.

14.3.2 Tax liability

Where a beneficiary is *absolutely entitled* to the income or income has been applied for the beneficiary's benefit, the decision in *Baker* v *Archer Shee* (see para. 14.2.1) indicates that the beneficiary should be assessed to income tax under the Schedule or Case appropriate to the source of the income as it arises. If the trustees have paid tax on the income at the basic rate, the amount received by the beneficiary is grossed up at the basic rate and included in the beneficiary's total income. The beneficiary's tax liability is calculated accordingly and he is then given a 'credit' for the tax borne by the trustee.[25]

However, although the sum received by beneficiary is grossed up, it will not necessarily be the same as the gross income of the trustees. This is because of the rule in *Macfarlane* v *IRC* 14 TC 532 that while trust expenses are not deductible in computing trustees income, such expenses are deductible in computing the taxable income of a beneficiary. This shows that it is not strictly correct to say that the tax paid by the trustees is available as a credit against the beneficiary's liability, for the amount paid by the trustees will be greater than that paid by the beneficiaries. For example, if in the 1997–98 year of assessment, a trust has trading income of £1,000 and trust expenses properly chargeable to income of £100, the amount of tax paid by the trustees will be £230 (since the trust expenses are not deductible). The beneficiary will only receive £670 from the trust (£1,000 − [£230 + £100]) and it is this £670 which is grossed up at 23% to £870.13. The amount of tax which may be 'credited' is 23% on £870.13, i.e., £200.13. Since the trustees paid £230 in tax, £29.87 has been 'lost' to the Revenue.

[25.] It is hard to find any authority for this proposition but it seems generally accepted in practice.

Income tax and trusts   411

It has been pointed out[26] that the Revenue may be wrong to apply the 'rule' in the *Macfarlane* case since it was based on an earlier case, *Murray* v *IRC* 11 TC 133. in which the Court of Session held that a beneficiary's income was the net income of the fund after deduction of the fund's administrative expenses. It was argued in *Macfarlane* that *Murray* had been overruled by the House of Lords decision in *Baker* v *Archer Shee* but the Court of Session refused to accept this. It appears that the basis of the decision is that trust expenses are incurred before the beneficiary ever receives any income and, as trustees are not agents of the beneficiary, the beneficiary cannot claim the benefit of their expenses. It is nonetheless extremely difficult to reconcile this with the view upheld in *Baker* v *Archer Shee* that trust income belongs to the beneficiary as and when it arises. The difficulty relates back to the basic problem, discussed in para. 14.2, of what should properly be regarded as the source of the income; the underlying assets or the chose in action which is the beneficiary's interest under the trust.

14.3.3 Accumulation or discretionary trusts

Although a beneficiary under a discretionary settlement is not assessable on the income of the settlement because he has no right to receive income or property until the discretion is exercised in his favour, once the discretion is so exercised, he will become assessable to tax on any income paid to him[27] and he will be assessed under Schedule D, Case III. The payment to him is treated as a net amount paid after deduction of the rate applicable to trusts. The tax so deducted is treated as paid by the beneficiary (s. 687(2)(a), TA) so he may reclaim any tax paid in excess of his liability to income tax on the income received. Conversely, if the beneficiary is a higher rate taxpayer, he will be liable for the excess tax. The 'expenses' problem discussed in para. 14.3.2 does not arise with accumulation or discretionary trusts as the legislation specifically provides that such expenses are deductible (s. 686(2)(d)).

14.3.4 Payments out of capital

The general principle that a person is only to be taxed on income applies equally to payments received from settlements. However, the fact that the trustees make the payment to the beneficiary out of the capital of the settlement rather than the income, will not, of itself, prevent the payment being income and taxable as such in the beneficiary's hands. The nature of

---

[26.] *Butterworths UK Tax Guide 1995–96*, para. 11.08.

[27.] No argument (based on cases such as *IRC* v *Whitworth Park Coal Company* (1959) 38 TC 531) exists that a payment by trustees of a discretionary trust cannot be an annual payment. Lord Wrenbury in *Drummond* v *Collins* [1915] AC 1011 at pp. 1019 to 1021 held that sums actually paid to a beneficiary under exercise of a discretion (whether express or statutory) are part of the beneficiary's total income. And it was held in *Lindus and Hortin* v *IRC* 17 TC 442 that the beneficiary is entitled to demand that the money is paid over to him as soon as the trustees exercise their discretion in his favour.

the trust power pursuant to which the payment is made appears to be decisive (*Stevenson* v *Wishart* – see para. 14.2.3). So if, for example, the trustees are directed to pay an annuity to a beneficiary and all or part of that annuity is paid out of trust capital, the payments will be treated as income (*Brodie's Trustees* v *IRC* (1933) 17 TC 432, *Jackson's Trustees* v *IRC* (1942) 25 TC 13 and *Cunard's Trustees* v *IRC* [1946] 1 All ER 159).[28]

14.4 NON-RESIDENT TRUSTS

The tax position of non-resident trusts in discussed in outline in Chapter 35.

[28.] The capital element of a purchased life annuity is, generally, excluded from the charge to income tax by s. 656, TA. However, this does not apply to 'any annuity purchased in pursuance of any direction in a will, or to provide for an annuity payable by virtue of a will or settlement out of income of property disposed of by the will or settlement (whether with or without resort to capital)', s. 657(2)(c).

CHAPTER FIFTEEN
Income tax anti-avoidance provisions on settlements – Part XV, TA

15.1 INTRODUCTION

A taxpayer who wishes to reduce his income tax bill may try to alienate part of his income at law, but in such a way that he, or his family, continues to benefit from the income. For example, he may create a trust and transfer income-producing assets to trustees so that the capital of the fund and the income from it no longer belongs to him in law, although he and his family may be beneficiaries of the trust. The Revenue obviously wish to strike down such arrangements and over the years a number of anti-avoidance provisions have been introduced. These were collected together in Part XV, TA. The anti-avoidance provisions were enacted in a piecemeal fashion, often in response to particular tax avoidance schemes entered into by taxpayers, and they did not form a coherent code. Over time, some of the provisions effectively became obsolete in the light of developments elsewhere in the tax system[1] and there was considerable overlap. Accordingly, in his 1994 Budget Speech, the Chancellor of the Exchequer announced that the Part XV rules would be simplified and new legislation was brought forward in clause 68 and sch. 17 of the Finance Bill 1995.

Clause 68 and sch. 17 of the Finance Bill 1995 were initially intended to replace the 'old' Part XV rules in their entirety. Three new charging provisions were proposed:

---

[1] The former distinction between provisions which deem trust income to be the settlor's for all tax purposes and those which treat trust income as the settlor's only for the purposes of charging higher rate tax, had already become redundant for post-1989 settlements following the enactment of s. 674A, TA. Similarly, the provisions rendering settlements which could not exceed six years ineffective in s. 660, TA had become redundant following the reform of the taxation of annual payments in 1988, except to the extent they applied to charitable covenants.

(a) a provision treating income arising under a settlement as the settlor's own where he or his spouse retained an interest in the settlement;
(b) a provision treating income payments to the settlor's minor unmarried child or children as the settlor's income; and
(c) a provision charging income tax on a notional rate of interest on any loan made by the trustees of a settlement to the settlor or his spouse or vice versa.

The charging provisions described at (a) and (b) above became law following the granting of Royal Assent to the Finance Bill 1995. The proposed tax charge on loans to settlors was, however, widely criticised and was eventually withdrawn. In its place the government 'reinstated' some of the 'old' Part XV rules, namely ss. 677 to 682, TA, with some modifications to take account of the Finance Act 1995 changes. In all cases, the rules apply from the 1995–96 year of assessment onwards and apply to 'settlements' whenever and wherever made (s. 74(2), FA 1995).

15.2 MEANING OF 'SETTLEMENT'

For these purposes, a 'settlement' is defined as including 'any disposition, trust, covenant, agreement, arrangement or transfer of assets' (s. 660G, TA).[2] The width of this definition is such that it is arguable that it is not a 'definition' at all.[3] Its scope can best be illustrated by examples which although concerned with the 'old' Part XV rules are still applicable in determining the meaning of settlement.

IRC v *Mills* [1974] STC 130 concerned the tax affairs of Hayley Mills, a film actress. When Hayley was 14 her father, John Mills, formed a company and settled shares of that company on trust for her absolutely on attaining 25. Hayley then signed a service contract giving the company the exclusive right to her services for an annual salary of £400. The company received substantial sums for the films she subsequently made and distributed those sums as dividends to the trustees of the settlement. The House of Lords held that the surtax assessment on Hayley was properly made. By entering into the contract with the company she had entered into an 'arrangement' which constituted a 'settlement' and by securing her earnings from films were paid to that company she had provided funds to that settlement and was a 'settlor' in relation to it (see para. 15.3).

In *IRC* v *Wachtel* [1971] Ch 573 the settlor transferred £1,000 to trustees. The trustees purchased shares for £7,691 borrowing the difference from a bank at 1% interest. The settlor guaranteed the loan and deposited an equal sum at the bank for no interest. The trustees gradually discharged the debt

---
[2.] This definition is applied to ss. 677 to 682, TA by s. 682A TA (inserted by para. 11, Sch. 17, FA 1995). By including a transfer of assets the definition of 'settlement' is extended. Formerly the phrase 'transfer of assets' was only included in the definition of settlement for the purposes of chapter II, Part XV, TA (settlements on children).
[3.] For example, in *Hood-Barrs* v *IRC* [1946] 2 All ER 768 Cohen LJ held that the phrase 'transfer of assets' could not be construed *ejusdem generis* with the other categories listed.

with trust money which, in turn, released the settlor's debt. The Court of Appeal held that this amounted to an 'arrangement'.

In *IRC v Buchanan* [1958] Ch 289 funds were settled on G for life with remainder to D for life with remainder to D's children. The will expressly provided that a life tenant could surrender his or her life interest only to those persons who would become entitled on the death of the life tenant. D surrendered her expectant life interest in favour of her children and the next day G surrendered his life interest. D was assessed to surtax on the income of the settlement which was used for the maintenance of her children. The assessments were upheld by the Court of Appeal. The destruction of D's interest constituted a 'disposition' and accordingly, a settlement existed for the purposes of the anti-avoidance rules. *IRC v Buchanan* was followed in *d'Abreu v IRC* [1978] STC 538 which held that the release of a contingent interest amounted to a disposition.

In *Hood-Barrs v IRC* [1946] 2 All ER 768 a father transferred shares worth £45,000 to his infant daughters. The Court of Appeal had no difficulty in holding that this constituted a 'transfer of assets' and so a settlement. Similarly in *Thomas v Marshall* [1953] AC 543 there was a transfer of assets where a father paid money into a Post Office savings bank account for his infant children.

There is, however, one limitation of the scope of 'settlement' for these purposes. The cases on the old Part XV rules had established that some element of bounty was an essential requirement of a settlement.[4] The reasons for such a requirement were set out by Lord Wilberforce in *IRC v Plummer* [1979] 3 All ER 775:

> [The anti-avoidance provisions] are designed to bring within the net of taxation dispositions of various kinds in favour of a settlor's spouse, or children [etc.] that Parliament considers it might be right to treat such income . . . as still the settlor's income. These sections, in other words, though drafted in wide, and increasingly wider language, are nevertheless dealing with a limited field, one far narrower than the totality of dispositions or arrangements or agreements which a man may make in the course of his life. Is there any common description which can be applied to this? The courts which, inevitably, have had to face this problem, have selected the element of 'bounty' as a necessary common characteristic of all the 'settlements' which Parliament had in mind.

The particular tax avoidance scheme upheld in *Plummer v IRC* was stopped by statute (s. 125, TA) and was not followed by the House of Lords in *Moodie v IRC* [1993] STC 188 on the grounds that the decision in *Plummer* was inconsistent with the *Ramsay* doctrine (discussed in Chapter 4). However, this does not affect the validity of the element of bounty test as espoused in *Plummer*. When the Finance Bill 1995 changes were announced the Revenue

---

[4.] The development of this limitation can be traced back to Lord Macmillan in *Chamberlain v IRC* [1943] 2 All ER 200. See also *IRC v Leiner* (1964) 41 TC 589 and *Bulmer v IRC* [1967] Ch 145.

stated that the new rules would only apply to settlements that involved an element of bounty (Inland Revenue Press Release, 4 January 1995).

In *Chinn* v *Collins* [1981] 1 All ER 189 Lord Roskill explained that the element of bounty test sought to:

> distinguish between those cases where the recipient has in return for that benefit which he has received accepted some obligation which he has to perform, either before receiving the benefit or at some stated time thereafter, and those cases where the recipient benefits without any assumption by him of any correlative obligation.

However, in the later case of *IRC* v *Levy* [1982] STC 442 Nourse J summarised the law as follows:

> [A] commercial agreement devoid of any element of bounty is not within the definition [of a settlement]. The absence of any correlative obligation on the part of him who is at the receiving end of the transaction may be material, but it is not conclusive, in determining whether it contains an element of bounty or not.

Thus *bona fide* commercial transactions are not caught by the anti-avoidance rules as they are not settlements. The result in *IRC* v *Levy* was that an interest-free loan made by a taxpayer to a company in which he owned 99% of the shares was not a settlement. The loan was made in order to keep the company afloat and both the Special Commissioners and Nourse J accepted that the loan was made for sound commercial reasons.

The 'element of bounty' limitation on the anti-avoidance legislation may be criticised on the grounds that a *bona fide* commercial transaction may have tax avoidance as its main object. As Viscount Dilhorne put it in his dissenting speech in *IRC* v *Plummer*: 'That there are some who carry on the business of devising schemes for tax avoidance is well known. Their activities may well be described as commercial.' It is odd that despite the existence of new legislation, the government were content to rely on the 'common law' rules rather than create an express exclusion for *bona fide* commercial transactions in the legislation.

The element of bounty test sometimes sits uneasily with some of the decided cases. For example, in *Yates* v *Starkey* [1951] Ch 465 it was held that a court order directing a father to make payments on trust for his child was a 'settlement' for the purposes of the anti-avoidance provisions, although it is hard to see an 'element of bounty' on the part of the father.[5] In *Harvey* v *Sivyer* [1985] STC 434 Nourse J suggested that the case could be rationalised on the basis that the 'natural relationship between a parent and a young child was one of such deep affection and concern that there must always be an element of bounty by the parent, even where the provision is on the face of things made under compulsion.' This justification is somewhat hard to accept

---

[5.] See also *Stevens* v *Tirard* [1939] 4 All ER 186.

but the difficulty is avoided in practice as maintenance payments made after 14 March 1988 are subject to a special tax regime (s. 347B, TA).

The element of bounty test has recently been applied in *Butler v Wildin* [1989] STC 22. In that case, the parents arranged for shares in their company to be held by their children. Vinelott J held that the necessary element of bounty was demonstrated by the fact that the children contributed nothing except trifling sums to the company and they were exposed to no risk. All the risks of the venture were in fact borne by the taxpayers who lent money to the company, guaranteed bank loans and gave their services as directors free of charge. Accordingly there was a settlement for the purposes of the Part XV rules and the dividends of the company were treated as income of the parents.

15.3 MEANING OF 'SETTLOR'

A 'settlor' is 'any person by whom the settlement was made' (s. 660G, TA). A person is deemed to have made a settlement if he or she:

> made or entered into the settlement directly or indirectly, and, in particular, but without prejudice to the generality of the preceding words, if he has provided or undertaken to provide funds for the settlement, or has made with any person a reciprocal arrangement for that other person to make or enter into the settlement (s. 660G(2)).

This definition is derived from, and is very similar to, the previous legislation and therefore the case law on the application of the phrase still seems applicable. This had established that a person makes a settlement if he or she carries out any steps of that settlement. So there will be a settlement if a taxpayer simply follows a scheme devised by his or her lawyers and accountants. Thus there was a settlement in *Crossland v Hawkins* [1961] Ch 537 where the taxpayer agreed to perform services for a company for which he was paid £900 but the company received the significantly larger sum of £25,000. The taxpayer's children were beneficiaries under a settlement created by their grandfather and the trustees of the settlement used the funds of the settlement to subscribe for 98% of the company's share capital. After receiving the £25,000 the company declared a substantial dividend which the trustees applied for the benefit of the taxpayer's children. It was held that the formation of the company, the taxpayer's agreement to perform services for the company and the grandfather's settlement all constituted an arrangement to which the taxpayer had contributed funds indirectly.[6]

Where there is more than one settlor in relation to the settlement, the rules apply as if:

[6.] See also *IRC v Mills* (in para. 15.2) although in that case the argument concerning *mens rea* is no longer applicable in the light of the new definition of 'settlement'. (The argument, which in any event failed, was that because the former wording required that funds be provided for the 'purpose' of the settlement, the settlor must have some knowledge of what he or she was doing. The House of Lords did not consider that any element of *mens rea* was necessary. The word 'purpose' no longer appears in the definition of settlor.)

(a) each settlor were the only settlor; but

(b) references in the legislation to 'property comprised in a settlement' apply only to property originating from that particular settlor, that is property which the settlor has provided directly or indirectly or which represents that property; and

(c) references in the legislation to 'income arising under the settlement' apply only to income originating from that particular settlor, that is income from property originating from the settlor or income provided directly or indirectly by the settlor; and

(d) in relation to s. 660B (children's settlements) only income originating from that particular settlor is taken into account in determining the income paid to or for the benefit of the settlor's child (ss. 660E(2), (3), (4) and (5)).

However, these rules may not apply to successive interests. For instance, in *IRC* v *Buchanan* income only accrued to D's children because *both* G and D released their life interests. Yet the Court of Appeal's decision in that case upheld the Revenue's contention that the income accrued to D's children because of D's disposition alone. The Revenue avoided argument as to whether G was a settlor in relation to the fund by only raising assessments under the anti-avoidance rules from the time of G's death. In the similar case of *d'Abreu* v *IRC* the two beneficiaries of a trust, J and A, both effected dispositions of their interests under a family trust. J released her power of appointment with the result that if she died childless, her interest in the fund would pass to A. A then released her interest in the fund contingent on J's death in favour of A's children. J died without issue and therefore the income of the trust accrued to A's children. The taxpayer argued that J and A were joint settlors and the only way of determining the income which originated from each of them was to make an actuarial apportionment of the trust fund at the time of the dispositions. Oliver J, however, held that even if J was a settlor in relation to the settlement created by the disposition(s), the direction to apply the anti-avoidance rules to each settlor as if she was the only settlor meant that the court had to consider what income had originated from A. Since income originating from the settlor encompassed income provided directly or indirectly by the settlor, the question to be answered was, why did the income become payable to A's children? Oliver J considered that the only answer to this question was: 'because [A] had disposed of her contingent reversionary interest in the income'. Had it not been for that disposition, the income would have comprised A's income so it must follow that the income had been provided directly or indirectly by her.

15.4 THE CHARGING PROVISIONS

15.4.1 Settlements where the settlor retains an interest

Section 660A(1), TA provides:

> Income arising under a settlement during the life of the settlor shall be treated for all purposes of the Income Tax Acts as the income of the settlor

and not the income of any other person unless the income arises from property in which the settlor has no interest.

A settlor is regarded as having an interest in property if that property, or any other property derived from it, is, or may become, payable or applicable for the settlor or his or her spouse (s. 660A(2)). A spouse of the settlor does not include:

(a) a person who the settlor may later marry;
(b) a separated spouse, which includes not only those who are separated under a court order or who have entered into a separation agreement, but also spouses 'in such circumstances that the separation is likely to remain permanent';
(c) the widow or widower of the spouse.

Settlors are not regarded as having an interest in the settlement if they can only benefit in unlikely contingencies such as the bankruptcy of the beneficiary or, in the case of a marriage settlement, only by the death of both parties to the marriage and all the children of the marriage. Settlements where the settlor can benefit only in the event of: (a) the death of the settlor's child who became beneficially entitled to settled property under the age of 25; or (b) the death of any beneficiary under the age of 25 during whose life the settlor could not benefit, are similarly excluded.

Since a settlor will have an interest in property if it 'may' become payable or applicable for himself or his spouse, interests in discretionary trusts are included. It will be enough if the trustees have a power to exercise their discretion in favour of the settlor or his spouse. The fact that the discretion is in fact exercised in favour of somebody else will not prevent the section from operating.

In recognition of the fact that spouses are separately taxed, s. 660A excludes gifts between spouses from which income arises unless:

(a) the gift does not carry the right to the whole of that income; or
(b) the property given is wholly or substantially a right to income (s. 660A(6)).

This allows one spouse to make outright gifts of property to the other with the result that the recipient spouse becomes liable to income tax on any income subsequently arising on that property. A gift is not an outright gift for these purposes if it is subject to conditions or if it may become payable or applicable for the benefit of the transferor.

The Revenue take the view that where ss. 660, 671 to 674A or 683 to 684 (covering dispositions for short periods, revocable settlements and settlements in which the settlor retained an interest) previously applied to a settlement, s. 660A will generally apply to that settlement under the new rules (Inland Revenue Press Release 4 January 1995). The reader is referred to Chapter 7 of *Trusts and UK Tax* (Shipwright, Key Haven, 1992) for a full discussion of the 'old' rules. However it should be noted that:

(a) some settlements to which the 'old' rules applied will be excluded from the new rules because the circumstances in which a settlor is treated as having retained an interest will be narrower;

(b) the new rules will apply to some settlements outside the scope of the previous rules because they apply to settlements whenever made and where income from the settlement is payable only to the settlor; and

(c) where the previous rules sometimes treated income as the settlor's only for higher rate tax purposes, the new rules will treat it as the settlor's for all tax purposes but will allow the settlor to claim reimbursement from the trustees for any tax paid (see para. 15.4.4).

Because the tax treatment of the settlor in the 1995–96 and subsequent years of assessment may differ from that of previous years, all trustees and settlors need to review their tax positions. Settlors are obliged to notify their tax office of any liability under the new provisions even if they do not normally receive a tax return. Where settlement income has not previously been treated as the settlor's but is treated as the settlor's under the new rules, the tax treatment of beneficiaries receiving income or payments from the settlement will also change. The income will no longer be treated as that of the beneficiaries for tax purposes. As a result, the beneficiaries will not be liable to tax on it nor, if they are lower rate or non taxpayers, will they be able to reclaim any of the tax already paid on that income. It has been pointed out that this involves an element of retrospection (*Taxes*, Issue 6, 10 February 1995).

15.4.2 Children's settlements

Section 660B, TA applies where there is a settlement in favour of a settlor's minor unmarried child, or children. In such circumstances, any payments of income made to, or for the benefit of, the child will be treated as income of the settlor provided that such income has not been treated as the settlor's under s. 660A as described in para. 15.4.1 (s. 660B(1)). Where income is retained or accumulated under the terms of the settlement, any subsequent payments to the child out of the settlement (whether income or capital) are deemed to be income of the settlor to the extent that the settlement has 'available retained or accumulated income' (s. 660B(2)). Retained or accumulated income is available to the extent that the income arising to the settlement since its creation exceeds the amounts which have been:

(a) treated as income of the settlor or beneficiary;

(b) paid (whether as income or capital) to, or for the benefit of, a beneficiary other than an unmarried minor child of the settlor; or

(c) applied in defraying the expenses of the trustees properly chargeable to income or which would have been so chargeable but for an express provision of the trust (s. 660B(3)).

'Child' includes both a stepchild and an illegitimate child of the settlor (s. 660B(6)(a)).[7] For the avoidance of doubt, the legislation provides that a minor child is a child under 18 years of age (s. 660B(6)(b)). There is *de minimis* exception so that where the total income paid to the child that could be treated as the income of the settlor under s. 660B does not exceed £100, it is ignored (s. 660B(5)).

15.4.3 Capital payments to settlors

As noted in para. 15.1, when the Chancellor of the Exchequer announced the changes to Part XV, TA he announced that new provisions relating to loans to settlors would be introduced. The Finance Bill 1995 accordingly contained draft legislation for a third new charging provision. Under the proposed new rules, where the trustees of a settlement made a loan to the settlor or the settlor's spouse, or where either of them made a loan to the trustees, the settlor would be charged to income tax on the 'annual value' of the loan, calculated by reference to an official rate of interest, less any interest which had actually been paid. This proposal was subject to a great deal of criticism.[8] It was argued that it was wrong in principle to impose a liability on notional income since this could result in a tax charge where the settlor did not actually receive any income, for example, where the settlor made an interest free loan as part of a *bona fide* arrangement.[9] Further, as the proposed new rules would apply to both existing *and* new loans the new rules would effectively be retrospective. In the light of these criticisms, the government decided to reconsider its proposals and tabled amendments to the Finance Bill 1995 which removed the proposed new charging provision. The previous rules in ss. 677 to 682, TA were accordingly 'reinstated' with some modifications to take into account the new ss. 660A and 660B.

Under s. 677, where a settlor, or the settlor's spouse, or a third party at the settlor's direction, receives capital payments from the settlement, the payments are treated as the settlor's income for tax purposes to the extent that they represent 'available income' of the settlement (ss. 677(1), (9)(b) and (10)). 'Available income' is elaborately defined but essentially comprises the total income arising to the settlement in that and the previous years of assessment which has not been distributed (s. 677(2)). Section 677 does not apply when the capital sum is paid in return for full consideration in money or money's worth, but loans are specifically excluded from this proviso. This exclusion prevents a settlor from claiming that his or her promise to repay the loan amounts to full consideration even though the trustees might not enforce

---
[7.] Adopted, but presumably not foster, children are included.
[8.] See, *inter alia*, The Law Society's Revenue Law Committee, *Memorandum on the Finance Bill 1995*; The Chartered Institute of Taxation, *Representations on the Finance Bill 1995*; and the Tax Faculty of the Institute of Chartered Accountants in England and Wales, *Memorandum on the Finance Bill 1995*.
[9.] For example, in a typical inheritance tax arrangement the settlor makes a loan to trustees to purchase a single premium life insurance policy on the settlor's life. Such arrangements were not affected by the 'old' Part XV rules, but under the proposed 'loans to settlors' rules an income tax charge would arise notwithstanding that there was no income in the settlement.

that promise (s. 677(9)(a)). This same proviso states that a 'capital sum' means both a sum paid by way of loan and by repayment of a loan, so the provisions of section 677 apply where trustees make a loan to the settlor (and/or his spouse or third party at the settlor's direction) and where the settlor makes a loan to the trustees which is subsequently repaid by the trustees at a time when there is available income in the settlement. Since s. 678 extends s. 677 to capital sums paid by corporate bodies connected with the settlement (s. 678(1)), it creates difficulties where the trust assets are shares in a family company, the trustees are accumulating dividend income and the settlor receives repayment of a loan he previously made to the company. Accordingly, s. 678 only applies where, in addition to the capital sum from the company, there has been an 'associated payment' by the trustees. An associated payment is a payment by the trustees to the company in the period of five years ending or beginning on the date that the capital sum was repaid to the settlor (s. 678(3)). The aim of this provision is to ensure that s. 677 only applies where the transactions give rise to a genuine benefit for the settlor.

15.4.4 Calculation of tax liability

When ss. 660A or 660B, TA apply, the income will be treated as Schedule D, Case VI income of the settlor taxed at his marginal rate of income tax (ss. 660C(1) and (3)). The settlor is entitled to recover the tax he pays on that income from the trustees of the settlement (s. 660D(1)(a)). To assist the settlor in his or her claim against the trustees, the settlor can require the Inland Revenue to provide a certificate of the amount of tax paid (s. 660D(1)(b)).

In the case of a capital payment to the settlor, the sum received is grossed up at the rate applicable to trusts and charged under Schedule D, Case VI (ss. 677(6) and (7)). Credit is given for tax previously paid on that income at the rate applicable to trusts (s. 677(2)). If the capital sum or loan made exceeds the settlement's available income for that year, the excess is carried forward and charged to the settlor in the next year of assessment to the extent that there is available income and so on up to a maximum of 11 years (s. 677(1)). However, once the whole of any loan has been repaid no part of it will be treated as the settlor's income for the subsequent years of assessment (s. 677(4)). So the settlor's tax liability will not be affected by any later accumulation of income in the settlement.

CHAPTER SIXTEEN
Income tax and death

16.1 DECEASED'S INCOME

Personal representatives are required to settle the income tax liability of the deceased in respect of the income that accrued to him during his lifetime (s. 74, TMA). The computation of income arising in the year of death generally follows normal principles but income arising after the date of death is taxed as income of the estate and not as income of the deceased (*IRC v Henderson's Executors* (1931) 16 TC 282; *Wood v Owen* (1940) 23 TC 541 and *IRC v Mardon* (1956) 36 TC 565). Income tax may be assessed and charged on any one or more of the personal representatives to whom it arises (s. 151, FA 1989).

The personal allowances that would have been available to the deceased during the year of assessment are available to the personal representatives in full. Where a married man dies and he was entitled to the married couple's allowance, his widow may claim that relief for the year of assessment in which he dies and (unless she remarries in the year of assessment in which he dies) for the following year of assessment (s. 262, TA).

16.2 INCOME ARISING AFTER DEATH

Where income arises to the estate after death, the personal representatives will be assessable to income tax in respect of that income in the usual way. However, since the personal representatives are 'persons' not 'individuals' they will only be liable to income tax at the basic rate (*IRC v Countess Longford, Pakenham and others* (1928) 13 TC 573). Since they receive the income in their capacity of personal representatives, the personal representatives may not use their own personal reliefs, nor any personal allowances not absorbed by the deceased's income, to reduce their tax liability.

When a personal representative vests a specific legacy (such as shares in X Ltd) in the legatee, intermediate income accruing during the administration is related back and assessed on the beneficiary at the time the income accrued to the property (*IRC* v *Hawley* (1927) 13 TC 327). This is because the specific legatee is entitled to the income from the date of the testator's death. Where a legacy carries interest, the beneficiary is liable to tax on that interest under Schedule D, Case III as if it had become his income. The interest income cannot be disclaimed if a specific sum had been set aside to pay the legacy (*Spens* v *IRC* (1970) 46 TC 276).[1]

The tax position of residuary beneficiaries is governed by Part XVI, TA.[2] The broad scheme of the legislation is to attribute residuary income of the estate to the persons who are interested in that residue to the extent that they receive payments on account of their interests. Different rules apply according to whether a beneficiary has a 'limited' or an 'absolute' interest in the residue. The Finance Act 1995 amended the previous legislation which deemed income to be spread over the period of the administration of the estate, and replaced it with new rules so that payments in respect of limited or absolute interests in residue are taxed, as income, in the year of receipt. It has been commented that this change is unfair to low income beneficiaries since a lump sum payment at the end of the administration could cause the beneficiary's income for that year to exceed his or her personal allowances or push them into a higher tax bracket.[3]

16.2.1 Limited interests in residue

Where a person has a limited interest in a United Kingdom estate, any sums paid in respect of the limited interest during the 'administration period' are grossed up[4] at the 'applicable rate' and treated as the beneficiary's income for the year of assessment in which the sum is paid (s. 695(2), TA).[5] A person has a limited interest if he would have a right to the income of the whole or part of the residue if the administration were complete (s. 701(3)).[6] The 'administration period' is the period between the death and the completion

---

[1] Cf. *Dewar* v *IRC* (1935) 19 TC 561.
[2] Part XVI, TA as amended by s. 75 and Sch. 18, FA 1995 overrides the common law rule that a residuary beneficiary is not taxable on the income of the estate in the course of administration; *Corbett* v *IRC* (1937) 21 TC 449.
[3] The Revenue Law Committee of the Law Society, *Memorandum on the Finance Bill 1995*, February 1995. The memorandum also notes potential compliance problems for beneficiaries under the new self-assessment regime (see Chapter 2).
[4] Benefits in kind must also be grossed up; *IRC* v *Mardon* (1956) 36 TC 565. Income from a foreign estate is grossed up only to reflect the UK tax paid; s. 695(5) TA.
[5] If the interest has ceased, the grossed up income is assessed to tax as income for the year in which the interest ceased.
[6] It is unclear whether a person has a 'limited interest' within the meaning of this section if this interest is vested subject to being divested. See *Stanley* v *IRC* (1944) 26 TC 12.

of the administration of the estate (s. 695(1)). The question whether the administration of the estate is complete is a matter of fact, the issue being whether the residue has been ascertained.[7] The 'applicable rate' means the basic or lower rate according to the type of income from which the amount is paid, i.e., basic rate for non savings income and lower rate for savings income (ss. 1A and 701(3A)). When the administration of the estate is completed on or after 6 April 1995 any amounts which remain payable in respect of the limited interest are deemed to have been paid to the beneficiary as income in that year of assessment (s. 695(3) inserted by para. 2(1), sch. 18, FA 1995).[8]

16.2.2 Absolute interests in residue

A beneficiary has an absolute interest if, on the hypothesis that the administration were complete, he would be entitled to the capital, or a part of it, in his own right (s. 701(2), TA).[9] Sums actually paid to the beneficiary during the administration period in respect of his or her absolute interest are deemed to have been paid to the beneficiary as income grossed up at the applicable rate for the year of assessment in which they are actually paid (s. 696(3), TA inserted by para. 3(1), sch. 18, FA 1995 and s. 686(4), TA). However, the payments will be excluded if, when added to all previous payments in respect of the beneficiary's absolute interest, they exceed the beneficiary's 'aggregated income entitlement' for that year. The aggregated income entitlement is the total payment that the beneficiary would have received if the personal representatives had paid over his or her entire entitlement to the 'residuary income' of that year less income tax at the applicable rate (ss. 686(3A) and (3B), TA inserted by para. 3(1), sch. 18, FA 1995). Residuary income is, broadly, income of the estate less any payments properly chargeable to income such as interest, annuities and trustees' expenses (s. 697(1), TA).[10]

When the administration of the estate is completed on or after 6 April 1995, any payments during the administration period in excess of the beneficiary's aggregated income entitlement are treated as having been actually paid immediately before the end of the administration period (s. 696(5), TA inserted by para. 3(2), sch. 18, FA 1995). However if, on completion of the administration, it appears that the aggregate of benefits received by the beneficiary in respect of his or her interest is less than the residuary income (or the beneficiary's share in it) for the administration

---

[7.] This is the position at common law and the legislation does not appear to have altered this. See *Wahl* v *IRC* (1933) 17 TC 744; *Daw* v *IRC* (1928) 14 TC 58; *IRC* v *Pilkington* (1941) 24 TC 160 and *George Attenborough & Son* v *Solomon* [1913] AC 76.

[8.] Previously the total sums paid out before and after completion were aggregated and treated as having accrued from day to day during the period. The result was that the residuary income was spread evenly over the administration period.

[9.] Query if a person who is entitled to the capital but subject to the payment of an annuity is entitled to the capital 'in his own right'.

[10.] If the deductions exceed the income, the excess may be carried forward and deducted from the income of the estate in the following year, s. 697(1A), TA inserted by para. 4(1), Sch. 18, FA 1995.

period, the residuary income for the year in which the administration of the estate is completed is reduced by the amount of the deficiency. If the residuary income of that year is insufficient to absorb the deficiency, the balance is carried back to the previous year to reduce that year's residuary income and so on until the deficiency is eliminated (s. 697(2), TA as amended by para. 4(2), sch. 18, FA 1995). Any assessments already made on the basis of sums received are opened up and adjusted (s. 700, TA).

If the residue is held on discretionary trusts, the scheme used for limited interests is deemed to apply (s. 698(3)).

CHAPTER SEVENTEEN
Income tax and UK land

17.1 INTRODUCTION

This chapter is concerned with the taxation of income from UK land.[1] This is now mainly found in Schedule A. However, changes have been made to Schedule A by FA 1995 for income tax purposes but not for corporation tax purposes. New rules apply for income tax (referred to as New Schedule A) and the old rules apply for corporation tax purposes (referred to as Old Schedule A). It is not immediately obvious why this should be the case. The new rules will be considered after some general comments and consideration of the Old Schedule A.

17.2 HISTORICAL MATTERS

As is often the case with UK tax some knowledge of the history of the charge helps in understanding it. Land has long been the subject of taxation.[2] The Doomsday Book was seemingly compiled to ease the collection of tax on land[3] and the eighteenth century land tax was a precursor of the modern income tax 'system'.[4]

[1.] See Whiteman, *Income Tax*, 3rd edn, 1988; *Simon's Taxes*; M. Gammie and J. Desouza, *Land Taxation*. The expression 'taxation of income' is used to cover income tax and corporation tax on income.

[2.] It is arguable that much of our feudal system of land tenure for service is tax based. Socage tenure is still the basis of English land law: see the Tenures Abolition Act 1660. Nb also heregeld, danegeld and scutage.

[3.] See Sabine, *Short History of Taxation*, Chapter 1.

[4.] Sabine, above, footnote 3 pp. 103 et seq. Its start date seems to be 1689 but it becomes more fully developed in the eighteenth century.

The 1803 Act charged income tax in respect of land under two schedules, Schedules A and B. Schedule A was originally a charge on the 'ownership' of land capable of actual occupation. An owner occupier was charged on the 'notional income' of the value of his occupation. It was because of this charge that mortgage interest was allowed as a deduction – it was treated as a cost of earning the 'notional income'. Schedule B was a charge on the occupation of land on the 'profits' from it.

Schedule A was charged by reference to the annual value of the land. This was intended to represent the open market value of letting on a landlord's full repairing lease after an allowance for repairs. It was charged on the occupier except to the extent that he paid rent to a landlord. An owner not in occupation was charged only to the extent that he received actual income. This system was abolished by FA 1963 and replaced by the present system, at first designated Schedule D, Case VIII but rechristened Schedule A from 1970–71. The tax is now based entirely on the income received, not on the benefit in kind of owning the land. Nevertheless, an example will show how it can be argued to be unjust to tax actual income but not benefit in kind. A and B each own a house worth £50,000. A occupies his house and thus pays no income tax in respect of it. B rents his house out for £5,000 per annum and himself pays £5,000 per annum rent for his home. B has exactly the same benefit in kind as A (use of a house) but has a cash deficiency equal to income tax on £5,000 at his marginal rates.

Schedule B came to be charged only on the income from commercial woodlands. It has now been abolished.

The FA 1995 introduced a new regime for the income taxation of land and a new charging section for income tax purposes. The old rules still apply for corporation tax and they will be considered first. The new system essentially charges income tax as the profits of a business.

(It should be noted that there are special rules for furnished holiday lettings in ss. 503–4, TA and for income under the 'rent-a-room' scheme in sch. 10, F (No. 2) A 1992 which are not discussed in this book for reasons of space.)

17.3 GENERAL MATTERS

Income from land may be subject to tax in one of four ways under:

(a) Schedule A in the case of most receipts;
(b) Case VI of Schedule D in respect of certain miscellaneous transactions in land which are not charged under Schedule A;
(c) Case I of Schedule D if the taxpayer is a dealer in land or is indulging in transactions having a trading nature; and
(d) Case V of Schedule D in the case of land outside the United Kingdom.

Corporation tax under the old Schedule A is charged on:

the annual profits or gains arising in respect of any such rents or receipts as follows, that is to say—

(a) rents under leases of land in the United Kingdom;
(b) rentcharges, ground annuals and feuduties, and any other annual payments reserved in respect of, or charged or issuing out of, such land;
(c) other receipts arising to a person from or by virtue of his ownership of an estate or interest in or right over such land or any incorporeal hereditament or incorporeal heritable subject in the United Kingdom.

The charge under the new Schedule A to income tax covers broadly the same matters but phrases it differently. It charges:

... the annual profits or gains arising from any business carried on for the exploitation, as a source of rents or other receipts, of any estate, interest or rights in or over land in the UK.

Transactions entered into for such exploitation are deemed to have been entered into in the course of such a business. This can include one-off transactions.

17.4 THE CHARGE UNDER THE OLD SCHEDULE A

17.4.1 Background

The charge under Schedule A is broadly concerned with income derived from land such as rent. As seen in para. 17.2 above, the notional value of the land is not charged so that occupiers are no longer taxable in respect of their occupation of properties.

The receipt of rent etc. in respect of land in the UK is taxed under Schedule A. This is set out in s. 15, TA (and see para. 17.3 above). Broadly, the person chargeable is the person receiving or entitled to the profits or gains taxable under Schedule A. The charge is on the amount which the taxpayer is entitled to receive in the period rather than the amount actually received (s. 15(1), para. 2). This is subject to adjustment under s. 41 where amounts to which a taxpayer has become entitled are not paid and the taxpayer is able to prove this and has taken reasonable steps to enforce payment or, if rent has been waived, that it was waived without consideration and to avoid hardship.

Where there is a furnished letting, tax in respect of payment for the use of the furniture it is chargeable under Schedule D, Case VI unless the taxpayer elects for taxation under Schedule A (see s. 15(1), para. 4, TA as amended).

The old Schedule A contains a list of certain minor exceptions from charge (s. 15(1), paras 3 and 4) which are not dealt with in this book.

The reference to 'annual profits or gains' in old Schedule A seems to connote no more than that the profits must be of an income nature though not necessarily recurrent (cf. Schedule D, Case I discussed in Chapter 10).

17.4.2 Interpretation

The old Schedule A taxes the rents from 'leases', 'rentcharges', 'ground annuals' and 'feuduties' and 'other receipts . . . from land'. The meaning of these words and phrases is discussed below.

17.4.3 'Lease'

A lease for these purposes includes an agreement for a lease and any tenancy (s. 24, TA). This reflects the English law position which, in equity, treats a lease which can be specifically enforced as generally equivalent to a formal lease duly sealed where appropriate (see *Walsh* v *Lonsdale* (1882) 21 Ch D 9). The distinguishing feature of a lease (as opposed to a licence) in English law seems to be exclusive possession (see *Street* v *Mountford* [1985] AC 809).

17.4.4 'Land'

Land is not defined specifically for these purposes. The Interpretation Act 1978 provides in sch. 1 that:

> 'Land' includes buildings and other structures, land covered with water, and any estate, interest, easement, servitude or right in or over land.

It should be noted that this definition of land only applies from 1 January 1979 but the previous definitions are preserved by para. 5, sch. 2 to the 1978 Act. It seems that the new definition applies to UK tax legislation notwithstanding the consolidatory nature of the acts (see para. 2.1.5).

17.4.5 'Rentcharge' etc.

'Rentcharges' are not further defined for these purposes. 'Ground annuals' and 'feuduties' are Scots terms for certain annual payments charged on land. The Rentcharges Act 1977 prohibits the creation of new rentcharges after 21 August 1977 subject to certain exceptions. Section 1 of the 1977 Act defines a 'rentcharge' as 'any annual or other periodic sum charged on or issuing out of land except rent reserved by a lease or tenancy or any sum payable by way of interest'.

17.4.6 'Other receipts ... from land'

The phrase 'other receipts ... from land' is wide and covers virtually all other income derived from UK land. It catches receipts of an income nature from land such as fishing and shooting rights and other *profits à prendre*. It would also catch licence fees and payments of an income nature for easements and similar rights (but cf. s. 120, TA and similar provisions). It can be important to determine whether a receipt is rent or an 'other receipt' from land, as different deduction rules can apply (see ss. 25 and 26 discussed in para. 17.5 below).

The phrase 'other receipts ... from land' was considered in *Lowe* v *J.W. Ashmore* (1970) 46 TC 597. A company owned land in Leicestershire on which it carried on the trade of farming. It was agreed that turf should be sold at £75 per acre for two years. The turf was cut and removed by the purchasers. The receipts were assessed under Schedule D. The Commissioners concluded that the receipts were of a capital nature and not assessable to income tax. Megarry J reversed this decision. He considered that the company was assessable under Schedule D, Case I. He also considered the sums assessable under what is now Schedule A (then Schedule D, Case VIII). On the Schedule A part of the case he said:

> The words 'other receipts arising to a person from, or by virtue of, his ownership of an estate or interest in or right over . . . land' in [s. 15(1), para. 1(c)] are wide, general and devoid of authority. I think that it is clear that the evidence adduced does not begin to support any contention that the contractors owned in equity any estate or interest in the unsevered turf greater than at most an equitable *profit à prendre* . . . The expression 'profits or gains arising . . . from payments for any easement over or right to use any land made to the person who occupies the land' formerly appeared verbatim in the Income Tax Act 1952 s. 179, and before that in the Finance Act 1948 s. 31(1). The authorities on these provisions show that 'the right to use any land' was construed as including all *profits à prendre*.

17.5 DEDUCTIONS AND OLD SCHEDULE A

17.5.1 General

As has been seen, s. 15, TA imposes the charge on 'the annual profits or gains' arising in respect of rents or other receipts. There are special rules about the deductions which may be made for Schedule A purposes from these rents or other receipts. These rules are found in Part II, TA, especially in:

(a) s. 25 which sets out the general rules;
(b) s. 26 which deals with land managed as one estate;
(c) s. 27 which deals with maintenance funds for historic buildings;
(d) s. 28 concerning deductions from receipts other than rent;
(e) s. 29 which deals with sporting rights;
(f) s. 30 where special rules as to expenditure on making sea walls are set out; and
(g) ss. 31–33B which deal with other miscellaneous matters.

17.5.2 Section 25

17.5.2.1 General Section 25(1), TA provides that certain deductions 'from rent to which [a person] becomes entitled under a lease' in a chargeable period are allowed in computing the profits or gains which are taxable. These are called 'permitted deductions' in the section and are set out in s. 25(2). There are four categories consisting of payments (other than interest) in respect of:

(a) maintenance, repairs, insurance and management;
(b) services which the landlord is obliged to provide but for which he receives no separate payment (e.g., porterage and central heating in a block of mansion flats);

(c) rates or other charges on the occupier which the landlord is obliged to pay (e.g., where the rent is inclusive of rates);
(d) any rent, rentcharge, ground annual, feu duty or other periodical payment in respect of the land or charged on or issuing out of the land.

Further provisions on deductibility are set out in subsections (3) to (9).

(a) Section 25(3) allows the deduction of permitted deductions from rent which the taxpayer becomes entitled to during the chargeable period. Deductions of permitted deductions from an earlier period are also allowed provided they fell due during the period of the lease in respect of premises subject to the lease. However, where the landlord is not the original lessor (e.g., because the reversion has been assigned), the general rule is that expenditure payable before the new landlord took over is not deductible as the periods before he became landlord are not to be treated as part of the currency of the lease (s. 25(4)).

(b) Section 25(5) makes further provision as to the 'currency of the lease' where a lease at a full rent has been entered into after a previous lease has expired. This allows permitted expenditure during a void or preceding lease to be deducted. Any necessary apportionments are to be made (s. 25(6)).

(c) Where there is a lease at a 'full rent' which is not a tenant's repairing lease (defined in s. 24(6)(c)) then instead of only being able to deduct expenditure relating to the particular lease's rent expenditure in respect of other properties let at a full rent may be deducted (s. 25(7)). Effectively excesses can be carried forward. If the leases are not at a 'full rent' then expenditure can only be set against rent from the lease to which it relates. If the lease is a tenant's repairing lease then in general there should not be much expense on the landlord for repairs and management other than the cost of collecting ground rent.

(d) Special provision is made in s. 25(9) for deduction in respect of expenditure on 'common parts' (such as lobbies etc.) which are retained by the landlord but are used for all the premises let (e.g., a block of flats). Without this there would be no deduction as, by definition, the common parts are not let.

17.5.2.2 Revenue view The Inland Revenue had published their view of what deductions they considered allowable in leaflet IR 27 (since withdrawn). They said in Appendix I of that pamphlet:

Appendix I
Note on expenditure on maintenance, repairs, insurance and management allowed as a deduction under Schedule A.

The kind of expenditure which can be allowed as a deduction in computing profits under Schedule A consists broadly of normal expenditure on maintenance, repairs, insurance and management of the property. Capital expenditure is not allowable, except where part of the cost of improvements, additions or alterations is allowable in the circumstances mentioned at the end of this Note. Expenditure attributable to the period before the taxpayer acquired the property, or to a period when he occupied the property himself, is also not allowable.

A problem could arise where a property is altered so that repairs and maintenance which would otherwise be done are not carried out but are 'obviated' by the alteration. This is dealt with by ESC B4. It reads:

1. Maintenance and repairs of property obviated by alterations etc: Schedule A assessments.
Where maintenance and repairs of property are obviated by improvements, additions and alterations, so much of the outlay as is equal to the estimated cost of the maintenance and repairs is allowed as a deduction in computing liability in respect of rents under Schedule A. This concession does not apply where:
   (i) the alterations, etc, are so extensive as to amount to the reconstruction of the property, or
   (ii) there is a change in the use of the property which would have made such maintenance or repairs unnecessary.

17.5.3 'Management'

This expression has been considered in some of the cases. The cases on s. 75, TA (management expenses of investment companies) should also be contrasted (see Chapter 26). In *IRC* v *Wilson's Executors* (1934) 18 TC 465, £1,600 was paid by the taxpayer in full settlement of disputed claims. He claimed to deduct this sum as an expense of management. The Commissioners allowed this deduction but were reversed by the Court of Session.

Lord President Clyde said:

> If 'management' means just administration, it follows that the cost of management includes some things which, from an accounting point of view, would constitute capital expenditure, as well as a great variety of things which, from an accounting point of view, would constitute revenue expenditure. In short, there is almost no end to the scope of the deductions which would become permissible under the Rule if the word 'management' is construed in the wide and general sense to which I have referred – a sense which, as I have said, is consistent with its ordinary use in popular language.
>
> There is, however, another meaning which the word 'management' will bear, much more restricted and also not inconsistent with the use of the word in popular language. . . .
>
> There are two aids to the choice between these alternative constructions of the Rule which occur to me. To the first of them . . . the alarmingly large scope of costs which would be included if the wider construction were adopted. I cannot think Parliament meant that. The other aid is that 'management' appears in the Rule alongside of 'maintenance', 'repairs' and

'insurance'. If 'management' were given its larger meaning, it would be superfluous to make special mention of maintenance, repairs and insurance, for these are merely particular heads of the cost of administering an estate. Since 'management' is put in as a separate head, it is natural to suppose that it was not intended to embrace the others, but, on the contrary, to designate something relatively as limited as each of the others, but different from them. The narrower construction of the Clause is consistent with this supposition. I wish I felt more confident than I do in drawing from these considerations a conclusion that the narrower construction is the preferable one.

In *Southern* v *Aldwych Property Trust Ltd* (1940) 23 TC 707 the company claimed to be allowed to deduct the cost of advertising for tenants for flats it owned as expenses of management within the meaning of what is now s. 75, TA. Deduction of any expense deductible in computing income for the purposes of Schedule A is not permitted under s. 75 (see s. 75(1)). Lawrence J said:

> The question is, is the cost of advertising a 'necessary disbursement' in managing property? In my opinion it is perfectly clear that it is. No property which is let can be managed in an ordinary business sense without advertisement of the property when it is about to become vacant . . . I do not think that the words 'maintenance', 'repairs' and 'insurance' form any class which excludes the word 'management' in the sense which I put upon that word; and I think that the word 'management' has its ordinary meaning and includes all the ordinary expenses of management of the property which falls to be taxed under Schedule A.

17.5.4 Section 26: land managed as one estate

This allows for a pooling of expenditure where certain conditions are fulfilled. The most important conditions are that the land was in one ownership and managed as one estate at the end of 1962–63 and an election has been made. There are also annual value limits on the rent against which the expenditure may be set.

17.5.5 Section 27: maintenance funds

This deals with contributions to maintenance funds for historic buildings allowing them to be deducted from rents provided certain conditions have been met.

17.5.6 Section 28: deductions from receipts other than rent

This section deals with deductions from receipts from land other than rent (see para. 17.4.6) and now applies only for corporation tax purposes. Thus revenue payments can be deducted from entitlement to payments for sporting

Income tax and UK land

rights, easements, rentcharges and the like provided these payments fall within the categories listed in s. 28(1), TA. These are:

(a) maintenance, repairs, insurance or management of the premises;
(b) and (c) sums reserved as an expense of the transaction;
(d) items deductible under (a), (b) or (c) above and which have been carried forward.

17.5.7 Section 29: sporting rights

This deals with the cost of maintaining land for granting 'sporting rights' (defined in s. 29(5), TA as rights of fowling, shooting, fishing or killing game, deer or rabbits). Where land is normally so let, but is not in a particular year, the costs may be deducted from rent from a notional lease at a full rent. If the owner uses the rights for himself then these expenses are to be reduced by the market value of the rights enjoyed by the owner or his guest. The charge is strictly on a year of assessment basis requiring apportionment of accounting periods. In practice an accounts basis may be allowed.

17.5.8 Section 30: sea walls

This allows capital expenditure on sea walls to protect the property to be deducted over a 21-year period at the rate of $\frac{1}{21}$st a year effectively as if it were repair expenditure.

17.5.9 Other matters

These are dealt with in ss. 31–33B. Section 31 and sch. 1 deal with transitional provisions for expenditure incurred before 1963–4. Section 33 deals with agricultural land.

Sections 33A and 33B deal with rents etc. payable between connected persons. This is to counter possible tax advantages by mismatching the deductibility and taxability of payments, for example within a group if rent were payable in arrears after the end of the chargeable period in which allowable expenditure was incurred.

17.6 PREMIUMS AND DEEMED PREMIUMS

17.6.1 Introduction

A lease may be granted for a consideration which is capital (a premium or fine) or income (a rent) or partly income and partly capital. It would thus be possible to avoid income tax by granting a succession of short leases at a high premium and a low rent. Sections 34–39, TA therefore tax premiums partly as capital and partly as income. The longer the lease granted the smaller the amount of the premium deemed to be income. When the lease exceeds fifty years the provisions no longer apply.

Thus ss. 34 to 38 can have the effect of treating sums as liable to income taxation rather than taxation on capital gains. This can be important as far as the use of losses and reliefs is concerned. If there are capital (allowable) losses available these cannot be used against income profits. Equally if it is hoped to make use of the replacement of business assets relief in TCGA (see Chapter 22) it is necessary that the gain fall within the capital gains tax regime if the relief is to be obtained. The possible recharacterisation of the gain as income is therefore a trap for the unwary.

Premiums paid on leases were treated as capital and as being not liable to income tax before the year of assessment 1963–64 (see, e.g., *Gillott and Watts v Kalhoun* (1884) 2 TC 76). Seemingly the converse was also true, i.e., a premium received by a landlord was treated as a capital sum (see the *Austin Reed* case reported in 1963 BTR but not elsewhere as it was a Special Commissoners' case). Consequently, as until the mid-1960s there was no capital gains tax, an item received as capital escaped the UK tax net unless there was some specific provision dealing with it.

It is the FA 1963 provisions to 'rectify' this that are now ss. 34–39, TA. Three areas in particular are covered. These are:

(a) Premiums on leases for 50 years or less. Section 34 effectively imposes an income tax charge (generally under Schedule A) on premiums etc. required on the grant of a lease not exceeding 50 years.

(b) Sale at undervalue. Section 35 provides that if no premium is charged, or a premium of less than the market value is charged, then an income tax charge arises in respect of the amount forgone.

(c) Sale with a right to reconveyance. Section 36 imposes an income tax charge in some circumstances where there is a sale with a right to reconveyance.

Sections 35 and 36 are anti-avoidance provisions. The general aim of these provisions is to stop persons turning income into capital and so avoiding tax or reducing their tax liability. Now that the marginal rates of income and capital gains tax have been harmonised this is much less of a problem.

FA 1995 made consequential changes to this legislation for income tax purposes following the introduction of the new Schedule A.

17.6.2 Section 34: Treatment of premiums etc. as rent or Schedule D profits

17.6.2.1 General Section 34, TA imposes an income (or corporation) tax charge where a premium is required under a lease, or under the terms subject to which the lease is granted, where the lease does not exceed 50 years. The landlord is treated for income (or corporation) tax purposes as becoming entitled to an amount by way of rent in addition to the actual rent receivable calculated in accordance with a formula.

The formula to calculate the amount of the premium liable to income (or corporation) tax is

Income tax and UK land

$$P - \frac{(P \times Y)}{50}$$

Where P is the premium; and Y is the number of complete periods of 12 months, other than the first, comprised in the duration of the lease.

There are special rules for calculating the duration of a lease discussed in para. 17.6.2.6. The effect of s. 34 is that there is a 2% deduction for each year of the unexpired duration of the lease except the first.

Example
Henry is the owner of the freehold in Whiteacre. He grants a lease for 46 years to B at a premium of £100,000. A will be liable to income tax in respect of the premium on an amount calculated in accordance with the formula, i.e.:

$$£100,000 - \left(£100,000 \times \frac{(46 - 1)}{50}\right) = £100,000 - £90,000 = £10,000$$

(This is equivalent to a deduction of 90%, i.e., 2% × 45 [46 − 1]. It seems that in practice this is the easier way to calculate the amount although this is not the statutory method.)

The £90,000 not liable to income tax (i.e., the amount deducted) may still be liable to capital gains taxation as a capital sum derived from an asset within s. 22, TGCA. (In working out the gain it should be remembered in appropriate cases (e.g., a lease and leaseback in respect of an original lease with now less than 50 years to run) that there is a curved line restriction on the acquisition expenditure which may be taken into account as the base cost on a lease with 50 years or less to run.)

17.6.2.2 Definitional questions Section 34, TA gives rise to a number of questions including the following.

(a) What is a 'premium'?
(b) When is a premium 'required'?
(c) What are the 'terms subject to which a lease is granted'?
(d) How is the 'duration of a lease' to be calculated?

These questions are considered next.

17.6.2.3 What is a 'premium'? 'Premium' is a word whose meaning can change according to its context. By s. 24(1), TA 'premium' includes any like sum, whether payable to the immediate or a superior landlord or to a person connected with the immediate or superior landlord.

It should be noted that the payment referred to here is a payment *to* the landlord *not* a payment *by* the landlord. The effect of this is that payments by the landlord, so-called 'reverse premiums', are not included as, by definition, they are payments to the tenant.

The approach that a premium is a payment to a landlord fits in with *Clarke v United Real (Moorgate) Ltd* [1988] STC 273 where Walton J said (at p. 299):

Now what is a premium? Having in mind the dictum of Lord Goddard CJ in *R v Birmingham (West) Rent Tribunal* [1951] 1 All ER 198 at 201, that 'The whole conception of the term is a sum of money paid to a landlord as consideration for the grant of a lease,' I venture to define a premium as any sum paid by the tenant to the landlord in consideration of the grant of the lease.

Section 24(2) contains a presumption that any sum (other than rent) paid on or in connection with the *granting* of a tenancy is a premium 'except insofar as other sufficient consideration for the payment is shown to have been given.' It is believed that by (unpublished) concession payment of the lessor's legal costs by the tenant is not normally treated as falling within s. 24(2).

The meaning of premium for these purposes is further extended by s. 34(2). The subsection provides:

> where the terms subject to which a lease is granted impose on the tenant an obligation to carry out any work on the premises, the lease shall be deemed for the purposes of this section to have required the payment of a premium to the landlord (in addition to any other premium) of an amount equal to the amount by which the value of the landlord's estate or interest immediately after the commencement of the lease exceeds what its then value would have been if those terms did not impose that obligation on the tenant.

Sums payable on surrender or variation of the lease may also be taxable.

17.6.2.4 When is a premium 'required'? Section 34(1), TA refers to premium being required under a lease or otherwise under the terms subject to which a lease is 'granted'. There is an argument that as a matter of English law this wording would not catch an agreement for a lease. The word 'grant' has a technical meaning in English law according to *City Permanent Building Society v Miller* [1952] Ch 840 as requiring a deed. However, this argument does not seem to be the generally accepted view for tax purposes. It seems that a technical English meaning of a word such as 'grant' should not be taken in a statute which applies to the whole of the United Kingdom (see, e.g., *IRC v City of Glasgow Police Athletic Association* (1953) 34 TC 76). This fits in with a purposive construction of the statute as well. By s. 24 'lease' includes an agreement for lease which would also support this approach.

17.6.2.5 'Terms subject to which a lease is granted' This phrase is potentially very wide. It would cover side letters to carry out building works as part of the terms on which a lease is granted. How much further does it go? Do the terms in question need to be legally enforceable? If a side letter fell foul of the Law of Property (Miscellaneous Provisions) Act 1989, would this mean that it was not one of the terms subject to which the lease is granted? These are very difficult questions on which there is no helpful authority. Such additional 'terms' should therefore be avoided where possible.

Income tax and UK land

17.6.2.6 'Duration of the lease' The provisions in s. 34 and s. 35, TA apply to a lease of a duration not exceeding 50 years. If there were no anti-avoidance provisions it would be relatively straightforward to avoid the application of s. 34 et seq by suitable drafting. For example by including break clauses in a 52 year lease or having 'funny rents' that cut in, e.g., at £1 million per square foot after the first five years of a 52 year lease when the period of the lease would exceed 50 years as a matter of law but the rental would be such that in the real world such a lease would not last that long. The draftsman thought of this and made provision for it in s. 38 by providing rules for the determination of the length of a lease essentially by reference to what is likely to happen viewed as at the date of the grant of the lease.

Broadly, the rules in s. 38 are as follows:

(a) Where it is unlikely for any reason that the lease will continue to its expiry date, the term of the lease is treated as being for a period from the date on which it is likely to end judged by reference to the circumstances prevailing at the time when the lease is granted (see s. 38(1)(a)).

(b) Where the lease provides for an extension by notice given by the tenant then account may be taken of any circumstances making it likely that the lease will be so extended (see s. 38(1)(b)).

(c) Where the tenant or a person connected with him is or may become entitled to a further lease or the grant of further lease (whenever commencing) of the same premises or of premises including the whole or part of the same premises, the term of the lease may be treated as not expiring before the term of the further lease (see s. 38 (1)(c)). Thus an option for a further lease may in fact take it over the 50-year period. This can be helpful in minimising stamp duty in some circumstances (e.g., by having a 34 year lease and an option) but not falling foul of these rules.

17.6.3 Sections 35 and 36, TA

17.6.3.1 General Sections 35 and 36 were introduced to deal with possible avoidance of s. 34 by assignment of a lease granted at an undervalue and transfer with a right to reconveyance, which could be structured to give the same benefit to the landlord as the payment of a premium without apparently falling within s. 34.

17.6.3.2 Section 35: sale at an undervalue This section was introduced to deal with a potential avoidance device of s. 34 which, as drafted, only applies to the *grant* of a lease (see para. 17.6.2.4) and not to an assignment of a lease. If a landlord wished to grant a lease to A at a premium of £1 million he might avoid tax under s. 34 (without the anti-avoidance provisions) by granting the lease to a controlled company at a small premium first and then arranging for the company to assign the lease to A for £1 million consideration, less the small premium. It is interesting to consider whether nowadays this might fall within the *Ramsay* doctrine discussed in Chapter 4. If so, s. 35 might today be otiose. However it is still there. The method of charging is to charge the amount of additional premium forgone by the landlord.

17.6.3.3 Section 36: transfer with a right of reconveyance

Section 36 is aimed at a further potential avoidance device where the landlord could disguise an intended grant of a lease at a premium as an 'outright' sale of the land with an option or requirement for a reconveyance or leaseback at a later date. The charge in these circumstances is on a notional premium consisting of the excess of the original sale price over the price on reconveyance or, if a lease is granted back, over any premium on the grant of the lease. The usual 2% rule discussed in para. 17.6.2.1 applies.

17.6.4 Section 87: deduction

Where there is a premium charge to income taxation the corollary is that an income deduction of an equivalent amount may be allowed. The allowance is a proportion each year of the amount of the premium charged in the landlord's hands. A premium paid for a lease is otherwise capital expenditure (see *Gillott and Watts* v *Kalhoun* (1884) 2 TC 76).

17.7 SERVICE CHARGES

The payment and receipt of service charges is a topic which can cause considerable problems.

17.7.1 What is a 'service charge' for tax purposes?

There is no special fiscal definition – like a monkey or an elephant one is supposed to recognise a service charge when one sees it.

Section 136 and sch. 19, Housing Act 1988 provides five pages worth of detail. In essence in that Act a service charge is an amount payable by a tenant as part of, or in addition to the rent, directly or indirectly, for services, repairs, maintenance, insurance or the landlord's costs of management.

17.7.2 Tax consequences

Since a service charge can take a number of different forms the tax consequences can differ radically. The correct legal analysis of what is paid for what is essential to understanding the tax treatment. If the service charge is reserved as rent this may also affect the indirect tax position, i.e., VAT.

17.7.3 Persons to consider

Broadly when service charges are involved there are three parties (other than the Revenue) to consider. These are:

   (a) the tenant who pays the service charge;

Income tax and UK land

(b) the landlord who receives the service charge; and
(c) the provider of services to the landlord.

In simple terms the income/corporation tax charges to consider can be represented as follows.

Provider	Landlord	Tenant
DI receipt	Schedule A receipt	
	DI receipt	
	DVI receipt	
	Schedule A deduction	Schedule A deduction
DI deduction	DI deduction	DI deduction
	(including capital allowances)	(including capital allowances)

The tax position of each of these needs to be considered in turn in order to understand tax charges.

17.7.4 The provider

The provider will generally be carrying on the trade of providing services so the usual trading rules will apply to charge the sums he receives to tax under Schedule D, Case I. Section 74 restricts any deductions the provider may claim to expenditure:

(a) incurred for the purpose of the trade;
(b) wholly and exclusively incurred;
(c) of a recurrent or 'income' nature.

17.7.5 The landlord

17.7.5.1 Payment for what? It is important to establish precisely what the payment by the tenant relates to as this affects what Schedule or Case applies to tax the receipt. The Schedule or Case under which the income is chargeable is important as it affects, e.g., the deduction rules and the date of payment of tax.

17.7.5.2 Possible heads of charge

17.7.5.2.1 Schedule A as rent A service charge reserved as rent and/or which forms part of the consideration for the grant of the lease will be taxed under Schedule A (s. 15, para. 1 and see *Property Holding Co. Ltd v Clark* [1948] 1 All ER 165). Section 25 deals with the permitted deductions from rent received under the old Schedule A and thus determines what costs incurred by the landlord in organising or providing the services may be deducted. Permitted deductions from rent include payments for maintenance, repairs, insurance and management (see para. 17.5.2).

17.7.5.2.2 Schedule A as other receipt Section 15, para. 1, TA also covers 'Other receipts arising to a person from, or by virtue of, his ownership of an estate or interest . . . in land'. There are slightly different applicable deduction rules for the old Schedule A in s. 28 (see para. 17.5.6).

17.7.5.2.3 Schedule D, Case I If the services provided by the landlord amount to a trade then there may be a Schedule D, Case I charge on the sums received in respect of them. The s. 74 deduction rules will then apply to any costs incurred by the landlord in connection with the provision of services.

17.7.5.2.4 Schedule D, Case VI This is a restrictive 'sweeper' charge which may apply if none of the others does. The rules as to deductions are unclear in this context but it seems that no capital allowances are available and there are restricted uses of losses.

17.7.6 Tenant

Deductibility of the service charges for the tenant will depend on whether or not there is a trade, when s. 74, TA may apply. Other cases will depend on the precise context.

17.7.7 Reserve funds

These can also cause great difficulty from a tax perspective. The tax position depends on a very careful analysis of the precise terms on which the reserve fund has been set up. Is there, for example, a trust? Is it valid? (NB, e.g., the perpetuity rules which may invalidate the purported trust). If there is a trust, what type of trust? Is its income taxable at 23% or 34%? Is the 'fund' actually an unincorporated association? Is it liable to IHT? These and other questions need to answered to decide the tax position.

17.8 CAPITAL ALLOWANCES

UK taxation disallows the deduction of depreciation as such for tax purposes. Instead the UK tax system provides 'capital allowances' which allow the deduction of certain capital expenditure in computing a taxpayer's liability to income tax. Capital allowances are discussed in Chapter 12. The Finance Act 1997 makes new provision for capital allowances to be computed on machinery or plant used for the purposes of a property letting business by pooling the expenditure.

17.9 SECTION 779, TA – SALE AND LEASEBACK: LIMITATION ON TAX RELIEFS

These provisions were introduced in 1964 to limit the advantage of sale and leaseback transactions at a time when there was no charge to UK capital gains and a high 'payout' rent provided the tenant with deductible expenditure for income tax purposes so giving a further advantage. The effect of s. 779 is to restrict the rent deductible for income tax purposes to a 'commercial rent'.

17.10 SECTION 780, TA – SALE AND LEASEBACK: TAXATION OF CONSIDERATION RECEIVED

The grant of a lease at a low rent gives a lease value so that, by assigning it, a capital sum can be received and deduction for rent paid on a subsequent leaseback obtained. This section reduces the benefit of such transactions.

17.11 LAND AS A TRADE

This is discussed in Chapter 9. Land can be held as trading stock and profits (or losses) on its sale or other exploitation fall within Schedule D, Case I. Thus a builder can hold land on which he is building houses to sell off at a profit as trading stock. Schedule A is not concerned with such activities. It should be noted that by s. 53(1), TA all farming (defined in s. 832) and market gardening is to be treated as trading and taxed accordingly. By s. 53(3) the occupation of land managed on a commercial basis and with a view to the realisation of profits is to be treated as trading and the profits or gains thereof taxed accordingly. By s. 55 the profits arising out of land in the case of mines, quarries etc. are also to be taxed under Schedule D, Case I.

17.12 NON-RESIDENTS AND INCOME FROM UK LAND AND FOREIGN LAND

Schedule A is a source-based charge to income tax. In other words the charge is on income arising from land or an interest in land in the UK. The charge therefore does not depend on the taxpayer's residence in the UK and so a non-resident is within the charge. This will usually be to income tax under the new Schedule A (see para. 17.13 below) as, unless a non-resident company is carrying on a trade in the UK through a branch or agency, there will not be a charge to UK corporation tax (see ss. 6 and 8, TA).

There is provision for the tax to be collected by deduction at source. Changes have been made to the liability of agents by ss. 126 and 127, FA 1995. This necessitated changes to the deduction at source rules in s. 43, TA. Section 43 is repealed by s. 40(3), FA 1995 from 1996–97. A new s. 42A is inserted into TA by which the Revenue have authority to allow gross payment and are given power to make appropriate regulations.

The provisions of ss. 34 to 36 and s. 780, TA (which apply charges under Case VI of Schedule D in certain circumstances) are not, it would seem, restricted to land or leases of land in the United Kingdom, but are presumably restricted to residents of the United Kingdom by the terms of s. 18(1) (which imposes a general territorial limit on the scope of Case VI). The charge under Case VI imposed by s. 776 in relation to 'artificial' transactions in land (see Chapter 4) applies to all persons, whether resident in the United

Kingdom or not, but is restricted to land situated in the United Kingdom (s. 776(14). This provision overrides s. 18(1) which is 'without prejudice' to other provisions charging tax under Case VI (s. 18(4)). Double tax relief may be available (see Chapter 35).

Schedule A applies only to land in the United Kingdom, and accordingly for land outside the United Kingdom, the income arises from a foreign possession and is assessable under Schedule D, Case V (discussed in Chapter 35). If income arises from trading in land situated abroad, then the taxpayer, if resident in the United Kingdom, will be liable to income tax under Schedule D, Case I if he takes an active part in the management of the trade, or under Schedule D, Case V if he takes no part in the management. Section 777(9) TA allows the Board to direct the withholding of income tax from consideration within s. 776 paid to a non-resident. In England this may not be of much help to the Revenue as land contracts are not usually public documents. Section 41, FA 1995 inserts a new s. 65A into the TA. The effect of this is that income from land situated outside the UK is to be computed in accordance with the new Schedule A.

17.13 THE NEW SCHEDULE A

17.13.1 General

As noted in the introduction to this chapter, Schedule A has been recast in its application other than for corporation tax for 1995–96 and subsequent years of assessment. The new Schedule A thus applies to individuals, partnerships, non-residents and other persons liable to income tax. A taxpayer may elect for the new rules to apply from 1994–95 to new sources arising in that year.

The purposes of the changes is to put Schedule A income tax on a 'formal current fiscal year basis of assessment' to make self-assessment easier. The computation of the income liable to income tax under Schedule A has been changed, allegedly to simplify it. Broadly, taxable income is to be computed on a Schedule D, Case I approach which generally will be an accruals basis instead of the previous receipts and payments basis.

There are special transitional provisions rules (see Tax Bulletin, Issue 20 December 1995, p. 268 and Inland Revenue Press Release of 10 February 1995). Income from furnished lettings is now to be liable to income tax under Schedule A rather than Schedule D, Case VI.

The most important changes for these purposes are that:

(a) Schedule A income is to be computed for income tax purposes on 'normal commercial accountancy principles'. (It is not clear why this should not also apply for corporation tax purposes); and

(b) profits are to be calculated on the tax year basis for income tax purposes, i.e., from 6 April one year to 5 April next (there is a special exception for some partnerships).

The income from sources within the old Schedule A rules (see para. 17.4) and from furnished lettings formerly within Schedule D, Case VI is now treated as income from a business. The profits of that business are to be computed broadly in the same way as profits from a trade.

17.13.2 New Schedule A charge for income tax

Section 39(1), FA 1995 inserts a new s. 15(1), TA for income tax purposes but not corporation tax. The new para. 1 provides:

> (1) Tax under this Schedule shall be charged on the annual profits or gains arising from any business carried on for the exploitation, as a source of rents or other receipts, of any estate, interest or rights in or over any land in the United Kingdom.
> (2) To the extent that any transaction entered into by any person is entered into for the exploitation, as a source of rents or other receipts, of any estate, interest or rights in or over any land in the United Kingdom that transaction shall be taken for the purposes of this Schedule to have been entered into in the course of such a business as is mentioned in sub-paragraph (1) above.
> (3) In this paragraph 'receipts' in relation to any land, includes—
>   (a) any payment in respect of any licence to occupy or otherwise to use any land or in respect of the exercise of any other right over land; and
>   (b) rentcharges, ground annuals and feu duties and any other annual payments reserved in respect of, or charged on or issuing out of, that land.

This wording has yet to be subject to judicial interpretation. However, in determining the meaning of some of the words and phrases used in the new Schedule A, reference should be made to the matters discussed in para. 17.4.

The new para. 2 of s. 15(1) excludes yearly interest, woodlands and wayleaves (cf. the old para. 3 and NB s. 98, TA on tied premises).

As with the old Schedule A, broadly the person chargeable is the person receiving or entitled to the profits or gains taxable under Schedule A.

17.13.3 Schedule 6, FA 1995 changes

17.13.3.1 General Essentially, the new Schedule A charges all sources of income within the old Schedule A. However, sch. 6, FA 1995 introduced a number of consequential changes following from the 'tax year accountancy' approach. Some of these will be considered below.

17.13.3.2 Land managed as one estate Section 26, TA which permits, in certain prescribed circumstances, owners of estates to elect for the expenditure incurred on the upkeep of one part of the estate to be set against the total income of the whole estate, is preserved under the new Schedule A by para. 5, sch. 6, FA 1995.

17.13.3.3 Maintenance funds Section 27, TA permits the deduction from rent for contributions to maintenance funds for historic buildings (see para. 17.5.5). By para. 6 of sch. 6, FA 1995, s. 27 is modified to bring it into line with the concept of a Schedule A business.

17.13.3.4 Sea walls Paragraph 7, sch. 6, FA 1995 similarly modifies s. 30, TA (see para. 17.5.8) which deals with capital expenditure on sea walls to bring it into line with the concept of a Schedule A business.

17.13.3.5 Premiums Finally, paras 9 to 14, sch. 6, FA 1995 modifies the premium and deemed premium provisions (discussed in para. 17.6 above) to bring them into line with the concept of a Schedule A business.

17.13.4 Computation

17.13.4.1 General All sources of income and expenses arising to a taxpayer within the new Schedule A are treated as a single business (see s. 21(4), TA). Except as otherwise provided, the profit or loss is to be computed as if the Schedule A business were a Schedule D, Case I trade (s. 21(3)) so that, generally, the Schedule D, Case I rules on deductible expenditure etc. will apply. There are, however, some special provisions, some of which are discussed below.

17.13.4.2 Interest Interest payable in respect of a Schedule A business is now deductible as a Schedule A business expense. This will include, for example, interest paid on loans to purchase let property to the extent that the expenditure is incurred wholly and exclusively for the purposes of the Schedule A business. Paragraph 17, sch. 6, FA 1995 modifies s. 368(3) and (4), TA to prevent the taxpayer from also claiming relief for the interest paid under s. 353, TA. If the loan is eligible for mortgage interest tax relief (see Chapter 13), the borrower will receive relief through MIRAS unless he or she elects to claim the interest paid as a deduction in computing the profits of the Schedule A business (s. 375A(1), TA).

17.13.4.3 Losses Paragraph 19, sch. 6, FA 1995 introduces a new loss relief by inserting s. 379A into the TA which allows losses to be carried forward and set against the Schedule A profits of the following year. If these are insufficient to absorb all the loss, the loss may be carried forward indefinitely against future Schedule A profits until it is exhausted. Where the loss is comprised of agricultural expenses and capital allowances, the loss may, subject to limits, be set against the taxpayer's *general* income for the year in which the loss occurred and the following year (s. 379A(2) and (3)).

17.13.4.4 Pre-trading expenditure Section 401, TA which deals with pre-trading expenditure is extended to cover expenditure incurred for the purposes of a Schedule A business (s. 401(1B), TA).

17.13.4.5 Expenses on entertainment, counselling etc. Modifications are made to bring the Schedule D, Case I deduction provisions into line with the concept of a Schedule A business. These include statutory redundancy payments, training courses and counselling.

17.14 EXEMPTIONS

Certain bodies are given specific exemption from tax under Schedule A. Thus by s. 505(1)(a), TA 'exemption from tax under Schedules A and D' is given 'in respect of any profits or gains arising in respect of rents or other receipts from an estate, interest or right in or over any land . . . vested in any person for charitable purposes and . . . applied for charitable purposes only.'

Other bodies are given exemption from all income tax. These include certain pension funds (cf. s. 592(2)).

CHAPTER EIGHTEEN
Schedule D, Case VI

18.1 INTRODUCTION

This chapter is concerned with Schedule D, Case VI, 'the sweeper' provision of income tax.[1] It charges tax on income from sources not already covered. Under s. 18(3), TA income tax under Schedule D, Case VI is charged on any annual profits or gains not falling under any other Case of Schedule D, and not charged by virtue of Schedule A or E. By s. 18(4) this is without prejudice to any other provision directing tax to be charged under Case VI.

Accordingly Schedule D, Case VI can be considered in two parts. These are what may be called:

(a) the general charge under s. 18(3); and
(b) the specific matters provided for charge under Schedule D, Case VI by s. 18(4).

18.2 THE GENERAL CHARGE

Schedule D, Case VI appears to be very wide in its ambit. However, there are limitations. First, Schedule D, Case VI only applies to income receipts. This can be illustrated by *Scott* v *Ricketts* [1967] 2 All ER 1009. The taxpayer was an estate agent. He was paid £39,000, in addition to his fees, to withdraw any claim that he might have had to participate in the development of a site whose purchase he had negotiated for a client. The Court of Appeal held that the payment to him was not assessable under Schedule D, Case VI, since it represented a capital sum.[2]

[1.] See generally Whiteman, *Income Tax*, Sweet & Maxwell, 3rd edn, 1988 and *Simon's Taxes*.

[2.] Any claim which the taxpayer had was not legally enforceable, and it is interesting to speculate whether such a receipt would now be subject to capital gains tax; cf. s. 22(1)(c), TCGA 1992, discussed in Chapter 20.

Schedule D, Case VI

Lord Buckmaster observed in *Jones* v *Leeming* [1930] AC 415 (see further below) that 'an accretion to capital does not become income merely because the original capital was invested in the hope and expectation that it would rise in value; if it does so rise, its realisation does not make it income' (cf. the comments of Lord Keith in *IRC* v *Reinhold* (1953) 34 TC 389).

The second limitation on Schedule D, Case VI is that the use of the words 'profits or gains' implies that the Case is confined to profits or gains *ejusdem generis* with the profits or gains in Cases I to V (cf. *Attorney-General* v *Black* (1871) LR 6 Ex 308). Thus, receipts which are not profits or gains, such as gifts, betting winnings and receipts by finding, are not within any Case of Schedule D, even Case VI (see Rowlatt J in *Ryall* v *Hoare* [1923] 2 KB 447).

In *Jones* v *Leeming*, the taxpayer and three others acquired separately two options to purchase adjoining rubber estates. Subsequently the two estates were sold to a company at a profit. The Commissioners found that the taxpayers were not engaged in an adventure in the nature of trade. In the Court of Appeal, Lawrence LJ said:

> I have the greatest difficulty in seeing how an isolated transaction of this kind, if it be not an adventure in the nature of trade, can be a transaction *ejusdem generis* with such an adventure and therefore fall within Case VI. All the elements which would go to make such a transaction an adventure in the nature of trade in my opinion would be required to make it a transaction *ejusdem generis* with such an adventure. It seems to me that in the case of an isolated transaction of purchase and resale of property there is really no middle course open. It is either an adventure in the nature of trade, or else it is simply a case of sale and resale of property.

Lord Buckmaster concluded: 'To that proposition I can see no adequate answer'. The House of Lords held that the profits were not assessable under Case VI as there was not a profit within Schedule D.

The effect of this is that Schedule D, Case VI applies for the most part to casual profits from isolated transactions which lack the 'source' of a trade, profession, vocation, office or employment to make them taxable under Schedule D, Case I or II or Schedule E. It must be remembered though that an isolated transaction may be an adventure in the nature of trade and so assessable under Case I.

A common form of transaction within Case VI is a contract for the performance of services in a situation where no profession or employment exists. In *Hobbs* v *Hussey* [1942] 1 KB 491, the taxpayer was a solicitor's managing clerk. He had never been an author, but he contracted with a newspaper to write his reminiscences. The contract involved the sale of the copyright in a series of articles to be written subsequently. Lawrence J said that 'the true question in such cases is whether the transaction in question is really a sale of property or the performance of services.' In holding the taxpayer's receipts under the contract to be assessable under Schedule D, Case VI, he said:

In my opinion, the true nature of the transaction was the performance of services. The appellant did not part with his notes or diaries or his reminiscences. He could republish the very articles themselves so long as they were not in serial form, and, on the whole, I am of opinion that the profits he received were of a revenue nature and not the realisation of capital.

Similarly, in *Housden* v *Marshall* [1958] 3 All ER 639, a jockey contracted to sell his reminiscences to a newspaper. He provided the newspaper with information, and a professional journalist then wrote the articles for the newspaper, which were vetted by the taxpayer. The first British serial rights were granted to the newspaper by the contract. Harman J held that the main purpose of the contract was the provision of services and it was immaterial that those services were of a trivial nature. He considered there was no sale of any property. The taxpayer's receipts under the contract were therefore taxable under Schedule D, Case VI (cf. *Alloway* v *Phillips* [1980] 3 All ER 138 discussed in para. 18.5).

The essential distinction is therefore between a sale of property and the performance of services. In *Hobbs* v *Hussey* above, Lawrence J explained the importance of the distinction:

> Any sale of property where no concern in the nature of trade is carried on must result in the realisation of capital ... and it is also true, in my opinion, that the performance of services, although they may involve some subsidiary sale of property ... are in their essence of a revenue nature since they are the fruit of the individual's capacity which may be regarded in a sense as his capital but are not the capital itself.

Thus, in *Trustees of Earl Haig* v *IRC* (1939) 22 TC 725, the trustees were authorised to publish the Earl's war diaries. At their request, the Earl's biography was then written making full use of the diaries. The Court of Session held that sums received as advances against royalties were in fact capital receipts for the partial realisation of an asset (the diaries), so that Case VI did not apply. (This may be a case that turns on its own specific facts as there were security concerns about publication of the diaries alone.)

For a payment to be taxable as a receipt for the performance of services, it must be clear what those services are. In *Dickinson* v *Abel* [1969] 1 All ER 484, the taxpayer had no interest in a farm held by trustees of his wife's grandmother's will, but because of his connection with the family he was approached by a prospective purchaser of the farm. He was offered £10,000 if the prospective purchaser bought the farm for £100,000 or less, although no services were ever specified. The taxpayer simply passed the offer for the farm to the trustees, and subsequently received £10,000 following the sale of the farm. Pennycuick J, in holding that the sum was not taxable, reached the conclusion 'with regret' that the evidence was:

> quite inconsistent with a contractual consensus, either expressed or tacit ..., that the £10,000 should be payable in return for some specified

service to be rendered by the taxpayer . . . On this evidence one is left with nothing but a conditional promise made without valuable consideration, which would have been unenforceable by the taxpayer. Conversely, once a contract for the performance of services exists, any receipt will be assessable even if, in the event, no services are in fact performed.

(Cf. *Brocklesby* v *Merricks* (1934) 18 TC 576 where fees paid to an architect for arranging a meeting between a landowner and a developer were held taxable under Schedule D, Case VI.)

18.3 SPECIFIC CHARGES

As was seen in para. 18.1, s. 18(4) provides for other charges to be made under Schedule D, Case VI. Some specific charges to income tax under Schedule D, Case VI are made (inter alia) in respect of:

(a) furnished lettings
(b) lease premiums paid to a person other than the landlord
(c) undervalued leases
(d) sales and reconveyance of property
(e) sales and lease-back
(f) artificial transactions in land
(g) certain sales of 'know-how'
(h) enterprise allowances
(i) certain balancing charges
(j) certain receipts after a change of accounting basis
(k) post-cessation receipts
(l) transactions in securities
(m) income from certain settlements treated as the settlor's
(n) transfers of assets abroad.

With the introduction of the 'new' Schedule A, some of these charges to income tax under Schedule D, Case VI will apply only where the 'old' Schedule A is in issue. For a discussion of the rules under 'new' and 'old' Schedule A, see Chapter 17.

18.4 BASIS OF ASSESSMENT

Income tax under Schedule D, Case VI is computed either on the full amount of the profits or gains arising in the year of assessment (s. 69, TA)[3] any apportionment being made on a straight-line (or time) basis (s. 72). Profits or gains do not 'arise' until they are received by the taxpayer; it is not sufficient that they are due and payable (see *Grey* v *Tiley* (1932) 16 TC 414 and *Whitworth Park Coal Co. Ltd* v *IRC* [1961] AC 31). Although s. 817(1)

[3.] For income sources which existed before 6 April 1994 the assessment may alternatively be made on the average of the profits of a period, not being greater than a year.

provides that 'in arriving at the amount of profits or gains' for the purposes of income tax, 'no other deductions shall be made than such as are expressly enumerated in the Tax Acts', and there is no express or even implied enumeration in relation to Case VI, the use of the words 'profits' and 'gains' is normally thought to be sufficient authority for the deduction of expenses incurred in earning the Case VI income. The existence of s. 392 providing for the relief of Schedule D, Case VI losses would not be necessary unless this were so, since if expenses could not be deducted no loss would ever arise to be relieved.

18.5 THE INTERNATIONAL ELEMENT

The international element of Schedule D, Case VI is based on UK residence or UK situs property (see s. 18(1), TA). Thus, if a person is resident in the United Kingdom, income will be chargeable under Case VI from any kind of property whatever, whether situated in the United Kingdom or elsewhere (s. 18(1), para. 1(a)(i)) whereas if a person is not resident in the United Kingdom, income will only be chargeable under Case VI if it arises from any property whatever within the United Kingdom (s. 18(1), para. 1(a)(iii)). For example, in *Alloway v Phillips* [1980] 3 All ER 138 the taxpayer lived in Canada. She entered into a contract with an English newspaper whereby in consideration for the supply of information for publication as newspaper articles relating to her husband (the 'Great Train Robber' who escaped, Charles Frederick Wilson) she would receive £39,000. The Inland Revenue assessed this sum under Case VI and the Court of Appeal upheld the assessment. The source of the income was not the information provided by the taxpayer, but her rights under the contract. Since such choses in action are situated in the country where they can be enforced (in this case England, the place where the newspaper was resident), she had received income from property situated within the United Kingdom and she was accordingly liable under Case VI.

PART III
Capital Gains Tax

CHAPTER NINETEEN
Capital gains tax – general principles

19.1 INTRODUCTION

This and the following five chapters deal with the taxation of capital gains, the analogue of the taxation of income. Although rates of income tax and capital gains tax have been harmonised, the tax bases have not. It is thus important to know whether a profit is of an income or a capital nature as different tax regimes apply. The most important differences between income tax and capital gains tax are as follows:

    (a) The bases of computation differ. For example, the indexation allowance (see para. 21.10) is available for capital gains tax but not for income tax.

    (b) There is an annual exempt amount for capital gains tax purposes of £6,500 for the 1997/98 year of assessment whereas the personal allowance available as a deduction from total income is £4,045 for a single person.

    (c) Income losses may be used more extensively than capital losses (compare Chapter 11 and para. 22.1).

    (d) A non-resident who does not carry on a trade in the UK through a branch or agency is not within the charge to capital gains tax. However, a UK source may be sufficient for an income tax charge to arise (compare paras 20.3 and 17.12).

    (e) Different reliefs apply for the purposes of the two regimes (compare Chapter 22 and, inter alia, para. 5.6).

19.2 POLICY

The two reasons usually given for taxing capital gains are equity and efficiency. Equity demands that capital gains are taxed because such gains add to a person's economic power. They are thus on a par with income from employment and all other sources of income liable to income tax. As James Callaghan, the then Chancellor of the Exchequer, said when he introduced capital gains tax (Hansard 1964 vol. 710 col. 245):

> Capital gains confer much the same kind of benefit on the recipient as taxed earnings more hardly won. Yet earnings pay full tax while capital gains go free. This is unfair to the wage and salary earner.

The point is made clearer if an economic definition of income is used, namely that 'income' includes all means by which economic power is increased.[1]

Efficiency demands the taxation of capital gains because the border line between income and capital can be shadowy. Prior to the introduction of capital gains tax a substantial number of cases were brought in an attempt to distinguish trading from investment. One motivation for doing so was that gains arising from trading were taxed as profits of the trade whereas gains arising from investment activity were not.[2] The cases rest on the notion that there is a distinction between income and capital and the obvious point that income tax 'is a tax on income'[3] can be made. However, as the early cases on the borderline between income and capital show, it is not always easy to determine what that distinction is. The introduction of capital gains tax has not entirely removed these difficulties since the UK's system of capital gains tax is critically dependent on income tax.

The legislation does not attempt to define what a 'capital' gain is and the differences between the UK's income and capital gains tax system may still make it desirable to realise capital gains rather than income profits.[4] Nevertheless the introduction of a capital gains tax reduces the risk of erosion of the tax base by taxpayers taking income benefits in capital form.[5]

19.3 HISTORY OF CAPITAL GAINS TAXATION

Prior to 1962 the UK had no system for the taxation of capital gains. The Royal Commission on the Taxation of Profits and Income in 1955 (Cmd 9474) had been split on the question of whether capital gains should be taxed. The majority rejected such a tax arguing that a tax on capital gains could not be expected to prove a tax of simple structure or one that would be free of a number of problems. In contrast, the minority considered that the exemption from tax for capital profits represented the most serious omission in the UK's tax system.

---

[1] Although the precise definition of 'income' has been disputed by economists for a number of years, the definition that is most generally accepted is an accretion to economic power, i.e., the accrual of wealth, see further Chapter 1.
[2] For example, *Wisdom v Chamberlain* (1969) 45 TC 92, *IRC v Reinhold* (1953) 34 TC 389, *Pickford v Quirke* (1927) 13 TC 251 and *Iswera v IRC* [1965] 1 WLR 663. See Chapter 9.
[3] *Per* Lord Macnaghten in *LCC v Attorney General* [1901] AC 26 at p. 35.
[4] Because of the wider range of exemptions and reliefs in the capital gains tax system and the differences in the payment dates.
[5] There may be other, economic benefits of a tax on capital gains, namely that such a tax on capital gains may reduce the attraction of investment in assets purely for their anticipated increases in value rather than for any productive purpose.

Capital gains tax – general principles

In 1962, a short-term gains tax was introduced in the UK on the acquisition and disposal, within specified periods, of land and shares. The periods were three years for land and six months for shares. Chargeable gains on these assets were defined as the difference between the cost price (or acquisition value) and the proceeds of disposal, after allowing for the expenses of sale and purchase. The gains were taxed as *income* under Schedule D, Case VII. This had an important effect on the structure of capital gains tax today. It was assumed that a gain was known and could be calculated without detailed provisions. Today there are still no detailed rules as to how to calculate a gain.

A universal capital gains tax was introduced in 1965. This was levied without reference to the length of time the asset had been owned and was designed to be distinct from income tax. Capital gains tax applied to all gains accruing on the disposal of assets after 6 April 1965. In the case of assets held on 6 April 1965, the charge was restricted to the gain referable to the period from that date to the date of disposal. Short-term gains tax continued to apply to disposals of assets within 12 months until it was abolished in 1971.

Under the new capital gains tax, capital gains accruing to individuals were taxed at 30% or at a lower rate in the case of individuals with moderate incomes. Exemptions were provided for an individual's own home, savings certificates and other national savings issues, chattels disposed of for £1,000 or less, and the proceeds of life assurance policies. The term 'disposal' did not refer merely to sales of assets but included gifts and virtually any situation in which a capital sum, including another asset, was received which was derived from an asset.

By the 1970s, however, inflation had become a real problem in the UK. The capital gains tax system then made no allowance for inflationary gains and taxpayers were thus subjected to tax on not only their real, economic gain, but also on their inflationary or 'paper' gain.[6] Inevitably, pressure for some kind of inflationary allowance began to mount. Initially, the government attempted to deal with the problem by allowing a certain amount of gains to be realised tax free in a year of assessment. This proved insufficient and in 1982 provisions for indexing the tax base were brought in. The legislation was extremely complex and was in many respects incomplete. The new provisions only adjusted the original cost of the asset for inflation after March 1982 and this indexation did not apply for the first year, so assets sold within a year gained no inflation adjustment.

Continued criticism of the 1982 indexation provisions resulted in further changes in 1985 and major changes to the tax structure were made in 1988. The rates of capital gains tax were brought into line with those of income tax, so that capital gains tax was charged at the taxpayer's highest income tax rate. The move was justified by the Chancellor of the Exchequer as follows (Hansard 15 March 1988 col. 1005):

> In principle, there is little economic difference between income and capital gains, and many people effectively have the option of choosing to a significant extent which to receive. And in so far as there is a difference, it

---
[6.] See, for example, *Secretan v Hart* [1969] 3 All ER 1196.

is by no means clear why one should be taxed more heavily than the other. Taxing them at different rates distorts investment decisions and inevitably creates a major tax avoidance industry. Moreover, at present, with capital gains taxed at 30% for everybody, higher rate taxpayers face a lower – sometimes much lower – rate of tax on gains than on investment income, while basic rate taxpayers face a higher rate of tax on gains than on income. This contrast is hard to justify.

The problem of inflationary gains between 1965 and 1982 which had not been tackled by the 1985 reforms, was also dealt with by treating assets as having been disposed of on 31 March 1982 and then reacquired at their then market value.

The capital gains tax system was then largely left alone until 1993, when the government again changed the rules on indexation so that the indexation allowance could not be used to create or increase an allowable loss for capital gains tax purposes. This introduced asymmetry into the system and has been widely criticised.[7] Nevertheless, apart from introducing some transitional reliefs, the government has resisted pressure to reverse the change.

19.4 PROBLEMS

It was noted in para. 19.3 that the Royal Commission on the Taxation of Profits and Income thought that any system of capital gains tax would be subject to a number of problems. Some of the difficulties with a capital gains tax are discussed below.[8]

19.4.1 A realisations or accrual basis?

The UK system of capital gains tax only taxes gains when they are realised. This can be criticised on three grounds.

First, on the grounds of horizontal equity, since the frequency with which gains are realised makes no difference to the fact that, as capital gains accrue, they add to an individual's economic power.

Secondly, if gains are taxed only when they are realised, a 'lock in' effect is generated under which the taxpayer is reluctant to realise gains and incur a tax liability. This lock in effect may be encouraged by the present system of capital gains tax in the UK which removes from capital gains tax completely assets held by taxpayers on death (see Chapter 23).

Thirdly, treating gains as taxable in the year in which the gain is realised results in inequality since some taxpayers realise their gains over several years, perhaps taking the benefit of each year's annual exemption, while others may realise their entire capital gain in one year.

Naturally the difficulty with any system that sought to tax accrued but unrealised gains is that it would be very complex. Annual valuations would

---

[7.] The Institute of Taxation, *Representations on the Finance Bill 1994*; The Tax Faculty of the Institute of Chartered Accountants in England and Wales, *Memorandum on the Finance Bill 1994*; the Revenue Law Committee of the Law Society, *Memorandum on the Finance Bill 1994* and see the criticisms made in Twelfth Sitting of Standing Committee A on the Finance Bill 1994.

[8.] See further Chapter 4, *Butterworths UK Tax Guide 1995–96 Policy Supplement*.

be required and this would be particularly difficult (and expensive) in the case of assets which do not have a readily available market. It also raises the question of whether it is desirable to force a taxpayer to sell an appreciating asset in order to pay tax due.

It seems therefore to have been decided that for reasons of administration, collection and enforcement, a tax based on the realisation of assets is the only workable one. However, in one sense there is taxation on an accruals basis and this is in relation to gifts of assets since the restriction of hold-over relief (see para. 22.3.1). The justification for the abolition of this relief, which allowed donor and donee of a gift to elect jointly that the donee take over the donor's acquisition cost, was that it was used as a method of tax avoidance. Realisation of the asset by the donee was rare; donees would retain the gifted asset, perhaps until their death, thus obtaining a capital gains tax uplift (see Chapter 23). Nevertheless the restriction on hold-over relief in 1989 can be criticised on the grounds that the gift of an asset does not give rise to a *realised* gain.[9]

19.4.2 What allowance should be made for inflation?

If no inflationary allowance is made, tax will be charged on the whole gain including the inflationary gain. This is perceived by taxpayers as unfair and may act as a disincentive to saving. However it has been noted by commentators that an allowance for inflation in capital gains taxation, while making no such allowance for those who live on fixed incomes, creates inequality since no allowance is made for the decrease in real terms of their income.

19.4.3 What are the economic risks in a capital gains tax?

The UK's solution to the lock in effect is to offer a number of exemptions and deferrals from capital gains tax. This may have led to investment distortions by channelling savings into privileged savings media and away from others. Of course, these difficulties must be set against the investment distortions that would arise from a system that exempted capital gains from tax completely,[10] but it is clear that some distortions have arisen particularly in relation to private housing.[11] It is unknown whether, and if so to what extent, tax on capital gains has raised the cost of capital since 1965.

---

[9] See, for example, the Law Society's representations on the Finance Bill 1989. Cf. the Institute for Fiscal Studies, *Death: The Unfinished Business* (1988) para. 3.4.2, which while accepting that no gain has been realised in the sense that the asset has been turned into cash, did not accept this as a justification for continuing the relief.

[10] Although this appears to be the current Conservative government's long term objective – see the Chancellor of the Exchequer's Budget Speech, 28 November 1995.

[11] The exemption of private housing from capital gains tax must be seen primarily as a political decision. It acts as an encouragement to put wealth into the family home and, when combined with mortgage interest tax relief, it has unquestionably contributed to private housing becoming one of the largest forms of personal saving, see IFS Report, *Reforming Capital Gains Tax* (1988). Nonetheless removal of the main residence exemption (see para. 22.2.3.2) would be politically difficult. Some form of roll-over relief would have to be offered in compensation and thus the change would have little economic impact.

Other criticisms of the UK's system of capital gains taxation are that its yield is not substantial in comparison to other taxes,[12] the legislation is unnecessarily complex and the extent of avoidance and evasion is unclear. The system contains a large range of exemptions and reliefs which may be argued to be illustrations of a system that is either unjust or unworkable. It has been noted[13] that capital gains tax carries with it significant compliance costs for taxpayers arising from the need to search out information, maintain investment records, compute liability and negotiate valuations. Further, the costs to the Revenue of collection are not insubstantial.

However, if it is accepted that some form of taxation of capital gains is desirable for the reasons given in para. 19.2, then it is difficult to devise modifications without radically rethinking the current UK tax system.[14] Since such reform is unlikely in the foreseeable future the deficiencies of the current UK system will, for the present, have to be accepted.

[12.] £912 million compared to the £63,002 million raised by income tax in 1994/95: Financial Statistics, HMSO May 1995.

[13.] C.T. Sandford, 1993, *Hidden Costs of Taxation*, Institute for Fiscal Studies.

[14.] The Mead Committee ((1978) *The Structure and Reform of Direct Taxation*, Institute for Fiscal Studies) proposed an expenditure tax in 1978 under which the purchase of a registered asset would be a deductible expense in the year of purchase and all proceeds from it would comprise a taxable receipt in the year of receipt. There would thus be no difference in the tax treatment of the proceeds of the asset and the income from it. To prevent the artificial generation of tax losses, most durable goods used for personal consumption would be unregistered assets. But the Committee considered that there would still be a need for a capital gains tax on the proceeds of sale from the disposal of potentially valuable assets treated as unregistered assets. Such a tax would be indexed and contain generous roll-over provisions. In 1988, the Institute of Fiscal Studies Report, *Reforming Capital Gains Tax* proposed a capital disposal tax which would levy tax on the difference between the amount received on the disposal of qualifying assets and the amount spent on acquisition of such assets in a tax year. Their proposal had many similarities to an expenditure tax.

CHAPTER TWENTY
Capital gains tax – the charge

20.1 THE CHARGING SECTION

The charge to capital gains tax is found in s. 1(1) of the Taxation of Chargeable Gains Act 1992 ('TCGA'):[1]

> Tax shall be charged in accordance with this Act in respect of capital gains, that is to say chargeable gains computed in accordance with this Act and accruing to a person on the disposal of assets.

There are therefore four important elements in a charge to capital gains tax:

(a) a *chargeable gain* must accrue
(b) to a *chargeable person* when an
(c) *asset* is subject to
(d) a *disposal*.

These elements are examined in the remainder of this chapter.

20.2 CHARGEABLE GAINS

By s. 15(2), TCGA:

> Every gain shall, except as otherwise expressly provided, be a chargeable gain.

[1.] In the next five Chapters all statutory references will be to the TCGA, but note that many of the *cases* will refer to the previous legislation in the Finance Act 1965 or the Chargeable Gains Tax Act 1979.

The term 'gain' is not defined and must therefore bear its ordinary meaning. In *Aberdeen Construction Group Ltd v IRC* [1978] STC 127 (at p. 131) Lord Wilberforce said:

> [A] general principle must underline any interpretation of the Act, namely, that its purpose is to tax capital gains and to make allowance for capital losses, each of which ought to be arrived at on normal business principles. . . . To paraphrase a famous cliché, the capital gains tax is a tax on gains; it is not a tax on arithmetical differences.

It will be seen in Chapter 22 that the TCGA distinguishes between gains which are not chargeable at all, gains which are not chargeable within certain limits and gains which, although they are chargeable gains, are not charged to tax until a later date. Even where a gain is chargeable, the precise amount of the gain will be computed by deducting certain allowable expenditure. This aspect is discussed in Chapter 21.

A chargeable gain must 'accrue' for a charge to arise. Again, there is no statutory definition of this word. In *Coren v Keighley* (1972) 48 TC 370 Ungoed-Thomas J said that it simply referred to the event of a capital gain or loss being made in accordance with the statute.

20.3 CHARGEABLE PERSON

Capital gains tax applies to persons who are resident or ordinarily resident in the United Kingdom (s. 2(1), TCGA). 'Resident' and 'ordinarily resident' have the same meanings as in the Income Tax Acts (s. 9(1) and see Chapter 1).

Individuals who are resident or ordinarily resident in the United Kingdom, but who are not domiciled in one of its constituent countries (England, Wales, Scotland etc.), are only chargeable in respect of gains arising on the disposal of assets situated outside the UK to the extent that those gains are remitted to the UK (s.12).

A non-resident person will be liable to capital gains tax in respect of UK assets used for the purposes of a trade carried on in the United Kingdom through a branch, or UK assets held for the purposes of the branch (s. 10(1)).[2] The taxation of non-UK domiciles and residents is discussed further in Chapter 35.

20.4 ASSETS

By s. 21(1), TCGA, all forms of property are assets for the purposes of the Act, whether situated in the UK or not, including:

(a) options, debts and incorporeal property generally;

---

[2] Section 10(5) extends this section to professions and vocations carried on by non-residents in the UK. Section 10(1) has recently been held by the Special Commissioners to apply to a business carried on under a partnership agreement in the UK by non-resident partners; *White v Carline* (1995) Sp C 33.

(b) any currency other than sterling;[3]
(c) any form of property created by the person disposing of it, or otherwise coming to be owned without being acquired.

Paragraph (a) of the definition is sufficient to include such assets as easements, shares, choses in action and other intangible rights and interests. Paragraph (c) includes such matters as patents, copyrights and the goodwill of a business.[4]

The meaning of 'asset' was considered by the House of Lords in *O'Brien v Benson's Hosiery (Holdings) Ltd* [1979] 3 All ER 652. The taxpayer company received £50,000 from its sales and merchandise director in consideration of the company releasing the director from his obligations under his contract of employment.[5] The contract had five years left to run. The House of Lords held that the sum received was derived from an asset. Lord Russell of Killowen said:

> If, as here, the employer is able to exact from the employee a substantial sum as a term of releasing him from his obligations to serve, the rights of the employer appear to me to bear quite sufficiently the mark of an asset of the employer, something which he can turn to account, notwithstanding that his ability to turn it to account is by a type of disposal limited by the nature of the asset.

In *Zim Properties Ltd v Procter* [1985] STC 90, Warner J commented that the House of Lords had regarded the word 'asset' as dominating and had paid little attention to the use of the word 'property'. This, Warner J thought, could mean either that, whatever else an asset might be, all forms of property are assets or that 'property' was not a precise term and could vary according to the context. Either way, he was prepared to hold that the right to bring a civil action that was neither frivolous nor vexatious could be an asset for capital gains tax purposes.

20.4.1 Illustrations of 'assets'

In *Marren v Ingles* [1980] STC 500 it was held that the right to receive a further sum on the happening of a future event, namely, the right to receive additional consideration for the sale of shares if those shares were subsequently floated, was an asset for capital gains tax purposes.

A beneficial interest under a trust is an asset just as much as the trust property itself.

Shares in a company are assets separate from the property owned by the company. In the case of unnumbered shares of the same class, it is not possible to identify which particular shares have been disposed of. The legislation deals with this problem by pooling the shares so that all the shares

---

[3.] Special rules for the taxation of currency fluctuations apply to corporate bodies; ss. 60, 92–95, 125–170 and Schs. 15–18, FA 1993.
[4.] There are some special rules which apply to capital sums and intellectual property, see Shipwright and Price, *UK Tax and Intellectual Property*, 2nd. Edn, 1996, Sweet and Maxwell.
[5.] A contract of employment without more is not capable of assignment; *Re Skinner* [1942] 1 All ER 32 and *Bean v Doncaster Amalgamated Collieries Ltd* (1944) 27 TC 296.

of the same class acquired by the same person in the same capacity are treated as a single asset which grows or diminishes when further shares are acquired or sold (ss. 104 et seq, TCGA). A disposal of some of the shares constitutes a part disposal of that asset. Part disposals are discussed in para. 20.9.

In other cases, particularly land, it is difficult to tell whether an estate is a single asset or several smaller parcels of land. Revenue practice (CCAB Press Release published in [1969] BTR 438) is to treat a single acquisition of land as a single asset even if it comprises distinguishable elements such as farmhouses, cottages, woodlands etc. However, the contrary view will be taken if the evidence shows that more than one asset was acquired, for instance, the land was offered for sale by auction in lots.

If the land is leased, the grant of the lease will constitute a part disposal of the freehold. That lease then becomes an asset in the hands of the leaseholder which may itself be disposed of. In *Bayley* v *Rogers* [1980] STC 544 a new business lease granted under the Landlord and Tenant Act 1954 was held to be a different asset from the old lease.[6]

20.5 DISPOSAL

Although in many circumstances a disposal is deemed to take place, the word 'disposal' is not defined in the TCGA and has not often been discussed in the case law. Where it has been discussed, the courts have been reluctant to supply a definition.[7] In an Inland Revenue leaflet, CGT 8, which has since been withdrawn, the Revenue attempted a definition as follows:

> An asset is disposed of whenever its ownership changes or whenever the owner divests himself of his rights in or interest over that asset, for example, by sale, exchange or gift.

It is thought that the transfer of legal but not beneficial ownership does not constitute a disposal in view of s. 60 which provides:

> In relation to assets held by a person as nominee for another person . . . this Act shall apply as if the property were vested in, and the acts of the nominee . . . in relation to the assets were the acts of, the person or persons for whom he is the nominee . . .

In contrast, a person who declares himself trustee of his property for the benefit of others makes a disposal of the entire property.[8]

[6.] Cf. ESC D39 which provides that the surrender and regrant of a new lease on the same terms save for the length of the lease and the rent, does not amount to a disposal for capital gains tax.
[7.] 'There is no limitation on the generality of the word disposal' *per* Lord Wilberforce in *Berry* v *Warnett* [1982] STC 396 at p. 399 and 'there is no legal definition of the word disposal and I can see no reason to define it as the first legal transfer in the ownership in property' *per* Lord Everleigh in *Floor* v *Davis* [1978] STC 436 at p. 445.
[8.] This accords with the statement of Slade LJ in *Welbeck Securities* v *Poulson* [1987] STC 468 at p. 473 that the word 'disposal' is 'plainly apt' to cover the transfer of beneficial title to property by one person in favour of another.

It is not necessary for the taxpayer to dispose of the entire asset because s. 21(2)(a) provides that references in the Act to a disposal include a part disposal. There is a part disposal whenever an interest or right in or over the asset is created and, generally, there is a part disposal of an asset when any part of the asset remains undisposed of (s. 21(2)(b)). Thus the grant of a lease out of a freehold will constitute a part disposal of the freehold interest.[9]

20.6 DEEMED DISPOSALS

The TCGA also contains a number of special rules where particular events are deemed to involve the disposal of assets. One of the most important of these is s. 22(1), under which there is a disposal of assets by their owner where any capital sum is *derived* from assets, notwithstanding that no asset is acquired by the person paying the capital sum. It is important that the sum received is a *capital* receipt; an assessment under s. 22 will fail if the payment is of a revenue nature.[10]

Section 22(1) can apply in a variety of circumstances. In *Marren* v *Ingles* [1980] STC 500 the taxpayer sold some shares in consideration for an immediate payment and the right to receive a further sum in the event of a flotation of the shares. The taxpayer subsequently received £2,825 per share following a flotation. The Inland Revenue claimed that this was a capital sum derived from an asset. The House of Lords held that the taxpayer's right to receive the further payment following the flotation was a chose in action and therefore an asset.[11] The sum which the taxpayer received was derived from that asset even though the payer acquired no asset in return.[12] Accordingly, the taxpayer was liable to capital gains tax under s. 22(1). Similarly in *Marson* v *Marriage* [1980] STC 177 the taxpayer entered into a contract for the sale of land under which he would become entitled to additional payments on the grant of planning permission. The taxpayer subsequently released the purchaser from this additional liability in consideration of a payment of £348,250. Fox J held that the taxpayer's rights under contract constituted a chose in action, and the sum of £348,250 was therefore a capital sum derived from this incorporeal asset and taxable.

Although these cases establish that a right to future payment can constitute an asset for capital gains tax, it must not be thought that every right to payment will give rise to a tax charge. For s. 22(1) to apply, it must be shown that the capital sum is 'derived' from an asset. In *IRC* v *Montgomery* [1975] 1 All ER 664 Walton J said:

[9.] Where the lease has less than 50 years to run, part of any premium paid for the grant will be chargeable under Schedule A and only the remainder will be chargeable to capital gains tax; see para. 17.6.

[10.] See, for example, *Lang* v *Rice* [1984] STC 172.

[11.] Incorporeal property is an asset for the purposes of capital gains tax; s. 21(1)(a). The chose in action was treated as a separate asset, so that the eventual receipt of £2,825 per share constituted a separate disposal from the original sale of the shares.

[12.] The taxpayer's argument that s. 22(1) could not apply if an asset was acquired in return was dismissed. Walton J's dictum in *IRC* v *Montgomery* [1975] STC 182 at p.189 on the meaning of 'notwithstanding' was disapproved of.

What . . . does 'derived' mean? The relevant dictionary meaning of 'derivation' is to trace or show the origin, and that is what I think it means here.

However, in interpreting s. 22(1), the view expressed by the House of Lords in *Aberdeen Construction Group* v *IRC* [1978] STC 127 (see para. 20.2), that 'normal business principles' ought to be applied, must be borne in mind. According to Warner J in *Zim Properties* v *Procter* [1985] STC 90 (at p. 107) the court must search for the *real* asset from which the capital sum is derived. If there is no asset there will be no charge to capital gains tax. The following paragraphs illustrate some of the difficulties that can arise.

In *Davis* v *Powell* [1977] 1 All ER 471 the taxpayer was paid compensation under the Agricultural Holdings Act for the surrender of some farmland leased to him. The Inland Revenue sought to assess the taxpayer to capital gains tax on the basis that the compensation was a capital sum derived from the lease within s. 22(1), TCGA. Templeman J held that the compensation was not derived from an asset at all. It was simply a sum which Parliament had decreed should be paid for the expenses and losses which were unavoidably incurred after the lease had been surrendered.

Davis v *Powell* was distinguished by Nourse J in *Davenport* v *Chilver* [1983] STC 426. The taxpayer received compensation in respect of some property which had once been owned by the taxpayer's mother and which had been seized by the USSR in 1940. The payment was made under the terms of the Foreign Compensation (USSR) Order 1969 resulting from a Treaty between the USSR and the UK. Nourse J held that the taxpayer's right under the 1969 Order could be described as an independent proprietary right since it gave the taxpayer a right to share in a designated fund, subject to proof of title and value. That right was an asset and the compensation was therefore a capital sum derived from that asset. Nourse J said that it had not been necessary to consider whether the statutory right to compensation was an asset in *Davis* v *Powell* because in that case the Revenue had claimed that the compensation was derived from the lease and not from the statutory right.

These apparently conflicting views came to be considered in the later case of *Drummond* v *Austin Brown* [1984] STC 321. The taxpayer received compensation of £31,384 under the Landlord and Tenant Act 1954 for the loss of a business tenancy. The first instance decision of Walton J was handed down very shortly after *Davenport* v *Chilver* and it appears that that case was not cited in argument. However, Walton J was invited to consider the point that the asset from which the capital sum was derived was the Landlord and Tenant Act 1954. This did not find favour, Walton J stating firmly that:

> Nor do I think the compensation is a capital sum derived from an asset. It seems to me it is a capital sum which is given to the tenant because he has lost the asset, not to compensate him in any way for the loss of that asset which is gone beyond all redemption, but for the purpose of enabling him to start up all over again, and I do not think that it can be brought fairly and squarely within the workings of [section 22].

Warner J thought that even if he had accepted that the asset derived from the Landlord and Tenant Act 1954 this did not assist the Crown. Either (a) the statutory right was acquired otherwise than by way of a bargain made at arm's length and there was therefore 'no real room for any appreciation' in the value of the asset to have taken place; or (b) the statutory right 'must be taken somehow to have been paid for in the terms of the lease'. On appeal, the Revenue simply advanced the argument that the £31,384 was derived from the lease. This enabled Fox LJ, in giving the judgment of the court in favour of the taxpayer, to say:

> In our opinion the £31,384 was not derived from the lease. The word 'derive' suggests a source. The right to the payment was, in our view, from one source only, namely the statute of 1954. The lease itself gives no right to such payment. The statute simply created an entitlement where none would otherwise have existed. And in creating that entitlement it did not require that any provisions were to be written into the lease. Thus, there is no deeming provision which would in any way require one to treat the lease as being the source of the entitlement.

Although cited in argument, *Davenport* v *Chilver* was not specifically mentioned in the Court of Appeal's judgment.[13]

The later case of *Pennine Raceway Ltd* v *Kirklees Metropolitan Council* [1989] STC 122 takes matters a little further but does not resolve the basic conflict. Pennine Raceway Ltd conducted dragracing on a disused airfield in accordance with a licence granted by the owner of that airfield, Mr Whitham. The grant of the licence was effectively dependent on the existence of planning permission from Kirklees Metropolitan Council to use the land for such purposes. This planning permission was eventually withdrawn and the licence became worthless. Pennine Raceway obtained compensation from Kirklees Metropolitan Council under the Town and Country Planning Act 1971 for its 'expenditure, loss or damage' resulting from the revocation of the planning permission. This compensation was paid net of income tax[14] but the Revenue subsequently indicated that the sum received might be assessable to capital gains tax under s. 22(1), TCGA. Pennine Raceway accordingly claimed that the compensation moneys should have been paid gross.

Pennine Raceway Ltd's claim was upheld by the Court of Appeal on the basis that the sum received would have been taxable under s. 22(1) if it was a capital sum.[15] However, although the Court of Appeal considered *Davis* v *Powell*, *Drummond* v *Brown* and *Davenport* v *Chilver*, each of the Lords Justices considered that the 'asset' from which the capital sum was derived for the purposes of s. 22(1) was the licence and not the Town and Country Planning

---

[13] Note that it was accepted by both Walton J and the Court of Appeal in *Drummond* v *Austin Brown* that the situation would be quite different if the tenant voluntarily surrendered the 'fag end' of a lease for a capital sum, since this would constitute the disposal of a chargeable asset. (Cf. the Inland Revenue's interpretation in *Tax Bulletin*, Issue 22, April 1996.)

[14] See *British Transport Commission* v *Gourley* [1956] AC 185.

[15] The question whether, on the facts, the sum was capital or income was not finally decided.

Act 1971. Warner J's dictum in *Zim Properties* v *Procter* [1985] STC 90 (at p. 107) that it was necessary to look for the 'real (rather than the immediate) source of the capital sum' was cited with approval. As Ralph Gibson LJ put it:

> In my judgment, the compensation paid to the company for the 'loss or damage . . . directly attributable to the revocation' of the planning permission for dragracing was 'derived from' the asset, that is to say the licence to use the land for dragracing.

And Stuart-Smith LJ said:

> In my judgment the capital sum derived from the licence, more specifically from the depreciation of the licence. The licence coupled with the planning permission for dragracing was a valuable asset; without planning permission it was worthless. The revocation of the planning permission turned the licence into a totally emasculated creature compared to what it was before; indeed although the licence continued in existence it could be likened to someone in a permanent coma.

It is thus clear that the analysis of the right(s) from which the capital sum is derived must be undertaken with some care. Not every right will constitute an 'asset' for the purposes of s. 22 but if the reality is that an asset was the true source of the payment a capital gains tax charge may arise.[16] For completeness, it should be noted that in the Inland Revenue's *Tax Bulletin* (Issue 22, April 1996), the Revenue stated that, following two Special Commissioners' decisions, where a tenant receives a notice to quit under the Agricultural Holdings or the Landlord and Tenant Acts and then enters into a surrender agreement, any payment which 'relates to' the statutory compensation will not be chargeable to capital gains tax. However, the Revenue will continue to seek to tax any amount 'that is not genuine statutory compensation'. Accordingly great care must be taken to establish the facts in any dispute with the Revenue.

The rule in s. 22 is said to apply 'in particular' to the receipt of a capital sum in four instances. The situations are:

(a) capital sums received by way of compensation for any kind of damage or injury to assets or for the loss, destruction or dissipation of assets or for any depreciation or risk of depreciation of an asset;

(b) capital sums received under a policy of insurance of the risk of any kind of damage or injury to, or the loss or depreciation of, assets;

(c) capital sums received in return for the forfeiture or surrender of rights, or for refraining from exercising rights; and

(d) capital sums received as consideration for the use or exploitation of assets.

In *Davenport* v *Chilver* Nourse J accepted the argument of the Revenue's counsel that the various sums referred to in paragraphs (a) to (d) were

---

[16] The potential application of ESC D33 must be borne in mind; see para. 20.6.1.

particular examples of sums which were deemed to derive from assets for the purposes of the general words. Accordingly, if a sum fell within one of paragraphs (a) to (d) there was no need to investigate whether it was derived from a capital asset. It is submitted that this is an incorrect construction of the section and the argument of the taxpayer's counsel in that case – that the particular sums referred to in paragraphs (a) to (d) are subject to a condition precedent that they should be capital sums derived from assets – is to be preferred. The approach of Nourse J potentially leads to absurd tax results. For instance, if Nourse J's judgment in *Davenport* v *Chilver* is right, then it ought to be enough for a charge within (say) s. 22(1)(c) if the Revenue could show that a capital sum had been derived from the forfeiture, surrender or non-exercise of a right and it would follow that the term 'right' should be determined by reference to things that could be surrendered, forfeited or not exercised. On this basis, a capital sum received by a church organist from grateful parishioners in return for his failure to exercise his 'right' to play golf on a Sunday morning could be taxable as a capital gain.[17]

A number of later cases suggest that Nourse J's view on the construction of s. 22(1) was mistaken. In *Zim Properties Ltd* v *Procter*, Warner J thought that paragraphs (a) to (d) described particular instances of the application of the principle enacted in the general words and that a case could not come within any of the lettered paragraphs if it did not also come within the general words.[18] At first instance in *Kirby* v *Thorn EMI plc* [1986] 1 WLR 851 a sum paid for entering into a restrictive covenant in connection with the sale of shares in subsidiary companies was held not to be a capital sum derived from an asset because the capital sum derived not from the shares but from the parent's freedom to trade through its subsidiaries.[19] This freedom to trade was not an asset.

20.6.1 Extra-statutory Concession D33

If capital sums are received by way of compensation for any kind of damage to, or loss of, assets there is a disposal of those assets and so a consequent gain or loss by reference to their acquisition cost. However, where the compensation or damages are received by way of settlement of a court action it was held in *Zim Properties* v *Procter* [1985] STC 90, that the 'asset' from

---

[17.] See Lord Denning in *Jarrold* v *Boustead* [1964] 3 All ER 76 at p. 80 confirming that such a payment would not be subject to income tax under Schedule E.
[18.] The two judges who considered the point in *Pennine Raceways Ltd* v *Kirklees Metropolitan Council* above took opposing views. Ralph Gibson LJ considered that the examples were intended to be within the deemed disposal provision without proof of any further requirement whilst Stuart-Smith LJ was content to assume that the construction favoured by Warner J in *Zim Properties Ltd* v *Procter* was correct.
[19.] However, on appeal it was held that although the freedom to trade was not an asset and therefore there could not be a capital gains tax charge on its disposal, the sum in question was partly received for Thorn EMI's agreement not to exploit the goodwill attaching to the group. Accordingly, there was a capital sum derived from an asset (the goodwill) and the case was remitted to the Commissioners for them to determine the proper capital gains tax computation. For further reading see Sparkes, 'The Derivation of Capital Sums' [1987] *BTR* 323.

which the capital sum is derived is the right of action, not the underlying subject matter of the action. So a capital sum received in settlement of a negligence action against a firm of solicitors resulting from the conveyancing of particular properties, stems from the right to sue and not from the properties themselves. Since in most cases the acquisition cost of the right of action is nil,[20] and therefore the potential capital gains tax liability very high, the Revenue have issued an Extra-statutory Concession, ESC D33. This provides that the gain arising from the disposal of the right of action will be assessed as though it was derived from the 'underlying asset'. Thus any exemptions and reliefs relating to the underlying asset can be claimed and the part disposal formula should be used where appropriate. In cases where there is no underlying asset, for example where the claim arises as a result of negligent professional advice, any gain accruing on payment of compensation or damages will be exempt from capital gains tax.[21]

20.6.2 Repair or replacement of assets

Since compensation moneys are generally used to repair or replace destroyed or damaged assets, provisions exist for the receipt of the capital sum not to be treated as a capital gains tax disposal.[22]

If the sum is wholly applied in restoring a damaged asset there is no disposal (s. 23(1)). There is also no disposal if all but a small part of the capital sum is used in restoring the asset. The word 'small' is not defined but the Revenue take it to mean no more than 5% (IR leaflet CGT 8 – now withdrawn). If the restored asset is later disposed of, the sums received are deducted from the allowable expenditure. If only part of the sum received is used in restoring the asset, that part will be deducted from the allowable expenditure on a subsequent disposal (s. 23(3)) but the remainder will be treated as consideration for an immediate part disposal of the asset. The taxpayer must claim the benefit of these provisions (ss. 23(1) and (3)).

Example
Larry purchased an oil painting for £3,000 in 1992. It was damaged by a fire in December 1995. The insurance company paid him £2,000 compensation in February 1996.

---

[20] This is certainly the case for rights which came into being on or after 10 March 1981 – see s. 17(2), TCGA which was inserted by the FA 1981. Rights arising before that date should have a market value acquisition cost but in most cases that value will be negligible.
[21] ESC D33 is particularly important in the context of the sale of shares in private companies. It is common in such transactions for the vendor to provide indemnities and warranties to cover any tax liabilities which arise after the sale has taken place but which relate to accounting periods before the sale. Paragraph 13 of ESC D 33 provides that the principle in *Zim Properties Ltd* v *Procter* is not applicable to payments by the vendor to the purchaser made under such warranties or indemnities if they were given as one of the terms of the sale. Instead the payment will be treated as an adjustment to the sale price of the shares and the appropriate capital gains tax adjustment made; s. 49(2), TCGA.
[22] If these provisions did not exist, taxpayers would suffer the injustice of having to replace their assets out of taxed funds.

Capital gains tax – the charge

(a) If Larry retains the £2,000 insurance moneys and does nothing to restore the picture, this will be a capital sum derived from an asset and hence will constitute a disposal in accordance with s. 22(1)(b). However, as Larry still retains the asset the disposal will be a part disposal (s. 21(2)(b)) and therefore the allowable expenditure to be deducted from the disposal consideration will be computed in accordance with the part disposal formula discussed in para. 21.9.3.

(b) If Larry spends £1,000 of the insurance moneys on restoring the painting he will be able to postpone his liability to tax on the sum expended. He will have an immediate liability to capital gains tax in respect of the remaining £1,000 which is not so used. His gain will be computed by reference to the part disposal rules.

(c) The £1,000 expended on restoration will be deducted from his allowable expenditure when the painting is eventually sold or otherwise disposed of (s. 23(3)). But as Larry actually spent the £1,000, Larry's allowable expenditure on the eventual disposal will be the balance of the £3,000 original acquisition cost (i.e., that part of the cost not taken into account under (b) above) plus £1,000 (the amount expended on restoring the asset) less £1,000 (the amount he must deduct under the replacement of assets rules).

The entire loss, destruction, dissipation or extinction of an asset is treated as a disposal of that asset under s. 24. This generally permits an allowable loss to be claimed on the occasion of the destruction etc. However, any insurance or compensation money received will be treated as a disposal under s. 22(1)(a) or (b) subject to the relief discussed below if those moneys are spent on acquiring a replacement asset. The logical result is that if the destruction occurs in one year and the receipt of compensation moneys in the next tax year, loss relief should be given immediately and there should be a taxable sum accruing on receipt of the compensation. However, the Revenue take the view that if no sum is received the disposal occurs at the time of destruction but if a payment subsequently accrues the disposal takes place at the time of the receipt (IR leaflet CGT 8 – now withdrawn).

As mentioned above, if the asset is lost or destroyed there is relief from capital gains tax if the compensation is spent on acquiring a replacement asset. The compensation must be applied in acquiring a replacement asset within one year of receipt although the taxpayer's inspector of taxes may allow a longer period (s. 23(4)). The consideration for the disposal of the old asset is then deemed to be such amount that neither a gain nor a loss accrues. The acquisition cost of the new asset is then reduced by the excess of the compensation (plus scrap value if any) over the deemed consideration for the disposal of the old asset.

If the asset is lost or destroyed and only part of the sum is used to replace it there is some relief provided the part not spent is less than the amount of the gain (s. 23(5)). In other words postponement of the tax liability is available only to the extent that it is necessary to make use of the gain on replacement. A claim must be made by the taxpayer in order to take the benefit of these provisions.

Example
Larry also owned a piece of antique furniture which was destroyed in the fire of 1995. It was worth £10,000 at the date of destruction. Unfortunately, the insurance company failed to pay him any money for the furniture until June 1996 when he received compensation in full of £10,000.

When the furniture is destroyed in 1995 there is a capital gains tax disposal under s. 24(1) and, strictly, a capital loss should accrue to Larry at that date as his disposal consideration is nil. However, there will also be a deemed disposal of the furniture in 1996, when the insurance moneys are received, under s. 22(1)(b). Applying the Revenue's practice, Larry will be liable to tax on the £10,000 received in 1996 less any allowable expenditure.

If Larry replaces the furniture with another piece using the insurance moneys he can have the disposal of the original furniture treated as taking place at such a consideration as to give rise to neither a chargeable gain nor an allowable loss. The consideration for the replacement asset is then reduced by the amount the insurance moneys received exceed the deemed disposal sum. So if the acquisition cost of the original furniture was £4,000, when Larry receives the insurance moneys he will be deemed to have disposed of the furniture for £4,000. If Larry then spends the insurance moneys of £10,000 on a replacement asset his acquisition cost of the replacement asset will be £4,000 (i.e., the £10,000 acquisition cost less the £6,000 gain that would otherwise have accrued).

These rules do not apply to wasting assets (s. 23(6) and see para. 22.2.2.4) and are expressed to be limited to the owner of the property (although insurance proceeds received by a lessee of land for fifty years or less are by concession exempt if the lessee is under an obligation to restore the property – ESC D1).

20.7 ASSETS OF NEGLIGIBLE VALUE

If an asset becomes of negligible value and the taxpayer's inspector of taxes is satisfied of this, there is a deemed disposal (s. 24(2). The legislation was previously strictly construed so that the notional sale and reacquisition only took place when the negligible value claim was made (*Williams* v *Bullivant* [1983] STC 107). Thus the allowable loss was realised when the claim was made not when the asset first became of negligible value. This could be unfair to the taxpayer since losses cannot be carried back.[23] The position was, however, remedied by Extra-statutory Concession D28 under which the claim could be related back to a date before the claim was made, provided the asset is then of negligible value and was of negligible value at the earlier date. The claim had to be made no later than 24 months after the end of the tax year in which the circumstances giving rise to the claim occurred. FA 1996 has now made this concession statutory – see s. 24(2)(b).

20.8 HIRE PURCHASE

Under the typical hire purchase agreement, a person uses an asset for a period in return for a fee calculated to cover the purchase price of the asset. At the

---
[23] Save on death, see para. 23.1.

end of that period the ownership of the asset passes to the hirer. In such a situation, the TCGA provides that there is a disposal of the entire asset at the beginning of the hire period, subject to an adjustment of tax if ownership does not in fact pass, because, for example, of a default in payments by the hirer (s. 27). If the taxpayer is in the business of offering hire purchase transactions, his profits will be subject to income tax under Schedule D, Case I as profits of his trade in the normal way and will not, therefore, be subject to capital gains tax.

In addition to referring to hire purchase agreements, the relevant legislation refers to 'other transactions' under which the use of property passes to a person at the end of a period. Thus in *Lyon* v *Pettigrew* [1985] STC 369 there was an entire disposal of assets when a taxpayer sold taxi-cabs together with their hackney licences on terms that the price would be payable in instalments over 150 weeks. The taxpayer was accordingly liable to capital gains tax as if the whole consideration was payable on the disposal.[24]

20.9 PART DISPOSAL

A part disposal is defined in s. 21(2)(b), as occurring where:

> an interest or a right in or over the asset is created by the disposal, as well as where it subsists before the disposal, and generally, there is a part disposal of an asset where, on a person making a disposal, any description of property derived from the asset remains undisposed of.[25]

Save where the context otherwise requires, all references in the legislation to a disposal include references to a part disposal (s. 21(2)(a)).

The definition of part disposal thus covers the sale of part of an asset, such as the sale of part of the grounds of a private house, and the creation of rights over an asset, such as the grant of a leasehold interest out of a freehold. In *Berry* v *Warnett* [1982] STC 396 Lord Wilberforce said that there could not be a part disposal where there was a 'clear total disposal', but where an event did not amount to a total disposal, the effect of the legislation was that it might be taxed as a part disposal. Thus there will be a part disposal if an asset is damaged (as opposed to being totally destroyed).

It may be difficult to decide whether there has been a part disposal or a total disposal. The matter is of importance since the method of computing the chargeable gain arising is quite different on a total as opposed to a part disposal (see para. 21.9.3). The question of whether there is a part or a total disposal will be a question of fact but in the case of land, where the difficulties of distinguishing a part disposal from a total disposal can be acute, the Revenue have issued a statement indicating that land is generally to be

---

[24] That part of the consideration that was attributable to the motor cars (as opposed to the licences) was exempt, see para. 22.2.2.11. In addition, the taxpayer might have been able to invoke the hardship provisions discussed in para. 20.16.

[25] This definition is partially repeated in s. 42 which sets out the formula for computing the allocation of allowable expenditure on a part disposal; see para. 21.9.3.

regarded as a single asset if it was subject to a single acquisition (CCAB Press Release published at [1969] BTR 438).

20.10 VALUE SHIFTING

The TCGA contains a number of provisions designed to ensure that capital gains tax is not avoided by means of value-shifting schemes whereby taxpayers attempt to move or shift value from chargeable to non-chargeable assets. The value-shifting provisions apply if a scheme has been effected or arrangements made, either before or after disposal, whereby the value of the asset has been materially reduced, and a tax-free benefit conferred (s. 30(1)). A benefit is conferred if a person becomes entitled to any money or money's worth, or the value of the asset in which he has an interest is increased, or he is wholly or partly relieved from any liability to which he is subject (s. 30(3)). A benefit is tax free if it is not required to be brought into account for the purposes of income tax, capital gains tax or corporation tax (s. 30(3)). The benefit must be conferred on the person making the disposal or a person connected with him[26] or on any other person if the main purpose or one of the main purposes of the scheme or the arrangements was the avoidance of tax (ss. 30(1)(b) and 30(4)). The section does not apply to disposals between spouses or by a personal representative to a legatee.

Additional provisions exist in relation to companies since it is relatively easy for a controlling shareholder to manipulate the capital value of his shares by requiring the company to pay out income dividends. If a person who has control of a company exercises his control in such a way that value passes out of shares in a company owned by him, or by a person connected with him, or out of rights over the company exercisable by him or by a connected person, and passes into other shares in or rights over the company, there is a disposal by him of the shares or rights out of which the value passes (s. 29(2)). It was held by a bare majority of the House of Lords in *Floor* v *Davis* [1979] 2 All ER 677 that the word 'person' included the plural, so control exists where a person exercises or is able to exercise, by himself or with others, direct or indirect control of the company, in particular by possessing or being able to acquire the greater part of the share capital or voting power of the company. So if an individual who owns 80% of the voting shares in a company (the remaining 20% being owned by his wife and children) passes a resolution so that the shares held by his wife and children carry four times the votes of his shares,[27] the value that passes is the value of control and the individual will be treated as though he had disposed of his shares.

20.11 DEBTS

Section 21(1)(a) specifically provides that a debt is an asset. When, therefore, the debt is repaid there is a disposal of the debt by the lender. This is unlikely

---
[26.] For the meaning of a connected person see para. 21.2.1.
[27.] So that voting power is now equally divided between himself on the one hand and the wife and children on the other.

Capital gains tax – the charge

to give rise to a gain but could give rise to a loss if (say) the debt is only partially repaid.[28] To prevent taxpayers from creating allowable losses by creating and forgiving debts, s. 251(1) provides that no chargeable gain or allowable loss arises on the disposal of the debt by the original creditor except in the case of a debt on a security. The phrase 'debt on a security' is said to be defined in s. 132 but this is erroneous. Section 132 merely defines a 'security' as including 'any loan stock or similar security whether of the government of the United Kingdom or of any other government, or any public or local authority in the United Kingdom or elsewhere, or of any company, and whether secured or unsecured'. It has been held that a mere contingent liability which might never actually become a debt is not 'a debt' (*Marson* v *Marriage* [1980] STC 177), and that a 'debt' must also be of an ascertainable amount payable at an ascertainable time (*Marren* v *Ingles* [1980] STC 500, HL). But this does not assist in defining a 'debt on a security'. However, the final words of the definition of a security in s. 132 ('whether secured or unsecured') led Lord Cameron in *Cleveley's Investment Trust Co.* v *IRC* (1971) 47 TC 300 to say that whatever else it may mean, the phrase 'debt on a security' is not a synonym for secured debt.

The possible meaning of a 'debt on a security' has been discussed in two House of Lords' cases, *Aberdeen Construction Group Ltd* v *IRC* [1978] STC 127, and *W.T. Ramsay* v *IRC* [1981] STC 174. These indicate that a debt on a security is a debt which is intended, from its inception, to be marketable (i.e., capable of being bought and sold). In the *Aberdeen Construction* case, the taxpayer company spent £114,024 on acquiring shares in a rock drilling company. Over the next ten years, the taxpayer company made a series of loans totalling £500,000 to the drilling company. The taxpayer then sold the shares for £250,000, and waived the loans. The taxpayer company was assessed to tax on the gain on the shares. One of its arguments against the assessment was that the loans constituted a debt on a security and they were within the charge to capital gains tax. Accordingly, an allowable loss had arisen on the disposal of the loans which could be offset against the gain on the shares. The taxpayer company did not succeed in this argument. Lord Wilberforce said:

> The only basis on which a distinction can be drawn is between a pure unsecured debt as between the original borrower and lender on the one hand and a debt (which may be unsecured) which has, if not a marketable character, at least such characteristics as enable it to be dealt in and if necessary converted into shares or other securities. This is indeed lacking in precision but no more can be drawn from the statutory provisions that the draftsmen have put in, and that is both meagre and confusing. In agreement with the Court of Session I can find nothing here except an unsecured loan subsisting as between the original debtor and creditor given the description of loan capital, whether correctly or not, but with no quality

---

[28] Note that since 1993 indexation allowance cannot be used to increase the size of the loss. See generally para. 21.10.

or characteristic which brings it within whatever special category is meant by debt on a security.

And Lord Russell of Killowen said:

> In my opinion this was not a case of loan stock, which suggests to my mind an obligation created by a company of an amount for issue to subscribers for the stock, having ordinary terms for the repayment with or without premium and for interest. The series of loans by the taxpayer company ... are not within that concept; nor can they fairly be described as 'similar security'. They were simply loans made by the taxpayer company.

In *W.T. Ramsay* v *IRC*, the taxpayer company offered to lend £218,750 to another company as part of what was subsequently found to be an ineffective tax avoidance scheme. The offer was accepted orally, but the taxpayer was subsequently provided with a statutory declaration made by one of the directors of the accepting company recording the acceptance. The taxpayer disposed of the loan about a week later to a finance company for its market value of £391,481 (the loan being repayable at par after 31 years and carrying interest at 22% in the meantime). The taxpayer contended that the consequent gain of £172,731 was not taxable because the loan was not a debt on a security. The House of Lords disagreed. Lord Wilberforce said of the debt:

> It was created by a contract the terms of which were recorded in writing; it was designed, from the beginning, to be capable of being sold, and, indeed, to be sold at a profit . . . [Section 132] includes within 'security' any 'similar security' to loan stock; in my opinion these words cover the facts. This was a contractual loan, with a structure of permanence such as fitted it to be dealt in and to have a market value.

He referred to the distinction which he drew in *Aberdeen Construction* and said:

> To this I would now make one addition and one qualification. Although I think that, in this case, the manner in which [the loan] was constituted, viz., by written offer, orally accepted together with evidence of acceptance by statutory declaration, was enough to satisfy a strict interpretation of 'security', I am not convinced that a debt, to qualify as a debt on a security, must necessarily be constituted or evidenced by a document. The existence of a document may be an indicative factor, but absence of one is not fatal . . . Secondly on reflection, I doubt the usefulness of a test enabling the debt to be converted into shares or other securities . . . for even a simple debt can, by suitable contract, be converted into shares or other securities.

20.12 OPTIONS

Notwithstanding that, on general principles, the grant of an option to buy or sell an asset could be considered to be a part disposal of that asset,[29] the TCGA provides that the grant of an option is a total disposal of an asset in its own right – so the grant of an option is a total disposal of that option (ss. 21(1)(a) and 144(1)).[30] However, the *exercise* of an option does not constitute a disposal of it although for the purposes of computing the taxpayer's liability to capital gains tax, the grant and exercise of the option are treated as a single transaction (s. 144(3)). Thus if the option binds the grantor to sell, any sums paid by the grantee for the option will be added to any sums paid on exercise of the option to ascertain the overall consideration for the transaction. If, on the other hand, the option binds the grantor to buy, any sums paid to the grantor for the option will be deducted from the sum received by the grantee when the option is exercised.

If the option is abandoned, the grant of the option will stand as a disposal and any sums received by the grantor will be taxed as a capital gain. However, for the grantee, the abandonment of the option is not treated as a disposal and so no allowable loss can arise (s. 144(4)).[31] Exceptions allow grantees of abandoned options to obtain loss relief where the option is:

(a) a quoted option to subscribe for shares in a company, meaning an option which at the time of the disposal is quoted on a recognised stock exchange;

(b) a traded or financial option which at the time of disposal is quoted on a recognised stock exchange (principally on the London Stock Exchange or any other exchanges designated by the Board of Inland Revenue);

(c) an option to acquire assets exercisable by a person intending to use them, if acquired, for the purposes of his trade (ss. 144(4), (8) and 288).

The provisions relating to options also apply to forfeited deposits of purchase money or other consideration given by a prospective purchaser in respect of a transaction which is subsequently abandoned (s. 144(7)). The recipient of the forfeited deposit will thus be liable to capital gains tax on the sum forfeited, but the payer will be unable to claim an allowable loss.

[29.] See, for example, *Strange* v *Openshaw* [1983] STC 416. Note the Revenue take the view that the treatment of an option as an asset only applies for the purpose of computing the gain on the grant of the option and it appears that reliefs from capital gains tax may be claimed in respect of the underlying asset; Inland Revenue Interpretation RI 11.

[30.] The practical result of this treatment is that the only allowable expenditure which may be deducted from any consideration received for the grant of the option is the cost of the grant. No expenditure relating to the underlying asset may be deducted.

[31.] Cf. *Golding* v *Kaufman* [1985] STC 152 (approved in *Poulson* v *Welbeck Securities Ltd* [1986] STC 423, CA) which held that although the abandonment of an option does not, of itself, give rise to capital gains tax, if a capital sum is given in return for the abandonment, that consideration is a capital sum derived from an asset and is subject to tax under s. 22(1).

20.13 TIME OF DISPOSAL

Where a contract for the disposal of an asset is entered into, for example, a contract for sale of the asset, the time at which the disposal is made is the time the contract is made and not (if it is different) the time at which the asset is conveyed or transferred (s. 28(1)).[32] It should be noted that s. 28(1) does not deem a disposal to have taken place at the date of the contract. Strictly, it deems the date of the disposal to be the date of the contract *if there has been a disposal*. This is a vital distinction since, if there is no disposal, issues of timing do not arise as there can be no charge to capital gains tax. This is particularly important if the contract is rescinded. If it can be shown that no transfer of beneficial title took place, there will have been no disposal and no capital gains tax charge can arise.[33]

Where, however, the contract is conditional, the time of disposal is the time when the condition is satisfied (s. 28(2)). In *Lyon v Pettigrew* [1985] STC 369 (at p. 380) Walton J said:

> The words 'contract is conditional' have traditionally, I think, been used to convey only two types of case. One is the 'subject to contract' contract, where there is clearly no contract at all anyway, and the other is where all the liabilities under the contract are conditional on a certain event. It would, for example, be possible for a hotelier to make a booking with a tour operator conditionally on the next Olympic Games being held in London. Then until it had been decided that the next Olympic Games were going to be held in London, there would be no effective contract: the whole contract would be conditional, the whole liabilities and duties between the parties would only arise when the condition was fulfilled.[34]

If, however, the fulfilment of the 'condition' is within the control of one of the parties, there is no conditional contract for the purposes of the capital gains tax legislation. Thus in *Eastham v Leigh London and Provincial Properties* [1971] Ch 871 an agreement for a building lease on the condition that the builder constructed an office block on the freeholder's land was not a 'conditional contract'. Russell LJ said:

[32.] Even if, strictly, the contract is unenforceable; *Thompson v Salah* (1971) 47 TC 559.

[33.] So it is argued in Shipwright, *Tax Planning and UK Land Development*, 2nd Edn (1990), Key Haven Publications plc, para. 3.6.7 that there will be no disposal for capital gains tax purposes if a contract for sale of land is rescinded before it becomes specifically enforceable. A contract for sale of land will only become specifically enforceable when the vendor is in a position to make title (or the purchaser agrees to accept title); *Lysaght v Edwards* (1876) 2 ChD. 449. In *Whittles v Uniholdings Ltd (No 3)* [1995] STC 767 the Special Commissioner held that if no foreign currency was actually acquired under a forward contract to purchase such currency, s. 28 could not apply.

[34.] This reasoning seems to suggest that if the contract is subject to a contingent condition subsequent, so that the happening of an event outside the parties' control causes the contract to terminate, the contract is a conditional contract. This view is taken by the authors of *Sumption Capital Gains Tax*, para. A1.11, but the conservative view is that such a contract is not a conditional contract within the meaning of s. 28(2).

Capital gains tax – the charge

What is provided for in the contract is not a condition of the contract at all; it is simply a provision that one party shall carry out certain works in consideration of a promise to grant a lease.

The TCGA specifically provides that where a contract is conditional on the exercise of an option, the contract will be a conditional contract (s. 28(2)).[35] It was held in *J Sainsbury Plc v O'Connor* [1991] STC 318, CA that the vendor will not lose beneficial ownership of an asset even if it is subject to 'cross options' whereby the vendor grants an option requiring him to sell and acquires an option from the purchaser requiring him to buy the asset. In such a case, the date of disposal will be the date when the options are exercised.[36]

20.13.1 Time of disposal in other cases

Where a capital sum is derived from an asset within the meaning of s. 22(1) (see para. 20.6), the time of disposal is the time when the capital sum is received (s. 22(2)).[37]

Where an interest in land is acquired, otherwise than under a contract, by an authority in exercise of its powers of compulsory purchase, the time of the disposal is the earlier of the time at which compensation for the acquisition is agreed or the time when the authority enters the land in pursuance of its powers (ss. 245 and 246).

Where an asset is gifted, the time of disposal is the time when the donor has done all that he can to enable the gift to be perfected (*Re Rose* [1952] Ch 499).

20.14 NON-DISPOSALS

Certain events which would, on the general principles discussed so far, be treated as disposals of assets, are treated as though they did not involve any disposal.

20.14.1 Mortgages

The conveyance or transfer of an asset, or of an interest or right in or over the asset, by way of security is not treated as involving any disposal or acquisition of the asset (s. 26(1)).[38] If the mortgagee is in possession of the

---

[35] Cf. *Spiro v Glencrown Properties Ltd* [1991] 1 All ER 600 at pp. 605–606 a case on the meaning of s. 2, Law of Property (Miscellaneous Provisions) Act 1989 in which Hoffmann J said: 'An option is not strictly speaking either an offer or a conditional contract. It does not have all the incidents of either of these concepts. To that extent it is a relationship *sui generis*.'

[36] Cross options are used so that the vendor can effectively force the sale to take place even though there is no contract to sell the asset.

[37] However, strictly, s. 22(2) only applies where there is a disposal within paras. (a) to (d) of s. 22(1). If there is a disposal of an asset because a capital sum is derived from an asset in a way not falling within one of these paras., it is a moot point whether the timing rule in s. 22(2) applies.

[38] Mortgages of land are no longer created by conveyance: a purported conveyance of land by way of mortgage operates as a demise; ss. 85(1) and (2), Law of Property Act 1925.

asset because of some default on the part of the mortgagor, any dealings of the mortgagee are treated as though they were the acts of the mortgagor's nominee (s. 26(2)).

20.14.2 Death

On a person's death, the assets vest in his or her personal representatives. However, there is no capital gains tax disposal by the individual on death and there is thus no charge to capital gains tax on the assets comprised in the deceased's estate at that time (s. 62(1)(b)). The liability of personal representatives to capital gains tax on the administration of the deceased's estate is discussed in Chapter 23.

20.15 RATES OF CAPITAL GAINS TAX

As mentioned in Chapter 19, when capital gains tax was first introduced in 1965, it was charged at the flat rate of 30%. However, since 1988, capital gains have been charged at the taxpayer's marginal rate of income tax (s. 98, FA 1988). This means that the taxpayer will pay capital gains tax at the highest rate of income tax applicable when his taxable income and chargeable capital gains are combined. The move towards taxing income and capital gains at the same marginal rate undermined the point of a number of tax planning considerations under which it was better for the taxpayer subject to high rates of income tax to receive capital gains which were taxed at the lower flat rate of 30%.[39] However, there will still be occasions where it is preferable for the taxpayer to receive capital gains rather than income because of the generous range of reliefs and exemptions that exist in the UK's capital gains tax system and the differences in the dates for payment of tax.

20.16 PAYMENT OF TAX

Following the introduction of self-assessment, capital gains tax is payable on or before 31 January following the year of assessment for which the gain accrues (s. 59B, TMA). Provision is made for payment of tax by instalments in certain circumstances. First, if all or part of the consideration for the disposal of the asset is payable by instalments over more than 18 months and the taxpayer can satisfy the Inland Revenue that he would otherwise suffer undue hardship, tax may be paid in instalments. The period over which the tax may be paid cannot exceed eight years and must end no later than the date of payment to the taxpayer of the last instalment (s. 280, TCGA).

Secondly, if a gift has been made and hold over relief is not available (see para. 22.3.1), the taxpayer may by written notice elect to pay the tax in ten equal yearly instalments (s. 281). Interest is payable on the instalments except in certain cases including that of agricultural land. These provisions only apply where the asset in question is:

[39.] See Venables, 'Capital Gains Tax Planning after the 1988 Budget', [1988] BTR 266.

Capital gains tax – the charge

(a) land or an estate or interest in land;
(b) shares or securities of a company which immediately before the disposal gave control of the company to the person by whom the disposal was made or deemed to be made; or
(c) shares or securities not falling under (b) and not quoted on a recognised stock exchange nor dealt with on the Unlisted Securities Market (now the Alternative Investment Market or AIM).

CHAPTER TWENTY ONE
Computation of gains and losses

21.1 INTRODUCTION

Oddly, there is no clear statement in the TCGA on how chargeable gains and losses should be computed. The Act simply details adjustments which may be made to the consideration received for the disposal of the asset and lists certain types of allowable expenditure which may be deducted from this consideration.

In *Harrison* v *Nairn Williamson* [1978] 1 All ER 608 Buckley LJ said:

> The policy of the . . . Act is to tax any increase in the capital value of the asset between acquisition of the asset by the taxpayer and his subsequent disposal of it, and to allow deduction in respect of any decrease in that capital value.

He continued:

> Broadly speaking, the method of computation so provided has the result that the gain which attracts tax is the excess of the proceeds of disposing of the asset over the cost to the taxpayer of the acquisition of the asset while in his ownership. So that to compute the taxable gain one has to ascertain two factors: the cost to the taxpayer and the receipts of the taxpayer when the asset is disposed of.

It was stated by Lord Wilberforce in *Aberdeen Construction Group Ltd* v *IRC* [1978] STC 127, that the guiding principle in the interpretation of the capital gains tax legislation was to tax capital gains and make allowances for capital

Computation of gains and losses 481

losses arrived at by applying normal business principles. Thus capital gains tax is a 'tax on gains' not a tax on arithmetical differences.

As was noted in Chapter 19, the rules for calculating a gain were substantially modified by the Finance Act 1988. The basic position is that an asset disposed of today, which was acquired by the person making the disposal before 31 March 1982, will be deemed to have been sold and reacquired at its market value on 31 March 1982. Only the gain arising since that date will then be liable to tax. This deemed sale and reacquisition is known as 'rebasing'. The reason for choosing 31 March 1982 as the relevant date was that an allowance for inflation, known as indexation relief, introduced to ensure that taxpayers only face capital gains tax on their 'real' not 'inflationary' or 'paper' gains, was made available from that date. Rebasing to 31 March 1982 makes the calculation of the indexation allowance simpler. The relevant legislation is now contained in s. 35, TCGA.

Example
Alex purchased Blackacre in 1980 for £25,000 and sold it in 1996 for £125,000. On the face of it he has made a gain of £100,000, but he is assumed to have sold and reacquired Blackacre on 31 March 1982. On that date Blackacre would have been worth £30,000. Alex's taxable gain (subject to indexation and any other available reliefs) is thus only £95,000.

Rebasing will not apply if its effect is to increase the gain or loss or turn a loss into a gain or if, apart from rebasing, no gain or loss would accrue (s. 35(3)(a)–(c)). In any event, if the effect of the rule is to turn a gain into a loss or a loss into a gain, it will be assumed that the asset was acquired for such consideration as results in neither a gain nor loss accruing on disposal of the asset (s. 35(4)). This requires taxpayers to keep a record of each asset's acquisition cost and 31 March 1982 market value. To avoid this administrative burden, a taxpayer may elect that *all* assets held by him on 31 March 1982 are rebased to their 1982 value (s. 35(5) which disapplies s. 35(3)). Such an election is irrevocable and must be made in writing within two years of the end of the year of assessment in which the taxpayer makes the first disposal to which these provisions apply (s. 35(6)).[1] In deciding when the first disposal is made, disposals which are not taxable are ignored (Inland Revenue Statement of Practice SP 4/92).

21.2 CONSIDERATION

'Consideration' is not defined in the TCGA but the following definition was accepted by both the taxpayer and the Revenue in *Fielder* v *Vedlynn* [1992] STC 553:[2]

> A valuable consideration in the sense of the law, may consist either in some right, interest, profit or benefit accruing to the one party, or some

---
[1.] The Inland Revenue may allow a longer time.
[2.] This definition was set out in the speech of Lord Lindley in *Fleming* v *Bank of New Zealand* [1900] AC 577 at p. 586, PC but dates back to the 17th century *Comyn's Digest*. Cf. the VAT position – *Customs and Excise Commrs* v *Apple and Pear Development Council* [1988] STC 221, ECJ.

forbearance, detriment, loss, or responsibility, given, suffered or undertaken by the other . . .

In most cases, the consideration brought into account is the price paid to the taxpayer for the disposal of the asset. Since capital gains tax is computed in sterling, any sums received in a foreign currency must be converted into sterling at the exchange rate prevailing at the date of payment.[3] As foreign currency is itself an asset for capital gains tax purposes (s. 21(1)(b)) this will involve a number of acquisitions and disposals. If payment is in kind (for example the transfer of shares, land or other property) the consideration will have to be valued. However, if the disposal of the asset takes place under a contract for a consideration expressed in terms of a sum of money but satisfied by the transfer of agreed property to the taxpayer, the monetary sum stated in the parties' agreement will be the taxpayer's consideration for the purposes of computing the chargeable gain, irrespective of the actual market value of the property transferred (*Stanton* v *Drayton Commercial Investment Co. Ltd* [1982] STC 585, CA). This rule only applies to genuine transactions where the parties are acting at arm's length. It cannot be relied upon to manipulate artificially a taxpayer's capital gains tax liability. In other cases, the consideration for the disposal is adjusted in accordance with the rules set out in the TCGA. These are considered below.

21.2.1 Substitution of market value

Section 17(1) of the TCGA provides:

> Subject to the provisions of this Act, a person's acquisition or disposal of an asset shall for the purposes of this Act be deemed to be for a consideration equal to the market value of the asset:
>
> (a) where he acquires or, as the case may be, disposes of the asset otherwise than by way of a bargain made at arm's length and in particular where he acquires or disposes of it by way of gift or on a transfer into settlement by a settlor or by way of distribution from a company in respect of shares in the company, or
>
> (b) where he acquires or, as the case may be, disposes of the asset wholly or partly for a consideration that cannot be valued, or in connection with his own or another's loss of office or employment or diminution of emoluments, or otherwise in consideration for or recognition of his or another's services or past services in any office or employment or of any other service rendered or to be rendered by him or another.

The provision does not apply to the acquisition of an asset if there is no corresponding disposal of it and there is no consideration in money or

---

[3.] *Bentley* v *Pike* [1981] STC 360 approved in *Capcount Trading* v *Evans* [1993] STC 11, CA. A special regime applies to companies engaged in foreign currency transactions; ss. 60, 92–96, 125–170 and Schs. 15–18, FA 1993.

Computation of gains and losses

money's worth or the consideration is of an amount lower than the market value of the asset (s. 17(2)). Thus, the acquisition cost of a client's right to sue a firm of solicitors for professional negligence will be nil, not the 'market value' of the action.

There is no definition of a 'bargain made at arm's length' but this will presumably be determined by, inter alia, the relationship of the parties and the terms and conditions of their agreement. Certain 'connected persons' are treated as parties to a transaction otherwise than by way of a bargain made at arm's length (s. 18(2)). Section 17 will thus apply to substitute market value for the consideration, if any, actually passing between the connected persons for the disposal of the asset regardless of whether that consideration is more or less than market value.[4]

The following rules determine whether two or more people are connected with each other:

(a) A person is connected with his or her spouse, spouse's relatives and the spouses of those relatives (s. 286(2)). Relatives means brothers, sisters, ancestors or lineal descendants (s. 286(8)). Collateral relatives such as aunts, uncles, nieces, nephews and cousins are therefore excluded.

(b) The trustee of a settlement is connected with the settlor, any person who is connected with the settlor and with any body corporate that is deemed to be connected with the settlement (s. 286(3)).[5]

(c) A person is connected with his partners and with the spouses or relatives of his partners, except in relation to 'acquisitions or disposals of partnership assets pursuant to *bona fide* commercial arrangements' (s. 286(4)).

(d) A company is connected with another company if:

(i) a person who has control[6] of one company is connected with others who control the other company, or

(ii) a group of two or more persons has control of each company, and the group either consists of the same people or could be regarded as consisting of the same people if any member of the group were replaced by a person with whom he is connected (s. 286(5)).

---

[4] Section 18(6) to (8) also provide that if the asset disposed of is subject to any right or restriction enforceable by the person making the disposal or by a person connected with him, the market value of the asset is the market value it would have if it were not subject to the right or restriction less the market value of the right or restriction (or the amount by which its extinction would increase the value of the asset, if that would be less). This does not, however, apply to a right of forfeiture or other right exercisable on breach of a covenant contained in a lease of land or other property, and does not apply to any right or restriction under a mortgage or other charge. The rule prevents taxpayers from artificially reducing the value of property by the imposing restrictions.

[5] 'Settlor' and 'settlement' have the meanings assigned to them by Chapter IA, Part XV, TA – see further Chapter 15.

[6] 'Control' for these purposes has the meaning given by s. 416, TA.

(e) A company is connected with another person if it is controlled either by that person alone or by that person together with others who are connected with him (s. 286(6)).

(f) If two or more persons act together to secure or exercise control of a company they are connected with each other and with any person who acts on the direction of any of them to secure or exercise control of the company (s. 286(7)).

It is submitted that if two people become connected because of a transaction, for example, the sale of assets to a company in return for a controlling interest in it, the act that connects them should not constitute a transaction between connected persons for the purposes of the market value rule. However, the Revenue do not appear to share this view.[7]

The rules deeming transactions to take place at market value can have harsh results for taxpayers who enter into gratuitous transactions without considering the tax consequences. For example, in *Turner* v *Follet* [1973] STC 148, the taxpayer gifted some shares to his children and was accordingly assessed to capital gains tax. His argument that, far from making a capital gain, he had actually made a capital loss of the value of the shares given away and, on the grounds of equity and natural justice, he should not be treated as having made a capital gain, failed. The Court of Appeal held that the legislation was quite clear; a gift of assets was a disposal for capital gains tax purposes and therefore the taxpayer's assessment to capital gains tax was valid.

21.2.2 Value shifting

As has been seen in para. 20.10, a reduction in the value of an asset which confers a tax free benefit on a person is a disposal of assets (s. 30, TCGA). In this event, the consideration for the disposal is increased by such amount as appears to the inspector to be 'just and reasonable' having regard to the scheme or arrangements and the tax free benefit in question (s. 30(5)).

If there is a disposal of assets because the taxpayer has exercised his control over a company so that value passes out of his shares in the company and into other shares, the consideration for the disposal is the consideration which the taxpayer could have obtained for the transaction had it taken place at arm's length (s. 29(2)).

21.2.3 Debts

No chargeable gain or allowable loss accrues when the person disposing of the asset is the original creditor (s. 251(1), TCGA). If the debt is satisfied, wholly or in part, by the transfer of property rather than cash, the creditor is

---

[7.] See Inland Revenue *Tax Bulletin*, Issue 6 February 1993 which states that the settlement of assets on trust is a transaction between connected persons so that the restriction on the use of losses in s. 18(3), TCGA applies (see para. 22.1.1). The Revenue's view on this aspect may, however, be justified by the wording of s. 286 and the authors submit that it does not affect their opinion of the operation of the section for other transactions.

Computation of gains and losses

deemed to acquire the property and the debtor is deemed to dispose of it, for its market value (s. 251(3)).[8] If the property is subsequently sold by the creditor for more than the amount of the debt, the chargeable gain is deemed not to exceed the gain that would have accrued if the property had actually been acquired for a consideration equal to the amount of the debt.

Example
Caroline is owed £5,000 by Diana. Diana transfers property then worth £4,000 to Caroline in full and final satisfaction of the debt. Caroline later sells this property for £6,000 but her chargeable gain (ignoring all other applicable reliefs) is restricted to £1,000 as her acquisition cost of the property is treated as being £5,000.

21.2.4 Options

As has already been seen in para. 20.12, the grant of an option constitutes the disposal of an asset, and the consideration to be brought into account on that disposal is the price paid for the grant of the option. However, if the option is subsequently exercised, the grantor is treated as though the grant of the option and the transaction entered into by him to comply with his obligation were a single transaction, and the consideration for the option is added to his consideration for the sale of the asset in respect of which the option was granted (s. 144(2), TCGA).

Example
Alex owns Blackacre. He grants an option to Brenda to buy Blackacre from him for £120,000. The cost of the option is £5,000. Brenda therefore pays £5,000 to Alex for the option, and when the option is exercised, she pays £120,000 for Blackacre. The grant of the option is not in practice treated as a separate disposal by Alex, so he will not be assessed to capital gains tax immediately; the Revenue will generally 'wait and see'. When Brenda exercises the option, Alex will be treated as though he had disposed of Blackacre for £125,000.

If the option is not exercised, the taxpayer will be assessed to capital gains tax on the full amount of the option price for the year of assessment in which the option is granted (*Strange* v *Openshaw* [1983] STC 416).

21.2.5 Appropriation to trading stock

Where an asset was acquired by a taxpayer otherwise than as trading stock and is subsequently appropriated by him to trading stock, he is treated as having sold the asset for its then market value (s. 161(3), TCGA).[9] The rationale for this was said by Pennycuick J in *Ridge Securities Ltd* v *IRC* [1964] 1 All ER 275 to be:

[8.] This rule prevents a creditor from generating an allowable loss by accepting property worth less than the debt and immediately selling the property in the open market.

[9.] This is the analogue of *Sharkey* v *Wernher* (1955) 36 TC 275; see para. 10.4.

If a trader starts a business with stock provided gratuitously, it would not be right to charge him with tax on the basis that the value of his opening stock was nil.

On the sale of the appropriated trading stock, the trader will be charged to income tax under Schedule D, Case I on the excess of the sale price over the market value of the stock at the time of appropriation. A capital gains tax charge will be imposed on any appreciation in the value of the stock up to the time of appropriation. However the taxpayer may, on election, reduce the amount entered into his trading accounts at the time of appropriation by the amount of the capital gain with the result that the whole gain is charged in the taxpayer's Schedule D, Case I computation (s. 161(3)).

Example
Thomas is an antiques dealer. In 1988 he bought an antique writing desk for his home for £1,500. In 1992, when the writing desk had appreciated in value to £2,250, he transferred it to his trading stock and in 1996 he sold the desk in the course of his business for £2,750. For income tax purposes, Thomas will be treated as though he had acquired the writing desk as trading stock for £2,250 and sold it for £2,750 giving him a trading profit of £500. For capital gains tax purposes, he will be assessable to capital gains tax on the appreciation in the value of the writing desk between acquisition for £1,500 and appropriation to trading stock when it was worth £2,250. His chargeable gain (before indexation relief) would therefore be £750. However, if Thomas wished, he could have elected to be treated for income tax purposes as though he had acquired the writing desk as trading stock for £1,500, thus giving him a trading profit on the sale of the desk of £1,250. Whether this would have resulted in an overall tax saving[10] depends on whether Thomas's income tax liability on his trading profit would be less than his combined capital gains and income tax liabilities without election.[11]

21.2.6 Negligible value claims

Where the taxpayer claims that the value of the asset has become negligible and the inspector allows the claim, the asset is deemed to have been sold and immediately reacquired at its now negligible value. Negligible value claims have been discussed in para. 20.7.

[10.] Clearly there will be a cash flow advantage to Thomas in making the election because he will not have to pay tax until he actually receives the proceeds of sale of the writing desk.
[11.] There may be an advantages in making the election if the asset is standing at a capital loss since a trading loss may be more use to a taxpayer than a capital loss, compare Chapter 11 and para. 22.1. However, attempts to manipulate the rules to taxpayers' advantage have been severely regarded by the courts which have held that, in order to qualify as an appropriation to trading stock, there must be a genuine trading purpose in mind and not simply a wish to gain a tax advantage; *Coates v Arndale Properties Ltd* [1984] STC 637 and *Reed v Nova Securities Ltd* [1985] STC 124, CA.

21.2.7 Rights of security

Assets are usually treated as though they are disposed of, and acquired free of, any security interest or right subsisting at the time of disposal or acquisition. This is because the vendor will normally discharge the liability out of the proceeds of sale. However, if the asset is acquired subject to the liability to discharge the interest or right, the full amount of that liability forms part of the consideration for the disposal and acquisition of the asset (s. 26(3), TCGA).

Example
Victoria sells property to Peter for £95,000. At the time, the property is security for a loan to Victoria of £30,000. In normal circumstances, Victoria would be treated as though she had disposed of the property for £95,000 and Peter as though he had acquired it for that amount. However, if Peter takes the property subject to the rights of security (by assuming the liability to discharge Victoria's loan) Victoria will be treated as though she had disposed of the property for £125,000 and Peter as though he had acquired it for £125,000.

21.2.8 Instalments and contingencies

It was seen in Chapter 20 that the right to receive a sum on the happening of a certain specified future event constitutes a chargeable asset. When therefore the right to receive the sum matures, the capital sum received is consideration derived from the disposal of an asset. This situation must be distinguished from an arrangement under which the consideration for the disposal of the asset is paid in instalments. In such a case, the taxpayer is taxed on the total instalments due at the outset. No discount is made for the fact that that the taxpayer has not yet received all the money due to him or for the risk that the consideration may not be paid in full.[12]

Furthermore, no allowance will be made in the first instance to the person making the disposal for the following contingent liabilities:

(a) the defaults of an assignee of a lease;
(b) breaches of covenants for quiet enjoyment of land given by the vendor on a sale of land;
(c) breaches of warranties or representations made by the donor on the disposal of property other than land (s. 49, TCGA).

However, if it is subsequently shown that any such contingent liability is being or has been enforced, an adjustment by way of discharge or repayment of tax will be made (s. 49(2)).

In *Randall* v *Plumb* [1975] STC 191, the taxpayer granted an option to a company to purchase part of his land. The company paid £25,000 to the

---
[12.] However, if the taxpayer's inspector of taxes is satisfied that the consideration has become irrecoverable, an adjustment will be made to the taxpayer's capital gains tax computation; s. 48, TCGA.

taxpayer in consideration for the grant of the option. This sum was repayable in certain circumstances, although if the option was exercised, it became a part payment of the purchase price. The option was not exercised and the taxpayer was assessed to capital gains tax on the £25,000. The taxpayer claimed the obligation to repay the £25,000 should have been taken into account in computing his consideration for the disposal of the option. The Inland Revenue disagreed, arguing that the obligation to repay the sum was assumed by the taxpayer as the vendor of the land within item (b) above and should not, therefore, be taken into account. Walton J found in favour of the taxpayer:

> I think that an obligation of a general nature of returning a deposit is not assumed by a person as vendor of land but, at the highest, as an incident of the contract under which he is hoping to become, but will never in the actual circumstances become, the vendor. It appears to me that this is miles away from the only kind of obligation mentioned – a covenant for quiet enjoyment – which is an incident of the completed relationship.

The Inland Revenue's alternative argument that, because this contingency was not expressly referred to in the legislation, it was to be disregarded altogether, was also rejected. Walton J said:

> I cannot accept this submission for one moment. I draw precisely the opposite conclusion; namely, that unless the contingency is one which is expressly mentioned in one or other of these sub-paragraphs . . . it must (if it can as a matter of valuation) be taken at once into account in establishing the amount of the consideration received by the taxpayer, this being the only possible method of arriving at a figure for the amount of the consideration which truly reflects the contingency to which the matter is subject.

Accordingly, the matter was remitted to the Commissioners for a valuation of the option subject to the stated contingencies.

21.2.9 Receipts taxed as income

The distinction between capital and income discussed in Chapter 1 means that, in theory, income receipts are subject to income tax and capital receipts are subject to capital gains tax. However, there are instances in income tax law of capital receipts being taxed as income[13] and it is therefore possible that the same receipt could be liable to both income and capital gains tax. There is no general rule against double taxation in these circumstances[14] but s. 37, TCGA provides that any money or money's worth chargeable to income tax is excluded from the consideration for the disposal for capital gains tax purposes.

[13.] For example, compensation moneys for the loss of an employment and off-market own share purchases which do not meet the conditions in ss. 219 to 224, TA.
[14.] See, for example, *IRC* v *Garvin* [1981] STC 344, HL and *Bye* v *Coren* [1986] STC 393.

However, money or money's worth taken into account in the making of a balancing charge or allowance in connection with capital allowances is not excluded from a charge to capital gains tax (s. 37(2)(a) and see Chapter 12). Nor are rights to income or payments in the nature of income over a period excluded (s. 37(3)).[15]

21.3 ALLOWABLE EXPENDITURE

Section 38(1), TCGA states that, except as otherwise expressly provided, the taxpayer's allowable expenditure is restricted to three headings:

(a) the amount or value of the consideration, in money or money's worth, given by him or on his behalf wholly and exclusively for the acquisition of the asset, together with the incidental costs to him of the acquisition or, if the asset was not acquired by him, any expenditure wholly and exclusively incurred by him in providing the asset,

(b) the amount of any expenditure wholly and exclusively incurred on the asset by him or on his behalf for the purpose of enhancing the value of the asset, being expenditure reflected in the state or nature of the asset at the time of the disposal, and any expenditure wholly and exclusively incurred by him in establishing, preserving or defending his title to, or to a right over, the asset,

(c) the incidental costs to him of making the disposal.

It will be appreciated that these headings deal with a number of different types of expenditure which arise at different stages. They will be referred to in this chapter as acquisition expenditure, production expenditure, enhancement expenditure, title expenditure and disposal costs.

A couple of general points should be noted. First, in the same way as sums taken into account in computing income tax liability are excluded from the taxpayer's capital gains tax computation (see para. 21.2.9), revenue expenditure is disallowed in computing the taxpayer's allowable expenditure for the purposes of computing his or her liability to capital gains tax. This principle is reinforced by two rules:[16]

(a) a sum is not an allowable expense if it is allowable as an expense in computing the profits or losses of a trade, profession or vocation or as a deduction in computing any other income for the purposes of the Income Tax Acts (s. 39(1)); and

(b) expenditure is not deductible for capital gains tax purposes if the expenditure would be deductible in computing the profits or losses of that trade for income tax purposes if the asset was employed as a fixed asset of a trade (s. 39(2)). Thus maintenance expenditure will not, generally, be

---
[15] This could be an example of double taxation.
[16] There are also rules confirming that payments of interest and premiums under insurance policies, which would in any case normally be classified as revenue expenses, are not deductible under s. 38(1) (ss. 38(3) and 205 but note s. 40, TCGA).

allowable, unless it can be shown that the asset has become so dilapidated that, unless rectified, the dilapidations will depress the capital value of the asset.[17]

Secondly, expenditure under s. 38(1)(a) and (b) can only be deducted from the disposal consideration if it is 'wholly and exclusively' incurred on the asset. It was said by Lord Reid in *IRC v Richard's Executors* (1971) 46 TC 626 at p. 635 that the phrase 'wholly and exclusively' must not be read too literally.[18] This interpretation is buttressed by the fact that the legislation permits apportionment of expenditure by any 'just and reasonable method' (s. 52(4)). Thus expenditure incurred by executors in preparing an inventory of the deceased's stocks and shares was incurred wholly and exclusively in establishing the executors' title to those shares, despite the fact that an incidental purpose of the expenditure was to enable the executors to pay the correct amount of estate duty on the deceased's death.

In *Cleveleys Investment Trust Co. v IRC (No. 2)* 51 TC 26, Lord Emslie explained *IRC v Richard's Executors* as follows:

In my opinion the view of the majority of their Lordships properly understood is not that the words 'wholly and exclusively' are to be denied their ordinary meaning in the English language but that they are to be construed reasonably so that where it is found that the expenditure has been laid out to achieve a particular object the fact that it also secured an incidental or ancillary object will not prevent it or a proportion thereof from being treated as having been 'wholly and exclusively' laid out for the particular object.

21.4 ACQUISITION EXPENDITURE

The cost of acquisition and any incidental costs of acquisition are allowable. The acquisition cost will normally be the price paid by the taxpayer to acquire the asset. If the asset was acquired before 31 March 1982, the acquisition cost will normally be rebased to its market value on that date (see para. 21.1).

Section 38(1)(a) refers to the 'value of the consideration . . . in money's worth' so that there will have to be a valuation of any consideration other than cash which is given for the acquisition of an asset. However, as has already been seen in para. 21.2, if the parties to a genuinely arm's length transaction agree a cash price for the sale of the asset to be satisfied by the transfer of specified property, the price stated in their agreement will be taken to be the purchaser's acquisition cost regardless of the market value of the property actually transferred. In contrast if the transaction is not by way of a bargain at arm's length, for instance if the parties are connected, market value may be substituted as the acquisition cost.

---

[17] For cases on the income tax deductibility of repair to dilapidated assets, see *Law Shipping Co. Ltd v IRC* (1924) 12 TC 621, *Odeon Associated Cinemas Ltd v Jones* (1971) 48 TC 257, *Whelan v Dover Harbour Board* (1934) 18 TC 55 and *Jackson v Laskers Home Furnishers Ltd.* (1956) 37 TC 69.

[18] Cf. s. 74, TA discussed at para. 10.5.

If a trader appropriates an item of trading stock to non-trading purposes, the rule in *Sharkey* v *Wernher* (see para. 10.4) will require him to enter the market value of that item in his accounts as a trading receipt. If the appropriation takes place on the discontinuance of the trade, s. 100, TA will similarly require the market value or the proceeds of realisation of the trading stock to be entered as a trading receipt. The trader will therefore be subject to income tax in respect of any increase in the value of the item up to the date of the appropriation or discontinuance. If the asset transferred out of trading stock is retained by the taxpayer, he is treated as having acquired the asset at the date of appropriation or discontinuance for a consideration equal to the amount entered into the accounts of the trade in respect of it. The taxpayer is therefore subject to capital gains tax on the disposal of the asset in respect of any increase in value in the asset after the date of the appropriation or discontinuance (s. 162(2), TCGA).[19]

21.4.1 Incidental costs of acquisition

The acquisition expenditure also includes the incidental costs of acquisition such as fees, commission or remuneration paid for the services of surveyors, valuers, auctioneers, accountants, agents and legal advisers (s. 38(2)).

A deemed disposal and reacquisition will not, of itself, result in any incidental costs of acquisition (s. 38(4)). However, it seems that if any expenditure is actually incurred it will be deductible. In *IRC* v *Chubb's Trustee* (1971) 47 TC 353 Lord President Clyde said:

> It is difficult to conceive of what expenditure would be incidental to the notional re-acquisition of the property . . . but if there was any it would be part of the cost of the whole disposal.

21.5 PRODUCTION EXPENDITURE

If the asset was not acquired by the taxpayer, but instead was created by him, for example a painting or a copyright, he may deduct under s. 38(1)(a) any expenditure wholly and exclusively incurred by him in providing the asset.

21.6 ENHANCEMENT EXPENDITURE

Expenditure wholly and exclusively incurred on 'enhancing the value of the asset' may be deducted from the consideration received on the eventual disposal of the asset. In *Emmerson* v *Computer Time International Ltd* [1977] 2 All ER 545, the company's liquidator sought to deduct arrears of rent in respect of a lease of land under this category. The claim was denied. Goff LJ said:

[19.] Unlike appropriations to trading stock, the taxpayer may not elect to defer the tax charge until the asset is sold. This is presumably because, as it is no longer trading stock, there is no guarantee that the asset will be sold and tax could be deferred indefinitely.

I do not see how rent can be said to be expenditure incurred on the premises, nor in my view did these payments enhance the value of the asset in any real sense. They merely restored it to what it ought to be, and was, before the company made default or went into liquidation.

Although there is no reference to 'money's worth' in s. 38(1)(b), TCGA, it appears that the expenditure must be incurred. A notional figure representing one's own efforts cannot be deducted. So in *Oram v Johnson* [1980] 2 All ER 1, the taxpayer was not allowed to deduct a notional figure of £1,700 representing the value of work carried out by him on the property which had increased its capital value. The taxpayer had valued his labour very modestly, at only £1 per hour. Nevertheless Walton J dismissed his claim saying:

> It is perhaps a matter of first impression based on the impression that the word 'expenditure' makes on one, but I think that the whole group of words 'expenditure', 'expended', 'expenses' and so on and so forth, in a revenue context, mean primarily money expenditure and, secondly, expenditure in money's worth, something which diminishes the total assets of the person making the expenditure, and I do not think that one can bring one's own work, however skilful it may be and however much sweat one may expend on it, within the scope of section [38(1)(b)].
>
> This may seem rather hard, and I am sure the taxpayer will think it hard, but I think that there is another side to the coin. Suppose the taxpayer were (as it were) to be able to charge the Revenue up in this way with his notional expenditure of £1,700 worth of work. Would it not then be just that the Revenue should charge the taxpayer up with his receipt of £1,700 as moneys earned by him in his subsidiary trade of a bricklayer, or whatever.[20]

Where the taxpayer claims that the expenditure should be deductible as enhancement expenditure, the expenditure must be reflected in the 'state or nature of the asset at the time of disposal'. It thus appears that the expenditure must make an identifiable change in the state or nature of the asset, so a payment to a valuer to determine the authenticity of some potentially valuable antique for insurance purposes will not be deductible although a valuer's fees can constitute incidental costs of acquisition and disposal if incurred at that time and for that purpose. Where an asset is disposed of under a contract, it follows from s. 28(1) (that the time of the disposal is the time that the contract is made) that expenditure incurred after the date of the contract is not material for the purposes of s. 38(1)(b). However, it was held in *Chaney v Watkis* [1986] STC 89 that notice *will* be taken of post-contract events. The taxpayer owned a house which his mother-in-law, Mrs Williams, occupied as a protected tenant. In 1981, the taxpayer entered into an agreement to sell the house and Mrs Williams agreed

---

[20]. Cf. the rule in *Sharkey* v *Wernher* under which taxpayers are taxed on notional receipts (para. 10.4).

to vacate the house in consideration of the taxpayer making a payment to her of £9,400. After exchange of contracts but before completion, Mrs Williams agreed to release the taxpayer from his obligation to pay the £9,400. In return, the taxpayer agreed to provide Mrs Williams with rent-free accommodation for life. The taxpayer then expended a substantial sum on constructing an extension to his house. The taxpayer claimed that the £9,400 represented the cost of obtaining vacant possession of the house and was therefore allowable expenditure under s. 38(1)(b) even though it was not actually paid but was exchanged for the obligation to provide rent-free accommodation. Nicholls J, in upholding the taxpayer's claim, said:

> In my view the context in which the phrase 'at the time of disposal' is found in section [38(1)(b)] compels the conclusion that the phrase does not exclude expenditure which is first reflected in the state and nature of the property after the date of contract but before completion.

He continued:

> The obligation to pay £9,400 was the price of obtaining vacant possession of the property. If payment in cash of that sum by the taxpayer would have been expenditure wholly and exclusively incurred on the asset by the taxpayer for the purpose of enhancing its value, so must have been the payment by the taxpayer for the like purpose made not in cash but by providing money's worth at his expense, regardless of the precise nature of the benefit provided in lieu of money.

The decision is, perhaps, another illustration that the courts must apply 'ordinary business principles' as opposed to a strictly literal approach to the construction of the TCGA.

21.7 TITLE EXPENDITURE

A sum will be deductible under this head if it has been spent on 'establishing, preserving or defending' title to the asset. Expenditure will not be deductible if, in reality, it relates to the *acquisition* of an asset. In *Passant* v *Jackson* [1986] STC 164, the taxpayer was a residuary legatee under his mother's will. The mother died and the taxpayer entered into an agreement with his mother's executor under which he would give up his residuary legacy in return for a house and a balancing payment (reflecting the fact that the house was worth considerably more than the taxpayer's entitlement to the residue). When the taxpayer eventually sold the house he sought to deduct the balancing payment made to the executor as allowable expenditure in computing his chargeable gain. The Court of Appeal rejected his claim. The effect of the agreement with the executor was to give the taxpayer, for the first time, title to the house which he did not have before. The balancing payment was a sum paid to enable him to acquire the house not to enable him to preserve or defend title to it.

It is also not possible to obtain a deduction under this head for payments one should have made. So in *Emmerson* v *Computer Time International Ltd* [1977] 2 All ER 545, the Court of Appeal refused the liquidator's claim that the payment of arrears of rent due in respect of a lease of land was made to preserve title to that lease. Goff LJ said:

> I do not think the expenditure can be said to have been incurred in preserving the title. The Crown suggested that the payment of arrears can be so regarded if paid under an immediate threat of forfeiture, but I cannot see how that can make any difference. If that limited submission be right, then surely one is also preserving one's title if one pays on the due date and so avoids the risk arising, but that conclusion is absurd. I would, therefore, hold that in paying rent one is not preserving one's title, but simply discharging the obligations under which one holds the property.

21.8 INCIDENTAL COSTS OF DISPOSAL

The incidental costs of disposal are defined in the same way as the incidental costs of acquisition discussed in para. 21.4.1. Although legal, accountancy and valuation fees are covered by this provision, the Revenue do not consider that the costs of negotiating the value of the asset with the Revenue are included ([1994] STI 271).

21.9 MODIFICATIONS

The general rule in s. 38, TCGA requires modification in certain situations.

21.9.1 Assets derived from other assets

Special provisions apply where a new asset is created out of a merger or division of the old asset (s. 43, TCGA). The scheme of the legislation is to trace through the allowable expenditure on the old asset and allow it on disposal of the new asset. However, there must be a change in the nature of the new assets. In *Aberdeen Construction Group Ltd* v *IRC* [1978] STC 127, the taxpayer company spent £114,024 on acquiring shares in a rock drilling company. Over the next ten years, the taxpayers lent some £500,000 to the drilling company. The taxpayers then sold the shares for £250,000 and waived the loan. One of the taxpayer company's arguments in resisting the assessment to tax on its capital gain was that the shareholding and the loan were assets which had merged on the sale of the shares and that the shares had derived part of their increased value from the waiver of the loan. Accordingly, the taxpayer company claimed that a proportion of the loan should be attributable to the sale of the shares. The argument on this point was unanimously rejected by the House of Lords. Lord Russell of Killowen said:

> If broad terms were legitimate in connection with any part of this compli-cated legislation one would say that the [legislation] is designed to provide

for computation of capital gains where one asset has gained in value at the expense of another asset in the same ownership. Had it been expressed in such broad terms it would be clear that in the circumstances the . . . shares asset had gained in value by the extinction of the taxpayer company's other asset, the debt. But the [legislation] has limiting factors or qualifying conditions for its operation. So far as presently relevant it was necessary for the taxpayer company to contend that the debt and the shares had been 'merged', or (perhaps) that the shares had 'changed their nature'. I find these contentions wholly unacceptable. Release of a company from its debt does not achieve anything that can be described as merger of the debt with the shares in the company; nor does it change the nature of those shares.

21.9.2 Wasting assets

The disposal of a 'wasting asset' (an asset having a predictable life of less than 50 years) which is also tangible moveable property is exempt from capital gains tax (s. 45(1), TCGA – see further para. 22.2.2.4). Disposals of other wasting assets are subjected to special provisions. These special provisions are needed because the value of a wasting asset will decrease during its useful life and therefore the consideration on disposal will almost certainly be far less than its acquisition cost. This will result in a capital loss, even though the taxpayer has had the benefit of the asset during its useful life. Accordingly, the special rules provide that the allowable expenditure on the wasting asset (after deducting the residual or any scrap value of the asset) is written off at a uniform rate from its full amount at the time of the acquisition to nothing at the end of its life (s. 46(1)).

Example
Alan acquires a piece of machinery with a useful life of 20 years for £100,000. It had an estimated scrap value of £20,000. The difference between the two figures (£80,000) is written off at a uniform rate over 20 years, that is at the rate of £4,000 a year. After ten years, Alan sells the machinery for £70,000. His chargeable gain will therefore be:

	£
Sale proceeds	70,000
Less acquisition cost	(60,000)
(£100,000 – £40,000 written off)	
Chargeable gain	10,000

The special writing down rules just discussed do not, however, apply to any asset which has been used since its acquisition solely for the purposes of a trade, profession or vocation and in respect of which the taxpayer has, or could have, claimed capital allowances for the expenditure allowable under s. 38(1) (s. 45(2)). If the asset has been used partly for business purposes and partly for other purposes, so that only part of the expenditure qualified for capital allowances, the expenditure will be apportioned (s. 45(3)).

21.9.3 Part disposals

If the taxpayer has made a part disposal, his allowable expenditure on the whole asset (that is, expenditure qualifying for deduction under s. 38(1)(a) and (b)) is apportioned between the part disposed of and the part retained. Expenditure which may be deductible under s. 38(1)(c) necessarily only relates to the part disposed of and not to the entire asset. Of course, if some of the allowable expenditure under s. 38(1)(a) or (b) relates only to the part retained or the part disposed of, no apportionment need be made (s. 42(4)).

Where an apportionment is required, s. 42(2) provides that:

The apportionment shall be made by reference—
   (a) to the amount or value of the consideration for the disposal on the one hand (call that amount or value A), and
   (b) to the market value of the property which remains undisposed of on the other hand (call that market value B),
and accordingly the fraction of the said sums allowable as a deduction in the computation of the gain accruing on the disposal shall be—

$$\frac{A}{A + B}$$

and the remainder shall be attributable to the property which remains undisposed of.[21]

Example

Brian purchased a plot of land for £50,000. He later sells part of the plot for £30,000. Legal fees on the sale amounted to £2,000. The remaining land is valued at £70,000.

Brian's acquisition cost is apportioned as follows:

$$£50,000 \times \frac{£30,000}{£30,000 + £70,000} = £15,000$$

So Brian's chargeable gain on the disposal is:

	£	£
Sale proceeds		30,000
Less: apportioned acquisition costs	15,000	
incidental costs	2,000	
		17,000
Chargeable gain		13,000

The costs of valuing the retained part will be an incidental cost of the part disposal of and therefore allowable under s. 38(1)(c). However, in the case

---

[21]. This method of apportionment is related to the proportion of the *value* given away rather than the proportion of the *asset* disposed of. This is perhaps logical for a tax which is based on increases or decreases in value.

Computation of gains and losses 497

of land, since the valuation of the retained part may be expensive, the Revenue will in practice accept any fair and reasonable method of apportioning the allowable expenditure (Statement of Practice D1, 22 April 1977).

If the consideration for the part disposal of the land does not exceed £20,000 or, if this was not full consideration, the market value does not exceed that amount, and that consideration does not exceed 20% of the market value of the entire holding of land immediately before the part disposal, the taxpayer can elect to postpone paying capital gains tax on the part disposed of. The consideration for the part disposal will be deducted from the allowable expenditure on any subsequent disposal of the holding (s. 242). Similar provisions exist if an authority compulsorily acquires part of the taxpayer's land and the compensation (or the market value, if the compensation is not full consideration for the acquisition) is small when compared with the market value of the entire holding immediately before the acquisition (s. 243). The Inland Revenue take 'small' to mean no more than 5% (CCAB Press Release, June 1965).

21.10 INDEXATION ALLOWANCE

It was noted in Chapter 19 that an indexation allowance exists to prevent taxpayers being subjected to capital gains tax on merely inflationary gains. Indexation allowance was first introduced in 1982 and was extended and amended in 1985. The allowance operates by increasing each item of expenditure that the taxpayer has incurred on the acquisition and enhancement of his assets by the rise in the retail price index between the date the expenditure was incurred and the date of disposal.[22] If the expenditure was incurred before 1 April 1982[23] indexation allowance is calculated by reference to the market value of the asset on 31 March 1982 (as opposed to the individual items of expenditure) if that gives a favourable result to the taxpayer (s. 55(1)). The market value on 31 March 1982 must be used if the taxpayer has made a rebasing election (s. 35(5) and see para. 21.1). Where several items of allowable expenditure are incurred at different times, the indexed rise is calculated separately for each and the aggregate becomes the indexation allowance. Monthly tables of the indexed rise since March 1982 are published in *Simon's Tax Intelligence*.

Example
Sally purchased an asset in July 1990 for £10,000. She sold the asset in December 1996 for £15,000. At the time of disposal, the indexed rise since July 1990 was 0.218. Sally's chargeable gain will therefore be:

[22.] The formula is $\frac{RD - RI}{RI}$ where RD is the retail price index for the month in which the disposal occurs and RI is the month in which the expenditure is incurred. The fraction has to be expressed as a decimal to the nearest three decimal places; s. 54.
[23.] And the asset is disposed of after 5 April 1988.

		£	£
Consideration for the disposal			15,000
Less: allowable expenditure		10,000	
indexation allowance £10,000 × 0.218		2,180	
			(12,180)
Chargeable gain			2,820

The indexation allowance may increase the allowable expenditure to the point where it exceeds the disposal consideration. However, as from 30 November 1993, indexation allowance may not be used to turn a gain into a loss or increase a loss (s. 53(1)). The reason given for this change was that indexation allowance was being exploited to increase capital losses when the underlying commercial loss was stable.[24] The extent of such 'abuse' is unknown and the result of this change is to introduce asymmetry into the UK's capital gains tax system. As a result of criticism of the unfair nature of this change, transitional relieving provisions were introduced. For individuals and trustees, relief for losses arising as a result of indexation was given on a transitional basis for the 1993/94 and 1994/95 years of assessment only (s. 93 and sch. 12, FA 1994). Relief was given by first using indexation losses to reduce a taxpayer's chargeable gains for 1993/94 with any unused balance being carried forward to 1994/95. Any remaining indexation losses after 1994/95 are lost. Transitional relief is limited to a maximum of £10,000 of indexation losses.

On a part disposal, the apportionment of allowable expenditure required by s. 42 must be made and the indexation allowance will be applied only to the apportioned expenditure allowable on the part disposal. Special rules apply where shares are pooled. Broadly the indexation allowance is applied to the whole pool of expenditure incurred on the shares whenever there is a transaction in relation to those shares such as a further acquisition, a disposal or a rights issue (ss. 104–114, TCGA).

21.11 ALLOWANCE FOR FOREIGN TAX

If one tax jurisdiction seeks to tax the taxpayer on his capital gains on the basis that he is resident or ordinarily resident or domiciled in that jurisdiction, and another seeks to tax him on the same gain on the basis that the asset in respect of which the gain accrues is situated in that other jurisdiction, potentially there will be a double charge to tax. If relief under an applicable double tax treaty is not available (see Chapter 35), s. 278, TCGA allows any foreign tax paid on the disposal of the asset to be deducted from the consideration for the disposal of the asset brought into account for capital gains purposes in the United Kingdom.

---

[24] Inland Revenue Budget Press Release IR 28, 30 November 1993.

CHAPTER TWENTY TWO
Capital gains tax – losses, exemptions and reliefs

22.1 LOSSES

Section 16(1), TCGA provides that:

> ... except as otherwise expressly provided, the amount of a loss accruing on disposal of an asset shall be computed in the same way as the amount of a gain accruing on a disposal is computed.

Thus a loss will arise if the actual or deemed consideration for the disposal of the asset is less than the allowable expenditure (i.e., the acquisition cost, any enhancement expenditure and the incidental costs of disposal). Such losses are designated 'allowable losses' if, had the computation given rise to a gain, that gain would have been a chargeable gain (s. 16(2)). As noted in Chapter 21, since 1993 indexation allowance cannot be used to increase a loss or turn a gain into a loss (s. 53(1)).

22.1.1 Use of allowable losses

Losses may be set off against capital gains of the same year (s. 2(2)(a)). Unrelieved losses may be carried forward to later years but not back to previous years save on death (ss. 2(2)(b) and 62(2)). It is thus preferable to realise losses sooner rather than later, although to prevent taxpayers creating losses artificially by entering into transactions with connected persons (spouses, parents, siblings etc.), losses incurred on a disposal of an asset to a connected person are subject to restrictions. Such losses may only be set against chargeable gains accruing to the same person on a disposal to the same connected person (s. 18(3)).[1]

22.1.2 Relief for loans to traders

Special provision is made for a taxpayer who loses money on a loan to a businessman. The loan must be a qualifying loan, that is, money lent to a borrower resident in the United Kingdom which is used by the borrower wholly for the purposes of his trade, profession or vocation (s. 253(1)). The loan must not constitute a debt on a security (see para. 20.11) and the taxpayer must not be in the business of lending money. If these conditions are met and the taxpayer can show that any outstanding amount of principal of the loan has become irrecoverable, that he has not assigned his right to recover it, that he will not obtain relief under the new loan relationships rules (see para. 26.9) and that he and the borrower are not spouses or companies which are members of the same group, he will be treated as though he had incurred an allowable loss of the amount outstanding (s. 253(3)). An amount is not irrecoverable for these purposes if it has become irrecoverable under the terms of the loan itself or in consequence of any arrangements of which the loan forms part or of any act or omission by the taxpayer (s. 253(12)).

Relief is also available to a taxpayer who has guaranteed a loan which is a qualifying loan (or which would be if it were not a debt on a security) and any outstanding amount of principal or interest has become irrecoverable. The taxpayer must have made a payment in respect of that amount under the guarantee and not assigned his right to recover that amount. The lender and the borrower or the taxpayer and the borrower must not be each other's spouses or companies in the same group (s. 253(4)). The allowable loss in this case is the amount of the payment made under the guarantee less any amount recovered from a co-guarantor.

If the amount which was shown to be irrecoverable and in respect of which relief was given is subsequently recovered, the taxpayer will be treated as though he had made a chargeable gain of the amount recovered (s. 253(5)).

22.1.3 Relief for losses on unquoted shares in trading companies

An individual who has subscribed for shares in a 'qualifying trading company' and who has incurred an allowable loss on the disposal of shares may, instead of setting the allowable loss against his current chargeable gains or carrying the loss forward to set off against future chargeable gains, claim loss relief against his *income* (s. 574, TA). The relief is only available to a subscriber, that is, an individual who has had shares issued to him by a company in consideration of money or money's worth (s. 574(3)(a)) or who has had shares transferred to him inter vivos by his spouse who subscribed for them

---

[1.] However, it is submitted that if it is the transaction which creates the loss which connects the transferor and transferee (such as the sale of assets to a company in return for a controlling interest in it) and the transferor and transferee were not connected before, any loss accruing to the transferor will not be subject to the 'connected persons' restriction.

(s. 574(3)(b)). The section does not apply unless the disposal giving rise to the allowable loss is either:

(a) by way of bargain made at arm's length for full consideration;
(b) by way of distribution in the course of dissolving or winding up the company; or
(c) a deemed disposal under s. 24(2), TCGA (i.e., a claim that the value of the asset has become negligible).

A 'qualifying trading company' is a company which:

(a) has been resident in the United Kingdom since its incorporation and has not had its shares quoted on a recognised stock exchange since its incorporation;[2] and
(b) is a trading company[3] on the date of the disposal, or has ceased to be a trading company not more than three years before that date; and
(c) has been a trading company throughout its life or for a continuous period of at least six years ending with the date of disposal or at the time when it ceased to be a trading company as above (ss. 576(4) and (5), TA).

Relief under these provisions is given in priority to relief under ss. 381 or 380, TA (see Chapter 11).

22.2 EXEMPTIONS

The following gains are not chargeable gains because they are exempt from charge. Some exemptions depend on the status of the taxpayer, others depend on the type of asset and the availability of others depends partly on the status of the taxpayer and partly on the nature of the asset.

22.2.1 Exemptions depending on the status of the taxpayer

22.2.1.1 Charities Any gain accruing to a charity and which is applied for charitable purposes is not a chargeable gain (s. 256(1), TCGA).[4] In addition, any gifts of property to a charity will be treated as being made for such consideration that neither a gain nor a loss accrues. Thus the liability for the unrealised gain is transferred to the charity and if that gain is subsequently

---

[2] Or, if later, one year before the shares disposed of were subscribed for.
[3] Defined in s. 576, TA as a company which exists wholly or mainly for the purposes of carrying on a trade and is not an 'excluded company'. An excluded company is defined as a company carrying on a trade consisting wholly or mainly of dealing in shares, securities, land, trades or commodity futures, or which has not been carried on on a commercial basis and in such a way that profits can reasonably be expected to be realised. Investment companies, i.e., companies whose businesses consist wholly or mainly in the making of investments and the principal part of whose income is derived therefrom are also excluded.
[4] In *IRC* v *Slater (Helen) Charitable Trust Ltd* [1981] STC 471, CA it was held that money would be 'applied' for charitable purposes if it was transferred outright to any charitable institution even if the transferee merely added the sums received to its general reserves.

realised by a disposal of the asset it can be expected to be exempt (s. 257(2)). However, if the property ceases to be held for charitable purposes there is a deemed disposal and reacquisition of the property at its then market value with the result that any accrued gain will be subjected to capital gains tax (s. 256(2)).

22.2.1.2 Annual exemption   Section 3(1), TCGA provides:

> An individual shall not be chargeable to capital gains tax in respect of so much of his taxable amount for any year of assessment as does not exceed the exempt amount for the year.

The exempt amount for the 1997/98 year of assessment is £6,500. Trustees are entitled to half the annual exemption (para. 2(2), sch. 1, TCGA). Since the 1990/91 year of assessment, husbands and wives have each been entitled to a (non-transferable) annual exemption. Previously only one relief was given for spouses living together, allocated between them pro rata to their net gains.

22.2.1.3 Death   The death of an individual results in a capital gains tax free uplift in the value of the assets comprised in his estate on death. The capital gains tax consequences of death are discussed further in Chapter 23.

22.2.2 Exemptions depending on the type of asset

22.2.2.1 Betting winnings   Winnings from betting, lotteries or games with prizes are not chargeable gains. Further, no chargeable gain accrues on the disposal of rights to winnings obtained by participating in any pool betting, lottery or game with prizes (s. 51(1), TCGA).

22.2.2.2 Compensation   Sums obtained by way of compensation or damages for any wrong or injury suffered by an individual in his person or in his profession or vocation are not chargeable gains (s. 51(2), TCGA). Thus damages received by an individual for breaches of contractual duties or torts (in Scotland delicts) are covered, as is compensation for unlawful discrimination, libel or slander. Although the exemption only applies to compensation for a wrong or injury suffered by an individual, by Concession, the Revenue extend the availability of the exemption to compensation received by relatives or personal representatives of a deceased individual (ESC D33).[5] This same Concession enables any gain arising on the disposal of a right to bring a court action to be computed by reference to the underlying asset or, if there is no underlying asset, to be treated as though it were exempt.

22.2.2.3 Gilt-edged securities and qualifying corporate bonds   Disposals of gilt-edged securities and qualifying corporate bonds are exempt

---

[5.] This Concession was introduced in response to the decision in *Zim Properties* v *Procter*; see para. 20.6.

from capital gains tax (s. 115(1), TCGA). Gilt-edged securities are listed in sch. 9 and qualifying corporate bonds are defined in s. 117. The Finance Act 1997 contains provisions to ensure that any gain accruing on a non-qualifying corporate bond remains chargeable if it subsequently becomes a qualifying corporate bond by (say) a change in its terms after it is issued.

22.2.2.4 Wasting assets No chargeable gain accrues on the disposal of, or an interest in, an asset which is both tangible moveable property and a wasting asset (s. 45(1), TCGA). A wasting asset is defined as an asset having a predictable life of less than 50 years (s. 44(1)). 'Life' means useful life having regard to the purpose for which the asset was acquired. Plant and machinery will be regarded as having a predictable life of less than 50 years and in estimating its life, it will be assumed that the asset's life will end when it is finally put out of use as being unfit for further use, and that it is going to be used in the normal manner and to the normal extent throughout its life (s. 44(1)(c)). However, the exemption for wasting assets does not apply to assets in respect of which capital allowances (see Chapter 12) were or could have been claimed nor for commodities dealt with on a terminal market (ss. 45(2)–(4)).

22.2.2.5 Foreign currency for personal expenditure Although foreign currency is an asset for capital gains tax purposes, no gain arises from the disposal of any foreign currency which was acquired by the taxpayer for personal expenditure abroad by him or his family or dependants (s. 269, TCGA).[6] 'Personal expenditure' includes any expenditure on the provision or maintenance of a residence abroad. Apart from this, currencies other than sterling are potentially liable to capital gains tax. This resulted in a number of difficulties for businesses involved in transactions with a foreign currency element and new legislation for companies has been implemented.[7]

22.2.2.6 Debts It was seen in Chapter 20 that an original creditor cannot make a capital gain or allowable loss on a debt unless the debt constitutes a 'debt on a security' (s. 251, TCGA and para. 20.11). However, if the original creditor assigns the debt for a price less than the amount of the debt, the assignee can make a capital gain if he recovers the original debt or himself assigns the debt for a greater price than he paid.

Since, strictly, moneys held in a foreign currency bank account constitute a debt owed by the bank in favour of the depositor, it is specifically provided that no exemption from tax applies in such a situation. However, that provision is itself subject to an exception, namely that there is an exemption from tax in respect of moneys held for the taxpayer or his family's personal expenditure abroad (see para. 22.2.2.5).

[6.] See s. 252(2) if the money is in a foreign bank account.
[7.] Sections 60, 92–96 and 125–170, FA 1993. For a fuller discussion see, inter alia, Choun and Taylor [1975] BTR 233; Pagan [1984] BTR 161; Pagan (1993) 14 Fiscal Studies 90; and Keeling [1995] BTR 122.

22.2.2.7 Assurance and annuities No chargeable gain accrues on the disposal of the rights under any policy of assurance or contract for a deferred annuity on the life of any person, unless the person making the disposal is not the original beneficial owner of the policy or contract and he acquired the rights or interest for a consideration in money or money's worth (s. 210(2), TCGA).

Section 237 provides that no chargeable gain will accrue to any person on the disposal of a right, or part of a right, to:

(a) any allowance, annuity or capital sum payable out of any superannuation fund, or under any superannuation scheme, established solely or mainly for persons employed in a profession, trade, undertaking or employment, and their dependants,

(b) an annuity granted otherwise than under a contract for a deferred annuity by a company as part of its business of granting annuities on human life, whether or not including instalments of capital . . . , or

(c) annual payments which are due under a covenant made by any person and which are not secured on any property.

The House of Lords held in *Rank Xerox Ltd* v *Lane* [1979] 3 All ER 657, that para. (c) is confined to gratuitous promises to make annual payments which are only enforceable because the agreement was under seal. Thus the taxpayer company was taxable on the gain arising from a disposal of a right to receive royalty payments.

22.2.2.8 Works of art Exemption from capital gains tax for gifts of works of art and other assets of national importance is given if the gift qualifies for certain inheritance tax exemptions. The reader is referred to the discussion of this subject in Chapter 31.

22.2.2.9 Shares held in personal equity plans Shares which form part of an investment which qualifies as a personal equity plan may be disposed of without any capital gains tax liability (s. 333, TA and reg. 17(1), Personal Equity Plan Regulations 1989).

22.2.2.10 Chattel exemption A gain accruing on a disposal of tangible moveable property is not a chargeable gain if the amount or value of the consideration for the property does not exceed £6,000 (s. 262(1), TCGA).[8] 'Tangible moveable property' refers to chattels, but the word 'tangible' will obviously exclude choses in action such as a bill of exchange or an insurance policy. The provision applies only to chattels that are not wasting assets since gains arising on wasting chattels are not chargeable gains at all.

If the consideration for the chattel exceeds £6,000 a marginal relief is given whereby the chargeable gain is limited to ⅗rds of the difference between the consideration and £6,000 (s. 262(2)).

[8.] Anti-avoidance provisions prevent exploitation by successive part disposals of an asset worth more that £6,000 or disposals of part of a set of articles to the same or a 'connected person'; ss. 262(4) and (5).

Example
Mary sells a chattel for £6,400 which she purchased for £5,500. Without the chattel exemption her gain on the disposal would be £900. However, with marginal relief her gain is limited to:

$$\frac{5}{3} \times £(6{,}400 - 6{,}000) = £666.66$$

If the disposal of the chattel gives rise to a loss and the consideration for the disposal was less than £6,000, the allowable loss is computed on the assumption that the consideration received for the disposal was £6,000 (s. 262(3)). This has the effect of restricting the taxpayer's allowable loss.

22.2.2.11 Passenger vehicles It is specifically provided that motor cars and other motor vehicles that can be used to carry passengers are not chargeable assets (s. 263, TCGA). Accordingly, no chargeable gain or allowable loss can arise on their disposal. Vehicles of a type which are not commonly used as private vehicles and are unsuitable for such use are excluded from exemption. Thus the exemption covers 'vintage cars bought as an investment, as well as the family car, but not an ambulance, a steam roller or a bus.'[9]

22.2.3 Exemptions depending partly on the status of the taxpayer and partly on the asset

22.2.3.1 Decorations for valour No chargeable gain arises from the disposal of a decoration for valour or gallant conduct unless the taxpayer acquired the decoration for a consideration in money or money's worth (s. 268, TCGA). A gain will therefore never arise to the original recipient of the decoration.

22.2.3.2 Private residence Despite the recent performance of the domestic housing market in the United Kingdom, the capital gain which the majority of taxpayers are likely to realise is the increase in the value of their homes. Exemption from capital gains tax is available to a taxpayer for a private residence if it is attributable to the disposal of, or an interest in:

 (a) a dwelling-house or part thereof which is, or has at any time in his period of ownership been, the taxpayer's only or main residence; or
 (b) land which the taxpayer has for his own occupation and enjoyment with that residence as its garden or grounds of an area up to 0.5 of a hectare (including the site of the house) or any larger area required for the reasonable enjoyment of the house (or part) as a residence having regard to the size and character of the house (ss. 222(1), (2) and (3), TCGA).

The rationale for this exemption was explained by Brightman J in *Sansom* v *Peay* [1976] 3 All ER 353 (at p. 379):

---

[9]. *Butterworths UK Tax Guide 1995–96*, para. 15:04.

The general scheme of [the legislation] is to exempt from liability to capital gains tax the proceeds of sale of a person's home. That was the broad concept. The justification for the exemption is that when a person sells his home he frequently needs to acquire a new home elsewhere. The evil of inflation was evident even in 1965. It must have occurred to the legislature that when a person sells his home to buy another one, he may well make a profit on the sale of one home and lose that profit, in effect, when he buys his new home at the new, inflated price. It would not therefore be surprising if Parliament formed the conclusion that, in such circumstances, it would be right to exempt the profit on the sale of the first home from the incidence of capital gains tax so that there was enough money to buy the new home.

22.2.3.3 Meaning of 'dwelling-house' It will usually be obvious whether or not a residence constitutes a dwelling-house, but border line cases sometimes arise, particularly where the 'dwelling-house' is argued to consist of a number of separate buildings. The principles that should be applied have been considered in a series of 'country house' cases. In *Batey* v *Wakefield* [1981] STC 521 the taxpayer built a bungalow for a married couple who acted as his housekeeper and caretaker within the grounds of his main residence but detached from the house. The bungalow had a separate access road and was separately rated. Eventually the taxpayer sold the bungalow with a small area of surrounding land and claimed that the gain was not chargeable to capital gains tax since he had disposed of part of his main residence. The Court of Appeal upheld his claim. Fox LJ (with whom Oliver and Stephenson LJJ agreed) said:

> [I]t seems to me that in the ordinary use of English, a dwelling house, or a residence, can comprise several buildings which are not physically joined at all. For example, one would normally regard a dwelling house as including a separate garage; similarly it would, I think, include a separate building such as a studio, which was built and used for the owner's enjoyment.

However, in *Markey* v *Sanders* [1987] STC 256, the taxpayer also built a bungalow for her domestic staff. The bungalow was situated 130 metres away from the main house and was screened from view by a belt of trees. The taxpayer eventually sold off the whole estate to a single purchaser and claimed that the gain accruing on the disposal of the bungalow was exempt as it constituted a single dwelling with the main house. The Commissioners allowed the taxpayer's claim but, on appeal, the Revenue's contention – that the house and bungalow were not a single dwelling because the bungalow was not 'closely adjacent to' the house – was upheld.

Markey v *Sanders* was itself doubted in *Williams* v *Merrylees* [1987] STC 445, although the facts of the later case were very similar. A country house with four bedrooms was set in one and a half hectares with stables and outbuildings, and with a one-storey lodge for domestic servants 200 metres from the house. Vinelott J held that separate buildings could be regarded as a single dwelling-house if they could be said to form an entity which could sensibly be described as a dwelling-house split up into different buildings performing different functions. The distance from the main house was a relevant factor but was not decisive.

More recent cases have taken a slightly different approach. In *Lewis* v *Lady Rook* [1992] STC 171, the taxpayer owned an estate of four and a quarter hectares which included a large house, an adjacent coach house and two cottages. The cottages were about 175 metres from the house. The taxpayer claimed the main residence exemption when one of the cottages was sold. The Crown's appeal that the taxpayer was not entitled to the exemption was allowed. The Court of Appeal did not consider the state of the authorities very satisfactory. It noted that the Shorter Oxford English Dictionary defined a dwelling-house as a place of residence, but that the Court was bound by the earlier decision in *Batey* v *Wakefield* that a dwelling-house could consist of more than one building, even if that other building itself constituted a separate dwelling-house. Balcombe LJ giving the judgment of the Court therefore proposed the following test:

> Where it is contended that some one or more separate buildings are to be treated as part of an entity which, together with the main house, comprise a dwelling house . . . no building can form part of a dwelling house . . . unless that building is appurtenant to, and within the main curtilage of, the main house.

Balcombe LJ thought this a 'helpful approach', since it involved 'the application of well recognised legal concepts and might avoid the somewhat surprising findings of fact in the earlier cases'. He cited Buckley LJ's dictum in *Methuen-Campbell* v *Walters* [1979] QB 525, that:

> . . . for one corporeal hereditament to fall within the curtilage of another, the former must be so intimately connected with the latter as to lead to the conclusion that the former in truth forms part and parcel of the latter.

Thus yards and passageways adjoining the land would be within the curtilage as would many ancillary buildings and areas such as garages, driveways and gardens. How far the curtilage would extend would depend on the 'character and circumstances of the items under consideration'. Balcombe LJ noted that this test coincided with the 'closely adjacent to' test referred to in the earlier cases.

Lewis v *Lady Rook* was followed in *Honour* v *Norris* [1992] STC 304, a case involving occupation of several flats in a London square. The taxpayer's argument that the decision in *Lewis* v *Lady Rook* was restricted to country estates was rejected. Thus the sale of one of a number of self-contained flats in the same square in London did not fall within the main residence exemption as it could not be described as being within the curtilage of the taxpayer's main residence.[10]

[10.] In *Tax Bulletin* Issue 12 (August 1994) the Revenue said that, in applying the test laid down in *Lewis* v *Lady Rook*, a wall, fence or road separating two buildings would normally prevent those buildings from being within the same curtilage.

It seems that a caravan can qualify as a dwelling-house. In *Makins* v *Elson* [1977] STC 46, the taxpayer acquired land with planning permission for the erection of a dwelling-house. He moved onto the site with his family and lived in a caravan which was connected to the water and electricity supplies and to the telephone network. The caravan wheels had not been removed but the caravan had been jacked up and was resting on bricks. Before the house was built, the taxpayer sold the land and the caravan, and claimed that the private residence exemption applied. The court upheld his claim. However, in *Moore* v *Thompson* [1986] STC 170, a caravan was held *not* to be a dwelling-house. The caravan was situated in the courtyard of a farmhouse and the taxpayer used the caravan while she and her husband were renovating the farmhouse. There was no electricity, water or telephone and the local authority did not treat the caravan as being in rateable occupation. The caravan was not jacked up but stood on its wheels. The General Commissioners held that the caravan was not a dwelling-house and Millett J agreed:

> It is clear that a caravan can be a dwelling house and that whether it is or is not a dwelling house is a question of fact which depends on a consideration of all the relevant facts proved or admitted before [the Commissioners]. I have no reason to think that [the Commissioners] failed to take account of any relevant fact which was in evidence before them and the conclusion which they came to was one to which the Commissioners were entitled to come.

22.2.3.4 Sales of part of a garden The sale of a part of the garden separate from the house can cause difficulties. It was held in *Varty* v *Lynes* [1976] 3 All ER 447, that land used as a garden could only qualify for the private residence exemption if it was sold prior to or at the same time as the dwelling-house. The taxpayer could not therefore claim exemption from capital gains tax when he had already sold the house and part of his garden and was now selling the retained part of the garden with planning permission. However, even advance sales of part of the taxpayer's garden may cause difficulties since if the garden is in excess of 0.5 of a hectare separate sales of parts of the garden may weaken the taxpayer's claim that the garden was required for the reasonable enjoyment of the house.[11]

22.2.3.5 More than one main residence If a taxpayer has more than one main residence, the question as to which one is his main residence for any period may be determined conclusively by the taxpayer giving written notice to his inspector of taxes within two years from the beginning of the period when the taxpayer occupies two or more dwellings as residences (s. 222(5)(a) and *Griffin* v *Craig-Harvey* [1993] STC 54). In the absence of

---

[11.] In *Tax Bulletin* Issue 2 (February 1992) the Revenue drew attention to du Parcq J's dictum in *Re Newhill Compulsory Purchase Order, 1937* [1938] 2 All ER 163 at p. 167 that 'required' meant that 'without it there will be such a substantial deprivation of amenities or convenience that a real injury will be done to the property owner . . .' It was more than simply meaning that the taxpayers would like to have the garden or would miss it if they lost it.

notice, the matter will be determined by the inspector, subject to an appeal to the Commissioners (s. 222(5)(b)). Spouses may have only one main residence for so long as they are living together and any notice concerning the choice of a dwelling-house as a main residence must be given by them both (s. 226(a)). Where one spouse transfers their only or main residence to the other when they are living together or when one spouse dies, the period of ownership during which the house was their only or main residence is attributed to the acquiring spouse (s. 227(a)). Where spouses have separated and one spouse leaves the matrimonial home, he or she may, by Concession, claim the benefit of the private residence exemption on a subsequent disposal to the other spouse as part of the financial arrangements on divorce provided the other spouse has lived in the house since the separation (ESC D6).

22.2.3.6 Period of occupation and apportionment It is sufficient that the dwelling-house was the owner's main residence at any time during the period of ownership. But full exemption only applies if the dwelling-house has been used throughout the period of ownership as the owner's main residence or throughout that period except for all or any part of the last 36 months of ownership (s. 223(1)). This allows the taxpayer time to sell his home if he has already acquired another. Partial exemption is given in other cases, the gain being apportioned rateably to the period of occupation as a main residence (s. 223(2)).

Example
Olive purchased Blackacre as her only residence on 1 January 1985 for £50,000. On 1 January 1991, Olive left Blackacre permanently. In 1993 she decided to sell Blackacre. This proved difficult. Olive finally sold Blackacre in January 1995 for £95,000.

Olive's chargeable gain on the disposal of Blackacre (ignoring indexation) is £45,000 (£95,000 − £50,000). She has owned the house for ten years but has only occupied it for six of those years. However, she will be deemed to have occupied the house for the last three years of her ownership. Thus Olive will be treated as though she had occupied Blackacre for nine out of her ten years of ownership. So:

$$\frac{9}{10} \times £45,000 \text{ will be exempt from capital gains tax, i.e., } £40,500$$

The balance of £4,500 will be chargeable.

Certain other periods of absence may be counted as periods of occupation, provided that the taxpayer has no other residence which is eligible for relief and the house was his only or main residence before and after the periods of absence.[12] These periods are:

[12.] This condition will be treated as satisfied where, after a period of absence resulting from the taxpayer's duties of employment, the taxpayer is unable to resume residence in his previous home because the terms of his employment require him to work elsewhere (ESC D4).

(a) any period or periods of absence not exceeding three years in all, and in addition;
(b) any period of absence of any length during which the taxpayer performed all the duties of an employment abroad; and in addition
(c) any period or periods of absence not exceeding four years in all throughout which the taxpayer was prevented from residing in his house because of the situation of his place of work or because of a condition that he should reside elsewhere reasonably imposed by the employer to secure the effective performance by the taxpayer of his duties (s. 223(3)).

Apportionment of the gain will also be made if part of the dwelling-house has been exclusively used for the purposes of a trade, profession or vocation. The part of the gain that can be attributed to the business use will be charged as a capital gain (s. 224(1)). Such apportionment can only be made when the part of the dwelling is permanently occupied; temporary occupation will not affect the taxpayer's ability to claim the exemption (*Tax Bulletin*, 12 August 1994).

The main residence exemption may also be available if the house has been occupied by a beneficiary under the terms of a settlement. This is discussed in Chapter 24.

22.2.3.7 Retirement relief Although called a 'relief', retirement relief, if applicable, comprises a full or partial exemption from capital gains tax. Retirement relief will be available if the taxpayer is at least 50 years old (even if he or she does not actually go into retirement) or if he has retired before that age on the grounds of ill health (s. 163(1), TCGA). A person who has retired on the grounds of ill health must submit medical evidence to the Revenue (para. 3, sch. 6, TCGA). Although the wording of the legislation permits an interpretation that a claim may be made by (say) a partner who gives up work to care for his or her unwell partner, the Revenue have stated that the retirement must be on the grounds of the claimant's ill health (Revenue Interpretation, RI 6). The Board must be satisfied that, because of his ill health, the claimant is incapable of engaging in work of a kind he previously undertook and he is likely to remain permanently incapable of engaging in such work. In the case of full-time working directors, the Board must be satisfied that the director is, and is likely to remain permanently, incapable of serving the company in a 'managerial or technical capacity' (para. 3, sch. 6, TCGA). There is no specific appeal procedure against the refusal of the Revenue to accept evidence of ill health. Presumably the taxpayer's 'remedy' is to challenge any subsequent capital gains tax assessment.

Retirement relief will be available if the individual makes a 'material disposal of business assets'. There will be a disposal of business assets if there is:

(a) a disposal of the whole or part of a business; or
(b) a disposal of one or more assets which, at the time the business ceased to be carried on, were used in the business; or

(c) a disposal of shares or securities of a company (s. 163(2)).

Thus, while relief may be available for any chargeable gain on the sale, at any time, of a part of the business, a gain on the sale of the assets of the business will only be available for relief if the assets are disposed of after the business has ceased. In the case of ongoing businesses, it is thus necessary to distinguish between sales of part of a business and sales of assets used in the business. In *McGregor* v *Adcock* [1977] STC 206, the taxpayer (aged 65) farmed 35 acres of land but, after he had farmed the land for ten years, he obtained planning permission to develop a 4.8 acre plot which he sold at a chargeable gain. The taxpayer claimed retirement relief on the grounds that the sale of the land was a sale of part of his farming business. Fox J, overturning the Commissioners, held that there was a clear distinction between a 'business' which connoted an activity and assets, such as land, used in the business. The mere occupation of land was not enough to constitute the business of farming and the nature of that business was not affected by the sale of the land. Thus retirement relief was not available.[13]

The disposal of a business or part of it is a 'material' disposal if the business has been owned by the individual for a least one year ending with the date of disposal (s. 163(3)) and on or before the date of disposal the individual has reached 50 or retired on the grounds of ill health. For disposals of business assets, the disposal should take place within one year of the cessation of the business or such longer time as the Revenue may, in writing, allow (s. 163(4) and para. 1(2), sch. 6). In contrast to the usual rule for disposals for capital gains tax purposes,[14] the date of disposal for all purposes of retirement relief may be taken as the date of completion where, pending completion, the business activities continue beyond the date of an unconditional contract for sale or transfer (ESC D31).

Alternatively, the business may have been owned for at least the preceding 12 months by a member of a group of trading companies of which the taxpayer's personal company is the holding company and the taxpayer is a full-time working officer or employee of the personal company or of one of the group or associated companies (s. 163(3)). A personal company is any company in which the individual can exercise not less than 5% of the voting rights (para. 1(2), sch. 6). A full-time officer or employee of the company is any officer or employee who is required to devote substantially the whole of his time to the service of that company in a managerial or technical capacity (para. 1(2), sch. 6).

Retirement relief is only available in respect of gains that arise on the disposal of 'chargeable' business assets. A chargeable business asset is defined as an asset (including goodwill but not shares or securities or other assets held as investments) which is used for the purposes of any trade, profession, vocation, office or employment carried on by the taxpayer, his personal

---

[13.] See also *Atkinson* v *Dancer, Mannion* v *Johnston* [1988] STC 758 and *Pepper* v *Daffurn* [1993] STC 466.
[14.] That the date of disposal is the date that an unconditional contract is entered into; s. 28 and see para. 20.13.

company or a member of its trading group, or a partnership in which the taxpayer is a member (para. 1(2), sch. 6). A recent decision of the Special Commissioner, *Durrant* v *IRC* (1995) Sp C 24), held that the exclusion for shares, securities or other assets held as investments should be read as excluding *all* shares even if the shares were held as part of the working capital of the business. In any event, an asset is not a chargeable business asset unless any gain which might arise on its disposal would be a chargeable gain. Thus an exempt gain, such as the gain accruing on the disposal of an item valued at less than £6,000 so qualifying for the chattel exemption (see para. 22.2.2.10), is not a chargeable business asset. If the disposal of chargeable business assets involves assets which give rise to allowable losses, those losses are set against the gains and only the net gains are available for relief.

Retirement relief is available on net chargeable gains up to £1,000,000. The first £250,000 of gains is wholly exempt from capital gains tax. Of the next £750,000, one-half is exempt and the whole of the excess over £1,000,000 is taxable (para. 13(1), sch. 6). Thus the maximum gain that may be relieved is £625,000 (provided a gain of £1,000,000 or more has been made), although the relief is available separately to spouses with the result that £1,250,000 of gains may be relieved.[15] Where the qualifying conditions have been satisfied for less than ten years, relief is reduced by the 'appropriate percentage'. This is a scale rising from 10% when the qualifying conditions have been satisfied for precisely one year to 100% when the conditions have been met for ten years. Thus the minimum relief (provided a gain of £1,000,000 or more has been made), for a qualifying period of exactly one year, is £25,000 completely exempt plus one-half of the next £75,000 of gains. Where retirement relief has been given on other disposals the maximum relief available is reduced (para. 15, sch. 6).

As mentioned above, relief is also available when the disposal is of shares or securities in a company owning the business and the company is a trading company which is either:

(a) that individual's personal company; or
(b) a member of a trading group of which the holding company is that individual's personal company.

Once again, the individual must be a full-time working officer or employee of that company or one or more of the companies in that group. The same maxima apply to the amount of gains which may be relieved and are related to the length of the qualifying period which must be at least one year. The qualifying period ends on the 'operative date' which is usually the date of the disposal (s. 163(5)). Where relief is available, it is restricted to a proportion of the aggregate gains accruing on the disposal of the shares or securities. That proportion is the value the company's (or trading group's) chargeable business assets bear to the company's (or trading group's) total chargeable assets (paras 7 and 8, sch. 6). Where the disposal is a deemed

---

[15.] The Revenue will not use the *Ramsay* principle (see Chapter 4) to challenge genuine gifts to spouses who subsequently claim retirement relief; Inland Revenue letter to the ICAEW of 25 September 1985.

Capital gains tax – losses, exemptions and reliefs

disposal on a company reorganisation, the taxpayer may elect that the normal rule treating the new shares as representing the old should not apply (seepara. 30.2). This will enable him to set the relief against the gains arising on the reorganisation (para. 2, sch. 6).

Retirement relief is available on the disposal of an asset by an employee where the asset is provided or held by him for the purpose of his office or employment (s. 164(1)). At the time of disposal or, if earlier, the end of his employment, the person must be over 50 or have retired from work through ill health. Relief is also available for 'associated disposals', i.e., disposals which take place as part of a withdrawal of the individual from a business carried on by a partnership or a company fulfilling the conditions for the principal relief. The asset must be a qualifying asset, have been in use in the business immediately before the withdrawal and have been used for the whole or part of the period (s. 164(7)). The gain eligible for relief is reduced if rent has been charged or if the individual has not been actively involved in the business throughout the period. The individual must have reached 50 or retired on the grounds of ill health. Finally, retirement relief is available to the trustees of a settlement who dispose of an asset used for business purposes (see para. 24.6).

Example Working of retirement relief rules
Assume A aged 65 disposes of his business which he has been running for 12 years on 1 June 1995. The gain after indexation allowance is £350,000. No earlier retirement relief has been given.

	£
Gain	350,000
Amount available for full relief	250,000
Therefore amount available for 50% relief	100,000
Total relief £250,000 + (£100,000 × 50%)	300,000
Thus	
Gain	350,000
Less retirement relief	300,000
Chargeable gain	50,000

Example
Assume B aged 62 disposes of her business which she has been running for precisely six years on 1 June 1995. The gain after indexation is £350,000. No earlier retirement relief has been given.

	£
Gain	350,000

Width of full relief band is:
£250,000 × appropriate percentage =
    £250,000 × 60% = £150,000

Amount available for 50% relief is:
£350,000[16] − £150,000 = £200,000
Amount of 50% relief = 50% × £200,000   £100,000

Total relief	250,000

Thus

Gain	350,000
Less retirement relief	250,000
Chargeable gain	£100,000

Example

Assume C aged 64 disposes of her business which she has been running for seven years on 1 June 1995. The gain after indexation is £800,000. No earlier retirement relief has been given.

Upper limit for 100% relief = 70% × £250,000	175,000
Upper limit for 50% relief = 70% × £1,000,000	700,000
Total of 100% relief	175,000
Total 50% relief	
= 50% × (£700,000 − £175,000) = 50% × £525,000	262,500
Total relief £175,000 + £262,500	437,500
Gain	800,000
Less retirement relief	437,500
	362,500

22.3 RELIEFS

The TCGA contains a number of provisions whereby gains on assets that would otherwise be immediately charged to capital gains tax may be deferred for a period of time. These type of reliefs are described as 'roll-over' reliefs or 'hold-over' reliefs.

22.3.1 Gifts of assets ('hold-over relief')

One of the drawbacks of assessing gifts to capital gains tax is that the donor of the gift may not have the funds to pay the tax due. The person who does have the funds (even if these can only be raised by selling the gifted asset) is the recipient. In the light of this, it used to be possible for the donor and recipient to elect jointly that the recipient would take over the donor's acquisition cost with the result that any accrued gain would be deferred or 'held over' until the recipient himself disposed of the asset (s. 79(1), FA

[16.] The computation of the 'appropriate percentage' of £1,000,000 has not been included since, that figure being £600,000 (60% of £1,000,000), the gain does not exceed it.

Capital gains tax – losses, exemptions and reliefs 515

1980).[17] However, the government became concerned that this 'hold-over relief' was increasingly being used as a method of tax avoidance.[18] It was therefore decided that relief should be restricted to:

(a) transfers of 'business assets' (s. 165, TCGA);[19]
(b) where the transfer may be subject to an immediate inheritance tax charge;[20] and
(c) certain exempt inheritance tax transfers, such as transfers by trustees of accumulation and maintenance settlements (s. 260). The interrelation of inheritance tax and hold-over relief is discussed in Chapter 31.

The capital gains tax liability accruing to an individual on a transfer of business assets otherwise than by way of bargain at arm's length, may be held-over provided that the asset transferred is:

(a) an asset (or an interest in an asset) used in the transferor's trade, profession or vocation; or
(b) an asset (or an interest in an asset) used in the transferor's personal company's trade, profession or vocation (or that of a member of a trading group of which the personal company is the holding company); or
(c) shares or securities in a trading company or the holding company of a trading group where the shares or securities are either not quoted on a recognised stock exchange nor dealt in on the Unlisted Securities Market (now the AIM) or the trading company or holding company is the transferor's personal company (s. 165(2)).

'Personal company' is defined in the same way as for retirement relief (see para. 22.2.3.7).

Both the transferor and the recipient must jointly elect for hold-over relief to apply (s. 165(1))[21] and both parties must be resident or ordinarily resident in the United Kingdom (s. 166(1)). If the recipient becomes non-resident within six years of the transfer, the held-over gain is deemed to accrue immediately before that event (s. 168). There are exclusions if the recipient emigrates to work abroad or if he resumes his residence in the United

---

[17.] Election was only possible if the recipient was resident or ordinarily resident in the United Kingdom. This condition was necessary to ensure that hold-over relief was not used as a way of transferring assets out of the scope of UK capital gains tax.

[18.] It seemed that the government were justified in this. See, for example, Institute of Fiscal Studies, *Reforming Capital Gains Tax* (1988) which notes at para. 1.4.33 that gift relief 'has become a device well used for avoiding CGT'.

[19.] This restriction to gifts of business assets has been criticised by, inter alia, the Law Society in its representations on the Finance Bill 1989 on the basis that gifts of non-business assets are now effectively taxed on an accruals, not a realisations, basis.

[20.] The reason for permitting hold-over relief where there is an immediate charge to inheritance tax on the transfer is to avoid the supposed 'double tax charge' of inheritance and capital gains tax. This ignores the fact that the policy underlying inheritance and capital gains tax is different, i.e., one aims to tax transfers of wealth while the other taxes increases in capital values.

[21.] However, if the recipients are the trustees of a settlement, only the transferor need make the election; s. 165(1)(b).

Kingdom without disposing of the asset within three years of the emigration (s. 168(5)).[22] The transferor may be made liable for any resulting tax which remains unpaid after 12 months (s. 168(7)).

Relief operates by reducing the amount of the transferor's chargeable gain and the recipient's acquisition cost by the amount of the held-over gain. If there is actual consideration for the transfer, the amount of the held-over gain is reduced by the amount by which the consideration exceeds the 'sums allowable as a deduction under section 38' of the TCGA. The taxpayer is thus taxed immediately on that part of his gain for which he has received consideration and only the balance is held over and passed to the recipient (s. 165(7)). As the held-over gain is not limited to the excess of the actual consideration over the *indexed* acquisition cost, the benefit of indexation is effectively transferred to the recipient. Apportionments will be made if the asset has not been used throughout the period of ownership for the purposes of the taxpayer's trade, profession or vocation (para. 5, sch. 7). As with retirement relief, in the case of share disposals, the proportion of the gain entitled to relief is that which the chargeable business assets bear to all the chargeable assets of the company (para. 7, sch. 7).[23]

Example
Andrew acquires an asset for £20,000 and uses it for the purposes of his business. He subsequently incorporates his business and sells the asset to the company for £24,000 at a time when the market value is £35,000. Suppose that since he acquired the asset 10% inflation has occurred. The held-over gain is therefore £35,000 − £(20,000 + 2,000) = £13,000. As, however, the actual consideration exceeds Andrew's acquisition cost of £20,000, the held-over gain is reduced by that excess, i.e., £13,000 − (£24,000 − £20,000) = £9,000. The gain arising immediately to Andrew is £13,000 − £9,000 = £4,000 and the acquisition cost of the asset acquired by the company is £35,000 − £9,000 = £26,000.

Since the recipient takes on the potential liability for capital gains tax, there may be cases where it is preferable not to elect for hold-over relief such as where the transferor has available his full annual exemption but the recipient is likely to use his exemption each year in respect of other asset disposals. Further, where the gain would have been reduced by the transferor's annual exemption or allowable losses there is a disadvantage as it is not possible to elect for partial hold-over. However, where retirement relief is available on the disposal of the asset, that relief is given first and only the balance of the chargeable gain is deducted from the recipient's acquisition cost (para. 8, sch. 7).

---

[22] Hold-over relief is not available if, at the outset, the transferee is not resident in the UK or is a company controlled by non-residents who are connected with the transferor; ss. 166 and 167.
[23] But this restriction only applies if the transferor could exercise at least 25% of the voting power at any time within the preceding 12 months or the company was his personal company at any time within the period.

22.3.2 Incorporation of a business

The incorporation of a business, whereby a business is transferred to a company in exchange for shares in that new company, is a disposal of chargeable assets so a chargeable gain may crystallise. To prevent tax considerations from discouraging individuals to incorporate their businesses, a roll-over relief is available (s. 162, TCGA). The relief applies where:

(a) the business (not just the assets of the business) is transferred to a company as a going concern;
(b) the business is transferred by an individual or individuals;
(c) the transfer is wholly or partly in exchange for shares issued by the company to the transferor; and
(d) the business is transferred with the whole of the assets of the business or the whole of the assets other than cash (s. 162(1)).[24]

The use of the word 'business' in this relief is slightly odd since the concept usually employed is 'trade, profession or vocation'.[25] There is no definition of 'business' in either the TA or the TCGA although it is a key term in the context of value added tax. In *American Leaf Blending Co. Sdn Bhd* v *Director General of Inland Revenue* [1978] STC 561 Lord Diplock said:

> 'Business' is a wider concept than 'trade'; and in the *Hanover Agencies* case ([1967] 1 AC 681) the Board uttered a warning against seeking to apply [judicial dicta on the meaning of the word 'trade'] outside the narrow context of British income tax law and in particular that of Schedule D.

But having said that business is a wider concept than trade, the question remains as to what activities fall within its scope apart from those that comprise a trade. In the context of excess profits duty Rowlatt J referred to business as 'an active occupation . . . continuously carried on' (*IRC* v *Marine Steam Turbine* (1920) 12 TC 171). This might mean that mutual trading activities which are not chargeable to tax under Schedule D, Case I (see para. 9.7) would constitute a business for the purposes of roll-over relief on incorporation.

Roll-over relief will only be available if the business is transferred as a going concern. Difficulties have arisen when businesses which have poor future prospects are incorporated. In a Scottish case, *Gordon* v *IRC* [1991] STC 174, the taxpayer farmed land in partnership with his wife. He decided that the business was not viable and that he should sell the land and purchase a smaller estate elsewhere. In order to buy out his brother (who was a part owner of the land) the partners formed a company and contracted to sell the farming business to it as a going concern, although in the meantime

---

[24.] The reason for the requirement that all the assets of the business must be transferred is to prevent the avoidance of stamp duty by excluding from the transfer assets which can only be transferred by means of a stampable document.
[25.] Cf. retirement relief which also uses the concept of 'business'; see para. 22.2.3.7.

negotiations were in progress for the sale of the farmland. Contracts for the sale of the land were concluded shortly afterwards with the result that, at the time the new company took over the farming business, it was known that the business of farming on that land would come to an end very shortly afterwards. It was held that the existence of a planned move of the entire assets of the business from one place to another was not inconsistent with the continuation of the trade. On the facts, the true and only reasonable conclusion was that the company had received the business as a going concern and had the ability to continue with it as it saw fit. The Lord President said:

> The words 'going concern' do not in themselves carry any implication about what may happen in the future or about the length of time which the business must remain in that condition once it has been taken over by the transferee. It has been said that: 'to describe an undertaking as a going concern imports no more than that, at the point of time at which the description applies, its doors are open for business, that it is active and operating, and perhaps also that it has all the plant etc. which is necessary to keep it in operation, as distinct from its being only an inert aggregation of plant.'

The Lord President also agreed with Widgery J in *Kenmir* v *Frizzell* [1968] 1 WLR 329 that the vital question was whether the transfer put the transferee in possession of a going concern such that the activities of that going concern could be carried on without interruption.

When roll-over relief on the incorporation of a business is available, the gain on the disposal of the business is deducted from the acquisition cost of the shares received in consideration for the transfer of the business. Where the consideration consists partly of shares and partly of other consideration, such as cash, the rolled-over gain is reduced. The whole gain is multiplied by the formula A/B where A is the cost of the shares received by the transferor and B is the value of the whole of the consideration received by the transferor in exchange for the business. The result of this calculation is allocated to the shares and is rolled-over. The unrelieved gain is allocated to the other consideration and is chargeable immediately. When the shares are eventually disposed of, the amount of the rolled-over gain is deducted from the cost of the shares and so becomes chargeable. Where more than one class of shares is issued the amount deducted must be apportioned in accordance with the market values of the shares at the time they are acquired by the transferor (s. 162(3)).

The assumption of any liabilities of the business by the company is not, in practice, treated as consideration for the transfer (ESC D32).[26] But the assumption of liabilities may affect the relief in another way since any gain may only be deferred to the extent that it is less than the cost of the shares.

---

[26] This Concession also makes it clear that if all the other conditions of s. 162 are satisfied, roll-over relief will not be precluded by the fact that not all liabilities of the business are taken over by the company.

Capital gains tax – losses, exemptions and reliefs

If the value of the business is reduced by the liabilities the company assumes with the result that the cost of the shares is reduced, full deferral may not be given.

Example
X purchased a retail business as a going concern in April 1982, paying £30,000 for the freehold premises, £10,000 for stock, debtors etc. and £5,000 for goodwill. In April 1988 X transferred his business to Y Ltd for a total consideration of £100,000 allocated as follows: £65,000 for the freehold premises, £23,000 for goodwill, and £12,000 for stock, debtors etc. The consideration was satisfied by 30,000 £1 preference shares in Y Ltd (market value par), 30,000 ordinary shares in Y Ltd (market value £2 per share) and £10,000 in cash. In March 1990, X sold his ordinary shares in Y Ltd for £70,000.

The chargeable gain on the disposal of chargeable assets (i.e., the land and the goodwill) to Y Ltd after indexation is £41,450. Using the A/B formula, the fraction is:

$$\frac{£30,000 + £60,000}{£100,000} \times £41,450 = £37,305$$

Thus X must pay capital gains tax on the transfer of his business on £4,145 (i.e., £41,450 – £37,305). On the subsequent disposal of the ordinary shares, part of the rolled-over gain of £37,305 will become chargeable. The £37,305 is apportioned between the ordinary and the preference shares. The 30,000 preference shares were valued at a total of £30,000 and the 30,000 ordinary shares were valued at £60,000, so £12,435 of the gain is apportioned to the preference shares and £24,870 to the ordinary shares. The acquisition cost of the 30,000 ordinary shares is accordingly £35,130 (i.e., £60,000 – £24,870) and on a disposal of those shares for £70,000 a gain of £34,840 arises.

22.3.3 Replacement of business assets

The rationale of roll-over relief was expounded by Goulding J in *Anderton* v *Lamb* [1981] STC 43):

> The general idea of relief is that if a trader disposes of trade assets and promptly applies the proceeds in the acquisition of new trade assets, generically similar to those disposed of, then the payment of tax in respect of any capital gain on the disposal of the old assets may be deferred or eliminated by, in effect, treating the new assets as substituted for and standing in the place of, the old.

Roll-over relief is available in relation to the following:

(a) a trade, profession, vocation, office or employment;
(b) the discharge of the functions of a public authority;
(c) the occupation of woodlands on a commercial basis;
(d) the activities of a body of persons which are carried out otherwise than for profit and are wholly or mainly directed to the protection or promotion of the interests of its members in the carrying out of their trade or profession;
(e) the activities of an unincorporated association or other body chargeable to corporation tax, being a body not established for profit whose activities are wholly or mainly carried on otherwise than for profit (s. 158(1)). This is extended by Concession to cases where assets are held by a company, the shares of which are held, wholly or apart from a very small proportion, by or on behalf of an unincorporated association or its members (ESC D15).

Relief will be available where a person carrying on one of the activities listed above disposes of an asset which has been used only for the purposes of that activity throughout his ownership of it and applies the consideration received to acquire a new asset for use only for the purposes of that activity.[27] The acquisition of the new asset must take place, or an unconditional contract for its acquisition must be entered into, during the period beginning 12 months before and ending three years after the disposal of the old asset (s. 152(3)).[28] The fact that the new asset may be acquired before the old asset is actually disposed of makes it clear that the requirement that the proceeds of sale be 'applied' in 'acquiring other assets' is not to be interpreted literally. According to the Revenue, it is sufficient if an amount equal to the disposal proceeds is reinvested in acquiring a replacement asset (Institute of Taxation Technical Information Release, October 1991). The method of financing the purchase of the new asset does not seem to be relevant. Where an unconditional contract is entered into within the specified time period, roll-over relief is given at once and the necessary adjustments to the taxpayer's assessment if, for example, the contract is subsequently cancelled, are made later (s. 152(4)).

Roll-over relief is only available for certain types of assets which must, in any event, be *capital* assets of the business. The assets which qualify for relief are:

(a) any building or part of a building and any permanent or semi-permanent structure in the nature of a building occupied (as well as used) only for the purposes of the trade;

---

[27] It was held in *Watton* v *Tippett* [1996] STC 101 that roll-over relief is not available on the disposal of part of a property purchased as a single asset. This is because the retained part of the property cannot be regarded as a 'new asset' for these purposes.
[28] The requirement that a new asset must be acquired has been substantially relaxed by Inland Revenue Concessions. For example, relief is available when: a qualifying partnership asset is partitioned on the dissolution of the partnership (ESC D23); the disposal proceeds are used to enhance an existing asset (ESC D22); and when proceeds are spent acquiring a further interest in an asset already used in the trade (ESC D25).

(b) any land occupied (as well as used) only for the purposes of the trade;
(c) fixed plant or machinery which does not form part of a building or of a permanent or semi-permanent structure in the nature of a building;
(d) ships, aircraft or hovercraft;
(e) goodwill;
(f) satellites, space stations and space vehicles (including launch vehicles);
(g) milk and potato quotas; and
(h) ewe and suckler cow premium quotas (s. 155).[29]

It is not necessary for the new and the old assets to be of the same type provided that both fall within one of the eight classes.

Full roll-over relief is available if the acquisition cost of the new asset equals or exceeds the actual disposal proceeds of the old asset so the consideration for the old asset is 'wholly applied' in acquiring the new asset. In such a case, the consideration for the disposal of the old asset is deemed to be such amount as ensures that neither a gain nor a loss accrues in respect of the old asset. The acquisition cost of the new asset is then reduced by the amount of the rolled-over gain.

Example

B buys a freehold trading premises in 1984 for £40,000. In 1990, B sold the premises for £95,000 and moved into new trading premises which cost him £150,000. In 1997 these second premises are sold off for £200,000. Ignoring any indexation allowances, B's capital gains tax liability will be:

	£
Proceeds of 1990 sale	95,000
Less acquisition cost	40,000
Gain	55,000

On this occasion, B will be treated as though he had sold the premises for £40,000 (resulting in no gain and no loss on the disposal) and the gain of £55,000 is rolled over.

	£
Proceeds of the 1997 sale	200,000
Less acquisition cost	150,000
held-over gain	55,000
	95,000
Chargeable gain	105,000

[29.] Land under (b) does not qualify if it is occupied for the purposes of a trade of dealing or developing land, unless the profit on the sale of the land would not constitute a profit of the trade; s. 156. This additional provision is arguably otiose since such non-qualifying land would constitute trading stock and would not fall within the capital gains tax regime on its disposal.

If the acquisition cost of the new asset is less than the disposal proceeds of the old asset so that the proceeds of disposal are only partly applied, a partial roll-over is available (s. 153). However, for a partial roll-over to be available at all, at least part of the gain must be used to acquire the other asset.[30] If no part of the gain is applied in acquiring the new asset, there is no roll-over relief. Where part of the gain has been so applied, the taxpayer may claim to be treated for capital gains tax purposes as if the actual gain on disposal of the old asset were reduced by the amount of the consideration applied in acquiring the new asset. So a tax charge arises on the amount of the gain not used to acquire the new asset and the acquisition cost of the new asset is reduced by the amount of the gain eligible for roll-over relief.

Example
S disposes of a qualifying business asset for £60,000, realising a chargeable gain (after indexation) of £20,000. He acquires a replacement asset for £50,000 and claims roll-over relief.

	£	£
Consideration not expended on new asset		60,000
		50,000
		10,000
Gain	20,000	
Less gain not expended on new asset	10,000	
Gain eligible for roll-over	10,000	
Adjusted base cost of new asset		
(£50,000 − £10,000)		40,000

The legislation contains no provisions for apportioning the gain when a gain is rolled-over against more than one item of qualifying expenditure. Presumably, the gain should be apportioned pro rata against the various items.[31] There is no requirement that either the new or the old assets are situated in the United Kingdom so a trader, who is within the charge to capital gains tax, may obtain roll-over relief in respect of the disposal or acquisition of non-UK assets.

The old asset must have been used throughout the period of ownership for the purposes of the qualifying activity. Mere intention to use the asset is insufficient. So in *Temperley* v *Visibell Ltd* [1974] STC 64 site visits coupled with an intention to occupy land were not sufficient to amount to using and occupying land for the purpose of this relief. An apportionment will be made if the asset has not been used for the purposes of the activity throughout the period of ownership (s. 152(7)) although if the taxpayer is carrying on two activities, either in succession or at the same time, they will be treated as a single activity for the purposes of this relief (s. 152(8)). The apportionment

---
[30] This is the consequence of the words 'less than the amount of the gain' in s. 153(1).
[31] *Butterworths UK Tax Guide 1995–96* para. 20:07 notes that this is the Revenue's favoured approach.

operates by notionally dividing the asset into two separate assets, one of which was wholly used in the trade, and applying the relief to that asset. Division is on the basis of time and the extent to which the asset was used.

Where the asset is acquired for use in the taxpayer's trade, it must not only be taken into immediate use in the trade[32] but must be acquired solely for that purpose and not, wholly or partly, for the purpose of realising a gain on its eventual disposal (ss. 152(1) and (5)).[33] Roll-over relief must be claimed and, as no time limit is specified in the TCGA, the time limits in s. 43, TMA will apply, so a six year claim period operates.

Where a taxpayer operates in a partnership, gains on his share of partnership assets can only be rolled over against his share of the consideration for the new assets. In *Todd* v *Mudd* [1987] STC 141 this principle became particularly apparent. The taxpayer disposed of an asset realising a chargeable gain. In a 75:25 partnership with his wife, he then purchased a property as tenants in common in the proportion of 75:25. The use of the property was 75% business and 25% personal. The taxpayer claimed to be able to set off his 75% contribution to the cost of the new asset. The Court held that he could not. As a tenant in common of the whole of the property, his roll-over relief was restricted to his 75% undivided share of 75% of the property used for the purposes of the business.

Where the trade is carried on by a personal company, but the person owning or replacing the asset is an individual, roll-over relief may be claimed (s. 157). The provision does not apply where the asset is held by another company (even a subsidiary of the personal company – *Taxline* 1991/26) nor if the company owns the asset and the individual carries on the trade. The old and new assets must both be used either for the trade of the individual or for the trade of the company. It is not possible to roll over gains realised by the individual against expenditure incurred by the company or vice versa.

Finally, roll-over relief is modified if the new asset is a depreciating asset, a wasting asset or one which will become a wasting asset within ten years (s. 154). In such a case the gain is not rolled-over but is deferred. The rolled-over gain will be triggered not only on the disposal of the new asset but on the tenth anniversary of its acquisition or on its ceasing to be used in the trade before disposal, whichever event comes first.

22.3.4 Reinvestment relief

A new relief from capital gains tax was introduced in 1993 for individuals who reinvest their chargeable gains in 'qualifying investments' (Chapter IA,

---

[32.] Again, the strictness of this requirement is relaxed in practice. By ESC D24, a new asset may still qualify for relief if the owner intends to incur capital expenditure in enhancing its value, and that work begins as soon as possible after the acquisition of the asset and will be completed in a reasonable time. The asset must be taken into use as soon as the improvements are completed and must not be used for any non-trading purpose in the interim.

[33.] This is a rather strange requirement since taxpayers will not, generally, be acquiring trading assets in the expectation that they will realise a loss on their eventual sale. The provision is perhaps simply directed at ensuring that the assets are not acquired as investments.

TCGA). Originally the gain had to be realised on the disposal of shares in specified categories of company, but the relief has been extended for disposals on or after 30 November 1993 and now applies in respect of any chargeable gain (s. 91 and sch. 11, FA 1994).

'Qualifying investments' are eligible shares in qualifying companies which are, broadly, ordinary shares in unquoted trading companies or in the holding company of a trading group (ss. 164A(8), 164G and 164I, TCGA). As with roll-over relief on the replacement of business assets, the reinvestment must take place one year before or three years after the disposal giving rise to the chargeable gain (s. 164A(9)). This means that there is no requirement that the actual disposal proceeds are used. All that is required is that an amount equal to the chargeable gain is reinvested. The previous prohibition on reinvestment in companies which hold more than half their assets in land or farming companies was lifted in the Chancellor's 1994 Budget.[34] Further relaxations were made in the Finance Act 1997 so that trading groups can contain a non-resident subsidiary (although the group as a whole must conduct its trade wholly or mainly in the UK) and the qualifying activities of the group members will be judged on a group, rather than company by company, basis. A clearance procedure has also been introduced so that companies can check in advance that their shares will qualify for relief. There is no longer a minimum holding of shares in order to take advantage of the relief. Reinvestment relief is given in priority to retirement relief (s. 164BA).

The deferred gain is brought into charge if the shareholder emigrates within three years of acquisition or if the company ceases to meet the qualifying conditions within three years of the investment being made (s. 164F). Relief is not available if at the outset:

(a) arrangements exist for the reacquisition or other disposal of the shares; or

(b) arrangements exist for the cessation of the company's trade or the disposal of a substantial amount of its business assets; or

(c) the shareholders are guaranteed a return of the whole or part of their investment (s. 164L(1)).

22.3.5 Spouses

As with income tax, since the 1990/91 year of assessment, spouses have been charged separately on their capital gains. Where assets are held jointly, each spouse is treated as owning a proportionate share and the proceeds and costs are apportioned accordingly.[35] Each spouse has a separate annual exemption and the capital losses of one spouse cannot be offset against the capital gains of the other spouse.

[34.] Section 46, FA 1995 which provides that s. 164H, TCGA is to be ignored for acquisitions of qualifying investments on or after 29 November 1994.
[35.] Where the couple have declared that any income from the property is held by them in unequal shares for the purposes of income tax the Revenue will presume that this split also holds for capital gains tax (Inland Revenue Press Release 21 November 1990).

Capital gains tax – losses, exemptions and reliefs

Where spouses transfer assets to one another, the general capital gains tax rules would say that as spouses are connected persons (s. 286(2), TCGA and see para. 21.2.1) any disposals between them are made at market value (ss. 17(1), 18(1) and (2)). However, if a married woman is living with her husband, a disposal from one to the other is treated as if the asset was acquired by the recipient spouse for a consideration which secures that no gain and no loss accrues to the disposing spouse (s. 58(1)).[36] Any indexation allowance is taken into account in computing the acquiring spouse's cost of acquisition (s. 56(2)).[37]

22.3.6 Venture capital trusts

The Finance Act 1995 contained provisions for the creation of a new type of investment company called a 'venture capital trust' to invest in unquoted trading companies. To qualify as a venture capital trust in its most recent accounting period:

(a) the company's income must have been derived wholly or mainly from shares or securities;
(b) at least 70% (by value) of the company's investments must have been in shares or securities in 'qualifying holdings';
(c) at least 50% of the qualifying holdings must have been in holdings of 'eligible shares' (broadly, shares carrying no preferential rights);
(d) no holding in any company (other than another venture capital trust) amounts to more than 15% of the value of the company's investments;
(e) the company's ordinary share capital is quoted on the London Stock Exchange;
(f) the company has not retained more than 15% of the income it obtained during the accounting period from shares or securities (s. 70(2), FA 1995).

Companies which meet all these conditions, and which continue to meet the conditions in the accounting period in which the application to become a venture capital trust is made, may be approved as venture capital trusts by the Inland Revenue (s. 70(3)). Once approved, individual investors who are aged 18 or over and who hold shares in a venture capital trust can take the benefit of various tax incentives. These include:

(a) exemption from capital gains tax on the disposal of shares in a venture capital trust;
(b) the ability to roll over gains into the acquisition cost of new shares in a venture capital trust provided that the acquisition of new shares is made in

---

[36] This section does not, however, apply to the disposal of an asset from trading stock of one of the spouses or if the disposal is by way of *donatio mortis causa*; s. 58(2).
[37] However, if the disposal by the disposing spouse would have resulted in a loss which is partly attributed to indexation, and the disposal is made after 30 November 1993, then the indexation allowance is deducted from the loss and the deemed consideration for the disposal adjusted accordingly.

the period beginning 12 months before and ending 12 months after the disposal which gave rise to the chargeable gain;

(c) income tax relief on dividends from ordinary shares to the extent that the shares acquired in each year do not exceed £100,000;

(d) income tax relief at 20% on up to £100,000 subscribed for new shares in any tax year provided the shares are held for at least five years.

CHAPTER TWENTY THREE
Capital gains tax on death

23.1 CAPITAL GAINS TAX ON DEATH

When someone dies their assets vest in their personal representatives. The personal representatives are treated as a single and continuing body of persons as distinct from the individuals who from time to time hold office (s. 62(3), TCGA). However, the assets are deemed not to have been disposed of by the deceased on death so no charge to capital gains tax arises (s. 62(1)(b)). The personal representatives of the deceased are deemed to acquire all the assets that the deceased was competent to dispose of at his death[1] for a consideration equal to their market value at the date of death (s. 62(1)(a)).[2] The result is that there is a tax free 'uplift' in the acquisition cost of assets comprised in the deceased's estate. Similarly, no chargeable gain accrues if a person disposes of assets by way of *donatio mortis causa* – that is, a gift by delivery of the asset in contemplation of death on the condition

---

[1.] This will include all assets which the deceased could have disposed of by will assuming that he or she was of full age and capacity, was domiciled in England and that the assets were situated in England. The severable share in any assets to which the deceased was beneficially entitled as a joint tenant immediately before his or her death are included; s. 62(10). However, in interpreting the phrase 'competent to dispose of at his death', it was held in *Marshall* v *Kerr* [1994] STC 638 that this did not include a settlement made by a residuary beneficiary while the administration of the estate was still in progress. This was because what the beneficiary had settled was a chose in action namely her right to the due administration of the estate, not any of the assets comprised within it.

[2.] If the asset has been valued for the purposes of a charge to inheritance tax on the death, the market value of the asset for capital gains tax purposes will be the inheritance tax valuation; s. 274, TCGA. If the value of the asset is not ascertained for inheritance tax purposes (because, for example, no inheritance tax is payable on the death) the normal capital gains tax valuation rules will apply; Inland Revenue, *Tax Bulletin*, April 1995, pp. 209–210.

(express or implied) that the gift becomes effective on the donor's death (s. 62(5)). The donee takes the gift at its market value at the date of death (ss. 62(4) and 64(2)).

If in the year an individual dies, he or she had allowable losses in excess of chargeable gains, those losses may be rolled back and set against the deceased's chargeable gains for the preceding three years of assessment taking later years first (s. 62(2)).

For the most part, a charge to inheritance tax will be imposed on the value of the deceased's estate and this is discussed in Chapters 31 to 34. However, the exemption from capital gains tax applies whether or not inheritance tax is imposed. This has not always been the position. Between 1965 (when capital gains tax was first introduced) and 1971, both capital gains tax and estate duty (a predecessor of inheritance tax) were payable on a person's death. The capital gains tax paid was then allowed as a deduction in computing the value of the estate for estate duty purposes. The current total exemption from capital gains tax on death has been criticised; it has been said that allowing an exemption from capital gains tax on death 'is equivalent to forgiving overdue income tax and is in the same sense illogical: capital gains tax is a payment in arrears of tax on income' (Institute for Fiscal Studies, *Death: The Unfinished Business* (1988), para. 1.4.2). Nevertheless it is not difficult to foresee the political difficulties that would arise for any government minded to reintroduce capital gains tax on death; particularly given that private housing forms a large proportion of inherited wealth and taxpayers have become used to the favourable tax treatment of such assets.

23.2 CAPITAL GAINS ACCRUING DURING ADMINISTRATION OF THE ESTATE

Since the disposal of assets to those entitled on the death is not an occasion of charge for capital gains tax purposes, no chargeable gain accrues when the personal representatives dispose of assets to a legatee (s. 62(4)(a)). The legatee is treated as if the personal representatives' acquisition of the asset had been his acquisition (s. 62(4)(b)). Thus, the legatee's acquisition cost is the market value of the asset at the date of the deceased's death. For these purposes, a 'legatee' includes any person taking under a will or codicil or on an intestacy or partial intestacy, whether he takes beneficially or as trustee (s. 64(2)) and an acquisition 'as legatee' includes any asset appropriated by the personal representatives in or towards satisfaction of a pecuniary legacy or any other interest or share in the property devolving under the will, codicil or intestacy (s. 64(3)). Any gain accruing while the asset is in the hands of the personal representatives will accordingly be charged on the legatee when he disposes of it.

Any other disposals by the personal representatives during the administration of the estate will give rise to capital gains tax charged on the personal representatives in the usual way. So if the personal representatives sell assets which have appreciated in value since the deceased's death, a capital gains tax charge will arise. The personal representatives' motives for the disposal are irrelevant. The tax charge will fall on the personal representatives unless a beneficiary is absolutely entitled to the asset as against the personal representatives (*Prest* v *Bettinson* [1980] STC 607).[3] The personal representatives are treated as having the same residence, ordinary residence and domicile as the deceased at the time of his death (s. 62(3)). However, they are not treated as individuals (s. 65(2)) and accordingly they pay capital gains tax only at the basic rate of income tax (s. 4(1)). By Extra-statutory Concession D5, personal representatives are entitled to the main residence exemption when they dispose of a house which before and after the deceased's death was used as the only and main residence of individuals entitled under the will or intestacy rules to the whole (or substantially the whole) of the proceeds of the house either absolutely or for life.

Personal representatives are entitled to the annual exemption from capital gains tax for the year the deceased dies and the two following years of assessment (s. 3(7)). For the 1997–98 year of assessment this annual exemption is £6,500. Any remaining tax due from personal representatives may be assessed and charged on any one or more of the personal representatives, excluding a person who is not resident or ordinarily resident in the United Kingdom (s. 65(1)). The personal representatives may deduct the tax paid by them from the assets and effects of the deceased (ss. 74 and 77, TMA).

23.2.1 Change of personal representatives

If there is a change of personal representatives, the assets held by the former personal representatives will have to be transferred to the new ones. However, as was noted in para. 23.1, s. 62(3), TCGA provides that personal representatives are treated as a single and continuing body of persons distinct from the persons who may from time to time hold office. There is thus no disposal of assets for capital gains tax purposes on a change of personal representatives.

23.2.2 Variations and disclaimers

The dispositions effected by the deceased in his will or by the law of intestacy may be varied or disclaimed by the legatees. Provided such variation or disclaimer is made by the legatees in a written instrument within two years of the deceased's death and the Inland Revenue are notified in writing within six months of the instrument being made (or such longer period as they may allow), the variation or disclaimer is not a disposal for the purposes of the TCGA. A variation is treated as though it had been effected by the deceased and a disclaimer is treated as though it resulted in the disclaimed benefit never having been conferred (s. 62(6) and (7)).[4] This provision does not apply, however, if the variation or disclaimer is made for money or money's worth (s. 62(8)).

[3.] It has been held that a residuary legatee is not absolutely entitled as against the personal representatives during the administration of the estate; *Cochrane* v *IRC* [1974] STC 335.

[4.] However these deeming provisions apply only to assets which the deceased was competent to dispose of at his death and does not affect other provisions of the TCGA; *Marshall* v *Kerr*, footnote 1 above.

CHAPTER TWENTY FOUR
Capital gains tax and settlements

24.1 INTRODUCTION

As with income tax, the policy underlying the capital gains taxation of trusts is not clear. Depending on the circumstances, either the settlor, the trustees or the beneficiaries may be taxed. Further the legislation talks in terms of 'settlements' as opposed to trusts, yet does not define what is meant by a settlement. Instead, there is a definition of 'settled property' and this definition is discussed in para. 24.2.

24.2 SETTLED PROPERTY

Section 68, TCGA provides:

> ... 'settled property' means any property held in trust other than property to which section 60 [of the TCGA] applies.

Property is therefore settled when it is held on trust, subject to exceptions. The difficulties arise with these exceptions. Section 60(1) provides:

> In relation to assets held by a person as nominee for another person, or as trustee for another person absolutely entitled as against the trustee, or for any person who would be so entitled but for being an infant or other person under disability (or for 2 or more persons who are or would be jointly so entitled), this Act shall apply as if the property were vested in, and the acts of the nominee or trustee in relation to the assets were the acts of, the person or persons for whom he is the nominee or trustee (acquisitions from

Capital gains tax and settlements

or disposals to him by that person or persons being disregarded accordingly).

The idea is that nominees and bare trustees are ignored for the purposes of capital gains tax. Nominees do not cause too much difficulty. Although not defined, presumably a person is a nominee when property is vested in him or her for the absolute benefit of another but he has no active duties to perform in relation to that property.

According to s. 60(1) there will be a bare trust when the beneficiary is 'absolutely entitled as against the trustee'. By s. 60(2), a person is absolutely entitled as against the trustees when he or she:

> . . . has the exclusive right, subject only to satisfying any outstanding charge, lien or other right of the trustees to resort to the asset for payment of duty, taxes, costs or other outgoings, to direct how that asset shall be dealt with.[1]

The following propositions may be formulated from the decided cases on the scope of s. 60.

24.2.1 A beneficiary is absolutely entitled if he has a right to call for a conveyance

The right to call for a conveyance of the trust property would seem to meet the test set out in s. 60. Where there is a single absolutely entitled beneficiary who is *sui juris*, or all the beneficiaries are absolutely entitled *sui juris* beneficiaries, they can direct the trustees to transfer the trust property to them and therefore the property is not settled property. However, where the person absolutely entitled only has a *share* in trust property, his right to call for that share to be transferred to him may depend on the nature of the trust property. In *Stephenson* v *Barclays Bank Trust Co. Ltd* [1975] STC 151, it was said by Walton J (at pp. 163–4):

> When the situation is that a single person who is *sui juris* has an absolutely vested beneficial interest in a share of the trust fund, his rights are not, I think, quite as extensive as those of the beneficial holders as a body. In general, he is entitled to have transferred to him . . . an aliquot share of each and every asset of the trust fund which presents no difficulty as far as division is concerned. This will apply to such items as cash, money at the bank or an unsecured loan, Stock Exchange securities and the like.

---

[1] It has been argued (see Thomas, *Taxation and Trusts*, Sweet & Maxwell (1981)) that this definition may be founded on a misconception. A beneficiary has no general right to direct a trustee how to deal with an asset even if he is 'absolutely entitled'. As a *sui juris* beneficiary he can terminate the trust on the *Saunders* v *Vautier* (1841) Cr. & Ph. principle, but as long as the trust continues in existence, he cannot direct the trustees how to act or control the exercise of their powers or discretions, *Re Londonderry's Settlement* [1965] Ch 918 and *Re Brockbank* [1948] Ch 206.

However, as regards land, certainly, in all cases, as regards shares in very special circumstances (see *In Re Weiner's Will Trusts* [1956] 1 WLR 579) and possibly (although the logic of the addition in fact escapes me) mortgage debts[2] (see *In Re Marshall per* Cozens-Hardy MR [1914] 1 Ch 192 at p. 199) the situation is not so simple, and even a person with a vested interest in possession in an aliquot share of the trust fund may have to wait until the land is sold and so forth before being able to call upon the trustees as of right to account to him for his share of the assets.

The basis of the exceptional treatment of land is that an 'undivided share of real estate never fetches quite its proper proportion of the proceeds of sale of the entire estate; therefore, to allow an undivided share to be elected to be taken as real estate by one of the beneficiaries would be detrimental to the other beneficiaries' (*Re Marshall* above). The exceptional circumstances which apply to shares include the case of a private company in which the trust holds the majority of shares so that the transfer to one beneficiary of his share might prejudice the interests of other beneficiaries (*Re Sandeman* [1937] 1 All ER 368 and *Re Weiner* above).

Thus in *Crowe v Appleby* [1975] STC 502[3] it was held, at first instance, that where a beneficiary under a settlement of real property was absolutely entitled to his share while others had only life interests, the property remained settled property. Goff J said that the case law showed 'a clear distinction' between trusts of realty and personalty.[4] Nevertheless, in *Stephenson v Barclays Bank Trust Co.* Walton J had commented that the scheme of the capital gains tax legislation was to 'treat all assets alike' and that it would be 'extremely curious' if, by reason of the different natures of the assets when a person becomes entitled to an aliquot share of a trust fund, some were treated in one way and some in another for the purposes of tax. It may well be that a higher court would take a different view if faced with the point again and some support for this can be gained from the later case law. In *Booth v Ellard* [1980] STC 555, 45% of the issued share capital in a family company held by members of the family was transferred to trustees. Restrictions were placed upon the disposal of the settled shares but it was nevertheless held that the shares were not settled property. Each beneficiary was entitled to the same rights as every other beneficiary in proportion to the size of his original holding and could direct the trustees how to exercise the voting rights attached to the shares. Each beneficiary could sell his interest subject to a right of pre-emption and the beneficiaries could, by unanimous act, put an end to the settlement at any time. In *Jenkins v Brown* [1989] STC 577 a father, his three sons and two daughters pooled 1,680 acres of land in a trust to which all

---

[2]. The addition of mortgages was explained by Goff J in *Crowe v Appleby* [1975] STC 502 at p. 510 as being because they include not only the debt but also the estate and powers of the mortgagee.

[3]. Affirmed *Crowe v Appleby* [1976] STC 301 on other grounds, the Court of Appeal declining to express a concluded view on this point.

[4]. Cf. the position under Scottish law where the right to bring an action for the division and sale of property is a necessary incident of common property so that beneficiaries in similar circumstances would be absolutely entitled as against the trustee.

were equally entitled. Later some of the contributors wished to recover some of the land they had contributed. This was done by deed of rearrangement. It was held by Knox J that the property was not settled because the interests of the beneficiaries as a mass precisely reflected their beneficial proprietary interests prior to the creation of the trust and those interests remained unaffected by the deed of rearrangement. Since the property had, by virtue of s. 60, always belonged to the beneficiaries there could be no disposal by them and no charge to capital gains tax.

In *Pexton* v *Bell* [1976] STC 301,[5] a decision on the meaning of what is now s. 72, TCGA, Sir John Pennycuick said that the Court could look to the reality of the situation and ignore the subtle technicalities of the law relating to the equitable interests of owners of undivided shares in land. This approach fits with that espoused by Lord Wilberforce in *Aberdeen Construction Group Ltd* v *IRC* [1978] STC 127, that the guiding principle underlying the interpretation of the TCGA ought to be to tax the gain arrived at by applying normal business principles.

24.2.2 A beneficiary is absolutely entitled if infancy is the only bar to his entitlement

Section 60(1), TCGA provides that property is not settled if it is held by the trustees for a person who would be absolutely entitled but for being an infant.[6] This does not, however, cover the common case where property is held on trust for an infant, contingent on attaining 18 years of age or marrying before that time. This is because it was held in *Tomlinson* v *Glyn's Settlement and Trustee Co.* [1970] Ch 112, that infancy must be the *only* bar to absolute entitlement. If the beneficiary's entitlement is subject to an additional contingency, such as reaching a certain age (even the age of majority), s. 60 does not apply and the property remains settled. Were the position to be otherwise, the infant could be charged to capital gains tax on the disposal of property he might never acquire since he might die before reaching 18. The correct approach according to Lord Denning MR in *Tomlinson* is to:

> take the time the capital gain was made and ask the question: 'if he was not an infant at that time, would he be absolutely entitled to call for his money so as to be able to give directions to the trustees and to give a good receipt to them?' In short: is infancy the only bar?[7]

[5.] A case joined with *Crowe* v *Appleby* on appeal. For discussion of the point decided in that appeal see para. 24.8.2.

[6.] Section 1(6), Law of Property Act 1925 provides: 'A legal estate is not capable of . . . being held by an infant.'

[7.] Query what would be the capital gains tax analysis if the beneficiary in this example had married at 17, thus satisfying the contingency while still an infant. The conservative view is that there is a disposal on his becoming absolutely entitled under s. 71(1), TCGA although the contrary has been argued (Wheatcroft [1969] *BTR* 63) on the basis that in *Tomlinson* Cross J took the view that a deemed disposal by a trustee under s. 71(1) must be construed by reference to s. 60(1) so that 'absolutely entitled' in s. 71(1) does *not* include the case of an infant whose interest became vested while he is still an infant.

24.2.3 Persons are absolutely entitled if they are jointly absolutely entitled

According to s. 60(1), TCGA, property will not be settled if two or more persons are jointly absolutely entitled or would be if they were not infants. In *Kidson v Macdonald* [1974] Ch 339, John and Edwin Mawle held land on trust for sale, to hold the net proceeds of sale on trust for themselves as tenants in common. It was argued that because they held the land as tenants in common rather than as joint tenants, they were not 'jointly' entitled for the purposes of s. 60(1). Foster J disagreed, saying that although the words 'as joint tenants' had a technical meaning, the word 'jointly' was not a term of art in English real property law and 'jointly' should be given its ordinary meaning, namely, concurrently or in common. John and Edwin were therefore jointly absolutely entitled and the property was not settled because between them they held the entirety of the beneficial interest.

The requirement that the joint entitlement be concurrent excludes successive interests such as a life interest and a remainder. As Walton J said in *Stephenson v Barclays Bank Trust Co. Ltd*:

> the definition says 'jointly'; it does not say 'together' . . . If property is settled upon A for life with remainder to B, A and B are 'together' entitled absolutely as against the trustees, but they are not so entitled 'jointly', 'concurrently' or as 'tenants in common'.[8]

24.2.4 An annuity charged on property can make it settled property

In *Stephenson v Barclays Bank Trust Co. Ltd* a testator appointed the trust company to act as trustee of his estate. He directed that some of his income from that estate be used to pay annuities to his wife and each of his three daughters during widowhood, the remaining income to be accumulated and held with the capital of the estate on trust for his grandchildren in equal shares contingently on attaining 21 years of age. Two grandchildren attained that age, and each of the three daughters was alive and widowed. Walton J held that the grandchildren did not become absolutely entitled to the property as against the trustee while the entire estate was charged with the payment of annuities since the beneficial interest in the fund was divided between the grandchildren and the daughters.[9]

---

[8]. The decisions in *Kidson v MacDonald* and *Stephenson v Barclays Bank Trust Co.* clearly give sensible results since they prevent property held by joint tenants being converted into settled property by the simple expedient of one joint tenant giving the other notice of severance and, at the same time, ensure that settlements for living beneficiaries are still regarded as settlements despite the fact that the beneficiaries acting together could terminate the trust under the rule in *Saunders v Vautier*. But it has been argued that it is difficult to reconcile the two cases in the sense that if Foster J was right in *Kidson v MacDonald* to say that 'jointly' should be given its ordinary meaning, it is difficult to see why the equally ordinary meaning of 'jointly' as 'together' should have been excluded in *Stephenson v Barclays Bank Trust Co.* Nevertheless *Stephenson v Barclays Bank Trust Co.* was followed and applied in the later case of *Booth v Ellard* [1980] STC 555.

[9]. The annuities could not be described as 'outgoings' so as to fall within the exception in s. 60(2). The grandchildren only became absolutely entitled as against the trustees when, under a deed of family arrangement, part of the trust fund was appropriated to paying the daughters' annuities. Once that had been done the grandchildren were jointly entitled to the remaining residue of the estate.

24.3 TRANSFER INTO A SETTLEMENT

When a settlement is created, there will be a disposal of assets by the settlor to the trustees so that, on general principles, a charge to capital gains tax will arise. It is not possible for a settlor who declares himself trustee of certain property or becomes a beneficiary under his own settlement to argue that there has been no disposal or only a part disposal.[10] This is because of s. 70, TCGA which provides that:

> A transfer into settlement, whether revocable or irrevocable, is a disposal of the entire property thereby becoming settled property notwithstanding that the transferor has some interest as a beneficiary under the settlement and notwithstanding that he is a trustee, or the sole trustee, of the settlement.

The settlor is deemed to have disposed of the assets transferred into the settlement for a consideration equal to their market value (s. 17). If this results in a loss, then the Revenue view is that because the settlor and the trustees of the settlement are treated as connected persons (s. 286(3) and Inland Revenue, *Tax Bulletin*, Issue 6 February 1993), the loss can only be set against a chargeable gain accruing to the settlor in respect of a subsequent disposal of assets to the trustees of the same settlement (s. 18(3)).[11] For the purposes of this rule 'settlement' and 'settlor' have the same meaning as in Chapter IA of Part XV, TA (see Chapter 15).

24.4 SETTLOR'S LIABILITY TO TAX ON THE CAPITAL GAINS OF THE SETTLEMENT

With the alignment of capital gains and income tax rates in 1988, it might be thought attractive for a settlor with a marginal rate of tax of 40% to put property into a trust so that gains on it would be separately taxable (at lower rates) in the hands of the trustees and not taxed in his hands. To prevent this, if at any time during a year of assessment the settlor or his spouse has had an interest in the trust property, and gains have accrued to the trustees on a disposal of settled property, which after deducting losses (but not the annual exemption) leave a chargeable amount, that amount of gains will be treated as accruing to the settlor rather than the trustees and will be taxed accordingly (s. 77(1)).[12] Interests in a trust are widely defined for these purposes. They include any direct or indirect interest, and any circumstances in which

---

[10] A part disposal argument would be based on the premise that as trustee he would have legal ownership of the settled property, and as beneficiary he would have beneficial entitlement to it.
[11] This restriction does not apply if the disposal is by way of gift to a settlement if the gift and the income from it are wholly or primarily applicable for educational, cultural or recreational purposes and the persons benefiting from the application for those purposes are confined to members of an association of persons for whose benefit the gift was made, not being persons all or most of whom are connected persons; s. 18(4).
[12] The settlor may, however, recover the tax paid from the trustees; s. 78.

property or income from the trust may become applicable for the benefit of the settlor or his spouse, subject to limited specific exemptions such as the bankruptcy of the beneficiary (s. 77(2) and (8)). However, the settlor may only be taxed with regard to chargeable gains accruing on the disposal of property which originated from him (s. 79).

24.5 DISPOSALS BY TRUSTEES

Once the settlement has been created, the trustees may make disposals of trust property on three separate occasions. First, trustees may dispose of assets in the course of their management of the trust. Secondly, the trustees will be deemed to dispose of trust assets when a beneficiary becomes absolutely entitled to trust property. Thirdly, there will be a deemed disposal on the termination of a life interest in possession by the death of the person entitled provided that the property does not then cease to be settled property. Depending on which type of disposal has occurred, a charge to capital gains tax or simply an adjustment to the trustees' acquisition cost of the asset may result. These three occasions are discussed in paras 24.6 to 24.8.[13]

24.6 DISPOSAL OF TRUST ASSETS BY THE TRUSTEES

In accordance with general principles, when the trustees dispose of investments or other assets held by them as trustees, they will be liable to capital gains tax on any chargeable gains arising in the usual way.[14] If the disposal gives rise to an allowable loss, that loss may be set against chargeable gains of the same or subsequent years. Since the trustees are not 'individuals' they are subject to capital gains tax only at the basic rate of income tax (s. 4(1)). However, if the trust is an accumulation or discretionary settlement the rate of tax is the 'rate applicable to trusts' which is currently 34% (s. 5, TCGA and s. 686(1A), TA). A trust is an accumulation or discretionary trust wherever:

(a) all or any part of the income arising to the trustees in the year of assessment is income to which s. 686, TA applies (see para. 14.2.3); or

(b) all the income arising to the trustees in the year of assessment is treated as the income of the settlor, but s. 686 would apply if it were not so treated; or

(c) all the income arising during the year is used in defraying expenses of the trustees in that year, but would otherwise be subject to s. 686; or

---

[13]. The potential liability of settlors mentioned in para. 24.4 should not be forgotten.
[14]. Note that the Court of Appeal recently held that a settlor could orally declare himself trustee of 5% of his shareholding in a company without identifying or ascertaining which shares were subject to the trust; *Hunter v Moss* [1994] 1 WLR 452. Criticised as being out of step with previous trust law authorities which require the segregation of assets (see, inter alia, Hayton (1994) 110 *LQR* 335 and Oliver *KCLJ* 5 (1994–95) 139) the case currently raises the difficulty of identifying which shares have been disposed of if part only of the shares are subsequently sold. For a fuller discussion of tax issues see Shipwright, *The Tax Journal*, 19 May 1994.

(d) no income arises to the trustees in the year of assessment, but that section would apply if there were such income and none of it were treated as the income of the settlor or applied as mentioned in (c).

As trustees are not individuals, they are not entitled to the annual exemption for capital gains tax. Instead they are entitled to a lower exemption calculated as half the annual exemption. For the 1997–98 year of assessment, the exemption for trustees is £3,250 (para. 2(2), sch. 1, TCGA and s. 3(2), TCGA).

The exemption from capital gains tax on the disposal of private residences is similarly restricted to individuals. However, it is extended to gains accruing to trustees by s. 225, TCGA if, during the period of ownership of the trustee, the dwelling-house has been the only or main residence of a person entitled to occupy it under the terms of the settlement. The words 'entitled under the terms of the settlement' were considered in *Sansom* v *Peay* [1976] 3 All ER 353. The taxpayers were the trustees of a discretionary settlement. They purchased a dwelling-house known as Wickwoods and allowed the beneficiaries to occupy it until it was disposed of by deed of exchange. On disposal, the trustees claimed the benefit of the main residence exemption. Brightman J upheld the claim saying:

> In this case the beneficiaries were in occupation of Wickwoods throughout the relevant period as their only or main residence. They were in occupation pursuant to the exercise by the trustees of a power expressly conferred by the settlement to permit those beneficiaries to go into occupation and remain in occupation. The trustees exercised that power, and the beneficiaries thereupon became entitled to go into occupation and continue in occupation until the permission was withdrawn. The trustees never did withdraw permission until they required vacant possession in order to complete the exchange. Therefore, in looking at the matter at the date of the disposal, the beneficiaries were persons who, in the events which happened, were entitled to occupy the house and did occupy it under the terms of the settlement.

Likewise retirement relief is extended to the trustees of a settlement who dispose of shares or securities in a company or an asset used or previously used for business purposes, provided that the shares, securities or asset form part of the settled property and certain other conditions are met (s. 164).[15] Extensions to the relief for gifts of business assets (para. 2, sch. 7,

---

[15] Broadly, the relief is available when a beneficiary who has an interest in possession (other than an interest for a fixed term) in the settled property retires at the age of 50 or before that age because of ill health and: (a) where the disposal is of shares or securities, the beneficiary was until his retirement a full-time working director of his personal trading company or his personal holding company of a trading group and the trustees are disposing of shares in that company; or (b) where the disposal is of a business asset, he was until his retirement carrying on the business in which the asset was used.

TCGA) and roll-over relief on reinvestment (s. 164B) are also available to trustees.

Capital gains tax in respect of chargeable gains accruing to trustees may be assessed and charged on any one or more of the trustees. But if tax is not assessed and charged on all the trustees, the persons assessed cannot include someone who is not resident or ordinarily resident in the United Kingdom (s. 65(1)).

24.6.1 Change of trustees

When the trustees of a settlement change, the settled assets will have to be transferred from the old trustees to the new trustees. There will therefore be a disposal of assets and, on general principles, a charge to capital gains tax could arise. Since it would be unfair to impose a charge to tax in such circumstances, s. 69(1), TCGA provides that:

> ... the trustees of the settlement shall for the purposes of this Act be treated as a single and continuing body of persons (distinct from the persons who may from time to time be the trustees) ...

Thus a disposal of trust assets by the old trustees to the new trustees is ignored for capital gains tax purposes.

24.7 ABSOLUTE ENTITLEMENT TO SETTLED PROPERTY

This is the second occasion of disposal by the trustees mentioned in para. 24.5. Section 71(1), TCGA provides:

> On the occasion when a person becomes absolutely entitled to any settled property as against the trustee all assets forming part of the settled property to which he becomes so entitled shall be deemed to have been disposed of by the trustee, and immediately reacquired by him in his capacity as a trustee within s. 60(1), for a consideration equal to their market value.

The reference in this subsection to absolute entitlement includes absolute entitlement but for infancy or other disability (s. 71(3)) and the meaning of absolute entitlement bears the meaning that it does in relation to settled property (s. 60(2)). A person will become absolutely entitled as against the trustee if settled assets are advanced to him either under the exercise of a discretion or pursuant to a power of advancement in the trust instrument or under s. 32, Trustee Act 1925. However, since the criterion is entitlement, not receipt, the person becoming absolutely entitled need not actually receive the trust assets. So if the beneficiary's interest is contingent on the happening of a certain event, such as attaining a specified age or being called to the Bar, the beneficiary becomes absolutely entitled as soon as the contingency is fulfilled even if the trustees do not actually transfer assets to him at that time.[16]

24.7.1 Creation of a new settlement

The decided cases on s. 71(1) have also established that the beneficiary need not become absolutely entitled as against the world. All that is required, as the section states, is that a person should become absolutely entitled 'as against the trustees' (*Hoare Trustees* v *Gardner* [1978] 1 All ER 791).[17] For example, in *Hart* v *Briscoe* (which was decided at the same time as *Hoare Trustees* v *Gardner* and is also reported at [1978] 1 All ER 791) the trustees of a settlement were directed to hold property for certain beneficiaries and they were given an absolute discretion to pay or apply any part of the capital for the benefit of any beneficiary. The settlor created a new settlement 17 years later with the same trustees as the original settlement. On the same day, the trustees of the original settlement declared that property subject to that settlement would thereafter be held on the trusts of the new settlement. The trustees were then assessed to capital gains tax under s. 71(1), on the basis that their declaration was a deemed disposal of assets of the original settlement. Brightman J held that the assessment had been correctly made; the trustees of the new settlement had become absolutely entitled as against themselves as trustees of the old settlement to the assets held under the original settlement.

The decision in *Hart* v *Briscoe* raises the spectre of a charge to capital gains tax under s. 71(1) whenever the trustees exercise their fiduciary powers so that the property is held on separate trusts for the benefit of a particular beneficiary or beneficiaries. However, since someone (usually the same or new trustees) needs to become absolutely entitled to all or part of the settled property as against the original trustees, a charge will only arise under s. 71 when the exercise of a fiduciary power constitutes the creation of a new settlement. The question which accordingly needs to be answered is: when is a new settlement created? Lord Wilberforce gave the following indication in *Roome* v *Edwards* [1981] 1 All ER 736:

> Since 'settlement' and 'trusts' are legal terms, which are also used by business men or laymen in a business or practical sense, I think that the question whether a particular set of facts amounts to a settlement should

---

[16.] Thus in *Stephenson* v *Barclays Bank Trust Co. Ltd* (para. 24.2.4) there was no absolute entitlement as against the trustees to the entirety of the fund where the fund was charged with the payment of an annuity. But when the fund was divided under the deed of family arrangement into two parts, one to provide the daughters' annuities and one to be held for the benefit of the grandchildren, Walton J held that the grandchildren became absolutely entitled as against the trustee to that part of the fund held for their benefit free from the payment of annuities.

[17.] The decision can be criticised since it is more natural to construe the phrase 'absolutely entitled' as requiring complete beneficial ownership in the property, and trustees can never be beneficial owners. This argument was rejected by Brightman J in *Hoare Trustees* v *Gardner* but his decision sits uneasily with cases such as *Stephenson* v *Barclays Bank Trust Co. Ltd* and *Tomlinson* v *Glyn's Settlement and Trustee Co.* (para. 24.2.2).

be approached by asking what a person, with knowledge of the legal context of the word under established doctrine and applying this knowledge in a practical and common-sense manner to the facts under examination would conclude. To take two fairly typical cases. Many settlements contain powers to appoint part or a proportion of the trust property to beneficiaries; some may also confer power to appoint separate trustees of the property so appointed, or such power may be conferred by law (see s. 37 of the Trustee Act 1925). It is established doctrine that the trusts declared by a document exercising a special power of appointment are to be read into the original settlement (see *Muir v Muir* [1943] AC 468). If such a power is exercised, whether or not separate trustees are appointed, I do not think it would be natural for such a person as I have presupposed to say that a separate settlement had been created, still less so if it were found that provisions of the original settlement continued to apply to the appointed fund, or that the appointed fund were liable, in certain events, to fall back into the rest of the settled property. On the other hand, there may be a power to appoint and appropriate a part or a portion of the trust property to beneficiaries and to settle it for their benefit. If such a power is exercised, the natural conclusion might be that a separate settlement was created, all the more so if a complete new set of trusts were declared to the appropriated property, and if it could be said that the trusts of the original settlement ceased to apply to it. There can be many variations of these cases each of which will have to be judged on its facts.

In *Bond v Pickford* [1983] STC 517, discretionary trustees allocated by deed part of the settled property to themselves to be held on trusts for some of the beneficiaries contingently on their attaining a specified age. The deeds of allocation expressly applied the terms of the original settlement relating to investment, the apportionment and remuneration of the trustees and the execution of the trusts and powers. The Court of Appeal held that the deeds did not render the trustees absolutely entitled as against themselves. Slade LJ said:

> ... there is in my opinion a crucial distinction to be drawn between (a) powers to alter the presently operative trust of a settlement which expressly or by necessary implication authorise the trustees to remove assets altogether from the original settlement (without rendering any person beneficially entitled to them); and (b) powers of this nature which do not confer on the trustees such authority. I will refer to these two different types of power as 'powers in the wider form' and 'powers in the narrower form'.

He continued:

> It is in my opinion particularly important to note the essential difference between the two 'fairly typical cases' mentioned by Lord Wilberforce [in *Roome v Edwards*], which I think is this. The first is the example of a fairly typical exercise of what I have described as a power in the narrower form.

The second is an example of a fairly typical exercise of a power in the wider form.

Following these decisions the Inland Revenue issued a Statement of Practice SP 7/84. This states that:

It is now clear that a deemed disposal under [s. 71(1), TCGA] cannot arise unless the power exercised by the trustees, or the instrument conferring the power, expressly or by necessary implication, confers on the trustees authority to remove assets from the original settlement by subjecting them to trusts of a different settlement. Such powers (which may be powers of advancement or appointment) are referred to by the Court of Appeal as 'powers in the wider form'. However, the Board considers that a deemed disposal will not arise when such a power is exercised and the trusts are declared in circumstances such that:

(a) the appointment is revocable; or
(b) the trusts declared of the advanced or appointed funds are not exhaustive so that there exists a possibility at the time when the advancement or appointment is made that the funds covered by it will on the occasion of some event cease to be held upon such trusts and once again come to be held upon the original trusts of the settlement.

Further, when such a power is exercised the Board considers it unlikely that a deemed disposal will arise when trusts are declared if duties in regard to the appointed assets still fall to the trustees of the original settlement in their capacity as trustees of that settlement, bearing in mind the provision in [s. 69(1), TCGA] that the trustees of a settlement form a single and continuing body (distinct from the persons who may from time to time be the trustees).

Finally, the Board accept that a power of appointment or advancement can be exercised over only part of the settled property and that the above consequences would apply only to that part.

24.7.2 Tax liability

Once a person has become absolutely entitled as against the trustee, the trustee is deemed by s. 71(1), TCGA to dispose of the assets to which that person is entitled and to reacquire the same assets for a consideration equal to their market value. The gain or loss arising on the deemed disposal and reacquisition is then computed in the usual way. The trustee reacquires the assets 'in his capacity as a trustee within s. 60(1)'. Since property held for a person absolutely entitled as against the trustee is not settled property for capital gains tax purposes, it is treated by s. 60(1) as though it were vested in the person absolutely entitled as against the trustee so there is no further charge to capital gains tax when the trustee actually transfers the assets to the person absolutely entitled. If tax payable by trustees is overdue by six months or more, and the asset in respect of which tax is due is transferred to a person who is absolutely entitled as against the trustees, that person may be assessed and charged to tax at any time within two years from the date when the tax became payable (s. 69(4)).

Some special situations must be noted. First, in accordance with the principle that capital gains are not chargeable as the result of a death, if the person who becomes absolutely entitled does so on the termination of a life interest in possession by the death of the life tenant, no chargeable gain is to accrue on the disposal (s. 73(1)(a)).[18] There will still be a deemed disposal and reacquisition of the assets at their then market value but that gain will not be chargeable. The person absolutely entitled on the death of the life tenant thus takes the benefit of the capital gains tax uplift discussed at para. 23.1 on the life tenant's death.[19] If the settled property reverts to the settlor on the death of the life tenant and the settlor becomes absolutely entitled as against the trustees, the deemed disposal is treated as though it were made for a consideration which resulted in neither a gain nor a loss (s. 73(1)(b)). Thus the unrealised gain is passed back to the settlor and is not absorbed tax free by the death of the life tenant.[20]

Secondly, when a person becomes absolutely entitled to settled property as against the trustee, any allowable but unrelieved losses which have accrued to the trustee in respect of that property can be passed on to the beneficiary who becomes absolutely entitled (s. 71(2)).[21]

24.8 TERMINATION OF A LIFE INTEREST IN POSSESSION ON DEATH

This is the third occasion of disposal by the trustees referred to in para. 24.5. The relevant provisions are contained in s. 72, TCGA and they apply 'on the termination, on the death of the person entitled to it, of a life interest in possession in all or any part of settled property'. The property must continue to be settled property after the death of the life tenant.

24.8.1 Meaning of 'life interest in possession'

A 'life interest', on general principles, means an interest in any income produced by the trust property which lasts for as long as the life of the beneficiary. Thus 'to A for life' means that A will benefit as long as he lives. Interests *pur autre vie* – 'to A for as long as B lives' so that A (or his estate) benefits for as long as B lives – are specifically included (s. 72(3)(a)). In these

---

[18.] Save where a chargeable gain was held-over on the creation of the settlement; s. 74.

[19.] If the life interest only affects part of the settled property, s. 73(1)(a) does not apply. Instead any chargeable gain is reduced in the proportion which that part of the settled property bears to the whole; s. 73(2).

[20.] This provision prevents the taxpayer from passing an asset which is likely to appreciate rapidly to an elderly life tenant so the taxpayer can take the benefit of the capital gains tax uplift on the life tenant's death.

[21.] Query how s. 18(3) which restricts the use of losses applies if the trustee and beneficiary are connected.

Capital gains tax and settlements 543

circumstances, however, s. 72(1) only applies to the death of the beneficiary (A) and not to the death of the 'life' or 'lives' (B) (s. 72(2)).

A right which is contingent on the exercise of the discretion of the trustee or of some other person is not a life interest so discretionary beneficiaries are excluded even if they receive an income from the settled property (s. 72(3)(b)).[22] Similarly, there can be no *life* interest in possession where the settlement is in favour of a beneficiary if (say) he attains 25 (although he will be entitled to the income of the settlement from the time he attains 18 under s. 31, Trustee Act 1925).

It is specifically provided that an entitlement to an annuity is not a life interest, even if it is payable out of or charged on the settled property unless (a) some or all of the settled property is appropriated by the trustees as a fund out of which the annuity is payable; (b) there is no right of recourse to settled property not so appropriated or the income thereof; and (c) during the lifetime of the annuitant the property so appropriated is treated for the purposes of s. 72 as settled property under a separate settlement (ss. 72(3)(c) and 72(4)).

An interest 'in possession' is not defined but generally a life interest is in possession when the person entitled to it has a present right of present enjoyment, that is, an immediate right to the income from, or the use or occupation of, the settled property in which the interest subsists. A duty or power to withhold income, such as a power to accumulate, negatives possession unless the accumulation is for the person with the interest.[23]

24.8.2 Tax liability

Where there is a termination of a life interest in possession on the death of the life tenant, the trustee is deemed to have disposed of the property remaining subject to the settlement and immediately reacquired it at its market value. However no chargeable gain accrues on the disposal. The effect of the application of s. 72 is thus a tax free uplift of the settled property. Since the property must remain settled after the death of the life tenant, s. 72 will not apply if the property leaves the settlement at that time. For example, if property is settled on A for life, to B for life, remainder to C absolutely, s. 72(1) will apply on A's death but not on B's death because on B's death C becomes absolutely entitled as against the trustees. C becoming absolutely entitled will cause the provisions of s. 71 (discussed in para. 24.7) to operate, but there will be no chargeable gain because C became entitled on the death of B (see para. 24.7.2).

Where the life interest comprises a right to part of the income of settled property, it is treated as an interest in the corresponding part of settled property (s. 72(1)(a)). So if the life tenant is entitled to half the

---
[22.] *Butterworths UK Tax Guide 1995–96*, para. 18:13, argues that s. 72(3)(b) may be otiose in view of the House of Lords decision in *Gartside* v *IRC* [1968] AC 553 that the objects of a discretionary trust do not have an interest in possession. Cf. *Sansom* v *Peay* [1976] STC 494 (see para. 24.6).
[23.] Cf. the inheritance rules at para. 34.4.

income of the settled property, when his life interest terminates, the trustees will be treated as though they had disposed of assets having a market value equal to half the market value of all the assets in the trust. In contrast, if the life tenant is entitled to the income from a specified part of the settled property and there is no right of recourse to the income of any other part of the settled property, the part in which the life interest subsists is treated for the purposes of s. 72 as settled property under a separate settlement (s. 72(5)). So if the life tenant is entitled to the income from half the settled fund which is appropriated to provide his income, when his life interest comes to an end the trustees will be treated as though they had disposed of the appropriated fund for its market value regardless of whether that part is more or less than half the market value of the entire fund at the date of termination.

The Revenue used to take the view that unless the beneficiary's interest subsisted in a separate, distinct piece of property, there was always a disposal of the entire fund when a life interest terminated. In other words, the Revenue view was formerly that the word 'part' did not apply where the beneficiary's interest was in an undivided share. This view was firmly rejected in *Pexton* v *Bell*; *Crowe* v *Appleby* [1976] STC 301. A testator had created a settlement by will giving each of his four daughters a life interest in one quarter of the settled property. The life interest of one of the daughters terminated at a time when the trustees had not appropriated property to her. The Inland Revenue claimed that because there had been no appropriation, the daughter was not entitled to 'part' of the settled property but had an interest in the whole of the property so that the whole of the fund should be deemed to be disposed of. In the Court of Appeal Sir John Pennycuick said:

> It seems to me that, on the natural construction of the words used in their context, the word 'part' in the subsection is apt to denote either a distinct item of property comprised in the entirety of the settled property or an undivided share of the entirety of the settled property.

Thus the daughter was to be treated as though her interest was in a separate settlement and therefore, on termination of her interest, the trustees disposed of that part of the settled property which was comprised in that settlement, i.e., one quarter of the whole.[24]

24.9 BENEFICIARIES

A person who is a beneficiary under a bare trust or for whom property is held by a nominee is treated as though the assets were vested in him and any disposals by the trustee or nominee were the beneficiary's disposals (s. 60(1)

[24.] The case was fought because the capital gains tax provisions used to impose a charge whenever and however a life interest terminated, for example, on death, under a provision in the settlement or on surrender. Since 5 April 1982 there has been no deemed disposal when the life interest terminates otherwise than on the death of the life tenant and, as has been seen, such a disposal does not give rise to a chargeable gain.

Capital gains tax and settlements

and see para. 24.2). Thus the trust is transparent for tax purposes and the beneficiary is in exactly the same position as any other taxpayer. If the beneficiary has become absolutely entitled to trust property, but the property remains in the hands of the trustees, he may direct the trustees to transfer the property to which he has become absolutely entitled to any other person. Such a transfer will be treated as the beneficiary's and accordingly he will be liable for any tax. On the other hand, the effect of s. 71 is that there is no charge to capital gains tax on the actual transfer of the assets to him by the trustees after the beneficiary has become absolutely entitled, since a charge will have been imposed on the trustees when he became absolutely entitled. If the asset has appreciated in value since the beneficiary became absolutely entitled, with the result that a gain accrues to him on his eventual disposal of the asset, any incidental expenditure within s. 38(2) incurred by him or his trustees in relation to the transfer of the asset to him by the trustees, is allowable as a deduction in computing the gain (s. 64). Further, any previously unrelieved losses of the trustees in relation to the property to which the beneficiary has become entitled can be passed to the beneficiary (s. 71(2)).

The disposal of beneficial interests under a settlement must be distinguished from disposals of the trust property. Where a person is entitled to an interest in settled property, he can dispose of his interest free of capital gains tax provided he did not acquire that interest for a consideration in money or money's worth (s. 76(1)).[25] The trust property must be settled at the time of the disposal of the beneficial interest (*Harthan* v *Mason* [1980] STC 94). In contrast, a beneficiary who acquired his interest for a consideration will be assessed on any gain that he makes from the disposal of that interest. The gain will be the difference between the actual consideration received for the disposal (provided it is a genuine arm's length transaction) and his allowable expenditure.[26] If the interest is retained until the acquirer becomes absolutely entitled as against the trustees, the consideration for the disposal of the interest will be deemed to be the settled property (s. 76(2)) but this is without prejudice to any gain accruing to the trustees on a deemed disposal under s. 71.

Example
Property worth £50,000 is transferred to trustees to be held by them on trust for Peter until he is 25 years old. When he is 22, Peter sells his beneficial interest to Andrew for £48,000. There is no capital gains tax liability at this time because Peter is the person for whose benefit the interest was created. In the 1997–98 year of assessment, when the property is worth £55,000, Peter becomes 25. At this time Andrew becomes absolutely entitled to the property as against the trustees and the trustees will be liable under s. 71 as follows (ignoring indexation and the effects of any exemptions and reliefs):

---

[25] Exchanges of beneficial interests do not count for these purposes.
[26] Although if the interest that has been acquired is a life interest and the predictable life expectancy of the life tenant is less than fifty years, it will be treated as a wasting asset so the costs of acquisition must be written down; s. 44(1)(d).

	£
Market value on deemed disposal	55,000
Less acquisition cost	50,000
Chargeable gain	5,000

Capital gains tax at 23% on £5,000 is £1,150 which the trustees pay, reducing the trust fund to £53,850.

Andrew is then treated as though he had disposed of his interest in the settled property in return for the settled property itself. His capital gains tax liability therefore is:

	£
Market value of settled property	53,850
Less acquisition cost of beneficial interest	48,000
Chargeable gain	5,850

Andrew will pay capital gains tax at his marginal rate of tax on £5,850.

24.10 CHARITABLE TRUSTS

The capital gains tax position of charities has already been discussed at para. 22.2.1.1. Where a life interest terminates otherwise than on the death of the life tenant and a charity becomes absolutely entitled to assets under s. 71, the trustees are deemed to dispose of and reacquire those assets for a consideration which results in neither a gain nor a loss (s. 257(3)). The unrealised gain is therefore passed to the charity, and will be realised tax free if applied by the charity for charitable purposes (s. 256(1)).

24.11 NON-RESIDENT TRUSTS

This topic is discussed in outline in Chapter 35.

PART IV
Companies and UK tax

CHAPTER TWENTY FIVE
Companies and UK tax – general matters

25.1 INTRODUCTORY MATTERS

25.1.1 General

Companies, as fiscal intermediaries, cause problems for any tax system as to how they should be treated for tax purposes.[1] As a matter of general law companies are treated as having a legal personality separate from their members.[2] However, a company is an *artificial* person and can only act through the agency of natural persons, namely its owners (the shareholders), or its managers (the directors). So, by its very nature, the company poses taxation problems, for instance, as to whom to tax and arguments as to double taxation. Should the company be ignored and only the shareholders taxed? Should receipts by the shareholders be taxed as well as receipts by the company? If so, should the shareholder be given credit for some or all of the tax paid by the company out of which, for example, the dividend was paid?[3] This last approach is sometimes called an imputation system. Company taxation raises difficult policy issues to which there are no absolutely clear answers.[4]

---

[1] See Bramwell, *The Taxation of Companies*, Sweet & Maxwell, 6th edn., 1994, *Simon's Direct Taxes*, Binder 5.
[2] See, e.g., *Salomon v Salomon & Co. Ltd* [1897] AC 22 and *Macaura v Northern Insurance* [1925] AC 619. Lord Macnaghten said in *Salomon* at p. 51: '. . . The Company is at law a different person altogether from the subscribers to the memorandum . . .'
[3] Cf. trustees and beneficiaries discussed at Chapters 14, 15, 24 and 34.
[4] See James and Nobes, *The Economics of Taxation*, 1996/97 edition, Prentice Hall, Chapter 12 and the difficulties in the European Union on agreement of a common corporation tax system recently discussed by Cnossen in *Fiscal Studies* (1996) vol. 17, no. 4, pp. 67–97.

25.1.2 UK partial imputation system

The present UK direct tax system for companies is somewhat of a compromise. In the fiscal jargon it is an 'imputation system' but only a partial one. Companies are usually liable to corporation tax rather than income tax and capital gains tax although corporation tax is calculated by reference to income tax and capital gains tax principles and practice. However, corporation tax has different rules for such matters as rates of tax, date of payment of tax, deductibility of charges on income and administration.

25.2 OUTLINE OF UK DIRECT TAX POSITION

In very general terms the UK direct tax position where companies are involved is as follows:

(a) a company is liable to UK corporation tax on its 'profits' (i.e., income and gains) to which it is beneficially entitled if it is UK resident or it is trading in the UK through a branch or agency (on profits attributable to the branch or agency). Otherwise, it may be liable to UK income tax and capital gains tax;[5]

(b) a distribution by a UK resident company, such as a dividend, attracts ACT, i.e., an advance or early payment of corporation tax;

(c) a company may set ACT against its mainstream corporation tax[6] subject to certain limits;

(d) a UK resident shareholder receiving a dividend from a UK resident company is subject to income tax under Schedule F[7] and broadly receives a tax credit equal to lower rate income tax;

(e) a non-resident recipient of a qualifying distribution does not generally receive a tax credit in cash unless a double tax treaty applies. Instead the credit in effect is treated as covering the recipient's liability to UK income tax at the lower rate on the distribution plus the credit;

(f) a UK resident shareholder receiving a dividend from a non-UK resident company is taxed on its gross amount (subject to a credit for foreign tax paid) under Schedule D, Case V.

25.3 HISTORY

25.3.1 History explains the current system

As with much UK taxation it helps, in understanding corporation tax, to know some of the historical background. The separate taxation of companies

---

[5.] See s. 6, TA. It may also be liable to foreign tax but this is not within the scope of this work. However, credit may be available in the UK for the foreign tax paid.

[6.] The usage of the term mainstream corporation tax varies. Here it is used to mean the liability on the taxable profits rather than the difference between that and ACT, i.e., the extra amount to be paid.

[7.] The receipt of a qualifying distribution such as a dividend by another UK resident company is not taxable; s. 208, TA (see Chapter 27).

is a comparatively recent matter in the UK. Companies were first taxed differently from individuals during the First World War and a new profits tax on companies partially financed rearmament during the Second World War. Companies also remained liable to income tax.

25.3.2 Classical system 1965–1972

In 1965 a 'classical system'[8] of corporation tax was introduced which 'discriminated' against distributed profits. This system treated the company as an entirely separate taxable entity from the shareholders. Consequently, for tax purposes, there was complete separation between a company and its shareholders and no tax credits between them. A company was taxed at 40% on its profits and in addition had to account for the income tax of its shareholders on distributions made to them. The effective rate of tax on profits could thus be more than 56%. It made it more tax efficient not to distribute profits as dividends etc. but to retain them within the company. The classical system also led to a greater use of loan stock (i.e., debt) in financing the company as the interest was deductible in computing taxable profits and so gave a lower effective rate of tax.

25.3.3 Reform and FA 1972 changes

The 1971 Conservative government decided to reform corporation tax, particularly to remove the 'discrimination' against distributed profits. A green paper (Cmnd 4630) was published which considered a number of systems but a House of Commons Select Committee reported in favour of the introduction of an imputation system of sorts. This was enacted by FA 1972 which took effect from April 1973. The FA 1972 reformed the 1965 provisions which still form the basis of corporation tax and are reflected in the drafting of the applicable legislation. Under the current partial imputation system, the company pays corporation tax on its profits and its shareholders receive a tax credit on the distributions made to them by the company reflecting part of the tax paid by the company. The government ensures that it has received sufficient corporation tax to cover the tax credit by a system of early (or advance) payment of corporation tax – see further Chapter 27.

25.4 PROBLEM AREAS

25.4.1 General

UK company taxation is not free from difficulties. The following is a selection of some of the problem areas. Many of them are linked.

25.4.2 Separate legal personality

As noted above, a company is a separate legal personality from its members; *Salomon* v *Salomon & Co Ltd* [1897] AC 22. It is an artificial construct or

---

[8.] For much of the recent period Germany had a classical system. Some have said its economic success owes much to this.

'moral person'. A company can only act through humans. Only humans can benefit from companies. As was said in the *Case of Sutton's Hospital* (1612) 10 Co Rep 1a by Coke CJ:

> ... a corporation aggregate of many is invisible, immortal, and rests only in intendment and consideration of the law ... They cannot commit treason, nor be outlawed, nor excommunicated, for they have no souls, neither can they appear in person but by attorney ... it is not subject to imbecilities [or] death of the natural body ...[9]

As has been seen above, this raises the question, who should be taxable? Should the company be ignored or not for tax purposes? This is a general problem of fiscal intermediaries. Here two particular problems need to be addressed.

25.4.2.1 Money box companies If the company is not taxed then distortion can arise as companies become used as 'money boxes' to accumulate income and gains tax free. This is also true if there is a differential tax rate between the receipts by a shareholder and the company. Such problems led to the apportionment provisions in the UK under which profits could be treated as distributed to shareholders if they were kept in a company under the close company legislation (see para. 25.6.6).

25.4.2.2 Double tier of tax If the company is made a taxable entity then the problem arises that the profits out of which dividends are paid are taxed on the company and the dividends are taxed on the recipient, so arguably giving rise to double taxation. This is true not only of income but also of a double tier of capital gains tax as the increase in value of a company's shares can be attributed to increases in value of a company's underlying assets.

25.4.3 Summary

The UK's partial imputation system addresses some of the problems mentioned above but not all. In particular it does not deal with the (alleged) double tier of capital gains tax. It is interesting to contrast the sale of an interest under a UK settlement which is not taxed on the original beneficiary with the sale of the underlying assets of the trust which are taxed on the trustees of the settlement (see Chapter 24). It may be that the same policy is being applied, as shares have to be paid up or a liability to do so assumed, whereas a settlement can be entirely voluntary.

25.4.4 Distributions

Profits can be kept within a company or distributed (e.g., by dividend – distribution is the generic description). The problem of whether to tax the

---

[9]. See also the *dicta* of Lord Loreburn LC in *De Beers Consolidated Mines Ltd* v *Howe* [1906] AC 455 set out at para. 25.6.2 below.

company and what comes out of it has already been met. If it is decided to tax dividends, then it has to be decided what is to be treated as a dividend for these purposes. Clearly a dividend declared as such and paid should fall within the dividend charge but what else? There are numerous ways in which value can be transferred to shareholders without there being a dividend in the classic sense. For example, a bonus issue could be made of redeemable shares which the next day are redeemed. Is this to be treated as a dividend? (See s. 211, TA for the UK solution.) The UK has enacted much legislation that is effectively anti-avoidance legislation describing what is a distribution for tax purposes (see, e.g., Chapter II, Part VI, TA).

25.4.5 Groups

Groups of companies are often run economically as one business but as a matter of law the group consists of a number of separate legal personalities (see above). For accounting purposes the accounts of the group may be consolidated which emphasises the 'one business' position. Should neutrality require that the tax position be the same whether the business is run through a number of divisions of one company or through a number of interlocking companies? If so, should one require a consolidated tax return for the group (as in, e.g., the USA), or should reliefs for losses, dividends, gains and the like be introduced to provide neutrality? The UK has adopted the second approach. A further difficulty then arises as to the definition of the group for these purposes. Is less than a 100% beneficial ownership to be sufficient? If so, what percentage should be sufficient and why? Should a group consist only of companies within the same tax net? For example, should a group only consist of UK resident companies (see s. 170(2)(a), TA)? Is such a provision contrary to EU law?[10]

25.4.6 Closely held companies

As was seen in para. 25.4.2.1 companies can be used as tax planning vehicles. If a company has a small number of shareholders who alone and/or by acting in concert can ensure that the company does what they want so that, in effect, the company is their creature, should the corporate veil then be lifted to prevent tax benefits being obtained? If so, how? The UK approach has changed here: see the discussion of close companies in para. 25.6.6 below.

25.4.7 Foreign element

Tax is a territorial matter whereas business is not. This raises problems as to who should have the taxing jurisdiction. Should credit be given for foreign tax paid which reduces the tax take of the country giving such credit? As a company is one legal personality, how should foreign branches be taxed and

---

[10.] See, inter alia, *European Law Review*, Vol. 20, No. 6, p. 580 and *The EC Tax Journal*, vol. 1, 1995/96, pp. 27–51.

on what? These are not purely questions relating to companies but they have in the main been dealt with by the UK in that context. These are questions that are very closely aligned with sovereignty. Raising tax is one of a government's most cherished powers that it is reluctant to give up (cf. Article 100a of the Treaty of Rome, as amended).

25.5 UK CORPORATION TAX – GENERAL MATTERS

25.5.1 Introduction

To understand UK corporation tax it is necessary to know where to find the relevant legislation. This is considered in this section.

25.5.2 What is the main legislation on UK corporation tax?

Like all UK taxes corporation tax is a creature of statute. Accordingly it is necessary to know where to find the legislation which is not particularly sensibly set out.[11] The main legislation dealing with UK corporation tax includes the following provisions:

TA
ss. 6–14 charge to tax, time for payment etc.
ss. 208–255 company distributions, tax credits etc.
ss. 337–347 computation
ss. 393–395 loss relief
ss. 402–413 group relief
Parts XI and XII close companies and special classes of companies and businesses

TCGA
ss. 139 and 170–192 reliefs from charge

25.5.3 Four essential questions

It is necessary to consider what UK corporation tax involves. The starting point for this is the charge to UK corporation tax. Section 8(1), TA provides that 'Subject to any exceptions provided for by the Corporation Tax Acts, a company shall be chargeable to corporation tax on all its profits whenever arising.'

There are thus (inter alia) four essential questions to consider in relation to the charge to UK corporation tax. These are as follows:

(a) Who is liable to UK corporation tax?
(b) What is liable to UK corporation tax?

[11.] Why, for instance, is ACT dealt with in s. 14, TA and distributions to which it relates in s. 209, TA? One theory is a computer crash when the consolidation was undertaken with 'the benefit of information technology'.

Companies and UK tax – general matters

(c) For what period?
(d) When is UK corporation tax due?

These questions will be considered in broad terms next. They are considered in further detail in the following chapters.

25.5.4 UK resident companies and companies trading in the UK liable to UK corporation tax

The broad answer to the question, 'Who is liable to UK corporation tax?' is that companies, as defined for this purpose in s. 832, TA, are liable to UK corporation tax. The definition of a 'company' is considered at para. 25.6.1 below. More particularly, UK resident companies and non-resident companies trading in the UK through a branch or an agency are liable to UK corporation tax. Questions of residence are considered in more detail at paras 25.6.2 and 25.6.3.

25.5.5 'Profits' charged to UK corporation tax

The broad answer to the question 'What is liable to UK corporation tax?' is that 'profits' as defined in s. 6, TA are taxed. The meaning of 'profits' is considered at para. 25.6.4 but it includes income and capital gains.

25.5.6 UK corporation tax charged on a current year arising basis

The broad answer to the question, 'What period?' is that the profits of a UK resident company are charged:

(a) on a current year basis, i.e., no preceding year basis or payments on account by reference to last year's tax as for income tax under Schedule D, Case I; and
(b) whether or not remitted to UK.[12]

The charge is by reference to the company's accounting period for profits and financial year for rates. This is discussed in more detail at para. 25.6.13 below.

25.5.7 Due date for corporation tax

The broad answer to the question 'When is corporation tax due?' is that corporation tax is due and payable nine months from the end of the company's accounting period. This is discussed in more detail at paras 25.6.13 and 25.9 below.

---

[12] On unremittable income see s. 585, TA. There are also special rules for controlled foreign companies; see *Strategic Tax Planning*, (ed. Shipwright) Gee Publishing Ltd in association with Sweet & Maxwell, 1995, Chapter H4.

25.6 SOME DEFINITIONS

There are a number of words and phrases which it helps to understand to comprehend UK corporation tax. Some of these are considered below. For the meaning of other words and phrases the reader is referred in the first place to the Glossary.

25.6.1 Company

The meaning of this word is important as UK corporation tax only applies to companies as defined for these purposes. Companies can include more than just limited liability companies.

'Company' by s. 832(1), TA means '. . . subject to subsection (2) below, any body corporate or unincorporated association but does not include a partnership, a local authority or a local authority association.'

Accordingly, it is not just corporate bodies that are companies liable to UK corporation tax. Unincorporated associations are included notwithstanding that most people would not think of unincorporated associations as companies. The effect of this is, for example, that clubs are liable to pay corporation tax rather than income tax and capital gains tax. This can be important because of different rates of tax and times of payment.

'Body corporate' is not specifically defined for these purposes. Broadly, it means an entity having a separate legal personality. In Sir Edward Coke's *Commentary upon Littleton* 'body corporate' is said (at p. 250a) to be, 'A succession or collection of persons having in the estimation of the law an existence and rights and duties distinct from those of the individual persons who form it from time to time.' It would thus cover companies formed under the Companies Acts and corporations formed by statute or by Royal Charter. It can also cover certain foreign entities which have no exact equivalent in UK law (e.g., an Anstalt – a Liechtenstein entity).

An 'unincorporated association' for these purposes is, according to Lawton LJ in *Conservative and Unionist Central Office v Burrell* [1982] 2 All ER 1:

> two or more persons bound together for one or more common purposes, not being business purposes, by mutual undertakings, each having mutual duties and obligations, in an organisation which has rules which identify in whom control of it and its funds rests and on what terms, and which can be joined or left at will.

The issue in *Conservative Central Office v Burrell* was whether or not Conservative Central Office was an unincorporated association. It was held that it was not.

If there is a business purpose and no separate personality but several parties, then it is likely that the parties are carrying on business in common with a view to profit and so are a partnership.[13] This was considered in the

---

[13.] Cf. s. 1, Partnership Act 1890. It might also amount to mutual trading if outsiders are not involved (see para. 9.7).

context of fund raising for charity in *Blackpool Marton Rotary Club* v *Martin* [1988] STC 823. It was held that there was not a partnership in that case but a club as partners were usually entitled to a proportion of the profits and liable for losses and whereas club members were not. Accordingly, as a club the taxpayer was an unincorporated association liable to corporation tax. Similarly a rugby club was held liable as a company in *Frampton and Another (Trustees of Worthing RFC)* v *IRC* [1987] STC 273.

The definition in s. 832(1), TA is subject to s. 832(2) which specifies exclusions from this definition of company. It provides that the definition '. . . does not apply when the context otherwise requires because some other definition of "company" applies.' The specific exclusions include:

    (a) Chapter I of Part XVII, TA (cancellation of tax advantages etc.) where s. 709(2) provides that company includes any body corporate (on the meaning of 'body corporate' see above);

    (b) ss. 774 to 777 (transactions between dealing company and associated company etc.) where again company is defined as including any body corporate (see ss. 774(4)(a) and 777(13));

    (c) s. 839, connected persons (see s. 839(8) which seems broadly similar to the s. 832 definition);

    (d) para. 15, sch. 3 (interest payable out of the public revenue of the Republic of Ireland etc.).

Section 832(1) excludes local authorities and local authority associations from the definition of 'company'. 'Local authority' is defined in s. 842A for the purposes of the Taxes Acts 'except so far as the context otherwise requires'. Broadly, it means a body having power to raise or participate in council tax or rates. Section 842A does not include companies set up by local authorities. This can be important in funding schemes for local authorities, as a tax charge can have a damaging effect on a budget.

'Local authority association' is defined in s. 519(3) and is an incorporated or unincorporated association of which all the members are local authorities etc. and whose primary object is the furtherance etc. of the interests of local authorities. (Section 519A exempts health service bodies from tax.)

Thrift funds and clubs formed annually to provide facilities for saving towards holidays are regarded as outside the scope of corporation tax (Extra-statutory Concession C3).

25.6.2 Residence of a company

The residence of a company is important in this context because UK corporation tax applies to companies resident in the United Kingdom, and to certain non-resident companies. The rules vary according to whether the company is UK resident or not. As with income tax, therefore, the critical test of liability to corporation tax is residence.

It should be noted that for corporation tax purposes there is no difference between residence and ordinary residence (see *Union Corporation Ltd* v *IRC*

[1953] AC 482). Further a company is domiciled in the country in which it was incorporated (*Gasque* v *IRC* [1940] 2 KB 80).

Previously the place of incorporation of a company did not matter greatly in determining a company's residence. There is now a distinction to be made between UK and non-UK incorporated companies as to the test of residence to be applied.

(a) Since 1988 a UK incorporated company is treated as UK resident by reason of its incorporation in the UK whether or not by other tests it would be resident outside the UK. If a company is incorporated in the UK it is UK resident by reason of that fact.[14]

(b) Other companies (i.e., companies incorporated outside the UK) are treated as resident where the 'centre of management and control' of the company is situated. This test applies both to parent and subsidiary companies (see SP 1/90). The meaning of the 'centre of management and control' is a matter of case law.

Where the case law test applies (i.e., to non-UK incorporated companies) the company resides where the company's central management and control of the company is or where its 'controlling brain' actually abides. In general terms this is concerned with broad strategy and policy rather than day-to-day management of the company.

In *De Beers Consolidated Mines Ltd* v *Howe* [1906] AC 455, Lord Loreburn, LC said:

In applying the conception of residence to a company, we ought, I think, to proceed as nearly as we can upon the analogy of an individual. A company cannot eat or sleep, but it can keep house and do business. We ought, therefore, to see where it really keeps house and does business.

The House of Lords therefore held that a company is resident where its real business is carried on, and in the words of Lord Loreburn, 'the real business is carried on where the central management and control actually abides'.

The powers of management and control in the strategic and policy sense are often vested in the directors of an incorporated company.[15] If this is the case, the company is controlled by the directors and not the shareholders according to *Automatic Self-Cleansing Filter Syndicate Co.* v *Cuninghame* [1906] 2 Ch 34.

The central management and control of a company normally 'abides' at the place where the directors hold their meetings. The residence of individual directors or shareholders or the place of the company's general (i.e., shareholders) meeting are usually irrelevant considerations. It does not matter in determining residence where the company's assets are situated. Thus, a company with assets in India could be resident in the United Kingdom if the

---

[14] See s. 66 and Sch. 7, FA 1988. There were transitional provisions but these have now expired.
[15] See reg. 70 of Table A: The Companies (Tables A to F) Regulations 1985, SI 1985/805.

board of directors met in the United Kingdom (*Calcutta Jute Mills* v *Nicholson* (1876) 1 Ex D 428). Conversely, a company with assets in Egypt would be resident there if the directors met there (*Egyptian Delta Land and Investment Co. Ltd* v *Todd* [1929] AC 1). The place of the company's incorporation is the decisive factor for domicile but is just one of the factors which may determine residence (other than for a UK incorporated company when it is decisive).

If it is clear that the powers of management and control of a company can revert to the shareholders in general meeting if there is no functioning board of directors, for example, where there is a deadlock on the board (*Barron* v *Potter* [1914] 1 Ch 895), or no effective quorum (*Foster* v *Foster* [1916] 1 Ch 532), or where the directors are disqualified from voting (*Grant* v *United Kingdom Switchback Railways* (1888) 40 Ch D 135), or certainly if there are no directors (*Alexander Ward and Co. Ltd* v *Samyang Navigation Co. Ltd* [1975] 2 All ER 424), this is a factor to be taken into account. But the place of the directors' meetings is still often the most important matter. However, the position depends on all the circumstances of the particular case (cf. *Kodak Limited* v *Clarke* (1903) 4 TC 549).

The Inland Revenue were worried for some time about the lack of a statutory definition of company residence, with many problems being raised by the international activities of companies. Accordingly they issued a Statement of Practice stating how they would interpret the test of company residence (SP 6/83, 27 July 1983; see now SP1/90 which has replaced it). This is still of importance for companies incorporated outside the UK.

If a company is no longer carrying on any business or is being wound up, but was regarded as being resident in the United Kingdom immediately before this, it will be regarded as continuing to be so resident (s. 66(2)).

The position on company residence may thus be broadly summarised as follows:

(a) subject to FA 1988 which deems UK incorporated companies to be UK resident, the place of incorporation of a company is merely a factor in determining its residence;

(b) the fact that a company is trading in the UK does not of itself make it UK resident;

(c) it is possible for a company to be resident in more than one place;

(d) a company may from time to time change its place(s) of residence;

(e) the centre of management and control test previously applied both to UK and non-UK incorporated companies (see *Egyptian Delta Land and Investment Co. Ltd* v *Todd* [1929] AC 1) but UK incorporation is now the alternative determinative test;

(f) the same tests apply for subsidiaries as for parent companies (see *Unit Construction* v *Bullock* [1960] AC 351). Subject to s. 66, FA 1988 the key indicator of residence remains the location of the superior and directing authority (see *Union Corporation* v *IRC* [1952] 1 All ER 646);

(g) shareholder control does not in general matter in determining the residence of a company (see *Kodak Ltd* v *Clarke* (1903) 4 TC 549);

(h) effective control of a local board does not guarantee non-UK residence (see *Swedish Central Railways* v *Thompson* [1925] AC 495).

25.6.3 Dual residence

Like an individual a company may be 'dual or multi resident'.[16] A company may thus be treated as resident in more than one country. This may give rise to double taxation. Double taxation treaties sometimes seek to deal with this potential problem (see Chapter 35). But this is not always the case. For example the UK/US Treaty does not provide for the dual residence of companies. This led to the use of dual resident companies to obtain deductions in respect of a particular expenditure both in the UK and in the US by means of having a US incorporated, but UK resident company.[17] This device has now been effectively stopped by s. 404, TA 1988 which denies group relief to dual resident companies.

In *Swedish Central Railways* v *Thompson* [1925] AC 495 a company was incorporated in the United Kingdom to build a railway in Sweden. At a time when the company was managed and controlled in Sweden, the directors formed a committee to transact administrative business in the United Kingdom (share transfers and the drawing of cheques on the company's English bank account). The Special Commissioners held that the company was resident in the United Kingdom, notwithstanding that it was controlled and managed abroad (which would be sufficient to make the company resident in Sweden). The House of Lords held, by a 4-1 majority, that a company could have more than one residence for tax purposes and that there was evidence to support the conclusion of the Commissioners.

In *Unit Construction Co. Ltd* v *Bullock* [1960] AC 351 Lord Radcliffe said:

> My Lords, I cannot avoid the opinion that the *Swedish Central Railway Co.* decision was an unfortunate one, having regard to the course of authority both before and after its date. . . . If the accepted test is that a company is resident in that country where its central management and control abide, and the facts are that at the material date that central management and control do not abide in England, it seems that in such cases the nature of the test itself precludes the conclusion that the company is nevertheless resident here . . . I am myself of the opinion that the best way of treating the matter is to regard . . . the 1925 decision of the House [as] no more than a decision on that special class of case . . . where the facts themselves are genuinely such as not to admit of a finding that central management and control are exercised in or from any one country.

It would therefore seem that a finding of dual residence can only be made where it is impossible on the facts to say that the 'superior and directing

---
[16.] Although an individual may be multi resident he or she can only have one domicile.
[17.] E.g., 'the Delaware Link' seeking interest deductions in both jurisdictions when the UK corporation tax rate was 52% and tax was 48% in the US. This would make borrowing remarkably cheap.

authority' of the company is to be found in one country. This will be rare. A company will now have dual residence, however, if, although incorporated and therefore resident in the United Kingdom, it operates in a country which treats management and control (or some criterion other than incorporation) as its test of residence. In such a case, however, the question may be resolved by the application of a 'tie-breaker' clause in a double tax treaty.

The Inland Revenue have been concerned for some time about the supposed loss of tax[18] attributable to the exploitation of dual resident companies. There are now limits on the availability of group relief to certain defined dual resident companies (s. 404, TA) to prevent tax avoidance. From 14 March 1989, if the assets of a dual resident company change (for example, due to a double taxation agreement) from being within the charge to United Kingdom tax to not being so liable, there will be a deemed disposal of its assets at that time at market value, so that unrealised gains will be charged to tax (s. 185, TCGA). There are also limits on the availability of roll-over relief on business assets for dual resident companies.

25.6.4 Profits

By s. 6(4)(a), TA 'profits' means income and chargeable gains. The effect of this is that UK corporation tax is charged on the income and chargeable gains of companies at the same rate. Income and capital gains are computed in accordance with income tax and capital gains tax principles and practice.

25.6.5 Small companies

The definition of small companies is to be found in s. 13, TA and is discussed in para. 25.8.

25.6.6 Close and close investment-holding companies ('CICs')

Provisions were included in the legislation from the 1920s to deal with closely held 'money box' companies (see para. 25.4.2.1). As they are not individuals, companies were not liable to surtax nor higher rate income tax (see s. 1(2), TA) but special apportionment treated the 'participators' as if they were. Section 103, FA 1989 abolished apportionment (ss. 423 to 430, TA) and introduced the concept of the close investment-holding company ('CIC'; discussed in para. 25.6.11).

Broadly, a close company is a UK resident company under the control of its directors or five or fewer participators. A company in general terms is close if:

(a) it is resident in the UK;[19]

---

[18] This was generally tax in a different jurisdiction which should be of no concern to the UK Revenue.
[19] A company not resident in the UK is not a close company under the general definition. Sometimes a company which would be close if UK resident is to be treated as close; see s. 414(5) and (6), TA.

(b) is under the control of either:

   (i) five or fewer participators; or
   (ii) participators who are directors or who possess or are entitled to acquire:

      (1) rights giving them the greater part of the assets available for distribution on a notional winding up; or
      (2) the greater part of the assets, disregarding rights *qua* loan creditor.

There are exceptions for companies controlled by the Crown (s. 414(1)(c), TA), companies controlled by non-close companies (s. 414(5), TA) and companies listed as to 35% or more[20] on a recognised stock exchange (see s. 841, TA). The rights of associates are to be taken into account in ascertaining control (see ss. 416 and 417, TA).

The concept of 'close company' is still relevant notwithstanding the abolition of apportionment for a number of purposes including the following.

25.6.6.1 Meaning of distribution By s. 418, TA certain payments to or for the benefit of participators are treated as distributions if made by a close company. This includes the expense of providing living accommodation, entertainment, domestic and other services.

25.6.6.2 Loans to a participator A loan to an individual who is a participator (or an associate) attracts a liability to corporation tax equal to ACT on a distribution of an equivalent amount, under s. 419, TA. It cannot be used in the same way as ACT (see Chapter 27) as it is not ACT but an amount equal to ACT. There is an exclusion for working participators up to £15,000 if they own less than 5% of the close company or any of its associated companies, but the loan may then fall within s. 160, TA (beneficial loan arrangements).[21] There are anti-avoidance provisions to catch indirect loans etc.

25.6.6.3 Capital gains tax Section 13, TCGA deems the gains of a non-resident company, which would be close if it were UK resident, to be the gains of the shareholders in the company at the time the gains accrue, if those shareholders are UK resident or ordinarily resident and, if those shareholders are individuals, are UK domiciled.

25.6.6.4 Small companies rate not available to CIC Sections 13 and 13A, TA denies the small companies rate to CICs; see paras 25.6.11 and 25.8.

[20.] By voting power; see s. 415, TA. This will normally be 35% of the share capital listed if the listing is on the International Stock Exchange of the UK and Republic of Ireland.

[21.] See s. 420, TA and note the company law position on loans to directors.

25.6.6.5 Profit distributions by CIC Section 106, FA 1989 inserted subsections 3A–3D in s. 231, TA, thereby allowing tax credits to be restricted where a CIC is involved. See para. 25.6.11.

25.6.7 Participator

By s. 417(1), TA a participator:

> is, in relation to any company, a person having a share or interest in the capital or income of the company and . . . includes—
> (a) any person who possesses, or is entitled to acquire, share capital or voting rights in the company;
> (b) any loan creditor of the company;
> (c) any person who possesses, or is entitled to acquire, a right to receive or participate in distributions of the company . . . or any amounts payable by the company (in cash or in kind) to loan creditors by way of premium on redemption; and
> (d) any person who is entitled to secure that income or assets (whether present or future) of the company will be applied directly or indirectly for his benefit.

Being entitled includes being entitled to do something at a future date (s. 417(1), TA).

25.6.8 Associate

This is defined in s. 417(3), TA. It includes any relative or partner of the participator, the trustees of a settlement of which the participator (or any relative of his, alive or dead) is the settlor and certain other trustees of settlements in which the participator is interested.

25.6.9 Loan creditor

This is defined in s. 417(7), TA as meaning:

> . . . a creditor in respect of any debt incurred by the company —
> (a) for any money borrowed or capital assets acquired by the company;
> or
> (b) for any right to receive income created in favour of the company; or
> (c) for consideration the value of which to the company was (at the time the debt was incurred) substantially less than the amount of the debt (including any premium thereon);
> or in respect of any redeemable loan capital issued by the company.

Again this is a wide definition.

25.6.10 Control

Section 416(2), TA provides that '. . . a person shall be taken to have control of a company if he exercises, or is able to exercise or is entitled to acquire, direct or indirect control over the company's affairs . . .' Particularised examples are then given as to control, including the greater part of the voting power in the company, the greater part of the income on distribution or the greater part of the assets on a liquidation available for distribution amongst the participators. This is a very wide definition particularly when put together with the wide ambit of associate. The effect is that control is actual control or the right to acquire control. The consequence of this is that more than one person can be treated as having control. (See also *EVC International NV v Steele* [1996] STC 785 in which control of the affairs of a company was held to mean control at the level of general meetings of shareholders.)

25.6.11 Close investment-holding company

The concept of the 'close investment-holding company' was introduced by the Finance Act 1989 for accounting periods beginning after 31 March 1989. A close investment-holding company is defined negatively by s. 13A, TA as a company which does not comply with specific conditions. Companies which can meet the conditions are designated 'relevant companies'.

The conditions are that the company should throughout the period in question exist wholly or mainly for any one or more of the following purposes:

(a) the purpose of carrying on a trade or trades on a commercial basis;
(b) the purpose of making investments in land or estates or interests in land in cases where the land is, or is intended to be, let to persons other than;
   (i) any person connected with the company; or
   (ii) any person who is the wife or husband of an individual connected with the company, or is a relative, or the wife or husband of a relative, or such an individual or the husband or wife of such an individual;
(c) the purpose of holding shares in and securities of, or making loans to, one or more companies each of which is a qualifying company or a company which:
   (i) is under the control of the relevant company or of a company which has control of the relevant company; and
   (ii) itself exists wholly or mainly for the purpose of holding shares in or securities of, or making loans to, one or more qualifying companies;
(d) the purpose of coordinating the administration of two or more qualifying companies;
(e) the purpose of a trade or trades carried on on a commercial basis by one or more qualifying companies or by a company which has control of the relevant company;
(f) the purpose of the making, by one or more qualifying companies or by a parent company, of investments as mentioned in paragraph (b) above.

A 'qualifying company' is one which is under the control of the relevant company or of a company which has control of the relevant company, and which exists wholly or mainly for the purposes mentioned in (a) or (b).

The results of being a close investment-holding company are first, that the small companies rate is not available (see para. 25.8) so that the company will pay tax at the full rate of corporation tax. Secondly, there is a restriction on the availability of tax credits under s. 231(3A), TA. An inspector has the power to limit a claim to credit for advance corporation tax paid by the company to such amount as appears just and reasonable in respect of a particular individual. This applies where, in any accounting period of a company at the end of which it is a close investment-holding company, it appears that:

(a) arrangements relating to the distribution of the profits of the company exist or have existed, the purpose or one of the main purposes of which is to enable payments, or payments of a greater amount to be made to one or more individuals; and

(b) by virtue of these arrangements, any eligible person receives a qualifying distribution of a payment made by the company on the redemption, repayment or purchase of its own shares, or receives any other qualifying distribution in respect of shares or securities of the company where the amount or value of this is greater than might have been expected but for the arrangements.

This power of the inspector will not apply to a payment made in respect of the company's ordinary share capital if that share capital consists of only one class of shares, and no person has waived or failed to receive any dividend which was due and payable to him during the accounting period (s. 231(3B)).

25.6.12 Investment company

By s. 130, TA 'In this Part of this Act [Part IV Schedule D Charge]' investment company 'means any company whose business consists wholly or mainly in the making of investments and the principal part of whose income is derived therefrom . . .'. It is to be noted that this definition has two limbs to it. These are that:

(a) the company's business consists of holding investments; and
(b) the principal part of its income is 'derived therefrom'.

Whether or not a company is an investment company is an important matter for deduction purposes. There are particular rules for trading companies and for investment companies (see para. 26.7). However, a third category is possible. A company may be neither a trading company nor an investment company as defined. If so, it falls within neither set of rules.

25.6.13 Financial year and accounting period

The rate of corporation tax is fixed for a 'financial year', i.e., 1 April one year to 31 March next year. Liability is by reference to an 'accounting period' for which a company makes up accounts but this period cannot exceed 12 months for tax purposes.[22] If a longer period is used then it is time apportioned. If the accounting period straddles financial years then the profits are to be time apportioned.

Section 12(2), TA provides that the start of an accounting period is:

(a) when a company comes within the charge to UK corporation tax 'by becoming resident in the UK or acquiring a source of income or otherwise'; and

(b) at the end of an accounting period without the company ceasing to be within the charge to UK corporation tax.

Section 12(3), TA provides that the end of an accounting period is generally twelve months from the start of an accounting period. An accounting period may also end:

(a) when a company ceases to be within the charge to UK corporation tax (s. 12(3)(e));

(b) when a company ceases to be UK resident (s. 12(3)(d));

(c) on a company beginning or ceasing to trade or to be within the charge to UK corporation tax in respect of its trade, or all its trades if more than one (s. 12(3)(c), TA);

(d) on an accounting date of the company, or where a company does not make up accounts for a period, the end of that period (s. 12(3)(b)).

25.7 RATES OF CORPORATION TAX

The rate of corporation tax is fixed for a financial year, i.e., from 1 April of one year to 31 March the next year. However, the assessments are made by reference to accounting periods (see para. 25.6.13). This means that where the accounting period straddles the end/beginning of a financial year, the amount of the profits arising in each of the two accounting periods covering the financial year must be apportioned (s. 8(3), TA).

The standard rate of corporation tax for the financial year 1997 is 33%. This rate is applicable to income and chargeable gains.[23] There is also a 'small companies' rate. This is a lower rate (currently 23%) for companies with small profits rather than being a reference to the size of the company in question.

[22.] See ss. 12 and 834, TA. Section 12 refers to an 'accounting period'. Section 834 provides that accounting period is to 'construed in accordance with s. 12'. Section 834 defines period of account and accounting date.

[23.] In the past the effective rates were different because only a proportion of chargeable gains was brought into charge.

25.8 'SMALL COMPANIES' RATE

The rate of corporation tax is lower for 'small companies' on their basic profits liable for corporation tax (s. 13(1), TA). The small companies rate for the financial year 1997 is 23% (the same as basic rate rax for the individual). The small companies rate is only available to a UK resident company according to the legislation,[24] which is not a close investment-holding company at the end of the period.[25]

A 'small company' is thus a UK resident company (which is not a close investment-holding company) with profits (including franked investment income from companies which are not in the same group) which do not exceed £300,000 in the accounting period. The limit of £300,000 must be apportioned if the company's accounting period is less than 12 months in length (s. 13(6), TA).

One cannot take advantage of the small companies rate by splitting the business between a group of companies in an attempt to obtain the small companies rate for each company, since the £300,000 limit is divided between the number of associated companies plus one (s. 13(3), (4) and (5)). A company is an 'associated company' of another if at the time in question one has control of the other or both are under the control of the same person or persons (s. 13(4)). The wide definition of control in s. 416 is to apply for these purposes (s. 13(4)). A dormant company may be disregarded for these purposes (see s. 13(4)).

If a company's profits exceed the limit of £300,000 but do not exceed £1,500,000, marginal relief is available (s. 13(2)). The relief is calculated by reducing the corporation tax payable at 33% on the company's profits by:

$$\frac{1}{40} \text{ of } (£1,500,000 - \text{profits}) \times \frac{\text{basic profits}}{\text{profits}}$$

The 'basic profits' are those liable to corporation tax, whereas for this calculation only 'profits' includes franked investment income (see para. 27.15).

Example
C Ltd, in its accounting period ending 31 March 1998, had £300,000 trading income and £30,000 chargeable gains. C Ltd had £70,000 of franked investment income. The corporation tax payable in respect of these profits would therefore be:

[24.] See s. 13(1)(a), TA. However, often the non-discrimination article in a double tax treaty will allow the rate to be given. It is at least arguable in the light of *Halliburton Services BV* v *Staatssecretaris van Financien* [1994] STC 655 that it would be discriminatory to refuse the rate to a company incorporated in an EC member state; see footnote 10 above. Overseas companies may qualify for the small companies rate in respect of its UK branches or agencies if it can benefit from the non-discrimination article in a double tax treaty, ICAEW Technical Release TR 500.
[25.] Section 13(1)(b). On the meaning of close investment-holding company see s. 13A and para. 25.6.11.

Profits will be:

Trading income	300,000
Capital gains	30,000
Franked investment income	70,000
	400,000

As franked investment income is exempt from corporation tax, C Ltd would expect to pay corporation tax at the rate of 33% on £330,000 which is £108,900.

However, as C Ltd's profits are less than £1,500,000 it is entitled to a reduction in its corporation tax bill in accordance with the above formula:

$$\frac{1}{40} \times (1,500,000 - 400,000) \times \frac{330,000}{400,000} = £22,687.50$$

C Ltd is therefore liable to corporation tax of £108,900 − £22,687.50 which is £86,212.50.

25.9 PAYMENT OF CORPORATION TAX

The introduction of the pay and file system has led to radical changes in the collection of corporation tax (ss. 82 to 90, FA (No. 2) 1987 and s. 10, TA).

Corporation tax for an accounting period is due and payable on the day following the expiry of nine months from the end of that accounting period (s. 10(1), TA). Although the final tax liability may not be known, the company will be able to pay an estimated amount of tax (and advance corporation tax may have been paid that will count towards the final bill). To encourage payment, interest will run from the date the tax is due (see ss. 85 and 86, FA (No. 2) 1987). If the company has grounds to believe, before final assessment, that it has paid too much on account, it can claim part repayment in writing (s. 10(3), TA). Tax overpaid will be repaid with interest (see ss. 87 and 88, FA (No. 2) 1987).

Tax can of course only be finally assessed when accounts have been submitted. The Taxes Management Act 1970 has been amended so that accounts should be submitted within one year of the end of the period of account to which they relate (see s. 11, TMA 1970). If the accounts are submitted late there will be penalties of up to £1,000, or if the accounts are more than 18 months late, a penalty of a percentage of the tax then due, being 10% of tax unpaid, or 20% if the accounts are more than two years late (see s. 94, TMA 1970).

The powers to collect information in connection with corporation tax returns have been widened by amendments in s. 91, FA 1990, and further amendments in connection with determining tax liability were made by ss. 97 to 100, FA 1990.

It should also be noted that the amount of corporation tax payable may be reduced by:

(a) the amount of income tax deducted at source in respect of payments to the company;
(b) double taxation relief by credit; and
(c) advance corporation tax.

CHAPTER TWENTY SIX
The charge to corporation tax

26.1 INTRODUCTORY MATTERS

This chapter is concerned with the charge to UK corporation tax.[1] The statutory authority for charging UK corporation tax is found in s. 6, TA. Section 6(1) provides 'Corporation tax shall be charged on profits of companies, and the Corporation Tax Acts shall apply, for any financial year for which Parliament so determines . . .' The meaning of 'company' for these purposes has been considered in Chapter 25 but it should be recalled that it includes unincorporated associations other than partnerships.

Like income tax, corporation tax is an annual tax like income tax. The Provisional Collection of Taxes Act 1968 applies to corporation tax (see s. 1(1), PCTA and Chapter 2).

26.2 WHAT IS CHARGEABLE TO CORPORATION TAX?

26.2.1 General principle

The general principle behind UK corporation tax is that a UK resident company is chargeable to corporation tax on all its profits (capital or income) wherever arising (see s. 8(1), in para. 26.2.2). In relation to non-resident companies, however, this general principle is modified so that only profits attributable to a branch or agency in the UK are taxed (see s. 11(2)).

26.2.2 The charge: s. 8, TA

Section 8(1), TA provides that 'Subject to any exceptions provided for by the Corporation Tax Acts, a company shall be chargeable to corporation tax on

---

[1] See Bramwell, *Taxation of Companies*, 6th edn, Sweet & Maxwell, 1994, Chapter 2.

all its profits whenever arising'. As has been seen in Chapter 25, 'profits' for these purposes means income and chargeable gains (s. 6(4)(a)). So far as 'chargeable gains' are concerned, s. 15(2), TCGA (as applied by s. 832(1), TA) provides that 'every gain shall, except as otherwise expressly provided, be a chargeable gain'. This is discussed in the context of capital gains tax in para. 26.4.

26.3 FIDUCIARY RECEIPTS

A company is not liable to corporation tax on fiduciary receipts. This is the effect of s. 8(2), TA which provides:

> A company shall be chargeable to corporation tax on profits accruing for its benefit under any trust, or arising under any partnership in any case in which it would be so chargeable if the profits accrued to it directly; and a company shall be chargeable to corporation tax on profits arising in the winding up of the company, but shall not otherwise be chargeable to corporation tax on profits accruing to it in a fiduciary or representative capacity except as respects its own beneficial interest (if any) in those profits.

Thus, a trust corporation, acting as such (i.e., in a fiduciary capacity), will not be liable to corporation tax on the trust's income or gains (see Chapter 14 for liability of trustees to income tax) though the trust corporation will be liable to corporation tax on the fees charged by it for acting as trustee (since these fees belong to it in its own right). A company will be liable to corporation tax if it is a beneficiary under a trust and such a beneficiary, if an individual, would be liable to income tax or capital gains tax.

26.4 EXCLUSION OF INCOME TAX AND CAPITAL GAINS TAX.

Where there is a liability to UK corporation tax there is an exclusion from income tax and capital gains tax. By s. 6(2), TA:

> The provisions of the Income Tax Acts relating to the charge of income tax shall not apply to income of a company (not arising to it in a fiduciary or representative capacity) if:
>
> (a) the company is resident in the United Kingdom; or
> (b) the income is, in the case of a company not so resident, within the chargeable profits of the company as defined for the purposes of corporation tax by section 11(2).

The effect of this is that a corporate trustee can be liable to income tax *qua* trustee but is not liable to corporation tax on those profits. Equally, if a company is not trading in the UK through a branch or agency, it can still be liable to UK income tax though not corporation tax. Thus an investment company holding let land in the UK can be liable to UK income tax (at basic rate as the company is not an individual) on the rent but will not be liable to corporation tax.

There is also an exclusion from capital gains tax. By s. 6(3), TA:

> A company shall not be chargeable to capital gains tax in respect of gains accruing to it so that it is chargeable in respect of them to corporation tax or would be so chargeable but for an exemption from corporation tax.

The effect of this is that a non-resident company not trading in the UK through a branch or agency will not be liable to capital gains tax or corporation tax on chargeable gains. Thus if the company in the above example were to sell the land no charge to UK tax would arise on a capital gain on the sale.

26.5 LIABILITY OF NON-UK RESIDENT COMPANY TO UK CORPORATION TAX

26.5.1 General position

The general approach so far has been to look at residence as the factor connecting the company to the UK for corporation tax purposes. However, as seen in para. 26.4 above, the source of the income can also be a connecting factor. Here liability depends on whether or not the company is carrying on a trade in the UK through a branch or agency. The authority for this is s. 11(1), TA. This provides:

> A company not resident in the United Kingdom shall not be within the charge to corporation tax unless it carries on a trade in the United Kingdom through a branch or agency but, if it does so, it shall, subject to any exceptions provided for by the Corporation Tax Acts [see Glossary], be chargeable to corporation tax on all its chargeable profits wherever arising.

Chargeable profits are defined in s. 11(2) discussed below.

26.5.2 Necessary conditions

There are thus two necessary conditions for UK corporation tax liability of a non-resident company:

(a) that the company is carrying on a trade in the UK;
(b) through a branch or agency.

The position may be modified by a double tax treaty (see Chapter 35). Such a treaty may limit business profits liable to UK corporation tax to those attributable to a 'permanent establishment'. The precise meaning of a permanent establishment will depend on the relevant double tax treaty but generally includes, inter alia, branches, agencies, factories and offices.

26.5.3 Matters to consider

There are a number of matters to consider. These include:

(a) What is a 'branch or agency'?
(b) What is meant by 'trading with or in the UK'?
(c) What profits are chargeable?

26.5.4 'Branch or agency'

By s. 834(1), TA 'branch or agency' means any factorship, agency, receivership, branch or management. It should be noted that by Part XXIII of the Companies Act 1985 a foreign company with a place of business in the UK is required to file certain information at the Companies Registry. An agent may also have to account for tax for the principal.

26.5.5 What is trade within the UK?

26.5.5.1 Trade with or in? In order for a non-resident company to be liable to UK corporation tax, it must be carrying on a trade *in* the UK through a branch or agency. A contrast is to be drawn between 'trading *with*' and 'trading *in*' the UK. Lord Herschell made this clear in *Grainger* v *Gough* [1896] AC 325 at p. 335. He said:

> ... there is a broad distinction between trading with a country and carrying on a trade within a country. Many merchants and manufacturers export their goods to all parts of the World, yet I do not suppose anyone would dream of saying that they exercise or carry on their trade in every country in which their goods find customers ... something more must be necessary in order to constitute the exercise of a trade within this country. How does a wine merchant exercise his trade? I take it, by making or buying wine and selling it again, with a view to profit. If all that a merchant does in any particular country is to solicit orders, I do not think he can reasonably be said to exercise or be carrying on his trade in that country. What is done there is only ancillary to the exercise of his trade in the country where he buys or makes, stores and sells his goods.

26.5.5.2 Fundamental approach Rowlatt J set out the fundamental approach in *F.L. Smith & Co.* v *Greenwood* (1922) 8 TC 193 at p. 198. He said:

> It seems to me that in these cases the question is whether the trade which it is sought to tax is exercised in the United Kingdom, or outside of it in the sense that it is supposed to have a single situation, and the question is

what that situation is. I do not think that the exercise of a trade mentioned in Schedule D can be said to be in the United Kingdom with a reservation that it may also perhaps take place outside of it. The scheme of this part of the Income Tax Act is to tax a foreign resident in respect of a source of income in the United Kingdom. The exercise of a trade produces a profit once, but not twice, and if that exercise takes place in the United Kingdom it cannot, in respect of the same profits and gains, take place elsewhere.

26.5.5.3 Importance of *locus contractus* Viscount Cave identified the importance for these purposes of the place of contracting, or *locus contractus*, in *Maclaine* v *Eccott* (1926) 10 TC 481. He said:

> The question whether a trade is exercised in the United Kingdom is a question of fact, and it is undersirable to attempt to lay down any laws to test what constitutes such an exercise of trade; but I think it must now be taken as established within the case of a merchant's business, the primary object of which is to sell goods at a profit, the trade (speaking generally) is exercised and carried on . . . at the place where the contracts were made. No doubt reference has sometimes been made to the place where the payment is made for the goods sold or to the place where the goods are delivered, it may be that in certain circumstances these are material considerations, but the most important and indeed crucial, is, where the contract of sale is made.

26.5.5.4 Place of contracting not conclusive Notwithstanding Viscount Cave's dictum in para. 26.5.5.3 above, the place of contracting is an important matter but is not conclusive and is not always apt outside the merchanting context, particularly as regards services and long term supplies. It seems that a better test is to ask, where in substance do the profits arise? This follows from Rowlatt J's dictum in *F.L. Smith & Co.* v *Greenwood* (1922) 8 TC 193 at p. 198, as approved and applied by Lord Radcliffe in *Firestone Tyre Co. Ltd* v *Llewellin* (1958) 37 TC 111. Rowlatt J said (8 TC at p. 203):

> The contracts in this case were made abroad. But I am not prepared to hold this test decisive. I can imagine cases where the contract of resale is made abroad, and yet the manufacture of the goods, some negotiations of the terms, and complete execution of the contract take place here. I think that the question is, where do the operations take place from which in substance the profits arise?

26.5.5.5 Three important issues It therefore seems that three matters are important in deciding whether or not a trade is carried on in the UK. These are:

(a) the place where the contract is made;
(b) the place where performance takes place; and
(c) the place of payment.

The charge to corporation tax 573

If all three of these elements take place outside the UK then generally the company will not be trading in the UK. The more that is done in the UK the more likely it is that there is a trade in the UK. However, it is a matter of fact and degree in each case.

It should be noted that the English law on the place of contracting is complicated. It is first necessary to decide what law governs the formation of the contract.[2] If the contract is made orally and *inter praesentes*, the place of notification of acceptance of the offer is the place of contracting.[3] If the contract is made by instantaneous communications such as telephone, telex etc., the place where the contract is made is the place where the acceptance is received.[4]

26.6 BASIS OF LIABILITY AND COMPUTATION

26.6.1 Current year arising basis

UK corporation tax is charged on a current year arising basis, i.e., on the income for the period in question whether or not remitted to the UK. (There is an exception for some unremittable income in s. 584, TA.) Income and capital gains are aggregated to form total profits from which charges on income are deducted (cf. income tax).

26.6.2 Income – s. 9, TA application of income tax principles

26.6.2.1 General Although companies are not liable to income tax (see s. 6(2), TA and para. 26.4 above), their income profits are generally computed in accordance with income tax principles. This is the effect of s. 9(1), TA. It provides:

> ... the amount of any income shall for purposes of corporation tax be computed in accordance with income tax principles, all questions as to the amounts which are or are not be to taken into account as income, or in computing income, or charged to tax as a person's income, or as the time when any such amount is to be treated as arising, being determined in accordance with income tax law and practice.

(As to the meaning of 'income tax law' see s. 9(2).)

Accordingly, one must compute the amount of any income which would be chargeable under the Schedule and Case (other than Schedules E and F which only apply to individuals) appropriate to the source of the income

---

[2.] Logically a choice of law clause without more cannot govern this as such a clause depends on there being a valid contract. See Contracts (Applicable Law) Act 1990 and *Albeko Scuhmaschinen v Kamborian* (1961) 111 LJ 619.

[3.] *Entores Ltd v Miles Far East Corporation* [1955] 2 QB 327 and *Brinkibon v Stahag Stahl* [1982] 1 All ER 293

[4.] *Entores* and *Brinkibon* (see footnote 3). If the contract is made by telegram or post, the place of proper posting is the place of formation; see *Adams v Lindsell* (1818) 1 B & Ald 681.

which accrues to the company. However, some specific points need to be mentioned.

26.6.2.2 Professional activities It is established that a company cannot carry on a profession (*William Esplen Son and Swainston Ltd* v *IRC* [1919] 2 KB 731). The company does not escape tax on professional activities, however, as it will be assessed to corporation tax in accordance with Case I of Schedule D in respect of its trade of hiring out the professional services of its employees or agents.

26.6.2.3 Dividends The United Kingdom system of corporate taxation operates by subjecting dividends and other distributions of resident companies to a separate regime. This subject is considered in detail in Chapter 27. The receipt of dividends and distributions of resident companies is not taken into account in computing income for the purposes of corporation tax (s. 208, TA), and the payment of a dividend or other distribution is not allowed as a deduction in computing that income (s. 337(2)(a)). These provisions achieve the separation of dividends from the charge to corporation tax, and have the necessary consequence that resident companies declare their dividends out of taxed profits. Dividends from non-UK resident companies may be taxable under Schedule D, Case IV or V.

26.6.2.4 Interest, annuities and annual payments Previously a company could deduct from its income any yearly interest payable in the United Kingdom on an advance from a bank carrying on a *bona fide* banking business in the United Kingdom (s. 337(3), TA unamended), but interest was not otherwise deductible in computing income from any source (s. 337(2)(b)). The FA 1996 amended this so that (subject to s. 337A) s. 337 no longer prevents interest paid other than to a bank from being deductible in computing the profits from any source. Annuities and annual payments are not deductible as trading expenses and may not be deducted in computing a company's schedular income (s. 337(2)(b), TA). However, where annuities and annual payments may not be deducted from income, they may be allowable as 'charges on income'. This was previously the case with annual interest.

A new s. 337A is inserted into TA by FA 1996. This provides that no interest shall be deductible in computing a company's income from any source other than in accordance with the loan relationship provisions (see para. 26.9).

26.6.2.5 Receipts net of income tax The fact that a company is the recipient of a payment from which income tax must be deducted does not affect the deduction by the payer (s. 7(1), TA). The income tax so deducted may be set against the company's liability to corporation tax, and if the company is wholly exempt from corporation tax, or is not liable to pay as much by way of corporation tax as has been deducted as income tax from payments to it, it may reclaim the income tax (s. 7(2)). The position is the

The charge to corporation tax 575

same for non-resident companies subject to corporation tax (s. 11(3)). If income tax is deducted from payments to non-resident companies not subject to corporation tax, generally no repayment may be claimed. Where a company makes payments from which it deducts income tax, as well as receiving income from which tax has been deducted, it may set the income tax deducted on its behalf against the income tax which it is liable to pay in respect of its own payments, rather than setting it against corporation tax in accordance with ss. 7(2) and 11(3) (see para. 5 of sch. 16).

26.6.2.6 Overview The company's income profits are the aggregate income chargeable in accordance with the Schedules (see s. 9(3), TA) and are subject to the special rules noted above. Any exemptions from income tax are also available to companies charged to corporation tax (see s. 9(4)) unless the exemption is restricted to 'individuals' (see s. 9(2)). Sections 1 to 5, 60 to 69, 256 to 336, 348 to 350 are not applied by s. 9 (these sections deal with the charge to income tax, payment, personal reliefs, aggregation of spouses' incomes, residence, the ss. 348, 349(1) and (2) procedures and small maintenance payments), together with ss. 60 to 73 (which deal with assessment under Schedule D; see s. 9(6)), In relation to mutual trading by companies, see ss. 486(10), 490 and 491.

26.6.3 Capital gains/chargeable gains

Just as a company's income profits are computed in accordance with income tax principles, so its capital profits are computed in accordance with capital gains tax principles. Thus, the amount to be included in respect of chargeable gains is, by s. 8, TCGA, to be computed in accordance with the principles applying for capital gains tax. All questions as to the amounts which are or are not to be taken into account as chargeable gains or as allowable losses, or charged to tax as a person's gain, or as to the time when any such amount is to be treated as accruing, being determined in accordance with the provisions relating to capital gains tax, although no account is taken of matters confined to 'individuals' (s. 8).

The provisions of s. 40, TCGA are particularly relevant to the liability of companies to capital gains tax. Where a company has incurred expenditure on the construction of any building, structure or works, and that expenditure is allowable under s. 38 in computing a gain accruing to the company on the disposal of the building, structure or work, or of any asset comprising it, and the expenditure was defrayed out of borrowed money, then the amount of the interest charged on that money before the disposal is also allowable under s. 38.

Until 17 March 1987 the chargeable gains of companies were treated differently from income in certain respects.

(a) whereas the whole of a company's income profits were subject to corporation tax, its capital profits were reduced so that the effective rate of corporation tax on chargeable gains was 30%, the same rate (at that time) as for individuals;

(b) the reduced rate of corporation tax for 'small companies' was not available in respect of chargeable gains;

(c) advance corporation tax could not be set against corporation tax on chargeable gains.

For accounting periods beginning on or after 17 March 1987 these differences have been removed (see s. 74, FA (No. 2) 1987).

26.7 DEDUCTIONS AND CHARGES ON INCOME

26.7.1 Introduction

The amount of any profits chargeable to corporation tax may only be reduced by deductions authorised by the Corporation Tax Acts (s. 12(1)). Some deductions are allowed in computing profits by the appropriate income tax and capital gains tax rules applied by s. 9, TA and s. 8, TCGA. The following deductions may (inter alia) also be available.

26.7.2 Trading expenses

In calculating the trading income of the company a balance of the profits is to be drawn which is to be done on the basis of 'the ordinary principles of commercial accountancy as modified by statute'. This is discussed in Chapter 10. It should be recalled that by s. 74, TA no expense is deductible in the computation of taxable profits unless incurred wholly and exclusively for the purposes of the trade. There is much case law on these requirements which has been discussed in Chapter 10. It is worth noting though that if there is a 'duality of purpose' in making a particular expenditure this may prevent deductibility.

There are special rules for the deductibility of interest (see para. 26.8.2). It should be noted that merely because an expense is deductible for profit and loss account purposes it does not make it deductible for tax purposes (e.g., depreciation – see para. 26.7.4 below).

26.7.3 Management expenses

If a company's income arises from trading activities, the expenses of managing the company are deductible under the provisions of Case I of Schedule D. If, however, the company's income arises from investments such as rents and dividends, the expenses of managing the investments themselves would be allowable, but the expense of managing the company would not. This restriction on deductibility would typically affect many parent and holding companies. Accordingly, s. 75, TA provides that sums disbursed as expenses of management (including commissions) may be deducted in computing the total profits of a resident investment company (unless those expenses are deductible for the purposes of Schedule A). An 'investment company' is a company whose business consists wholly or mainly in the making of

The charge to corporation tax

investments and the principal part of whose income is derived therefrom. The definition includes a savings bank (s. 130). Section 75 will not prevent the deduction as a management expense of the cost of temporarily seconding an employee to charity (cf. s. 86(1)).

There is no definition of 'expenses of management', but the term will include administrative expenses, including salaries and wages, although the commissions referred to above will not include stockbrokers' commissions on a change of investments (*Capital and National Trust v Golder* [1949] 2 All ER 956 and see *Hoechst Finance Ltd v Gumbrell* [1983] STC 150, CA and the discussion at para. 28.5.1). However, expenses of management which represent business entertainment expenses may not be deducted (s. 577(1)(a)). If the management expenses of a taxable period exceed the profits against which they may be set, the excess may be carried forward to the next taxable period, and be treated as management expenses for that next period (s. 75(3)). The provisions of s. 75 are extended to certain life assurance companies (see s. 76 and s. 432 et seq).

26.7.4 Depreciation and capital allowances

The United Kingdom disallows depreciation in computing taxable profits. Any depreciation shown in the profit and loss account is to be added back for tax computation purposes. The UK does, however, have a system of capital allowances which in effect give a deduction for depreciation. In the main these are now on the basis of a 25% writing-down allowance (restricted to 6% for certain 'long life' assets in the FA 1997). The system of first year allowances at 100% has been withdrawn. Chapter 12 contains a discussion of the UK's capital allowance rules.

A company is entitled to the same allowances and is subject to the same charges as an individual in relation to capital expenditure for which relief may be claimed under the Capital Allowances Act 1990. The 'chargeable period' for companies (by reference to which allowances are given) is the accounting period (s. 161, CAA 1990). For corporation tax purposes, writing-down and balancing allowances are normally treated as business expenses, and balancing charges are normally treated as business receipts (s. 144). A company is not obliged to take all the capital allowances to which it is entitled. It may disclaim a writing-down allowance or claim a reduced allowance (s. 24 and see *Ellis v BP Oil Northern Ireland Refinery Ltd* [1985] STC 722).

In relation to claims for capital allowances by companies, s. 145A and sch. 17, CAA 1990 came into effect with the pay and file provisions for corporation tax. Claims by companies are assimilated to claims by individuals by amendments in s. 103 and sch. 17, FA 1990. Some allowances are given effect by discharge or repayment of tax, primarily against a specified source of income (cf. s. 9, CAA 1990). In such a case, this is achieved for a company by deducting the allowance from the specified income for the accounting period in question (s. 145). If there is no, or insufficient, income from the specified source, the unrelieved amount can be carried forward indefinitely to succeeding accounting periods and treated as capital allowances for those periods. Alternatively, the unrelieved amount may, subject to certain conditions, be used to reduce the profits of the preceding accounting period (or, exceptionally, the period before that).

If a company is the landlord of an industrial building for which it can claim a capital allowance, a balancing charge will be treated as income taxed under Schedule A (s. 9, CAA 1990). Similarly, a balancing charge on an equipment lessor will be treated as income from equipment leasing (s. 73, TA). It may happen that a non-resident company is within the charge to corporation tax in respect of its trading activities within the United Kingdom, but within the charge to income tax in respect of other assets (for example, rents or interest) and is entitled to capital allowances against both charges. In this event, capital allowances in respect of the income chargeable to income tax must be set against that income, and capital allowances in respect of income chargeable to corporation tax must be set against that income (s. 149, TA).

The provisions relating to capital allowances for the provision of machinery or plant also apply to machinery or plant provided for use or used for the purposes of the management of the business of an investment company or a life assurance company. If effect cannot be given to the capital allowances by setting them against the income of the investment or insurance company, they can instead be treated as expenses of management except in the case of a close holding investment company (s. 75(4), TA).

26.8 CHARGES ON INCOME ETC. AND CORPORATION TAX

26.8.1 General matters

We are concerned here with what used to be termed 'charges on income' but is now termed 'allowance of charges on income and capital' (s. 338 et seq, TA). This differs from the position of an individual who only gets a deduction against income as opposed to income and capital gains, i.e., profits (s. 338 et seq). Charges on income used to include annual interest but this has been changed by the loan relationship provisions in FA 1996 discussed in para. 26.9 below. Matters which are likely to fall within the revised provisions include:

(a) annuities, annual payments and patent royalties; and
(b) charitable donations.

Charges on income are a deduction from 'profits' (i.e., income and capital gains) as opposed to a deduction in computing a taxable amount in accordance with a particular Schedule. Charges on income must be deducted after all other reliefs other than group relief (s. 338(1)). This can be important (see, e.g., *Willingale* v *Islington Green Investment Co.* [1972] 3 All ER 849).

A distribution is not a charge on income. The consequence is that if the company pays a dividend etc. more is taxable on the company than if the payment constituted a charge on income, e.g., an annuity.

For income tax purposes, it will be remembered that certain payments require the deduction of income tax. No charge on income is allowed on payments of annuities etc. to a person not resident in the UK unless a withholding of income tax is made or treated as such.

26.8.2 Allowable charges

The following types of payment are allowable deductions as charges on income:

(a) Interest is now dealt with by the loan relationship provisions and is no longer a charge on income as such. The position was formerly that any yearly interest, and any other interest payable in the United Kingdom on an advance from a bank carrying on a *bona fide* banking business in the United Kingdom or from a person who, in the opinion of the Inland Revenue, was *bona fide* carrying on the business of a discount house, or was carrying on business as a member of a stock exchange in the United Kingdom, was allowable (s. 338(3), TA). However, it had to be shown that the company existed wholly or mainly for the purposes of carrying on a trade or vocation, or that the payment of the interest was wholly and exclusively laid out or expended for the purposes of a trade or vocation carried on by the company and that the company was not a close investment-holding company, or that the company was an investment company, or that the payment of interest would qualify for interest relief if made by an individual in respect of a loan for the purchase or improvement of land, on the assumption that if the land was occupied by the company the conditions in s. 355 were satisfied if the land either was not used as a residence, or as an individual's main or only residence (and that the £30,000 restriction applied only if the land was used as an individual's main or only residence) (s. 338(6)). Interest charged to capital which would have come within s. 338 if not so charged was also allowable (s. 338).

(b) Any annuity or other annual payment, any patent royalty or other sum paid in respect of the user of a patent, and any mining rent or royalty (s. 338(3)(a), TA). The payment of any annuity, annual payment, patent royalty, or mining rent or royalty to a person not resident in the United Kingdom is not a charge on income unless the paying company is resident in the United Kingdom and either:

  (i) the company deducts income tax in accordance with s. 349(1) or (2) and accounts for the tax so deducted; or
  (ii) the payment is payable out of income brought into charge to tax under Class IV or Case V of Schedule D.

(c) A 'qualifying donation' or a 'covenanted payment' to charity. These terms are defined and discussed in para. 26.8.4 below.

26.8.3 Excluded charges

The following (inter alia), in addition to interest, are not charges on income:

(a) Any payment which is deductible in computing Schedular profits (s. 338(2), TA); this will include all provisions for the deduction of expenses. This is because charges on income are deductible after profits have been computed.

(b) Any dividends or other distributions made by the company (s. 338(2)(a)); this is because dividends and distributions are subject to the separate system of taxation discussed in Chapter 27.

(c) Any annual payment charged on land (s. 338(3)(a)); these payments are chargeable in the recipient's hands under Schedule A but have not had income tax deducted from them.

(d) Any payment charged to capital (s. 338(5)(a)); obviously a payment charged to capital cannot normally be treated as a charge on income (cf. *Fitzleet Estates Ltd v Cherry* [1977] 3 All ER 996).

(e) A payment that is not ultimately borne by the company (s. 338(5)(a)); in other words, the payment must be a charge on the company's income in the sense that the ultimate liability remains with the company, there being no right of reimbursement or other form of substituted liability.

(f) A payment that is not made under a liability incurred for valuable and sufficient consideration and, in the case of a non-resident company, incurred wholly and exclusively for the purposes of a trade or vocation carried on by it in the United Kingdom through a branch or agency (s. 338(5)(b)). Thus, a voluntary or gratuitous charge does not qualify. In *Ball v National and Grindlays Bank Ltd* [1973] Ch 127, the company made annual payments under a covenant to an educational trust for the benefit of the employees' children. The Court of Appeal held that to constitute 'sufficient consideration' for the payment, there must be an adequate *quid pro quo* for the liability incurred (in the law of contract sense). Since the company's payments ensured only the goodwill of the employees, they were not made under a liability incurred for valuable and sufficient consideration. (It seems that such payments may in certain circumstances qualify as trading expenses; cf. *Heather v P-E Consulting Group Ltd* [1973] Ch 189 and would not for that reason qualify as charges on income; see para. (a).)

(g) Annual payments made in return for non-taxable consideration (see s. 125).

26.8.4 Charitable donations

26.8.4.1 General There are two ways in which a charitable donation may qualify as a charge on income:

(a) it may be a 'covenanted payment to charity'; or
(b) it may be a 'qualifying donation'.

26.8.4.2 Covenanted payments to charity A 'covenanted payment to charity' is 'a payment made under a covenant made otherwise than for consideration in money or money's worth in favour of a body of persons or trust established for charitable purposes only whereby the like annual payment (of which the payment in question is one) becomes payable for a period which may exceed three years and is not capable of earlier termination under any power exercisable without the consent of the persons for the time being entitled to the payments' (s. 347A(7), TA). There is no requirement that the charity must have some connection with the business.

The company must deduct tax at the basic rate on making the payment and account for it (s. 349, TA and see SP 3/87). There is no restriction on the maximum amount that may be covenanted.

Where a charity wishes to carry on a trade in circumstances such that the profits would not be exempt from tax under s. 505(1)(e), it is usual for the trustees to form a company to carry on the business and for the company to covenant to pay an amount equal to its annual trading profits to the charity. In this way, the amount of the covenanted payment eliminates any liability to corporation tax on the company, and the annual payments received by the trustees are exempt from tax under s. 505(1)(c)(ii), provided the charity exercises an expenditure policy which does not prevent the exemption applying. The only point to watch is that charges on income are deductible from the profits of the accounting period in which they are paid provided they are paid out of those profits. Thus, the terms of the covenant have to be such as to permit the annual payment.

26.8.4.3 Donations to charity Donations to charity which are allowable as trading expenses are not charges on income. If the donation is not a trading expense, however, it will qualify as a charge on income if it is a 'qualifying donation to charity', which can include a one-off donation to charity which is neither deductible as a trading expense nor a covenanted payment to charity (ss. 338(1) and 339). The relief is given by allowing companies which are resident in the United Kingdom to deduct qualifying donations as charges on income (ss. 338(1) and 339(1) and (2)). The company must deduct basic rate income tax from any payment it makes, and account to the Inland Revenue for the amount deducted (s. 339(3) and (4)); if the charity is not liable to pay tax on the donation, it can reclaim the amount deducted.

26.9 LOAN RELATIONSHIPS

26.9.1 Introduction

26.9.1.1 General Chapter II Part IV, FA 1996 has made important changes to the corporation tax treatment of interest and the like. This follows the review of interest paid and received by companies announced by the Chancellor of the Exchequer in the November 1993 Budget. Following reaction to the consultation on the topic (which had suggested the inclusion of some individuals in the proposals) it was announced in the November 1995 Budget that the new rules would be confined in general to companies. The new rules apply from 1 April 1996.

26.9.1.2 Objectives The Treasury Minister in the Standing Committee debates described the changes as follows.

The basic rules are, first, that the tax system should recognise all debit and credit that arise from borrowing and lending, although in more complex deals, it does not necessarily do that. Secondly, they should be calculated according to authorised accounting methods. We have spoke particularly of accruals because far and away the vast majority of businesses account in that way. Thirdly, the figures should follow those that are produced for non-tax purposes wherever they are acceptable . . . it means we can have one set of accounts . . . We are moving to a more simplified method of ensuring that debits, credits and taxation follow accounts.

In broad terms the objectives of the new loan relationships rules were:

(a) to simplify the tax system by removing unnecessary distinctions between different ways of meeting the cost of borrowing and between loans from different types of lender;
(b) to allow interest shown in the commercial accounts as a deduction for tax purposes;
(c) to remove the need to apportion the return on securities between capital and revenue;
(d) to rationalise the treatment of cross border flows;
(e) to make it easier for businesses to comply with their taxation responsibilities (cf. 1993 Budget statements).

26.9.2 Taxation of loan relationships

Section 80, FA 1996 introduces the loan relationships provisions. It sets the general rules for the taxation of loan relationships. Subsection (1) provides that for corporation tax purposes all profits and gains from a company's loan relationships are to be chargeable to tax as income under the provisions of the Loan Relationships Chapter of FA 1996. These rules are the only ones to apply for corporation tax purposes in the absence of 'any express provision to the contrary' (s. 80(5)). The section deals with loan relationships for trading etc. purposes which are to be brought into account in computing the profits of the trade etc. (s. 80(2)) and with loan relationships that are not for trading etc. purposes which are to be dealt with under Schedule D, Case III (a new s. 18(3A) to cover this was inserted by FA 1996). Deficits are also dealt with by allowing relief even where none of the company's loan relationships falls to be regarded as a source of income under these provisions (see ss. 82 and 83, FA 1996 discussed in paras 26.9.4 and 26.9.6).

26.9.3 What is a 'loan relationship'?

26.9.3.1 General meaning Section 81, FA 1996 deals with the meaning of 'loan relationship'. By s. 81(1):

a company has a loan relationship . . . wherever—

(a) the company stands (whether by reference to a security or otherwise) in the position of a creditor or debtor as respects any money debt; and
(b) that debt is one arising from a transaction for the lending of money . . .'

Associated terms are to be construed accordingly.

The language of the section in the main is reasonably obvious as to meaning but, as would be expected, is likely to cause problems at the margins. We shall have to await interpretation by the courts. For example, precisely what is meant by 'that debt is one arising from a transaction for the lending of money . . .'?

Other provisions in the FA 1996 add some flesh to the basic position. Thus s. 100 provides that certain payments are to be treated as loan relationships notwithstanding that technically there is no loan and/or relationship. This includes payment of interest on judgments and payments subject to the transfer pricing provisions. Section 101 and sch. 12 amend the financial instrument provisions of FA 1994 to integrate them with the loan relationship provisions. Section 102 and sch. 13 provide for the income tax treatment of discounted securities on transfer or redemption.

26.9.3.2 What is a money debt? 'Money debt' is defined in s. 81(2). It provides:

. . . a money debt is a debt which falls to be settled—
(a) by the payment of money; or
(b) by the transfer of a right to settlement under a debt which is itself a money debt.

Money in this context 'includes money expressed in a currency other than sterling' (s. 81(6)). Thus not only obligations in sterling but in foreign currencies such the US $ are covered (as is seemingly the Euro).

Subsection (3) extends the meaning of money debt by providing that:

. . . where an instrument is issued by any person for the purpose of representing security for, or the rights of a creditor in respect of, any money debt, then (whatever the circumstances of the issue of the instrument) that debt shall be taken . . . to be a debt arising from a transaction for the lending of money.

This is to deal (inter alia) with situations where there was not a loan as a matter of general law. However, this does not apply to '. . . a debt arising from rights conferred by shares in a company' (s. 81(4)). This deals with the problem that could otherwise arise from the treatment in a company's accounts of shares as, in effect, an amount owed by the company to the shareholder.

26.9.4 Accounting for profits and deficits

26.9.4.1 General As noted above, the broad intention behind the loan relationship provisions is to treat loans and interest on an accounts basis. Section 82, FA 1996 sets out the provisions dealing with the 'Method of bringing amounts into account'. The profits and gains and the deficits from a company's loan relationships are to '. . . be computed in accordance with this section using the credits and debits given for the accounting period in question by the following provisions of this Chapter' (s. 82(1)). A distinction is drawn in the drafting between a 'loan relationship of a company . . . to which it is a party for the purposes of a trade carried on by it' (called here a trading relationship) and other loan relationships (called here non-trading relationships).

Share premium accounts are not included in the profits, gains and losses of the company's loan relationships but reserves made in accordance with normal accounting principles are included (s. 84(2)).

26.9.4.2 Trading relationships By s. 82(2), FA 1996, for any accounting period, to the extent that a loan relationship of a company is a trading relationship, the credits and debits are to be treated as receipts or expenses of the trade, as the case may be. Most of the rest of the provisions elaborate on this broad proposition. The general effect is that such relationships will be dealt with under Schedule D, Case I.

26.9.4.3 Non-trading relationships To the extent that a loan relationship of a company is a non-trading relationship it is to be dealt with under Schedule D, Case III. Credits and debits not dealt with as trading receipts or expenses are called in the section 'non-trading credits' and 'non-trading debits' (s. 82(3)). The 'non-trading credits' and 'non-trading debits' are each to be aggregated and the aggregate of 'non-trading debits' is to be subtracted from the aggregate of 'non-trading credits' (s. 82(3)). That difference is to be:

(a) if it is positive, the amount chargeable for the accounting period under Schedule D, Case III as the profits or gains arising from the company's loan relationships;

(b) if it is negative, the amount of the company's 'non-trading deficit' for the accounting period.

Thus if the aggregate non-trading debits were £1,000 and the non-trading credits were £3,000 then the difference would be +£2,000 which would be taxable under Schedule D, Case III. If the figures were reversed, then the difference would be (−£2,000) which would be the 'non-trading deficit' for the accounting period. What can be done with a 'non-trading deficit' is discussed in para. 26.9.6.

26.9.4.4 Debits and credits brought into account The credits and debits to be brought into account in respect of a company's loan relationships

The charge to corporation tax

are the sums computed in accordance with 'an authorised accounting method' which for the accounting period in question fairly represent:

(a) all profits, gains and losses of the company including those of a capital nature of a company from its loan relationships and related transactions (other than interest, expenses etc.)

(b) all interest under the company's loan relationships and expenses under or for the purposes of its loan relationships and related transactions (s. 84, FA 1996).

A related transaction '. . . in relation to a loan transaction is any disposal or acquisition (in whole or part) of rights or liabilities under that relationship' (s. 84(5)). A disposal or acquisition for these purposes includes the transfer or extinction of such rights and liabilities by any sale, gift, exchange, surrender, redemption or release (s. 84(6)).

'An authorised accounting method' is one which complies with s. 85. There are broadly two authorised accounting methods. These are:

(a) an accruals basis; and
(b) a mark to mark basis.

The rest of s. 85 and s. 86 provide guidance as to how these methods are to be applied. However, where there is a connection between the parties to a loan relationship as creditor or debtor then an authorised accruals method is to be used (s. 87). This is subject to the exemptions provided for in s. 88.

Provision is made in ss. 89 and 90 to ensure that no debits or credits fall out of account as a result of a change in, or inconsistent application of, accounting methods.

Schedule 9 sets out further special computational provisions. These are very detailed and cannot be considered in depth here for reasons of space. However, some general points can be made. Distributions (such as dividends) are excluded from these provisions (para. 1). Where there is a delay in the payment of interest the accounting method may sometimes be adjusted to take that into account (para. 2). Paragraph 3 provides special rules where an accruals method is used but a contingency is involved. Exchange rate fluctuations are ignored for these purposes but not for the purposes of the special rules on the taxation of currency fluctuations in the FA 1993 (para. 4).

Paragraph 5 provides for bad debts relief where an accruals method is used. This is subject to para. 6 which provides for the accruals method to apply (rather than para. 5 relief) where the parties are connected (as to which see s. 87), unless, broadly, the debt is discharged in consideration of shares which are part of the company's ordinary share capital provided there was no previous connection between the parties.

Various anti-avoidance provisions are included. For example, para. 10 restricts loss relief relating to periods when the loan relationship is not within the charge to UK tax. Paragraph 11 sets out special provisions for transactions not at arm's length. A number of other technical provisions are included to deal with such matters as 'repo' and stock lending arrangements (see para. 15).

Receipts of interest subject to deduction of tax are dealt with by s. 91. Broadly, the company receives a tax credit for the income tax deducted by the payer.

26.9.5 Special cases

As would be expected, special provision is made for certain matters. These include:

(a) convertible securities (s. 92) when capital treatment may apply;
(b) securities etc. linked to the value of chargeable assets (s. 93) where only an authorised accruals basis may be used;
(c) indexed gilt-edged securities (s. 94) where regulations may make provision for the indexed adjustment;
(d) gilt strips (s. 95) where regulations may be made;
(e) certain other gilts (s. 96): interest on $3\frac{1}{2}$% Funding Stock 1999–2004 and $5\frac{1}{2}$% Treasury Stock 2008–2012 are to be dealt with on an authorised accruals basis;
(f) manufactured interest (s. 97) is effectively to be treated as real interest and dealt with accordingly;
(g) collective investment schemes (s. 98 and sch. 10);
(h) insurance companies (s. 99 and sch. 11).

26.9.6 Deficits

Trading deficits are treated as expenses of the trade. Accordingly, any excess will be dealt with in the normal way (see Chapter 11). However, without special provision non-trading deficits could be unrelieved. Section 83 and sch. 8, FA 1996 thus make provision for the relief of a non-trading deficit for an accounting period.

The company may claim (see s. 83(2)) for the whole or part of the deficit:

(a) to be set off against any profits of the company (of whatever description) for the deficit period, i.e., an accounting period where there is a non-trading deficit on a company's loan relationships;
(b) to be treated as eligible for group relief;
(c) to be carried back to be set off against profits for earlier accounting periods;
(d) to be carried forward and set against non-trading profits for the next accounting period. It seems this carry forward may be repeated in successive years.

Different claims may be made in respect of different parts of a non-trading deficit (s.83(8)). Where no claim is made under s. 83(2) the deficit is carried forward and treated as a non-trading debit (expense) for the next accounting period (s. 83(3)). Subsection (4) provides that no claim may be made under heads (a) to (c) in respect of so much of a non-trading deficit as is equal to the amount by which that deficit is greater than it would have been if any carried-forward debit for that period had been disregarded. Claims must be made within two years from the end of the 'relevant period' as defined (s. 83(6) and (7)).

Paragraph 1 of sch. 8 sets out the sequence of relief where non-trading deficits are carried across for set off against other profits of the deficit period under s. 83(2)(a). Paragraph 2 deals with group relief (s. 83(2)(b)). Paragraph 3 sets out how a deficit is to be carried back under s. 83(2)(c). Paragraph 4 deals with claims to carry forward under s. 83(2)(d).

CHAPTER TWENTY SEVEN
Advance Corporation Tax ('ACT') and distributions

27.1 PURPOSE OF CHAPTER

The purpose of this chapter is to consider tax and distributions by companies and in particular 'qualifying distributions'. Qualifying distributions give rise to a potential ACT liability on the payer and an income charge on the recipient under Schedule F.[1]

27.2 ADVANCE CORPORATION TAX ('ACT')

When a company makes a distribution, for example, it pays a dividend, it has to make an early payment of its corporation tax liability, hence the name 'Advance Corporation Tax'. Under the UK's partial imputation system, the ACT paid is available as a tax credit for the shareholder (see paras 24.17 et seq below). This ACT may also, subject to limits, be set against the company's liability to mainstream corporation tax (see Chapter 25). There are special rules for dividends which the company has elected to be dealt with under the Foreign Income Dividend ('FID') scheme.[2] ACT is discussed further below.

27.3 DISTRIBUTIONS

27.3.1 Transfers

Where there is a transfer of assets or liabilities by a company to its members (the shareholders) there is a potential income tax charge on the member as

---

[1] For the position of individuals see para. 27.18; for UK resident companies see para. 27.15 and for non-UK resident companies see para. 27.17.
[2] See Chapter VA of Part VI (ss. 246A to 246Y), TA inserted by FA 1994. Foreign income dividends are not discussed further in this book for reasons of space.

receiving a distribution. Where the company is a UK resident company this transfer of assets etc. may amount to a qualifying distribution with ACT consequences for the company and a tax credit for the recipient in so far as it is not a return of capital.

27.3.2 Wide definition of distribution

The Taxes Act contains a wide definition of 'distribution'. This is found mainly in s. 209, TA et seq. The provisions are broadly drafted seemingly to prevent people circumventing the tax regime by making payments which are in essence dividends but in form something different. Thus the distribution provisions are essentially anti-avoidance provisions and should be approached as such. It should be noted that by s. 209(1) 'references in the Corporation Taxes Acts to distributions of a company shall not apply to distributions made in respect of share capital in a winding-up'. Accordingly, payments in a liquidation will not be distributions for income tax purposes but may be capital distributions within s. 122, TCGA. There are special rules for certain payments of dividends in shares rather than cash (sometimes called stock dividends or scrip dividends) in ss. 230 and 240, TA. Dividend payments in shares can be useful devices for companies particularly when cash is short and have been fashionable of late.

By s. 254(3) distribution includes 'anything distributed out of the assets of the company (whether in cash or otherwise) in respect of shares in or securities of another company in the group.' A group here means a 90% subsidiary and its parent. The idea of something distributed out of the assets of the company (whether in cash or otherwise) in respect of shares in, or securities of, a company is what s. 209 et seq is really concerned with. The impact of a distribution on the company's or group's accounts should also be borne in mind.

27.4 IMPORTANCE OF COMPANY LAW

The relevant company law is very important in this context.[3] As a matter of British company law 'a company shall not make a distribution except out of profits available for the purposes' (s. 263(1), CA 1985). 'Distribution' is widely defined in s. 263. By s. 263(3):

> . . . a company's profits available for distribution are its accumulated, realised profits, so far as not previously utilised by distribution or capitalisation, less its accumulated, realised losses, so far as as not previously written off in a reduction or reorganisation of capital duly made . . .

Special provisions apply in ss. 265 to 267 for investment and companies whose principal business consists of investing in securities, land or other assets.[4]

[3.] The law of the place of incorporation will often determine what can be distributed by the company.
[4.] Dividends in specie may benefit from the special rules in s. 276, CA in effect allowing any increase in the value of the non-cash asset to be taken as realised profits.

Section 277 provides that if the distribution was unlawful the recipient of the distribution will have to repay the company if he knew or should have known that the distribution was unlawful. For a case on the effect of illegal dividends, see *Precision Dippings Ltd* v *Precision Dippings Marketing Ltd* [1986] Ch 447.

27.5 WHEN IS A DISTRIBUTION PAID?

For the purposes of the Corporation Tax Acts,[5] dividends shall be treated as paid on the date when they become due and payable (see s. 834(3), TA). The question when dividends become due and payable was considered in *Potel* v *IRC* (1970) 46 TC 658. This case concerned interim dividends. The dividend was declared during the 1964–65 tax year (31 March 1965) but payment was not made until the tax year 1965–66 (29 May 1965). The dividend was treated as paid in the tax year 1965–66 as an interim dividend did not create a debt before the payment was made.

Brightman J set out (at p. 667) the following principles:

(1) If the articles of association of a company contain an article similar to article 80 [i.e., the directors may exercise such powers of the company as are not by the Companies Act or articles required to be exercised by the company in general meeting[6]] directors who recommend a final dividend have power at the same time to stipulate the date on which such dividend shall be paid: *Thairlwall* v *Great Northern Railway Co* [1910] 2 KB 509.

(2) If a final dividend is declared by a company without any stipulation as to the date for payment, the declaration of the dividend creates an immediate debt: *In re Severn and Wye and Severn Bridge Railway Co* [1896] 1 Ch 559.

(3) If a final dividend is declared and is expressed as payable at a future date a shareholder has no right to enforce payment until the due date for payment arrives. This was assumed to be correct in *In re Kidner* [1929] 2 Ch 121, and, despite a submission to the contrary, in Brightman J's view, it was clear beyond argument.

(4) In the case of an interim dividend which a board has resolved to pay, it is open to the board at any time before payment to review its decision and resolve not to pay the dividend: *Lagunas Nitrate Co Ltd* v *Schroeder & Co.* (1901) 85 LT 22 (see also *Hurll* v *IRC* (1922) 8 TC 292). Therefore an interim dividend is only due and payable when it is actually made.

27.6 IMPORTANT DEFINITIONS

In order to help our understanding of a distribution there are a number of definitions which need to be considered.

[5.] See s. 831(1)(a), TA and the Glossary. They include 'the enactments relating to the taxation . . . of company distributions (including provisions relating also to income tax) . . .'

[6.] Note article 125, 'The Directors may from time to time pay to the Members or any class of Members, such Interim Dividends as appear to the directors to be justified by the profits of the Company.'

Advance Corporation Tax ('ACT') and distributions

27.6.1 'In respect of shares or securities'

Since the intention of the legislation is to prevent companies avoiding dividend treatment (i.e., ACT), the relevant legislation refers to matters being done in respect of shares in the company, or in respect of securities of the company. By s. 254(12), TA something is to be regarded as done in respect of a share if it is done to persons being the holder of a share, or having at a particular time been the holder, or is done in pursuance of a right granted or offer made in respect of a share. Shareholder for these purposes is to include the personal representatives of a deceased shareholder. By s. 254(2) this provision is extended to 90% groups of companies.

27.6.2 'Shares and securities'

The word 'shares' is to include stock for these purposes.[7] 'Security' for these purposes includes securities creating or evidencing a charge on assets, and any interest paid by a company or money advanced without the issue of a security for the advance or other consideration given by the company for the use of the money so advanced are to be treated as paid in respect of a security (s. 254(1), TA). This is a very wide definition.

27.6.3 'New consideration'

One way of getting value to shareholders in a company is by issuing shares or securities without requiring the holders to make any contribution for the shares. If the holders do make a contribution for the shares or securities issued, this contribution is referred to as 'new consideration'. New consideration means consideration not provided directly or indirectly out of the assets of the company and, in particular, does not include amounts retained by the company by capitalising distributable profits, for example, on a bonus issue of shares.[8] If company A has 1,000 shares in issue and £100 of profits available it might decide to use the profit to pay up 100 £1 shares and issue those shares to its holders on a one for ten basis. This would be a bonus issue by way of capitalisation. Consideration is treated as provided out of the assets of a company if the cost falls on the company (s. 254(9)).

By s. 254(5), TA where share capital has been issued at a premium representing new consideration, any part of that premium afterwards applied in paying up share capital is to be treated as new consideration for that share capital unless already taken into account.

By s. 254(6) no consideration derived from the value of share capital or securities is to be regarded as new consideration unless it consists of:

[7.] Section 254(1), TA. Shares that are fully paid up may be converted into stock (ss. 121 and 122, CA). This is unusual. For a discussion of the relationship between shares and stock see Lord Cairns in *Morrice* v *Aylmer* (1874) 10 Ch App 148 at p. 154.

[8.] Section 254(1), TA. A company might use distributable profits to pay up shares it issues to existing shareholders. This is sometimes called a bonus issue and the profits are said to be capitalised.

(i) money or value received from the company as a qualifying distribution;

(ii) money received from the company as a payment which for those purposes constitutes a repayment of that share capital or of the principal secured by the security; or

(iii) the giving up of the right to share capital or security on its cancellation, extinguishment or acquisition by the company.

No amount is to be regarded as new consideration on repayment or extinction of a share or security so far as it exceeds any new consideration received by the company for the issue of the share capital or security in question, or where there was a qualifying distribution on issue of a share capital on nominal value of the share capital (s. 254(7)). Thus if shares in company B were cancelled in return for the issue of new shares the amount treated as new consideration would be the amount paid up as new consideration on the issue of the first shares.

Reciprocal arrangements are dealt with by s. 254(8). Thus if company A makes a distribution to the shareholders in company B this can be treated as a distribution by company B.

27.7 MATTERS WHICH CAN BE DISTRIBUTIONS

There are essentially seven groups of matters which are included as distributions. These are as follows:

27.7.1 Any dividend paid by the company including a capital dividend

'Dividend' is not defined for these purposes. Broadly it is a share in the profits of the company. It has been said to be the amount of a company's distributed profits expressed in terms of the nominal value of share capital which must usually be paid out of distributable profits (see para. 27.4 and cf. article 118 old Table A Articles of Association).

A simple example of something falling within this category is the payment of a cash dividend out of distributable profits of the company.

A capital dividend was something previously known to UK law but most capital dividends these days are likely to be made in the course of a liquidation and so will fall within s. 122, TGCA. A capital dividend is not the same thing as a dividend paid out of capital: a capital dividend could arise when the company realises a fixed capital asset and distributes the profit to shareholders and this is not prohibited by company law.[9]

---

[9]. See *Foster* v *New Trinidad Asphalt Co.* [1901] 1 Ch 208 and cf. s. 263(3), Companies Act 1985 and *IRC* v *Reid* (1949) 30 TC 431 where a dividend paid out of capital profits was held by the House of Lords not to be income in the particular circumstances and cf. also *Re Doughty* [1947] Ch 263.

27.7.2 Any distribution out of the assets of the company etc.

This includes any distribution out of the assets of the company, whether in cash or otherwise, in respect of shares in the company except in so far as it:

(a) represents a repayment of capital on the shares; or
(b) is made for new consideration.

This is potentially a very wide heading but there are exclusions for transfers of assets and liabilities between certain UK resident companies (s. 209(5), TA et seq).

This head of distribution accords with the company law position (cf. s. 263(1) and (2), CA 1985). Obviously, if a shareholder provides new consideration for a distribution to him, the assets of the company are not reduced overall, so that there can be in this sense no 'distribution'.

27.7.3 Redeemable shares or securities

This head catches redeemable share capital or any securities issued in respect of shares or securities of the company except in so far as the issue is applicable to new consideration other than stock dividends (s. 209(2)(c)). Without this provision, the issue of bonus redeemable shares and bonus securities would be a simple way of converting income into capital and so disguising income as capital. Section 209(8), TA deals with the question of the value of such a distribution. However, the issue of bonus redeemable shares or bonus securities may not amount to a 'qualifying distribution' (see para. 27.8).

27.7.4 Any interest or other distribution out of assets of the company in respect of the securities of a company except in so far as it represents principal secured

This head only applies to:

(a) bonus securities;
(b) unquoted securities which are convertible into shares in the company or carry a right to receive shares in or securities of the company unless issued on terms reasonably comparable to a quoted security;
(c) securities under which the interest payable by the company depends to any extent on the results of the company's business or represents more than a reasonable commercial rate;
(d) securities issued by a UK company to its 75% or more parent or fellow subsidiary. This may be modified by an applicable double tax treaty (see for example the UK/USA treaty and note the changes made by s. 87, FA 1995 discussed below);
(e) connected securities, i.e., securities connected with shares in the company.[10]

[10.] It might otherwise be possible to get the best of both worlds by having such linked holdings. By paying interest a deduction of interest and avoidance of ACT might be sought.

These provisions seem to be concerned with the servicing but not repayment of loans. The thinking seems to be that in the circumstances described in paragraphs (a) to (e) above payment is more akin to a dividend than interest and so should not be deductible in computing the company's taxable profits and should attract ACT. The application of distribution treatment to such payments can cause problems for payments between companies where the recipient company is resident in a country with which the United Kingdom has no double tax treaty enabling the tax credit to be reclaimed such as Hong Kong. Broadly, the excess interest etc. over what would be paid on an arm's length basis is treated as a distribution.

27.7.5 Transfer of assets or liabilities

Where there is a transfer of assets or liabilities between the company and its members there will be a distribution except to the extent that the amount or value distributed does not exceed new consideration provided by the member.

27.7.6 Bonus issue on or after repayment of share capital

See para. 27.7.7 below.

27.7.7 Repayment of share capital preceded by a bonus issue of shares

The purpose of classifying the transactions noted at paras 27.7.6 and 27.7.7 as distributions seems to be to prevent a company from escaping distribution treatment by making the distribution out of reserves in the guise of a bonus issue.

27.8 QUALIFYING DISTRIBUTIONS

Only qualifying distributions paid by a UK resident company attract ACT. By s. 14(2), TA: 'qualifying distribution' means any distribution other than:

(a) a distribution which, in relation to the company making it, is a distribution by virtue only of s. 209(2)(c); or

(b) a distribution consisting of any share capital or security which the company making the distribution has directly or indirectly received from the company by which the share capital or security was issued and which, in relation to the latter company, is a distribution by virtue only of s. 209(2)(c).

Section 209(2)(c) is noted in para. 27.7.3.

Thus, a qualifying distribution is any distribution by the company except a non-distribution (see para. 27.9 below) and a distribution which is, or represents, bonus redeemable share capital or a bonus security.

Advance Corporation Tax ('ACT') and distributions

Example

Company A Ltd makes £100 profit (but is taxable at the 33% rate).

It distributes £67 which is received by B, a UK resident shareholder, who is beneficially entitled to all the shares in A Ltd.

	£
(1) *Overall Tax Bill*	
Profits	100
Tax @ 33%	33
Available for distribution	67
(2) *Franked Payment*	
If A Ltd declares a dividend of 67	67
ACT of ¼ of 67 is	16.75
(see para. 27.11)	67
(3) *Company A's Position*	
Tax on 100 @ 33%	33
Less ACT paid	16.75
Net amount due as mainstream corporation tax	16.25
(4) *B's Position*	£
B receives dividend of	67
Plus a tax credit of	16.75
Taxable on	83.75
Tax at 40% on 83.75	33.5
Less credit	16.75
Leaving tax to pay of	16.75
Total tax paid by A Ltd and B is 33 + 16.75 =	49.75
Net receipt	50.25
Total	100.00

27.9 'NON-DISTRIBUTIONS'

The following do not constitute distributions, so that no question of their being qualifying or non-qualifying arises:

(a) A distribution in a winding-up (s. 209(1), TA; cf. s. 263(2)(d), CA 1985). By concession, this exclusion is extended to small distributions to the members of a non-trading social or recreational club on its dissolution (Extra-statutory Concession C15). It is also extended in some cases to dissolutions under s. 652, CA 1985 which is strictly not a winding up but a striking off (see Extra-statutory Concession C16).

(b) A repayment of capital (s. 209(2)(b), TA).

(c) The provision of assets to the extent that new and valuable consideration is given (ss. 209(2)(b), (c), (3) and 210(1)(b)).

(d) A transfer of assets or liabilities between a parent company and subsidiaries (s. 209(5).

(e) A covenanted donation to charity (s. 339(6)), such a payment is a charge on income rather than a distribution.

(f) A payment for group relief (s. 402(6)(b)).

(g) A payment (in limited circumstances) by an unquoted trading company on the redemption, repayment or purchase of its own shares (s. 219 and cf. ss. 162 to 181, CA 1985 and see Chapter 30).

(h) Certain payments of interest or other 'distributions' to another company (s. 212, TA). This is, in essence, an anti-avoidance provision. Companies which, because of their corporation tax position, could not make use of the tax deduction for interest paid, might otherwise attempt to treat the interest payment as a qualifying distribution. The lender would then receive franked investment income (rather than taxable profit) and, if this was of benefit to the lender, might share this benefit with the borrowing company by charging a lower interest rate. Section 212 prevents such arrangements.

27.10 STOCK DIVIDENDS[11]

Section 230, TA provides that a stock dividend is not a distribution if it falls within s. 249. It is also apparently not to be treated as paid up for new consideration for the purposes of ss. 210 and 211. Section 249 taxes such stock or scrip dividends as income receipts. The chief advantage to the company in paying stock dividends is that no ACT will become due (because it is not a qualifying distribution – see para. 27.8). For the recipient shareholder, there is no charge to lower rate income tax but the receipt is treated as having borne tax at the lower rate. This lower rate tax is not recoverable (as no ACT has been paid).[12] The recipient is taxable on an amount net of the lower rate of tax equal to the 'appropriate amount in cash'. By s. 251(2) this is the amount of the cash alternative to the stock dividend if not substantially different,[13] and in other cases it is the market value. Thus if a stock dividend worth £80 is received, the taxpayer will be treated as receiving £80 (i.e., 100 less 20%) together with a non-recoverable tax credit of 20%. There are difficulties with trustees and scrip dividends.[14]

[11.] 'A company may offer its shareholders the option of taking additional shares rather than a cash dividend. Such issues of shares are described in the statute as stock dividends, although they are also commonly known as scrip dividends. Where the number of shares issued is deliberately set so that their market value exceeds the cash alternative, the issue is known as an enhanced stock dividend (or enhanced scrip dividend).' Paragraph 2, SP 4/94.

[12.] This is unattractive to an exempt institution such as a pension fund which may otherwise be able to recover ACT. Hence the use of enhanced scrip dividends giving more in value terms if the scrip is taken.

[13.] 'Substantially different' is a difference of 15% or more (SP A8).

[14.] See *Sinclair* v *Lee* [1993] STI 844. The problem is whether the scrip dividends are to be treated as capital or income for trust purposes and the effect of this for tax. See also SP 4/94, 17 May 1994.

27.11 ADVANCE CORPORATION TAX

As was seen above where a company resident in the United Kingdom makes a 'qualifying distribution' the distributing company is liable to pay advance corporation tax in addition to the dividend. Under s. 14(3), TA advance corporation tax is payable 'on an amount equal to the amount or value of the qualifying distribution'.[15] The rate of advance corporation tax for a financial year is to be fixed by a fraction set out in s. 14 (3). The fraction is:

$$\frac{\text{income tax at the lower rate}}{(100 - \text{income tax at the lower rate})}$$

For 1997–98 the fraction therefore is:

$$\frac{20}{(100 - 20)} = \frac{20}{80} = \frac{1}{4}$$

This maintains the link with the lower rate of income tax. At a 20% lower rate the dividend will be 80% of the dividend plus credit. Consequently, the credit will be ¼ of the dividend so that it is ⅕ of the dividend plus credit.

27.12 REDUCTION OF CORPORATION TAX

The UK's partial imputation system allows part of the corporation tax paid by the company to be a credit for the shareholder. However, it also requires early payment of some of the company's tax on declaring a dividend in order to finance the granting of the tax credit to the shareholder. There is therefore a need for a 'set off' between the early payment of advance corporation tax and the company's full liability to tax. Accordingly, s. 239(1) provides that:

> advance corporation tax paid by a company (and not repaid) in respect of any distribution made by it in an accounting period shall be set against its liability to corporation tax on any profits charged to corporation tax for that accounting period and shall accordingly discharge a corresponding amount of that liability.

The credit is now against the full profits of the company. Before 17 March 1987 it was only against the tax on the income of the company.

Example
C Limited declares a dividend of £80,000. It will therefore be liable to pay advance corporation tax of £20,000. C Limited's profits in the same accounting period are subsequently computed at £2,200,000, of which £200,000 is chargeable gains. The company's corporation tax liability will therefore be:

[15.] This is why it is in addition to the distribution. If a company pays a dividend of £80 it is required to pay £20 (¼ of £80) in addition to the dividend.

Corporation tax on £2,200,000 @ 33%	£726,000
Less advance corporation tax	(£20,000)
Amount extra to pay	£706,000

The existence of this reduction in liability to corporation tax might tempt companies to declare a dividend out of accumulated profits or out of capital profits in the hope of reducing the company's liability to corporation tax as much as possible. There is, however, a maximum limit to the amount of advance corporation tax that can be set against corporation tax on profits (this latter is often referred to as 'mainstream corporation tax').

This limit is imposed by s. 239(2), TA the tortuous language of which will not be repeated here. Section 239(2) presupposes a notional distribution by the company. The amount of this notional distribution plus the advance corporation tax which the company would be liable to pay on a notional distribution of that amount must together equal the amount of the company's actual profits. The amount of the advance corporation tax on such a notional distribution is the maximum amount of advance corporation tax that the company may set against its mainstream corporation tax.

For example, if a company has profits of £200,000, its mainstream corporation tax will be £66,000. The assumption required by s. 239(2) is that the notional distribution plus the advance corporation tax on it equals £200,000. The maximum set off for this company is the amount of advance corporation tax which would be payable on the notional distribution. The amount of advance corporation tax is 20% of a gross distribution. The figure for profits (£200,000) is a gross figure because s. 239(2) assumes that it includes tax and so the amount of advance corporation tax is 20% of the profits. In this example, it will be £40,000 (£200,000 × 20%).

The result of this calculation is that if the company declares a dividend in excess of £160,000 (so that the advance corporation tax is more than £40,000) the company's mainstream corporation tax liability of £66,000 cannot be reduced by more than £40,000 and there will be a surplus of advance corporation tax.

27.13 USES OF SURPLUS ADVANCE CORPORATION TAX[16]

The result of declaring an 'excessive dividend', that is a dividend of an amount which results in the s. 239(2), TA limit being exceeded so that the full amount of advance corporation tax paid is not relieved by a reduction of corporation tax liability, is that a surplus of advance corporation tax will arise. There will, in effect, be an element of double taxation because the same profits will be bearing both mainstream and advance corporation tax: this should act as a deterrent to the payment of large dividends by over-ambitious directors. All is not lost, however, if a surplus of advance corporation tax arises. That surplus may be relieved in one of three ways:

[16.] There are some limits on the uses of surplus advance corporation tax in specific circumstances, e.g., oil companies (ss. 497 to 499, TA).

27.13.1 Carry-back

The company may elect within two years of the end of the accounting period in which a surplus arises to treat the surplus or any part of it as if it were advance corporation tax of any accounting period beginning within the six[17] years preceding the period in which it arises. The surplus may then be set against the mainstream corporation tax for a previous accounting period (subject to the s. 239(2), TA limit for those earlier periods). More recent accounting periods will be relieved before more remote ones. The company may claim to have the mainstream corporation tax so relieved repaid under s. 239(3). Any claim for carry-back must be properly and specifically claimed (*Procter & Gamble Ltd* v *Taylerson* [1990] STC 624).

27.13.2 Carry-forward

If the surplus ACT cannot be relieved under s. 239(3), TA, it may be carried forward indefinitely and treated as advance corporation tax of succeeding accounting periods until it has been relieved. The amount usable in subsequent accounting periods will also be subject to the s. 239(2) limit (see s. 239(4)).

27.13.3 Surrender

The company may surrender the whole or part of the surplus to a subsidiary company (s. 240, TA). This is considered in para. 29.8. The acquisition of a company with accumulated surpluses of previously surrendered advance corporation tax would be of benefit to a company which could use the company to take over a profitable part of the business. Sections 245 to 245B attempt to stop such schemes by disallowing the use of the surplus in certain circumstances. These anti-avoidance provisions are also considered in para. 29.8.

27.14 UK TAX AND RECIPIENTS OF DISTRIBUTIONS FROM UK COMPANIES

Shareholders may be:

(a) companies or individuals or trustees;
(b) who are resident or non-resident in the United Kingdom.

This status may affect their UK tax position.

Shareholders may receive distributions from companies which are either resident or non-resident. Where a foreign element is involved, double taxation relief may be available (see Chapter 35). This gives rise to a number of permutations. However, this chapter is only concerned with receipts from UK companies.

---

[17] Two years for accounting periods ending before 1 April 1984; see s. 52(2), FA 1984.

27.15 RESIDENT CORPORATE SHAREHOLDERS

A company resident in the United Kingdom may receive distributions from another UK resident company. By s. 208, TA corporation tax is not chargeable on dividends and other distributions of a company resident in the UK and they are not to be taken into account in computing the recipient company's income for corporation tax.

If a company receives a dividend or other qualifying distribution from another company resident in the United Kingdom, the distributing company will have paid advance corporation tax on the distribution. It will be recalled that the object of the imputation system is for the company to pay tax on behalf of the shareholders. Accordingly, s. 231(1) and (2) provide that a resident corporate shareholder in receipt of a qualifying distribution is entitled to a tax credit equal to the amount of the advance corporation tax on that distribution. For example, if company A declares a dividend of £80,000 in favour of company B on which it pays advance corporation tax of £20,000, company B receives the amount of the dividend direct from company A and is entitled to a tax credit of £20,000.

The amount of the distribution received plus the tax credit (£100,000 in the example) is known as 'franked investment income' (s. 238(1) or, in other words, a gross distribution received by the company).

If a company is declaring dividends on which it is liable to pay advance corporation tax and is receiving distributions in respect of which it is entitled to tax credits, the company ought only to be required to pay advance corporation tax if its liability to advance corporation tax exceeds its entitlement to tax credits. This is because, to the extent of the tax credits, the Inland Revenue already have money to which the company is entitled and which can be used to discharge its liability to advance corporation tax. Such a situation will only arise if the company's 'franked payments' (i.e., its qualifying distributions plus the ACT thereon) exceed its franked investment income. Section 241(1) deals with this. It provides:

> Where in any accounting period a company receives franked investment income the company shall not be liable to pay advance corporation tax in respect of qualifying distributions made by it in that period unless the amount of the franked payments made by it in that period exceeds the amount of that income.

For example, if a company declares a dividend of £160,000 on which it is liable to pay advance corporation tax of £40,000, and receives a distribution of £80,000 in respect of which it is entitled to a tax credit of £20,000, its franked payment is £200,000 and its franked investment income is £100,000. The company is liable to pay advance corporation tax in accordance with s. 241 because the franked payment exceeds the franked investment income by £100,000.

There should sensibly be a set off and the amount of advance corporation tax due from the company should be £20,000, the difference between the total liability to advance corporation tax and the entitlement to the tax credit.

The Inland Revenue would then hold the tax credit of £20,000 and would receive a further £20,000 from the company, giving the total of £40,000 which is needed to confer tax credits on the company's own shareholders. However, common sense and simplicity is not the hallmark of tax legislation. Instead, s. 241(2) requires the assumption of yet another notional distribution (as for the ACT limit discussed in para. 27.12). This time it is of a notional distribution of an amount which, together with the advance corporation tax that would be due on a distribution of that amount, equals the excess of the franked payments over the franked investment income. Thus, in the example above, the excess is £100,000. Section 241(2) requires the assumption that the notional distribution plus the advance corporation tax on it equals £100,000. It is that amount of advance corporation tax that the company must actually pay to the Inland Revenue. As before, the amount of the advance corporation tax is 20% of the gross distribution. Since the excess is itself an excess of gross payments, that is, of amounts which include tax, it must necessarily be a gross amount. The amount of the advance corporation tax is therefore 20% of the excess (in the example, this is, not surprisingly, £20,000).

Payment of advance corporation tax in accordance with s. 241(1) is required every quarter, that is for the periods ending 31 March, 30 June, 30 September and 31 December.[18]

27.16 SURPLUS FRANKED INVESTMENT INCOME

Here a company receives more by way of dividend that it declares for its own shareholders. In this situation, there will be a surplus of franked investment income ('FII'). A surplus of franked investment income may be relieved in one or more of four ways which are discussed below.

27.16.1 Repayment where FII after ACT payment

The requirements of sch. 13, TA that the company should account quarterly for its franked payments and franked investment income may mean that a surplus arises in one quarter after the company has declared its own dividends and paid advance corporation tax for an earlier quarter. Such a surplus may be relieved by having the tax credit comprised in the excess of the franked investment income over the franked payments for the same quarter (or the whole of the tax credit in the franked investment income if there are no franked payments in that quarter) repaid to the company (see para. 4 of sch. 13) if it is within the same accounting period.

27.16.2 Carry forward

Where there is a genuine surplus of franked investment income over franked payments at the end of an accounting period (rather than an artificial surplus

---

[18.] Para. 1 of Sch. 13 (though no return need be made for a quarter in which there are no franked payments because necessarily no advance corporation tax can be payable). One would have thought that staggered dates as for VAT would help with cash flow and administration.

created by the quarterly returns), that surplus may be carried forward indefinitely to succeeding accounting periods and treated as franked investment income of those periods (see s. 241(3), TA). The company may therefore make franked payments up to the amount of the surplus so carried forward without being liable to pay any advance corporation tax to the Inland Revenue.

27.16.3 Set off of losses etc. against FII

Section 242, TA allows surplus franked investment income from the same (but not an earlier) accounting period to be treated as though it were profits for that period against which losses etc. may be set. The company may therefore have the tax credit in the surplus so treated repaid to it.

A claim under s. 242 may only be made in respect of the following matters:

(a) the relief of a trading loss by the reduction of present profits under s. 393A(1). The claim must be made within two years from the end of the accounting period in which the trading loss was incurred (see s. 242(8));

(b) the deduction of charges on income under s. 338. The claim must be made within six years from the end of the accounting period in which the charges were paid (s. 242(8));

(c) the deduction of management expenses under ss. 75 and 76. The claim must be made within six years of the end of the accounting period in which the expenses were incurred (s. 242(8));

(d) the relief of certain capital allowances given by discharge or repayment of tax under s. 145, CAA. Such a claim must be made within two years from the end of the accounting period for which the allowances fall to be made (s. 242(8), TA);

(e) the relief of a loss on unquoted shares in trading companies. Such a claim must be made within two years from the end of the accounting period in which the loss was incurred (s. 242(8));

(f) the setting against non-trading deficits on loan relationships under s. 83, FA 1996. The claim must be made within two years of the end of the relevant period (s. 242(8), TA and para. 26.9.6).

It is also possible to set off surplus FII against carried forward trading losses under s. 393(1) (s. 243).

It may happen that after a claim under s. 242 has been made, franked payments are made against which there is no surplus of franked investment income to be set. If the s. 242 claim had not been made, the franked investment income would have reduced the franked payments and there would still be unrelieved losses, charges on income, management expenses, capital allowances and non-trading deficits on loan relationships. To prevent this relief being lost, s. 242(5) allows the unrelieved loss, expense, allowance and non-trading deficits on loan relationships (but not charge) to be treated as a loss, expense or allowance for the accounting period immediately before that in which the franked payment is made, of an amount equal to the lesser of the excess of the franked payments over franked investment income or the amount in respect of which relief was given under s. 242.

27.16.4 Share dealer

Where the company is a share dealing company, the exclusion of distributions received from corporation tax by s. 208, TA prevents the company relieving its trading losses against the distributions received. Section 243 remedies this situation by allowing the surplus franked investment income to be treated as trading income for the purposes of s. 393(1). A claim under s. 243 (which may be instead of or in addition to a claim under s. 242) must be made within six years from the end of the accounting period for which the claim is made under s 393(1) or six years from the time when the company ceases to carry on the trade if the claim relates to (the now repealed) s. 394, TA (s. 243(6), TA).

It should be noted that where the company is entitled to claim repayment of the tax credit comprised in a surplus of franked investment income which is relieved, the repayment is not made by cheque from the Inland Revenue, but by reduction of advance corporation tax due from the company in the future (s. 244(2), TA).

27.17 NON-RESIDENT CORPORATE SHAREHOLDERS RECEIVING DISTRIBUTIONS FROM UK RESIDENT COMPANIES

A distribution made by a resident company may be a qualifying distribution and if it is, a payment of advance corporation tax will be required. However, tax credits are conferred only on resident recipients (cf. s. 231(1), TA), and so the non-resident company in receipt of the dividend or distribution will not be entitled to reclaim any tax (whether or not the company is within the charge to corporation tax under s. 11) unless the qualifying distribution is the income of a colonial pension fund of, or of the government of, any sovereign power, or of any organisation of sovereign powers (s. 232(3)).

If the recipient company is resident in a country with which the United Kingdom has a double tax treaty, the terms of that treaty may provide for the repayment of the tax credit (though this will usually be subject to the deduction of withholding tax); (cf. ss. 812 to 816).

27.18 OTHER RESIDENT SHAREHOLDERS

The receipt of a distribution of a resident company by a resident shareholder other than a company is chargeable to income tax under Schedule F. This charge applies whether the distribution is a qualifying distribution or not. However, if the distribution is a qualifying distribution, the company will have paid advance corporation tax in respect of it, and the recipient shareholder will be able to claim a tax credit equal to the amount of the advance corporation tax on his distribution (s. 231(1), TA).

To the extent of the tax credit[19] the shareholder will be absolved of his liability to income tax on the distribution. If his circumstances are such that he is not liable to pay lower rate income tax on the whole of the distribution, that part of the tax credit which represents overpaid tax may be repaid to him (s. 231(3)). If the recipient is a lower or basic rate taxpayer, the tax credit will wholly satisfy his income tax liability and he will have no further tax to pay on the distribution.

Alternatively, if he is liable to higher rate tax or additional rate tax on the distribution, he must pay the amount of the extra tax due under Schedule F. It should be borne in mind that if any provision of the Income Tax Acts deems the dividend or distribution to be the income of a person who does not actually receive it, the question of whether a tax credit is to be given must be determined by reference to the residence of the person whose income the distribution is deemed to be and not that of the actual recipient (s. 231(4)). Such credits are only available in limited circumstances in the case of a close investment holding company (s. 231(3A) to (3C) and see para. 25.6.11).

If the distribution is not a qualifying distribution, the shareholder is not entitled to a tax credit because no advance corporation tax is due in respect of it, and therefore may not claim to have any amount repaid to him. If the shareholder is a higher rate taxpayer, he is liable for that extra tax on the net amount of the distribution, though he is not liable to lower rate income tax (s. 233(1)).

27.19 OTHER NON-RESIDENT SHAREHOLDERS

A distribution by a resident company may be a qualifying distribution and if it is, a payment of advance corporation tax will be due in respect of it. However, tax credits are conferred only on resident shareholders (cf. s. 231(1), TA), and so the non-resident shareholder will not be entitled to reclaim any tax in respect of the distribution, unless he is entitled to claim personal reliefs in accordance with s. 278(2) (see s. 232(1) and (2)). The shareholder will be liable to income tax on the distribution under Schedule F.

If the shareholder is resident in a country with which the United Kingdom has a double tax treaty, the terms of that treaty may allow the shareholder to claim some or all of the tax credit,[20] though this will usually be subject to the deduction of withholding tax. A non-qualifying distribution does not in any event confer a tax credit (because it does not require the payment of advance corporation tax), but the shareholder is not liable to pay basic rate income tax in respect of it: liability is restricted to higher rate tax (s. 233(1)).

---

[19] Which broadly represents lower rate income tax on the gross amount of the distribution, though before 1993–94 it was the equivalent of basic rate tax; see s. 77, FA 1993.
[20] See, e.g., Article 11 UK/US double tax treaty.

CHAPTER TWENTY EIGHT
Losses

28.1 INTRODUCTION

28.1.1 General

As with any business losses[1] as well as profits may be made by a company. When losses are made the question arises as to how they are to be dealt with for tax purposes. Broadly, the UK's approach is to allow them as a reduction against what is taxed. However, not all losses are treated in the same way. There are, for example, differences in treatment between income and capital losses. The corporation tax rules are also different from those for income tax and capital gains tax. There are special rules for investment companies. These are discussed in para. 28.5.

In considering losses in this context it is important to distinguish between;

(a) trading losses etc.;
(b) allowable losses, i.e., losses for capital gains tax purposes;[2]
(c) surplus charges on income etc. of a trading company;
(d) surplus management charges etc. of an investment company;
(e) Schedule D, Case VI losses.

The reason for this is that different rules apply to different types of loss. It must also be remembered that corporation tax, like income tax, is charged

---

[1] See Bramwell, *Taxation of Companies*, Sweet & Maxwell, Chapter 7; *Simon's Direct Taxes* Part D2.4 passim.
[2] See s. 16, TCGA. By s. 8, TCGA an allowable loss for corporation tax purposes does not include a loss which, if it been a gain, would be exempt.

under different Schedules with their varying rules. This can have the effect (inter alia) of restricting losses under one Schedule being used against profits or gains under another Schedule or against capital gains in future periods. There are also special restrictions on the use of Schedule D, Case VI losses (see below).

28.1.2 How do losses arise?

Losses depend on the deductions available. The expenses incurred by the company in respect of a particular source of income may exceed the income from that source, thereby occasioning a loss in respect of that source. Thus, if the overheads of a trade exceed its receipts there will be a loss for accounting purposes and probably for tax purposes as well. Accordingly, the rules for deduction under the appropriate Schedule are important. Further, some matters are deducted after the Schedular income has been computed. These are called charges on income and were discussed in Chapter 26.

28.1.3 How are losses computed?

By s. 393(7), TA, 'The amount of a loss incurred in a trade in an accounting period shall be computed for the purposes of this section in the same way as trading income from the trade in that period would have been computed.' Section 393A(9)(a) is to the same effect. By s. 9 income tax principles are to be applied to the computation of income for corporation tax purposes except as otherwise provided. Similar provision is made for corporation tax on chargeable gains in s. 8, TCGA. Section 8(3), TCGA specifically refers to allowable losses in the context of corporation tax.

28.1.4 What can be done with losses?

In general terms the use of losses depends on the type of loss involved. The following is a brief summary.

28.1.4.1 Losses incurred by pre-trading expenditure
By definition no trade is carried on by the company but it may incur what would otherwise be tax deductible expenditure in its preparations to trade. Accordingly, special provision is made in s. 401, TA for pre-trading expenditure (see para. 28.2).

28.1.4.2 Trading losses
Trading losses can be:

(a) carried forward against profits of the same trade (s. 393(1));
(b) carried across against other profits of that accounting period (s. 393A);
(c) carried back against profits of previous accounting periods if the company was trading then (s. 393A);
(d) set off against franked investment income (s. 242).

Losses

28.1.4.3 Capital allowances
Capital allowances can be treated as giving rise to a trading loss for a trader in some cases.

28.1.4.4 Allowable losses
These can be used in broadly the same way as for capital gains tax purposes, i.e., against capital gains of that or future periods. There is no ability to carry across such losses against trading profits etc.

28.1.4.5 Groups
Group relief may allow trading losses etc. to be surrendered within a UK group of companies in some circumstances. This is discussed in Chapter 29.

28.2 COMMENCEMENT LOSSES

The relief for commencement losses in s. 381, TA (discussed in Chapter 11) applies only to 'individuals' and is not therefore available to companies. This is because the company will not normally have any previous income against which a commencement loss may be set (though such a situation may arise if an existing company begins trading activities some time after its formation).

Special provision is nevertheless made in s. 401 to give relief for pre-trading expenditure. Expenditure incurred in the seven years before the commencement of the trade which is not then deductible but would have been had the trade been started, is treated as incurred on the day the trade is first commenced.

28.3 TRADING LOSSES

28.3.1 Introductory matters

The provisions dealing with 'Trade etc. losses' are to be found in Chapter II Part X, TA (ss. 393–396) inclusive). These provisions have been amended, particularly by FA 1990.

28.3.2 What can be done with trading losses?

Trading losses can be used in the following ways. They can be:

(a) carried forward against profits of the same trade in future accounting periods (s. 393(1), TA);
(b) carried across against other profits of the same accounting period;
(c) carried back against profits of previous accounting period(s) if the company was trading then;
(d) set off against franked investment income (s. 242).

Losses under head (a) can be set off against 'trading income' as defined in s. 393(8).[3] This is broadly '. . . the income which falls or would fall to be

---

[3] For a recent case on the meaning of 'trading income' in this contect see *Nuclear Electric* v *Bradley* [1996] STC 405.

included in respect of the trade in the total profits of the company . . .' It therefore includes interest or dividends which would be trading income but for being received under deduction of tax.

There are some special anti-avoidance provisions, see, e.g., ss. 343 and 768 and restrictions are placed on the use of Schedule D, Case VI losses and 'uncommercial trade' losses.

It should be remembered that 'accounting period' by s. 834(1) 'shall be construed in accordance with s. 12'. This is discussed in Chapter 25 above.

28.3.3 Carry-forward against profits of the same trade without time limit

28.3.3.1 Statute Section 393, TA allows unused trading losses to be carried forward against profits of the same trade without time limit. It provides (so far as relevant):

> (1) Where in any accounting period a company carrying on a trade incurs a loss in the trade, the loss shall be set off for the purposes of corporation tax against any income from the trade in succeeding accounting periods; and (so long as the company continues to carry on the trade) its trading income from the trade in any succeeding accounting period shall then be treated as reduced by the amount of the loss . . .

Accordingly, by s. 393(1), a trading loss may be carried forward without time limit and set against future trading profits (but not chargeable gains or income from sources other than trading: cf. Extra-statutory Concession B19) for as long as the company continues to carry on the same trade. Where the company is in receipt of interest or dividends on investments which are trading receipts (for example, because the company is a share-dealing company) but which have had tax deducted from them at source, the gross amount of the interest or dividends may be treated as trading profit for future accounting periods if the profits of those periods are otherwise insufficient to relieve a loss in a trade falling within Case I or Case V of Schedule D (s. 393(8)).

Further, if a company has charges on income, which are payments made wholly and exclusively for the purposes of the trade carried on by the company and which exceed the amount of the profits against which they are deductible, the excess may be treated as a trading expense for the purpose of computing a loss to which s. 393(1) applies: such an excess is therefore effectively treated as a trading loss (s. 393(9)) (cf. *Scorer* v *Olin Energy Systems Ltd* [1984] STC 141).

28.3.3.2 Requirements to carry forward The current requirement to carry forward a trading loss of a company (within the charge to corporation tax) is a loss in the trade. The income against which the trading losses can be carried forward is income from the same trade in the future.

Losses

Example

Year 1	Schedule D	Loss	(£1,000)		
Year 2		Breakeven			
Year 3		Profit	£3,000	Taxable	£2,000
					(£3,000 − £1,000)

28.3.3.3 Carry-forward and Schedule D, Case V Losses Schedule D, Case V losses can be carried forward against profits of the same trade as that in which they arise. Whether or not the same trade is being carried on is primarily a question of fact – see, for example, cases such as *Gordon & Blair Ltd v IRC* (1962) 40 TC 358.

28.3.4 Carry-across – reduction of present and previous profits

28.3.4.1 General Where a company incurs a trading loss, that loss may be set against profits of any description (that is, both income and chargeable gains) of the same accounting period (s. 393A(1)(a)) and, provided that the company was then carrying on the same trade, of previous accounting periods (s. 393A(1)(b)). From 1991–92 and onwards it is possible for a loss to be set against the profits of the three previous years (s. 393A).

Section 393A(1) provides (so far as relevant):

> where in any accounting period ending after 1 April 1991 a company carrying on a trade incurs a loss in the trade, then (subject to subsection (3) below) the company may make a claim requiring that the loss be set off for the purposes of corporation tax against profits (of whatever description)—
>
> (a) of that accounting period, and
>
> (b) if the company was then carrying on the trade and the claim so requires, of preceding accounting periods falling wholly or partly within the period specified in subsection (2) . . .

Subsection (2) of s. 393A provides that the period for subsection (1) purposes is to be a period of three years immediately preceding the accounting period in which the loss was incurred. If there is a 'straddle' the profits are to be apportioned. Subsection (3) of s. 393A excludes profits from trades falling within Schedule D, Case V and trades that are not being carried on on a commercial basis with a view to the realisation of a gain.

Accordingly s. 393A(1) splits into two parts, namely;

(a) carry-across against income and chargeable gains of the same accounting period; and

(b) carry-back against income and chargeable gains of previous accounting periods (up to three years).

These will each be considered separately.

28.3.4.2 Carry-across – general As noted in para. 28.3.4.1, s. 393A(1)(a) allows losses to be carried across against income and chargeable gains of the same accounting period.

28.3.4.3 Requirements to carry across The requirements to carry across are as follows:

(a) a trading loss (under Schedule D, Case I);
(b) in the year in question;
(c) other profits 'of whatever description' (i.e., chargeable gains or other income;
(d) in the same accounting period;
(e) claim made to carry across within two years (s. 393A(10)).

Example
In its current accounting period company A made a trading loss of £50,000 and a chargeable gain of £150,000. The loss could be set against the capital gain as follows:

Schedule D, Case I	(£50,000)
Chargeable gain	£150,000
Taxable profit	£100,000

Since the relief is given only against present or previous profits, if the gain had been realised in an accounting period after the trading loss arose the loss could not generally be set against the gain.

28.3.4.4 Schedule D, Case V Subsection (1) of s. 393A, TA does not apply to a Schedule D, Case V trade (s. 393A(3)).

28.3.5 Carry-back to preceding accounting period

28.3.5.1 General matters As was noted in para. 28.3.4.1, s. 393A(1)(b), TA allows losses to be carried back against profits for up to 36 months of the accounting periods immediately preceding the one in which the loss in question arose. Section 393A(1)(a) allows a loss to be carried across against profits of the current accounting period. This was considered in the preceding paragraphs. This time limited carry-back against all profits (provided only that the company was then carrying on the trade) contrasts with the unlimited carry-forward against profits but only of the same trade. It is interesting to consider the underlying policy rationale for such differences.

Section 393A(1) provides (so far as relevant):

> where in any accounting period ending after 1 April 1991 a company carrying on a trade incurs a loss in the trade, then (subject to subsection

Losses

(3) below) the company may make a claim requiring that the loss be set off for the purpose of corporation tax against profits (of whatever description)—

. . .

(b) if the company was then carrying on the trade and the claim so requires, of preceding accounting periods falling wholly or partly within the period specified in subsection (2) . . .

Subsection (2) of s. 393A provides that the period for subsection (1) purposes is to be a period of three years immediately preceding the accounting period in which the loss was incurred. If there is a 'straddle' the profits are to be apportioned.

It is understood that the Revenue consider that a loss should first be set against current profits 'and then' carried back. This has yet to be tested in the courts.

28.3.5.2 Requirements to carry back The requirements to carry back are a company carrying on the trade in:

(a) the current accounting period; and
(b) the preceding period(s) in question up to a total of 36 months;
(c) with a surplus trading loss incurred in the current period; and
(d) which makes a claim within two years (s. 393A(10)).

Example

Accounting Period	4 (current)	Loss	(£10,000)	Taxable Nil
Accounting Period	3	Breakeven		Taxable Nil
Accounting Period	2	Profit	£4,000	Taxable Nil: £4,000 of loss used
Accounting Period	1	Profit	£5,000	Taxable Nil: £5,000 of loss used

In these circumstances £1,000 of losses (£10,000 less (£4,000 + £5,000) would not attract relief.

28.3.5.3 Carry-back and Schedule D, Case V losses Section 393A(1) does not apply to trades falling within Schedule D, Case V, i.e., profits of a trade carried on wholly overseas (s. 393A(3)).

28.3.6 Terminal losses

There were formerly special provisions dealing with terminal losses in s. 394, TA. These were repealed by FA 1991 for accounting periods ending on or after 1 April 1991. The rules used to provide that where a company incurred a trading loss in any accounting period wholly or partly within the last 12 months during which the trade was carried on by the company, that loss could be set against the trading income of the company for an accounting period falling wholly or partly within the period of three years preceding those 12 months. At that time other losses could normally only be carried back for 12 months. When the general position was changed by s. 393A the separate provisions in s. 394 became unnecessary and were repealed. Section 393A allows trading losses to be carried back on a termination (or otherwise) for three years as described above.

28.4 SURPLUS CAPITAL ALLOWANCES

Surplus capital allowances can be treated as losses in some circumstances (see s. 393A(5), TA).

28.5 INVESTMENT COMPANIES

28.5.1 General

The meaning of investment company is considered at para. 25.6.12. There are special rules as to deductions for investment companies since investment companies cannot fall within the trading rules as, by definition, such companies are not trading. These rules are to be found essentially in s. 75, TA. (Special rules for insurance companies are to be found in s. 76.) By s. 75(1) expenses of management can be deducted in computing profits (i.e., income and chargeable gains) unless otherwise deductible, e.g., under Schedule A.

28.5.2 Expenses of management

The expression 'expenses of management' is not defined in the statute for these purposes. It has been the subject of judicial disagreement. Are they expenses 'of' management or expenses incurred 'by' management. The case law conflicts. Thus in *Capital and National Trust* v *Golder* (1949) 31 TC 265 stockholders commission was not allowed as an expense of management. Wider views were expressed in *Sun Life* v *Davidson* (1958) 37 TC 330 that if the expense was part of the revenue cost of investment then it was to be allowed. Effectively this allows all revenue expenses incurred by a company in managing its business to qualify for relief. This would include staff costs and would permit repairs and maintenance etc. to be deducted. (See further para. 26.7.3.)

Capital expenditure is not allowed for these purposes unless it is expenditure which qualifies for capital allowances.

Expenses of management are reduced by amounts derived from sources not otherwise taxed except franked investment income, foreign income dividends, group income and regional development grants.

28.5.3 Surplus expenses of management

By s. 75(3), TA surplus expenses of management can be:

Losses

(a) carried forward; and
(b) treated as incurred in that subsequent period for most purposes.

28.5.4 Capital allowances

An investment company may be entitled to capital allowances (s. 28, CAA). By s. 75(4), TA surplus capital allowances can be added to an investment company's management expenses and carried forward subject to the succeeding accounting period.

28.6 SECTIONS 242 AND 243 AND FRANKED INVESTMENT INCOME

Sections 242 and 243, TA allows losses etc. to be set off against surplus franked investment income. The point of this is to allow the tax credit in the surplus franked investment income to be repaid: see para. 27.16.3. (For non-residents, see SP 2/95.) Section 244 deals with the subsequent ACT position.

28.7 CASE VI LOSSES – SECTION 396, TA

Where a company incurs a loss in a transaction within Case VI of Schedule D the loss may only be set against the profits of Case VI transactions of the same or any subsequent accounting period (s. 396(1)). This does not, however, apply to transactions falling within ss. 34, 35 and 36 (s. 396(2) and see para. 17.6).

28.8 OTHER LOSSES

Losses incurred in respect of rented property may be carried forward and set against future rents. Other types of charges do not, by their nature, generally give rise to losses.

28.9 HIVEDOWNS ETC.

The Taxes Act has provisions to deal with losses where a trade is transferred to another company. If the transfer is to a company under common ownership with the transferor, then the losses etc. may continue to be available for carry-forward under s. 343, TA. If the transfer is to a company without such common ownership, carry-forward may be excluded under s. 768. Broadly, by s. 343, where on a reconstruction the beneficial ownership of 75% or more of a trade (within the requisite time limits) is held by the same persons, the trade is not treated as discontinued nor a new trade set up. Consequently the losses and capital allowances are carried across to the successor company.

There is a restriction on allowable amounts if liabilities left are behind. This section is most commonly used in hivedowns (see Glossary).

Section 768 and other complex anti-avoidance loss provisions are not dealt with in detail in this book for reasons of space.

28.10 ALLOWABLE LOSSES

Allowable losses in respect of capital transactions may be taken into account in computing chargeable gains. If there is an excess of allowable losses over chargeable gains, the excess may not be carried back, but may be carried forward indefinitely (see s. 8, TCGA). Certain investment companies may claim relief for losses on unquoted shares in trading companies (see s. 573, TA).

There is no 'grouping' (i.e., surrender of losses to other group companies) of allowable losses for corporation tax purposes as there is for current trading losses (see para. 28.11 and Chapter 29). This leads to the use of 'sink companies' within groups. All intended capital transactions are routed through one company, the sink company, so that all the losses and gains arise in one company, thereby avoiding the need for grouping. The Revenue do not, generally, seek to attack such tax planning under the *Ramsay* doctrine (see Chapter 4 and [1985] STI 568 but cf. s. 177A, TCGA discussed at para. 29.10).

28.11 GROUP RELIEF

A company within a group may (inter alia) surrender current year trading losses within the UK group. This is discussed further in Chapter 29.

CHAPTER TWENTY NINE
Groups

29.1 INTRODUCTORY MATTERS

29.1.1 Business v legal approach

Economically a group of companies[1] is often, in effect, one business notwithstanding that as a matter of law[2] each company has a separate legal personality and so prima facie is a separate taxable entity. A company may choose to set up subsidiary companies (rather than operate through divisions) for commercial (rather than tax) reasons or to allow the title of director to be given to certain employees.

29.1.2 Possible treatments

The question therefore arises as to how a tax system should deal with the tension between the separate legal personality of group companies and the commercial reality of one business. A number of ways could be adopted including the following:

(a) ignore it (as in some tax havens);
(b) tax by reference to consolidated (i.e., group) accounts (cf. USA);
(c) mitigate the effects of separate legal personality for tax purposes by special provisions dealing with specific matters so as to provide neutrality in those areas between a company operating through divisions and a group.

[1.] See Bramwell, *Taxation of Companies*, Sweet & Maxwell, Part II, Chapters 21–6 and see *Simon's Direct Taxes*, Division D2.6, passim.
[2.] The company law background must be noted and in particular cases such as *Re Aveling Barford* [1989] BCLC 122, *Aveling Barford* v *Perion* [1989] BCLC 626 and the Insolvency Act 1986.

The UK has adopted the last of these.

29.1.3 Consortia

Where a company is owned by a consortium of companies (cf. e.g., s. 402(3) and (4), TA) who are co-operating with each other, it has problems similar to those of a group of companies. Accordingly the legislation deals with consortia in a similar way to the groups and broadly the same provision is made. This is discussed at para. 29.11.

Broadly, a company is owned by a consortium if 75% or more of its ordinary share capital (in the main all shares other than fixed rate preference shares) is owned beneficially by UK resident companies none of which owns less than 5% (see s. 413 and s. 247).

29.2 OUTLINE OF UK APPROACH

As noted above, for some purposes the UK corporation tax system takes account of the economic reality that a group of companies is really one business. This may be summarised in broad terms as follows.

29.2.1 If there is a 75% relationship between UK resident companies

In this case:

(a) assets may be transferred between group members on a no gains/no loss basis, subject to a clawback on the recipient company leaving the group within six years (ss. 171 and 179, TCGA);
(b) surplus losses and capital allowances can be relieved within the group on a current year basis (s. 402, TA);
(c) certain other reliefs may be available on a group basis, e.g., roll-over relief for business assets (s. 175, TCGA).

29.2.2 If there is a 51% relationship between UK resident companies

In this case:

(a) group income may be paid without ACT if an election is in force (s. 247, TA);
(b) ACT may be surrendered within the group.

(On the meaning of 75% and 51% subsidiaries see s. 838, TA discussed in para. 29.4.2.)

29.2.3 Consortia

Certain of these reliefs are extended to consortia. For example loan interest and surplus capital allowances may be surrendered in proportion to share

Groups

holdings by and to members of the consortium. This is discussed at para. 29.11.

29.3 AREAS COVERED IN THIS CHAPTER

This chapter is concerned with groups and consortia. The areas covered include the following matters.

29.3.1 Groups

(a) group income (ss. 247–248, TA);
(b) group relief (ss. 402–413, TA);
(c) surrender of ACT (s. 240, TA);
(d) transfer of assets within a group (s. 170 et seq, TCGA).

29.3.2 Consortia

(a) group income (s. 247);
(b) group relief (s. 402).

29.4 GENERAL MATTERS

29.4.1 Introduction

There are a number of definitions which it is important to understand in this context. The first is, what is a group? A group for these purposes consists of a parent and its subsidiary(ies) (cf. s. 170, TCGA). The UK tax system usually requires the companies to be UK resident[3] for these provisions to apply.

29.4.2 Percentage ownership

The provisions require a different level of ownership for different purposes. Section 838, TA provides that the meaning of the different percentage of ownership of subsidiaries is by reference to beneficial ownership of ordinary share capital.[4] The effect of the definitions is as follows.

(a) A 51% subsidiary is one where *more* than 50% of its ordinary share capital is owned by another body corporate (not defined but see Chapter 25).

[3.] It is arguable that this is in breach of EC law; see, inter alia, [1995] European Law Review, Vol. 20, No. 6, p. 580, [1996] BTR 573 and note the referral of *ICI v Colmer* [1996] STC 352 to the European Court of Justice.

[4.] Section 832, TA, i.e., all the issued share capital by whatever name called other than capital whose holders have a right to a dividend at a fixed rate but no other rights to share in the profits of the company. This excludes fixed rate dividend shares with no other rights. A right in addition to a share in a liquidation surplus would seemingly make the shares ordinary share capital. See also *Tilcon Ltd v Holland* [1981] STC 365.

Thus if A Ltd owns 501 of B Ltd's 1,000 issued shares (all of the same class), B Ltd is a 51% subsidiary of A Ltd.

(b) A 75% subsidiary is one where 75% or more of its ordinary share capital is owned by another body corporate. Thus if C Ltd owns 75 of D Ltd's 100 issued shares (all of the same class), D Ltd is a 75% subsidiary of C Ltd.

(c) A 90% subsidiary is one where 90% or more of its ordinary share capital is owned by another body corporate. Thus if E Ltd owns 900 of F Ltd's 1,000 issued shares (all of the same class), F Ltd is a 90% subsidiary of E Ltd.

29.4.3 'Ordinary share capital'

These percentages are determined by reference to ordinary share capital. By s. 832(1), TA 'ordinary share capital' is to mean '. . . all the issued share capital of the company other than capital the holders of which have a right to a dividend at a fixed rate but have no other right to share in the profits of the company' (see *Tilcon Ltd v Holland* [1981] STC 365). This covers virtually all share capital. The exception is fixed rate dividend shares with no other rights. It is therefore possible to create 'funny shares' that are ordinary share capital for tax purposes but economically are not part of the real equity in the company. For example, shares could be created which had a right to share in the company's profits once £1 million per share of another class had been distributed in any one accounting period. This has led to the imposition of extra conditions for some purposes.

29.4.4 Beneficial ownership for percentages

The percentages of share capital definitions are concerned with beneficial ownership.[5] In determining whether there are 51% and 75% subsidiaries one can look to shares 'owned directly or indirectly'.[6] This is discussed further below.

29.4.5 Rules for determining amount of share capital held

29.4.5.1 Introduction If all the share capital of one company is owned by another company there is no difficulty in working out what percentage of the first company is owned by the second. What if the share holding is more complicated and/or indirect? Rules dealing with this are set out in s. 838, TA. Subsection (4) is important in showing that ownership can be traced through a number of companies and that direct and indirect holdings can be aggregated. This can be illustrated as shown in *Figure 29.1*.

---

[5] Section 838(3), TA and cf. *Hawks v McArthur* [1951] 1 All ER 22; *Wood Preservation v Prior* [1969] 1 All ER 364; *J. Sainsbury v O'Connor* [1991] STC 318 and see 15 November 1991 Inland Revenue Press Release.

[6] Section 838(2), 'In subsection (1)(a) and (b) above "owned directly or indirectly" can take into account shares owned through other bodies corporate.'

Groups

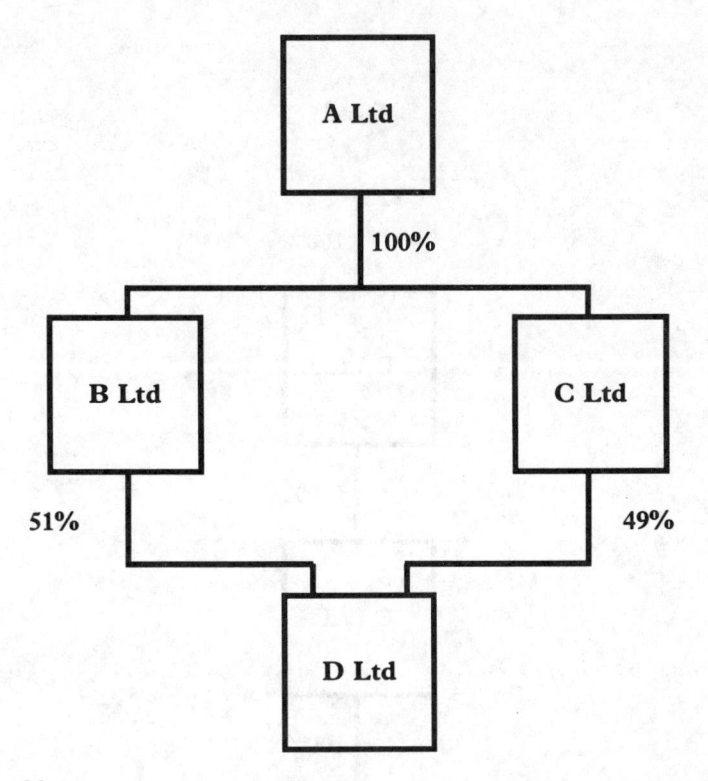

```
                    ┌─────────┐
                    │  A Ltd  │
                    └────┬────┘
                       100%
            ┌────────────┴────────────┐
       ┌────┴────┐               ┌────┴────┐
       │  B Ltd  │               │  C Ltd  │
       └────┬────┘               └────┬────┘
          51%                        49%
            └────────────┬────────────┘
                    ┌────┴────┐
                    │  D Ltd  │
                    └─────────┘
```

Figure 29.1

D Ltd is a 100% subsidiary of A Ltd because the 51% and 49% can be aggregated through B Ltd and C Ltd.

29.4.5.2 Direct ownership Section 838(5), TA provides:

> Where, in the case of a number of bodies corporate, the first directly owns ordinary share capital of the second and the second directly owns ordinary share capital of the third, then for the purposes of this section, the first shall be deemed to own ordinary share capital of the third through the second, and, if the third owns directly ordinary share capital of a fourth, the first shall be deemed to own ordinary share capital of the fourth through the second and third, and the second shall be deemed to own share capital of the fourth through the third and so on.

This makes it clear that one can trace through direct ownerships. It may be illustrated as follows:

A Limited owns ordinary share capital in B Limited.
B Limited owns ordinary share capital in C Limited.
C Limited owns ordinary share capital in D Limited.

```
                    ┌─────────┐
                    │  A Ltd  │
                    └────┬────┘
                         │ 100%
                    ┌────┴────┐
                    │  B Ltd  │
                    └────┬────┘
                         │ 100%
                    ┌────┴────┐
                    │  C Ltd  │
                    └────┬────┘
                         │ 100%
                    ┌────┴────┐
                    │  D Ltd  │
                    └─────────┘
```

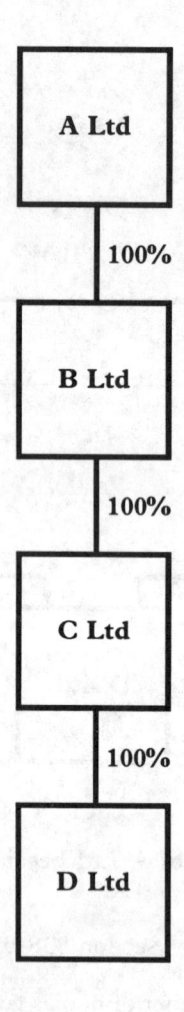

Figure 29.2

A Limited is deemed to own ordinary share capital in D Limited.
B Limited is also deemed to own ordinary share capital in D Limited.
C Limited owns ordinary share capital in D Limited.

29.4.5.3 Tracing definitions and rules Various definitions are set out in s. 838(6), TA. These provisions set out the rules as to how ownership may be traced but they do not deal with the question of what percentage is to be treated as owned in calculating what type of subsidiary is involved.

The rules depend on whether there is:

(a) 100% ownership in all the companies involved in the chain or series when s. 838(7) applies; see para. 29.4.5.4;

(b) where one of the companies in the chain is owned as to less than 100% when s. 838(8) may apply; see para. 29.4.5.5;

Groups

(c) where there is a more complex ownership when s. 838(9) and (10) apply; see para. 29.4.5.6.

29.4.5.4 100% ownership chain This is dealt with by s. 838(7), TA. Where there is 100% relationship throughout the chain then the first company in the chain is treated as owning all the share capital of the last company in that chain. This may be illustrated as follows:

A Limited owns all the ordinary share capital in B Limited.
B Limited owns all the ordinary share capital in C Limited.
C Limited owns all the ordinary share capital in D Limited.

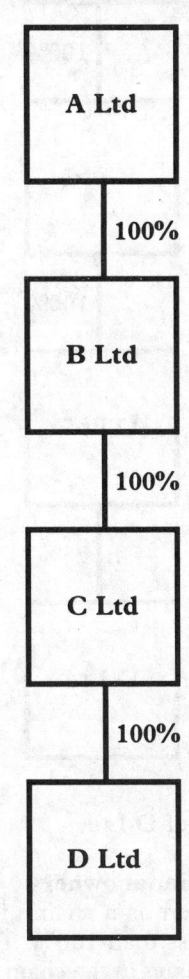

Figure 29.3

A Limited is deemed to own all the ordinary share capital in D Limited.
B Limited is also deemed to own all the ordinary share capital in D Limited.
C owns all the ordinary share capital in D Limited.

29.4.5.5 All but one 100% owner Where one owner in the chain owns less than 100% the position is dealt with by s. 838(8), TA. The first company is treated as owning the fraction owned by the last link in the 100% chain. This may be illustrated as follows:

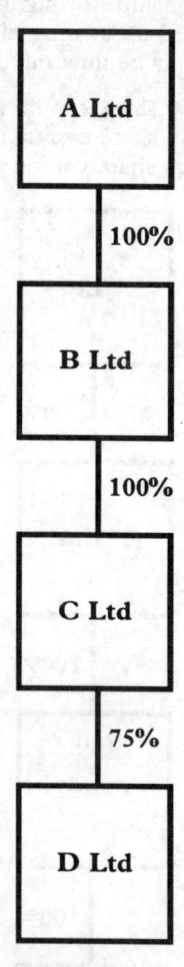

```
           ┌─────────┐
           │  A Ltd  │
           └────┬────┘
              100%
           ┌────┴────┐
           │  B Ltd  │
           └────┬────┘
              100%
           ┌────┴────┐
           │  C Ltd  │
           └────┬────┘
               75%
           ┌────┴────┐
           │  D Ltd  │
           └─────────┘
```

Figure 29.4

A Ltd is deemed to own 75% of D Ltd.

29.4.5.6 Two or more fractional owners The question then arises as to how much is owned where there is a chain of companies but two or more companies in the chain own less than 100%. This is dealt with in s. 838(9), TA. Where two or more companies in the chain own a fraction of the ordinary share capitals less than the whole, then the superior company is treated as owning '. . . such fraction . . . as results from the multiplication of those fractions . . .' This is best understood from an example.

Groups

Example
A Limited owns 100% of B Limited.
B Limited owns 90% of C Limited.
C Limited owns 80% of D Limited.
D Limited owns 70% of E Limited.
E Limited owns 60% of F Limited.

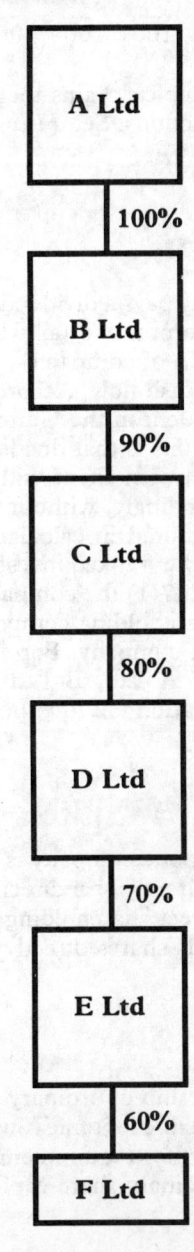

Figure 29.5

C Limited is a 90% subsidiary of A Limited.
D Limited is owned as to $\frac{(90 \times 80)}{(100 \ \ 100)} = 72\%$ by A Limited.
E Limited is owned as to $\frac{(90 \times 80 \times 70)}{(100 \ \ 100 \ \ 100)} = 50.4\%$ by A Limited.
F Limited is owned as to $\frac{(90 \times 80 \times 70 \times 60)}{(100 \ \ 100 \ \ 100 \ \ 100)} = 30.24\%$ by A Limited.

If the chain is still more complex chains then s. 838(10), TA applies and in effect one aggregates the fractions. See *Figure 29.1* above.

29.5 GROUP INCOME

29.5.1 Introductory matters

Generally, when a UK company pays a dividend to a shareholder, it must also make a payment of advance corporation tax which becomes a tax credit for the shareholder. Within a group of companies, this can be an administrative inconvenience and may affect cash flow. Accordingly, s. 247, TA allows two companies which are both resident in the United Kingdom to make a group income election. The effect of this is that dividends, but not other qualifying distributions, may be paid between them without accounting for advance corporation tax and, correspondingly, without giving rise to any tax credit. Similarly, the dividends are ignored in calculating the franked payments of the distributing company and the franked investment income of the recipient company. To qualify under s. 247(1) the company paying the dividends must be a 51% subsidiary of the shareholding company, or both companies must be 51% subsidiaries of a third company. For example, if B Ltd and C Ltd are both 51% subsidiaries of A Ltd, B Ltd may pay dividends without accounting for advance corporation tax to either A Ltd or C Ltd. See *Figure 29.6* for an illustration of this.

29.5.2 UK residence

When deciding whether or not one company is a 51% subsidiary of another, share capital which is owned directly or indirectly in a non-resident company must be ignored, and an indirect shareholding cannot be established where an intermediary company holds shares directly as a share dealer (s. 247(8), TA).

29.5.3 Anti-avoidance

Because of concern that ownership of ordinary share capital (as defined) did not necessarily reflect the real economic ownership of a company, the Finance Act 1989 added a further requirement (s. 247(8A), TA). Even if a company owns 51% of the ordinary share capital of another, it will only be

Groups

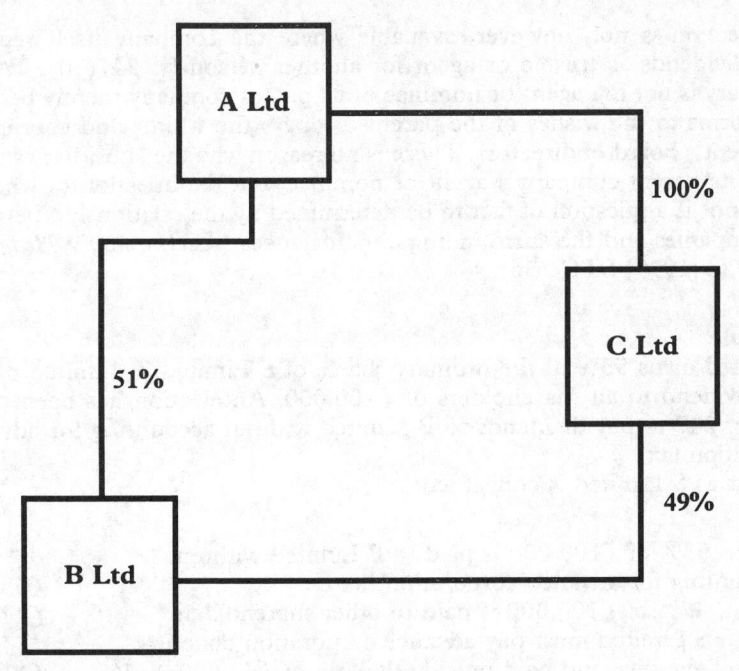

```
         ┌─────────┐
         │  A Ltd  │
         └─────────┘
         ╱         ╲
      51%          100%
       ╱              ╲
                    ┌─────────┐
                    │  C Ltd  │
                    └─────────┘
                         │
                        49%
                         │
   ┌─────────┐           │
   │  B Ltd  │───────────┘
   └─────────┘
```

Figure 29.6

treated as a subsidiary if the parent company would also be beneficially entitled to more than 50% of the profits available for distribution to 'equity holders' of the subsidiary company, and the parent company would be beneficially entitled to more than 50% of the assets of the subsidiary company available for distribution to equity holders on the winding-up of the company. 'Equity holders' and other related terms are elaborately defined in sch. 18, TA.

29.5.4 Dividend by parent to subsidiary

There is no provision for a parent company (A Ltd) to pay dividends without accounting for advance corporation tax to its subsidiaries (B Ltd or C Ltd) because, under British company law, subsidiaries generally are prevented from holding shares in their parent company (s. 23, CA 1985).

29.5.5 Capital holding not trading stock

The shareholding company to which the dividends are paid must not be holding the shares in question as part of its trading stock such that a profit on the sale of the shares would be treated as a trading receipt, if the group income election is to be available (s. 247(5), TA). However, payment may be made under a group income election where the dividends are not received directly by the company concerned but are paid to a trustee or agent for it.

The election is not, however, available where the company itself receives those dividends as trustee or agent for another person (s. 247(10), TA). A subsidiary is not the agent or nominee of its parent company merely because it conforms to the wishes of the parent or obeys the whims and caprices of the parent's board of directors. There is no reason why the subsidiary should not be its parent company's agent or nominee, but the question of whether it is or not is a question of fact to be determined by the relationship between the companies and the surrounding circumstances (see *Burman v Hedges & Butler Ltd* [1979] STC 136).

Example
P Limited owns 53% of the ordinary shares of S Limited. S Limited pays a total dividend to all shareholders of £100,000. An election has been made under s. 247 to pay dividends to P Limited without accounting for advance corporation tax.

As far as S Limited is concerned:

(a) 53% of £100,000 is paid to P Limited without accounting for advance corporation tax £53,000
(b) 47% of £100,000 is paid to other shareholders £47,000
(c) S Limited must pay advance corporation tax on 47% of the dividend paid outside the group: £47,000 × ¼ £11,750
Total payment £111,750

As far as P Limited is concerned, it will receive a dividend of £53,000. This is not franked investment income, but group income. P Limited will not receive the benefit of any tax credit on the dividend, because S Limited did not pay any advance corporation tax on it.

29.5.6 Temporary disapplication

Companies might sometimes find it to their benefit to make payments outside the group income election. For example, where the company paying the dividends has considerable surplus franked investment income, this will absorb any advance corporation tax that would otherwise be payable. Temporary disapplication of the group income election is therefore given provided the paying company gives notice to the Revenue (s. 247(3)). In these circumstances, the paying company (S Limited in the last example) does not actually pay any advance corporation tax even though there is a s. 247 election: the advance corporation tax due in respect of the dividend is absorbed by the surplus franked investment income. The recipient company (P Limited in the last example) obtains franked investment income which it can use to offset advance corporation tax on any dividends which it might pay. In effect, therefore, surplus franked investment income is transferred from one group company to another where it might be better used.

29.6 DEDUCTIBLE PAYMENTS

Payments made by companies which are deductible payments (such as charges on income) are generally required to be paid under deduction of income tax (see Chapter 26). This is inconvenient for payments between group companies. Accordingly, s. 247(4), TA allows two group companies that are both resident in the United Kingdom to elect to make payments between them without deduction of income tax if certain conditions are met. The election may be made between two UK companies where one is a 51% subsidiary of the other, or where both companies are 51% subsidiaries of a third company (s. 247(4)(a)). Unlike the group income election, the group charges election is available for payments up and down between parent and subsidiary. Share capital owned directly or indirectly in a non-resident company is to be ignored in deciding whether or not the paying or recipient companies are 51% subsidiaries. A direct shareholding of an intermediary company holding shares as a share dealer is also to be ignored (s. 247(8)). An election cannot be made in respect of payments received by a company on any 'investments', if a profit on the sale of those investments would be treated as a trading receipt of the recipient company (s. 247(5)). As with group income, payments do not have to be received directly by the company concerned but can be paid to its trustee or agent, though correspondingly any payments which the company receives as trustee or agent for another cannot be the subject of an election (s. 247(10)).

29.7 GROUP RELIEF

29.7.1 Introduction

Sections 402 to 413, TA provide for certain losses and other deductions to be surrendered within a 75% UK group. This is intended to provide neutrality between subsidiaries and divisions. It is known as group relief. Group relief is available in respect of certain losses, excess charges on income, surplus minor capital allowances and excess management expenses. The relief operates by allowing one company within a group (the claimant company – see ss. 402(1) and 413(2)) to claim these items from another group member (the surrendering company), and to set them against its total profits for corporation tax purposes (s. 402(1) and (2)).

29.7.2 75% relationship

For the purposes of group relief, two companies are members of the same group if one is the 75% subsidiary of the other, or both are 75% subsidiaries of a third company (s. 413(3)(a), TA). On the meaning of a 75% subsidiary see para. 29.4.2. In deciding whether one company is a 75% subsidiary of another, the following is ignored (s. 413(5)):

    (a)   any share capital which is owned directly as a share dealer; or

(b) any share capital which is owned indirectly, but which is owned directly by an intermediary company as a share dealer; or

(c) share capital which is owned directly or indirectly in a non-resident company. Both the surrendering and the claimant companies must be resident in the United Kingdom (s. 413(5)).

In order to prevent the exploitation of group relief by the formation of artificial groups, provisions were introduced in 1973 which, in addition to the 75% subsidiary requirement discussed in para. 29.4.2, require two further conditions to be satisfied for a company to be a 75% subsidiary. These are as follows (see s. 413(7)).

(a) the shareholding company must be beneficially entitled to at least 75% of any profits available for distribution to equity holders of the subsidiary; and

(b) the shareholding company would be beneficially entitled to at least 75% of any of the subsidiary's assets which would be available for distribution to equity holders on a winding-up.

Detailed rules in sch. 18 define the elements of these additional requirements. A claim for group relief must be clear and specific to be effective (see *Farmer v Bankers Trust International Ltd* [1990] STC 564).

29.7.3 Losses etc. available for group relief

The following matters are available for group relief:

(a) a loss of the surrendering company available for relief under s. 393A(1) (see para. 28.3.4, s. 403(1) and (2), TA);

(b) certain types of capital allowances whether by discharge or repayment of tax are given primarily against a specified class of income, and where the surrendering company has insufficient relevant income against which to set those allowances, the excess may be surrendered (s. 403(3));

(c) where the surrendering company is an investment company (this is often likely to be a holding company) with a surplus of management expenses deductible under s. 75(1), the excess may be surrendered whether or not the claimant company is an investment company (s. 403(4), (5) and (6)); and

(d) if the surrendering company's charges on income exceed its profits, that excess may be surrendered (s. 403(7) and (8)).

29.7.4 Current accounting period

Items to be surrendered by way of group relief purposes must be items of the surrendering company's current accounting period. The surrendered amounts may be set off for the purposes of corporation tax against the total profits of the claimant company for its corresponding accounting period (s. 403, TA). Where the accounting periods of the claimant and surrendering companies coincide, then they are also corresponding accounting periods (s. 408(1)). If they do not coincide, then any accounting period of the claimant company which overlaps the surrendering company's relevant accounting period in whole or in part is a corresponding accounting period (s. 408(1)).

Thus, for any given accounting period of the surrendering company there will usually be two corresponding accounting periods of the claimant company (unless the two companies have matching accounting periods). However, if the accounting periods do not coincide, the following fraction of the surrendered amount is available for set-off (s. 408(2)(a)):

$$\frac{\text{the length of the period common to the two accounting periods}}{\text{the length of the surrendering company's accounting period}}$$

The amount to be surrendered is to be set against the following fraction of the claimant company's total profits (s. 408(2)(b)):

$$\frac{\text{the length of the period common to the two accounting periods}}{\text{the length of the claimant company's corresponding accounting period}}$$

Either of these fractions may therefore impose a maximum limit on the amount available for surrender. For example, if A Ltd wishes to surrender £12,000 of group relief in its accounting period to 31 March to B Ltd, which has total profits of £10,800 in its accounting period to 31 January, the period common to both accounting periods is the ten months from April to January. The amount which A Ltd can surrender is therefore restricted to $^{10}/_{12}$ths of £12,000, which is £10,000, and the amount which B Ltd can claim is restricted to $^{10}/_{12}$ths of £10,800, which is £9,000. In this case, therefore, the maximum amount which can be surrendered by A Ltd to B Ltd is £9,000.

Where a company joins or leaves a group, an accounting period is deemed to begin or end at that time (s. 409). If for any reason the claimant company's accounting period is shorter than 12 months, or is deemed by the operation of s. 409 to be shorter than 12 months, the fractions in s. 408(2) could exceed 1 (thereby increasing the relief beyond the surplus actually available). In this case, the fractions are limited to 1 (s. 408(2)).

Group relief is given to the claimant company on the assumption that the company makes all relevant claims to other reliefs to which it may be entitled, except reliefs which are derived from subsequent accounting periods such as loss relief carried back under s. 393A(1)(b), or relief for the minor capital allowances carried back under s. 145(3) CAA 1990 (s. 407, TA).

29.7.5 Anti-avoidance

In order to prevent the exploitation of group relief by the formation of temporary groups, s. 410, TA may apply in certain circumstances to deny the existence of a group in circumstances where group relief would otherwise be available. Section 410 assumes the existence of two companies within a group, and will then treat them as not being members of the same group if 'arrangements' are in existence. These are arrangements by virtue of which:

(a) the first company (or its successor) could cease to be a member of the same group as the second and could become a member of a different group of companies; or

(b) any person has, or any persons together have, or could obtain, control (within the meaning of s. 840, TA) of the first company but not of the second; or

(c) a third, non-group, company could begin to carry on the whole or any part of a trade which is carried on by the first company.

This is an extremely wide provision. Statement of Practice SP 3/93 (which replaced SP 5/80) sets out the Revenue's views. Despite some inept drafting in s. 410, and the mandatory effect of its provisions, the Inland Revenue apply the section only to accounting periods in which the arrangements exist, even though on a strict reading, once arrangements are found to exist, the section could be applied to any accounting period which ends on or after 6 March 1973 (SP 5/80, para. 3). (This reassurance is no longer contained in SP 3/93 but since para. 1 of SP 3/93 states that omissions do not indicate a more restrictive approach on the part of the Revenue, this is still thought to be the position.)

The expression 'arrangements' cannot be defined, but will be given a very wide meaning. In particular, the Inland Revenue believe that an arrangement may exist between parties even though it is not legally enforceable (SP 3/93, para. 10: in the light of *Furniss* v *Dawson* [1984] STC 153 this seems reasonable). However, in the case of a straightforward sale of the company, arrangements will not normally exist before the date of the acceptance of the offer, and if the transaction requires the approval of shareholders, arrangements will not come into existence until that approval has been given (SP 3/93, paras 6 and 7). Where the sale of a company is being negotiated, the fact that the potential vendor does not pursue alternative offers would not be sufficient to bring an arrangement into existence between him and a prospective purchaser, unless perhaps there is an understanding between them that an offer would remain open for some time, thus allowing the prospective purchaser to choose the most favourable time to him at which to finalise the bargain. Where negotiations have broken down, this will be a strong indication they did not reach a stage at which arrangements could be said to have come into existence. The Inland Revenue previously stated that where a company mortgages shares as security for a loan, there will be no arrangement within s. 410 as long as the company retains full power to exercise or control the exercise of the voting rights attaching to those shares.

Section 410 was considered by the House of Lords in *Pilkington Brothers Ltd* v *IRC* [1982] STC 103. Initially, Pilkington had two wholly-owned subsidiaries, Hello TV Ltd and Villamoor Ltd. A shipping company, Manchester Liners Ltd, with a wholly-owned subsidiary (Golden Cross Line Ltd),

Groups 631

wanted to build a ship. The ship would be owned by Golden Cross, which would be entitled to capital allowances in respect of its expenditure on the ship, but the profits of the Manchester Liners group could not absorb those allowances. Pilkington was willing to finance the building of the ship providing that the capital allowances were surrendered to it in cash by Golden Cross. The surrender would only be possible, of course, if Pilkington and Golden Cross were members of the same group and the surrender of the allowances was made by way of group relief. Pilkington and Manchester Liners therefore entered into a scheme as a result of which the group structure was as shown in *Figure 29.7*.

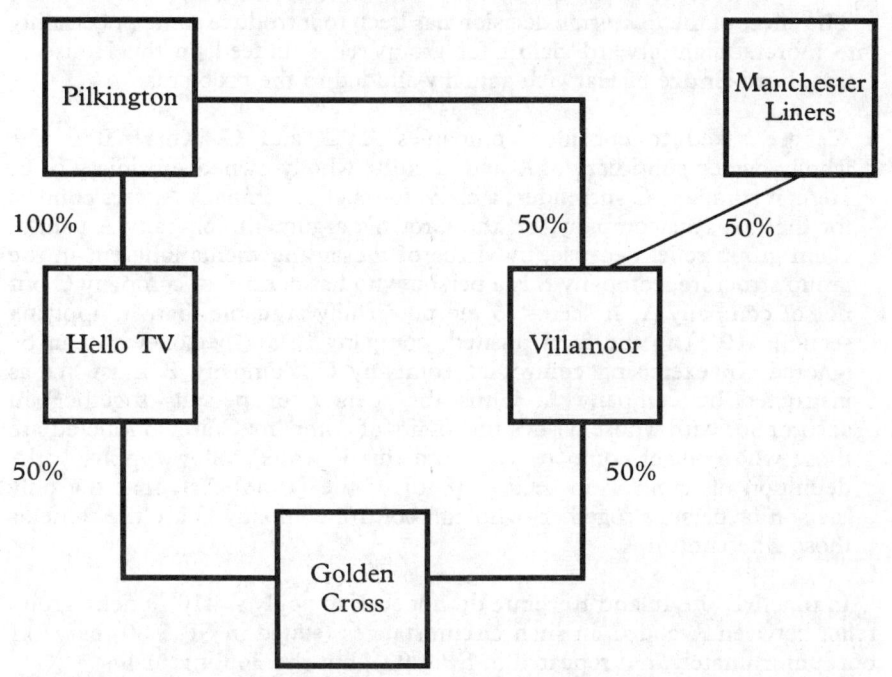

Figure 29.7

These arrangements resulted in Golden Cross becoming a 75% subsidiary of Pilkington (through Hello TV, Pilkington held 50%, and through Villamoor it held 25%). The scheme went ahead, and group relief was claimed between Golden Cross and Pilkington. The Inland Revenue refused the claim on the basis that arrangements were in existence by virtue of which persons together (i.e., Pilkington's shareholders) had control of Pilkington but not of Golden Cross. Through Hello TV, Pilkington's shareholders could control 50% of Golden Cross, but that would not be sufficient for them to ensure that Golden Cross's affairs were conducted in accordance with their wishes (s. 840). Because Villamoor was owned as to 50% by Manchester Liners, it was a deadlocked company in that neither Manchester Liners nor Pilkington could control the remaining 50% interest in Golden Cross. Pilkington's shareholders therefore could not control Golden Cross, though they could of course control Pilkington itself. Nevertheless, the Inland Revenue still had to point to the 'arrangements' which resulted in this state of affairs. They argued that Pilkington's memorandum and articles of association were part of an arrangement between the company and its shareholders, and this argument found favour with the House of Lords. It was irrelevant that the arrangements had been in existence for many years before this particular scheme was entered into: it was sufficient that they existed at the relevant time. Nor did it matter that the arrangements applied only to one of the companies involved, and not to both. Group relief was therefore denied.

The effect of the *Pilkington* decision has been to introduce some uncertainty into more straightforward claims for group relief. Indeed, in the House of Lords, Lord Bridge of Harwich actually alluded to the problem:

> We are asked to consider companies A, B and C, where B is the wholly-owned subsidiary of A and C is the wholly-owned subsidiary of B. Here, if company C surrenders a claim to relief to company A, says counsel for the taxpayer company, on the Crown's argument company A cannot claim group relief because, by virtue of the arrangements inherent in the group structure, company B is a person who has control of company C but not of company A. It seems to me powerfully arguable that, in applying section 410(1) to the facts posited, company B is a person who can be ignored. In exercising control of company C, company B must act as instructed by company A. Thus the 'person or persons together' in accordance with whose wishes the affairs of company C are conducted are those who control company A. From this it would follow, applying the definition of 'control' in section [840] of the [1988] Act, that the only 'person or persons together' who can control company C are the same as those who control A.

In practice, the Inland Revenue do not seek to apply s. 410 to deny group relief between A and C in such circumstances (stated in SP 5/80, para. 11 but, unfortunately, not repeated in SP 3/93), but the doubt remains.

Section 410 was also applied to deny group relief in *Irving v Tesco Stores (Holdings) Ltd* [1982] STC 881, where a similar arrangement existed as in the *Pilkington* case and which resulted in a company being deadlocked. In the *Tesco* case, Walton J rejected a suggestion that the court must look simply at the situation which happened. He said that s. 410 required the court to look at the arrangements which were in existence, and not just to the extent to which those arrangements were in fact implemented.

On a separate matter it has been held that if the transactions of a subsidiary which generate the losses are not genuine trading transactions, they will have no fiscal effect, so no group relief can be claimed (*Overseas Containers (Finance) Ltd v Stoker* [1987] STC 547). There are also limits on the availability of group relief to certain defined dual resident companies (s. 404), to prevent tax avoidance.

29.7.6 Claims

Group relief must be claimed by the claimant company (s. 402(1) and (2), TA). The procedure for making a claim is set out in s. 412 and sch. 17A. The claim should normally be made within two years of the end of the period to which the claim relates, but may in certain circumstances be made within six years, so long as the tax assessment is not final and conclusive, or after six years if there is an appeal in respect of the assessment. The company does not have to claim the full amount of relief available, and the surrendering company must consent.

A claim may be in a general form (*Gallic Leasing Ltd* v *Coburn* [1992] 1 All ER 336). Where a claim for group relief is made within a consortium, then in addition to the claim by the claimant company and the consent of the surrendering company, the consent of every other consortium member must also be notified to the inspector (para. 10(2), sch. 17A). However, a claim cannot be made for consortium relief if the consortium member's shareholding in the relevant accounting period in the surrendering trading or holding company is nil or if a profit on a sale of the shares would be a trading receipt of the consortium member (that is, the consortium member is holding the shares as a share dealer; s. 402(4)).

Although the claimant and surrendering companies must be members of the same group or consortium at the time the surrendered loss or excess arises, they do not need to be members of the same group or consortium at the time the claim for relief is made (*A. W. Chapman Ltd* v *Hennessey* [1982] STC 214).

Where there are several ways of giving relief for a particular loss or excess of charges on income, management expenses or capital allowances, relief cannot be given more than once in respect of the same amount (s. 411(1)). This is a reasonable restriction, but the situation may become complicated because more than one company is allowed to make claims relating to the same surrendering company and to the same accounting period of that surrendering company (s. 402(5)). Where this happens, the claimant companies together cannot obtain in all more relief than could be obtained by a single claimant company (s. 411(2)). Companies must therefore co-ordinate their claims to make sure that maximum relief is given, and that the minimum amount of time is wasted in making overlapping claims for the same amount.

Within a consortium, it is possible that a holding company and its 90% trading subsidiaries could qualify for group relief on ordinary principles, in addition to claims for consortium relief (see para. 29.11) between consortium members and the holding or trading companies. In these circumstances, the claims for group relief and consortium relief must be carefully worked out. Where a claim for group relief by one company does not fully absorb the total amount which could be surrendered, the unabsorbed amount may be the subject of a further claim for relief by another group company. Similarly, consortium relief may be claimed by different companies until the total amount available for consortium relief has been absorbed. Further, the restriction in s. 411(9) which prevented consortium relief and group relief from applying to the same amount was removed by the Finance Act 1985 in relation to claims relating to the accounting periods of surrendering companies which begin after 31 July 1985 (s. 39(2)(a), FA 1985). In addition, new rules were introduced by the Finance Act 1985 to extend group relief in circumstances where a consortium member also belongs to a group, and to allow group relief within a consortium to 'flow through' a consortium member to and from other companies in the consortium member's group (see ss. 403(10), 405, 406 and 409(5) to (8), TA).

If an inspector discovers that any group or consortium relief which has been given is or subsequently becomes excessive, the excess may be recovered by an assessment to corporation tax under Case VI of Schedule D (s. 412(3)).

Amounts which are surrendered by way of group or consortium relief do not have to be accompanied by a corresponding payment by the claimant company to the surrendering company. However, occasionally the claimant company will pay an amount to the surrendering company.[7] Provided the payment does not exceed the amount surrendered, and is paid pursuant to an agreement between the claimant and surrendering companies, such a payment is left out of account in computing the profits or losses of both companies for corporation tax purposes, and is not treated as a distribution or charge on income (s. 402(6)). There are therefore no tax consequences to the making of a payment for group or consortium relief (VAT is not normally charged).

29.8 SURRENDER OF ADVANCE CORPORATION TAX

29.8.1 Introduction

A company which has declared a dividend and paid advance corporation tax in respect of that dividend may surrender the whole or part of the advance corporation tax to one or more of its UK-resident 51% subsidiaries (s. 240(1) and (10), TA. In addition to satisfying the 51% share capital requirements discussed above, a company will not be a subsidiary unless the parent company is also beneficially entitled to more than 50% of any of the subsidiary's profits available for distribution to equity holders and would be beneficially entitled to more than 50% of the subsidiary's assets available for distribution to equity holders on a winding-up (s. 240(11)(b)). 'Equity holder' and related terms are defined in sch. 18, TA. Further, share capital which the parent company holds as a share dealer must be ignored; as must capital which it owns indirectly, but which is held directly by an intermediary subsidiary as a share dealer; and as must share capital owned by the parent company which is owned directly or indirectly in a non-resident company (s. 240(10)). The subsidiary must be a 51% subsidiary throughout the parent company's accounting period in which it paid the surrendered advance corporation tax (s. 240(1)).

29.8.2 Dividends only

Section 240, TA applies only to advance corporation tax paid by a holding company in respect of a dividend or dividends (s. 240(1)), and will not

---

[7.] For instance, in *Pilkington Brothers Ltd* v *IRC* in para. 29.7.5, Pilkington paid 87% of the amount surrendered by Golden Cross.

Groups

therefore be available in respect of all advance corporation tax paid by it if some relates to qualifying distributions which were not dividends. The section is, however, extended to advance corporation tax paid in respect of distributions made on the redemption, repayment or purchase by the parent company of its own shares (s. 240(9), although following the Finance Act 1997 changes, no ACT will be paid in respect of such distributions (see para. 30.10.1)).

29.8.3 Change of ownership

A restriction on the use of s. 240, TA is made by s. 245A. Where there is a change in the ownership of a company which has had advance corporation tax surrendered to it before that change, and there is within a period of six years, commencing three years before the change, a major change in the conduct or nature of the business of the company which surrendered the advance corporation tax, then no advance corporation tax surrendered before the change of ownership can be used in accounting periods after the change of ownership. This is intended to prevent the indirect sale of advance corporation tax by surrendering it to a subsidiary before making a major change in the business of the surrendering company. The Inland Revenue's interpretation of the term 'a major change' in the nature of the business is set out in a Statement of Practice (SP 10/91).

A further restriction is contained in s. 245B and is designed to prevent companies purchasing a subsidiary with surplus advance corporation tax and then transferring assets to it shortly before they are sold, so that the unrelieved advance corporation tax can be set against the gain on the assets. Where there is a change of ownership of a company with unrelieved advance corporation tax, following which that company acquires any asset subject to s. 171, TCGA (no gain/no loss group transfer – see para. 29.9) and a chargeable gain accrues on the disposal of that asset within three years of the change of ownership, then when the gain accrues, the amount of advance corporation tax that can be set off will be reduced by the lower of the advance corporation tax that would have been payable on a distribution equal to the amount of the chargeable gain and the amount of unrelieved advance corporation tax which passed on the change of ownership.

29.8.4 Use of surrendered payments

Where the parent company has paid only one dividend, or has paid several dividends on the same day, the subsidiary to which advance corporation tax is surrendered is treated as though it had paid advance corporation tax equal to the surrendered amount on a distribution which it had itself made on that same day (s. 240(2)(a), TA). Where the parent company has paid dividends on different days, the subsidiary is treated as though it had paid advance corporation tax in the proportion which the parent company's dividends for each date bear to the total of all its dividends which relate to the surrendered advance corporation tax (s. 240(2)(b) and (3)). For example, suppose that the parent company declares dividends of £8,000 and £16,000 respectively on 1 April and 1 October, and pays advance corporation tax in respect of those dividends of £2,000 and £4,000. If it surrenders £3,000 of its advance corporation tax to a subsidiary, the subsidiary will be treated as having paid advance corporation tax of, respectively, £1,000 and £2,000 on notional distributions by it on 1 April and 1 October.

A subsidiary to which advance corporation tax has been surrendered may set the surrendered amount against its liability to mainstream corporation tax. Further, in determining the amount of any surplus for carry-back or carry-forward purposes, the surrendered advance corporation tax is treated as though it were set against mainstream liability before advance corporation tax on the subsidiary's own distributions (s. 240(4)). However, no surrendered advance corporation tax can be relieved by carrying it back to earlier accounting periods (s. 240(4)). Any claim to carry surrendered advance corporation tax forward will be lost if, in the subsidiary's accounting period in question, it is not (or ceases to be) a subsidiary of the parent company which made the surrender (s. 240(5)) unless both companies remain subsidiaries of a third company, after 14 March 1989 (s. 97, FA 1989). There are also limits on carry-back within the oil industry (s. 498, TA). Advance corporation tax surrendered by a parent company to a subsidiary is no longer treated as having been paid by the parent (s. 240(7)). Finally, if the parent company has already elected to carry any surplus advance corporation tax back to its own previous accounting periods, the amount carried back is no longer available for surrender under s. 240 (s. 240(7)).

29.8.5 Anti-avoidance provisions

The parent-subsidiary relationship will be denied if arrangements are in existence by virtue of which any person has, or any persons together have, or could obtain, control of the subsidiary but not of the parent (s. 240(11)(a), TA and control has its s. 840 meaning; s. 240(11)). This anti-avoidance provision mirrors those which exist for group relief purposes, and the Inland Revenue apply similar criteria in considering whether or not arrangements exist for the purposes of s. 240 as they do for s. 410 (Statement of Practice SP 3/93, para. 2).

29.8.6 Claims

The surrender of advance corporation tax by the parent company must be pursuant to a claim made by it, and where a surrender is made to two or more subsidiaries, the parent company decides the proportion in which the surrender is made (s. 240(1), TA). The claim must be made within six years after the end of the parent company's relevant accounting period, and the subsidiary or subsidiaries involved must notify their consent to the surrender to the inspector (s. 240(6)).

29.8.7 Payments

In the same way that payments for group relief are ignored, any payment made by a subsidiary to its parent in pursuance of an agreement between them which does not exceed the amount surrendered, is ignored in computing the profits and losses of both companies, and is not to be treated as a distribution or charge on income (s. 240(8)). In the past, it was possible for companies to obtain a tax advantage in that when surrendered advance corporation tax was set against the subsidiary's tax liability, tax was repaid with interest, but the surrendering company would only have to pay interest on its own increased corporation tax liability from 30 days after the date of assessment. This advantage was removed by s. 102, FA 1989, which charges interest on the corresponding increase in the tax liability of the parent company.

29.9 GROUPS AND CHARGEABLE GAINS

29.9.1 Introduction

For the purposes of corporation tax on chargeable gains, a company resident in the United Kingdom (called the 'principal company') and all its resident 75% subsidiaries form a group (s. 170(3)(a), TCGA). Where a subsidiary has 75% subsidiaries, the group will include them and their 75% subsidiaries (s. 170(3)(a)).

Example
For example, if B Ltd is a 75% subsidiary of A Ltd, and B Ltd has a 75% subsidiary, C Ltd, then B Ltd and C Ltd form a group; and because B Ltd

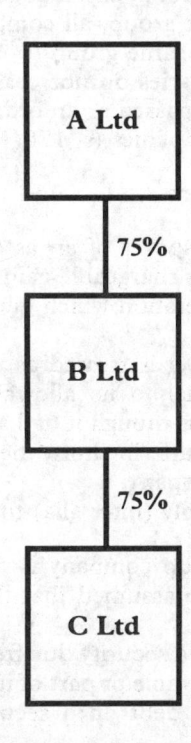

Figure 29.8

is itself a 75% subsidiary of A Ltd, all three companies together form a group. This is very different from group relief, where both B Ltd and C Ltd would have to be 75% subsidiaries of A Ltd in order for all three companies to form a group. For capital gains purposes, all three companies constitute a group even though C Ltd is only a 56.25% subsidiary of A Ltd.

29.9.2 Effective 51% subsidiary requirement

The definition of a group was modified from 14 March 1989 to provide that a group does not include any company that is not an effective 51% subsidiary of the principal company of the group (s. 170(3)(b), TCGA). Nor can a company be a principal company in a group in which it is itself a 75% subsidiary, though it may still be a principal company of another group. A company cannot be a member of more than one group (s. 170(6)). If it is potentially a member of more than one group, statutory rules will be applied to decide to which group it actually belongs. Those rules relate to entitlement to distributions and to assets (s. 170(6)).

29.9.3 Changes

A group remains the same group for as long as the same company remains the principal company of the group, and if at any time the principal company becomes a member of another group, all companies in the expanded group are treated as members of the same group (s. 170(10), TCGA). A principal company and its 75% subsidiaries do not cease to be members of a group simply because a resolution is passed or an order made for the winding-up of a member of the group of companies (s. 170(11)).

29.9.4 Intra-group transfers

Where one group member disposes of an asset to another group member, both companies are treated for chargeable gains purposes as though the asset were disposed of for a consideration which gives rise to neither a gain nor a loss (s. 171, TCGA).

The disposing group member is treated as though it had disposed of the asset for a consideration equal to its allowable expenditure etc. and the acquiring company is treated as though it had acquired the asset for the same amount of allowable expenditure: in short, the acquiring company stands in the shoes of the disposing company.

This treatment does not apply (inter alia) to:

(a) situations where a group company is deemed to have disposed of a capital asset (when it must be assumed that the disposal was made outside the group; s. 171(1));

(b) a disposal of a debt on a security due from a group member by paying off or otherwise satisfying the whole or part of it (s. 171(2)(a)). This provision does not refer in terms to a debt on a security, but other debts are not chargeable assets;

(c) a disposal of redeemable shares on the occasion of their redemption (s. 171(2)(b));

(d) a disposal by or to an investment trust (s. 171(2)(c));

(e) a deemed disposal of an interest in shares arising from the receipt of a capital distribution (s. 171(2));

(f) compensation for any kind of damage or injury to assets, or for the destruction or dissipation of assets, or for anything which depreciates or might depreciate an asset, since the asset in these circumstances is treated as being transferred to the person who ultimately bears the burden of paying that compensation (whether as insurer or otherwise) (s. 171(4)); and

(g) a transaction treated by virtue of ss. 127 and 135 as not involving a disposal by the company making the disposal within a group (after 15 March 1988) (s. 171(3) and see Chapter 30);

Where a group member acquires an asset as trading stock from another group member which did not hold the asset as trading stock, the acquiring group member is treated as having acquired the asset otherwise than as trading stock and immediately appropriated it as trading stock (s. 173). This will mean that the acquiring group member will either have an immediate capital gain or, if the election is made, a future trading profit if the market value of the appropriated asset exceeds its allowable expenditure (see s. 161).

Generally speaking, capital losses sustained by a company can only be set against its own chargeable gains as there is no 'grouping' of allowable losses for corporation tax purposes as there is for current trading losses (see Chapter 28). However, s. 173(1) makes it possible for a capital loss in one company to be converted into (effectively) a trading loss of another group company, which loss can then be relieved as a trading loss of the other group company or be surrendered by way of group relief. Such conversions are perfectly legitimate, but the frequent stumbling block is the acquisition of the asset 'as trading stock'.

For example, in *Coates v Arndale Properties Ltd* [1984] STC 637, Sovereign Property Investments ('SPI') carried on business as a property developer. It acquired a lease of certain land and developed the site at a total cost of £5,300,000. The market value of the lease was £3,100,000, and SPI thus faced a potential capital loss of £2,200,000. If this loss was realised by SPI it could only be set off for corporation tax purposes against its own chargeable gains. Arndale Properties was a fellow subsidiary of SPI and carried on business as a property dealer. Thus, any losses incurred by Arndale Properties in carrying on its business were trading losses which could be set off against its own trading profits or those of any other group member. Accordingly, SPI assigned its lease to Arndale Properties for £3,090,000. On the same day, Arndale Properties assigned the lease for £3,100,000 to a third subsidiary, Arndale Property Trust Ltd ('APTL'), which carried on business as an investment company. Thus, the assignment to Arndale Properties was made to allow a capital loss to be converted into a relievable trading loss within the group, and the assignment to APTL was to ensure that the lease became a capital asset of APTL and therefore remained a capital asset of the group as a whole.

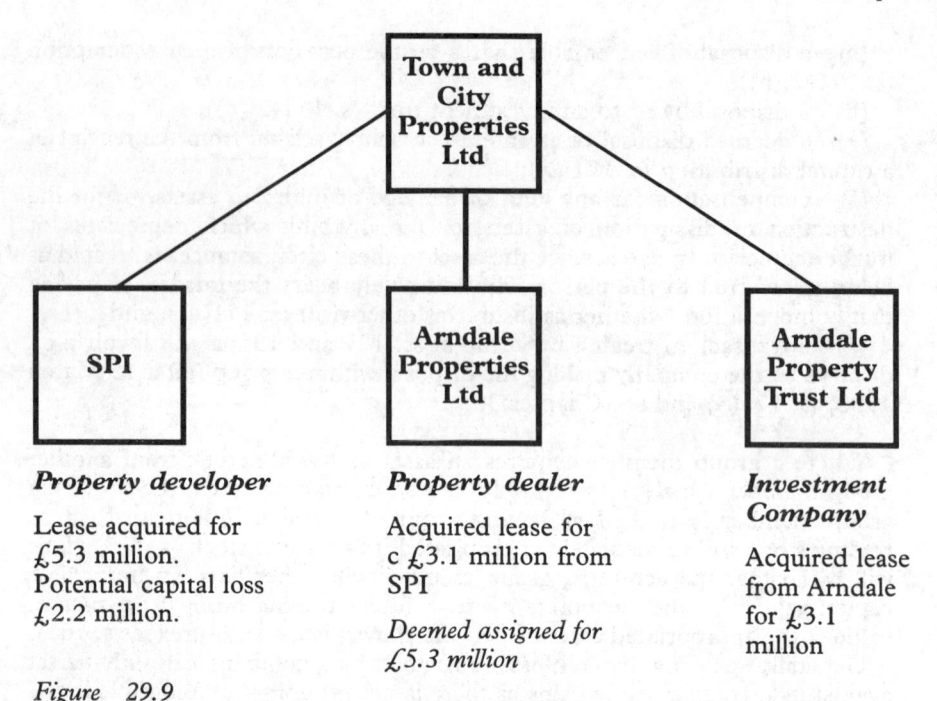

```
                    ┌──────────────┐
                    │  Town and    │
                    │    City      │
                    │ Properties   │
                    │    Ltd       │
                    └──────┬───────┘
              ┌────────────┼────────────┐
        ┌─────┴─────┐ ┌────┴─────┐ ┌────┴─────┐
        │           │ │ Arndale  │ │ Arndale  │
        │    SPI    │ │Properties│ │ Property │
        │           │ │   Ltd    │ │Trust Ltd │
        └───────────┘ └──────────┘ └──────────┘
```

Property developer   *Property dealer*   *Investment Company*

Lease acquired for   Acquired lease for   Acquired lease
£5.3 million.   c £3.1 million from   from Arndale
Potential capital loss   SPI   for £3.1
£2.2 million.   million
                                Deemed assigned for
                                £5.3 million

Figure 29.9

In the House of Lords, Lord Templeman referred to ss. 161 and 173 and said:

> Thus, if Arndale purchased the lease from SPI 'as trading stock' for the purposes of the property dealing trade of Arndale then Arndale may elect that the acquisition cost of the lease shall be entered in its trading accounts as £5,300,000 and not £3,100,000 and thus when Arndale sold the lease to APTL for £3,100,000 Arndale for corporation tax purposes would suffer a trading loss of £2,200,000 . . . In my opinion Arndale never decided to acquire, and never did acquire, the lease as trading stock. The group's advisers procured the transfer of the lease from SPI to Arndale and from Arndale to APTL with the object of obtaining group relief of £2,200,000 trading loss without in fact changing the lease from a capital asset to a trading asset. The group seeks the advantage of treating the lease as trading stock while ensuring that the group retains the lease as a capital asset at all times. Arndale followed instructions and lent to the transaction its name and description as a property dealing company. Arndale did not trade and never had any intention of trading with the lease. In order to give the whole transaction a faint air of commercial verisimilitude, the trading company Arndale was awarded the modest sum of £10,000 for entering into two assignments of property worth over £3,000,000 . . . The profit of £10,000 was a timid veil designed to conceal the fact that the lease was not being traded. Moreover, all three companies being wholly-owned subsidiaries of

the same parent, the £10,000 was a book entry which had no material effect on the overall financial position of the group.

Similarly, in *Reed v Nova Securities Ltd* [1985] STC 124, Littlewoods acquired shares in a German company (Medaillon) for £1,512,599, and also acquired that company's bank debts amounting to £2,424,166. Subsequently, Littlewoods disposed of the shares and debts to Nova Securities, a share dealing company, for their market value of £30,000. This consideration was apportioned into a payment of £10 for the shares and a payment of £29,990 for the bank debts. In the House of Lords, Lord Templeman said: 'In the result Littlewoods sustained an actual capital loss of £1,512,589 resulting from the purchase and sale of the Medaillon shares and £2,394,176 resulting from the purchase and sale of the Medaillon bank debts.' However, because of what is now s. 171, Littlewoods did not sustain an allowable capital loss.

Lord Templeman continued:

Thus for corporation tax purposes Littlewoods, having acquired the Medaillon shares for £1,512,599, are deemed to have sold those shares and Nova is deemed to have purchased those shares not for the actual price of £10 but for the price of £1,512,599. Similarly, Littlewoods, having acquired the Medaillon bank debts for £2,424,166, are deemed to have sold those bank debts and Nova is deemed to have purchased those bank debts not for the actual price of £29,990 but for the price of £2,424,166. If s. [171] had stood alone the potential allowable loss of Littlewoods in respect of the Medaillon shares and bank debts amounting in the aggregate to £3,906,765 would simply have been transferred to and become the potential allowable loss of Nova. But if Nova, a trading company, acquired the Medaillon shares and the Medaillon bank debts as 'trading stock' then Nova became in a position to convert the potential capital allowable loss into a trading loss.

So far as the bank debts were concerned, the House of Lords held that they were acquired as trading stock. Nova Securities was a trading company which had bought property of a kind in which it was authorised to deal. The company's directors had considered as a commercial matter the profit that the company was likely to make on the transaction, and it was conceivable that Nova Securities might have decided to acquire similar bank debts from a source unconnected with the group in the hope of making a profit either by resale or by waiting until the debts were repaid. As for the shares, Lord Templeman explained:

Different considerations apply, however, to the Medaillon shares. Medaillon's assets were valued at not more than £200,000. Medaillon's debts amounted to £8,700,000. The shares were worthless. There was no commercial justification for the acquisition of the shares by Nova. There was no conceivable reason, apart from s. [173], why the shares should change hands at all. In my opinion no reasonable tribunal could have concluded that the shares were acquired by Nova as trading stock . . . Counsel for Nova urged that the shares were purchased as part of a package deal; Nova could not acquire the Medaillon bank debts without also acquiring the Medaillon shares. But assuming this to be so, the shares were not acquired as trading stock just because they were acquired in connection with bank debts which were so acquired.

Finally, s. 173(1) applies to the acquisition of an asset as trading stock. Section 173(2) applies where a member of a group of companies disposes of an asset which formed part of its trading stock to another group member which acquires it otherwise than as trading stock. In these circumstances, the disposing group member is treated as having immediately before the disposal appropriated the asset for purposes other than use as trading stock. The acquiring group member will then be treated as though it had acquired the asset for a consideration equal to the amount brought into the disposing group member's trading accounts in respect of the appropriation (s. 161(2)).

29.9.5 Transfers outside the group

Where a group member disposes of an asset outside the group which it has previously acquired from another group member, s. 174, TCGA treats the entire group as a single person for the purposes of:

(a) establishing 31 March 1982 values (group assets will be treated as having been acquired on the earliest date on which any member of the group acquired them); and

(b) deduction of capital allowances under s. 41, TCGA except in so far as they have been taken into account in relation to earlier disposals by group members;

(c) where business assets are replaced by the application of the proceeds of an old asset being reinvested in the purchase of a new asset, roll-over relief is available to prevent an immediate charge on the disposal of the old asset. For the purposes of this relief, all the trades carried on by members of a group of companies are treated as a single trade (except in the case of an intra-group transfer, when the rules discussed in para. 29.9.4 apply (s. 175)). Thus, provided the conditions for relief are otherwise fulfilled, if a business asset used by one group member is disposed of and replaced by another qualifying business asset which is then used by another group member, roll-over relief is still available. (This provision does not, however, apply to dual resident investment companies, s. 175(2), TCGA and s. 404, TA.)

29.9.6 Recovery of tax from group members

If a chargeable gain accrues to a group member and that member is more than six months late in paying any corporation tax due from it, the corporation tax attributable to the chargeable gain may be assessed and charged (s. 190, TCGA):

(a) on the group member's principal company; and
(b) on any other company which at any time within two years before the accrual of the chargeable gain was a group member and owned the whole or any part of the asset disposed of (or if the asset disposed of is an interest or right in or over another asset, owned the interest or right in or over the other asset in which the interest or right subsisted, or any part thereof).

Such an assessment must be made within two years from the time at which the corporation tax should have been paid (s. 190(1)).

Where a group member, other than the principal company, is charged under s. 190(1), that company may recover the tax which it pays either from the defaulting company or from that company's principal company. If the principal company is charged under s. 190(1), or reimburses another group member under s. 190(3), the principal company may recover any amount paid from the defaulting company, or, failing this, in respect of reimbursements under s. 190(3) only, from any other group member which has owned the asset disposed of (or, in the case of an interest or right in or over an asset, the interest or right or the underlying asset itself) or any part of it. The principal company is entitled to recover the proportion of the unrecovered amount as is just having regard to the value of the asset at the time when the asset (or the interest or right in or over it) was disposed of by that group member: s. 190(3).

29.9.7 Company leaving group

Where a company leaves a group, having previously acquired an asset by way of intra-group transfer, the company leaving the group is treated as though it had sold and immediately reacquired the asset for its market value at the time of its acquisition from the other group member. This treatment applies only to the company leaving the group (s. 179(1) and (3), TCGA) and applies only to assets acquired on or after 6 April 1965 or within six years before the time when the company concerned leaves the group (s. 179(1) and (3)), and only if the asset (or, in the case of business assets qualifying for roll-over relief on replacement, the new asset) is held otherwise than as trading stock (s. 179(3)).

For the purposes of s. 179, a company does not cease to be a member of a group by being wound up or dissolved or in consequence of another group member ceasing to exist (s. 179(1)). It is understood that the Revenue consider this to be of narrow ambit and applies only to the final act of liquidation of the company.

If a principal company leaves a group, its 75% subsidiaries will necessarily leave with it. In these circumstances s. 179(1) and (3) apply to assets owned by the 75% subsidiaries as they did to assets owned by the principal company (s. 179). However, s. 179 does not apply where the original intra-group transfer was between associated companies (s. 179(2) and (10)) and they are still associated companies on leaving the group.

For the purposes of s. 179, assets can be 'traced' in that if the value of a second asset is derived in whole or in part from the first asset, they are treated as the same asset, particularly where the second asset is a freehold and the first asset was a leasehold and the lessee has acquired the freehold reversion (s. 179(10)(c)).

The application of s. 179 will result in the recomputation of liability to corporation tax, and any necessary adjustments will be made (s. 179(13)). If any of the corporation tax assessed on a leaving company under s. 179 is not paid within six months of the due date, then that tax may be assessed and charged within two years of the due date on a company which on that date was the leaving company's principal company (or became its principal company after it left the group), or on a company which owned the asset on the due date or when the company left the group (s. 179(11)).

Section 179 does not apply where a company ceases to be a group member as part of a merger carried out for *bona fide* commercial reasons and where tax avoidance is not the main or one of the main purposes of the merger (s. 181). There will also not be a charge when a company leaves a group purely because the principal company in the group becomes a member of another group, provided certain conditions are satisfied (s. 179(5)–(9)).

29.10 ANTI-AVOIDANCE

Provisions exist to prevent the transfer of share ownership of a subsidiary by exploiting the beneficial capital gains tax treatment on amalgamations or reconstructions (s. 181, TCGA), the creation of artificial capital losses by depreciatory transactions (s. 176), and the allowance of capital losses attributable to dividend stripping (s. 177). Provisions also exist to restrict the use of allowable losses when a company with allowable losses is acquired by a group. Broadly such 'pre-entry' losses will only be available for use against gains arising on the subsequent disposal of assets held by the company when it joined the group or assets which it acquired from outside the group and used in its trade (s. 177A). These rules limit the market that would otherwise exist between companies wishing to sell subsidiaries with allowable losses and groups with, as yet, unrealised gains, wishing to purchase such subsidiaries to use the losses to off-set their gains.

29.11 CONSORTIA

29.11.1 Introduction

The group income and group deductions elections and group relief are also available within a consortium. In a consortium, a number of companies may together want to carry out a single trading operation. To do this, they can form a trading company of which the consortium members are shareholders. Sometimes, there may be more than one trading company involved, in which case the shares in those companies may be held by a single holding company and the consortium members will hold shares in the holding company.

29.11.2 Group income etc.

For the purposes of group income and group deductions elections, dividends or, for instance, charges on income may be paid gross by a UK-resident trading company or the UK-resident holding company to a consortium member provided at least 75% of the ordinary share capital of the trading or holding company is beneficially owned by the consortium members, and that each member is resident in the United Kingdom and owns at least 5% of that ordinary share capital (s. 247(1)(b), (4)(a) and (9)(c), TA). Each member must also be beneficially entitled to at least 5% of any profits available for distribution to equity holders of the company, or be beneficially entitled to at least 5% of the assets of the company available for distribution to equity holders on winding-up (s. 247(9)(c)). 'Equity holders' and associated terms are, again, as defined in sch. 18, TA. Further, where a holding company is involved, the trading companies must be its 90% subsidiaries and the holding company's business must consist wholly or mainly in the holding of the shares or securities of those subsidiaries (s. 247(9)(a)). There is an exclusion from relief under s. 247(1)(b) if the paying company is a 75% subsidiary of another company, or there are written arrangements to make it so (s. 247(1A)).

29.11.3 Group relief

Group relief is also available within a consortium provided that the companies concerned are resident in the United Kingdom (ss. 402(3) and 413(5), TA). If there is no holding company, group relief is available between a consortium member and a trading company owned by the consortium which is not a 75% subsidiary of any single company (s. 402(3)(a)).

Where a holding company is involved, group relief is available between a consortium member and the holding company provided the latter is not a 75% subsidiary of any single company (s. 402(3)(c)). In this situation, group relief is also available between a consortium member and a trading company which is a 90% subsidiary of the holding company owned by the consortium but which is not a 75% subsidiary of any other company (s. 402(3)(b)). For this purpose, the 90% subsidiary requirement must be met not only as to share capital, but also in relation to beneficial entitlement to profits available for distribution to equity holders and as to beneficial entitlement to the subsidiary's assets available for distribution to equity holders on a winding-up (s. 413(7)). A trading company or holding company will be owned by a consortium if at least 75% of its ordinary share capital is beneficially owned by the consortium members, provided that each member's share of that capital is at least 5% (s. 413(6)).

The same kinds of group relief are available within a consortium as are available to groups. However, consortium relief is more restricted than group relief by virtue of s. 403(9). Where the claimant company is a consortium member, the amount surrendered can only be a fraction of the total amount available for surrender (s. 403(9)(a)). Similarly, where the surrendering company is a consortium member, the amount surrendered can only be set against a fraction of the claimant company's profits (s. 403(9)(a)). In both cases, the fraction is equal to the consortium member's share in the consortium and, of course, this fraction will be further reduced by the rules relating to corresponding accounting periods in s. 408 (s. 403(9) and see para. 29.7.4). A consortium member's share in the consortium (which will need to be determined in relation to the relevant accounting period of the surrendering company) is the lowest of the following percentages in that period:

(a) the percentage of the holding or trading company's ordinary share capital which is beneficially owned by the consortium member;

(b) the percentage of the holding or trading company's trading profits available for distribution to equity holders to which the consortium member is beneficially entitled; or

(c) the percentage of the holding or trading company's assets available for distribution to equity holders on a winding up to which the consortium member would be beneficially entitled;

and if any of these percentages has fluctuated during the accounting period, the average percentage must be taken (s. 413(8) and (9)).

The anti-avoidance provisions of s. 410 (discussed at para. 29.7.5) apply to claims for group relief within a consortium. Thus, by s. 410(2) relief will be denied if arrangements are in existence by virtue of which:

(a) the holding or trading company (or its successor) could become a 75% subsidiary of a third company; or

(b) any person who owns, or any persons who together own, less than 50% of the holding or trading company's ordinary share capital has or together have, or could obtain, control of the company; or

(c) any person, either alone or together with connected persons within s. 839, holds or could obtain, or controls or could control the exercise of at least 75% of the votes which may be cast on a poll taken at a general meeting of the holding or trading company (though in the case of a trading company, which must be the 90% subsidiary of any holding company, the holding company is excluded when considering the arrangements); or

(d) a non-consortium company could begin to carry on the whole or any part of a trade which is carried on by the trading company.

If the consortium members have entered into an arrangement under which, where one member wishes to dispose of his shares, it must first offer them to other consortium members in proportion to their existing shareholdings, and without the transferee being given the right to dictate either the terms or the date on which the sale takes place, this will not be regarded as an arrangement for the purposes of s. 410 (Extra-statutory Concession C10).

CHAPTER THIRTY
Reorganisations, reconstructions and repurchases

30.1 INTRODUCTION

The purpose of this chapter is to bring together and consider some of the provisions on company reorganisations, reconstructions and repurchases.

30.2 CGT AND REORGANISATION OF SHARE CAPITAL ETC., SS. 126 AND 127, TCGA

30.2.1 General

The TCGA contains in ss. 126 and 127 provisions which are aimed at providing neutrality for reorganisations of a company's share and other capital. Section 127 sets out the general rule. This rule is that such a reorganisation must not be treated as involving any disposal of the original shares on the acquisition of the new holding or part of it, but the original shares (taken as a single asset) and the new holding (taken as a single asset) are to be treated as the same asset acquired as the original shares were acquired. Since there is no disposal there can be no capital gains tax charge as one of the necessary conditions for a charge is a disposal.

30.2.2 'Original shares' and 'new holding'

By s. 126(1)(a), TCGA 'original shares' means the shares held before and concerned in the reorganisation. By s. 126(1)(b) 'new holding' means, in relation to any original shares, the shares and the debentures of the company which, as a result of the reorganisation, represent the original shares (including such, if any, of the original shares as remain).

30.2.3 Meaning of 'reorganisation'

Section 126(2), TCGA deals with the meaning of 'reorganisation' for these purposes. It provides:

> The reference in subsection (1) above to the reorganisation of a company's share capital *includes* [emphasis added]—
> (a) any case where persons are, whether for payment or not, allotted shares in or debentures of the company in respect of and in proportion to (or as nearly as may be in proportion to) their holdings of shares in the company or of any class of shares in the company; and
> (b) any case where there are more than one class of share and the rights attached to shares of any class are altered.

What is the effect of the word 'includes' in this context? In *Dunstan v Young, Austen and Young* [1989] STC 69 the Court of Appeal (inter alia) had to consider whether or not s. 126 was an exhaustive definition of reorganisation. They considered it was not. Balcombe LJ, delivering the judgment of the Court, said that the phrase 'reorganisation of a company's share capital' was 'not a term of art either in fiscal or company law'. He said (at p. 75):

> An increase of share capital can be a reorganisation of that capital notwithstanding that it does not come within the precise wording of [s. 126(2)(a), TCGA] provided that the new shares are acquired by existing shareholders because they are existing shareholders and in proportion to their existing *beneficial* holdings [emphasis supplied].

The reference to beneficial holdings is important especially where nominees are involved and is apparently an application of s. 60, TCGA which deems the acts of the nominee to be the acts of the beneficial owner. The Court also considered that if the shares had been allotted to the shareholders in exact proportion to their existing holdings (for example on a bonus issue of shares) this would have fallen clearly within the s. 126(2)(a) wording. It seems therefore that either route can be used.

30.2.4 'New consideration'

If consideration is given by the shareholder for the new holding then s. 128, TCGA applies. The effect of this is broadly that the consideration is treated as having been given as additional consideration for the original shares. It will therefore form part of the acquisition cost of the new holding as s. 127 provides that the new holding is treated as the same asset as the original shares and acquired at the same cost as the original shares. However, for the purposes of indexation, indexation allowance will only be available from the date the consideration is actually paid (s. 131).

30.2.5 Disposal with a liability attaching

By s. 128, TCGA where there is a disposal of the new holding with a liability attaching, e.g., to pay up the share capital, the consideration for the disposal of the new holding is to be adjusted. The relationship to s. 38(1)(a) is not entirely clear (on this see further Lord Fraser in *IRC* v *Burmah Oil Co. Limited* [1982] STC 30).

Subsections 128(3) and (4) deal with consideration received by the *shareholder*. By s. 128(3) where consideration is received on a reorganisation in addition to the new holding the shareholder will be treated as though he had first made a part disposal of his original shares for the consideration received and only then will the original shares and the new holding be treated as the same asset in accordance with s. 127. Section 129 deals with the apportionment of the acquisition cost of the original shares on such a part disposal.

30.3 PAPER FOR PAPER TRANSACTIONS – SS. 135 AND 136, TCGA

30.3.1 Exchange of securities for those in another company – s. 135

30.3.1.1 General Section 135, TCGA provides for neutrality by giving a roll-over relief for the shares or debentures disposed of where one company has, or obtains control of, a substantial interest in another company. Section 135 applies s. 127 (the reorganisation provision – see para. 30.2) to the situation where one company issues shares or debentures in exchange for shares in or debentures of another company and certain other conditions are fulfilled. The result then is that there is no disposal and so no charge to capital gains tax and the new holding is equated with the original shares.

The operation of s. 135 is subject to the qualifying corporate bond and loan relationship legislation in ss. 115–117B (especially s. 117) and ss. 80–105, FA 1996. This is a very complex area outside the scope of this book but is very important in practice.

Section 135 applies where:

(a) a company issues shares or debentures to another person in exchange for shares or debentures in another company and holds, or as a result of the exchange holds, more than 25% of the ordinary share capital of the other company ('the 25% test'); or

(b) a company issues shares or debentures in exchange for shares in another company as a result of a general offer to the members of the target company conditional in the first instance on the issuer obtaining control ('the general offer test'); or

(c) a company holds or will hold in consequence of the exchange the greater part of the voting power in the target company.

In all these cases an 'exchange' is needed. 'Exchange' is not defined for these purposes. The *Shorter Oxford English Dictionary* defines it (inter alia) as:

1. The action, or an act, of reciprocal giving and receiving. 2. *Law*, 'A mutual grant of equal interest, the one in consideration of the other'. Blackstone 1574.

This seems to require a 'swap' of broadly equal value. The position is not clear if there is a mismatch – presumably the roll-over would not be available.[1] But what is needed – is it a bad bargain or something more?

30.3.1.2 25% control test
This test applies where the issuer either:

(a) holds *more* than 25% of the ordinary share capital;[2] or
(b) will as a result of the exchange hold *more* than 25% of the ordinary share capital.

The 25% test is only concerned with the issuer and more than 25% of the ordinary share capital is needed for the relief to apply – 25% exactly will not be sufficient.[3] There is no provision for groupings of holdings. If A Ltd held 17% of the target company and A's subsidiary held 9% of the target, the 25% test would not be satisfied notwithstanding that the A Group owned 26%.

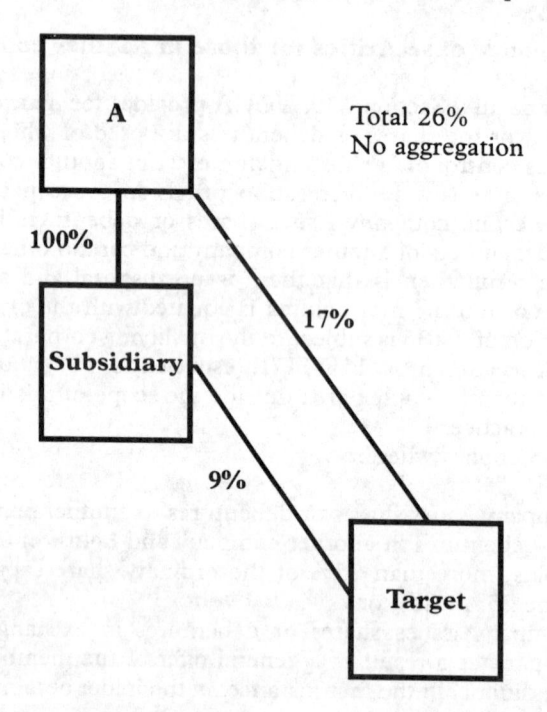

Figure 30.1

---

[1] Though if the mismatch is done to crystallise an allowable loss, the *Furniss* approach might deny the loss; see Chapter 4.
[2] As defined in s. 832, TA; broadly all shares other than fixed rate preference shares with no other rights.
[3] If a company has 100 shares in issue, 25 shares will not be sufficient for the relief to apply: 26 shares would be needed to comply with the *more than* 25% requirement.

If the 9% were just transferred to A Ltd before the exchange so that it owned 26%, the test would be satisfied.

Section 135, TCGA requires 'more than one-quarter' of the ordinary share capital to be held or acquired. The percentage acquired or held is calculated by reference to the nominal value of the shares in question. This is thought to follow from *Canada Safeway v IRC* [1972] 1 All ER 666, a stamp duty case where it was held that the concept to be applied is that of a 'share capital which is divided into shares of a fixed amount' (at p. 671 relying on the 1948 Companies Act, s. 2(4) and see now s. 2(5), 1985 Act). The word 'capital', it was considered, would be inapt if it was intended to convey the idea of actual values. It seems very hard to distinguish this case. It is understood that in practice the Revenue generally take this approach.

30.3.1.3 General offer test This limb only applies to an issue in exchange for shares in the target not for debentures. Where debentures are involved in an offer, s. 135(1)(a), TCGA may often be applicable to the debentures if the offer is for debentures as well as shares, or where more than 25% of the ordinary share capital is already owned.

There is no definition of general offer for this purpose although the general offer must be made to members of the target company or any class of them. On the meaning of class, see *Re Hellenic & General Trust Limited* [1975] 3 All ER 382.

30.3.1.4 Greater part of the voting power This was introduced by s. 35, F (No. 2) A 1992. It provides for roll-over relief where the acquirer will hold the greater part of the *voting* power of the target as a result of the exchange. Thus if a company has non-voting shares they do not need to be acquired as well.

30.3.2 Section 136, TCGA

30.3.2.1 Introduction Section 135, TCGA does not deal with all the ways of reconstructing and amalgamating companies. Accordingly, s. 136 supplements s. 135. Section 136 deals with the more complex types of reconstruction and amalgamation and applies the reorganisation provisions in ss. 127 to 131 to them (see further para. 30.2).

30.3.2.2 Necessary conditions For s. 136, TCGA to apply:

(a) there must be an arrangement between a company and its shareholders or a class of them and/or its debenture holders etc.;
(b) this must be in connection with a scheme of reconstruction or amalgamation (see above);
(c) the arrangement must involve the issue of shares or debentures by the acquiring company to the holders in the company being reconstructed;
(d) the issuer must issue the shares or debentures in proportion to the holdings in the company being reconstructed or amalgamated;

(e) the shares or debentures in the company being reconstructed etc. must either be retained by the holders or cancelled.

30.3.3 Anti-avoidance and clearance

Sections 135 and 136, TCGA are both subject to s. 137. This provides that the roll-over relief is not to apply unless the transaction:

(a) is effected for *bona fide* commercial reasons; and
(b) does not form part of a scheme or arrangements of which the main purpose or one of the main purposes is the avoidance of liability to CGT or corporation tax.

The application of this provision is discussed at para. 30.7 below in the context of s. 139, TCGA. Section 138 provides for advance clearance to be sought.

30.4 SECTION 132, TCGA AND SECTION 473, TA: CONVERSION OF SECURITIES

'Reorganisation' in s. 126, TCGA (see para. 30.2.3) on its wording only applies to share capital. This would not cover a reorganisation in respect of a conversion of loan stock etc. into shares in the company. Sections 132 to 134 accordingly deal with conversion of securities. The effect of the sections applying is that there is to be no disposal of the original securities or acquisition of the new holding and the two holdings are treated as being the same asset acquired at the same time and at the same price.

Section 132(3)(a) provides that a 'conversion of securities' includes:

(i) a conversion of securities of a company into shares in the company, and

(ii) a conversion at the option of the holder of the securities converted as an alternative to the redemption of those securities for cash, and

(iii) any exchange of securities effected in pursuance of any enactment . . . which provides for the compulsory acquisition of any shares or securities and the issue of securities or other securities instead.

Section 133 deals with premiums paid by the company on conversion. If the premium is small, i.e., less than 5%, it may be treated as a deduction from the acquisition cost and not as a part disposal.

Section 473, TA deals with the conversion of securities held as circulating capital. This provides similar relief for banks, insurance companies and share dealers where ss. 126 to 136, TCGA would otherwise apply.

30.5 DEMERGERS

30.5.1 Introduction

Demergers are a method of dividing the businesses carried on by a company between the shareholders in the company. There are a number of ways in which this can be done (see paras 30.5.3 and 30.5.4).

If there were no special legislation, the distribution by a company of shares owned by it and/or trading activities carried on by it could give rise to a number of UK tax charges. These would include:

(a) ACT if there were distributions;
(b) income tax charges on the shareholders; and
(c) capital gains tax charges on the shareholders.

A measure of relief was therefore introduced by FA 1980. These provisions are now to be found in ss. 213-218, TA and s. 192, TCGA.

The government's policy in 1980 was that demergers should be fiscally neutral so that decisions on corporate grouping and demergers could be taken on purely commercial grounds. It was their intention that both the corporate structure and the whole sphere of business operations in which companies operate could be loosened. However, they decided to approach this problem cautiously so as not to give scope for tax avoidance (see Official Report, Standing Committee A, 1 July 1980, cols. 986-88) and the demerger provisions are the result. Relief from advance corporation tax, income tax, and capital gains tax for the shareholders is given where the provisions apply. It is not entirely clear why this was not done by defining a reconstruction to include demergers. This might have fitted in better with the relevant company law. In any event difficulties may still arise in distributing assets etc. because of restrictions in the Companies Act 1985 on distributions.

30.5.2 Application of the demerger provisions

These provisions apply to 'exempt distributions'. By s. 213(2), TA 'exempt distributions' are distributions which fall within s. 213. The section deals with two types of transactions. The first of these is a distribution to shareholders, the second is the transfer of assets to another company.

30.5.3 Distribution to shareholders

Where a company distributes shares in a 75% subsidiary or subsidiaries to all or any of the parent's shareholders, this is an exempt distribution. This may be represented diagrammatically as follows:

```
                        SHAREHOLDERS
         ┌─────────────→         ←─────────────┐
         │                                      │
    SHARES                                   SHARES
         │           ┌──────────────┐           │
         │           │ Distributing │           │
         │           │   Company    │           │
         │           └──────────────┘           │
         │             75%    75%               │
    ┌─────────┐                           ┌─────────┐
    │Subsidiary│                          │Subsidiary│
    │    1    │                           │    2    │
    └─────────┘                           └─────────┘
```

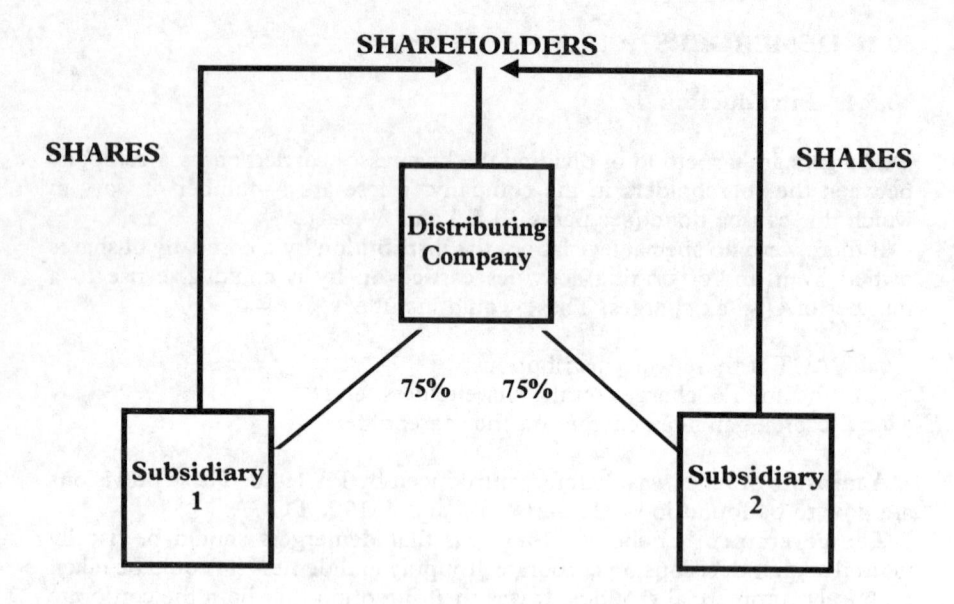

Figure 30.2

On the wording of s. 213(3)(a) there is no need for the distribution to be to all the shareholders or even pro rata. However, it is highly desirable that it is and is generally a requirement of the Stock Exchange.

30.5.4 Distribution to another company

Section 213(3)(b), TA applies to two circumstances where assets are transferred to one or more companies in return for the issue of shares in the transferee company to members of the transferor company. The transferee company does not need to be a newly formed company.

The first of these circumstances is the transfer by one company of a trade or trades to another company. This can be represented as follows:

Reorganisations, reconstructions and repurchases 655

```
                    SHAREHOLDERS
                         ▲
                         │         SHARES
                    ┌────────┐
                    │Distributing│
                    │ Company │
                    │    Y    │
                    └────────┘
                    │      ╲
                    │       ╲        ┌──────┐
                    │        ╲       │ Newco │
                    │         ╲      │   X   │
                 Trade 1    Trade 2  └──────┘
                 e.g. land  e.g. garden
                            centre
```

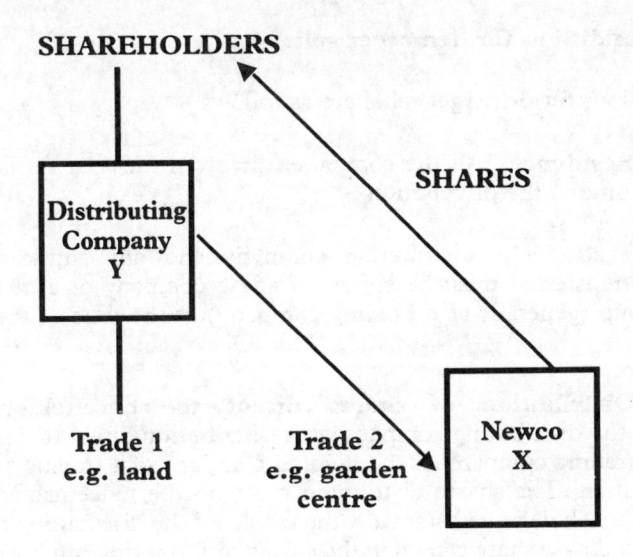

Figure 30.3

(It is assumed that the divisions are taxed separately and regarded as distinct.)

The second of these circumstances is the transfer of shares in a 75% subsidiary or subsidiaries to a new company in return for shares issued to members. This can be represented as follows:

```
                    SHAREHOLDERS
                         ▲
                         │         SHARES
                    ┌────────┐
                    │Distributing│
                    │ Company │
                    └────────┘         ┌──────┐
                    │    │    ───────▶ │ Newco │
                  75% │  75%           └──────┘
                    │    │                │
              ┌────────┐ ┌────────┐
              │Subsidiary│ │Subsidiary│
              │    1    │ │    2    │
              └────────┘ └────────┘
```

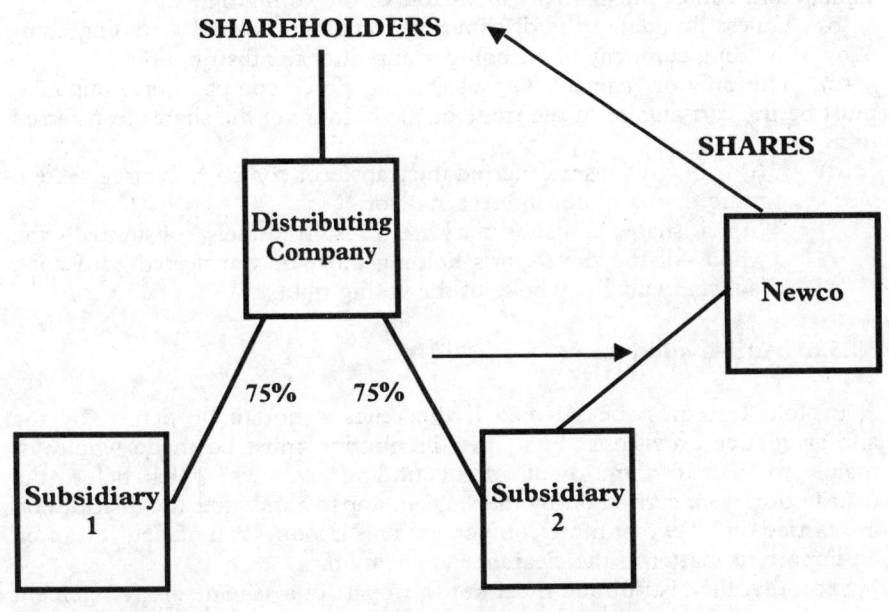

Figure 30.4

30.5.5 Conditions for demerger relief

The conditions for demerger relief are as follows.

30.5.5.1 Residence All the companies involved must be resident in the UK at the time of the distribution.

30.5.5.2 Trade The distributing company and any subsidiary whose shares are transferred must be either a trading company or a member of a trading group (generally as a holding company) at the time of the distribution.

30.5.5.3 Distribution of shares direct to shareholders Unless liquidated, the distributing company on a distribution direct to shareholders must be a trading company or the holding company of a trading group after the distribution. The shares distributed must not be redeemable and must constitute the whole or 'substantially the whole' of the distributing company's holding of ordinary share capital in the subsidiary. It is not entirely clear what 'substantially the whole' means here.

30.5.5.4 Distribution to another company

(a) The shares issued by the transferee company must: not be redeemable; be the whole or substantially the whole of its issued ordinary share capital; and confer substantially the whole of the voting rights.
(b) Unless liquidated the distributing company must be a trading company or holding company of a trading group after the distribution.
(c) The only or main activity of the transferee company or companies must be the carrying on of the trade or the holding of the shares transferred to it.
(d) (i) if a trade is transferred the transferor company must not retain more than a minor interest in it; or
 (ii) if shares in a subsidiary are transferred then 'substantially the whole' of the transferor's holding must be transferred conferring 'substantially the whole' of the voting rights.

30.5.6 Anti-avoidance

A twofold test must be satisfied if the relief is not to be denied by the anti-avoidance provisions. First, the distribution must be made wholly or mainly to benefit 'some or all of the trading activities' which before the distribution were carried on by the single company and after the distribution are carried on by two or more companies. This is a question of fact. It is often an important matter in the clearance application.

Secondly, the distribution must not form part of a scheme or arrangement where one of the main purposes is:

Reorganisations, reconstructions and repurchases

(a) tax avoidance; or
(b) the making of a 'chargeable payment' (see below); or
(c) the passing of control to persons other than members of the distributing company; or
(d) the cessation of the trade or its sale after the distribution.

Further anti-avoidance provisions are contained in s. 214, TA. If a payment (called a chargeable payment) is made otherwise than for *bona fide* commercial reasons or for tax avoidance purposes within five years, tax relief is lost or is withdrawn by a charge under Schedule D, Case VI. These are very complex provisions to which specific reference must be made. A normal dividend is seemingly not caught.

30.5.7 Clearance procedure

Application can be made for advance clearance which if granted, will render the transfer or payment an exempt distribution or not a chargeable payment as the case may be. Appeal against refusal of clearance lies to the Special Commissioners.

30.5.8 Capital gains tax

Section 192(2), TCGA provides:

> Where a company makes an exempt distribution which falls within section 213(3)(a) of the Taxes Act—
> (a) the distribution shall not be a capital distribution for the purposes of section 122; and
> (b) sections 126 to 130 shall, with the necessary modifications, apply as if that company and the subsidiary whose shares are transferred were the same company and the distribution were a reorganisation of its share capital.

The effect of this is that there is no capital gains tax charge on the shareholders.

30.6 SECTION 139, TCGA

30.6.1 General

Section 139, TCGA provides that for UK capital gains tax purposes there is a roll-over (i.e., a disposal is on a no gain/no loss basis) of the chargeable assets comprised in the transfer of a business where:

(a) a scheme of reconstruction or amalgamation is in effect which involves the transfer of the whole or part of a company's business to another company;
(b) the transferor and transferee companies are both resident in the UK; and

(c) the transferor company receives no consideration for the transfer of the business or part of the business other than because the transferee company assumes some or all of the transferor company's liabilities.

30.6.2 Definitions

30.6.2.1 General
Subject to the anti-avoidance provisions discussed below this provision raises a number of definitional questions including:

(a) What is a business?
(b) What is a scheme of reconstruction?
(c) What is a scheme of amalgamation?
(d) When does a company receive consideration for the transfer?

These questions (inter alia) are discussed in the following paragraphs (cf. s. 110, Insolvency Act 1986 discussed at para. 30.8).

30.6.2.2 'Business'
The section applies to a transfer of a company's business. The word 'business' is not defined for these purposes. Case law provides some general guidance. In *American Leaf Blending Co. Sdn Bhd* v *Director General of Inland Revenue* [1978] 3 All ER 1185 (a Privy Counsel case on the meaning of 'business' in the Malayasian Income Tax Act 1967) Lord Diplock said (at p. 1189) '"business" is a wider concept than "trade"'. He continued:

> In the case of a private individual it may well be that the mere receipt of rents from property that he owns raises no presumption that he is carrying on a business. In contrast, in their Lordships' view, in the case of a company incorporated for the purpose of making profits for its shareholders any gainful use to which it puts any of its assets prima facie amounts to the carrying on of a business. Where the gainful use to which a company's property is put in letting it out for rent, their Lordships do not find it easy to envisage circumstances that are likely to arise in practice which would displace the prima facie inference that in doing so it was carrying on a business.
>
> The carrying on of 'business', no doubt, usually calls for some activity on the part of whoever carries it on, though, depending on the nature of the business, the activity may be intermittent with long intervals of quiescence in between.

This implies a wide definition for business in s. 139 of the 1992 Act. In practice, it is believed the Revenue often take a wide view but this approach should not be assumed (cf. SP 5/85 discussed at para. 30.6.2.3.2 below).

30.6.2.3 Meaning of scheme of reconstruction or amalgamation

30.6.2.3.1 General In a reconstruction the business is transferred to a new company in return for shares issued to the shareholders in the old company.

Reorganisations, reconstructions and repurchases

In form an amalgamation appears often to be the reconstruction of a number of companies to a new company, though in substance it is the rolling of businesses together.

Section 139(9), TCGA provides that 'scheme of reconstruction or amalgamation' means a scheme for the reconstruction of any company or companies or the amalgamation of any two or more companies.

'Scheme' is a word that can be quite elastic in its meaning and so can provide the courts with a useful control device.

This phrase 'scheme of reconstruction or amalgamation' has been used in a number of taxing and stamp duty statutes but without any strict definition. Its meaning has therefore emerged from the case law. Many of these cases have been in connection with stamp duty, e.g., s. 55, FA 1927. One of the most recent cases has also been in this context. This is the case of *Swithland v IRC* [1990] STC 448 mentioned below.

30.6.2.3.2 Reconstruction Before *Cotman v Brougham* [1918] AC 514 objects of companies were often limited and companies sometimes had fixed 'lives'. It was not uncommon at the turn of the century for a company to transfer its undertaking and assets to a new company in consideration of the issue of shares in the new company to the shareholders in the old company. The business of and shareholders in the new company were substantially the same as the old company's business and shareholders. It seems that it is because of this that 'substantial identity' between the shareholders in the old company and new company is required for a reconstruction.

As Pennycuick J said in *Brooklands Selangor Holdings Ltd. v IRC* [1970] 2 All ER 76 at p. 86 (quoted with approval by Ferris J in *Swithland*; see para. 30.6.2.3.1):

> ... In ordinary speech the word reconstruction is, I think, used to describe the refashioning of any object in such a way as to leave the basic character of the object unchanged. In relation to companies, the word 'reconstruction' has a fairly precise meaning which corresponds, so far as the subject matter allows, to its meaning in ordinary speech. It denotes the transfer of the undertaking or part of the undertaking of an existing company to a new company with substantially the same persons as members as were members of the old company.

Buckley J said in *Re South African Supply and Cold Storage Co. Ltd* [1904] 2 Ch 268 at p. 286:

> What does 'reconstruction' mean? To my mind it means this. An undertaking of some definite kind is being carried on, and the conclusion is arrived at that it is not desirable to kill that undertaking, but that it is desirable to preserve it in some form, and to do so, not by selling it to an outsider who shall carry it on – that would be mere sale – but in some altered form to continue the undertaking in such manner that the persons now carrying it on will substantially continue to carry it on. It involves, I

think, that substantially the same persons shall carry it on. But it does not involve that all the assets shall pass to the new company or resuscitated company, or that all the shareholders of the old company shall be shareholders in the new company or resuscitated company. Substantially the business and the persons interested must be the same. Does it make any difference that the new company or resuscitated company does or does not take over the liabilities? I think not . . . It is not, therefore, vital that either the whole assets should be taken over or that the liabilities should be taken over. You have to see whether substantially the same persons carry on the same business; and if they do, that, I conceive, is a reconstruction.

What seems to emerge from the case law is the requirement of 'substantial identity' before and after the transfer. (Plowman J also took a similar approach in *Baytrust Holdings Ltd* v *IRC* [1971] 3 All ER 76.) This can be illustrated diagramatically as follows:

The business of Company A is rolled into Company B in return for an issue of shares in Company B to the shareholders in Company A.

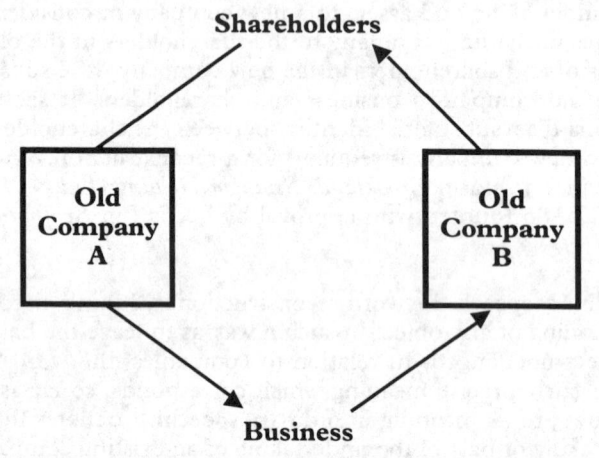

Figure 30.5

The transfer of the business would fall within s. 139, TCGA as a reconstruction and the issue of the shares would fall within s. 136, TCGA.

Alternatively, Company A has two businesses which it wishes to split. The businesses could be transferred to different companies in exchange for shares.

Reorganisations, reconstructions and repurchases

Before

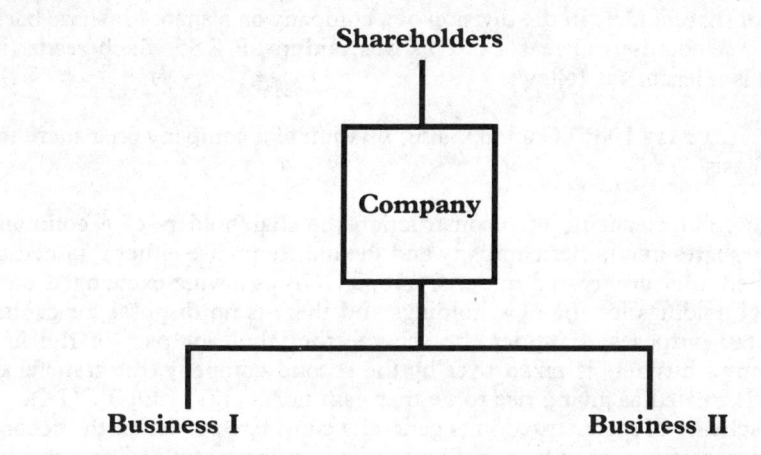

```
            Shareholders
                 |
              Company
             /        \
      Business I    Business II
```

Figure 30.6

This assumes that all the shareholders want to own part of both businesses. Problems could arise if one group of shareholders wanted one business and another group of shareholders wanted the other business. If one group of shareholders had all the shares in one company and the other group had all the shares in the other company, then it would seem that the 'substantial identity' test would not be satisfied.

After

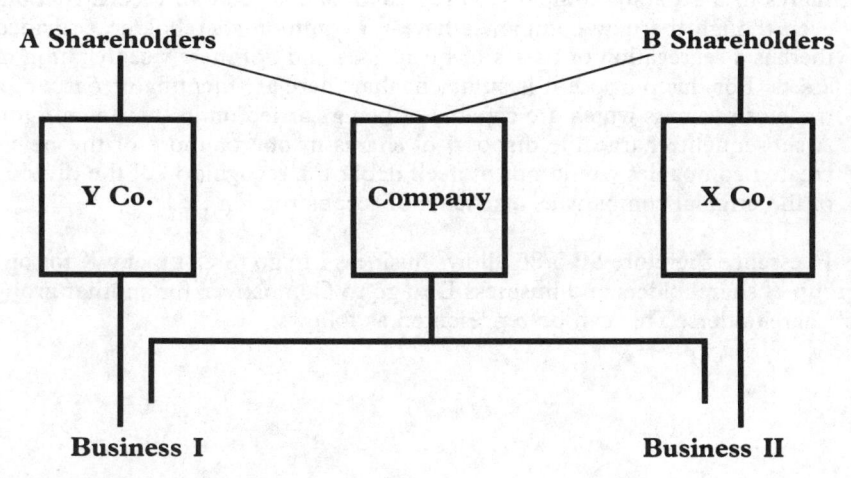

```
 A Shareholders                    B Shareholders
       |           \      /              |
     Y Co.        Company              X Co.
                     |
            /                \
      Business I         Business II
```

Figure 30.7

However, the Revenue in practice will not always insist on complete identity of shareholders in the division of a company on a share for share basis for *bona fide* commercial reasons. This was said in SP 5/85 which reads (in so far as is relevant) as follows:

SP5/85 (21 May 1985) Capital Gains: division of a company on a share for share basis.

1   Where in a scheme of reconstruction the shareholders of a company receive shares in another company and the old shares are either retained or cancelled, they are treated under s. 136, TCGA as having exchanged their original holdings for the new holdings and there is no disposal for capital gains tax purposes. If under the scheme the whole or part of the first company's business is taken over by the second company, the transfer of assets is treated as giving rise to neither gain nor loss (s. 139, TCGA).
2   A scheme of reconstruction is generally considered to entail the second company carrying on substantially the same business and having substantially the same members as the first. [Accordingly] the division of the company's undertaking into two or more companies owned by different sets of shareholders (e.g., separate family groups) would not rank as a reconstruction. In practice, however, for capital gains tax and for the corporation tax charge on capital gains, identity of shareholders in the old and new companies is not insisted upon in the case of a division carried out for *bona fide* commercial reasons.
3   A scheme whereby the shares are reorganised into separate classes, new companies are formed to take over the separate parts of the undertaking allocated to the different classes and each group of shareholders receives shares in a separate company, is regarded as a scheme of reconstruction, even though the new companies have no common shareholder, provided there is a segregation of trades or businesses and not merely segregation of assets. For this purpose it is sufficient that there are identifiable parts of a trade or business which are capable of being carried on in their own right. A subsequent chargeable disposal of shares in one or more of the newly created companies would not of itself debar the recognition of the division of the original company as a scheme of reconstruction . . .

In essence therefore SP 5/85 allows business I to go to Company X for one group of shareholders and business II to go to Company Y for another group of shareholders. This can be represented as follows:

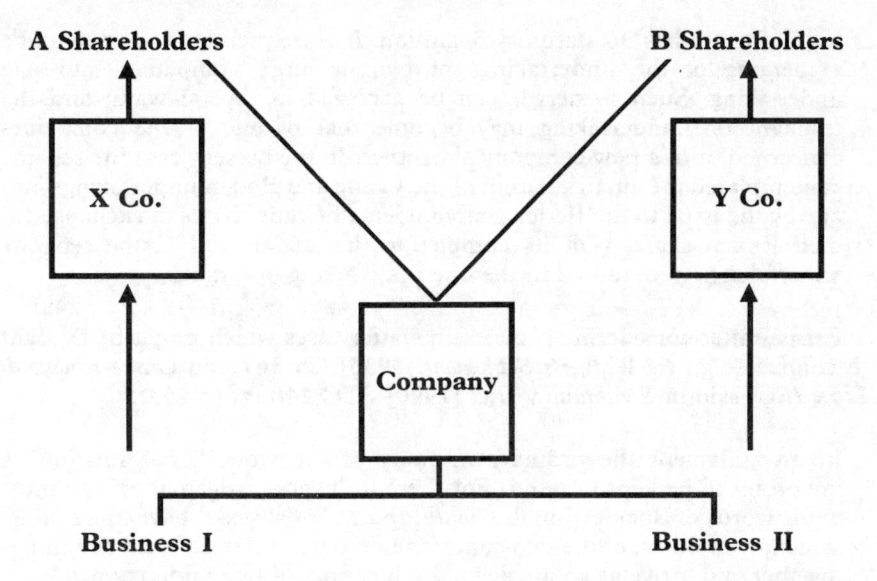

```
   A Shareholders                          B Shareholders
         ↑                                        ↑
   ┌──────────┐                             ┌──────────┐
   │　        │                             │　        │
   │　X Co.   │                             │　Y Co.   │
   │　        │                             │　        │
   └──────────┘                             └──────────┘
         ↑           ┌──────────┐                ↑
         │           │          │                │
         └───────────│ Company  │────────────────┘
                     │          │
                     └──────────┘
                    ┌─────┴─────┐
                    │           │
              Business I    Business II
```

Figure 30.8

30.6.2.3.3 Scheme of amalgamation Buckley J considered the meaning of this phrase in *Re South African Supply and Cold Storage Co. Ltd* [1904] 2 Ch 268. He said (at p. 287):

> Now what is an amalgamation? An amalgamation involves, I think, a different idea [from a reconstruction]. There you must have the rolling, somehow or other, of two concerns into one. You must weld two things together and arrive at an amalgam – a blending of two undertakings. It does not necessarily follow that the whole of the two undertakings should pass – substantially they must pass – nor need all the corporators be parties, although substantially all must be parties. The difference between reconstruction and amalgamation is that in the latter is involved the blending of the two concerns one with the other, but not merely the continuance of one concern. An amalgamation may take place, it seems to me, either by the transfer of undertakings A and B to a new corporation, C, or by the continuance of A and B by B upon terms that the shareholders of A shall become shareholders in B. It is not necessary that you should have a new company. You may have a continuance of one of the two companies upon the terms that the undertakings of both corporations shall be substantially merged in one corporation only.

In *Crane-Fruehauf Ltd* v *IRC* [1975] 1 All ER 429 Scarman LJ said (at p. 437):

> Although 'amalgamation' is a technical term in the sense that it is frequently used by technicians in the field of company law, it is not a legal

term of art; it has no statutory definition. It is frequently used to describe a merging of the undertakings of two or more companies into one undertaking. Such a merger can be achieved in several ways; and the resultant one undertaking may become that of one of the companies concerned or of a new company altogether. In the present case the scheme contemplated the amalgamation of the Crane and Boden undertakings into one by the issue to the Boden shareholders of Crane shares in exchange for their Boden shares. On its completion the Boden and Crane separate undertakings were united in the one undertaking of Crane.

Ferris J after considering some of the latter cases which might be thought to conflict (e.g., *Re Walker's Settlement* [1935] Ch 567 and *Crane-Fruehaulf Ltd v IRC*) said in *Swithland v IRC* [1990] STC 448 (at p. 463):

In my judgment the ordinary meaning of the word 'amalgamation' is important to be kept in mind. For there to be an amalgamation you must in the words of Buckley J in the *South African Supply* case, have 'the rolling, somehow or other, of the two concerns into one. You must weld two things together and arrive at an amalgam – a blending of two undertakings.'

30.6.2.4 Specific exclusions from s. 139 Section 139, TCGA does not apply to trading stock or unit trust etc. recipients.

30.6.2.4.1 Trading stock I.e., the assets held as or to be held as trading stock (s. 139(2)). The definition in s. 100, TA of trading stock applies. This reads:

. . . 'trading stock', in relation to any trade—
(a) means property of any description, whether real or personal, being either—
(i) property such as is sold in the ordinary course of the trade, or would be so sold if it were mature or if its manufacture, preparation or construction were complete; or
(ii) materials such as are used in the manufacture, preparation or construction of such property as is referred to in subparagraph (i) above; and
(b) includes also any services, article or material which would, if the trade were a profession or vocation, be treated, for the purposes of s. 101, as work in progress of the profession or vocation, and references to the sale or transfer of trading stock shall be construed accordingly.

Although trading stock falls outside s. 139, TCGA, s. 100(1), TA provides that if a trade is discontinued and it is sold for valuable consideration which falls to be included in a UK trader's computation (e.g., as opening stock) then that value is to be used and, if not, open market value is to be used. The parties can thus control the value of what is to be included.

Reorganisations, reconstructions and repurchases

However, usually in these circumstances there will be no discontinuance because s. 343, TA applies and the 'substantial identity' test for a reconstruction under s. 139, TCGA will mean that the requirements in s. 343(1), TA that 'a three-fourths share' in the transferred trade 'belongs to the same persons' is automatically satisfied (see further para. 28.9).

30.6.2.4.2 Unit trust etc. recipients I.e., a transfer to:

(a) a unit trust for exempt unit holders within s. 100, TCGA;
(b) an authorised unit trust within s. 468, TA; or
(c) an investment trust within s. 842, TA.

30.7 ANTI-AVOIDANCE

30.7.1 Introduction

Anti-avoidance provisions were introduced into what is now s. 139, TCGA by FA 1977 at the same time as for paper for paper transactions (s. 40, FA 1977 now s. 137, TCGA). Section 139(5) provides that the relief is not to apply unless:—

(a) the reconstruction or amalgamation is effected for *bona fide* commercial reasons; and
(b) the reconstruction or amalgamation does not form part of a scheme or arrangements of which the main purpose, or one of the main purposes, is the avoidance of liability to corporation tax, capital gains tax or income tax.

This is very widely worded but must have some limits to it if the section is to have any application at all. If taken too literally the fact that relief were sought at all would deny the application of the section. This cannot have been the intention of Parliament.

30.7.2 '*Bona fide* commercial reasons'

The words '*bona fide* commercial reasons' are not defined for these purposes. Discussion of the phrase in the first line of the text of s. 139(5) is generally outside the scope of this book for reasons of space but broadly it helps if there is a sensible business reason for the transfer. The Revenue do not consider saving tax a *bona fide* commercial purpose notwithstanding that many businessmen would. *Bona fide* commercial reasons might include:

(a) reorganising a group structure to make it more 'logical' and more akin to the management and reporting and/or operating structure of a group;
(b) reorganising a group recently acquired to retain the core business and sell off the non-core businesses in suitable, more readily saleable corporate vehicles;

(c) separating businesses in a company with a view to floating one on the Stock Exchange and retaining the other one.

It is suggested that if one method is adopted which saves tax as compared with others, it does not cease to be '*bona fide* commercial' if the overall objective is *bona fide* commercial. This ties in to the second limb of s. 139(5) (cf. the *Shepherd* v *Lyntress* [1989] STC 617 approach in connection with the *Furniss* doctrine discussed in Chapter 4).

30.7.3 'Avoidance of tax'

The second limb of the test in s. 139(5), TCGA is that the reconstruction or amalgamation should not form part of a scheme or arrangements of which one of the main purposes is avoidance of liability to corporation tax, capital gains tax or income tax. It is clear from this wording that the contemplated 'scheme or arrangements' are wider than just the reconstruction or amalgamation, so that the wider perspective has to be looked at to see if that wider matter has, as one of its main purposes, the avoidance of tax.

'Avoidance' of tax is not defined for these purposes. However, it implies a comparative, that is to say, the tax must be *less* than would otherwise be the case if the 'scheme or arrangements' were not put in place, if there is to be avoidance. Even if tax is 'saved' on this comparative basis it does not mean that s. 139 should be disapplied. Avoidance of tax must be a *main* purpose of the wider 'scheme or arrangement'.

It is therefore necessary to identify the wider 'scheme or arrangements' of which the reconstruction or amalgamation is part and then seek out the 'main' purpose of the wider scheme or arrangements. These will often tie into the *bona fide* commercial purposes for the arrangements; cf. the predominant purpose for civil conspiracy discussed in *Crofters* v *Veitch* [1942] AC 435. Thus, if what is proposed is the acquisition of a group of companies and to concentrate on its core business and dispose of non-core businesses, then it would seem:

(a) the 'scheme or arrangements' is the whole of the acquisition, restructuring and disposals;

(b) the question to ask is whether one of the main purposes of this whole arrangement is the avoidance of tax. This does not mean that the use of s. 139 so that the heaviest tax burden is not attracted makes tax avoidance one of the main purposes. If it did, s. 139 could never apply. The taxpayer does not have to adopt the most expensive route in tax terms to demonstrate that the main purpose is not tax avoidance;

(c) although in the circumstances it is to be assumed that the application for clearance would not be made until the acquisition was unconditional (as until then it would be a hypothetical case), the comparison needs still to be made as regards the *whole* scheme (i.e., including the acquisition) and not just what remains to be done.

As s. 139 must have been designed to allow persons to avoid or more accurately, to defer tax, so facilitating corporate restructuring and the like without precipitating a tax charge on unrealised capital gains, it is suggested that, unless the restructuring is part of a wider matter one of whose main purposes is the avoidance of tax, s. 139 relief should be available.

A similar anti-avoidance test is used for s. 137 and the mere fact that capital gains tax may also be deferred would not, of itself, be a main purpose of avoidance of tax. Each case turns on its precise circumstances but as Lord Wilberforce said (albeit in a different context) in *Ramsay* v *IRC* [1981] 1 All ER 865 at p. 873 'The capital gains tax was created to operate in the real world, not that of make believe . . .' He was echoing what he had said in *Aberdeen Construction* v *IRC* [1978] 1 All ER 962 (at p. 986) namely '. . . the Courts should hesitate before accepting results which are paradoxical and contrary to business sense . . .'

30.8 CONSIDERATION FOR THE TRANSFER

Section 139(1)(c), TCGA provides that if the relief is to be obtained the transferor company amalgamated or reconstructed must 'receive no part of the consideration for the transfer'. There is an exception for the assumption of the debts and liabilities of the transferring company by the acquiring company.

'Consideration' is not defined in this context. Tax statutes apply to the whole of the UK and must be construed in this light so that the technical English contract law meaning would seem not to be the right interpretation. It is suggested that here it means more than the *quid pro quo* (which may not be that different from English contract law).

One potentially difficult problem is the relationship between the wording of s. 110, Insolvency Act 1986 and s. 139, TCGA. In the writers' experience most transactions to which s. 139 apply take place under s. 110, Insolvency Act 1986. Section 110(2) permits the liquidator (with the requisite sanction of a special resolution) to receive in compensation or part compensation for the transfer or sale of the whole or part of the company's business to another company 'shares, policies or other like interests in the transferee company for distribution among the members of the transferor company.'

Shares are usually used but in practice it is unusual for the shares to be issued to the liquidator. Rather they are issued directly to the shareholders. If the shares issued for the transfer discharge obligations in the liquidation there is an argument that this is consideration. This could be argued to be a benefit to the transferor company and so in breach of s. 139(1)(c), TCGA. This does not seem to be the Revenue's view. In the writers' opinion the Revenue's view is correct because analytically it is not the transferor that receives the consideration.

The requirement that the transferor should receive no part of the consideration for the transfer must be borne in mind in drafting documentation, particularly 'further assurances' as to, e.g., land and intellectual property where registries expect to see a figure for consideration paid.

30.9 RELATIONSHIP TO OTHER TAX PROVISIONS

Section 139, TCGA does not give any indication of how it is to relate to other sections in the tax legislation. For example, does s. 139 take precedence over s. 171, TCGA? If not on a disposal of the shares of a reconstructed company can a s. 178, TCGA charge arise?

This is best illustrated by way of an example. Company A acquires Company T, a holding company with three business groups below it.

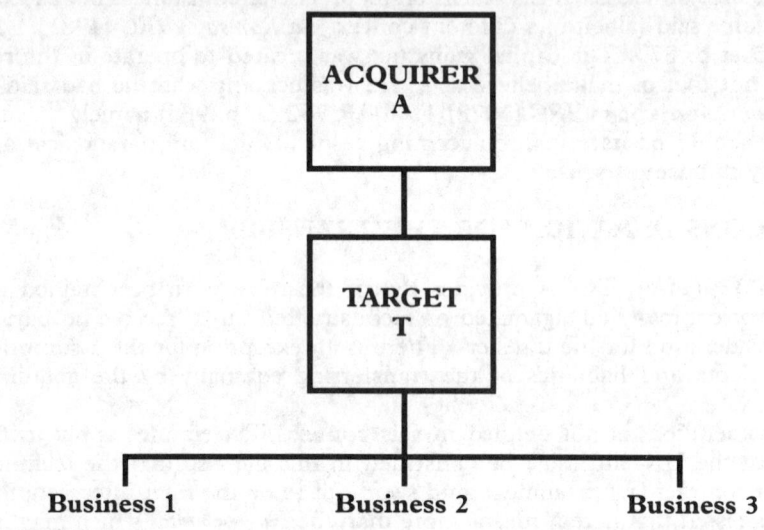

```
          ACQUIRER
             A
             |
           TARGET
             T
    _____|_____
   |         |         |
Business 1  Business 2  Business 3
```

Figure 30.9

If Company T were reorganised under s. 110, Insolvency Act 1986, then the post-reorganisation structure might be as set out below.

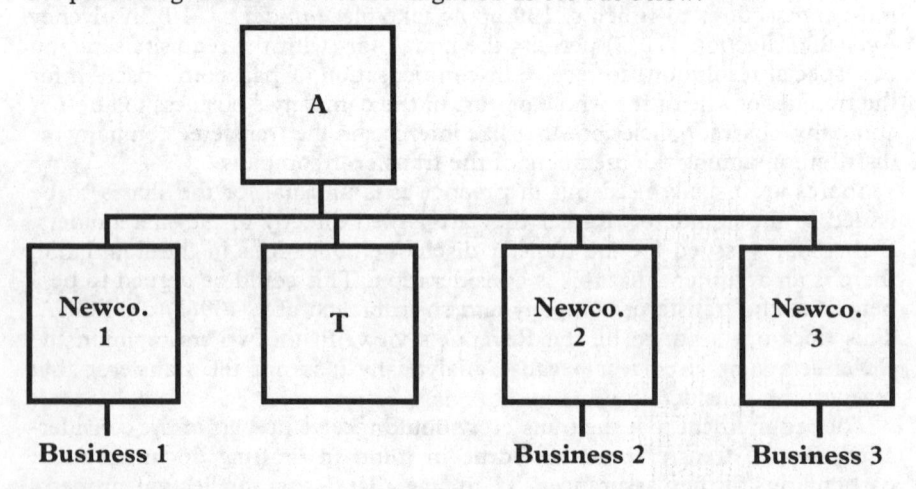

```
                    A
         _____|_____
        |      |         |        |
     Newco.    T      Newco.    Newco.
       1                2          3
        |              |           |
   Business 1    Business 2   Business 3
```

Figure 30.10

30.10 UK TAX AND REDEMPTION AND PURCHASE OF OWN SHARES

30.10.1 Introduction

The possibility of a British company purchasing its own shares is a fairly recent phenomenon. The Companies Act 1981 allowed a British company to purchase its own shares for the first time. Sections 53 to 56 and sch. 9, FA 1982 dealt with the tax position.

The effect of s. 53, FA 1982, now s. 219, TA, is that there is not a 'distribution' where an unquoted trading company, or the holding company of a trading group, redeems or purchases its own shares provided certain conditions (set out below) are fulfilled. Broadly, the effect of these provisions is that the redemption or purchase of shares is treated as liable to capital gains tax rather than a distribution attracting ACT and income tax under Schedule F.

In the absence of these provisions there would be a distribution on the purchase of its shares at more than par by a company. This is because there would be a transfer of assets to the shareholders and the amount in excess of the consideration originally given for the shares woud be a distribution (see s. 209(2)(b) and (4), TA). Following the enactment of the Finance Act 1997, where distribution treatment applies to the redemption or purchase of a company's own shares, the distribution is treated as though it was a 'foreign income dividend'. This means that no tax credit will be available on the dividend (although any ACT paid in respect of it can be reclaimed from the Revenue). An exception is made for 'pre-sale dividends' defined as distributions made within 14 days of 75% of the share capital of the company changing ownership.

The conditions for capital gains tax treatment in s. 219, TA depend on whether the redemption or purchase is:

(a) for general purposes; or
(b) to pay IHT on death within two years of death which could not otherwise have been paid without undue hardship.

There is a clearance procedure under s. 225, TA.

30.10.2 'Unquoted trading company'

The provisions as to purchase or redemption of shares only apply to shares in an unquoted trading company or the holding company of a trading group. An 'unquoted company' is defined in s. 229(1), TA as a company which is neither a quoted company nor the 51% subsidiary of a quoted company. A 'quoted company' is a company any class of whose shares is listed in the official list of a stock exchange (s. 229(1)). By SP 18/80 shares dealt in on the USM (now the AIM) are not listed or quoted.

There are a number of further definitions for the purposes of these provisions, set out in s. 229.

(a) Section 229(1) provides that a 'trading company' is a company whose business consists wholly or mainly of the carrying on of a trade or trades. There are exceptions for dealing in shares, securities, land or futures with the result that s. 219 is inapplicable.

(b) By the same section a 'holding company' is a company whose business (disregarding any trade it carries on) is the holding of shares or securities in one or more companies which are its 75% subsidiaries.

(c) Similarly a 'trading group' is defined as a group (i.e., a holding company and its 75% subsidiaries) whose 'business' consists 'wholly or mainly' in the carrying on of a trade or trades. This could exclude a group with a mixture of trading and investment subsidiaries. However, it seems the Revenue's view is that a subgroup which is a trading group can qualify.[4]

30.10.3 Redemption or purchase – general conditions

Section 219(1), TA provides that there is not to be a 'distribution' on the redemption or purchase of shares if the conditions in ss. 219 et seq are satisfied. The conditions are that:

(a) The company is unquoted; and
(b) It is either:

(i) a trading company; or
(ii) the holding company of a trading group (s. 219(1)(a)).

(c) The redemption or purchase is made 'wholly or mainly' for the purpose of 'benefiting a trade' carried on by the company or any of its 75% subsidiaries. The meaning of 'benefiting a trade' was raised during the Committee stage debate on the bill.[5] The Financial Secretary to the Treasury commented that 'Both among the public [sic] and the Government there is no doubt about its intention'. However, he said the Revenue would issue a statement of practice on the 'benefiting of the trade' test. It is not clear on its wording whether it is a 'motive' or 'results' test. It seems the better view is that it is a 'motive' test probably of a subjective character in theory though effectively objective in practice. The Revenue's views are set out in SP 2/82.

(d) The redemption or purchase of the shares does not form part of a 'scheme or arrangement' the main purpose or one of the main purposes of which is either:

(i) to enable the owner of shares to participate in the 'profits' of the company without receiving a 'dividend'. The phrase 'profits' is not defined. Does it include capital gains for these purposes? (Cf. s. 6(4), TA.) What is a 'dividend' for these purposes is also not defined; or

---
[4.] See para. 54 of the Consultative Committee of Accountancy Bodies (CCAB) [1982] STI 281.
[5.] Hansard 8 June 1982, col 440 et seq.

(ii) the avoidance of tax. There is no guidance as to the meaning of this. Does tax here include, for example, IHT? (Cf. s. 832(3), TA.)

(e) The vendor is UK resident and ordinarily resident in the year of the assessment in question (i.e., the vendor is liable to capital gains tax) (see s. 220(1)). The legislation is generally concerned with 'beneficial ownership' (see s. 229(2)). However, if the shares are held through a nominee the nominee must also be UK resident (s. 220(1)). Trustees are to be treated in the same way as they are for capital gains tax (see s. 69, TCGA). Personal representatives are to have the same residence and ordinary residence as the deceased immediately before the death. Residence only, and not ordinary residence, is to be taken into account for a company (s. 220(4)).

(f) The vendor must have owned the shares for the five years before the purchase or redemption (s. 220(5)). When shares were transferred by one spouse to another while they were living together, then the other spouse's period of ownership can be included in calculating the period of ownership unless the spouses are alive but living apart (s. 220(6)). Personal representatives are treated as owning the shares during periods when the deceased did (s. 220(7)). The period is reduced to three years from five for personal representatives. Where shares of the same class have been acquired at different times shares acquired earlier are to be taken into account before shares acquired later. Any previous disposal is to be treated as a disposal of shares acquired later. The capital gains rules as to timing of acquisitions or reorganisation etc. apply.

(g) The vendor's interest (if any) immediately after the redemption or purchase as a shareholder must be 'substantially reduced' as compared with his interest before (s. 221). A vendor's interest will be 'substantially reduced' if and 'only if' the nominal value of his holding immediately after the redemption or purchase does not exceed 75% of his holding before. However, if on a distribution of all profits available for distribution (broadly the Companies Act meaning), he would be entitled to more than 75% of the profits after the redemption on purchase than he would before, then his holding will not be taken to be substantially reduced. This provision is only concerned with beneficial entitlement except where trustees or personal representatives are involved in that capacity.

(h) The combined interests of the vendor and his associates must also be 'substantially reduced' (s. 221(3)). Section 227 defines 'associates'. They include spouses living together, parents and minor children, and a company they 'control' (see s. 228; inter alia entitlement to acquire 30% of voting power is sufficient). Trustees are associated with the settlor and beneficiaries.

(i) Where a group of companies is involved the vendor's interest in the group must be substantially reduced, as must the combined interest of himself and his associates (s. 222). 'Group' is specifically defined for these purposes in s. 222(9) as a company and its 51% subsidiaries.

(j) The vendor must not be 'connected' (as defined in s. 228) with the purchasing company or its group member after the purchase etc. (s. 223).

If the conditions set out in (g)–(j) above are not satisfied in relation to the vendor, but the taxpayer agreed to the purchase or redemption so that the combined interests are reduced, he can still benefit from the s. 219 tax regime (s. 224).

(k) As a further anti-avoidance measure, it is provided that the purchase or redemption must not be part of a 'scheme or arrangement' which is 'designed or likely to result' in the vendor or any associate having interests in any company such that if he were treated as having those interests immediately after the redemption or purchase any of the other conditions would not be satisfied. This is to prevent compliance in fact but not in spirit by changing interests after the redemption or purchase. There is no time limit provided. 'Scheme or arrangement' is not defined. The Revenue have indicated that the Statement of Practice on Group Relief and arrangements would be relevant. It is not entirely clear what degree of probability 'likely to result in' requires.

30.10.4 Purchase or redemption to pay IHT on death

Section 219(1)(b), TA provides that if a redemption or purchase is made to pay a person's liability to IHT on death within two years there will be no distribution if:

(a) the company is unquoted;
(b) it is either:

   (i) a trading company; or
   (ii) the trading company of a trading group;

(c) the whole or substantially the whole of the payment is used to discharge the vendor's (which can include personal representatives) liability to IHT at a death and is so applied within two years of the death. The payment for these purposes is to be considered net if any of it is used to pay capital gains tax on the redemption etc.

The Revenue have said that in their view 'substantial' means 'nearly all'. The relaxation is not to apply to the extent that the liability to IHT could 'without undue hardship' have been discharged without a redemption or purchase (s. 219(2)).

30.10.5 Clearance

Section 225, TA provides for a clearance procedure. The Revenue have issued a press release dated 1 June 1982 which sets out the type of information they require to be included on application. An application and consent only gives clearance under s. 219. Other provisions may still be applicable (e.g., s. 703, TA discussed at para. 4.16.2).

PART V
Inheritance tax

CHAPTER THIRTY ONE
Inheritance tax – general principles

31.1 INTRODUCTION

Inheritance tax[1] fulfils two functions. First, it acts as a tax on gifts made during a person's lifetime, although certain favoured transfers will either be completely exempt from tax or 'potentially' exempt and will not be charged to tax at all if the taxpayer survives for seven years after making the gift. Secondly, inheritance tax acts as a tax on death, imposing a charge on the value of a deceased's estate, cumulated with certain other property of which he had not completely divested himself, and other transfers of wealth made in the last seven years of his life (unless those transfers were exempt from inheritance tax when they were made).

Inheritance tax thus acts as a tax on the transfer of wealth as opposed to a tax on the mere holding of wealth.[2] Wealth transfer taxes may be divided according to whether they are 'donor' or 'donee' based. The United Kingdom has traditionally imposed donor based systems of wealth taxation. These systems treat the donor of the wealth as the taxable person and calculate the liability to tax upon the total amount being given away. In contrast, donee based systems treat the recipient of the wealth as the taxable person and compute the tax liability according to the circumstances of the recipient.[3]

---

[1] See, generally, *Foster's Inheritance Tax*, Butterworths.
[2] 'Annual wealth taxes' have been proposed for the United Kingdom, most notably by the then Labour government in 1974 (*Wealth Tax*, Cmnd. 5704) but have never been adopted. For a discussion of wealth taxes and their advantages and disadvantages see Chapter 1 and James and Nobes, *The Economics of Taxation*, 1996/97 edn, Prentice Hall, paras. 10.7 to 10.10.
[3] Donee based systems of wealth taxation are often labelled 'accessions taxes'. The case for an accessions tax and how it might be operated is made out by Sandford et al, *An Accessions Tax*, Institute for Fiscal Studies (1973).

31.2 HISTORY

Modern legislation dates from the introduction of estate duty in 1894 which imposed a testator based system of taxing transfers of wealth. Under estate duty, lifetime gifts were not taxed at all, but in order to prevent gifts being made 'in contemplation of death' it was necessary to include death bed gifts in the taxpayer's estate. As taxpayers began to gift at least part of their estate in advance of their anticipated deaths, successive governments began to extend the length of the period before death during which gifts were taxable. Eventually this period was extended to seven years.

One major weakness with estate duty from the government's point of view was that the rules concerning settled property were limited to situations where beneficiaries had beneficial interests under trusts. Thus discretionary trusts could be used to reduce significantly a taxpayer's liability to estate duty. In 1969 attempts were made to close this 'loophole' by notionally attributing the property within the settlement to the discretionary beneficiaries and taxing them accordingly. However, it was still possible to use trusts judiciously to save estate duty.

In 1975, estate duty was transformed into capital transfer tax. Capital transfer tax was also a donor based tax but, in contrast to its predecessor, it sought to tax *all* transfers of wealth whenever made as well as the value of the estate on death. It was thus an integrated lifetime gift and death tax. The rate of tax was determined by cumulating the transfers made over a lifetime, the aim being to stop taxpayers avoiding the tax by making 'early' lifetime gifts. Special rates of tax applied to trusts. However, the rate of capital transfer tax on lifetime gifts was less than the rate paid on death, allegedly to help with the problems of lifetime transfers of small private businesses.

Once the Conservative government came to power in 1979, the scope of capital transfer tax was considerably narrowed in successive Finance Bills by raising thresholds, granting concessions to agriculture and industry and, in particular, removing the general tax on lifetime gifts. In 1986 capital transfer tax was replaced with inheritance tax. The Capital Transfer Tax Act 1984 was renamed the Inheritance Tax Act 1984 ('IHTA') and all references to capital transfer tax, whether in the statute itself or any document(s) 'executed, made, served or issued' before the introduction of inheritance tax, must now be read as references to inheritance tax (s. 100(1)(b), FA 1986).[4] The legislation has undergone some modification to take account of the move to inheritance tax, most notably by introducing the concept of the potentially exempt transfer which is only liable to inheritance tax if the transferor dies within seven years of making the gift. However, the modifications have been done in a hurry and this has not always led to the clearest of drafting.[5]

---

[4] Save where the reference to capital transfer tax relates to a liability to tax arising before 25 July 1986; s. 100(2), FA 1986.

[5] For example, the provisions relating to potentially exempt transfers use the word 'gift' which does not fit with the drafting in the remainder of the IHTA. The wording was derived from estate duty which employed different concepts from those in use in the IHTA.

31.3 POLICY

The present system of inheritance tax is subject to a number of criticisms. First, under the present system those who, looked at over a lifetime, are equally well off do not always pay the same amount of tax. This is because the amount of inheritance tax paid can vary enormously – between zero on the whole amount to 40% on the whole amount above £215,000 (at current rates) depending on the timing and to whom (and in what form) dispositions are made by the taxpayer. The possibility of making potentially exempt transfers means that wealthy and well-advised taxpayers will pass on assets as early in life as they can afford to do so. Should the transferor live for seven years after the gift, the transfer of wealth will escape tax altogether.[6] In contrast, the estate of a person who dies wholly unprepared, for example in an accident, and who has not divested himself of any of his wealth may incur considerable inheritance tax liabilities.[7] If the individual had previously sold assets pregnant with capital gains, the subsequent inheritance tax liability will fall on top of his capital gains tax bill. Moreover, even if the taxpayer had taken advice and given away as much of his wealth as he could afford to, but is unlucky enough to die within seven years, inheritance tax will be payable on those lifetime gifts. The overall result is that there can be significant inequities as between similarly placed taxpayers depending on whether they happen to have received good tax advice and whether they live for seven years after making any substantial transfers of wealth.

Secondly, unlike capital transfer tax which had the redistribution of wealth from rich to poor as one of its aims, inheritance tax, when introduced, was justified by the government as a revenue raising tax. However, the contribution made by inheritance tax to total tax revenues is small.[8] This is because, by making use of trusts and lifetime giving, the very rich and well-advised can (if they choose) escape paying inheritance tax at all, and can effectively pass on substantial chunks of wealth tax-free. Inheritance tax, like its progenitor estate duty, is therefore often described as a 'voluntary' tax. Thus, to the extent that revenue is raised by inheritance tax, it will be 'proportionally more from the comparatively wealthy' and 'from the badly-advised rather than the well-advised' (*Death: The Unfinished Business*, Institute for Fiscal Studies, para. 2.3.34).

Thirdly, inheritance tax contains a number of reliefs and exemptions from tax, in particular the transfer of much business and agricultural property is entirely removed from tax. It has been argued[9] that this structure actually creates inequalities between individuals, since people are taxed differently not according to the amount of wealth that they hold, but the form in which they

---

[6.] Although capital gains tax may have been paid.
[7.] Although his capital gains tax liabilities will be removed.
[8.] £1,333 million in 1993/94 compared with £58,442 million raised by income tax, (Board of Inland Revenue, Report for year ending 31 March 1994). The estimated yield from inheritance tax in 1997/98 is only £1,550 million (Budget Press Release, 26 November 1996).
[9.] By Sandford, 'Death Duties: Taxing Estates or Inheritances', 1987, *Fiscal Studies*, vol. 8, no 4, pp. 15 to 23.

hold it. The effect may be to generate investment distortions. Further, it is argued, as market prices adjust to reduce the differences in net of tax returns from assets, the price of, for example, farmland may be raised, ultimately harming future farm owners who are discouraged from acquiring farms because of high prices.

Fourthly, the interaction of capital gains tax and inheritance tax is a complex area of tax policy and the current rules are not internally consistent. Strictly, capital gains tax and inheritance tax are taxing different things so there is no overlap between the two. Although both arise when an asset is transferred, capital gains tax is taxing the increase in the capital value of the asset since it was acquired whereas inheritance tax is taxing the total capital value of the asset. Nevertheless a number of steps have been taken to ensure that taxpayers do not pay capital gains tax and inheritance tax in respect of the same transaction. These may be summarised as follows:

(a) When a taxpayer dies his or her personal representatives are deemed to acquire the deceased's assets at their then market value; but there is no corresponding disposal of those assets by the deceased and no capital gains tax charge can arise (s. 62, TCGA). This rule applies whether or not the deceased's estate is subject to inheritance tax.[10]

(b) Although there may be a liability to capital gains tax if an individual gifts an asset during his or her lifetime, the gift is likely to be classified as potentially exempt for inheritance tax purposes so that no inheritance tax will be chargeable if the transferor survives for seven years after making the gift (s. 3A, IHTA). If inheritance tax does become chargeable (because the transferor dies within the seven years) no account is taken of the capital gains tax previously paid by him or her in assessing the liability of the transferor's estate for inheritance tax.[11] Where, however, the gift is not potentially exempt for inheritance tax purposes, for example because it is made to the trustees of a discretionary settlement (see Chapter 33), the transferor and transferee may claim hold-over relief thus postponing the capital gains tax that would otherwise accrue on the gift until the transferee disposes of the asset (s. 260(2)(a), TCGA). Hold-over relief may be claimed even if no inheritance tax is actually payable, because (say) the transfer is within the transferor's 0% rate band for inheritance tax (see para. 33.4). If inheritance tax is payable, the amount of inheritance tax paid can be used to reduce the transferee's liability to capital gains tax when the transferee disposes of the gift even though the inheritance tax was charged on the transferor (s. 260(7), TCGA).[12]

---

[10] As noted in Chapter 23, this has not always been the position. Between 1965 (when capital gains tax was first introduced) and 1971, both capital gains tax and estate duty were payable on a person's death. The capital gains tax paid was then allowed as a deduction in computing the value of the estate for estate duty purposes.

[11] Cf. s. 165(1), IHTA whereby an adjustment can be made if the capital gains tax is borne by the transferee.

[12] Inheritance tax can only be deducted up to the amount of the chargeable gain so that this provision cannot be used to create an allowable loss for capital gains tax purposes.

Nevertheless, there are some attractions to the current system of inheritance tax. The tax is principally imposed on death and, as property generally has to be valued on death for the purposes of administration, the tax is comparatively simple to calculate for both the Inland Revenue and the executors and relatively hard to evade. Inheritance tax is also said by some to be less affected than alternative taxes might be by the intricacies of will and settlements.[13]

[13.] A number of options for reform have been suggested. The Institute for Fiscal Studies Capital Taxes Group in the publication, *Death: The Unfinished Business* recommended extending income tax so as to include gifts and inheritances. An accessions tax has been proposed by, among others, Sandford although such taxes tend to raise less revenue. Alternatively the recommendations of the Mead Committee which proposed an annual wealth tax, or a combination of a wealth and accessions tax, could be adopted.

CHAPTER THIRTY TWO
Inheritance tax – the charge

32.1 THE CHARGE

Section 1, IHTA provides that:

> [Inheritance] tax shall be charged on the value transferred by a chargeable transfer.

Section 2(1), IHTA provides that:

> A chargeable transfer is a transfer of value which is made by an individual but which is not . . . an exempt transfer.

There are therefore three important elements in a charge to inheritance tax:

(a) a transfer of value;
(b) which is not an exempt transfer;
(c) as a result of which value is transferred.

These elements are examined in this and the next chapter, together with the computation of liability to the tax. The inheritance tax provisions relating to trusts are discussed in Chapter 34. Throughout these chapters the word 'transferor' is used to describe the person making the transfer of value and the word 'transferee' is used to describe the recipient. It will, however, be noted that the IHTA uses the words 'donor' and 'donee' in addition to transferor and transferee when describing transfers of value.

32.1.1 Territorial limits

Inheritance tax applies to anyone with assets in the United Kingdom and to United Kingdom residents who are also domiciled in the United Kingdom.[1] For inheritance tax purposes, domicile is given an extended meaning (s. 267, IHTA). A person not otherwise domiciled in the United Kingdom will be deemed to be domiciled here if:

(a) He was domiciled in the United Kingdom within the three years immediately preceding the time at which his domicile falls to be determined for inheritance tax purposes. Thus, a person will continue to have a United Kingdom domicile for inheritance purposes for three years after having acquired a new foreign domicile on general principles.

(b) He was resident in the United Kingdom for not less than 17 of the 20 years of assessment ending with the year of assessment in which his domicile falls to be determined for inheritance tax purposes. Residence for these purposes is determined in the same way as for income tax.[2]

If an individual is not domiciled in the United Kingdom, any assets which are situated outside the UK will be classified as 'excluded property' and fall outside the scope of inheritance tax (ss. 3(2) and 6(1), IHTA).

32.2 TRANSFERS OF VALUE

Section 3(1), IHTA provides that:

> a transfer of value is a disposition made by a person (the transferor) as a result of which the value of his estate immediately after the disposition is less than it would be but for the disposition.

The meaning of the words 'disposition' and 'estate' and the circumstances in which a transferor's estate will be reduced are discussed in paras 32.2.1 to 32.2.4.

32.2.1 Disposition

The word 'disposition' is not defined save that it 'includes a disposition effected by associated operations' (s. 272) and s. 3(3), IHTA provides that an omission to act is a disposition if it results in a diminution of the taxpayer's estate and an increase in value in another's. Examples of such omissions include: the failure to exercise an option to purchase property at a favourable price; a failure of a landlord to exercise a rent review clause; and a failure of one shareholder in a family company to take up rights under a rights issue. Associated operations are discussed below.

---

[1] For a general discussion of domicile, see Chapter 1.
[2] For a description of the income tax rules, see Chapter 1.

The *Concise Oxford Dictionary* defines a disposition as, among other things, a 'bestowal by deed or will' or a 'disposal'. While the extended meaning given to a disposal for the purposes of the capital gains tax legislation cannot be imported into the inheritance tax legislation, it is submitted that the deliberate destruction of an interest will be a disposition for these purposes.[3]

There are no longer any express provisions concerning the tax treatment of the free use of property or money. But if the lender permits such free use, his or her estate will be reduced by the value of the loss of the use of the property or money, i.e., the rent or interest that would be charged in the open market.[4] Since in order to use the property or money it must be transferred to the borrower, there must be a disposition and therefore the requirements for a 'transfer of value' for inheritance tax purposes exists. This conclusion is bolstered by the fact that some of the exemptions from inheritance tax are specifically extended to such 'free loans' – see paras 32.8.2 and 32.8.4.

It has already been noted that a disposition includes a disposition effected by associated operations. This is inheritance tax's own anti-avoidance provision. Its relationship with the *Ramsay* doctrine (see Chapter 4) is still not fully worked out although it is now clear that the *Ramsay* principle applies to inheritance tax in circumstances where the associated operations rule does not apply.[5] Associated operations are defined by s. 268(1) as:

> any two or more operations of any kind, being—
> (a) operations which affect the same property, or one of which affects some property and the other or others of which affect property which represents, whether directly or indirectly, that property, or income arising from that property, or any property representing accumulations of any such income, or
> (b) any two operations of which one is effected with reference to the other, or with a view to enabling the other to be effected or facilitating its being effected, and any further operation having a like relation to any of those two, and so on,
> whether those operations are effected by the same person or different persons, and whether or not they are simultaneous; and 'operation' includes an omission.

The commonly cited example of the operation of s. 268(1)(a) concerns the transfer of land worth (say) £100,000. If the transferor grants the intended transferee a lease of the land at a full market rent that will reduce the value of the transferor's interest to (say) £75,000. The grant of the lease will not

---
[3.] Cf. s. 24, TCGA and *IRC v Buchanan* [1957] 2 All ER 400 in the context of Part XV, TA. There have been arguments over the meaning of the word 'disposition' in other contexts, most notably in s. 53(1)(c), Law of Property Act 1925. For a review of the case law see Green, 1984, *MLR*, vol. 47, no. 4, pp. 385–421.
[4.] The lender's estate is not reduced by the value of the property itself because legally it still belongs to him.
[5.] *Fitzwilliam v IRC* [1993] STC 502, HL. Lord Browne-Wilkinson expressly left open the question of how the *Ramsay* principle and the associated operations rules would interact in a case where both could apply.

Inheritance tax – the charge

be a transfer of value if the transferee gives full consideration for it. The transferor could subsequently transfer the reversion to the lessee and claim that the value transferred is only £75,000 as opposed to £100,000. The associated operations rule in s. 286(1)(a) prevents this. Section 268(3), IHTA provides that the associated operations are treated as made at the time of the last transaction and the transfer is thus treated as a transfer of the fee simple valued at £100,000 to the transferee made at the time of the transfer of the reversion.[6]

Section 268(1)(b) is directed at a chain of events, one or more of which may not be a transfer of value, but which ultimately reduces the value of a person's estate, particularly through the exploitation of the exemptions. A typical example here might be a husband with a 60% shareholding first transferring a 30% stake to his wife and then transferring the balance to their son, his wife later transferring her 30% stake to their son. The aim would be to exempt the value of the transferor's loss of his controlling interest in the company (as transfers between spouses are exempt from inheritance tax – see para. 32.7.1) thus reducing the value transferred to his son. The associated operations rule would treat the transfer of value as occurring when the wife transferred her 30% stake to the son, so that tax would be paid as if the transferor had transferred his 60% shareholding directly to the son.[7] It is a moot point *who* actually makes the reconstructed transfer – the transferor or his spouse.

32.2.2 Estate

For a disposition to result in a transfer of value there must be a reduction in the value of the transferor's estate. For inheritance tax purposes, 'a person's estate is the aggregate of all the property to which he is beneficially entitled' (s. 5(1)), and 'property' includes rights and interests of any description (s. 272).

32.2.3 Reduction in the transferor's estate

It may seem an obvious point that the reduction has to be in the value of the estate of the *transferor*. For the most part, there will be little or no difference between the loss in the value of the transferor's estate and the increase in value to the transferee's estate. However, situations do arise where the difference is considerable. A typical example concerns transfers of shares in a family company. If a transferor holding 60% of the voting shares in a company gives one-third of his holding to the transferee, the transferee's estate will increase by the value of a 20% minority shareholding, but the transferor's estate will reduce by more than the value of a 20% holding

---

[6.] This tax avoidance scheme is still possible if the transfer of the reversion takes place more than three years after the grant of the lease; see s. 268(2), IHTA.

[7.] Hansard Vol. 888, 10 March 1975 col. 55, reproduced in *Foster's Inheritance Tax* X6.01. The related property rules (see para. 33.2.1) would also catch the first transfer but they would not apply to the later transfer by the wife.

because the transferor will also be parting with control of the company. A similar situation occurs if the transferor gives away one item from a complete set of articles. The value of the set may be reduced far more by being incomplete than simply the value of a single article from the set.

The measure of the reduction in the value of a person's estate is a question of valuation, and this is considered in Chapter 33.

32.2.4 Void and voidable transfers

Where a transfer is void, there is no loss to the transferor's estate and so no transfer of value occurs. The same could be said of voidable transfers where the transferor could rescind the transfer and recover the property, or transfers subject to a condition precedent whereby the property does not pass until the condition is fulfilled. However, the legislation proceeds on the basis that such transfers are effected, and the tax computations are adjusted if the transfer is rescinded or the condition unfulfilled (s. 150).

32.3 TRANSACTIONS WHICH ARE NOT TRANSFERS OF VALUE

Certain dispositions are deemed by the IHTA not to be transfers of value. These are discussed in paras 32.3.1 to 32.3.8.

32.3.1 Non-gratuitous transfers

Clearly, there will be no reduction in the value of the transferor's estate if he receives full consideration for the transfer. However, *full* consideration may not have been given, perhaps because the transferor made a bad commercial bargain, even though no gift was intended. To meet this problem, s. 10(1), IHTA provides that:

> A disposition is not a transfer of value if it is shown that it was not intended, and was not made in a transaction intended, to confer any gratuitous benefit on any person and either:
> (a) that it was made in a transaction at arm's length between persons not connected with each other,[8] or
> (b) that it was such as might be expected to be made in a transaction at arm's length between persons not connected with each other.

A 'transaction' in s. 10(1) includes a series of transactions and any associated operations. This prevents a transferor from dividing a transaction into several parts, each of which takes place for full consideration (for example, separate sales of items comprising a set), when the overall objective is to make a

---

[8.] The meaning of 'connected persons' is that applied by s. 286, TCGA save that the definition of 'relative' is extended to include uncles, aunts, nephews and nieces and the words 'settlement', 'settlor' and 'trustee' bear their inheritance tax, not their capital gains tax meanings; s. 270, IHTA.

transfer of the whole set at less than its full market value (because the set as a whole is worth more than the individual items).

Additional requirements apply to sales of unquoted shares or unquoted debentures. Section 10(1) will only apply if the sale took place for a freely negotiated price at that time or if the price was such that might be expected to have been freely negotiated at that time. These conditions might be difficult to satisfy if the company's articles of association state the price at which the shares are to be offered on a sale.

32.3.2 Maintenance of family

Section 11(1), IHTA provides that a disposition is not a transfer of value if it is made by one party to a marriage in favour of the other party or of a child[9] of either party and is either for the maintenance of the other party[10] or for the maintenance, education or training of the child until he or she reaches 18 or, if later, ceases to undergo full-time education or training.

Payments to an ex-spouse will not be transfers of value if made 'on the occasion of' the dissolution or annulment of the marriage. It is understood that the Inland Revenue interpret the words 'on the occasion of' liberally so, provided the disposition is made within a reasonable time of the dissolution or annulment of the marriage, s. 11(1) will apply.[11] If the disposition is much later, reliance will have to be placed on s. 10(1). Presumably, periodical payments in favour of a former spouse or a child will be exempt from inheritance tax as normal expenditure out of income (see para. 32.8.3).

A disposition is also not a transfer of value if it is made in favour of a child who is not in the care of his or her parent and is for the child's maintenance, education or training until he or she attains 18, or if before then the child has for substantial periods been in the care of the person making the disposition, until the child ceases to undergo full-time education or training after the age of 18.

Finally, a disposition is not a transfer of value if it is made in favour of a dependent relative and is reasonable provision for the relative's care or maintenance (s. 11(3)).[12] A dependent relative for these purposes is a relative of the transferor or his spouse who is incapacitated by old age or infirmity from maintaining him or herself, or is the mother of the transferor or his spouse who is widowed or living apart from her husband or has not remarried following a decree of divorce or annulment (s. 11(6)).[13]

The dispositions under s. 11 have to be 'in favour of' the particular transferee. This clearly covers a direct transfer and a transfer on trust to an

---

[9.] Defined to include a step-child and an adopted child; s. 11(6), IHTA. Illegitimate children are also covered by this exemption; s. 11(4).

[10.] This provision is supplemented by the exemption from inheritance tax for transfers between spouses discussed in para. 32.7.1. However, s. 11 is necessary because the spouse exemption is limited when the transferee is not domiciled in the United Kingdom.

[11.] See *Foster's Inheritance Tax* C1.51 citing the *New Law Journal*, 2 December 1976, p. 1183.

[12.] Strictly 'relative' is not defined although see s. 270, IHTA.

[13.] Extra-statutory Concession F12 provides that a disposition is also exempt if the child's unmarried mother (although not incapacitated) is genuinely financially dependent on the child making the disposition.

absolutely entitled beneficiary. It may also cover a transfer to a beneficiary on trust for life but it is difficult to describe a transfer to a discretionary trust under which the transferee is merely a potential beneficiary as being in that beneficiary's favour since that beneficiary will be only one of a number of potential beneficiaries.[14]

32.3.3 Dispositions allowable for income tax

A disposition is not a transfer of value if it is allowable in computing the transferor's profits or gains for the purposes of income or corporation tax (s. 12(1)). The provision is not limited to expenses that may be deducted in computing trading income, but extends to sums which may be deductible under other Schedules or Cases. However, if an income tax deduction is specifically disallowed under the TA, the transferor cannot rely on this provision to exclude a transfer of value, although there may not be a transfer of value in any event because (say) s. 10, IHTA applies.

32.3.4 Pension plans

Contributions by an employee to an approved retirement benefits scheme or personal pension plan are not transfers of value (s. 12(2), IHTA).

32.3.5 Waiver of remuneration

The waiver or repayment of remuneration is not a transfer of value if, apart from the waiver or repayment, that remuneration would be assessable to income tax under Schedule E and would have been deductible in computing the taxable profits of the payer (s. 14, IHTA).

32.3.6 Waiver of dividends

The waiver of any dividend on shares of a company within twelve months before any right to the dividend has accrued is not a transfer of value (s. 15, IHTA). A dividend will accrue when it is declared even if not paid until a later date (*Re Severn and Wye and Severn Bridge Railway* [1896] Ch 559 and *Re Kidner* [1929] 2 Ch 121; cf. *Potel* v *IRC* [1971] 2 All ER 504 if the dividend is specifically stated to be payable at a future date).[15]

32.3.7 Grant of agricultural tenancies

The grant of a tenancy of agricultural property in the United Kingdom, the Channel Islands or the Isle of Man for use for agricultural purposes is not a

---

[14.] Query if a disposition to a discretionary trust could be within s. 11 if all the potential beneficiaries of the trust meet the criteria specified.
[15.] The position is otherwise for interim dividends which do not accrue until actually paid; see *Lagunas Nitrate Co. Ltd* v *Schroeder and Co.* (1901) 85 LT 22. See further Sims [1977] *BTR* 28 and Baxter [1978] *The Conveyancer* 294. See Chapter 27.

transfer of value if made for full consideration in money or money's worth (s. 16, IHTA).[16]

32.3.8 Transfer to a trust for the benefit of employees

A transfer by a close company (see para. 25.6.6) to trustees on trust for the benefit of a member of a class of employees or officers of that company is not a transfer of value (ss. 13 and 86(1), IHTA). It should be noted that the trustees can be given discretion as to whom to benefit.

32.4 TRANSFERS OF VALUE ON DEATH

Section 4(1), IHTA provides that:

> On the death of any person tax shall be charged as if, immediately before his death, he had made a transfer of value and the value transferred by it had been equal to the value of his estate immediately before his death.[17]

A person's estate immediately before his death does not include excluded property, but it will include property subject to a reservation and potentially exempt transfers made within seven years before death. The meaning of excluded property was discussed in para. 32.1.1. Gifts of property subject to a reservation and potentially exempt transfers are discussed in paras 32.5 and 32.9 respectively.

The IHTA does not say to whom the transfer of value on death is made, however, it is taken to be the person who becomes entitled to the deceased's estate under the will or on an intestacy. The exemption for a spouse and other exemptions from inheritance tax may therefore be applicable to transfers on death.

32.5 GIFTS WITH RESERVATION

If a person has given away property during his lifetime, which immediately before his death is 'subject to a reservation', that property is deemed to form part of the deceased's estate on death. Property is treated as property subject to a reservation if an individual made a gift of that property after 17 March 1986 and either:

(a) the transferee does not *bona fide* assume possession and enjoyment of it within seven years before the transferor's death; or

---

[16.] This provision is needed because the system of protected tenancies of agricultural land invariably means that a grant of such a tenancy reduces the value of the transferor's estate even if made for full consideration.

[17.] Section 4, IHTA does not apply where the deceased was a member of the armed forces on active service who died from a wound or disease resulting from that service. Thus such a person's estate does not bear inheritance tax on his death; s. 154.

(b) the gifted property is not enjoyed to the entire exclusion, or virtually the entire exclusion, of the transferor at any time within seven years before the transferor's death (s. 102, FA 1986).

The purpose of these rules is to counter avoidance devices that might otherwise be employed by taxpayers to 'give away' their property at least seven years before their anticipated deaths while still retaining a benefit from that property.[18] The rules are very similar to the old estate duty rules so some of the authorities on estate duty are relevant in determining whether (or not) a gift is subject to a reservation.

It is vital to the application of the gift with reservation rules that the transferor retains a benefit from something which he has purported to give away. If a transferor simply retains something, he cannot fall within the gift with reservation rules. As Lord Simonds put it in *St Aubyn* v *AG* [1952] AC 15 at p. 29:

> if A gives B all his estates in Wiltshire except Blackacre, he does not except Blackacre out of what he has given; he just does not give Blackacre.

Such 'carving out' or 'shearing' of property before transferring the remainder to the transferee can be exploited in inheritance tax planning since it need not necessarily involve a physical division of the property but can involve the legal separation of interests in a property, such as the carving out of an equitable interest in the property. Two cases may illustrate this point. In *Ingram & another* v *IRC* [1995] 4 All ER 334, Lady Ingram owned land in Berkshire. She transferred the entire property to her nominee who granted two leases back to Lady Ingram and then conveyed the reversion to trustees on trust for various members of Lady Ingram's family. It was held that the gift with reservation rules did not apply. Although the leases were invalid because a person cannot contract with himself,[19] the trustees took the legal estate on the basis that it was subject to purported leases to Lady Ingram who thus had interests in equity co-extensive with those she thought she had at law. What had therefore been conveyed to the trustees was a freehold interest shorn of a leasehold interest. This meant that when the transfer of the freehold interest became chargeable on Lady Ingram's death, it was subject to a lower valuation as a freehold encumbered by two leases.[20]

By way of contrast, if the transferor gives away the unencumbered freehold on the understanding that the transferee will then grant him a lease of it, the gifted property (the *unencumbered* freehold) is subject to a benefit reserved to the transferor. So in *Chick* v *Stamp Duty Commissioner* [1958] AC 435 a father made an absolute gift of land to his son. A year later the son brought the land

---

[18.] Thus the policy underlying these provisions is directly analogous to that underlying Part XV, TA discussed in Chapter 15.

[19.] The English court followed the decision of the Scottish Court in *Kildrummy (Jersey) Ltd* v *IRC* [1990] STC 657 on this point.

[20.] See also *Munro & others* v *Commissioner of Stamp Duties* [1934] AC 61 and *Stamp Duties Commissioner of New South Wales* v *Perpetual Trustee Co. Ltd* [1943] AC 425.

into a farming partnership with his father and another brother. The Privy Council held that the son had not retained possession and enjoyment to the exclusion of the transferor, so when the father died, the land was included as part of the father's estate for estate duty purposes.

The decision in *Chick* was particularly harsh given that the farming partnership was a *bona fide* arm's length arrangement. As a result, a relaxation was made to the estate duty gift with reservation rules and this relaxation has been incorporated into the inheritance tax rules. Where the property is an interest in land or a chattel, the retention or assumption by the transferor of actual occupation of the land, or actual enjoyment of an incorporeal right over the land (for example, a right of way or fishing rights), or actual possession of the chattel, will be disregarded in determining whether the property was enjoyed to the entire exclusion of the donor if it was retained or assumed for full consideration in money or money's worth (para. 6(1)(a), sch. 20, FA 1986). So, a gift of an unencumbered freehold to the transferee on the condition that the transferor is given a lease of the property, will not be treated as being subject to a reservation if a lease is subsequently granted for a full market value rent.

In addition, the words 'virtually to the entire exclusion' of the transferor in s. 102, FA 1986 impart a *de minimis* exception into the gift with reservation rules. And if the gifted property is an interest in land, the transferor's occupation of the land, or of any part of it, will be ignored in determining whether he has been excluded from benefit if:

(a) his occupation results from an unforeseen change in the transferor's circumstances, which occurs at a time when the transferor has become unable to maintain himself because of old age, infirmity or otherwise; and

(b) the transferee is a relative[21] of the transferor or his spouse, and providing the occupation represents reasonable provision for the care and maintenance of the transferor (para. 6(1)(b), sch. 20, FA 1986).

If property is subject to a reservation it will remain part of the transferor's estate for inheritance tax purposes. Accordingly, provisions exist to 'trace' the transferor's property into its exchange products. The rules provide that the value of the gift with reservation is traced through to property substituted for the gift and into all accretions to the gifted property (para. 2, sch. 20, FA 1986). Substituted property includes any benefit received by the transferee by way of consideration on a sale, exchange or other disposition of the gifted property, any benefit received by him in or towards satisfaction or redemption of any debt or security, and any property acquired pursuant to an option. However, this provision does not apply if the gifted property was a sum of money (since the value transferred is clear, at least in the case of gifts of sterling) or was a gift into settlement (since settlements have their own rules; see Chapter 34).

Unless the transferee gives the property back to the transferor, any gift or other voluntary disposition by the transferee of the gifted property without

---
[21] 'Relative' is not defined.

consideration in money or money's worth will be ignored because the transferee will be treated as though he continued to have the possession and enjoyment of the property (para. 2(4), sch. 20).[22] Further, the transferee will be treated as though he had voluntarily divested himself of the gifted property without consideration if that property is merged or extinguished in another interest which he subsequently holds or acquires (for example, the merger of a leasehold interest into the freehold when the transferee as a tenant acquires the reversion).

If the gifted property was shares or debentures, and the transferee is subsequently granted an option to acquire further shares or debentures, or a rights or bonus issue is made, the new shares or debentures are treated as part of the original gifted property (in addition to the original shares and debentures), unless the original shares or debentures were exchanged for the new ones such as on a take-over or merger (paras 2(6) and (7), sch. 20).

32.6 EXEMPT TRANSFERS

Several provisions exempt transfers of value from inheritance tax. It is convenient to divide the exemptions into four categories:

(a) those available at any time;
(b) those available during lifetime only;
(c) those which are potentially exempt; and
(d) those which are conditional.

The gifts with reservation rules discussed in para. 32.5 do not apply if the transfer of the gifted property is an exempt transfer unless the transfer is exempt because it falls within the annual or small expenditure out of income exemptions (s. 102(5), FA 1986). Provisions exist to apportion the exemption where the transfer is only partially exempt (ss. 36 to 42, IHTA).

32.7 ALL TRANSFERS

The following exemptions are available in respect of all transfers of value whether made during a transferor's lifetime or on his or her death.

32.7.1 Spouses

Transfers of value between spouses are exempt (a) to the extent that the value transferred is attributable to property which becomes comprised in the estate of the transferor's spouse; or, (b) so far as the value transferred is not so attributable, to the extent that the transferor spouse's estate is increased (s. 18(1), IHTA). This makes it clear that all transfers of value between spouses are covered by the exemption even where the value transferred to the transferee is less than the loss to the transferor or where no asset is

---

[22.] Thus the transferor cannot avoid having the gifted property treated as part of his estate on death by ensuring the transferee agrees to give the property away without receiving anything to substitute in return.

Inheritance tax – the charge

transferred.[23] A 'spouse' is not defined but will clearly not include a former spouse once a decree of divorce or nullity has become absolute.

To qualify for exemption the disposition must take effect immediately after the transfer of value and not on the termination of any other interest. So a gift of property to a spouse for life, with remainder to their children, will be covered by the exemption but a gift of property to a third party, with remainder to the spouse will not (s. 18(3)(a)). Exemption is also not available if the disposition by which the property is given depends on a condition which is not satisfied within 12 months of the transfer (s. 18(3)(b)). Thus a survivorship period (i.e., that property left on death to a spouse only passes if the spouse survives the deceased for a pre-determined period) must not exceed one year.

If the transferor is domiciled in the United Kingdom but his spouse is not, the exemption is limited to £55,000 (s. 18(2)). Were it not for this provision a taxpayer could transfer foreign assets to his or her non-UK domiciled spouse using the spouse exemption who could then transfer the foreign assets without paying inheritance tax since the property would then be excluded property (see para. 32.1.1).

32.7.2 Gifts to charities

Transfers of value are exempt if the property transferred becomes the property of a charity or is held on trust for charitable purposes only (s. 23, IHTA).[24]

32.7.3 Gifts to political parties

Gifts to qualifying political parties are exempt from inheritance tax (s. 24, IHTA).[25] A political party qualifies for exemption if at the last general election immediately preceding the gift, either two members of the party were elected to the House of Commons, or one member of that party was elected to the House of Commons and not less than 150,000 votes were given to candidates of that party. Thus gifts to the Monster Raving Loony Party or other fringe political parties will not qualify for exemption.[26]

32.7.4 Gifts to housing associations

Gifts to 'registered housing associations', within the meaning of the Housing Associations Act 1985 or Part VII of the Housing (Northern Ireland) Order 1981, are exempt (s. 24A, IHTA).

[23.] The exemption will cover, inter alia, the transfer of a single item from a valuable set or the payment by one spouse of another's debts.

[24.] The exemption also applies to the use of property or money for charitable purposes; s. 29(5), IHTA.

[25.] The reader may care to consider whether there is such as thing as the Conservative 'Party', see *Conservative Central Office v Burrell* [1980] STC 400. Gifts by will are usually made to the local Conservative Association.

[26.] The current qualifying political parties are: Conservative, Labour, Social and Liberal Democratic, Ulster Unionist, Plaid Cymru, Scottish Nationalist, Social Democrat, Democratic Unionist and Social Democratic and Labour; *Foster's Inheritance Tax* D2.16.

32.7.5 Gifts for national purposes

A transfer of value is an exempt transfer to the extent that the value transferred by it is attributable to property which becomes the property of:

(a) The National Gallery, the British Museum, the National Museums of Scotland, the National Museum of Wales, the Ulster Museum and any other similar national institution which exists wholly or mainly for the purpose of preserving for the public benefit a collection of scientific, historic or artistic interest and which is approved by the Treasury;

(b) any museum or art gallery in the United Kingdom which exists wholly or mainly for that purpose and is maintained by a local authority or university in the United Kingdom;

(c) any government department or local authority;

(d) any university or university college in the United Kingdom, and any library which serves the teaching and research needs of a university in the United Kingdom;

(e) The Historic Buildings and Monuments Commission for England, the National Trust, the Nature Conservancy Council for England, Scottish National Heritage, the Countryside Council for Wales; the Historic Churches Preservation Trust, the National Art Collections Fund, the Friends of the National Libraries, the Trustees of the National Heritage Memorial Fund, and any health service body (s. 25 and sch. 3, IHTA).

32.7.6 Gifts for the public benefit

A transfer of value is an exempt transfer to the extent that the value transferred by it is attributable to property which becomes the property of a body not established or conducted for profit, and the Treasury agree that the transfer should be exempt (s. 26, IHTA). Gifts for the public benefit include:

(a) land which in the Treasury's opinion is of outstanding scenic or historic or scientific interest and the body to which it is transferred is an appropriate one to be responsible for the preservation of its character;

(b) a building which in the Treasury's opinion should be preserved because of its outstanding historic or architectural or aesthetic interest and the Treasury are satisfied that the body to which is it transferred is an appropriate one to be responsible for its preservation;

(c) land used as the grounds of a building within (b) above and any objects which at the time of the transfer are ordinarily kept in, and are given with, such a building;

(d) property given as a source of income for the upkeep of any property mentioned above unless, in the Treasury's opinion, the property will produce more income than is needed for such upkeep (within a reasonable margin);

(e) a picture, print, book, manuscript, work of art or scientific collection which in the Treasury's opinion is of national, scientific, historic or artistic interest, and the body to which it is transferred is an appropriate one to be responsible for its preservation.

Inheritance tax – the charge

The Treasury may require undertakings from parties involved in the transfer to secure the preservation of the property or its character and ensure that members of the public are given reasonable access to it. Such undertakings may be varied and enforced by injunction or interdict or petition in Scotland (ss. 26(4), (5) and (6)).

32.7.7 Restrictions on exemption

Exemption for gifts to charities, political parties, housing associations, or for national purposes or for the public benefit is not available for any property if (ss. 23(2) to (5), 24(3) to (4), 24A(3), 25(2) and 26(7), IHTA):

(a) the disposition by which it is given is defeasible (although any disposition not defeated 12 months after the transfer of value and thereafter incapable of being defeated is treated as not defeasible);

(b) the property is an interest in other property and that interest is less than the transferor's (to be decided 12 months after the transfer of value), or the property is given for a limited period. This does not, however, prevent exemption for a gift for national purposes if the property consists of the benefit of an agreement restricting the use of land;

(c) the property is land or a building and is given subject to the right of the transferor, his spouse, or a person connected with him, to possession or occupation of the whole or any part of the property rent-free or at less than a true market rent;

(d) the property is not land or a building and is given subject to an interest reserved or created by the transferor (to be decided 12 months after the transfer of value) other than an interest created by him for full consideration in money or money's worth, or an interest which does not substantially affect the enjoyment of the property by the transferee;

(e) the disposition takes effect on the termination of any interest or period (for example, a remainder interest).

32.8 LIFETIME TRANSFERS

The following exemptions are available to a transferor during his or her lifetime but not on death.

32.8.1 Annual exemption

Transfers of value made by a transferor in a year of assessment are exempt to the extent that the value(s) transferred (without grossing-up, see para. 33.2) do(es) not exceed £3,000 (s. 19(1), IHTA). Where the transferor transfers less than £3,000 the difference between that amount and the amount actually transferred may be carried forward to the next year of assessment (s. 19(2)). However, the unused exemption may only be carried forward for one year. Any unused exemption at the end of the second year is lost.

Where the transfers of value in a year of assessment exceed £3,000, the exemption is attributed to earlier transfers rather than later ones. If the transfers were made on the same day, the exemption is apportioned between them (s. 19(3)).

32.8.2 Small gifts

Outright gifts by a transferor are exempt if the value transferred by them (without grossing-up) does not exceed £250 (s. 20, IHTA). A transfer of value that arises from the use of property or money is treated as made by outright gift, so interest free loans qualify for this exemption (s. 29(3)).

This exemption applies only to outright gifts and not, for example, to gifts in settlement.[27] The annual exemption and the small gifts exemption are not cumulative, so that the taxpayer will have to make separate transfers in order to utilise both exemptions. The small gifts exemption is intended as a *de minimis* provision and cannot be used to exempt the first £250 of a larger transfer.

There are no provisions for carrying forward to the next year of assessment any unused part of the small gifts exemption.

32.8.3 Normal expenditure out of income

A transfer of value is an exempt transfer if it is:

(a) made as part of the transferor's normal expenditure; and
(b) made out of income; and
(c) after allowing for all transfers of value forming part of the transferor's normal expenditure, the transferor is left with sufficient income to maintain his usual standard of living (s. 21(1), IHTA).

In *Bennett & others* v *IRC* [1995] STC 54 Lightman J held that 'normal expenditure' connoted expenditure which, at the time it took place, accorded with the settled pattern of expenditure adopted by the transferor. The existence of a settled pattern of expenditure might be established either by regular, quantifiable payments over a period of time or by establishing that a pattern was intended to remain in place for more than a nominal period. Thus 'death bed' resolutions to make periodical payments for life would not suffice. However, if it was genuinely expected that the payments would continue (because, for example, they were made under a covenant or in accordance with a direction to the transferor's solicitors), they would constitute normal expenditure out of income even if the actual period over which they were paid was very short. So, on the facts of the case itself, surplus income paid by an elderly widow to her three sons constituted normal expenditure out of income. The fact that her surplus income had suddenly increased and that the payments were only made for two years because of her sudden death did not prevent the payments constituting normal expenditure out of income.

[27.] Presumably a transfer to trustees to hold as bare trustees for an absolutely entitled *sui juris* beneficiary would constitute an outright gift for these purposes as the beneficiary could demand the transfer of the property to him on the *Saunders* v *Vautier* (1841) Cr. & Ph. 240 principle.

32.8.4 Gifts in consideration of marriage

Gifts of up to £5,000 made in consideration of marriage by a parent of one of the parties to the marriage are exempt (s. 22(1), IHTA).[28] Thus up to £20,000 may be transferred to the couple free of inheritance tax if each parent of the couple utilises his or her exemption to the full. Grandparents or remoter ancestors may claim up to £2,500 as an exemption for the same types of gifts. The bride and groom may each claim up to £2,500 for an outright gift to the other or for a settled gift.[29] Any other person may claim exemption up to £1,000 for an outright gift to either the bride or the groom or a settled gift. The marriage gift exemption may be increased by any unused annual exemption and may be supplemented by a *separate* outright gift of up to £250 each to the bride and groom.

To qualify for exemption, a gift must be made in 'consideration of marriage'. A gift will not necessarily satisfy this requirement for exemption if it is made on the occasion of the marriage or is contingent on the marriage taking place. The question is one of fact and must be looked at in the light of the surrounding circumstances. The real question to be addressed is whether the purpose of the gift was to encourage, celebrate or facilitate the marriage, or whether it was really being made as part of a plan to avoid inheritance tax so as to benefit the family as a whole not just the parties to the marriage (*IRC v Lord Rennell* [1964] AC 173 and *Re Park (deceased) (No. 2)* [1972] Ch 385).

As with the small gifts exemption, use of property or money is treated as made by outright gift so interest free loans qualify for exemption (s. 29(3)).

32.9 POTENTIALLY EXEMPT TRANSFERS

For inheritance tax purposes, many transfers of value which are not otherwise exempt will be 'potentially exempt'. A potentially exempt transfer is a transfer of value made by an individual after 17 March 1986 which would otherwise be a chargeable transfer – that is, no exemptions apply, or the transfer of value exceeds the exemption available. The transfer must either be a gift to another individual or a gift into an accumulation and maintenance trust or a trust for persons with disabilities (s. 3A(1), IHTA and see Chapter 34). If the transferor survives for seven years, the transfer becomes completely exempt from inheritance tax. If he does not, the transfer becomes chargeable on his death (s. 3A(4)). For as long as a transfer is treated as potentially exempt it is assumed for inheritance tax purposes that it will ultimately prove to be completely exempt (s. 3A(5)). Potentially exempt transfers will not therefore affect a transferor's cumulative total of lifetime chargeable transfers (see para. 33.4.2).

A few points can be made. First, the definition of potentially exempt transfers talks in terms of 'gifts'. However, it is generally accepted[30] that it

---

[28.] Parents may claim the relief in respect of their illegitimate, adopted or step-children, but presumably not their foster children; s. 22(2), IHTA.
[29.] This exemption may be of use in creating (free of inheritance tax) settlements for any future children of the marriage.
[30.] See, for example, *Foster's Inheritance Tax* C3.11 which notes that the Revenue take this view.

will include sales of assets at an undervalue which can, in any case, be viewed as a gift to the extent of the price forgone.[31]

Secondly, a transfer of value is only potentially exempt to the extent that:

(a) the value transferred is attributable to property which becomes comprised in the estate of the transferee; or

(b) If (a) above is not satisfied, the estate of the transferee is increased (s. 3A(2)).

Care must therefore be taken if the purpose of the transfer is to meet the expenses of the transferee, since if the transferor pays these directly, the property will neither become comprised in, nor increase the estate of, the transferee. The solution is to transfer the property to the transferee first, who then uses the property to discharge the expenses since both conditions (a) and (b) will then be satisfied albeit only transiently.

Potentially exempt transfers are normally left out of account when considering the transferor's annual exemption (s. 19(3A)(a)). However, if the transferor dies within seven years and the transfer becomes chargeable, any unused annual exemption for the year in which the potentially exempt transfer was made can be used to exempt the now chargeable transfer (s. 19(3A)(b)).

If property which has been property subject to a reservation ceases to be so before the transferor's death, the transferor is treated as though the property was then disposed of by a potentially exempt transfer (s. 102(4), FA 1986). So, if the transferor survives for seven years after the property ceases to be property subject to a reservation, inheritance tax will be avoided.

32.10 CONDITIONALLY EXEMPT TRANSFERS

A transfer of value is a conditionally exempt transfer to the extent that it is attributable to property which is so designated by the Treasury and the requisite undertakings are given by the people the Treasury consider appropriate in the circumstances (s. 30(1) and (2), IHTA). Conditional exemption is available for transfers on death, but not for lifetime transfers unless the transferor or his spouse (or the two of them between them) have been beneficially entitled to the designated property for a period of six years immediately before the transfer, or the transferor acquired the property on a death and the transfer was then conditionally exempt (s. 30(3)). Conditional exemption is not available if the transfer of value is exempt as a transfer to a spouse or to a charity (s. 30(4)).

The Treasury may designate the following property for the purposes of conditional exemption (s. 31(1)):

[31.] This view is taken by *Butterworths UK Tax Guide 1995–96*, para. 38:02.

(a) any pictures, prints, books, manuscripts, works of art, scientific collections or other things not yielding income which appear to the Treasury to be of national, scientific, historic or artistic interest;

(b) any land which in the Treasury's opinion is of outstanding scenic, historic or scientific interest;

(c) any building which in the Treasury's opinion should be preserved because of its outstanding historic or architectural interest;

(d) any area of land which in the Treasury's opinion is essential for the protection of the character and amenities, or any object which is historically associated with, a building qualifying under (c) above.

In the case of property within category (a), the requisite undertaking is that, until the person beneficially entitled to the property dies or the property is disposed of by sale or gift or otherwise, the property will be kept permanently in the United Kingdom, will only leave the United Kingdom temporarily for a purpose and period approved by the Treasury, and agreed steps will be taken for the preservation of the property and for securing reasonable access to the public (s. 31(2)).[32]

In the case of land, buildings and objects within categories (b) to (d), the requisite undertaking is that, until the person beneficially entitled to the property dies or the property is disposed of by sale or gift or otherwise, agreed steps will be taken, in the case of land within category (b), for the maintenance of the land and the preservation of its character, and, in the case of any other property, for the maintenance, repair and preservation of the property. In the case of objects within category (d), an additional undertaking to keep the object(s) associated with the building concerned is required. In all cases, an undertaking securing reasonable access to the public must be given (ss. 31(4) to (4G)).

Conditionally exempt property is only exempt until the happening of a 'chargeable event' (s. 32(1)). There are three chargeable events:

(a) a failure to observe the requisite undertaking in a material respect (s. 32(2));

(b) the death of the person beneficially entitled to the property (s. 32(3)(a));

(c) the disposal of the property by sale or gift or otherwise (s. 32(3)(b)).[33]

Inheritance tax is then payable by reference to the value of property at the time of the chargeable event or, if the chargeable event is a disposal on a

---

[32] If the Treasury is satisfied that any documents designated under category (a) contain information which ought to be treated as confidential for personal or other reasons, it may exclude those documents either altogether or to such an extent as it thinks fit from the undertaking relating to public access; s. 31(3), IHTA.

[33] Presumably a 'disposal' bears its ordinary meaning of transferring or parting with property, so that the concepts of deemed disposal in (say) s. 22(1), TCGA when insurance proceeds are received in respect of damage to the property, would not be employed. However, the authors consider that a deliberate destruction of property would constitute a disposal for these purposes (cf. s. 24(1), TCGA).

genuine arm's length sale, the sale proceeds (s. 33(1)(a) and (3)).[34] However, the death or disposal will not be a chargeable event if:

(a) within three years of death the personal representatives dispose of the property to a body specified for the purposes of the exemption for gifts for national purpose or to the Inland Revenue in satisfaction of inheritance tax. Lifetime transfers to such persons will similarly not be chargeable events (s. 32(4)); or

(b) the transfer is on death or otherwise than by sale and either is itself a conditionally exempt transfer of the property or the undertaking previously given is replaced by a corresponding undertaking given by such person as the Treasury think appropriate in the circumstances (s. 32(5)).

---

[34] If the transferor is still alive the rate of tax is that which would have been payable on the date of the chargeable event. If the transferor is dead, the rate is that applicable on the transferor's death if the value transferred had been added to the value of his or her estate on death; s. 33(1)(b), IHTA.

CHAPTER THIRTY THREE
Inheritance tax – computation

33.1 INTRODUCTION

The first step in determining the amount of inheritance tax to be paid is to calculate the value transferred by the chargeable transfer. This is discussed in paras 33.2 and 33.3 below.

33.2 VALUE TRANSFERRED

The value transferred by a lifetime chargeable transfer is the amount of the reduction in the transferor's estate due to the transfer. This will require a valuation of the property concerned. The general valuation rule is set out in s. 160, IHTA which provides:

> Except as otherwise provided by this Act, the value at any time of any property shall for the purposes of this Act be the price which the property might reasonably be expected to fetch if sold in the open market at that time; but that price shall not be assumed to be reduced on the ground that the whole property is to be placed on the market at one and the same time.

Since tax is levied on the *reduction* in the value of the transferor's estate, any consideration given by the transferee will automatically be taken into account. For example, if the transferor transfers an item of property worth £100 to the transferee for £30, the value transferred by the transferor will be £70 (the reduction in value of his estate).

The 'open market' value of the property can usually be agreed with the Inland Revenue which has specialist valuation divisions for this purpose.

However, if the parties cannot agree the matter will be resolved by the Special Commissioners or, in the case of land, the Lands Tribunal with appeal in the usual way on questions of law, where expert evidence and evidence of actual transactions can be led (s. 222). It will be for that body to decide what weight should be given to that evidence (*IRC* v *Stenhouse's Trustees* [1992] STC 103).

In determining the open market value of the transferred property, it is unclear whether account should be taken of so-called 'special purchasers' who are prepared to pay over the odds for a particular asset because of some reason peculiar to themselves. The case law on this point is somewhat divergent. The existence of a special purchaser was taken into account in *IRC* v *Clay* [1914] 3 KB 466 and *Glass* v *IRC* [1915] SC 449 to inflate the open market value but apparently excluded in *IRC* v *Crossman* [1937] AC 26.[1]

The fact that some restriction on the transfer of the property[2] means that the property cannot actually be sold in the open market, does not prevent the property having an 'open market' value for inheritance tax purposes. However, the open market value is determined on the basis that once the property is acquired by the hypothetical purchaser, the purchaser becomes subject to the same restrictions on the future transfer of the property (*IRC* v *Crossman* [1937] AC 26; *Lynall* v *IRC* [1972] AC 680 and *Alexander* v *IRC* [1991] STC 112). Clearly this will result in a lower valuation than the transfer of the property not subject to such restrictions. To prevent transferors avoiding tax by imposing artificial restrictions on the transfer of property, a restriction is only taken into account if it was acquired for actual consideration in money or money's worth (s. 163).[3]

Liabilities are taken into account provided they have been incurred for a consideration in money or money's worth or are imposed by law (s. 5(3) and (5)). Thus the voluntary adoption of a liability, or a liability incurred for a nominal consideration or for a consideration which is not money or money's worth will not be taken into account. If the transfer is made during the transferor's lifetime and the transferor bears the inheritance tax due on the transfer, the tax payable is taken into account since the payment of tax diminishes the value of the transferor's estate. The net transfer must therefore be grossed up to take account of the inheritance tax due.

Example
Alex makes a chargeable transfer of £20,000. No exemptions or reliefs from inheritance tax apply. Alex has previously made chargeable transfers in excess of the nil rate band, so inheritance tax is chargeable at 20% (see para. 33.4). The £20,000 will have to be grossed up to determine the value transferred so that £20,000 is the sum left after inheritance tax has been paid. This is done by multiplying £20,000 by:

[1.] See also Harman J's explanation of the case in *Lynall* v *IRC* (1971) 47 TC 375.
[2.] Such as pre-emption rights affecting shares whereby the other shareholders in the company have a right to purchase the shares for a pre-determined price.
[3.] However, the decision in *Midland Bank Trust Co. Ltd* v *Green (No 2)* [1981] 1 All ER 153 suggests that the court will not enter into an examination of the adequacy of the consideration.

Inheritance tax – computation

$$\frac{100}{(100 - \text{Rate of inheritance tax})} \quad \text{i.e.} \quad \frac{100}{100-20}$$

$$£20,000 \times \frac{100}{80} = £25,000$$

Thus the value transferred by Alex is £25,000.

Obviously, there will be no need to gross up the value of the property transferred if the *transferee* agrees to bear the tax due, since the transferor's estate will be unaffected by the payment of the tax. There is also no need to gross up transfers on death since inheritance tax is paid on the property left by the deceased not added to it.

The transferor's liability for other taxes and duties on the transfer of the property (such as capital gains tax or stamp duty) is not taken into account in calculating the value transferred (s. 5(4)). The reason for this is to ensure that the transferor is in the same position regardless of whether he gifts an asset to the transferee and incurs a capital gains tax liability as a result, or, alternatively, the transferor sells the asset, pays the capital gains tax and transfers the net proceeds to the transferee. A similar logic applies to incidental expenses incurred by the transferor on the transfer of property such as solicitors' or valuers' fees. If these expenses were taken into account they would increase the reduction in the transferor's estate and therefore the value transferred. It is thus provided that, in determining the value transferred, expenses incurred by the transferor in making the transfer are to be left out of account if they are borne by him. If the expenses are borne by the transferee, they will reduce the value transferred (s. 164).

A liability which is an incumbrance on property (such as a mortgage) reduces the value of that particular property on a transfer (s. 162(4)). So if the transferor gives a house worth £100,000 to his son at a time when there is an outstanding mortgage on the house of £30,000, the value transferred is £70,000.

The liability is valued at the time at which it is taken into account and not as at the time of actual discharge if later (s. 162(2)). It seems, however, that if the liability is unenforceable (for example, because it is a gaming debt or is statute barred) it cannot be deducted even if it is actually paid.[4] Similarly if the transferee will not become liable to pay the debt, it cannot be deducted (*Re Barnes* [1939] 1 KB 316). And if the transferor has a liability in respect of which there is a right to reimbursement, that liability will be taken into account only to the extent that reimbursement cannot be reasonably expected to be obtained (s. 162(1)).

Finally, where a liability is owed to a person not resident in the United Kingdom which does not fall to be discharged in the United Kingdom and is

---

[4.] Although *Foster's Inheritance Tax* Division C2.35 notes that the Revenue practice is to allow a deduction in the case of a statute barred debt which is actually paid. See also *Norton v Frecker* (1737) Atk 524.

not an incumbrance on property in the United Kingdom, that liability is first taken to reduce the value of foreign property (s. 162(5)).

33.2.1 Related property

The rules concerning related property are set out in s. 161, IHTA and are best illustrated with an example. If the transferor owns 60% of the shares in a company, a gift of a 20% holding to his son would reduce the transferor's estate by more than the market value of the shares representing the 20% holding because the transferor is also giving away his majority shareholder control over the company. If, however, the transferor first gave a 12% holding to an exempt transferee (such as his wife) thus reducing his stake to 48%, the value of the transfer of control would be exempt from inheritance tax. He could then transfer a 20% holding to his son and the value transferred to his son would simply be the market value of the shares comprised in such a holding.

The tax advantages of such a transaction are countered by the 'related property' provisions. For these purposes, property is related to other property if:

(a) it is comprised in the estate of a spouse; or
(b) it is, or has within the preceding five years, been the property of a body mentioned in the exemptions for charities, political parties, national purposes or public benefit and became so by an exempt transfer of value by the transferor or his spouse after 15 April 1976 (s. 161(2)).

Where the transferor transfers property which is related to other property, the value transferred is not less than the 'appropriate portion' of the aggregate value of the property of the transferor and the related property. The appropriate portion is the proportion which the value of the property transferred bears to the aggregate value of the property of the transferor and the related property (ss. 161(1) and (3)).

Example
Edward owns 70% of X Ltd. He wants to give 20% to his son, but in an (unsuccessful) attempt to reduce the value transferred to his son, he first transfers 30% to his wife, Flora. Edward then transfers 20% of his shareholding in X Ltd to his son, Graham. The related property rules apply and as the value transferred to Graham of a 20% holding is less than the appropriate portion of Edward's and Flora's combined holdings (i.e., $^{20}/_{70}$ of a 70% holding) the value of the property transferred to Graham will be $^{20}/_{70}$ of the value of Edward's and Flora's combined holdings.

The related property rules apply most commonly to shares transfers in family companies, but the rules are not restricted to shares and apply with equal vigour to other assets where the sum of the parts is less than the value of the whole, such as sets of valuable objects.

33.2.2 Death

On death, inheritance tax is charged as if, immediately before the deceased's death, he had made a transfer of value equal to the open market value of his estate immediately before his death (ss. 4(1) and 160). 'Estate' is defined as the aggregate of all the property to which the deceased was beneficially entitled less any liabilities (s. 5). It will therefore include both the value of any potentially exempt transfers which become chargeable on death because the transferor did not survive for seven years after making the transfer and any gifts subject to a reservation in favour of the transferor.

Provisions exist to prevent transferors creating debts during their lifetimes in the hope that they will reduce the value of their estates on death, by making gifts to a creditor from which the creditor can make a loan to the transferor. A debt or incumbrance on the deceased's estate will not be taken into account to the extent that any consideration given for the debt or incumbrance consisted of property derived from the deceased (s. 103(1), FA 1986). So if a transferor gives money to his son during his lifetime, and the son then loans the money back to the transferor, that loan cannot be deducted in valuing the transferor's estate on death. If the deceased in his lifetime paid or applied money or money's worth in or towards satisfying, discharging or reducing a debt or incumbrance to which these provisions would have applied on his death, the payment or application of the money or money's worth is treated as a potentially exempt transfer so that he must survive for seven years to escape an inheritance tax liability (s. 103(5), FA 1986).

Certain property is not included in the deceased's estate:

(a) self evidently, 'excluded property' such as the foreign assets of a deceased who was not domiciled in the UK for inheritance tax purposes (s. 5(1), IHTA);

(b) an annuity which becomes payable under an approved personal pension scheme to a widow, widower or dependant of the deceased, and the terms of the scheme were such that at the deceased's option a sum of money might instead have become payable to his personal representatives (s. 152);

(c) certain overseas pensions (s. 153);

(d) where the deceased was not domiciled, resident or ordinarily resident in the United Kingdom immediately before his death, his estate is to be valued without taking into account the balance to which he was beneficially entitled on any non-sterling account with a recognised bank or the Post Office (s. 157);

(e) pensions or annuities under various types of superannuation funds or approved personal pension plans (s. 151);

(f) works of art which qualify for conditional exemption from inheritance tax and exempt transfers (see paras 32.7 and 32.10); and

(g) on election, the value of land on which trees or underwood are growing if the deceased was beneficially entitled to the land throughout the five years immediately preceding his death or became beneficially entitled to it other than for a consideration in money or money's worth, for example, by inheritance.[5] The land must be situated in the United Kingdom.[6] This 'woodlands relief' operates as a deferment of inheritance tax. When all or some of the trees are subsequently disposed of, inheritance tax is levied on the net proceeds of sale if the sale is made for full consideration in money or money's worth, or, if not, on the net value of the trees or underwood at the time of the disposal. The rate of tax is the rate which would have applied if the chargeable amount had been the highest part of the value transferred on the deceased's death (ss. 126 to 128). References to the 'net' proceeds of sale or value are to the proceeds of sale or value after deduction of any expenses incurred in the disposal of the trees or underwood or in replanting within three years replacement trees and underwood, provided these expenses are not allowable for income tax purposes (s. 130). Where the subsequent disposal of the trees or underwood is itself a chargeable transfer, the value transferred by that transfer is reduced by the amount of the inheritance tax payable by reference to the deceased's death (s. 129).

The position if the deceased was a beneficiary under a settlement is discussed in Chapter 34.

In determining the value of an estate immediately before death, changes in the value of the estate which have occurred by reason of the death (for example, payments to the estate under pension or compensation schemes) are taken into account as if they had occurred before the death rather than on or after it (s. 171(1)). However, the deceased's interest in a joint tenancy which passes by survivorship is not deemed to have passed before death and the value of the deceased's interest in it is therefore included in the value of the deceased's estate (s. 171(2)). This means tax will be payable as each joint tenant dies (unless, for example, the spouse exemption is available) on a progressively larger value until the death of the sole surviving joint tenant, when the whole of the value of the property will be included in his estate.

Allowances will be made in the valuation of the estate for reasonable funeral expenses (s. 172),[7] including the cost of a tombstone (Statement of Practice SP 7/87), and for the expenses incurred in administering or realising property situated outside the United Kingdom up to a maximum allowance of 5% of the value of the foreign property (s. 173).

The related property valuation provisions discussed in para. 33.2.1 do not apply to a 'qualifying sale' of property comprised in the estate immediately before death if the sale takes place within three years after the death (s. 176). A qualifying sale is an arm's length sale at a freely negotiated price by vendors who are the personal representatives or other persons in whom the property vested immediately after death. The sale must not be made in conjunction with a sale of the related property, the purchaser must not be connected with

---

[5.] Since the definition of agricultural property for the purposes of agricultural property relief includes woodland if occupied with agricultural land or pasture, woodlands relief does not apply if agricultural property relief is available; s. 125(1)(a), IHTA.

[6.] There is no extension to include the Channel Islands and the Isle of Man.

[7.] Including a reasonable amount for mourning for the family and servants; Extra-statutory Concession F1.

the vendors and the vendors must have no rights to reacquire the property or obtain any interest in it.

33.3 THE VALUATION OF PARTICULAR ASSETS

The general 'open market' valuation rule is modified in relation to transfers of value of particular assets.

33.3.1 Debts due to the transferor

It is assumed that any debt owed to the transferor will be duly discharged in full except to the extent that recovery of the sum is impossible or not reasonably practicable *and* has not become so by any act or omission of the person to whom the sum is due (s. 166).

33.3.2 Life policies

The market value of a policy of life assurance during the life of the assured is normally the surrender value. As this is low during the early years of the policy, s. 167(1), IHTA provides that the value transferred on any transfer of such a policy is not less than the total premiums paid under the policy at the time of the transfer. Any sums received under policy prior to the transfer (such as cash bonuses) may be deducted from the premiums paid since these form part of the transferor's estate in any event.

On the death of the life assured, the value transferred will be the proceeds of the policy actually paid out (s. 171). If the policy is owned by the life assured, this amount will be part of the transfer of value the deceased is deemed to have made immediately before his death. If the policy is owned by others (for example, the policy was written in trust for the deceased's children) the amount will not form part of the estate of the deceased on death.

33.3.3 Shares

There are no provisions relating to the valuation of shares quoted on the Stock Exchange but in practice the Revenue apply the capital gains tax rules. So the market value of quoted shares is the lower of:

(a) the lower of the two prices quoted in *The Stock Exchange Daily List* plus one-quarter of the difference between the two figures; or

(b) half the difference between the highest and lowest prices at which bargains were recorded on the day on which the transfer took place (s. 272(3) and (4)).[8]

The IHTA grants special relief for falls in the value of quoted shares following the transferor's death. If the aggregate value of all quoted securities

---

[8.] 'Quoted' for inheritance tax purposes includes any shares or securities quoted on a recognised stock exchange or dealt with on the Unlisted Securities Market (now the AIM); s. 272, IHTA.

comprised in the deceased's estate immediately before his death exceeds the aggregate proceeds of sale of those securities within twelve months of the date of death or, if higher, the best consideration which could reasonably have been obtained for them at the time of the sale, the value transferred on death may be reduced by the difference in value (ss. 178 to 189).[9]

The valuation of shares in private companies is more problematic. The general rule that such shares are to be valued at the price they might reasonably be expected to fetch if sold in the open market continues to apply, but s. 168 additionally provides that in determining the value of such shares in the open market, it must be assumed that prospective purchasers have all the information which a prudent purchaser would reasonably require if he were proposing to purchase the shares in a private, arm's length sale.

33.3.4 Land

A reduction in the 'open market' value transferred is permissible in the case of land which has fallen in value since the date of the transferor's death. If an interest in land[10] which was comprised in the estate of the deceased immediately before his death is sold within four years of the date of death, the value of the land for inheritance tax purposes is the proceeds of sale or, if greater, the best price that could reasonably have been obtained at the time of sale, provided that the difference between the proceeds or consideration and the value of the interest on death exceeds the lesser of £1,000 and 5% of the value on death (ss. 190 to 198).

33.3.5 Agricultural property

Agricultural property (like business property – see para. 33.3.6) is subject to favourable inheritance tax treatment. Provided certain conditions are met, the 'agricultural value' of 'agricultural property' is eligible for relief by way of reduction in the value transferred. Agricultural property is defined in s. 115(2), IHTA as:

> ... agricultural land or pasture and includes woodland and any building used in connection with the intensive rearing of livestock or fish if the woodland or building is occupied with agricultural land or pasture and the occupation is ancillary to that of the agricultural land or pasture; and also includes such cottages, farm buildings and farmhouses, together with land occupied with them, as are of a character appropriate to the property.[11]

The agricultural property must be situated in the United Kingdom, the Channel Islands or the Isle of Man (s. 115(5)). The 'agricultural value' of agricultural property is the value of the property if it were subject to a

---
[9.] Cancelled or suspended shares within the relevant time are deemed to have been sold for the purposes of this provision; ss. 186A and 186B, IHTA.
[10.] This does not include any estate, interest or right of way by mortgage or other security.
[11.] This will include stud farms; s. 115(4), IHTA and, as from 26 November 1996, farmland which has been dedicated to wildlife habitats.

perpetual covenant prohibiting its use otherwise than as agricultural property (s. 115(3)). So any part of the value of land which is due to (say) its potential for development for residential housing is excluded from relief.

Agricultural property relief is only available if the agricultural property has been:

(a) occupied by the transferor for agricultural purposes throughout the period of two years ending with the date of transfer (s. 117(a)). This condition is treated as satisfied if the agricultural property occupied by the transferor on the date of the transfer replaced other agricultural property and all the properties were occupied by the transferor for agricultural purposes for a total of at least two out of the five years preceding the transfer (s. 118(1)); or

(b) owned by the transferor throughout the period of seven years ending with the date of the transfer and was throughout the period occupied (by him or someone else) for agricultural purposes (s. 117(b)). This condition is treated as satisfied if the agricultural property owned by the transferor on the date of the transfer replaced other agricultural property and all the properties concerned were both owned by the transferor and occupied (by him or someone else) for agricultural purposes for a total of at least seven years out of the ten years preceding the transfer (s. 118(2)).

For these purposes, occupation by a company which is controlled by the transferor is treated as occupation by him (s. 119(1)). A transferor has control of a company if he can exercise a majority of votes on all questions affecting the company as a whole (s. 269).

If the transferor became entitled to agricultural property on the death of another person, he is deemed to have owned the property (and if he subsequently occupies it, to have occupied it) from the date of the death. If the deceased was the transferor's spouse, the transferor is deemed to have occupied the property for agricultural purposes and to have owned it for any period for which the deceased's spouse so occupied and owned it (s. 120).

Where the relief may be claimed, the value transferred may be reduced by either 100% (so that no value passes for inheritance tax purposes) or 50%. 100% relief may be claimed if:

(a) the transferor has the right to vacant possession of the agricultural property or the right to obtain it within the next 12 months; or

(b)(i) the transferor has been beneficially entitled to his interest since before 10 March 1981; and

(ii) if he had disposed of his interest immediately before 10 March 1981, he would have been entitled to the agricultural property relief under the legislation then in force;[12] and

---

[12.] For a description of the legislation in force prior to 10 March 1981 see *Foster's Inheritance Tax* Division G2.

(iii) the transferor's interest has not at any time since 10 March 1981 carried a right to vacant possession of the land (or a right to obtain it within 12 months);

(c) the property is let on a tenancy beginning on or after 1 September 1995.

The extension of 100% relief to land let after 1 September 1995 was intended to bolster the government's reform of the law of agricultural tenancies. The government hoped to 'reverse the decline in agricultural tenancies' in order to 'help younger people without much capital take on farm tenancies' (Inland Revenue Press Release 27 January 1995). If 100% relief cannot be claimed, 50% relief is available.

Relief may not be claimed if, at the time of the transfer, the transferor has entered into a binding contract for the sale of the agricultural property, unless the sale is to a company and is made wholly or mainly in consideration of shares in or securities of the company which will give the transferor control of the company (s. 124(1)).

Where agricultural land is owned by a company, agricultural property relief may be available in respect of any transfer involving shares in that company. The agricultural property must (a) form part of the company's assets; (b) part of the value of the company's shares or securities must be attributed to the agricultural value of the agricultural property; and (c) the shares or securities must have given the transferor control of the company immediately before the transfer (s. 122(1) and (2)). It must also be shown either that the agricultural property was occupied by the company for agricultural purposes, and the shares or securities were owned by the transferor throughout the period of two years preceding the transfer, or that the agricultural property was owned by the company (and occupied for agricultural purposes by the company or someone else) and the shares or securities were owned by the transferor throughout the period of seven years preceding the transfer (s. 123(1)). If these conditions are satisfied, 100% relief is available. 50% relief will be available in any other case.

Where a potentially exempt transfer becomes chargeable or a lifetime chargeable transfer becomes subject to additional tax on the transferor's death within seven years (see para. 33.4.3), agricultural property relief is not available unless (ss. 124A and 124B):

(a) the agricultural property or shares in an agricultural company were owned by the transferee throughout the period between the time of transfer and the transferor's death (or, if the transferee dies before the transferor, the transferee's death); and

(b) in the case of agricultural property, the property is agricultural property immediately before the death, and has been occupied throughout the period mentioned in (a) above for agricultural purposes either by the transferee or someone else;

(c) in the case of shares in an agricultural company, the agricultural property must have been owned by the company and occupied by the company or someone else for agricultural purposes throughout the period mentioned in (a).

If these conditions are satisfied for only part of the agricultural property, the relief is proportionately reduced.

If a person has made a gift of agricultural property or of shares in an agricultural company subject to a reservation, inheritance tax will become payable if the transferor dies while the property is subject to that reservation. If the property ceases to be subject to a reservation during the transferor's lifetime, there will then be a potentially exempt transfer of the property, and inheritance tax will become payable if the transferor dies within seven years of the reservation ending. Since in these circumstances the property will have passed to the transferee (albeit that, for at least part of that time, some benefit in the property was reserved to the transferor) special rules are needed to determine whether agricultural property relief can be claimed in respect of the tax due on the transferor's death. Accordingly, para. 8 of sch. 20, FA 1986 provides that for the purposes of determining whether agricultural property relief is available, the transfer made by the transferor at the time of his death or at the time the reservation ends is treated as made by the *transferee*. The transferor's period of ownership and any occupation are treated as periods of ownership and occupation by the transferee. In the case of shares in an agricultural company, relief will be available provided it was available for the transferor's original gift to the transferee and the transferee owned the shares throughout the period between the gift and the transferor's death or the time the reservation ended. If the transferee dies before the transferor or while the property is still the subject of a reservation, these rules apply with the substitution of the transferee's personal representatives or the person who became entitled to the property under the transferee's will or the intestacy rules.

33.3.6 Business property

Where the whole or part of the value transferred is attributable to the value of any 'relevant business property', that value transferred may be reduced by 100% or 50% (s. 104, IHTA). Relevant business property is defined in the following paragraphs.

If the value transferred is attributable to property consisting of a business or an interest in a business the value transferred may be reduced by 100% (ss. 104(1)(a) and 105(1)(a)).[13] However, a business is not relevant business property if the business consists wholly or mainly of dealing in securities, stocks or shares, land or buildings or making or holding investments, unless the business concerned is that of a market maker[14] or discount house and is carried on in the United Kingdom (s. 105(3), (4) and (7)).

---

[13] The value of a business for these purposes is the value of assets used in the business, including goodwill, less the aggregate amount of any liabilities incurred for the purposes of the business; s. 110, IHTA.

[14] Meaning a person who is recognised by the Council of the Stock Exchange as holding himself out at all normal times as willing to buy and sell securities, stocks or shares in accordance with the Stock Exchange's rules at a price specified by him.

In his 1995 Budget Speech the Chancellor of the Exchequer announced his intention to extend 100% business property relief to all holdings of unquoted shares. Accordingly, s. 184, FA 1996 amended s. 105, IHTA so that 100% business property relief is available for holdings of all shares in qualifying unquoted companies.[15] Quoted shares which, either by themselves or together with other shares or securities owned by the transferor, gave the transferor control of the company immediately before the transfer qualify for relief at 50% (s. 105(1)(cc)). A person has control of a company if he is able to cast a majority of votes capable of being cast on all questions affecting the company as a whole.

Shares are not relevant business property for these purposes if the business carried on by the company consists wholly or mainly of dealing in securities, stocks or shares, land or buildings or making or holding of investments. However, shares in a holding company will qualify for relief provided the businesses of its subsidiaries do not consist of prohibited activities (s. 105(3) and (4), IHTA).[16]

If the value transferred is attributable to any land or building, machinery or plant which, immediately before the transfer, was used wholly or mainly for the purposes of the business carried on either: (a) by a company controlled by the transferor; or (b) by a partnership of which the transferor was a member, the value transferred may be reduced by 50% (ss. 104(1)(b) and 105(1)(d)). However, these assets are not relevant business property unless the shares or securities of the company or the partnership's business are relevant business property in relation to the transfer (s. 105(6)).

In all cases, in order to qualify as relevant business property, the property must either have been owned by the transferor throughout the two years immediately preceding the transfer or it must have replaced other property (which was relevant business property at the time of replacement) so that it and the replacement property were owned by the transferor for at least two years falling within the five years immediately preceding the transfer. If the transferor acquired the property on a person's death, he is deemed to have owned the property since the date of death. If the deceased was a spouse, the transferor's period of ownership includes the deceased's spouse's period of ownership (ss. 106 to 108).[17]

Where a binding contract for the sale of a business or an interest in a business has been entered into at the time of transfer, the property will not qualify for relief unless the sale is to a company which is to carry on the business and is made in consideration wholly or mainly of shares in or

---

[15] Shares dealt in on the Unlisted Securities Market (now the AIM) count as unquoted companies for these purposes; s. 105(1ZA), IHTA.

[16] Shares are also not relevant business property if at the time of the transfer a winding-up order has been made in respect of the company or the company is in the process of liquidation, unless the business of the company is to continue to be carried on after a reconstruction or amalgamation; s. 105(5), IHTA.

[17] Additional provisions exist in s. 112, IHTA to ensure that the reduction in the value transferred by application of this relief only applies to assets which have been used in the business for the last two years prior to transfer or assets which were required for future use in the business.

Inheritance tax – computation

securities of the company (s. 113(a)). This provision ensures that relief will continue to be available if a transferor incorporates his business.[18]

As with agricultural property relief, if a potentially exempt transfer becomes chargeable, or a lifetime transfer becomes subject to additional tax on the transferor's death within seven years, business property relief will only be available if (ss. 113A and 113B):

(a) the business property (or business property which replaced it) was owned by the transferee throughout the period between the time of the transfer and the transferor's death (or, if the transferee dies before the transferor, the transferee's death); and

(b) if the transferee had made a transfer of the property (or replacement property) immediately before his death, it would then have been qualifying business property (apart from the requirement of having been owned for at least two years).

If these conditions are satisfied for only part of the business property, the relief is proportionately reduced. Identical rules to those relating to agricultural property also apply if the transferor of business property dies while the property is still subject to a reservation in the transferor's favour or within seven years of the ending of the reservation (para. 8, sch. 20, FA 1986).

If the property transferred qualifies for both agricultural property relief and business property relief, only agricultural property relief is given (s. 114(1), IHTA).

33.4 RATES OF TAX

Inheritance tax is a cumulative tax, and the rates of tax differ according to the transferor's cumulative total and whether the transfer is made during the transferor's lifetime or on his death. As from the 1997/98 year of assessment, there are three rates of inheritance tax. There is a wide 0% rate band for chargeable transfers of up to £215,000 and a single rate of 40% thereafter. However, if the chargeable transfer is made during the transferor's life, as opposed to being made on death, the rate applied to any transfers of value in excess of £215,000 is 20% (s. 7(2) and sch. 1, IHTA).

33.4.1 Cumulation

The principle of cumulation is that the inheritance tax due on the present transfer must take account of any previous chargeable transfers made by the transferor (s. 7(1), IHTA). When originally enacted, capital transfer tax applied to the cumulative values transferred during the transferor's lifetime and on his death. However, the principle of lifetime cumulation was abandoned in 1981 and the cumulation period is now only seven years as it was for estate duty.

---

[18] Relief will also be available if the sale is made for the purposes of reconstruction or amalgamation; s. 113(b), IHTA.

33.4.2 Lifetime transfers

Inheritance tax on lifetime transfers is restricted to those chargeable transfers which are not exempt, potentially exempt or conditionally exempt and so fall to be charged immediately. The rate of tax payable is determined by cumulating all the transferor's chargeable transfers in the last seven years. Since the payment of inheritance tax is a liability which is included in the value transferred, the net transfer must be 'grossed up' to take account of the transferor's tax liability.

Example
Betty, who has made no previous chargeable transfers, makes a chargeable transfer of £190,000. The tax chargeable will be nil because the transfer is within her nil rate band. However, Betty's cumulative total is now £190,000. If Betty makes a further chargeable transfer of £61,000 her cumulative total will be £251,000. The excess over £215,000 must be charged to inheritance tax at the lifetime rate of 20%. Assuming Betty pays the tax, this value transferred must be grossed up so that the inheritance tax due is:

$$£(251,000 - 215,000) \times \frac{100}{100 - 20} = £45,000 \text{ (the value transferred)}$$

Inheritance tax of 20% on £45,000 is £9,000.

33.4.3 Transfers on death

On a person's death, the value of his estate immediately before his death is added to the total of his lifetime chargeable and potentially exempt transfers made by the transferor in the seven years preceding his death. Once the nil rate band of £215,000 has been exceeded, the rate of tax is 40%. Grossing up does not occur on death because the transfer that takes place necessarily includes the tax due. Inheritance tax is paid out of the property left by the deceased, and not added to it.

Lifetime chargeable transfers made within seven years of the transferor's death are subject to the rates of tax applicable on death (s. 7(1), IHTA). As such transfers will already have been taxed at lifetime rates, only the additional tax due because of the death will be payable. Potentially exempt transfers made within seven years of death will also have become chargeable at the rates applicable on death (ss. 3A(4) and 7(1)). In both cases agricultural and business property relief may be claimed if the qualifying conditions are met at that time (see paras 33.3.5 and 33.3.6).

Example
Charles gave £150,000 to Diane and then gave £125,000 to Eleanor. Shortly afterwards Charles dies penniless. Both these potentially exempt transfers will become chargeable at the rates of inheritance tax applicable on Charles's death. So the gift to Diane (assuming Charles had made no previous chargeable or potentially exempt transfers) will fall within Charles's nil rate

Inheritance tax – computation

band but his cumulative total will be £150,000. The gift to Eleanor will increase his cumulative total to £275,000 so that the inheritance tax payable is:

£(275,000 − 215,000) × 40% = £24,000

Because the potentially exempt transfer has itself become chargeable by reference to the date it was made, the tax liability of any subsequent lifetime chargeable transfers will have to be recalculated (as the transferor's cumulative total will have increased by the amount of the potentially exempt transfer).

In addition, transfers made within seven years of death and which become subject to the rates of inheritance tax applicable on death, are liable at the following percentages of those rates (s. 7(4)):

100% if the death occurs within 3 years of the transfer;
80% if the death occurs within 4 years but after 3 years;
60% if the death occurs within 5 years but after 4 years;
40% if the death occurs within 6 years but after 5 years; and
20% if the death occurs within 7 years but after 6 years.

Thus the longer the transferor survives after making a lifetime chargeable or potentially exempt transfer, the lower the charge to tax on his or her death.[19]

Example
Alex died in June 1997 leaving an estate valued at £500,000. In January 1992 he made a potentially exempt transfer of £100,000. The tax attributable to this potentially exempt transfer of £100,000 × 40% = £40,000 is itself reduced by 40% because the gift was made five and a half years before Alex's death. Thus the tax on the potentially exempt transfer is 40% of £40,000 = £16,000.

33.4.4 Relief for a decline in value

Where tax becomes payable on a potentially exempt transfer, or additional tax becomes payable on a lifetime chargeable transfer, because of the death of the transferor within seven years of the transfer, that tax is generally calculated by reference to the value actually transferred at the time the transfer was made. This will be unfair if the value of the property has declined in value between that date and the date of the transferor's death or has been sold in the open market for a lower figure. Accordingly, the inheritance tax legislation provides relief if either:

(a) when the property was transferred it was transferred to, and has been continuously held by, the transferee or his spouse; or

(b) the property was sold by the transferee or his spouse before the death of the transferor in a 'qualifying sale' (s. 131(1), IHTA).[20]

---

[19] The reduction in tax under s. 7(4), IHTA cannot be used to reduce the tax payable on a lifetime transfer to below the amount already paid (or which would have been payable at lifetime rates) at the time the transfer was made; s. 7(5), IHTA.
[20] This complex formulation is necessary because the value transferred by the transferor at the time of the earlier transfer may have been different from its market value at that time.

A qualifying sale is a sale at arm's length for a freely negotiated price, provided that the vendor is not connected with the purchaser and there is no provision for the vendor to reacquire the property or to have some interest created in or out of it (s. 131(3)). If available, the relief operates by reducing the value transferred by the difference between the 'market value' of the transferred property at the time of death or the time of the qualifying sale and the market value at the time of the earlier transfer (s. 131(2)). The market value is the price which the property would fetch if sold in the open market. In the case of unquoted shares, an identical valuation rule is adopted as described in para. 33.3.3. However, the market value of any shares will be increased by any capital payments received by the transferee or his spouse in respect of the shares (s. 133) and decreased by the amount of any calls paid on the shares (s. 134). With property other than shares, as like must be compared with like, the market value of the property at the time of death or the qualifying sale, as appropriate, is increased by the difference between the market value at the time of the earlier transfer and what the market value would have been if the circumstances prevailing at the time of the death or qualifying sale had prevailed at the time of the earlier transfer (ss. 137 and 139(1)–(3)).

The relief is not available if the transferred property is tangible moveable property (such as a chattel but not a chose in action) which is a wasting asset, that is, an asset which immediately before the earlier transfer, had a predictable useful life of no more than 50 years, having regard to the purpose for which it was held by the transferor (s. 132).[21]

33.5 QUICK SUCCESSION RELIEF

To prevent inheritance tax being suffered twice in respect of the same property, albeit by different taxpayers, when a person who has received property by way of a chargeable transfer (for example, by inheritance) dies shortly afterwards, quick succession relief exists. The relief applies if the value of the deceased's estate was increased by a chargeable transfer to him within five years before his death. In such circumstances the inheritance tax chargeable on the deceased's death which is attributable to the increase in the deceased's estate by the chargeable transfer is reduced by the following percentage of the tax charged on the earlier transfer (s. 141, IHTA):

100% if the death occurs within a year;
 80% if the death occurs within 2 years but after 1 year;
 60% if the death occurs within 3 years but after 2 years;
 40% if the death occurs within 4 years but after 3 years; and
 20% if the death occurs within 5 years but after 4 years.

However, as the reduction is made in the tax attributable to an increase in the *deceased's* property, the inheritance tax paid at the time of the first transfer

---

[21.] Machinery and plant are deemed to have a predictable life of less than 50 years for these purposes.

Inheritance tax – computation

is excluded since this increases the coffers of the Treasury not the estate of the deceased. For example, if the deceased received property valued at £1,000 on which £250 tax was paid, the increase in the deceased's estate was £1,000 on a value transferred of £1,250. If, therefore, the deceased dies within four years of the earlier transfer, the tax attributable to the increase is £1,000/£1,250 (four-fifths) of the tax attributable to the value transferred. Thus only four-fifths of £250 may be relieved on death. The quick succession relief will therefore be 40% of £200, which is £80, and this amount may be deducted from the tax chargeable on death.

33.6 AGGREGATION

Where more than one item of property is the subject of a chargeable transfer, for example, all the items of property forming the transferor's estate on death, the tax payable on the value transferred is attributed to the different items of property in the proportion their values bear to the aggregate value (s. 265, IHTA).[22]

33.7 PAYMENT OF TAX

33.7.1 Lifetime transfers

The persons liable for the tax on lifetime chargeable transfers are (s. 199(1) and (2), IHTA):

(a) The transferor or, in the case of a potentially exempt transfer, the transferor's personal representatives. To prevent transferors from making exempt transfers of wealth to their spouses, so that they have nothing left with which to pay the tax, s. 203 provides that where the transferor is liable for any tax and, by another transfer of value, property becomes the property of his spouse, the spouse is liable for so much of the tax due as does not exceed the market value of the property transferred to him or her.[23]

(b) The transferee. If the transferee pays the inheritance tax, no grossing up is necessary.

(c) Any person in whom the property transferred is vested (whether beneficially or otherwise) at any time after the transfer.

[22.] If two transfers take place on the same day, one which requires grossing up, the other which does not, more tax may be payable if the transfer which requires grossing up is the later transfer because the transferor's cumulative total will be increased by the earlier transfer. However, s. 266(1), IHTA avoids this consequence by providing that the transfers may be treated as made in the order which results in the lowest chargeable value. Subject to this, the rate of tax applicable to transfers made on the same day is averaged out between the transfers; s. 266(2), IHTA. These rules do not apply to transfers on death; s. 266(3), IHTA.

[23.] If the property was transferred to the spouse before the chargeable transfer in respect of which the transferor is liable, the spouse's liability is limited to the market value of the property transferred at the date of the chargeable transfer, if that figure is lower than the market value at the time of the inter-spouse transfer; s. 203(2), IHTA. Likewise, if the spouse has sold the property in an arm's length sale to an unconnected purchaser and there is no provision for the spouse to reacquire the property or have some interest in or over it, the market value at the time of sale may be taken if it is lower than the market value at the time of the inter-spouse transfer; s. 203(3), IHTA.

Inheritance tax is due six months after the end of the month in which the chargeable transfer is made or, if the transfer is made after 5 April and before 1 October in any year, at the end of April in the next year (s. 226(1)). Where a person is liable under (b) or (c) above, he or she is liable only if the tax remains unpaid after it ought to have been paid by the transferor and the liability is limited to the tax due if the transfer had not been grossed up (s. 204(6)).

33.7.2 Transfers within seven years before death

If a lifetime chargeable transfer has become subject to additional tax, or a potentially exempt transfer has become chargeable because it was made within seven years of death, the persons liable for the tax or any additional tax are those persons referred to in items (a), (b) and (c) in para. 33.7.1 with the substitution of the transferor's personal representatives for the transferor (s. 199(2), IHTA). The personal representatives are only liable, however, if no other person is liable to pay the tax, or if the tax remains unpaid twelve months after the end of the month in which the transferor dies. In any event, the personal representatives' liability is limited to the assets which they have received as personal representatives or which they should have received but for their neglect or default (s. 204(8)). The effect is that the primary liability for payment of the tax is placed on the transferee and the tax or any additional tax must be paid six months after the end of the month in which the transferor dies (s. 226(3) and (3A)).

33.7.3 Transfers on death

Where the chargeable transfer is made on a person's death, the following persons are liable for the tax (s. 200(1), IHTA):

(a) The deceased's personal representatives.[24] Where the deceased's estate includes property treated as part of the estate because it is property subject to a reservation, the personal representatives are only liable for the inheritance tax attributable to that property if it remains unpaid 12 months after the end of the month in which the transferor died. The personal representatives are only liable to the extent of the assets received by them or which might have been received by them but for their neglect or default (s. 204(9)).

(b) Any person in whom the property transferred on death is vested (whether beneficially or otherwise) at any time after the death. This will include both absolutely entitled beneficiaries and the trustees of a settlement created by the deceased's will. Such persons are only liable to the extent of the property vested in them (s. 204(3)). If the person in whom the property is vested is a purchaser, or a person deriving title from such a purchaser, he is only liable for tax due in respect of that property if it is subject to an Inland

---

[24.] Liability cannot be avoided by the appointment of personal representatives who are not resident in the United Kingdom; *IRC v Stannard* [1984] STC 245.

Revenue charge (s. 200(2)). Inland Revenue charges are discussed in para. 33.8.3.

Generally, the personal representatives must make an account of the property forming the estate of the deceased person (s. 216).[25] This account must be delivered before the grant of representation can be obtained. Tax is payable when the personal representatives deliver their account to the Inland Revenue (s. 226(2)). The account is due within 12 months of the end of the month in which the death occurs or, if later, within three months of the personal representatives first acting as such (s. 216(6)). Since tax has to be paid before probate is obtained, the personal representatives may have difficulty raising the necessary money. They will be unable to sell many of the assets of the deceased's estate because they will be unable to prove title to a purchaser. In practice, this problem may be dealt with by the personal representatives obtaining a loan from the beneficiaries or a bank.[26]

The personal representatives may at the same time pay any part of the tax chargeable on the death for which they are not liable, if the persons who are liable for the tax request them to do so (s. 226(2)). If such a request is not made, then the tax is due from such persons six months after the end of the month in which the death occurs (s. 226(1)).

Where personal representatives pay any tax due in respect of the deceased's death, they will normally pay it out of the residue of the estate (s. 211(1)).[27] Thus the deceased's residuary estate will be reduced by the amount of the inheritance tax payable. However, tax will not be paid out of residue if the deceased left directions in his will that a particular gift should bear its own tax (s. 211(2)).[28]

33.7.4 Miscellaneous

33.7.4.1 Conditionally exempt transfers
If the chargeable event in relation to a conditionally exempt transfer is a failure to observe an undertak-

---

[25] Certain estates are excepted from this requirement. As from 1 July 1995 an estate will be excepted if, inter alia, the gross value of the estate is less than £145,000, the deceased was domiciled in the UK at the date of his death and the estate consists only of property passing by the deceased's will or intestacy, or by nomination or survivorship; SI 1995/1459, 1995/1460 and 1995/1461.

[26] Where because of restrictions imposed by a foreign government, the personal representatives are unable to transfer to the United Kingdom sufficient of the deceased's foreign assets for the payment of inheritance tax attributable to them, they will be given the option of deferring payment until the transfer can be effected. If the sterling amount that the personal representatives finally succeed in bringing to the United Kingdom is less than the amount of the tax payable, the Inland Revenue will waive the balance (Extra-statutory Concession F6).

[27] Prior to the passing of this section, this rule had been accepted by a Scottish court in *Re Dougal* [1981] STC 514, although see *Foster's Inheritance Tax* Division K2.01A for criticism of the correctness of that decision and the Inland Revenue's interpretation of its effect.

[28] Where there is a specific gift of property situated outside the United Kingdom, inheritance tax is not paid by the personal representatives out of the residue, but must be paid by the beneficiary in addition to any foreign tax due on it. However, the beneficiary will normally be able to claim double tax relief by credit.

ing or is a death, the person liable for the tax is the person who, if the property were sold at the time of the chargeable event, would be entitled to receive the proceeds of sale or any income arising from them. If the chargeable event is the disposal of property, the person liable for the tax is the person by or for whose benefit the disposal is made (s. 207(1) and (2), IHTA).[29] Tax due in respect of a chargeable event is due six months after the end of the month in which the chargeable event occurs (s. 226(4)).

33.7.4.2 Woodlands If trees or underwood left out of account for the purposes of a transfer on death, are subsequently disposed of, the person liable for the tax chargeable on the disposal is the person entitled to the proceeds of sale or who would be so entitled if the disposal were a sale (s. 208, IHTA). The tax is due six months after the end of the month in which the disposal occurs (s. 226(4)).

33.8 METHODS OF PAYMENT

Inheritance tax must normally be paid in full on or before the due date for payment. However, the Inland Revenue may accept payment of tax in instalments if the value transferred is attributable to 'qualifying property' namely (s. 227, IHTA):

(a) Land of any description wherever situated.
(b) Shares or securities of a company which gave the transferor control of the company immediately before the transfer.
(c) Shares or securities not falling within (b) above and which are unquoted if the Inland Revenue are satisfied that the tax cannot be paid in one sum without undue hardship or, in the case of a transfer on death, that not less than 20% of the total tax chargeable and for which the payer is liable in the same capacity is attributable to the value of shares or securities or such other tax as may be payable by instalments.
(d) Shares of a company not falling within (b) above and which are unquoted, provided that the value transferred attributable to the shares exceeds £20,000, and the nominal value of the shares is not less than 10% of the nominal value of all the company's shares at the time of transfer.
(e) A business or an interest in a business.[30]

If the chargeable transfer giving rise to the inheritance tax liability is a lifetime transfer, payment may only be made by instalments if the tax 'is borne by the person benefiting from the transfer' (s. 227(1)). If the chargeable transfer is a transfer on death, the first instalment of tax is due six months after the end of the month in which the death occurs. In any other case, the first instalment is due at the time at which the tax would have been

---
[29.] The liability is based on receipt of the proceeds and not beneficial entitlement.
[30.] Since transfers of interests in businesses will generally qualify for 100% business property relief, the option to pay tax by instalments need only be considered if the business does not qualify for business property relief because, for example, the business consists of dealing in land and buildings or has not been owned for the qualifying time period (see para. 33.3.6).

Inheritance tax – computation

due were it not payable by instalments (ss. 227(3)). If the qualifying property is sold the unpaid tax becomes payable immediately (s. 227(4)).

33.8.1 Unpaid tax

If tax remains unpaid at any time after payment has become due, interest is charged. Where tax is payable in instalments, interest is due on the instalment from the date on which it becomes payable (s. 234(1), IHTA). However, where the chargeable transfer was a transfer of shares or securities of a company whose business consists wholly or mainly of dealing in securities, stocks or shares, land or buildings, or the making or holding of investments, interest is due on the whole amount of the tax still outstanding, unless it is shown that the company's business consists wholly or mainly in being a holding company for one or more companies that do not carry on those activities, or the company's business is that of a market maker or discount house and is carried on in the United Kingdom (s. 234(2) to (4)).

33.8.2 Acceptance of property

As an alternative to the payment of tax in cash or, in appropriate cases, by instalments, the Inland Revenue may accept certain property in satisfaction of all or part of the inheritance tax due. The property which may be accepted is set out in the IHTA namely (s. 230):

(a) such land as may be agreed upon by the taxpayer and the Inland Revenue;

(b) any objects which are or have been kept in any building if the Secretary of State and the Chancellor of the Duchy of Lancaster consider it desirable for the objects to remain associated with the building, provided the building:

(i) has been or will be accepted by the Inland Revenue in satisfaction of tax, or

(ii) belongs to the Queen in right of the Crown or the Duchy of Lancaster, to the Duchy of Cornwall, to a government department, or to one of the bodies specified in the national purposes exemption, or

(iii) is an ancient monument under the guardianship of the Secretary of State;

(c) any picture, print, book, manuscript, work of art, scientific object or other thing, or any collection or group thereof, which the Secretary of State and the Chancellor of the Duchy of Lancaster think is pre-eminent for its national, scientific, historic or artistic interest.

33.8.3 Inland Revenue charge

If any tax and any interest on it is unpaid, a charge for that amount arises in favour of the Inland Revenue on any property to which the value transferred is wholly or partly attributable (s. 237(1), IHTA).[31] Incumbrances (such as mortgages) which are deductible in valuing the value transferred take priority over any Inland Revenue charge and no charge arises on a deceased's personal or moveable property in the United Kingdom if the charge has arisen on death. For this purpose, leaseholds and undivided shares in land held on trust for sale are personal property.[32]

Potentially exempt transfers can be caught by the Inland Revenue charge. However, where the property subject to the potentially exempt transfer was sold to a *purchaser* before the transferor's death, the property itself will not be subject to a charge, but any property which represents it at the time of the transferor's death will be subject to the charge (s. 237(3A)).

Once a charge has arisen any subsequent disposition of that property will be subject to that charge (s. 237(6)). However, the charge will lapse if the property or an interest in it is sold off to a purchaser and, in the case of land in England and Wales, the charge was not registered as a land charge or protected by notice on the register, or, in the case of other property, the purchaser had no notice of the facts giving rise to the charge. In such a case any property representing the disposed property, such as the sale proceeds, continues to be subject to the charge (s. 238(1)). The charge will also lapse on the later of six years after the tax became due or an account of the tax due was delivered to the Inland Revenue.

33.9 VARIATIONS AND DISCLAIMERS

The dispositions made by the deceased on his or her death may be varied or disclaimed by the beneficiaries.[33] In such circumstances, s. 142(1), IHTA provides that there will be no transfer of value if the variations or disclaimers are contained in a written instrument executed by all those affected by the variation or disclaimer within two years of the death. A variation is then treated as though it had been made by the deceased and a disclaimer is treated as though the benefit had never been conferred. This allows beneficiaries to make the best use of the inheritance tax rules in operation at the date of the deceased's death to reduce the inheritance tax payable. Written notice of the variation or disclaimer must be given to the Inland Revenue within six months of the date of the instrument. Only one instrument varying or disclaiming beneficiaries' entitlements can be effected (*Russell* v *IRC* [1988] STC 195 and *Seymour* v *Seymour, The Times*, 16 February 1989)[34] and it is irrevocable ([1985] STI 298).

Section 142(1) does not apply to variations or disclaimers made for any consideration in money or money's worth, other than consideration which

---

[31] Provision is made for replacement property; s. 237(2), IHTA.
[32] The property must, however, have vested in the deceased's personal representatives; s. 237(3), IHTA.
[33] Such variations and disclaimers are made possible by Court Order under the Variation of Trusts Act 1958.
[34] However, supplemental variations which merely increase the beneficiaries' rights or which rectify an error are permissible; *Schnieder* v *Mills* [1993] STC 430 and *Lake* v *Lake* [1989] STC 865.

consists of the making of a variation or disclaimer in respect of another interest under the will or right in the intestacy (s. 142(3)). So s. 142(1) does not apply if one of the beneficiaries agrees to sell his benefit to another.[35] Section 142(1) also does not apply to property which is deemed to form part of the deceased's estate, because he had an interest in possession in it or because a previous disposition of it was subject to a reservation (ss. 142(5) and 49(1), IHTA and s. 102, FA 1986). However, section 142(1), IHTA will apply whether or not the administration of the estate is complete and whether or not any of the property involved has been distributed in accordance with the original dispositions (s. 142(6)). It also covers variations or disclaimers of excluded property.

Where a testator expresses a wish (which is not legally binding) that property bequeathed by his will should be transferred by the legatee to someone else, and the legatee transfers any of the property in accordance with that wish within two years of the testator's death, the transfer is not a transfer of value for inheritance tax purposes. Instead the property transferred is treated as though it had been bequeathed by the will to that other person (s. 143). This prevents a double charge to tax arising on the death of the deceased and subsequent transfer by the legatee.[36]

If the surviving spouse of a deceased who died intestate elects to be paid the capital value of the life interest in part of the deceased's residuary estate that he or she would otherwise be entitled to, there is no transfer of value. For inheritance tax purposes, the surviving spouse is treated as though he or she had become entitled to a sum equal to the capital value of the life interest rather than the life interest itself (s. 145).

Where a successful application has been made under the Inheritance (Provision for Family and Dependants) Act 1975 for financial provision out of the deceased's net estate, the property is treated as though it had passed on the deceased's death in accordance with the court order (s. 146). Where under Scottish law a child is entitled to claim legitim[37] and a bequest to the deceased's spouse reduces the child's rights, the executors may assume either that full rights of legitim will be claimed or that the will will be allowed to stand. The necessary adjustments to the inheritance tax paid will be made when the child reaches 18 (s. 147).

---

[35] Although s. 142(1) will apply if the beneficiaries' agree to 'swap' their benefits even though this amounts to consideration for their own variation or disclaimer.
[36] Legally binding directions to transfer to a third party will be treated as having been made by the deceased in any event.
[37] Broadly, certain rights in the deceased parent's estate which cannot be renounced while the child is still a minor.

CHAPTER THIRTY FOUR
Inheritance tax and settlements

34.1 SETTLEMENT

It will come as no surprise to the reader to learn that inheritance tax has its own definition of 'settlement'. Section 43(2), IHTA provides that a settlement is any disposition or dispositions of property, whether effected by instrument, parol, or operation of law, or partly in one way and partly in another, whereby property is for the time being:

    (a)   held in trust for persons in succession or for any person subject to a contingency; or
    (b)   held by trustees on trust to accumulate the whole or part of any income of the property or with power to make payments out of that income at the discretion of the trustees or some other person, with or without power to accumulate surplus income; or
    (c)   charged or burdened (otherwise than for full consideration in money or money's worth paid for his own use or benefit to the person making the disposition) with the payment of any annuity or other periodical payment payable for a life or any other limited or terminable period.

Thus 'typical' trusts such as 'to A for life remainder to B' or 'to C contingent on his reaching 25 years of age' will be caught by the provisions described in this chapter as will property held on discretionary or accumulation trusts or charged with an annuity or other periodical payment (unless full consideration was given for it).

The definition of a 'settlement' for these purposes is further extended by s. 43(3) which provides that 'a lease of property which is for life or lives, or

Inheritance tax and settlements

for a period ascertainable only by reference to a death, or which is terminable on, or at a date ascertainable only by reference to a death' is treated as a settlement unless the lease was granted for full consideration in money or money's worth. Thus property will be settled if a lease of it is granted to A for life.[1]

34.2 SETTLORS

The inheritance tax liability on a transfer of value which creates a settlement is determined in accordance with the general principles set out in Chapters 31 to 33. So transfers of value in favour of exempt transferees such as a spouse will be exempt from inheritance tax[2] whereas a trust created on death by the settlor's will will be chargeable. The lifetime creation of a discretionary trust by a settlor will usually be a chargeable transfer. It cannot be potentially exempt because the gift is not made to an individual. However, there are some special rules which are specifically relevant to the creation of settlements. Transfers by individuals during their lifetimes into accumulation and maintenance settlements and into trusts for people with disabilities are deemed to be potentially exempt transfers and transfers into a trust in which an individual other than the settlor has an 'interest in possession' (see para. 34.4) are potentially exempt to the extent of the interest (s. 3A(1)(c), IHTA).[3] Thus the creation of accumulation and maintenance trusts, trusts for people with disabilities and interest in possession trusts are potentially exempt and no inheritance tax will be payable by reference to the settlor's transfer of value if the settlor survives for seven years after making the transfer.

A 'settlor' in relation to a settlement is defined in s. 44(1) as:

> any person by whom the settlement was made directly or indirectly, and in particular (but without prejudice to the generality of the preceding words) includes any person who has provided funds directly or indirectly for the purpose of or in connection with the settlement or has made with any other person a reciprocal arrangement for that other person to make the settlement.

This definition bears a close resemblance to the definition in Part XV, TA discussed in Chapter 15 save that the definition in the IHTA includes the additional words 'for the purpose of or in connection with' the settlement. In *Fitzwilliam* v *IRC* [1993] STC 502 at p. 516 Lord Keith said:

> The words 'for the purpose of or in connection with' connote that there must be a conscious association of the provider of the funds with the

---

[1] A lease for life at a rent or in consideration of a fine takes effect by virtue of s. 149(6), Law of Property Act 1925 as a lease for a term of 90 years determinable after the death of the original lessee, or of the survivor of the original lessees.
[2] As will be seen in para. 34.4.2, a person who is beneficially entitled to an interest in possession is treated as beneficially entitled to the property in which the interest subsists. So a gift of property to a spouse for life, remainder to their children will be covered by the spouse exemption.
[3] The property must become comprised in, or increase, the estate of that individual; s. 3A(2) IHTA.

settlement in question. It is clearly not sufficient that the settled funds should historically have been derived from the provider of them. If it were otherwise anyone who gave funds unconditionally to another which that other later settled would fall to be treated as the settlor or as a settlor of the funds.[4]

If more than one person is a settlor in relation to one settlement, the IHTA applies as if the settled property were comprised in separate settlements 'where the circumstances so require' (s. 44(2)). In *Hatton v IRC* [1992] STC 140 Chadwick J said:

Circumstances in which [this provision] is commonly found to apply include those in which two or more persons have separately provided funds from their own independent resources to be held on the trusts of the same settlement. In such a case the effect of [this provision] is, I suspect, generally thought to be that the settled property is treated as if a proportionate or identifiable part were held in one settlement and other proportionate or identifiable parts were held in other, separate settlements: each notionally separate settlement having its own single settlor. But examination of [the legislation] shows that there may well be more than one person who is a settlor in relation to the settlement in circumstances in which the settled property cannot sensibly be apportioned or partitioned amongst a series of notionally separate settlements. In such a case, as it seems to me [the legislation] requires that [the IHTA is] to apply as if there were a number of separate settlements each of which with its own single settlor and each comprising the whole of the settled property.

34.2.1 Gifts subject to a reservation

Gifts into settlement are subject to the rules about property subject to a reservation which results in gifted property being treated as part of the settlor's estate on death. However, when similar provisions applied for estate duty purposes, a resulting trust in favour of the settlor because he had failed to dispose fully of his beneficial interest was not treated as a reserved benefit. The Privy Council held that the property given was the property less the settlor's remainder interest, so the remainder interest had not been reserved to the settlor, it had simply not been given away (*Commissioner of Stamp Duties* v *Perpetual Trustee Co. Ltd.* [1943] AC 425, PC).[5] In contrast, it would seem that if the settlor is one of the objects of a discretionary trust, there will be a reserved benefit sufficient to make the settled property subject to a reservation.[6]

[4.] Cf. *IRC* v *Mills* [1974] STC 130 on the 'old' Part XV, TA rules noted at footnote 6 to Chapter 15.
[5.] It is stated in *Butterworths UK Tax Guide 1995–96*, para. 40:07, that the same argument might apply if a settlor who was a trustee of a settlement had the benefit of a remuneration clause, but cf. *Oakes* v *Commissioner of Stamp Duties* [1954] AC 57, PC.
[6.] Revenue correspondence with Touche Ross and Co. published in *Law Society's Gazette*, (1986) vol. 83, p. 3728 and see *Attorney-General* v *Farrell* [1931] 1 KB 81.

34.3 TRUSTEES AND BENEFICIARIES

The policy of the inheritance tax legislation relating to settlements is to distinguish between settlements in which there is an 'interest in possession', and settlements in which there is no such interest. This being the case, reversionary interests[7] are treated as though they did not exist for inheritance tax purposes. This is achieved by providing that a reversionary interest is excluded property so no account is taken of the value of the excluded property when calculating the value transferred on a transfer of value (ss. 3(2) and 48(1), IHTA). So if the property is settled on A for life, remainder to B no account will be taken of B's remainder interest in computing the value transferred on B's death if B dies before A. The reason for this is that A will be treated as beneficially entitled to the *whole* of the property in which his life interest subsists and the value of the property will be included in A's estate on his death.

To prevent exploitation, the following reversionary interests are not treated as excluded property:

(a) reversionary interests which have at any time been acquired, whether by the person entitled to it or by a person previously entitled to it, for a consideration in money or money's worth; or

(b) reversionary interests to which either the settlor or his spouse is, or has been, beneficially entitled; or

(c) reversionary interests expectant on the determination of a lease for lives.

34.4 INTERESTS IN POSSESSION SETTLEMENTS

Surprisingly, an 'interest in possession' is not defined in the IHTA. In an estate duty case, *Gartside* v *IRC* [1968] AC 553, Lord Reid said (at p. 607):

> To have an interest in possession does not mean that you possess the interest. You also possess an interest in expectancy, for you may be able to assign it and you can rely on it to prevent the trustees from dissipating the trust fund. 'In possession' must mean that your interest enables you to claim now whatever may be the subject of the interest. For instance, if it is the current income from a certain fund your claim may yield nothing if there is no income, but your claim is a valid claim, and if there is any income you are entitled to get it; but a right to require trustees to consider whether they will pay you something does not enable you to claim anything. If the trustees do decide to pay you something, you do not get it by reason of having the right to have your case considered; you get it only because the trustees have decided to give it to you.

[7.] A reversionary interest is defined as a future interest under a settlement, whether vested or contingent; s. 47, IHTA. A mere hope of obtaining an interest by, for example, the exercise by the trustees of an overriding power of appointment in the beneficiary's favour will not be a reversionary interest for these purposes.

It is therefore sufficient for an interest in possession that the beneficiary has a present right to the income (say) dividends on shares as and when the dividends are paid or the rent from property as and when the property is leased. However, an interest in possession may also arise if the beneficiary is entitled to the use and enjoyment of the settled property, for example, the right to occupy a dwelling house as his or her own home (see para. 34.4.1). A typical example of an interest in possession is a life interest in settled property. In contrast, a beneficiary under a discretionary trust can never have an interest in possession, even if that beneficiary was, at that time, the only person who qualified as a member of the class of discretionary objects (*Moore & Osborne* v *IRC* [1984] STC 236).

The Inland Revenue outlined their interpretation of an interest in possession in a Press Release dated 12 February 1976:

> [A]n interest in possession in settled property exists where the person having the interest has an immediate entitlement (subject to any prior claim by the trustees for expenses or other outgoings properly payable out of income) to any income produced by that property as the income arises; but that a discretion or power, in whatever form, which can be exercised after the interest arises so as to withhold it from that person negatives the existence of an interest in possession. For this purpose a power to accumulate income is regarded as a power to withhold it, unless any accumulations must be held solely for the person having the interest or his personal representatives. On the other hand the existence of a mere power of revocation or appointment, the exercise of which would determine the interest wholly or in part (but which, so long as it remains unexercised, does not affect the beneficiary's immediate entitlement to income) does not in the Board's view prevent the interest from being an interest in possession.

The distinction between a power to accumulate and a power of revocation or appointment is that the former prevents a present right to present enjoyment of income arising whereas the latter is simply a power to terminate such a right. Although at first sight this appears a clear-cut distinction, most trusts contain a number of powers which do not readily fall into either of these two categories. For example, a trust may confer on trustees wide powers to pay or apply income to meet the costs of improvements to trust property or to pay taxes, fees or other expenses properly incurred by the trustees. If the payment of such costs and expenses swallows up the whole of the trust income in a particular year, is the life tenant's interest in possession 'negatived'? The Revenue's answer in their Press Release is 'no', but as Fox J put it at first instance in *Pearson* v *IRC* [1978] STC 627:

> If the answer is no, what realistic difference is there between such a power and a power to accumulate . . .

The *Pearson* case revealed some of the difficulties inherent in the distinction between powers of accumulation and powers of revocation or appointment.

In that case, the settlor created a settlement for one or more of his children and their issue as the trustees should appoint. Until the power of appointment was exercised, the trustees were to accumulate the trust income for 21 years subject to which the trustees were to hold the capital and income for such of the settlor's children as attained 21 in equal shares absolutely. The question was whether the beneficiaries had an interest in possession before the power was exercised. The House of Lords held, by a bare 3:2 majority, that they did not: *Pearson* v *IRC* [1980] STC 318),[8] overruling Fox J and the Court of Appeal. The majority affirmed that the words 'interest in possession' meant a present right of present enjoyment. According to Viscount Dilhorne:

> A distinction has in my opinion to be drawn between the exercise of a power to terminate a present right to present enjoyment and the exercise of a power which prevents a present right of present enjoyment arising.

Thus the existence of the power to accumulate the income for twenty-one years prevented the beneficiaries from having an interest in possession during the accumulation period. A distinction was drawn between 'administrative' and 'dispositive' powers so that a power given to trustees to pay trust expenses out of income would not, of itself, prevent the beneficiaries from having an interest in possession. Unlike a dispositive power, it was argued that such an administrative power could not prevent a present right to present enjoyment from arising.[9]

The decision in *Pearson* therefore supports the view of the Inland Revenue in their Press Release although the decision can be criticised on a number of grounds. Little guidance was given as to which types of powers would be regarded as dispositive and which as administrative[10] and the decision blurs the distinction between trust powers (which must be exercised) and mere powers (which may or may not be exercised). Lord Russell in his dissenting speech had concluded that the trustees had a mere power to accumulate as opposed to a trust duty to accumulate. Thus the beneficiaries were entitled to the trust income as it accrued, subject to the possibility that the trustees might divert it from them by a decision to accumulate. However, the majority accepted the Revenue's argument that, at least for these purposes, there was no material distinction between a duty to accumulate and a power to accumulate.

34.4.1 Occupation of a dwelling-house

If the terms of the settlement give the trustees power to allow a beneficiary who does not have an interest in possession to occupy a dwelling-house

---

[8.] The reasoning is not entirely clear. There may in fact be three lots of two Lords agreeing; see further Shipwright, *Solicitors Journal*, 535, (1980) vol. 124.

[9.] Because, according to Viscount Dilhorne, the beneficiary is only entitled to the income net of expenses etc.

[10.] This part of their Lordships' decision was followed in *IRC* v *Miller* [1987] STC 108 where the Court of Session held that a power to use such proportion of the trust income as the trustees thought proper to meet any depreciation in the capital value of the trust was an administrative power. Thus even though the trustees could theoretically use all the income in this way, the life tenant was entitled to any income that was not so used and therefore had an interest in possession.

forming part of the trust property on such terms as they think fit, the Revenue's practice is set out in Statement of Practice SP 10/79. The Inland Revenue will not regard the exercise of such a power as creating an interest in possession if the effect is merely to allow non-exclusive occupation or to create a contractual tenancy for a full consideration. The Inland Revenue also take the view that no interest in possession arises on the creation of a lease for a fixed term at less than full consideration, although this will normally give rise to a charge to inheritance tax. On the other hand, if the power is sufficiently wide to permit the beneficiary to occupy the property exclusively as his or her home whether for a definite or indefinite period, the Revenue will normally regard the exercise of the power as creating an interest in possession. If the trustees exercise their powers to grant a lease for life for less than full consideration, this is also regarded as creating an interest in possession.

34.4.2 Beneficial entitlement

A person who is 'beneficially entitled' to an interest in possession in settled property is treated as beneficially entitled to the property in which the interest subsists (s. 49(1), IHTA). The IHTA does not define beneficial entitlement but unlike the capital gains tax provisions, the IHTA does not distinguish between entitlement as against the trustee or as against anyone else (see Chapter 24). It is therefore thought that the entitlement must be as against the world.

If a beneficiary is so entitled, the effect of this provision is that if the beneficiary gives away his interest in possession or sells it or the interest comes to an end, the beneficiary will be deemed to make a transfer of value of the whole of the settled capital. For example, if A gratuitously assigns his life interest in a settled fund of £100,000 he will make a transfer of value of £100,000.[11] If a beneficiary is only entitled to a part of the income from the settled property, his interest in possession is taken to subsist in that part of the settled property which corresponds with his share of the income (s. 50(1)). So if A is only entitled to one quarter of the income produced by the settled fund he will make a transfer of value of £25,000.

If a person is entitled to a specified amount of the income produced by the settled property, or the whole of the income less a specified amount, he is treated as though his interest in possession corresponds with that part of the property which produces that amount of income (s. 50(2)). So if A is entitled to £10,000 a year from the settled fund of £100,000, and that fund actually generates an income of £15,000, A will be treated as though his interest in possession subsisted in 10,000/15,000 of £100,000, so the value transferred on a gratuitous assignment of his interest will be £66,666. Since the effect of this rule is that the value transferred varies with the income yield of the settlement and this yield may be deliberately managed, the Treasury prescribe maximum and minimum yields for these purposes (ss. 50(3) and (4)).

[11.] Since in equity A is only entitled to the income of the settled fund, the actuarial value of A's life interest will obviously be considerably less than £100,000.

Since the use and enjoyment of settled property can give rise to an interest in possession, provisions are needed to determine the extent of the beneficial entitlement if more than one beneficiary is allowed to use the property. The formula used by the IHTA is that the beneficiary's estate will be increased by the proportion the annual value of his interest bears to the total annual values of all interests (s. 50(5)). There is no definition of annual value for these purposes, but it is unlikely that an actual valuation would be needed. The example given in *Foster's Inheritance Tax* is three people who have the right to occupy jointly a house forming part of the settled property. In such a case, it is argued, it is clear that they will each have an interest in possession of one-third of the house.

If, instead of a right to use and enjoy Blackacre, A has been granted a lease of it for life at less than a full market rent, A's interest will subsist in the whole of Blackacre less an amount equal to the landlord's interest. The landlord's interest is the proportion which the consideration given for the grant of the lease bears to the value of the property at that time (ss. 50(6) and 170). Thus if the landlord grants a lease for lives for ¼ of the full market rent, the landlord is treated as owning ¼ of Blackacre and A is treated as owning ¾.

34.4.3 Termination of an interest in possession during the beneficiary's lifetime

Section 52(1), IHTA provides:

> Where at any time during the life of a person beneficially entitled to an interest in possession in settled property his interest comes to an end, tax shall be charged . . . as if at that time he had made a transfer of value and the value transferred had been equal to the value of the property in which his interest subsisted.[12]

Since s. 52(1) specifies the amount of value transferred there is no grossing up. The deemed transfer is potentially exempt if another individual becomes entitled to the property in which the interest subsisted, or to an interest in possession in it, or if the property passes into an accumulation and maintenance trust or a trust for people with disabilities (s. 3A(2)). If the property passes into a discretionary trust it will be fully chargeable.

An interest in possession can come to an end during the beneficiary's lifetime in a variety of ways, for example: the exercise of a power of advancement in favour of the remainderman; where the interest is given only for a limited period and that period comes to an end; or where the interest is an interest on the life of another and that other person dies.

Example
Sally settles £100,000 on Albert for life, remainder to Brenda absolutely. If the trustees exercise their powers of advancement to advance £20,000 to

---

[12.] If an interest is only partially terminated, tax is charged on the corresponding part of the value of the property; s. 52(4), IHTA.

Brenda, Albert's interest in possession in that £20,000 will terminate. Albert will be treated under s. 52(1) as though he had made a transfer of value of £20,000. The transfer will be potentially exempt since Brenda becomes entitled to the property and so will be inheritance tax free if Albert survives for seven years after the appointment. If Albert dies before that time, the £20,000 will be added to his lifetime chargeable transfers and the amount of inheritance tax due will be determined in the usual way.

If, the beneficiary disposes of his interest in possession for a consideration in money or money's worth, the value transferred (i.e., the beneficiary's interest in the settled property) will be reduced by the amount of the consideration (s. 52(2)). So there will be no inheritance tax charge if a beneficiary sells his interest to an unconnected purchaser in a genuine arm's length transaction.

34.4.4 Depreciatory transactions

Provisions exist to counter attempts to reduce the value of property comprised in the settlement shortly before the anticipated termination of an interest in possession by, for example, selling settlement assets at an undervalue to someone connected with the beneficiary or the settlement. Section 52(3), IHTA provides that if the value of the settled property in which the beneficiary's interest subsists is reduced by a transaction made between the trustees of the settlement and a person who is connected with any beneficiary of the settlement or for whose benefit any of the settled property may be applied, a corresponding part of the interest is deemed to have come to an end. Thus, if the value of the interest in possession is reduced by (say) £10,000 as a result of such an arrangement, the beneficiary is treated as though his interest has come to an end to that extent and he has made a transfer under s. 52(1) of £10,000.[13]

34.4.5 Termination of an interest in possession on death

The death of a person results in a transfer of all the property to which he was beneficially entitled immediately before his death. This will include the settled property to the extent of his interest, so if A has a life interest in a settled fund of £100,000, the value of A's estate will include the £100,000 value of the fund (ss. 4(1) and 49(1), IHTA).

34.4.6 Exceptions

There are some situations in which no charge to inheritance tax arises on the termination of an interest in possession. The exceptions in paras 34.4.7 and 34.4.8 apply whether the interest terminates during the beneficiary's life or

---

[13.] There is an exclusion from charge if the transaction would not constitute a transfer of value if the trustees were beneficially entitled to the property, for example, there was no intention to confer a gratuitous benefit such that s.10, IHTA would apply. An illustration of the provisions in operation can be seen in *Macpherson v IRC* [1988] STC 362, HL.

on death. The exceptions in paras 34.4.9 to 34.4.12 only apply if the interest in possession terminates in the prescribed way during the beneficiary's lifetime. However, it should not be forgotten that the general exemptions from inheritance tax will also apply, so if the interest in possession is transferred to the beneficiary's spouse or to a charity, a political party or one of the specified public bodies (see Chapter 32) it will be exempt from tax. Further the annual, small gifts, normal expenditure out of income and gifts in consideration of marriage exemptions may be claimed in respect of charges under s. 52 (s. 57, IHTA). Business property relief at 50% is available to a beneficiary if the property transferred is any land or building, or machinery or plant which, immediately before the transfer, was used wholly or mainly for the purposes of a business carried on by him and was settled property in which he was then beneficially entitled to an interest in possession (ss. 104(1)(b) and 105(1)(e)).

34.4.7 Reversion to settlor

If an interest in possession comes to an end and the property in which the interest subsisted reverts to the settlor or his spouse, inheritance tax is not chargeable unless either of them acquired the reversionary interest for a consideration in money or money's worth. This relief extends to the settlor's widow or widower if the settlor died less than two years before the interest in possession came to an end (s. 53(3) to (6)).[14]

34.4.8 Trustees' annuities

Tax is not chargeable under s. 52(1), IHTA if the person entitled to the interest in possession is a trustee entitled to the interest by way of remuneration for his services as a trustee, except to the extent that the interest represents more than a reasonable amount of remuneration (s. 90).

34.4.9 Where the beneficiary becomes entitled to settled property

No inheritance tax is chargeable under s. 52, IHTA if the beneficiary becomes beneficially entitled to the settled property when his interest in possession terminates (s. 53(2)).[15] The reason for this is obvious. Prior to the termination, the beneficiary is deemed to be entitled to the settled property; when that beneficiary actually becomes entitled to that property, he will only be receiving what he has been assumed to have had all along.

The exception will thus apply where a beneficiary with an interest in possession receives the property as a result of the trustees' exercise of a power

---

[14] The spouse must be domiciled in the United Kingdom at the time of the reversion so the property cannot thereby become excluded property, see para. 32.1.1. The purpose of this relief is to encourage settlors to provide life interests for their relatives; *Foster's Inheritance Tax* E2.52.
[15] There will also not be a charge to inheritance tax if the beneficiary becomes entitled to another interest in possession in the settled property except to the extent that the value of the interest to which he was previously beneficially entitled exceeds the value of the property or interest to which he has now become entitled.

of advancement, or where a beneficiary who is absolutely entitled to the settled property provided he attains the age of 25 (and he has a life interest before that date) reaches 25.

34.4.10 Disclaimers

Where a person who becomes entitled to any interest in settled property disclaims the interest, he will be treated as though he had never been entitled to the interest provided that the disclaimer is not made for a consideration in money or money's worth (s. 93, IHTA).[16] There is no time limit by which the disclaimer must be made[17] but an interest cannot be disclaimed once it has been accepted.

34.4.11 Inheritance (Provision for Family and Dependants) Act 1975

Compliance with a court order under the Inheritance (Provisions for Family and Dependants) Act 1975 does not give rise to a charge under s. 52(1), IHTA (s. 146(6), IHTA).

34.4.12 Family maintenance

A disposition of an interest in possession which qualifies as a disposition for the maintenance of the beneficiary's family is not treated as the termination of an interest in possession (ss. 11 and 51(2), IHTA and see para. 32.3.2).

34.4.13 Potentially exempt transfers – special rates of charge

If there is a potentially exempt transfer of settled property, followed within seven years by a deemed disposal under s. 52, IHTA, special rates of charge apply (ss. 54A and 54B). The purpose of these rules is to prevent settlors avoiding or reducing the inheritance tax charge on the creation of discretionary settlements by first settling the property on an interest in possession settlement which will later lapse in favour of the discretionary trusts. Without these provisions the transfer into the interest in possession trust would be potentially exempt, and although the termination of the beneficiary's interest in possession in favour of the discretionary trust would be a chargeable transfer, if the beneficiary is chosen with care, he or she will have a lower lifetime cumulative total than the settlor and the eventual inheritance tax bill will be lower.

Therefore a special rate of inheritance tax applies if the settlor makes a potentially exempt transfer into a trust with an interest in possession after 17 March 1987 but the interest in possession ends under s. 52 or on the death of the beneficiary within seven years while the settlor is still alive, and the property passes into a trust in which there is no interest in possession (other

---

[16.] See *Re Paradise Motor Co. Ltd* [1968] 2 All ER 625, a case concerning the winding-up of a company.

[17.] Cf. the two year rule for disclaimers on death; s. 142, IHTA and para. 33.9.

than an accumulation and maintenance trust). In such a case inheritance tax is calculated off the settlor's cumulative total at the time the settlement was created and if that amount is higher than the tax calculated in the normal way, the higher amount is taken.

34.4.14 Quick succession relief

Quick succession relief is available as described in para. 33.5 in respect of a charge under s. 52, IHTA which arises on the beneficiary's death. If the charge under s. 52 arises during the beneficiary's life, quick succession relief will still be available provided that the property is settled property in which the beneficiary had an interest in possession and the earlier transfer was either the creation of the settlement or some subsequent event (s. 141).

34.5 SETTLEMENTS WITHOUT INTERESTS IN POSSESSION

A separate inheritance tax regime applies to trusts where there is no 'qualifying interest in possession'. A qualifying interest in possession means an interest in possession to which an individual[18] is beneficially entitled (s. 59, IHTA). Since an interest in possession is not further defined, the discussion in para. 34.4 of what constitutes an interest in possession is equally relevant here. Thus discretionary trusts, trusts where the income from the settled property is accumulated or trusts where there is a power to accumulate will all be dealt with in accordance with the rules described in the following paragraphs.

Since no one person is beneficially entitled to the use or enjoyment of the property or income of such settlements, the inheritance tax regime applicable to interest in possession trusts cannot operate here. Rules have therefore been devised to tax such 'non' interest in possession trusts periodically and when trust property is distributed. Accordingly, s. 64 imposes a charge to inheritance tax on the settlement every ten years where, immediately before the ten year anniversary, all or part of the property in the settlement comprised 'relevant property'. Relevant property is settled property in which there is no qualifying interest in possession (i.e., property held on discretionary trusts or trusts to accumulate income) other than certain favoured settlements (s. 58). These favoured settlements are discussed in para. 34.6. In addition to the ten year charge on discretionary trusts, inheritance tax is imposed on the happening of certain chargeable events.

34.5.1 The ten year charge

This charge will first arise on the tenth anniversary of the date on which the settlement commenced, and on subsequent anniversaries at ten year intervals (s. 61(1), IHTA). The date on which the settlement commenced is the date property first became comprised in the settlement (s. 60). However, where

---

[18.] And certain types of company; s. 59(2), IHTA.

the settlor or the settlor's spouse, widow or widower is beneficially entitled to an interest in possession in the property immediately after it becomes comprised in the settlement, the property is not treated as having become comprised in the settlement at that time. Instead the property is treated as becoming comprised in a separate settlement made by, and at the time when, the last of the settlor or the settlor's spouse, widow or widower ceased to be beneficially entitled to an interest in possession in that property (s. 80).

When a ten year charge arises, tax will be charged on the value of the relevant property at that time (s. 64). In order to determine the rate of inheritance tax, a hypothetical cumulative total must be calculated. The cumulative total is hypothetical as no one beneficiary has sufficient interest in the settlement to enable his or her actual cumulative total to be used. Similarly, since there is no actual transfer of value on the date of the ten year anniversary, a hypothetical value transferred must be computed. The rate of inheritance tax payable is then 30% of the 'effective rate'. The effective rate is the inheritance tax chargeable on the hypothetical value transferred at lifetime rates based on the hypothetical cumulative total, expressed as a percentage of the hypothetical value transferred (s. 66).

The hypothetical value transferred is the value of the relevant property immediately before the ten year anniversary (s. 66(3)(a) and 66(4)(a)). To this amount is added the value of any property immediately after it became comprised in the settlement which was not then, and has not since become, relevant property (s. 66(4)(b)) – for example, a life interest – and the value of any property immediately after it became comprised in another settlement made by the same settlor on the same day that settlement in issue was made (ss. 62(1) and 66(4)(c)). However, where the whole or part of the value of the relevant property immediately before the ten year anniversary is attributable to property which was not relevant property (for example, it was subject to an interest in possession) or was not comprised in the settlement for some part of the preceding ten year period, the rate at which tax is charged is reduced by one-fortieth for each successive quarter[19] in that ten year period which expired before the property became relevant property comprised in the settlement (s. 66(2)).

The hypothetical cumulative total is the aggregate of (s. 66(3)(b) and (5)):

(a) the values transferred by chargeable transfers made by the settlor in the seven years ending with the commencement of the settlement (excluding values transferred on the day of the commencement of the settlement); and

(b) the amounts on which any charges to tax were imposed under s. 65(1) on the happening of any chargeable events in the preceding ten years (see paras 34.5.3 to 34.5.9).

The rule in (a) above is subject to modification if, after 8 March 1982 but before the ten year anniversary, the settlor has made a chargeable transfer which has increased the value of the settlement. In such a case, the hypothetical cumulative total is the aggregate value transferred by chargeable

---

[19.] A period of three months; s. 63, IHTA.

Inheritance tax and settlements

transfers by the settlor in the seven years ending with the day on which the addition occurred, but disregarding transfers made on that day, if that gives a higher total than that calculated under (a) above (s. 67(3)).

Example

Sally, having made chargeable transfers of £201,000 in the seven years prior to 1 January 1988, settled £30,000 half on Andrew for life and the other half on discretionary trusts. On 1 January 1998, the discretionary trust is worth £50,000 and Andrew is still alive. The hypothetical value transferred is:

	£
The value of the relevant property immediately before the ten year anniversary	50,000
The original value of Andrew's life interest	15,000
Any other settlement created on the same day	nil
	65,000[20]

The notional cumulative total is:

	£
The settlor's chargeable transfers in the seven years prior to the creation of the settlement	201,000
Tax on the occurrence of chargeable events	nil
	201,000

The rate of tax applied is then:

Tax at the lifetime rate of 20% on a hypothetical value of £65,000 transferred by a transferor with a hypothetical cumulative total of £201,000 (after allowing for the nil rate band of £215,000) is £10,200 (i.e., 20% × £51,000).

This gives an effective rate of tax of $\frac{10,200}{65,000}$ % which is 15.69%.

30% of the effective rate is 4.7% and this is the rate to be applied to the value of the relevant property on 1 January 1998 giving a total tax due of:

4.7% × £50,000 = £2,350

34.5.2 Settlements created before 27 March 1974

The rules described in para. 34.5.1 apply to settlements created after 27 March 1974. For settlements created before that date a simpler regime

---

[20] This illustrates the obvious planning point that when a settlor wishes to create non-discretionary and discretionary settlements they should be made by separate settlements created on different days to prevent aggregation of values.

applies. The hypothetical value transferred on the tenth anniversary of such settlements is simply the value of the relevant property on that date and the hypothetical cumulative total is simply the sums charged under s. 65, IHTA on the happening of a chargeable event (s. 66(6)).

34.5.3 Other chargeable events

Apart from the ten year charge, a charge to inheritance tax may be levied on a discretionary settlement in two other situations, subject to exceptions. These are noted in paras 34.5.4 and 34.5.5.

34.5.4 Property no longer subject to a discretionary trust etc.

Inheritance tax is chargeable when the settled property, or any part of it, ceases to be relevant property, for example, by becoming subject to an interest in possession or by ceasing to be settled property on the exercise of a power of advancement in favour of a beneficiary absolutely (s. 65(1)(a), IHTA).

34.5.5 Reduction in value

Where a charge on a discretionary settlement is about to arise, the trustees might consider it to be to the trust's advantage to reduce its value thereby reducing the amount on which a charge could be levied. In this situation a charge may arise even though the property continues to be relevant property (s. 65(1)(b), IHTA). However, inheritance tax is not chargeable if the disposition is such that, if the trustees had been beneficially entitled to the settled property, the disposition would not have been a transfer of value because it was the grant of an agricultural tenancy or because there was no intention to confer a gratuitous benefit (s. 65(6) and see paras 32.3.7 and 32.3.1).

Neither of the charges described in para. 34.5.4 and this paragraph applies if:

(a) the event in question occurs within three months after the day on which the settlement commenced or a ten year anniversary (s. 65(4)); or

(b) the trustees make a payment;

　(i) in respect of costs or expenses fairly attributable to the relevant property; or
　(ii) which is income of the recipient for income tax purposes or would be if the recipient was resident in the United Kingdom (s. 65(5));[21]

(c) the event in question is the result of complying with a court order under the Inheritance (Provision for Family and Dependants) Act 1975 (s. 146(6), IHTA).

[21.] 'Payment' for these purposes includes a transfer of assets; s. 63, IHTA.

34.5.6 Amount and rate of tax on a chargeable event

The amount subject to inheritance tax is the reduction in the value of the settlement as a result of the chargeable event. If the inheritance tax is paid by the trustees out of other relevant property in the same settlement, the reduction in value must be grossed up (s. 65(2), IHTA).

The calculation of the rate of inheritance tax payable in respect of the chargeable event depends on whether the chargeable event takes place before the first ten year anniversary or between ten year anniversaries.

34.5.7 Rate before the first ten year anniversary

Where a chargeable event takes place before the first ten year anniversary, the rate of inheritance tax payable in respect of that event is the 'appropriate fraction' of the effective rate (s. 68(1), IHTA). The effective rate is, again, the inheritance tax chargeable on a hypothetical value transferred at lifetime rates based on the hypothetical cumulative total, expressed as a percentage of the hypothetical value transferred. The hypothetical cumulative total is the value of any chargeable transfers made by the settlor during the seven years ending with the commencement of the settlement excluding values transferred on the day of the commencement of the settlement (s. 68(4)).

The hypothetical value transferred is the sum of (s. 68(5)):

(a) the value of the settled property immediately after the settlement commenced;

(b) the value of any property in a settlement made by the same settlor on the same day; and

(c) the value, immediately after it became comprised in the settlement, of any property which became comprised in the settlement before the chargeable event under s. 65 but after the commencement of the settlement whether that property has remained in the settlement or not.

Once again, simpler rules apply for calculating the rate of inheritance tax if the settlement was created before 27 March 1974 (s. 68(6)).

The 'appropriate fraction' is the number of complete successive quarters in the period from the commencement of the settlement to the day before the chargeable event (the 'chargeable period') divided by forty and multiplied by 30% (s. 68(2)). So if the settlement has been in existence for five years (i.e., 20 complete quarters) when the chargeable event occurs, the appropriate fraction will be:

$$\frac{20}{40} \times 30\% = 15\%$$

Adjustments are made to the number of quarters if the property was not comprised in the settlement for some part of the chargeable period or was previously not relevant property. Quarters expiring before the day on which the property became relevant property are not counted although if that day fell in the same quarter as that in which the chargeable period ends, that quarter is counted whether it is complete or not (s. 68(3)).

34.5.8 Rate between ten year anniversaries

Where a chargeable event takes place between two ten year anniversaries, inheritance tax payable in respect of that event is charged at the appropriate fraction of the rate of inheritance tax used to calculate the last ten year charge (s. 69(1), IHTA). The appropriate fraction is the number of complete successive quarters in the period from the last ten year anniversary to the day before the chargeable event. However, if the property was not comprised in the settlement at the time of the last ten year charge or was not at that time relevant property, the rate of tax is the rate at which the ten year charge would have been levied if that property had been comprised in the discretionary settlement when the ten year charge was last applied (s. 69(2)).[22]

Where the rates of inheritance tax have been reduced since the time of the last ten year charge, the rate of tax payable on the chargeable event is to be calculated as if the reduced rates had been in force at the time the ten year charge was last applied (para. 3, sch. 2, IHTA).

34.5.9 Exemptions

It would seem that trustees of 'non' interest in possession settlements are not entitled to claim the annual, small gifts, normal expenditure out of income, or gifts in consideration of marriage exemptions in respect of the ten year and other inheritance tax charges, although they can, apparently, claim other relevant exemptions.[23]

Agricultural property relief and business property relief may be claimed. The hypothetical value transferred is treated as the value transferred and the trustees are treated as the transferor (ss. 115(1) and 103(1)).

34.6 FAVOURED SETTLEMENTS

As was noted in para. 34.5, certain 'non' interest in possession trusts are afforded favourable treatment.

34.6.1 Property held for charitable purposes

Property held for charitable purposes only is not relevant property for the purposes of the provisions discussed above (s. 58(1)(a), IHTA).[24] Such trusts

---

[22.] The value to be attributed to such property for these purposes is the value when it first became relevant property of the settlement; s. 69(3), IHTA.
[23.] Cf. the position with regard to interest in possession settlements; s. 57, IHTA.
[24.] Where the trusts on which property is held only require that part of the income of the property is applied for charitable purposes, a corresponding part of the settled property will be regarded as being held for charitable purposes; s. 84, IHTA.

Inheritance tax and settlements

will therefore escape the ten year charge although if the charitable trust is 'temporary', i.e., the property is only held for charitable purposes until the end of a period, a charge will arise when the property ceases to be subject to the charitable trusts (s. 70(1)). A charge will also arise if the trustees make a disposition as a result of which the value of the temporary charitable trust is less than it would have been but for the disposition (s. 70(2)(b)).[25] In such circumstances, inheritance tax is charged on the amount by which the value of the temporary charitable trust has been reduced, although where the tax is paid out of the funds of the temporary charitable trust, the reduction in value must be grossed up (s. 70(5)). The rate at which tax is chargeable is the aggregate of (s. 70(6)):

(a) 0.25% for each of the first forty complete successive quarters;
(b) 0.20% for each of the next forty;
(c) 0.15% for each of the next forty;
(d) 0.10% for each of the next forty; and
(e) 0.05% for each of the next forty.

The relevant period is the period beginning with the later of 13 March 1975 and the day on which the property became subject to the temporary charitable trust and ending with the day before the event giving rise to the charge (s. 70(8)).[26] So the maximum rate of 30% is reached only when the property has been held on temporary charitable trusts for 50 years or more before the event giving rise to the charge. Since the earliest the relevant period can have begun was 13 March 1975, this maximum rate cannot be reached until 13 March 2025.

Example
Property becomes held on temporary charitable trusts on 1 January 1982. A chargeable event occurs on 1 January 1997. The property has been held on temporary charitable trusts for 15 years or 60 complete quarters. The rate at which tax will be charged on the chargeable event is therefore:

	%
First 40 quarters at 0.25% a quarter = 40 × 0.25	10
Remaining 20 quarters at 0.20% a quarter = 20 × 0.20	4
Rate of tax	14

34.6.2 Accumulation and maintenance trusts

Property which is subject to accumulation and maintenance trusts is not relevant property (s. 58(1)(b), IHTA). An accumulation and maintenance settlement will exist if (s. 71(1) and (2)):

[25.] Exemptions from charge apply if the payment is made in respect of costs or expenses or the payment will be income in the hands of the recipient; s. 70(3), IHTA.
[26.] See s. 70(9), IHTA for some transitional rules for property becoming held on temporary charitable trusts between 9 December 1981 and 9 March 1982.

(a) one or more of the beneficiaries will, on or before attaining a specified age not exceeding 25, become beneficially entitled to the trust property or an interest in possession in it. If no age is specified in the trust instrument but it is clear that the beneficiary will become entitled before the age of 25, the Inland Revenue will accept that this condition is satisfied (Extra-statutory Concession F8). If s. 31, Trustee Act 1925 applies to the settlement, the condition will be satisfied since s. 31 grants the beneficiary the right to the intermediate income at 18. However, if the settlement gives the trustees power to revoke the trusts in whole or in part it is not possible to say that any beneficiary will become entitled as required and the trust will not qualify as an accumulation and maintenance trust (*Lord Inglewood* v *IRC* [1983] STC 133, CA);[27]

(b) no interest in possession subsists in the settled property and the income is accumulated so far as it is not applied for the maintenance, education or benefit of a beneficiary. The income must be accumulated; a mere power to accumulate is not sufficient to comply with this condition. Again if s. 31, Trustee Act 1925 applies to the trust this condition will be satisfied; and

(c) that either:

(i) no more than 25 years have elapsed since the commencement of the settlement or, if later, the time at which conditions (a) and (b) were satisfied; or

(ii) all the people who are, or have been, beneficiaries are, or were, *either* grandchildren of a common grandparent *or* children, widows or widowers of such grandchildren who were themselves beneficiaries but died before becoming entitled.

Condition (c) prevents 'generation skipping'. However, it applies to unborn children provided that there is, or has, been a living beneficiary, and the word 'children' includes illegitimate, adopted children and step-children (s. 71(7) and (8)).

Since accumulation and maintenance trusts do not comprise relevant property no ten year charge can arise. In addition, the IHTA provides that there will be no charge when a beneficiary becomes beneficially entitled to the settled property or an interest in possession in it on or before attaining the specified age, nor will there be a charge if a beneficiary dies before attaining the specified age (s. 71(4)).[28] These provisions explain the popularity of such trusts with settlors. However, an inheritance tax charge will arise if the property ceases to be subject to an accumulation and maintenance trust or where the trustees make a disposition as a result of which the value of the accumulation and maintenance trust is less than it would have been but for the disposition (s. 71(3)).

[27.] Of course, the happening of events inherent in the contingent interest itself, such as the beneficiary's death or bankruptcy, will not prevent the trust from fulfilling this condition.

[28.] If the beneficiary dies after attaining an interest in possession but before obtaining a vested interest in the capital, there will be a charge under s. 4, IHTA in the usual way.

Inheritance tax and settlements 739

If inheritance tax becomes due it is payable in respect of the same value and at the same rates as set out in para. 34.6.1 (s. 71(5)).

34.6.3 Property becoming held by exempt bodies

Generally speaking, no inheritance tax charges arise if the settled property becomes indefeasibly property held for charitable purposes only, or a qualifying political party, or a housing association or for national purposes or the public benefit (s. 76(1), IHTA). This general exemption from tax is lost if the property or any part of it becomes applicable for purposes other than those listed.

34.6.4 Maintenance funds for historic buildings

Settlements for the maintenance of historic buildings are not relevant property, and an inheritance tax charge will only arise when trust property leaves the settlement other than for the maintenance of such buildings (s. 58(1)(c) and sch. 4, IHTA).

34.6.5 Superannuation schemes and employee trusts

Property which is held for the purposes of certain approved pension plans will not be treated as relevant property for the purposes of the ten year and other charges (ss. 58(1)(d) and 151, IHTA). Similarly property which is subject to employee trusts is not relevant property for these purposes (ss. 58(1)(b) and 86).

34.6.6 Trusts for disabled persons

If property is held on trust for a disabled person who has no interest in possession in the settled property but the terms of the trust provide that not less than half of the settled property will be applied for that person's benefit, that person is treated as having an interest in the trust property so that the normal charges on 'non' interest in possession trusts will not apply (s. 89, IHTA).

34.6.7 Property comprised in a trade or professional compensation fund

Property comprised in such a fund is not relevant property (s. 58(1)(e), IHTA). A 'trade or professional compensation fund' is (s. 58(3)):

> a fund which is maintained or administered by a representative association of persons carrying on a trade or profession and the only or main objects of the fund are compensation for or relief of losses or hardship that, through the default or alleged default of persons carrying on the trade or profession or of their agents or servants, are incurred or likely to be incurred by others.

34.7 PAYMENT OF TAX

Tax due on the creation of a settlement will be payable in accordance with the principles discussed in Chapter 33. In relation to inheritance tax arising during the life of the settlement, the persons liable for the tax are (s. 201(1), IHTA):

(a) The trustees of the settlement, but only to the extent of the property they have actually received or disposed of or have become liable to account for to the persons beneficially entitled, and so much of any other property as is for the time being available in their hands as trustees for the payment of tax or which would have been available but for their own neglect or default (s. 204(2)).

(b) Any person entitled, whether beneficially or not, to an interest in possession in the settled property, but only to the extent of that property and only if the tax remains unpaid after it ought to have been paid (s. 204(3) and(6)).

(c) Any person for whose benefit any of the settled property or income from it is applied at or after the time of the charge, but only to the extent of the amount of the property or income applied (reduced in the case of income by the amount of any income tax borne by him in respect of it), and only if the tax remains unpaid after it ought to have been paid (s. 204(5) and (6)).

Tax may be paid in instalments if the settled property meets the conditions set out in para. 33.8. If the tax or any interest thereon incurred on the creation of the settlement or in relation to a 'non' interest in possession trust is unpaid, the Inland Revenue charge is imposed on *any* property comprised in the settlement (s. 237(1)).

Where the charge to tax arises on the death of a person beneficially entitled to an interest in possession, the trustees of the settlement are liable for the tax (s. 200(1)(b)). If part of the property to which a deceased was beneficially entitled immediately before his death is at any time after the death vested in another person or another person has an interest in possession in it, that person is liable for the tax attributable to that property, but only to the extent of the property in which his interest subsists (ss. 201(c) and 204(3)).

Inheritance tax is generally due from trustees within six months of the end of the month in which the chargeable transfer takes place.[29] However, where the trustees become liable to pay additional tax because the settlor died within seven years of a chargeable transfer, the additional tax is due six months after the end of the month in which the settlor died (s. 226(3B)) and interest is charged on any amount of tax overdue from trustees in these circumstances (ss. 233 and 236(1A)).

[29.] Or, in the case of a transfer made after 5 April and before 1 October in any year otherwise than on death, the tax is due at the end of April in the following year; s. 226(1), IHTA.

PART VI
Foreign element

CHAPTER THIRTY FIVE
The foreign element

35.1 INTRODUCTION

It was seen in Chapter 1 that a liability for UK tax on foreign income and gains may arise if the taxable person is resident or ordinarily resident in the UK. This chapter will look at the rules which apply if a UK resident or ordinarily resident taxpayer receives income or gains from a source outside the UK. It will discuss the beneficial tax regime (known as the 'remittance basis') which is available to those who are so resident or ordinarily resident in the UK but who are domiciled in a foreign country. The chapter will also briefly discuss the rules that apply if a UK resident or ordinarily resident taxpayer attempts to reduce his or her liability to UK tax on foreign source profits and gains by creating an 'offshore' trust, i.e., a trust with non-UK resident trustees. Finally, the chapter notes the possibility of double tax relief and certain miscellaneous provisions.

35.2 UK RESIDENTS WITH FOREIGN INCOME AND GAINS

UK residents or ordinary residents may be liable to tax on their foreign income and gains under, inter alia, any of the following provisions:

(a) Schedule D, Case IV: income from securities outside the UK, and Schedule D, Case V: income from possessions outside the UK (s. 18(3), TA).
(b) Schedule E: income from overseas employments (s. 19(1), TA).
(c) Capital gains tax on the disposal of foreign situs assets (s. 2(1), TCGA).
(d) Schedule D, Case VI: tax in respect of any annual profit or gains not falling under any other Case of Schedule D and not charged by virtue of Schedules A or E (s. 18(3), TA).

The tax liability arising under heads (a) to (c) is discussed in this chapter. The tax liability arising under head (d), namely Schedule D, Case VI, is discussed in Chapter 18.[1]

35.3 SCHEDULE D, CASES IV AND V

Section 18(3), TA provides that Schedule D, Case IV charges income tax in respect of 'income arising from securities out of the United Kingdom'.[2] Schedule D, Case IV also covers income paid or deemed to be paid to beneficiaries from foreign estates in the course of their administration (ss. 695(4)(b) and 696(6), TA). 'Securities' normally involve 'a right to resort to some fund or property for payment' or 'some form of secured liability' (*per* Viscount Cave LC in *Williams* v *Singer* [1921] 1 AC 41). Case IV therefore applies to interest on mortgages and debentures where the property charged is situated abroad. However, the term has been held to extend to a personal guarantee so that foreign source interest is not assessable under Schedule D, Case III, but under Case IV as income arising from a security out of the United Kingdom (*National Bank of Greece S.A.* v *Westminster Bank Executor and Trustee Co. (Channel Islands) Ltd* [1971] AC 945).[3]

Section 18(3) provides that Schedule D, Case V charges income tax in respect of 'income arising from possessions out of the United Kingdom, not being income consisting of emoluments of any office or employment'. Offices and employments with a foreign element are considered in para. 35.4.

The phrase 'income arising from possessions' outside the UK has been held to include any foreign source of income (*per* Lords Herschell and Macnaughten in *Colquhoun* v *Brooks* (1889) 14 App Cas 493).[4] It thus includes income from a foreign trade,[5] profession or vocation and certain foreign pensions and annuities (s. 58). Income paid by trustees of an overseas trust fund to a beneficiary is within Case V.[6]

Neither Schedule D, Case IV nor Case V will apply if the taxpayer is not UK resident or ordinarily resident. This is because UK tax is only chargeable

---

[1.] A Schedule D Case VI charge will arise, inter alia, when an offshore income gain arises to an investor disposing of a material interest in an offshore fund; ss. 757 to 764, TA (as amended). A discussion of these provisions is outside the scope of this book.

[2.] This used to exclude income charged under Schedule C, but Schedule C was effectively repealed by the FA 1996. Schedule C covered payments out of public revenues, i.e., interest, public annuities or dividends payable out of the revenue of any government or public authority whether of the UK or another state.

[3.] See Revenue Interpretation 58 (*Simon's Taxes* Division H5.4) on the location of the source of the interest.

[4.] It is sometimes stated that Schedule D Case V cannot include income falling within Case IV but it is submitted that such income can also fall within Case V and that the Revenue may choose which Case to apply. For the reasons set out in para. 35.3.3, where income potentially falls within both Case IV and Case V and is taxable on the remittance basis, the Revenue will usually choose to treat the income as Case IV income.

[5.] If, however, the trade is only partially carried on overseas it will be taxable under Schedule D Case I in the usual way.

[6.] Unless the beneficiary is 'absolutely entitled' to the income so that he or she is taxable under the Schedule or Case appropriate to the income as it arises; *Baker* v *Archer Shee* [1927] AC 844 and see Chapter 14.

if either the taxpayer or the income producing asset is situated in the UK (*National Bank of Greece S.A.* v *Westminster Bank Executor and Trustee Co. (Channel Islands) Ltd* and see the discussion in Chapter 1).

35.3.1 Assessment

The basis of assessment for Cases IV and V of Schedule D is the same whatever the nature of the income. Generally, income tax under either of these Cases is taxed on an 'arising' basis. However, a special basis of tax, known as the 'remittance basis', applies to those individuals who are resident or ordinarily resident in the UK but who are not domiciled in one of the UK's constituent countries. These bases are discussed in the following paragraphs.

35.3.2 Arising basis

Section 65(1), TA provides that income tax under Case IV or V is charged on the 'full amount of the income arising in the year of assessment, whether the income has been or will be received in the United Kingdom or not'. Income 'arises' when it is received by the taxpayer or credited to him (*Whitworth Park Coal Co. Ltd* v *IRC* [1961] AC 31; *Dunmore* v *McGowan* [1978] STC 217 and *Peracha* v *Miley* [1990] STC 512; cf. *MacPherson* v *Bond* [1985] STC 678). This follows from Rowlatt J's dictum in *Leigh* v *IRC* [1928] 1 KB 73 that 'receivability without receipt is nothing'. If the income is payable by cheque or in some other conditional form, the income is not 'received' until the cheque is cleared or payment otherwise becomes unconditional and the money is credited to the taxpayer's account (*Parkside Leasing Ltd* v *Smith* [1985] STC 63). However, it is not necessary for the Case IV or V income to be received in the United Kingdom for the arising basis to apply, so the crediting of funds in a foreign bank account will be sufficient receipt for these purposes.

The same deductions and allowances that would have been made if the income had been received in the United Kingdom may be made (s. 65(1)(a)).

If the taxpayer becomes liable to pay income tax on income which has arisen abroad but:

(a) the taxpayer is prevented, despite reasonable endeavours on his part, from transferring the income to the United Kingdom, either by the laws or executive action of the government of the jurisdiction in which the income arises or by the impossibility of obtaining foreign currency there; and

(b) he has not realised the overseas income elsewhere in sterling or some other currency which he could transfer to the United Kingdom,

relief is available (s. 584). The income tax liability is postponed until the taxpayer brings the income into the UK or the conditions for relief cease to be satisfied. If by the time the assessment is made the taxpayer has died, the tax is charged on his personal representatives and is a debt due from and payable out of his estate.

35.3.3 Remittance basis

The arising basis does not apply to anyone who can satisfy the Inland Revenue that:

(a) he or she is not domiciled in the United Kingdom; or
(b) he or she is not ordinarily resident in the UK and is a Commonwealth citizen or a citizen of the Republic of Ireland (s. 65(4), TA).

In such cases the remittance basis applies. For Case IV income, the charge is made on the full amount of the sums received in the United Kingdom in the year of assessment, without any deduction (s. 65(5)(a)).[7] For Case V income, tax is computed (s. 65(5)(b)):

'on the full amount of the actual sums received in the United Kingdom in the year of assessment from remittances payable in the United Kingdom, or from property imported, or from money or value arising from property not imported, or from money or value so received on credit or on account in respect of any such remittances, property, money or value brought or to be brought into the United Kingdom.

So a liability to tax will arise if income from a foreign possession is brought into the UK directly and also if that foreign income is used to purchase an asset which is brought into the UK and then sold.[8] The only deductions allowed in computing the tax liability under Schedule D, Case V are those which are allowed for profits chargeable under Schedule D, Case I (s. 65(5)(b)).

When deciding whether income has been remitted to the UK, it is possible to trace the income through a series of transactions. So in *Harmel* v *Wright* [1974] STC 88[9] income was remitted when a taxpayer with overseas income purchased shares in a company which he controlled and that company made an interest free loan to an independent company which in turn made a loan to the taxpayer in the UK.

However, it was held in *IRC* v *Gordon* [1952] 1 All ER 866 that there was no remittance of income if what the taxpayer actually did was export his debt. The taxpayer had opened a bank account in the UK which he was allowed to overdraw. When his overdraft reached £500, the overdraft was transferred to a foreign branch of the same bank and the overdraft was satisfied by payments to the foreign branch out of the taxpayer's foreign income. The House of Lords held that no income was remitted to the UK. No property had been imported and there was no receipt in the UK of sums of money or

---

[7.] For this reason, if income falls within both Case IV and Case V, the Revenue will usually elect to charge the *full* amount of the income under Schedule D Case IV.
[8.] This is the consequence of the words taxable on the 'actual sums received' 'from property imported'.
[9.] The case actually concerned income liable to tax under Schedule E Case III but it is submitted that the same principle applies to Schedule D Cases IV and V.

value arising from property not imported. Accordingly, the taxpayer was not liable to UK tax on the foreign income.

Legislation now exists to prevent taxpayers 'exporting' debts. Income will now be subject to tax under Cases IV or V if the foreign source income is applied towards the repayment of a loan (s. 65(6) to (9)).[10] The legislation was applied in *Thomson v Moyse* [1961] AC 967. A taxpayer who was entitled to certain income in a New York bank account was taxable in the United Kingdom on a remittance basis. He drew cheques on the New York account and sold them to a bank in the United Kingdom. The UK bank then sold the dollar cheques to the Bank of England and the taxpayer's UK bank account was then credited with the sterling equivalent. The cheques were cleared on the New York bank and the proceeds credited to the account of the Bank of England with the Federal Reserve Bank. The taxpayer was assessed to tax under Schedule D, Case V. He argued that the sterling sums received by him in the UK were not remittances of US income but arose from contracts concluded by him in the UK. The House of Lords unanimously rejected this argument, their Lordships taking the view that the taxpayer's UK income had increased and his US income had decreased. The technical mechanism by which the dollars were converted into sterling was therefore irrelevant.[11]

Despite the width of the remittance basis, it is relatively easy for taxpayers who wish to avoid remitting income to do so. If, for example, the taxpayer makes an *outright* gift of the income to his spouse or adult child (so that he no longer has any claim over it) the fact that the income is subsequently brought into the United Kingdom by the recipient does not lead to a remittance of the taxpayer's overseas income (*Carter v Sharon* [1936] 1 All ER 720). Alternatively, the overseas income can simply be spent abroad (by, for example, financing overseas holidays) so that it is never remitted to the UK and no UK tax charge can arise.[12]

35.3.4 Delayed remittances

Taxation on the remittance basis is usually favourable to the taxpayer since no tax is payable until the overseas income is received in the United Kingdom. If, however, a taxpayer wishes to remit his or her foreign income annually but is unable to do so for some reason, the sudden receipt of a large amount of accrued income when the taxpayer is able to remit the income could be disadvantageous as it could push the taxpayer into a higher income tax bracket for that year of assessment. The TA therefore provides relief in such circumstances if:

(a) the income arose in previous years but the taxpayer was unable to transfer the income to the United Kingdom;

[10.] These provisions apply to taxpayers who are ordinarily resident in the UK.
[11.] See the criticism of the case in *Butterworths UK Tax Guide 1995–96*, para. 34:23.
[12.] Other methods include opening separate accounts for capital and income and remitting only from the capital account.

(b) the inability of the taxpayer to transfer the income was due to the laws or executive action of the government of the jurisdiction in which the income arose, or to the impossibility of obtaining foreign currency there; and

(c) the inability to remit the income was not due to any lack of any reasonable endeavours on the taxpayer's part (s. 585, TA).

If these conditions are met, when the income is finally remitted, or the conditions can no longer be satisfied, the income of earlier years is not assessed as income of the year of actual remittance, but is treated as though it had been received in the year of assessment in which it in fact arose in the overseas jurisdiction.

35.3.5 Basis of assessment

Historically (as with Schedule D, Case III – see Chapter 13), assessment under Schedule D, Cases IV and V has been on a preceding year basis. However, as from the 1996/1997 tax year assessment is on a current year basis. Foreign sources of income which arose for the first time after 6 April 1994 were already assessed on a current year basis (Chapter IV, Part IV, FA 1994).

A special regime of deduction at source applies to banks (and others) who organise the payment of foreign dividends on behalf of the payer, although this was amended in the FA 1996 in response to representations that the scheme was 'outdated' and imposed 'serious compliance problems'.[13] 'Foreign dividends' are defined as any interest, dividends or annual payments payable out of, or in respect of, the stock, funds, shares or securities of any body of persons not resident in the United Kingdom (s. 118A).

Where foreign dividends are entrusted to any person in the United Kingdom for payment to any person, the person making the payment must deduct income tax at source and account for it to the Inland Revenue on the payee's behalf (s. 118E). Exemption from this regime is available to certain non-UK resident recipients (s. 118G(4)). In addition, the rules do not apply if the foreign dividends are paid in respect of stocks, funds, shares or securities held in a recognised clearing system.

Tax under Schedule D, Cases IV and V will usually be payable at the taxpayer's marginal rate of income tax. However, if the income is a dividend or other savings income, the income will be charged under Schedule D, Cases IV or V at the lower (20%) rate of tax (s. 77(2), FA 1993 and s. 1A, TA)).

35.4 INCOME FROM OVERSEAS EMPLOYMENTS

35.4.1 Schedule E, Case I

Schedule E, Case I covers:

> any emoluments for any year of assessment in which the person holding the office or employment is resident or ordinarily resident in the United

---
[13.] Budget Press Release Rev 26, 28 November 1995.

Kingdom, subject however to section 192 [of the TA] if the emoluments are foreign emoluments (within the meaning of that section) and to section 193(1) [of the TA] if in the year of assessment concerned he performs the duties of the office or employment wholly or partly outside the United Kingdom.

'Foreign emoluments' are emoluments received by a taxpayer who is not domiciled in the United Kingdom and who is employed by a non-resident person, other than a person resident in the Republic of Ireland (s. 192(1), TA). Taxpayers in receipt of foreign emoluments are excepted from tax under Schedule E, Case I if the foreign emoluments are received in respect of the duties of an office or employment performed wholly outside the United Kingdom (s. 192(2)). Such foreign emoluments will be subject to tax under Schedule E, Case III (discussed at para. 35.4.3).

Section 193 provides that a total exemption from income tax under Schedule E, Case I is available if the duties of the office or employment are performed wholly or partly abroad during a 'qualifying period' of at least 365 days.[14] A 'qualifying period' is either (para. 3(1) and (2), sch. 12):

(a) a period of days of absence from the United Kingdom; or

(b) a period of days of absence and days of presence, provided the days of presence, if consecutive, do not exceed 62 and in any event do not account for more than one-sixth of the total period in question.[15]

A day is not a day of absence unless the taxpayer is absent from the United Kingdom at the end of the day (para. 4, sch. 12). The effect of this rule is that the day of return to the United Kingdom is not a day of absence, although the day of departure from the UK is.[16] Careful planning is required to take advantage of this rule. For example, if the taxpayer is abroad for 140 consecutive days, present in the UK for 30 consecutive days, absent for 130 consecutive days and then present for 60 consecutive days, relief can be claimed because the periods of presence in the UK do not exceed 62 consecutive days and the total number of days of presence in the UK (90 days) do not exceed one-sixth of the total number of days in question (600 days). However, if the taxpayer in this example had stayed a mere 11 extra days on his first visit (so that he spent a total of 101 days in the UK) or three extra days on his second visit (so that he spent 63 consecutive days in the UK), he would have failed to qualify.

The amount of a taxpayer's emoluments which qualify for this relief is the amount remaining after the deduction of all deductible expenses (para. 1A,

---

[14.] The mechanism for the exemption is that, in computing the liability to tax under Schedule E Case I, the whole amount of the emoluments attributable to the qualifying period is allowed as a deduction (s. 193(1), TA).

[15.] The rules have been significantly relaxed for seafarers who can stay up for up to 183 consecutive days in the UK and those periods in the UK can amount to up to one half of the total qualifying period (para. 3(2A), Sch. 12, TA).

[16.] The possibility that someone who is consistently absent from the UK between 23.59 and 00.01 hours every night is absent from the UK for these purposes is noted in *Butterworths UK Tax Guide 1995–96*, para. 6:05.

sch. 12). This prevents taxpayers from setting a full year's expenses against their UK taxable income while claiming relief from UK tax on the gross earnings from abroad.

In deciding where the duties of the office or employment are performed the following rules apply:

(a) Where the taxpayer normally performs the whole or part of his duties in the UK, his emoluments for any period during which he is absent from his office or employment are treated as emoluments for duties performed in the UK (thus excluding them from relief) unless it is shown that they would have been emoluments for duties performed abroad had the taxpayer not been absent from the UK (s. 132(1)).

(b) Where the duties of the office or employment in substance fall to be performed abroad, any incidental duties performed in the UK are normally treated as performed abroad. However, this rule does not apply for the purposes of the exception for tax under s. 193 so that emoluments attributable to incidental duties performed in the UK will not qualify for a reduction (s. 132(2) and (3)).[17]

35.4.2 Schedule E, Case II

If the emoluments of the officeholder or employee do not fall to be taxed under Schedule E, Case I they may fall to be taxed under either Schedule E, Case II or Schedule E, Case III. Schedule E, Case II covers:

> any emoluments, in respect of duties performed in the United Kingdom, for any year of assessment in which the person holding the office or employment is not resident (or, if resident, not ordinarily resident) in the United Kingdom, subject however to section 192 [of the TA] if the emoluments are foreign emoluments (within the meaning of that section).

Thus non-UK residents will only be charged to UK tax on the income from their offices or employments if those offices or employments are performed in the United Kingdom in accordance with the rules set out in para. 35.4.1.[18]

35.4.3 Schedule E, Case III

Schedule E, Case III covers:

> any emoluments for the year of assessment in which the person holding the office or employment is resident in the United Kingdom (whether or not ordinarily resident there) so far as the emoluments are received in the United Kingdom.

---

[17] Once again, special rules apply to seafarers (s. 132(4)(b), TA). Special rules also apply to civil servants (s. 132(4)(a) and Extra-statutory Concession A25).
[18] On the allocation of earnings where the duties are performed partly in the UK and partly outside, see Statement of Practice SP 5/84.

Schedule E, Case III will thus primarily catch the foreign emoluments (as defined in para. 35.4.1) paid in respect of duties performed wholly outside the UK by taxpayers who are resident in the UK. The effect of the words 'so far as the emoluments are received in' the UK is to apply the remittance basis (discussed in relation to Schedule D, Cases IV and V in para. 35.3.3) to income falling within Schedule E, Case III. It thus continues the favourable UK tax treatment of non-UK domiciles who are living in the UK.

Emoluments are treated as received in the UK if they are 'paid, used or enjoyed in, or in any manner or form transmitted or brought to, the United Kingdom' (s. 132(5)).[19] The provisions introduced in the context of Schedule D, Cases IV and V to prevent taxpayers 'exporting debts' rather than remitting income are specifically applied to Schedule E, Case III (ss. 65(6) to (9) and 132(5)). Relief as described at para. 35.3.4 is available if the taxpayer wishes to remit income but is unable to do so in a particular year of assessment (s. 585).

Where income is taxed under Schedule E, Case III, the general rule relating to the deductibility of expenses in s. 198(1) is excluded. Instead, emoluments charged under Case III may only be reduced by 'the amount of expenses defrayed out of those emoluments, and of any other expenses defrayed in the United Kingdom' for any year of assessment in which the taxpayer was resident in the UK, being in any event expenses for which a deduction would have been allowed under s. 198(1) (s. 198(3)).

Since the remittance basis is generally a favourable method of taxation, non-UK domiciled employees who work for a foreign employer and perform duties in both the UK and abroad are likely to find it advantageous to work under 'split contracts' whereby their services are split into services to be carried out in the UK and services to be carried out abroad. This will allow the taxpayer to claim the benefit of the remittance basis in respect of the income from work carried out abroad.

35.4.4 Expenses in connection with duties performed abroad

Sections 193 and 194, TA make special provision for expenses incurred in connection with work performed abroad. These rules only apply to taxpayers who are resident and ordinarily resident in the UK and are therefore restricted to income which is taxable under either Schedule E, Case I or III and which does not constitute foreign emoluments. Section 195 contains additional rules which apply to employees who are not domiciled in the UK but who are assessed under Schedule E, Case I or II in respect of emoluments for duties performed in the UK.

Sections 193 and 194 provide that:

(a) Where duties are performed wholly outside the UK, s. 198(1) of the TA extends to the expenses of travelling from any place in the UK to take up

---

[19.] However, since there is no requirement that 'actual sums' be received in the UK, the drafting is wider than that applicable to Schedule D Cases IV and V.

the overseas employment and of travelling to any place in the UK on its termination. An apportionment will be made if the expenditure is incurred partly for employment purposes and partly for other purposes (s. 193(2) and (3)).[20]

(b) Where the taxpayer holds two or more offices or employments, the duties of at least one of which are performed wholly or partly abroad, the cost of travelling from one place to another may be deducted from the emoluments of the duties the taxpayer performs on arrival (s. 193(5) and (6)).

(c) When the duties are performed wholly outside the UK, the cost of any board and lodging incurred for the purpose of enabling the employee to perform his or her duties and which is reimbursed to the employee or borne by the employer (so falling to be included in the employee's emoluments) may be deducted provided that the emoluments are taxable under Schedule E, Case I (s. 193(2) and (4)). If the taxpayer is absent from the UK for at least 60 consecutive days, the travel costs of the taxpayer's spouse and/or any minor children of the taxpayer incurred by them in visiting the taxpayer and which are either reimbursed or borne by the taxpayer's employer may be deducted (s. 194(1) and (2)).

(d) Where the duties are performed partly outside the UK and the employee makes a journey wholly and exclusively for the purpose of performing those duties or returning to the UK after performing them, his or her travel costs may be deducted provided the taxpayer's emoluments are subject to tax under Schedule E, Case I and the duties could only be performed abroad (s. 194(3) and (4)). Similarly, if duties are performed wholly and exclusively abroad, the travel costs of any journey to or from the UK may be deducted (s. 194(5) and (6)).

It was noted above that special rules apply to employees who are not domiciled in the UK but who are assessed under Schedule E, Cases I and II in respect of employment for duties performed in the UK. Such employees can claim a deduction for travel costs borne by the employer or reimbursed to the employee if the cost relates to a journey from the taxpayer's usual place of abode to the place of performance of the duties of the office or employment (s. 195(5) and (7)). Travels costs incurred by the taxpayer's spouse or minor children are similarly deductible if the taxpayer has been in the UK for 60 or more consecutive days (s. 195(6)). These rules only apply if, on the date the taxpayer arrives in the UK to perform the duties, he or she has not been resident in the UK for the two preceding years, or the taxpayer has not been in the UK for any purpose during the two year period immediately preceding arrival. These rules then only apply for five years beginning with that date (ss. 195(2) and (3)).

35.5 CAPITAL GAINS TAX

A person is chargeable to UK capital gains tax if he or she is resident or ordinarily resident in the UK (s. 2(1), TCGA). If he or she is not so resident,

---

[20]. These provisions constitute a partial reversal of *Ricketts v Colquhoun* [1926] AC 1 – see para. 8.3.2.1.

a liability to capital gains tax only arises in respect of assets situated in the UK and used for the purposes of a trade carried on in the UK through a branch or agency (s. 10). It has been noted that these rules 'preserve the basic premise that a person is taxable either because he is resident or because the source is here but curiously restricts the source to one type – through a branch or agency'.[21] Residence and ordinary residence have the same meanings as for income tax (s. 9(1) and see Chapter 1). Someone who is resident here for some temporary purpose only and not with a view to establishing residence in the UK is treated as resident here only if his period of residence in the UK exceeds six months (s. 9(3)).

A more favourable capital gains tax regime applies to those who are either resident or ordinarily resident in the UK but who are not domiciled in one of its constituent countries. Such people are only taxable in respect of the chargeable gain accrued on the disposal of foreign situs assets to the extent that the gain is remitted to (i.e., received in) the UK (s. 12(1)). If the asset has been acquired and disposed of in a foreign currency, the acquisition cost and disposal proceeds are calculated in sterling by converting the foreign currency into sterling at the exchange rates prevailing at the date of acquisition or disposal (*Bentley* v *Pike* [1981] STC 360 affirmed in *Capcount Trading* v *Evans* [1993] STC 11).

Clearly, the taxation of gains on a remittance basis can be problematic. If, for example, the taxpayer sells a house in France for £75,000 having acquired it for £25,000, his gain, ignoring indexation and any other applicable reliefs, will be £50,000. If the taxpayer then remits £25,000 to the UK the question arises as to what has been remitted – part of the taxpayer's chargeable gain of £50,000 or the whole of the taxpayer's acquisition cost? It is understood that, in practice,[22] the Revenue treat the taxpayer as though gain has been remitted in proportion to the disposal consideration received, so in the example given the taxpayer will be liable to capital gains tax on:

$$\frac{£50,000}{£75,000} \times £25,000 = £16,666$$

It is unclear whether the Revenue will accept that gain has not been remitted if the taxpayer specifies the nature of the receipt by splitting it into two bank accounts (one for the 'allowable expenditure' and one for the 'gain') while still in the foreign country and remitting only from the 'allowable expenditure' account.[23]

Another consequence of the remittance basis is that it is, obviously, not possible to remit a capital loss. To avoid losing the benefit of capital losses a well advised taxpayer should, where possible, bring the asset standing at a loss into the UK before disposal to ensure that the loss will be available for set off against subsequent capital gains.

[21.] *Butterworths UK Tax Guide 1995–96*, para. 34:48.
[22.] See Sumption, *Capital Gains Tax*, Butterworths, Division A3.05.
[23.] Cf. *Kneen* v *Martin* 19 TC 33 which held that, in the income tax context, the Revenue could not assume that what had been remitted was income and not capital.

Since the remittance basis applies to foreign situs assets it is necessary to have a list of rules setting out where assets will be deemed to be located for tax purposes. A detailed list is, accordingly, set out in s. 275, TCGA.

Finally, a similar relief to that available for Schedule D, Case IV and V income (see para. 35.3.4) is available in respect of capital gains tax if the remittances to the UK are delayed (s. 279).

35.6 OFFSHORE TRUSTS

Since neither UK income tax nor capital gains tax will be charged if the income or capital gains arise to a non-UK resident from assets situated outside the United Kingdom, a UK resident taxpayer might try to escape tax by transferring assets to non-resident trustees who would be directed to hold the assets for the benefit of the settlor or his family. The perceived tax advantages of such a transaction are, however, countered by the application of the rules discussed in paras 35.7 to 35.9 below.

35.7 INCOME TAX AND OFFSHORE TRUSTS

The residence of the settlor, trustees and beneficiaries for income tax purposes will be determined in accordance with the general principles set out in Chapter 1. In the case of trustees, however, these rules are overridden by a statutory provision if the settlement has a mix of UK resident and non-resident trustees.[24] Section 110, FA 1989 provides that where the trustees of a settlement include at least one trustee who is not resident in the United Kingdom, as well as at least one trustee who is so resident, the non-resident trustees will be treated as being resident in the UK if at the 'relevant time' the *settlor* is resident or ordinarily resident or domiciled in the United Kingdom. Anyone who provides or undertakes to provide funds for the settlement will be treated as a settlor in applying these provisions. The 'relevant time' in the case of a settlement set up by will or on an intestacy is the time of death and, in any other case, is the time when the settlor provided funds for the settlement. If the settlor is not resident, ordinarily resident or domiciled in the UK at the relevant time, the UK resident trustees of the settlement will be treated as non-resident.

35.7.1 Transfer of assets abroad

A special anti-avoidance provision, set out in s. 739, TA, applies whenever an individual who is ordinarily resident in the United Kingdom transfers assets abroad and, as a consequence of that transfer, that individual has power to enjoy the income of, or receives a capital sum from, a person resident or domiciled out of the United Kingdom to whom income becomes payable (for example, non-resident trustees). In such circumstances the individual is

---

[24.] This provision was introduced to reverse the decision in *Dawson* v *IRC* [1989] STC 473, HL which held that the presence of a single UK resident trustee was insufficient to enable the unremitted foreign income of the trust to be taxed in the UK.

treated for income tax purposes as though the income were his assessable under Schedule D, Case VI (s. 743(1)). This means that an individual who is ordinarily resident in the UK cannot avoid UK income tax by the simple expedient of transferring income producing assets to non-resident trustees with powers to apply the income or capital for the individual's benefit.

In *Vestey* v *IRC* [1980] STC 10, the question arose as to whether the requirement in s. 739 that income is enjoyed by 'such an individual' referred to any individual who was ordinarily resident in the United Kingdom or to the individual who actually transferred the assets abroad. The House of Lords held that both interpretations were possible, but ruled that the second interpretation was preferable and should be followed.[25] The effect of this decision is that s. 739 only permits the Revenue to assess the settlor and not any other beneficiaries of the settlement resulting from the transfer of assets abroad. Since the settlors in *Vestey* v *IRC* had no power to enjoy the trust income, the income tax assessments on the discretionary beneficiaries were invalid. It also follows from the decision in *Vestey* that the transferor must be ordinarily resident in the UK at the time the transfer is made and this argument was upheld by the Court of Appeal in *IRC* v *Willoughby* [1995] STC 143.

The Finance Act 1997, however, makes provision for s. 739 to be amended so that it applies whatever the ordinary residence status of the individual when the transfer was made. The amendments are made in order to 'clarify the application of the legislation' (see HM Treasury Notes on Clauses January 1997) despite the fact that the House of Lords is not due to hear the Revenue's appeal of *IRC* v *Willoughby* until May 1997. For the purposes of the amendments, it is irrelevant when the transfer took place, but the changes will only catch income arising on or after 26 November 1996.

Unsurprisingly, the government were not content with the outcome in *Vestey* v *IRC*, and a new provision (now s. 740) was introduced. Section 740 applies where, 'by virtue or as a consequence of a transfer of assets' abroad, income becomes 'payable to a person resident or domiciled outside the United Kingdom' (such as non-resident trustees) and an individual who is ordinarily resident in the United Kingdom and who is not liable to tax under s. 739 'receives a benefit provided out of assets which are available for the purpose by virtue or in consequence of the transfer'. If that income is not otherwise chargeable to income tax in the hands of the recipient, it is subject to income tax under Schedule D, Case VI up to the amount of the trust's income in the year of receipt. If the benefit exceeds the trust's income it is carried forward and taxed in later years to the extent of the trust's income in those later years.

Where income may be assessed under both ss. 739 and 740, the Inland Revenue can claim tax only once. Where more than one person may be assessed, the Inland Revenue may choose to whom, and in what proportions,

---

[25]. The effect of this decision was to overrule the principal *ratio* of a previous House of Lords decision, *Congreve* v *IRC* [1948] 1 All ER 948. The subsidiary *ratio* in *Congreve*, namely that where the taxpayer engineered the transfer abroad by the settlor, the taxpayer could be treated as though she was the settlor in relation to the settlement, remains intact.

the income is to be attributed as appears to them 'just and reasonable' (s. 744(1)).

It should be emphasised that ss. 739 and 740 are not limited to the creation of trusts and may affect a wide range of transactions. For example, in *IRC* v *Brackett* [1986] STC 521 the taxpayer was resident in the United Kingdom. He retired from the firm of chartered surveyors in which he was a partner and continued as a 'consultant', with the fees being paid to a Jersey company which paid them to him as salary in accordance with an agreement with the taxpayer. It was held that he could be assessed on those fees under s. 739 which should not be narrowly construed.

Sections 739 and 740 do not apply if:

(a) avoidance of tax was not one of the reasons for the transfer of assets abroad; or

(b) the transfer was a *bona fide* commercial transaction and was not designed for the purpose of tax avoidance (s. 741).

In *IRC* v *Willoughby* [1995] STC 143, the taxpayer, who was a professor of law at the University of Hong Kong, became entitled to a lump sum payment on his retirement. He decided to invest the money with an insurance company which was resident in the Isle of Man. The advantage in investing with such an offshore company was that the taxpayer was able to take advantage of a special tax regime whereby the income on his investments could be rolled up free of income tax. The Inland Revenue raised assessments under s. 739. The taxpayer challenged these assessments on the grounds that, inter alia, the investment was not made with tax avoidance in mind. The taxpayer succeeded in his claim in the Court of Appeal. The Court held that the choice of such offshore investments could not be regarded as tax avoidance. The Revenue's argument that this was tax avoidance as described by Lord Templeman in *IRC (New Zealand)* v *Challenge Corporation* [1986] STC 548,[26] was dismissed. Morritt LJ delivering the judgment of the Court held that the taxpayer had genuinely paid the premium for his insurance policies and had complied with all the other conditions so that the taxpayer qualified for the benefit of the beneficial tax treatment. The transfer of assets abroad did not amount to tax avoidance merely on the ground that the taxpayer might have invested his money in a different way which would have subjected him to less favourable tax treatment.

The Finance Act 1997 also contains an amendment to s. 739 so that the legislation will apply regardless of whether the avoidance of an income tax liability was one of the purposes for which the transfer was effected. The Revenue have stated that this means that s. 739 will apply when the purpose of the transfer is to avoid any form of direct taxation (HM Treasury Notes on Clauses January 1997).

[26.] The argument was that while a taxpayer was free to mitigate his liability, tax was avoided when a tax advantage accrued without involving the taxpayer in the loss or expenditure that would have entitled him to that reduction, see further Chapter 4.

35.8 CAPITAL GAINS TAX AND OFFSHORE TRUSTS

In order to be liable to UK capital gains tax, the person making the disposal must be either resident or ordinarily resident in the United Kingdom. The residence and ordinary residence of settlors and beneficiaries will be determined in accordance with the income tax rules discussed in Chapter 1. However, trustees are treated as a single and continuing body, and that body is treated as being resident in the United Kingdom unless the general administration of the trust is ordinarily carried on outside the United Kingdom and the majority of the trustees are not resident or ordinarily resident in the United Kingdom (s. 69(1), TCGA).[27] This means that it is relatively easy to constitute a trust with non-resident trustees. Since such trustees can dispose of assets pregnant with gain outside the scope of UK capital gains tax, special provisions exist to restrict such tax planning opportunities. These provisions are discussed below.

35.8.1 Attribution of trust gains to beneficiaries

These rules apply if:

(a) a settlor who is domiciled and either resident or ordinarily resident in the United Kingdom;
(b) creates a settlement with non-resident trustees (s. 87(1), TCGA).

In such circumstances any gains which would have been chargeable to UK capital gains tax if the trustees had been UK resident or ordinarily resident are treated as accruing to the beneficiaries of the settlement if those beneficiaries are domiciled in the United Kingdom and receive capital payments from the trustees (s. 87(2), (4) and (7), TCGA). The assessment on the beneficiaries is made in proportion to the capital payments received but cannot exceed the amount received (s. 87(5)). Thus the beneficiaries' maximum liability at current rates of capital gains tax is 40% of the capital sum received. However, increased tax is due if the capital gains were made in an earlier year of assessment and the capital sum is paid sometime after 6 April 1992 (s. 91(1)). The purpose of these provisions is to prevent trustees from retaining capital gains within the trust. The tax is increased by an amount equal to the amount of interest that would be chargeable on the tax due for a period beginning on 1 December in the year of assessment in which the gain accrued and ending on 30 November in the year of assessment following that in which the capital payment is made. The rate of interest for these purposes is currently 10%. However, the increased tax cannot exceed the amount of the capital payment (s. 91(2)).

[27.] A special rule applies for professional trustees who manage trust property here but are not themselves UK residents if the whole of the settled property derives from a non-UK domiciled, resident or ordinarily resident settlor (s. 69(2), TCGA).

35.8.2 Migrant settlements

If a UK settlement is 'exported' (that is, the trustees become non-resident or not ordinarily resident in the United Kingdom after having been resident or ordinarily resident) capital payments to beneficiaries made while the trustees were UK resident or ordinarily resident are ignored for the purposes of the attribution rule discussed in para. 35.8.1. This saving provision is overridden if the capital payments were made in anticipation of a future disposal of trust assets by the trustees once they have become non-resident (s. 89(1), TCGA). Where the converse occurs so that a settlement with non-resident trustees and undistributed capital gains arising from the last year of non-residence is 'imported', the trust gains may be charged on United Kingdom domiciled beneficiaries who subsequently receive capital payments from the trust (s. 89(2)).

35.8.3 Trustees ceasing to be liable to UK tax

If a trust is exported there is a deemed disposal and reacquisition at market value of the 'defined assets' and a consequent charge to capital gains tax (s. 80(1) and (2), TCGA). The defined assets are all the assets of the settlement excluding:

(a) assets situated in the UK which are held for the purposes of a trade carried on in the UK by the trustees through a branch or agency; and
(b) assets which would not be subject to UK tax at that time because of the existence of a relevant double tax treaty (s. 80(3), (4) and (5)).

The effect of this provision is to charge capital gains tax on any accrued gains up to the date of export on all assets which will cease to be subject to capital gains tax after the trust is exported.

35.8.4 Disposal of beneficial interests

The discussion in the foregoing paragraphs has concentrated on the gains arising when trust property is disposed of. However, a beneficiary under a trust can dispose of his beneficial interest by sale or gift. It was seen in Chapter 24 that the disposal by a beneficiary of his or her beneficial interest will not usually give rise to a charge to capital gains tax, and that tax will generally only arise when the beneficiary becomes entitled to all or part of the trust property (ss. 71 to 76, TCGA).[28] This exemption from tax will not apply, however, if at the time of the disposal of the beneficial interest the trustees are not resident in the United Kingdom (s. 86(1)). If the trust has previously been exported so that a charge as described in para. 35.8.3 has arisen, the tax on the later disposal of the beneficiary's interest will be

---

[28.] The exemption from tax on disposals of beneficial interests will not apply if the beneficiary acquired the beneficial interest for a consideration in money or money's worth.

calculated on the assumption that it was acquired for its market value at the date of exportation (s. 85(2) and (3)).

35.8.5 Attribution of trust gains to the settlor

Finally special rules apply if a UK domiciled and resident or ordinarily resident settlor has an 'interest' in a non- (or dual) resident 'qualifying' settlement. These rules provide that the gains made by the settlement are attributed to the settlor in the year of assessment in which the gains arise. The settlor has an indemnity against the trustees for any resulting tax charge (s. 86 and sch. 5, TCGA).

A settlement is a qualifying settlement if, broadly, it was created on or after 19 March 1991 or it was created before that date and sometime afterwards either:

(a) property is provided for that settlement otherwise than by way of bargain at arm's length; or
(b) the trust emigrates or acquires non-resident status under a double tax treaty; or
(c) inter alia, the settlor, his or her spouse or their children or their children's spouses benefit, or become entitled to benefit, under the settlement for the first time.

A settlor will have an interest in the settlement if property or income of the settlement becomes payable to, or applicable for the benefit of, the persons mentioned in (c) above or any company controlled by them.

35.9 INHERITANCE TAX AND OFFSHORE TRUSTS

For completeness, the inheritance tax rules applicable to offshore trusts should be noted. Section 48(3), IHTA provides that if property comprised in a settlement is situated outside the UK, the property (but not a reversionary interest in it) is excluded property and hence outside the scope of UK inheritance tax unless the settlor was domiciled in the UK at the time the settlement was made.[29] The deemed domicile provisions will apply unless the settlement was made before 10 December 1974 (s. 267). A reversionary interest in settled property situated abroad will be excluded property if the person beneficially entitled to it is an individual domiciled outside the UK (ss. 6(1) and 48(3)).

Where settled property is not excluded property, the normal inheritance tax rules relevant to settlements apply. However, no inheritance tax will be charged if the settled property ceases to be situated in the United Kingdom and, because the settlor was domiciled outside the UK at the time the settlement was made, as a result the settled property becomes excluded property (s. 65(7)).

[29.] Thus subsequent changes in the settlor's domicile will not affect the inheritance tax treatment of the settlement.

If an inheritance tax charge arises on the settled property at a time when the trustees are not resident in the United Kingdom, the settlor is liable for the tax (s. 201(1)(d))[30] but only if the tax remains unpaid after it ought to have been paid (s. 204(6)). For these purposes, the trustees of a settlement are not resident in the United Kingdom if the administration of the settlement is ordinarily carried on outside the United Kingdom and the majority of the trustees are resident outside the United Kingdom (s. 201(5)).

35.10 DOUBLE TAX RELIEF

A UK resident is normally subject to UK tax in respect of income and gains from an overseas source, but since that income or gain is likely to have been subjected to foreign tax in the country of origin, the income or gain will be doubly taxed if UK and foreign tax are both levied. Conversely, a similar double tax charge is likely to arise when non-UK residents have taxable UK source income or gains on disposal of UK assets used in a trade carried on in the UK through a branch or agency. Such double taxation is thought to be objectionable because, by making overseas profits more 'expensive' in tax terms than domestic profits, it discourages taxpayers from trading overseas and so reduces the attractions of international trade.

Tax systems can avoid double taxation of income and other profits in a variety of ways. The most obvious is to decline to tax overseas profits.[31] However, such a strategy is obviously undesirable to governments which, generally speaking, like to extend their jurisdiction to impose tax as widely as possible. Three other alternatives therefore exist.

(a) The foreign tax can be deducted from the gross receipt in the same way as any other allowable or deductible expenditure. Such treatment is permitted in the UK in the income tax context by s. 811, TA and in the capital gains tax context by s. 278, TCGA. The effect of this is to give some credit for the foreign tax paid. For example, if Alfred, a UK resident higher rate taxpayer, is entitled to £100 of foreign income which has been subject to foreign tax at 30%, his UK liability will be as follows:

	£
Foreign income	100
Less foreign tax	30
	70
UK tax liability @ 40% of £70	28

[30.] But see also s. 201(3),(3A) and (4), IHTA.

[31.] The UK effectively operated such a system prior to 1914 when all income accruing to a UK resident taxpayer from a foreign source was taxed on the remittance basis, i.e., it was not subjected to tax until the income was received in the UK. The benefit of the remittance basis was restricted after that date and now remains of importance only for those not domiciled in one of the UK's constituent parts (see para. 35.3.3).

(b) The foreign tax can be allowed as a credit against the domestic tax liability (so called 'unilateral relief'). Such treatment is permitted in the UK for income tax by s. 790, TA and will be relevant where no double tax treaty (see (c) below) exists between the UK and the foreign country or, if a treaty does exist, it does not cover the particular tax charge. Unilateral relief is made available in the context of capital gains tax by s. 277, TCGA.[32] Unilateral relief will generally be more favourable to the taxpayer than claiming that foreign tax as a deductible expense as in (a) above. In Alfred's case, for example, his tax position under unilateral relief would be as follows:

	£
UK tax @ 40% on £100	40
Less credit for foreign tax	30
UK tax liability	10

(c) The two countries can enter into a double taxation agreement to establish which has taxing rights over the relevant income or gain.[33] In the UK, effect is given to such agreements by s. 788, TA.[34] The Fiscal Commission of the Social and Economic Council of the UN first published a model double tax convention in 1946. That model and the later Organisation for Economic Co-operation and Development ('OECD') models, first published in 1963 and revised in 1972, 1977 and 1992, have been used as the pattern on which the UK government has based its negotiations for double taxation agreements.[35] The UK currently has double taxation agreements with over 100 countries. It must, however, be emphasised that although the model conventions may have been used as a starting point in the negotiations, each treaty is unique and reflects the bargain that has been struck between the contracting states. Generally speaking, double tax treaties operate by granting exemption from tax for some income or gains and granting tax credits in other cases.

35.11 MISCELLANEOUS

The preceding paragraphs of this chapter have concentrated on the individual taxpayer with foreign income or gains. However, a couple of specific provisions which apply more particularly to the corporate sector should be noted

---

[32] See Statement of Practice SP 6/88 for the Revenue's interpretation of s. 277, TCGA. Unilateral relief is also available in respect of inheritance tax by s. 159, IHTA.
[33] See generally Baker, *Double Taxation Agreements and International Tax Law*, 2nd edn, Sweet & Maxwell, 1994.
[34] Applied for capital gains tax purposes by s. 277(1), TCGA. Double tax treaties made in relation to estate duty now apply to UK inheritance tax on death by s. 158(6), IHTA.
[35] These models have been criticised as being biased in favour of the country of residence rather than the country of source and have been argued by some to have caused difficulties for developing countries. In 1988 the UN published a model treaty specifically for the benefit of less developed countries.

although a discussion of these provisions is outside the scope of this book. The first provision relates to so-called 'transfer pricing' (s. 770, TA). This provision allows the Revenue to adjust the sale price of property to the true arm's length price (i.e., market value) where one of the parties to the sale (such as a UK resident parent company) has control over the other (such as a non-resident subsidiary). The purpose of this provision is, broadly, to prevent a sale taking place at a price which creates a loss for the UK resident seller and a tax free profit for the non-resident purchaser. A full discussion of transfer pricing is set out in Chapter H4 of *Strategic Tax Planning* (ed. Shipwright, Gee Publishing Ltd in association with Sweet & Maxwell).

The second provision affects so-called 'controlled foreign companies', i.e., companies that are resident outside the UK but which are controlled by persons resident in the UK (s. 747(1) and (2)). The controlled foreign company provisions apply if the foreign company is subject to a lower level of taxation (as defined) in its country of residence than it would be if it was resident in the UK. When the provisions apply they permit the Revenue to apportion the company's chargeable profits for an accounting period to the persons who had an interest in the company during that period (s. 747(3)). A full discussion of these provisions is contained in Chapter H5 of *Strategic Tax Planning* (ed. Shipwright).

Index

Abuse of rights doctrine 71
Accountancy basis
  accounting date 334
    change 335
  anticipation 288
  basis period 333
  bills delivered 287
  capital 5–8
  cash 287
  change of basis 287–8
  commencement date 333
  commencement provisions 334–5
  corporation tax 573
  current year 331
    charge on 333
  current year arising 573
  discontinuance 335–6
  documents 9
  earnings 285–7
  expenditure 8–9
  general rules 334
  importance of capital/income
    distinction 7–8
  income 3–5
  inheritance 9
  new rules 333–6
  old system
    general rule 331–2
    opening years 332
  overlap relief 336
  payment of tax 336

Abuse of rights doctrine – *continued*
  preceding year 330–1, 380–2
  Schedule D, Cases I and II 284–8,
    330–6
  Schedule D, Case III 380–2
  transactions 9
  wealth 8
  year of assessment 333
Accountancy costs 322
Accounting date
  change 335
  Schedule D, Cases I and II 334,
    335
Accounting period, companies 564
Actors 167
Administration period 424–5
  chargeable gains during 528–9
  income tax 424–5
  see also Death of taxpayer
Administration of tax 31–3
  appeals *see* Appeals
  assessment 33
  Board 32–3
  collector of taxes 33
  inspector of taxes 33
  judicial review *see* Judicial review
  payment *see* Payment of tax
  personal returns 34–5
  self-assessment 34–6
  see also Inland Revenue

Advance corporation tax (ACT)
  distributions 588–9
    bonus issue 594
    dividends 592
    foreign element 599
    legislation 589–90
    new consideration 591–2
    non-corporate shareholders 603–4
    non-distributions 595–6
    non-resident corporate shareholders 603
    non-resident non-corporate shareholders 604
    out of assets of company 593
    qualifying 594–5
    redeemable shares or securities 593
    repayment of share capital 594
    share dealers 603
    shares and securities 591
    transfer of assets or liabilities 594
    when paid 590
    in winding up 595
  franked investment income 600–1
    carry-forward 601–2
    losses 613
    set off against 602–3
    repayment after ACT payment 601
    surplus 601–3
  non-distributions 595–6
  Pigott v *Staines Investment Co* 102–9
  residence 599, 600–1
  stock dividends 596
  surplus 598–9
    carry-back 599
    carry-forward 599
    surrender 599
  surrender
    groups 634–7
    surplus 599
  tax avoidance 102–9
  transfer of assets or liabilities 588–9
Adventure *see* Income tax, Schedule D, Cases I and II (trades, professions and vocations)
Agency workers 166
Agricultural property
  grant of tenancy 684–5

Agricultural property – *continued*
  valuation for inheritance tax 704–7, 709
Alienation of income 362, 396
Amalgamations
  anti-avoidance 665–7
  bona fide commercial reasons 665–6
  capital gains tax 651–2, 657–8, 663–7
  consideration for transfer 667
  meaning 663–4
  necessary conditions 651–2
  trading stock 664–5
  unit trusts 665
Annual payments
  corporation tax 574, 578, 579
  income tax *see* Income tax, Schedule D, Case III (interest, annuities and annual payments)
Annuities
  capital gains tax 503
  corporation tax 574, 578, 579
  income tax *see* Income tax, Schedule D, Case III (interest, annuities and annual payments)
  reverse 80
Appeals
  against assessment 33, 37
  Chancery Division 38–9
  courts 36
  direct tax appeals 36–8
  further 40
  general commissioners 37–8
  judicial review *see* Judicial review
  jurisdiction 37–8
  law and fact distinction 39–40
  other remedies 40
  special commissioners 37, 38
  tribunals 41
  valuations 38
  VAT tribunals 41
Architects 287
Assessment
  appeals against 33
  income tax 149
  self-assessment
    enquiries into returns 36
    payment 35
    personal returns 34–5
Assets
  capital gains tax meaning 460–2

Index

Assets – *continued*
  derived from other assets 494–5
  disposal 462–3
    conditional contracts 476–7
    deemed 463–70
    incidental costs 494
    non-disposals 477–8
    part disposal 471–2, 496–7
    time of 476–7
  gifts 514–16
  hire purchase 470–1
  licence grant 465–6
  negligible value 470
  repair or replacement 468–70
  wasting 495, 503
Assurance, capital gains tax 503
Avoidance *see* Tax avoidance

Bad debts 328–30
Badges of trade 261–76
  business knowledge 275–6
  circumstance for realisation 263, 271–2
  fact/law distinction 263–4
  length of ownership period 262, 268–9
  motive 263, 271, 272–5
  number of transactions 262, 269–70
  supplementary work 262, 270–1
Bank interest 386–7
Barristers
  cash basis 287
  textbooks and capital allowances 352
Base *see* Accountancy basis
Bayliss v *Gregory* 88
Beneficiaries 544–6
Benefits in kind 174–7
  additional accommodation charge 222–3
  cars 233–5
    fuel 235
    parking 216
  cash vouchers taxable under PAYE 218
  common law 179–80
  company directors 223–39
    assets placed at disposal 232–3
    beneficial loans 236–7
    benefits in Code 229

Benefits in kind – *continued*
  car fuel 235
  cars 233–5
  cash equivalent 228, 229–30
  chargeable expense 228
  costs of benefit 230
    transfer of asset 230–2
  definition 225
  employee shareholdings 237–8
  expenses payments 228
  general charge 228
  living accommodation expenses 238
  mobile telephones 235–6
  scholarships 238–9
  tax paid by employer 238
  vans 235
  credit tokens 216–18
    by reason of employment 217
    chargeable expense 217
    exemptions 218
    provided for employee 217
    reductions 218
  entertainment 216
  expense payments 228
  higher paid employees 223–39
    meaning 226
    see also company directors
  holiday stamp 213
  living accommodation 218–23
    amount charged 220
    by reason of employment 220
    directors' expenses 238
    exceptions 221–2
      additional accommodation charge 222–3
    provided in any period 220
    reductions 221
  mobile telephones 235–6
  scholarships 238–9
  statutory modifications 211–39
  trading stamp 213
  transport vouchers 216
  valuation 177–9
  vans 235
  vouchers 213–18
    by reason of employment 214
    car parking 216
    chargeable expense 214–15
    entertainment 216
    holiday stamp 213

Benefits in kind – *continued*
  non-cash 213–16
  provided for employee 213–14
  received by employee 214
  reduction in amount chargeable 215–16
  trading stamp 213
  transport vouchers 216
  see also Fringe benefits
Betting winnings 502
Blind persons' relief 146
Bonus issue 594
Bonuses
  cricketers 193–4
  footballers 195, 206–7
Bowater Property Developments Ltd 87–8
Building society interest 386–8
Burmah Oil schemes 83–5
Business entertainment expenses 253
Business property, valuation for inheritance tax 707–9
Business purpose test 72

Capital, income distinguished 289
Capital allowances
  allowances 347–8
  availability 347–8
  balancing allowance 348–9
  balancing charge 348–9, 357
  companies 577–8
    investment companies 613
    surplus 612
  dredging 360
  income tax Schedule E 253
  industrial buildings 345–9
  investment companies 613
  know-how 360
  machinery and plant 349–60
    belonging 353–5
    disposal value 356
    expenditure on provision of 353
    hire purchase 359
    leasing 359–60
    for letting business 442
    meaning 349–52
    non-business use 357
    pool 355–60
    short and long life assets 358
    textbooks 352
    wear and tear 358

Capital allowances – *continued*
  mines 360
  motor cars 358
  oil wells 360
  patents 360
  pool 355–7
    separate 357–60
  reducing balance basis 356
  relevant interest 347–8
  scientific research 360
  ships 359
  textbooks 352
  writing down allowance 355
Capital base 5–8
Capital gains tax
  accrual basis 456–7
  amalgamations 657–8
    anti-avoidance 665–7
    bona fide commercial reasons 665–6
    consideration for transfer 667
    meaning 663–4
    necessary conditions 651–2
    trading stock 664–5
    unit trusts 665
  annuities 504
  appropriation to trading stock 485–6
  assets 460–2
    derived from other assets 494–5
    gifts of 514–16
    hire purchase 470–1
    negligible value 470
    repair or replacement 468–70
    wasting 495, 503
    see also disposals
  assurance 504
  bargain at arm's length 482–3
  betting winnings 502
  chargeable gains 459–60
  chargeable person 460
  charging section 459
  charities 501–2
  chattels 504–5
  companies 560, 575–6
    exclusion 569–70
  compensation payments 465–8, 502
  computation 480–91
    see also consideration; expenditure

Capital gains tax – *continued*
  consideration
    appropriation to trading stock 485–6
    bargain at arm's length 482–3
    contingencies 487–8
    debts 484–5
    gratuitous transactions 484
    instalments 487–8
    market value substitution 482–4
    meaning 481–2
    negligible value claims 486
    options 485
    receipts taxed as income 488–9
    rights of security 487
    for transfer of business 667
    value shifting 484
  contingencies 487–8
  death of taxpayer 378, 502
    disclaimers 529
    donatio mortis causa 527–8
    gains during administration 528–9
    personal representatives 527–8
    change 529
    variations 529
  debts 472–4, 484–5, 503
  decorations for valour 505
  demergers
    anti-avoidance 656–7
    clearance procedures 657
    conditions for relief 656
    distribution
      to another company 654–5, 656
      to shareholders 653–4, 656
    exempt distributions 653
    meaning 653
    residence condition 656
    trade condition 656
  disposals 462–3
    conditional contracts 476–7
    deemed 463–70
    incidental costs 494
    non-disposals 477–8
    part disposal 471–2, 496–7
    time of 476–7
  economic risks 457–8
  exemptions
    annual 502
    charities 501–2

Capital gains tax – *continued*
    partly on status partly on asset 505–14
    status of taxpayer 501–2
    type of asset 502–5
    see also charities; *individual exemptions eg* betting winnings
  expenditure
    acquisition 490–1
    allowable 489–90
    enhancement 491–3
    production 491
    title 493–4
  extra-statutory concession D33 467–8
  foreign currency 503
  foreign tax 498
  future payment rights 463
  gilt-edged securities 502–3
  gratuitous transactions 484
  hire purchase 470–1
  history 454–6
  incidental costs of disposal 494
  indexation 454, 455
  indexation allowance 497–8
  inflationary gains 454, 455, 457
  inheritance tax and 676
  instalments 487–8
  international elements 750–2
  losses
    relief for loans to traders 500
    unquoted shares in trading companies 500–1
    use of allowable 499–500
  market value 482–4
  meaning 481–2
  modifications
    assets derived from other assets 494–5
    part disposals 496–7
    wasting assets 495
  mortgages 477–8
  negligible value claims 486
  non-disposals 477–8
  offshore trusts 755–7
    attribution of gains
      to beneficiaries 755
      to settlor 757
    disposal of interests 756–7
    migrant settlements 756

766 Index

Capital gains tax – *continued*
  trustees ceasing to be liable to UK tax 756
  options 475, 485
  passenger vehicles 505
  payment 478–9
  personal equity plan shares 504
  policy issues 453–4
  private residence 505–6
    apportionment 509–10
    dwelling house meaning 506–8
    more than one residence 508–9
    period of occupation 509–10
    sale of part of garden 508
  purchase of own shares 669–71
    clearance procedure 669, 672
    general conditions 670–2
    to pay IHT on death 672
    unquoted trading company 669–70
  qualifying corporate bonds 502–3
  rates 478
  on realisation 456–7
  receipts taxed as income 488–9
  reconstructions 657–8
    anti-avoidance 665–7
    bona fide commercial reasons 665–6
    consideration for transfer 667
    exclusions 664–5
    meaning 659–62
    substantial identity test 659–62
    trading stock 664–5
    unit trusts 665
  redemption of own shares 669–71
    to pay IHT on death 672
    see also purchase of own shares
  reliefs
    gifts of assets 514–16
    hold over relief 514–16
    incorporation into business 517–19
    reinvestment relief 523–4
    retirement relief 510–14
    roll-over relief
      incorporation into business 517–19
      replacement of business assets 519–22
    spouses 524–5
    venture capital trusts 525–6

Capital gains tax – *continued*
  reorganisations
    25% control test 650–1
    anti-avoidance 652
    clearance 652
    conversion of securities 652
    disposal with liability attaching 649
    exchange of securities 649–51
    general offer test 651
    greater part of voting power 651
    meaning 648
    necessary conditions 651–2
    new consideration 648
    new holding 647–8
    original shares 647–8
    paper for paper transactions 649–52
    roll-over relief 649–51
  retirement relief 510–14
  rights of security 487
  settlements
    absolutely entitled
      disposal by trustees 538–42
      infancy only bar to inheritance 533
      jointly 534
      right to call for conveyance 531–3
      tax liability 541–2
    beneficiaries 544–6
    change of trustees 538
    charitable trusts 546
    creation of new settlement 539–41
    disposals by trustees
      absolute entitlement to property 538–42
      termination of life interest on death 542–4
      trust assets 536–8
    life interest in possession 542–3
    settled property 530–4
      annuity charge on property 534
    settlor's liability 535–6
    termination of life interest on death 542–4
    transfer into 535
  tax avoidance 118, 131–4
  trading losses set against 344

Capital gains tax – *continued*
  transfer of business   657–67
    meaning of business   658
    see also amalgamations;
      reconstructions
  value shifting   472, 484
  wasting assets   503
  works of art   504
Capital transfer tax   674
  avoidance   94–8
Cars   233–5
  benefits in kind   233–5
  fuel   235
  parking   216
Carter Commission (Canada)   10
Case law   26
  employment meaning, *Hall* v *Lorimer* 168–9
  income tax Schedule D, *Strong* v *Woodfield* rule   316
  income tax Schedule E
    Pook v *Owen*   244–5
    Rickets v *Colquhoun*   243–4
    Taylor v *Provan*   246–7
  tax avoidance
    Bayliss v *Gregory*   88
    Bowater Property Developments Ltd   87–8
    Burmah Oil schemes   83–5
    Craven v *White*   87, 88, 90–1
    Duke of Westminster case   78–81
    Ensign Tankers v *Stokes*   91–2
    Fitzwilliam case   94–8, 100
    Furniss v *Dawson*   85–7
    McGuckian   100–2
    old approach   78
    Pigott v *Staines Investment Co* 102–9
    pre-*Ramsay*   79–81
    Ramsay doctrine   81–3
    Shepherd v *Lyntress Ltd*   91
    time and change   77
    Whittles v *Uniholdings Ltd*   98–100
Causation test   187–9
Chancery Division, appeals   38–9
Channel Islands   14
Charitable donations
  corporation tax and   578, 579, 580–1
  covenanted payments   580–1
  income tax   394–5

Charitable donations – *continued*
  inheritance tax   689
Charitable trusts   546
Charities
  capital gains tax   501–2
  property held for charitable purposes 736–7
Chattels   504–5
Circular transactions   81–3
Citizens' Charter   40
Classification
  capital base   5–8
  direct and indirect   3
  documents base   9
  expenditure base   8–9
  income base   3–5
  inheritance base   9
  transactions base   9
  wealth base   8
Clearances   27
  capital gains tax
    demergers   657
    paper for paper transactions   652
    purchase of own shares   669, 672
  tax advantage cancellation   130
Clergy cases   192
Close companies   559–61
Close investment-holding companies (CICs)   559–61
  meaning   562–3
  profit distributions by   561
Closely held companies   551
Clothes   322–3
Clubs
  identity requirement   281
  mutual trading   280–2
Collection of taxes
  income tax   149
  statutes for   24–5
Collective investment schemes   586
Collector of taxes   33
Commissioners of Inland Revenue 32–3
Companies
  accounting period   564
  artificial person   547
  associate   561
  capital allowances
    investment companies   613
    surplus   612
  capital gains tax   560, 575–6

Companies – *continued*
  close 559–61
  close investment-holding companies (CICs) 559–61
    meaning 562–3
  closely held companies 551
  control 561
  controlled foreign companies 760
  definition 554–5
  distributions 550–1
    by CICs 561
    meaning 560
    otherwise than as dividend 124–6
  double tier of tax 550
  financial year 564
  foreign element 551–2
  groups *see* Groups
  imputation system 547, 548, 550
  insurance 586
  international elements 759–60
  investment companies 563
    capital allowances 613
    expenses of management 612
      surplus 612–13
  loan creditor 561
  loans to participator 560
  losses
    allowable 607, 614
    capital allowances 607
    commencement 606, 607
    computation 606
    deductions and 606
    franked investment income 613
    group relief 614
    groups 607, 628
    hivedowns 613
    pre-trading expenditure 606, 607
    Schedule D, Case VI 613
    terminal 611–12
    trading *see* trading losses
    uses 606–7
  money box companies 550
  participator 561
  professional activities 574
  residence 555–8
    dual 558–9
    international activities 557
    management and control 556–7
    place of incorporation 556
  separate legal personality 549–50
  small 559, 560

Companies – *continued*
  corporation tax rate 565–6
  surplus capital allowances 612
  trading losses 606, 607–8
    carry-across
      general 610
      reduction of present and previous profits 609–10
      requirements 610
      Schedule D, Case V losses and 610
    carry-back
      requirements 611
      Schedule D, Case V losses and 611
      to preceding accounting period 610–11
    carry-forward
      against profits without time limit 608
      requirements 608–9
      Schedule D, Case V losses and 6–9
    uses 607–8
    see also Corporation tax
Company directors, benefits in kind 223–39
  assets placed at disposal 232–3
  beneficial loans 236–7
  benefits in Code 229
  cars 233–5
    fuel 235
  cash equivalent 228, 229–30
  chargeable expenses 228
  costs of benefit 230
    transfer of asset 230–2
  definition 225
  employee shareholdings 237–8
  expenses payments 228
  general charge 228
  living accommodation expenses 238
  mobile telephones 235–6
  scholarships 238–9
  tax paid by employer 238
  vans 235
Compensation funds, inheritance tax 739
Compensation payments
  cancellation of contracts 291–3
  capital gains tax 465–8, 502

Index

Compensation payments – *continued*
  filling a hole in profits 293
  income tax 289–93
  sterilisation of assets 290–1
Consideration
  appropriation to trading stock 485–6
  bargain at arm's length 482–3
  contingencies 487–8
  debts 484–5
  gratuitous transactions 484
  instalments 487–8
  market value substitution 482–4
  meaning 481–2
  negligible value claims 486
  options 485
  receipts taxed as income 488–9
  rights of security 487
  for transfer of business 667
  value shifting 484
Consortia 616–17, 644–6
  group income 645–6
  group relief 645–6
Construction workers 166–7
Contracts
  cancellation payments 291–3
  of and for service 161–2, 163–5
Conversion of securities 652
Convertible securities 586
Corporate bonds 502–3
Corporation tax
  1965–1972 classical system 549
  1972 changes 549
  accounting basis 573
  advance *see* Advance corporation tax (ACT)
  allowable charges 579
  annual payments 574, 578, 579
  annuities 574, 578, 579
  capital allowances 577–8
  capital gains 575–6
    tax exclusion 569–70
  charge to 568–87
  chargeable gains 575–6
  charges on income and 578–81
    allowable 579
    excluded 579–80
  charitable donations 578, 579, 580–1
  close companies 559–61

Corporation tax – *continued*
  close investment-holding companies 559–61
  collective investment schemes 586
  company defined 554–5
  computation 573–6
  consideration, new 591–2
  convertible securities 586
  current year arising 573
  deductions 576–8
  deficits 586–7
  depreciation 577–8
  distribution, meaning 560
  dividends 574
  due date 553
  excluded charges 579–80
  fiduciary receipts 569
  franked investment income 600–1
    surplus 601–3
  gifts 586
  gilt strips 586
  gilt-edged securities 586
    indexed 586
  history 548–9
  income tax exclusion 569–70
  income tax principles application 573–4
  insurance companies 586
  interest 574
  legislation 552
  liability
    due date 553
    period 553
    what is liable 553
    who is liable 553
  loan relationships 581–7
    accounting for profits and deficits 584–6
    anti-avoidance provisions 585–6
    authorised accounting method 585
    meaning 582–3
    money debt meaning 583
    non-trading relationships 584–6
    trading relationships 584
  management expenses 576–7
  manufactured interest 586
  non-UK resident company liability
    branch or agency 571
    locus contractus 572–3
    necessary conditions 570–1

Corporation tax – *continued*
  trade within UK   571–3
  patent royalties   578, 579
  payment   566–7
  principle behind charge   568
  profits, definition   559
  rates   564
  receipts net of income tax   574–5
  reduction   597–8
  Schedule D, Case III   399
  securities   586
  small companies   559, 560
  trading expenses   576
  see also Companies
Costs, legal and accountancy   322
Council tax   13
Craven v *White*   87, 88, 90–1
Credit tokens   216–18
  by reason of employment   217
  chargeable expense   217
  exemptions   218
  provided for employee   217
  reductions   218
Cricketers   193–4
Criminal activities, trade meaning and   277–9
Current year basis, Schedule D, Cases I and II   331, 333

Death of taxpayer
  capital gains tax   378, 502
    disclaimers   529
    donatio mortis causa   527–8
    gains during administration   528–9
    personal representatives   527–8
      change   529
      variations   529
  income tax
    absolute interest in residue   425–6
    administration period   424–5
    deceased's income   423
    income arising after   423–6
    limited interests in residue   424–5
    personal allowance   423
    personal representatives
      allowances available to   423
      persons not individuals   423
    residuary beneficiaries   424
    specific legatees   424
  inheritance tax   701–3

Death of taxpayer – *continued*
  allowable expenses   702–3
  market value at   701
  property not included in estate   701–2
  transfers of value   685
  transfers of value on   685
Debt on a security   473–4
Debts
  bad   328–30
  capital gains tax   472–4, 484–5, 503
  employees, discharge by third party   181–3
  released   298–301
Decorations for valour   505
Deductible expenditure *see* Expenses
Demergers
  anti-avoidance   656–7
  clearance procedures   657
  conditions for relief   656
  distribution
    exempt   653
    to another company   654–5, 656
    to shareholders   653–4, 656
  meaning   653
  residence condition   656
  trade condition   656
Deposit takers   387
Deposits, unclaimed   298–301
Depreciation   577–8
Differentiation   136
Directors *see* Company directors
Disabled persons trusts   739
Discounts, Schedule D, Case III   367, 380
Discretion, avoidance and   74
Disposal of assets   462–3
  capital gains tax   462–70
  conditional contracts   476–7
  deemed   463–70
  incidental costs   494
  non-disposals   477–8
  part disposal   471–2, 496–7
  time of   476–7
Distributions   550–1, 588–9, 592–4
  ACT   588–9
  advance corporation tax   588–9, 592–4
  bonus issue   594
  dividends   592
  foreign element   599

Distributions – *continued*
  legislation 589–90
  new consideration 591–2
  non-corporate shareholders 603–4
  non-distributions 595–6
  non-resident corporate shareholders 603
  non-resident non-corporate shareholders 604
  otherwise than as dividends 124–6
  out of assets of company 593
  qualifying 594–5
  redeemable shares or securities 593
  repayment of share capital 594
  share dealers 603
  shares and securities 591
  transfer of assets or liabilities 594
  when paid 590
  in winding up 595
Dividend stripping 111, 114
Dividends 363, 574
  distribution by company otherwise than as 124–6
  as distributions 592
  groups ACT surrender 634–5
  stock 596
  waiver 684
Documents base 9
Donatio mortis causa 527–8
Double taxation 758–9
Dredging 360
Duke of Westminster case 78–81
Dwelling house
  inheritance tax 725–6
  meaning 506–8
  see also Private residence

Education expenses 182–3
Emoluments 156, 157
  causation test 187–9
  foreign 209–10
  Hochstrasser test 185–8, 190
  'therefrom' 184–7
  under common law 168–9
  see also Overseas employments
Employee shareholdings 237–8
Employee theft 330
Employee trusts 685, 739
Employment
  contracts of and for service 161–2, 163–5

Employment – *continued*
  Schedule E meaning 161–6
  statutory meanings 166–7
Enquiries into returns 36
Ensign Tankers v *Stokes* 91–2
Entertainment expenses 447
  business entertainment 253
  Schedule D deductible expenditure 326–7
  vouchers 216
Estate duty 674, 675
European Court 68
European law 49
  Community legal order 63–4
  direct application 63, 64
  directive 62, 64, 66, 67
  directly effective 62
  interpretation of statute and 61–4
  proportionality 65
  regulation 62, 64
Evasion *see* Tax avoidance; Tax evasion
Exclusivity test 314–16
Expenditure
  capital gains computation 489–94
    acquisition 490–1
    allowable expenditure 489–90
    enhancement 491–3
    production 491
    title 493–4
  payment by taxation 9
  see also Expenses
Expenditure base 8–9
Expenses
  accountancy costs 322
  bad debts 328–30
  business entertaining expenses 253
  capital allowances 253
  capital test 316–20
  clothes 322–3
  concessions 252–3
  conditions to be met 249–52, 313
  duality of purpose 314–16
  duties performed abroad 749–50
  earning of profits requirement 316
  employee theft 330
  entertainment 447
    business entertainment 253
    Schedule D deductible expenditure 326–7
    vouchers 216
  exclusivity test 314–16

Expenses – *continued*
  fines 327–8
  foreign travel 253
  funeral 702
  general rule 312–13
  improvements 323–5
  'in performance of duties' 250–1
  income nature 311
  interest on loan for plant 253
  legal costs 322
  living accommodation 238
  losses generally 321–2
  management 576–7
  ministers of religion 253
  'necessarily obliged' 249–50
  necessary 241–2
  personal benefit from 252
  remoteness test 314
  removal 253
  rent 323
  repairs 323–5
  revenue capital test 316–20
  salaries 325–6
  Schedule D 311–20
  Schedule E 240–53
  Strong v *Woodfield* rule 316
  subscriptions to professional bodies 253
  tort damages 321–2
  trading 576
  travel 242–9, 320–1
    foreign 253
    Pook v *Owen* 244–5
    quantum 248
    Rickets v *Colquhoun* 243–4
    Schedule D 320–1
    site bases employees 247–8
    Taylor v *Provan* 246–7
    triangular travel 247–8
  'wholly, exclusively and necessarily' 251–2
Extra-statutory Concessions 26, 28–9

Fact, law and fact distinction 39–40
Farming 260
  fluctuating profits 303–4
  see also Agricultural property
Finance Acts 24–5
Financial year 564
Fines, Schedule D expenditure 327–8
Fitzwilliam case 94–8, 100

Footballers 195, 206–7
Foreign currency 503
Foreign emoluments 209–10
  see also Overseas employment
Foreign travel expenses 253
Franked investment income 600–1
  carry-forward 601–2
  losses 613
    set off against 602–3
  repayment after ACT payment 601
  surplus 601–3
Fringe benefits 174–7
  compensation for loss or withdrawal 183–4
  trade-in value 171–2
  see also Benefits in kind
Funeral expenses 702
Furnished holiday lettings 428
Furniss v *Dawson* 85–7

General commissioners 37–8
Gifts with reservation 685–8
  settlements 722
Gilt strips 586
Gilt-edged securities
  capital gains tax 502–3
  corporation tax 586
  indexed 586
'Golden handshakes'
  non-money consideration 205
  prior agreement 201–2
  statute 204–7
  variation payments 199–201
'Golden hello' 196–9
Golden rule 53, 56–7, 59
Graduation 136
Group income
  anti-avoidance 624–5
  capital holding and trading stock 625–6
  consortia 645
  deductible payments 627
  dividend to subsidiary 625
  election 625–6, 627
  temporary disapplication 626
  UK residence 624
Group relief
  75% relationships 627–8
  anti-avoidance 629–32
  claims 633–4
  consortia 645–6

Index

Group relief – *continued*
  current accounting period 628–9
  losses available for 628
  trading losses 614
Groups 551
  ACT surrender
    anti-avoidance provisions 636
    change of ownership 635
    claims 636
    dividends only 634–5
    payments 636–7
    use of surrendered payments 635–6
  chargeable gains 637–44
    51% subsidiaries 638
    75% subsidiaries 637–8
    anti-avoidance 644
    changes within group 638
    company leaving group 643–4
    intra-group transfers 638–42
    recovery of tax from members 642–3
    transfers outside group 642
  consortia 616–17, 644–6
    group income 645
    group relief 645–6
  deductible payments 627
  direct ownership 619–20
  losses 607
  ordinary share capital 6–8
  percentage ownership 617–18
    51% relationship 616, 617–18
    75% relationship 616, 618
      group relief 627–8
    90% subsidiary 618
    beneficial ownership 618
  separate legal personalities 615
  share capital determination 618–24
    100% ownership chain 621
    all but one 100% owner 622
    direct ownership 619–20
    tracing 620–1
    two or more fractional owners 622–4
  trading stock 639–42
  see also Group income; Group relief

Hall v *Lorimer* 168–9
Hansard 30–1, 61
Higher paid employees
  benefits in kind 223–39

Higher paid employees – *continued*
  meaning 226
  see also Company directors
Hire purchase 470–1
Historic buildings, maintenance funds 446, 739
History
  capital gains tax 454–6
  corporation tax 548–9
  differentiation 136
  income tax 135–7
    earned income 136
    Schedule E 154–6
    unearned income 136
  inheritance tax 674
  land 426–8
  taxation in general 1–2
Hivedowns 613
Hochstrasser test, emoluments 185–8, 190
Holiday lettings 428
Housing associations 689

Illegal trading 277–9
Improvements, Schedule D deductible expenditure 323–5
Imputation system 597
Income base 3–5
Income tax
  alienation of income 142–3, 362, 396
  annual profits or gains 139
  assessment 149
    Schedule D, Case III 380–2
    Schedule D, Case VI 451–2
    when assessable 172–4
  capital/income distinction 138
  charge 138, 142–3
  computation 140–2, 283–336
  charging provisions 150–2
  collection 149
  companies exclusion 569–70
  death
    absolute interest in residue 425–6
    administration period 424–5
    deceased's income 423
    income arising after 423–6
    limited interests in residue 424–5
    personal allowance 423
    personal representatives
      allowances available to 423

Income tax – *continued*
    persons not individuals 423
    residuary beneficiaries 424
    specific legatees 424
  graduation 136
  history 135–7
    Schedule E 154–6
  income
    alienation 142–3, 362, 396
    capital/income distinction 138
    charges on 142–3
    earned 136
    grossed up 141
    meaning 137
    total 140–1
    unearned 136
  land *see* Income tax, Schedule A (land)
  offshore trusts 752–4
  professions *see* Income tax, Schedule D, Cases I and II (trades, professions and vocations)
  rates 147–9
    basic rate 147, 148
    higher rate 147, 148–9
    lower rate 147, 148
    trusts 149
    unified system 147
  reliefs
    additional personal 145
    blind persons' relief 146
    claim requirement 143
    index linked 144
    medical insurance 146–7
    non-residents 147
    not set against charges on income 143–4
    'one-parent' families 145
    personal 144
      additional 145
      aged 75 and over 144
    'qualifying child' resident 145
    widow's bereavement allowance 146
  Schedules
    mutual exclusivity 139–40
    see also individual Schedules
  settlements, anti-avoidance provisions 412–22
    bona fide commercial transactions 416

Income tax – *continued*
    calculation of liability 422
    capital payments to settlors 421–2
    charging provisions
      children's settlements 420–1
      settlor retaining interest 418–20
    element of bounty test 415–17
    settlement meaning 414–17
    settlor meaning 417–18
    transfer of assets requirement 415
  situs 138
  source doctrine 137–40, 173
  supertax 136
  surtax 136
  tax avoidance *see* Tax avoidance: settlements, anti-avoidance provisions
  temporary tax 25
  territorial scope
    domicile 15, 20–2
    dual residence 16, 19
    locus classicus 14–15
    ordinary residence 15, 19–20
    residence 15, 16–18
  trade profits *see* Income tax, Schedule D, Cases I and II (trades, professions and vocations)
  trusts 400–12
    accumulation and discretionary trusts 405–7, 411
    beneficiaries' liability
      absolute entitlement 401, 408–10
      accumulation or discretionary trusts 411
      infant beneficiary 409
      payments out of capital 411–12
    non-resident 412
    rates of tax 149
    trustees' income liability 401–8
      accumulation or discretionary trusts 405–7
      actual receipt or control 401–2
      assessment 404–5
      bases for assessment 403
      failure to deduct from beneficiaries 407–8
      mistakes 407–8

Income tax – *continued*
  see also settlements, anti-avoidance
    provisions
  vocations see Income tax, Schedule
    D, Cases I and II (trades,
    professions and vocations)
  year of assessment 139
Income tax, Schedule A (land)
  capital allowances 442
  furnished holiday lettings 428
  historical matters 426–8
  interest, new Schedule A 446
  international aspects 443–4
  land as trade 443
  leases
    duration 439
    terms 438
    see also premiums and deemed
      premiums
  losses, new Schedule A 446
  maintenance funds 446
  MIRAS 446
  new Schedule A 444–7
    charge 444
    computation 446–7
    entertainment expenses 447
    exemptions 447
    FA 1995 changes 445–6
    interest 446
    land as one estate 445
    losses 446
    maintenance funds 446
    persons applicable 444
    premiums 446
    pre-trading expenditure 446
    sea walls 446
  non-residents 443–4
  old schedule A charge
    background 429
    deductions
      Inland Revenue view 432–3
      receipts other than rents 434–5
      rents 431–4
    interpretation 429–31
    land 430
    land managed as one estate 434
    lease 430
    maintenance funds 434
    maintenance and repairs 432–3
    management expenses 433–4
    other receipts 430–1

Income tax, Schedule A (land) –
  continued
  rentcharge 430
  sea walls 435
  sporting rights 435
  as one estate 434, 445
  premiums and deemed premiums
    435–40
    deduction 440
    meaning 437–8
    new Schedule A 446
    as rent 436–8
    sale at undervalue 439–4
    transfer with right of reconveyance
      440
    when required 438
  sale and leaseback
    consideration received 443
    limitation on reliefs 442–3
  sea walls 435, 446
  service charges
    heads of charge 441–2
    landlord 441
    meaning 440
    persons to consider 440–1
    provider 441
    reserve funds 442
    tax consequences 440
    tenant 442
Income tax, Schedule B 428
Income tax, Schedule D, Cases I and II
  (trades, professions and vocations)
  254–360
  accountancy costs 322
  accounting approach 284
  accounting bases 284–8
    anticipation 288
    bills delivered basis 287
    cash basis 287
    change of basis 287–8
    earnings basis 285–7
  adventure see trade
  bad debts 328–30
  badges of trade 261–76
    business knowledge 275–6
    circumstance for realisation 263,
      271–2
    fact/law distinction 263–4
    length of ownership period 262,
      268–9
    motive 263, 271, 272–5

Income tax, Schedule D, Cases I and II
(trades, professions and vocations)
– *continued*
  number of transactions 262, 269–70
  subject matter of realisation 262, 265–8
  supplementary work 262, 270–1
 basis period rules 330–6
  accounting date 334
   change 335
  basis period 333
  'commencement date' 333–6
  commencement provisions 334–5
  current year basis 331
   charge on 333
  discontinuance 335–6
  general rules 334
  new rules 333–6
  old system, general rule 331–2
  opening years 332
  overlap relief 336
  payment of tax 336
  preceding year basis 330–1
  year of assessment 333
 capital allowances
  allowances 347–8
  availability 347–8
  balancing allowances 348–9
  balancing charge 348–9, 357
  dredging 360
  industrial buildings 345–9
  know-how 360
  machinery and plant 349–60
   belonging 353–5
   disposal value 356
   expenditure on provision of 353
   hire purchase 359
   leasing 359–60
   meaning 349–52
   non-business use 357
   pool 355–60
   short and long life assets 358
   textbooks 352
   wear and tear 358
  mines 360
  motor cars 358
  oil wells 360
  patents 360
  pool 355–60

Income tax, Schedule D, Cases I and II
(trades, professions and vocations)
– *continued*
   separate 357–60
  reducing balance basis 356
  relevant interest 347–8
  scientific research 360
  ships 359
  textbooks 352
  writing down allowance 355
 Cases 256
 charging provisions 255
 clothes 322–3
 clubs 280–2
 compensation payments 289–93
  cancellation of contracts 291–3
  filling a hole in profits 293
  sterilisation of assets 290–1
 computation 283–336
 deductible expenditure 311–20
  accountancy costs 322
  bad debts 328–30
  capital test 316–20
  clothes 322–3
  conditions for deductibility 313
  duality of purpose 314–16
  earning of profits requirement 316
  employee theft 330
  entertainment expenses 326–7
  exclusivity test 314–16
  fines 327–8
  general rule 312–13
  improvements 323–5
  income nature 311
  legal costs 322
  losses generally 321–2
  remoteness test 314
  rent 323
  repairs 323–5
  revenue capital test 316–20
  salaries 325–6
  Strong v *Woodfield* rule 316
  tort damages 321–2
  travelling expenses 320–1
 employee theft 330
 entertainment expenses 326–7
 farming 260
 fines 327–8
 fluctuating profits 303–4
 general rule 283–4

Index

Income tax, Schedule D, Cases I and II
  (trades, professions and vocations)
  – *continued*
  illegal trading   277–9
  improvements   323–5
  know-how payments   301
  land as trade   443
  legal approach   284
  legal costs   322
  losses   337–44
    carry across against other income   339–42
    carry back against profits of preceding years   344
    carry back in opening years   338–9
    carry forward against future profits   342–4
    commencement losses   338–9
    set against capital gains tax   344
    trading loss meaning   338
    uses   337
  market gardening   260
  market value
    determination   295–7
    see also Sharkey v Wernher rule
  moneys worth not cash   286
  mutual trading   280–2
  occupation of land   260–1
  one-off transactions   259
  profession meaning   255–7
  profits
    fluctuating   303–4
    and gains   284
  receipts less expenses   283–4
  released debts   298–301
  rent   323
  repairs   323–5
  salaries   325–6
  Sharkey v Wernher rule   304–11
    exceptions   309–11
  stock, meaning   297–8
  Strong v Woodfield rule   316
  taxable income   288–304
    capital/income distinction   289
    compensation *see* compensation payments
    'derived from trade'   289
  tort damages   321–2
  trade
    asset stripping   276–7

Income tax, Schedule D, Cases I and II
  (trades, professions and vocations)
  – *continued*
  dividend stripping   276–7
  illegal trading   277–9
  land as   443
  meaning   259–60
  mutual trading   280–2
  statute   260–1
  tax avoidance motive   276–7
  see also badges of trade
  trading receipts *see* taxable income
  trading stock   294–7
  transfer pricing   301
  travelling expenses   320–1
  unclaimed deposits   298–301
  vocation meaning   257–8
    calling meaning   257–8
  work-in-progress   294–7
Income tax, Schedule D, Case II   154
Income tax, Schedule D, Case III
  (interest, annuities and annual payments)   361–99
  agreement not to deduct   395–6
  alienation of income   362, 396
  annual payments   367, 369–76
    deduction at source   390–1
  annuities   367, 368–9
    deduction at source   390–1
  assessment basis   380–2
  avoidance schemes   396–8
  binding legal obligation requirement   370–1
  changes 1988   366–7
  changes 1996   399
  charge   362, 364–5, 366–7
  charities   373, 394–5
  deduction at source   182–7, 363
    annual payments   390–1
    annuities   390–1
    bank interest   386–7
    building society interest   386–8
    interest   384–6
    MIRAS   385, 388–90
  discounts   367, 380
  free of tax clause   395–6
  income and capital payment   374–6
  interest   367, 376–80
    deduction at source   384–6
    meaning   377–8
    MIRAS   385, 388–90

Income tax, Schedule D, Case III (interest, annuities and annual payments) – *continued*
  premium distinguished 379–80
  short 378–9
  yearly 378–9
  international element 399
  MIRAS 385, 388–90
  mortgage interest 365
    see also MIRAS
  payment of tax 398
  payments out of profits or gains
    brought into charge 391–3
    not brought into charge 393–4
  persons chargeable 398
  preceding year basis 380–2
  pure income payment 371–2, 374
  reverse annuity schemes 372–3
Income tax, Schedule D, Cases IV and V
  UK residents with foreign income or gains 741, 742–6
    arising basis 743
    assessment 743
    basis of assessment 746
    delayed remittances 745–6
    remittance basis 744–5
Income tax, Schedule D, Case V 155
  foreign possessions 155
Income tax, Schedule D, Case VI 448–52
  assessment basis 451–2
  general charge 448–51
  income receipts only 448
  international element 452
  losses 613
  performance of services 449–50
  profits or gains 449
  specific charges 451
Income tax, Schedule E (income from employment) 153–253
  assessment 172–4
  benefits in kind 174–7
    additional accommodation charge 222–3
    cars 233–5
      fuel 235
    cash vouchers taxable under PAYE 218
    company directors *see* company directors' benefits in kind

Income tax, Schedule E (income from employment) – *continued*
    expense payments 228
    higher paid employees 223–39
      meaning 226
      see also company directors
    mobile telephones 235–6
    scholarships 238–9
    statutory modifications 211–39
    valuation 177–9
    vans 235
    see also credit tokens; living accommodation; vouchers
  bonus cases 193–5
    cricketers 193–4
    footballers 195, 206–7
  cars 233–5
    fuel 235
    parking vouchers 216
  Case I 208–9, 746–8
  Case II 208–9, 748
  Case III 208–9, 748–9
  cash vouchers taxable under PAYE 218
  charge under 156–8
  clergy cases 192
  company directors' benefits in kind 223–39
    assets placed at disposal 232–3
    beneficial loans 236–7
    benefits in Code 229
    cars 233–5
      fuel 235
    cash equivalent 228, 229–30
    chargeable expenses 228
    costs of benefit 230
      transfer of asset 230–2
    definition 225
    employee shareholdings 237–8
    expenses payments 228
    general charge 228
    living accommodation expenses 238
    mobile telephones 235–6
    scholarships 238–9
    tax paid by employer 238
    vans 235
  contractual conditions 180–1
  credit tokens 216–18
    by reason of employment 217
    chargeable expense 217

Index

Income tax, Schedule E (income from employment) – *continued*
  exemptions 218
  provided for employee 217
  reductions 218
 deductions from wages 171
 deferral 172
 discharge of debt to third party 181–3
 education expenses 182–3
 emoluments 156, 157
  Case I to Case III 208–9
  causation test 187–9
  foreign 209–10
  Hochstrasser test 185–8, 190
  'therefrom' 184–7
  under common law 168–9
 'employment'
  actors 167
  agency workers 166
  construction industry 166–7
  Hall v *Lorimer* 168–9
  meaning 161–6
  North Sea divers 167
  statutory meanings 166–7
 expenses 240–53
  business entertaining expenses 253
  capital allowances 253
  concessions 252–3
  conditions to be met 249–52
  foreign travel 253
  'in performance of duties' 250–1
  interest on loan for plant 253
  ministers of religion 253
  'necessarily obliged' 249–50
  necessary expenses 241–2
  personal benefit from 252
  removal expenses 253
  subscriptions to professional bodies 253
  travelling expenses 242–9
   Pook v *Owen* 244–5
   quantum 248
   Rickets v *Colquhoun* 243–4
   site bases employees 247–8
   Taylor v *Provan* 246–7
   triangular travel 247–8
  'wholly, exclusively and necessarily' 251–2
 extra-statutory concessions 184

Income tax, Schedule E (income from employment) – *continued*
 footballers 195, 206–7
 foreign possessions 155
 fringe benefits 174–7
  compensation for loss or withdrawal 183–4
  trade-in value 171–2
 'golden handshakes'
  armed forces personnel 205
  before obligations ceased 202–3
  common law 199–204
  non-money consideration 205
  prior agreement 201–2
  statute 204–7
  variation payments 199–201
 'golden hello' 196–9
 history 154–6
 illegality 167–8
 inducements
  to take up office 196–9
  see also 'golden handshakes'
 living accommodation 218–23
  amount charged 220
  by reason of employment 220
  directors' expenses 238
  exceptions 221–2
   additional accommodation charge 222–3
  provided in any period 220
  reductions 221
 mobile telephones 235–6
 new rules 173–4
 Nicoll v *Austin* rule 181–3
 'office' 158–60
  as asset of trade or profession 160
  meaning 158–60
 old rules 172–3
 'perquisites whatsoever' 174–7, 178
 place of performance of duties 210
 reality rules 169–70
 redundancy payments 206
 retirement benefits 2–6, 205
 scholarships 238–9
 source doctrine 173
 superannuation scheme payments 205
 tax avoidance 167
 third party payments
  anticipation of payment 195
  bonus cases 193–5

Income tax, Schedule E (income from employment) – *continued*
  clergy cases 192
  cricketers 193–4
  exceptional nature of payment 195
  footballers 195, 206–7
  relationship of recipient to payer 195–6
  tips 191–2
  transfer benefits 195
  voluntary payment 195
tips 191–2
trade-in values of benefits 171–2
vans 235
vouchers 213–18
  by reason of employment 214
  car parking 216
  chargeable expense 214–15
  entertainment 216
  holiday stamp 213
  non-cash 213–16
  provided for employee 213–14
  received by employee 214
  reduction in amount chargeable 215–16
  trading stamps 213
  transport vouchers 216
waiver 172
Indexation allowance 497–8
indexed gilt-edged securities 586
Industrial buildings 345–9
Ineffective transactions 72
  substance over form 72
Inheritance base 9
Inheritance tax
  aggregation 713
  agricultural tenancy grant 684–5
  annual exemption 691–2
  capital gains tax and 676
  charge 678–9
  computation 697–719
  conditionally exempt transfers 694–6
  death 701–3
    allowable expenses 702–3
    market value at 701
    property not included in estate 701–2
  dependents 683–4, 719
    settlements 730

Inheritance tax – *continued*
  disclaimers 718–19
  dispositions 679–81
    allowable against income tax 684
  estate
    meaning 681
    transferor's, reduction of 681–2
  exempt transfers 688–96
    conditionally 694–6
    lifetime transfers 691–3
    potentially 675, 693–4, 730
    restrictions 691
    see also individual transfers eg gifts to charities; spouses
  family maintenance 730
  free loans 680
  functions 673
  gifts in consideration of marriage 693
  gifts for national purposes 690
  gifts for public benefit 690–1
  gifts with reservation 685–8
    settlements 722
  gifts to charities 689
  gifts to housing associations 689
  gifts to political parties 689
  history 674
  interests in possession settlements 723–31
    beneficial entitlement 726–7
    beneficiary becoming entitled 729–30
    dependents 730
    depreciatory transactions 728
    disclaimers 730
    exceptions 728–9
    family maintenance 730
    Inland Revenue interpretation 724
    occupation of dwelling house 725–6
    potentially exempt transfers 730–1
    quick succession relief 731
    reversion to settlor 729
    termination 727–8
    termination on death 728
    trustees' annuities 729
  liabilities for other taxes 699
  lifetime transfers 691–3
  maintenance of family 683–4

Index

Inheritance tax – *continued*
  market value at death 701
  non-gratuitous transfers 682–3
  normal expenditure out of income 692
  offshore trusts 757–8
  payment of tax
    acceptance of property 717
    conditionally exempt transfers 715–16
    Inland Revenue charge 717–18
    instalments 716–17
    lifetime transfers 713–14
    methods 716–18
    transfers on death 714–15
    transfers within seven years before death 714
    woodlands 716
  pension plans 684
  policy 675–7
  potentially exempt transfers 675, 693–4
  settlements 730
  purchase of own shares to pay 672
  quick succession relief 712–13, 731
  rates of tax
    cumulation 709
    lifetime transfers 710
    relief for decline in value 711–12
    transfers on death 710–11
  reduction of transferor's estate 681–2
  related property 700
  settlements
    accumulation and maintenance trusts 737–9
    beneficiaries 723
    charitable purposes 736–7
    compensation funds 739
    disabled persons trusts 739
    employee trusts 739
    gifts subject to reservation 722
    maintenance funds for historic buildings 739
    payment of tax 740
    possession *see* interests in possession settlements
    property held by exempt bodies 739
    settlement meaning 720–1
    settlors meaning 721–2

Inheritance tax – *continued*
    superannuation schemes 739
    trustees 723
    without interests in possession 731–6
      ceasing to be settled property 734
      created before 22 March 1974 733–4
      rates 735–6
      reduction in value 734–5
      ten year charge 731–3
  small gifts 692
  spouses 688–9
  territorial limits 679
  transfer to trust for benefit of employees 685
  transfer of value 679–82
    on death 685
    transactions which are not 682–5
    value transferred 697–703
  transfer of wealth 673
  unpaid tax 717
  valuation of assets
    agricultural property 704–7, 709
    business property 707–9
    debts due to transferor 703
    land 704
    life policies 703
    shares 703–4
  variations 718–19
  void and voidable transfers 682
  waiver of dividends 684
  waiver of remuneration 684
  woodlands relief 701–2
  works of art 701
Inland Revenue
  collector of taxes 33
  Decisions 29
  discretion 74
  Extra-statutory Concessions 26, 28–9
  inspector of taxes 33
  Interpretations 29
  Press Releases 26, 30
  Statement of Practice 29
  tax avoidance statements 110–11
Inspector of taxes 33
Insurance companies 586
  corporation tax 574
  manufactured 586

Insurance companies – *continued*
  see also Income tax, Schedule D, Case III (interest, annuities and annual payments)
Interest schemes 80
International elements
  capital gains tax 750–2
    allowance for foreign tax 498
  companies 551–2, 759–60
    controlled foreign companies 760
    transfer pricing 760
    see also corporation tax
  corporation tax
    branch or agency 571
    locus contractus 572–3
    necessary conditions 570–1
    trade within UK 571–3
  double tax relief 758–9
  foreign emoluments 209–10
  income tax *see* offshore trusts; overseas employments; UK residents with foreign income or gains
  income tax
    non-UK residents 138, 147
    see also Schedules A, D and E
  land transaction 134, 443–4
  offshore trusts
    capital gains tax 755–7
    income tax 752–4
    inheritance tax 757–8
    transfer of assets abroad 752–4
  overseas employment
    absence from UK 747, 748, 749
    expenses 749–50
    place of performance 210
  Schedule A land 443–4
  Schedule D, Case III 399
  Schedule D, Cases IV and V 741, 742–6
    arising basis 743
    assessment 743
    basis of assessment 746
    delayed remittances 745–6
    remittance basis 744–5
  Schedule D, Case VI 452
  Schedule E 209–10
  Schedule E, Case I 746–8
  Schedule E, Case II 748
  Schedule E, Case III 748–9
  transfer of assets abroad, tax

International elements – *continued*
  avoidance 113, 130–1
  UK residents 740–1
  unilateral relief 759
Interpretation of statute 29, 50–68
  ambiguity 60–1
  charging sections 59
  complexity of language 51
  consolidation 58
  courts 53–4
  deeming provisions 59
  diversity of approach 51
  European Court 68
  European law 61–4
  European principles 65–7
  golden rule 53, 56–7, 59
  grammar 57
  Hansard 61
  latin tags 58–9
  legal theory 52–3
  length of statutes 52
  literal rule 53, 54–5
  machinery sections 59
  mischief rule 53, 55–6
  obscurity 60–1
  ordinary meaning 57
  pari materia 59
  presumptions against retrospection 60
  punctuation 58
  reading words in 59
  standing committee on taxation 51
  statutory meaning 57
  territorial scope 59
Investment companies 563
  capital allowances 613
  expenses of management 612
    surplus 612–13
  meaning 563
Isle of Man 14
Isles of Scilly 14

Joint ventures 93–4
Judicial review 41–9
  alternative remedies 47–8
  illegality 46
  irrationality 46
  legitimate expectation doctrine 45, 49
  locus standi 44
  procedural fairness 48–9

Index

Judicial review – *continued*
  procedural impropriety 46–7
  remedies 43–4
  testing rulings 42–3
  time limits 44
'Just price' theory 304

Know-how
  capital allowances 360
  payments 301

Land
  artificial transactions 131–4
  indirect realisation 134
  non-UK residents 134
  occupation as trade 260–1
  see also Income tax, Schedule A (land); Leases
Leases
  agricultural tenancy grant 684–5
  duration 439
  premiums and deemed premiums 435–40
    deduction 440
    meaning 437–8
    new Schedule A 446
    as rent 436–8
    sale at undervalue 439–4
    transfer with right of reconveyance 440
    when required 438
  terms 438
Legal costs 322
Legislation
  consolidating acts 26
  distributions 589–90
  Finance Acts 24–5, 51
  interpretation *see* Interpretation of statute
  tax as creature of statute 23–6
  UK statutes 24
Legitimate expectation doctrine 45, 49
Literal rule 53, 54–5
Living accommodation 218–23
  amount charged 220
  by reason of employment 220
  directors' expenses 238
  exceptions 221–2
    additional accommodation charge 222–3

Living accommodation – *continued*
  provided in any period 220
  reductions 221
  see also Private residence
Loans
  beneficial 236–7
  interest charge 236–7, 253
    for plant 253
  as transactions in securities 115
  writing off charge 237
Local taxes 13
Locus classicus 14–15
Losses
  allowable 607, 614
  capital allowances 607
  capital gains tax
    relief for loans to traders 500
    unquoted shares in trading companies 500–1
    use of allowable 499–500
  carry-across
    general 610
    reduction of present and previous profits 609–10
    requirements 610
    Schedule D, Case V losses and 610
  carry-back
    requirements 611
    Schedule D, Case V losses and 611
    to preceding accounting period 610–11
  carry-forward
    against profits without time limit 608
    requirements 608–9
    Schedule D, Case V losses and 609
  commencement 606, 607
  companies 605–14
    trading losses 606, 607–8
  computation 606
  deductions and 606
  franked investment income 613
  group relief 614
  groups 607, 628
  hivedowns 613
  pre-trading expenditure 606, 607
  Schedule D, Case VI 613
  terminal 611–12

Losses – *continued*
  trading 606, 607–11
  uses 606–8
'Lump' system 166–7

Machinery and plant *see* Capital allowances
Maintenance funds
  historic buildings 446, 739
  Schedule A (land) 432–3
  new 446
Management expenses
  investment companies 612–13
  old schedule A charge 433–4
Manufactured interest 586
Market gardeners 260, 303–4
Market value
  determination 295–7
  disposal consideration 482–4
  see also Sharkey v *Wernher* rule
Marriage gifts 693
Meade Report 12–13
Medical insurance 146–7
Mines, capital allowances 360
MIRAS 385, 388–90, 446
Mischief rule 53, 55–6
Mistakes, law and fact distinction 39–40
Mitigation 75, 76–7
Mobile telephones 235–6
Moneys worth 286
Mortgages
  capital gains tax 378
  MIRAS 385, 388–90, 446
Mutual trading, identity requirement 281

Nairn Williamson schemes, reverse 80, 83–5
National purpose gifts 690
Nicoll v *Austin* rule 181–3
Non-UK resident company liability
  branch or agency 571
  locus contractus 572–3
  necessary conditions 570–1
  trade within UK 571–3
Non-UK residents
  income tax 138
  income tax reliefs 147
North Sea divers 167
Northern Ireland 13, 14

Office
  as asset of trade or profession 160
  Schedule E meaning 158–60
Offshore rollovers 80
Offshore trusts
  capital gains tax 755–7
    attribution of gains
      to beneficiaries 755
      to settlor 757
    disposal of interests 756–7
    migrant settlements 756
    trustees ceasing to be liable to UK tax 756
  income tax 752
  inheritance tax 757–8
  transfer of assets abroad 752–4
Oil wells 360
One-off transactions 259
Options 475, 485
Overlap relief, Schedule D, Cases I and II 336
Overseas employments
  absence from UK 747, 748, 749
  expenses 749–50
  Schedule E, Case I 746–8
  Schedule E, Case II 748
  Schedule E, Case III 748–9

Part disposals 471–2, 496–7
Participator 561
Passenger vehicles 505
Patents
  capital allowances 360
  royalty payments 391–3, 578, 579
Payment of tax
  capital gains tax 478–9
  corporation tax 566–7
  inheritance tax
    acceptance of property 717
    conditionally exempt transfers 715–16
    Inland Revenue charge 717–18
    instalments 716–17
    lifetime transfers 713–14
    methods 716–18
    settlements 740
    transfers on death 714–15
    transfers within seven years before death 714
    unpaid 717
    woodlands 716

Index

Payment of tax – *continued*
  Schedule D, Cases I and II 336
  Schedule D, Case III 398
  under self-assessment 35
Pension plans 684
'Perquisites whatsoever' 174–7, 178
Personal equity plan shares 504
Personal representatives 527–8
  change 527–8
  see also Death of taxpayer
Pigott v *Staines Investment Co* 102–9
Plant *see* Capital allowances, machinery and plant
Political party gifts 689
Pook v *Owen*, travelling expenses 244–5
Preceding year basis
  Schedule D, Cases I and II 330–1
  Schedule D, Case III 380–2
Premiums 379–80
Preordained transactions *see* Series of transactions
Press Releases 26, 30
Pricing, transfer 301, 760
Private residence
  apportionment 509–10
  capital gains tax 505–6
  dwelling house meaning 506–8
  more than one residence 508–9
  period of occupation 509–10
  sale of part of garden 508
  see also Dwelling house
Professions *see* Income tax, Schedule D, Cases I and II (trades, professions and vocations)
Profits, fluctuating 303–4
Proportionality 65
Public benefit gifts 690–1
Purchase of own shares
  capital gains tax 669–72
  clearance procedure 669, 672
  general conditions 670–2
  to pay IHT on death 672
  unquoted trading company 669–70

Quick succession relief 712–13, 731

Ramsay doctrine 81–3
  pre-*Ramsay* case law 79–81
Rates of tax
  capital gains tax 478

Rates of tax – *continued*
  corporation tax 564
    small companies 565–6
  income tax 147–9
    basic rate 147, 148
    higher rate 147, 148–9
    lower rate 147, 148
    trusts 149
    unified system 147
  inheritance tax
    cumulation 709
    lifetime transfers 710
    relief for decline in value 711–12
    transfers on death 710–11
Reconstructions
  anti-avoidance 665–7
  bona fide commercial reasons 665–6
  capital gains tax 657–67
  consideration for transfer 667
  exclusions 664–5
  meaning 659–62
  substantial identity test 659–62
  trading stock 664–5
  unit trusts 665
Redistribution of wealth 9–10
Reinvestment relief 523–4
Reliefs
  capital gains tax
    gifts of assets 514–16
    hold over 514–16
    incorporation into business 517–19
    reinvestment 523–4
    retirement 510–14
    roll-over
      incorporation into business 517–19
      replacement of business assets 519–22
    spouses 524–5
    venture capital trusts 525–6
  double tax 758–9
  group *see* Group relief
  hold over 514–16
  income tax
    additional personal 145
    blind persons' 146
    claim requirement 143
    index linked 144
    medical insurance 146–7
    non-residents 147

Reliefs – *continued*
   not set against charges on income 143–4
   'one-parent' families 145
   personal 144
     additional 145
     aged 75 and over 144
   'qualifying child' resident 145
   widow's bereavement allowance 146
  overlap 336
  quick succession 712–13, 731
  reinvestment 523–4
  retirement 510–14
  roll-over
   incorporation into business 517–19
   paper for paper transactions 649–51
   replacement of business assets 519–22
   unilateral 759
   woodlands 701–2
Remittances
  delayed 745–6
  Schedule D, Cases IV and V 744–6
  Schedule E, Case III 749
Remoteness test, deductible expenditure 314
Removal expenses 253
Remuneration, waiver 684
Rent
  rent-a-room scheme 428
  Schedule D deductible expenditure 323
Reorganisations
  25% control test 650–1
  anti-avoidance 652
  clearance 652
  conversion of securities 652
  disposal with liability attaching 649
  exchange of securities 649–51
  general offer test 651
  greater part of voting power 651
  meaning 648
  necessary conditions 651–2
  new consideration 648
  new holding 647–8
  original shares 647–8
  paper for paper transactions 649–52

Reorganisations – *continued*
  roll-over relief 649–51
  see also Demergers
Repairs
  expenses Schedule A (land) 432–3
  Schedule D deductible expenditure 323–5
Residence 15, 16–18
  domicile 15, 20–2
  dual 16, 19
  ordinary 15, 19–20
Residence of company 555–8
  dual 558–9
  international activities 557
  management and control 556–7
  place of incorporation 556
Retirement relief 510–14
Reverse annuities 80, 372–3
Reverse *Nairn Williamson* schemes 80, 83–5
Rickets v *Colquhoun* 243–4
Roll-over relief
  incorporation into business 517–19
  paper for paper transactions 649–51
  replacement of business assets 519–22
Rollovers, offshore 80
Royalty payments 391–3, 578, 579
Rulings 27

Salaries, deductible expenditure 325–6
Sale and leaseback
  limitation on reliefs 442–3
  taxation of consideration received 443
Scholarships 238–9
Scientific research 360
Scotland 13, 14
Sea walls 435, 446
Securities
  conversion 652
  corporation tax 586
  transactions in 115–16
Self-assessment
  enquiries into returns 36
  payment 35
  personal returns 34–5
Series of transactions 70–1, 88–94
  step transactions doctrine 72

Index

Service charges (land)
  heads of charge 441-2
  landlord 441
  meaning 440
  persons to consider 440-1
  provider 441
  reserve funds 442
  tax consequences 440
  tenant 442
Services, contracts of and for 161-2, 163-5
Settlements
  absolutely entitled
    disposal by trustees 538-42
    infancy only bar to inheritance 533
    jointly 534
    right to call for conveyance 531-3
    tax liability 541-2
  accumulation and maintenance trusts 737-9
  beneficiaries 544-6
  capital gains tax
    absolutely entitled
      disposal by trustees 538-42
      infancy only bar to inheritance 533
      jointly 534
      right to call for conveyance 531-3
      tax liability 541-2
    beneficiaries 544-6
    change of trustees 538
    charitable trusts 546
    creation of new settlement 539-41
    life interest in possession 542-3
    settled property 530-4
      annuity charge on property 534
    settlor's liability 535-6
    termination of life interest on death 542-4
    transfer into 535
    see also disposals by trustees
  charitable purposes 736-7
  charitable trusts 546
  compensation funds 739
  creation of new settlement 539-41
  disposals by trustees

Settlements – *continued*
  absolute entitlement to property 538-42
  termination of life interest on death 542-4
  trust assets 536-8
  income tax
    anti-avoidance provisions 412-22
    bona fide commercial transactions 416
    calculation of liability 422
    capital payments to settlors 421-2
    charging provisions
      children's settlements 420-1
      settlor retaining interest 418-20
    element of bounty test 415-17
    settlement meaning 414-17
    settlor meaning 417-18
    transfer of assets requirement 415
  inheritance tax
    accumulation and maintenance trusts 737-9
    beneficiaries 723
    charitable purposes 736-7
    compensation funds 739
    disabled persons trusts 739
    employee trusts 739
    gifts subject to reservation 722
    interests in possession settlements 723-31
      beneficial entitlement 726-7
      beneficiary becoming entitled 729-30
      dependents 730
      depreciatory transactions 728
      disclaimers 730
      exceptions 728-9
      family maintenance 730
      Inland Revenue interpretation 724
      occupation of dwelling house 725-6
      potentially exempt transfers 730-1
      quick succession relief 731
      reversion to settlor 729
      termination 727-8
      termination on death 728

Settlements – *continued*
    trustees' annuities   729
    maintenance funds for historic
        buildings   739
    payment of tax   740
    property held by exempt bodies
        739
    settlement meaning   720–1
    settlors meaning   721–2
    superannuation schemes   739
    trustees   723
    without interests in possession
        731–6
        ceasing to be settled property
            734
        created before 22 March 1974
            733–4
        rates   735–6
        reduction in value   734–5
        ten year charge   731–3
    life interest in possession   542–3
    settled property   530–4
        annuity charge on property   534
    settlor's liability   535–6
    termination of life interest on
        death   542–4
    transfer into   535
    see also Trusts
Sham transactions   72, 75–6
Shareholders
    employee   237–8
    substantial identity test   659–62
Shares
    bonus issue   594
    purchase and redemption of own
        669–71
    value shifting   472
Sharkey v *Wernher* rule   304–11
    exceptions   309–11
Shepherd v *Lyntress Ltd*   91
Ships   359
Small companies   559, 560, 565–6
Smith, Adam   11–12
Solicitors   287
Sources of law
    accountancy practice   30
    cases   26
    Europe   49
    Extra-statutory Concessions   26,
        28–9
    Hansard   30–1, 61

Sources of law – *continued*
    law and fact distinction   39–40
    Press Releases   26, 30
    reports   26
    see also Inland Revenue; Legislation
Special commissioners   37, 38
Sporting rights   435
Spouses
    capital gains tax relief   524–5
    inheritance tax exemption   688–9
Standing committee on taxation   51
Statement of Practice   29
Step transactions doctrine   72
Stock   297–8
Stock dividends   596
Strong v *Woodfield* rule   316
Subscriptions   253
Substantial identity test   659–62
Superannuation schemes   739
Supertax   136
Surplus capital allowances   612
Surtax   136

Tax advantage
    cancellation   113, 114–30
        clearance procedure   130
        commercial reasons   128–9
        exemptions   128–30
        main object   129–30
        ordinary course of investing   129
    meaning   116–18
Tax avoidance   69–134
    abuse of rights doctrine   71
    advance corporation tax (ACT)
        102–9
    business purpose test   72
    capital gains tax   118, 131–4
        amalgamations   665–7
        demergers   656–7
        reconstructions   665–7
    capital transfer tax   94–8
    case law
        Bayliss v *Gregory*   88
        Bowater Property Developments Ltd
            87–8
        Burmah Oil schemes   83–5
        Craven v *White*   87, 88, 90–1
        Duke of Westminster case   78–81
        Ensign Tankers v *Stokes*   91–2
        Fitzwilliam case   94–8, 100
        Furniss v *Dawson*   85–7

Tax avoidance – *continued*
    McGuckian 100–2
    old approach 78
    Pigott v *Staines Investment Co* 102–9
    pre-*Ramsay* 79–81
    Ramsay doctrine 81–3
    Shepherd v *Lyntress Ltd* 91
    time and change 77
    Whittles v *Uniholdings Ltd* 98–100
  circular transactions 70–1, 81–3
  complex corporate schemes 80
  complexity of statute language and 51
  corporation tax 585–6
  discretion 74
  distribution otherwise than as dividend 124–6
  dividend stripping 111, 114
    abnormal dividend 119
    share dealers 119–20
  group relief 629–32
  groups 624–5
    ACT surrender 636
    chargeable gains 644
  income tax
    Schedule D, Case III 396–8
    Schedule E 167
  ineffective transactions 72
  interest schemes 80
  joint ventures 93–4
  judicial approach 90–1
  judicial doctrines 72–3
  legislative doctrines 73–4
  loan relationships 585–6
  meaning 69–71
  ministerial discretion 74
  non-taxable consideration 126
  object and spirit of legislation 72–3
  official statements 110–11
  offshore rollovers 80
  prescribed circumstances 118–26
    circumstance A 119
    circumstance B 119–20
    circumstance c 120–4
    circumstance D 124–6
    circumstance E 126
  present law position 109–10
  quasi-trading profits into capital profits 131–4
  reorganisations 652

Tax avoidance – *continued*
  reverse annuities 80
  reverse *Nairn Williamson* schemes 80, 83–5
  rules 73–4
  series of transactions 70–1, 72, 88–94, 97–8
  settlements
    income tax 412–22
      bona fide commercial transactions 416
      calculation of liability 422
      capital payments to settlors 421–2
      charging provisions
        children's settlements 420–1
        settlor retaining interest 418–20
      element of bounty test 415–17
      settlement meaning 414–17
      settlor meaning 417–18
      transfer of assets requirement 415
  sham transactions 72, 75–6
  statutory anti-avoidance 111–34
    general application 112
    specific provisions 112–13
    see also individual areas eg dividend stripping
  statutory principles 74–5
  step transactions doctrine 72
  substance over form 72
  tax advantage cancellation 113, 114–30
    clearance procedure 130
    commercial reasons 128–9
    exemptions 128–30
    main object 129–30
    ordinary course of investing 129
  tax advantage meaning 116–18
  trading and 276–7
  transactions in securities 115–16
  transfer of assets abroad 113, 130–1
  uncertainties 110
Tax evasion 70
  sham transactions 75, 76–7
Tax mitigation 75, 76–7
Taxation
  administration *see* Administration of tax
  aims 9–12

Taxation – *continued*
  bases *see* Accountancy basis
  classification *see* Classification
  criteria for 'good' 10–13
  definition difficulties 2–3
  history 1–2
  redistribution by 9–10
Taylor v *Provan* 246–7
Terminal losses 611–12
Termination payments *see* 'Golden handshakes'
Territorial scope
  income tax
    domicile 15, 20–2
    dual residence 16, 19
    locus classicus 14–15
    ordinary residence 15, 19–20
    residence 15, 16–18
  interpretation of statute and 59
  local taxes 13
  national 13
  United Kingdom meaning 13–14
  whole UK context 13
  see also International elements
Textbooks 352
Theft by employees 330
Third party payments
  anticipation of payment 195
  bonus cases 193–5
  clergy cases 192
  cricketers 193–4
  exceptional nature of payment 195
  footballers 195, 206–7
  relationship of recipient to payer 195–6
  tips 191–2
  transfer benefits 195
  voluntary payment 195
Tips 191–2
Trade profits *see* Income tax, Schedule D, Cases I and II (trades, professions and vocations)
Trading
  illegal 277–9
  losses *see* Trading losses
  mutual 280–2
Trading losses
  carry-across
    general 610
    reduction of present and previous profits 609–10

Trading losses – *continued*
    requirements 610
    Schedule D, Case V losses and 610
  carry-back
    requirements 611
    Schedule D, Case V losses and 611
    to preceding accounting period 610–11
  carry-forward
    against profits without time limit 608
    requirements 608–9
    Schedule D, Case V losses and 609
  companies 606, 607–8
  uses 607–8
Transactions
  artificial, in land 131–4
  business purpose test 72
  circular 70–1, 81–3
  gratuitous 484
  ineffective 72
  number of 262, 269–70
  one-off 259
  in securities 115–16
  series 70–1, 72, 88–94
  sham 72, 75–6
  step transactions doctrine 72
  uncertainties 110
Transactions base 9
Transfer pricing 301, 760
Transport vouchers 216
Travelling expenses 242–9, 320–1
  foreign 253
  Pook v *Owen* 244–5
  quantum 248
  Rickets v *Colquhoun* 243–4
  Schedule D 320–1
  Schedule D deductible expenditure 320–1
  site bases employees 247–8
  Taylor v *Provan* 246–7
  triangular travel 247–8
Trusts
  accumulation and maintenance trusts 405–7, 411, 737–9
  beneficiaries' liability
    absolute entitlement 401, 408–10

Index

Trusts – *continued*
  accumulation or discretionary trusts 411
  infant beneficiary 409
  payments out of capital 411–12
  charitable 546
  compensation funds 739
  disabled persons 739
  discretionary trust 405–7, 411, 737–9
  employee 685, 739
  income tax 400–12
  non-resident 412
  offshore *see* Offshore trusts
  rates of tax 149
  trustees' income liability 401–8
    accumulation or discretionary trusts 405–7
    actual receipt or control 401–2
    assessment 404–5
    bases for assessment 403
    failure to deduct from beneficiaries 407–8
    mistakes 407–8

United Kingdom, meaning 13–14

Valuations, appeals 38
Value shifting schemes 472, 484
Van 235
VAT tribunals 41
Venture capital trusts 525–6

Vocations *see* Income tax, Schedule D, Cases I and II (trades, professions and vocations)
Vouchers 212–18
  by reason of employment 214
  car parking 216
  chargeable expense 214–15
  entertainment 216
  holiday stamp 213
  non-cash 213–16
  provided for employee 213–14
  received by employee 214
  reduction in amount chargeable 215–16
  trading stamp 213
  transport vouchers 216

Waiver, Schedule E assessment 172
Wasting assets 495, 503
Wealth base 8
Wealth redistribution 9–10
Whittles v *Uniholdings Ltd* 98–100
Widow's bereavement allowance 146
Wills, variations and disclaimers 529
Woodlands 260
  relief 701–2
Work-in-progress 287, 294–7
Works of art
  capital gains tax 504
  inheritance tax exemption 701
Writing down allowance *see* Capital allowances